The Law of
Public and Utilities
Procurement

AUSTRALIA
The Law Book Company
Brisbane – Sydney – Melbourne – Perth

CANADA
Carswell
Ottawa – Toronto – Calgary – Montreal – Vancouver

Agents
Steimatzky's Agency Ltd, Tel Aviv
N.M. Tripathi (Private) Ltd, Bombay
Eastern Law House (Private) Ltd, Calcutta
M.P.P. House, Bangalore
Universal Book Traders, Delhi
Aditya Books, Delhi
MacMillan Shuppan KK, Tokyo
Pakistan Law House, Karachi, Lahore

THE LAW OF
PUBLIC AND UTILITIES
PROCUREMENT

Sue Arrowsmith
B.A.(Oxon), D.Jur.(Osgoode Hall)
Professor of Law, University of Wales, Aberystwyth

London
Sweet & Maxwell
1996

Published in 1996 by
Sweet & Maxwell Limited of
South Quay Plaza,
183 Marsh Wall,
London E14 9FT

Computerset by LBJ Enterprises Ltd
Aldermaston and Chilcompton

Printed and bound in Great Britain by
Butler & Tanner Ltd, Frome and London

No natural forests were destroyed to make this product;
only farmed timber was used and re-planted.

A CIP catalogue record for this book is available from the British Library

ISBN 0421 444 606

PREFACE

The aim of this book is to provide a comprehensive and structured analysis of the law of public and utilities procurement as it applies in England and Wales. It covers both the purely "domestic" dimension, notably the rules on Compulsory Competitive Tendering, and the increasingly important obligations under European Community law and under various international agreements such as the World Trade Organisation Agreement on Government Procurement. I have sought not merely to provide a detailed exposition of the legal rules — although this is an important aspect of the work since there is little existing material — but also to scrutinise the policy background, to identify the practical difficulties which the rules have created for purchasers, and to examine the prospects for future development.

There is significant uncertainty over many of the rules, not least because some matters of current importance — such as the operation of the rules in relation to privatisation, and to the government's Private Finance Initiative — were not contemplated when the procurement rules were originally devised. Further, even within the context of a relatively simple procurement, numerous issues may arise which have not been specifically addressed in the legislation, but which are likely to be the subject of obligations developed by the judiciary to fill out the skeletal legislative (and common law) framework — for example, the position when a purchaser seeks to waive express tendering formalities. I have tried to identify these areas of difficulty, and to provide a structure for analysis by setting out the possible solutions and their merits.

This work has been a long time in gestation and I am greatly indebted to numerous individuals and organisations who have assisted me over the last few years. In particular, I am grateful to many government officials in the United Kingdom (especially in H.M. Treasury) and the European Commission, who have provided invaluable assistance and information. I would also like to thank those other colleagues and friends who took time to discuss ideas with me, to provide materials and/or to read parts of the manuscript, in particular Roger Bickerstaff, Rosemary Boyle, Adrian Brown, Brian Clark, Professor Keith Hartley, Jose Maria Fernández Martín, Christopher McCrudden, Nuala O'Loan, and Peter-Armin Trepte. I have also gained many valuable insights into the practical operation of the law from discussions at conferences and seminars with lawyers and procurement officers from across Europe. Although they may not know it, I have benefited too from the input of the students at the University of Wales, Aberystwyth who have taken my postgraduate or undergraduate courses on procurement or conducted research in the field, and the enthusiasm of some of them for such a specialised field of the law has been a great encouragement in my work. Finally, I would like to thank Yvonne Williams and Mark Slater, who worked diligently and efficiently as research assistants on this project, and all the staff at the Aberystwyth law library, especially Lillian Stevenson and Meirion Derrick, for their invaluable assistance — always cheerfully provided — which I suspect often goes beyond the call of duty.

The work is up to date, so far as published sources are concerned, up to October 31, 1995, and I have also included material not published at that date but available then from unpublished sources. (Unfortunately the High Court decision of June 6, 1995 in *R. v. Portsmouth City Council, ex parte Bonaco*, which deals with the works Regulations, was not available to me at the time.) Material after that date has not been included, with the important exception that the manuscript was updated at a very late stage to take in the new Utilities Contract Regulations 1996. The text is written on the basis of a draft of these regulations as at March 1, 1996 (which was expected to be formally adopted within the following few days), as if those regulations were in effect. I am grateful to all those at Sweet & Maxwell who put themselves out to make this last minute update possible.

This work is dedicated to my partner and colleague, Peter Cartwright, in recognition of his unfailing support and encouragement.

Sue Arrowsmith,
Aberystwyth,
February 1996.

CONTENTS

Chapter 17 ... 847

DEFENCE PROCUREMENT

1. Defence procurement in the United Kingdom

TABLE OF U.K. CASES

TABLE OF E.C. CASES

CHRONOLOGICAL TABLE

ALPHABETICAL TABLE

l

TABLE OF U.K. LEGISLATION

STATUTES

li

STATUTORY INSTRUMENTS

TABLE OF E.C. LEGISLATION

RECOMMENDATIONS AND DECISIONS

OPINIONS

ABBREVIATIONS

The following abbreviations are used extensively:

Directive 93/36/EEC, [1993] O.J. L199/1	Supply Directive
Directive 93/37/EEC, [1993] O.J. L199/54	Works Directive
Directive 92/50/EEC, [1992] O.J. L209/1	Services Directive
Directive 89/665/EEC, [1989] O.J. L395/33	Remedies Directive
Directive 93/38/EEC, [1993] O.J. L199/84	Utilities Directive
Directive 92/13/EEC, [1992] O.J. L76/7	Utilities Remedies Directive
Agreement on Government Procurement, Annex 4 to the Agreement Establishing the World Trade Organisation, [1994] O.J. L336/273	GPA
Public Works Contracts Regulations 1991, 1991 S.I. 1991 No. 2680	Works Regulations
Public Services Contracts Regulations 1993, S.I. 1993 No. 3228	Services Regulations
Public Supply Contracts Regulations 1995, S.I. 1995 No. 201	Supply Regulations
Draft Utilities Contracts Regulations 1996	Utilities Regulations

CHAPTER 1

INTRODUCTION

The term "procurement" refers to the function of purchasing goods or services from an outside body. Generally this takes place through contractual arrangements although the term may also be used to cover acquisition arrangements which are not strictly contractual.[1] It can be used, first, in a broad sense to refer to the whole of the contract process from specification through to the administration and termination of the contract. It can also be used in a narrow sense to cover merely specification and placing of the contract.

The subject of this book is the special law which governs the procurement of the public sector, using the term procurement in its narrow sense of the process leading up to a contract. The book also covers the law relating to the procurement of certain entities in the "utilities" sectors of water, energy, transport and telecommunications, even though entities in this sector are now privately owned and not generally regarded as "public" bodies. The reason for covering these entities as well as the public sector is that they have been included in the procurement regime established by the European Community in order to open up European markets. This was felt to be necessary on the basis that the purchasing practices of such utilities present the same problem as public purchasing from the perspective of the open European market – that is, a tendency to favour national industry.[2] Although this regulatory regime is still often referred to as the regime of "public procurement" this is misleading given the private character of some of the regulated entities and this book will use instead the phrase "regulated procurement" when referring to the procurement of regulated entities in general.[3]

The regulated market forms a significant part of the economy in most industrialised nations. The most comprehensive examination of the size of such markets in the United Kingdom and other European countries is the Atkins study,[4] carried out for the European Commission, which

---

[1] For example, it is sometimes used to include also the acquisition of public utility services which are supplied under statutory arrangements rather than under a contract.

[2] The reasons for this are considered at p. 56.

[3] The professional association set up in the United Kingdom to bring together professionals interested in the field is named "the United Kingdom Association for Regulated Procurement".

[4] W.S. Atkins Management Consultants, *The Cost of Non-Europe in Public Procurement* (1988) (hereafter the Atkins study).

estimated that the annual value of procurement of government and nationalised industries[5] of the twelve states who were members of the Community in 1985 was about 450 billion ECUs at 1984 prices, amounting to about 15 per cent of Community Gross Domestic Product (GDP) as a whole, and 21.8 per cent of GDP in the United Kingdom.[6] More recently, in the Government's 1995 White Paper on procurement strategy, *Setting New Standards: a Strategy for Government Procurement,* the annual procurement expenditure of U.K. central government alone was estimated at nearly £40 billion per annum (excluding National Health Service purchasers of around £20 billion).[7] Spending on procurement has steadily increased in the last few years as a proportion of all government spending,[8] partly because of increased contracting out to the private sector of services formerly carried on by government "in-house".

For the purposes of control and regulation, procurement is frequently divided into three categories – "supplies", "services" and "works". These categories are often used in legislation and international agreements on procurement, although the boundaries between them are far from clear-cut and these categories are often given a slightly different scope in different legal provisions. "Supplies" procurement by regulated purchasers – basically the acquisition of products – covers a whole range of transactions, from the purchase of simple "off the shelf" items such as stationery and office furniture, through to complex computer systems, power generation equipment and military equipment. "Works" refers to construction and engineering activities, such as the building of roads, bridges or buildings. The term "services" is generally used to refer to the provision of non-construction services – although construction is a type of service and the term "services" is sometimes used, including in legal provisions, to cover in a broad sense both construction and non-construction services. "Services" covers manual services, such as gardening or street cleaning, and "white collar" services such as advertising, auditing and legal work.

The activity of procurement is of concern to a wide range of groups and interests. In particular, it affects the interests of those who fund the activity (taxpayers in the case of government); the citizens or consumers who benefit from the products or services acquired; businesses which supply the products or services; and also the economy as a whole, since effective purchasing can play an important role in promoting economic activity. The legal rules considered in this book are concerned with, and affect, all these different goups. Before considering these rules in detail it is proposed in the remainder of this introduction to highlight some of the main concerns and objectives behind the regulatory provisions.

---

[5] In the United Kingdom many of the enterprises studied have since been privatised, but most are subject to regulation in their private form: see further Chap. 9.

[6] The Atkins study, Vol. 5A, p. 26. This figure included non-tradeable and purchases in non-competition markets.

[7] *Setting New Standards: a Strategy for Government Procurement* (1995) Cm. 2840, at p. 2.

[8] *Ibid.*

From the perspective of those who fund the purchaser, control of expenditure is the primary concern. This arises, first, in deciding *what* to purchase, when decisions must reflect appropriate political or business priorities. (Should the government widen a road or build a new library?) Whilst, as explained in Chapter 2, legal rules impose some outside limits on the subject matter of government contracts – for example, local authorities may generally engage only in activities and projects authorised in their enabling legislation – determination of priorities between different projects here is largely a matter of the operation of the political process within a wide area of legal discretion.

Once a decision to spend funds on a particular project or service has been taken, the question arises of how to obtain value for money in providing the project or service. One issue here is whether these needs can be best met through "in-house" provision or by contracting out the work to the market (which will usually, although not invariably, mean the private sector). In both government and the private sector there has been an increasing move towards contracting out in recent years, either as a strategic decision, or because this is felt to offer the most efficient method of meeting government needs. In cases where the function is one traditionally carried out in-house, often a decision to contract out will be taken following a competition through competitive bidding between an existing in-house unit and potential outside providers. In the United Kingdom, as will be seen, the law has become involved in this process at local government level to ensure that the competition between the in-house and external bidders is fairly conducted – one of the few areas in which the law has played an important role in procurement in the United Kingdom. These rules are the subject of Chapters 12–14 of this book.

The pursuit of "best value" is also a key concern in designing the form of any contract and in choosing a provider to carry out the work. For larger contracts, both the public and private sectors have traditionally relied on competitive tendering, whilst for smaller contracts it is usual to seek informal quotes from a number of different providers. Traditionally, the practice of public bodies in implementing such procedures has tended to be more bureaucratic than that of the private sector, and, in particular, there has been a heavy reliance on compliance with general rules, monitored through a hierarchical structure, as a way of ensuring efficient purchasing. In some states many of the applicable rules – especially those governing tendering procedures – have been enacted, in a greater or lesser amount of detail, into law, and sometimes aggrieved firms, as well as other interested parties, are given a right to enforce the rules to ensure that they are complied with. This is the case with the United States, for example, where the government procurement system is based on a myriad of complex and technical legal provisions. This has not, however, been the tradition in the United Kingom, at least in central government, where rules designed to secure value for money have been imposed through administrative directions and guidelines from the Treasury rather than enacted in legislation.[9] Such rules as do exist in the United Kingdom for this purpose are noted in Chapter 2.

The complex and formal procurement structures found within government are sometimes explained by a simple reference to the importance of obtaining "value for taxpayers' money". This does not mean, however, that value for money is a more important objective in the public sector than in the private sector, nor that formal and bureaucratic purchasing is the best way of achieving this objective: it appears that often best value can be obtained most effectively by conferring a wide discretion on professional purchasers, as often occurs in private sector firms. The special nature of government procurement probably arises from a combination of factors. These include, for example, the absence of accountability to the market; the less professional approach traditionally adopted to the recruitment and development of purchasing personnel; the greater weight placed on ethical standards and fair treatment of providers (considered further below); and the perceived need in some cases to eliminate the influence of concerns "secondary" to best value such as political gain or national preference (also considered further below), which are more likely to arise in the public sector. The gap between government's traditional approach to purchasing and private sector "best practice" has widened even further in recent years with the increased private sector recognition of purchasing as a skilled profession and changes to procurement strategies – notably, the increased use of "partnering" (development of long-term relationship with trusted providers) to replace the adversarial tendering approach.

The government in the United Kingdom has, in procurement as in other areas, sought to learn from the private sector as far as possible, and has increasingly recruited procurement staff with private sector experience. The 1995 White Paper on procurement strategy, referred to above, shows a commitment to the development of central government procurement in line with best practice,[10] and places special emphasis on development of professional training and skills for government procurement personnel.[11] This indicates clearly that the way forward for obtaining value for money in government procurement is not seen in further legal regulation. In fact, whilst legal regulation may be appropriate as a first step to reform for states with an underdeveloped procurement system and which lack trained and experienced personnel,[12] it

---

[9] On central government purchasing see further Turpin, *Government Procurement and Contracts* (1989). Local authorities have been required to adopt their own standing orders governing competitive tendering, but even these rules are at a rather general level: see p. 29.

[10] *Setting New Standards*, above, p. 1.

[11] *Setting New Standards*, above, Chap. 5.

[12] The United Nations has sought to encourage such states to develop their procurements systems, including through legal regulations, by issuing a Model Law on public procurement for states wishing to adopt, or improve, their regulatory systems: see further p. 776. Another aim of the Model Law is to improve opportunities for such states to open up their procurement markets to outside states and to participate in international liberalisation agreements, for which legal regulation may be more necessary: see the discussion in the text below.

seems likely that to achieve value for money internally a move away from legal and bureaucratic controls is generally appropriate for a more advanced system. Even within less developed systems, it may be more useful to focus on training and the development of skills than on the development of rigid procedural controls. So far as the United Kingdom is concerned, however, the flexibility to develop best practice is limited by the requirement to follow strict legal rules for the award of major contracts which have been adopted by the European Community in order to open European markets, as explained below.

Apart from best value, another important concern in regulated procurement is the elimination of corrupt practices, such as acceptance of bribes in return for favours from procurement officials or nepotism. Such practices do, of course, affect the value for money objective itself. However, this is not the only concern raised, at least so far as public bodies are concerned: honesty and fairness in government activity can be perceived as independent values in their own right, and also important in upholding public confidence in government. This is explicitly recognised in the Government's 1995 White Paper on procurement strategy which refers to the importance of supporting ethical standards.[13] More cynically, the problem of corruption may receive more attention than it deserves in the government context because of the disproportionate political damage which small incidents of corruption can inflict on the administration and this may help to explain the traditionally bureaucratic nature of government purchasing. Similar concerns also make it important to avoid the appearance of unfairness or any conflict of interest and legal rules have sometimes been adopted to address these concerns.

The fair treatment of those doing business with government is also often regarded as an independent objective of procurement strategy and this objective has also been explicit acknowledged in the Government's 1995 White Paper.[14] To an extent this objective is consistent with and contributes to the attainment of best value: for example, providers who are fairly treated are more likely to participate in future competitions, and giving reasons for decisions, for example, may enable them to compete more effectively in future. However, this will not always be the case. There is some debate over how far the government can be expected to go in considering the interests of providers independently from the government's own interests, whether the standards expected of government in its dealing with firms should be higher than that expected of private businesses and whether the law should play a role in enforcing such standards. The view taken in this book is that higher standards should be maintained and that legal and political controls protecting the interests of citizens in general, such as judicial review and review by the Ombudsmen, should apply equally to procurement, although this is not

---

[13] *Setting New Standards*, above, note 7, para. 2.60.
[14] *Setting New Standards*, para. 2.60.

always the case at present. Related to the issue of fair treatment is that of fair and equal access to government business: the recent White Paper notes that competition is important not only as an aid to value for money "but because it provides fair access to work paid for by the taxpayer".[15]

Procurement policy also has a wider importance for economic strategy. In general, efficient purchasing by government and the utilities has the effect of promoting industrial growth and development, by encouraging competition and ensuring that the most competitive providers flourish in the market. Quite apart from its sheer size, regulated purchasing is important in this respect because of its dominance in many of the technology sectors, which are particularly important to the economy and where competition is of special importance for an efficient industry. However, whilst the objectives of obtaining best value and promoting economic development largely coincide so far as domestic industry is concerned, states have frequently sought to favour their own industry against that of other states, which may involve a compromise of best value. Further, the short-term economic gains of such an approach may be outweighed by the long-term disadvantages in terms of lack of efficiency and competitiveness which may arise where national industry is shielded from full competition; gains from this approach are in general cancelled out, at least, by similar policies followed by other states; and overall there is a net loss of welfare as a result of such policies. Even where states are aware of this and would prefer not to adopt a protectionist approach from an economic perspective, political considerations – the visibility of individual decisions to purchase from abroad – may lead governments to make protectionist decisions.

The main recent development in public procurement in the industrialised states has been the emergence of co-operative efforts by states to eradicate national protectionism, in order to maximise overall economic welfare. In this respect the lead has been taken by the European Community which has implemented a detailed internal procurement regime which seeks to eradicate protectionist purchasing within Europe. This has involved a requirement for all individual Member States, including the United Kingdom, to adopt legal rules on the award of major contracts in both the public sector and utilities sector, which seek to ensure fair treatment and opportunities for providers from throughout Europe. These rules, which are enforceable by providers as well as by the European Commission through the European Court, are the most significant legal rules on procurement in the United Kingdom and their implementation marks a major departure from the domestic tradition of non-legal control of procurement. The greater part of this book – Chapters 3–11, as well as parts of other chapters – comprises an analysis of these rules. As has already been noted above, the existence of these

---

[15] *Setting New Standards,* above, para. 2.54.

provisions reduces the flexibility of the government to follow best private sector practice, and the rules have been a source of frustration to some purchasers. However, this problem of protectionist purchasing marks an important distinction between the regulated and non-regulated sectors, and it is submitted that, despite the difficulties which these rules may cause, some regulation similar to that which is in place is justified, in order to deal with the problem. The Community is also now party to a number of agreements with third countries providing for mutual liberalisation of procurement through rules and procedures similar to those of the Community's internal market regime, and these are also enforceable in law against purchasers within the United Kingdom.

Finally, it may be noted that in the past, procurement has often been used as a tool to promote social policies, in particular by threatening to withhold contracts from firms which do not meet requirements set by government in fields such as equal opportunities and fair labour conditions. However, this use of procurement has now been largely curtailed as a side effect of the European Community's procurement regime, and by legislation adopted by the central government specifically to prevent local authorities using procurement in this way. This issue is examined more closely in Chapter 16.

CHAPTER 2

THE COMMON LAW AND STATUTORY FRAMEWORK

1. INTRODUCTION

The procurement contracts of the entities considered in this book are in principle subject to the ordinary private law of contract. Thus the ordinary private law rules of liability apply – for example, in determining whether a contract has been formed, whether a breach of contract has occurred and the remedies available for enforcing the contract – and disputes are resolved in the ordinary private courts. This position contrasts with that in France where many (although not all) government procurement contracts are designated as *contrats administratifs* and are subject to a conceptually distinct body of contract law, applied by special administrative courts.[1-2]

However, the public character of one of the parties may influence the approach of the courts in construing the parties' intentions, as is illustrated, for example, by the rules on warranty of authority, discussed below.[3-4] Further, there is a whole body of special rules, both under the common law and in legislation, which concern the procurement activity of public bodies and of bodies closely associated with government. In some cases these special provisions may affect the private law liability of the contracting parties – for example, the rules limiting capacity, which may render an agreement unenforceable against the government, and the rules on Crown immunities, which may affect the contractual remedies available to the other party to a Crown contract. It is with this special "public law" on procurement that this book is concerned.

As was noted in Chapter 1, today much of this special law is concerned with the procedures which public bodies and utilities must follow in awarding their procurement contracts, and most of this book is taken up with a discussion of the detail of the main legislation on award procedures. In this chapter, however, it is first necessary to outline the general "public law" framework for the procurement activities of these

---

[1-2] See Brown and Bell, *French Administrative Law* (4th ed., 1993), Chap. 6.
[3-4] See p. 23. On the other hand, in *Great Northern Railway v. Witham* (1873) L.R. 9 C.P. whilst the public character of one party was cited by the court the conclusion would have been the same in the case of private parties. See also the discussion of the cases on implied contracts governing the tendering process, discussed at pp. 37-40.

regulated entities, as well as to introduce the main areas of legislation which are examined in later chapters.

We will first consider the rules which affect the *subject matter* of procurement contracts, in particular the general capacity to make such contracts; the authority to conclude contracts; the rules governing Parliamentary appropriations; and the limitations on contracts imposed by competition law. We will then outline the legal constraints affecting the procurement *award process*, including both legislative rules (such as requirements to advertise contracts) and common law rules, notably the principles of judicial review and the implied contract which governs the tendering process. Finally, we will note briefly the privileges of the Crown so far as they affect procurement.

2. GENERAL LIMITATIONS ON THE SUBJECT MATTER OF PROCUREMENT CONTRACTS

(1) THE CAPACITY TO CONTRACT

With all contracts it is necessary to ensure (i) that the entity which is party to the contract has the legal capacity to make the contract and (ii) that the human agent(s) who purport to conclude the contract have the authority to enter into the contract on behalf of that entity. Capacity is considered in this section, and authority in section (2) below.

(a) CAPACITY OF THE CROWN AND CROWN AGENTS

(i) THE CROWN

In the field of contract, it was held in *The Bankers' Case*[5] (which concerned a contract to borrow money) that the Crown has all the powers of a natural person, including the power to enter into contracts. Thus it was concluded that the Crown could make a contract for any purpose without obtaining the approval of Parliament. The reasoning on which this case is based – that the Crown cannot be distinguished from the natural person of the monarch of the day – is now open to doubt,[6] but the existence of the Crown's general and unlimited contract power is itself generally accepted.[7]

---

[5] (1700) 90 E.R. 270.
[6] The alternative view is that the Crown in public affairs is a corporation distinct from the natural person of the monarch: see further, Arrowsmith, *Civil Liability and Public Authorities* (1992), at pp. 6–8.
[7] See also *J.E. Verrault v. Quebec* [1977] 1 S.C.R. 41; *Quebec v. Labrecque* [1977] 1 S.C.R. 1057; *New South Wales v. Bardolph* (1934) 52 C.L.R. 455 *per* Evatt J. at pp. 474–475; Turpin, *Government Procurement and Contracts* (1989), pp. 83–84; Hogg, *Liability of the Crown* (1989), at pp. 163–164; Aronson and Whitmore, *Public Contracts and Torts* (1982), pp. 187–188.

Parliament may, of course, restrict the scope of the Crown's powers by statute.[8] Where a statutory power to contract is conferred on the Crown the common law power will by implication be subsumed into the common law power,[9] and any restrictions governing the statutory power must thus be observed – they may not be evaded by recourse to the common law.[10]

(ii) CROWN AGENTS

Public authorities which are agents of the Crown, such as Ministers of the Crown and Crown corporations,[11] have *authority* to make contracts on behalf of the Crown in connection with their activities.[12] Do they also, however, have an independent *capacity* to make contracts?

There are three main possibilities:

(a) That Crown agents generally have no independent capacity to contract and thus cannot be liable themselves on any contract which they negotiate or award. On this view the Crown is the only entity which is party to the contract.

(b) That Crown agents have a capacity to undertake contractual liability towards the other party to the contract, who may thus sue the Crown agent where he has chosen to contract in his own name; but that the *primary* liability under the contract remains with the Crown.

(c) That Crown agents have the capacity to enter into contracts within the area of their jurisdiction in the same way as other non-natural persons (such as local authorities). In this regard Crown agents may choose to make contracts on behalf of the Crown, as its agent, should they wish, but may alternatively make contracts in an independent capacity to which the Crown is not party and for which the Crown bears no responsibility.

If either proposition (a) or (b) is correct, the question also arises of the principles of construction to be adopted in deciding who is party to the contract in any particular case.

Clearly Crown agents have no need in practice for a separate contractual capacity, since they may exercise the capacity of the Crown

---

[8] *Att.-Gen. v. De Keyser's Royal Hotel* [1920] A.C. 508.

[9] *De Keyser's Royal Hotel*, above; *C.O. Williams Construction v. Blackman* [1995] 1 W.L.R. 102, *per* Lord Bridge at p. 108. In *Williams* the Judicial Committee of the Privy Council held that the exercise of specific functions in a contract award procedure which were conferred upon the Cabinet of Barbados, involved the exercise of statutory power rather than the Crown's common law power and thus were made "under an enactment" for the purposes of judicial review under the Barbados Administration of Justice Act. It is submitted, however, that this does not mean that the power to contract is itself derived from the legislation and that the common law power is subsumed, but merely that the functions of *awarding* the contract are carried out in a statutory capacity where these functions are conferred by statute.

[10] *New South Wales v. Bardolph*, above, *per* Rich J. at 496.

[11] As to who is a Crown agent see Arrowsmith, *Civil Liability and Public Authorities* (1992), pp. 16–18.

[12] See pp. 21-22.

for the purpose of making any contracts which are appropriate for carrying out their functions: for example, if the Ministry of Defence wishes to purchase helicopters it may enter into a contract for this purpose on behalf of the Crown and so obtain the helicopters which it needs. However, some earlier decisions on this subject indicated that Crown agents – at least those which have corporate status – may have an independent capacity to contract and also that they are to be considered in the same way as private persons in deciding whether that capacity has been exercised (and on this basis are normally party to the agreement).[13] These decisions were prompted by the desire of the courts to evade the rule which used to apply that the Crown itself could be held accountable in contract only through the special petition of right procedure, which would not apply if the party to the contract were the Crown agent rather than the Crown itself. Whilst this rule has now been abolished the Crown still enjoys certain special priviliges and immunities in contract which are regarded by many as anomalous[14] and there is some support today for the view that the Crown agent should be considered as possessing an independent capacity *and* that the Minister and not the Crown should be presumed to be the contracting party, to allow the courts to avoid applying Crown immunities.[15]

However, such an approach was rejected by the House of Lords in *Town Investments v. Department of the Environment*[16] The question in issue was whether a lease was within the scope of legislation giving protection from rent increases, which applied only where the "tenant" and "occupier" were the same person. The Department of the Environment, which had responsibility for providing accommodation for the government, had negotiated the lease and the premises were occupied by another department. The landlord argued that the Minister of the Environment was the "tenant" and thus the tenant and occupier were different. The argument was based on a view that Ministers and the Crown are separate entities with a separate legal capacity, and that the relationship between them is one of principal and agent. It was argued that the Minister of the Environment could conclude the lease in his own name; that whether he had done so was to be determined by ordinary private law rules concerning construction of contracts; and that, applying these rules, the Minister and not the Crown had undertaken liability and was the "tenant".

In the leading judgment Lord Diplock, with whom Lord Edmund Davies agreed, rejected this view and concluded that acts done by

---

[13] See, in particular, *Graham v. Public Work Commissioners* [1901] 2 K.B. 781 and *International Railway Co. v. Niagara Parks Commission* [1941] A.C. 328, discussed further in Arrowsmith, *Civil Liability and Public Authorities* (1992), at pp. 56–57.

[14] See pp. 41–42.

[15] See, for example, Harlow, "'Public' Law and 'Private' Law: Definition without Distinction" (1980) 43 M.L.R. 241 at pp. 244–248; and the note by Wade (1991) 107 L.Q.R. 5.

[16] [1978] A.C. 359. The view that a Crown agent with corporate status may contract in an independent capacity was later stated by Dillon L.J. in *McLaren v. Home Office* [1990] I.R.L.R. 338, but *Town Investments* was not referred to.

Ministers are acts of the Crown, and that the Crown was the tenant in this case. Lord Kilbrandon reached the same conclusion. It is not clear whether these views were based on the premise that the Minister possesses no independent capacity to contract, and that there is a presumption in public law (which differs from private law rules of construction) that he does not intend to use such a capacity. However, the decision in any case appears inconsistent with the view that the Crown agent is *normally* the contracting party.

To ascribe an independent capacity to a Crown agent is an artificial device, and, whilst it has been done in other contexts (for example, to hold Ministers amenable to certiorari and prohibition), it is particularly unsatisfactory in relation to contract, where cases will turn upon the capacity in which the agent has chosen to act in that case.[17] It is submitted that the better view, a view which is consistent with *Town Investment*,[18] is that Crown agents do not normally have any independent capacity to contract at all, unless such a capacity is clearly and expressly provided by legislation.[19] The mere fact that a Minister has a statutory power to conclude a specific type of contract should not suffice: it is submitted that such provisions are generally concerned to confer *authority* on the agent to make contracts on behalf of the Crown.[20]

(b) BODIES WHICH ARE NOT CROWN AGENTS

(i) THE SCOPE OF THE POWER TO CONTRACT

Most public bodies, whether central or local, which are not Crown agents, have been created by statute and are usually given corporate identity. Such bodies are referred to as "statutory corporations". Such corporations possess only those powers specifically conferred upon them by legislation.[21] The principle applies as equally to contract as to other powers; thus they do not, like the Crown or natural persons, enjoy a general capacity to contract. Its application was recently, and famously, illustrated in the context of local government in *Hazell v. Hammersmith*

---

[17] See further Arrowsmith, "The Contractual Liability of the Crown and its Agents" (1990) 28 Osgoode Hall L.J. 572.

[18] The only other possible interpretation—that agents have a separate capacity but are presumed not to exercise it—has no merits at all: it does not avoid any immunities and creates unnecessary complexity.

[19] As, for example, in the National Health Service Act 1977, Sched. 5, para. 15(1) which provides that an authority may enforce obligations and incur rights as if it were a principal, even where acting on behalf of the Secretary of State.

[20] See further pp. 21–22. However, it should be mentioned that the government itself has taken the view that, even though the Crown is the employer, the relevant government department is a party to any contract of employment with a civil servant, a view which assumes that departments enjoy a capacity to contract: see Freedland [1995] P.L. 224 at pp. 230–231.

[21] *Att.-Gen. v. Manchester Corporation* [1906] 1 Ch. 643; *Att.-Gen. v. Fulham Corporation* [1921] 1 Ch. 44.

and Fulham L.B.C.[22] In this case Hammersmith had – like a number of other authorities at that time – entered into a number of "interest rate swap" transactions. These were, in essence, speculative financial transactions which would lead to a profit for the authority if interest rates moved down, but a loss if they should rise. In fact interest rates rose significantly and the authority stood to lose a sum amounting to several times its annual budget should the contracts be enforceable against it. The auditor sought a declaration to determine whether the contracts were within the power of the authority. The House of Lords held that they were not, since no statutory authority could be found for local authorities to conduct transactions of this type.

The precise scope of each body's power to contract depends on the details of the relevant legislation in each case. Sometimes a power to enter a contract for a very specific purpose is clearly and expressly conferred by the legislation. For example, the Local Authorities (Goods and Services) Act 1970 expressly authorises agreements between certain public bodies for the procurement of goods and services from each other. Such precise provisions are not essential, however: it has been stated that "whatever may fairly be regarded as incidental to, or consequential upon, those things which the legislative has authorised ought not (unless expressly prohibited) to be held by judicial construction, to be *ultra vires*".[23] Under this principle if an authority is authorised to carry out a particular activity or project – for example, the construction of roads or the hosting of a music festival – the authority will have the power to enter procurement contracts in connection with that activity, even though no express power of procurement is contained in the legislation. For local authorities, section 111 of the Local Government Act 1972 confers a power to do anything which is calculated to facilitate, or is conducive or incidental to, the discharge of its functions, which may be considered a statutory embodiment of the general common law principle.[24]

Any contract which is entered into other than to further an authorised activity is unlawful, as is illustrated by *Hazell v. Hammersmith*. In that case the House of Lords held that local authorities have no power to enter into an interest rate swap transaction in any circumstances. Many transactions, on the other hand, are of a type capable of being lawful but are unlawful because of the purpose for which they are made. Thus a contract for the purchase of computer equipment will be lawful if the equipment is intended for use in connection with the authority's lawful

---

[22] [1991] 2 W.L.R. 372. In *Hammersmith* itself, the authority was actually created by Crown charter pursuant to statute; but it was held that the statute only permitted the creation of corporations with the same limited powers as statutory local authorities, so that the same principles applied.

[23] *Att.-Gen. v. Great Eastern Railway* (1880) 5 App.Cas. 473 at p. 478.

[24] *Hazell,* above, *per* Lord Templeman at p. 554.

functions, but not if it is purchased specifically for a project which is itself *ultra vires*.[25]

(ii) THE LEGAL CONSEQUENCE OF AN UNLAWFUL AGREEMENT

Where a public body proposes or has concluded an unlawful agreement, an interested party with standing in public law will be able to restrain an authority from entering into the agreement or seek a declaration that it is unlawful. In the case of a local authority such a declaration may be sought by the auditor, as happened in the *Hammersmith* case, noted above.

A more problematic question is whether either of the parties may enforce the unlawful agreement once it has been made, and whether a third party may seek to prevent their going ahead.

So far as actions against the authority are concerned, in *Ashbury Carriage and Iron Co. v. Riche*[26] the House of Lords held, in the context of an unlawful agreement concluded by a private statutory corporation, that the agreement could not be enforced *against* the corporation. This principle was assumed to apply in the same way to unlawful agreements of public bodies,[27] and this was recently confirmed by Colman J. in *Credit Suisse v. Allerdale B.C.*[28] In this case Allerdale sought to build a swimming pool for the local population but was unable to finance the project without exceeding its borrowing limits. These it sought to evade by setting up a company to carry out the project and take out the loan, the council guaranteeing the loan. The company also undertook the development of time shares as part of the transaction with the intention that the sale of these would provide finance for the pool. The time shares failed to generate the expected revenue, however, and the company collapsed. The authority claimed that its own guarantee of the loan could not be enforced on the basis that the guarantee agreement was unlawful. The judge agreed that the agreement was unlawful, both because it was entered into for an improper purpose (to evade the restrictions on local authority borrowing requirements) and because it was "tainted" by the time share project which was wholly outside the authority's powers. He also accepted that this rendered the guarantee unenforceable against the authority. The judge specifically rejected an argument that a transaction which could on its face be lawful but which is unlawful because it is entered into for an improper purpose, or

---

[25] See, for example, *Credit Suisse v. Allerdale B.C.* judgment of May 6, 1994 (concerning a contract of guarantee), noted by Cane (1994) 111 L.Q.R. 514.

[26] (1875) LR 7 HL 653.

[27] It was applied by the Supreme Court of Canada in *Sydney v. Chappel Bros.* [1910] 43 S.C.R. 478. See also the English cases concerned with procedural *ultra vires* discussed at pp. 895–897 below.

[28] Judgment of May 6, 1994. This decision was followed in *Morgan Grenfell v. Sutton L.B.C.*, *The Times*, March 23, 1995, noted by Arrowsmith (1995) 4 P.P.L.R. CS134.

because it is irrational, should be held to be unenforceable against the authority only where the other party to it is aware of the unlawful purpose. He also rejected a suggestion that an agreement made in breach of public law is not to be treated as void automatically but that its enforceability should instead be subject to judicial discretion, thus allowing the court to uphold the transaction where the other party has acted in good faith.[29] The policy behind the approach in these cases is to uphold the interests which are protected by the limitations imposed by the law. In the case of a private company this is the interests of shareholders and investors who have contributed funds on the basis that they will be used for authorised purposes, whilst in public law the rule generally protects public funds from dissipation on unlawful ventures.

Applied in the context of procurement, this principle means that firms who have supplied a statutory authority with goods or services will be unable to enforce the agreement if it turns out to be unlawful. This will apply whether the illegality is obvious because of the nature of the project – for example, a contract to erect a leisure centre which the authority has no power to operate – or because the goods or services, whilst capable of being used for lawful purposes are destined for use in an unlawful venture. The provider will be unable to claim any damages for loss of profits, and may not claim under the contract itself for work done and goods delivered or expenditure already incurred.

The case law also indicates that no remedy is available in restitution for the value of work done pursuant to the agreement – for example, for work done on an unlawful construction project. The law of restitution generally permits a claim for work done for another, based on the principle of unjust enrichment, when it can be shown that this work constitutes a benefit and that it would be unjust for that other to retain that benefit. Where one party does work for another in the course of performing an agreement which turns out to be invalid, there is generally a claim for the reasonable value of the work.[30] Such work can be shown to constitute a benefit by virtue of the fact that it was requested by the plaintiff when the contract was made, and it has been held that it is unjust for the defendant to retain it when the consideration for the benefit (the plaintiff's own part of the bargain) has failed. However, the courts have denied such claims in the context of work done for public bodies in contravention of public law rules, where to allow a claim would infringe the policy behind the rule in question (that is, the same policy which leads the courts to deny that the contract itself is enforceable).[31]

---

[29] This argument was based on the view that the public law remedies are discretionary and thus private law rights which depend on public law issues should be subject to the same discretion.

[30] See Arrowsmith, "Ineffective Transactions and Unjust Enrichment: a Framework for Analysis" (1989) 9 L.S. 121.

[31] See further Arrowsmith, *Civil Liability and Public Authorities* (1992) at pp. 290–296; Arrowsmith, "Ineffective Transactions, Unjust Enrichment and Problems of Policy" (1989) 9 L.S. 307.

Thus in *Young v. Royal Leamington*[32] the House of Lords held that there could be no claim for work on the construction of a waterworks for a local authority, where this was done pursuant to a contract which was invalid for breach of a statutory requirement to fix the corporate seal to the contract. The purpose of the statutory requirement was to ensure that proper consideration was given to the decision to enter the contract, and to require the authority to pay for the works when the existence of such consideration was not evidenced by the seal would contravene the policy of the legislation. The same reasoning will apply *a fortiori* where the contract is one which the authority had no power to make at all, or which it had no power to make for the purpose in question.

With goods supplied under an invalid agreement it appears that the property will pass to the authority.[33] If the goods have not been consumed it would appear they should be restored, but if already consumed for an unlawful purpose[34] it would appear that, based on the reasoning in *Young*, no claim in restitution is possible: this would effectively require payment for something the authority is forbidden to purchase.

If the contract cannot be enforced *against* the authority it seems clear that where it is still executory it cannot be enforced *by* that authority since there is no consideration for the promise of the other party. Thus the authority may not require the provider to deliver the promised goods and services. If the authority has already made some payment under the contract this may generally be recovered under the law of restitution.[35] It has been stated that recovery is permitted only where there is a total failure of consideration which indicates that recovery is not possible where part of the work has been performed by the provider,[36] but this limitation is illogical and may be discarded by the courts.[37] Where the provider has incurred expenses in preparation or performance of the contract, arguably he may retain part of any sum paid to meet these expenses, on the basis of a defence of change of position.[38]

---

[32] (1883) 8 App.Cas. 517. In *Westdeutsche Bank v. Islington L.B.C.* [1994] 1 W.L.R. 938 a bank was permitted to recover payments made to an authority, but in this case the objections of public policy referred to in the text had no application.

[33] *Ayers v. South Australian Banking Co.* (1871) LR 3 PC 548; *Breckenridge Speedway v. The Queen* [1970] S.C.R. 175; *Stocks v. Wilson* [1913] 2 K.B. 335 (contract vitiated by the incapacity of a minor; although for a contrary view see *Sinclair v. Brougham* [1914] A.C. 398 at *per* Viscount Haldane at p. 414, *per* Lord Dunedin at p. 435 and *per* Lord Parker p. 441 and also *Westdeutsche Landesbank*, above, where it was accepted that property does not pass in equity. The better view is that property does pass since passage of property does not depend on the contract itself, and—as is illustrated by *Stocks v. Wilson*—is not generally vitiated by a mistake of "motive" (here, as to the validity of the contract) as opposed to a mistake of identity regarding the other party.

[34] If the goods have been purchased for an unlawful purpose but applied to a lawful purpose then there is no objection of policy to a restitutionary claim and recovery should be allowed.

[35] *Brougham v. Dwyer* (1913) 108 L.T. 504.

[36] Fibrosa Spolka Akyjna v. Fairbairn Lawson [1943] A.C. 32.

[37] See Arrowsmith, note p. 31, above at pp. 134–135. The point was left open in *Westdeutsche Landesbank*, above.

[38] This defence was recognised in *Lipkin Gorman v. Karpnale* [1991] 3 W.L.R. 10, for the case where the defendant has acted in reliance on a receipt.

The principle that unlawful contracts may not be enforced against a public authority is open to criticism because of the prejudice which this may cause to the other party to the contract. The interests which this party has arising from the agreement are generally protected by the private law of contract and it is submitted that such interests normally outweigh the general public interests which are embodied in the *ultra vires* rule. It is thus submitted that such agreements should be enforceable against the authority, provided that the other party to the contract does not know that the agreement is unlawful.[39] It can be noted that a similar solution has now been provided by statute for unlawful contracts made by private companies,[40] and also for contracts of loan with local authorities, which may be enforced even where not authorised by statute.[41] Further, in legislation imposing procedural requirements for public contracting it has generally been stated that breach of these requirements should not invalidate the contract, thus giving priority to the interests protected by the private law of contract.[42] Whilst the old rule in *Ashbury* has been applied recently in the High Court it is possible that the appeal courts may in future decline to apply the rule in public law.[42a] In this respect it is noteworthy that the House of Lords in *Hammersmith* did not pronounce upon the question of whether the contract was enforceable but confined itself to considering whether the contract was lawful in its substance.

Finally, if the contract is indeed unenforceable, it seems clear that an interested third party could seek a remedy to prevent the parties from proceeding with the agreement.

(2) AUTHORITY TO CONTRACT

(a) GENERAL PRINCIPLES

As indicated above, where a public body has capacity to make a particular contract the question still arises of whether a particular person, or persons, who purport to conclude the contract on behalf of that body have the authority to do so. This problem arises in all cases

---

[39] Of course, with an unlawful contract the court would decline to award specific performance or an injunction, but would limit the other party to a remedy in damages for loss of profits.

[40] Companies Act 1935, s.35(1), as amended by Companies Act 1989, s.108, and Companies Act 1985, s.122A, as inserted by Companies Act 1989, s.109.

[41] Local Government Act 1972, Sched. 13, para. 10.

[42] See further pp. 896–897. It can also be pointed out that where a corporation is created under the Crown's common law powers and exceeds the limitations on its powers to contract which are imposed by its charter, the contract in question is still enforceable against the corporation: *Sutton's Hospital Case* (1612) 77 E.R. 937.

[42a] Whilst in *Baroness Wenlock v. The River Dee Co.* (1885) 10 A.C. 355 the House of Lords held that the *Ashbury* principle was not limited to companies created under the Companies Act 1862, the House was considering only the limits on the power to contract, and not the effect of exceeding the statutory limitations.

where an artificial legal entity enjoys a capacity to contract: such an entity must always be represented in practice by natural persons. The starting point for both private[43] and public bodies[44] is to apply the ordinary rules of private law concerning authority to act for another.

Under these rules a purchaser is bound, first, if the agent has actual authority. This may be express – that is, expressly conferred by some individual or organ which has the power to confer such authority. Alternatively, it may be implied. Where a person has been appointed to an office – for example, head of purchasing – it is implied that that person has all the authority which normally goes with an office of that kind, unless the contrary is specifically provided. Where "Next Step" agencies have been created to carry out functions within the responsibility of a Minister the relevant agencies will no doubt have authority to make contracts for the purpose of carrying out those functions.

A contract may also bind an authority by virtue of the doctrine of ostensible authority. This doctrine renders a contract binding on an entity where that entity has represented to the other party that the person concluding it has authority to do so, even though no actual authority exists (for example, because the person concluding it has been privately told he may not conclude the type of transaction in question).

Officials or organs of a purchasing entity will possess express authority to the extent that this has been conferred upon them by statutory provisions. Express authority also exists where this has been specifically delegated by persons having authority to make such a delegation. Implied actual authority will exist where persons have been properly appointed to an office or organ of the authority to allow such persons to bind the authority in exercising functions normally associated with that office or organ, provided no specific instructions are issued to the contrary.[45] In both cases actual authority is negated, however, where legislation provides that the authority or organ in question is not authorised to bind the entity to certain acts: this, it is submitted, makes it legally impossible for any actual authority to be created. Thus, for example, if a statute states that a particular function of a local authority can be exercised only by the Chief Executive in person, then an individual officer could not bind the authority in carrying out the act in question under the doctrine of actual authority, even if the Chief Executive purported to delegate the authority to him.

Ostensible authority will exist where a representation is made to the other party to the contract by a person concerned with managing the relevant part of the purchaser's business[46] – for example, expressly telling the other party to the contract that a particular person is authorised to

---

[43] *Freeman and Lockyer v. Buckhurst Park Properties (Mangel)* [1964] 2 Q.B. 480.
[44] *Att.-Gen. for Ceylon v. A.D. Silva* [1953] A.C. 461; *North West Leicestershire D.C. v. East Midlands Association* [1981] W.L.R. 1396.
[45] *North West Leicestershire S.C.,* above.
[46] *Freeman and Lockyer,* above, *per* Lord Diplock at p. 506.

conclude contracts. In many cases there will be both ostensible and actual authority for a transaction: in particular, where a person is appointed to an offfice which normally carries authority to make certain purchases there will be both implied authority as explained above, and also ostensible authority since allowing the person to act in that office constitutes a representation to third persons that he has the usual authority of the office. Where actual authority exists there is no need to rely on ostensible authority. However, ostensible authority will be invoked where the usual implied authority of the office holder has been negated by express instructions, but these have not been communicated to the third party who deals with the individual.

It was suggested above that actual authority cannot exist where an officer is precluded by legislation from carrying out a particular trans-action. In this case it is probably also not possible to rely on the doctrine of ostensible authority. This can be deduced from the more general principle that estoppel cannot operate to hold a party to a representation where this is contrary to statute.[47] Thus in *Western Fish Products v. Penwith D.C.*[48] a planning officer represented to the plaintiff that planning permission would not be required for the plaintiff's proposed use of a factory since it was covered by an established user right. However, the Council to which the decision on this matter was entrusted by statute, concluded that permission was in fact necessary and refused to grant it. It was held that the earlier representation of the office could not bind the Council to permit the development, even if the Council had represented that the officer had power to act in this matter, since the delegation of authority to the officer was contrary to the statute. The same principle will apply in relation to the authority to conclude contracts.[49] The principle can be criticised, since it automatically gives primacy to the public interest reflected in the statutory provision to the detriment of the private interests of the party to whom the representa-tion has been made.[50] Arguably, in the case of representations relating to the scope of authority to contract, priority should generally be given instead to the private interests of the other party to the contract, and the contract should be enforceable by way of a damages claim, although not necessarily through specific performance or an injunction. The consid-erations applicable are exactly the same as those in favour of enforcing contracts where the contract is beyond the *capacity* of the entity concerned[51] – in both cases the question is whether private interests should be sacrificed in favour of the interest protected by the legislative rule which has been breached.

---

[47] See generally Craig, *Administrative Law* (3rd ed., 1994), Chap. 18.
[48] [1981] 2 All E.R. 204.
[49] See Hilliard (1976) 54 Can Bar Rev. 401.
[50] See Craig, above.
[51] See pp. 15–18.

(b) THE CROWN AND CROWN AGENTS

Some special consideration is required of the authority of Crown servants and agents to bind the Crown.

First, it is necessary to consider how the principles of agency apply to government Ministers. A ministerial office may be created at common law or by statute. Whichever is the case, Ministers generally have many statutory powers conferred on them in their own name, rather than in the name of the Crown. It is not clear to what extent the acts of Ministers may bind the Crown in contract.

The widest view is that *any* contract made by a Minister in a public capacity will bind the Crown. Some support for this approach can be found in dicta in the House of Lords in *Town Investments v. Department of the Environment*[52] (the facts of which were discussed above[53]) stating that a Minister has no legal identity separate from the Crown. In particular, Lord Simon compared the position of the Crown and a Minister with that of the body and a hand[54]: all acts of the hand are by necessity also acts of the body. This could apply in relation to the doctrine of authority to suggest that any act of the Minister is automatically an act of the Crown. However, this approach has not been adopted in other Commonwealth jurisdictions, which have for this purpose treated a Minister as a separate legal person who must be vested with actual or ostensible authority to act.[55] These ordinary agency concepts have also been applied in the United Kingdom to servants of the Crown who are not Ministers.[56]

Applying these private law principles it is clear that express actual authority exists where the contract relates to functions conferred upon the agent by statute.[57] It was suggested above that such provisions do not confer on the agent any independent *capacity* to make contracts; thus, it is submitted, that in the area of contract the sole function of such provisions is to confer *authority* on such entities to conclude agreements on behalf of the Crown.[58]

It is unclear if there is any room for the doctrine of usual authority in relation to Crown agents, at least those whose functions are in general defined by statute. It appears from the Privy Council decision in *Attorney General for Ceylon v. A.D. Silva*[59] that where an agent's functions are set out in statute then, prima facie, the statute is to be regarded as laying

---

[52] [1978] A.C. 359.
[53] See p. 12.
[54] [1978] A.C. 359 at p. 400.
[55] *J.E. Verrault v. Quebec* [1971] A.C.R. 41 and *R. v. C.A.E. Industries* (1985) 5 W.W.R. 481 (Canada); *Meates v. Att.-Gen.* [1979] 1 N.Z.L.R. 415 (New Zealand).
[56] *Att.-Gen. for Ceylon v. A.D. Silva* [1953] A.C. 461.
[57] *A.D. Silva*, above.
[58] Such statutes confer capacity on agents to exercise the functions in question in their own name (as *persona designata*); however, the contractual capacity which these persons enjoy in carrying out these activities is that of the Crown .
[59] Above, note 56.

down in an exhaustive manner the scope of the matters in relation to which that person may contract on behalf of the Crown. That case concerned a sale by a customs officer, who was an agent of the Crown, of some silver plate which, unknown to him, belonged to the Crown itself. Under the customs legislation he had the power to sell certain property but this authority did not extend to the sale of Crown property. It was held that the purported sale did not bind the Crown: there was no authority in the legislation, and no ostensible authority. The Privy Council rejected the contention – which seems to have been based on some concept of usual authority – that the officer had the authority to bind the Crown simply by virtue of his position as a customs officer. On the other hand, in the New Zealand case of *Meates v. Attorney General*,[60] it was suggested, although without any specific discussion, that a Minister could enjoy usual authority. It is submitted that the approach in *A.D. Silva* is to be preferred. The concept of usual authority is inappropriate for the unique "offices" of public bodies, the scope of which is generally defined by statute.

However, although relevant statutory provisions should be regarded as prima facie exhaustive of the scope of an agent's authority, it is submitted that this may be extended without the need of further legislation, provided this is done expressly by action by the Crown. This seemed to be contemplated in *A.D. Silva*, where it was said that authority could be conferred by statute "or otherwise".[61] It is not clear who or what is the proper organ of government for conferring such authority: it might be argued that an Order in Council or at least a decision of the Cabinet is necessary, or alternatively that a decision of the Prime Minister or other relevant Minister would suffice. In Canada it was held by the federal court in *R. v. CAE Industries*[62] that the cabinet could confer authority on a government Minister without the need for an Order in Council.

It was accepted in *A.D. Silva* that agents of the Crown, like other public officials, may make arrangements which bind the Crown under the doctrine of ostensible authority. Where a representation is made that a person has authority beyond that given in statute, such a representation will be binding only if given by those with the responsibility for the area of activity in question (that is, who could, if they choose, confer express authority on the agent in accordance with the principles outlined above). There is no difficulty with this if, as indicated, the statutory provisions are considered merely to empower the agent and not to impose any actual restrictions on his activities. (Where legislation does purport to impose restrictions, on the other hand, the doctrine of ostensible authority cannot be used to evade those restrictions, as was explained above.)

---

[60] Above, note 55.
[61] Above, note 56, at p. 479.
[62] Above, note 55.

(c) BREACH OF WARRANTY OF AUTHORITY

In general, where a servant purports to contract for a principal but exceeds the scope of his authority to do so, he is liable to the other party to the agreement for breach of an implied warranty that he has the authority to bind the principal. It was held in *Dunn v. MacDonald*,[63] however, that no such warranty of authority was to be implied in the case of a servant of the Crown (although he may make himself liable by express terms should he wish). This different rule for Crown service was justified on the ground that without such a rule persons would be unwilling to act as agents for the Crown. The rule has been criticised, for it is difficult to see why the Crown should be treated differently from any other public authority.[64]

(d) PERSONAL LIABILITY

When an agent makes a contract on behalf of a principal there is a presumption that the agent does not also undertake personal liability. This also applies to public servants.[65]

(3) THE RULE ON PARLIAMENTARY APPROPRIATIONS

All expenditure by the Executive is required to be authorised by Parliament.[66] Funds are "appropriated" by Parliament for different areas of government activity in the annual Appropriation Acts which cover expenditure in the year ahead, with supplementary acts if required.[66a] In practice, appropriations are voted to cover broad areas of activity rather than specific projects or items. Where expenditure is to be made under a contract it is sufficient that its purpose falls under one of the general heads in the appropriations; it is not necessary that funds be appropriated specifically for that contract.[67]

Some dicta in early cases appeared to suggest that an absence of an appropriation at the time the contract is made for the amount which is

---

[63] [1897] 1 Q.B. 555.
[64] For a possible narrower explanation of the decision see Arrowsmith, *Civil Liability and Public Authorities* (1992) at p. 71.
[65] *MacBeath v. Haldimand* (1786) 99 E.R. 1036; *Gidley v. Lord Palmerston* (1822) 129 E.R. 1290.
[66] *Auckland Harbour Board v. R.* [1924] A.C. 318 at 326–7.
[66a] On proposed reforms of this system see the White Paper, *Better Accounting for the Taxpayer's Money*.
[67] *New South Wales v. Bardolph* (1934) 52 C.L.R. 455. Where expenditure under a contract is partly attributable to some "secondary" consideration rather than for the primary object of the contract (for example, where additional cost is incurred under a defence contract in order to support a deprived region of the country rather than purchasing from the best value provider) it is not clear whether such expenditure should be set off against sums appropriated for the secondary purpose rather than those appropriated for the general subject matter of the contract.

due under the contract would render the contract null and void.[68] However, in *New South Wales v. Bardolph*[69] it was held that the absence of an appropriation cannot affect the initial validity of a contract, and this view is generally considered to represent the law in the United Kingdom.[70] Any other view would clearly be impractical since the funds are appropriated each year for payments falling due that year, whilst contracts often extend for many years. If sums needed to be appropriated for the whole contract at the time it is made, this would involve significant changes in Parliamentary practice. Further, appropriations made at the start of the contract could well be spent on other projects in the same field before the amount under the contract becomes due, so that a rule requiring all money to be appropriated at the start would not be helpful.

What is the position if there is no appropriation to cover contract expenditure at the time it falls due? In *New South Wales v. Bardolph* the court stated that the contract would not be enforceable but did not explain precisely what was meant by this. If a judgment were given against the Crown, it would appear that it would in principle be unlawful[71] to meet that judgment in the absence of an appropriation, and that any sum which was paid out could be recovered from the recipient in an action in restitution.[72] Turpin has suggested that in such a case the courts should still give judgment against the Crown in the ordinary way, on the assumption that funds will be made available, unless there is clear evidence that Parliament does not intend to make such funds available. In fact there is no good reason to refuse to give a judgment even where it is clear that funds will be denied; judicial decisions should not be affected by speculation about the future conduct of Parliament.

Hogg has argued that in any case in the United Kingdom section 25 of the Crown Proceedings Act, which places an obligation on the Crown to meet all judgment debts, constitutes a continuing statutory appropriation for all such debts.[73] If this is correct, once any judgment is given an appropriation comes into existence under section 25, and the position of the other party to the contract is not affected at all by the absence of an appropriation.

In practice, appropriations do not cause problems, first because it will rarely arise that a contract payment is not covered and, secondly because, should this be the case, the money will generally be voted by Parliament.

---

[68] *Churchward v. R.* (1865) L.R. 1 Q.B. 173 *per* Shee J. at p. 209; *Commercial Cable Co. v. Newfoundland* [1916] 2 A.C. 610 *per* Viscount Haldane at p. 617.

[69] Above, note 67.

[70] See, for example, Hogg, *Liability of the Crown* (2nd ed. 1989), at pp. 164–166, Street, *Government Liability* (1953) at p. 91; Turpin, *Government Procurement and Contracts* (1989) at pp. 91–94.

[71] There could in any case be no execution against the Crown or attachment of the debt since this is the general rule in proceedings against the Crown: Crown Proceedings Act 1947, s.25(4).

[72] *Auckland Harbour Board v. R.* [1924] A.C. 318.

[73] Hogg, *Liability of the Crown* (2nd ed., 1989), at pp. 164–166.

(4) FETTERING OF DISCRETION BY CONTRACT[74]

It is a general principle of public law that a public body must retain the freedom to exercise its discretionary powers as required from time to time in the public interest, and one aspect of this rule is that it may not fetter by contract its discretion to act in future. For example, in *Ayr Harbour Trustees v. Oswald*[75] harbour trustees, appointed for the purpose of acquiring land to develop and improve a harbour, covenanted with the former owner of a piece of land which they had acquired not to obstruct his access to the harbour from the land which he retained. This was held to be an invalid fetter on the exercise of the trustees' statutory power to develop the harbour land.

Of course, any contract limits future freedom of action. However, it is clear that not all contracts are prohibited, since the ability to enter binding contracts (including procurement contracts) is essential in order for authorities to carry out their functions. The rule on fettering by contract has thus developed to allow authorities to make, as far as possible, those contracts which are useful, whilst prohibiting those which *unreasonably* interfere with their discretion. The question of which contracts are permitted is resolved, essentially, by weighing up the utility of particular types of contract against the detriment of the particular fetter on discretion.

As to whether procurement contracts may be affected by this doctrine, it was stated by Rowlatt J. in the case of *The Amphitrite*[76] that the doctrine does not apply to a "commercial contract" as opposed to an assurance as to what the government's executive action would be in the future. This might indicate that the doctrine does not apply to procurement contracts. Procurement contracts may in practice fetter the government's powers to act on important issues of public interest – for example, a contract could bind the government to a major and expensive weapons system which has now become obsolete. However, it is submitted that the balance of interests involved suggests that all procurement contracts should be regarded as outside the doctrine since the likelihood of interference with future discretion is unlikely and the advantages of holding such contracts fully effective in all cases considerably outweigh the disadvantages of the remote possibility of a conflict. In practice the central government includes in its major supply contracts clauses – referred to as "termination for convenience clauses" – which allow it to cancel the contract at any time subject to the payment of certain compensation.[77]

---

[74] See generally Mitchell, *The Contracts of Public Authorities* (1954); Street, *Governmental Liability* (1953) Chap. 3; Rogerson, "On the Fettering of Public Powers" [1971] P.L. 288; Turpin, *Government Procurement and Contracts* (1989), pp. 85–90; Arrowsmith, *Civil Liability and Public Authorities* (1992), pp. 72–78; Craig, *Administrative Law* (3rd ed., 1994), pp. 699–707.

[75] (1883) 8 A.C. 623.

[76] *Rederiaktiebolaget Amphitrite v. R. (The Amphitrite)* [1921] 3 K.B. 500, at p. 503.

[77] See Turpin, *Government Procurement and Contracts* (1989), pp. 243–246.

(5) LIMITATIONS ON THE POWER TO "CONTRACT OUT" GOVERNMENT FUNCTIONS

Even where the government has the power to carry out a particular activity it may not have the power to engage an independent contractor to carry out that activity on its behalf. This is particularly relevant to statutory powers to provide public services or to make decisions or to take an action which directly affects members of the public (such as collecting and enforcing taxes), where sometimes there is an express or implied requirement that the power is to be carried out only by a specific person, or persons, or body designated by the statute. This will preclude authorities from engaging an outside provider to perform the function in question.

However, in support of the general presumption which the government has adopted in favour of contracting out the performance of government functions wherever this appears more efficient than carrying out such functions in-house, Parliament has recently enacted the Deregulation and Contracting Out Act 1994. *Inter alia*, this Act provides for the removal of legal obstacles to contracting out.

The Act[78] operates by allowing for the possibility of a Ministerial order to authorise the contracting out of most public functions, including in those cases where this is at present subject to legal obstacles. For statutory functions of Ministers and office holders[79] such orders are provided for in section 69 of the Act, whilst for functions of local authorities[80] they are provided for by section 70.[81] The order may authorise contracting out of the whole of the function or merely a specified part, and may relate to the function in general or merely to specified areas.[82] The possibility of contracting out may be made subject to specified conditions.[83] Several orders have already been made pursuant to these provisions authorising contracting out of, for example, certain functions of the Official Receiver[84]; functions of the Registrar of Companies and of the Secretary of State relating to company registration[85]; and various functions of the Secretary of State for Transport which relate to highways.[86]

---

[78] See further Craig, *Administrative Law* (3rd ed., 1994), pp. 734–738; Department of Trade and Industry, *Deregulation and Contracting Out Act 1994: an Explanatory Guide* (November 1994); Freedland, "Privatising *Carltona*; Part II of the Deregulation and Contracting Out Act 1994" [1995] P.L. 21.

[79] These terms are defined in Deregulation and Contracting Out Act 1994, s.79(1).

[80] As also defined in Deregulation and Contracting Out Act 1994, s.79(1).

[81] Procedure for the orders is set out in Deregulation and Contracting Out Act 1994, s.7. Where orders are made authorising contracting out of functions of an office holder that person must be consulted (s.69(3)), whilst with orders relating to functions of local authorities the Minister must in England and Wales consult "appropriate" representatives of local authorities: s.70(3).

[82] Deregulation and Contracting Out Act 1994, ss.69(4) and 70(4).

[83] Deregulation and Contracting Out Act 1994, ss.69(4) and 70(4).

[84] Contracting Out (Functions of the Official Receiver) Order 1995, S.I. 1995 No. 1386.

[85] Contracting Out (Functions in Relation to the Registration of Companies) Order 1995, S.I. 1995 No. 1013.

[86] Contracting Out (Highways Functions) Order 1995, S.I. 1995 No. 1986.

Certain functions, however, are wholly excluded from the possibility of contracting out under these provisions; these are cases where for policy reasons it is thought appropriate that full control and responsibility for performance of the function must be retained in-house. These exclusions, set out in section 71, are as follows:

(i) Where the exercise of the function would constitute the exercise of jurisdiction of a court or tribunal exercising the judicial power of the state;

(ii) Where the exercise or failure to exercise the function would necessarily interfere with or affect the liberty of an individual;[87]

(iii) The exercise of powers or rights of entry, search or seizure of property (with the exception of certain powers to enforce taxes, charges etc., which are set out expressly in section 71(3));[88]

(iv) The power or duty to make subordinate legislation.[89]

In the case of functions contracted out under the Act's provisions, the contract must be limited to ten years, and the contract period must always be specified.[90] Further, it is provided that the contract may be rescinded at any time by the public authority letting the contract.[91] However, it is expressly provided in section 73(2) that in such a case (or where the Minister himself revokes the order authorising the function to be contracted out) the authority is to be treated as repudiating the contract. Thus the provider's private law rights to sue for damages for non-performance of the contract by the public body will not be affected by the decision to override the contract in the public interest.

The possibility of contracting out many of the functions potentially subject to this provision gives rise to some concern over whether there will be adequate protection given to citizens whose interests are affected by the function in question – for example, whether judicial review will be available against the private service provider. Such issues also arise with other contracted-out functions. These concerns are addressed in Chapter 12, which considers general issues relating to contracting out versus in-house provision.[92]

(6) LIMITATIONS IMPOSED BY COMPETITION LAW

In awarding procurement contracts public bodies, like private firms, must ensure that such contracts do not infringe the restrictions imposed by competition law. So far as domestic law is concerned, agreements to

---

[87] With the exception of functions of the official receiver attached to a court: s.71(2).
[88] With the exception of functions of the official receiver attached to a court: s.71(2).
[89] As defined in Interpretation Act 1978 (Deregulation and Contracting Out Act 1994, s.79(1)).
[90] Deregulation and Contracting Out Act 1994, ss.69(5)(a) and 70(4).
[91] Deregulation and Contracting Out Act 1994, ss.69(5)(b) and 70(4).
[92] See further pp. 626–630.

purchase all or a large part of a requirement from a particular provider for a long period might potentially constitute an anti-competitive practice under section 2(1) of the Competition Act 1980.[93] The rules under the Act only cover conduct "in the course of a business", but it is expressly stated that the provisions apply to local authorities, so that the procurement activities of these bodies are clearly covered.[94] It might be suggested that the requirement for a "course of conduct" precludes the application of the rules to a single contract, but it is submitted that the continued application of a contract over a period of time would suffice. As to which contracts may be caught by the Act, this will no doubt depend on the exact nature and duration of the contract, the nature of the product market, and the significance of the contract for the market as a whole, as well as the method by which the contracting partner was selected.[95]

If it appears that a contract may be caught by the Act the Director General of Fair Trading (DGFT) may launch an investigation to determine if this is the case and, if it is, may refer the matter to the Monopolies and Mergers Commission. This body may in turn, if it considers there may be harm to the public interest, request the DGFT to negotiate an undertaking for the entity to desist. Ultimately, the Secretary of State has a power under section 10 of the Act to prohibit the practice and order the entity to remedy any adverse effect on the public interest.

Where the agreement has an appreciable effect on trade within the European Community the agreement may also infringe Article 85 E.C., in which case the agreement is automatically void and sanctions may be imposed.[96]

A procurement agreement might also potentially infringe the common law doctrine of restraint of trade when it is either unreasonable in view of the public interest, or unreasonable as between the parties.[97]

3. CONTRACT AWARD PROCEDURES

(1) INTRODUCTION

As noted in Chapter 1, there are a variety of interests involved in the contract award process, either relating to the concerns of particular

---

[93] On these provisions see further Whish, *Competition Law* (3rd ed., 1993), especially Chap. 4. The Director General of Fair Trading has found the Act to cover exclusive concession arrangements in certain cases: see *British Railways Board/Brighton Taxis*, OFT, 24/11/82; *British Railways Board/Godfrey Davis*, OFT, 9/2/83; *British Airports Authority*, OFT, 22/2/84. According to the Office of Fair Trading, no complaints relating to ordinary procurement contracts had been made at the time of writing, so that the potential application of the Act here remains untested.

[94] Competition Act 1980, s.2(8).

[95] See *British Airports*, above, where the existence of competition in the selection process was said to be a relevant factor.

[96] On Article 85 E.C. see further pp. 95–99. Similar rules apply under the European Economic Area Agreement.

[97] See Whish, above, pp. 140–141 and pp. 575–576.

individuals or to the general public interest. To deal with these concerns the United Kingdom has adopted some legislation which is either specific to public bodies or (in the case of the "utilities" rules deriving from Community law) is justified by reference to the special privileged position of the purchaser.[98-99] This legislation is outlined in section (2) below. The most significant provisions are dealt with in detail in subsequent chapters of this book. In addition, principles developed by the common law may be invoked to protect the interests of firms involved in contract award procedures and these are examined in sections (3)–(4). Finally, section (5) notes the possible role of the government ombudsmen in relation to procurement.

(2) LEGISLATION GOVERNING AWARD PROCEDURES

As noted in Chapter 1, some states have sought to promote value for money and other interests which are affected by the procurement process through legal regulation, but this has not been the traditional approach in the United Kingdom. However, there is some limited legislation on these issues.

So far as value for money is concerned, local authorities are required under section 135(2) of the Local Government Act 1972 to make their own standing orders for use of competitive procedures in the award of larger procurement contracts. The nature of the procedures and the thresholds above which they will apply is for authorities to determine, although it is expressly stated that thresholds may be set below which competition is not required. Such procedures have in practice generally been based on models produced by the Department of the Environment.

There is also legislation on competition in the particular area of local authority waste disposal. This is an activity which the authority may not undertake itself but is required to contract out.[1] So ensuring that the body regulating waste disposal and the waste disposal operator are not the same person. However, the authority is permitted to form a company in which it is a shareholder to bid for the contracts. To ensure there is no discrimination in favour of the local authority company, and to attract competition, section 51 of the Environmental Protection Act 1990 requires contracts for the keeping, treatment or disposal of controlled waste to be awarded in accordance with a procedure set out in Part II of

---

[98-99] See p. 56.

[1] Environmental Protection Act 1990, s.32. See further Rees, "Section 51 of the Environmental Protection Act 1990: the Impact on Waste Disposal Arrangements in the Public Sector" (1995) 4 P.P.L.R. CS106. Authorities are not excused from complying with the provisions by the fact of the Secretary of State's approval for setting up a local authority company in a particular form pursuant to approval requirements under other provisions of the Act: *R. v. Avon County Council, ex p. Terry Adams, The Times,* January 20, 1994.

Schedule 2 to the Act. This requires the authority to invite tenders through at least two trade publications and to allow a reasonable time for response,[2] and also contains provisions relating to the ready availability of specifications.[3] At least four of those responding must be invited to bid (or all those interested, if fewer than four respond). The procedure for selecting the provider following receipt of tenders is not prescribed in detail, but it has been held that the contract must be awarded "in consequence" of the tendering procedure.[4] This entails certain implied requirements: for example, that an authority may not choose a bidder whose initial tender does not comply with significant requirements of the tendering procedure,[5] or the contract specifications (such as those concerning the service to be provided).[6] It is not clear whether authorities may engage in post tender negotiations prior to selection, to allow those providers to revise and improve their bids (for example, on price);[7] but most contracts subject to the EPA are in any case subject to the European Community procurement rules, which probably prohibit such negotiations.[8] The authority's control over the bidder is to be disregarded,[9] and authorities must frame contract terms

---

[2] Environmental Protection Act 1990, Sched. 2, para. 20.

[3] *Ibid.*

[4] *Mass Energy v. Birmingham City Council*, September 3, 1993: *R. v. Avon County Council, ex p. Terry Adams, The Times*, January 20, 1994.

[5] Terry Adams, above, holding that the authority could not have regard to a qualification in a provider's bid stating that the authority must accept that provider's bids for all six contracts to be awarded in the procedure, or for none at all, where the rules of the tendering procedure provided that each contract was to be treated as distinct. Such a prohibition on accepting non-responsive bids also exists under the European Community procurement rules (see pp. 234–235), which also now apply to most contracts which are subject to the EPA. It is suggested in Chap. 6, however, that under the European rules an authority may, if it chooses, permit a bidder to correct its bid to bring the bid into compliance, and it is submitted that it is desirable to construe the tendering procedure under the EPA in the same manner. It is also suggested in Chap. 6 that under the E.C. rules authorities should be able to waive certain *minor* formalities, and again it is submitted that the same principle should apply in construing the EPA. It can be noted that in *Mass Energy*, above, Scott L.J. suggested that an authority could give a bidder an extension of time for submission of a bid, something which probably is not, however, allowed under the E.C. rules, since adherence to the time limit is a requirement deriving from express provisions of the legislation (see p. 235).

[6] *Mass Energy*, above. The Court of Appeal in *Terry Adams* held that an authority may negotiate changes to the specifications with a winning provider *after* that firm has already been selected in accordance with the rules of the tendering procedure—something which is probably also permitted under the European rules (see pp. 249–250). However, under both the EPA and European rules any such change is subject to an obligation to readvertise the contract if the change in specifications is substantial: see Chap. 11, on the European rules, and the judgment of Ralph Gibson L.J. in *Terry Adams*, indicating that there is a breach of the obligation to advertise the nature of the work if the changes made are such as may affect the decision of particular providers on whether or not to bid for the contract.

[7] In *Mass Energy*, above, Scott L.J. expressed the view that such negotiation is permitted with any provider, provided that that provider's bid complies with the contract specifications; but Glidewell L.J. confined his comments on the permissibility of negotiations to the case where the successful provider has already been selected and negotiations are carried out to improve the terms of the winning bid.

[8] See pp. 247–249.

[9] Environmental Protection Act 1990, Sched. 2, para. 21.

and conditions to avoid "undue discrimination" in favour of one "description" of waste contractor over another (whether or not the favoured provider is a local authority company).[10] There are no express provisions on award criteria, although where the contract also falls within the European Community legislation the European rules on award criteria will apply.[11]

For local government there are also some legislative provisions to regulate conflicts of interest. This is necessary not merely to prevent corruption[12] or other conduct which might prejudice value for money, but also to secure the appearance of fairness which is itself an important concern. So far as elected members of the Council are concerned, section 94(1) of the Local Government Act 1972 provides that any member with a pecuniary interest (direct or indirect)[13] in a contract or proposed contract, who is present at a meeting where this contract is the subject of consideration, must disclose the interest at the meeting as soon as practicable.[14] The member may then take no further part in the consideration or discussion of the contract.[15] Under section 94(2) failure to comply with section 94(1) is a criminal offence, unless the member can prove he did not know the matter was the subject of consideration. Section 105 of the same Act applies these same principles, with slight modifications, to persons who are members of local authority committees and are present at committee meetings where contracts are discussed. Section 117 further requires any officer of the council to declare – in writing and as soon as practicable – any direct or indirect

---

[10] Environmental Protection Act 1990, Sched. 2, para. 18. It is submitted that discrimination occurs where measures favour one type of firm above another and they cannot be justified on commercial grounds relating to the contract. It has been held that discrimination is "undue" where its effect "was such that it was likely to have had a significant effect upon the competitive tendering for the contract which the statute requires": *Terry Adams*, above, *per* Ralph Gibson L.J. In this case it was held in breach of this provision to formulate the contract terms in such a way as to require use of assets which were in practice available only to one provider, where this could have been avoided.

[11] See pp. 236–247. It was held in *Terry Adams*, above, that an express provision in EPA, Sched. 2, para. 19, permitting the inclusion of contract terms relating to the minimisation of pollution and the recycling of waste, does not preclude authorities from taking into account such matters as *relative* criteria for evaluating bids. The court also indicated in this case that it would not interfere with the authority's own judgment in balancing cost with environmental concerns. Consideration of environmental factors as criteria for award may, however, be limited under the European Community rules: they may not be considered unless they relate to the actual subject matter of the contract: see pp. 237–239.

[12] On corruption in local government contracting, which seems not to be too widespread in the United Kingdom, see Cirell and Bennett, "Fraud in Public Sector Contracting" (1995) 139 Sol.J. 38.

[13] On what counts as an interest for this purpose see L.G.A. 1972, s.95 which lists (non-exhaustively) certain matters caught by the provision.

[14] s.96 provides for the possibility of a general disclosure of interests.

[15] For the possibility for the removal of the disability, however, see L.G.A. 1972, s.97. s.94(4) also states that authorities may provide in standing orders for the exclusion of the member in question from the meeting, but this is up to each authority and is not required by the legislation.

pecuniary interest in a contract or proposed contract of the authority or one of its committees, where it comes to his knowledge that he has such an interest. This applies regardless of any involvement in the actual award or administration of that contract. Section 117 also makes it a criminal offence to accept any fee or reward other than the officer's proper remuneration.

Failure to implement efficient procurement procedures by local government could also be a breach of the general "fiduciary duty" owed to ratepayers and taxpayers.[16] However, given the current prevalence in the private sector of partnering arrangements, as opposed to competitive tendering, as a method of achieving value for money,[17] failure to use competitive tendering should not necessarily constitute a breach of this duty.

At central government level, the value for money objective has been promoted mainly through advice, guidance and directions from the Treasury, through the Treasury's Central Unit on Purchasing.

Apart from the specific provisions on competition under the Environmental Protection Act, the competition and conflict of interest provisions described above have existed in a similar form for many years. As was noted in Chapter 1 the most significant body of law now, however, is that which implements the procurement rules laid down by the European Community. The aim of this legislation is not the same as that of most domestic legislation in the Member States, which is concerned with value for money in a domestic context; rather, the Community regime seeks to open up opportunities for cross-border competition. Thus this legislation covers only those contracts with a value significant enough to create cross-border interest: for example, with works contracts the threshold is 5 million ECUs, which is far above the level for regulation of works contracts in most domestic systems. It is also concerned only with those aspects of award procedures which are particularly significant for non-domestic providers (such as requirements for Europe-wide advertisement) or which require regulation in order to prevent authorities from disguising discriminatory decisions (as with the detailed rules on award criteria) and does not contain rules which might be expected in domestic systems concerned with value for money, such as obligations to assess the financial status of bidders or to obtain performance bonds. However, the basic rules on the use and conduct of competitive tendering procedures do to a large extent overlap with those which are characteristic of domestic "value for money" systems.

In practice, it can be doubted whether the rules will have much effect on participation by non-domestic firms in many of the fields to which they apply.[18] Their main effect may thus be to sharpen tendering practice

---

[16] On this see further Craig, *Administrative Law* (3rd ed., 1994), pp. 435–438.
[17] See further pp. 290–292.
[18] See pp. 71–76.

for the benefit of domestic interests and domestic providers in cases where this was needed or, according to one perspective, to restrict and straitjacket the efforts of some purchasers to achieve value for money through efficient and professional purchasing in those cases where best practice was already in place.[19] Domestic firms are permitted to enforce the rules as part of the incentive to compliance for purchasers and, whilst such firms are not the main intended beneficiaries, the rules clearly improve the legal position of domestic providers aggrieved over the conduct of a tendering process.

The European Community rules and the regulations which implement these rules in domestic law are the subject of detailed examination in Chapters 3–11 and in the relevant parts of other chapters, notably Chapter 17 on defence procurement and Chapter 18 on remedies.

The other main area of law regulating tendering procedures is also of recent origin and is concerned with mandatory market testing – "compulsory competitive tendering" or "CCT" – in local government. The legislation on this subject is contained in the Local Government Planning and Land Act 1980 (LGPLA 1980) and the Local Government Act 1988 (LGA 1988) and associated legislation. These rules require local authorities who wish to provide certain services in-house to submit their own bid for providing these services in competition with the private sector, to ensure that in-house provision is only undertaken if this offers the best value for money. Legislation was considered necessary because of opposition from local government to voluntary implementation of such a policy. The policy behind these rules and the detailed award procedures which they impose are examined in Chapters 12–14.

Finally, the LGPLA 1980 and LGA 1988 also contain provisions concerned with the undertaking of work by local authority in-house units for *other* bodies, including for other local authorities. The rules on CCT as such regulate the role of authorities as *purchasers*, to ensure that the authority's own work is contracted out rather than given to the in-house unit where contracting out would be more efficient. This other legislation aims to ensure that in-house units do not do work for *other* bodies where this would not be the most efficient option. These rules are considered briefly at the end of Chapter 14.

(3) THE COMMON LAW PRINCIPLES OF JUDICIAL REVIEW[20]

The courts of England and Wales have developed a body of principles which control the exercise of administrative powers, referred to as the

---

[19] On this issue see further pp. 290–293.
[20] See further Arrowsmith, *Government Procurement and Judicial Review* (1988); Arrowsmith, "Judicial Review and the Contract Powers of Public Authorities" (1990) 106 L.Q.R. 277.

principles of judicial review. The most significant include[21] a requirement that persons affected by administrative decisions should generally be given a hearing before a decision is made (the principle of "natural justice" or "fairness"), the requirement that authorities should not act "arbitrarily" or "unreasonably" and the obligation to take into account only relevant considerations (that is, those contemplated by any enabling statute) in exercising administrative power. In relation to procurement, the existence of a common law fiduciary duty could also be important, as noted in the previous section.

There is some doubt over whether these principles apply at all to the exercise of the contractual powers of government in general, and the power of procurement in particular. In the past there has been some reluctance to apply such principles to contract. In relation both to the award of contracts and the exercise of contractual rights the courts have often stated that there may be no review unless there is some special "public law" element to the decision. Such statements have been made, for example, in the context of decisions to terminate a contractual licence for a market stall, the award of contracts for a television franchise and cases on public employment[22] (where this element may be found, for example, in an express statutory requirement to appoint or dismiss a servant).

However, in several cases in which procurement decisions were held to be reviewable the courts did not mention any requirement for an element of public law. Thus in *R. v. Lewisham London Borough Council, ex p. Shell U.K.*[23] it was held that a decision not to deal with firms having South African connections, which was motivated by a desire to put pressure on the apartheid system, was reviewable because it was made for a purpose not contemplated by the statute conferring the authority's procurement powers; and Neill L.J. indicated that in general authorities may not exercise procurement powers in a way which involves procedural impropriety or unfairness. Further, in *R. v. Enfield London Borough Council, ex p. Unwin*[24] a decision by a local authority to suspend a contractor from its approved lists was considered subject to judicial review for breach of natural justice. These cases support the view that procurement powers are reviewable in principle in the same way as any other government function.[25]

---

[21] For a detailed account see Craig, *Administrative Law* (3rd ed., 1994), Pt. II.

[22] On these cases see Arrowsmith, "Judicial Review of the Contract Powers of Public Authorities", above, and, more recently *R. v. Birmingham City Council, ex p. Dredger and Paget* [1993] C.O.D. 340.

[23] [1988] 1 All E.R. 938, discussed further at pp. 814–815.

[24] [1989] C.O.D. 466.

[25] See also *C.O. Williams Construction v. Blackman* [1995] 1 W.L.R. 102, where the Judicial Committee of the Privy Council indicated that a procurement award was an "administrative act" for the purpose of judicial review under the Barbados Administration of Justice Act. The scope of review under the Act need not, however, be the same as under the common law. The relationship between the two was not discussed although some of the English cases, including *Hibbit and Sanders*, were cited in argument. Support for a

On the other hand, in the most recent cases in which providers have sought to review procurement decisions, in which the issue of reviewability has been expressly raised, the court have insisted on the requirement of a special element of public law. This approach was adopted, for example, in *R. v. Hibbit and Sanders, ex p. the Lord Chancellor's Department*.[26] This case concerned an award by the Lord Chancellor's Department of a contract for court reporting services. The applicant was a disappointed bidder who challenged the award decision in an application for judicial review on the basis of the Department's failure to adhere to certain procedures which the applicants claimed they were led to believe would be followed: it was claimed that the Department had negotiated with bidders after receipt of tenders, contrary to statements in the tender documents, and also that it had acted contrary to expectations in allowing some bidders, but not the applicant, to submit bids according to altered specifications. This, it was claimed, was a breach of the public law principle protecting "legitimate expectations" created by the dealings of public authorities.[27] The court took the view that legitimate expectations had indeed been infringed, but that the application should fail since there was no element of public law sufficient to render the decision amenable to judicial review. Rose L.J.,[28] relying on the decisions concerning public employment, stated that judicial review applied "only in relation to those [of the Lord Chancellor's decisions] which are either in some way statutorily underpinned or involve some other sufficient public law element".[29]

This approach can be criticised. It is submitted that contract should in fact be reviewable in principle in the same manner as any other government power,[30] even where the type of contract has an analogy in

---

general argument that it is not necessary to search for a special element of public law in contract cases can also be derived from the decision of the Court of Appeal in *Jones v. Swansea City Council* [1990] 1 W.L.R. 54; affirmed [1990] 1 W.L.R. 1453. In this case, concerned with the Council's contractual power as a landlord of commercial premises to refuse consent to a change of user, the Court cast doubt on the view that contract powers are prima facie outside the scope of public law, and refused to apply the restrictive approach used in some of the judicial review cases in determining what is a "public" power for the purpose of the tort of misfeasance in public office.

[26] The Times March 12, 1993 and Lexis; noted by Arrowsmith (1993) 2 P.P.L.R. CS 104; Oliver [1993] P.L. 214. The approach in *Hibbit and Sanders* was also supported by the Court of Appeal in *Moss Energy Ltd v. Birmingham City Council*, September 3, 1993. See also *R. v. Walsall M.B.C., ex p. Yapp* [1994] I.C.R. 528, where, in the context of an action by members of the DSO, the Court of Appeal doubted where the legitimate expectations doctrine could apply (although the point was not raised by the Council). Since this case concerned the DSO, however, it is an "employment" rather than a "procurement" case.

[27] See *R. v. Home Secretary, ex p. Asif Khan* [1984] 1 W.L.R. 1337; *R. v. Secretary of State for the Home Department, ex p. Ruddock* [1989] 1 W.L.R. 1482. For an outline of the principle see Cane, *Introduction to Administrative Law* (2nd ed., 1992), pp. 141–143 and the works cited there.

[28] See p. 13 of the transcript.

[29] Waller J. also pointed specifically to the contractual nature of the present decision as a reason for regarding it, prima facie, as unreviewable.

[30] On the arguments see further Arrowsmith, "Judicial Review and the Contract Powers of Public Authorities", above; Arrowsmith, *Government Procurement and Judicial Review* (1988). A contrary view is expressed by Craig, *Administrative Law* (ed.), pp. 567–568.

private law, as in the case of procurement. It is appropriate to apply such principles both because of the public interests involved and also because even where it is exercising these types of functions, a public body should be held to the high standards of treatment of citizens which are imposed in the exercise of other, peculiarly "governmental", powers. The fact that the relationship of the parties is affected to some degree by private law does not make it inappropriate to apply public law in addition to or alongside that law.

Even if judicial review were to be applicable in principle, it would be necessary to examine the facts of each case to determine the precise content of a party's rights. For example, in the *Enfield* case, discussed above, the court held that a firm was entitled to a hearing prior to suspension from a tender list, and also prior to a decision not to renew a specific contract which the firm already held. However, it is doubtful if the principles of natural justice would permit a hearing to a party simply because his bid has failed or because he has been denied an invitation to bid: a hearing is not, in general, permitted simply because a benefit is refused.[31]

Another question to be considered if judicial review were to be available in principle is how far such review may apply to bodies outside the traditional state and local government sector. As explained in Chapter 9, the European Community's regime for the regulation of procurement extends very widely, covering not only the traditional public sector bodies but, in the "utilities" sectors of water, transport, energy and telecommunications, even state-owned industries and purely private enterprises enjoying "special or exclusive rights" granted by the state. In *Mercury Energy Ltd v. Electricity Corporation of New Zealand*[32] the Privy Council held that a state-owned enterprise, which was required to be run in general along commercial lines although subject to consideration of certain social responsibilities, was subject in principle to judicial review. However, even if public law review is available against such entities it is perhaps unlikely that it would be extended to enterprises which are under private ownership – as is the case with most of the utilities in the United Kingdom (such as the privatised water and electricity companies and BT) especially if those enterprises operate in a competitive market.

Even where review is available in principle in such cases, it can be noted that Lord Templeman also stated in the Mercury case that "it does not seem likely that a decision by a state enterprise to enter into or determine a commercial contract to supply goods or services will ever be the subject of judicial review in the absence of fraud, corruption or bad faith".[33] This indicates a very narrow scope of review for contractual

---

[31] See *McInnes v. Onslow-Fane* [1978] 1 W.L.R. 1520 (contrasting "application" cases with cases involving termination of, or failure to renew, an existing benefit).

[32] [1994] 1 W.L.R. 521. See further Taggart, "Corporatisation, Contracting and the Courts" [1994] P.L. 351.

[33] [1994] 1 W.L.R. 521 at p. 529.

activities of a commercial nature. It could be argued, however, that a review of entities such as Mercury operating in general according to commercial principles should in fact be less stringent than that applying to government bodies engaged in other activities, especially if the enterprise must compete against private industry – which is not subject to review – in the market. The standard of review of the contractual activities of government departments or local authorities should, arguably, be more stringent.

The legislation which now exists to regulate procurement award procedures may sometimes confer rights on aggrieved firms which obviate the need for reliance on common law judicial review. For example, the regulations implementing the European Community rules give a right to reasons for many types of decision, as well as a right to hearing before certain decisions – such as decisions to reject a bid as "abnormally low"—are taken by the authority.[34]

(4) THE IMPLIED "BLACKPOOL" CONTRACT

Apart from the possibility of judicial review, some protection of the interests of firms seeking government contracts is afforded in an implied contract which governs the award process, at least where there is a formal tendering procedure. The existence of such a contract was established by the Court of Appeal in *Blackpool Aero Club v. Blackpool Borough Council*.[35] That case concerned an invitation issued by the Council to a number of air operators to seek tenders for a concession contract[36] for the operaton of pleasure flights. The plaintiff submitted a bid which was mistakenly treated as late and excluded from consideration. It was held that this refusal to consider the bid constituted a breach of an implied contract under which any party submitting a bid before the deadline had a right to have that bid considered. It is not clear whether such a contract arises only in tendering procedures by public authorities or whether it is a doctrine of general application. The fact that the purchaser was a public authority was mentioned as a relevant factor in the *Blackpool* case, but it is difficult to see any justification for distinguishing between public and private tendering procedures in this respect.

---

[34] See p. 244 and pp. 281–282.

[35] [1990] 1 W.L.R. 1195. The existence of such a contract seems also to have been argued in the earlier case of *Burroughes Machine Tools v. Oxford Area Health Authority*, judgment of July 21, 1983, but the issue was not expressly addressed by the court. The existence of an implied contract governing the tendering process had already been recognised in Canada, although the decisions have not been considered by the English courts: see, in particular, *R. v. Ron Engineering & Construction (Eastern) Ltd* [1981] 1 S.C.R. 111, and for discussion Fridman, "Tendering Problems" (1987) 66 Can.B.R. 582 and Arrowsmith, *Government Procurement and Judicial Review*, at pp. 323–327.

[36] This is a contract where the remuneration of the contractor consists (at least in part) of the revenue collected by operating the concession. Often a concessionaire will have to pay the authority for the concession, rather than receiving any payment for a promise to operate it.

The court also did not examine the precise scope of the contract. First, it is not clear whether it will apply to all tendering procedures. *Blackpool* itself concerned a procedure where only those specifically invited were permitted to submit tenders, and this factor was mentioned. However, the courts might be prepared to apply it also to a procedure where any interested party is permitted to bid in response to a general advertisement, and it is submitted that it would be anomalous not to do so. On the other hand, it seems clear that it could not be applied in a procedure which does not involve tendering to a set deadline.

The Court of Appeal also did not examine the exact nature of the authority's obligations under the contract. However, if the implied contract is designed to give effect to the commercial expectations of the parties, as stated in *Blackpool*, it could be extended beyond an obligation merely to *consider* the bid, to require that bids be evaluated in accordance with an expected procedure. Bingham L.J. contemplated such an extension, indicating that the authority might be obliged to reject late bids.

This possibility was confirmed by the Court of Appeal in a recent unreported case, *Fairclough Building Ltd v. Port Talbot Borough Council*.[37] Here the plaintiffs had been placed on a list of firms invited to participate in a two-stage procedure for the award of a contract for the construction of a civic centre, the procedure consisting of an appraisal of proposals followed by a formal tendering stage. However, before the completion of the process of assessing first stage tenders it was decided to remove the plaintiff from participation on the grounds of existence of a conflict of interest: the local director of the plaintiff firm was married to the Borough Council's Principal Architect. The Court accepted that an implied contract arose under which the Council must act "reasonably" in removing the plaintiff from the competition. Thus it was clearly contemplated that the court may exercise control over the criteria and procedures for considering the bids. In this particular case the removal was held to be lawful.

It remains to be seen exactly how the courts will develop the contract to control the operation of tendering procedures by a purchaser.[38] Clearly the contract could be "interpreted" widely to provide generous protection for bidders, although, to the extent that procedures are not laid out expressly in the tender documents, this would create considerable uncertainty in the law pending development of the courts' ideas on what may be expected in different types of tendering procedure. One important issue in this context is whether the contract contains an implied term that a purchaser will adhere to any relevant regulatory

---

[37] Decision of July 16, 1992; see [1992] *Construction Industry Law Letter* 779. And see the comments of Scott L.J. in *Mass Energy Ltd v. Birmingham City Council*, September 3, 1993.
[38] On this see further Arrowsmith, "Protecting the Interests of Bidders of Public Contracts: the Role of the Common Law" (1994) 53 C.L.J. 104, pp. 126–132.

legislation, such as the Works, Supply Services and Utilities Regulations, or the legislation on CCT. This could be important if remedies for enforcing the implied contract are more favourable than those for enforcing the legislation. It is suggested, however, that such a term cannot be implied; any intention to follow the regulations arises from their legislative status, not from an intention to incorporate them into any contract which might exist.

Another issue is the exact nature of the contract and the point at which the contractual obligations arise. It is probable that the court in *Blackpool* envisaged a unilateral contract arising when the bid is submitted, the tenderer's consideration for the authority's obligations being the actual submission of the bid. On this basis the bidder himself undertakes no obligations. Another possibility is that there is a bilateral agreement, under which the authority undertakes to consider the bid in the manner provided and the bidder also undertakes an obligation, which could perhaps be an obligation not to withdraw the bid. However, in *Southampton City Council v. Academy Cleaning Services London*,[39] it was held, although the *Blackpool* case was not expressly considered, that there is no obligation to keep a bid open where the bid is not made under seal.

A breach of the implied contract will give a bidder damages to put him in the position in which he would have been had the contractual obligation not been breached. In the present context, his position depends on whether he would have succeeded if the procedure had been properly conducted. If the breach has not affected his position he will recover nothing, not even bid costs.[40] If he would have obtained the contract, however, he will be able to recover the profits[41] which he would have made. Usually, a plaintiff must prove his loss on the balance of probabilities. Obviously, however, this may create difficulties, because of the uncertainties over both which bidder would have won and what the profits would have been, difficulties which also arise in attempting to claim damages for breachs of legislative rules on procurement.[42]

This implied contract provides a flexible tool to give effect to the commercial expectations of the parties. However, it is submitted that[43] in

---

[39] *The Times*, June 11, 1993.

[40] If the plaintiff would have succeeded he will obtain the difference between what it would have cost to perform and the contractual payment. This sum minus his bid costs will be the net profit.

[41] Using the term to refer to the contractual payment minus costs of performance.

[42] With regard to the first uncertainty the court might invoke the rule in *Chaplin v. Hicks* [1911] 2 K.B. 786 to claim damages for "loss of a chance". Secondly, the courts could adopt a presumption that these would have been at least equivalent to the amount spent in bidding on the contract. On these possibilities see further the discussion on remedies for breach of legislative rules in Chap. 18.

[43] See Arrowsmith, *Government Procurement and Judicial Review* (Toronto 1988), pp. 325–328, discussing the Canadian case law; and the notes on the *Blackpool* case by Adams and Brownsword (1991) 54 M.L.R. 281; and Phang (1991) J. of Contract L. 46. A different view, though, is taken by Davenport, in his note in (1991) 107 L.Q.R. 201.

the tendering situation there is no element of bargain – an exchange based on consideration from both sides—which is normally required for a binding contract; nor any intention to create legal relations. There is merely a creation of expectations of how the tendering process will be conducted, which may have been relied upon.[44] The use of a contractual approach to protect bidders is thus questionable. Although this was expressly denied by Bingham L.J., the court appears to be manipulating contractual principles simply to provide a remedy where it felt one ought to be given by some means. It is submitted that it would be more appropriate for the courts to develop a remedy for this situation based directly on the need to protect legitimate expectations in the bargaining process, or alternatively through the development of existing principles of estoppel.[45]

In practice, purchasers now often seek to exclude "*Blackpool*" liability by inserting exclusion clauses into the tender documents.

(5) THE "OMBUDSMEN" IN CONTRACT AWARD PROCEDURES

The Parliamentary Commissioner for Administration and the Commissioners for Local Administration provide a means for the investigation of citizens' complaints of "maladministration" by central government and local government respectively and, in the case of central government although less so at local level, have proved an effective forum for achieving redress in individual cases (as well as prompting improvements in the system of administration in some cases).[46] The government's procurement activities, however, are generally excluded from the jurisdiction of the Ombudsmen. In relation to the Parliamentary Commissioner, procurement is covered by a general exclusion for "action in matters relating to contractual or other commercial transactions".[47] This has always been interpreted by the Commissioner as excluding matters relating to the relationship between the government and its providers. For the local Commissioners there is a similar exclusion for "action taken in matters relating to contract or other commercial transactions".[48] It is then stated that this does not apply to "transactions in the discharge of any functions under any public general Act"; but this latter provision is subject to an exclusion for transactions "required for the procurement of goods and services needed to discharge those functions".[49]

---

[44] The argument was considered but rejected by Bingham L.J. His reasoning, however, was largely confined to asserting the existence of the expectations and the need to protect them, and did not address the need for an intention to embody the expectations in a contractual relationship.

[45] On these possibilities see further Arrowsmith, "Protecting the Interests of Bidders for Public Contracts: the Role of the Common Law" (1993) 53 C.L.J. 104.

[46] See Craig, *Administrative Law* (3rd ed., 1994), pp. 127–141.

[47] Parliamentary Commissioner Act 1967, s.5(3), and Sched. 3.

[48] Local Government Act 1974, s.26(7) and 5, para. 3.

[49] Local Government Act 1974, para. 3(3).

The exclusion of contractual activities, including procurement, has been heavily criticised, including by the Commissioners themselves, by the Select Committee on the Parliamentary Commissioner and by many government commissions,[50] and seems clearly unwarranted. Even as regards the conduct of the government towards its providers as part of the business relationship there is no reason why matters of "maladministration" – for example, corruption or careless conduct such as losing bids or firms' documents – should not be subject to investigation by the Commissioners. Questions relating to such matters can be raised in the House of Commons and it would be useful if Members of Parliament were able to call upon the Commissioner for assistance in their investigations. Any fear that the Commissioners would interfere with the commercial aspects of procurement is unfounded since they are limited to investigating "maladministration". This does not cover policy decisions and would clearly exclude investigations of the merits of particular award decisions or decisions on the qualifications of bidders, for example.

It appears that the Ombudsmen may investigate complaints about the administration of public services by government contractors, who administer the service on behalf of the government, even where there is no direct maladministration by government employees but only by employees of the contractor.[51]

4. CROWN IMMUNITIES

(1) THE IMMUNITIES OF THE CROWN [52]

Since 1947 the Crown has been liable to suit in contract in the ordinary way.[53] The Crown enjoys a number of privileges and immunities which may affect procurement.

First, in civil proceedings the Crown is immune from the remedies of specific performance and injunction, a rule stated in section 21(1) of the Crown Proceedings Act 1947. Under section 21(2) of the Act these remedies also may not be granted against an officer (including a servant) of the Crown where the effect would be to give relief against the Crown

---

[50] On these criticisms see further Arrowsmith, "Government Contracts and Public Law" (1990) 10 L.S. 231 at pp. 240–243.

[51] See p. 626.

[52] See further Craig, *Administrative Law* (3rd ed., 1994), at pp. 723 and 732); Arrowsmith, *Civil Liability and Public Authorities* (1992), at pp. 13–16, and the works cited there.

[53] Formerly proceedings could only be brought through a petition of right which required the permission ("fiat") of the Crown. However, the Crown Proceedings Act 1947, s.1 rendered the Crown liable in all cases where the petition of right was formerly available. It is the relevant Minister, however, and not the Crown as such, who must be named in the action, even if in law it is the Crown who is party to the action: see Crown Proceedings Act 1947, s.17.

which is not available against the Crown directly. It was suggested above that contracts made by government departments are generally made on behalf of the Crown and that only the Crown is party to the contract. If this is the case, then clearly under section 21 specific performance or an injunction will not be available to enforce the contract. If, however, the view is taken that officers of the Crown may undertake liability in an independent capacity and that the Crown is sometimes not party to the contract, where this is done the immunity will not apply.[54] It is less clear what the position would be should a Minister or other agent undertake liability in the agent's own name, under a contract made on behalf of the Crown. Even were a remedy sought against the agent, this could be regarded as having the effect of relief against the Crown and therefore forbidden under section 21(2).

The Crown is also immune from the burden of statutes, unless the contrary is provided either expressly or by "necessary implication".[55] However, this rule is not of great importance since in practice the major statutes which affect procurement, such as the Sale of Goods Act 1979, the Supply of Goods and Services Act 1982 and the Unfair Contract Terms Act 1977, all expressly bind the Crown.

Proceedings relating to procurement may also potentially be affected by the rule in section 25(2) of the Crown Proceedings Act which states that there may be no execution of judgment or attachment against the Crown.

(2) APPLICATION OF IMMUNITIES TO CROWN CONTRACTORS

A question relevant to procurement is the extent to which firms engaged in work for the Crown as independent contractors may partake of the immunities enjoyed by the Crown itself. This may be particularly important in relation to the rule that the Crown is not bound by statute, which providers may wish to invoke to avoid the burden of regulatory legislation.

It is clear that the Crown's immunity is shared by its servants,[56] but in general it appears that it does not extend to independent contractors, who are thus bound by legislation when carrying out their work. The leading authority is *Dixon v. London Small Arms Company*.[57] In this case the Crown had engaged the defendant to manufacture rifles and in so doing the defendant had infringed a patent of the plaintiff. It was assumed that the Crown would not have been restricted by the patent had it decided to manufacture the rifles itself, on the basis that patents,

---

[54] See *M v. Home Office* [1993] 3 All E.R. 537.
[55] *B.B.C. v. Johns* [1965] Ch. 32; *Lord Advocate v. Dumbarton D.C.* [1990] 2 A.C. 580.
[56] *Cooper v. Hawkins* (1904) 2 K.B. 164.
[57] (1875–6) 1 App.Cas. 632.

like statutes, are presumed not to bind the Crown. The House of Lords held that the defendants did not share any Crown immunity, and seemed to regard this as a general principle. It is submitted that this general approach is correct, on the basis that the decision whether or not to take advantage of Crown immunities should in all cases[58] rest with the Crown and not with the independent contractor who carries out the work. Since the Crown has no general right to control the way a provider carries out his work, a general rule allowing that provider to benefit from Crown immunities would mean that the decision whether to invoke them is effectively transferred to the provider.

The rule denying the benefit of immunities to providers could prejudice the Crown's interests by making the work more difficult or expensive. However, it is submitted that the Crown should be able to invest the external provider with its immunity should it choose to do so, a point which seems to have been accepted in *Dixon*.[59] The court should be slow to find that it has done so, however. Thus the immunity should only normally apply where it is conferred expressly, or where it arises by necessary implication from the contract on the basis that the contract could not otherwise be fulfilled in a lawful manner.

---

[58] For the most part the Crown does *not* decline to adhere to relevant legislation, even if not strictly bound.

[59] Above, at pp. 641, 642 and 645, where it is stated that the firm could have enjoyed this immunity if appointed the Crown's "agent" for the purpose. This appears to mean no more than that it is open to the Crown to designate a firm as having Crown status for the purpose of Crown immunities where that person carries out work for the Crown. This interpretation can be supported by the fact that Lords Cairns, Hatherley and Penzance emphasised that in the case before them it was possible for the work to have been done without infringing the patent, indicating that immunity may have applied if that had not been possible. This can be explained on the basis that had performance not been possible without an infringement, then it could be implied from the terms of the contract that immunity should be enjoyed. See further Arrowsmith, *Civil Liability and Public Authorities* (1992), pp. 83–84.

CHAPTER 3

EUROPEAN COMMUNITY POLICY ON PROCUREMENT [1]

1. INTRODUCTION

As explained in Chapter 1, much of the legislation applying to procurement in the United Kingdom derives from European Community law and relates to the Community's policy of opening procurement markets to Europe-wide competition. This chapter explains the background to this legislation – the objectives of Community policy, its development up to the present day, and prospects for the future. The details of the legal rules which implement this policy are examined in Chapters 4–11.

2. THE OBJECTIVES OF COMMUNITY PROCUREMENT POLICY

The European Communities consist of three separate Communities established under three separate Treaties. The most significant so far as procurement is concerned, since its covers most purchases by governments and the utilities, is the European Community (E.C.), first established under the first Treaty of Rome in 1957 (and prior to 1993 referred to as the European Economic Community (EEC)).[2] The others are the

---

[1] For general works on Community procurement rules and policy see Cox, *The Single Market Rules and the Enforcement Regime after 1992* (1993); Lee, *Public Procurement* (1992); Trepte, *Public Procurement in the EEC* (1993); Weiss, *Public Procurement in European Community Law* (1993); Bright, *Public Procurement Handbook* (1994). On implementation in the United Kingdom see Digings and Bennett, *E.C. Public Procurement: Law and Practice* (looseleaf); Geddes, *Public Procurement: a Practical Guide to the U.K. Regulations and Associated Community Rules* (1993). Specifically on the case law of the Court of Justice see Arrowsmith, *A Guide to the Procurement Cases of the Court of Justice* (1992); Millett, "The Role of the European Court of Justice in Relation to Public Procurement" (1992) 1 P.P.L.R. 70; Brown "An Overview of the Court of Justice Case Law on the E.C. Public Procurement Rules" (1993) 2 P.P.L.R. CS34; Fernández Martín, "Recent Cases on Procurement before the Court of Justice" (1994) 3 P.P.L.R. CS200.

[2] The name was changed following the coming into effect of the Maastricht Treaty, to reflect the wider purposes of the Community. The "European Union" is an umbrella name, covering the three communities, plus other Treaty powers governing the relationship of the Community Member States which are exercised on an intergovernmental basis rather than through the three Communities. "European Community" policy on procurement is used here in a broad sense to refer to the procurement policies of all three communities.

European Coal and Steel Community, the first of the Communities, which was set up under the Treaty of Paris of 1951; and the European Atomic Energy Community (Euratom), set up under the second Treaty of Rome of 1957. These Communities were established with the primary goal of promoting co-operation, and consequent prosperity, in the economic sphere, but they also envisaged the development of co-operation in other areas. The impetus arose mainly from the hope that economic co-operation would contribute towards the maintenance of peace in Europe, following the devastation of the Second World War.[3] Since 1965 the three Communities have shared common governmental institutions. The Communities currently have fifteen members – the six founding states of Belgium, France, Germany, Italy, Luxembourg and the Netherlands; Denmark, Ireland and the United Kingdom, who became members in 1973; Greece, a member from 1981; Spain and Portugal, who joined in 1986; and Austria, Finland and Sweden who acceded only in 1995.

One of the key objectives of the Communities has been to create a free internal market within the areas of the Member States, which requires the elimination of barriers to the free trade of goods between states and also of barriers to the movement of business, labour and capital. This is intended to improve overall economic welfare and growth: increased competition tends to lead to lower prices and to encourage improved performance and innovation; the larger market allows firms to take advantage of economies of scale and to restructure to achieve maximum efficiency; and specialisation in areas of comparative advantage is facilitated. In the context of the European Community's single market, it is hoped that such improvements will enable European industry to become more competitive with firms from outside the Community, particularly in the high technology sectors where the benefits of the free market are likely to be most significant.[4] The barriers to trade which had grown up to impede free trade – whether deliberately erected as protectionist measures, or otherwise – were numerous and varied; they include customs duties, discriminatory taxation, bans on foreign products or investment, quota systems and subsidies to domestic industry.

When entities follow procurement practices which do not allow for fair competition between firms who seek to do business with that entity, these practices also operate as barriers to trade – in the Community context, they effectively prevent interested firms from having access to all parts of the Community market. Restrictive procurement practices have been a particular problem with public bodies and those subject to public influence.

---

[3] For an outline history of the establishment and development of the Communities see Wyatt and Dashwood, *European Community Law* (3rd ed., 1993), Chap. 1.

[4] However, in most areas Europe has indicated that it is willing to open its own markets to other states on the basis of "reciprocity": see further Chap. 16.

Such practices arise, first, because governments often seek deliberately to favour their own industry in allocating contracts. This may be for economic reasons – either to give general support to domestic industry, or to promote specific industrial objectives such as the development of a new technology or regional development.[5] Even where the government is disinclined to protectionism it may be difficult to resist political pressure to buy national goods and services, especially those visible to the public (such as cars) and in industries threatened with specific job losses. Such nationalistic puchasing has been carried out not only by government itself, but also by entities susceptible to government control or government influence, especially if those entities (as with many of the utilities) do not operate under competitive conditions, so that there is no commercial pressure to resist government demands. Apart from the effect of deliberate discrimination, trade barriers may also arise from a tendency to source solely from known domestic providers because of conservatism and lack of initiative – a particular tendency of government and other entities which do not operate in competitive markets, since they do not face the same commercial pressure as most private firms. The Atkins study of procurement carried out for the European Commission (published in 1988) offered as evidence of restrictive measures in public procurement the fact that the rate of import penetration was much lower for public procurement than for the market as a whole. For example, in the United Kingdom it was 22 per cent for the market as a whole and only 4 per cent for public procurement.[6]

These trade barriers are significant to the market, since purchases of government, together with industries which are susceptible to government control or influence, accounts for a high proportion of economic activity. The Atkins study estimated that the annual value of procurement of government and nationalised industries of the twelve states who were members of the Community at that time was about 450 billion ECUs at 1984 prices, amounting to about 15 per cent of Community Gross Domestic Product (and with a figure of 21.8 per cent for the United Kingdom).[7] Part of this consisted of non-tradeable purchases or purchases for which there was no competitive market (such as gas, electricity and postal and telecommunications services), or of procurement which was too insignificant to be carried out under formal award procedures. However, it was estimated that between 170–250 billion ECUs (6–10 per cent of GDP) was purchasing suitable for competitive procedures.[8] It is also important to note that government purchasers are active in many high technology sectors – such as telecommunications and information technology – which are of particular significance for the

---

[5] On the use of procurement as an industrial development tool see Chap. 16.
[6] W.S. Atkins Management Consultants, *The Cost of Non-Europe in Public Procurement* (1988) (hereafter the Atkins study), vol. 5A, p. 12.
[7] Vol. 5A, p. 26.
[8] *Ibid.*, pp. 24–26.

economy. In many such sectors they dominate the market, so that public purchasing strategies are a key factor in shaping the industry as a whole.

Similar features are seen in the public procurement of many industrialised countries and elimination of restrictive public procurement[9] is an important issue in world trade. Community procurement policy aims to eliminate such restrictive practices so far as they affect trade between Member States, and so to realise the full benefits of a single market in those sectors affected by public procurement.

More specifically, the Atkins Study carried out for the Commission identified the potential benefits of open public procurement to the (twelve-member) Community of the 1980s as follows:

(i) The "static trade effect"
This referred to the savings for government purchasing arising from the increased purchase of low cost imports, rather than more expensive domestic products. Such savings were estimated at 4–9 billion ECUs per annum.

(ii) The "competition effect"
This referred to savings from lowering of prices by domestic firms, which would arise in response to the need to compete with non-domestic firms previously excluded from the market. Such savings were expected to be significant in markets dominated by the public sector, and were estimated to total between 1–3 billion ECUs per annum. (Where there is a substantial – and competitive – private sector market alongside the public market, competition will tend to result in lower prices.)

(iii) The "restructuring" effect
This is the effect expected as a result of the restructuring of industry and the consequent economies of scale. It was anticipated that the advent of the single market would result, in particular, in a large number of mergers and takeovers, leading in turn to economies of scale through rationalisation of production (elimination of excess capacity, or investment in larger plant) and the avoidance of duplication in research and development (R & D), marketing etc. These benefits were expected mainly in industries where the government is a significant purchaser and where there is room for economies of scale (for example, because of high R & D or equipment costs). In particular, in many such industries European states had used their purchasing to support large and inefficient national operators – "national champions" – who were insulated from competition in national markets and unable to take advantage of

---

[9] This phrase is here used loosely to refer to government bodies and those subject to government control or potential government influence. These purchases are regulated because of the effect of government control/influence which – especially where combined with absence of commercial pressure – causes the problems outlined in the text. It is not generally considered necessary to regulate private purchasing – although it is not unknown for private purchasers to choose national products and firms, even when these are not the best value for money.

economies of scale by selling to other European governments. With the opening up of procurement it was predicted that such market structures would break down, with larger, more efficient firms emerging to serve a wider market. The savings from this effect were estimated to amount to 3–5 billion ECUs per annum.

(iv) Savings for private sector purchasers

Although many of the benefits of opening government markets were expected to arise in industries in which the government is the dominant or only purchaser, it was anticipated that leverage from public sector purchasers might lead to some private sector savings in markets such as office equipment and construction, which are common to both public and private sectors. The study did not, however, attempt to quantify these gains.

(v) Effect on innovation and growth

The study also suggested that the larger market would stimulate more effective use of R & D and marketing expenditure, which could improve innovation, investment and growth in the industries affected. However, again this was not quantified.

(vi) External effects

Finally, it was suggested – although again the benefits were not quantified – that the improved competitiveness of industry resulting from the above changes could enable European firms to compete more effectively against third countries, both in the Community itself and in markets outside; and in some cases might even be essential to the survival of certain European industries.

The significance of these conclusions can be seen in the fact that the savings anticipated under the first three headings – that is, those which were quantified – amounted to $^{1}/_{2}$ per cent of *total* Community GDP.[10] As is apparent from the analysis, however, these savings would not be spread evenly through industrial sectors. They would be concentrated particularly in those sectors – such as railways, power generation and telecommunications equipment – with a government-dominated market and significant investment costs which produced high barriers to market entry and potential for economies of scale; whilst in others, such as certain types of office equipment, no gains could be expected at all.

The study itself acknowledged the existence of wide margins of error and the accuracy of the figures given in this and other studies on the potential impact of open market reforms have been much debated.[11] In particular, the impact of such reforms may depend on how far competition law, combined with the effect of opening Community markets to

---

[10] Atkins Report, *op cit.,* vol. 5A, p. 54.
[11] For a summary of the debate see Tsoukalis, *The New European Economy* (2nd revised ed., 1993), pp. 91–94.

third countries,[12] proves adequate to deal with problems of monopoly or oligopoly situations within the European market which may potentially result from the restructuring of industry – such a scenario may mean that such entities fail to operate efficiently and/or that costs savings from economies of scale are not passed on to purchasers.[13] Further, the figures for savings above do not take account of the need for expenditure by the Community itself to assist those regions which will be the losers from the competition of the single market. However, it is generally accepted that, however difficult it may be to calculate precise benefits, the savings to be made from opening up procurement markets are certainly significant.

Whilst the benefits are considerable, however, their realisation has presented special difficulty, both for political reasons – the reluctance of Member States to give up their powers to use procurement to promote domestic industry or to obtain political support – and the practical difficulties of proving discrimination in procurement. It is not surprising, therefore, that the opening up of public procurement has been seen as an important part of the Community's single market policy, and that extensive legislation has been adopted to promote this objective.

3. DEVELOPMENT OF COMMUNITY PROCUREMENT POLICY [14]

(1) THE TREATY PROVISIONS AND LIBERALISATION DIRECTIVES

Public procurement practices are, first, affected by certain provisions in the Community Treaties themselves. Unlike the Stockholm Convention which created the European Free Trade Area,[15] they do not contain special provisions on public procurement,[16] but this activity falls within the general provisions of the treaties concerned with creation of the single market. These provisions prohibit, *inter alia*, discrimination by government against firms and products from other Member States, and

---

[12] On the opening of procurement markets see Chap. 16.

[13] For discussion in the context of procurement see Cox, *The Single Market Rules and the Enforcement Regime after 1992* (1993), pp. 269–271; Konstadakopulos, "The Limited Oligopoly Concept in the Single European Market: Recent Evidence from Public Procurement" (1995) 4 P.P.L.R. 213.

[14] For a detailed account of the historical development of Community procurement policy see Cox, *The Single Market Rules and the Enforcement Regime after 1992* (1993) and Weiss, *Public Procurement in European Community Law* (1993).

[15] See Weiss, "The Law of Public Procurement in EFTA and the EEC: The Legal Framework and Its Implementation" (1987) 7 Y.E.L. 59.

[16] The original EEC Treaty mentioned procurement only in the context of contracts financed by the Community in certain overseas countries and territories: see Article 132(4) EEC/E.C. The E.C. Treaty now also mentions public procurement in Article 130 on industrial policy.

can be invoked to prevent discriminatory procurement practices, as is explained in Chapter 4. The most important are Article 30 E.C., which prohibits restrictions on the free movement of goods – including purchasing decisions which discriminate against products from other Member States; Article 59 E.C., which prohibits restrictions on those seeking to provide services, including restrictions on those seeking government contracts; and Article 52 concerned with "freedom of establishment" (the right to set up business in another state), which, *inter alia,* protects firms established in a state of which they are not nationals who wish to participate in government contracts there.

These provisions did not have direct effect immediately they were adopted, since it was impractical for the states to abolish all restrictions straightaway. So far as Article 30 was concerned, this was to have direct effect only on expiry of a transitional period ending on January 1, 1971. Articles 32–33 EEC provided for the gradual abolition during this period of measures caught by Article 30, whilst states were also to refrain from introducing new ones (Article 32 E.C.). In relation to procurement and certain other measures[17] Article 33(7) EEC provided for abolition through the adoption of directives, which were to set out a timetable and procedures for abolition of particular kinds of restrictions. In the case of measures restricting the procurement of products from other Member States, this was done through a "liberalisation" directive, Directive 70/32. This forbade measures requiring that the whole or part of a particular government requirement should be met by domestic products or providing for advantages or preferences for domestic products,[18] and listed in detail various restrictive practices in procurement which were considered to contravene the free movement of goods principle. In fact, this directive was adopted only just prior to the expiry of the transition period. Now that the period has expired, procurement practices which limit the free movement of goods are automatically forbidden under Article 30 and this prohibition is directly enforceable against Member States by those affected. Directive 70/32 is now merely relevant as an illustration of the kind of procurement measures which the Commission has considered to be caught by Article 30, and may be used as a guide to its interpretation.

Similarly,[19] Articles 52 and 59 did not require immediate abolition of restrictions affecting the right to establish and to provide services in other Member States: the Treaty merely provided for programmes to be drawn up for their gradual abolition, to be implemented through

---

[17] Those categorised as measures having equivalent effect to quantitative restrictions: on this see further Chap. 4.
[18] Directive 70/32/EEC [1970] O.J. L13/1. On this see further Weiss, *Public Procurement in European Community Law* (1993), Chap. 3, esp. pp. 34–35; Turpin, "Public Contracts in the EEC" (1972) C.M.L.Rev. 411.
[19] See further Weiss, above, Chap. 3, esp. pp. 28–39; Turpin, above.

directives.[20] In 1964 directives were adopted which forbade public authorities to require their contractors to discriminate on grounds of nationality in choosing subcontractors.[21] However, states remained free to adopt discriminatory policies in choosing their own providers, and it was not until 1971 that this discretion was limited with the adoption of the liberalising Directive 71/304[22] which prohibited practices in public works contracts which favoured national providers over those from other Member States – effectively, doing for public works what Directive 70/32 did for supplies.[23] No comparable directive was adopted for non-construction services. However, both Articles 52 and 59 have had direct effect since the end of the transitional period,[24] so that procurement practices which restrict access to services contracts for providers from other Member States (Article 59), or which restrict access to any government contracts for non-nationals established in the awarding state (Article 52) may be caught by the Treaty without the need for any directive to prohibit such conduct. Directive 71/304 is thus generally redundant; but it may be used as a guide to interpretation of the Treaty.[25]

(2) THE CO-ORDINATION AND REMEDIES DIRECTIVES

(a) THE NEED FOR CO-ORDINATION DIRECTIVES

It was always clear, however, that trade barriers in procurement would not be removed simply by prohibiting positive conduct which favours domestic providers or products. This is inadequate, first, because of the difficulties of proving discriminatory treatment. For example, where several firms have bid and the contract is given to a national firm it is often impossible to establish whether the true reason was commercial (that is, based on the merits of the bid) or national preference. Similarly, as mentioned above, trade barriers do not arise only because of discriminatory conduct, but also from inefficient sourcing practices – such as the habit of seeking bids from a limited number of providers: these are probably not caught by the Treaty provisions where they do not

---

[20] A General Programme for the elimination of restrictions under each of these Articles was adopted in 1961: see General Programme for the Abolition of Restrictions on Freedom of Establishment [1962] J.O. 36; General Programme for the Abolition of Restrictions on Freedom to Provide Services [1962] J.O. 32.

[21] Directive 64/429/EEC, O.J. 1880/64; and Directive 62/427/EEC, O.J. 1863/64.

[22] [1971] O.J. L185/1. This entered into force on August 1, 1972.

[23] Directive 70/32 already, however, applied to supplies used in performing public works contracts.

[24] Case 2/74, *Reyners v. Belgian State* [1974] E.C.R. 631 (Article 52); case 33/74, *Van Binsbergen v. Bestuur van de Bedrijfsvereniging voor de Metaalsnijverheid* [1974] E.C.R. 1299.

[25] See case 389/92, *Ballast Nedem Groep v. The State (Belgium)* [1994] 2 C.M.L.R. 836.

involve deliberate discrimination. They also arise for structural reasons, notably from the use of different standards for products and services in different Member States.

To deal with these difficulties, the Community has adopted specific directives on procurement – sometimes referred to as the "co-ordination directives" – to regulate award procedures for major contracts. These embody two main principles, which reflect the two problems mentioned above – the difficulties of proving discrimination, and the absence of concrete opportunities for non-domestic providers. First, they seek to ensure that no discrimination occurs in award procedures, by regulating and structuring the award procedure so that it is more difficult to hide discrimination. (For example, criteria to be used in choosing between bids must be set out in advance, so that the justification for particular award decisions can more easily be held up to scrutiny.[26-27]) Secondly, the directives require certain positive steps which improve access to contracts from providers from outside the awarding state. In particular, contracts must as a general rule be advertised in the *Official Journal of the European Communities.* They do not apply to all contracts, but only those above a certain threshold, since cross-border trade is likely only with larger contracts. Smaller contracts, however, may still be subject to the Community Treaties. The directives also deal expressly with the issue of standards in regulated procurement.

(b) THE ORIGINAL CO-ORDINATION DIRECTIVES – 71/305 (WORKS) AND 77/62 (SUPPLIES)

The need for co-ordination directives to regulate award procedures was recognised even during the transitional period when Articles 30, 52 and 59 E.C. did not have direct effect. In the case of public works such a directive, Directive 71/305, was adopted at the same time as Directive 71/304 (the liberalisation directive), and a similar directive on supplies, Directive 77/62, was adopted six years later.[28] These are the predecessors of the existing public sector directives which are described below.[29]

Like the current public sector directives, they covered traditional public bodies such as government departments, regional government (in Member States which recognise this level of government) and local authorities, as well as certain other authorities of a public nature. They did not, however, cover the nationalised industries. Further, four important industrial sectors – water, transport, energy and telecommunications

---

[26-27] See p. 239 (public sector) and pp. 509–510 (utilities).

[28] Directive 71/305/EEC, [1971] O.J. L185/1; Directive 77/62/EEC [1977] O.J. L13/1. Directive 77/62 was amended in 1980 by Directive 80/767, [1980] O.J. L215/1 to adjust the Community regime in light of the "GATT" Agreement on Government Procurement (the GPA), which came into effect in 1980. (On the reason for these adjustments see pp. 61–62.) For details of these original directives see further Weiss, above, Chap. 4; Cox, above, pp. 32–53.

[29] See pp. 57–59.

– were largely excluded from their scope, even where these activities were carried out by public authorities. The main reason for this was that these activities were carried out in some states by public bodies and in other states by private authorities. Since it would have been inequitable to regulate such activities in some states but not others, it was decided to exclude these sectors from regulation. Initially, these were known as the "excluded sectors", but they are now covered by a separate directive (as explained below) and are referred to today as the "utilities" sectors.

The award procedures under these original directives on public sector works and supplies directives in essence still apply under the current public sector directives, as outlined in section (d) below. However, as will be explained, their content has to some extent been modified and extended in recent years.

(c) THE 1985 WHITE PAPER AND EXTENSION OF THE PROCUREMENT REGIME

Unfortunately, the original procurement directives were widely disregarded, whether deliberately or through ignorance of their existence, and little attempt was made to enforce the rules.[30] Further, as indicated above, they failed to cover large areas of the market – notably the utilities sectors – in which discriminatory or inefficient purchasing was common, and where the potential for significant savings existed. These factors meant that the original public procurement legislation had only a marginal impact, if any at all, in opening up the European market.

Procurement policy – along with other aspects of the Community's single market policy – received a new lease of life, however, with the publication of a White Paper by the Commission in 1985. The failure of procurement policy merely reflected a more general malaise afflicting the Community's single market policy, and the 1985 White Paper sought to rejuvenate this whole area by setting out an ambitious plan for completion of the single market by 1992.[31] The Paper highlighted public procurement as one of the key areas for action and prompted major legislative initiatives (supplemented by other measures) which were designed to "complete" Community procurement policy before the 1992 deadline.

The legislative measures which were adopted following the White Paper initiative can be divided into four categories.

(i) Measures to improve the existing public sector directives
First, measures were adopted to improve the operation of the existing directives on procurement – that is, Directive 71/305 on public works

---

[30] On the impact of this legislation see, for example, COM (84) 717 Final and COM (84) 747 Final.

[31] *White Paper from the Commission to the Council on Completing the Internal Market* COM (85) 310 Final.

contracts and Directive 77/62 on public supply contracts. These changes were introduced through two new directives – Directive 89/440 on public works, which amended the original directive on works, and Directive 88/295 on public supplies, which amended the original directive on supplies.[32] The new provisions included a new procedure – the negotiated procedure – for certain contracts which had previously been exempt from the rules altogether[33]; an extension of the rules on specifications to require use of European standards by public bodies[34]; and an extension of the minimum time-limits given to potential bidders to respond to advertisements and to submit their bids. The new directives also brought in a requirement to advertise intended purchases in advance (now referred to as the Prior Information Notice (PIN),[35] to give the market maximum time to prepare for bidding; this was an addition to the existing requirement to advertise contracts at the start of each individual award procedure. There was also introduced a new requirement to publish a notice giving details of contract awards once an award was made ("award notices"). In the case of the directive on works (although not supplies) there was also introduced for the first time a general and comprehensive definition of bodies caught by the directive, to ensure that there were no loopholes – a definition now incorporated in all the public sector directives (that is, on works, supplies and services).[36] The 1989 directive also extended the works rules to cover concession contracts (to a limited extent), and also certain contracts awarded by the private sector but funded by the government.[37]

Directive 89/440 and 88/295 merely amended the original works and supplies directives and did not implement a consolidated text. The extensive amendments introduced by these new directives, combined with lesser amendments introduced by other provisions, meant that the texts were very difficult to piece together. Thus in 1993 new directives were adopted with the aim of consolidating the existing rules in a single text, to make them more accessible. These are Directive 93/37[38] on public works contracts and Directive 93/36 on public supply contracts,[39] which are the directives currently in force. Whilst the main aim was consolidation, however, it was decided at the same time to introduce

---

[32] Directive 89/440/EEC [1989] O.J. L210/1 and Directive 88/295/EEC [1988] O.J. L127/1. On these directives see further Weiss, above, Chap. 5; Cox, above, Chaps. 3–4.
[33] On the negotiated procedure, see pp. 255–281. The directive on supplies also introduced a new requirement that preference should be given to the "open" procedure above the "restricted" procedure; but this was removed again in 1993.
[34] On this rule see Chap. 11.
[35] See further pp. 182–191.
[36] See pp. 112–115.
[37] At the same time, however, the threshold for applying the works rules was increased from 1 million ECUs to 5 million ECUs (the present figure), to reflect the increased cost of building work and the fact that cross-border trade was considered unlikely for smaller works contracts.
[38] Directive 93/37 [1993] O.J. L199/54 ("the Works Directive").
[39] Directive 93/36 [1993] O.J. L199/1 ("the Supply Directive").

some minor amendments to the rules on supplies, to eliminate some anomalies between the works and supply rules. Thus, for example, the general definition of "bodies covered by public law" used in the works rules was incorporated into the supply rules.[40]

(ii) Extension of the public sector regime to cover non-construction services

The original directives covered only public works and supplies; there was no regulation of services other than construction. In 1992, however, a new directive, Directive 92/50,[41] was adopted to extend the regime to services. This directive largely follows the same approach as the supply and works directives (in their revised form). However, it should be noted that not all services are fully regulated – in general, the rules governing award procedures only apply to certain services specifically listed in the directive. Others (including, for example, legal and catering services) are subject only to very limited obligations.

(iii) Extension of regulation to the utilities sector

As has been mentioned, the original procurement directives did not apply to many activities in the important "utilities" sectors of water, energy, transport and telecommunications. In any case, in many Member States these activities were not carried out by government itself, but by separate commercial entities, some of which were not even subject to public ownership or control but were wholly in the private sector.

However, the procurement practices of entities in these sectors constituted important barriers to trade. Discriminatory practices occurred because many of these entities were subject to government control or, if in the private sector, were still susceptible to public influence because of their dependence on government (for example, for exclusive licences). Further, the absence of competition in the supply of these utility services meant that many of these entities were not subject to competitive pressure to procure efficiently. Many of these are, however, the very industries – government dominated, and with high R & D and equipment costs – in which the greatest savings can be realised by an open market.

After 1985 the political will emerged amongst Member States to sacrifice their own short-term interests and to bring these industries within the open procurement regime. This was first done by Directive 90/531,[42] which regulated the procurement of supplies and works. Services were brought into the regime three years later by Directive 93/38.[43] (This was done at the same time as the consolidating directives for public sector works and supplies were adopted.) Directive 93/38 did

---

[40] For details of the amendments see Servenay, "The New Provisions of Supplies Directive 93/36" (1994) 3 P.P.L.R. 163.
[41] [1992] O.J. L209/1 ("the Services Directive").
[42] [1990] O.J. 297/1.
[43] [1993] O.J. L199/84 ("the Utilities Directive").

not merely bring services within the utilities regime, but also consolidated in a single text along with services rules the works and supplies rules which had been adopted under Directive 90/531. Thus today the single text of Directive 93/38 governs all utilities procurement.

(iv) Measures to improve enforcement

One important reason identified by the Commission for lack of compliance with the procurement rules was the absence of effective enforcement mechanisms. It is commonly stated that before the White Paper, Community law did not give affected firms any right to enforce the rules on procurement, and that hence legal actions were only available if permitted under the law of individual states. In fact, this was not strictly true: general principles of Community law, as developed by the Court of Justice do in fact give persons affected by Community law certain rights to enforce the law in the courts of the state which is in breach, and these could have been used in procurement cases.[44] However, they were not much used in practice. An important reason for this was ignorance about the possibility of legal action and doubts over the extent of the rights and their effectiveness; this resulted from the fact that their existence depended on the interpretation of case law of the Court of Justice, which was not commonly known to those in the industry and was not entirely clear in its requirements. The Commission itself also possesses a general power to enforce Community law which could have been used in procurement cases, but the Commission had not previously concerned itself much with procurement.

Following the 1985 White Paper, specific directives were adopted to deal with enforcement – Directive 89/665,[45] which deals with remedies for enforcing the public sector rules, and Directive 92/13,[46] which deals with remedies in the utilities sector. Both directives aim mainly to ensure that effective remedies are available to providers affected by a breach of the rules and to ensure that these are known to affected parties, and also contain some other provisions on enforcement, including some on the powers of the Commission.[47]

In addition to these legislative measures, it should be mentioned that after 1985 the Commission made much more aggressive use of its powers to enforce the rules, and has since that time played a significant role in ensuring that the rules are properly enforced and implemented.[48]

(d) THE CURRENT REGIME – THE PUBLIC SECTOR

As explained above, procurement in the public sector is now regulated by four different directives. These are:

---

[44] See further pp. 902–903.
[45] [1989] O.J. L395/33 ("the Public Sector Remedies Directive").
[46] [1992] O.J. L76/14 ("the Utilities Remedies Directive").
[47] See further pp. 933–934.
[48] See further pp. 920–935.

(i) Directive 93/36, which regulates supply contracts made by public bodies – hereafter "the Supply Directive";

(ii) Directive 93/37, which regulates works contracts entered into by public bodies – hereafter "the Works Directive";

(iii) Directive 92/50, which regulates contracts for services made by public bodies – hereafter "the Services Directive"; and

(iv) Directive 89/665, which deals with remedies for enforcing Community rules in relation to contracts covered by the Supply, Works and Services Directives – hereafter "the public sector Remedies Directive".

As already explained, these directives regulate, broadly, all major contracts awarded by public bodies, except those in the sectors of water, energy, transport and telecommunications (which are the subject of the separate Utilities Directive). There are also certain other specific exclusions, including contracts for military equipment. The exact scope of the directives, in terms of the authorities and contracts covered, is described in Chapter 5 (with certain special cases being dealt with in Chapter 8).

As indicated, the directives, first, require that advance notices ("PINs") should be published, to give the market as much notice as possible of an authority's future requirements. Most importantly, however, they lay down rules to regulate the award procedures for individual contracts made by the authority.

In general these must be awarded in accordance with formal tendering procedures as laid out in the directives. Authorities may choose between either an "open procedure" or a "restricted procedure". Under the open procedure, the authority must advertise the contract in the *Official Journal of the European Communities*, and must consider bids from any interested party who responds. Under the restricted procedure the contract must also be advertised in the *Official Journal*, and all interested parties invited to contact the authority; however, not all interested persons need be invited to bid, but the authority may select (in accordance with rules in the directives) a limited number of bidders from amongst those who reply. Under both procedures, there are minimum time-limits for firms to respond, to ensure that firms from other Member States are not disproportionately disadvantaged by short deadlines. Once bids have been received, the authority must select either the lowest price bid *or* the one which is the most economically advantageous (taking account, for example, of quality, delivery date or running costs, as well as initial price). Where the latter is chosen, the criteria must be stated in advance. Contracts must be awarded to the best bidder in accordance with these rules – it is not permitted, for example, to negotiate with bidders to get them to lower their prices.

In exceptional cases, contracts may be awarded in accordance with a more informal procedure – the negotiated procedure – which does not require the submission of formal bids by a set deadline but permits discussions between the authority and interested firms. However, where there is more than one party to negotiations the usual commerical criteria (lowest price or most economically advantageous offer) must be applied to choosing the successful provider following the negotiations. There are two types of negotiated procedure, and they may be used only in the very limited circumstances set out in the directives. One is the negotiated procedure with advertisement, where the contract must be advertised in the *Official Journal* to select several parties for negotiations. This applies where a formal procedure is not suitable, but it is still appropriate to have competition. For example, it applies to procurement of services where formal competition is impossible because specifications cannot be formulated in advance; here an informal competition is the best way to obtain value for money. The second type of negotiated procedure is the negotiated procedure without advertisement, which applies where competition is not appropriate – for example, in cases of extreme urgency, or where there is only one provider able to do the work because of exclusive rights to relevant technology.

For all procedures, there are limitations on the grounds on which providers may be excluded from the bidding process (that is, designated as "unqualified"): they may be excluded for inadequate financial capacity or technical ability and for certain other reasons, but not on other grounds not mentioned in the directives. There are also strict rules governing the evidence which may be used to assess qualification.

Other provisions which apply to all types of award procedure regulate the way in which specifications are drawn up – for example, requiring reference to European standards where these exist for the product or services in question.

Finally, at the end of any award procedure, authorities must give reasons for their decisions where these are requested, and must publish a notice to publicise any award (or to explain why none was made).

In general, the obligations are the same regardless of whether it is the Works, Supply or Services Directive which applies, and hence the rules in these three directives can be considered together. They are examined further in Chapter 6 (general procedures), Chapter 7 (the qualification process) and Chapter 11 (specifications), with certain special cases (such as concessions) considered in Chapter 8.

A general feature of the procedures is that they are very rigid, allowing little discretion to public authorities in the way procurement is carried out. This has been done to minimise opportunities for abuse or inefficiency, and ensure that decisions can be easily monitored. However, in the case of a conscientious purchaser who genuinely seeks value for money, such procedures appear to impose unnecessary costs and to inhibit practices such as post-tender negotiations and long-term partnering arrangements which may be the best way of obtaining value for money. There is much debate over whether the public sector rules have struck the right balance between these competing considerations, an issue which is examined further in Chapter 6 once the procedures have been discussed in more detail.[49]

---

[49] See pp. 290–295.

(e) THE CURRENT REGIME – UTILITIES

As explained, contracts in the utilities sectors of water, energy, transport and telecommunications are governed by a separate directive, Directive 93/38 – hereafter "the Utilities Directive". Remedies for enforcing these rules are dealt with by Directive 92/13 – hereafter "the Utilities Remedies Directive". This covers contracts for works, supplies and services which are made by utilities.

As already observed, activities in these sectors are carried out by both public and private entities. It would have been inequitable to subject them to regulation only where carried on directly in the public sector, and also inadquate to achieve Community objectives, since restrictive procurement practices were exhibited by many entities in these sectors where operating as nationalised industries and even where operating wholly in the private sector. Hence, the Utilities Directive regulates not only public authorities themselves (when engaged in these activities) but also (i) "public undertakings" – that is, undertakings dominated in some way (for example, through financial control) by government and (ii) bodies with special or exclusive rights to carry on activities in these sectors (for example, monopoly rights to operate, or special powers), since these were also considered susceptible to government influence. The exact authorities covered, and also the exact extent of the relevant activities, are examined in Chapter 9.

As with the public sector, utilities must publish an advance notice of their contracts (a PIN) in the Official Journal of the European Communities, to alert the market to the purchaser's requirements as soon as possible, and it also – like the public sector directives – regulates the award of individual contracts. However, whilst all the directives have the same basic objectives – to prevent purchasers from making and hiding discriminatory decisions, and to force them to reach out to the market beyond their own state – the award procedures in the Utilities Directive are different from those in the public sector directives; they are less rigid, and permit more discretion to purchasers. Thus in balancing, on the one hand, the flexibility required for a conscientious purchaser to obtain best value for money with, on the other, the need to structure discretion to eliminate abuse and guard against development of inefficient practices, the Utilities Directive gives greater weight to the former interest. One view is that the rules in this directive achieve a better balance in this respect than the very rigid public sector rules.[50]

One important difference is that the Utilities Directive allows authorities a free choice between the open procedure, the restricted procedure and a competitive form of negotiated procedure; thus purchasers under this directive are not tied into a rigid and formal tendering procedure. Further, there is more flexibility in the way contracts are publicised:

---

[50] See pp. 290–295.

whilst the public sector directives requires publication of an advertisement for each individual contract which is to be subject to a competitive procedure this is not required under the Utilities Directive. Instead, authorities may either publicise contracts through a general PIN, or may advertise a "qualification system", under which providers may register their general interest in contracts of a particular type.[51] Another significant difference is that the rules on qualification are less rigid. In particular, the Utilities Directive does not impose the same limitations on the criteria for qualification, nor the evidence which may be used – one aspect of this being that contracts may be restricted to those who have already registered on qualification lists (or "approved" lists), something which is not permitted under the public sector rules.[52] Other differences include[53] more flexibility in choosing who is to be invited to bid in restricted or negotiated procedures;[54] more flexible time limits; and greater scope for using procedures which do not require any advertisement or competition (in particular, to take advantage of liquidations and similar events, which is not permitted under the public sector rules).[55]

These procedures are examined in detail in Chapter 10, with those on specifications (which are similar, though not identical, to those in the public sector) being considered separately in Chapter 11.

(3) PROPOSALS TO AMEND THE DIRECTIVES

The Commission has recently submitted two proposals for new directives, to amend the existing directives in the light of the new World Trade Organisation Agreement on Government Procurement (GPA). One proposal deals with amendments to the public sector directives,[56] and another deals with the directives on utilities.[57]

The GPA is an international agreement for liberalisation of procurement[58] to which the Community Member States are party, under which those states guarantee access to Community procurement markets to

---

[51] On these forms of publicity see further pp. 479–482.
[52] See pp. 244–247.
[53] It can also be noted that the Utilities Directive expressly permits the use of "framework agreements", whilst it is not clear if these are allowed under the public sector rules: see further pp. 177–179.
[54] See pp. 497–500.
[55] See pp. 488–489.
[56] Proposal for a European Parliament and Council Directive amending Directive 92/50/EEC relating to the co-ordination of procedures for the award of public service contracts, Directive 93/36/EEC co-ordinating procedures for the award of public supply contracts, and Directive 93/37/EEC concerning the co-ordination of procedures for the award of public works contracts, COM(95) 107, Final.
[57] Proposal for a European Parliament and Council Directive amending Directive 93/38/EEC co-ordinating the procurement procedures of entities operating in the water, energy, transport and telecommunications sector, COM(95) 107, Final.
[58] On this Agreement see Chap. 16.

certain third countries whilst those countries in turn undertake similar obligations towards Member States (and to each other). The GPA does not, however, govern the relationship of the Community states *inter se* – this is left to the Community Treaties and Directives. The original GPA (negotiated under the auspices of GATT) covered only central government supply contracts, but a new Agreement in force from January 1, 1996 extends the regime to sub-federal government and to works and services, and also to some utilities. This Agreement is discussed further in Chapter 15. In some respects, it gives access to procurements markets on terms which are more favourable than the Community directives – for example, as explained in Chapter 15, the thresholds for access to central government services contracts are lower under the GPA than under the public sector Services Directive, and in certain respects more stringent award procedures apply. The situation could thus result that third country signatories to the GPA receive better access to the markets of Community states than Member States enjoy in relation to each other.

The Commission's proposals are primarily designed to ensure that rights which Member States enjoy under Community law are no less favourable than those which third countries enjoy against Community states under the GPA.[59] They also ensure that compliance with the procedures in the directives automatically ensures compliance with the GPA.[59a] Between January 1, 1996, when the GPA comes into force, and the time when the proposed new directives come into force, firms from third countries covered by the GPA will, however, continue to enjoy better access to E.C. markets than E.C. firms will enjoy to the markets of other Member States. It can be noted that the United Kingdom regulations contain express provisions stating that E.C. providers must be as favourably treated as any third country providers,[59b] so that the benefit of the more stringent GPA award procedures must be extended to E.C. providers in the United Kingdom. However, this applies only to contracts within the regulations, and does not affect contracts which are covered by the GPA but which are outside the directives.

The Commission's proposals are not confined to amendments which are essential to harmonise the E.C. and GPA regimes but go further, in particular by applying the more stringent obligations which are imposed on some entities under the new Agreement to *all* entities covered by the E.C. regime. Most signficantly, the new GPA only covers utilities which are "public undertakings" and not those subject to the Utilities Directive merely because they enjoy "special and exclusive rights"; but the

---

[59] The Supply Directive was amended in 1980 for the same purpose when the original GPA came into effect in that year: see note 28 above.

[59a] However, as explained in Chapter 15, Member States themselves have a duty to implement the GPA; the amendment to the directives do not as such implement the GPA but affect only access of E.C. providers.

[59b] Works Regulation 4(2); Supply Regulation 4(2); Service Regulation 4(2); Utilities Regulation 4(3).

Commission proposes to apply any additional requirements for utilities under the new GPA to *all* types of entity covered by the Utilities Directive. However, such extensive amendments to the directives may provoke opposition, and it is not clear whether all the Commission's proposals will be accepted.

The details of these proposed amendments are explained in the course of the analysis of the existing rules in Chapters 5–11.

(4) LEGISLATION IMPLEMENTING THE DIRECTIVES IN THE UNITED KINGDOM

Directives are not intended to take effect automatically: under Article 189 E.C. they must be implemented by Member States into their own legal systems. What exactly is required by way of implementation depends on the nature of the directive in question: the general principle is that national law must provide for measures which are effective to secure the objectives of the particular directive. In the context of rules which are intended to be enforceable in law by third parties, a method of implementation is required which provides for such legally enforceable rights within the domestic system. Generally, this will involve the enactment of legislation. Other methods of implementation, such as administrative circulars of a type which are *not* generally enforceable in domestic law, are not adequate.[60]

Most of the rules in the procurement directives fall into this category since they are intended to be enforceable by aggrieved providers.[61] Initially, the United Kingdom (like many other Member States) failed properly to implement the directives: the original Works and Supply Directives were implemented only by means of administrative circular, which was not adequate.[62] However, the directives have now been implemented by means of regulations, enacted under section 2 of the European Communities Act 1972, which allows for the implementation by delegated legislation of most Community measures. The current directives and the corresponding regulations are summarised in the table on page 65. In interpreting the regulations it must be borne in mind that this enabling provision allows the government to enact regulations only so far as is necessary to give effect to Community law. It was not intended in the regulations to impose obligations more stringent or extensive than those actually required by the directives.

---

[60] Case 239/85, *Commission v. Belgium* [1986] E.C.R. 3645; case C–59/89, *Commission v. Germany* [1991] E.C.R. I–2607.

[61] See the discussion on direct effect at pp. 902–903 (which shows clearly that the rules were intended to be legally enforceable even before the specific directives on remedies were adopted). As to the few procurement rules which are not enforceable in this way see pp. 900–901.

[62] During that time the rules could, however, be enforced by relying on the doctrine of direct effect: see pp. 902–903.

In the public sector the directives are implemented through three separate sets of regulations. These are:

(i) The Public Works Contracts Regulations 1991.[63] These implement the rules on public sector works, and also the rules on remedies in Directive 89/665 so far as these affect works contracts.

(ii) The Public Supply Contracts Regulations 1995.[64] These implement the rules on public supply contracts in the Supply Directive 93/36, and also the rules on remedies in Directive 89/665 so far as these affect supply contracts.

(iii) The Public Services Contracts Regulations 1993.[65] These implement the rules on public services contracts in Directive 92/50, and also the rules on remedies in Directive 89/665 so far as these affect services contracts.

The rules on utilities purchasing are contained in the (draft) Utilities Contracts Regulations 1996.[66] These implement both the substantive rules contained in the Utilities Directive 93/38, and also the rules on remedies contained in the Utilities Remedies Directive 92/13.

As noted in section (3) above, it is proposed to amend the directives in the near future to ensure that the Community rules are at least as stringent as those giving rights to third countries under the GPA, and to make certain other incidental changes. To the extent that these proposals are adopted it will be necessary to amend the United Kingdom regulations to give effect to the amendments.

As well as being subject to the directives themselves, which require rights to be conferred on providers from other Community Member States, the United Kingdom is also bound by various international agreements negotiated by the Community, which oblige it to confer access to United Kingdom procurement on firms from certain states outside the Community. A number of these, such as the European

---

[63] S.I. 1991 No. 2680 (as slightly amended by the Utilities Supply and Works Contracts Regulations 1992, S.I. 1992 No. 3279, s.32 and the Public Supply Contracts Regulations 1995, S.I. 1995 No. 201, s.31). These regulations were enacted in 1991 following the revision of the original directive on works in 1989. It was not necessary to make any amendments following adoption of Directive 93/37 on works, since this did not alter the substance of the relevant rules but was merely a consolidating measure.

[64] S.I. 1995 No. 201. The rules in the original directive on supplies as amended in 1980 and 1988 (as to which see pp. 53–56) were implemented by the Public Supply Contracts Regulations 1991, S.I. 1991 No. 2679. Following the adoption of the new Supply Directive 93/36 in 1993, which both consolidated and amended the supply rules, the entire new directive was enacted through the 1995 regulations, which repealed the 1991 regulations.

[65] S.I. 1993 No. 3228.

[66] ("Utilities Regulations"). The rules on works and supply contracts of utilities originally adopted under Directive 90/531, plus the rules on remedies affecting these contracts, were originally implemented through the Utilities Supply and Works Contracts Regulations 1992, S.I. 1992 No. 3279. Following the addition of rules on services and the consolidation of all the utilities rules in a single directive through Directive 93/38, the entire new directive will be enacted through the Utilities Regulations 1996, which will repeal the 1992 regulations.

THE CURRENT PROCUREMENT DIRECTIVES AND IMPLEMENTING MEASURES

DIRECTIVES	UNITED KINGDOM IMPLEMENTING MEASURES
Works Directive (93/37/EEC), [1993] O.J. L199/54	Public Works Contracts Regulations 1991 (S.I. 1991 No. 2680), as am. by Utilities Supply and Works Contracts Regulations 1992, S.I. 1992 No. 3279, Public Supply Contracts Regulations 1995 (S.I. 1995 No. 201), and draft Utilities Contracts Regulations 1996.
Supply Directive (93/36/EEC), [1993] O.J. L199/1	Public Supply Contracts Regulations 1995 (S.I. 1995 No. 201), as am. by draft Utilities Contracts Regulations 1996.
Services Directive (92/50/EEC), [1992] O.J. L209/1	Public Services Contracts Regulations 1993 (S.I. 1993 No. 3228) as am. by Public Supply Contracts Regulations 1995 (S.I. 1995 No. 201) and draft Utilities Contracts Regulations 1996.
Remedies Directive (89/665/EEC), [1989] O.J. L395/33, as am. by the Services Directive, above	Public Works Contracts Regulations, above; Public Supply Contracts Regulations, above; Public Services Contracts Regulations, above.
Utilities Directive (93/38/EEC), [1993] O.J. L199/84 as am. by Directive 94/22/EEC, [1994] O.J. L164/3	Draft Utilities Contracts Regulations.
Utilities Remedies Directive (92/13/EEC), [1992] O.J. L76/7	Draft Utilities Contracts Regulations, above.

Economic Area Agreement (EEA) and Association Agreements with central and eastern European states, confer the same procedural rights on providers as do the Community directives and, like the directives, are – according to Community law – probably enforceable by those providers under the same remedies regime as applies under the directives.[67] The United Kingdom regulations have given effect to these identical obligations relating to third country providers as well as the directives themselves, in so far as such obligations were in effect when the regulations were adopted. Thus providers from the non-E.C. EEA states (Norway, Liechtenstein and Iceland) and from several Eastern and Central European states are expressly provided to have a right to enforce the regulations and providers from other states who obtain the benefits of similar agreements in the future will also be able to enforce the regulations, under the doctrine of direct effect, even though they are not mentioned expressly.[68]

The WTO Agreement on Government Procurement (GPA), in effect January 1, 1996, confers legal rights relating to products and firms from additional non-Community countries. The United Kingdom regulations will be amended in due course to reflect these obligations, as explained in Chapter 15.[69] Probably, these rules again have direct effect, so that they may be enforced even prior to any amendment to the regulations.[69a]

Apart from the measures adopted to implement obligations to third countries, the United Kingdom regulations are concerned only with implementing the Community directives. There are other Community provisions which affect procurement, notably the Treaty provisions and the "IT Standards Decision"[70]; these, however, do not require any implementation measures. Procurement obligations arising under domestic law – such as those on Compulsory Competitive Tendering – have not been incorporated into the regulations but remain subject to separate legislation.[71]

(5) PRACTICAL INITIATIVES TO SUPPORT THE OPEN MARKET

Action by the Community to open up procurement is not confined to the implementation and enforcement of the legislative measures referred to above. Within the framework of the legislation, and by way of supplement to its provisions, the European Commission has taken a number of practical initiatives to improve the workings of the internal procurement market.

---

[67] See further pp. 938–939.
[68] See further pp. 941–942.
[69] See pp. 781–782.
[69a] See pp. 938–939.
[70] See further Chap. 11.
[71] See further Chaps. 13–14.

(a) COMMUNITY POLICY ON SMEs

One area of activity is the improvement of opportunties for small- and medium-sized enterprises (SMEs) in the open procurement market. SMEs are considered important to the Community economy for a variety of reasons – for example, their particular potential for innovation and their flexibility to respond to new market requirements – and measures to promote SME participation in procurement markets is just one aspect of a more general policy directed at supporting SMEs in the single market.[72] Article 130f(2) E.C. now expressly provides that, in pursuing the aim of strengthening the scientific and technological base of industry, the Community shall encourage enterprises to co-operate to take advantage of the opportunties of the single market, *in particular* those provided (*inter alia*) through the opening up of public markets. This special need for action to help SMEs in public procurement has been perceived partly because of a concern that certain features of the open procurement legislation may have an adverse effect on SME participation. For example, provisions in the legislation which require separate contracts for identical or similar requirements to be valued as a single contract and awarded under the directives are likely to encourage purchasers to aggregate requirements into larger contracts which may be beyond the reach of SMEs[73]; whilst the increased bureaucracy of the new procedures is likely to deter SMEs disproportionately.

In contrast with the United States, and also with the policy of some of its own Member States, the Community does not require any preferential treatment for SMEs – for example, by requiring that a certain proportion of contracts (or subcontracts) be set aside for such entities, or (less restrictively) that certain work should be subcontracted by main contractors to provide greater opportunities for SMEs. Instead it has provided assistance and encouragement to enable SMEs to participate in the market on a competitive basis. In this respect, general measures to improve the flow of information or reduce the burden of qualification in procurement contracts (which are discussed below) are one aspect of SME policy, since the heavy costs of participating in government markets place disproportionate burdens on SMEs. More general Community measures to assist SMEs also, of course, help their participation in procurement markets – for example, the Community networks to facilitate contacts between firms with different expertise or local knowledge for the purpose of partnerships or subcontracting (such as the Business Co-operation Network – or BCNET). In addition, there have

---

[72] See O'Brien, "Public Procurement and the Small or Medium Enterprise" (1993) 2 P.P.L.R. 82; Mardas, "Subcontracting, Small and Medium Enterprises (SMEs) and Public Procurement in the European Community" (1994) 3 P.P.L.R. CS19; Cox, *The Single Market Rules and the Enforcement Regime after 1992* (1993), pp. 272–276; Business International, "Public Procurement in Europe: How E.C. Rules Will Open Up Cross Border Markets" (1991), Chap. 7.
[73] On this point see pp. 167–175 and 446–452.

been specific measures directed at procurement,[74] such as training programmes to highlight the opportunities in government markets. The Commission has also encouraged action by Member States over issues such as the setting up of insurance or guarantee schemes to assist SMEs in providing the financial guarantees necessary to compete on government contracts, and the avoidance of late payment for work done on government contracts, which can cause particular hardship for SMEs.[75] The United Kingdom has itself recently undertaken a review to identify ways of improving access to the public market for SMEs.[76]

(b) IMPROVING THE INFORMATION SYSTEM [77]

Another important aspect of the Commission's recent policy has been an attempt to improve the systems for providing information on contracts, mainly through an initiative referred to as SIMAP (*Système d'Information Marchés Publics*). As explained above, under the directives purchasers must publish (i) PIN notices giving advance details of proposed purchases, (ii) notices advertising all major contracts which they seek to award (which may be either individual contract notices or, in the utilities sector, notices of qualifications systems or detailed PIN notices) and (iii) notices giving details of award procedures once these have been completed. These are sent to the Community's Office of Official Publications which publishes the notices in both the hard copy of the *Official Journal of the European Communities* and in the electronic database version of the journal, Tenders Electronic Daily (referred to as TED). Either the full version of the notice or a summary of the main details (according to the type of notice) appears in all the Community languages. Firms may subscribe to TED individually or obtain information from TED through agents, in particular from "Euro-Info Centres" set up to provide assistance to businesses in all regions of the Community.

Under the SIMAP project the Community has sought to improve the operation of these systems, to provide better quality and more accessible information for providers; to make the systems easier to use for purchasers: and to provide better information for use by the Commission in monitoring compliance.

---

[74] See the articles cited in note 72.
[75] On this issue see Arrowsmith, "The United Kingdom Government Policy on Prompt Payment of Government Contractors and Sub-contractors" (1994) 3 P.P.L.R. CS124.
[76] See further n.16 on p. 802.
[77] See Moitinho, "The E.C. Public Procurement Information System – A Case for Simplification" (1992) 1 P.P.L.R. 189; Department of Trade and Industry, *Public Procurement Review* (1994), paras. 15–36.

One important project has been the development of a *Common Procurement Vocabulary* (CPV).[78-79] This provides a detailed standard nomenclature and numbered reference system for identifying products and services. A sample of the draft CPV, relating to the headings of "Seats and parts thereof" and "Other office and shop furniture" is set out on page 70. The CPV is designed for use in describing products and services in notices in the *Official Journal* and also for other purposes such as use in reports and statistical returns sent by states to the Commission. The description of products and services in this way should make it easier for providers to identify from a large amount of information in the *Official Journal* which individual contracts are of interest and also to extract general market information[80] – in particular, it should greatly facilitate electronic searches by use of key words and reference numbers. It will also enable notices to be easily translated; and will make it easier for the Commission to collect accurate and detailed information on purchases to assist in the monitoring process. The draft CPV has been used in practice by the *Official Journal* from early 1995, and at the time of writing the Commission was expected to adopt a Recommendation for its use from January 1996. Although initially its use will not be mandatory, it may be made so in due course.

Other initiatives under SIMAP include the development of standard formats for notices[81] in the *Official Journal*, and promoting the use of E-mail between purchasers and providers and between purchasers and the *Official Journal*. (Pilot projects in this latter area have just been launched.) There have also been moves to increase the publication of notices for contracts which are below the threshold of the directives, which may be published in the *Official Journal* on an optional basis.

[78-79] This is based on the Community's *Classification of Products According to Activities* (CPA), which is in turn based on the United Nations *Central Product Classification* (CPC), which is used for classifying products and services worldwide, including under the GATT and WTO Agreements on Government Procurement. On the CPV see further Street, "The Common Procurement Vocabulary (CPV): Development of the Community Nomenclature" (1995) 4 P.P.L.R. CS86; Laudat, "Advantages of a Common Product Nomenclature in Public Procurement" (1995) 4 P.P.L.R. CS112.

[80] The Department of Trade and Industry (DTI) has recently suggested that the greatest use of the improved Community information systems may be to extract such general information which will allow firms to develop a long-term strategy in public markets: DTI, *Public Procurement Review* (1994), paras. 24–29. The Report suggests that the time periods in the directives are often too short to facilitate bidding on specific work which comes to light for the first time only through the O.J., and that improvements on the availability of information on individual contracts is thus of limited value.

[81] See Commission Recommendation 91/561/EEC, [1991] O.J. L305/19.

DRAFT COMMON PROCUREMENT VOCABULARY 1994

DIVISION 36—FURNITURE; OTHER MANUFACTURED GOODS N.E.C.

36.11.10.00–2	SEATS AND PARTS THEREOF
36.11.11.00–3	Seats, primarily with metal frames
36.11.11.00–6	Seats for civil aircraft
36.11.11.30–2	Seats for motor vehicles
36.11.11.50–8	Swivel seats
36.11.11.91–7	Classroom chairs
36.11.11.98–6	Ejector seats
36.11.11.99–3	Theatre seats and others seats n.e.c.
36.11.12.00–4	Seats, primarily with wooden frames
36.11.12.20–0	Dining chairs
36.11.12.40–6	Armchairs and settees
36.11.12.60–2	Bench seats
36.11.12.80–8	Deck chairs and other seats with wooden frames n.e.c.
36.11.13.00–5	Other seats n.e.c.
36.11.13.10–8	Seats of plastic
36.11.13.90–2	Other seats n.e.c.
36.11.14.00–6	Parts of seats
36.12.10.00–5	OTHER OFFICE AND SHOP FURNITURE
36.12.11.00–6	Metal furniture of a kind used in offices
36.12.11.10–9	Tables (metal)
36.12.11.23–3	Cupboards (metal)
36.12.11.30–5	Desks (metal)
36.12.11.40–8	Metal office shelving
36.12.11.60–4	Other metal office furniture n.e.c.
36.12.11.61–1	Filing cabinets (metal)
36.12.11.62–8	Card-index cabinets (metal)
36.12.11.69–7	Metal trolleys and other metal office furniture n.e.c.
36.12.11.80–0	Maintenance and repair services of metal office furniture
36.12.12.00–7	Wooden furniture of a kind used in offices
36.12.12.22–7	Tables (wood)
36.12.12.23–4	Cupboards (wood)
36.12.12.30–6	Desks (wood)
36.12.12.40–9	Wooden office shelving
36.12.12.60–5	Other wooden office furniture n.e.c.
36.12.12.61–2	Filing cabinets (wood)
36.12.12.62–9	Card-index cabinets (wood)
36.12.12.69–8	Wooden trolleys and other wooden office furniture n.e.c.
36.12.12.80–1	Maintenance and repair services of wooden office furniture
36.12.13.00–8	Wooden furniture for shops
36.12.13.10–1	Display cases
36.12.13.90–5	Counters and other wooden shop furniture n.e.c.

(c) SIMPLIFICATION OF AWARD PROCEDURES AND MUTUAL RECOGNITION

Finally, it should be emphasised that the operation of the open procurement market, especially for SMEs, will be considerably enhanced if the complexity and cost of participating in award procedures can be reduced. The directives themselves have attempted this to some extent – for example, the public sector rules seek to reduce the burdens of qualification by limiting the information which purchasers may demand from providers.[82] However, qualification and other burdens of participating in new markets remains significant. An important recent initiative to deal with such difficulties is the placement by the Community of a mandate with CEN and CENELEC, two European standardising institutions,[83-84] to develop a voluntary standard for qualification procedures for works contracts. This could provide the basis for mutual recognition of qualification lists amongst states applying the same voluntary standard, so removing the need for providers to qualify separately in each state. Initiatives to develop voluntary standards for other aspects of procurement procedures could provide an initial basis for increased harmonisation of contract award procedures between different Member States, and could ultimately provide the foundation for further harmonisation under the directives.

(6) A CRITIQUE OF COMMUNITY POLICY[85]

Whilst it is generally accepted that there is scope for substantial savings from open procurement, there are some doubts as to whether the rules adopted will succeed in opening the market. It is at this point too early to draw any firm conclusions about the actual impact of the procurement legislation on the market[86]; but some general points may be considered about the prospects for success.

---

[82] See generally Chap. 10.
[83-84] On these bodies see further Chap. 11.
[85] On these issues see, in particular, Cox, *The Single Market Rules and the Enforcement Regime after 1992* (1993); Cox, "Implementing 1992 Public Procurement Policy; Public and Private Obstacles to the Creation of the Single European Market" (1992) 1 P.P.L.R. 139; Fernández Martín, *A Critical Analysis of E.C. Public Procurement Legislation: Present Limitations and Future Prospects* (1993), Ph.D. thesis, pp. 201–221; Business International, "Public Procurement in Europe" (1991), Chaps. 5–8; von Bael, "Public Procurement and the Completion of the Internal Market" [1989] L.I.E.I. 21; Nicholson, "Europe-wide Public Procurement: the Gainers and the Losers" (1989) 1 European Business Law Journal 15.
[86] There have been a few small studies, including some consideration of the rules' impact on purchasing patterns: see, for example, Department of Trade and Industry, *Public Procurement Review* (1994); Hartley and Uttley, "The Single European Market and Public Procurement Policy: the Case of the United Kingdom" (1994) 3 P.P.L.R. 114. It is likely that substantial economic impact studies will be carried out for the European Commission in the next few years.

A first question is whether the rules – which were widely ignored before 1985 – will now be followed. Whilst there has been increased compliance with at least some of the rules (as shown by the increase in notices sent to the Official Journal) some recent studies suggest that non-compliance is still prevalent.[87] One issue here is the adequacy of the enforcement system: in particular, whether the remedies available to aggrieved providers are really effective; whether, in any case, they will be prepared to use such remedies; and (related to this) whether there is a need to improve enforcement mechanisms which do not depend on action by aggrieved firms – for example, by introducing external auditing or increasing the powers and resources of the Commission. These issues are examined further in Chapter 18. Another problem is the uncertainty over what is required of purchasers. As will be explained, on certain key issues, such as the permissible criteria for shortlisting,[88] the operation of the aggregation rules[89] and the use of framework agreements in the public sector,[90] the requirements are unclear. Such uncertainty reduces both the prospects for compliance by purchasers and the likelihood of legal actions by providers.

Another concern affecting the possibility of non-compliance is that certain breaches remain virtually impossible to prove. Whilst the directives, especially the public sector directives, have sought to minimise discretion, areas remain where there is much scope for subjective assessment and thus potential for abuse. For example, the directives seek to preclude the influence of "national" considerations at the award stage by requiring that evaluation criteria are notified in advance in order of preference. However, where a variety of criteria are listed it is difficult to show that an award decision is based on improper considerations, such as nationality – provided the selected bidder has at least one of the "lawful" criteria in its favour (such as the earliest delivery date) the authority can cite that to justify its decision. However effective the remedies system, it is unlikely to be of much use for either redress or deterrence with breaches which involve an abuse of discretion, as opposed to non-compliance with formal rules such as those requiring publication of notices.[91] This is probably an inherent limitation of legal

---

[87] See, for example, Department of Trade and Industry, *Public Procurement Review* (1994), paras. 37–41; Hartley and Uttley, above, pp. 119–121. Both found a low publication rate for notices advertising contracts, but it is difficult to draw clear conclusions without knowing exactly which contracts *should* have been advertised. Extensive non-compliance was found in the publication of award notices: the Department of Trade and Industry Review found, for example, that only three of the 12 Member States of 1994 published notices for more than 50 per cent of advertised contracts (Denmark, Luxembourg and the United Kingdom); and in some states the figure was less than 10 per cent.

[88] See pp. 217–222.

[88] See pp. 167–175.

[90] See pp. 175–179.

[91] This problem can be dealt with only by providing an appeal to a higher body which would be allowed to overturn award decisions on their merits; but this would involve an unacceptable interference with the commercial discretion of purchasers.

regulation of procurement; it is probably impossible to stop purchasers who are determined to discriminate.

Whilst this may be the case, however, it would probably be wrong to conclude that purchasers will not generally comply with the rules. For states and individual authorities who still seek to discriminate, the threat of legal action is likely to impose considerable restraints and to reduce the opportunities for doing so, even if abuse cannot be entirely eliminated. For the rest (probably the majority) who do not seek positively to favour domestic industry there may still be reluctance to comply, because of the additional procedural burdens and because the rules may preclude preferred procurement methods such as long-term "partnering" arrangements.[92] However, such tendencies are likely to be overcome as monitoring by the Commission and Member States themselves becomes more widespread, and, perhaps, as providers become aware of their rights. Further, compliance should increase as more information becomes available, as governments become more used to operating the rules and systems are established, and as measures to make the rules more "user-friendly" – such as the use of standard nomenclature – are put in place. The experience of non-compliance before 1985 cannot be taken as an indication of likely future behaviour, especially since there was at that time widespread ignorance by many purchasers even about the existence of the rules, let alone what compliance entailed.[93]

As well as the issue of whether purchasers will indeed comply with the rules, the question arises as to whether, even if they do, the market will really become more competitive – will providers respond to the opportunities to bid on public contracts in other states? As Cox has noted, "Firms often lack the size, the financial resources, the staff, the language expertise and the entrepreneurial flair to behave as the textbooks on supply and demand suggest they ought to."[94] Factors which may inhibit participation in practice – but which could be overcome – include language barriers; lack of familiarity with the purchasing structure and procedures in other states; the burdensome nature of those procedures, and the high costs of bidding; lack of familiarity with the applicable private law; and the difficulty of obtaining information about contracts. Many of these barriers apply in private markets, and since Atkins calculated potential participation in foreign public procurement markets by comparing existing participation in those markets with participation in foreign markets as a whole, some of these barriers have been taken

---

[92] On this see further pp. 290–293.

[93] In particular, before the reforms of the1980s many of those who were Member States at that time – including, as explained above, the United Kingdom – had not even implemented the public sector rules into national law: see D'Hooghe *et al.*, "Special Feature: Implementation of the Public Procurement Directive in the 12 States of the E.C." (1992) 1 P.P.L.R. 167 and 251.

[94] Cox, *The Single Market Rules and the Enforcement Regime after 1992* (1993), p. 274.

into account in the Atkins analysis of potential savings. However, certain of the barriers may be more significant in public sector than private sector markets, because of the especially bureaucratic nature of government purchasing. It is important that they should not be overlooked, since the public procurement legislation may be rendered much more effective if steps are taken to deal with these issues. As noted above, the Community has already taken some action in this area, including providing assistance to SMEs, and improving the accessibility of information on public contracts.

Another issue which has concerned some critics has been the nature of the rules themselves: as noted above, it has been questioned whether the rigid and costly tendering system under the public sector regime, in particular, is really the most appropriate one for obtaining value for money. This issue is examined in further detail in Chapter 6 on the public sector procedures. Briefly, however, it may be noted here that whilst it can be accepted that rigid competitive tendering is often not the best method of procurement for a conscientious purchaser who operates under commercial constraints and seeks solely to obtain value for money, often government purchasers do not fall into this category; this is, indeed the main reason why it has been necessary to regulate public, but not private, procurement. To avoid abuse and inefficiency there is a need for a rule-based system under which decisions can easily be monitored, and this will inevitably be more restrictive than an "ideal" system for the private sector. However, the difficult question is exactly how the balance should be struck between rules and discretion. As is explained in Chapter 6, it is the author's view that in many respects the Utilities Directive strikes a better balance than the public sector regime.[95]

Finally, it should be mentioned that whilst the programme on procurement envisaged in the 1985 White Paper is now complete, there are still calls for its further extension. Most notably, procurement of military equipment is outside the regime, although this is an area with enormous potential for savings; this issue is considered further in Chapter 17 on defence procurement. Further, the scope of the procurement regime so far as it affects services is also affected by the fact that some services are not yet fully covered by the rules[96] and by the fact that many services are carried out by Member States "in-house",[97] which means that they are not open to Europe-wide competition as they would be if contracted out to the private sector. Both these limitations relating to services are to be considered by the Commission in its review of the Services Directive in 1996, as noted at (7) below.

---

[95] See pp. 290–295.
[96] See pp. 132–138 and 421–422.
[97] On the in-house provision of services see further Chap. 12.

(7) PROVISIONS FOR REVIEW OF THE DIRECTIVES

It has already been explained that the Commission has recently made proposals to amend the directives in light of the new World Trade Organisation Agreement on Government Procurement.[98] More generally, the directives themselves provide for states to furnish the Commission with various pieces of information on the operation of the rules, and for the Commission to undertake a review of the position.

In relation to the public sector, Article 29(1) of the Supply Directive requires the Commission to examine the application of the directive in consultation with the Advisory Committee for Public Contracts and where appropriate to submit proposals to the Council with the aim, in particular, of harmonising the implementation measures of Member States. Article 43 of the Services Directive also provides for a review by the Commission, with a deadline of July 1, 1996, in consultation with both the Advisory Committee for Public Contracts and the Advisory Committee on Telecommunications Procurement, and to make appropriate proposals for revisions. The Commission is specifically required to consider the effects of the existing rules; the possibility of extending the full provisions of the directive to those services which are presently not fully covered (the "non-priorty" services); and the effects of in-house provision of services on the opening of markets. Whilst there is no express provision for review in the Works Directive this directive is likely to be reviewed by the Commission at the same time as those on supplies and services.

At the very least, any review may result in consolidation of the works, supplies and services rules in a single directive. Consolidation would itself eliminate a number of anomalies. In particular, at present many of the rules are drawn up on the basis that supply contracts cover only provision of supplies, works contracts works only and services contracts services only. In fact supply contracts often have significant elements of services (for example, contracts for products plus some maintenance element) and services contracts a substantial element of supplies. This leads to gaps which do not exist under the Utilities Directive, where works, supplies and services are generally dealt with under the same provisions. For example, the qualification rules under the Supplies Directive allow authorities to call for product samples; but this is not mentioned under the services rules (it being assumed that services contracts do not involve supplies), although samples might be useful in relation to products furnished under services contracts. Any review process will also no doubt involve the elimination of other minor and obvious anomalies.

It is too early to predict the extent to which any review may lead to more substantial revisions, such as relaxation of some of the rigid

---

[98] See pp. 61-63.

tendering rules and, even, closer approximation of the utilities and public sector rules. It seems unlikely at the present time that there will be any extension of the services rules to non-priority services or any regulation of in-house service provision, but this cannot be said with certainty. It is also unclear whether the rules are likely to be amended to clarify their operation: as already noted, their effect remains unclear in a number of important respects.[99]

Article 44 of the Utilities Directive provides for a review by the Commission of both the scope of the directive and its operation, and for necessary proposals for amendments. This is to be carried out by July 1998, in consultation with the Advisory Committee for Public Contracts and (in the case of entities operating in the sphere of telecommunications) the Advisory Committee on Telecommunications Procurement. There is a specific direction to consider the progress made in opening up markets and the actual level of competition. Again, it is too early to anticipate what significant changes, if any, may result from such a review.

---

[99] See p. 72.

CHAPTER 4

PROCUREMENT UNDER THE E.C. TREATY

1. INTRODUCTION

This chapter considers the application of the E.C. Treaty[1] to procurement decisions. The Treaty does not expressly mention procurement, except in the context of contracts financed by the Community in certain overseas countries and territories,[2] but it has been accepted from the very beginning that a number of its general provisions are relevant to procurement. The most significant are as follows:

Article 30: This forbids measures which hinder or discourage free trade in *goods*. This includes measures which restrict access of goods to government contracts – for example, a ban on the use of imported products in such contracts.

Article 52: This is concerned with "freedom of establishment" – the right for firms from one state to set up and carry on a business in other Member States on a permanent basis. This covers restrictions on access to government contracts which affect the activities of non-nationals established in the state in question.

Article 59: This deals with restrictions on those who wish to provide services on a temporary basis in another Member State, including persons wishing to participate in contracts for services awarded by government.

Article 6: This is a general prohibition on discrimination on grounds of nationality, which covers certain acts of discrimination not within other specific articles of the Treaty (such as Articles 30, 52 and 59). As is explained below, it is not clear if it has a role in the procurement field.

Article 85: This prohibits restrictive trade agreements, and prevents procuring entities from entering into purchasing arrangements – such as long-term exclusive supply agreements – which unduly restrict possibilities for competition.

---

[1] Some purchases are subject not to the E.C. Treaty but the ECSC or Euratom Treaties, although most fall within the E.C. Treaty. The provisions of the E.C. Treaty apply to products covered by the other two Treaties where there is no conflict with those Treaties. Additional relevant provisions are Articles 4 and 86 ECSC and Article 93 Euratom (which deal with free movement of goods) and Article 97 Euratom (supplementing Articles 52 and 59 E.C.).
[2] In Article 132(4).

Article 86: This prohibits undertakings from abusing a dominant market position, and operates to prevent purchasers who are dominant in their markets from abusing that power in the way they treat their providers.

Article 90(1): Article 90(1) E.C. gives Member States responsibility in connection with "undertakings" in their own states over which they have some control, or to which they have granted special privileges, to ensure the proper functioning of the free market. This may be used to hold the state responsible where such undertakings adopt restrictive measures relating to government contracts.

It should be noted that similar rules sometimes apply in relation to firms and products from states outside the Community, under international agreements concluded with those states; these are considered further in Chapter 16.

Major contracts are, of course, subject to detailed regulation under the Community directives and implementing legislation, as described in Chapters 5–11 below. The Treaty principles are relevant, however, in supplementing this legislation. The Treaty is also important in relation to contracts not caught by the directives, such as those below the threshold, or which are excluded for certain other reasons; as explained below such contracts may still sometimes be caught by the Treaty provisions.

2. ARTICLE 30 E.C.: FREE MOVEMENT OF GOODS [3]

(1) GENERAL PRINCIPLES

Article 30 E.C. seeks to ensure that goods[4] can move without restriction from one Member State to another. Essentially it prohibits government measures which have the effect of hindering trade between these states. More specifically, it provides that: "Quantitive restrictions on imports and all measures having equivalent effect shall . . . be prohibited between member states."

The sort of measures which are most obviously damaging to trade are those which prohibit altogether the import of goods from other member states, or impose quotas – these are examples of the "restrictions" on imports forbidden by Article 30. However, it is not only these direct restrictions which are forbidden, but also other measures which have

---

[3] See further Wyatt and Dashwood, *European Community Law* (3rd ed., 1993) Chap. 8; and for a detailed discussion Gormley, *Prohibiting Restrictions on Trade within the EEC* (1985) and Oliver, *Free Movement of Goods* (2nd ed., 1988).

[4] Goods covered are those originating in the E.C. or which have been placed in free circulation on the Community market: on this see further Chap. 15.

"equivalent effect" to restrictions on imports. This concept of measures of "equivalent effect" has been widely defined: according to a famous statement of principle by the Court of Justice in *Dassonville* it covers "all trading rules enacted by member states which are capable of hindering, directly or indirectly, actually or potentially, intra-Community trade."[5] It covers a variety of restrictions which may have the effect of hindering such trade by affecting the access of imports to the domestic market. Examples include rules on the quality or safety of products, or the packaging which may be used: such measures can restrict trade, since their effect is to prevent the sale of imports which do not meet those standards.

Article 30 E.C. is generally invoked in relation to measures which affect the domestic market as a whole – for example, bans on imports, or the imposition of general safety standards. However, it applies equally to conduct which merely restricts opportunities for the supply of imports in the *government* market. Thus, for example, it contravenes Article 30 to adopt a rule that government bodies may buy a particular type of product only from domestic producers. The type of measures caught are considered in further detail below.

Article 30 applies to restrictions on products supplied under any public contract. This may be a contract which is primarily for the supply of goods, but the provision also covers restrictions on products to be used or supplied in the performance of contracts for works or non-construction services. This was established by the Court of Justice in *Dundalk*,[6] a case arising out of a call for tenders relating to the construction of a water main by an Irish municipal authority. The specifications for the pipes to be used in the construction were held to discriminate in favour of Irish products, and the Court held that use of such discriminatory specifications constituted a breach of Article 30. It was argued that because the contract was primarily one for services,[7] it should be assessed only under the provisions of the Treaty dealing specifically with services, notably Article 59 E.C. However, the Court rejected this argument, holding that both the goods and services provisions of the Treaty were applicable to the contract, within their appropriate spheres of operation.[8]

Article 30 covers measures which may *potentially* hinder trade, which clearly may apply where products are excluded from the government

---

[5] Case 8/74, *Procureur du roi v. Dassonville* [1974] E.C.R. 837, [1974] 2 C.M.L.R. 436.

[6] Case 45/87, *Commission v. Ireland* [1988] E.C.R. 4929; and see the notes by Arrowsmith, *A Guide to the Procurement Cases of the Court of Justice*, at 7 and Gormley, (1989) 14 E.L.Rev. 156.

[7] The term "services" is used here in its wide sense, as used in the Treaty, to include contracts for works, as well as contracts for other types of services. In the procurement directives and implementing legislation the concept of a services contract is narrower, the term being used to refer only to contracts not already regulated by the directives on works and supplies, and hence excluding works contracts.

[8] Para. 17 of the judgment. For discussion of the judgment on this point see further Arrowsmith, *A Guide to the Procurement Cases of the Court of Justice* (1992) at 7.4.2.

market or any part of it. However, a question relevant for procurement is whether there is a *de minimis* rule which excludes Article 30 where the potential effect is negligible. This would not affect the Article's application to general measures, such as legislation or administrative guidance laying down a "Buy National" policy, but might take outside its scope conduct which relates only to an individual contract. This issue was raised in *Dundalk* but not specifically addressed by the Court. Advocate General Darmon suggested that, given the importance of contracts with public bodies for suppliers in the industry in question, and the importance of the particular contract, the effect of the measure was sufficiently significant that a limit of this kind would not apply; and the Court's finding of an infringement of Article 30 could rest on this view. It is widely accepted, however, that in general no *de minimis* rule applies in the context of Article 30,[9] and it is submitted that this is the better view.

A further limitation might arise out of the fact that Article 30 applies only to "measures". The Court has stated that to constitute a "measure", conduct must exhibit a degree of consistency and generality and, if this is so, this also could exclude from Article 30 restrictions relating solely to individual contracts. This was accepted by Advocate General Darmon in *Dundalk* who concluded, however, that the specification should not be treated as an isolated act because it was a "specific manifestation of a general practice" of referring to Irish national standards in Irish government contracts. In subsequent cases, *Re Data Processing* (Article 59 E.C.),[10] *Storebaelt* (Article 30 E.C.)[11] and case C–359/93, *Commission v. Netherlands*,[12] discussed below, the Court of Justice has found breaches of the Treaty arising from acts connected with specific contracts. However, in none of these cases was the issue specifically discussed, and in each one the action was in any case a manifestation of a more general practice. It is difficult to see, however, the justification for an approach which limits the application of the Treaty to purchasing practices of a general nature where these involve a definite and positive act such as a restrictive description of products or the express exclusion of foreign providers.

(2) CONDUCT COVERED [13]

Article 30 E.C. generally applies, first, to measures which *discriminate directly* between domestic and imported products. This covers, for

---

[9] See for example, Gormley, above, p. 3, esp. note 5; Oliver, above, p. 74.
[10] Case C–3/88, *Commission v. Italy* [1989] E.C.R. 4035.
[11] Case C–243/89, *Commission v. Denmark* judgment of November 17, 1992.
[12] Judgment of January 24, 1995.
[13] On this see also Directive 70/32/EEC, [1970] O.J. L13/1, which may provide assistance in interpretation. As explained in Chap. 3 (see pp. 50–52) this directive was adopted to eliminate restrictive procurement practices affecting goods prior to the time when Article 30 became directly effective. See further Weiss, *Public Procurement in European Community Law* (1993), Chap. 3, esp. pp. 34–35; Turpin, "Public Contracts in the EEC" (1972) C.M.L.Rev. 411.

example, decisions to buy certain products only from the domestic market, or a policy which gives a preference to domestic products – for example, by purchasing products from other states only when they are more than 10 per cent cheaper. This is illustrated by case C–263/85, *Commission v. Italy*,[14] in which the Court of Justice ruled to be unlawful measures which required Italian public authorities to purchase motor vehicles of domestic manufacture, as a condition of eligibility for certain subsidies; and also by the *Storebaelt* case, in which the Court held contrary to Article 30 a clause in a Danish construction contract requiring the use of Danish materials as far as possible.

Another illustration is *Du Pont de Nemours*.[15] This case concerned Italian legislation which required certain public authorities to reserve 30 per cent of their supplies purchases for undertakings which had establishments and fixed plant in the *Mezzorgiorno* (southern) region of Italy, and which offered products which had been processed at least partly in that region, the aim of the policy being to promote the industrial development of the *Mezzorgiorno*. Procurement decisions based on this legislation were challenged before the Italian courts. In response to a request for a preliminary ruling, the Court ruled that the policy discriminated against imported products and was thus incompatible with Article 30.[16] It is also prohibited to impose special conditions on providers who wish to use imported products for the contract – for example, an authority may not require a special security bond from providers whose bids involve imported products, which does not apply to those offering domestic products.[17]

Secondly, Article 30 also covers measures which apply equally to domestic and imported products ("indistinctly applicable" measures), but which *have the effect of favouring domestic products* – that is, measures which are discriminatory in their effect. A measure of this type was held to be contrary to Article 30 in *Dundalk*.[18] The contract specifications in that case required that certain pipes to be used in the construction work should comply with an Irish national standard. The requirement was indistinctly applicable – the same standard applied to both imported and domestic products – and in theory could be met by

---

[14] Judgment of May 16, 1991.
[15] Case 31/88, *Du Pont de Nemours Italiana SpA v. Unita Sanitaria Locale No. 2 Di Carrara* [1990] I–E.C.R. 889, analysed in Arrowsmith, *A Guide to the Procurement Cases of the Court of Justice* (1992; Earlsgate) at p. 10. The Court's ruling relating to the application of Article 30 was confirmed in case 351/88, *Laboratori Bruneau Srl v. Unita Sanitaria Locale RM/24 de Monterondo* July 11, 1991, which concerned the application of the same Italian legislation: see Arrowsmith, *A Guide to the Procurement Cases of the Court of Justice* (1992), at 15.
[16] It was irrelevant that the policy did not merely discriminate against products from other states, but also discriminated against *Italian* products from outside the *Mezzorgiorno*; it was sufficient that all the products favoured were domestic products: see paras. 12–13 of the judgment.
[17] See Article 3(2) of Directive 70/32, above.
[18] Case 45/87, *Commission v. Ireland* [1988] E.C.R. 4929, [1989] 1 C.M.L.R. 225, analysed further in Arrowsmith, above, note 15, at 7.

products produced anywhere in the E.C. In practice, however, as the Court pointed out, only one firm, an Irish firm, produced products complying with the standard. Specifications which refer to a national standard will generally be discriminatory since it is more likely that products from the state concerned will be manufactured to comply with that standard.[19]

It is not clear how far measures which tend to favour national *suppliers* may be considered to discriminate indirectly against imported *products*. This issue arose in the *Lottomatica* case,[20] which concerned a contract for the computerisation of the Italian national lottery system, including the supply of computer equipment. The Commission argued that legislation which restricted participation in the contract to firms in the ownership of the Italian government infringed Article 30. The Court of Justice held that the measure infringed Article 59 E.C., since it tended to favour Italian firms.[21] However, the Court did not consider whether it also infringed Article 30, since the Commission had not explained how such a measure hindered the use of foreign products in the contract.[22]

It would appear, however, that measures favouring domestic providers for contracts do also favour domestic products, since providers are more likely to use and supply products from their own state[23]; in particular, such measures are likely to hit the products of manufacturers who wish to bid to sell their own products directly to governments in other Member States. Thus it is submitted that measures directed at providers rather than directly at products may still infringe Article 30; and this applies equally whether the contract is wholly for supplies, or simply involves provision of supplies in the course of, or ancillary to, the provision of services (for example, products used in public works contracts).[24] This will mean that conditions imposed on suppliers – for example, those relating to financial and technical standing – which

---

[19] This area is considered more fully in Chap. 11, which considers the application of both the Community Treaties and other measures to contract specifications.

[20] Case C–272/91, *Commission v. Italy,* judgment of April 26, 1994.

[21] On this point, see further p. 91.

[22] See paras. 15–17 of the judgment.

[23] This arises even if it can be assumed that providers take into account only commercial, and not nationalistic considerations, in deciding which products to use or purchase, since commercial factors, such as language considerations, the existence of long-term "partnering" arrangements with local providers, or transport costs, will tend to result in purchases from local providers in most cases.

[24] This, of course, applies only where the items provided in the course of carrying out services contracts are products of the type which fall under Article 30, and not where they are items which are so inextricably linked with the provision of services that they do not fall within Article 30 at all (as, for example, case C–275/92, *Commissioners of Customs and Excise v. Schindler,* judgment of March 24, 1994, where the Court of Justice ruled that Article 30 did not apply to a measure restricting the right to run lotteries in the United Kingdom (held to constitute the provision of services), even though this had the effect of restricting the import and sale of lottery tickets from other Member States, where the sole purpose of the import and distribution of the products was to allow participation in services.

The rule advocated in the text has the effect that many restrictions directed at providers seeking public services contracts fall within Article 30 as well as Article 59.

operate, directly or indirectly, in a discriminatory manner, infringe Article 30. Likewise, it is contrary to Article 30 to give preference to national suppliers in other ways – for example, by giving priority to such suppliers in deciding which providers are to be selected to bid on a contract.

Thirdly, Article 30 applies to some measures which are *neither directly or indirectly discriminatory*[25] – that is, which hinder equally both imports and domestic products. It is generally accepted that Article 30 applies to such measures where they relate to the characteristics of the goods – for example, safety or quality standards in legislation.[26] There has been controversy over how far Article 30 applies to other types of measures which affect domestic and imported products equally – for example, restrictions on the marketing or advertising of products, or the conditions in which the goods are produced (such as the working conditions of employees).[27] Following the Court of Justice decision in *Keck* and subsequent similar cases, however, it is now considered that measures which do not relate to product characteristics are only generally caught by Article 30 if they discriminate, directly or indirectly.[28] The same appears to apply to measures of a fiscal nature or measures concerned with general economic management, which have the effect of restricting the market generally[29] – for example, measures restricting the availability of credit. Thus non-discriminatory policies of this type are entirely within the discretion of Member States.

In relation to government procurement, the above principle entails that contract specifications covering health, safety and other product characteristics must not be defined in a way which is unduly restrictive and which denies suitable products access to government markets. This was indicated by the Court of Justice in case C–359/93, *Commission v. Netherlands*,[30] in which it held that a requirement for use of the "UNIX" operating system in a contract for the supply of an information technology system infringed Article 30. Such a specification did not appear to favour providers from the Netherlands in any way, but was held unlawful simply because it excluded providers using systems other than UNIX which were, however, equally suitable in meeting the government's operational requirements.[31-32] On the other hand, it

---

[25] This was established following the reasoning of the Court of Justice in the landmark decision in the "Cassis de Dijon" case, case 120/78, *Rewe-Zentral v. Bundesmonopolverwaltung für Branntwein* [1979] E.C.R. 649. On this point see Wyatt and Dashwood, above, pp. 221–224; Gormley, above, pp. 262–264; Oliver, above, p. 89.

[26] This does not mean that such standards are not permitted: they are allowed where they can be justified under one of the limitations on Article 30 discussed at pp. 84–86 below.

[27] On this controversy see Wyatt and Dashwood, above, pp. 212–213, and the academic works cited there.

[28] Cases C–267 and C–268/91, *Keck & Methouard,* [1993] I E.C.R. 6097; confirmed by subsequent case law of the Court of Justice.

[29] Case 238/82, *Duphar* [1984] E.C.R. 523, can be explained on this basis.

[30] Judgment of January 24, 1995.

[31-32] The implications of this decision are considered more fully in Chap. 11.

appears that conditions for participation in government contracts which relate to "secondary" policy issues, such as a supplier's equal opportunities record, are not covered by Article 30 unless their effect is to discriminate, directly or indirectly, against foreign providers. The position of measures which concern the qualifications of providers to participate in government contracts is considered in Chapter 7.

(3) LIMITATIONS ON ARTICLE 30[33]

Some measures which restrict the freedom to sell products may be needed to protect legitimate interests: for example, restrictions on products which are unsafe. Where there are no appropriate Community measures, the Treaty preserves the discretion of states to take their own measures in certain areas, even though these restrict trade.

First, Article 36 E.C. provides for derogations from Article 30 on grounds of "public morality, public policy or public security; the protection of health and life of humans, animals or plants; the protection of national treasures possessing artistic, historic or archeological value; or the protection of industrial and commercial property". To invoke these it must be shown that there is no "arbitrary" discrimination[34] – that is, that any distinction between domestic and imported goods is justifiable on objective grounds;[35] and that there is no "disguised restriction on trade".[36] Further, the measure must be limited to what is necessary, and if its objective may be achieved by a less restrictive means, that means should be used instead.[37]

Secondly, Article 30 may also be inapplicable where a measure can be justified on the basis of one of a number of other public interest grounds ("mandatory requirements") recognised by the Court,[38] such as protection of consumers, environmental protection, the effectiveness of fiscal supervision and improvement of working conditions (a non-exhaustive list which may be added to by the Court). This applies, however, only to indistinctly applicable measures – that is, those which do not draw a direct distinction between domestic and imported products. In addition, such measures must be proportionate to the objective sought.[39]

In relation to procurement, the mere fact that the subject matter of a procurement contract is concerned with one of the matters falling under

---

[33] On these limitations see Wyatt and Dashwood, above, pp. 225–232.

[34] Article 36 E.C.

[35] Case 4/75, *Rewe-Zentralfinanz v. Landwirtshaftskammer* [1975] E.C.R. 843.

[36] Article 36 E.C. This appears to mean that where the motive is protectionist, there is a presumption that the measure is not justified: see Oliver, *Free Movement of Goods* (2nd ed., 1988), pp. 170–171; *Bourgoin v. Minister of Agriculture, Food and Fisheries* [1986] Q.B. 716.

[37] Case 104/75, *Officier van Justitie v. de Peijper* [1976] E.C.R. 613.

[38] "Cassis de Dijon", above. In theory these are not *derogations* from Article 30, but limitations on its scope.

[39] Case 261/81, *Rau* [1982] E.C.R. 3961.

Article 36 or mandatory requirements will not exempt all action relating to that contract from the scope of Article 30. This issue was raised in *Re Data Processing*,[39a] in which the Court of Justice held unlawful, as contrary to Articles 52 and 59 E.C., Italian legislation providing that only firms with the majority of their shares in Italian public ownership could be eligible for certain contracts to supply data processing systems to the Italian government. These Articles are subject to similar derogations as Article 30, including on grounds of health, public policy and public security.[40] It was suggested that because some of the systems related to the functions of public security (such as systems concerned with the fight against organised crime) and health (systems concerned with health-care service), measures relating to these contracts were exempt from Article 30. This argument was, however, rejected.[41] As Advocate General Mishco pointed out, it must be shown that the particular measure – participation of firms not in Italian ownership – would actually prejudice the relevant interest, such as public security or public health. The same will apply with mandatory requirements.

There are cases, however, where governments may be able to justify restrictive procurement measures. For example, the "security" derogation could be invoked to restrict government purchases to national providers in order to ensure the survival of a national capability in a product or technology in the defence industry; or to secure the continuation of other industries vital to the national economy.[42]

Authorities might also seek to invoke the security derogation to protect the confidentiality of security-related information (such as details of criminal or terrorist activity, or details of defence purchases); or where there is a need to ensure that sensitive supplies (such as equipment which could be useful to criminals, or drugs) are not diverted to improper uses. However, in *Re Data Processing* the Court rejected an argument by the Italian government that the need for confidentiality in relation to data to which providers would have access[43] justified restrict-

---

[39a] Case C–3/88, *Commission v. Italy* [1989] E.C.R. 4035.

[40] See further pp. 000–000 below.

[41] It was not expressly considered, but its rejection is implicit in the Court's ruling that the derogations were inapplicable.

[42] See case 72/83, *Campus Oil* [1984] E.C.R. 2727, in which the Court of Justice upheld an Irish measure requiring importers of refined petroleum products to purchase oil from an Irish refinery, where the measure was directed at securing the security of supply for oil in Ireland. Restrictive *government* purchasing to the same end is probably justified. This objective was upheld under Article 36 because of the importance of oil to a country's "institutions, its essential public services and the survival of its inhabitants". It was held to be irrelevant that the security objective was to be achieved through economic means – supporting national industry – even though the support of national industry for purely economic reasons is prohibited. It is unclear what other products may be treated in this way; but in the defence arena the courts are likely to defer to states on what defence capability should be maintained: see further Chap. 17.

[43] It is not clear which of the derogations could have applied here (except in the case of crime data, which could be treated as relating to security). Confidentiality concerns not covered by these derogations could be dealt with by mandatory requirements.

ing contracts to firms in Italian public ownership. The Court considered that this could be achieved by less restrictive measures, in particular by imposing a duty of secrecy on the provider's staff with possible criminal sanctions, the effectiveness of which the Court considered would not be affected by whether or not the company was under Italian public ownership.[44] Similarly, in *R. v. Secretary of State for the Home Department, ex p. Evans*[45] the Court suggested that the interest in preventing unauthorised diversion of drugs purchased by public authorities could be safeguarded adequately by taking into account a firm's relative abilities to apply security measures as a criterion in awarding the contract.[46] This suggests that confidentiality and security concerns of this type do not normally justify restrictive purchasing.

It should also be noted that restrictive procurement measures designed to promote domestic industry – for example, by maintenance of employment or development of new technology – cannot be justified under these provisions. This issue of using procurement to promote industry is considered further in Chapter 16.

In addition to Article 36 and mandatory requirements, a further limitation which is significant for procurement, arises under Article 223 E.C., which exempts from the E.C. Treaty certain measures relating to defence equipment (such as tanks and missiles), and Article 224 E.C. These are examined in Chapter 17 on defence procurement.

(4) AUTHORITIES COVERED

Article 30 E.C. is not of general application – it does not apply to ordinary private persons.[47] Clearly it covers the "traditional" government bodies, such as central government departments and local authorities in the United Kingdom, but, beyond this, there is room for debate. The problem of drawing an exact line between a "public" and "private" sphere of activity for the purpose of public law rules is often a difficult one in light of the variety of institutional arrangements in the modern state. It is a problem which occurs in relation to a number of rules of

---

[44] Para. 11 of the judgment.

[45] [1995] I-E.C.R. 563.

[46] Para. 49 of the judgment. This statement was made in considering the scope of the "security" derogation in the Supply Directive (as to which see pp. 152–154). In relation to Article 36 itself the Court emphasised that the measures taken must be no more restrictive than necessary to achieve their objective, but did not comment on how this test applied to either the general product licensing scheme which was in issue in that case, or to restrictive government purchasing. However, in relation to restrictive purchasing, the same considerations will surely apply in construing Article 36 as in construing the directive.

[47] This has been assumed in the cases cited below concerning the scope of Article 30 E.C. This must be correct; otherwise private individuals would be prohibited from giving preference to British products which was surely not intended. To apply Article 30 E.C. to all persons would also drive a coach and horses through the European Community competition law rules: see Weatherill and Beaumont, *E.C. Law* (1993), p. 389.

domestic law in the United Kingdom.[48] It also arises in other contexts in Community law. In particular, the courts have considered which bodies are sufficiently associated with "the state" for the application of the principle of the direct effect of Community directives,[49] and also which bodies are sufficiently linked to government for a Member State to be held responsible for their conduct in actions brought by the Commission under Article 169 E.C.[50] The Court of Justice has not indicated whether these different rules have exactly the same ambit, but it is likely that their scope is similar, and cases in one context may thus be useful in predicting the Court's approach in other areas.

In a case brought by the Commission against Ireland, the Court of Justice ruled that Article 30 was applicable to a "Buy Irish" campaign conducted by a private company limited by guarantee, where the management committee was appointed by public authorities and its objectives set by those authorities, and the body was government funded.[51] It is submitted that in fact Article 30 will probably apply to all bodies which are covered by the public sector procurement directives as "contracting authorities", including all those which are covered simply because they are *either* financed *or* appointed *or* controlled by the state or by local authorities.[52] In addition, Article 30 applies to bodies set up by the state to exercise regulatory functions, or entrusted by the state with the exercise of regulatory power, based on the "public" nature of their activity.[53] On this basis Article 30 might cover some bodies which are not subject to the public sector directives since the requirements of funding, control or appointment are not satisfied, and which are also not regulated by the Utilities Directive, since they are not involved in "utility" activities. However, where Article 30 applies merely because of the exercise of some public function, and not because of any characteristics of the authority such as public funding, it might be argued that it is only that function which is subject to Article 30, and not the functions of that body which are not of a regulatory nature, such as purchasing.

According to the view above, bodies covered by the Utilities

---

[48] See Arrowsmith, *Civil Liability and Public Authorities* (1992), pp. 1–6.

[49] See pp. 902–903.

[50] On this see pp. 922–924.

[51] On the scope of the Article in this respect see case 249/81, *Commission v. Ireland* [1982] E.C.R. 4005.

[52] On the definition of "contracting authorities" see pp. 105–106. In cases C–24/91, *Commission v. Spain* [1994] 2 C.M.L.R. 621 (paras. 8–13 of the Opinion) and case C–247/89, *Commission v. Portugal* [1991] E.C.R. I–3659 (paras. 20–21 of the Opinion) Advocate General Lenz appeared to take the view that all "contracting authorities" are bodies for whose actions the state is responsible under Article 169 E.C.

[53] Case 222/82, *Apple and Pear Development Council v. Lewis* [1983] E.C.R. 4083; case 266/87, *Re the Pharmaceutical Society, ex p. A.P.I.* [1989] E.C.R. 1295 1295. See also case 36/74, *Walrave and Koch v. Association Union Cycliste Internationale* [1974] E.C.R. 1405, in the context of the Treaty rules prohibiting discrimination on grounds of nationality, discussed below at p. 94.

Regulations as "public authorities" or "public undertakings" (that is, undertakings over which public authorities exercise a dominant influence)[54] will also be subject to Article 30. This view is reinforced by the decision in *Foster v. British Gas,*[55] in which the Court of Justice ruled that the direct effect of directives applies to bodies responsible for providing a public service, where that service is under the control of the state, and the body enjoys special powers in providing the service. On this basis the House of Lords held that British Gas, a nationalised industry subject to state control and direction (since privatised), was subject to the doctrine.[56] More recently, the High Court decision in *Griffin v. South West Water*[57] indicates that the *Foster* test extends direct effect to private utilities which are not owned, financed or appointed by the state, because of the degree of regulatory control over the provision of their services, where they provide a public service using special powers. It is not clear if this decision will be upheld nor, if so, whether it will apply to Article 30. If so, however, Article 30 will in the United Kingdom cover many entities which are subject to the Utilities Regulations simply because they enjoy "special or exclusive rights" as well as those which are "public authorities" or "public undertakings", since the regulatory regimes which govern such entities are similar to those applying in the water industry.

There are certain other bodies covered by the procurement regulations which are purely private, notably private bodies holding works concesssions; those awarding contracts which are funded by more than 50 per cent from the public purse – which public authorities must subject to the same procurement rule as they follow themselves; and those which enjoy special or exclusive rights to provide services.[58] Article 30 will not generally apply to these bodies. However, Advocate General Lenz has indicated, in the context of actions under Article 169 E.C., that a state might be considered responsible for the procurement decisions of such bodies if the *particular contract* was under state control, even where the state is not responsible for the activities of that body as a whole.[59] A similar approach could be adopted with Article 30, to hold it applicable to some contracts of private bodies, including those which are state funded and, as such, subject to the procurement regulations.

---

[54] On these definitions see pp. 385–387.
[55] Case C–188/89, [1990] E.C.R. I–3313.
[56] [1991] 2 A.C. 306.
[57] Judgment of August 25, 1994.
[58] On these provisions see Chap. 8
[59] See note 52.

3. ARTICLES 52 AND 59 E.C.: FREEDOM OF ESTABLISHMENT AND FREEDOM TO PROVIDE SERVICES [60]

(1) GENERAL PRINCIPLES

Article 52 E.C. guarantees the right of Community nationals and firms to set up business in other Member States, whilst Article 59 is concerned with the right to provide services in other Member States without necessarily setting up business there. Similar rules apply to the two provisions.

Article 52 is concerned with "freedom of establishment" – the right of nationals of all Member States to set up business in other states of the Community. The right applies to individuals who are nationals of Member States and also to "Community" companies – companies which are set up under the law of one of the Member States *and* which have their registered office, central administration or principal place of business in the Community.[61] This provision means that individuals who are self-employed[62] in business or the professions may set up operations in another part of the Community, and that companies may establish subsidiaries or branches in other States. For example, it will cover a United Kingdom company manufacturing computer hardware which wishes to establish an additional factory in Germany, or a United Kingdom software consultancy which desires to set up a branch in Germany to provide its services to the German market.

The Article covers government measures which hinder these individuals and companies from "establishing" themselves (setting up) in other States, or which hinder their activities once they are established. This includes measures relating to general market access, but also covers measures which restrict the access which non-nationals established in the state have to *government markets* – for example, by preventing them from bidding on public contracts.

Article 59 is concerned with the "freedom to provide services". It seeks to open up markets for persons established in one Community state who seek to provide services in another on a temporary basis – for example, an engineering firm based in Paris acting as consultant on a

---

[60] On these Articles generally see further Wyatt and Dashwood, *European Community Law* (3rd ed., 1993), Chap. 8. See also Directive 71/304, [1971] O.J. L185/1, which is relevant as a guide to interpreting these provisions in the context of public works: on this see pp. 53–54 above.

[61] Article 58(1) E.C. Where a firm relies merely on the fact that its registered office is in the Community it must also have a "real and effective link" with the Community economy: see "General Programme for the abolition of restrictions on freedom to provide services" [1962] J.O. 32; English Special Ed. 2nd series IX, p. 7.

[62] Article 48 guarantees free movement for those who wish to undertake work in the employment of another, as opposed to working in a self-employed capacity.

specific project in London, without setting up a permanent office or branch. This includes those who may wish to base themselves temporarily in the state where the services are provided, in order to carry out the work.[63] Like Article 52 it may be invoked by either individuals who are Community nationals or Community companies (those set up under the law of one of the Member States and which have their registered office, central administration or principal place of business in the Community[64]).

Like the other provisions it applies where a government restricts access to the market in general – for example, by banning foreign firms from providing services in the state, or making access subject to payment of a fee which does not apply to domestic firms. Like the other provisions, however, it also applies to such measures relating solely to the *government* services market – for example, forbidding foreign firms from bidding on government services contracts.

Article 59 can apply to any government contracts involving services, including construction, which is a service for this purpose (although construction is treated separately under the procurement directives). Since it is concerned only with services it has no relevance to contracts which are solely for the supply of products. However, it may apply to contracts which are partly for products and partly for services, even where products are the greater part; thus, it may apply to some contracts within the Supply Directive.

In relation to Article 30 it was suggested above that there is no *de minimis* rule, nor any requirement that measures covered should be of a general nature. In these respects it is appropriate to apply the same rules to Articles 52 and 59 E.C.

(2) CONDUCT COVERED

Article 59 will be infringed, first, by conduct hindering access to government contracts which discriminates directly on the basis of the nationality of providers. It also covers any measures which discriminate against firms not established in the awarding state.

Most obviously, this covers measures which limit contracts to providers who are nationals of, or established in, that state, or which gives such persons any form of preference – such as a price preference, or preferential treatment in deciding whom to invite to tender. For example, in case 360/89, *Commission v. Italy*,[65] the Court of Justice held

---

[63] See Article 60.

[64] Article 58(1) and 66 E.C. Where a firm relies merely on the fact that its registered office is in the Community it must have a "real and effective link" with the Community economy to invoke Article 52, since the Article applies only where the firm is already "established" in a Member State, a requirement which is not satisfied simply by the existence of a registered office: see "General Programme for the abolition of restrictions on freedom to provide services" [1962] J.O. 32; English Special Ed. 2nd series, IX, p. 7.

[65] Judgment of June 3, 1992; noted by Arrowsmith, (1992) 1 P.P.L.R. 408.

contrary to Article 59 Italian legislation requiring contractors for certain public works to reserve a proportion of the works for subcontractors who had their registered office in the region of the works – this discriminated against firms established outside Italy (it being irrelevant that some firms established in Italy were also affected).[66] Discriminatory conditions for qualification are also caught – for example, requirements for foreign, but not domestic, contractors to be registered on an approved list, to provide a guarantee or to obtain a special permit.

Also forbidden, as under Article 30, are measures which discriminate indirectly – that is, which are indistinctly applicable but have the *effect* of favouring firms which are nationals of or established in the awarding state. This is illustrated, for example, by *Re Data Processing*,[67] which concerned Italian legislation limiting participation in contracts for certain data processing systems to firms whose shares were wholly or mainly in Italian public ownership. The Court held this to be discriminatory and contrary to Article 59: although in theory non-Italian firms might be owned by the Italian government, in practice all data processing firms in Italian public ownership at that time were Italian.[68] Another example is case 360/89, already mentioned above, in which the Court also held to be contrary to Article 59 Italian legislation giving preference in choosing contractors to bid to consortia and joint ventures involving the participation of firms whose main activity was in the region of the works. This was held to favour enterprises established in Italy who were more likely than other enterprises to have their main activities in the region concerned.[69]

Another form of indirect discrimination considered by the Court of Justice is the application of conditions which make it more difficult for non-nationals than for domestic providers to use their own labour force. This includes any requirements for firms to employ local labour – in the *Storebaelt* case[70] a clause requiring use of Danish labour as far as possible was held to be contrary to Article 59. It also covers any limitations on bringing the provider's own labour force into the host state in order to

---

[66] The Court did not specify the exact nature of the discrimination. The Advocate General noted that it could discriminate in two ways – first, against subcontractors from other states who would be excluded from participating in the reserved works – the ground on which he preferred to rest his opinion – and, secondly, possibly, against main contractors from other states, who could not do the works themselves.

[67] Case C–3/88, *Commission v. Italy* [1989] E.C.R. 4035. And see also case C–272/91, *Commission v. Italy* (the *Lottomatica* case) [1995] 2 C.M.L.R. 504.

[68] Para. 9 of the judgment. As Advocate General Mishco pointed out (para. 13 of the Opinion), it would of course be sufficient if the effect was to disadvantage *primarily* other nationals; it was thus not necessary that there should be no non-national firms who qualified.

[69] Para. 12 of the judgment.

[70] Above.

work on the contract – Article 59 requires that firms be permitted to bring their existing workers.[71]

It has been explained that Article 30 E.C. applies to certain restrictions, such as those relating to the characteristics of goods, which discriminate neither directly nor indirectly against non-domestic goods, but affect domestic and imported goods in the same way. The Court of Justice has recently indicated that it will adopt the same approach as with restrictions relating to goods, bringing some restrictions of this type within Article 59.[72] This suggests that, as with goods, unduly restrictive specifications for services are prohibited even where not discriminatory in their effect.[73] Whether measures of this type relating to qualification of providers may be covered is considered in Chapter 7.[74]

Measures relating to access to government contracts which discriminate directly or indirectly between providers on grounds of nationality will infringe Article 52, as well as Article 59, where they hinder non-nationals established in the awarding state. For example, in *Re Data Processing*, the Italian legislation limiting certain data-processing contracts to firms in Italian government ownership was held to infringe Article 52: such legislation affects non-Italian firms established in Italy in their opportunities to obtain business in that country more than it affects Italian firms.

(3) LIMITATIONS ON ARTICLES 52 AND 59

The Treaty provides express derogations from Articles 52 and 59 E.C. on grounds of public policy, public health or public morality[75] – derogations which also apply to Article 30 under Article 36. Although the list here is not as extensive as under Article 36,[76] the additional grounds mentioned

---

[71] Case C–113/89, *Rush Portuguesa v. Office national d'immigration* [1990] E.C.R. I–1417, where the Court of Justice ruled to be unlawful requirements that foreign nationals working on contracts in France should either hold a special permit or be recruited through the national labour office. Although the case concerned a public works contract, the requirement was general; obviously, though, similar restrictions applying only to government contracts (for example, imposed by the awarding authority) are equally unlawful. Such limitations may also infringe Article 48 on the free movement of workers, although this was not so in *Rush Portuguesa* because this provision was not at that time in effect in relation to the Portuguese workers concerned. See also case C–43/93, *Vander Elst v. Office des Migrations Internationales* [judgment of August 9, 1994], upholding the right under Article 59 to "import" for contract work workers who are not Community nationals who are "lawfully and habitually" employed by the provider.

[72] See, in particular, case C–384/93, *Alpine Investments B.V. v. Minister van Financiën* [1995] 3 C.M.L.R. 209 and also case 205/84, *Commission v. Germany* [1987] 2 C.M.L.R. 69; case C–275/92, *Commissioners of Customs and Excise v. Schindler* [judgment of March 30, 1994]; case C–288/89, *Stichting Collective Antennevoorziening v. Commissariat voor de media* [1991] E.C.R.–I 4007; *Vander Elst*, above.

[73] On the application of the Treaty to such qualification rules see further Chap. 7.

[74] See p. 352.

[75] See Articles 55 and 56 (listing the derogations applicable to Article 52) and 66 (applying these provisions to Article 59).

[76] See pp. 84–86.

in that Article can be relevant as grounds of general interest, as outlined below. Similar conditions regarding justification apply. The possible application of these derogations in relation to procurement, whether under Article 30 or Articles 52 or 59, has already been considered.[77]

For Articles 52 and 59 there is also a further derogation: they do not apply to activities which "are connected, even occasionally, with the exercise of official authority".[78] In relation to procurement, the Court of Justice indicated in *Re Data Processing* that the derogation may apply only to providers who participate in activities involving a "direct and specific" connection with the exercise of such official authority, and that it could not apply to contracts for the provision of data-processing systems in connection with the exercise of official functions, since these were of a purely "technical" nature.[79] Thus it is clear that the derogation does not cover those supplying support services to those engaged in the exercise of official authority. Further, in *Lottomatica* the Court rejected an argument that a contract for the computerisation and operation of the Italian national lottery system fell within this derogation.[80] It is not clear how the line will be drawn between the provision of support by providers to government and the actual exercise of official authority, since the Court of Justice has not attempted any positive definition of "official authority". The potential scope of the derogation could be important in the United Kingdom as functions traditionally carried out by the government in-house, including, for example, the collection of taxes and the operation of prisons, are being increasingly contracted out to the private sector.[81] It is submitted, however, that the scope of the derogation is very narrow, and is likely to cover only the actual exercise of judicial and legislative powers, and the making of high-level policy decisions, such as the levels of taxation or policies governing the treatment of prison inmates, rather than day-to-day operation and management of such activities.[82] Since functions of this nature are unlikely to be contracted out, the derogation is unlikely to be relevant to government procurement.

In addition, Articles 52 and 59, like Article 30, are inapplicable so far as distinctly applicable measures are concerned, where the measures can be justified by general interest requirements recognised by the Court of Justice as impliedly limiting the scope of those provisions[83] – for

---

[77] See pp. 84–86.
[78] Article 55 (derogation from Article 52 on freedom of establishment); Article 66 (applies Article 55 to Article 59 on freedom to provide services).
[79] Case C–3/88, *Commission v. Italy* [1989] E.C.R. 4035, para. 13.
[80] Case C–272/91, *Commission v. Italy* (the *Lottomatica case*) [1995] 2 C.M.L.R. 504.
[81] See further Chap. 12.
[82] In the case of Lottomatica, above, the Court noted that the rectification and verification of winning tickets, and the making of prize payments, remained with the public authority. However, it is submitted that even this had been done by the outside provider, the contract would still not have involved participation in the exercise of official authority.
[83] See Wyatt and Dashwood, above, pp. 311–312.

example, protection of intellectual property rights or protection of the interests of the recipients of services. Measures affecting services may also sometimes be excluded under Article 223 or Article 224 E.C., which are discussed in Chapter 17.

(4) AUTHORITIES COVERED

The question arises, as with Article 30, as to which authorities are subject to the rules in Articles 52 and 59. It is submitted that the application of these provisions to purchasing functions should be exactly the same as that under Article 30. This issue, and the relevant jurisprudence, was discussed above.[84] It can be noted that in *Walrave and Koch*[85] the Court of Justice indicated that the Treaty provisions prohibiting discrimination on grounds of nationality, including Articles 6 (formerly Article 7 EEC), 48 and 59, applied to all rules "regulating in a collective manner" gainful employment or the provision of services, whether or not adopted by public authorities. To apply Article 59 to such rules is consistent with the approach of the cases discussed in relation to Article 30, although it was suggested above that where an authority is covered by the free movement rules merely because it exercises regulatory functions, rather than because of its association with the state, those rules might apply only to the authority's regulatory functions and not to its purchasing.

4. ARTICLE 6 E.C.: DISCRIMINATION ON GROUNDS OF NATIONALITY

Article 6 E.C. (formerly Article 7 of the EEC Treaty) provides that within the scope of application of the Treaty, any discrimination on grounds of nationality is prohibited.[86] This covers both direct discrimination on the basis of nationality, and indirect discrimination. Articles 30, 52 and 59 implement this principle within their respective spheres of operation, however, and where it is possible to invoke one of these provisions Article 6 does not apply (although it may serve as a guide to interpretation of the more specific provisions).

Discriminatory procurement is generally covered by Article 30, Article 52 and Article 59, so that Article 6 will not be invoked.[87] It has been

---

[84] See pp. 84–86.
[85] Case 36/74, *Walrave and Koch v. Association Union Cycliste Internationale* [1974] E.C.R. 1405.
[86] See further Weiss, above, pp. 20–23.
[87] Article 7 EEC (the predecessor of Article 6 E.C.) was expressly referred to by the Court of Justice in case 31/87, *Gebroeders Beentjes B.V. v. Netherlands* [1988] E.C.R. 4635, para. 30 of the judgment, in which the Court indicated that a requirement for a works contractor to employ a certain number of long-term unemployed persons would infringe the provision if it could be satisfied only by domestic tenderers, or if tenderers from other Member States would find it more difficult to satisfy. However, it appears that any action on this basis would have to be brought on the basis of Article 59 or Article 30.

suggested that Article 6 might apply to private bodies, and thus operate to forbid discrimination in procurement by certain authorities not caught by these other Articles.[88] However, it seems unlikely that it will apply to private persons, unless they exercise functions of a public nature such as would also be caught by Articles 30, 52 and 59; it was surely not intended that the Treaty should prohibit all private persons – including private individuals – from discriminating in their contracting against nationals from other states.[89] The directives themselves appear to be based on this restrictive view of Article 6; thus the Utilities Directive contains an express provision forbidding discrimination for contracts falling within its scope,[90] and the "public sector" directives – which extend to a limited extent to private sector bodies – also prohibit discrimination in making certain types of decisions.[91] These seem to have been included in order to extend the prohibition to authorities subject to the directives but not to Articles 30, 52 and 59; they are unnecessary if all discriminatory procurement is under Article 6.

5. ARTICLE 85 E.C.: RESTRICTIVE PRACTICES [92]

(1) CONDUCT COVERED

Article 85 E.C. is concerned with collusive arrangements between actors in the common market where these restrict competition. Article 85(1) prohibits any agreements between undertakings, decisions of associations of undertakings, or concerted practices which affect trade between Member States and which have as either their object or their effect the "prevention, restriction or distortion of competition within the common market". Under Article 85(2) such restrictive arrangements are void. However, restrictive arrangements may sometimes have beneficial effects which outweigh their disadvantages, and in recognition of this the Commission has a power to grant exemptions from Article 85(1), under certain conditions laid down in Article 85(3).

Article 85(1) may affect purchasers[93] by rendering unlawful procurement agreements which tie up the market for a product or service in an

---

[88] This seems to be the view, for example, of Winter, "Public Procurement in the E.C." (1991) C.M.L.Rev. 741, p. 762.

[89] That Article 6 is circumscribed in the same way as other provisions is assumed by Weiss, *op. cit.*, pp. 22–23.

[90] See p. 462.

[91] See, for example, p. 368.

[92] On Article 85 generally see Wyatt and Dashwood, *European Community Law* (1993) Chap. 14.

[93] Article 85(1) also has an impact on procurement by restricting the possibility of collusive action on the supply side (for example, agreements by providers to refrain from bidding in competition with each other and instead to "take turns" at government business); but consideration of activities on the supply side is outside the scope of this book. On this see Trepte, "Public Procurement and the Community Competition Rules" (1993) 2 P.P.L.R. 93, *Public Procurement in the E.C.* (1993), pp. 61–87 and "Partnering: Political Correctness or False Modesty" (1993) 14 E.C.L.R. 204.

unduly restrictive manner and so remove that market from competition.[94] The provision has been held to apply to arrangements under which a purchaser agrees to obtain its requirements exclusively from one provider over a relatively long period of time; it has been suggested that any exclusive arrangement extending beyond three years may be doubtful.[95] The provision may also apply where the arrangement is not exclusive; thus in the *Carlsberg* case the Commission held that an agreement for an organisation to buy specified quantities of lager from Carlsberg for an 11-year period, where the volume in question represented over half the organisation's annual purchases of the product, was caught by Article 85(1).[96] It can also cover agreements to purchase a large requirement from a single provider, even over a period as short as a year.[97] Exactly which arrangements will be caught will depend on the nature of the product and market.

The Article will obviously catch agreements in the form of binding contracts, but may also cover "framework agreements" – that is, agreements under which parties set the terms of future dealings between them with an expectation that contracts will be made, but which involve no legal commitment.[98] It may, further, cover arrangements which, whilst of limited duration or scope, contemplate the possibility of indefinite renewal. Such arrangements will be publicly known for purchases covered by the procurement rules, since it appears that if the parties wish to renew an arrangement, without the need to follow a new award procedure under the regulations, the intention and potential duration of the renewal must be stated in the original contract notice.[99]

It is likely that arrangements regarded as restrictive under Article 85(1) will not be able to claim any exemption under Article 85(3).[1]

Article 85(1) targets only arrangements which affect trade between Member States: restrictive practices which have only an internal effect are left to national law. (In the United Kingdom they may be caught by the Competition Act 1980.[1a]) The provision may apply to any arrangement which distorts patterns of trade between Member States, whether its effect is direct or indirect, and actual or potential. However, the effect must be "appreciable"; thus where the arrangement affects only a small

---

[94] See the views of the Commission in *BP Kemil/DDSF*, [1979] 3 C.M.L.R. 684. On Article 85 and procurement see also Broomhall and Lomas, "Partnering: An Acceptable Strategy for Utilities?" (1993) 2 P.P.L.R. 221, pp. 233–255; Trepte, "Partnering: Political Correctness or False Modesty" (1993) 14 E.C.L.R. 204, pp. 210–213.
[95] Trepte, "Political Correctness or False Modesty", above, p. 210.
[96] [1985] 1 C.M.L.R. 735.
[97] See *BP Kemil/DDSF*, above.
[98] On framework agreements see further pp. 175–179.
[99] See pp. 119–121.
[1] On this see Trepte, "Partnering: Political Correctness or False Modesty", above, pp. 212–213.
[1a] See pp. 27–28.

part of the market it is not covered.[2] The position in this respect is different from that under the free movement provisions, under which it appears no such limit applies.[3] This *de minimis* rule raises the possibility that certain restrictive procurement arrangements are not covered, because of their insignificance in the market as a whole: for example, it is difficult to see that an agreement between a small local authority for the purchase of its stationery requirements would be covered, however restrictive. Even arrangements which exceeds the threshold for the application of the procurement directives could fall outside the rules under this test. (Conversely, the provisions may catch some contracts which are not subject to the directives, where these are manifestations of a more general practice.[4]) It is interesting that the nature of the market deemed relevant in applying this *de minimis* rule may be affected by the open procurement market: the market in which purchasers operate will be increasingly a European market rather than a purely national market.[5]

An interesting question is the relationship between the restrictions under Article 85(1) and those in the procurement directives. It may be noted, first, that the utilities rules expressly provide that framework agreements may not be used to "hinder, limit or distort competition".[6] It is not clear if this should be considered merely as an express statement of requirements already implicit in Article 85(1), or whether it applies more widely than Article 85. It is submitted that, in view of the ambitious aim of the directives of subjecting to regular competition all purchasing arrangements above the thresholds, it may be wider in two respects. First, it should be applied to all agreements covered by the directive, without any additional *de minimis* test: the directives, unlike Article 85, are not restricted to purchasing arrangements which have an "appreciable" effect on trade, but identify their target by reference to a general threshold value. Secondly, it may (although this is more debatable) cover agreements which are not sufficiently restrictive in terms of

---

[2] On what is an appreciable effect see, in particular, Commission Notice of September 3, 1986, which states that Article 85 does not apply where the products and services covered do not exceed 5 per cent of the relevant market and the parties' turnover does not exceed 200,000 million ECUs; and, in general, Wyatt and Dashwood, above, pp. 413–417.

[3] See pp. 79–80.

[4] This is indicated by Commission Decision 92/204, [1992] O.J. L92/1, in which the Commission rejected an argument that Article 85 could not apply to a supply-side cartel which controlled the public works market because many of the contracts covered fell below the Works Directive's threshold.

[5] The Court of Justice has already considered the impact of the open procurement rules for determining the market in which particular providers operate, in the context of the Community legislation on mergers, under which it is necessary to consider the dominance of undertakings in particular markets, and also the effect which a potential merger may have on competition in that market; on this see, in particular, Brown, "High Hopes for Competitive Supply Markets: The Impact of Public Procurement on E.C. Merger Control" (1994) 3 P.P.L.R. 16.

[6] See further pp. 457–458.

length, scope or duration to fall under Article 85, but which go beyond what is acceptable in light of the directives' aim of ensuring regular competition. It should be remembered here that the directives impose procedures which are more burdensome than those which would normally be followed by purchasers as a matter of "best practice", to limit discretion and improve monitoring: this is justified by the special position of regulated purchasers who may be subject to pressure to "buy national" and/or may be immune to some extent from the stimulus of competition. Thus it may be accepted that the directives impose requirements on utilities purchasers which are more stringent than those imposed on entities generally by virtue of Article 85 E.C.

There is no corresponding provision on framework agreements under the public sector rules (although it may be that this is because framework agreements are not permitted under those rules)[7]; nor is there any provision under either the public sector or utilities rules to deal with long-term arrangements which take the form of simple understandings (for example, regarding the renewal of existing agreements) or binding contracts. Such arrangements may be covered by Article 85 as outlined above; but the question arises as to whether any further restrictions are implied under the directives/regulations themselves. It is suggested in Chapter 5 that where provision is made for renewal of agreements these must be treated as new contracts and so subjected to competition under the directives/regulations, except to the extent that such renewals reflect the normal and appropriate commercial practice in that industry.[8] This limitation will certainly apply to all purchases covered by the rules, the Article 85 *de minimis* test being irrelevant. In addition, the standard for what is acceptable practice may be stricter than that which applies in determining whether the arrangement infringes Article 85. It is not clear whether the Court of Justice will also imply limits on the length of contracts or framework arrangements which sidestep the *de minimis* tests and/or are more stringent than the limits under Article 85.[9]

(2) AUTHORITIES COVERED

The concept of an "undertaking" covers a body with legal capacity involved in an "economic" or "business" activity, whether or not it is carried out for profit. It is clear that it covers nationalised industries involved in providing services to the public in return for payment, and thus the procurement activities of these bodies, including the regulated utilities are clearly caught, as is the state when it engages in these sorts of activities. It is submitted, further – although this has not been considered by the Court – that Article 85 is also likely to apply to

---

[7] See further pp. 175–179.
[8] See pp. 119–121.
[9] On this see further pp. 457–458.

procurement activities of the state and other public authorities even where they relate to governmental functions which are not entrepreneurial in nature: these government bodies must be treated as acting as "undertakings" for this purpose whenever they undertake procurement.[10] There is no justification to exempt such contracts from the usual competition rules – particularly in view of the importance to the market of certain fields of government procurement.

6. ARTICLE 86 E.C.: ABUSE OF A DOMINANT MARKET POSITION [11]

Article 86 E.C. prohibits abuse by one or more undertakings of a dominant position in the common market or a substantial part of it, so far as that abuse affects trade between Member States. An undertaking is regarded as dominant in a market where it has a position of economic strength such as enables it to behave to an appreciable extent independently of its competitors, customers and consumers.[12] As with Article 85, the question of what is the "market" in which an entity operates may be affected by the impact of the procurement rules themselves in replacing national markets with wider, even Community-wide, markets. This means that it may become less likely that public and utility purchasers will exercise a dominant market power.

Article 86 may apply where an undertaking exercises a dominant position as a purchaser in a particular market.[13] For example, the Court of Justice has stated in the *CICCE* case that it could constitute a breach of Article 86 where an undertaking (or group) uses a dominant position to impose unreasonably low prices on providers.[14] A price established through a tendering procedure under the procurement rules is no doubt prima facie to be considered acceptable, although this may not be the case if the price is reduced after further negotiations with bidders[15] or if unfairly low prices result from the purchaser's previous practices of

---

[10] This is regarded as an open question by Bellamy and Child, *Common Market Law of Competition* (4th ed. 1993), p. 42. However, in *French State/ Suralmo* the Commission treated a patent licence granted by the French state as subject to the competition rules: see European Commission, *Ninth Report on Competition Policy* (1980), point 14.

[11] On Article 86 generally see Wyatt and Dashwood, above, Chap. 15 and 16.

[12] Case 27/76, *United Brands Co. v. Commission* [1978] E.C.R. 207 at p. 277.

[13] See Trepte, "Public Procurement and the Community Competition Rules" (1993) 2 P.P.L.R. 93, pp. 105–109 and Trepte, *Public Procurement in the E.C.* (1993) pp. 74–78 (which consider also the impact of Article 86 on the supply side).

[14] Case 293/83, *Comité des Industries Cinematographiques des Communautes européenes (CICCE) v. Commission* [1985] E.C.R. 1105 (in which, however, both the Commission and Court found there had been no breach on the facts).

[15] Such negotiations are permitted under the negotiated procedure, although under the open and restricted procedures (which must normally be used by the public sector) negotiations on price are probably permitted only once the winner has been chosen: see pp. 247–250.

"bargaining down" winning bidders. The Commission has also held, in *Eurofima,* that there is an abuse of a dominant position in imposing unreasonable terms and conditions.[16] It has also been suggested that discrimination, whether on nationality or other grounds, between different providers, or even a failure to follow the legal obligations in the procurement directives, may also constitute a breach of Article 86.[17]

As with Article 85, this provision will probably apply to procurement activities of all authorities, including those in the traditional state sector, as well as those engaged in industrial activities.

A breach of Article 86 E.C. might also occur where a provider abuses its own dominant position to secure a contract with a regulated purchaser which is unreasonable in its effect on competition.

7. ARTICLE 90(1) E.C. [18]

(1) CONDUCT COVERED

Article 90 E.C. is concerned with the obligations of Member States in relation to enterprises which are state-owned or controlled, or which enjoy special privileges. Such enterprises are important in the utilities sectors of water, transport, energy and telecommunications, as well as many other areas. They present particular difficulties for a free market since state influence over their actions, or the fact that they depend on the state for their rights, render them susceptible to government pressures – for example, to "buy national" – and they may also have a degree of market dominance which immunises them from commercial pressure and allows them to act in a non-competitive way. For these reasons such enterprises present a special problem for the Community. Article 90 E.C. was adopted specifically to deal with these problems.

Article 90(1) provides that Member States shall neither enact nor maintain in force with respect to "public undertakings" or undertakings given "special or exclusive rights", measures which are contrary to the E.C. Treaty. Thus, the state is held to act unlawfully under Article 90(1) where it requires or encourages relevant undertakings to breach the Treaty rules. For example, it would be liable under this provision for directing an undertaking to follow a "buy national"policy, or by failing to remove existing directions. This will also usually constitute a breach of Article 30 or Article 59 E.C., and possibly, of Article 52 E.C., by the state itself. It also renders the state liable for encouraging or promoting a breach by such an undertaking of the competition rules in Article 85 or

---

[16] European Commission, *Third Report on Competition Policy,* paras. 68–69.
[17] See the two pieces by Trepte cited in n.13 above.
[18] On this provision generally see Wyatt and Dashwood, *European Community Law* (1993), Chap. 19.

Article 86 (or failing to remove measures which have this effect) – for example, by requiring utilities to enter into restrictive long-term contracts. In this case the action would not itself be a breach of Article 85 or 86, but the state is responsible solely under Article 90(1).[19]

The provision does not, on the other hand, render the state itself in breach of the Treaty for unlawful measures put into effect by undertakings on their own initiative. For example, where a public undertaking decides itself to enter into a long-term contract which contravenes Article 85 E.C. or to give a preference to British providers the state is not held responsible under Article 90(1) if it has not required or encouraged such behaviour.[20] In some cases, however, where that entity is sufficiently associated with the state, the state may be held responsible for that undertaking's actions, in proceedings under Article 169 E.C.[21]

It is not clear whether "measures" for the purpose of Article 90(1) includes an isolated act, such as discrimination in the award of an individual procurement contract. It has been suggested earlier that such actions should fall within Article 30, and it is likewise submitted that Article 90(1) should apply to this case.

Under Article 90(3) the Commission has a power to adopt directives defining specific conduct which is prohibited under Article 90(1).[22]

(2) ENTITIES FOR WHICH THE STATE IS RESPONSIBLE

Article 90(1) makes the state responsible for undertakings which are either "public" or which possess "special or exclusive" rights granted by the state.

An undertaking is any legal person engaged in an economic activity and, as suggested above, appears to cover any entity so far as it is involved in procurement, no matter what the nature of its other activities.[23]

As to which undertakings are "public", the Commission has defined the concept of a "public undertaking" in Article 2 of the so-called "transparency directive" issued under Article 90(3)[24] (which is concerned with preventing unlawful State Aids to public undertakings and to this end sets out requirements to make the financial relationships between states and their public undertakings more transparent). The same

---

[19] Case 30/87, *Bodson v. SA Pompes funèbres des regions libérées* [1987] E.C.R. 2479.

[20] Joined cases C–271/90, C–281/90 and C–289/90, *Spain, Belgium and Italy v. Commission*, judgment of November 17, 1992.

[21] See pp. 922–924.

[22] However, it may not adopt directives which are directed at specific acts of certain states: the legality of specific existing measures must be tested through proceedings under Article 169 E.C. (case C–202/88, *France v. Commission* [1991] I–E.C.R. 1223).

[23] See pp. 98–99.

[24] Directive 80/723, [1980] O.J. L195/35, as amended by [1985] O.J. L229.

definition has now been adopted in the directive on procurement by utilities[25] – which, like Article 90, also applies to "public undertakings" and undertakings enjoying "special or exclusive rights". The definition covers undertakings over which public authorities exercise, directly or indirectly, a dominant influence, by virtue of ownership, financial participation, or the rules governing the entity. This is to be presumed where the government holds a majority of its subscribed capital, controls a majority of the votes attaching to its shares or can appoint more than half of its administrative, managerial or supervisory body (although these are not exhaustive of the cases where a dominant influence will exist). The Court of Justice has accepted this definition in the context of Article 90, although it has indicated that it might be extended even further.[26]

As regards "special or exclusive rights", these appear to be separate concepts.[27] It is generally considered that an exclusive right exists where a single entity is given a right to the exclusion of others – for example, a right to operate to the exclusion of others: here special problems arise both because of the monopoly which insulates from competition, and because of dependence on the state for operating rights. A "special" right, on the other hand, will cover a right which is conferred on a limited number of entities.[28] If a right is open to be claimed by everyone, without any conditions at all, then clearly it cannot be regarded as "special".[29] The same may also be the case where the right is open to *all* who meet certain minimum objective conditions, since in this case ordinary conditions of competition are applicable, and entities will also not be susceptible to pressure by Member States where the standards applied to applicants are objective and verifiable. However, it is difficult to draw a precise line between objective conditions and subjective criteria for the grant of rights – even apparently objective criteria, such as financial stability, involve discretion in their application, and, thus, the potential for abuse.

Rights conferred on undertakings will most often be licences to operate in the market in question. However, rights may take other forms, such as privileges to carry out certain acts – such as appropriation of property – in the course of operations.

---

[25] On this see further pp. 386–387.

[26] Joined cases 188–190/80, *France, Italy and the U.K. v. The Commission* [1982] E.C.R. 2545.

[27] This was assumed to be the case in case 202/88, *Commission v. France* [1991] E.C.R. I–1223, in which a challenge was made to a Commission Directive adopted under Article 90(3) EEC, which required states to remove certain special and exclusive rights in the telecommunications sector. The part concerning "special" rights was struck down on the basis that the relevant rights were not defined with sufficient precision, whilst the part concerned with exclusive rights was left standing, a distinction thus being assumed to exist between the two. The Court of Justice did not, however, attempt to define the two concepts.

[28] This view was stated by Advocate General Jacobs in joined cases C–271, 281 and 289/290, *Spain, Belgium and Italy v. Commission,* above.

[29] Case 13/77, *Inno v. ATAB* [1977] E.C.R. 2115, where the Court stated that no special or exclusive rights exist where they have been conferred upon the undertaking as a member of a class carrying on an activity which is open to everyone.

Since the scope of the utilities rules on procurement is defined by reference to the same criteria as Article 90(1), that Article obviously covers the regulated utility purchasers. However, it also renders states responsible for the procurement activities of public undertakings and undertakings with special or exclusive rights which operate in other – non-regulated – sectors.

CHAPTER 5

THE PUBLIC SECTOR REGULATIONS: SCOPE

1. INTRODUCTION

This chapter examines the scope of the Public Works Contracts Regulations 1991, the Public Supply Contracts Regulations 1995 and the Public Services Contracts Regulations 1992.[1] As has been explained in Chapter 3, these regulations were originally adopted to implement the European Community directives which seek to open up the public procurement market in Europe. The regulations have also subsequently been adapted to implement the government's international obligations to open up its procurement to certain countries from outside the Community, under the European Economic Area Agreement and under Association Agreements with certain central and eastern European states, by applying the rules in the regulations to providers from those states, and expressly conferring upon those providers a right to enforce the rules.[1a]

To decide whether an award procedure is covered, the first question is whether the purchaser is a body subject to the regulations. All three sets of regulations apply to bodies which are "contracting authorities" which covers, broadly, public bodies of a non-commercial nature. Precisely which bodies are "contracting authorities" is considered in section 2 of this chapter. (In addition, some obligations under the regulations apply to bodies which are not contracting authorities, including some purely private entities; these special cases are considered separately in Chapter 8.)

Where a body is a contracting authority, it is then necessary to consider whether the particular award is covered. Here a number of issues arise.

First, the regulations only apply to an arrangement which is "a contract in writing for consideration". This requirement is considered in section 3.

---

[1] S.I. 1991 No. 2680, S.I. 1995 No. 201 and S.I. 1992 No. 3228. The award procedures under these regulations are considered in Chaps. 6, 7 and 11, and enforcement in Chap. 18; the history and background to the regulations was discussed in Chap. 3. Special rules apply to design contests, concessions, to some subsidised contracts and to government suppliers who enjoy special or exclusive rights. These are considered separately in Chap. 8.

[1a] The regulations will be further adapted in due course to implement any new agreements, and also to implement obligations under the GPA. On these issues see further pp. 773–774, 780–781 and 784–786.

Secondly, it is necessary to determine whether the contract is for works, supplies or services, in order to know whether it is the Works Regulations, Supply Regulations or Services Regulations which apply; this is considered in section 4. This is important for determining whether the contract is regulated at all – in particular, the thresholds are different under the different regulations – and, in addition, there are a few differences in the award procedures under each set of regulations.

It must then be considered whether there is any specific exemption under the relevant regulations. These exemptions are explained in section 5.

Finally, only contracts above a certain threshold are regulated. The relevant thresholds are examined in section 6.

2. WHICH PURCHASERS ARE SUBJECT TO THE REGULATIONS?

(1) GENERAL PRINCIPLES

The public sector procurement rules cover, broadly, public bodies of a non-commercial nature, the aim being to regulate authorities likely to be subject to significant pressure to "buy national". This obviously includes central government departments and local authorities, the traditional forms of government authority. In view of the diverse organisational forms employed by government in Europe,[2] however, it is necessary to go beyond this, and to formulate a more sophisticated definition of the public sector. The way in which this has been done for the purpose of applying the general obligations in the procurement directives is considered below. Those public authorities which are generally covered by the rules are referred to in both the directives and regulations as "contracting authorities".[3]

As noted above, the regulations also impose some obligations on entities which are not "contracting authorities". Thus, the Works Regulations and Services Regulations apply to contracts subsidised by contracting authorities which are awarded by private bodies; the Works Regulations impose obligations on private entities holding public works concessions; and certain obligations apply under the Supply Regulations to private sector suppliers who enjoy special or exclusive rights. These special cases are discussed in Chapter 8.

---

[2] On the variety of institutional forms in the United Kingdom see generally Craig, *Administrative Law* (3rd ed. 1994), Chap. 3.

[3] On these directives see Chap. 3.

(2) DEFINITION OF CONTRACTING AUTHORITY[4]

"Contracting authority" is defined in regulation 3 of each set of regulations.[5] It covers a) certain public bodies expressly listed in the regulations; b) other authorities falling within a general definition in the regulations, which is designed to catch any non-commercial public bodies not expressly listed; and c) joint associations involving the participation of bodies under a) and b). These provisions are the same in all three sets of regulations.

In addition, the Supply Regulations (though not the other regulations) includes an express provision to bring in d) authorities covered by GATT but which do not fall under a)–c).

(a) AUTHORITIES EXPRESSLY LISTED IN THE REGULATIONS

The authorities listed expressly in the regulations are as follows[6] (regulation numbers apply to all three sets of regulations). Those listed are essentially the traditional and most easily identifiable types of government entity.

(i) A Minister of the Crown (regulations 3(1)(a)). This is defined in regulation 2 as meaning "the holder of an office in Her Majesty's Government in the United Kingdom" and is stated as including the Treasury. The Crown itself is not expressly listed, although it appears that it is the Crown which is in fact the party to a contract entered into through a Minister.[7] However, it is clear that the specific reference to officers of the Crown – in addition to government departments – is intended to bring within the regulations contracts awarded for the Crown by its officers.[8]

(ii) A government department (regulation 3(1)(b)).[9]

---

[4] See Harden, "Defining the Range of Application of the Public Sector Procurement Directives in the United Kingdom" (1992) 1 P.P.L.R. 362; Lewis, "Works, Supplies and Services Contracts: Coverage of United Kingdom Contracting Authorities and Entities" (1995) 4 P.P.L.R. 128.

[5] See also regulation 2(1) of each set of regulations, the "definitions" section, which provides in each case that "contracting authority" is to have the meaning given in regulation 3.

[6] Works Regulation 3(1), Supply Regulation 3(1), Services Regulation 3(1).

[7] See the discussion at pp. 10–13.

[8] These are all contracts made by the Crown in its public capacity; contracts made by the Queen in her private capacity are not covered. This has apparently lead to complaints, where computer contracts for the Queen's private household which are above the regulations' threshold have not been advertised (see *The Independent*, October 19, 1992); but the view that such contracts are not covered seems correct.

It could also be suggested (although it appears unnecessary to rely on this) that the Crown is a public body by virtue of the general provision in regulation 3(1)(r), discussed below.

[9] This is not defined, except that regulation 2 states that it shall include a Northern Ireland Department or head of such Department.

(iii) The House of Commons (regulation 3(1)(c)), the House of Lords (regulation 3(1)(d) and Northern Ireland Assembly (regulation 3(1)(e)).
(iv) A local authority (regulation 3(1)(f)).[10]
(v) A fire authority[11] (regulation 3(1)(g)).
(vi) A police authority[12] (regulation 3(1)(i)).
(vii) Certain authorities established under the Local Government Act 1985. These are: an authority established under section 10 of the Act; a joint authority established by Part IV of the Act; and any body established pursuant to an order under section 67 of the Act (regulation 3(1)(m)).
(viii) The Broads Authority (regulation 3(1)(n)).
(ix) A joint board, of which the constituent members consist of local authorities, fire authorities, police authorities, the authorities mentioned under (vi) above or the Broads Authority (regulation 3(1)(o)).
(x) A joint or special planning board constituted for a National Park under the Local Government Act 1972 (paras. 1 or 3 of Schedule 17) (regulation 3(1)(p)).
(xi) A joint education board under Part I of the First Schedule to the Education Act 1994 (regulation 3(1)(q)).

(b) BODIES COVERED BY THE GENERAL DEFINITION IN THE REGULATIONS

All three sets of regulations also contain, in regulation 3(1)(r), a definition in general terms of bodies which are to be treated as "contracting authorities". Bodies within this definition are covered by the regulations, even though not expressly listed.[13]

The definition covers a body which meets three main conditions:
(i) It must have been set up "for the specific purpose of meeting needs in the general interest". It is not required that the body must have been set up *by the government,* to meet these needs; thus a body set up privately (for example, a self-regulatory body) might be covered, where the

---

[10] Defined in regulation 3(2) in relation to England and Wales as a county council, district council, London borough council, a parish council, a community council, the Council of the Isles of Scilly, and the Common Council of the City of London in its capacity as local authority or police authority. (In relation to Scotland it means a regional islands or district council or any joint board or joint committee within the meaning of Local Government (Scotland) Act 1973 (c. 65), s.235; in relation to Northern Ireland it means a district council within the meaning of the Local Government Act (Northern Ireland) 1972 (c. 9 (N.I.)).

[11] As constituted by a combination scheme under the Fire Services Act 1947, c. 41. The Fire Authority for Northern Ireland is also listed: regulation 3(1)(h).

[12] This refers to a police authority constituted under the Police Act 1964 (c. 48), s.2, or combined police authority established by an amalgamation scheme under the Act. (Also expressly included is the Police Authority for Northern Ireland: regulation 3(1)(j)).

[13] Those bodies which are expressly listed also, in fact, fall within the general definition; obviously, however, it is not necessary to rely on the definition in such cases.

government becomes involved (so that condition ii) is satisfied) at a later point.[14]

(ii) One of the following must apply: a) the body must be financed wholly or mainly by another contracting authority; or b) it must be subject to management supervision by another contracting authority; or c) more than half of its board of directors or its members, must be appointed by another contracting authority (or, where it is a group of individuals, half of those individuals must be appointed by another contracting authority). In other words, the definition covers bodies which are either financed, supervised or appointed by government.

A variety of legal bodies have been established, mainly since the 1970s, to carry out public-interest activities outside the normal departmental structure – though often subject to a degree of direction by Ministers – and most are covered by this definition. Examples are the Equal Opportunities Commission, the Development Board for Rural Wales, and the Health and Safety Executive. Many such bodies satisfy all three tests a), b) and c) above, although it is necessary to satisfy only one. The definition also covers most schools, universities and other educational institutions, which generally obtain most of their funding from government (although this is not necessarily true of all universities).[15] A whole variety of other bodies may also satisfy one of these tests, and each case must be considered on its facts.

It is not clear whether an entity is "financed" by a contracting authority where it is funded by work awarded under contracts. Arguably, contracts won in competition would not count as "government-financed", on the basis that "financing" implies an element of subsidy.[16] More questionable, however, is the position of a body funded by contracts not placed in a competitive manner, either because no competition is available, or because the government wishes to maintain that institution[17]; this might apply to an independent research institution set up to do government work.

---

[14] However, in the most common case of this kind, where the government becomes involved with an existing regulatory body by giving it legislative powers to carry out some or all of its functions (or new regulatory functions), it is rare that condition ii) below is satisfied.

[15] Annex I to the Works Directive indicates that universities are covered. (On the relevance of this Annex see pp. 112–115 below.) The Treasury has so far taken the view that most are covered because of public funding, which appears to be correct since income generally comes from grants and fees paid by government (although the Committee of Vice Chancellors and Principals has disputed this: see *Government Purchasing*, April 1995, p. 1). However, the private University of Buckingham and institutions with a private income which provides most of their funding (such as some Oxford and Cambridge colleges) may not be covered, and the Teasury has indicated that it will seek an amendment to the Annex to reflect the view that not *all* university bodies are necessarily covered: *Government Purchasing*, April 1995, p. 1.

[16] Many private firms involved in government work would not fall under condition i). However, it is difficult to see this would not apply to a company set up solely to do government work, such as street cleaning, unless condition i) is not satisfied by bodies whose aim is private profit.

[17] This is probably permitted under the E.C. rules on state aid, which probably do not preclude assistance for basic, as opposed to applied, research.

(iii) A third condition is that the body must not have an "industrial or commercial character". This appears intended to exclude bodies involved primarily in providing services in return for revenue, on the basis that such bodies are subject to commercial pressure and are less likely to discriminate in favour of national products or firms. However, the fact that an entity sells to the market clearly does not immunise it from pressure: nationalised industries have been some of the worst perpetrators of discriminatory practices. Certainly it is not appropriate to exclude all authorities charging for services – for examples, museums charging a nominal admission fee. It is submitted that it is necessary to examine closely the extent to which an entity is subject to real market disciplines, including the extent of competition, the stringency of financial targets and the availability of subsidies, before this limitation may be relied on.

In practice, this limitation is not of much importance in the United Kingdom. Many activities concerned with meeting public needs which are industrial or commercial are specifically excluded from the public sector regulations, because they fall under the Utilities Regulations[18] and the Post Office, which can also probably take advantage of this provision, is covered under the Supply Regulations as a "GATT" contracting authority.[19]

Where a body meets the three conditions above, its legal form is not relevant. Traditionally, public bodies have been established by statute or (more rarely) Royal Charter; the regulations apply equally, however, to those set up under the ordinary Companies Acts, such as the companies set up to administer student loans, which were established to meet needs in the general interest and satisfy the relevant criteria, or certain private companies set up by local authorities.[20] It is expressly stated in regulation

---

[18] See pp. 151–152. This regime does apply to public bodies involved in commercial/industrial activities; moreover, it also applies to many other bodies which would not be contracting authorities under the public sector rules, so that most activities in these sectors are now regulated: see Chap. 9.

[19] See pp. 111–112. Some "Next Steps" agencies, which are formally part of government departments but operate as independent units, are involved in activities which might be regarded as industrial or commercial, selling services to other government bodies and/or the private sector, and operating on a "trading fund" basis, which generally requires costs to be provided from revenue – for example, HMSO. As is pointed out, however, by Harden, above, p. 367 such bodies are subject to the regulations, since their activities are in law those of an entity expressly listed in the regulations – a government department or Minister – and with entities expressly listed, the commercial/industrial character test is irrelevant. Even if it were, it can be argued that no exemption would apply, since it is only these functions which are of a commercial nature, not those of the entity as a whole.

It is also not clear whether the industrial/commercial limitation can be relied on to exclude from the rules a body which is a distinct legal entity but is wholly owned and controlled by a contracting authority. In such circumstances it may be that the entity concerned is to be regarded as a part of the contracting authority, and so subject to the rules, even though it has a legally separate entity.

[20] For example, all companies which are "controlled companies" under Local Government Act 1989 s.68 satisfy condition (ii) and will be regulated where set up to meet needs in the general interest and not of an industrial or commercial character.

3(1)(r) that the definition covers either a corporation, or a group of individuals appointed to act together – that is, a body without legal personality.

The directives themselves may need to be considered in borderline cases, as an aid to interpretation. In particular, the directives contain a list of covered authorities, which is intended to provide guidance (though it is not conclusive) on which bodies are regulated. This point is considered further below.[21]

The definition of contracting authority does not, of course, necessarily correspond to those bodies desginated as "public bodies" for the purpose of other public law rules, such as the rules on the availability of judicial review.[22] For example, self-regulating bodies entrusted with regulatory functions by statute are often susceptible to judicial review,[23] but many are neither financed, supervised nor appointed by government, and are therefore not contracting authorities.

(c) ASSOCIATIONS OF MORE THAN ONE BODY

An association[24] of, or formed by, any one or more of the bodies covered under (a) or (b) above, is also itself a contracting authority for the purpose of the regulations (regulation 3(1)(s)).[25] It appears that "association" (which is not defined) may cover either a contractual joint venture, or a separate entity such as a company formed jointly by more than one body. An example would be a purchasing consortium formed by a number of contracting authorities to purchase on a centralised basis: where such a body itself enters into legally binding contracts, it is covered by the regulations.[26] The provision covers, however, not merely associations comprised wholly of bodies within the above list but also associations involving these bodies together with one or more purely private entities.

(d) GATT CONTRACTING AUTHORITIES

In addition, under the Supply Regulations a body which is a GATT contracting authority is also covered,[27] reflecting the position under the

---

[21] See pp. 112–115.

[22] There are a variety of "public law" rules in the United Kingdom, whose scope differs according to the particular context: see further Arrowsmith, *Civil Liability and Public Authorities* (1992), pp. 1–4.

[23] *R. v. Panel on Take-Overs and Mergers, ex p. Datafin plc* [1987] Q.B. 815.

[24] The term "association" is used in the directives themselves.

[25] Joint bodies constituted by certain bodies of a local nature are specifically included in the list under (a), above.

[26] This would include a framework arrangement which is of a legally binding nature (for example, obliging members of the consortium to purchase all supplies from the chosen supplier, and for the supplier to supply these as required). It is unclear what is the position with an arrangement which merely establishes terms on which contracts may be made in the future, and leaves individual members to enter into any binding commitments: see further pp. 175–179.

[27] Supply Regulation 3(1)(t).

Supply Directive. A GATT contracting authority is one which is subject to the GATT Agreement on Government Procurement[28] and such authorities are expressly listed in Schedule 1 to the Supply Regulations.[29] The reason for applying the E.C. rules to all GATT contracting authorities, was to ensure that authorities opening up their procurement to countries outside the E.C. should also open up that procurement to other Member States: the GATT Agreement (and the new WTO Agreement which largely supersedes it) does not achieve this itself, since it only governs relations of the Member States with outside countries, and not the relationship between the Member States themselves.

The GATT Agreement applied at the time the Supply Regulations were adopted only to government departments and certain other authorities of central government, and most bodies covered by the GATT Agreement are in any case subject to the regulations under categories (a)–(c) above, so that it is not necessary to rely on Schedule 1. The only body which appeared not to be covered by these provisions,[30] but is covered under the Supply Regulations by the GATT Agreement and hence listed in Schedule 1, is the Post Office, in relation to its postal business.[31]

At the time of writing, the GATT Agreement applies only to supplies. However, from January 1, 1996 it will be largely superseded by a new Agreement on Government Procurement, part of the World Trade Organisation (GPA). This new agreement applies to works and services as well as supplies,[32] and also extends coverage to a variety of authorities outside central government. The Commission has submitted a Proposal for a directive amending the public sector procurement directives to align them with the WTO Agreement,[33] but, suprisingly, this does not contain a provision to include all "GPA authorities" in the Works or Services Directives.

(e) RELEVANCE OF THE DIRECTIVES

Where the regulations are ambiguous, they must be interpreted in the light of the directives which they implement. Further, where interpreted

---

[28] On this Agreement see pp. 774–782.

[29] Supply Regulation 2 defines a "GATT contracting authority" as one listed in Schedule 1.

[30] It is not covered by the general definition in regulation 3(1)(r) since its activities are of an "industrial or commercial nature".

[31] Schedule 1 states that coverage of the Post Office is limited to its postal business only, as under the GATT Agreement itself. Thus contracts connected with any other activities of the Post Office are unregulated. The Post Office was included in the GATT Agreement to ensure an overall balance of coverage in light of the entities put forward for coverage by other signatory states.

[32] See pp. 774–776.

[33] Proposal for a European Parliament and Council Directive amending Directive 92/50/EEC relating to the co-ordination of procedures for the award of public service contracts, Directive 93/36/EEC co-ordinating procedures for the award of public supply contracts, and Directive 93/37/EEC concerning the co-ordination of procedures for the award of public works contracts, COM (95) 107, Final.

in this way they still fail properly to implement the directive, a contracting authority is still obliged to follow the directive, which can be enforced against it where the directive has direct effect.[34] Thus it is relevant to consider the scope of the directives themselves.

The Works, Supply and Services Directives all apply to[35] i) the State, ii) regional or local authorities and iii) "bodies governed by public law", as well as iv) associations formed by one or more of such bodies.

Categories i) and ii) are not defined, but the concept of "the State" has been interpreted widely by the Court of Justice in *Beentjes,* in the context of the Works Directive to cover, at least, a body "whose composition and functions are laid down by legislation and which depends on the authorities for the appointment of its members, the observance of the obligations arising out of its measures and the financing of the public works contracts which is its task to award".[36]

Category iii), "bodies governed by public law",[37] covers a body with legal personality which is "established for the specific purpose of meeting needs in the general interest", is not of "an industrial or commercial character" and either a) is financed for the most part by the State, a regional or local authority or some other body governed by public law; b) is subject to management supervision by the State, regional or local authorities or bodies governed by public law; or c) has an administrative, managerial or supervisory board more than half of whose members are appointed by the State, regional or local authorities or bodies governed by public law. As an aid to interpreting the concept of "bodies governed by public law", the directives provide for a list to be drawn up of relevant bodies in each Member State; the list is to be "as exhaustive as possible", and may be updated. The list is found in Annex I of the Works Directive, but it applies to all three directives.[38] It is for guidance only: thus bodies not in the list but within the general definition are still covered, and, conversely, those in the list but not within the general definition would not appear to be included. Clearly there is a substantial overlap between the categories – many bodies will be both part of the State or a local authority and also a body governed by public law (though the Annex to the Works Directive lists as bodies governed by public law only those not obviously part of the State).

---

[34] Most of the procurement rules are of the kind which have direct effect, and contracting authorities are all bodies against which the principle may be invoked. Where a directive has direct effect, it does not normally matter where authorities are brought within the rules by purposive interpretation of the regulations, or through the direct effect doctrine, thus relying on the directive itself.

[35] Works Directive Article 1(b), Supply Directive Article 1(b), Services Directive Article 1(b).

[36] Case 31/87, *Gebroeders Beentjes B.V. v. The Netherlands* [1988] E.C.R. 4635, para. 12 of the judgment.

[37] *Ibid.*

[38] Supply Directive Article 1(b); Services Directive Article 1(b) and Works Directive Article 36(2) and Annex VIII.

The general definition in the United Kingdom regulations is clearly intended to include all authorities which are "bodies governed by public law" under the directives (and not expressly listed in the regulations[39]); in fact, the United Kingdom provisions parallel the directives' own definition of "bodies governed by public law".[40] It may therefore be deduced that the regulation 3(1)(r) seeks to cover, at least the bodies listed in Annex I to the Works Directive. Where there is doubt, it should thus be construed to cover bodies in the current version of this list, unless these have since changed their status or were wrongly included in the list itself.[41]

Where an authority is a "body governed by public law" under the directives, there will be no difficulty in construing regulation 3(1)(r) to cover such a body since the wording is so similar. The only difficulty in interpreting the regulations to comply with the directive may arise if the concepts of "the State", or "regional and local authorities", are extended to cover entities which are not in the express list in the regulations, and are not within the general definition. This might apply, for example, if the directives were held to cover bodies entrusted with statutory regulatory functions, but not appointed, controlled or funded by government. Such authorities are not covered by the definition of "the State" given in *Beentjes*, and it is perhaps unlikely that the Court of Justice would extend

---

[39] The express list is concerned mainly with bodies which would be considered as part of "the State", or as regional or local authorities. In view of the wide definition of "the State" adopted by the European Court in *Beentjes*, however, as outlined in the text above, the regulations do not appear to list all such bodies; thus the general definition in regulation 3(1)(r) must be relied on to ensure that all such bodies are covered in the United Kingdom.

[40] It is not, however, limited to this: it expressly includes bodies without legal personality, which are not within the definition of "bodies governed by public law" under the directives, though potentially within the directives as part of "the State", or as regional or local authorities.

[41] The list presently covers a number of specific bodies and agencies: the Central Blood Laboratories Authority; the Design Council; the Health and Safety Executive; the National Research Development Corporation; Public Health Laboratory Services Board; Advisory, Conciliation and Arbitration Service; Commission for the New Towns; Development Board for Rural Wales; English Industrial Estates Corporation; National Rivers Authority, Northern Ireland Housing Executive; Scottish Enterprise; Scottish Homes; and the Welsh Development Agency. Also listed are several catagories of body: universities and polytechnics; maintained schools and colleges; National Museums and Galleries; Research Councils; Fire Authorities; National Health Service Authorities; Police Authorities; New Town Development Corporations; and Urban Development Corporations. Clearly many of these – for example, police and fire authorities – are covered by the specific list in the regulations in any case.

The list is not entirely up to date – for example, in the reference to polytechnics, which have now converted to university status. It also does not include certain non-departmental bodies – for example, the Equal Opportunities Commission – which are clearly within the definition. This has arisen because the list applied originally only to the Works Directive, and the United Kingdom sought to include in the United Kingdom list only those bodies involved in works procurement above the relevant threshold, and it has not since been significantly revised.

the definition this far; but it is not inconceivable.[42] In such a case, it may be necessary to rely on the principle of direct effect to enforce the rules.

(f) ENTITIES WITHOUT LEGAL PERSONALITY

An entity need not possess legal personality to be caught by the regulations; indeed, as noted above, the general definition of regulated bodies in regulation 3(1)(r) expressly provides that such a body may be either a corporation or a group of individuals acting together.

Regulation 3(5) of each set of regulations provides that where an entity falling with regulation 3(1) (which defines "contracting authority") does not have the capacity to enter into a contract, the contracting authority in relation to that entity is the person whose function it is to enter into contracts for that entity. This seems to refer to the capacity to make a legal contract (as opposed to the power to undertake the mechanics of the procurement process).

A distinct unit which lacks legal capacity is often part of a larger entity which does have legal capacity and is itself a contracting authority – for example, most "Next Steps" agencies do not have separate legal personality, but are legally part of a government department. Regulation 3(5) makes it clear that the separate unit is not a separate contracting authority distinct from the department itself.

A group of persons acting together as a distinct unit which meets the definition in regulation 3(1) may be a sub-unit of a larger legal body which is not itself, however, within regulation 3(1) – for example, where the sub-unit is dependent on government funding but the body as a whole is not. It is not clear whether it is intended to bring such sub-units within the regulations. One view is that the test in regulation 3(1)(r) is applied to the legal entity as a whole. Another view, however, is that "a group of persons acting together" may include a group performing a distinct function within a larger body; if so, the larger body could be treated as a contracting authority to the extent that it awards contracts on behalf of the regulated sub-unit.

In the case of a group of persons acting together and lacking legal personality altogether, the effect of regulation 3(5) appears to be that the contracting authority is the individual(s) who concludes contracts on its behalf.[43] Proceedings to enforce the rules will thus presumably be brought against such persons.

---

[42] It is submitted that the general definition of bodies governed by public law is intended to set the boundaries for the type of authorities which are subject to regulation *outside* the traditional structure of government, and that the court should not move the boundaries through a very broad definition of the State. Thus the definition of "the State" in this context is probably narrower than the definition for other purposes, such as the jurisdiction of the European Court of Justice or the direct effect of directives.

[43] For a different view see Harden above, p. 27, who suggests that regulation 3(5) does not prevent the group as such being treated as a contracting authority. The view expressed in the text, however, is more consistent with the wording, and avoids problems with remedies which might arise if the body lacking legal personality were itself the contracting authority.

(3) CONTRACTS LET BY AGENTS

(a) CONTRACTS LET ON BEHALF OF A CONTRACTING AUTHORITY

A contracting authority may engage an agent to let contracts on its behalf; the contracting authority becomes the principal party to the contract, but the actual award process is carried out by the agent. This sometimes occurs, for example, in relation to major works procurements, where the award procedures are carried out by a company engaged by the authority, but in the name of the authority itself. In this case, the regulations clearly will apply to the award,[43a] and the authority would be advised to insert into its contract with the agent a clause providing for the rules to be followed.

(b) CONTRACTS LET BY A CONTRACTING AUTHORITY AS AGENT

It is not clear whether the regulations apply where a contracting authority awards a contract as agent for an entity which is not itself a contracting authority – that is, where the other entity is the principal party to the agreement, and the authority merely conducts the procedure. It is submitted that the regulations ought not to apply here.

Whatever the general position, however, it is clear that an award procedure is covered where awarded by an officer of the Crown on behalf of the Crown.[44]

3. REQUIREMENT OF "A CONTRACT IN WRITING FOR CONSIDERATION"

(1) REQUIREMENT FOR A CONTRACT

The Works Regulations, Supply Regulations and Services Regulations apply, respectively, when a contracting authority seeks offers in relation to a proposed "public works contract", "public supply contract" or "public services contract".[45] This involves a requirement for a proposed arrangement which is a "contract".[46]

(a) THE PROVISION OF SERVICES THROUGH NON-CONTRACTUAL ARRANGEMENTS

This, first, has the consequence that the regulations may not cover certain needs procured through arrangements of a non-contractual

---

[43a] See, in particular, note 81 below.
[44] See p. 107.
[45] Works Regulation 5; Supply Regulation 5; Services Regulation 5.
[46] See the definitions in Works Regulation 2(1) (public works contract); Supply Regulation 2(1) (public supply contract); Services Regulation 2(1) (public services contract).

nature. In English law the courts have tended to conclude that no contract exists with respect to the provision of services and products such as gas, electricity or water under a statutory framework, and also the provision of mail services.[47] If the scope of the regulations is determined by reference solely to the concept of a "contract" under domestic law, the acquisition of such services and products will not be subject to regulation where these are obtained from an entity which supplies on a non-contractual basis. However, the regulations would need to be followed if the authority were to consider any providers who do supply the product or services under contractual arrangements, as well as those who do not.

However, it seems unlikely that the concept of a "contract" is to be determined solely by reference to national law.

First, it is almost certain that the European Court will require that certain arrangements for acquiring goods and services must be treated as contracts under the directives and regulations, regardless of their general classification under domestic law. If this is not the case, it would be too easy to avoid the procurement rules by providing for a special non-contractual regime for public procurement, even for items such as vehicles or furniture which are subject to traditional competitive purchasing arrangements. If authorities wish to depart from the traditional contractual approach to acquisition – as, for example, has sometimes been done during wartime in order to ensure satisfactory terms or security of supply – it will surely be necessary to rely on one of the specific exemptions (such as the "security" exemption).[48]

On the other hand, there may be some acquisition arrangements which need not be regarded as contracts. In this respect it can be noted that the Atkins study carried out for the Commission on potential savings from opening up procurement markets excluded from the definition of "contractual procurement", and hence from the scope of the study, products and services regarded as "non-competitive" and "non-tradeable", under which categories it included, *inter alia*, gas, electricity, postal services and telecommunications[49] – those very cases which the English courts have tended to treat as non-contractual. It might be argued, even if not expressly excluded,[50] that these kind of purchases are intended to be outside the procurement regime and should either be subject to a general implied exclusion (regardless of whether there is a contract with any provider), or, alternatively, excluded

---

[47] See Arrowsmith, *Civil Liability and Public Authorities* (1992) pp. 49–50. See also *Norweb plc v. Dixon* [1995] 1 W.L.R. 636, where the court affirmed the view that the relationship between a tariff customer and an electricity supplier was non-contractual, although indicating that this may not be the case with customers with whom a special agreement has been concluded under the relevant statute.

[48] See pp. 152–154.

[49] Commission of the European Communities, *The Cost of Non-Europe in Public Sector Procurement* (1988), Vol. 5, P. A, pp. 16–17.

[50] Some such services, notably voice telephony (see p. 139) are excluded.

on the basis of the absence of a contract where acquired from a specific provider with whom there is no contract under domestic law. However, it is submitted that this is an unsatisfactory approach. Such products have not traditionally been the subject of competitive procurement simply because no competitive market has previously existed, not because the application of competitive award procedures is inherently inappropriate; this is now changing, however, with the increased introduction of measures, both by national governments and by the Community itself, to introduce competition in these markets. Already there is competition in areas of the United Kingdom telecommunications market, and the European Community is also moving towards liberalisation in this field. If it is open to states to properly classify any acquisition arrangements as "non-contractual" for the purpose of the directives and regulations, then it is submitted that this should apply only for products and services for which the nature of the market is such as to render competitive tendering procedures inappropriate.[51]

As indicated above, situations may arise where some bidders will, if successful, supply under contractual arrangements, whilst others will not. In this case, there is a proposed contract since a contract is one possible outcome of the procedure; thus the regulations must be followed. Another important case of this kind is where bids may be submitted by an in-house team; this is considered under (b) below.

(b) APPLICATION TO IN-HOUSE AWARDS

Where work is awarded to an in-house service provider which is legally part of the purchasing authority, there is in law no contract, and the work may thus be awarded to the in-house unit without following the regulations. This applies even if the in-house unit operates in practice on a largely independent basis, and even where it is normally required to compete for such work with the private sector. The degree of market openness in different states is obviously affected significantly by the extent to which work is contracted out – when it must be advertised Europe-wide – or retained in-house; this issue is discussed further in Chapter 12.

If for specific work the authority does seek external offers, a contract is in contemplation, and there is then a "proposed contract" for the purpose of the regulations[52]; the regulations must then be followed. Thus the regulations apply where an in-house unit is required to compete for work with outside bidders.

---

[51] An alternative approach would be to apply the rules to all contract-type acquisition arrangements, regardless of their contractual status under domestic law. This would mean that even where there is no competitive market, the award procedures under the regulations would have to be followed. However, in such a case the purchaser would be able to conclude a contract through the negotiated procedure without advertisement, because there is only one possible provider.

[52] The regulations then require the in-house bid to be treated in the same way as external bids: see further p. 242.

Where work is awarded to another public authority which is a separate legal entity, the award will take the form of a contract, and the regulations must thus be followed. However, the Services Regulations provide an exemption which effectively allows states to set up exclusive service provision arrangements between separate public sector bodies – for example, to allow a separate government accounting agency to provide accounting services to other public bodies, without competing for the work. This is considered further below.[53]

(c) RENEWALS, EXTENSIONS AND AMENDMENTS

Another important question is when a proposed extension, renewal or amendment to a contract is a new "contract" for the purpose of the regulations. Where this is the case, it is not permissible simply to place the work with the existing contracting party: it must be awarded in accordance with the regulations. Neither the regulations nor directives give clear guidance on this; nor has the position been clarified by case law.

As is explained below, it appears that mutually agreed extensions and variations will often need to be treated as new contracts. In practice, however, these are difficult to challenge: direct challenge is generally precluded when the agreement has been concluded, and an aggrieved competitor is unlikely to be able to prove loss for the purpose of obtaining damages.[54]

(i) EXTENSION BY MUTUAL AGREEMENT

One case is where there is an existing contract for either a specified time period or a specified amount, and it is sought to extend the time or amount. For example, an authority may place a contract for all its stationery for a year, and then seek an agreed extension for six months; or it may place an order for thirty photocopiers, and then request another ten on the same terms.

The most straightforward case is where the possibility of extension was not referred to in any previous advertisement, and the parties simply negotiate an extension. This involves the conclusion of a completely new "contract" under the regulations. They must thus be followed if the estimated value of the extension exceeds the threshold. This will often apply under the supply and services rules even where the addition is of very low value, because of the aggregation rules.[55]

This will apply regardless of whether the original contract was subject to the regulations, since it is the value and status of the new contract, not the original contract, which is relevant.

---

[53] See pp. 156–157.
[54] On the remedies available see further Chap. 15.
[55] See pp. 167–175.

This means that in practice it is not possible to operate by agreeing extensions to existing contracts on an ad hoc basis. In practice, for products for which exact needs are not known, it will be necessary instead to conclude a contract for a set period but without specifying the quantity, or to give the authority a unilateral option to increase or decrease any fixed amount. Another possibility might be conclusion of a "framework agreement", under which terms are set but goods or services ordered under binding arrangements only when they are required (if such arrangements are permitted under the public sector rules which, as will be explained below, is not entirely clear).[56]

Where the original contract was awarded in an open or restricted procedure[57] and the possibility of agreeing an extension was mentioned in the notice,[58] it might be suggested that the new agreement is a continuation of the previous one. It is submitted, however, that in principle this is incorrect: since if the addition requires the agreement of both parties, it is generally a new agreement. Any other view would provide a simple method for a purchaser to continue purchasing indefinitely from a single favoured enterprise, subject only to any restraints imposed by competition rules, and this is unlikely to be accepted by the Court of Justice in view of the objective of the directives of opening public sector markets to regular competition.[59]

However, a limited exception might be made for certain types of contract where continuation through agreed renewals is the normal and appropriate commercial practice: for example, with contracts of insurance, contracts with auditors or bankers, or hire contracts. It is unlikely that the directives intended to prohibit the traditional approach to purchasing in these cases, and here a common sense approach might override the usual formal test to suggest that the extended arrangement, whilst depending on mutual agreement, can nevertheless be treated as part of the existing arrangement. However, this should be permitted only where the possibility of renewal was mentioned in the original notice, and to the extent that the extension is for a reasonable period. This period should be determined in the light of the nature of the subject matter, taking into account factors such as the expense and inconve-

---

[56] See pp. 175–179.

[57] The question is unlikely to arise with a contract awarded by the negotiated procedure, since the nature and duration of the contract is limited to that prescribed by the regulations.

[58] This would not add to the parties' legal powers under private contract law, since it is always possible to extend a contract by mutual agreement.

[59] This is supported by the provisions in the Works and Services Regulations allowing use of the negotiated procedure for repeated works within three years, as discussed in the text below, which seem to assume that agreed extensions normally constitute new contracts; the provisions appear unnecessary if the regulations do not apply to renewals. These provisions can be seen as defining an exceptional case where an agreed renewal is regarded as commercially reasonable under the procurement rules.

    The above arguments are not affected by the fact that an agreed extension is provided for in the contract itself, nor by the fact that the length or nature of the extension is specified.

nience of changing providers (which may be a factor, for example, in contracts with a banker) – the greater this is, the longer the appropriate period.

Where the regulations apply, the additional work required must generally be placed through either an open or restricted procedure. However, in some cases the public sector regulations allow use of the negotiated procedure to conclude an agreement with the existing provider. Under the Works and Services Regulations[60] this may be used for unforeseen additional works or services where for technical or economic reasons it is unduly inconvenient to use a different firm, or if the works or services are necessary to the later stages of the contract. It also applies in certain cases to the repetition of works or services foreseen at the time, within three years of the original, provided that the possibility of an extension was mentioned in the contract notice.[61] Under the Supply Regulations, a new contract for addition to, or partial replacement of, existing goods (or an installation) may be negotiated with the existing provider in certain cases, to avoid incompatibility or technical difficulties.[62] The exact conditions for these exceptions are considered in Chapter 6.[63] The negotiated procedure may also be used in an emergency, although only where this was not foreseeable and was not the authority's fault[64] (which is unlikely where it has failed to prepare in time for supplying needs of an on-going nature). The use of the negotiated procedure in these cases constitutes, in substance, an agreed extension. However, in law this is a new procedure, and the usual requirements for the negotiated procedure without advertisement – such as publication of award notices – must be followed.

(ii) CONTRACTS SUBJECT TO TERMINATION AT THE OPTION OF EITHER PARTY

Another form of agreement is a contract which may be terminated at the option of either party, at any time, or after a certain period. For example, parties may agree that the authority will purchase, and the supplier provide, all the authority's stationery needs for an indefinite period, but that either may terminate the agreement on a month's notice. This produces, in practical terms, the same effect as a contract subject to renewal by consent: it permits extension beyond the period or quantity to which the parties are committed, but only by mutual agreement.

It can be argued that, although in form this appears a continuation of an existing agreement, it is the substance which is crucial, and that this

---

[60] Works Regulation 10(2)(g) and 10(4), Services Regulation 10(2)(h) and 10(4).
[61] Works Regulation 10(2)(h) and 10(5), Services Regulation 10(2)(i) and 10(5).
[62] Supply Regulation 10(2)(f) and 10(4).
[63] See pp. 262–265.
[64] See pp. 260–262.

should thus be treated in the same way as an agreed extension. On this view, once the period or quantity to which the parties are committed had expired, any continuation would normally constitute a new contract. As with the case of an agreed extension, however, an exception could be made for certain contracts where the arrangement in question is the normal and appropriate commercial practice.

(iii) CONTRACTS SUBJECT TO UNILATERAL EXTENSION (OPTIONS)

Another situation is where one party – usually the purchaser – has an option to extend the agreement unilaterally. Such an option is most likely to be for a specified period or quantity – for example, an agreement to purchase fifty photocopiers with an option for the purchaser to require an additional ten – although it could be indefinite.

In form, the exercise of an option is merely the exercise of a right under an existing agreement: the legal right to obtain the new goods or services does not depend on a new mutual agreement. An option is also subject to inherent limitations, arising from the fact that one party is legally bound to the extension without the need for further agreement: in practice, firms are unlikely to commit themselves to a long, binding relationship which is at the option of the other party alone, and hence an option does not present the same threat to competition as an agreed renewal.[65] Thus it appears that the exercise of an option should not be treated as creating a new contract.

(iv) CONTRACTS SUBJECT TO UNILATERAL TERMINATION (OPTION TO TERMINATE)

A contract under which one party only may terminate, is in substance the same as an agreement which may be extended at the option of one party. It should, therefore, be treated in the same way, as outlined at (iii) above.

(v) AGREED CHANGES TO THE SPECIFICATIONS

Parties sometimes wish to change by agreement the specifications for the goods, works, or services which form the subject matter of the contract.

---

[65] On the other hand, it can be pointed out that it is usually the reticence of the purchaser and not the other party, which will limit any agreement, and if the option is one for the purchaser, extensive agreements may still result. Such agreements may be unlawful under the competition provisions of Article 85 E.C., as to which see Chap. 4. However, it is possible that the Court of Justice could imply limitations under the directives on the potential duration of rights created through options, which go beyond those of Article 85, to ensure that markets are regularly opened to competition under the directives' procedures. At the very least the Court may imply that limitations equivalent to those under Articles 85 E.C. should apply to *all* contracts governed by the directives, even if the *de minimis* test which normally applies under Article 85 E.C. is not met.

This sometimes occurs, for example, with civil engineering work, where changes to methods are demanded by unforeseen ground conditions; with high technology contracts where specifications need to be adapted to new technology; or where a purchaser wishes to introduce improvements suggested by the other contracting party. Alterations to the price and other terms will be agreed to take account of such changes.

It is explained in Chapter 11 on specifications that changes may probably be made to the advertised specifications prior to the actual award decision, or between the award decision and actual conclusion of the agreement, provided these are not "substantial".[66] It is logical to apply the same test where the parties wish to alter specifications after concluding the contract, to determine whether the altered work should constitute a new contract and so require a new award procedure. Where a change is substantial, if any additional value attributable to the work is above the relevant threshold, the regulations apply.

(vi) UNILATERAL CHANGES TO THE SPECIFICATIONS

It is also common for contracts to contain a clause allowing unilateral changes to the specifications, generally at the option of the purchaser; the standard conditions used for most central government contracts include a clause allowing unilateral variations.[67] Probably such clauses are subject to implied limitations, allowing only amendments which are within the scope and objectives of the original agreement.[68] Such clauses will generally provide for an appropriate price adjustment.

It is submitted that a variation under such a clause is to be treated in the same way as an option to extend the contract.[69] Thus, such changes are probably not generally covered by the regulations, even where the change involves increasing the value of the contract by an amount which exceeds the relevant threshold.

(2) REQUIREMENT FOR WRITING

The definitions of public works contract, public supply contract and public services contract cover only contracts which are in writing[70]; hence, the regulations apply only to written contracts. In theory it is thus possible to avoid the regulations by concluding a verbal contract, although this is unlikely. This provision could also give rise to difficulties

---

[66] See Chap 11.
[67] See generally Turpin, *Government Procurement and Contracts* (1989) pp. 186–190.
[68] Turpin above, p. 187.
[69] On these see p. 122.
[70] Works Regulation 2(1), Supply Regulation 2(1), Services Regulation 2(1).

of interpretation – for example, as to the position where a verbal contract refers to some standard written terms.

The requirement is of little practical importance. Nevertheless, to avoid the difficulties just mentioned, it would have been better if the application of the regulations had not been limited to written contracts.

(3) REQUIREMENT FOR CONSIDERATION

For a contract to be a public works, supply or services contract under the regulations it is also provided that it must be "for consideration".[71] It is expressly stated that this may be consideration of any kind. Thus, for example, contracts of exchange or part-exchange are covered.

The extent to which this provision brings concession contracts within the regulations is considered in the separate section on concessions.[72]

4. THE SCOPE OF "WORKS", "SUPPLY" AND "SERVICES" CONTRACTS

(1) INTRODUCTION

As explained, the Works Regulations apply to a "public works contract", the Supply Regulations to a "public supply contract" and the Services Regulations to a "public services contract".[73]

It is important to know whether a contract falls within one of these definitions, and so potentially is subject to regulation, and also *which* set of regulations applies. This is relevant to whether the award procedure is regulated at all, since the regulations have different thresholds and exclusions. Of particular importance is the distinction between works, on the one hand, and supplies or services on the other, since the threshold for the Works Regulations is much higher than for the other regulations. Classification also affects the details of the award procedure, since the procedural rules vary in small respects.

(2) PUBLIC WORKS CONTRACTS

"Public works contract" is defined in Works Regulation 2(1) to cover i) contracts for the carrying out of a work or works, and ii) contracts under which the authority engages a person to procure a work "by any means".

---

[71] Works Regulation 2(1), Supply Regulation 2(1), Services Regulation 2(1).
[72] See Chap. 8.
[73] Works Regulation 5, Supply Regulation 5, Services Regulation 5.

(a) THE CARRYING OUT OF WORKS OR A WORK

First, the definition covers a contract for the "carrying out" of "works" or "a work".

"Works" is defined in Works Regulation 2, as meaning any of the activities specified in Schedule 1 to the regulations. This Schedule is reproduced on pages 126–127. The Schedule refers to the Community's old general classification of economic activities, NACE. This is out of date: the United Nations CPC (Central Product Classification) and the Community's own CPA classification based on this are now generally used, including in the Community supplies and services rules, and in the WTO Agreement on Government Procurement (for supplies, services and works).

Schedule 1 covers, in brief, general building and civil engineering work; construction of buildings; construction of roads, bridges and railways; demolition work; installation work such as plumbing and the installation of heating and electrical equipment; and "building completion work" such as plastering, papering and tiling.

There has been some debate over the position of exterior maintenance since, apart from restoration and repair of outside walls, this is not expressly listed. However, building maintenance is not listed under the services rules, and if such work is not covered by the works rules it appears that it would be subject, at most, to limited regulation as a non-priority (Part B) service under the category of "other services". Its omission from the services rules probably reflects an assumption that such work is covered by the works rules. The Court of Justice is likely to adopt a broad construction of the works rules to rectify the omission, and it was assumed in the High Court in *General Building and Maintenance v. Greenwich Borough Council*[74] that the works rules apply.

Maintenance of, as opposed to installation of, plumbing, heating and electrical work is also not expressly referred to; probably this is not intended to be covered, for it is expressly listed as a priority service under the Services Regulations.

In relation to installation, where the goods to be installed are provided by the supplier the contract to supply and install is defined under the Supply Regulations as a public supply contract. This provision probably takes such a contract outside the works rules in some cases even where the value of installation exceeds the value of the goods supplied; this point is considered further below.[75]

The regulations cover, as indicated, any contract for carrying out such activities. This clearly does not require that the contractor should do the

---

[74] [1993] I.R.L.R. 535.
[75] See pp. 147–148.

PUBLIC WORKS CONTRACTS REGULATIONS – SCHEDULE 1

ACTIVITIES CONSTITUTING WORKS

Classes	Groups	Subgroups and items	Descriptions
50			BUILDING AND CIVIL ENGINEERING
	500		General building and civil engineering work (without any particular specialisation) and demolition work
		500.1	General building and civil engineering work (without any particular specialisation)
		500.2	Demolition work
	501		Construction of flats, office blocks, hospitals and other buildings, both residential and non-residental
		501.1	General building contractors
		501.2	Roofing
		501.3	Construction of chimneys, kilns and furnaces
		501.4	Waterproofing and damp-proofing
		501.5	Restoration and maintenance of outside walls (repainting, cleaning, etc.)
		501.6	Erection and dismantlement of scaffolding
		501.7	Other specialised activities relating to construction work (including carpentry)
	502		Civil engineering construction of roads, bridges, railways etc.
		502.1	General civil engineering work
		502.2	Earth-moving (navvying)
		502.3	Construction of bridges, tunnels and shafts, drilling

	502.4	Hydraulic engineering (rivers, canals, harbours, flows, locks and dams)
	502.5	Road-building (including specialised construction of airports and runways)
	502.6	Specialised construction work relating to water (i.e. to irrigation, land drainage, water supply, sewage disposal, sewerage, etc.)
	502.7	Specialised activities in other areas of civil engineering
503		Installation (fittings and fixtures)
	503.1	General installation work
	503.2	Gas fitting and plumbing, and the installation of sanitary equipment
	503.3	Installation of heating and ventilating apparatus (central heating, air conditioning, ventilation)
	503.4	Sound and heat insulation, insulation against vibration
	503.5	Electrical fittings
	503.6	Installation of aerials, lightning conductors, telephones, etc.
504		Building completion work
	504.1	General building completion work
	504.2	Plastering
	504.3	Joinery, primarily engaged in on the site assembly and/or installation (including the laying of parquet flooring)
	504.4	Painting, glazing, paper hanging
	504.5	Tiling and otherwise covering floors and walls
	504.6	Other building completion work (putting in fireplaces, etc.)

127

work itself – merely that he is responsible for securing that they are provided; this may be done wholly or partly through subcontractors.[76]

"Carrying out" is defined in Works Regulation 2 to refer not merely to construction itself,[77] but also to design and construction, making it clear that contracts involving both design and construction are covered. (A contract solely for the design of works is covered as a priority service under the Services Regulations.)

"Work" means the *outcome* of any of the above works such as is of itself "sufficient to fulfil an economic or technical function".[78] This covers, for example, a complete public building, such as a theatre or town hall, or a complete engineering work such as a bridge or tunnel; on the other hand, a roof for a building clearly does not of itself constitute a work (although it involves "works", which are subject to the regulations as explained above). Other cases create more difficulty: for example, it is unclear whether a swimming pool which is part of a larger leisure complex, or an individual house or apartment block which is part of a larger estate, is a separate work; or whether a demolition job which clears land in preparation for a new structure is a work by itself.

The precise definition of "work" is not important in relation to the first part of the definition of public works contract, as one for the carrying out of works or a work. This is because since the reference to a "work" in this first part of the definition of public works contract does not add anything to the reference to "works": carrying out a "work" involves, by definition, the carrying out of "works". However, the concept of a "work" is relevant to the second part of the definition ((ii) below), and also for the application of the threshold rules.[79]

(b) PROCUREMENT OF A WORK BY ANY MEANS

Also within the definition of public works contract is one under which a contracting authority "engages a person to procure by any means the carrying out for the authority of a work corresponding to specified

---

[76] Case C–389/92, *Ballast Nedem Groep N.V. v. The State (Belgium)* [judgment of April 14, 1994]. In case C–331/92, *Gestion Hotelera Internacional SA v. Communidad Autonoma de Canarias* [1994] E.C.R. I–1329, Advocate General Lenz stated that an agreement for a firm to renovate an hotel to an amount of 1 million pesetas could not be a contract for works. One relevant factor was stated to be that the winning bidder was not permitted to realise the renovation itself, but only through other parties. It is not clear from the report whether the contracts to do the work were to be concluded with the contracting authority itself or the winning bidder; it is submitted that the Advocate General's remark on this particular issue is compatible only with the first possibility.

[77] It is interesting that regulation 2 in defining "carrying out" refers to the construction of the works. Here "works" is being used to refer to the end product of the activities in Schedule 1, whereas in the definition of "public works contract" and the definition of "works" itself "works" is used to refer to an activity (such as construction itself), not the end product of the activity.

[78] Works Regulation 2(1).

[79] See pp. 172–173.

requirements".[80] This brings within the works rules any arrangement whereby the authority draws up a specification for a work, and the contractor is entrusted with the task of providing it.

This was intended to bring within the works rules a contract whereby an authority engages a provider to act as agent for the authority in letting contracts in connection with a particular work.[81] Without this provision such a contract would be a services contract, since it consists solely of the provision of services. The threshold for applying the Works Regulations is much higher than the Services Regulations, and such management contracts may by themselves be well below the 5 million ECUs works threshold, although they are above the threshold which would apply to them if they were caught by the services rules. However, they do not escape regulation, since their value must be aggregated with the value of the contracts for actual construction of the works, under the aggregation rules set out below.[82] Thus if the value of the work itself is approaching 5 million ECUs, the management contract for those works will be covered.

The provision also appears to catch an arrangement under which a builder or developer arranges for the construction of a work on land not owned by the authority, and undertakes to transfer or lease the land and structure to the authority at a later point. Without this provision, such a contract might not be covered since arguably it could be regarded as one for the sale of land, which would not be subject to any of the regulations, rather than one for the carrying out of works, even though the works need to be carried out before the sale can be completed. The provision applies only where a structure is erected to the authority's specification: it does not apply, for example, to an arrangement whereby an authority agrees to buy land along with structures on the land, on condition that an investment is made in improvements without specifying the nature of the improvements. It is not clear whether it would apply to a contract for the purchase of a building not yet erected, which is to be built to a specification set by the developer which the authority has accepted.[83]

The definition of "work", discussed above, is important in relation to this provision, since the provision applies only where the authority procures from the other party a complete "work". It is suggested that the Court of Justice is likely to give a wide meaning to "work", to bring

---

[80] Works Regulation 2(1).

[81] This refers to the case where the contracts let by the agent are let *on behalf of* the authority, so that the authority itself becomes the principal contracting party. Where the provider managing the work lets the contracts on his own behalf, this is probably an ordinary contract for the carrying out of works done through subcontractors, so that it is not necessary to rely on this provision. However, the provision, which was introduced only in the 1989 review of the Works Directive, does at least clarify that contracts of the latter type are covered, in case there is any doubt over whether it may be classified as one for the carrying out of works.

[82] See pp. 172–173.

[83] For further consideration of the position of contracts of this type see p. 156.

within the rules most transactions which are likely to occur in practice involving the transfer of land following the carrying out of some kinds of works.

(3) PUBLIC SUPPLY CONTRACTS

"Public supply contract" is defined in Supply Regulation 2(1).

It covers, first, a contract for the purchase of goods or the hire of goods. It also covers a contract for the purchase or hire of goods, together with the siting or installation of those goods – for example, where a plumbing firm contracts to fit washrooms with fittings supplied by the plumber (as opposed to fittings already acquired by the authority under a separate contract). Installation work is generally caught by the Works or Services Regulations, but this provision appears to bring within the Supply Regulations installation contracts which also involve the supply of products installed.[84]

"Purchase" includes both the case where the consideration is given in instalments and where it is not.[85] It includes a purchase conditional upon the occurrence of a particular event. This could be an external event, or the exercise of an option by the buyer or seller under the contract.

"Hire" is expressly stated to cover both the case in which the authority becomes the owner of the goods after the period of hire (for example, a contract of hire purchase) and where it does not.

The regulations do not attempt an exhaustive definition of "goods".[86] However, Supply Regulation 2(1) states that "goods" *include* electricity; substances, growing crops and things attached to and forming part of the land which are agreed to be severed before the purchase or hire under the supply contract; aircraft; vehicles; and ships.[87]

One issue is whether something should be classified as goods where it is a concrete item which is the product of an activity other than simple manufacture: for example, a film commissioned by the authority or a product designed specifically for the authority such as bespoke computer software. In the case of *Re Data Processing*[88] it was assumed by both the European Court of Justice and Advocate General Mischco that an initial order for bespoke software was not an order of goods. It is likely that "goods" in this context will be interpreted in the same way as for the purpose of Article 30 E.C.[89] The distinction is of particular importance

---

[84] See further pp. 143–144 and 147–148.
[85] Supply Regulation 2(1).
[86] The term "goods" and the similar term "products" have been used in other English statutes. However, domestic definitions are unlikely to be helpful, since the meaning of goods in this context is probably a matter of European law to which existing domestic definitions are not relevant.
[87] Ship is further defined in the same regulations as a boat or other description of vessel used in navigation.
[88] Case C–3/88, *Commission v. Italy* [1989] E.C.R. 4035.
[89] See p. 82, n.4.

where the alternative to defining the item as "goods" is that its provision is treated as a service in the non-priority category; if it is treated as goods, regulation will be much more stringent.

"Goods" does not naturally include land, and the express reference to things severed from the land also indicates that land itself is not included.[90]

(4) PUBLIC SERVICES CONTRACTS

(a) CONCEPT OF A PUBLIC SERVICES CONTRACT

A public services contract is defined as one under which the authority "engages a person to provide services".[91] The concept of "services" is not expressly defined.

Certain contracts are expressly excluded from the definition, and thus are not "public services contracts" even though they may involve provision of services.[92]

First, public works contracts and public supply contracts within the meaning of the Works and Supply Regulations are excluded.[93] Thus, although the carrying out of works clearly involves the provision of services, contracts for works are not "public services contracts". Contracts which are for goods are not covered, as they are public supply contracts.[94]

Also excluded is "a contract of employment or other contract of service". A contract of employment (or contract of service) is often contrasted with a contract for *services* in United Kingdom law – the

---

[90] On the position of contracts for land see p. 156.
[91] Services Regulation 2(1). The Services Directive itself does not define public service contracts by reference to provision of services, but simply provides that it shall apply to all contracts not expressly excluded (Article 1(a)). This is curious, since it seems to bring within the ambit of the directive contracts which do not involve procurement, such as contracts to settle legal disputes, which were obviously not intended to be covered and which there is no authority to regulate since the legal basis of the directive is the Treaty provisions on services and establishment. It is thus likely the Court of Justice would construe the directive as impliedly excluding contracts which obviously do not involve procurement. The concept of "services" in the Services Regulations must be construed to include all matters within the directive.
[92] In addition to the exclusions mentioned in this text, also excluded from the regulations through the means of exclusion from the definition of "public services contract" are contracts covered by the utilities rules, as to which see pp. 151–152 and services concessions, on which see p. 366.
[93] Services Regulation 2(1), definition of "public services contract", items (b) and (c).
[94] Strictly speaking, there could be an overlap between "goods" and "services", since they are not defined as mutually exclusive. It is not necessary to consider this point; anything which is goods is under the supply rules because of the express provision to this effect, so that the only question in defining the relationship between the two sets of regulations is the definition of "goods". In practice, "services" is likely to be construed to cover only things which are not goods.

distinction is sometimes phrased as one between a contract with an employee and a contract with an "independent contractor". The distinction is employed in a number of contexts, notably in establishing vicarious liability (a person is generally liable for the torts of employees but not those of independent contractors),[95] and in determining a party's tax and social security position. It depends on factors such as the extent to which the engagor has the right to control the manner of performance of the work and the allocation of risk of profit or loss.[96] In the context of the procurement directives it is likely that the meaning of "employee" is a matter of European law for resolution by the Court of Justice,[97] so that these national rules are not directly relevant, although the approach of European law is likely to be similar to that of English law. The distinction will not surface often in practice, but may do so occasionally. For example, heads of certain large public corporations have sometimes claimed to be self-employed consultants for tax purposes; such a claim now raises the question of whether the post should be advertised under the regulations!

Finally, contracts for certain services, such as voice telephony services, are excluded from the regulations, even though they fall within the definition of a "public services contract".

(b) THE DISTINCTION BETWEEN "PART A" AND "PART B" SERVICES CONTRACTS

(i) NATURE AND EFFECT OF THE DISTINCTION

The Services Regulations do not apply in the same way to all public services contracts. They apply in their entirety only to contracts designated "Part A services contracts".[98] Other contracts – those for "Part B" services – are subject only to very limited regulation.

A Part A services contract is one for the services listed in Part A of Schedule 1 to the regulations.[99] The classification used is the United Nations Central Products Classification (CPC). Part A covers, *inter alia,* maintenance and repair of equipment and vehicles; some transport services; financial services[99a]; computer services; research and develop-

---

[95] See, for example, Jones, *Textbook on Torts* (4th ed., 1993), pp. 268–289.
[96] It is probably the same in each context: *Calder v. H. Kitson Vickers* [1988] I.C.R 232 *per* Ralph Gibson L.J.
[97] European law itself also contemplates distinctions of this kind, notably in European employment protection legislation: see, for example, Directive 75/117/EEC, [1975] O.J. L45/19 on equal pay; and Directive 76/207/EEC, [1976] O.J. L39/40 on equal treatment in access to employment. It is not clear whether the line will be drawn in the same place in different contexts in European law.
[98] Services Regulation 5(1).
[99] Services Regulation 2(2)(a).
[99a] On issues relating to financial services see Goris, "The Position of Financial Instruments under E.C. Public Procurement Rules" (1994) 9 Butterworths Journal & International Banking and Finance Law 213.

ment for the authority's own purposes; accounting services; management consultancy; computer services; architectural and planning services; advertising; building cleaning and property management; publishing and printing; and sewerage and sanitation services. The full list is set out on pages 134–135. Details of which services are considered by the Community to fall into these categories may be ascertained by consulting the Community's proposed Common Procurement Vocabulary (CPV), which currently exists in draft form.[1] All the listed services are Part A services *except* in so far as the categories cover services which are excluded from the Services Regulations altogether under Services Regulation 6.[2] (For example, research and development services are listed in Part A, but some of these services are within the regulation 6 exclusion and so are not covered at all.) Part A services are also often referred to as "priority services".

The other type of public services contract is a "Part B services contract". This is defined as a contract for those services listed in Part B of Schedule 1[3] (sometimes referred to as "non-priority services"). Since this list includes a reference to "other services" (item 27 of the Schedule), in the sense of all services not expressly listed in the Schedule, a service which is not listed in Part A automatically falls within Part B (although again it should be pointed out that services in the Part B list which are excluded services under Services Regulation 6 are not regulated at all). The only obligations applying to the award procedure for Part B contracts[4] are those in regulation 8 on technical specifications[5]; those in regulation 22 on contract award notices[6]; and those under regulation 27(2) concerning submission of statistical reports,[7] for transmission to the Commission.[8]

---

[1] On the CPV see pp. 69–71.
[2] On the excluded services see pp. 138–140.
[3] Services Regulation 2(2)(b).
[4] Listed in Services Regulation 5(2).
[5] See Chap. 11.
[6] See pp. 283–286.
[7] On this see pp. 288–290. Also relevant is Services Regulation 29, containing the rules on notices. Regulation 29(5) provides that an authority may send a notice to the *Official Journal* relating to a services contract, even though this is not required.
[8] It is expressly stated in Services Regulation 2(2) that the rules in regulation 28 on responsibility for obtaining reports are to apply.

PUBLIC SERVICES CONTRACTS REGULATIONS 1993, SCHEDULE 1 – PART A AND PART 13 SERVICES

PART A

Category	Services	CPC Reference
1.	Maintenance and repair of vehicles and equipment	6112, 6122, 633, 886
2.	Transport by land, including armoured car services and courier services but not including transport of mail and transport by rail	712 (except 71235), 7512, 87304
3.	Transport by air but not transport of mail	73 (except 7321)
4.	Transport of mail by land, other than by rail, and by air	71235, 7321
5.	Telecommunications services other than voice telephony, telex, radiotelephony paging and satellite services	752
6.	Financial services	81 (Part) 812, 814
	(a) Insurance services (b) Banking & investment services other than financial services in connection with the issue, sale, purchase or transfer of securities or other financial instruments, and central bank services	
7.	Computer and related services	84
8.	R&D services where the benefits accrue exclusively to the contracting authority for its use in the conduct of its own affairs and the services are to be wholly paid for by the contracting authority	85
9.	Accounting, auditing and bookkeeping services	862
10.	Market research and public opinion polling services	864
11.	Management consultancy services and related services, but not arbitration and conciliation services	865, 866

12.	Architectural services; engineering services and integrated engineering services; urban planning and landscape architectural services; related scientific and technical consulting services; technical testing and analysis services	867
13.	Advertising services	871
14.	Building-cleaning services and property management services	874 82201 to 82206
15.	Publishing and printing services on a fee or contract basis	88442
16.	Sewerage and refuse disposal services: sanitation and similar services	94

PART B

Category	Services	CPC Reference
17.	Hotel and restaurant services	64
18.	Transport by rail	711
19.	Transport by water	72
20.	Supporting and auxiliary transport services	74
21.	Legal services	861
22.	Personnel placement and supply services	872
23.	Investigation and security services, other than armoured car services	873 (except 87304)
24.	Education and vocational education services	92
25.	Health and social services	93
26.	Recreational, cultural and sporting services	96
27.	Other services	

Part A services are those on which the open market regime is likely to have the most impact, taking into account factors such as the potential for cross-border trade, economic importance, and the availability of savings. Another relevant factor was the extent of information available about each service. In its review of the Services Directive under Article 43 of the directive,[9] the Commission is obliged to consider the pos-

---

[9] See further pp. 75–76.

sibilities for applying all the provisions of the directive to Part B services. As indicated above, statistical information is being collected on Part B contracts, and this should assist in any revision.

(ii) CLASSIFICATION OF CONTRACTS INVOLVING BOTH PART A AND PART B SERVICES

I. General

Where a contract involves both Part A and Part B services, its classification is determined by ascertaining the value of the consideration attributable to the Part A services on the one hand, and to the Part B services on the other. If the value of Part A services is greater than that of the Part B services it is a Part A contract; if equal to or less than the value of Part B services, it is a Part B contract.[10]

This can be criticised. If Part A services of a value above the threshold are purchased in conjunction with Part B services of equal or greater value, the effect is to exempt the Part A services from the full rigours of the procurement rules, although all the rules would apply if the Part A services were purchased separately. This is difficult to justify: it would be better to treat a contract as a Part A services contract wherever the value of the Part A services is above the threshold. It is immaterial that this would involve the full regulation of Part B services: Part B services are lightly regulated merely because there are insufficient proven reasons *for* regulation, not because there are positive reasons not to regulate (as there are, for example, with contracts caught by the security exemption).[11] Indeed, such services are subject to the rules where combined with other purchases, such as Part A services, where those other purchases are of greater value. The position advocated may be the one applicable under the new WTO Agreement on Government Procurement: under that Agreement it is arguable that a contract for non-regulated services (which are the same as those regulated under the Community rules as Part B services), together with regulated services

---

[10] Services Regulation 2(2).

[11] The approach advocated in this paragraph was the one adopted by the Court of Justice in case C-3/88, *Commission v. Italy* (*Re Data Processing*) [1989] E.C.R. 4035, in considering an analagous situation of contracts partly for supplies (regulated under the Supply Directive) and partly for services (not regulated at that time). This can be compared directly with a contract partly for Part A services (fully regulated) and partly for Part B services (regulated only to a limited degree). The Court held that contracts involving supplies of a value above the threshold were regulated, even if the value of services under the contract was greater than the value of the supplies. This ruling covered the position where the purchases of supplies and services could be separated; Advocate General Mischo expressed the view that it should apply also even if the two could not be purchased separately. It is submitted that this is correct; the position where there is both a regulated and non-regulated element should be the same whether or not it is reasonable or possible to separate the purchases.

which alone exceed the threshold value, is under the Agreement, even where the value of the non-regulated services is the greater.[12]

Whether the position under the Services Regulations is different if Part A and Part B services are deliberately packaged together to limit the application of the rules to Part A services, is considered under (III.) below.

II. Contracts divided into lots

An award may sometimes be divided into lots in such a way as to give firms the choice of bidding/negotiating either for both the Part A and Part B services, or for the Part A or Part B services alone. In this case it appears that there are several possible "proposed contracts" for the purpose of the regulations – the "mixed" contract, which will be either a Part A or Part B contract, depending on the relative value of the different services; a separate Part A services contract, for the Part A services alone; and a separate Part B contract for the Part B services alone. If the value of the Part A services exceeds that of the Part B services, the "mixed" contract is a Part B contract and subject only to limited regulation; but it appears that the Part A services nevertheless must be advertised under the regulations as a separate Part A contract.[13]

(iii) PACKAGING AND SEPARATION OF PART A AND PART B SERVICES

The different treatment of Part A and Part B services may appear to create some, limited, opportunities for reducing the impact of the regulations, through the way in which contracts are packaged.

First, where for commercial reasons an authority would normally wish to advertise both types of services in a single contract, with the value of Part A services exceeding the value of Part B services, an authority may be tempted to advertise the Part B services separately, to avoid the full application of the rules to the Part B services. This is probably permitted.

A provision which might be cited in favour of a contrary view is Services Regulation 7(11), which provides that a contracting authority "shall not enter into separate public services contracts ... with the intention of avoiding the application of these Regulations to those

---

[12] See the unadopted GATT Panel Report on Procurement of a Sonar Mapping System (*European Community v. United States*) of April 23, 1992, noted by Footer (1993) 2 P.P.L.R. C5193, ruling that the old GATT Agreement applied to a contract for both supplies, which were regulated at that time, and services, which were not, even though the services were of greater value than the supplies, where the value of the supplies exceeded the threshold. This could be applied by analogy to the case referred to in the text.
[13] It is submitted that this case is different in principle from the case where it is the nature of the purchases – rather than the nature of the contract – which is not known at the start of the award procedure: on the former case see p. 148.

contracts". On a literal reading this could be interpreted to cover the deliberate split referred to above.[14] On the other hand, the provision did not contemplate this kind of case: the remainder of regulation 7, in which it appears, is concerned only with the threshold rules, and the wording of Services Directive Article 7(3), which it implements, clearly prohibits only contract splitting designed to avoid the threshold rules, and not splitting aimed at avoiding other rules. Even so, it might still be argued that, even if splitting a contract to avoid advertising non-priority services is not expressly forbidden by the directive, it is forbidden by implication by analogy with Article 7(3).

However, such a split, it is submitted, does not infringe the policy of the procurement rules: they do not seek to ensure the full regulation of non-priority services. This case is different from splitting of contracts relating to subject matter which the directive *does* seek to regulate, in order to avoid that regulation. Thus, such a split is in principle unobjectionable. Of course, if it is done in order to favour a domestic service provider (for example, to award the Part B services to that firm without advertising), this would be a breach of the relevant Community Treaty.[15]

A second way in which an authority may utilise the Part A–Part B distinction is by packaging Part A services, which are valued above the threshold and would otherwise have been purchased separately, along with Part B services of the same or greater value. (Opportunities for such packaging are of course limited in practice, but may occasionally arise.) There is nothing in the regulations which expressly prohibits such packaging. The Court of Justice may, however, be willing to adopt a purposive approach to the rules and imply such a limitation, by analogy with Services Directive Article 7(3), implemented by Services Regulation 7(11), which prohibits *splitting* contracts (simply the reverse of joining contracts together) to avoid the threshold. Of course, it will often be difficult to prove that purchases have been joined together simply to avoid the rules; but it may be possible, in particular where the packaging involves a departure from the authority's own previous practice.

(c) EXCLUDED SERVICES

(i) THE EXCLUDED SERVICES

Services Regulation 6 provides that the Services Regulations are not to apply to public services contracts for certain specified services. Services contracts are thus effectively divided into three types – those for Part A services, which are subject to full regulation; those for Part B services,

---

[14] "Avoiding the application" of the regulations could be construed to cover avoiding the application of certain parts of the regulations to a contract, as well as the regulations as a whole.

[15] See Chap. 4.

which are subject to very limited rules; and those for "excluded" services which are not subject to regulation at all.

The excluded services are divided into six categories as set out below.

(i) Broadcasting services

Services Regulation 6(b) excludes contracts for the "acquisition, development, production or co-production of programme material for radio or television by a broadcaster". This excludes the purchase by a contracting authority responsible for broadcasting (for example, the British Broadcasting Corporation) of programmes, sound recordings, etc., for broadcast on its channels, as well as the purchase of advertisements. It also excludes contracts for the purchase of broadcasting time *by* contracting authorities.

(ii) Voice telephony and other communications services

Services Regulation 6(c) excludes contracts for voice telephony, telex, radiotelephony, paging and satellite services. These have been excluded because the Community's general market liberalisation programme for communications does not yet extend to these kind of services.

(iii) Arbitration or conciliation services

Services Regulation 6(d) excludes contracts for arbitration services, and conciliation services.

(iv) Certain financial services

Financial services, namely insurance services and investment services, are generally listed as Part A services. However, Services Regulation 6(e) excludes from the regulations altogether contracts for financial services in connection with the issue, purchase, sale or transfer of securities or other financial instruments.[16]

(v) Central banking services

Regulation 6(f) excludes contracts for "central banking services". This wording differs from Article 1(a)(vii) of the Services Directive which it seeks to implement, the directive referring to central "bank" services rather than central "banking" services. The concept of "central banking" services could be interpreted literally to cover the services provided by the central clearing banks, as well as those special to the central bank, the Bank of England. Clearly, however, the exclusion in the regulation must be construed more narrowly, in line with the directive. It may also be noted that the list of Part A services in Schedule 1 to the regulations expressly excludes from its scope central "bank" services.

(vi) Research and development services

Services Regulation 6(g) generally excludes contracts for research and development services. This provision seeks to exclude from the rules

---

[16] The list of Part A services in Schedule 1 also states that these services are excluded from the Part A list.

research activities funded or assisted by public bodies for general public benefit.

The exclusion does not apply where two conditions are satisfied:

(a) The first condition is that the benefits of the research and development are to accrue exclusively to the contracting authority for use in its own affairs. This means that the regulations may sometimes cover contracts for the development of equipment or techniques, where these are sought for the authority's own use. For example, an authority may engage a body to investigate the possibilities of developing new surveillance equipment for the government's own use in combatting terrorism, and this may be covered. It is not clear whether the position is affected by the fact that the firm is permitted to keep the intellectual property rights, so as to exploit its finds in the market generally.

At the other end of the spectrum, funding of research which seeks to develop products or technology for the benefit of the market as a whole, and for which the authority itself has no requirements, is clearly excluded from the regulations. This will apply to much research funded by government in research institutions, universities, etc., but also applies where such "public benefit" research is contracted out to private profit-making firms. However, in the case of "applied" research – that is, research with a potential market application – contracts may need to be let under open competitive procedures, in order to avoid the possibility that such contracts are unlawful State Aid under Articles 92–93 E.C.

(b) The second condition is that the services are to be wholly paid for by the contracting authority. Thus, even where benefits of the services accrue exclusively to the authority, the services are still excluded where the service provider, or some other body which is not a contracting authority, assists in funding.

Those research and development services which do not fall within the scope of the exclusion are Part A services.

(ii) PUBLIC SERVICES CONTRACTS FOR BOTH EXCLUDED AND NON-EXCLUDED SERVICES

A single contract could involve the provision of both regulated services, and those excluded by Services Regulation 6 (hereafter "excluded services"). For example, a single contract might be awarded for a variety of research activities, of which some are excluded and others not. Neither the directives nor regulations give express guidance on how such contracts should be treated.

It is submitted that the correct approach depends on the justification for excluding the services in question. First, services may be excluded because the award procedures laid down are inappropriate: the preamble to the Services Directive indicates that this is the case for broadcasting and arbitration/conciliation services. In this case – as also, for example, with purchases excluded from the directives for secrecy reasons – there is a positive reason not to regulate the purchases. Another possibility, however, is that the directive and implementing regulations are "neutral" over the regulation of the excluded service – it has not been included because there is no positive reason to regulate (for example, there is no real prospect of cross-border transactions), but there is no positive reason to exclude the procedures in the directive. Probably voice telephony, etc. (category ii) above) falls into this category. It is not entirely clear how the other exclusions should be categorised: perhaps most should be regarded as excluded for some positive reason, since where no such reason exists for exclusion, services are generally categorised as Part B services.

Where a service is one excluded for a positive reason, then it is submitted that it should be treated in the same way as services falling within the secrecy/security exemptions where it is part of a "mixed" contract. This issue is discussed below,[17-18] where it is suggested that the whole contract is excluded, provided that it would involve some inconvenience or financial cost to purchase the two elements of the contract separately, and that this should apply regardless of whether the excluded or non-excluded element constitutes the greater part of the contract. However, this may be at odds with the approach to be adopted with a contract for supplies and excluded services, which appears to be regulated wherever the value of the goods acquired exceeds the value of the excluded services.

If, on the other hand, the directive may be regarded as "neutral" as to the treatment of the excluded service, the contract as a whole should be treated as within the regulations, when the value of the regulated service exceeds the value of the excluded service: where the excluded service is merely incidental in this way, the contract is not one "for" an excluded service, so the exclusion does not apply. In addition, it is submitted that a contract should be regulated even where the excluded service constitutes the greater part of the contract, *where the value of the regulated services is by itself above the threshold*; the fact that the regulated services are packaged with excluded services does not justify the exclusion of services which would be regulated if let separately. Admittedly, a different approach is adopted in the case of contracts for both Part A and Part B services, where the purchase of Part A services above the threshold may escape regulation if packaged with Part B services of greater value; but that rule was criticised above.

Since the courts have not yet considered this issue, however, the correct approach remains open to debate.

[17-18] See pp. 153–154.

(5) CONTRACTS FOR TWO OR MORE OF GOODS, WORKS AND NON-CONSTRUCTION SERVICES

(a) INTRODUCTION

A single contract may be one for both goods and services; for both goods and works; for works and other services; or even for goods, works and other services together. In all these cases the contract must be classified as a public supply contract, public works contract or public services contract: it cannot fall within more than one set of regulations.

(b) THE BOUNDARY BETWEEN SUPPLY AND SERVICES CONTRACTS

Many contracts involve the purchase of both goods and non-construction services which, if purchased separately, would be governed by different regulations. For example, a contract for a data processing system may cover both hardware, which constitutes "goods" under the Supply Regulations, and bespoke software, purchase of which probably does not constitute "goods". Another example is a contract for both the supply of products – for example, vehicles – and their maintenance.

Classification of such a "mixed" contract as either a supply contract or a services contract may affect whether the contract is subject to regulation at all. In particular, the services threshold is presently higher than the supply threshold for central government (although there is a Proposal to charge this, in line with the thresholds in the new GPA).[19] Classification may also affect procedures. With a contract for goods and Part A services the procedural differences are minor; however, where the services are Part B services, the differences are important, since if the contract is a services contract it is a Part B contract and regulated only in a limited way.

The general rule is that the contract is a supply contract if the value of the consideration attributable to the goods (or the goods plus installation) is equal to or greater than the value attributable to the services.[20] If, on the other hand, the value of the goods (or goods plus installation) is less than or equal to the value of the services, the contract is a public services contract. Thus, for example, a contract involving the provision of

---

[19] See p. 162.
[20] Supply Regulation 2(1) which provides that where services as well as goods are provided a contract is only a public supply contract where the value attributable to the goods (or goods plus their installation) is equal to or greater than that attributable to the services. Where the contract is not a public supply contract under this definition – as where the value of the services exceeds the value of the goods (or goods plus installation) it then falls under the definition of a public services contract in Services Regulation 2(1): as explained above, this covers any contract involving some provision of services which is not a public supply contract (or other excluded contract).

goods worth 300,000 ECUs and maintenance services worth 200,000 ECUs is a supply contract; but if the position is reversed and the maintenance is worth 300,000 ECUs and the goods only 200,000 ECUs, it is a services contract. If both are worth 250,000 ECUs it is a services contract.

This rule for classifying applies regardless of whether the services are Part A or Part B services.[21]

One consequence of this is that where goods of a value above the threshold are purchased along with Part B services of greater value, the purchase of goods is subject only to the limited regulation applicable to Part B services contracts. This is similar to the case of a contract for both Part A and Part B services, where the rule has the effect of taking the Part A services out of the full regime. The rule was criticised in that context, above; and the same criticism is valid in relation to a contract for goods plus Part B services. It was queried above whether the rule would apply where Part A and B services are packaged together deliberately to remove the Part A services from the full application of the regulations; no doubt the same position will prevail where a package is designed specifically to avoid full regulation of a supplies purchase.

The position may, as with contracts partly for regulated and partly for non-regulated services, be different under the WTO Agreement on Government Procurement: under that Agreement a contract for non-regulated services (which are equivalent to Part B services), together with regulated goods which alone exceed the threshold value for supply contracts, appears to be regulated under the Agreement, even where the value of the non-regulated services exceeds that of the goods.[22]

Theoretically, a single contract might involve goods, Part A services, and Part B services. The literal wording of the Services Regulations and Directive suggest that such a contract must first be classified as either a supply contract or a services contract, according to whether the predominant element is the goods, or the services (the Part A services and Part B services together).[23] Where the value of the services is greater, so that the contract is a services contract, the wording of the rules indicate that its classification as a Part A or Part B services contract is then determined by the respective value of the Part A and Part B services.

It is possible in such a case that the value of the Part A services plus the goods -- elements upon which the Community seeks to apply the full rules – is greater than the value of the Part B services – that is, the element which the Community does not seek to regulate fully. However,

---

[21] This is made clear in Article 2 of the Services Directive, which expressly refers to "services within the meaning of Annexes IA and IB" (which correspond to Part A and Part B services under the regulations). Following this, Services Regulation 2(1) does not distinguish in setting out the rules between Part A and Part B services.

[22] See note 12 on p. 137.

[23] This is implied by the literal wording of both Services Regulation 2(2), and Services Directive Article 10 which the regulation is intended to implement.

the outcome is that the contract is not subject to full regulation, but only to the limited regime applying to Part B services. The Court of Justice may seek to avoid such a conclusion by departing from the literal wording of the rules, and classifying such a contract as a Part A services contract. Such a purposive interpretation is consistent with the policy reflected in the rules on contracts involving Part A and Part B services only, which is to apply the full regime of the regulations wherever the "fully regulated" element constitutes the greater part of the contract.

There is a special rule for supply of goods together with their installation, since Supply Regulation 2(1) indicates expressly that a contract for the supply of goods together with their installation is a supply contract. It appears that this overrides the usual rules and applies even when the value of the installation services is greater than the value of the products.

A firm may be permitted to bid for goods and services in separate lots, as well as together: for example, with an award for the supply and maintenance of equipment, firms may be given the choice of bidding for both, or bidding for either supply or maintenance only. In such a case it appears that there is a separate proposed supply contract (for the equipment) and services contract (for the maintenance), as well as the "mixed" contract (for both the equipment and its maintenance). Thus, for example, where the mixed contract is a services contract because the services element predominates, the contract is subject to the Services Regulations; but if the goods may be bid for separately, the Supply Regulations will apply in relation to the purchase of the goods. This is significant where the services are Part B services, since the obligations under the Supply Regulations are in that case much more stringent than those under the Services Regulations.

(c) THE BOUNDARY BETWEEN WORKS/SERVICES CONTRACTS AND WORKS/SUPPLY CONTRACTS

(i) The works/services boundary

As explained above, public works contracts are defined as contracts for carrying out works or a work, and the procurement of a work to the authority's specification by any means[24]; whilst public services contracts are contracts for the provision of services which are not public works contracts (or other excluded contracts).[25] In contrast with the express rules on the status of a contract involving both goods and non-construction services the directives and regulations do not deal expressly with the status of a contract for both works and other services. The issue

---

[24] See pp. 124–130.
[25] See pp. 131–132.

is important, because the threshold for regulation is much higher under the works rules.

The issue was considered by the Court of Justice, in its recent decision in *Gestion Hotelera Internacional*,[26] which concerned a contract to renovate a hotel and fit out a casino, and then to operate both for a period of time. The Court ruled that a contract is not one "for" carrying out works, where the works are "incidental" to the services provided. However, it did not specify what it meant by "incidental".

In argument, two possible meanings of incidental were suggested by the Commission. One is that works are "incidental" to services where the value of the consideration attributable to the works is less than the value attributable to the services – the same test as applies in distinguishing a supply from a services contract. The other possibility is that the contract is characterised by considering what is the main object of the contract: is it to acquire services – in which case it is a services contract – or to obtain a work or works? A contract for building a leisure facility or housing estate (works), which a provider is to manage and operate for ten years (services) and then return it to the use of the authority would probably be a works contract, at least where the concession arrangement is designed solely for the purpose of remunerating the provider, since the main object of the contract is to provide a leisure facility or public housing for indefinite public use under the authority's control. On the other hand, an agreement whereby a provider is to operate prison services for the authority for ten years under an agreement which includes an obligation to build a prison for this purpose, but which contains no obligation to transfer this to the authority at the end of the ten-year term, would be a services contract, since the works are merely carried out for achieving the main object of providing prison services. The two tests will often, though not always, give the same result.[27]

The Treasury in its introductory guidance on the procurement rules

---

[26] Above, note 76.

[27] Whatever the definition of "incidental", the Court's approach in using this concept at all is based on a purposive rather than literal interpretation of the directives: a literal reading suggests that a contract involving works is a works contract, even if *other* services are also provided and are of greater value and greater importance than the works, since it falls within the definition of a works contract, and there is no express provision to take the contract out of that category and place it under the services rules. Clearly the Court's interpretation is a better one: in view of the higher works threshold the literal approach would take many significant purchases of services outside the regulations, simply because they are packaged along with a works element – even though services are the greater element and the main object of the contract, and their value exceeds the threshold for the services rules. For example, a contract involving construction and repair works of 1 million ECUs, along with services to manage the repaired works of a value of 2 million ECUs, would not be regulated at all: the 2 million ECUs of management services easily exceeds the threshold for regulation for public services contracts, but the contract as a whole does not exceed the 5 million ECUs works contract threshold.

has taken the view that it is the "main object" test which applies.[28] This test is clearly sensible where services are provided in the course of producing a work, or carrying out work.[29] (There is unlikely to be any interest from firms which provide the relevant services but do not themselves do works; only works contractors will be interested, which makes the works thresholds appropriate). In other cases, however, it may be difficult to apply in practice, even where the works and services are connected, since it cannot be said that the transaction has a main purpose. For example, a contract to build and operate a prison facility may be structured as such because an authority may both wish to obtain the "work" – a prison (which the contract may provide to be transferred to it at some point) and also to find a provider to run the prison. It is hard to see that one of these objectives is the main objective of the contract any more than the other. Further, in some cases the works and services may be unconnected to each other but packaged together because some firms are involved in both, and an authority feels it may get better value from a package deal. Even if the purpose test is to be applied in general, in these types of cases it may be necessary to fall back on a "greater value" test.

In all those cases where the services are not provided in the course of the works, both the services and the works elements may attract interest from firms in the relevant field, and it can be argued that the Community rules ought to apply if the works alone exceed the threshold of the Works Regulations, or if the services alone exceed the threshold of the Services Regulations, at least if the two elements could reasonably be separated. Under the present rules, however, where the contract is classified as a works contract it remains unregulated if the total contract value does not exceed the high works threshold, even if the value of the services element is much greater than the normal threshold for services. For example a contract for 1 million ECUs of works plus 500 000 ECUs of services would be unregulated if a works contract, since the total value of 1 500 000 ECUs is well below the 5 million ECUs works threshold, although the 500 000 ECUs paid for services is well above the services threshold. Under the Utilities Regulations services are regulated in such a case: whenever the services are not "necessary" for the works with which they are packaged in a works contract, the Utilities Regulations

---

[28] H.M. Treasury, *An Introduction to the E.C. Procurement Rules.*

It can also be pointed out that where the main object of the contract is the procurement of a complete work which is built to the authority's specifications, such a contract might in any case be regarded as a works contract by virtue of the provision in the works rules which designate as a works contract a contract which seeks to procure "a work by any means".

A contract for design and construction is also expressly stated to be a works contract. This will presumably apply even if the relative value test applies and (in a rare case) the design element is greater than the works element. Under the "main object" test such a contract is a works contract without the need for any express provisions.

[29] The utilities rules expressly state that services necessary for the execution of the works are treated as part of works contract.

expressly provide that they are regulated where their value alone exceeds the "services" threshold[29a]. It would be desirable to adopt such a provision for the public sector also.

An authority should, however, be wary of deliberately packaging works and services together to avoid applying the regulations to the services – for example, by adding together with works services which are totally unrelated. This is because, whilst the rules do not expressly prohibit such practices, the Court of Justice might imply such a restriction, by analogy with the express rules on contract splitting. Indeed, it may even go further and apply the Services Regulations where there is no commercial justification for the approach adopted to packaging the works and services, producing a rule which is similar to that applied expressly in the utilities sector.

In practice, contracts which involve both works and services are often contracts of "concession", under which the provider is given the right to exploit the works – for example, a contract to build, operate and maintain a leisure centre under which the provider is permitted to charge and retain user fees, as payment for its work and services. Such concession contracts are subject to special rules, as explained in Chapter 8. In this context, the distinction discussed above between works and services contracts is of particular importance, since works concession contracts are subject to some regulation, whilst services concession contracts probably are not.[30]

(ii) THE WORKS/SUPPLY BOUNDARY

It has been explained that a contract involving the carrying out of works, or the procurement, by any means, of a work to the authority's specifications, is a public works contract, whilst a contract for the acquisition of goods, or of goods plus installation, is a supply contract. A contract involving both works and goods thus falls prima facie within both the Works and Supply Regulations; but clearly this was not intended, since that would involve the regulation of contracts involving any kind of works – which almost invariably involve some provision of products – at the very low Supply Regulations threshold.

As with contracts for both works and services, the test of whether the products are incidental to the works is probably to be adopted. In general a predominant purpose test seems appropriate here. Thus if a builder provides both material and labour in erecting a building, this appears to be a works contract regardless of whether the value of materials exceeds the value of the labour.

As has been noted, a contract for supply and installation of goods is expressly stated to be a supply contract. This is consistent with a general

---

[29a] See pp. 441–442.
[30] See further Chap. 8.

predominant purpose test: if the supply of goods can be seen as the main object of the contract it is a contract for supply and installation, and is a supply contract regardless of the respective value of the goods and any works activities carried out in their supply.[31] For example, a contract to install a lightning conductor will be a supply contract, since the purpose is the supply of conductor; however, a contract to build a wall is not, since it can be said that the objective of the contract is the erection of a wall, not the supply of bricks.

A contract which involves works plus the supply of unrelated goods is unlikely in practice, but if it should occur it is probably to be classified in principle by applying a relative value test, since a "purpose" test is meaningless. As with services, the Court of Justice might be prepared to "sever" the works and supply elements of such a contract when the works and supplies have been packaged together to evade the rules, or even where the packaging cannot be justified on a commercial basis.

(d) CONTRACTS FOR SUPPLIES, WORKS AND OTHER SERVICES

Some contracts involve provision of goods, works *and* other types of services – for example, a contract for the design and construction of a public work along with its management for a specified period.[32] If, as suggested above, the Court generally prefers a "predominant value" test for classifying "mixed" contracts, then the status of a contract for the provision of all three is likely to depend on which of the three elements is the most significant. In practice, this is normally the works.

(e) POSITION WHERE THE NATURE OF THE CONTRACT IS NOT KNOWN AT THE START OF THE PROCEDURE

It is possible that it is not known at the start of the award procedure whether the contract will be a supply, works or services contract. This may be the case, for example, in a procedure to purchase computer software, where the specifications allow for variations and the authority's needs could be met by either off-the-shelf software (goods) or bespoke software (which is probably services). The situation can also arise where a firm is required to invest a certain sum in renovation and repair of

---

[31] The European Commission in its 1987 *Guide to the Community rules on open government procurement* [1987] O.J. C351/1, p.16, suggests that the position will depend on the relative value of the goods and installation works. This statement probably assumes that the general principle for drawing the line between goods and works is the "relative value" test. However, as noted in the text, an alternative is the "main object" test. Further, even if the "relative value" test is correct, it is submitted that it does not apply to a contract for the supply of products involving installation works in view of the express provision that a contract for supply plus installation is a supply contract.

[32] It is assumed here that the management is not on a concessionary basis.

property, but their nature is not specified: such a contract may involve provision of both works and services, but their respective value will not be known. The directives and regulations assume, however, that contracts can be classified prior to commencing the award procedure. It is submitted that it is acceptable to classify the contract by means of the category in which it is most likely to fall.

(6) ASSET SALES AND OTHER TRANSACTIONS INVOLVING WORKS/SUPPLIES/SERVICES PLUS OTHER CONSIDERATION

A particular arrangement for which the application of the procurement rules causes difficulty is an arrangement for the sale of an authority's in-house service unit accompanied by a guarantee of future work from the authority. Such sales have increased recently in the United Kingdom, as a result of the central government's own privatisation programme, and also the general expansion of market testing: the fact that work can no longer be guaranteed to the in-house unit has prompted a number of local authorities who might otherwise have preferred to retain an in-house capability to sell off these units to the private sector. Such sales generally involve a sale of assets, along with agreements for existing staff to be retained, and also guarantees of work from the authority. Thus, the sale of a local authority Direct Labour Organisation, for example, which formerly performed construction and maintenance work for the authority, may include provision for the buyer to do all the authority's construction and maintenance work. Such guarantees may be necessary to ensure the viability of the new enterprise and hence to secure the sale, but may also go further than necessary to achieve this, in order to provide security for the authority's former staff. The buyer in such a case is often a company set up for the purpose by senior management of the in-house unit (or more rarely, other authority employees) – with or without participation from private enterprise; or the sale may be to an existing private sector organisation.

Prima facie, such an arrangement appears to fall within the procurement rules, since it involves a legal agreement – a contract – with a contracting authority, for the provision of works or other services (or, rarely, supplies), for consideration; this satisfies the general definition of a work, supply or services contract. Further, there is no specific provision to exempt agreements which meet these conditions simply because they are part of a more extensive business arrangement. However, it has been argued that where the agreement on work, supplies or services is part of a business sale, it is not caught by the rules.[33]

One argument for such a view might be that the definitions of a public

---

[33] See Cirell and Bennett, *Compulsory Competitive Tendering*, section B, Chap. 6A.

works, supply or services contract do not apply where the agreement for provision of works, goods or services is only one element – and incidental to – a wider transaction which is not itself subject to regulation, and cannot be severed from that transaction. In such a case it can be said that the "non-regulated" element of the transaction – the sale of the assets – predominates and that the contract is not therefore one for works, goods or services. On this basis, the Court of Justice may be prepared to permit guarantees of work as part of an asset sale, provided they go no further than is necessary to secure the sale. However, it is not clear whether this would be accepted.

An alternative argument might be used where work has already been won in-house, *in accordance with an award procedure under the regulations.* This will often apply in the United Kingdom, where internal bidders are required to compete with outside firms and to have their bids dealt with in accordance with the regulations.[34] In these cases it could be suggested that, although technically there is no contract with the in-house unit and a contract only arises where the work is later transferred to the outside bidder, in substance the award of work to the in-house bidder should be treated as the award of a "contract" under the regulations; thus it is not necessary to run a new award procedure when the work is transferred. To permit this work to be transferred with the assets would not undermine the policy of the procurement rules. However, whilst it will adopt a purposive approach to interpretation to prevent avoidance, the Court is less willing to do so in favour of the regulated party, and probably would be unwilling to regard an in-house award as a contract where this is not a legal agreement. Further, even if accepted, this argument can be used only to provide guarantees in relation to work already won by the in-house team: it cannot assist an authority which wishes to privatise the in-house unit because it is not at present sufficiently competitive to win work in open competition.

At present, the legal position is uncertain, and any authority which makes guarantees of work without following the regulations risks challenge. The uncertainty is unsatisfactory, and it would be desirable to introduce express provisions to deal with this important issue.

There are also other types of transactions similar to asset sales in that they involve the provision of works, supplies or services in the context of a wider transaction. For example, following the implementation of compulsory competitive tendering for housing management,[35] some local authorities have sought to sell off unwanted housing stock to external bodies, and have included contracts for the purchaser to manage the authority's remaining (wanted) housing stock, as an inducement for the purchaser to agree to buy the unwanted stock.[36] Such transactions

---

[34] See Chaps. 12–14.

[35] As to which see Chaps. 13–14.

[36] For a discussion of the European Community issues relating to these transactions see also Diamond, "Issues Relating to the Transfer of Housing Stock Together with a Housing Management Contract" (1995) 4 P.P.L.R. CS121.

involve the same issues as asset sales, and, it is submitted, must be resolved in accordance with the same principles.

5. EXCLUDED CONTRACTS

(1) GENERAL PRINCIPLES

A number of contracts are expressly excluded from the regulations under Works Regulation 6, Supply Regulation 6 and Services Regulation 6, as set out below. In accordance with the usual principles applying to derogations from Community law rules, these derogations must be interpreted strictly.[37]

In addition to the exclusions listed in the directives, if restrictive action by a purchaser could be justified under one of the Treaty derogations, that derogation cannot be relied upon to claim exemption from the procurement legislation since these directives may not restrict the power of Member States to rely on derogations under the Treaty provisions.[38]

(2) CERTAIN CONTRACTS COVERED BY THE UTILITIES REGULATIONS

A first exclusion covers certain contracts in the water, energy, transport and telecommunications sectors. Bodies carrying out these activities are generally subject to the Utilities Regulations. It was decided that the more flexible utilities regime should normally apply to such contracts even where made by bodies which are "contracting authorities" and therefore subject, with most of their contracts, to the public sector regime. In this way, the same regulatory regime is generally applied to utilities activities, regardless of the public or private status of the body engaged in such activities in a particular state.

To give effect to this principle, Works Regulations 6(a)[39] and Supply Regulation 6(a)[40] state that the relevant regulations are not to apply where the contracting authority is a "utility" under the Utilities Regulations, and the services to be provided under it are for the purposes of

---

[37] Case C–328/92, *Commission v. Spain* [1994] E.C.R.–I 1569; case C–324/93, *R. v. Secretary of State for the Home Department, ex p. Evans Medical,* judgment of March 28, 1995, para. 48.

[38] This was not permitted in Case C–71/92, judgment of November 17, 1993, but this was because the derogation claimed in that case was too general: see para. 15 of the judgment and para. 15 of the opinion of Advocate General Gulmann.

[39] As amended by Utilities Supply and Works Contracts Regulations, 1992, S.I. 1992 No. 3279 reg.32(1)(a).

[40] As amended by Utilities Supply and Works Contracts Regulations, 1992, reg.32(20(a).

carrying out an activity in the Part of the Schedule in which the utility is specified.[41] The general effect of this is to take contracts covered by the Utilities Regulations out of the public sector rules, and to leave them to be regulated under the Utilities Regulations. Where a body which is a contracting authority carries out both "utilities" and "non-utilities" activities, it is thus subject to the utilities regime for some contracts, and the public sector regime for others. The same result is achieved under the Services Regulations by excluding contracts covered by the Utilities Regulations from the definition of "public services contract" under Regulation 2(1).[41a]

A contract may relate both to excluded and non-excluded activities – for example, a contract for the construction of administrative offices used for all the authority's activities. This situation is not expressly dealt with, but is likely to be resolved by considering whether the contract is related mainly to activities covered by the public sector regime or mainly to "utilities" activities. This could involve a test either of what is the "main object" of the contract, or of whether the greater part of the use relates to the utility sector.

(3) SECRECY AND SECURITY EXEMPTIONS

Works Regulation 6(d), Supply Regulation 6(c) and Services Regulation 6(i) contain exemptions concerned with secrecy and security, as set out below. It is likely that these will be construed in a similar way to the security and other derogations to the E.C. Treaty provisions on free movement[42]: thus they may probably be invoked only for measures which are objectively justified and proportionate to their objectives, which includes a requirement that these could not be achieved by less restrictive means.

(i) First, the regulations do not apply to contracts "classified as secret". This might apply, for example, to an order of dual-use equipment (blankets, tents etc.) for military purposes, where to publicise the requirements would betray military information. The need for secrecy is not necessarily confined to security concerns but might arise, for example, for commercial reasons, as where an authority is developing a new product which it wishes to keep secret from competitors.

(ii) Secondly, the regulations are not to apply where the work, goods or

---

[41] Works Regulation 6(a), as am. by 1992 Utilities Regulations, reg.32(1)(a) and Utilities Regulations 1996, reg. 35(1)(c); Supply Regulation 6, as am. by 1992 Utilities Regulations, reg.32(2)(a) and Utilities Regulations 1996, reg. 35(3).

[41a] Services Regulation 2(1)(d) as substituted by Utilities Regulations 1996, reg. 35(2)(a)(i).

[42] As to which see Chap. 4.

services provided under the contract[43] "must be accompanied by special security measures in accordance with the laws, regulations or administrative provisions of any part of the United Kingdom". As with the Treaty's security derogations, this is not confined to defence: it might cover, for example, measures relating to the delivery of sensitive supplies, such as equipment for combatting crime or terrorism, which could be diverted to improper purposes. However, in *R. v. Secretary of State for the Home Department, ex p. Evans Medical*[44] the Court of Justice indicated that this exclusion would not cover a contract for delivery of drugs: the Court suggested that the objective of preventing improper diversion could be achieved in an open or restricted procedure by taking account of a firm's ability to provide adequate security as an award criterion.[45] Alternatively, authorities could perhaps simply write stringent security standards into the minimum specifications. The same arguments probably apply for other sensitive equipment.

(iii) Thirdly, the regulations do not apply "when the protection of the basic interests of the security of the United Kingdom require it". This exclusion is, no doubt, to be interpreted as covering the same circumstances as the security derogations from the E.C. Treaty's free movement provisions; again it may be invoked either for defence reasons, or reasons of internal security. It could be relied on, for example, where an authority wishes to make a purchase from a domestic firm, in order to preserve a domestic capability in an industry or technology, whether for defence reasons or other reasons.[46]

The existence of an exemption from the regulations does not necessarily mean that there is an exemption from the Treaty. For example, the need to keep a contract secret may justify not advertising publicly through the *Official Journal*, so that the exemption in the regulations may be invoked. However, the same need for secrecy may not be sufficient to invoke the security derogation in the Treaty to impose a condition that only domestic providers will be considered, since it may be possible to ensure secrecy even where the work is awarded to providers in other states, by including secrecy clauses in the contract.

It is possible that only part of a contract's consideration may be affected by secrecy or security considerations. For example, to achieve economies from bulk purchasing, an authority may wish to make a single contract covering equipment which must be delivered in accordance with

---

[43] Strictly speaking, the Works Regulations only apply where the security measures relate to the work or works carried out; the Supply Regulations where they relate to the goods supplied; and the Services Regulations where they relate to services provided (though this would seem to include works, since services is a general term covering works and all other services). Since a works, supply or services contract may contain all three types of consideration – works, goods or services – it would be better to provide that the exemption applies wherever consideration provided under the contract must be accompanied by such measures.

[44] Case C–324/93, judgment of March 28, 1995.

[45] Para. 45 of the judgment.

[46] On the Treaty derogations see Chap. 4.

special security arrangements, together with other equipment made by the same manufacturers, which does not need special arrangements. Where it it totally impossible to contract separately for the different elements, it must be possible to invoke the exclusion for the contract as a whole: it is necessary to do so in order to protect the relevant secrecy or security interest, and this applies even where the value of that part of the contract affected by these considerations is less than the part which is not.

However, this will be rare: the two elements will normally be packaged together for purely commercial reasons.[47] It is not clear whether in such a case the whole contract may be exempt. According to the general principles suggested above, this depends on the extent to which an action may be considered to be "objectively justified". This does not necessarily require that the objective could have been achieved *only* by the action taken – here the alternative of splitting the contract is possible – but requires some consideration of the costs of the alternative. It is not clear what weight would be given here to commercial costs; however, in view of the possible dangers of abuse, and the principle that derogations must be strictly construed, it is likely that to rely on the exemption an authority would be required to show that tangible and significant costs would occur from splitting the contract.[48]

Where such a contract is subject to the regulations, it seems that the value of all the consideration under the contract is to be counted for threshold purposes: the threshold rules contain nothing to exempt that part of the consideration which may be affected by secrecy or security, where the contract as a whole is covered.

(4) CONTRACTS COVERED BY ARTICLE 223 E.C.

The Supply Regulations and Services Regulations contain exclusions relating to contracts for defence equipment, which is covered by Article 223 E.C. Since this exclusion relates almost wholly to purchasing for defence purposes, it is considered in the separate chapter on defence procurement.[49]

(5) CONTRACTS PURSUANT TO INTERNATIONAL AGREEMENTS INVOLVING OTHER STATES

Works Regulation 6(e)(i), Supply Regulation 6(e)(i) and Services Regulation 6(j)(i) exclude contracts pursuant to an international agreement to

---

[47] If the motive was simply to avoid applying the regulations to the non-exempt part, the courts would probably adopt a presumption that "objective justification" does not exist and the exemption cannot be invoked, although probably the issue of motive is not relevant in itself.

[48] An analogy might be drawn here with certain other derogations in the regulations – for example, the provisions allowing an authority to decline to use European specifications where this would involve "disproportionate" costs or difficulties (see Chap. 11).

[49] See Chap. 18.

which the United Kingdom and a state which is not a "relevant" state are both party,[50] where the contract is for purchase of goods, works or other services which are for the joint implementation or exploitation of a project pursuant to that agreement.[51] The exemption applies even if the contract is made solely by a United Kingdom contracting authority.[52] It will apply, for example, to placement of research contracts pursuant to ad hoc partnerships with other states to develop new high technology equipment for government use.

The exemption applies only where different procedures govern the award of the contract. Thus it appears that the regulations apply where it is intended that their procedures should govern, or where no other formal procedures have been set out.

It appears that such contracts awarded by United Kingdom authorities are still, however, subject to the E.C. Treaty rules prohibiting discrimination, as well as similar rules in other relevant international agreements.

(6) CONTRACTS PURSUANT TO INTERNATIONAL AGREEMENTS ON THE STATIONING OF TROOPS

Works Regulation 6(e)(ii), Supply Regulation 6(e)(ii) and Services Regulation 6(j)(ii) exclude from the regulations a contract entered into pursuant to an international agreement relating to the stationing of troops, where awarded under different procedures. Again, it would appear that such contracts are still, however, generally subject to the rules in the E.C. Treaties.

(7) CONTRACTS OF INTERNATIONAL ORGANISATIONS

Works Regulation 6(e)(iii), Supply Regulation 6(e)(iii) and Services Regulation 6(j)(iii) further exclude agreements made in accordance with the contract award procedures of international organisations – that is, organisations of which only states are members. The exclusions also covers organisations of which only international organisations are mem-

---

[50] On which states are relevant states see Chap. 15. Certain other states are also entitled to benefit from the regulations, but are not referred to since their rights were conferred after the regulations were adopted. Thus the exemption cannot be relied on in relation to these states.

[51] Works Regulation 6(e)(i), as amended by Supply Regulation 31(1)(b); Supply Regulation 6(e)(i); Services Regulation 6(j)(i), as amended by Supply Regulation 31(2)(b).

As in many other cases, the Works Regulations refers only to works, the Supply Regulations only to goods and the Services Regulations only to services, even though contracts covered by each set of Regulations may involve all three types of consideration.

[52] If it is made by a consortium set up for the purpose, or solely by an entity from the partner state, any United Kingdom authority involved in the project would not in any case generally be a contracting authority.

bers. This covers, for example, contracts awarded according to the procedures of the European Space Agency, United Nations, or the World Bank. Contracts awarded by the organisations themselves are arguably not covered in any case, on the basis that they are not contracting authorities within the definitions in the procurement directives and implementing regulations.

Again, it appears that the rules in the Treaties still apply where the contract is awarded by a United Kingdom authority. It appears that it may also be a breach of Community Treaty obligations by the United Kingdom where its rules are not followed by an organisation of which the United Kingdom is a member, as for example, where the European Space Agency allocates contracts according to the principle of "fair returns" whereby Member States receive work under contracts in proportion to the amount which they have contributed to the agency's projects.[53]

(8) CONTRACTS FOR THE ACQUISITION OF LAND

Contracts for land and rights related to land are generally excluded from regulation. They are expressly excluded from the Services Regulations[54]: regulation 6(a) provides that the regulations do not apply to contracts "for the acquisition of land, including buildings and other structures, land covered with water, and any estate, interest, easement, servitude or right in or over land". Such contracts are clearly not contracts for "goods" under the Supply Regulations, and are also not generally works contracts. However, they may be under the Works Regulations in limited cases: this applies where the main object of the contract is to acquire a "work" under the Works Regulations (as defined in the Works Regulations) built to the authority's specifications, as where a developer erects a building to the authority's requirements on his own land, and then transfers it to the authority.[55]

A difficulty arises with contracts to purchase a building and land from another where the building is not built at the time of contract, and is to be built not to specifications set by the authority but to those already set by the developer. If this case is not covered by the works rules, it is certainly not covered by those on supplies, and in the United Kingdom is also excluded from the Services Regulations, which, as noted above, exclude all purchases of buildings. However, it can be noted that the

---

[53] See further p. 801.

[54] It was probably unnecessary to include this exclusion in the Services Regulations, since they only apply to contracts for "services", and provision of land and related rights would not appear to be services. The exclusion is taken from the Services Directive, where it is necessary, since the prima facie definition of public service contract in the Services Directive is not limited to contracts for services but covers all contracts which are not public supply contracts or public works contracts.

[55] See pp. 129–130.

Services Directive excludes only *existing* buildings, which might suggest that the present case should thus be covered by the services rules, if it is not within works. This was probably not intended – if such a contract is covered at all, it is the works rules which are appropriate. One possibility is that the works rules should be construed to cover not merely the case where an authority commissions a work to its own specifications, but also where it accepts specifications set by another. If this is not the case, it is submitted that the concept of "existing" buildings should be construed to cover those which exist at the time of transfer, not just at the time of contract, so that such a purchase is excluded from regulation altogether.

(9) PROVISION BY ANOTHER CONTRACTING AUTHORITY PURSUANT TO EXCLUSIVE RIGHTS

Services Regulation 6(k)[56] excludes a public services contract under which services are provided by another contracting authority[57] which has either (i) an exclusive right to provide the services or (ii) an exclusive right which is necessary for their provision. This right must be given pursuant to any published law, regulation or administrative provision (which must be compatible with the E.C. Treaty).

It has already been mentioned that an authority may choose to provide a service in-house without following the regulations, since this does not involve a proposed *contract*. The exclusion in Services Regulation 6(k) effectively extends this to where the service is provided through the government itself, but by a *different* contracting authority. The only limitation is that there must be a published measure establishing the exclusive right to service provision (whether legislation, or a simple published circular or guideline from the relevant public authority). It is not clear whether this could be invoked on an ad hoc basis for a particular contract, or whether there must be a right to exclusive provision on a general basis.

This first part of the exemption could be relied on, for example, to require all government bodies to purchase services from an independent centralised purchasing authority from which public bodies are obliged by law or administrative direction to purchase certain types of requirements.[58] The second part of the exemption will cover, for example, the

---

[56] As amended by Supply Regulation 31(2)(b).
[57] This may be a contracting authority from either the United Kingdom or some other "relevant state". On which states are "relevant states" see Chap. 15.
[58] Although that authority will be a contracting authority, required to follow the regulations in its own purchases, if it relies on private sector providers. In practice the United Kingdom has moved away from "tying" government bodies to centralised purchasers, or other public sector service providers, preferring to allow maximum competition in service provision. Further, in central government many apparently separate entities (including, probably, the different government departments, as well as agencies within them) are not legally distinct entities for the purpose of making contracts, so that the procurement regulations do not apply in relation to agreements between them.

case where a provider has special statutory powers to carry out work under the contract. For example, in the United Kingdom the Department of Transport enjoys certain special powers in relation to highway works, which may be exercised instead by local authorities where the works are contracted to these authorities, but may not be exercised by private contractors. The exemption permits the Department to contract out the work to local authorities which are able to take advantage of the special powers, without following the regulations.

An authority might, theoretically, wish to include within a single contract both services to which this exemption applies, and other consideration. The courts should adopt the same approach in deciding whether such a contract would be excluded from the regulations as it adopts in relation to a contract which is partly for consideration affected by security/secrecy exemptions, and partly for other consideration. This issue was discussed above,[59] where it was suggested that the exemption will be available only where exceptional costs would result from splitting the work.

There is no similar exemption for any exclusive right to provide supplies or works. Thus such arrangements are incompatible with the regulations.

(10) PUBLIC HOUSING SCHEME WORKS CONTRACTS

Under Works Regulation 24 authorities proposing to enter into a works contract for the design and construction of a public housing scheme are exempt in certain circumstances from applying some of the provisions of the Works Regulations. This is not a complete exemption but rather provides a special award procedure for these contracts, and this is considered further in Chapter 8.

6. FINANCIAL THRESHOLDS

(1) PURPOSE OF THE THRESHOLDS

The Community Treaty provisions can affect *all* public procurements, however small.[60] The regulations, on the other hand, apply only to contracts above a certain value: there is an administrative cost in applying the procedures, and their application can only be justified where the benefits are likely to outweigh these costs.

---

[59] See pp. 153–154.
[60] It was suggested in Chap. 4 that there is no *de minimis* requirement for the free movement provisions, although there is for the application of competition law rules. However, even where such a requirement applies, small contracts may be affected – for example, they may be awarded under general legislation which is itself caught by the Treaty provisions.

The thresholds are set with a view to identifying contracts for which there is likely to be cross-border competition, since the directives are concerned only with cross-border trade. In many states, a legal obligation to use specified competitive procedure is imposed to promote "domestic" objectives such as value for money and prevention of corruption: and for these rules – in view of their different objectives – thresholds are generally well below those of the directives. In implementing the directives, however, the United Kingdom has not departed from the tradition of non-legal control of procurement, and the regulations use the same thresholds as the directives being aimed, like the directives, only at opening cross-border trade.

(2) THE APPLICABLE THRESHOLDS

The threshold figures are generally stated in the directives and regulations in European Currency Units (ECUs),[61-62] rather than in pounds sterling. The sterling equivalent (as well as the equivalent in other Community currencies) is calculated every two years and published in the *Official Journal*.[63]

The one exception is for the supply contracts of central government: here thresholds are stated by reference to the ECU equivalent of Standard Drawing Rights (SDR). This was done to ensure that the Community rules do not differ from those in the GATT Agreement on Government Procurement which refers to SDRs.[64] From January 1, 1996 the existing GATT Agreement of Procurement is largely superseded by the World Trade Organisation Agreement on Government Procurement (GPA), which covers sub-central authorities, and also works and services.[65] As noted below, a Commission Proposal to align the directives to this new Agreement proposes amendments so that other thresholds will also be expressed by reference to SDR.

[61-62] An "ECU" is defined in Works Regulation 2(1), Supply Regulation 2(1) and Services Regulation 2(1) as meaning the European Currency Unit as defined in Council Regulation 318/78/EEC [1978] O.J. L379/1, as amended by Council Regulation 2626/84/EEC [1984] O.J. L247/1 and Council Regulation 1971/89/EEC [1989] O.J. C189/1.

[63] Works Regulation 2(2), Supply Regulation 2(2), Services Regulation 2(3), which refer back to the directives. The rates are based on the average of the daily exchange rates between each currency and the ECU over a period of 24 months prior to the date the rate is set, terminating on the last day of August immediately preceding the revision date: Works Directive Articles 6(2)(a); Supply Directive Article 5(c); Services Directive Article 7(8). The relevant provisions require the new exchange rate to be published in the *Official Journal of the European Communities* in the November before the changes take effect. It was provided for this method of calculation to be reviewed two years from its initial application (January 1992 for works, January 1988 for supplies) by the Advisory Committee for Public Contracts: Works Directive 6(2)(b); Supply Directive 5(c); Services Directive 6(2)(b).

[64] This does not apply to the relationship of Community Member States *inter se*, but it is thought desirable that the same rules should apply within the Community as under the Agreement: see pp. 61–63.

[65] See pp. 774–782.

(a) WORKS REGULATIONS

(i) THRESHOLDS IN THE CURRENT REGULATIONS

The Works Regulations generally apply only to contracts with an estimated value of 5 million ECUs or more, net of Value Added Tax (Works Regulation 7(1)).[66] For 1994–95 the sterling equivalent was £3,743,203, but this was to be revised again as from January 1, 1996.

(ii) PROPOSED AMENDMENTS RELATING TO THE GPA

Under the new WTO Agreement on Government Procurement (GPA) referred to above, works have been regulated for the first time, with a threshold of 5 million SDR (converted into ECUs). The GPA itself governs only the relationship of the United Kingdom and other Member States, on the one hand, with the other signatories, on the other; it does not affect the relationship of the Community Members States *inter se*, which is governed solely by the Community Treaties and secondary legislation, notably the directives. Thus, the GPA thresholds have no direct relevance to the directives. However, the Commission has taken the view that it would be inconvenient to apply slightly different thresholds under the GPA and directives. In a Proposal for adjusting the directives to take account of the need for consistency with the GPA, it has therefore proposed to align the thresholds under the two regimes, by amending the Works Directive to refer to a threshold value of not less than the equivalent in ECUs of 5 million SDR.[67] This will not produce substantial differences in terms of the relevant value in Member State currency. If the change is adopted in the directive, the Works Regulations will eventually need to be amended to reflect this change.

(b) SUPPLY REGULATIONS

(i) THRESHOLDS IN THE CURRENT REGULATIONS

Under the Supply Regulations the threshold varies according to whether or not the offer is sought by a contracting authority regulated by the

---

[66] In the original version of the Works Directive the threshold was much lower at 1 million ECUs but it was raised when the Directive was amended by Directive 89/440, partly to take account of the impact of inflation since the original 1971 directive on works but also because of the limited opportunities for cross border competition for smaller works contracts.

[67] Proposal for a European Parliament and Council Directive amending Directive 92/50/EEC relating to the co-ordination of procedures for the award of public service contracts, Directive 93/36/EEC co-ordinating procedures for the award of public supply contracts, and Directive 93/37/EEC concerning the co-ordination of procedures for the award of public works contracts, COM (95) 107 Final, Article 3(1).

The Proposal provides that the value of the threshold in ECUs and in national currencies is to be revised every two years with effect from January 1, 1996. The calculation of the values is to be based on the average daily value of the ECU expressed in SDR, and of the national currencies expressed in ECUs, over the last 24 months, terminating on the last day of August immediately preceding the January 1 revision.

"GATT" Agreement on Government Procurement ("GATT Agreement"), which is the predecessor of the current GPA.

For bodies not subject to the GATT Agreement the current threshold is 200,000 ECUs.[68] In 1994–95 the sterling equivalent was £149,728, but this was to be revised from January 1, 1996.

For awards by contracting authorities subject to the GATT Agreement – "GATT contracting authorities" – as well as the E.C. rules, the Supply Regulations apply when the estimated value of the contract, net of VAT, is the ECU equivalent of 130,000 SDRs, or above (Supply Regulation 7(1) and (2)).[69] At the time of writing the sterling equivalent was £96,403, but was to be revised from January 1, 1996. (With contracts awarded by the Secretary of State for Defence, this threshold applies only to some contracts; this is explained further in the chapter on defence procurement.[70]) A list of GATT contracting authorities is set out in Schedule 1 to the Supply Regulations.[71] These are all government departments and bodies closely associated with these.

The reason for this lower threshold, and also the fact that it is expressed by reference to SDRs, is to apply the same threshold under E.C. rules as applies under the GATT Agreement: prior to 1980, when the GATT Agreement came into force, the relevant threshold in the Supply Directive was 200,000 ECUs for all authorities, but was changed in that year for the GATT contracting authorities to bring it into line with the GATT threshold. Since the old GATT Agreement, like the new GPA, did not apply between Member States but only as between Member States and signatory third countries, if this had not been done E.C. Member States would have been required to open contracts awarded by GATT contracting authorities to third countries at a lower threshold than those contracts were required to be opened to other Member States under the E.C. rules.

(ii) PROPOSED AMENDMENTS RELATING TO THE GPA

Under the new GPA, the threshold remains at the ECU equivalent of 130,000 SDR for central government departments and associated bodies, and there is therefore no need of any change of substance to the existing

---

[68] Supply Regulation 7(2)(b).

[69] What constitutes the ECU equivalent of SDR 130,000 is determined every two years as from January 1, 1988, and the figure published in the *Official Journal of the European Communities* in the November: Supply Directive Article 5(c). The figure for 1994–1995 is 128,771 ECUs ([1993] O.J. C341/11). (The sterling equivalent of this ECU figure is calculated as explained in the text above).

[70] See pp. 868–869.

[71] "A GATT contracting authority" is defined in Supply Regulation 2(1) as one of the entities listed in Schedule 1 "being entities" for which special provision is made in the regulations to comply with the GPA.

threshold in the Supply Directive and Regulations, which is already the same.[72]

The new GPA, unlike the old GATT Agreement, now also covers local authorities. For these bodies the GPA threshold is the ECU equivalent of 200,000 SDR. This is similar to the 200,000 ECUs of the E.C. procurement directives, and hence there is no need for a substantial change in the directives to ensure that access for Community suppliers under the Supply Directive is similar to that of third country suppliers under the new GPA. However, as with works, for simplicity and convenience the Commission has proposed changing the Supply Directive to express the directive's threshold as the ECU equivalent of 200,000 SDR.[73] Again, any changes to the directive in this respect will need eventually to be reflected in changes to the Supply Regulations.

(c) SERVICES REGULATIONS

(i) THRESHOLDS IN THE CURRENT REGULATIONS

At the time of writing the Services Regulations apply to contracts of 200,000 ECUs or above.[74] For 1994–1995 the sterling equivalent of this was £49,728, but as with the other thresholds this was to be revised from January 1, 1996.

(ii) PROPOSED AMENDMENTS RELATING TO THE GPA

Under the new GPA services which are Part A services under the Services Regulations – with the exception of research and development services – are regulated for the first time. Part B services are not covered. The threshold for applying GPA to regulated services is the equivalent in ECUs of 130,000 SDR for most central government departments and associated bodies, and the equivalent in ECUs of 200,000 SDR for others.

In the Proposal for adapting the Community rules to align them with the GPA, referred to above, the Commission has proposed changing the thresholds in the Services Directive to bring them into line with those in the GPA.[75]

This will involve, first, a reduction of the threshold for regulation of services for GPA authorities (central government) from 200,000 ECUs to the ECU equivalent of 130,000 SDR, for contracts for Part A services.

---

[72] However, in its Proposal referred to above the Commission proposes a slight modification to Supply Directive Article 5(1)(a), setting out this threshold, to refer directly to the "equivalent in ECU of 130,000 SDR"; at present the Article refers to "the threshold fixed pursuant to the GATT Agreement".
[73] Commission Proposal, above, Article 2(1).
[74] Services Regulation 7(1).
[75] Commission Proposal, above, Article 1(1).

This ensures that the GPA rules for third countries are not more favourable than those under the Community's regime. The current Proposal in addition goes further than required to align the E.C. and GPA rules, proposing, for the sake of a single threshold for all services contracts awarded by these authorities, that this lower threshold should also apply to Part B services contracts and contracts for research and development services, which are not covered by the GPA.[76] However, this latter aspect of the Proposal is controversial and appears unlikely to be adopted.

Secondly, for other contracts covered by the directives, thresholds will be the ECU equivalent of 200,000 SDR, rather than 200,000 ECUs as at present. This does not represent a substantial change in monetary value but ensures absolute consistency between the two regimes.

Amendments to the Services Regulations will be needed to give effect to any changes to the Services Directive.

THRESHOLDS UNDER THE PUBLIC SECTOR DIRECTIVES

	Works Directive	Supply Directive		Services Directive	
	All authorities	*Authorities listed in Annex 1 of the Supply Directive**	*Other authorities*	*Authorities listed in Annex 1 of the proposed new directive*	*Other authorities*
Current Thresholds	5 million ECUs	Equivalent in ECUs of 130,000 SDR*	200,000 ECUs	200,000 ECUs	200,000 ECUs
Thresholds proposed in COM (95) 107 final	Equivalent in ECUs of 5 million SDR	Equivalent in ECUs of 130,000 SDR*	Equivalent in ECUs of 200,000 SDR	Equivalent in ECUs of 130,000 SDR†	Equivalent in ECUs of 200,000 SDR

Notes
* For contracts awarded by the Secretary of State for Defence, this applies only to some contracts: see pp. 868–869.
† It is proposed that this will apply both to priority (Part A) and non-priority services; but its application to non-priority services and to priority research and development services, all of which are outside the GPA, is controversial and seems likely to be rejected.

[76] *Ibid.*

(3) VALUATION OF CONTRACTS

(a) GENERAL PRINCIPLES

The value of the contract for the purpose of the threshold rules is its *estimated value* net of value added tax,[77] the time for estimation being the *time at which a contract notice would be sent to the Official Journal* if such a notice were required.[78]

As a general rule the estimated value refers to the "value of the consideration" which the authority expects to give under the contract[79] – that is, the expected price. This must be estimated at the time for the notice, even though this may difficult – as, for example, with a contract for the design and execution of works, where the value of the contract depends upon the nature of the design. For cases where value is difficult to estimate because of the unknown *duration* of the contract certain special provision is made, as outlined below.

In the case of a public works contract, where the authority intends to provide any goods to the contractor for the purpose of carrying out the contract, the value of the consideration is to be calculated to include the estimated value of those goods.[80] Thus, for example, if the authority is to supply building materials worth, 1,000,000 ECUs and expects to pay the contractor 4,500,000 ECUs the contract would be subject to the regulations, even though the anticipated price is less that the 5,000,000 ECUs threshold, since the value of the price plus the goods – 5,500,000 ECUs – exceeds the threshold. There is no requirement for services provided by the authority to be taken into account (for example, electricity or security services); this is anomalous (and differs from the position under the utilities rules).[81] There is, further, no provision under the Supply or Services Regulations for taking account of the value of goods or services provided by the authority, which is also anomalous: an authority might provide services, for example, to a supplier installing goods under a supply contract.

In the case of a public services contract, it is expressly stated that, where appropriate, the authority shall, in determining the value, take account of the premium payable for insurance services; the fees, commissions or other remuneration payable for banking and financial services; and the fees or commission payable for design services.[82] There

---

[77] Works Regulation 7(1), Supply Regulation 7(1), Services Regulation 7(1).

[78] Works Regulation 7(7), Supply Regulation 7(11), Services Regulation 7(12). A notice is not actually required for a contract subject to the negotiated procedure without advertisement.

[79] Works Regulation 7(2), Supply Regulation 7(3), Services Regulation 7(2).

[80] Works Regulation 7(6). The value of these goods is also to be estimated as at the time the contract notice would be published in the *Official Journal* if required: Works Regulation 7(6)).

[81] See p. 443.

[82] Services Regulation 7(3).

is, anomalously, no such requirement in the Works or Supply Regulations although such fees, etc., could be payable under works or supply contracts, including in connection with any services provided under those contracts.

In a procedure under which firms may bid for all or part of a requirement, the relevant value is that of the whole of the requirement: this is a proposed contract for that requirement, even if such a large contract will not necessarily be awarded.

(b) PUBLIC WORKS CONCESSIONS

Special provision is made for a public works concession[83] – that is where at least part of the contractor's remuneration consists in revenues obtained from exploiting the service. Here it is expressly provided that the estimated value is "the value of the consideration which the contracting authority would expect to give for the carrying out of the work or works if it did not propose to grant a concession".[84]

(c) OPTIONS

Under the Supply and Services Regulations, there is special provision for certain cases where the precise value of the consideration is not known because the contract includes one or more options.[85] In this case, the estimated value is the highest amount which could be payable[86]: in other words, the consideration is calculated on the assumption that all the options will be exercised. Thus, for example, the Supply Regulations cover a contract for purchase by a government department of four machines at 20,000 ECUs each (total 80,000 ECUs), with an option to purchase a further four at the same price (overall total 160,000 ECUs). Although the value of the purchase to which the authority is bound – 80,000 ECUs – is below the threshold, the regulations apply since the value of the contract if the option is exercised – 160,000 ECUs – is above the threshold. There is no corresponding provision for works, presumably because option provisions are not common; however, such a provision would be useful for completeness, especially since there may be options relating to non-construction services provided under a works contract.

(d) SERVICES CONTRACTS AND HIRE CONTRACTS OF UNCERTAIN DURATION

There are also special provisions under the Supply Regulations for contracts for hire which are of indefinite duration, or when the duration

---

[83] See further pp. 353–366.
[84] Works Regulation 7(5).
[85] In practice, this is almost always an option for the authority to purchase additional goods or services, although the rules could also apply if a provider is given an option to provide additional goods or services.
[86] Supply Regulation 7(9); Services Regulation 7(10).

is not fixed at the time of the contract (for example, because the hire is to terminate on the happening of a certain event, or is for an indefinite period subject to termination at the option of one or both parties). Similar provisions apply under the Services Regulations for services contracts of indefinite duration. In these cases, rather than requiring a speculative estimate of the likely length, and hence value, of the contract, the estimated value is to be the value of the consideration which the authority expects to give in each month of the hire, or service provision, multiplied by 48.[87]

Where there is a contract for the hire of goods, or for services, for a definite period along with an option to renew for an indefinite or uncertain period, the value of the contract is assessed as if the option were exercised, as explained at (c) above. Thus the contract is one for an indefinite or uncertain period, and the "four-year rule" applies to valuation. For example, a contract for the hire of goods for six months, with an option for the hirer to extend the period indefinitely, falls within this provision, and the consideration is thus calculated by multiplying the monthly hire fee by 48. If the option did not exist, the consideration would, of course, be calculated as the value of the hire fee for the six months.

Where a "contract" is indefinite because it is provided that it may be renewed on the agreement of both parties, it was argued above that it generally constitutes a new contract for the purpose of the regulations, and must be readvertised.[88] In addition, such a renewal does not appear to fall under this provision on indefinite/uncertain contracts.[89] Instead it is treated as a separate contract, and subject to the aggregation rules which are discussed at (3) below.[90] Thus, with a hire contract for six months renewable on the agreement of parties, the value of the consideration is merely six months hire charge; however, if the agreement is renewed, the consideration under the new agreement must be added to the consideration under the original agreement, in accordance with the aggregation rules.

There is no provision corresponding to that set out in the first sentence of this section for contracts of purchase (as opposed to hire) of indefinite or uncertain duration; thus it is necessary to estimate the likely actual duration of the contract.[91]

---

[87] Supply Regulation 7(8); Services Regulation 7(9).
[88] See pp. 119–120.
[89] This is not expressly stated. However, it may be deduced from the fact such a contract is in essence a new contract, and also from the fact that the aggregation rules are expressly stated to apply to renewable contracts: this would not be appropriate if such contracts were treated as single contracts of indefinite duration.
[90] This means that a *renewable* contract is treated differently from one which is of *indefinite duration subject to termination by either party*, though it is effectively similar in its substance, since a contract subject to termination by either party does appear to be caught by the "four-year" rule.
[91] See pp. 444–445.

As explained above, where the indefinite or uncertain nature of the contract arises because of the existence of an option for one party to extend, it must be assumed that the option is exercised to its maximum effect. Thus the value of a six-month hire contract with an option for renewal by one party for a further four and a half years, is the value of five full years' hire payments.[92]

A "contract" of purchase which is of uncertain or indefinite duration because of the stated possibility of renewal on mutual agreement appears, like a hire contract of this kind, to be regulated under the aggregation rules discussed below.[93]

(e) SERVICES CONTRACTS WHICH EXCEED FOUR YEARS

For a services contract under which services are to be provided over a period exceeding four years, even where the duration of the contract is certain, the estimated value of the contract is to be the value of the consideration which the authority expects to give in each month, multiplied by 48.[94] Thus a contract is treated as one for only four years. There is no equivalent provision for supply contracts of more than four years.

(4) REQUIREMENTS FOR AGGREGATION OF THE VALUE OF SEPARATE CONTRACTS

(a) PURPOSE OF THE AGGREGATION RULES

In principle, the relevant value for threshold purposes is based on the value of each individual contract. However, in certain cases an authority must add together the value of purchases made under a number of similar contracts, and the regulations will apply if the value of these taken together exceeds the threshold. These "aggregation" rules make it difficult for authorities to evade the regulations by splitting their purchases into separate contracts, each of which fall below the threshold. There is an express prohibition against deliberate "contract splitting", as is explained at (5) below. However, it is difficult to prove that an authority has deliberately packaged contracts to avoid the rules. The aggregation rules avoid the need for proving motive, by applying the regulations in certain "objective" situations where it is reasonable for the authority to make its purchases in the form of a single large contract. In

---

[92] If this were a services contract, probably it would be treated as a contract exceeding four years, and its value then calculated in accordance with the rule set out at (c) below.

[93] As with hire, this means that such a contract is treated differently from one which is indefinite or uncertain because both parties have an option to terminate.

[94] Services Regulation 10(9).

this respect the aggregation rules have a potentially important role in securing the effectiveness of procurement rules. Unfortunately, however, the significance of the provisions is in practice undermined by the considerable uncertainty over when aggregation is actually required, as is explained in the following paragraphs.

The rules ensure that the regulations are not rendered inoperative by *inefficient* purchasing, as well as by deliberate evasion. Their effect is that where there is a package of work which is likely to attract the attention of a single firm and which is sufficiently large to warrant Europe-wide advertisement, all that work must be awarded under the regulations. The need to identify and advertise all such work operates as an incentive for authorities to award it in a single package which might attract cross-border competition.

It should be emphasised that where reuirements must be aggregated under the rules, this does not entail that the whole requirement must be advertised in a single contract. Thus purchasers may split up the requirement into smaller periodic contracts if for example, it is felt this will be more attractive to the market or if, the purchaser wishes to encourage participation by small or medium-sized enterprises. The important point, however, is that all the relevant contracts, however small, must be awarded in accordance with the regulations, unless some specific exemption applies.

(b) AGGREGATION: GOODS AND SERVICES[95]

Rules on aggregation apply where a purchaser has a requirement over a period of time for goods and services of a particular "type", and enters into a series of contracts to obtain those goods or services.[96] This applies, for example, when an authority buys paper clips each month, placing a new contract each time. In this case the value of the separate contracts must be "aggregated" together, and if the collective value exceeds the threshold, then all the purchases must be awarded according to the regulations, even though each individual contract is below the threshold. The same principle applies where there is a single contract which is stated to be "renewable" (referring to the case where the renewal needs the consent of both parties, in contrast to where there is an extension through exercise of an option)[97]; thus renewals are treated, for the purpose of the aggregation rules, as a series of separate contracts.

---

[95] A process of aggregation of similar goods or services is also required for deciding whether authorities should publish a Prior Information Notice (PIN). On the relationship between the basis of aggregation for the purpose of a PIN and for the purpose of applying the regulations' award procedures, as discussed in the present section, see pp. 187–189.

[96] Supply Regulation 7(5) and (6); Services Regulation 7(6) and (7).

[97] *Ibid.* Where a contract is extended through the exercise of an option, the provision on aggregation of contracts is redundant, since the *whole* value of purchases under the option is already taken into account under the express provision on options discussed above.

This "aggregation" may be done in one of two ways[98]:

(i) The first method provides for aggregating the value of the consideration given under public supply or public services contracts for the acquisition of goods or services of that "type" in the previous year, adjusted to take account of any expected changes in quantity and cost in the next twelve months (commencing from the time in which the notice for the present contract would be published in the *Official Journal*, if required).[99] The previous year may be taken either as the twelve months ending immediately before the time the notice would be published, or the last financial year ending before this time. This method is relevant only where the authority has had previous requirements for the same type of product.

(ii) The second method is by estimating the amount of the consideration to be paid in the next twelve months, where the contract is for an indefinite term, or is for a definite term of twelve months or less. The twelve-month period is calculated from the time of the first date for delivery under the contract.

Under this second method, when the contract is for a definite term of more than twelve months, it is necessary to take account of the consideration during the whole period of the contract, not just during one year. For example, a local authority may place two contracts for stationery, each to run for three years, with sums of 40,000 ECUs to be paid out under each contract each year. Under this valuation method it is necessary to take the value of both contracts over the three-year period, to decide whether the purchases are subject to the regulations. In this example, the regulations do apply, since the total consideration is 240,000 – above the 200,000 threshold. If the one-year amounts were aggregated the contract would not be above the threshold.

Which of these two methods is to be used is a matter for the contracting authority.[1] However, it is expressly provided that an authority is not to exercise a choice of method with the intention of avoiding the application of the regulations.[2]

It should be noted that under both the Supply Regulations and Services Regulations it is the aggregate value of the consideration given under the contracts as a whole which is relevant. Thus under the Supply Regulations, for example, it is necessary to take into account the value of any services provided under supply contracts – for example, for maintenance of the products supplied – and not just the value of the products themselves.

---

[98] Supply Regulation 7(6); Services Regulation 7(7).

[99] Supply Regulation 7(6) and 7(11); Services Regulation 7(7) and 7(12).

[1] The regulation simply says that the value "shall be the amount calculated by applying one of these methods", but it seems obvious that the choice is intended to be left to the authority and this is assumed by the wording of Regulation 7(10), discussed in the text immediately below.

[2] Supply Regulation 7(10); Services Regulation 7(11).

Example: A local authority enters into two contracts to purchase product X in a single year. Each contract is valued at 110,000 ECUs, made up of product X to the value of 90,000 ECUs together with services for the maintenance of X valued at 20,000 ECUs. Both these contracts fall within the regulations: they must be aggregated and their total value (including the ancillary services) is 220,000 ECUs, which exceeds the 200,000 ECUs threshold. (If only the value of the product itself were aggregated the result would be different: the total value of the products alone is only 180,000 ECUs, which is below the threshold).

On the other hand, it is not required to include the value of products of that type which are purchased under works or services contracts, rather than supply contracts. The same principle applies, *mutatis mutandis,* under the Services Regulations.

The rules discussed above apply, as indicated, only to purchases of goods or services of the same "type".[3] There is some debate as to what is meant by a "type" of good or service for this purpose. Probably goods or services are to be treated as of the same "type" where they are typically available from the same supplier or service provider. Thus, for example, pens, rubbers and typing fluid could be regarded as products of the same "type", since they are all generally supplied by individual stationery firms; whilst certain different types of vehicles – such as street sweeping vehicles and fire engines – are probably different "types" of product since they are normally available only from different specialist enterprises. Such a test reflects the objective of the rules, which is to ensure that purchases are advertised when it is commercially reasonable for those purchases to be packaged in a single contract which exceeds the threshold. Services will generally need to be aggregated only at much lower levels than the "categories" of services listed in Schedule 1 to the Services Regulations (which is included for the purpose of categorising services as Part A and Part B services); many of these categories cover a wide range of services which would not typically be provided by a single firm. For example, repair and maintenance of vehicles, and of equipment, are both listed in category 1 of Part A, but different specialist firms are concerned with different sorts of vehicles and equipment and it is clear that work repairing, say, fire engines, photocopying machines and cleaning equipment, need not be aggregated. Generally, it is desirable that the courts should not be too strict, and should not insist on aggregation where there is a reasonable commercial argument for splitting requirements.

However, it should be emphasised that, although this has appeared to most commentators to be the most sensible test, there is as yet no

---

[3] See further Brown, "Getting to Grips with Aggregation under the E.C. Public Procurement Rules" (1993) 2 P.P.L.R. 69.

guidance from the Court of Justice on how these aggregation rules are to be applied. Further, even once a general principle has been established its application to particular products and services may still create difficulty. In view of the importance of the aggregation rules the uncertainty which exists is a significant problem in achieving an open market, as well as causing practical problems for purchasers.

The aggregation rules apply only to contracts "with similar characteristics". The appropriate test here appears to be whether the same providers would be likely to be interested in the contracts. This could depend on many factors – for example, on whether the contract is for hire or for purchase (which may, in some industries, be covered by different providers), or on the applicable terms, which may be very different for regular needs and for one-off special projects and may thus attract different types of provider. Another factor might be whether additional subject matter is included – for example, a contract for both supply and maintenance may interest different providers from a simple supply contract.

In addition, the Supply Regulations provide that where a "single requirement" for goods or services is divided into separate contracts, the value of the separate contracts must be aggregated.[4] This implements a provision in the Supply Directive requiring aggregation where a single procurement for "supplies of the same type" may lead to the award of separate contracts "at the same time"[5]: thus the reference to a "single requirement" seems to refer to a requirement for goods of the same type at a particular point in time (although not necessarily under the same award procedure). This ensures that the aggregation rules are applied to contracts awarded at the same time, as well as those awarded at different times. A similar provision applies under the Services Regulations where the authority has a single requirement for services.[6] This implements a provision of the Services Directive requiring aggregation where "the services are subdivided into several lots",[7] which also appears to contemplate separate contracts awarded at the same time.

The effect of aggregation is that where an authority decides to meet its requirements for identical or related purchases by placing several separate contracts, it must apply the regulations to contracts below the thresholds. In practice, this may encourage the award of a single contract, or the division of the requirement into lots to be awarded in a single procedure, so that authorities may avoid applying the regulations to lots of small contracts. This discourages inefficient ad hoc purchasing. It also, however, discourages authorities from breaking up procurements to encourage participation by smaller firms. There is, however, an exception to the rules to allow for this possibility with services, as explained at (d) below.

---

[4] Supply Regulation 7(4); Services Regulation 7(4).
[5] Supply Directive Article 5(4).
[6] Services Regulation 7(4).
[7] Services Directive Article 7(4).

(c) AGGREGATION: WORKS

There is no equivalent in the Works Regulations to the requirement in the Supply Regulations that purchases of the same "type" must be aggregated. This means, for example, that – on the assumption that exterior maintenance constitutes works – authorities need not aggregate separate maintenance contracts, even where these are for identical work on different buildings. This is, however, subject to a general prohibition on splitting contracts to avoid the regulations.[8]

It is provided, however, that an authority must aggregate the value of separate public works contracts entered into for the purpose of carrying out a single "work".[9] For example, a university erecting a new hall of residence which lets separate contracts for different phases of the building must aggregate the value of each separate contract; thus it must advertise them if the total costs of the building exceeds the five million ECUs threshold, even if the value of each separate contract is below that amount. Clearly the definition of a "work" is important in this context.[10]

(d) EXCEPTION TO AGGREGATION FOR WORKS AND SERVICES CONTRACTS DIVIDED INTO LOTS

There are some exceptions to the requirements to aggregate the value of separate contracts under the Works Regulations and Services Regulations.

Under the Works Regulations, where the value of the contract relating to a particular "work" is less than one million ECUs,[11] the value of that contract may be calculated without taking into account the value of other contacts relating to the same work. The authority may take advantage of this exemption for contracts worth up to 20 per cent of the total value of the work.[12]

Thus, for example, an authority may decide to produce a particular "work", such as a bridge, by awarding one contract worth four million ECUs and four contracts of 500,000 ECUs each. Generally, the aggregation rules require the value of all the contracts to be added together. This gives the result that all must be advertised, since the total is six million ECUs, which exceeds the five million ECUs threshold. However, under this exemption two of the contracts worth 500,000 ECUs may be valued without reference to the work as a whole; thus they are not subject to the regulations, since their value is only 500,000 ECUs. The exemption can only be applied, however, to two of the lots; if it were applied to three, the exempt amount would be worth 1,500,000 ECUs, which is 25 per cent of the six million total, thus exceeding the 20 per cent limit.

---

[8] See p. 175.
[9] Works Regulation 7(3).
[10] On this see p. 128.
[11] Works Regulation 7(4).
[12] *Ibid.*

These provisions appear to affect only the exempt lots themselves: the value of the exempt lots may not be disregarded in determining the value of the non-exempt part of the contract.[13] Thus, in the above example, if the authority decided not to apply the Works Regulations to two of the 500,000 ECUs lots, the value of these lots would still need to be aggregated to decide whether the four million ECUs contract should be subject to the regulations. The result is that it will be regulated, since the total value of the work is five million ECUs. If these lots were not required to be added it would probably not be covered.

The Services Regulations also contain a limited exemption from the aggregation rules where a "single requirement" for services is divided into lots. It was suggested above that a "single requirement" for services exists where the services are of the same type, and the contracts are awarded around the same time. This exemption applies to contracts with an estimated value of less than 80,000 ECUs and like the works exemption applies only when the value of the exempt lots is less than 20 per cent of the whole requirement. For example, if a requirement for building-cleaning services worth 400,000 ECUs were divided into eight lots worth 50,000 ECUs each, one of these lots could be awarded without following the regulations, but not two of them (since this would amount to 25 per cent of the total). As with works contracts, it appears that the value of exempt lots must be taken into account in assessing the value of the non-exempt lots for threshold purposes.

These exemptions encourage authorities to retain some part of their work for small- and medium-sized enterprises (SMEs),[14] which the Community itself has sought to promote and support. This limits the general effect of the aggregation rules in encouraging the grouping of work into large contracts, a grouping which is, of course, generally detrimental to SMEs.

(e) THE AGGREGATION RULES AND DISCRETE OPERATIONAL UNITS

In some cases a public body which is a single legal entity may function in practice as a number of independent units. An example in the United Kingdom is the case of schools which have opted out of local authority control; these remain legally part of the local authority but function in an independent manner with a separate budget, and carry out their own procurement. The question arises as to whether the purchases of all the

---

[13] This is not clear from the directive, but it is unlikely that it was intended to affect the rest of the work, and the view stated in the text is given effect in the Works Regulations, which provide that the usual rule on aggregated value in Works Regulation 79(3) is not to apply to a public works contract where "that contract" is less than one million ECUs, etc., this indicates that the exemption is relevant only in valuing that particular contract and not others awarded for the same work. This view is also stated by Brown, above pp. 73–74.

[14] See pp. 67–68.

units must be aggregated in such a case. To do this is inconvenient: if the principle of the unit's autonomy and control over procurement is to be retained, the effect is that units are required to follow the regulations in the award of a number of small contracts. The issue is likely to arise only with supplies and services.[15]

The directives do not deal expressly with this, but the Supply Regulations and Services Regulations effectively provide that the aggregation rules are not to require the aggregation of contracts awarded by independent units.[16] This applies where the following conditions are met:

(i) there is a purchase by a "discrete operational unit" (DOU). It is not clear what this means, but it probaly covers only a unit with budgetary and managerial autonomy.

(ii) the goods or services are acquired solely for the purpose of that unit;

(iii) the decision over whether to purchase has been wholly devolved to the unit; and

(iv) that decision is taken independently of any other part of the contracting authority (which probably involves a requirement that it should not be subject to approval).

There is some debate over whether these provisions on DOUs are lawful.

It can be pointed out that the aggregation rules do not state clearly that aggregation must be carried out at the level of the contracting authority rather than the purchasing unit: it is merely provided, for example, that "regular" contracts must be aggregated, and it could be suggested that contracts are only "regular" where awarded by the same part of the authority. Considerations of policy support this view. There are good reasons why purchasing authority may be delegated to separate units – for example, to improve accountability, to reduce overheads (where economies of scale are outweighed by extra bureaucratic costs from centralising the purchasing function), or to improve responsiveness of purchasers to user needs. To preclude such appropriate administrative organisation (or, as is the alternative, to require advertisement of a large number of small contracts by the separate units) is an unacceptable cost to impose for the benefit gained for the open market policy. Further, it emphasises form, rather than substance: it is often purely chance whether or not a body which is effectively independent has a separate legal identity. The Commission has indicated unofficially in a working document that it may accept provisions on DOUs in relation to the

---

[15] Aggregation of works is required only where contracts relate to a single work, and autonomous units do not each tend to let different contracts relating to the same work!

[16] Supply Regulation 7(7); Services Regulation 7(8). The exception applies both for aggregation rules relating to contracts made over a period of time and renewable contracts, and also to those made at the same time. The issue is likely to arise only in the context of the rules relating to separate contracts over a period of time; contracts are in practice only awarded at the same time where this is done by a common purchaser.

utilities rules[17] and also accepted the provisions on DOUs in the United Kingdom regulations when it considered the United Kingdom draft of the Supply and Services Regulations. Where the concept of a separate unit is clearly defined, the possibility of abuse should be precluded.

Another view, however, is that the directives require aggregation of all purchases made by a contracting authority which is a single legal entity, and that the United Kingdom provisions on DOUs are incompatible with the directives. The Commission indicated in 1993, in reply to a question from the European Parliament that this is the case.[18] If this is correct, authorities are obliged to ignore the provisions on DOUs, and if they fail to do so may be the subject of legal action.[19]

The correct interpretation remains to be determined by the Court of Justice. It is to be hoped that the Court favours an interpretation which does not require aggregation of the purchases of separate units. However, it may be reluctant to do so without a specific provision in the directives, because of the uncertainty this would create, and the possibility for abuse where the concept of a distinct unit is not carefully defined in the directives themselves. It would be desirable to adopt provisions to introduce an exemption for DOUs when the directives are reviewed.

(5) THE PROHIBITION ON CONTRACT SPLITTING

All three sets of regulations state that a contracting authority shall not enter into separate contracts with the intention of avoiding the application of the regulations.[20] This is directed at the case where an authority which might have awarded one single contract of a value above the relevant threshold seeks to award instead two or more distinct contracts, to avoid applying the regulations. In practice, many situations which result from this sort of conduct are now caught by the aggregation rules. The express provision on contract splitting, however, may catch some deliberate splits which are not caught by those rules. Obviously, it is difficult in practice, however, to prove an authority's motive in packaging work in a particular way.

7. FRAMEWORK ARRANGEMENTS UNDER THE PUBLIC SECTOR RULES

(1) THE NATURE OF FRAMEWORK ARRANGEMENTS

"Framework arrangement" is a term which can be used to refer to an arrangement whereby a purchaser and seller agree in advance to the

---

[17] See pp. 450–451.
[18] [1993] O.J. C207/38.
[19] Since most of the regulations have direct effect aggrieved providers can mount a challenge in the United Kingdom courts based on the directive itself: see pp. 902–903.
[20] Works Regulation 7(8); Supply Regulation 7(10); Services Regulation 7(11).

terms of any future dealings between them, without committing themselves to any specific orders. Such arrangements are useful where a purchaser has a recurring need for an item or service: framework arrangements allow those needs to be met simply by placing orders under the arrangement, without the cost of negotiating a new agreement on each occasion. They are often used, for example, for purchases of office equipment such as computer equipment or photocopiers where additional or replacement equipment, or spares, are likely to be required. They are also used to procure services or works – for example, for repair or maintenance of buildings over a period of time. Framework arrangements can be divided into two types.

The first is an arrangement whereby the parties undertake legal obligations with respect to the purchase and supply of the product or service covered by the arrangement. This covers an arrangement whereby, although no exact quantities are specified, the purchaser is committed to obtaining its requirements when they arise (or a certain amount or proportion of these) from the provider in question, and the provider is committed to deliver[21] – for example, an agreement for an authority to buy all the paper clips which it requires over the next year from that provider. Such a legally binding arrangement may be referred to as a "framework contract".

The second type is an arrangement under which the parties undertake no legal commitment, but merely set out the terms of possible future contracts. In other words, should the purchaser decide to make a purchase of the product or service covered by the arrangement, he may choose to place the order under the framework arrangement, but is not obliged to do so; and the provider is not bound to accept orders placed under it. The arrangement in this case does not itself constitute a contract between the parties; a contract arises only when a specific order is made.[22] An arrangement of this type can be referred to as a "framework agreement". A purchaser may prefer to enter into a framework agreement, which does not tie him to a specific provider, rather than a framework contract, which does, so that he is able to look

---

[21] Where only one party is bound to the arrangement this is not a binding contract in English law, because of absence of consideration. Such an arrangement could be binding if made under seal. It is not clear whether such an arrangement – where either the purchaser is obliged to buy, or the supplier to supply, but not both – is a contract "for consideration" under the regulations. If it is not, the contract for consideration will arise when an order is made or accepted.

[22] Such an arrangement may be in the form of a "standing offer", under which the provider is bound to fulfil an order once made, although the offer may be withdrawn at any time. Here the conclusion of the arrangements constitutes an offer by the provider and the placing of an order a acceptance of the offer by the purchaser, so that a contact arises when the order is placed. This construction of framework arrangements is the one generally adopted by the courts: see *Percival v. London County Council Asylums and Mental Deficiency Committee* (1918) 87 LJKB 677; *Great Northern Railway Co. v. Witham* (1873) L.R. 9 CP 16. Alternatively, the parties could provide that an offer occurs only when an order is placed, and that a contract arises only where the order is accepted by the provider.

elsewhere if the arrangement no longer offers value for money – for example, because a new and competitive provider has entered the market. At the same time, the arrangement still offers some security of supply for the purchaser, and some expectation of business for the provider and, as mentioned above, saves transaction costs for both parties.

(2) FRAMEWORK ARRANGEMENTS UNDER THE REGULATIONS

Where an authority enters into an arrangement which is a framework contract, in the sense explained above, this is to be treated under the regulations in the same way as any other contract. Thus, it must be advertised and awarded in accordance with the regulations' procedure, and a contract award notice must be published. Placing a specific order under the arrangement does not itself constitute the award of a new contract, and hence the regulations do not apply to such an order. Thus, the authority is free to place orders under a framework contract which has itself been properly awarded, without advertising those orders or following any other rules, and does not need to publish a specific contract award notice to cover each order.

There is, on the other hand, some doubt about how framework agreements – *i.e.* framework arrangements which do not constitute contracts for consideration – are to be treated for the purpose of the public sector procurement rules.

One view is that such agreements are not themselves "contracts" for the purpose of the regulations, whilst individual orders placed under those agreements, which are contracts under English private law, *are* distinct contracts for this purpose. On this view, each order falls within the regulations where its value exceeds the applicable threshold, and must be awarded in accordance with the regulations' procedures: it cannot simply be placed with a pre-selected provider under a framework agreement. This applies even if the framework agreement itself has been awarded in accordance with the regulations' procedures, since there is nothing to exempt contracts placed under such an agreement from the regulations' normal requirements.

> **Example:** An authority has a recurrent need for computer spares and enters into a framework agreement with provider A. This sets the terms for possible future contracts for A to supply such spares. However, the authority wishes to order spares worth 300,000 ECUs. On the view outlined above it must advertise this order under the Supply Regulations: the order is a proposed new contract, and is covered by the Supply Regulations since it exceeds the threshold. Thus it is not able simply to place the order with A under the framework arrangement.

If the above view is correct, the regulations effectively render impossible the use of non-binding framework agreements for orders covered by the regulations. It can be noted that in practice even small orders are generally covered, because of the effect of aggregation rules.[23] Support for this view might be seen in the fact that the Utilities Directive and Regulations contain express provisions authorising the use of framework agreements, and lay down certain conditions and ancillary rules relating to their use,[24] but that no corresponding provisions are contained in the public sector directives.

An alternative view, preferred by the Treasury,[25] is that where a framework agreement is awarded in accordance with the procedures in the regulations, these procedures need not be repeated for the award of any contract placed under the agreement: such a contract has already been awarded in accordance with the regulations, albeit through the intermediate step of a framework agreement. In other words, it is suggested that the award of the arrangement should be treated as an award of several contracts (those later placed under the arrangement) through a single award procedure. The possibility of several contracts being awarded in a single procedure is certainly contemplated by the regulations – which expressly refer, for example, to the possibility of an award being divided into separate lots. It is true that with a framework agreement there may be a delay before the contracts themselves are actually concluded, and indeed, that the authority may decide not to enter into any contracts at all, but the same applies to any award procedure: there is no minimum period within which an advertised contract must be concluded, nor is an authority obliged to conclude a contract once a procedure has been opened or an award made.

In favour of such an approach is the utility of such arrangements for both purchaser and provider, as explained at (1) above. Further, it can be pointed out that authorities which are not permitted to operate through non-binding framework arrangements may instead, rather than awarding a number of separate contracts, choose to enter into a binding framework contract – an arrangement which is less conducive to competition. As noted above, the use of framework agreements is permitted in the utilities sector and seems no less appropriate for the public sector.

On the other hand, it can be pointed out that framework arrangements might be used to remove a section of the market from competition for an unjustifiably long period of time. Contractual arrangements do not pose so much of a problem in this respect, since the binding nature of the relationship will act as some deterrent to agreements of excessive length.[26] Some limitations are imposed by the general Com-

---

[23] On these see pp. 169–175.
[24] See pp. 452–460.
[25] HM Treasury, *An Introduction to the E.C. Procurement Rules* (1995), para. 2–11.
[26] It is not clear whether the Court of Justice may imply into the directives effective limits on the duration for which contracts may run before being reopened to competition under the directives' rules, which go beyond those which may apply under Community competition law: on this see p. 96.

munity rules on competition,[27] but whilst these may cover the most serious abuses, more stringent limitations may be needed to achieve the objectives of the directives of opening up public markets. Under the utilities rules this problem is dealt with by express rules prohibiting agreements which hinder or distort competition.[28] In the absence of express rules for the public sector, the Court of Justice may prefer to construe the directives in a literal manner to prohibit the use of framework arrangements; on the other hand, it may feel that the issue is adequately dealt with through the competition rules, or may even be prepared to imply limitations on time into the directives themselves.

In conclusion, it may only be said that at present the legality of the practice of placing contracts through framework agreements is open to question, and that, even if the Commission does not wish to take action, purchasers who do this face legal challenges from aggrieved providers. It is hoped, however, that the non-binding framework agreements will be accepted by the Court of Justice, and that ultimately the directives will be amended to make it clear that they may be used.

If framework agreements are accepted then it appears the threshold must be calculated at the level of individual contracts, since there is no express provision for valuation of all purchases under a framework agreement. In practice, both methods would in fact produce the same result, since different contracts awarded under the same framework agreement will normally be aggregated together in any case, under the general aggregation rules. However, this is not always the case – for example, if a framework arrangement is made by a consortium and contracts are placed by members of the consortium who are separate contracting authorities, it is arguable that it is not, under the existing rules, required to aggregate the purchases of the different authorities.[29] The result is different under the utilities rules which require aggregation of all purchases under a framework agreement.[30]

---

[27] See Chap. 4.

[28] It is suggested that these may impose more stringent requirements than the competition rules: see pp. 457–458.

[29] On the other hand, if it is accepted that discrete operational units may aggregate contracts at the level of the purchasing unit and not the legal entity it may be argued that, conversely, purchases of *different* legal entities should be aggregated where they operate together in their purchasing.

[30] See p. 459.

CHAPTER 6

THE PUBLIC SECTOR REGULATIONS: AWARD PROCEDURES

1. INTRODUCTION

This chapter examines the steps which must be followed by a contracting authority in awarding a contract which is subject to the Public Works Contracts Regulations 1991, the Public Supply Contracts Regulations 1995 or the Public Services Contracts Regulations 1993.[1] The detailed rules relating to qualification of providers (Chapter 7) and specifications (Chapter 11) are considered separately.

The procedures in these regulations are likely shortly to be amended, to introduce new procedural obligations which apply in dealings with certain third country providers under the new WTO Agreement on Government Procurement (GPA).[1a] Even before these amendments are made, however, authorities covered by the GPA must apply these obligations as from January 1, 1996 when the GPA comes into force. The Commission has also proposed a directive to apply these obligations to Community, as well as third country, providers.[2] Whilst this directive has not yet been adopted, in the United Kingdom Community providers may nevertheless benefit from these additional rules as from January 1, 1996 by virtue of regulation 4(2) of the Works, Supply and Services Directives, which state that providers who are nationals of and established in a Member State are to be treated no less favourably than those who are not. Because of these rules, authorities thus need to apply not merely the rules set out in the regulations themselves, but also any additional procedural rules deriving from the GPA. These rules, as well as those in the regulations, will be noted in the course of this Chapter.

Further, in addition to the specific obligations in the directives and implementing regulations, the Court of Justice has stated in the *Storebaelt* case[2a] that there is a fundamental principle of "equality of treatment" of providers underlying the Community rules. The exact

---

[1] Respectively S.I. 1991 No. 2680, S.I. 1995 No. 201 and S.I. 1992 No. 3228. The definition of contracting authorities, and the question of which contracts are subject to the regulations, are examined in Chap. 5. The background to the regulations is discussed in Chap. 3 and enforcement in Chap. 18.
[1a] On this Agreement see pp. 774-782.
[2] See further pp. 61–63.
[2a] Case 243/89, *Commission v. Denmark*, judgment of June 22, 1993.

requirements of this principle have yet to be elaborated by the Court, but it would appear to mean that providers in the same position must be treated in the same manner, unless there is a good commercial justification for a difference in treatment (as there is, for example, in limiting the number of qualified providers invited to bid in restricted procedures). Clearly the principle has a potentially important application both in aspects of award procedures covered by the Community rules, and in those aspects which are not regulated expressly.

2. PRIOR INFORMATION NOTICES (PINs)

(1) THE REQUIREMENT FOR A PRIOR INFORMATION NOTICE

Individual contracts falling within the Works Regulations, Supply Regulations or Services Regulations must normally be advertised at the start of the award procedure, so that interested parties are informed about the contract and are able to participate as explained later in this Chapter. In addition, there is a requirement to publish advance notices of purchases which the authority intends to make in the future, referred to as Prior Information Notices (PINs).[3] This requirement seeks to ensure that potential bidders are given as much time as possible to prepare for participation.

The PIN requirements are useful to providers. However, whilst a provider may compel an authority to publish a PIN, there is probably no effective remedy for a provider whose chance of obtaining a particular contract has been affected by non-publication of a PIN.[4] In practice the most useful method of enforcement is through monitoring of *Official Journal* notices by the European Commission,[5] to check that specific authorities are publishing PINs in a systematic way.

Publication of a PIN does not, of course, bind the authority to make the purchases referred to in the notice.[6]

(2) PRIOR INFORMATION NOTICES FOR WORKS

Prior Information Notices for works contracts are dealt with under Works Regulation 9. This provides that when an authority intends to seek offers in relation to a public works contract it must send a notice to

---

[3] The directive refers to them as "indicative notices": Works Directive Article 11(1); Supplies Directive Article 9(1).

[4] See p. 901.

[5] See pp. 920–926.

[6] Even advertisement of a contract at the start of the award procedure does not commit the authority to making an award: see pp. 254–255.

the Office of Official Publications of the European Communities "as soon as possible after the decision approving the planning of the work or works".[7] This will be published in the *Official Journal of the European Communities* in its paper form and also in the Tenders Electronic Daily (TED) data bank in all the official Community languages,[8] the cost being borne by the Community.[9] The obligation to submit a notice applies for all individual works contracts covered by the regulations – that is, which are above the threshold and which are not excluded. This includes some contracts which individually are below the 5,000,000 ECUs threshold, but which are brought within the Works Regulations by the aggregation rules because they relate to a larger "work" which itself exceeds the threshold.[10]

It is not clear what constitutes "approval" of the award for this purpose. In view of the purpose of a PIN, of giving useful advance warning of contracts, and the low costs of compliance, it is likely that a work will be considered to be "approved" for this purpose once the purchaser has decided that it wishes to carry out the work, even though this decision may be subject to veto or ratification by a superior authority or where it is subject to external factors such as the award of planning permission.

The notice must be in a form "substantially corresponding" to the model PIN notice in Part A of Schedule 2 of the Works Regulations, and must contain the information which is specified in the model.[11] This model is set out at page 184. As with other notices, the PIN may not contain more than 650 words.[12] As regards the description of the work(s) in the PIN, the Commission is likely shortly to adopt a recommendation that authorities should make reference to the Community's Common Procurement Vocabulary (CPV), although this will not be mandatory.[13]

---

[7] As with other notices, the notice must be despatched by the "most appropriate means." (Works Regulation 30(1)), and the authority must retain proof of despatch (Works Regulation 30(3). The Office of Official Publications must publish the notice within 12 days of despatch: Works Directive 11(10).

[8] Works Directive 11(8). The original version alone is authentic.

[9] Works Regulation 11(3).

[10] On these aggregation rules see pp. 171–173. The view that the obligation to publish a PIN applies to such contracts is taken by the Treasury in its note, "The European Community Procurement Rules: Aggregation".

[11] Works Regulation 9.

[12] Works Regulation 30(2). Article 11(3) of the Works Directive which this implements differs slightly, providing that the notice must not exceed one page of the *Official Journal*, of *approximately* 650 words.

[13] On the CPV see pp. 69–70.

PUBLIC WORKS CONTRACTS REGULATIONS 1991, SCHEDULE 2, PART A – FORM OF PRIOR INFORMATION NOTICE

1. The name, address, telegraphic address, telephone, telex and facsimile numbers of the contracting authority.

2. (a) The site.
   (b) The nature and extent of the services to be provided and, where relevant, the main characteristics of any lots by reference to the work.
   (c) If available: an estimate of the cost range of the proposed services.

3. (a) Estimated date for initiating the award procedures in respect of the contract or contracts.
   (b) If known: estimated date for the start of the work.
   (c) If known: estimated timetable for completion of the work.

4. If known: terms of financing of the work and of price revision and/or references to the provisions in which these are contained.

5. Other information.

6. Date of despatch of the notice.

As is explained below, contract notices (those advertising the contract at the start of the procedure) may not be published in the national press prior to despatch to the Official Journal, nor may they contain more information than the Official Journal notice. There is, however, no equivalent provision relating to PINs.[14-15]

[14-15] This is based on the view that such a prohibition is not required by the Works Directive. In fact, the directive is ambiguous. Article 11(11) containing such prohibitions refers only to "notices": this could include PIN notices, which are also dealt with in Article 11. However, it could be confined by implication to other notices, since it follows on from other provisions which do not apply to PINs. The Utilities Directive, on the other hand, in Article 25(5), makes it clear that the restrictions do not in general apply to PIN notices, and probably the same rules were intended to apply in the public sector, so that the United Kingdom interpretation is correct.

PUBLIC SUPPLY CONTRACTS REGULATIONS 1995, SCHEDULE 3, PART A – FORM OF PRIOR INFORMATION NOTICE

1. Name, address, telegraphic address, telephone, telex and facsimile numbers of the contracting authority and of the service from which additional information may be obtained.

2. Nature and quantity or value of the goods to be supplied. CPA reference number.

3. Estimated date of the commencement of the procedures leading to the award of the contract(s) (if known).

4. Other information.

5. Date of despatch of the notice.

PUBLIC SERVICES CONTRACTS REGULATIONS 1993, SCHEDULE 2, PART A – FORM OF PRIOR INFORMATION NOTICE

1. Name, address and telephone, telegraphic, telex and facsimile numbers of the contracting authority and of the service from which additional information may be obtained.

2. For each category of services in Part A of Schedule 1, the total quantity in value to be provided.

3. For each category of services in (2), the estimated date of the commencement of the procedures leading to the award of the contract(s) (if known).

4. Other information.

5. Date of despatch of the notice.

Where a PIN has been published for a works contract which is later awarded under an open or restricted procedure, the authority may in certain cases shorten the usual time-limits for submission of bids.[16]

(3) PRIOR INFORMATION NOTICES FOR SUPPLIES AND SERVICES

(a) THE BASIC PRINCIPLES

Prior information notices relating to supply contracts are dealt with in Supply Regulation 9,[17] and those relating to services contracts in Services Regulation 9. These provisions require a notice to be sent to the Office of Official Publications as soon as possible after the commencement of each financial year,[18] which contains information about supply or services contracts in respect of which the authority intends to seek offers during that financial year.[19] This will then be published in the *Official Journal of the European Communities* in hard copy and in the TED data bank in all the official languages of the Community,[20] the cost being borne, as with other notices, by the Community itself.[21] In contrast with the obligation relating to works, the requirement is not to supply advance information of individual contracts as they arise, but rather to give a general indication of the authority's likely needs for goods and non-construction services in each year.

With services, as works, publication of a PIN may again sometimes allow an authority to shorten the usual minimum time periods for award procedures.[22]

(b) THRESHOLDS AND EXCLUSIONS

In relation to supply contracts, the obligation to publish an annual notice applies only where an authority expects (at the date of despatch of the notice) that in the relevant financial year the value of supply contracts awarded[23] in a particular "product area" will be equal to or greater than

---

[16] See pp. 204–205 and pp. 225–226.

[17] Implementing Supply Directive Article 9(1) and Services Directive 15(1).

[18] As with other notices, the notice must be despatched by the "most appropriate means" (Supply 27(1) and Services Regulation 29(1)), and the authority must retain proof of despatch (Supply Regulation 27(3) and Services Regulation 27(3)).

[19] Supply Regulation 9(1); Services Regulation 9(1).

[20] Supply Directive 9(6); Services Directive 17(3). It is provided in both cases that the text in the original language alone is authentic. Supply Directive 9(8) and Services Directive 17(5) require publication by the Office of Official Publications within 12 days of despatch.

[21] Supply Directive 9(11); Services Directive 17(8).

[22] See pp. 204–205 and pp. 225–226.

[23] The wording of Regulation 9(1) itself does not make it clear whether the reference is to contracts for which offers are sought in the relevant year, or contracts which are expected to be actually awarded in the relevant year. The wording of Article 9(1) of the Supply Directive, however, indicates that the reference is to those contracts which are expected to be awarded in that year.

750,000 ECUs.[24] The information for each "product area" must be given in a separate subdivision of the notice[25] which ensures that the information is presented in a form useful to potential providers.

An important question is when goods are to be regarded as falling within the same "product area". For example, are pens within the same "product area" as pencils? The Supply Directive provides that the question of classification of products by "product area" shall be expressed by reference to the *Classification of Products According to Activities* (CPA) which is the Community's own nomenclature for products and activities.[26] It also further provides that the Commission shall – with the assistance of the Advisory Committee for Public Contracts – determine how the nomenclature shall be used to give a definition of product area.[27] However, this has not yet been done, and in the meantime authorities have no direct guidance as to how a product area is to be defined.

It has been explained that the Supply Regulations, under regulation 7, require aggregation of separate contracts for goods of the same "type" to determine whether individual contracts fall within the threshold for the application of the Supply Regulations[28]. It was suggested that, in light of the purpose of the rule, which is to apply the regulations where it is commercially reasonable for an authority to combine the purchases in a single contract, the test for whether goods are of the same type in that context is whether a typical supplier is generally able to supply all those goods. The concept of "product area" likewise must be considered in light of its function.

The function of the PIN notice is to provide information which will be of use to individual suppliers, where the market for those suppliers is sufficiently large to justify the burden of publishing such notices. Thus the concept of product area should not cover products which are so diverse they are not likely to be supplied by the same firm. On the other hand, it is not desirable to require publication of notices relating to very specific goods within the area of interest of single suppliers: this would be burdensome both for authorities to publish and for suppliers to use. In light of these points, the appropriate test is probably the same as that which it was suggested should be used to determine product "type"

---

[24] Supply Regulation 9(2)(b). The sterling equivalent for January 1, 1994 to December 31, 1995 is £561,480, but this figure will be revised as from January 1, 1996: the value of the ECU threshold in national currencies is revised every two years, commencing January 1, 1988. It is calculated based on the average daily value of each currency expressed in ECUs over the 24 months ending on the last day of August prior to the date for revision: Supply Directive Article 5(1)(c). The new amount must be published in the *Official Journal* at the beginning of the November prior to the date of revision: Supply Directive Article 5(1)(d).

[25] Supply Regulation 9(2)(b).

[26] Supply Directive Article 9(1). This is based on the *Central Products Classification* (CPC) nomenclature, produced by the United Nations.

[27] The procedure to be followed is specified in Supply Directive Article 32(2).

[28] See pp. 168–171.

under Supply Regulation 7 – that is, whether a typical supplier is able to supply all the products concerned. This is also the test suggested in relation to the almost identical provision in the Utilities Directive in a document published by the Commission and approved by the Advisory Committee for Public Contracts.[29] The document suggests that this can normally be achieved by aggregating at the level of four CPA digits, although it is stressed that this may sometimes be too wide and sometimes too narrow, and that authorities should use their own knowledge of the market to determine whether the four-digit approach reflects adequately the capacities of a typical supplier.[30] It can be expected that a similar approach will be adopted in relation to the guidelines to be issued by the Commission pursuant to the Supplies Directive.[31]

In relation to services, the obligation to publish a PIN applies only in respect of Part A services.[32] It is only necessary to publish a notice where the value of contracts[33] in the relevant financial year for the provision of services in a particular Part A category is expected to be equal to or greater than 750,000 ECUs.[34] Information must be given separately in the notice for each category of service.

A "category" of service refers to one of the categories used in Part A of Schedule 1 to the Services Regulations, which are very broad. It was suggested earlier that the test of whether services are the same "type" of service for the purposes of determining whether individual contracts fall within the regulations should be whether the type of service is one typically provided by a single provider, and that this frequently involves classes of services much narrower than those listed in the Schedule.[35] The Services Directive's use of these very broad categories in the Schedule in relation to aggregation of services, for the purposes of PINs, may be criticised. In many cases it requires authorities to aggregate services which are very diverse and unlikely all to be of interest to single providers. Thus "management consultancy services" is a single category, but includes a wide variety of activities carried out by different types of specialists – for example, marketing, personnel services and provision of

---

[29] *Policy Guidelines Defining the Term "Product Area" in Periodic Indicative Notices for Directive 93/38/EEC"*; see para. 7.

[30] *Ibid*, para. 9.

[31] If the test is indeed the same as for aggregation for applying the rules on the award of individual contracts, then the guidance published in relation to annual notices will also be useful in that other context.

[32] On the concept of priority services see pp. 132–135.

[33] As with the corresponding supply rule, Services Regulation 9(2) is ambiguous as to whether it refers to contracts for which offers are sought in the relevant year, or contracts actually awarded, but again the directive indicates that the reference should be construed as one to contracts expected to be awarded: Services Directive Article 15(1).

[34] As for supply contracts, the sterling equivalent for January 1, 1994 to December 31, 1995 is £561,480, but this figure will be revised as from January 1, 1996. The sterling equivalent of the ECU sum is calculated in the same way as for the supply rules, as described in note 24, commencing first in 1994: Services Directive 7(8).

[35] See pp. 134–135.

safety advice. This means that PIN notices must be published for services falling into the category where the value of the category as a whole exceeds 750,000 ECUs, although only very small amounts of the individual types of services are purchased. It also means that it is difficult for potential providers to use PINs to obtain useful information: the existence of a demand for "management consultancy", for example, does not tell a provider whether the authority has a need for his particular expertise. A better test would be whether the services are likely to be provided by a typical provider.

It is expressly provided that the obligation relating to PIN notices does not apply to contracts which are excluded from the regulations under Supply Regulation 6[36] or Services Regulation 6[37] (for example, contracts affected by security considerations),[38] nor to those excluded because they fall below the thresholds in regulation 7.[39] Thus these need not be publicised, nor need they be taken into account in determining whether the threshold of 750,000 ECUs is met.

For the purpose of the rules on PINs, the purchases of the authority as a whole must be aggregated. In deciding, under Supply Regulation 7 or Services Regulation 7 whether individual contracts meet the threshold for the regulations to apply, this is not always the case: where an authority is divided into independent "discrete operational units" which make their purchases separately, regulation 7 provides that only the purchases of that unit need to be aggregated, and not those of the authority as a whole.[40] There is no similar provision, however, relating to aggregation for the purpose of a PIN notice. Thus, in deciding whether the 750,000 ECUs threshold is met the value of contracts of all discrete units within the authority are included – provided, however, those contracts are themselves covered under the threshold rules in regulation 7.

Examples:

(These examples assume that the paper stationery products purchased are products of a single type, falling within a single "product area".)

(1) There are three "discrete operational units", X, Y and Z, within a local authority. Each makes, in a year, similar contracts for the purchase of paper stationery, to a value of 100,000 ECUs each. The authority purchases a further 500,000 ECUs' worth of paper stationery for its other operations, under similar contracts.

---

[36] Supply Regulation 9(2)(a).
[37] Services Regulation 9(2)(a).
[38] For the list of exclusions see pp. 150–158.
[39] Supply Regulation 9(2)(a). This latter exclusion is not expressly stated in the Supply Directive, but the United Kingdom provision appears to be a correct interpretation: Article 5(1)(a) of the directive states that the obligations in Title III, which include the obligations relating to PINs, are to apply *to contracts above the threshold.*
[40] On discrete operational units see pp. 173–175. (It is assumed in the above analysis that the discrete operational units exemption is valid; there is in fact some debate over this, as explained in the pages just cited.)

In this case, the total value of contracts for paper stationery which are covered by the Supply Regulations is 500,000 ECUs. The contracts by units X, Y and Z are not covered because, under regulation 7, they are not to be aggregated with the purchases of other units, or of other parts of the authority, and, individually, are below the 200,000 ECUs threshold. Hence the total value of purchases is below 750,000, and no PIN notice is required.

(2) There is only one discrete operational unit, X, within the authority. The unit makes, in a year, contracts for the purchase of paper stationery to a value of 300,000 ECUs. The authority purchases a further 500,000 ECUs' worth of paper stationery for its other operations, under similar contracts.

A PIN notice is required in this case, since the total value of contracts covered by the Supply Regulations amounts to 800,000 ECUs: the contracts of unit X, at 300,000 ECUs, exceed the threshold, as do the purchases of the rest of the authority, at 500,000 ECUs.

The regulations provide for the relevant figure to be determined by reference to the value of relevant *contracts* rather than simply to the value of relevant *goods or services*. Thus the Supply Regulations provide that the authority must take account of the *total consideration under all proposed supply contracts for the purchase or hire of goods in a product area*; whilst the services regulations provide for the aggregation of *the total consideration of all proposed services contracts for each service category*.

In relation to a supply contract, this means, first, that in calculating whether the threshold is reached, the authority must take into account the value of any services to be provided under supply contracts.

Example:
An authority proposes to award during the year three separate supply contracts, each consisting of similar machinery with an estimated value of 200,000 ECUs together with machine maintenance services with an estimated value of 100,000 ECUs. In this case a PIN notice must be published, because the total value of the contracts (900,000 ECUs) exceeds 750,000 ECUs.

On the other hand, the above rule means that the authority need not take into account the value of products within the same product area which are provided under services contracts.

Example:
An authority proposes to award during the year a contract for machine maintenance services, of estimated value 300,000 ECUs, together with the provision of some new machinery, with an estimated value of 200,000 ECUs. This is a services contract since the value of the services exceeds that of the products. It also intends to award a

later supply contract for 600,000 ECUs' worth of new machinery of the same kind. It is not necessary to publish a PIN notice: although the total value of the machinery (800,000 ECUs) exceeds the 750,000 threshold, only the machinery included in the supply contract need be considered.

The same principles apply *mutatis mutandis* to the treatment of services contracts.

It is not clear whether this faithfully implements the Supply Directive and Services Directive. Article 9(1) of the Supply Directive requires a PIN where the "total procurement by product area" meets the threshold, and Article 15(1) of the Services Directive requires a PIN where the "intended total procurement in each of the service categories" equals or exceeds the relevant amount. This might mean that all goods or services in the relevant area or category are included, whatever the type of contract under which they are supplied. However, it is unlikely, since it would even require inclusion of supplies and other services provided under works contracts, which cannot have been intended. Since the directives in general apply only to supply and service contracts respectively, the rules in the directive might in fact have an even narrower scope than those in the regulations: it could be suggested that under the Supply Directive only goods provided under supply contracts are included (and no services at all), and under the Services Directive only services provided under services contracts (and no supplies at all). If this is correct, then the United Kingdom approach exceeds the requirements of the directives. Alternatively, the United Kingdom provisions might be an exact interpretation of the directives.[41]

The nature of the particular contract under which the goods or services to be provided is not relevant to aggregation. For example, goods provided under all supply contracts must be considered, whether they are contracts of hire or contracts of purchase.

(c) FORM OF NOTICES

The PIN notices must be in a form which "substantially corresponds" to the model notices in Supply Regulations Schedule 3, Part A, and Services Regulations Schedule 1, Part A; and they must contain the information which is specified in the model notices.[42] These models are set out on pages 184–185. As with other notices, a PIN notice for supply and services contracts may not contain more than 650 words.[43]

---

[41] It may be noted that the wording of the Utilities Directive indicates that it is the value of the consideration under the relevant supply or services which is relevant (see p. 466). This provides support for the United Kingdom interpretation of the public sector directives, since it is unlikely that the position was intended to be different from that which applies in the utilities sector.

[42] Supply Regulation (1); Services Regulation 9(1).

[43] Works Regulation 30(2); Supply Regulation 27(2); Services Regulation 29(2). Article 11(3) of the Works Directive, Article 9(11) of the Supply Directive and Article 17(8) of the Services Directive which these provisions implement differ slightly, providing that the notice must not exceed one page of the *Official Journal*, of *approximately* 650 words.

In relation to supply contracts, a single notice may refer to a variety of products, but as indicated above, the notice must be subdivided to give separate details of each "product area".[44] The model notice indicates that the relevant CPA reference number must be provided. It is not, however, necessary to indicate the nature of the contract – for example, whether the goods are to be purchased or hired.

In relation to services, it is notable that it is necessary only to indicate the categories of services to be purchased and the estimated value of each category. As already explained, information provided in this way is sometimes of limited use to service providers. In practice, it will be useful for authorities to break down services into more detailed classes within a particular category.

In relation to both supply and services contracts, as with works contracts, the Commission is likely shortly to adopt a recommendation that products and services should be described in PIN notices by reference to the Community's Common Procurement Vocabulary (CPV).[45]

(d) PIN NOTICES IN THE NATIONAL PRESS

As with works, contract notices for supply and services contracts cannot be published in the national press prior to their despatch to the *Official Journal*, nor may they contain more information than the *Official Journal* notice. However there is again no equivalent provision in the regulations relating to PIN notices.[46-47]

3. THE THREE AWARD PROCEDURES

Contracting authorities must use one of three types of procedure. These are:

(i) *The "open" procedure*. This is a formal tendering procedure, under which the contract is publicly advertised and all interested parties are able to tender.

---

[44] For supply contracts it is necessary only to supply details of goods supplied and for services contracts of the services provided. It is not necessary to give details of ancillary services to be provided with any goods in a supply contract, or goods ancillary to services under a services contract.

[45] On the CPV see pp. 69–70.

[46-47] Like the Works Directive, the Supply and Services Directives are ambiguous: Supply Directive 9(9) and Services Directive 17(6), imposing such limitations, refer merely to "notices", which could include PIN notices, but could be confined by implication to other notices, since as with works these provisions immediately follow other provisions which are inapplicable to PIN notices. In enacting the regulations the government has taken the view that the limitations are not applicable to PIN notices. That this is probably correct is indicated by the fact that the restrictions do not generally apply to PINs in the Utilities sector: see Utilities Directive Article 25(5).

(ii) *The "restricted" procedure.* This is also a formal tendering procedure, whereby the contract is publicly advertised to invite potential providers to express an interest. Tenders are then invited from a limited number of persons selected by the authority.

(iii) *The "negotiated" procedure.* Under this procedure, the authority simply selects potential contractors with whom to negotiate, and awards the contract to one of these firms without necessarily following any formal tendering procedure. There are two types of negotiated procedure:
(a): the negotiated procedure with advertisement, under which the authority must advertise to find suitable firms with which to negotiate; and
(b): the negotiated procedure without advertisement, whereby the authority is permitted to select a person or persons with whom to negotiate without any advertisement.

As a general rule, authorities must use either the open or the restricted procedure.[48] The negotiated procedure, on the other hand (both with or without advertisement) is an exceptional procedure, which may be used only in a limited number of carefully defined cases – for example, extreme urgency, or certain situations where only one possible provider exists. These are explained below in the section on negotiated procedures.[49]

These three procedures are described in detail in the following pages. A summary of the main steps for each procedure and the time limits for response by providers is provided at pages 296–300.

4. OPEN AND RESTRICTED PROCEDURES

(1) CHOOSING THE PROCEDURE

The public sector regulations generally give an authority a free choice over whether to use a restricted or open procedure. This choice will, however, be subject to judicial review according to the usual principles of administrative law which will require, in particular, that the choice must be made on bona fide commercial grounds. It is also subject to any other requirements of domestic law: for example, the rules on compulsory competitive tendering generally require the use of restricted procedures.[50]

In practice, the open procedure provides for the maximum possible competition. However, where a large number of firms are interested in

---

[48] Works Regulation 10(1), Supply Regulation 10(1), Services Regulation 10(1).
[49] See pp. 256–269.
[50] See Chap. 14.

participating, the costs of such a procedure – for example, costs for the authority in supplying documents and assessing bids, and overall costs for tenderers of bid preparation – may outweigh any benefits from greater competition, especially where the procurement is complex so that bid and assessment costs may be quite high. Costs may also be wasted by the submission of bids from unqualified persons, since under the open procedure the authority cannot insist on assessing the qualifications of bidders prior to the receipt of bids.[51] These factors often lead authorities to prefer the restricted procedure, under which only specific invited firms may submit bids.

Despite the possible disadvantages of an open procedure, some procurement regimes have designated this as the preferred method. In particular, the *UNCITRAL Model Law on Procurement of Goods, Construction and Services*,[52] which is designed as a model for countries wishing to develop or improve procurement systems, provides for a procedure similar to the open procedure (though with a possibility for prequalification) as the normal method for the procurement of goods and works.[53] This is because restricted procedures provide greater opportunities for abuse, through the manner of selection of the persons who are permitted to tender. (For example, an authority may decline to select a particular competitive provider, in order to protect a favoured provider from competition.) There has been some debate as to whether the priority for the open procedure is appropriate under the Community regime, and prior to 1993 the open procedure was given a preferred status under the supplies rules. However, this was dropped in the 1993 Consolidated Supply Directive, and the open and restricted procedures now have equal status under all the public sector regulations. In its record of the award procedure, however, an authority is still required to justify its decision to choose a restricted rather than an open procedure.[54]

(2) OBTAINING TENDERS: THE OPEN PROCEDURE

(a) ADVERTISEMENT OF THE CONTRACT

The steps to be followed under the open procedure are set out in Works Regulation 11, Supply Regulation 11 and Services Regulation 11. They

---

[51] See Chap. 7.
[52] On the Model Law see Wallace, "UNCITRAL Model Law on Procurement of Goods and Construction" (1994) 1 P.P.L.R. CS2; Wallace, "The UNCITRAL Model Law on the Procurement of Goods, Construction and Services: the Addition of Services" (1994) 3 P.P.L.R. CS218; Westring, "Multilateral and Unilateral Procurement Regimes: to which Camp does the UNCITRAL Model Law on Procurement Belong?" (1994) 3 P.P.L.R. 142. See also United Nations Commission on International Trade Law, *Guide to Enactment of UNCITRAL Model Law on Procurement of Goods, Construction and Services*.
[53] Article 18(1) of the Code. A restricted procedure is provided for, but it is provided that its use should be justified on specific grounds stated in the Code.
[54] Works Regulation 22(2)(c); Supply Regulation 23(2)(c); Services Regulation 23(2)(c).

include important provisions concerning the advertising of contracts, designed to ensure that information on the contract is available throughout Europe.

The authority must advertise its intention to seek offers by sending a notice (the "contract notice")[55] to the Office for Official Publications for the European Communities.[56] That Office must publish the notice (at the expense of the Community) not later than 12 days after its despatch.[57] It must be published in full in the original language in the *Official Journal of the European Communities* in hard copy and also in the Tenders Electronic Daily data bank, and a summary of its important elements must be published in the other official Community languages.[58]

The notice must be sent "as soon as possible" after the authority has formed its intention to seek offers,[59] and must be sent by the "most appropriate means".[60] Authorities are required to retain proof of the date of despatch of the notice.[61]

Authorities may not place any notice in the press or other "like" publications in the United Kingdom before the date on which the notice is despatched to the Office of Official Publications, and advertisements in the United Kingdom must not contain information additional to that sent to the Office of Official Publications.[62] These provisions are designed to prevent domestic firms obtaining an unfair advantage through better access to information about award procedures. However, since the directives give the Office 12 days to publish the notice after despatch, the rules are not wholly adequate, since an additional 12 days is a significant period. The rule may be justified, however, by the fact that it is convenient for an authority to despatch all relevant notices at the same time, and the best solution would be to reduce the time taken to publish notices in the *Official Journal*. Provided these rules are followed, there appears to be no problem in publishing a notice in the national press: there is no breach of the Treaty, since there can be no restriction on trade where the relevant information is also available in the *Official Journal*.

As well as providing for additional advertisements, there is also no reason why an authority should not draw the contract to the attention of

---

[55] See the definition of "contract notice" in Works Regulation 2(1), Supply Regulation 2(1), Services Regulation 2(1).
[56] Works Regulations 11(2) and 30(1); Supply Regulations 11(2) and 27(1); Services Regulations 11(2) and 29(1).
[57] Works Directive Article 11(10); Supply Directive Article 9(8); Services Directive 17(5).
[58] Works Directive Article 11(9); Supply Directive Article 9(7); Services Directive 17(4). It is stated that only the text in the original language is authentic.
[59] Works Regulations 11(2); Supply Regulation 11(2); Services Regulation 11(2).
[60] Works Regulations 30(1); Supply Regulation 27(1); Services Regulation 29(1). What is the most appropriate means is not further specified, except that in certain urgent cases, as explained, it is expressly provided that telex, telegram or facsimile shall be used, which seems to suggest that this method is not required as a general rule.
[61] Works Regulation 30(3); Supply Regulation 27(3); Services Regulation 29(3).
[62] Works Regulation 30(4); Supply Regulation 27(4); Services Regulation 29(4).

particular firms, provided that this does not involve deliberate discrimination in favour of domestic firms. It would be advisable, however, not to include in such a communication information additional to that sent to the *Official Journal*, nor to send it prior to the date of despatch of the *Official Journal* notice: although this is not expressly prohibited under the directives, the European Court might imply such a prohibition, drawing on the analogy of the rules on advertisements. Further, to contact firms at an earlier date would indicate a breach of the obligations to send the contract notice to the *Official Journal* as soon as the authority has formed an intention to seek offers.

Notices must be in a form "substantially corresponding" to the models set out in Schedules to the Regulations, and must contain all the information specified in the models.[63] These model notices are set out on pages 197–202. As with other notices, they may not contain more than 650 words.[64]

The model notices omit some of the information which the regulations require to be included and obviously this information must be inserted along with that in the model. Thus, the notices relating to works and services omit provision for a statement justifying any derogation from available European specifications, which is required under the regulations,[65] and the notice for services does not include provision for stating the deadline for receipt of tenders, although this is a requirement under Services Regulation 11(3). Further, whilst the models indicate that the detailed award criteria should be stated in the notices where they do not appear in the contract documents, they do not indicate that these should be listed where possible in order of priority, as is required by other provisions of the regulations.[66]

There are some anomalous differences between the models. Thus the works and supplies notices contain requirements for authorities to state an address for submission of tenders, the language for tenders, the type of award procedure to be followed and a reference to any previous PIN (or reason for non-publication of a PIN), which are not found in the services notice; whilst the supply and services notices require statement of a final date for any request for documents which are not found in the works notice.

With regard to the description of the subject matter of the contract, the model notice for supplies requires reference to the CPA nomen-

---

[63] Works Regulation 11(2); Supply Regulation 11(2); Services Regulation 11(2). The model notices are found in Part B of Schedule 2 of the Works Regulations, Part B of Schedule 3 of the Supply Regulations and Part B of Schedule 2 of the Services Regulations. All the specified information must be included and is not optional: case C–359/93, *Commission v. Netherlands*, judgment of January 24, 1995, para. 20.

[64] Supply Regulation 27(2) and Services Regulation 29(2). Article 9(11) of the Supply Directive and Article 17(8) of the Services Directive which these provisions implement differ slightly, providing that the notice must not exceed one page of the *Official Journal*, of *approximately* 650 words.

[65] On this see pp. 65–67. The model Supply Regulation notice does refer to this.

[66] See p. 239.

PUBLIC WORKS CONTRACTS REGULATIONS 1991, SCHEDULE 2, PART B – FORM OF OPEN PROCEDURE NOTICE

1. The name, address, telephone number, telegraphic address, telex and facsimile numbers of the contracting authority.

2. (a) the award procedure chosen.
   (b) Nature of the contract for which tenders are being requested.

3. (a) The site.
   (b) The nature and extent of the services to be provided and general nature of the work.
   (c) If the work or the contract is subdivided into several lots, the size of the different lots and the possibility of tendering for one, for several or for all of the lots.
   (d) Information concerning the purpose of the work or the contract where the latter also involves the drawing up of projects.

4. Any time-limit for completion.

5. (a) Name and address of the service from which the contract documents and additional documents may be requested.
   (b) Where applicable, the amount and terms of payment of the sum to be paid to obtain such documents.

6. (a) The final date for receipt of tenders.
   (b) The address to which they must be sent.
   (c) The language or languages in which they must be drawn up.

7. (a) Where applicable, the persons authorised to be present at the opening of tenders.
   (b) The date, hour and place of such opening.

8. Any deposit and guarantees required.

9. Main terms concerning financing and payment and/or references to the provisions in which these are contained.

10. Where applicable, the legal form to be taken by the grouping of contractors to whom the contract is awarded.

11. Minimum standards of economic and financial standing and technical capacity required of the contractor to whom the contract is awarded.

12. Period during which the tenderer is bound to keep open his tender.

13. The criteria for the award of the contract. Criteria other than that of the lowest price shall be mentioned where they do not appear in the contract documents.

14. Where applicable, prohibition on variants.

15. Other information.

16. Date of publication of the prior information notice in the *Official Journal of the European Communities* or references to its non-publication.

17. Date of despatch of the notice.

PUBLIC SUPPLY CONTRACTS REGULATIONS 1995, SCHEDULE 3, PART B – OPEN PROCEDURE NOTICE

1. Name, address, telegraphic address, telephone, telex and facsimile numbers of the contracting authority.

2. (a) Award procedure chosen;
   (b) form of contract for which offers are invited.

3. (a) Place of delivery;
   (b) nature and quantity of the goods to be supplied: CPA reference number;
   (c) indication of whether the suppliers can tender for some and/or all of the goods required;
   (d) derogation from use of European specifications.

4. Time-limit for delivery, if any.

5. (a) Name and address of the service from which the contract documents and additional documents may be requested;
   (b) final date for making such requests;
   (c) where applicable, the amount and terms of payment of any sum payable for such documents.

6. (a) Final date for receipt of tenders;
   (b) address to which they must be sent;
   (c) language(s) in which they must be drawn up.

7. (a) Person authorised to be present at the opening of tenders;
   (b) date, time and place of opening.

8. Where applicable, any deposits and guarantees required.

9. The main terms concerning financing and payment and/or references to the relevant provisions.

10. Where applicable, the legal form to be taken by a grouping of suppliers winning the contract.

11. The information and formalities necessary for an appraisal of the minimum standards of economic and financial standing and technical capacity required of the supplier.

12. Period during which the tenderer is bound to keep open his tender.

13. Criteria for the award of the contract. Criteria other than that of the lowest price shall be mentioned if they do not appear in the contract documents.

14. Where applicable, prohibition on variations.

15. Other information.

16. Date of publication of the prior information notice in the *Official Journal* or references to its non-publication.

17. Date of despatch of the notice.

PUBLIC SERVICES CONTRACTS REGULATIONS 1993, SCHEDULE 2, PART B – OPEN PROCEDURE NOTICE

1. Name, address and telephone, telegraphic, telex and facsimile numbers of the contracting authority.

2. Category of services and description. CPC reference number.

3. Place of delivery.

4. (a) Indication of whether the provision of the services is reserved by law, regulation or administrative provision to a particular profession;
   (b) Reference to the law, regulation or administrative provision;
   (c) Indication of whether legal persons should indicate the names and professional qualifications of the staff to be responsible for the provision of the services.

5. Indication of whether services providers can tender for some or all of the services required.

6. Where applicable, prohibition on variants.

7. Period of contract or time-limit, if any, for completion.

8. (a) Name and address of the service from which the contract and additional documents may be requested;
   (b) Final date for making such requests;
   (c) Where applicable, the amount and terms of payment of any sum payable for such documents.

9. (a) Where applicable, the persons authorised to be present at the opening of tenders;
   (b) Date, time and place of opening.

10. Any deposits and guarantees required.

11. The main terms concerning financing and payment and/or references to the relevant provisions.

12. Where applicable, the legal form to be taken by the grouping of services providers to whom the contract is awarded.

13. The information and formalities necessary for an appraisal of the minimum standards of economic and financial standing, ability and technical capacity required of the services provider.

14. Period during which the tenderer is bound to keep open his tender.

15. Criteria for the award of the contract. Criteria other than that of the lowest price shall be mentioned where they do not appear in the contract documents.

16. Other information.

17. Date of despatch of the notice.

---

clature and that for services to the CPC. (The model notice for works does not refer to any specific nomenclature.) It is expected that the Commission will shortly adopt a recommendation for use of the Common Procurement Vocabulary (CPV) in such notices.[67] It can be noted that the provisions on description of subject matter are not exhaustive: the Works Regulations require a description only of work(s), the Supply Regulations only of goods and the Services Regulations only of services, although – for example – a significant amount of services may sometimes be provided under supply contracts and so on.

(b) THE DESPATCH OF CONTRACT DOCUMENTS

Following the advertisement, interested parties will contact the authority to obtain the detailed documents which they will need in order to be

---

[67] On the CPV see pp. 69–70.

able to bid. To ensure firms can take advantage of the periods specified for them to prepare their tenders,[68] the regulations require the contract documents[69] to be sent within six days of receipt of a request.[70] A fee may be charged for the documents, which must be stated in the contract notice.[71] The obligation to supply the documents applies only where the request is accompanied by any relevant fee.[72]

Under the Supply Regulations and Services Regulations a time-limit for receipt of requests for documentation must be stated in the contract notice.[73] The Supply Regulations provide that the obligation to supply documents arises only where the request is received within this time.[74] The Services Regulations state that the request must be received "in good time",[75] which presumably also refers to the time stated in the contract notice. Under the Works Regulations the request must also be made "in good time".[76] In this case there is no requirement to specify a date for receipt in the contract notice, although presumably if one is specified a request made at a later date is not "in good time".

(c) OBLIGATION TO PROVIDE FURTHER INFORMATION

Authorities must provide any additional information relating to the contract documents which is requested by providers, where the request is reasonable, and it is made in time for the authority to supply the information no later than 6 days before the specified date for receipt of tenders.[77]

---

[68] As to which see pp. 204–205.

[69] The contract documents refer here to the contract conditions, the specifications or descriptions of the subject-matter of the contract and any supplementary documents: see the definition of "contract documents" in Works Regulation 2(1), Supply Regulation 2(1) and Services Regulation 2(1).

[70] Works Regulation 11(5); Supply Regulation 11(4); Services Regulation 11(5). The receipt itself is not counted in calculating this period: Works Regulation 2(3)(a); Supply Regulation 2(3)(a); Services Regulation 2(4)(a). If the day on which the period would expire is not a working day it must be extended to include the next working day: Works Regulation 2(3)(c); Supply Regulation 2(3)(c); Services Regulation 2(4)(c). Further, the period must include at least two working days: Works Regulation 2(3)(b); Supply Regulation 2(3)(b); Services Regulation 2(4)(b).

[71] See the model notices at pp. 197–202 above.

[72] Works Regulation 11(5); Supply Regulation 11(4); Services Regulation 11(5).

[73] See the model notices at pp. 197–202.

[74] Supply Regulation 11(4).

[75] Services Regulation 11(5).

[76] Works Regulation 11(5).

[77] Works Regulation 11(6); Supply Regulation 11(5); Services Regulation 11(6). The day of despatch is not counted and the period must include at least two working days: Works Regulation 2(3)(a); Supply Regulation 2(3)(a); Services Regulation 2(4)(a). When the period ends on a day which is not a working day it must be extended to include the next working day: Works Regulation 2(3)(c); Supply Regulation 2(3)(c); Works Regulation 2(4)(c).

(d) TIME-LIMIT FOR RECEIPT OF TENDERS

It will take interested firms some time to obtain the documents and to prepare a tender, and this time period is likely to be longer for non-domestic firms – for example, there may be a need to obtain translations of documents. The regulations prescribe a minimum time period for submission of tenders, to prevent authorities from setting a short period which would constitute an unreasonable barrier to participation by non-domestic firms. In general, the last date for receipt of tenders must be not less than 52 days from the date of despatch of the contract notice.[78]

A longer period must be allowed when (i) the contract documents and related documents are too bulky to be supplied within the usual time; (ii) providers need to be given the opportunity to inspect the site; or (iii) providers need to be given the opportunity to inspect documents which are related to the contract documents but do not form part of them. In these cases the minimum period must be extended to allow for the supply or inspection in question.[79] This will require an adequate opportunity for the supply or inspection in the context of the particular procurement.

There is also provision for a reduction of the above periods under the Works Regulations and Services Regulations when the authority has already published a Prior Information Notice (PIN),[80] which relates to the contract in question. In this case the 52-day period may be reduced to 36 days (extended as necessary for supply of bulky documents and inspections, in accordance with the provisions just outlined).[81] There is currently no equivalent provision in the Supply Regulations, but the Commission has proposed inclusion of such a provision, as explained further below.

In relation to these reduced periods, the WTO Agreement on Government Procurement (GPA), in force from January 1, 1996, imposes more stringent requirements. First, advance notice allows reduction of the period from a standard 40 days under the GPA to a lesser period only when the advance notice is published no more than 12 months, and at least 40 days, before the notice advertising the specific contract.[82] In addition, to be relied on for reducing the time limits the PIN must contain certain additional information on the specific contract which is not normally required in a PIN. The Commission's Proposal for aligning the Community regime with that under the GPA[83] includes a provision requiring the advance notice to be published within the same

---

[78] Works Regulation 11(3); Supply Regulation 11(3); Services Regulation 11(3). The time periods are calculated as stated in note 77.
[79] Works Regulation 11(3); Supply Regulation 11(6); Services Regulation 11(7).
[80] On PINs see pp. 182–192.
[81] The same rules apply in calculating this period as set out in note 00: Works Regulation 2(3); Services Regulation 2(4).
[82] GPA Article XI(3).
[83] On this Proposal see generally pp. 61–63.

time limits and to contain the relevant addition information if it is to be relied up to reduce the time limits for tendering under the Community regime.[84] This ensures that the PIN gives providers a reasonable opportunity to prepare for the procurement after reading the PIN. The present rule is open to abuse, since under the literal wording of the directives authorities may publish a PIN just before the contract notice – although it is likely that the Court of Justice would in fact imply an obligation to publish the PIN a reasonable time before the contract notice if that PIN is to be relied upon to reduce the time for tenders. If this suggested amendment is adopted, the regulations will need to be amended to reflect this. Regardless of any amendment, however, the more stringent obligation under the GPA will need to be adhered as from January 1, 1996.[85]

The Commission's proposal also provides for the possibility of providers to rely on publication of a PIN to reduce the time limits for submission of tenders under the Supply Directive.[86] Such a possibility was omitted previously from the Supply Directive because the old GATT Agreement did not allow for that possibility; but it is now permitted under the new GPA.

(e) PROPOSALS ON THE FORM OF TENDERS

The Commission's Proposal for aligning the Community directives with the GPA includes certain proposals concerning the form of tenders. These are discussed below.[86a]

(3) OBTAINING TENDERS: RESTRICTED PROCEDURES

The steps required to be followed to obtain tenders under the restricted procedure are set out in Works Regulation 12, Supply Regulation 12 and Services Regulation 12.

---

[84] Proposal for a European Parliament and Council Directive amending Directive 92/50/EEC relating to the co-ordination of procedures for the award of public service contracts, Directive 93/36/EEC co-ordinating procedures for the award of public supply contracts, and Directive 93/37/EEC concerning the co-ordination of procedures for the award of public works contracts, COM (95) 107 Final, Articles 3(4) and 1(6). It may be noted that the relevant date, as under the GPA, is to be the date of publication of the notice, instead of the date of despatch which is usually the relevant date for time limits under the directives. The relevant additional information is such of the information listed in the open procedure model notice as is available at the time the advance notice was published.

[85] These will need to be adhered to both by GPA providers, under the GPA, and Community providers: see p. 181.

[86] Commission Proposal, above, Article 2(4). The conditions and effect of its use will be the same as are to apply under the Services Directive (as that directive will apply when amended by the new Proposal).

[86a] See pp. 226–227.

(a) ADVERTISEMENT OF THE CONTRACT

As with the open procedure, authorities must send a notice (the "contract notice")[86b] to the Office for Official Publications of the European Communities.[87] That office must normally publish the notice within 12 days of its dispatch, in full in the original language in the *Official Journal* and Tenders Electronic Daily data bank, and in summary form in the other official Community languages.[88] Where the authority proposes to use the special "accelerated" version of the restricted procedure which is available in cases of urgency,[89] the usual 12 days for publication is reduced to 5 days.

As with open procedures the notice must be sent as soon as possible following the decision to seek offers,[90] and by the "most appropriate means".[91] In the case of use of the special accelarated procedure referred to above, it is expressly provided that the notice must be sent by telex, telegraph or facsimile.[92] In all cases, evidence must be retained by the authority to prove the date of despatch.[93]

As with open procedures, publicity for the contract in the national press is not permitted until the date of despatch of the *Official Journal* notice, and national notices may not contain more information than is found in that notice.[94] Provided these rules are complied with, however, notices may be published elsewhere in addition. It also appears acceptable to inform specific firms about the contract, provided this is not done at an earlier time nor additional information provided.[95]

The notice must be in "substantially" the same form as model notices which are set out in Schedules to the regulations, and must contain all the information in those model notices.[96] These models are set out at pages 208–213. As with other notices, they may not contain more than 650 words.[97]

Like the model notices for open procedures, the restricted procedure models do not contain all the information required to be published, and

---

[86b] See the definition of "contract notice" in Works Regulation 2(1), Supply Regulation 2(1) and Services Regulation 2(1).
[87] Works Regulation 12(2); Supply Regulation 12(2); Services Regulation 12(2).
[88] Works Directive, Article 11(10); Supply Directive, Article 9(8); Services Directive 17(3).
[89] On this accelerated procedure see p. 214.
[90] Works Regulation 12(2); Supply Regulation 12(2); Services Regulation 12(2).
[91] Works Regulation 30(1); Supply Regulation 27(1); Services Regulation 29(1).
[92] *Ibid.*
[93] Works Regulation 30(3); Supply Regulation 27(3); Services Regulation 29(3).
[94] Works Regulation 30(4); Supply Regulation 27(4); Services Regulation 29(4).
[95] On this see pp. 195–196.
[96] Works Regulation 12(2); Supply Regulation 12(2); Services Regulation 12(2). The models are found in Part C of Schedule 2 to the Works Regulations; Part C of Schedule 3 to the Supply Regulations; and Part C of Schedule 2 to the Services Regulations.
[97] Supply Regulation 27(2) and Services Regulation 29(2). Article 9(11) of the Supply Directive and Article 17(8) of the Services Directive which these provisions implement differ slightly, providing that the notice must not exceed one page of the *Official Journal*, of *approximately* 650 words.

this information needs to be added to the list in the model. Thus, only the supplies model contains provision for reasons for derogating from the obligation to use European specifications, although reference is required to such derogations in relation to works and services contracts also,[98] whilst none of the models makes reference to the necessity for listing award criteria in order of preference where this is not done in the contract documents.[99] As with the open procedure model notices there are also anomalies (although affecting only minor requirements), notably that the services notice unlike the others makes no provision for stating the award procedure to be used, or for reference to any previous PIN notice (or reason for non-publication of a PIN). There is also an anomaly, again found also in the open procedure notices, that the obligation to describe the subject matter of the contract in the notice is not comprehensive, applying with supply contracts to products supplied only, with services contracts to services only, and with works contracts to work(s) only: the obligation does not extend, for example, to services provided under supply contracts together with the products, nor services provided under works contracts.

---

[98] See pp. 590–596.
[99] On this requirement see p. 239.

PUBLIC WORKS CONTRACTS REGULATIONS 1991, SCHEDULE 2, PART C – RESTRICTED PROCEDURE NOTICE

1. The name, address, telephone number, telex and facsimile numbers of the contracting authority.

2. (a) the award procedure chosen.
   (b) Where applicable, justification for the use of the shorter time-limits.
   (c) Nature of the contract which tenders are being requested.

3. (a) The site.
   (b) The nature and extent of the services to be provided and general nature of the work.
   (c) If the work of the contract is subdivided into several lots, the size of the different lots and the possibility of tendering for one, for several or for all of the lots.
   (d) Information concerning the purpose of the work or the contract where the latter also involves the drawing up of projects.

4. Any time-limit for completion.

5. Where applicable, the legal form to be taken by the grouping of contractors to whom the contract is awarded.

6. (a) The final date for receipt of requests to participate.
   (b) The address to which they must be sent.
   (c) The language or languages in which they must be drawn up.

7. The final date for despatch of invitations to tender.

8. Any deposit and guarantees required.

9. Main terms concerning, financing and payment and/or provisions in which these are contained.

10. Information concerning the contractor's personal position and minimum standards of economic and financial standing and technical capacity required of the contractor to whom the contract is awarded.

11. The criteria for the award of the contract where they are not mentioned in the invitation to tender.

12. Where applicable, prohibition on variants.

13. Other information.

14. Date of publication of the prior information notice in the *Official Journal of the European Communities* or reference to its non-publication.

15. Date of despatch of the notice.

PUBLIC SUPPLY CONTRACTS REGULATIONS 1995, SCHEDULE 3, PART C – RESTRICTED PROCEDURE NOTICE

1. Name, address, telegraphic address, telephone, telex and facsimile numbers of the contracting authority.

2. (a) Award procedure chosen;
   (b) where applicable, justification for use of the shorter time-limits;
   (c) form of contract for which offers are invited.

3. (a) Place of delivery.
   (b) nature and quantity of goods to be delivered: CPA reference number;
   (c) indication of whether the supplier can tender for some and/or all of the goods required;
   (d) derogation from the use of European specifications.

4. Time-limit on delivery, if any.

5. Where applicable, the legal form to be assumed by a grouping of suppliers winning the contract.

6. (a) Final date for the receipt of requests to participate;
   (b) address to which they must be sent;
   (c) language(s) in which they must be drawn up.

7. Final date for the dispatch of invitations to tender.

8. Any deposits and guarantees required.

9. Information concerning the supplier's own position, and the information and formalities necessary for an appraisal of the minimum standards of economic and financial standing and technical capacity required of him.

10. Criteria for the award of the contract if these are not stated in the invitation to tender.

11. If known, the number or range of numbers of suppliers which will be invited to tender.

12. Where applicable, prohibition on variations.

13. Other information.

14. Date of publication of the prior information notice in the *Official Journal* or references to its non-publication.

15. Date of despatch of the notice.

PUBLIC SERVICES CONTRACTS REGULATIONS 1993, SCHEDULE 2, PART C – RESTRICTED PROCEDURE NOTICE

1. Name, address and telephone, telegraphic, telex and facsimile numbers of the contracting authority.

2. Category of services and description. CPC reference number.

3. Place of delivery.

4. (a) Indication of whether the provision of the services is reserved by law, regulation or administrative provision to a particular profession;
   (b) Reference to the law, regulation or administrative position;
   (c) Indication whether legal persons should indicate the names and professional qualifications of the staff to be responsible for the provision of the services.

5. Indication of whether the services provider can tender for all or part of the services required.

6. If known, the number of services providers which will be invited to tender or the range within which that number is expected to fall.

7. Where applicable, prohibition on variants.

8. Period of contract or time-limit, if any, for completion of the services.

9. Where applicable, the legal form to be assumed by the grouping of services providers to whom the contract is awarded.

10. (a) Where applicable, justification for the use of shorter time-limits;
    (b) Final date for the receipt of requests to participate;
    (c) Address to which they must be sent;
    (d) Language(s) in which they must be drawn up.

11. Final date for the despatch of invitations to tender.

12. Any deposits and guarantees required.

13. The information and formalities necessary for an appraisal of the minimum standards of economic and financial standing, ability and technical capacity required of the services provider.

14. Criteria for the award of the contract. Criteria other than that of lowest price shall be mentioned where these do not appear in the contract documents.

15. Other information.

16. Date of despatch of the notice.

In the description of the subject matter, the model notice for supplies requires reference to the CPA nomenclature and the model notice for services to the CPC. (The model notice for works does not refer to any specific nomenclature.) It is likely that the Commission will shortly adopt a recommendation for use of the Common Procurement Vocabulary (CPV) in such notices.[1]

(b) THE SUBMISSION OF REQUESTS TO BE INVITED TO TENDER

The purpose of the contract notice under the restricted procedure is not to solicit bids directly, but to obtain information about firms who may be interested in bidding, from which the authority may select a limited

---

[1] On this see pp. 69–70.

number to bid. Thus, following the notice, the next step is for interested firms to contract the authority, to request that they may be invited to bid on the contract.

As under open procedures, non-domestic enterprises may need more time to prepare their response, and a minimum time is provided for making a request, to ensure that non-domestic firms are not unreasonably excluded. As a general rule authorities must allow a period of 37 days[2] from despatch of the contract notice.[3]

There is a special accelerated form of the restricted procedure when compliance with the usual time-limits is "rendered impracticable for reasons of urgency". In this case the 37-day period may be replaced by a period of not less than 15 days.[4] Where this procedure applies the time-limits for submission of tenders following the invitation is also reduced.[5] Reasons for using the accelerated procedure must be set out in the contract notice, as is provided in the model notices. In cases, of extreme urgency, where even this accelerated restricted procedure involves undue delay, an authority may sometimes, instead, use the negotiated procedure without advertisement.[6]

As regards the form of requests, it is expressly provided that a request shall not be refused on the grounds that it is made by letter; nor because it is made by telegram, telex, facsimile or telephone, provided in these cases that it is confirmed by letter prior to the closing date for receipt of tender.[7] Apart from this, there are no express provisions relating to the form of requests. It is submitted that an authority may specify in the contract notice the form of the request (for example, the language to be used in requests), and may reject requests which do not meet these formalities. It should be able to waive these should it choose to do so, since they are specified for the benefit of the authority, provided, however, that all persons making requests are treated equally[8]

In relation to the content of requests, there is no reason why authorities should not provide in the contract notice that firms making a request must provide certain information which is relevant to selecting those to be invited to bid (for example, information on their financial standing). However, it can be implied from the regulations that information sought must be limited to that which may lawfully be taken into

---

[2] Works Regulation 12(3); Supply Regulation 12(3); Services Regulation 12(3).

[3] This is calculated to exclude the day of despatch: Works Regulation 2(3)(a); Supply Regulation 2(3)(a); Services Regulation 2(4)(a). Where the period ends on a day which is not a working day it is extended to include the next working day: Works Regulation 2(3)(c); Supply Regulation 2(3)(c); Services Regulation 2(4)(c).

[4] Again, this is calculated from the day of despatch of the notice, and where it ends on a non-working day is extended to the next working day: Works Regulations 2(3); Supply Regulation 2(3); Services Regulation 2(4).

[5] See pp. 204–205.

[6] See further pp. 260–262.

[7] Works Regulation 12(16); Supply Regulation 12(15); Services Regulation 12(16).

[8] This arises from the fundamental principle of the equality of treatment of providers, laid down in case C–243/89, *Commission v. Denmark* judgment of June 22 1993.

account in selecting those who are to be invited to tender.[9] In practice, authorities will often seek this information after requests to be invited to tender have been received, rather than requiring firms to provide the information along with the request.

It is not clear whether requests to tender may be excluded from consideration for failure to meet formalities (such as language requirements) where these have not been stated in the contract notice. Arguably it is to be implied that firms may not be rejected in such a case, in view of the rules' underlying purpose of eliminating unstructured discretion which might be abused. It could at least be implied that firms should be permitted to alter their requests to comply where the formalities have not been stated in advance.[10]

(c) SELECTING PROVIDERS TO BE INVITED TO TENDER

Once applications to be invited to tender have been received, the authority must decide which of the enterprises responding is to be invited to bid.

(i) THE GROUP FROM WHICH SELECTION MAY BE MADE

There is nothing in the directives or regulations to prevent an authority from considering for an invitation to tender providers of whom it is aware by reason other than their response to the contract notice (for example, those with which it has had previous deadling). However, if such providers are to be included in the group from amongst which invitees to tender are to be drawn, it would be advisable to ask these providers to confirm their interest before issuing an invitation to tender. If this is not done, then such firms probably may not be included in calculating whether a sufficient number of firms have been invited to tender in accordance with the rules in (ii) below: this must probably be assessed by reference to firms who have expressed an interest in the specific contract and are, therefore, reasonably likely to bid. Further, if such firms are not required to confirm their interest it may be argued that they are being treated more favourably than those firms which rely on the contract notice, in breach of the principle of equality of treatment. (Of course, it is clearly a breach of this principle to give

---

[9] On this see pp. 215–222.

[10] It is not clear how this principle would operate in relation to method of transmission, on which there are express provisions noted above. One view is that these merely limit the authority's discretion to reject on certain grounds, but do not affect any obligation to state these grounds in the contract notice if they are to be relied on; but another might be that they *confer* a discretion to reject certain forms of request where not confirmed by letter, even where the requirement for a letter is not stated in the contract notice.

known firms preference in deciding which firms should be issued with invitations.)

(ii) THE NUMBER OF INVITATIONS

The number of firms invited to bid must in all cases be "sufficient to ensure genuine competition".[11] Subject to this principle, the number will be set by balancing the advantages of more bidders in terms of greater competition, against the disadvantages, such as costs of assessment and preparation. Factors such as the likelihood of invitees actually choosing to bid will be relevant in making the decision. The regulations expressly state that the range for the number of invitees may be set in advance, provided that this range is specified in the contract notice.[12] In this case, the number must be between five and 20, and must be set in the light of the nature of the contract.[13] Where the number is not stated in advance there are no such limitations. Probably a minimum of three must be invited for adequate competition in complex procurements – perhaps more in procurements which are more straightforward.

In some cases the number of firms requesting invitations might not meet the number stated in the contract notice and might not be sufficient for adequate competition even if all qualified providers are invited. In this case, it is probably not necessary to open a new restricted or open procedure, however. This can be implied from the fact that where no tenders are received at all the authority may use the negotiated procedure without advertisement[14]; thus where at least two firms express an interest, but the number is insufficient for adequate competition under a restricted procedure, it also seems appropriate to allow the authority to go ahead with the existing procedure without the need to recommence a new one. Probably the authority must continue with the restricted procedure when at least two providers reply and may not resort to negotiation (although it could make contact with other known providers to increase the number of interested firms). However, if only one provider replies to continue with formal tendering would be pointless unless other interested providers are found, and arguably in this case the authority could negotiate with the single provider, even though the express provisions of the regulations permit use of the negotiated procedure only where there are no responses. On the other hand, where there are sufficient for adequate competition but less than the number stated in the notice, the best solution is to permit the authority to go ahead with the existing restricted procedure in the normal way – there is no reason to use negotiation where the restricted procedure can still proceed on a reasonable basis.

---

[11] Works Regulation 12(7); Supply Regulation 12(7); Services Regulation 12(7).
[12] Works Regulation 12(6); Supply Regulation 12(6); Services Regulation 12(6).
[13] *Ibid.*
[14] See pp. 250–251.

(iii) THE METHODS FOR SELECTING INVITEES ("SHORTLISTING")[15]

Sometimes the number of firms requesting to be invited to tender is greater than the number which it is appropriate to invite. There are a number of methods a purchaser may wish to use in practice to draw up a "shortlist" of those to invite.

(a) **Financial and technical position.** Purchasers will wish to ensure that a firm's technical capability and financial position are adequate for it to complete the contract. Frequently, this is checked before invitations are issued and firms not meeting minimum standards are eliminated from the list of potential invitees.

Where more firms meet the minimum acceptable levels than are to be invited to bid authorities may wish to use *relative* financial and technical standing to select potential bidders, to reduce the risk of non-completion as far as possible.

(b) **External factors affecting completion.** An authority may also wish to take account of factors external to the provider which might affect completion, such as strikes or political unrest.

(c) **The contract award criteria.** Purchasers also sometimes shortlist by assessing which providers are likely to submit the best tender by reference to the award criteria. For example, if price is the only factor (that is, the "lowest price" criterion is used), the authority may assess which firms are most likely to offer the best price – for example, by considering previous bids for similar work or the firm's list price. If the criterion is the "most economically advantageous tender" and, for example, quality is relevant, it may wish to look at the quality of the provider's products or services.[16] This can be particularly important for services where quality is a key factor and the quality offered by different providers may vary significantly – the outcome is likely to be much more satisfactory if the "best" providers can be selected to submit bids.

(d) **Other factors relating to purchasing efficiency.** A purchaser may also wish to consider factors relating to the efficiency of its purchasing arrangements which do not, however, concern the subject-matter of the immediate contract. For example, it may wish to give priority to certain firms with the objective of building up a long-term co-operative relationship with those firms ("partnering"); this may bring long-term savings by, for example, more amicable dispute resolution.[17]

---

[15] See further the notes by Arrowsmith (1993) 2 P.P.L.R. CS92 and (1992) 1 P.P.L.R. 408; and Boyle, "EC Public Procurement Rules – a Purchaser Reflects on the Need for Simplification" (1994) 3 P.P.L.R. 101.

[16] This may involve the same issues as *relative* technical capacity: for example, one aspect of technical capacity is the firm's ability to meet the quality standards in the specifications, whilst the quality of different bidders' products or services is also often a factor to be evaluated at the award stage.

[17] On partnering see further pp. 290–295.

(e) Secondary factors. Purchasers may also consider factors which do not relate to their own purchasing at all ("secondary" factors): for example, the promotion of gender or racial equality. As with financial and technical matters, standards relating to secondary issues can be laid down merely as minimum requirements – where, for example, all firms with an adequate equal opportunities policy are considered equally; or (alternatively, or additionally) firms' relative standing on these matters may be assessed – for example, by priority being given to those with the best equal opportunities policies.

(f) Random selection. Purchasers also often seek to produce a short list by random selection – for example, drawing names from a box.

(g) Rotation. Finally, another possibility is a "rotation" system whereby preference is given to providers who have not previously had opportunities to bid.

Unfortunately, the directive, and the implementing regulations, are not clear as to which of these criteria may be used. The relevant provisions state as follows:

"The contracting authority may exclude [a provider] from those persons from whom it will make the selection of persons to be invited to tender only if [the provider] may be treated as ineligible on a ground specified in regulation 14 or if [the provider] fails to satisfy the minimum standards of economic and financial standing and technical capacity required of [providers] by the contracting authority; for this purpose the contracting authority shall make its evaluation in accordance with regulations 14, 15, 16 and 17". (Works Regulation 12(4)[18]; Supply Regulation 12(4); Services Regulation 12(4)[19]

"The contracting authority shall make the selection of [providers] to be invited to tender in accordance with regulations 14, 15, 16 and 17; and in making the selection and in issuing invitations the contracting authority shall not discriminate between [providers] on the grounds of their nationality or state of establishment". (Works Regulation 12(5); Supply Regulation 12(5); Services Regulation 12(5).)

Regulations 15, 16 and 17 are the provisions which govern the way in which qualification on, *inter alia*, financial and technical grounds, is to be carried out.[20]

---

[18] As amended by the Utilities Supply and Works Contracts Regulations 1992, regulation 32(1)(c).

[19] In addition, the services provision includes a reference to "ability" after technical capacity: on this see further p. 312.

[20] The exact scope of these provisions and the procedures for qualification are considered in Chap. 8.

These provisions make it clear that authorities may eliminate at this early stage firms whose lack of financial status or technical resources indicate an unacceptable risk of non-completion.[21] It may, in fact, be *necessary* to consider these matters before inviting firms to tender, since under the restricted procedure the regulations do not appear to allow the introduction of tests for financial and technical qualification at a later stage.[22] They also make it clear that firms may be eliminated for failing to meet criteria referred to in Works Regulation 14, Supply Regulation 14 and Services Regulation 14 (hereafter "the regulation 14 criteria").[23] These regulations list a variety of grounds on which firms may be excluded from award procedures: they include bankruptcy or winding-up; grave professional misconduct; conviction of an offence relating to the business; non-payment of social security and tax contributions; and misrepresentation in supplying information.[24] Some of these relate to the likelihood of performance (for example, the existence of a winding-up order), and others to "secondary factors" (for example, the tax and social security provisions).

One view is that these express criteria of economic and financial standing, technical capacity and the regulation 14 criteria are the *only* relevant criteria, a view supported by the Court of Justice decision in case C–360/89, *Commission v. Italy*.[25] This case concerned an Italian law providing that where more than 15 providers sought to be invited to tender for a works contract at least fifteen were to be invited, and that in choosing invitees preference should be given to joint ventures and consortia involving firms whose main activities were in the region of the works. The Commission challenged this as an unlawful criterion under the Works Directive.[26] The directive states that selection must be based on information relating to either financial or technical status or the provider's "personal position".[27] The Court of Justice held that this requires the authority to make its choice only on economic and financial

---

[21] In case C362/92, *Commission v. Italy* [1993] E.C.R. I–000, Advocate General Lenz seemed to suggest that the directives do not permit providers to be rejected for non-compliance with substantive financial and technical criteria at the invitation stage but only once bids are submitted. This seems clearly wrong. The wording of the directives does not indicate this result and it would be most inconvenient, since it is desirable for unqualified firms to be eliminated from the procedure at the earliest possible stage. (See the note by Arrowsmith and Fernández Martín, (1993) 2 P.P.L.R. CS2.) Thus it is submitted that the regulations interpret the directive correctly.

[22] See further pp. 229–231.

[23] Works Regulation 12(4) (as amended by the Utilities Supply and Works Contracts Regulations 1992 No. 3279, regulation 32(1)(c)); Supply Regulation 12(4); Services Regulation 12(4).

[24] For a full discussion see pp. 331–340.

[25] Case C–360/89, *Commission v Italy*, judgment of July 3, 1992; noted by Arrowsmith in (1992) 1 P.P.L.R. 412.

[26] The provision was also held to constitute a breach of the E.C. Treaty.

[27] The provisions in question were those of the 1971 Works Directive, Articles 17 and 22. The current directives differ only very slightly in wording and no alterations from the previous position appears to have been intended: see now Works Directive Article 22(1), Supply Directive Article 19(1) and Services Directive 27(1).

grounds or on the basis of the "regulation 14 criteria" ("personal position" presumably referring to the provider's position under these criteria). Thus other considerations – such as approximation to the award criteria ((c) in the list above), and social policies (except where covered by regulations 14–16)[28] – appear to be excluded. The regulations were interpreted in conformity with this view in *General Building and Maintenance v. Greenwich Borough Council*,[29] holding that a firms' health and safety record can be taken into account in shortlisting only to the extent that this affects technical capacity.[30]

Neither case considered whether it is permitted to consider providers' *relative* financial or technical status as a way of reducing numbers where more than the desired number of providers meet the original minimum requirements on these matters. This seems to be contemplated by the regulations, however, which, in regulation 12(5) envisage a separate stage of selection in accordance with these criteria, once firms which fail to meet minimum standards have been eliminated under regulation 12(4); and this approach is certainly consistent with the wording of the directives. If this is permitted, it is submitted that it applies only to the extent that the relative status bears some relationship to the likelihood of the firm's successfully completing the particular contract: firms whose status is such that there is no risk of default should not be excluded. To do this would be entirely arbitrary, and, moreover, would conflict with the Community's policy of encouraging the participation of small and medium – sized enterprises in public contracts, by favouring large firms.[31]

Even if the decisions in case C–360/89 and *Greenwich* are correct in principle, in limiting substantive selection criteria to those in regulations 14–16, it is arguable that these decisions do not necessarily rule out the use of random methods of reducing the shortlist – that is, methods which are not based on a positive "selection" process – such as drawing of lots or a rotation system. If such methods are not permitted, then where there are an excessive number of firms who exceed the financial and technical requirements originally stipulated there is no way to reduce the number further.

An alternative view might be that these cases are wrong in their reasoning. One possibility is that there are no limits to the factors which may be taken into account, provided that these comply with other Community rules such as those in the Community Treaties. Another is that it is permitted, at least, to consider the matters in regulations 14–16 *plus* how firms are likely to perform by reference to the award criteria

---

[28] On this see Chap. 16.

[29] [1993] I.R.L.R. 535. Case 360/89 was not, however, referred to.

[30] On this point see further pp. 315–316 and Chap. 16.

[31] To allow consideration of such factors to exclude firms which are clearly able to meet the minimum requirements enables authorities to consider by the back door which firms best satisfy the award criteria. For example, where quality of personnel is an award criterion, to allow consideration of relative technical capacity appears to permit consideration of the issue of relative quality of personnel.

(This would mean that case C360/89 is correct on its facts in excluding secondary policies, although not on its reasoning.) This is consistent with the wording of the directives and regulations.[32] It is difficult to see that the additional discretion which this would give would present greater opportunities for discrimination than are afforded, by, for example, the discretion to assess financial and technical status, whilst the application of such criteria would be very useful for purchasers. Community legislation to clarify these important issues is urgently required.

Whatever the correct principle, regulation 12(5) of each set of regulations provides, as stated above, that selection must be made without discriminating on grounds of nationality or the state of establishment.[33] This applies in relation to firms which are nationals of, and established in, the European Community or the European Economic Area, as well as to firms from certain other states with which the Community has concluded international agreements giving access to procurement.[34] Thus, for example, authorities may not limit the shortlist to United Kingdom firms, or to firms from a particular disadvantaged region of the United Kingdom, since this would involve discrimination against firms from other states. For contracting authorities such discrimination is, in any case, forbidden under the general principles of the Community Treaties,[35] or – in relation to firms from certain states outside the Community – under the relevant international agreements.[36]

There is no requirement for authorities to indicate in advance – for example, in the contract notice – which criteria are to be used for shortlisting. Such a requirement would be useful, both to reduce the possibilities for abuse, and because firms may find such information useful in deciding whether to respond to the contract notice.

In assessing compliance with some of the relevant criteria (for example, financial or technical status), authorities will need to obtain information about potential bidders. The contract notice could require this to be sent with the request to be invited to tender, but in practice such information is often solicited at a later time.

---

[32] It is a possible interpretation of Works Regulation 12(5), Supply Regulation 12(5) and Services Regulation 12(5): the requirement to make the selection in accordance with regulations 14, 15, 16 and 17 might simply mean that where the authority chooses to use relative standing in relation to criteria referred to in these provisions, the limitations set out in these provisions (for example, on the evidence which may be used) must be adhered to.

[33] Works Regulation 12(5); Supply Regulation 12(5); Services Regulation 12(5).

[34] See the definition of "relevant state" in Works Regulation 2(1), as am. by Supply Regulation 31(1) and Utilities Regulation 35(1), and Works Regulation 4(1), as am. by Utilities Regulation 35(1); Supply Regulation 2(1) and 4(1), as am. by Utilities Regulation 35(1); Services Regulation 2(1), as am. by Supply Regulation 32(1) and Utilities Regulation 35(1) and Services Regulation 4(1), as am. by Utilities Regulation 35(1); Utilities Regulation 2(1) and 4(2).

[35] See generally Chap. 4. The inclusion of this provision in the regulations ensures that a remedy is available to enforce this principle against private bodies which are required to follow the award procedures in the regulations but are not subject to the Treaty.

[36] See further Chap. 15.

(d) SENDING THE INVITATIONS TO TENDER

Invitations must be sent to each of the firms selected to bid[37] and must be in writing.[38] Where the special accelarated version of the restricted procedure is used, the invitations must be sent by "the most rapid means possible".[39] It is not clear whether this refers to the most rapid *written* means, or constitutes a waiver of the usual requirement for writing. In view of the importance of certainty and transparency it is suggested that writing is required: this might include telex, facsimile, telegraph, and, possibly, electronic means.

Invitations must be issued simultaneously to all those selected,[40] to ensure no provider selected is unfairly disadvantaged. Although the requirement is designed for their benefit, providers should not be permitted to waive it: this might lead to abuse, with authorities sending invitations earlier to favoured firms, and leaving others with a choice of accepting a late invitation or receiving none at all.

Works Regulation 12(5), Supply Regulation 12(5) and Services Regulation 12(5), which as explained above prohibit discrimination against firms from relevant states[41] in selecting invitees, also prohibit discrimination in the way invitations to bid are issued. As with selecting bidders, such discrimination is in any case forbidden under the Community Treaties or under agreements with the relevant third countries.[42]

The following information must be included in invitations to tender:[43]
(i) The address to which providers should send requests for the contract documents[44] (that is, the contract conditions, specifications and descriptions of the subject-matter, and any supplementary documents[45]). The final date for making such a request must also be given, as well as the amount and terms of any fee payable for the documents. This obligation applies only if these documents have not already been sent with the invitation to tender. The same information must also be given in respect of any further information relating to the contract documents.
(ii) The final date for receipt of tenders; the address to which they must be sent; and the language(s) in which they must be drawn up.
(iii) A reference to the contract notice advertising the restricted procedure.
(iv) An indication of the information requested by the authority under regulations 15, 16 and 17 of the relevant regulation which is to be sent

---

[37] Works Regulation 12(8); Supply Regulation 12(8); Services Regulation 12(8).
[38] Works Regulation 12(9); Supply Regulation 12(9); Services Regulation 12(9).
[39] Works Regulation 12(14); Supply Regulation 12(14); Services Regulation 12(15).
[40] Works Regulation 12(9); Supply Regulation 12(9); Services Regulation 12(9).
[41] On the meaning of "relevant states" see p. 785.
[42] See further Chap. 16.
[43] Works Regulation 12(10); Supply Regulation 12(10); Services Regulation 12(10).
[44] This is stated in regulation 12(8) of each regulation as well as in the list of information in regulation 12(10).
[45] Works Regulation 2(1); Supply Regulation 2(1); Services Regulation 2(1).

with the tender. This refers to the information required of the bidder to verify his financial and economic standing and technical capacity (and, with services, ability).[46] It is illogical that there is no similar requirement to indicate the information sought in relation to an assessment under regulation 14.

(v) The criteria for the award of the contract.[47] The authority may, however, have opted to give this information in the contract notice itself, in which case it is not necessary to provide such information in the invitation to tender.

(e) DESPATCH OF THE CONTRACT DOCUMENTS

Under a restricted procedure the purchaser may choose to despatch the contract documents with the invitation to tender, or may require interested invitees to request the documents specifically. Where the documents are not sent, the authority must include with the invitation to tender, as noted above, the address for obtaining them, any time – limit for making the request, and the amount and conditions of any charges.

Under open procedures, the documents must be sent within six days of any request. No similar obligation is stated for restricted procedures; however, the court will no doubt imply that the documents must be sent within a reasonable period, to give effect to the purpose of the rules providing for minimum time – limits for response.

In some cases, where complex supplies or services are involved, authorities might wish to consult with interested bidders before preparing the precise specifications. This may be particularly useful for complex supplies – for example, computer systems where it is difficult for the authority to define its needs without reference to what the available market is able to supply. In such a case, it is not generally permitted to use the negotiated procedure, although this is possible with services contracts where the authority is unable to define specifications precisely at the outset.[48]

It is not clear whether such consultations are permitted. Since there is nothing to forbid this it can be argued that such consultations may take place, provided that all providers are equally treated.[49] Another view, however, is that the directives and regulations indicate a procedure in which substantial contact between purchaser and provider is carried out on the basis of documentation alone in order to minimise the difficulties for foreign providers. (For example, distance and language may be significant barriers to these providers if discussions occur.) According to this view, such discussions are by implication prohibited.

---

[46] On this process see Chap. 7.
[47] On the nature of the information required here see further pp. 237–239.
[48] See pp. 265–267.
[49] This is required by the general principle of equality of treatment laid down in case C–243/89, above.

If such consultations with bidders are allowed at this stage, authorities must take care to comply with the rules on drafting of specifications in consultation with bidders, which are discussed in Chapter 11.[49a]

(f) OBLIGATION TO PROVIDE FURTHER INFORMATION

Authorities must provide any additional information relating to the contract documents which is requested by providers, provided the request is reasonable, and is made in time for the authority to supply this information no later than six days before the date for receipt of tenders.[50] When the authority takes advantage of the special accelarated procedure, which applies when compliance with the usual time periods is "impracticable for reasons of urgency", a period of not less than four days is substituted.[51]

(g) TIME-LIMITS FOR RECEIPT OF TENDERS

The regulations prescribe a minimum time period for submission of tenders, to prevent authorities from setting a short period which would constitute an unreasonable barrier to the participation of non-domestic firms.

In general, the last date for receipt of tenders must be not less than 40 days from the date of despatch of the invitation to tender.[52]

A longer period must be allowed when (i) the contract documents and related documents are too bulky to be supplied within the usual time; (ii) providers need to be given the opportunity to inspect the site; or (iii) providers need to be given the opportunity to inspect documents which are related to the contract documents but do not form part of them. The period must then be extended to allow for the supply or inspection,[53] which no doubt requires an adequate chance for the supply/inspection in the context of the particular procurement.

As under the open procedure, the Works Regulations and Services Regulations allow for reduction of the usual periods when the authority

---

[49a] See pp. 615–616.

[50] Works Regulation 12(13); Supply Regulation 12(13); Services Regulation 12(14). The time periods are calculated as explained in note 3 above.

[51] Works Regulation 12(14); Supply Regulation 12(14); Services Regulation 12(15). The provisions actually state that such a period "may" be substituted. This is odd, since the purpose of the provision is to stipulate a *maximum* period for any cut-off date for requests, and a shorter period here is to the advantage of the provider; thus the authority clearly has the power to prescribe a shorter period in any event. It would seem that "may" is here to be read as "must", thus "requiring" the authority to shorten the period, and so ensure that adequate protection is given to bidders in the shortened procedure.

[52] Works Regulation 12(11); Supply Regulation 12(11); Services Regulation 12(11). The day of despatch is not included, and where the period ends on a non-working day it must be extended to the next working day: Works Regulation 2(3); Supply Regulation 2(3); Services Regulation 12(15).

[53] Works Regulation 12(14); Supply Regulation 12(14); Services Regulation 12(15).

has already published a Prior Information Notice (PIN),[54] which relates to the contract in question. In this case the 40-day period may be reduced to 26 days (extended as necessary for supply of bulky documents and inspections, in accordance with the provisions just outlined). The same rules apply to calculating this period as to calculating the 40 days.[55] There is currently no equivalent provision in the Supply Regulations, although the Commission has proposed that such a provision be introduced, as explained further below.

As has been mentioned, a special accelerated form of the restricted procedure is available where the usual time-limits are impracticable for reasons of urgency. In this case the usual period for submitting bids may be reduced to not less than ten days.[56-57] As indicated earlier, it appears that the period may only be reduced to the extent required by the particular circumstances: ten days is the *minimum* allowed, and is not necessarily appropriate in all cases where acceleration of the procedure is needed.

In relation to these reduced periods, the WTO Agreement on Government Procurement (GPA), in force from January 1, 1996, imposes more stringent requirements. First, advance notice allows reduction of the period from a standard 40 days under the GPA to a lesser period only when the advance notice is published no more than 12 months, and at least 40 days, before the notice advertising the specific contract.[58] In addition, to be relied on for reducing the time-limits the PIN must contain certain additional information on the specific contract which is not normally required in a PIN. The Commission's Proposal for aligning the Community regime with that under the GPA[59] includes a provision requiring the advance notice to be published within the same time limits and to contain the relevant additional information if it is to be relied on to reduce the time-limits for tendering under the Community regime[60]. As with the open procedure, this ensures that the PIN gives providers a reasonable opportunity to prepare for the procurement

---

[54] On PINs, see pp. 182–192.

[55] Works Regulation 2(3); Services Regulation 2(4).

[56-57] Works Regulation 12(14); Supply Regulation 12(14); Services Regulation 12(15). Again, this does not include the date of despatch of the invitations, and the periods must be extended to the next working day where it ends on a non-working day: Works Regulations 2(3); Supply Regulation 2(3); Services Regulation 2(4).

[58] GPA Article XI(3).

[59] On this Proposal see generally pp. 61–63.

[60] Proposal for a European Parliament and Council Directive amending Directive 92/50/EEC relating to the co-ordination of procedures for the award of public service contracts, Directive 93/36/EEC co-ordinating procedures for the award of public supply contracts, and Directive 93/37/EEC concerning the co-ordination of procedures for the award of public works contracts, COM (95) 107 Final, Articles 3(5) and 1(7). It may be noted that the relevant date, as under the GPA, is to be the date of publication of the notice, instead of the date of despatch which is usually the relevant date for time limits under the directives. The relevant additional information is such of the information listed in the restricted procedure model notice as is available at the time the advance notice was published.

through the PIN. If this suggested amendment is adopted, the regulations will need to be amended to reflect this. Regardless of any amendment, however, the more stringent obligation under the GPA will need to be adhered to as from January 1, 1996.[61]

The Commission's Proposal also provides for the possibility of providers to rely on publication of a PIN to reduce the time-limits for submission of tenders under the Supply Directive.[62] As with the open procedure, such a possibility was omitted previously from the Supply Directive because the old GATT Agreement did not allow for the possibility, but it is now permitted under the new GPA.

It is not clear whether these minimum time periods may be waived by agreement of all the parties selected to tender. This is expressly permitted under the utilities rules.[63] Whilst there is no express provision in the public sector rules, the possibility of waiver might be implied here also, since the rule is primarily for the benefit of bidders.[64]

(h) PROPOSALS ON THE FORM OF TENDERS

A Proposal by the Commission, which proposes a number of adjustments to the directives in light of the entry into force of the World Trade Organisation Agreement on Government Procurement (GPA), includes provisions for amending the public sector directives to include certain rules on the form of tenders[65] This is largely to incorporate in the directives rules found in the GPA.[66]

First, it is proposed that all tenders should be in writing and that telephone bids should not be acceptable.

Secondly, it is proposed to state expressly that *if* the authority chooses to permit bids by telegram, telex, fax or electronic means they must include all information necessary for tender evaluation; and, for open or restricted procedures must, in particular, include a statement that the

---

[61] The provision may be enforced by both GPA providers, under the GPA, and Community providers: see further p. 181.

[62] Commission Proposal, above, Article 2(5). The conditions and effect of its use will be the same as are to apply under the Services Directive (as that directive will apply when amended by the new Proposal).

[63] These Rules provide a minimum time period only when the parties cannot agree a suitable period: see p. 502.

[64] On the other hand, a short period may prejudice third parties who wish to intervene, such as those not invited to bid, and it can be argued that the usual period should be maintained for their benefit. This is not so significant under the utilities rules where there is not normally a public call for competition before a procedure.

[65] Proposal for a European Parliament and Council Directive amending Directive 92/50/EEC relating to the co-ordination of procedures for the award of Public Service Contracts, Directive 93/37/EEC co-ordinating procedures for the award of Public Supply Contracts and Directive 93/37/EEC concerning the co-ordination of procedures for the award of Public Works Contracts, COM (95) 107 Final, Article 1(8), Article 2(6) and Article 3(6), proposing amendments/additions to Services Directive Article 23, Supply Directive 15 and Works Directive 18, respectively.

[66] GPA Article XIII(1).

bidder agrees to the terms, conditions and provisions of the invitation. This is curious, since there is no corresponding express requirement for tenders submitted by letter or directly in writing, but it is difficult to see why the rules on these matters should vary according to the method of tender.

Thirdly, it is proposed that where tenders are submitted by the above means, with the exception of electronic mail, they must be confirmed by letter despatched before the time limit for receipt of tenders.

(4) OPENING OF TENDERS

In open procedures authorities must indicate in the contract notice the date, time and place for the opening of tenders.[67] There is no equivalent provision for restricted procedures.

As regards the opening of tenders, the question may be raised as to whether tenders should be opened in public or whether, at least, providers have a right to attend the opening. The regulations contain some reference to attendance: in open procedures the works and services notices require authorities to indicate in the contract notice who may be present at the tender opening *where applicable*, whilst the supply notice provides in unqualified terms for authorities to state who may be present.[68] In his Opinion in case C–359/93, *Commission v. Netherlands*,[69] which concerned a supply contract, Advocate General Tesauro seemed to suggest that providers must be permitted to be present because of the importance of transparency and openness under the Community procedures.[70] However, it is difficult to see that such a principle can be implied into the directives in general, since (as with the regulations) the Works and Services Directives provide for authorities to state who has a right to attend the opening only *where applicable*, indicating that in some cases authorities may refuse to allow attendance. The difference in the wording between these and the Supply Directive seem purely fortuitous and it is submitted that is anomalous to construe the Supply Directive alone as conferring a right of attendance. It is submitted that the correct view is that in all types of procedures the decision whether to permit providers to attend the opening is not affected by the directives and regulations.[71]

---

[67] See the model notices at pp. 208–213.
[68] See the model notices at pp. 208–213.
[69] Judgment of January 21, 1995.
[70] Para. 8 of the Opinion of November 17, 1994.
[71] The issue of a right of attendance was not actually raised in the *Netherlands* case; the only issue relating to this provision was whether the information on who may attend was required to be included in the notice, which the court answered in the affirmative. Where no persons are permitted to be present the notice provision can be construed as requiring authorities simply to state that attendance is not permitted.

(5) CHOOSING THE PROVIDER FOLLOWING RECEIPT OF TENDERS

(a) THE GENERAL PRINCIPLES

Once the closing date for receipt of tenders has passed, in both open and restricted procedures the authority will proceed to select between those providers who have submitted tenders. This process is closely regulated: the authority must make its choice in accordance with objective criteria, designed to ensure that there is no discrimination, and that any authority inclined to discriminate cannot easily hide its discriminatory decisions.

In outline, the rules allow an authority to exclude firms which do not have adequate financial status, or technical capacity/ability (see section (b)); which do not meet any relevant "regulation 14" criteria (see section (c)); and which do not comply with relevant conditions in the tender documents (see section (d)). Bids may not be excluded on other grounds (see (e)). The authority must then proceed to evaluate the bids of all firms not excluded under these rules (discussed in section (f)). At this stage the authority is required to choose either the lowest price bid or that which is the "most economically advantageous". In the latter case, it must be stated in advance that this basis will be used and the specific factors which it is intended to take into account (for example, price, quality or delivery date) must also be stated in advance. The only major exception is that the authority may refuse to accept any bid which is "abnormally low". In conducting the evaluation, the purchaser must consider the bids as submitted: these may not be altered in post tender negotiations (see section (g)).

The strict rules on award criteria do not mean that the authority is bound to award a contract to the best bidder: it may choose to cancel the award procedure. However, if it does wish to go ahead, it must make the award in accordance with the rules above, or must commence a new award procedure (see section 6 below).

(b) EXCLUSION FOR LACK OF FINANCIAL STANDING, OR TECHNICAL CAPACITY/ABILITY

An authority may wish to exclude some firms from consideration, on the basis that, for either financial or technical reasons, the particular bidder will be unable to perform the contract.

A power to exclude such firms after submission of tenders is essential in open procedures, where there has been no previous opportunity for authorities to eliminate firms which do not meet the required minimum standards.[72] Works Regulation 11(7), Supply Regulation 11(7), and

---

[72] There appears to be no objection to any form of prequalification procedure which is optional for providers, to which providers could submit to establish their qualification in advance. However, the rules seem to preclude the possibility of rejecting a firm which does not prove its qualification prior to submission of bids; the directives and regulations envisage that providers can be excluded on financial and technical grounds only following receipt of bids.

Service Regulation 11(8) state expressly that authorities may exclude bids from the evaluation process where the bidder fails to satisfy the minimum standards of financial and economic standing and technical capacity (or, for services contracts, "ability").[73]

These provisions do not impose any obligation on authorities to assess the financial and technical status of providers in open procedures; they are merely permissive. This is because the Community rules have only the limited objective of preventing unjustifiable *exclusion* of providers, with the aim of providing open access to procurement markets. In practice, a financial and technical assessment is essential to efficient procurement, and will normally be carried out; but this a matter left to states and is thus not covered by the regulations.

In restricted procedures an authority will have had an opportunity at the invitation to tender stage to exclude providers who do not meet minimum financial and technical requirements. Under the regulations[74] it appears that an assessment *must* in fact be carried out at this earlier stage. This is because there is no provision for exclusion after receipt of tenders: regulation 15(1) and 16(1) of each set of regulations, which permit exclusion on financial and technical grounds respectively, refer only to the possibility of exclusion at the stage of selecting firms to be invited to tender and, further, whilst in open procedures the regulations expressly state that the authority may decline to consider bids on such grounds (as noted above), there is no corresponding provision relating to restricted procedures. Such a requirement to invite only qualified firms is beneficial to providers, who are able to know whether their qualifications are acceptable before incurring the expense of submitting a tender.

On the other hand, the regulations require authorities to state in the invitation to tender any information which firms must provide on financial and economic standing.[75] This implies that such information

---

[73] The precise meaning of these concepts, and the procedures for assessing compliance, are considered in Chap. 7.

[74] It can be argued that the directives themselves permit assessment at the later stage, since they merely provide in general terms for exclusion based on absence of financial or technical standing, without prescribing when this shall be done: Works Directive Article 18; Supply Directive Article 15; Services Directive Article 23. This view finds support in case 31/87, *Gebroeders Beentjes B.V. v. Netherlands* [1988] E.C.R. 4635 in which the Court of Justice stated expressly that suitability and bid evaluation – though distinct processes – could take place at the same time (para. 16 of the judgment), and did not draw any express distinction in this respect between open and restricted procedures. Further, in case C–362/92, note 21 above, Advocate General Lenz, stated that qualification on financial and technical grounds must be considered at the bid evaluation stage (although this view that assessment at the earlier stage is actually ruled out is, it is submitted, incorrect: see note 21, above).

On the other hand, it is also a possible interpretation of the directives that any financial and technical assessment must be carried out at the selection stage, based on the provisions on selection of invitees: these provide that authorities "shall" select invitees on the basis of financial and technical considerations, which could mean that these factors must be considered at this stage if they are to be taken into account (Works Directive Article 22(1), Supply Directive Article 19(1) and Services Directive 27(1).

[75] See pp. 236–239.

may be considered *after* the invitations have been issued. This does not, however, necessarily contradict the view stated above that an assessment of standing must be carried out before the invitations are issued. It can be suggested that, whilst firms must be informed of the relevant financial and technical criteria and must confirm that they meet the relevant criteria, the factual accuracy of the information provided can be verified later. The information referred to in relation to the invitation to tender is thus the information required for the authority to verify the provider's position. This is a sensible interpretation of the rules: it still fulfils the function of allowing firms to know in advance whether their qualifications are adequate, but at the same time avoids unnecessary delays whilst factual matters are verified. Further, it is desirable to allow factual checks to be made after receipt of bids, since changes to the firm's status, particularly its financial status, may occur between the time of invitation to tender and contract award, and the authority will wish to take these changes into account.

As under open procedures, an authority is not *required* by the regulations to consider financial and technical standing at all; however, it will almost invariably wish to do so in practice.

Authorities may not take account of financial standing and technical capability as a factor to be weighed in relative terms, alongside the merits of bids. For example, an authority awarding a contract for basic supplies on the basis of price only, may decide that it is worth taking a risk on a firm whose financial resources are borderline in terms of the authorities usual requirements, only if that firm quotes a *much* cheaper price (for example, at least 10 per cent cheaper) than firms whose financial standing is clearly adequate. Under the regulations this is not possible, however: providers must be assessed against each other solely by reference to the merits of their bids.[76] Thus, in the scenario envisaged above, the authority must decide whether or not the firm has adequate resources to be considered at all; and if it does, its bid must then be accepted if it is the lowest, however small the margin of advantage.

(c) EXCLUSION UNDER THE REGULATION 14 CRITERIA

Under the open procedures, following the receipt of bids authorities may also disqualify firms from consideration on the grounds listed in Works Regulation 14, Supply Regulation 14 and Services Regulation 14[77], which include, inter alia, bankruptcy; grave professional misconduct; conviction

---

[76] This sharp distinction between the processes of qualification (assessment of suitability) and award is highlighted, for example, by Advocate-General Darmon in case 31/87, *Gebroeders Beentjes B.V. v. Netherlands* [1988] E.C.R. 4635 and by Advocate General Gulmann in case C–71/92, *Commission v. Spain*, judgment of June 30, 1993, para. 63 of the Opinion.

[77] Works Regulation 11(7); Supply Regulation 11(7); Services Regulation 11(8).

of an offence related to the business; non-fulfilment of social security and tax obligations; and misrepresentation in supplying information.[78] As with financial and technical requirements, there is under the open procedure no opportunity prior to receipt of bids to exclude firms which do not meet such requirements, since under open procedures any interested party may submit a bid.

In restricted procedures the authority has an opportunity to assess for compliance with any relevant regulation 14 criteria when issuing invitations. Regulation 14(1) of each set of regulations indicates that the authority cannot leave consideration of such matters solely to a later point: in authorising exclusion regulation 14 refers in relation to restricted procedures only to the earlier stage of selecting firms to tender. (Further, as with financial standing, exclusion on these grounds following receipt of bids is expressly authorised in relation to open procedures but there is nothing corresponding to this for restricted procedures.) However, it was suggested above in relation to financial and technical status that authorities may leave until a later point the verification of factual information provided by firms in connection with any earlier assessment. This is also appropriate in the context of regulation 14, particularly since a firm's status (for example, on payment of taxes) may change before the time of the award.[79]

In selecting the party for the contract, an authority may not consider the regulation 14 criteria as factors to be weighed alongside the respective merits of bids. It is merely permitted to impose set conditions of eligibility in relation to such matters, and all firms which meet these minimum conditions must then be considered for the contract solely on the basis of the merits of their bids.

The regulations do not *require* authorities to apply any of the regulation 14 criteria; they merely authorise this possibility, at the authority's discretion.

(d) NON-RESPONSIVE OFFERS

(i) NON-COMPLIANCE WITH SPECIFICATIONS AND OTHER SUBSTANTATIVE REQUIREMENTS

Tenders are sometimes submitted which do not comply with substantive requirements of the contract – that is, which offer products or services which are not in accordance with the specifications, or which do not comply with other requirements relating to contract performance, such as provision of a performance bond. This may arise where enterprises have misunderstood, or cannot meet, the authority's requirements. It

---

[78] For a detailed consideration see pp. 333–340.
[79] Authorities are not, however, required to refer in the invitation to tender to information sought under regulation 14, as they are with information sought under regulations 15 (financial standing) and 16 (technical capacity): see p. 331.

may also arise either when products are "equivalent" to those sought but are made to different technical specifications; or where enterprises proffer solutions which differ from those in the specifications, but which the tenderer believes are superior.

I. The discretion to accept non-responsive offers

An authority may sometimes wish to accept a non-responsive offer – for example, where that offer is so much better than other offers that the authority is prepared to forego some of the minimum requirements which it previously specified in the contract documents.

To accept a non-responsive tender is, however, generally prohibited under the directives. This was made clear by the Court of Justice in case C–243/89, *Commission v. Denmark*[80] (the *Storebaelt* case). In this case a contract for the construction of a bridge across the western channel of the Great Belt had been awarded by a Danish contracting authority in a procedure falling within the Works Directive. The specification proposed three possible construction methods. It also stated that the authority would consider other alternatives proposed by contractors themselves, subject to certain conditions, one of which was that the contractor would assume responsibility for the details of the alternative design. The authority accepted a tender which involved such an alternative proposal, but which did not, however, meet this condition. The Court ruled that to accept this tender infringed the directive, since any tender accepted must comply with the conditions in the contract documents. The Court based its conclusion on the existence of a principle of equality in the treatment of tenderers underlying the procurement directives[81]: clearly it is unfair to accept a bid which does not comply with the specifications, since other firms will have drawn up their bids on the basis of the specifications.

It thus appears that purchasers may not generally accept bids which diverge from the specifications and other conditions – for example, where the provider cannot deliver by the date specified for delivery, or provide the specified financial guarantees; or where the product offered does not conform to the safety or performance requirements laid down. The Court in *Storebaelt* did note that the condition in that case was a "fundamental" condition, which might indicate that there are some conditions which are not "fundamental", and to which the rule prohibiting acceptance of non-responsive bids would not apply. It is submitted, however, that in relation to conditions concerning contract performance, tenders must comply fully to be considered, and that the only conditions which are not "fundamental" for this purpose are certain conditions relating to the formalities of the bid process. (See (ii) below.)

This principle does not, however, preclude purchasers from taking advantage of the expertise of firms which are able to propose solutions

---

[80] Judgment of June 22, 1993; noted by Fernández Martín in (1993) 2 P.P.L.R. CS153.
[81] Paras. 37–39 of the judgment.

which are superior to those in the specifications. This is because the regulations expressly permit authorities to consider "variants", in those cases where the criterion for contract award is "the most economically advantageous tender".[82] Thus, in *Storebaelt* the authority would have been permitted to accept the alternative suggestion for construction of the bridge, *if* the alternative tenders had complied with the conditions laid down in the specifications for such alternative tenders. The rules on variants, including the conditions which apply where the authority wishes to rely on these rules, are considered further in Chapter 11 on specifications.

A question which did not arise in *Storebaelt* is whether a non-responsive tender (which does not fall within the rule on variants) can be accepted *if* other tenderers are first given the opportunity to revise their bids, either to comply with the specification offered by the non-responsive bidder, or (where applicable) to put forward their own alternative solution. This would still, however, be unfair, since other tenderers have already wasted expenditure in bidding, which might have been avoided had the possibility of an alternative tender been made clear at the outset.[83] Thus it is likely that the rules will be interpreted to require exclusion of the non-responsive bid, regardless of whether other firms are permitted to revise their own bids.

It is not clear whether an authority may permit a provider to amend a non-responsive bid to comply with the contract requirements.[84] Probably this should be permitted provided, of course, that all bidders are treated equally in accordance with the general principle of equality of treatment referred to above.

II. The discretion to exclude non-responsive tenders

Although, as explained above, a contracting authority is not normally *permitted* to accept bids which do not meet the exact contract requirements, in certain limited cases it is *required* to do so.

First, the Services Regulations provide that an authority may not reject a tender for a public services contract on the grounds that it offers variations which would result in the conclusion of a public supply contract instead.[85] For example, an authority which advertises a contract

---

[82] Works Regulation 20(4); Supply Regulation 21(4); Services Regulation 21(4).

[83] The authority itself may probably change the specifications to a limited extent, including before close of tenders, provided this does not "substantially" alter the nature of the contract (in which case a new procedure is required): see pp. 617–618. Likewise this may be done once tenders have been received but in this latter case only firms submitting responsive bids should be permitted to revise the bid to avoid giving an unfair advantage to a bidder who submits a non-responsive bid which leads the authority to amend the specifications: see pp. 617–618.

[84] If the procedure is one under which bids are opened as soon as they are received, before the deadline for receipt of bids, there is no reason why a firm should not be told of the defect and permitted to revise its bid before the deadline.

[85] Services Regulation 21(5).

for software under the services rules on the basis that the contract is likely to be one for bespoke software, and thus probably a services contract cannot decline to accept a bid which offers suitable off-the-shelf software, which may mean that the contract actually concluded is a supply contract.[86] Similarly, the Supply Regulations forbid rejection of bids on the grounds that these would lead to the award of a public services contract.

Secondly, authorities are forbidden to reject tenders which have been drawn up according to certain standard specifications, even if these differ from the specifications in the contract documents. This applies to tenders drawn up in accordance with "European specifications", or by reference to certain types of national standards. They will also be required by the E.C. Treaty to accept other "equivalent" tenders which are not in precise conformity with the specifications. These rules are considered in further detail in Chapter 11 on specifications.[87]

(ii) NON-COMPLIANCE WITH FORMALITIES

Offers may fail to comply not only with substantive requirements but also with the tendering formalities. For example, they may be submitted late; they may fail to meet requirements relating to the form of bids, such as language or number of copies; or may omit required information. This situation raises the questions of, first, whether the authority may choose to accept a non-compliant bid, and, secondly, whether there is ever any obligation to do so.

I. The discretion to accept non-responsive offers

The situation where a purchaser wishes to accept a bid which fails to comply with formalities, either in the form in which it is submitted, or following correction of the defect (for example, where a bidder who omits information from the original bid supplies this at a later date), is quite common. Formalities are imposed for the authority's own convenience and it may argued that they should thus be open to waiver by the authority. Clearly it is wasteful if purchasers must reject advantageous bids whenever there is a breach of some minor formal requirement. It is also harsh on providers for their bids to be excluded in such a case.

On the other hand, the same objection may arise in the case of breach of formalities as with non-compliance with substantive requirements, that acceptance of a non-responsive bid may result in an unfair advantage for the bidder concerned. For example, if a bid is accepted late or in a different language from that stipulated, the bidder may have

---

[86] This result does not mean that the contract should have been awarded under the Supply Regulations: the applicable regulations are determined by the anticipated outcome of the procedure, not the actual outcome (see p. 148).
[87] Supply Regulation 21(5).

benefited in terms of time and costs in comparison with other bidders, and also gains an advantage over firms who were deterred from bidding by the relevant formalities. Further, a discretion to waive formalities also creates the potential for abuse, since it may be exercised only for favoured providers.

Since most breaches of formalities will not create any significant inequity between bidders, it is submitted that the general principle should be that authorities retain the right to waive compliance. However, by way of exception it may be implied that with certain important formalities contemplated in the procurement legislation itself, strict compliance is necessary for a bid to be considered. This should apply to the deadline for submission of bids, which is a matter of importance under the legislation; and it might also extend to other formalities which the legislation requires to be dealt with in the contract documents (such as, in some cases, the address for submission, and language of the tender).[88] The general principle of equality of treatment referred to in *Storebaelt* may also require compliance with other formalities prescribed by the authority, where their particular nature and importance is such that to waive compliance might lead to unfairness between providers.[89] In the absence of decided cases, however, it is difficult to predict the approach which the courts will take to the issue of formalities.

If the authority does retain discretion to waive compliance with formal requirements, the equal treatment of bidders which was articulated in *Storebaelt* will require that this is exercised in the same manner for all bidders. Thus, if a particular requirement is waived for one bidder, it must generally also be waived for others whose bids breach that requirement.

Whether or not a power to waive formalities is expressly reserved in the contract documents should not affect the position. In general, it is suggested, the power of waiver referred to above should normally exist even if not expressly reserved. Where, on the other hand, waiver is forbidden under the specific legislation or the general equality principle, this prohibition, like others in the legislation, should not be subject to voluntary exclusion.

II. The discretion to exclude non-responsive offers

Though an authority may not be *required* to reject bids which do not comply with formalities, it must be implied that it generally has a discretion to do so: otherwise, bidders would be free to disregard requirements imposed to ensure the smooth functioning of the tender

---

[88] See the model notices at pp. 197–202 and 207–213 above. This might also apply to compliance with the rules on form of tenders which have been put forward for inclusion in the directives in the Commission's Proposal for aligning the directives with the GPA: see pp. 226–227.

[89] In some cases this inequity might be capable of removal by belated compliance; but this would depend on the facts of each case.

process. Thus, in general, it is submitted that the procurement legislation does not affect an authority's discretion in this matter. Any such discretion will, however, be subject to the general *Storebaelt* principle of equal treatment of tenderers. Thus, if a tender from one firm is rejected for non-compliance with a requirement, other tenders which fail to comply must also be rejected.

(e) EXCLUSION ON OTHER GROUNDS

Apart from the grounds mentioned above, there is no other basis to exclude bids from the bid evaluation process.

So far as open procedures are concerned, Works Regulation 11(7), Supply Regulation 11(7) and Services Regulation 11(8) state clearly that firms may have their bids excluded from consideration *only* on the grounds specified above. This makes it clear that other matters – for example, secondary "policy" concerns, such as a provider's general commitment to equal opportunities – cannot be grounds for exclusion.[90]

With restricted procedures there is no provision permitting the exclusion of a responsive bid which has been submitted by a party selected to receive an invitation to tender. Thus, it appears that all such bids must be brought into the evaluation process, subject to the possibility mentioned above that authorities may check the accuracy of information received from bidders, and may disqualify bidders where this information is incorrect or no longer applicable.

(f) EVALUATION OF OFFERS

(i) THE BASIC PRINCIPLE: LOWEST PRICE OR MOST ECONOMICALLY ADVANTAGEOUS OFFER

The process of selecting the successful bid from those which are not excluded under the rules outlined above is regulated by Works Regulation 20, Supply Regulation 21 and Services Regulation 21. The basic principle is that the contract must be awarded either (a) to the enterprise which offers the lowest price or (b) to the enterprise whose bid is "the most economically advantageous to the contracting authority".[91] Thus it is sought to ensure that contracts are awarded on the basis of objective commercial criteria, and that discriminatory decisions cannot be disguised. In an open procedure, the authority must state in the contract notice whether the award is to be based on lowest price or most economically advantageous offer.[92] In a restricted procedure, this must be stated in either the contract notice or the invitation to tender.[93]

---

[90] On this issue see further p. 302 and Chap. 16.
[91] Works Regulation 20(1); Supply Regulation 21(1); Services Regulation 21(1).
[92] See the model notices for the open procedure at pp. 197–202 above.
[93] Works Regulation 12(10)(e); Supply Regulation 12(10)(e); Services Regulation 12(10)(e).

(ii) LOWEST PRICE

Where the applicable principle is "lowest price", the bidder offering the lowest price must be awarded the contract. The only important exception[94] is that the authority may reject bids which are "abnormally low". (See (g) below.) The "lowest price" basis is rarely used in practice, except for simple, off-the-shelf supplies.

(iii) MOST ECONOMICALLY ADVANTAGEOUS OFFER

I. Factors relevant to economic advantage

Where the authority chooses the most economically advantageous offer as the basis for the award it may take into account other factors as well as (or instead of) price: for example, quality, delivery date or product life.

This is the award principle chosen for most contracts, especially for complex products or services, where there is wide variation in what is offered from different providers; in this case it is not appropriate to compare what is available on the basis of price alone. Thus, for example, an authority purchasing a machine such as a photocopier could specify minimum requirements for all relevant features (speed of copying; variety of functions available; running and maintenance costs; expected life; etc.) and then choose the lowest price from amongst those bidders whose products meet these requirements. However, it is more likely that it will prefer to compare the different machines on offer in light of a variety of these factors, and determine which offers the best value for money overall. In the example above it will probably specify a minimum standard for some or all characteristics – particularly those relating to quality and performance, to ensure that all demands placed on the product can be met – and then compare all those which meet the minimum requirements by reference to their relative merits in several areas. Usually these will include price, running/maintenance costs and product life (to give the overall cost), and perhaps also the extent to which the product exceeds the minimum requirements on matters such as turnover and reliability – a product with exceptional performance in these areas may, for example, be preferred to one with lower overall costs. With some purchases – for example, of professional services – non-cost factors, notably the quality of the service, are generally much more important than cost.

By way of illustration, the regulations list a number of criteria which may be taken into account where most economically advantageous offer

---

[94] The Works Directive provides for an exception for certain preference schemes but these are not of practical importance.

is used as the basis for the award.[95] Under the Works Regulations these are "price, period for completion, running costs, profitability and technical merit"[96]; under the Supply Regulations, "delivery date, running costs, cost effectiveness, quality, aesthetic and functional characteristics, technical merit, after sales service, technical assistance and price"[97]; and under the Services Regulations, "period for completion or delivery, quality, aesthetic and functional characteristics, technical merit, after sales service technical assistance and price".[98-99] The rules make it clear, however, that these lists are not exhaustive. Thus, for example, aesthetic characteristics are referred to only in the Supply Regulations and Services Regulations, but could also be taken into account in relation to a works contract. Similarly, commitments in relation to spare parts and security of supply (expressly mentioned as illustrations in the Utilities Regulations) may be taken into account in awarding public sector contracts, even though the public sector rules do not mention them expressly. It is also permissible to consider criteria which are not mentioned in the regulations at all.

It is not, however, any criteria which are relevant to the authority from an economic point of view which may be considered, but only criteria which relate to *the contract awarded*. This can be deduced from the fact that all the criteria listed as illustrations are criteria of this type.[1] Thus a purchaser may not take into account the potential benefits of developing a long-term relationship with a particular firm – for example, prospects for collaborative research of mutual benefit, or the award of discounts on the firm's other products. However, benefits which arise out of a prior relationship may provide an economic advantage which relates to the contract being awarded: for example, a firm's knowledge of the authority or its premises gained from previous contracts may allow the firm to perform the new contract more efficiently, or the existence of a computerised link for transmitting orders, set up for a previous contract, may cut the purchaser's costs of business with that provider under the new contract. These considerations may legitimately be taken into account.

It is also forbidden under the regulations, to consider the *relative* financial and technical status of firms at this stage: once firms have been deemed to be qualified as providers, their bids must be evaluated solely by reference to the merits of the bid.[2]

---

[95] The illustrative lists are taken from the Directives themselves: Works Directive Article 30(1)(b); Supply Directive 26(1)(b); Services Directive Article 36(1)(a).

[96] Works Regulation 20 (2).

[97] Supply Regulation 21 (2).

[98-99] Services Regulations 21(2).

[1] It is stated in the European Commission's *Guide to the Community rules on open government procurement* [1987] O.J. C 358/1 at 36 that " . . . it is clear from the examples given that only objective criteria may be used which are strictly relevant to the particular project". See also the view of Advocate-General Darmon in case 31/87, *Gebroeders Beentjes B.V. v Netherlands* [1988] E.C.R. 4635 in paras. 35–37 of the Opinion, where he states, in particular, that the award criteria concern "the qualities of the service [the provider] can offer".

[2] See pp. 230–231.

II. Requirement for advance notice of factors to be considered

When an authority intends to use "most economically advantageous offer" as the basis for the award it must state the specific factors to be taken into account (price, quality, etc.) in advance[3] and, where possible, in descending order of importance. This must be done in either the contract notice or the contract documents.[4] (In the restricted procedure it is thus not necessary to include this detail at the earlier stage of the invitation to tender, although, as explained above, it must be stated in either the contract notice or invitation to tender which of the two basic criteria – lowest price or most econmically advantageous offer – is to be used.) It appears that the authority is then bound by these criteria in making the award.[5] This requirement seeks to make it difficult to disguise discriminatory decisions. It also has the result of enabling interested persons to formulate their bid in the most appropriate manner.

If the authority fails to state the relevant criteria, then if it wishes to continue with the procedure it is probably required to award the contract to the lowest bidder.[6] It is possible as an alternative to commence a new procedure,[7] but obviously this will delay the procurement.

III. The obligation to exercise a discretion

A further issue is the extent to which an authority's discretion to determine and apply the relevant criteria may be limited in advance. In case 274/83, *Commission v. Italy,*[8] the Court of Justice considered an Italian law which required contracts to be awarded to the provider whose tender equalled the average price of tenders, or, in the absence of a tender meeting this requirement exactly, came closest to the average price. The Italian government argued that this was an objective method

---

[3] Works Regulation 20(3); Supply Regulation 21(3); Services Regulation 21(3). Provision is also made for this in the model contract notices, set out at pp. 197–202 and 207–213 above.

[4] *Ibid.*

[5] The relevant provisions state that the authority must state the factors which the authority *intends* to consider. Probably this must be interpreted to mean that the authority must adhere to the factors which it lists in the notice or contract documents and apply them in the order stated, and cannot later change its decision, to add or remove criteria from the list. This view is supported by the Commission's *Guide to the Community rules on open public procurement*, above, at 36. Consistently with this the authority could not later change the order of preference of the criteria. This allows the stated criteria to be used as a benchmark against which to review the authority's decision where it is alleged that an improper motive has influenced the decision. If it were permitted to change either the criteria or their order it would be too easy to rationalise discriminatory decisions *ex post facto*.

[6] See the opinion of Advocate General Darmon in case 31/87, *Gebroeders Beentjes BV v. Netherlands* [1988] E.C.R. 4635, para. 38 of the Opinion; and also para. 35 of the judgment of the Court of Justice.

[7] See pp. 254–255.

[8] [1985] E.C.R. 1077.

for identifying the most economically advantageous tender. The Court held, however, that this law contravened the Works Directive, which required authorities to exercise discretion "on the basis of qualitative criteria that vary according to the contract in question".[9]

This suggests, first, that the criteria must be set with reference to the specific type of contract. It is not clear how far this would permit general legislation, or guidelines, for the evaluation of certain *types* of contract – for example, a rule that quality should always be taken into account in awarding contracts for professional services – or whether is is necessary that the relevant factors should be determined by reference to the facts of each individual contract. Whatever the correct view, it may be noted that in practice authorities frequently list a large number of factors, including all those mentioned in the regulations, without any regard to the nature of the contract, making it difficult to know what the authority is looking for. In light of case 274/83, however, it can be suggested that this practice breaches the rules.

Secondly, in referring to "qualitative criteria", case 274/83 may indicate that purchasers must consider factors relating to the particular merits of bids submitted, rather than relying on an objective formula. Thus it is probably not permitted to use the "average price" formula relied on in that case even where the decision to do so is based not on general legislation but on a decision that this formula is appropriate for the particular contract. This view is also supported by the Court's jurisprudence on abnormally low bids, which denies the possibility of rejecting bids as abnormally low without considering the individual circumstances.[10] The argument in favour of formulae such as those used in case 274/83 is that, being wholly objective, they preclude abuse of discretion; but this advantage is outweighed by the danger of reaching decisions which are not justifiable on a commercial basis (thus denying the contract to the best bidder), because a formula cannot take adequate account of the facts of the particular case.

IV. The difficulty of enforcing the rules

Even where the rules are properly applied it is difficult to prove whether a particular decision has actually been based on the listed criteria. Often award decisions involve subjective judgment, and there is more than one "reasonable" choice available. Thus, for example, where both price and quality are relevant, firm A may offer the lowest price, and firm B a higher price but a better quality product. Here, an award to either A or B might be a reasonable commercial choice, and if the decision *is* based on some non-commercial factor, this will be hard to prove. Thus it may be difficult to challenge an evaluation decision in the courts, which are

---

[9] Para. 25 of the judgment.
[10] See p. 246.

likely to review only on the basis that the decision was not made bona fide by reference to the stated criteria.

V. The exception for abnormally low offers

An exception to the above rules[11] allows the authority to reject offers which, whilst appearing to be the the most economically advantageous, are "abnormally low". The rules on such offers are considered at (g) below.

VI. Alternative offers

There is nothing in the regulations to prevent providers from submitting more than one tender. Thus, for example, where price and quality are both relevant factors, a provider might seek to improve its chances of winning by offering both a good quality product at a high price, and a lower quality product at a lower price. It appears that in such a case the authority is required to consider both tenders, unless the conditions of tendering allow submission of one tender only.

(iv) PROCEDURES INVOLVING SEPARATE LOTS

Contracts are sometimes advertised in lots, with bidders able to bid for one or more lots. For example, an authority may have a requirement for three different types of machine, A, B and C. There may be some firms in the market which specialise in one type of machine, but some which make two or all three. In this case the authority is likely to advertise its requirements for all three in a single procedure, allowing providers to bid to supply all three types; just two; or just one.

In evaluating bids here it is submitted that, in principle, it is necessary to accept that combination of bids which offers either the lowest overall price or (where the most economically advantageous offer basis is used) the best overall "economic advantage". However, as an alternative a purchaser should be permitted to evaluate each lot as a wholly separate contract (or to retain a discretion to do so) where this is indicated in the documents setting out the award criteria. It appears that a purchaser could give a preference to a single bid covering the whole requirement (which it may wish to do because of a saving on administration costs), even if not the lowest/most economically advantageous, only if it indicates this possibility in advance. In other words, the award procedure must effectively proceed as two (or more) procedures in parallel – one for a series of separate contracts and one for a single (or several) larger contract(s).

---

[11] The Services Directive states that this is without prejudice to any national measures governing the remuneration of certain services. This is not mentioned in the regulations, apparently because it is considered that no relevant rules exist in the United Kingdom.

(v) TREATMENT OF IN-HOUSE BIDS

A bid by another part of the same authority – that is, by an in-house provider – is required to be treated as an "offer" for the purpose of the evaluation rules.[12] Thus, it must be evaluated against external bids in accordance with the rules outlined above.

However, as is explained in section (5) below, the regulations do not generally preclude authorities from terminating an award procedure for any reason. This includes the case where an authority decides not to award a contract to an external provider, but instead to retain the work in-house. There is nothing in the rules on evaluation of in-house bids to affect the position in this respect. Thus, if an in-house bid is not the "winning" bid in accordance with the rules on bid evaluation outlined above, it is still open to the authority to terminate the award procedure, and instead award the work in-house. This does not require a new award procedure under the regulations, since the in-house award is not a "contract" under the regulations.[13]

In the case, however, of work awarded by local authorities which falls under the legislation on compulsory competitive tendering (considered in Chapters 12–14) as well as under the regulations, it is not permitted to award the work in-house without inviting external bidders. This means that it is not possible to award the work in-house without following the regulations, since these must apply whenever there is a possibility of an award to an external provider.[14] The result is that in all cases the internal bid must be evaluated against the external bids in accordance with the principles laid down in the regulations (as well as the rules applying under the CCT regime).[15] Thus the internal provider cannot receive the work unless it offers the lowest/most economically advantageous bid. An authority is probably permitted to take into account "external" factors which affect the cost of accepting the in-house bid such as redundancy payments or costs of supervision of an outside provider, since these are economic advantages offered by the internal bid. However, these criteria, like others, must be referred to in the contract notice or invitation to tender.

(vi) THE PROCEDURE FOR EVALUATION

Under open procedures, an authority may proceed by evaluating all bids received in accordance with the bid criteria, and then assessing the qualifications (on financial and technical grounds, and under regulation 14) of the provider submitting the most favourable bid. If this provider is not qualified, the authority will then consider the qualification of the

---

[12] Works Regulation 20(8); Supply Regulation 21(9); Services Regulation 21(9).
[13] See pp. 118–119.
[14] See Chap. 14.
[15] On these see pp. 723–735.

next most favourable bidder and so on. Alternatively, it may prefer first to assess the qualifications of all bidders, and then to evaluate the bids, taking into consideration only those submitted by qualified providers. Either approach is permitted: the procurement legislation does not regulate the order in which qualification and evaluation processes are carried out.[16]

Under restricted procedures it has been noted that under the regulations the qualification process must be carried out before firms are invited to tender, and invitations limited to qualified firms; however, the authority may check information received on qualification matters after sending the invitation. Here, again, it would appear that this verification could be carried out either before or after the process of bid evaluation.

(vii) THE RIGHT TO REASONS FOR A DECISION

Providers who are unsuccessful in the evaluation process are entitled to know the reasons for the authority's decision. This obligation is considered in further detail below.[17]

(g) ABNORMALLY LOW OFFERS

(i) THE PROBLEM OF ABNORMALLY LOW OFFERS

Sometimes an offer appears to give little or no opportunity of profit for the bidder, or may even suggest that the provider will incur a loss. In this case the purchaser may fear that the contract will not be properly performed, or that the provider will later demand an increase in price. Low offers may also be possible because the provider is in receipt of state aid which is unlawful under Articles 92–93 E.C., and the contract could then be jeopardised by the provider's being required to repay the unlawful aid. Because of these possibilities purchasers may be unwilling to accept such low offers. However, there are a number of reasons why an offer which appears low may in fact result in a reasonable profit – for example because the bidder has obtained materials at a bargain price, or, with bidders from another state, because of lower costs in that state. Further, the fact that the enterprise is unlikely to make a profit does not necessarily pose a threat to the interests of the purchaser: for example, a low offer may be submitted by a solvent and reputable firm which prefers to keep its workers temporarily employed at a loss, rather than to lay them off. The regulations contain express provisions to deal with the problem of "abnormally low offers".

---

[16] *Beentjes*, above (para. 16 of the judgment).
[17] See pp. 281–282.

(ii) THE OBLIGATION TO SEEK AN EXPLANATION

First, it is provided that before rejecting any abnormally low offer, a purchaser must request in writing an explanation of the offer or of those parts which it considers contribute to the offer being abnormally low.[18] This ensures that the authority is appraised of the full facts before making any decision.[19] A right to a hearing would probably not be available in such a case under common law principles of judicial review, even assuming that these apply to procurement at all.[20] The inclusion of such a provision in the Community legislation was motivated primarily by the desire to ensure that purchases do not reject bids from other states which appear low in the awarding state, but reflect the cost advantages of that other state; this would defeat the object of the procurement rules.[21] A corresponding provision in the Utilities Directive and Regulations requires also that the bidder is given a reasonable time to respond to the request; this is not expressly stated in the public sector rules, but it is clear that such an obligation must be implied.

(iii) DISCRETION TO ACCEPT OR REJECT ABNOR-MALLY LOW OFFERS

It is less clear what the purchaser's obligations are in dealing with such bids. It is stated as a general principle in Works Regulation 20, Supply Regulation 21 and Services Regulation 21 that where the offer is abnormally low the purchaser *may* reject it.[22] However, this apparent discretion over when, and whether, to reject such a bid appears to be qualified to some extent, as is explained below.

I. Awards based on the lowest price criterion
Where the principle for the contract award is lowest price, the general rules on evaluation of bids normally require that the offer must be accepted if it is the lowest offer received. However, the express provision that such offers may be rejected, referred to above, provides an exception to this principle, allowing for the possibility of rejection. It is further provided, however, that the offer may only be rejected where the

---

[18] Works Regulation 20(6); Supply Regulation 21(7); Services Regulation 21(7).
[19] The Court of Justice has rejected an argument that it is not necessary to seek explanations in a case where the tender is so low as to bear no relation to reality: it is not for contracting authorities to decide when it would be useful to seek explanations, but they must be sought in all cases: case 76/81, *S.A. Transporoute v Minister of Public Works* [1982] E.C.R. 417. For discussion see Arrowsmith, A *Guide to the Procurement Cases of the Court of Justice* (1992) at 3.3.2.
[20] See pp. 33–37.
[21] See the Commission proposal for a Directive on the excluded sectors, Bulletin of the European Communities Supplement, p. 94, section 103.
[22] Works Regulation 20(6); Supply Regulation 21(7); Services Regulation 21(7).

purchaser has examined the details of all offers, taking into account any explanations given to it of any abnormally low offers.[23] It is also expressly stated that in considering the explanation the purchaser "may take into account explanations which justify the offer on objective grounds", including the economy of the construction or production method or method of service provision; the technical solutions suggested; the exceptionally favourable conditions available for the performance of the contract; or the originality of the goods, works or services proposed. This thus requires the purchaser, in making its decision, to consider the reasons why the offer is so low. Such an examination may reveal that the offer is in fact the most favourable, in that it is the lowest, and there does not appear to be a risk of default. This will be the case when there is an "objective" explanation of the type noted above – for example, an innovative production method, or the availability of cheap labour – which reflects the provider's superior competitive position. Probably the receipt of *lawful* state aid falls into this category. (The utilities rules expressly state that when aid has been notified to or approved by the Commission a bid may not be rejected because it is affected by such aid[24] and it would appear that the same applies in the public sector by implication). In such a case there is no commercial justification for rejecting the offer, and to do so would be contrary to the very purpose of the legislation, which seeks to ensure that the most competitive provider wins the contract. Thus although it is not expressly provided that the purchaser *must* accept a low offer in these circumstances – merely that explanations must be taken into account – it can be argued that this is implied: not to do so would be an abuse of the purchaser's apparent discretion.[25]

On the other hand, the offer may also be the lowest, and there may be no risk of default, in circumstances which do not reflect an advantageous commercial position, such as where the bidder is pursuing the contract at a loss in order to damage the position of competitors, or to provide continued employment for its workforce or because the firm is in receipt of *unlawful* state aid. Since it is not the purpose of the rules to support such enterprises, presumably an authority may choose to reject the bid, even though it would be the most advantageous to the authority. In practice, however, an authority will often choose to accept such a bid. There is nothing to suggest that the authority is *obliged* to reject the bid, even when the bidder is in receipt of unlawful state aid.

Where, on the other hand, consideration of the reasons for the low bid leads to the conclusion that there is an unacceptable risk of non-

---

[23] *Ibid.*

[24] See pp. 515–518.

[25] The original proposal for the Utilities Directive did expressly state that such bids could not be rejected: see Article 22(5) of the original proposed directive.

performance, it is clear that the general discretion to reject the bid applies.[26]

In all cases where the authority rejects an abnormally low bid in an award procedure based on the lowest price criterion, it is required to send to the Treasury a report justifying the reasons for its decision, for transmission to the Commission.[27]

It should also be noted that in deciding whether a bid should be rejected, the authority may not take this decision based on the application of an objective mathematical formula – for example, by rejecting all bids which fall below the average price offered by more than a certain percentage[28]; it must consider the explanations offered by the bidder in the individual case, and take a decision based upon the specific facts. This applies even though a formula is more objective and precludes any discrimination against individual bidders, since such a formula cannot properly take account of the exact merits of individual cases.

II. Awards based on the most economically advantageous offer

Where the principle for the contract award is the most economically advantageous offer, the authority must take any explanation into account in assessing which offer is the most advantageous.[29] In particular, as with the case of the lowest price criterion, it must consider "objective" factors justifying the low offer, such as the economy of the method, the technical solution suggested, exceptionally favourable conditions, or the originality of the proposal.[30]

Where the purchaser concludes that the offer is the most advantageous, the normal rules on evaluation prima facie require acceptance of the offer. However, as noted above, Works Regulation 20, Supply Regulation 21 and Services Regulation 21 expressly state that abnormally low bids may be rejected, raising the possibility that such a bid may be rejected, by way of exception to the usual rule. As with the case where lowest price is the criterion, it is suggested that this permits rejection of the bid where it does not reflect an objective competitive advantage held by the bidder. On the other hand, where the bid does reflect such an

---

[26] It might even be argued that the bid should be rejected. On the other hand, there is no requirement to assess firms' financial and technical standing, and to reject on those grounds; thus it could be accepted that likewise there is no requirement to reject a provider because the nature of the bid itself suggests a risk of default. If, however, an authority is required to reject such a bid where the most advantageous offer criterion is used (as to which see the text, below), for consistency the same rule should apply where the criterion is lowest price.

[27] Works Regulation 20(7); Supply Regulation 21(8); Services Regulation 21(8).

[28] Case 103/8, *Fratelli Costanzo v. Commune di Milano* [1989] E.C.R. 1839, [1990] 3 C.M.L.R. 239 and case 295/89, *Impresa Dona Alfonso di Dona Alfonso et Figli s.n.c. v. Consorzio per lo sviluppo industriale del Commune di Monafalcone*, judgment of June 18, 1991.

[29] Works Regulation 20(6); Supply Regulation 21(7); Services Regulation 21(7).

[30] *Ibid.*

advantage, as in those cases referred to above, it can again be argued that it is an abuse of discretion not to accept it.

When consideration of the reasons for the low offer lead to the conclusion that there is an acceptable risk of non-performance, clearly the discretion to reject the offer will apply. It might be suggested that the bid *must* be rejected in such a case, on the basis that such an offer cannot be the most economically advantageous. However, it is submitted that the concept of the most economically advantageous offer encompasses only factors relating to the content of the offer, not the prospects of performance. Thus it appears that it is for the authority to decide whether such a bid should be accepted, in the same way as it is for the authority itself to decide whether or not to disqualify bidders on financial or technical grounds.

As with an award based on the lowest price, the purchaser must consider the facts of each specific case, and cannot reject bids by applying a general mathematical formula, for example, relating the bidder's price to the general average bid price.[31]

There is no requirement to send a report to the Treasury where an abnormally low bid is rejected in a procedure based on the the most economically advantageous offer, although, as noted above, this is required when a bid is rejected in a procedure based on lowest price.

(iv) THE MEANING OF "ABNORMALLY LOW"

Neither the regulations nor directives on which they are based indicate what is meant by an "abnormally low" offer, for the purpose of the above rules. It is submitted, in light of the purpose of the rules, that such an offer is one which appears to offer the particular bidder no reasonable opportunity of making a profit.

(v) THE RIGHT TO REASONS FOR THE DECISION

A provider whose bid is rejected as abnormally low is entitled to request reasons for that decision. This obligation is considered in further detail below.[32]

(h) ALTERATIONS TO OFFERS PRIOR TO THE AWARD ("POST TENDER NEGOTIATIONS")

Although this is not expressly stated in the regulations, once the deadline for submission of bids has passed, it can be implied that there is no *general* power for the authority to allow alterations to bids: if this were the case, the open and restricted procedures would be barely distinguish-

---

[31] See the cases cited in note 28.
[32] See pp. 281–282.

able from the negotiated procedure. Thus, bids submitted cannot be treated merely as a basis for negotiations between the purchaser and bidders. On the other hand, it does not necessarily follow that no alterations are permitted at all.

A declaration has been made on this subject by the Council and Commission of the European Communities.[33] This relates specifically to the Works Directive but is also likely to be applied to the Supply Directive and Services Directive since there is no material difference between the directives. The view taken is that under open and restricted procedure "all negotiations with candidates or tenderers on fundamental aspects of contracts, variations in which are likely to distort competition, and in particular on prices, shall be ruled out". It is also provided, however, that discussions may be held with such persons "but only for the purpose of clarifying or supplementing the content of their tenders or the requirements of contracting authorities, and provided this does not involve discrimination".

This indicates, first, that purchasers may not permit amendments to aspects of the bid which are relevant to bid evaluation. Price is expressly mentioned, but this would apply equally to other factors, such as delivery date, which are assessment criteria in a procedure based on the "most economically advantageous offer". This rules out the practice of "post-tender negotiations", whereby purchasers negotiate with all or some bidders (for example, those submitting the best bids), or even conduct a second tendering exercise, to get firms to improve their offers. The merits of this practice in obtaining value for money are much debated; whilst bids may be improved, where providers' profit margins are squeezed too much there is a danger of unsatisfactory performance. In the context of the procurement regulations, however, the main justification for prohibiting negotiations is that it eliminates possibilities for abuse, by reducing the discretionary elements of the selection process. Such a rule appears implicit in the directives, which require the award to be made to the provider offering the best bid submitted, and do not leave any room for a further procedure to be carried out before the provider is selected. An alternative approach, which would preserve transparency but give authorities greater flexibility, could have been to allow for a second stage of the procedure, where bidders may submit revised bids according to a second formal deadline.

It can be argued, however, that the prohibition against allowing alterations should not apply where the effect is to make the bid less competitive – for example, by *increasing* the price. A provider might wish to make an alteration which has this effect where some mistake has been

---

[33] Statement concerning Article 7(4) of Public Works Directive 93/37 [1994] O.J. L111/114. The statement, whilst not legally binding, was referred to with approval by Advocate General Tesauro in case C–243/89 *Commission v. Denmark*, above, para. 19 of the Opinion of November 17, 1992. This he regarded as an aspect of the general principle of equality of treatment approved by the court in that case, as to which see pp. 181–182.

made – for example, in arithmetical calculations, or over the legal application of the TUPE regulations.[34] It can also be suggested that amendments of bids, whether to make them more favourable or less so, should be permitted in the case of a mistake which is apparent on the face of the bid. This would cover the cases of arithmetical or "TUPE" errors of all kinds.

A provider may also wish to alter the bid where it fails to comply with formalities or with minimum substantive requirements – for example, where it is submitted in the wrong language, or the product offered does not meet the specifications. In relation to formalities, it was suggested above that with certain exceptions, including late bids, authorities may choose to accept bids which do not comply with procedural requirements which it has set, and that this includes a power to accept such bids conditional on their alteration to comply with formalities, where appropriate.[35] So far as concerns bids which fail to meet substantive requirements, it was suggested above that these may not generally be accepted as they stand.[36] However, there appears to be no objection to allowing the authority to permit correction of a bid to meet substantive requirements provided, however, that the bidder is not also permitted to alter the content of the offer in relation to the evaluation criteria – for example, by lowering the price.

The regulations do not appear to prevent authorities from seeking, and bidders from providing, additional information on the bid, whether this was required originally and omitted, or was not originally requested. For example, the authority may require a bidder to specify in more precise terms how he proposes to organise a particular service, or request further details of the bidder's product. This is indicated by the second part of the statement of the Council and Commission above.

The position may also arise where the authority itself wishes to change its requirements after the bid deadline. This issue is dealt with in Chapter 11 on specifications, where it is suggested that changes to the specifications are permitted at this stage, provided that they are not "substantial".[37] In this case it will be necessary to give all bidders a reasonable and equal opportunity to revise their bids.

(i) NEGOTIATIONS WITH THE MOST FAVOURABLE BIDDER

It is not clear whether purchasers may negotiate with the winning bidder to seek an improvement to the bid. Negotiations to improve the winning offer are not open to abuse in the same way as negotiations with several bidders; there is no opportunity to favour a particular provider. The

---

[34] On the TUPE regulations see pp. 636–648.
[35] See p. 235.
[36] See pp 232–233.
[37] See pp. 617–618.

disadvantage of such a practice, as mentioned above, is that providers may be unduly squeezed and may not perform the contract properly. However, this question of value for money for purchasers is not a concern of Community law, which seeks only to provide for fair and equal access to contracts. There is nothing specific in the directives or regulations to limit an authority's powers once the winning bidder has been selected, so that it is possible to argue that negotiations with the most favourable bidder are permitted. However, since the rules clearly require the contract to be awarded to that bidder, if at all, it follows that if negotiations are not successful the only option for the purchaser is to commence a new award procedure.[38]

On the other hand, any agreement prior to the contract which benefits the provider – for example, an increase in price – must, by implication, be ruled out. This would enable favoured firms to win contracts by submitting very favourable bids, based on an understanding with the purchaser that these would later be revised in the provider's favour.

The position where the authority itself wishes to alter the specifications at this point – for example, because of changed requirements – is considered more fully in Chapter 11 on specifications. It is suggested there that non-substantial changes are permitted, and that the parties may then negotiate to change the terms of the agreement to reflect the changes.[39]

(6) PROCEDURES WHICH FAIL TO PRODUCE SATISFACTORY BIDS

In some cases an open or restricted procedure fails to produce a result which is satisfactory for the purchaser. This may be because no offers are submitted at all; or because those submitted are either non-responsive (for example, do not meet the specifications), are from unqualified providers, or are rejected as abnormally low. In other cases the purchaser may be dissatisfied because of a very limited response – for example, if only one or two bids are received – or simply because those received do not offer sufficient value for money. What is the position in these circumstances?

(a) ABSENCE OF TENDERS

Where an authority receives no offers at all under an open procedure, it is permitted to find a provider by using the negotiated procedure without advertisement[40]: since an advertisement has already been made which

---

[38] On this point see further pp. 254–255.
[39] See pp. 617–618.
[40] Works Regulation 10(2)(d), as amended by Utilities Supply and Works Contracts Regulations 1992, S.I. 1992 No. 3279, regulation 32(1)(b)(ii), and Works Regulation 13(1); Supply Regulation 10(2)(b) and 13(1); Services Regulation 10(2)(d) and 13(1).

has failed to produce an adequate response, it is considered inappropriate to require the authority to advertise the contract again (although it may, of course, choose to do so.)[41]

This right to use the negotiated procedure applies, however, only if the terms of the contract remain "substantially unaltered" from those originally advertised.[42] Where substantial alterations occur, it is necessary to begin a new open or restricted procedure – there is, in effect, a new contract which demands a new award procedure. This is consistent with the more general rule which, it is submitted, applies in open and restricted procedures, that an authority must always open a new procedure if it wishes to make a substantial change to the specifications or other terms.[43] What constitutes a substantial change should be the same for both purposes.[44]

Where an authority uses a negotiated procedure because an open or restricted procedure did not produce any tenders, it must send a report to the Treasury, for transmission to the Commission.[45] This monitoring provision was included because of the potential for abuse: it was thought that authorities might deliberately make the specifications and other terms unattractive, hoping to deter any bids and thus leaving the authority free to negotiate the contract with a particular favoured provider.

(b) WHERE ALL BIDS ARE NON-RESPONSIVE ("IRREGULAR") OR FROM UNQUALIFIED PROVIDERS

The regulations also make provision[46] for the case where an open or restricted procedure does not dictate the choice of provider because all bidders are excluded on the basis of the "regulation 14 criteria"[47] or for failing to meet minimum financial and technical requirements, or bids submitted are "irregular". The concept of irregular tenders is defined[48] as including those which fail to meet the technical specifications[49]; those

---

[41] Placing a voluntary advertisement does not entail that the authority must then follow the other formal requirements of the open procedure, restricted procedure, or negotiated procedure with advertisement – the only legal constraints remain those of the negotiated procedure without advertisement (case 45/87, *Commission of the European Communities v. Ireland* [1988] E.C.R. 4929).

[42] Works Regulation 10(3); Supply Regulation 10(3); Services Regulation 10(3).

[43] See pp. 617–618.

[44] On this see further pp. 617–618.

[45] Works Regulation 10(7); Supply Regulation 10(6); Services Regulation 10(7).

[46] Works Regulation 10(2)(a), as amended by Utilities Supply and Works Contracts Regulations 1992, S.I. 1992 No. 3279, regulation 32(1)(b)(ii); Supply Regulation 10(2)(a); Services Regulation 10(2)(a). It is expressly provided that this definition is not exhaustive. It is not clear which other tenders might be included: possibly, the provision could cover abnormally low tenders, as to which see p. 253.

[47] On these see pp. 331–340.

[48] Works Regulation 10(2)(a), as amended by Utilities Supply and Works Contracts Regulations 1992, above, regulation 32(1)(b)(ii); Supply Regulation 10(2)(a); Service Regulations 10(2)(a).

[49] On the precise definition of technical specifications see pp. 573–575.

which offer variations on the requirements of the contract documents where this is not permitted; and those which fail to meet other requirements in the contract documents – which could include a failure to comply with formalities (such as the language for bids).[50]

Where all bids are excluded for these reasons,[51] the authority is permitted, as where no tenders at all are received, to choose a contractor through a negotiated procedure,[52], rather than commencing a new open or restricted procedure.

The negotiated procedure *without* advertisement may be used.[53] This only applies, however, where the authority includes in the negotiations all those providers who submitted bids under the original open or restricted procedure, and who have not been excluded under the regulation 14 criteria or for failure to meet minimum financial and technical requirements[54]. If the authority does not wish to consider all qualified providers who bid under the original procedure, it must use the negotiated procedure with advertisement. This involves advertising the contract in the *Official Journal* as well as a number of other formalities.[55]

As with the case where there are no tenders at all, the negotiated procedure in any form may be used only where the terms of the contracts are "substantially unaltered" from those of the original open or restricted procedure.[56].

In this case, in contrast with the position where there are no tenders at all, there is no requirement to submit a special report to the Treasury on the use of the negotiated procedure.

(c) ABNORMALLY LOW BIDS

Authorities may exclude a bid where it is abnormally low[57] as well as because it is non-responsive or the bidder is unqualified. The regulations

---

[50] It was suggested above at pp. 232–236 that authorities have a general power to reject bids which are non-responsive in the above senses, and indeed in some cases (including non-compliance with substantive specifications) must do so. The provisions on irregular tenders do not affect any discretion which authorities otherwise have in these matters, but merely provide what is to be the position where authorities choose to exercise their discretion by rejecting non-responsive bids.

[51] The provisions set out below may also apply where one or more of the bids received is rejected as abnormally low: see p. 253.

[52] Works Regulation 10(2)(a), as amended by Utilities Supply and Works Contracts Regulations 1992, above, regulation 32(1)(b)(ii); Supply Regulation 10(2)(a); Services Regulation 10(2)(a). It is expressly provided that this definition is not exhaustive. It is not clear which other tenders might be included: possibly, the provision could cover abnormally low tenders, as to which see p .253.

[53] See pp. 269–279.

[54] Works Regulation 13(1); Supply Regulation 13(1); Services Regulation 13(1). The directives require participation only of those who have submitted bids in accordance with "formal requirements" of the tendering procedure.

[55] This procedure is explained at p. 253.

[56] Works Regulation 10(3); Supply Regulation 10(3); Services Regulation 10(3). On this requirement see pp. 617–618.

[57] See pp. 243–247.

are not clear as to the position where only abnormally low bids are received.

One view could be that such a bid is an "irregular tender", and is thus to be treated like a non-responsive bid, as outlined at (b) above. If this is correct, it means that, where a procedure fails because the only bids received are either non-responsive, from unqualified bidders or abnormally low, it is permitted to invoke the negotiated procedure without advertisement only where abnormally low bidders, as well as those submitting irregular bids, are brought into the negotiations. This seems an appropriate outcome although, on the other hand, an abnormally low bid does not easily fit with the usual understanding of the word "irregular".

The regulations also make provision for tenders which are classified as not "appropriate": the provisions discussed at (a) above which apply where there are no tenders at all, apply also where the only tenders received are not "appropriate".[58-59] These provisions allow use of the negotiated procedure without advertisement, provided that the terms of the contract are not substantially altered. An alternative view of abnormally low tenders might be that they are tenders which are not "appropriate". If this is correct, where the *only* bids received are abnormally low, the authority is permitted to use the negotiated procedure without advertisement *without* inviting providers who submitted those bids to participate in negotiations. Where the authority receives one or more bids which are abnormally low *and* one or more bids which are non-responsive, on the other hand, it might be thought that the abnormally low bidder should be included in the negotiations, since the rules applying where some non-responsive bids are received require *all* firms participating in the orginal procedure to be brought into the negotiations. However, it is illogical to do this if such persons do not need to be invited where they are the *only* bidders.

(d) WHERE THE BEST BID DOES NOT GIVE SUFFICIENT VALUE FOR MONEY

A purchaser may be dissatisfied with an award procedure because the best bid does not offer good value for money. This is especially likely where it is felt that the number of bids actually received provides inadequate competition – for example, where there is only a single responsive bid.

It was suggested above that it is arguable, although not clear, that in these circumstances the authority may negotiate with the winning bidder for an improvement to the bid.[60] On the other hand, it is not permitted

---

[58-59] Works Regulation 10(2)(d), as amended by Utilities Supply and Works Contracts Regulations 1992, above, regulation 32(1)(b)(ii); Supply Regulation 10(2)(b); Services Regulation 10(2)(d).
[60] See pp. 249–250.

to negotiate with other bidders.[61] Thus if the negotiations with the winning bidder are not successful, the only option is to decline to award the contract to any of the bidders.[62] If the authority still wishes to go ahead with the project and to search for new providers, it must then commence a new open or restricted procedure under the regulations; there is no basis for relying on the negotiated procedure in such a case.[63]

(7) TERMINATION OF THE PROCEDURE WITHOUT AN AWARD

For a variety of reasons a purchaser may wish to terminate an award procedure without awarding a contract. It may decide to abandon the project altogether – for example because changed circumstances mean that the goods or services are no longer required, or because it feels, after seeing the offers, that the project will be too expensive. In other cases, it may decide to begin a new award procedure; this might happen, for example, where the authority is dissatisfied with the offers submitted but feels that a second procedure would produce better results, or where some mistake has been made in the first procedure, such as omitting to list the applicable award criteria. There is nothing in the directives or regulations to prevent termination of a procedure in such cases, and the fact that this is permitted can be deduced from express provisions stating that where no contract is awarded the *Official Journal* must be informed and reasons given to providers.[64]

Another reason for failing to award a contract may be that the authority decides to do the work in-house, instead of contracting it out. This will normally happen following a market testing exercise, in which the in-house provider submits the most advantageous bid in competition with external providers.[65] However, an authority may also eventually decide to retain the work for strategic reasons, even where there is no in-house bid or where that bid is not the most favourable. The position in this case was discussed above, where it was explained that, under the regulations, there is nothing to prevent a procedure being terminated so that the work can be kept in-house.[66-67] For local authorities, however, this possibility may be precluded by the rules on compulsory competitive

---

[61] See pp. 247–249.
[62] See s.(7) below.
[63] It might be argued that tenders which do not offer sufficient value – for example, which exceed budget requirements – are tenders which are not "appropriate", under the rules discussed at p. 253. However, this leads to the conclusion that the authority can negotiate freely with providers offering these tenders, or with other providers. This cannot have been intended: it would completely undermine the principle that post-tender negotiations, with bidders or other providers, are not permitted (as to which see pp. 247–249).
[64] See pp. 281–286.
[65] On this see further Chap 12.
[66-67] See p. 242.

tendering, which require the work to be awarded to the best bidder in the procedure.

Where a purchaser decides that it will neither award a contract, nor seek new offers for that purpose, it is required, under Works Regulation 22(4), Supply Regulation 23(4) and Services Regulation 23(4), to inform the *Official Journal of the European Communities* of that fact. Further, the same provisions require that reasons should be supplied for this decision, where these are requested either by a party who has submitted a bid, or by a provider who has applied to be included amongst those from whom the authority will select persons to be invited to bid.[68] No minimum time is stated either for the submission to the *Official Journal*, or for replying to firms requesting reasons, but it is no doubt to be implied that this must be done within a reasonable time. A maximum reasonable period of 48 days and 15 days respectively could be suggested, by analogy with the time-limits which apply under the regulations to the publication of award notices (48 days), and the giving of reasons for other decisions relating to the procurement process (15 days).[69]

These obligations will apply where, for example, the purchaser decides to abandon the project altogether, or to award the work in-house. They are not relevant, on the other hand, where it is decided to commence a new procedure to find providers, whether an open, restricted or negotiated procedure.

5. NEGOTIATED PROCEDURES

(1) INTRODUCTION

The open and restricted procedures outlined above are very formal, and impose strict and detailed rules designed to ensure that discriminatory considerations cannot be taken into account, and to make it difficult for the authority to disguise discriminatory decisions. There are, however, a variety of circumstances in which it is not desirable to use these procedures, even for major contracts. This may apply, for example, because of the particular nature of the purchase (for example, because specifications cannot be precisely defined, or there is only one possible provider); because the advantages of the procedure are outweighed by the disadvantages in the circumstances (as in cases of extreme urgency); or where formal procedures have been tried but failed to produce satisfactory results. In some of these cases the regulations allow use of more informal procedures, referred to as negotiated procedures.

There are two types of negotiated procedures. Under the first the authority may simply negotiate a contract with one or more providers,

---

[68] This right seems to apply even to those who have applied to be included but who have been rejected as unqualified under regulation 14 or for financial or technical reasons.
[69] On these obligations see pp. 723–735.

without the need for any formal advertisement: this will be referred to as the "negotiated procedure without advertisement". In other cases, the contract must be advertised, and the parties for the negotiations selected from those who respond to the advertisement: this will be referred to as the "negotiated procedure with advertisement". The precise rules which govern each type of negotiated procedure are discussed in sections (3) and (4) below.

(2) GROUNDS FOR USING NEGOTIATED PROCEDURES[70]

(a) GENERAL CONSIDERATIONS

The negotiated procedures as set out in the directives do not offer the same guarantees of objectivity and transparency as the more formal restricted and open procedures. The public sector directives have thus been concerned to limit their use to those circumstances in which they are considered to be strictly necessary.[71] These circumstances are set out in detail in the procurement directives and implementing regulations. The European Court of Justice has emphasised that the provisions authorising their use should be strictly interpreted.[72] Further, the contracting authority has the burden of proving that the circumstances justifying use of the derogation have been met.[73]

Authorities may sometimes wish to combine in a single contract (i) purchases for which the negotiated procedure could be invoked and (ii) other purchases, for which the negotiated procedure could not be invoked had they been purchased separately. For example, it might be thought appropriate in purchasing certain urgent supplies, which fall within the exception (iv) below, to add to the contract an order for further supplies of the same kind, because it is felt that to buy all these supplies together is likely to produce better value for money (for example, allowing economies of scale to the supplier). The situation here is similar to that where an authority wishes to purchase under a single contract both products, services or works which are exempt from the regulations (for example, on security grounds) and products, works or

---

[70] See Mawrey, "Public contracts: pitfalls with the negotiated procedure" (1992) 136 *Solicitors Journal* 708 and 730; Trepte, *Public Procurement in the EC* (1993), pp. 123–130.

[71] However, under the utilities rules it has been determined that these procedures do in fact provide sufficient objectivity to permit their general use: see Chap. 10.

[72] Case 199/85, *Commission v. Italy* [1987] E.C.R. 1039, para. 14 of the judgment; case C–71/92, *Commission v. Spain*, judgment of November 17, 1993, para. 36 of the judgment; case C–328/92, *Commission v. Spain* [1994] E.C.R. I–1569, para. 15 of the judgment; case C–57/94, *Commission v. Italy* judgment of May 18, 1995.

[73] Case 199/85, above, para. 14; case C–328/92, above, para. 16; case C–57/94, above. These statements were made in the context of proceedings in the European Court under Article 169 E.C., but probably national courts are required to take the same approach in actions in the national courts.

services which are non-exempt. This situation was discussed in Chapter 5. It was suggested there that such a contract would be exempt from the regulations only if it would cause very serious inconvenience to sever the two purchases, or where severance is impossible.[74] The same test seems appropriate in the present context: as noted, the Court of Justice has held that the provisions allowing use of the negotiated procedure are to be interpreted strictly.

When authorities choose to use the negotiated procedure, the record of the procedure must include information on the reasons why this type of procedure was selected.[75]

When the negotiated procedure is permitted the authority may always use a more stringent procedure than is required. Thus, for example, an authority choosing the negotiated procedure without advertisement on the grounds that a previous restricted procedure did not result in any tenders, may nevertheless decide that it wishes to re-advertise the contract, and to follow most of the steps of the restricted procedure. This would not, however, be treated as a restricted procedure under the regulations: the only rules which the authority would be *obliged* to follow would be those of the negotiated procedure without advertisement.[76] Thus if, for example, the authority chose in this case to negotiate with bidders over prices after bids had been submitted, this would be unobjectionable, since, whilst prohibited under the restricted procedure, it is permitted under the negotiated procedure.

(b) GROUNDS FOR USING THE NEGOTIATED PROCEDURE WITHOUT ADVERTISEMENT

The negotiated procedure without advertisement may be used on the grounds outlined below, and on these grounds only.

It may be noted that under the utilities rules a purchaser is permitted to negotiate a contract without advertising it in certain additional cases where a particularly advantageous bargain is available – for example, in a sale arising because of an insolvency.[77] It would probably be appropriate to allow public sector purchasers to do likewise, by adding these situations to the list set out below.

(i) CONTRACTS FOR RESEARCH AND DEVELOPMENT (SUPPLIES)

For contracts covered by the Supply Regulations an authority may use the negotiated procedure without advertisement "when the goods to be

---

[74] See p. 157.
[75] Works Regulation 22(2)(c); Supply Regulation 23(2)(c); Services Regulation 23(2)(c). On these records see further pp. 286–288.
[76] See case 45/87, *Commission v. Ireland* [1988] E.C.R. 4929, paras.10–11 of the judgment.
[77] See pp. 488–489.

purchased or hired under the contract are to be manufactured purely for the purpose of research, experiment, study or development".[78] This is intended to refer to the purchase of a prototype product using, for example, a new technique or materials.[79] This could apply, for example, where the government seeks a new type of surveillance equipment to assist the police: it may use the negotiated procedure to choose a provider who is to develop the prototype.

The provision does not apply, however, when the goods are to be acquired to establish their commercial viability or to cover research and development costs. This is intended to exclude the case where the authority purchases a quantity which is sufficient to enable the product to be marketed commercially or for the developer to recover costs, rather than confining itself to the acquisition of the original prototype. If further items than the original prototype are required it is necessary for these to be obtained through an open or restricted procedure. Thus the new product on offer must compete with other similar products which may be in the market.

(ii) ONLY ONE POSSIBLE PROVIDER (WORKS, SUPPLIES AND SERVICES)

Works Regulation 10(2)(c), Supply Regulation 10(2)(d) and Services Regulation 10(2)(e) allow use of the negotiated procedure without advertisement, where the works, goods or services can only be provided by "a particular" provider for either "technical" reasons, "reasons connected with the protection of exclusive rights" or "artistic reasons".[80]

"Technical reasons" could be that there is only one enterprise with the expertise to do the work, or which produces the product sought; or that only one firm has the capacity to complete on the scale required.[81] However, as indicated above, the burden of proving this is on the authority, and it is likely to be very difficult to demonstrate in a positive way that there is no other firm – or potential consortium – which could meet the requirements. This argument might be made in relation to certain professional services where an authority seeks the skills of a specific well known individual; but even in this case is likely to be treated with caution.

---

[78] See Supply Regulations 10(3)(c) and 13(1).

[79] It is not intended to refer to products and works whose *function* is the carrying out of research, etc. – for example, laboratory equipment. Although this is one possible interpretation of the literal wording of the provision it is clearly not the correct one: "for the purpose of" refers to the purpose of the manufacture, not the purpose of the end product!

[80] See Works Regulations 10(2)(e) and 13(1); Supply Regulation 10(2)(d) and 13(1).

[81] Technical reasons might also be invoked where the work is an addition to existing work and can only be done by the existing provider. This was argued in case C–296/92, *Commission v. Italy* judgment of January 12, 1994, but rejected by Advocate-General Gulman on the facts (paras. 12–17 of the Opinion); the issue was not considered by the Court since the action was held inadmissible.

In case 199/85, *Commission v. Italy*,[82] in relation to a contract for a waste disposal plant, the Court of Justice made it clear that it is insufficient to demonstrate that a particular provider is able to produce the most *efficient* performance, but it is required to show that *only* he can produce what is required.[83] It is submitted, however, that in deciding whether alternatives are available the court must have regard to the authority's subjective definition of its own needs, provided this reflects a genuine choice of the authority and is not merely designed to evade the regulations. Thus if, for example, only one firm is able to produce a waste disposal plant to the performance standards required by the authority (for example, capacity or safety standards), and these are specified bona fide as minimum standards, the exception could, in theory, be invoked.[84] However, to prevent abuse, the onus must be on the authority to demonstrate bona fides, which will require it to produce convincing reasons for its choice. An even stricter approach might require the authority's approach to be reasonable, and not merely bona fides; but it is submitted that this would involve undue interference by the courts in authorities' commercial decisions.

The provision on "exclusive rights" envisages the case where for legal reasons only one enterprise can perform the contract. This will apply, in particular, when the subject-matter of the contract is protected by intellectual or industrial property rights such as patents, trademarks or copyright. It is insufficient for the authority to show that it desires to purchase a particular product or service which is protected by such rights[85] – it is necessary also to show that there is no available "equivalent" to that product or service, since, again, the question is not whether one provider is *preferable* but whether there is an alternative. Again the question arises as to what is an "equivalent" product or service. This should be answered, as explained above, by reference to the authority's own subjective requirements,[86] although again the authority would be required to demonstrate bona fides by providing convincing reasons for its choice.

Even in the rare case where the authority's needs can be met only by a product or process protected by exclusive rights, if use of these rights is licensed to more than one producer then it cannot, of course, be said that there is only one possible provider.

---

[82] Above.

[83] Case 199/85, *Commission v. Italy*, above.

[84] If the authority specifies in a way which is unduly restrictive in the light of its bona fide requirements, this is also a breach of the Treaty: see pp. 582–585.

[85] See case 199/85, above; and see also case C–57/94, *Commission v. Italy* judgment of May 18, 1995, emphasising that it is only when it is "absolutely essential" that the contract be awarded to one particular firm that the derogation may be relied upon.

[86] A similar issue again arises in relation to the Community Treaty provisions, where the Court has held that to specify a product by reference to a particular proprietary standard where equivalents may exist is a breach of Article 30 E.C., as its restricts access of suitable products which do not meet those requirements: see the discussion at pp. 582–585.

The need for a particular provider for artistic reasons could apply where an authority wishes to purchase a unique work of art, or to engage (on an external basis) a particular artist or performer – for example, a photographer, or an artist for painting murals. It is difficult to draw a line in objective terms between a work of art or service which is unique in nature, and one for which "equivalents" are available. Whilst on the one hand a purchase of a particular painting by Picasso has no equivalent, could the same be said of the works of local artists? As with technical reasons and reasons connected with exclusive rights, it is submitted that the question of whether there is an equivalent can be determined only by reference to the authority's subjective needs, and thus that courts must respect the authority's bona fide judgment as to the unique nature of work on artistic grounds. Even if an objective test of what is an equivalent is to be applied to the "technical reasons" and "exclusive rights" exceptions, a subjective approach should certainly be taken to the artistic grounds exception. The issue will not generally arise, however, in relation to artistic *services*, since these are generally Part B services to which the award procedures under the Services Regulations have no application.

(iii) URGENCY (WORKS, SUPPLIES AND SERVICES)[87]

Because of the minimum time-limits for certain phases of the open and restricted procedures these take some time to complete. Urgency may, however, sometimes require a shorter procedure. Works Regulation 10(2)(f), Supply Regulation 10(2)(e) and Services Regulation 10(2)(g) permit use of the negotiated procedure without advertisement where for reasons of "extreme urgency" it is "strictly necessary" to depart from the usual open and restricted procedures.[88] The provisions may be relied on, however, only where the event giving rise to urgency is "unforeseeable" by the contracting authority, and is not "attributable to" that authority.

Whether there is urgency requiring departure from the usual procedures is assessed in light of the consequences of applying the usual procedures. Clearly, if any potential danger or difficulties can be avoided within the time scale of the usual procedures, the derogation cannot

---

[87] See further the note by Fernández Martín, (1994) 3 P.P.L.R. CS13.

[88] It is not expressly stated that this urgency ground for using the negotiated procedure without advertisement can be invoked where the procedure which would otherwise be relevant is the negotiated procedure *with* advertisement. This may arise, for example, with a purchase of services for which the negotiated procedure with advertisement would normally be appropriate because detailed specifications cannot be formulated in advance (on which see pp. 265–266), where the procedure with advertisement is not appropriate because the services are urgently required. The negotiated procedure without advertisement could still be used, however, since the condition is still satisfied that urgency renders the open or restricted procedure inappropriate (even though they are already inappropriate for other reasons).

apply. In this context, it should be remembered that there is a special "accelerated" version of the restricted procedure, which may be used instead of the normal form of that procedure where urgency exists, and which allows the award procedure to be completed in only 25 days, by providing for a mere 15-day time-limit for response to the contract notice, and ten days for submitting offers.[89] The negotiated procedure can be invoked only where this accelerated procedure is not adequate. Thus, for example, in a case brought by the Commission against Italy, the Court of Justice rejected an argument that a contract for construction of an avalanche barrier required use of the negotiated procedure, since the authority had not shown why the barrier could not be completed by the start of winter by using the accelerated restricted procedure, given that the report on the need for the barrier was produced in August.[90]

Where difficulty cannot be avoided entirely by using the accelerated restricted procedure, in assessing whether there is an urgency to justify departing from this procedure the courts will consider the nature and extent of the interest to which the contract relates and the likelihood of prejudice to that interest if delay occurs. Presumably the highest priority will be given to interests in health and safety, and in preventing damage to property.[91] With certain other interests, however, the court may be less willing to countenance use of the negotiated procedure. One case which did not involve health and safety or property damage was case C–24/91, *Commission v. Spain*,[92] where Madrid University relied on the negotiated procedure for a contract to construct a new faculty building, on the basis that overcrowding might result if it were not completed by the start of the new academic year. However, since the derogation was held not to apply for other reasons, the Court did not discuss whether such an interest would suffice. Even where health and safety is at stake, use of this derogation might be denied when the likelihood of damage during the period of delay is low. In case C–328/92, concerning proceedings by the Commission against Spain for use of the negotiated procedure for the purchase of pharmaceutical products, the Court of Justice ruled that the procedure could not be relied upon merely to ensure security of supply so as to prevent future shortages of certain products, but only where a shortage actually occurred.[93]

As noted above, the burden of proving the factual circumstances giving rise to the urgency is on the authority.[94]

---

[89] See p. 214.

[90] Case 107/92, *Commission v. Italy*, judgment of August 2, 1993; and see also case C–24/91, *Commission v. Spain* [1992] I–E.C.R. 1989.

[91] In case C–107/92, above, Advocate General Gulmann indicated that the urgency exception could potentially be invoked where either of these interests is affected.

[92] Above.

[93] [1994] E.C.R. I–1569. In case C–107/92, above, the Commission argued that construction of the avalanche barrier could not be considered urgent as there had been no avalanche since 1975. The issue was not considered by the Court.

[94] Case 199/85, above.

As indicated, it is also necessary that the event giving rise to urgency was not foreseeable by the authority. Thus if the authority is aware of the problem earlier but has delayed in getting the work underway, the derogations cannot be used.[95] It is also required that the urgency should not be due to the fault of the contracting authority. In such cases, the need for the work in question is subordinated to the overall policy of the public procurement rules.

(iv) FURTHER CONTRACTS WITH AN EXISTING PROVIDER (SUPPLIES, WORKS AND SERVICES)

In certain cases the regulations provide for use of the negotiated procedure for concluding a follow-on contract with an existing contracting partner. It was explained in Chapter 5 that as a general principle it is not permitted simply to negotiate a new agreement with an existing partner. This is possible only where this is the usual commercial practice with that type of contract (for example, insurance contracts) *and* the possibility has been referred to in the contract notice[96]; in other cases, the usual open or restricted procedure must be used to select a new provider. The rules in this section provide, however, exceptions to that principle in certain defined cases, where there is a justification for continuing the relationship with the old provider.

I. Additional works and services which were unforeseen
Under Works Regulation 10(2)(g) and Services Regulation 10(2)(h), authorities may use the negotiated procedure without advertisement[97] to award work to an existing provider, where this is additional to work under the previous contract that arises from "unforeseen circumstances". The negotiated procedure may be used in two such cases.

The first is where, for "technical or economic reasons" the new works or services cannot be carried out separately without "great inconvenience" to the authority. This might apply, for example, where an extension is required to works on an existing site on which a contractor is already present and it would be very troublesome and expensive to remove that contractor and replace him with a new one. In accordance with the general rule on interpreting derogations "great inconvenience" will be narrowly construed.

The second case is where the new works or services *can* be carried out separately but they are "strictly necessary" to the later stages of the

---

[95] In case 194/88R, *Commission v. Italy* [1988] E.C.R. 4547 ("La Spezia"), the President ruled on an application for interim relief in Article 169 proceedings, that there was a prima facie case of breach in using the negotiated procedure for a contract relating to renovation of an incinerator, where need for the renovation had been apparent for a long time but no action taken.

[96] See pp. 119–121.

[97] Works Regulation 13(1); Services Regulation 13(1).

original contract. This could apply, for instance, when prior to completion of a structure such as a bridge a safety report reveals a need for alterations to the original structure; or where an unexpected landslip during the course of construction work gives rise to the need for earthmoving services not envisaged in the original contract, in order for the construction to be completed. In this case it is arguable that the work could be carried out by the original contractor under this derogation, without the need to prove that there would be "great inconvenience" in carrying out the new work with a different contractor.

In these cases the objective circumstances make it almost certain that the existing provider will offer best value for money for the additional work, and it thus appears inappropriate to advertise the contract. Thus it is justified to make an exception to the usual principle that the negotiated procedure cannot be used simply because it can be shown which provider will give best value for money.

The provision can only be relied upon where the consideration for the additional works does not exceed 50 per cent of the value of the consideration under the original contract.[98-99] In valuing the consideration under either contract it is necessary to include not only the price paid but also the value of any goods which the authority provides to the other contracting party for carrying out the contract.[1]

Where the need for the works or services was foreseen, then, as noted above, this provision cannot be relied upon. In this case, where it is considered that it may be appropriate to award the later work to the same provider, the authority should indicate this in the contract notice, and use the derogation for additional work referred to in the contract notice, described at (II). below. If it fails to do so, it may be able to use (ii) above, which applies where for technical reasons the existing provider is the *only* party able to carry out the new work.

II. Additional works or services referred to in the contract notice

Under the Works Regulations and Services Regulations, the negotiated procedure without advertisement may also be used to make a contract with a previous provider, where an authority wishes to obtain works or services which are a repetition of those under the original contract, and which relate to the project for the purpose of which the original contract was made.[2] This might apply, for example, where a contractor has been awarded a works contract to build houses in the first phase of development of an estate, to allow the authority to award that contractor the work of building identical houses under a second phase of the develop-

---

[98-99] Works Regulation 10(4); Services Regulation 10(4). This limitation does not currently apply under the Utilities Regulations.
[1] *Ibid.* The same rule applies in valuing the contract for threshold purposes.
[2] Works Regulations 10(2)(h) and 13(1); Services Regulations 10(2)(i) and 13(1).

ment. Probably it is not necessary for the work to constitute a "repetition" that it should be identical to previous work in every detail, but it must no doubt be substantially similar. There may also be debate as to what constitutes a single "project"; there is as yet no guidance on this in the case law.

The provision applies only when the contract notice expressly mentions the possibility of the additional work being awarded by negotiated procedure to the same provider.[3] This enables firms to know the full scope of work which they may receive, and hence to judge whether it is worth submitting a bid. It is also required that the new award procedure should begin within three years of the date of entry into force of the original contract.[4]

As already noted, it is generally not possible to simply negotiate a contract with a previous provider even where this possibility is referred to in the contract notice: to allow this as a general rule would create unlimited opportunities for extending the relationship with an existing favoured provider, and hence such an "extension" is normally treated as a new contract.[5] The present exception allows for this, however, in a limited case, where it is commercially reasonable and the limiting conditions minimise the possibilities for abuse. This exception will not be needed for those exceptional cases – for example, insurance contracts – where renewal of an agreement which is renewable by its terms is treated as an extension to the existing contract, rather than as a new contract.[6]

III. Additional purchases from a previous supplier

Under the Supply Regulations,[7] in certain cases authorities may use the negotiated procedure without advertisement to award a contract to an existing (or previous) supplier, when the contract is for goods required as a partial replacement for existing goods or installations, or is for goods which are required as an addition to existing goods or installations. The derogation applies where to use someone other than the existing/previous supplier would oblige the authority to acquire goods having "different technical characteristics", and this would result in either (i) incompatibility with the existing goods/installation or (ii) "disproportionate technical difficulties" in their operation and maintenance. This exception, like exception (I.) above, identifies specific circumstances where it is objectively very likely that the previous supplier will offer the best value for money.

The provision may only be invoked if the term of the contract or of any other contract entered into for the same purpose is for three years or less. However, there is an exception where to exceed three years is

---

[3] Works Regulation 10(5); Services Regulation 10(5).
[4] *Ibid*.
[5] See pp. 119–121.
[6] See pp. 119–121.
[7] Supply Regulation 10(2)(f) and Supply Regulation 13(1).

"unavoidable"[8] – for example, where the nature of the contract makes a longer period a necessity for economic reasons.

It is not necessary that the need for replacement or additions should be unforeseen for this provision to be invoked. Further, if the need for replacement or additions is foreseen, it is not required that this should be indicated in the original advertisement.

Where an existing partner is the *only* party able to meet the needs of the authority at all, the derogation explained at (ii) above may be used.

(v) FAILURE OF OPEN OR RESTRICTED PROCEDURES (WORKS, SUPPLIES AND SERVICES)

Sometimes open or restricted procedures may fail to produce a satisfactory outcome. This may arise, for example, where no tenders are received; or where those received are non-responsive, are abnormally low, or are from ineligible providers. Where the authority still wishes to continue with the project, it is not normally required to commence a new open or restricted procedure, but it may use the negotiated procedure without advertisement provided, as a general rule, that all the qualified providers who submitted a bid in the original procedure are included in the negotiations. These provisions were considered in more detail above.[9]

(vi) PROCEDURES FOLLOWING A DESIGN CONTEST (SERVICES)

Under Services Regulation 10(2)(f) authorities may also use the negotiated procedure without advertisement where a design contest has been held to select potential providers, and the contract is negotiated with those providers who were successful in the contest. This provision is considered further in the section on design contests.[10]

(c) GROUNDS FOR USING THE NEGOTIATED PROCEDURE WITH ADVERTISEMENT

The negotiated procedure with advertisement may be used in the following cases (and in the following cases only).

(i) WHERE SPECIFICATIONS CANNOT BE DRAWN UP (SERVICES)

The open and restricted procedures envisage that specifications will be drawn up which are sufficiently detailed to enable providers to compete

---

[8] Supply Regulation 10(4).
[9] See pp. 250–256.
[10] See pp. 378–379.

on the basis of the specification. In certain cases, however, it is difficult to define requirements in detail because these cannot be precisely measured in terms of the end product. For example, an authority may wish to obtain advice on improving its management system. Probably it will not be possible to define the result to be achieved at the end of the service in the same way as with, for example, a refuse collection service. For example, in the above case the authority may not be able to specify the result in terms of cost savings, nor tasks to be carried out, since it may have no idea of what is possible until advice has been received on these issues from the consultant selected. In this case, to make a reasonable comparison of services on offer, it may be necessary to consult potential providers about possible solutions before making a final selection. This situation is particularly likely to apply to services involving a significant creative and discretionary element, such as certain types of consultancy, advertising, legal services or research and development.

The Services Regulations allow use of the negotiated procedure with advertisement in cases where the nature of the services is such that "specifications cannot be drawn up with sufficient precision to permit the award of the contract using the open or restricted procedure".[11] It is stated that this may apply "in particular" to "intellectual services", and to those specified in category 6 of Part A of Schedule 1 to the regulations – that is, financial services.[12] "Intellectual services" is not defined. Certainly it would be limited to white-collar services, where the services involved make use of intellectual rather than manual skills. However, use of the provision may not be apt for some white-collar services. Whether all professional services can nevertheless be categorised as "intellectual" services is not, however, critical: the specific (but non-exhaustive) reference to these services simply means that the courts are likely to be sympathetic to attempts to invoke the derogation in these cases.

This exception will apply only where the condition is met that specifications cannot be drawn up with sufficient precision to use the other procedures. In some circumstances, it may be possible to use the open or restricted procedure to obtain tenders based on hourly rates or even based on fixed rates for specific tasks. It is interesting to note that under the compulsory tendering regime applying to professional services it is assumed that a detailed specification *can* be drawn up at the start of the award procedure.[13]

No similar derogation is provided under the Works Regulations and Supply Regulations; thus it is assumed that specifications can always be drawn up in such cases with sufficient provision to allow meaningful competition. This assumption can be criticised. For example, an author-

---

[11] Services Regulations 10(2)(c) and 13(1).
[12] Services Regulation 10(2)(c).
[13] See p. 714.

ity seeking to procure a complex information technology system under a supply contract may find it difficult to draw up precise specifications without consulting potential providers and it would be useful to make the negotiated procedure with advertisement available in such a case. National systems often provide for more flexible procedures in such cases, and it can be noted that the UNCITRAL Model Law on Procurement of Goods, Construction and Services[14] – designed to serve as a model for national procurement laws – provides for such special procedures (as an exception to the usual formal tendering procedure) for any type of contract where it is "not feasible for the procuring entity to formulate detailed specifications."[15] At present, where this situation arises in a case covered by the directives it is probably necessary to use a form of the restricted procedure where discussions are held with all invitees before the specifications are issued.[16]

The difficulty of formulating specifications is no reason why the authority should not seek providers from the widest possible market; it merely renders inappropriate selection through a very formal and rigid procedure. Hence, an advertisement is required where the negotiated procedure is used on this ground.

(ii) RESEARCH AND DEVELOPMENT (WORKS)

The Works Regulations[17] provide for use of the negotiated procedure with advertisement where the work(s) to be carried out are purely for research, experiment or development; this does not apply, however, where they are to be carried out to establish viablity, or to recover research and development costs. This is a parallel to provisions in the Supply Regulations, the meaning of which has been discussed above.[18] It may apply, for example, where a work is to be constructed for the authority using an experimental technique to test the suitability of that technique for future works.

Under the Supply and Services Regulations no advertisement is required when the negotiated procedure is used for this reason. There is no sensible explanation for the difference in treatment under the Works Regulations.

---

[14] On the Model Law see p. 766.
[15] Article 19(1)(a) of the Model Law. There are three types of procedure suggested: "two stage tendering" (Article 46) which involves considering suggestions by providers, followed by formal tendering based on specifications; "request for proposals" (Article 48), involving initial proposals from different providers, followed by submission of formal offers based on their own proposals; and "competitive negotiations" (Article 49), which does not involve any formal second stage. Any of the three approaches could be adopted when using the European Community's "negotiated procedure".
[16] See pp. 615–616.
[17] Works Regulation 10(2)(b) and 13(1).
[18] See p. 258.

(iii) OVERALL PRICING NOT POSSIBLE (WORKS AND SERVICES)

Under the Works Regulations and Services Regulations a contract may be awarded by the negotiated procedure with advertisement where the nature of the work(s) or services, or the risks attaching to performance, are such "as not to permit overall pricing".[19]

This exception does not apply merely because the *exact* price is not fixed – provided the *method* of pricing is fixed the regulations will apply. Thus the regulations will apply to a "cost plus" contract (where the provider is paid his costs plus an additional amount, such as fixed fee or percentage of costs) or to a "target cost" contract.[20] The exception may be invoked, however, where even the *structure* of the pricing arrangement cannot be set without negotiations with providers. The exception is particularly relevant for complex infrastructure projects where there are many ways in which risk under the contract could be divided between the authority and the contractor, and different contractors will wish to suggest their own solutions (according, for example, to the different sources of finance available to them). This exception will, in some cases, permit authorities to negotiate on this point with a number of providers, rather than committing themselves in advance to a particular price structure. However, it should be pointed out that the provision may be relied on only when overall pricing is not possible, and not simply because it is considered desirable not to fix the price structure in order to widen competition. This considerably narrows the potential for using this derogation in the context of the government's "private finance" initiatives.

There is no equivalent to these provisions in the Supply Regulations.

(iv) FAILURE OF OPEN OR RESTRICTED PROCEDURES (WORKS, SUPPLIES AND SERVICES)

When an open or restricted procedure fails to result in an award because all bids from qualified bidders are unacceptable (for example, because they are non-responsive), an authority may use the negotiated procedure *without* advertisement, provided that all qualified providers who bid are brought into the negotiations.[21] In some cases, however, the authority may not wish to negotiate with all such providers. In this case, it is not necessary to open a new open or restricted procedure; the authority may award the contract by negotiated procedure *with* an advertisement.[22]

---

[19] Works Regulations 10(2)(c) and 13(1); Services Regulation 10(2)(b) and 13(1).
[20] On the different types of pricing methods in common use see Turpin, *Government Procurement and Contracts* (1989), Chap. 6.
[21] See further p. 252.
[22] Works Regulations 10(2)(a) and 13(1); Supply Regulations 10(2)(a) and 13(1); Services Regulations 10(2)(a) and 13(1).

(3) THE NEGOTIATED PROCEDURE WITH ADVERTISEMENT

(a) ADVERTISEMENT OF THE CONTRACT

The negotiated procedure with advertisement is available, as explained, where the formal and rigid requirements of the open and restricted procedures are not appropriate, but it is nevertheless useful to advertise the contract so that the purchaser can consider competitive enterprises from across Europe. The rules governing the advertisement are similar to those for open and restricted procedures.

As with those procedures, the authority must advertise the award procedure by sending a notice to the Office for Official Publications of the European Communities as soon as possible after forming the intention to seek offers.[23] This must be published no later than 12 days after its despatch.[24] This period is reduced to five days where a special "accelarated" version of the negotiated procedure is used,[25] which applies where the time periods of the usual procedure are rendered impracticable for reasons of urgency.[26] The notice must be published in full in the original language in the hard copy of the *Official Journal* and also in the Tenders Electronic Daily data bank, and in summary form in the other official Community languages.[27] The notice must be sent by the "most appropriate means", which in the case of the accelerated procedure means that it must be sent by telex, telegraph or facsimile.[28] Evidence must be retained by the authority to prove the date of despatch.[29]

The same rules apply to advertisement in national publications as apply in open and restricted procedures – they are permitted, but not before the date of despatch of the "European" notice, and they may not contain more information than is found in the European notice.[30] As with other procedures, it is probably permitted to send the information to particular providers known to the authority, although additional information should not be sent, nor should such communications be sent before the date of despatch of the "European" notice.[31]

The notice must be in "substantially" the same form as the model notices which are set out in Schedules to the regulations, and must

---

[23] Works Regulation 13(1), 13(2) (as amended by Utilities Supply and Works Contracts Regulations 1992, S.I. 1992 No. 3279, regulation 32(1)(d)(ii)) and 30(1)); Supply Regulation 13(1), 13(2) and 25(1); Services Regulation 13(1), 13(2) and 29(1).

[24] Works Directive Article 11(10); Supply Directive Article 9(8); Services Directive Article 17(5).

[25] *Ibid.*

[26] See p. 274.

[27] Works Directive Article 11(9); Supply Directive Article 9(7); Services Directive Article 11(4).

[28] Works Regulation 30(1); Supply Regulation 27(1); Services Regulation 29(1).

[29] Works Regulation 30(3); Supply Regulation 27(3); Services Regulation 29(3).

[30] Works Regulation 30(4); Supply Regulation 27(4); Services Regulation 29(4).

[31] On this point see pp. 195–196.

contain all the information set out in those models.[32] These models are set out on pages 271–273. As with other notices, the notice must not contain more than 650 words.[33]

Like the models for other procedures, these models do not contain all the information required to be published, and additions may thus be required to the list in the models. Thus, only the supplies model contains provision for reasons for derogating from the obligation to use European specifications, although reference is also required to such derogations in relation to works and services contracts,[34] and there is no reference to the award criteria for an award based on the most economically advantageous tender, though these must be included in either the notice or contract documents.[35] There is also an anomaly, found also in the model notices for other procedures, that the obligation to describe the subject-matter of the contract is not comprehensive, applying with supply contracts to products only, with services contracts to services only, and with works contracts to work(s) only: it does not extend, for example, to services provided under supply contracts together with the products.

The model notice for supplies requires reference to the CPA nomen-clature and the model notice for services to the CPC. It is likely that the Commission will shortly adopt a recommendation for the use of the Common Procurement Vocabulary (CPV) in such notices.[36]

(b) TIME-LIMITS FOR SUBMISSION OF REQUESTS TO BE INVITED TO NEGOTIATE

Providers wishing to be considered for participation in a negotiated procedure need time to prepare their requests, and short time periods are likely to disproportionately disadvantage firms from outside the awarding state. Thus a minimum period for response is prescribed, which is the same as with restricted procedures: requests must be received not less than 37 days from despatch of the contract notice.[37] The deadline must be stated in the contract notice.[38]

---

[32] Works Regulation 12(2); Supply Regulation 12(2). The models are found in Part D of Schedule 2 of the Works Regulations, Part D of Schedule 3 of the Supply Regulations, and Part D of Schedule 2 of the Services Regulations.

[33] Supply Regulation 27(2) and Services Regulation 29(2). Article 9(11) of the Supply Directive and Article 17(8) of the Services Directive which these provisions implement differ slightly, providing that the notice must not exceed one page of the *Official Journal*, of *approximately* 650 words.

[34] See pp. 590–596.

[35] On this requirement see p. 239.

[36] On this see pp. 69–70.

[37] Works Regulation 13(1) and 13(3); Supply Regulation 13(1) and 13(3); Services Regulation 13(1) and 13(3). The period is calculated so as to exclude the date of despatch itself, and when the period ends on a day which is not a working day it is ext nded to include the next working day: Works Regulation 2(3)(c); Supply Regulation 2(3)(c); Services Regulation 2(4)(c).

[38] Works Regulation 13(1) and 13(3); Supply Regulation 13(1) and 13(3); Services Regulation 13(1) and 13(3).

PUBLIC WORKS CONTRACTS REGULATIONS 1991, SCHEDULE 2 PART D – NEGOTIATED PROCEDURE NOTICE

1. The name, address, telegraphic address, telephone, telex and facsimile numbers of the contracting authority.
2. (a) The award procedure chosen.
   (b) Where applicable, justification for the use of the shorter time-limits.
   (c) Nature of the contract for which tenders are being requested.
3. (a) The site.
   (b) The nature and extent of the services to be provided and general nature of the work.
   (c) If the work or the contract is subdivided into several lots, the size of the different lots and the possibility of tendering for one, for several or for all of the lots.
   (d) Information concerning the purposes of the work or the contract where the latter also involves the drawing up of projects.
4. Any time-limit.
5. Where applicable, the legal form to be taken by the grouping of contractors to whom the contract is awarded.
6. (a) Final date for receipt of tenders.
   (b) The address to which they must be sent.
   (c) The language or languages in which they must be drawn up.
7. Any deposit and guarantees required.
8. Main terms concerning financing and payment and/or the provisions in which these are contained.
9. Information concerning the contractor's personal position and information and formalities necessary in order to evaluate the minimum standards of economic and financial standing and technical capacity required of the contractor to whom the contract is awarded.
10. Where applicable, prohibition on variants.
11. Where applicable, the names and addresses of suppliers already selected by the awarding authority.
12. Where applicable, date(s) of previous publications in the *Official Journal of the European Communities.*
13. Other information.
14. Date of publication of the prior information notice in the *Official Journal of the European Communities.*
15. Date of despatch of the notice.

PUBLIC SUPPLY CONTRACTS REGULATIONS 1995, SCHEDULE 3, PART D – NEGOTIATED PROCEDURE NOTICE

1. Name, address, telegraphic address, telephone, telex and facsimile numbers of the contracting authority.

2. (a) Award procedure chosen;
   (b) where applicable, justification for use of the shorter time-limits;
   (c) where applicable, form of contract for which offers are invited.

3. (a) Place of delivery;
   (b) nature and quantity of goods to be delivered: CPA reference number;
   (c) indication of whether the suppliers can tender for some and/or all of the goods required;
   (d) derogation from the use of European specifications.

4. Time-limit on delivery, if any.

5. Where applicable, the legal form to be assumed by a grouping of suppliers winning the contract.

6. (a) Final date for the receipt of request to participate;
   (b) address to which they must be sent;
   (c) language(s) in which they must be drawn up.

7. Any deposits or guarantee required.

8. Information concerning the supplier's own position, and the information and formalities necessary for an appraisal of the minimum standards of economic and financial standing and technical capacity required of him.

9. If known, the number or range of numbers of suppliers which will be invited to tender.

10. Where applicable, prohibition on variations.

11. Where applicable, the names and addresses of suppliers already selected by the awarding authority.

12. Date(s) of previous publications in the *Official Journal.*

13. Other information.

14. Date of despatch of the notice.

PUBLIC SERVICES CONTRACTS REGULATIONS 1993, SCHEDULE 2, PART D – NEGOTIATED PROCEDURE NOTICE

1. Name, address and telephone, telegraphic, telex and facsimile numbers of the contracting authority.
2. Category of services and description. CPC reference number.
3. Place of delivery.
4. (a) Indication of whether the provision of the services is reserved by law, regulation or administrative provision to a particular profession;
   (b) Reference to the law, regulation or administrative provision;
   (c) Indication of whether legal persons should indicate the names and professional qualifications of the staff to be responsible for the provision of the services.
5. Indication of whether services providers can offer some or all of the services required.
6. If known, the number of services providers which will be invited to tender or the range within which that number is expected to fall.
7. Where applicable, non-acceptance of variants.
8. Period of contract or time-limit, if any, for completion of the services.
9. Where applicable, the legal form to be assumed by a grouping of services providers to whom the contract is awarded.
10. (a) Where applicable, justification for use of the shorter time-limits;
    (b) Final date for the receipt of requests to participate;
    (c) Address to which they must be sent;
    (d) Language(s) in which they must be drawn up.
11. Any deposits and guarantees required.
12. The information and formalities necessary for an appraisal of the minimum standards of economic and financial standing, ability and technical capacity required of the services provider.
13. Where applicable, the names and addresses of services providers already selected by the contracting authority.
14. Other information.
15. Date of despatch of the notice.
16. Date(s) of previous publications in the *Official Journal of the European Communities*.

The regulations also provide for a specially expedited negotiated procedure when compliance with the usual time-limits is "rendered impracticable for reasons of urgency."[39] In this event the 37-day period may be replaced by a period of not less than 15 days.[40] The authority must state in the contract notice the justification for using such an expedited procedure, as is clear from the model notices. Where even this period is too short, and certain other conditions are satisfied, the authority may dispense with advertisement altogether and use the negotiated procedure without advertisement, as explained above.[41]

As to the form of requests, as with restricted procedures it is stated that a request must not be refused on the grounds that it is made by letter, nor because it is made by telegram, telex, facsimile or telephone, provided in these last four cases that it is confirmed by letter prior to the closing date for receipt of requests.[42] Apart from this, as with restricted procedures there are no further express provisions on the form of requests. It was suggested in considering restricted procedures that in general an authority may reject requests which do not meet formalities stated in the contract notice – for example, on language – but may waive these, provided the principle of equal treatment is respected.[43] The same rules should apply to negotiated procedures.

In relation to content, as was suggested with restricted procedures, authorities should be able to provide in the contract notice that firms making a request must submit information which is relevant to bid selection – for example, on financial standing – provided that it is information which may lawfully be taken into account in making the selection. In practice, however, authorities generally seek this information after receiving the requests to be invited to negotiate.

It is not clear whether requests for tender may be excluded from consideration for failure to meet requirements (as to form or content of requests) where these have *not* been stated in the contract notice. The same rules should be applied here as in the context of restricted procedures, as discussed above.[44]

(c) SELECTING PROVIDERS TO BE INVITED TO NEGOTIATE

(i) THE NUMBER OF INVITATIONS

The regulations state that where there is a sufficient number of providers who are suitable to be selected to negotiate, then at least three must be

---

[39] Works Regulation 13(1) and 13(4); Supply Regulation 13(1) and 13(4); Services Regulation 13(1) and 13(4).

[40] *Ibid*. Again this period is calculated from the date of dispatch of the notice, excluding the date of despatch itself, and when it ends on a working day is extended to include the next working day; Works Regulation 2(3)(c); Supply Regulation 2(3)(c); Services Regulation 2(4)(c).

[41] See pp. 260–262.

[42] Works Regulation 13(6); Supply Regulation 13(5); Services Regulation 13(6).

[43] See pp. 181–182.

[44] See pp. 214–215.

invited.[45] It may probably be implied from this, although it is not expressly stated, that where there are only two who are suitable, both should be invited. "Suitable" appears to cover those who meet minimum financial and technical standards and who are not excluded for failing to meet the regulation 14 criteria.

There is no indication of whether an in-house bid is included in the three. Since the purpose of the rules is to provide for independent competition to prevent favouritism it can be suggested that three *external* bids should be necessary.

(ii) THE METHODS FOR SELECTING INVITEES

In deciding who to invite to bid, factors which the authority may wish to consider will be similar to those discussed above in relation to restricted procedures – for example, financial and economic standing; the likely merits of the provider's offer; secondary policy considerations; or random selection.[46] The authority's discretion in this respect is, however, restricted by the regulations.

The relevant provisions are contained in Works Regulations 13(7) and (8), Supply Regulations 13(7) and (8), and Services Regulations 13(7) and (8), and are effectively identical to those governing selection in restricted procedures, which have already been discussed.[47] They[48] make it clear that firms may be excluded from any possibility of selection for failing to meet minimum financial and technical requirements, and also on the basis of the "regulation 14 criteria".[49] (Indeed, it appears that it is necessary to lay down any relevant requirements on these matters at the invitation stage, since this cannot be done at a later stage of the tendering process.)[50] The rules on selection further state that in selecting providers there should be no discrimination on grounds of nationality.[51] Apart from this, as with the provisions on restricted procedures, their effect is not entirely clear. It was suggested above that selection according to *relative* financial and technical status is probably permitted (provided that these relate to some extent to what is required for the particular contract) as are random selection methods. On the other hand, selection according to the likely merits of the offer or secondary policy considerations is probably not acceptable. For further consideration of these issues reference should be made to the discussion of the restricted procedure.[52]

---

[45] Works Regulation 13(5); Supply Regulation 13(6); Services Regulation 13(5).
[46] See further pp. 217–218.
[47] See pp. 217–222
[48] Works Regulation 13(7); Supply Regulation 13(7); Services Regulation 13(7).
[49] On these see Chap. 7. For the procedures for excluding firms on financial and technical grounds see also Chap. 7.
[50] See further p. 278.
[51] Works Regulation 13(8); Supply Regulation 13(8); Services Regulation 13(8).
[52] See pp. 217–222.

(d) SENDING INVITATIONS TO NEGOTIATE

It has been noted above that in the case of restricted procedures, the regulations require invitations to tender to be be issued simultaneously to all invitees and to be in writing; and they also prescribe certain information to be included in invitations.[53] The regulations contain no similar requirements relating to invitations to negotiate in negotiated procedures. However, the Works and Services Directives appear to apply these requirements to both negotiated and restricted procedure,[54] and thus it is necessary for authorities awarding contracts under the Works or Services Regulations to adhere to these requirements despite their omission from the regulations.[55] The details of these obligations, including the information which must be included, were discussed above in the context of restricted procedures.[56] Some of the information, however, is not pertinent to negotiated procedures – for example, the closing date for tenders – and presumably may be omitted.

As with restricted procedures, the regulations state expressly that invitations must be sent by "the most rapid means possible" where the accelarated form of the negotiated procedure is used.[57] Since there is an obligation to communicate by written means, this should be construed as referring to the most rapid written means, which presumably excludes mail, but could include facsimile, telex, telegraph, and, possibly, electronic means.

(e) DESPATCH OF THE CONTRACT DOCUMENTS AND PROVISION OF FURTHER INFORMATION

The rules contain no provisions on despatch of the contract documents, such as are found in relation to open procedures. However, it was suggested above that for restricted procedures an obligation must be implied that these documents will be sent within a reasonable time, and clearly this should also apply to negotiated procedures.[58]

---

[53] See pp. 222–223.

[54] Works Directive 13(2); Supply Directive 11(2); Services Directive 19(2). These provisions apply to invitations sent to "candidates". This term is defined to cover persons seeking to participate in either a restricted or negotiated procedure, under the Works Directive (Article 1(h)) and Services Directive (Article 1(c)). Under the Supply Directive, it is defined to refer only to those seeking to participate in restricted procedures (Article 1(c)), which is anomalous.

[55] The regulations might be broadly interpreted to include such obligations; alternatively, if this goes beyond the legitimate bounds of "interpretation", the rules can in any case be enforced against contracting authorities on the basis of the principle of the direct effect of directives (as to which see pp. 901–902). It appears that these requirements were omitted because it was originally considered that the directives did not apply them to negotiated procedures, but it is now accepted that this view may be erroneous: they have been included for negotiated procedures under the Utilities Regulations which implement requirements in the Utilities Directive which are worded in the same way as those in the public sector directives (see pp. 528–529).

[56] See pp. 222–223.

[57] Works Regulation 13(4); Supply Regulation 13(4); Services Regulation 13(4).

[58] See p. 223.

There is also no specific regulation relating to provision of further information on the contract documents, such as that which applies in both restricted and open procedures, where it is required that such additional information reasonably requested shall be provided at least six days before the tender deadline. However, the directives appear to apply such an obligation to negotiated procedures,[59] and if this is correct, authorities are obliged to adhere to such an obligation despite its absence from the regulations. In this case the obligation needs to be construed as referring to a time period six days prior to the final opportunity for making offers, since there may be no formal "tender" involved.

(f) CHOOSING THE PROVIDER FROM THOSE INVITED TO NEGOTIATE

Once invitations have been issued, the authority will proceed to negotiate with each of the invitees, with a view to concluding a contract.

In selecting the successful provider the authority must adhere to the principle in Works Regulation 20, Supply Regulation 21 and Services Regulation 21 that the contract should be awarded on the basis of either lowest offer or "most economically advantageous" offer: this principle is not limited to open and restricted procedures. In negotiated procedures the offers which are to be evaluated are not necessarily identified through a formal tender process[60] but are those which emerge from each invitee at the end of the period of negotiations. The meaning of the most economically advantageous offer was discussed above in relation to open and restricted procedures,[61] and exactly the same provisions apply in negotiated procedures. The same rules also apply to the treatment of abnormally low offers[62] and of in-house bids.[63]

In contrast with the position in restricted procedures there is no express obligation to state in the contract notice or the invitation which basis – lowest price, or most economically advantageous offer – is to be applied nor is there a reference in the model notices to this requirement. However, the directives themselves provide for this to be stated in the invitation to tender where not included in the notice,[64] and it appears that authorities must thus adhere to this requirement even though it is

---

[59] Works Directive Article 13(6); Supply Directive Article 11(5); Services Directive 19(6).
[60] The provisions of the directive itself on evaluation refer to "tenders" which seems apt only in relation to open and restricted procedures; since negotiated procedures need not involve "tenders" in the traditional sense; but it is clear that the same principles of evaluation were intended to apply to negotiated procedures.
[61] See pp. 237–239.
[62] Works Regulation 20(6) and (7); Supply Regulation 21(7) and (8); Services Regulation 20(7) and (8). For detailed discussion see pp. 243–247.
[63] Works Regulation 20(8); Supply Regulation 21(9); Services Regulation 21(9). For discussion see p. 242.
[64] Works Directive 13(2); Supply Directive 11(2); Services Directive 19(2).

omitted from the regulations. As with other procedures, where the most economically advantageous offer basis is used, the authority must state in either the notice or the contract documents which precise criteria (price, quality, etc.) are to be taken into account, where possible in order of preference.[65]

There are no express rules on how negotiations should be conducted. Often, these may take the form simply of informal discussions with each invitee. However, an authority may equally prefer to use a tendering procedure involving formal submission of bids to a deadline. For example, where the reason for using the procedure is that the specifications cannot be precisely defined the authority could ask bidders to submit their own proposals and follow consideration of these proposals with either a formal tendering procedure based on a favoured proposal, or a formal request for "final" offers with each provider making a bid on the basis of its own proposal. Should an authority choose a form of tendering it would appear not to be bound by the precise rules applying to open and restricted procedures – for example, the rule forbidding post – tender negotiations with bidders.

In all types of negotiations, however, constraints may arise from the operation of the general principle of "equality of treatment" for providers articulated in the *Storebaelt* case.[66] It is submitted, for example, that it would be a breach of this principle to provide information for one invitee on the offers made by the other invitees but not to give equivalent information to the other invitees. Further, where the authority does choose to conduct a formal procedure as part of the "negotiations", behaviour which would infringe the equality principle in open and restricted procedures may also infringe that principle in negotiated procedures – for example, extending the tender deadline for one provider only. It should not, on the other hand, be considered a breach of this principle to select the providers with the best proposals and to negotiate on price with those providers alone in a second stage of negotiations: here the different treatment is based on a material distinction between providers.

Normally the authority will wish to eliminate providers on the basis of regulation 14 or on financial or technical grounds at the stage at which it selects providers to negotiate. In relation to restricted procedures it was suggested above that the regulations appear to allow authorities to eliminate providers for these reasons *only* at this earlier stage, and regulation 14 to 16 of each set of regulations seems to contemplate that in negotiated procedures, also, this can be done only at the selection stage. However, as with restricted procedures, it is submitted that authorities could still, at any stage prior to the award, verify the accuracy of factual information provided to them, or check that the factual position of the provider has not changed in the intervening period.[67]

---

[65] Works Regulation 20(3); Supply Regulation 21(3); Services Regulation 21(3).
[66] See pp. 180–181.
[67] See further pp. 229–230.

(g) UNSATISFACTORY PROCEDURES

An advertised negotiated procedure may, like an open or a restricted procedure, prove unsuccessful in producing a suitable contracting partner. Under open or restricted procedures, where this is the case because no tenders are received at all or because the only responses are from providers who are unsuitable, an authority may proceed to award the contract through a negotiated procedure without advertisement.[68] However, there is no similar provision for the case where a negotiated procedure *with* advertisement fails for these reasons. This appears to be a gap in the rules. For example, where an authority advertises a services contract under the negotiated procedure because specifications cannot be precisely formulated, and does not receive any replies, it is appropriate to allow the authority to search for a provider without readvertising, as it could do if it had originally used the open or restricted procedure.

(h) TERMINATING THE PROCEDURE WITHOUT AN AWARD

For a number of reasons an authority may wish to terminate a procedure without awarding a contract – for example, because it decides to abandon the project or to make an award in-house. There is nothing in the regulations to prevent the authority from terminating the procedure at any time and for any reason, although it may be required to publish a notice in the *Official Journal*. In these respects the rules are the same as with open and restricted procedures, as discussed above.[69]

(4) THE NEGOTIATED PROCEDURE WITHOUT ADVERTISEMENT

(a) POSITION WHERE THE PROVIDER IS ALREADY DETERMINED

Under the negotiated procedure without advertisement there is no requirement to publicise the contract. In most cases where this procedure is permitted this is because there is only one possible provider or because the work is being awarded to a previous contracting partner. In this case, the provider is already determined and negotiations will seek merely to settle the terms and conditions of the contract.

(b) POSITION WHERE THERE IS A CHOICE BETWEEN PROVIDERS

In some cases, however, there may be a choice between providers: for example, in a case of urgency an authority may quickly carry out

---

[68] See pp. 251–281
[69] See pp. 254–255.

negotiations with several providers. Here it will generally contact known providers directly to initiate negotiations. In some cases where this procedure is used – because open or restricted procedures have failed or where a design contest has been held – the negotiating parties are already predetermined, being those qualified providers who bid in the original procedure, or those selected through the design contest. In these cases the rules impose some constraints on the procedure to be followed.

First, in principle the provisions on exclusion of providers in Works Regulations 13(7) and (8), Supply Regulations 13(7) and (8) and Services Regulations 13(7) and (8) apply. As noted above, these[70] make it clear that potential providers may be excluded for failing to meet minimum financial and technical requirements and also on the basis of the "regulation 14 criteria", and that there should be no discrimination on grounds of nationality.[71] They also seem to contemplate that selection according to *relative* financial and technical status is permitted, as are random selection methods; whilst selection according to the likely merits of the offer or secondary policy concerns is not. Although these principles are applicable, however, in situations where providers have not submitted specific requests for consideration it is difficult to review the authority's discretion in selecting invitees since specific firms cannot show that they are entitled even to be considered.[72] Where providers have been predetermined through a design contest or previous open or restricted procedure, assessment for suitability will normally have been carried out already. When providers are invited to bid, there appear to be no express formalities relating to issue of invitations.[73]

Secondly, in selecting a provider from those invited to negotiate in accordance with the rules above, the authority must, as with all other types of procedures, adhere to the principle stated in Works Regulation 20, Supply Regulation 21 and Services Regulation 21, that the contract should be awarded on the basis of either lowest offer or "most economically advantageous" offer and must follow the other rules in those regulations, which apply to the treatment of abnormally low offers

---

[70] Works Regulation 13(7); Supply Regulation 13(7); Services Regulation 13(7).
[71] Works Regulation 13(8); Supply Regulation 13(8); Services Regulation 13(8).
[72] The main importance of the provisions in this context is that where an authority contemplates using a specific provider but decides to exclude that provider for reasons relating to financial or economic status or the regulation 14 criteria, the regulations' procedural and evidential rules governing such assessments will apply: on this see further Chap. 7.
[73] Under the negotiated procedure with advertisement invitations must be issued simultaneously to all invitees, must be in writing, and must (at least with works and services contracts) contain certain specified information: see p. 276. One view might be that this obligation applies to all types of negotiated procedure. However, the relevant provisions, whilst referring in general terms to invitations to participate, without expressly excluding the negotiated procedure without advertisement, follow immediately from other provisions which are limited to restricted procedures and negotiated procedures with advertisement; and it is suggested that this limit is implied into the rules on formalities also: see Works Directive 13(2); Supply Directive 11(2); Services Directive 19(2).

and to in-house bids.[74] As with other procedures, the authority must state in the contract documents which precise criteria (price, quality, etc.) are to be taken into account, where possible in order of preference.[75]

Finally, the general principle of "equality of treatment" for providers, articulated in *Storebaelt* will apply in the same way as it applies to negotiated procedures with advertisement, in order to ensure that all invited firms are treated equally.[76-77]

(c) TERMINATING THE PROCEDURE WITHOUT AN AWARD

As with other award procedures, there is nothing to prevent an authority terminating the procedure at any time and for any reason without awarding a contract.

Where other award procedures are terminated and a new procedure commenced a notice must be sent to the *Official Journal* giving details of the termination decision.[78] However, this does not apply to the negotiated procedure without advertisement since these obligations apply only where the procedure was originally advertised by a contract notice.[79]

6. INFORMATION AND RECORD KEEPING

(1) DUTY TO GIVE INFORMATION TO UNSUCCESSFUL PROVIDERS

Under Works Regulation 22(1), Supply Regulation 23(1) and Services Regulation 23(1) authorities which have awarded a contract under the regulations must, within 15 days of the receipt of a request,[80] inform an unsuccessful provider of the reasons why he was unsuccessful. This right to information applies to those rejected as ineligible under regulation 14 or for failing to meet minimum financial or technical requirements; to those not invited to tender or negotiate for other reasons; and to those who were unsuccesful in the evaluation process, including those whose bids were rejected as abnormally low. In addition, where a provider was rejected in the evaluation of offers (including because the bid was

---

[74] On these rules see pp. 236–247
[75] Works Regulation 20(3); Supply Regulation 21(3); Services Regulation 21(3).
[76-77] See pp. 180–181.
[78] See p. 255.
[79] Works Regulation 22(4); Supply Regulation 23(4); Services 23(4).
[80] Not including the day of receipt. It must include two working days, and if it expires on a non-working day must be extended to the next working day. See Works Regulation 2(3); Supply Regulation 2(3); and Services Regulation 2(4).

abnormally low) he must be informed of the name of the successful provider.[81] There is no provision for those whose bids are rejected as non-responsive unless it can be implied that an assessment of responsiveness is part of "evaluation", which seems unlikely.

Where legislation imposes an obligation to give reasons for a decision, it is generally implied under English law that reasons should be intelligible, and adequate to allow parties to decide whether to challenge a decision; and for cases where a right to put a case has been given, they must deal with the substance of points raised at the hearing.[82] Where a provider is excluded under regulation 14 or on financial or technical grounds, the obligation to provide reasons thus probably requires some detail of the basis of the decision – for example, that the firm's manpower is inadequate and in what respect – rather than a simple statement of the grounds for the exclusion. With an abnormally low bid, it would be necessary to explain why any explanation offered by the provider was rejected. Where reasons are sought by a bidder whose bid was not selected as the most advantageous, it should be necessary to inform him of the ways in which the bid selected was more favourable, in terms of the relevant award criteria.

The Commission Proposal to amend the procurement directives to align them with the GPA proposes the inclusion of an amended version of these debriefing provisions, which would expressly require bidders to be told the "characteristics and relevant advantages of a tender selected" in an award procedure involving tenders.[83] It is unclear how far this adds to the implied requirements of the existing directives but in any case, as noted above, this information is probably required under existing United Kingdom rules. The Commission's Proposal also includes a specific provision allowing purchasers to decline to provide certain information on the contract award when this would impede law enforcement or otherwise be contrary to the public interest, would prejudice the "legitimate commercial interest" of particular providers or might prejudice fair competition between providers[84] – the same reasons as currently allow authorities to omit information from a contract award notice.

The obligation to provide reasons facilitates the monitoring and enforcement of the rules: it may both discourage purchasers from acting unlawfully, and aid providers in deciding whether to challenge decisions.

---

[81] Works Regulation 22(1); Supply Regulation 23(1); Services Regulation 23(1).
[82] See Craig, *Administrative Law* (3rd.ed., 1994), pp. 311–312. A similar principle is no doubt in any case to be implied into the directives on which the regulations are based, and the regulations must thus in any case be interpreted to include such an obligation.
[83] Proposal for a European Parliament and Council Directive amending Directive 92/50/EEC relating to the co-ordination of procedures for the award of public service contracts, Directive 93/36/EEC co-ordinating procedures for the award of public supply contracts, and Directive 93/37/EEC concerning the co-ordination of procedures for the award of public works contracts, COM (95) 107 Final, Articles 1(3), 2(2) and 3(2).
[84] *Ibid.*

(2) OBLIGATION TO PUBLISH A CONTRACT AWARD NOTICE

Under Works Regulation 21, Supply Regulation 22 and Services Regulation 22, an authority which has awarded a contract under the regulations – by whatever procedure – must send a notice to the Office of Official Publications of the European Communities[85] no later than 48 days after the award.[86] The notice must be published in full in all official Community languages, in the *Official Journal of the European Communities* and the Tenders Electronic Daily (TED) data base.[87] In the case of services contracts, notices must be sent for both Part A and Part B services contracts. However, in the case of Part B services contracts it is provided that the authority must state in the notice whether or not it agrees to publication,[88] thus indicating that publication is voluntary for these contracts.

If framework agreements may lawfully be used under the public sector rules, the position regarding award notices where such agreements are relied on is that a notice is necessary under the public sector rules[89] whenever a contract is placed under the agreement, but not following the award of the framework agreement itself. It would be useful to require a notice concerning the award of the agreement itself, to inform other providers of the exact outcome of the procedure in which they participated, as well as for contracts placed under the agreement.

The notice must be in a form "substantially corresponding" to the model notices set out in the Schedules to the regulations.[90] These model notices are set out on pp. 284–286. The notices sent must contain all the information listed in the model. Although the order in which the information is set out differs between the notices under each set of regulations the information is essentially the same.[91]

The information specified need not, however, be included in the following cases.[92]

(i) Where publication would impede law enforcement.

---

[85] Works Regulation 21(1); Supply Regulation 22(1); Services Regulation 22(1). Notice must be sent by the "most appropriate means" (Works Regulation 29(3); Supply Regulation 29(3); Services Regulation 29(3); and the authority must retain evidence of the date of despatch (Works Regulation 30(3); Supply Regulation 27(3); Services Regulation 29(3).

[86] Works Regulation 21(1); Supply Regulation 22(1); Services Regulation 22(1).

[87] Works Directive 11(8); Supply Directive 9(6); Services Directive 17(3). The same provisions state that the original language alone is authentic. The Office must publish the notice no less than 12 days after its despatch: Works Directive 11(10); Supply Directive 9(8); Services Directive 17(4).

[88] Services Regulation 22(3).

[89] On this see p. 179.

[90] Works Regulations, Part E of Schedule 2; Supply Regulations, Part E of Schedule 3; Services Regulations, Part E of Schedule 2.

[91] Except that a services notice referring to a Part B contract must include the statement on agreement to publication, referred to above.

[92] Works Regulation 21(2); Supply Regulation 22(2); Services Regulation 22(2).

(ii) Where publication would "otherwise be contrary to the public interest".

(iii) Where publication would prejudice the "legitimate commercial interests of any person". This includes the interests of the authority, of providers or of any third party.

(v) Where publication might prejudice competition between providers.

As with other notices sent to the Office of Official Publications, contract award notices must not contain more than 650 words.[93]

PUBLIC WORKS CONTRACTS REGULATIONS 1991, SCHEDULE 2, PART E – CONTRACT AWARD NOTICE

1. Name and address of contracting authority.
2. Award procedure chosen.
3. Date of award of contract.
4. Criteria for award of contract.
5. Number of offers received.
6. Name and address of successful contractor(s).
7. Nature and extent of the services provided, general characteristics of the finished structure.
8. Price or range of prices (minimum/maximum) paid.
9. Where appropriate, value and proportion of contract likely to be subcontracted to third parties.
10. Other information.
11. Date of publication of the tender notice in the *Official Journal of the European Communities.*
12. Date of despatch of the notice.

---

[93] Supply Regulation 27(2) and Services Regulation 29(2). Article 9(11) of the Supply Directive and Article 17(8) of the Services Directive which these provisions implement differ slightly, providing that the notice must not exceed one page of the *Official Journal*, of *approximately* 650 words.

PUBLIC SUPPLY CONTRACTS REGULATIONS 1995, SCHEDULE 3, PART E – CONTRACT AWARD NOTICE

1. Name and address of contracting authority.
2. (a) Award procedure chosen;
   (b) where appropriate, justification for the use of the negotiated procedures.
3. Date of award of contract.
4. Criteria for award of contract.
5. Number of offers received.
6. Name(s) and address(es) of supplier(s).
7. Nature and quantity of goods supplied, where applicable, by supplier. CPA reference number.
8. Price or range of prices paid or to be paid.
9. Where appropriate, value and proportion of the contract which may be subcontracted to third parties.
10. Other information.
11. Date of publication of the tender notice in the *Official Journal.*
12. Date of despatch of the notice.

PUBLIC SERVICES CONTRACTS REGULATIONS 1993, SCHEDULE 2, PART E – CONTRACT AWARD NOTICE

1. Name and address of contracting authority.
2. (a) Award procedure chosen;
   (b) Where applicable, justification for the use of the negotiated procedure.
3. Category of services and description. CPC reference number.
4. Date of award of contract.
5. Criteria for award of contract.
6. Number of offers received.
7. Name(s) and address(es) of services provider(s).
8. Price or range of prices paid or to be paid.
9. Where appropriate, value and proportion of the contract which may be sub-contracted to third parties.
10. Other information.
11. Date of publication of the contract notice in the *Official Journal of the European Communities*.
12. Date of despatch of the notice.
13. In the case of contracts for services specified in Part B of Schedule 1, agreement by the contracting authority to publication of the notice.

---

(3) RECORDS OF THE AWARD PROCEDURE

Works Regulation 22(2), Supply Regulation 23(2) and Services Regulation 23(2) require authorities to keep a record of all award procedures. These must contain the following information:

(i) the name and address of the contracting authority; the work(s), goods or services to be provided[94]; and the consideration to be given;

---

[94] The Works Regulations require information only on works, the Supply Regulations only on supplies, and Services Regulations only on services. This leaves a gap, since works, supplies and services could be supplied under all three types of contract.

(ii) the names of all providers whose offers were admitted to the evaluation process under Works Regulation 20, Supply Regulation 20(1) and Services Regulation 20(1)[95];

(iii) the names of providers who were excluded as ineligible under regulation 14, or for failing to meet minimum financial and technical requirements; plus the names of any other providers who sought to be invited to participate in restricted or negotiated procedures but were not selected to tender/negotiate;

(iv) the name of the successful provider;

(v) the reasons for choosing the successful provider;

(vi) the where the negotiated procedure is used, the reasons for selection of this procedure, and the grounds relied on for using that procedure (that is, which of the grounds listed in Works Regulation 10(2), Supply Regulation 10(2) or Services Regulation 10(2) was invoked by the authority); and

(vii) if known to the authority, which part of the contract if any the successful provider intends to subcontract.

Under the directives the Commission may request that it be provided with a written report containing the above information.[96] Where such a request is made, the authority must send the information in a written report to the appropriate United Kingdom authority, for eventual onward transmission to the Commission.[97] For government departments or Ministers of the Crown, their report must be sent to the Treasury[98]; for other authorities the report must be sent to the Minister responsible for that authority,[99] who must pass the information to the Treasury.[1]

Authorities must also keep records of certain specific decisions:

(i) Where an authority invokes one of the derogations to the obligation to use European specifications,[2] it must keep a record of the grounds for the derogation.[3] Where requested by either the European Commission or another Member State, the authority must send this information to the Treasury, either directly or via the the appropriate responsible Minister as noted above, for transmission to the Commission or to the Member State which requested it.[4]

---

[95] On this evaluation stage see pp. 236–247.

[96] Works Directive 8(3); Supply Directive 7(3); Services Directive Article 12(3).

[97] Works Regulation 22(3); Supply Regulation 23(3); Services Regulation 23(3).

[98] *Ibid.*

[99] Works Regulation 29(1); Supply Regulation 26(1); Services Regulation 28(1). This means the Minister of the Crown whose areas of responsibility are most closely connected with the function of the authority, as determined by the Treasury, whose determination is final: Works Regulation 29(2); Supply Regulation 26(2); Services Regulation 28(2). The obligation to provide the report is enforceable by the responsible Minister by mandamus: Works Regulation 29(3); Supply Regulation 26(3); Services Regulation 28(3).

[1] Works Regulation 29(2); Supply Regulation 26(2); Services Regulation 28(2).

[2] On this see pp. 590–596.

[3] Works Regulation 8(6); Supply regulation 8(6); Services Regulation 8(6).

[4] *Ibid.*

(ii) Where the negotiated procedure is used because no tenders at all, or no appropriate tenders, were received in restricted or open procedures,[5] a report recording the use of the negotiated procedure must be prepared.[6] This may be requested by the European Commission, and where such a request is made the report must be passed to the Treasury – either directly or by way of the responsible Minister as noted above – which will send the report on to the Commission.[7]

(iii) Where an award is based on the lowest price criterion but the lowest bid is rejected as abnormally low,[8] the authority must send a report justifying the rejection to the Treasury, or to the relevant responsible Minister as noted above, for transmission on to the Commission.[9] In this case, the information must be provided automatically, and is not dependent on a request by the Commission. The purpose of the provision is to alert the Commission to the possibility that unlawful state aid has been granted to the abnormally low bidder.

(4) OBLIGATION TO PROVIDE STATISTICAL REPORTS

Under Works Regulation 28, Supply Regulation 25 and Services Regulation 27 authorities are required to provide statistical reports on contracts awarded. The purpose of these provisions is to allow the Commission to assess the actual impact of the operation of the directives.[10]

Reports must generally be provided in all "odd" years (1995, 1997, 1999 etc.).[11] "GATT" contracting authorities,[12] however, must prepare a report for every year[13]: this is required by the GATT Agreement on Government Procurement.[14] In the Commission's Proposal for a new directive to align the existing directives with the GPA it is proposed that commencing October 31, 1997, reports will be required annually of all authorities covered by the directives, as is required under the GPA which covers all these authorities from January 1, 1996.[15]

Currently the reports cover the year preceding the year in which the report is required, and must contain, in relation to each public contract falling within the regulations, the following information[16]:

---

[5] On the situations covered by this provision for use of the negotiated procedure see pp. 250–254.
[6] Works Regulation 10(7); Supply Regulation 10(6); Services Regulation 10(7).
[7] Ibid.
[8] On these rules see pp. 243–247.
[9] Works Regulation 20(7); Supply Regulation 21(8); Services Regulation 21(8).
[10] See Works Directive Article 34; Supply Directive Article 31; Services Directive Article 39.
[11] Works Regulation 28(1); Supply Regulation 25(2); Services Regulation 27(1).
[12] See pp. 111–112.
[13] Supply Regulation 25(1).
[14] See generally Chap 15.
[15] Commission Proposal, note 83, Articles 1(10), 2(8) and 3(8).
[16] Works Regulation 28(1); Supply Regulation 25(1) and (2); Services Regulation 27(1).

(i) The value of the consideration (estimated if necessary).

(ii) The "type of goods", "principal category of works" or category of services (as set out in Part A of Schedule 1) covered by the contract. It is not clear how "type" of goods is to be defined, and this has led to some difficulties for authorities trying to compile the relevant statistics. It is suggested that the concept of "type" is probably the same as "type" for the purpose of applying the rules on aggregation of contracts.[17] The Commission's Proposal for aligning the directives with the GPA provides for reference to the nomenclature in Annex 1 of the Services Directive, Annex II of the Works Directive and Article 9(1) of the Supply Directive, and also for the category of product to be identified as in Article 9(1) of the Supply Directive.[18]

(iii) Whether the open, restricted or negotiated procedure was used, and, if the last, which ground under the regulations was relied on. Under the Commission's new Proposal, this obligation is to be extended to works and service contracts, as well as supplies, reflecting the fact that these contracts are now also covered by the new GPA and that under its provisions such reports are now required for these contracts. However, although the GPA now covers additional purchasers, including local authorities, these oblogations are not applied by the GPA, nor the proposed new directive, to these other authorities.

Again reflecting the GPA, the Proposal also requires for central government bodies to include details on the number and value of contracts under the various derogations from the rules, and for other authorities to report the value of contracts awarded under such derogations.

(iv) The nationality of the successful provider.

Reports by GATT contracting authorities under the Supply Regulations must also specify:

(v) The aggregate value (estimated if necessary) of contracts excluded from the regulations as below the relevant thresholds.[19] In the case of central government authorities the Commission's proposed new directive is to require states to break down the number and value of contracts awarded under each ground for use of the negotiated procedure. This is to improve monitoring of use of the negotiated procedure, abuse of which has been a significant problem in the past.[20]

The directives themselves provide that the Commission may take measures to require provision of information additional to that stated

---

[17] See pp. 168–171.
[18] Commission Proposal, note 83, Articles 1(10), 2(8) and 3(8). On the relevant nomenclature see pp. 188–189 and 125.
[19] Supply Regulation 25(1)(b).
[20] Commission Proposal, above, Articles 1(10), 2(8) and 3(8). The exact authorities to which this provision is to apply are to be listed in Annex I of the proposed new directive.

above.[21] The regulations thus require that authorities shall also supply such other information as the Treasury shall from time to time require for the purpose of informing the Commission (including information on contracts excluded from the regulations).[22]

Reports must be submitted by July 13 of each relevant year.[23] For government departments or Ministers of the Crown, their report must be sent to the Treasury[24]; for other authorities the report must be sent to the Minister responsible for that authority[25] who must pass the information to the Treasury.[26] On the basis of these reports the Treasury must prepare a statistical report covering all contracting authorities, which must be sent to the European Commission by 31 October of the relevant year.[27]

7. EVALUATION OF THE PUBLIC SECTOR AWARD PROCEDURES[28]

The Community's procurement regime has attracted criticism for a variety of reasons: in particular, as was explained in Chapter 3, doubts have been expressed over whether it will achieve its objectives in light of, for example, problems in ensuring that the rules are followed, and other trade barriers which will remain even if fair award procedures are implemented (such as the reluctance of providers to participate in bureaucratic government procedures). This section focuses on concerns relating to the content of the public sector procedures themselves. The main criticisms have centred on the rigid and inflexible nature of the rules. It has sometimes been claimed that, rather than improving the efficiency of purchasing, the rules often *inhibit* efficient purchasing practices and involve considerable costs which cannot be justified.

One criticism is that the rules are largely incompatible with that approach to procurement referred to as "partnering" or "partnership

---

[21] Additional information is to be determined by the Commission in consultation with the Advisory Committee for Public Contracts: Works Directive 34(3); Supply Directive 31(3); Services Directive 39(3). The Commission's Proposal, above, also provides that States shall provide any additional information which, under this Advisory Committee Procedure, it is determined is required under the GPA.

[22] Works Regulation 28(3); Supply Regulation 25(3); Services Regulation 27(3).

[23] Works Regulation 28(1); Supply Regulation 25(1) and (2); Services Regulation 27(1).

[24] *Ibid.*

[25] Works Regulation 29(1); Supply Regulation 26(1); Services Regulation 28(1). This means the Minister of the Crown whose areas of responsibility are most closely connected with the function of the authority, as determined by the Treasury, whose determination is final: Works Regulation 29(2); Supply Regulation 26(2); Services Regulation 28(2). The obligation to provide the report is enforceable by the responsible Minister by mandamus: Works Regulation 29(3); Supply Regulation 26(3); Services Regulation 28(3).

[26] Works Regulation 29(2); Supply Regulation 26(2); Services Regulation 28(2).

[27] Works Directive Article 31(1); Supply Directive Article 31(1); Services Directive Article 39(1).

[19] Supply Regulation 25(1)(b).

sourcing" which is popular in the private sector.[29] These terms generally refer to arrangements which go beyond the life of a particular project to provide a framework for dealing with the longer term expectations of a purchaser and provider – whether indefinitely or for a set period. Such arrangements are, almost by their nature, characterised by a co-operative rather than an adversarial relationship and can offer a number of advantages. First, they provide a degree of security of supply to the purchaser and of security of orders for the provider, which is of itself beneficial to long-term planning and efficiency. Secondly, the expectation of long-term commitment may facilitate co-operation in matters such as research and training, as well as a general pooling of expertise, to the benefit of both sides. Such a relationship is also generally conducive to an amicable and less costly resolution of disputes (and indeed the arrangement may provide expressly for a particular form of dispute resolution to avoid litigation); whilst awarding contracts to a pre-selected provider of known reliability also avoids the considerable expense of competitive tendering.

There are, of course, problems which purchasers must be astute to avoid: for example, the guarantee of work may induce complacency and inhibit innovation by the provider; the purchaser may be unaware of, or unable to take advantage of increased competitiveness elsewhere in the market; and competitive tendering may be unjustifiably precluded in circumstances where this form of competition could produce substantial savings. A purchaser must thus design a partnering arrangement which, in light of the particular product or service and the nature of the market, secures the best balance between the benefits of long-term co-operative arrangements and the problems arising from complacency and a lack of competition. This might involve, for example, combining a partnering arrangement for part of a requirement for a product with the use of competitive tendering for the other part of the requirement, so that the purchaser remains abreast of market developments; or the conclusion of partnering arrangements with more than one provider, so that an element of competition is introduced. It is widely considered, however, that where carefully designed, partnering arrangements may constitute the most efficient method of purchasing certain needs.

Often a legally binding contract is not sufficiently flexible to deal with all potential purchases under a partnering arrangement, for the reason that these cannot necessarily be anticipated at the outset. (Development of new products over the period of the agreement may be contemplated,

---

[29] See, for example, *Partnering: Contracting without Conflict* (1991), Report by the Construction Industry Sector Group of the National Economic Development Council; Saunders, *Strategic Purchasing and Supply Chain Management* (1994) esp. Chap. 9; MacBeth and Ferguson, *Partnership Sourcing* (1994). On partnering and the procurement rules see Broomhall and Lomas, "Partnering: An Acceptable Strategy for Utilities?" (1993) 2 P.P.L.R. 221; Trepte, "Partnering: Political Correctness or False Modesty?" (1993) 14 E.C.L.R. 204; Furlong, Lamont and Cox, "Competition or Partnership?" (1994) 1 *European Journal of Purchasing and Supply 37.*

for example). Further, even where future needs can be defined, the parties may not wish to commit themselves to long-term binding arrangements, but may prefer a relationship based on a more informal understanding – for example, a purchaser may feel it necessary to keep open the possibility of using other providers as a deterrent to complacency by its "partner". Thus the parties will often contemplate an arrangement involving a number of distinct contracts over a period of time. Arrangements of this type are, however, precluded for contracts covered by the public sector procurement rules, since these generally require each individual contract to be put out to tender through an open or restricted procedure. Potential long-term benefits from a relationship cannot be considered in deciding which bidder should be awarded a particular contract[30] and nor can an authority even improve a particular provider's chances by taking account of such considerations in choosing parties to bid in restricted or negotiated procedures.[31] An authority cannot, therefore, offer the reasonable expectation of future business to a specific provider which is essential for a partnering arrangement. An opportunity for a limited form of partnering may be provided by framework agreements[32]: under these agreements, contracts may be awarded pursuant to an understanding between the parties, and an expectation of future business dealings thus created, without any binding commitment which might lead the purchaser otherwise to eschew such an arrangement. However, such agreements, even if permitted by the public sector directives,[33] are useful only in those limited cases where the nature of future purchases is known since they require the terms of the agreement to be firmly settled.

Curtailment of partnering opportunities appears inevitable, however, if awards are to be regulated in a manner which can be monitored and enforced by judicial means. Partnering in its widest sense depends on the exercise of a wide discretion, involving a balance between the benefits of a competitive as against a non-competitive approach in relation to individual contracts and product/services areas: its operation is not susceptible to regulation by general objective rules. The whole Community procurement regime rests on an assumption that such a wide discretion will result in favouritism, or, at least, in limited opportunities for foreign providers because of complacency in public purchasing (a factor which is also inimical to effective partnering). If this assumption is accepted, loss of the benefits of full partnering for public purchasers who would otherwise have used this strategy in an effective way seems a necessary price for the benefits of an open market.

However, whilst complete discretion to adopt partnering arrangements seems undesirable, some modifications to the existing regime might be

---

[30] See pp. 236–239.
[31] See pp. 217–222.
[32] See pp. 175–179.
[33] There are some doubts about this: see pp. 175–179.

useful to allow purchasers to reap some of the benefits of close relationships with providers. Under the utilities regime this is possible to some degree first, because awards may be limited to those on "qualification" lists[34] and, secondly because there is flexibility in choosing invitees from the lists to compete on individual contracts.[35] Thus competition can be confined to a limited number of "key" providers with whom a relationship can be developed – although future work can never be guaranteed since it is still necessary for providers to compete for individual contracts. These features of the utilities regime, whilst providing more discretion for purchasers, nevertheless do not significantly affect the transparency of award procedures, since selection of providers for lists and for participation in contracts must be justified by reference to objective factors, as must the final award decision.

Of course, whilst the possibilities for arrangements which extend beyond the lifetime of a contract are limited by the current rules, partnering in the narrow sense of fostering a relationship built on trust rather than an adversarial approach may still be sought within the confines of an award made pursuant to the Community rules. The value of a "partnership" in this sense has been emphasised by the government in its recent White Paper on central government procurement strategy.[36]

Apart from the difficulties of building up provider relationships, criticism has also been directed at certain other difficulties flowing from the mechanical and rigid nature of the open and restricted procedures, such as the difficulties of involving providers in the development of specifications for complex procurements[37] and the apparent prohibition on post-tender negotiations.[38] Under the utilities rules, purchasers may use the negotiated procedure in any circumstances[39] and the question may be raised as to why this is not also appropriate for the public sector rules. However, it cannot be denied that the negotiated procedure, because of its unstructured nature, is much more susceptible to abuse than other procedures and the general priority given to open and restricted procedures may be justified.

On the other hand, some adjustments to the existing procedures would certainly be desirable. In particular, extension of the negotiated procedure to allow its use where there is difficulty in formulating specifications for complex supply and works contracts is a necessary and important reform.[40] In relation to advertising, the requirement to publish a separate notice for each contract imposes heavy burdens for little return, since it appears that advance market information is more

---

[34] See pp. 544–545.
[35] See pp. 497–500.
[36] *Setting New Standards: a Strategy for Government Procurement* (1995) Cm. 2840, especially at paras. 3.24–3.26 and 7.4–7.5.
[37] See pp. 615–616.
[38] See pp. 247–249.
[39] See Chap 10.
[40] On this see pp. 265–266.

important than details of individual contracts and response to *Official Journal* notices is often poor[41]; thus it would be useful to allow publicity through a PIN or advertisement of a qualification list as is permitted in the utilities sector.[42] It is also desirable that the directives should be amended to make it clear that contracting authorities may place contracts through the means of advertised framework agreements.[43] Further, the present criteria for shortlisting in restricted and negotiated procedures unreasonably inhibit authorities in obtaining the best value especially since they do not appear to permit an authority to consider how likely it is that a provider will offer value for money. The introduction of more flexibility in time-limits to allow authorities to take into account the nature of the specific procurement would also be a valuable reform. It would also be useful to extend the possibility of using the negotiated procedure *without* advertisement to certain additional cases where this is already permitted under the utilities rules such as to allow authorities to take advantage of bargains arising from special circumstances such as liquidations.[44]

In addition, there is an urgent need for clarification of the procedures. The exact scope of permissible negotiations under the open and restricted procedures,[45] and the permissible criteria for shortlisting[46] are just some of the vital procedural issues where the rules are unclear. These add to the interpretive difficulties relating to the scope of the directives which were discussed in Chapter 5 (for example, on the practical operation of the aggregation rules and on the position of framework agreements, discrete operational units and asset sales). Some of these uncertainties – such as those on shortlisting – are the result of inadequate drafting, whilst others – such as the problems with asset sales – arise out of changed policies and circumstances which were not anticipated when the directives were drafted. Whatever their source, however, such uncertainties greatly contribute to the dissatisfaction felt by many purchasers with the procurement rules.

Finally, it should be mentioned that the idea has recently been mooted that the rules-based regulation of procurement which currently exists should be replaced by a system based on *general principles*, such as "open access" and "equality of treatment", which would leave purchasers with much greater flexibility to seek value for money, but at the same time safeguard the fundamental principles underlying the present regime. This would provide purchasers with the more flexible options which have been suggested above on time limits, use of negotiation, etc. and would

---

[41] See Department of Trade and Industry, *Public Procurement Review* (1994), paras. 24–29.
[42] This would require modification to the existing qualification rules which do not allow authorities to insist on registration on qualifications lists.
[43] See pp. 175–179.
[44] See further pp. 488–489.
[45] See pp. 247–249.
[46] See pp. 217–222.

also permit them to engage in partnering or other more flexible forms of purchasing arrangements. It would also have the advantage of allowing the regime to adapt to new political and economic developments, such as privatisation through asset sales and innovative private finance techniques, so avoiding the need for revision of the directives to take account of such new developments. Further, it could provide a way to extend the scope of regulation for procurements which are below the thresholds in the current directives.

However, whilst this might be a reasonable approach once states have clearly accepted the need for non-discriminatory procurement, and the profession of purchasing has become more highly developed in the public sector across the Community, it is submitted that at present a more rule-based system is appropriate to ensure that abuses and inefficiencies are eliminated: as has already been noted above, the loss of the full benefits from flexible purchasing seems at present a necessary price for the greater benefits to be gained from a more open market. It can also be pointed out that a system based on broad principles would involve considerable uncertainty, which could cause greater problems for both purchasers and providers than the existing system, and render enforcement actions much less likely. Further, the requirements of the principles would eventually be filled out to some extent by the Court of Justice, and inappropriate rules might develop as a result: whilst the Commission, which has formulated the present rules, has been criticised for failing to draw sufficiently on relevant expertise, this danger would be even more acute if the requirements of open purchasing were to be established judicially. Further, from a practical perspective, such a change at Community level will be rendered significantly more difficult by the Community's participation in international agreements for the liberalisation of procurement, such as the GPA. These currently operate as rule-based systems and it is difficult to see that any other approach is possible if such agreements are to embrace countries which do not have developed systems for the operation of procurement and for the training and development of the purchasing profession. Thus it is submitted that at present it would be neither helpful nor practical to move to an approach based on principle, and attention should instead be focused on introducing appropriate reforms to the present rule-based system.

MAIN STEPS IN THE OPEN PROCEDURE – PUBLIC SECTOR REGULATIONS

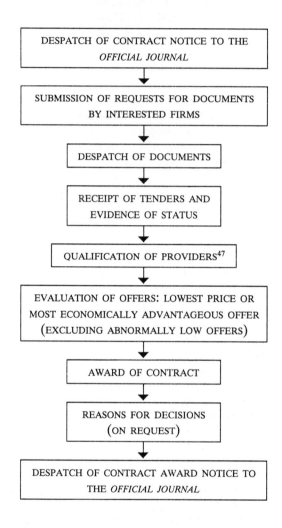

DESPATCH OF CONTRACT NOTICE TO THE *OFFICIAL JOURNAL*

SUBMISSION OF REQUESTS FOR DOCUMENTS BY INTERESTED FIRMS

DESPATCH OF DOCUMENTS

RECEIPT OF TENDERS AND EVIDENCE OF STATUS

QUALIFICATION OF PROVIDERS[47]

EVALUATION OF OFFERS: LOWEST PRICE OR MOST ECONOMICALLY ADVANTAGEOUS OFFER (EXCLUDING ABNORMALLY LOW OFFERS)

AWARD OF CONTRACT

REASONS FOR DECISIONS (ON REQUEST)

DESPATCH OF CONTRACT AWARD NOTICE TO THE *OFFICIAL JOURNAL*

---

[47] Optional, and may be done after, or alongside, evaluation of offers.

MAIN STEPS IN THE RESTRICTED PROCEDURE – PUBLIC SECTOR REGULATIONS

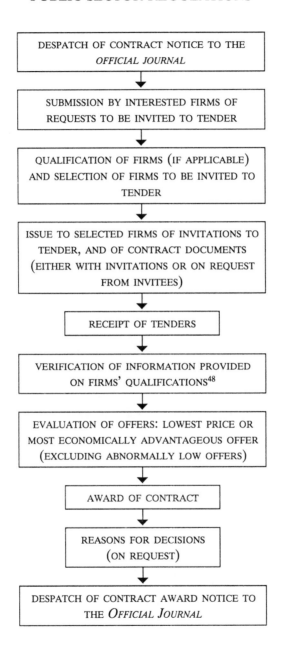

DESPATCH OF CONTRACT NOTICE TO THE *OFFICIAL JOURNAL*

SUBMISSION BY INTERESTED FIRMS OF REQUESTS TO BE INVITED TO TENDER

QUALIFICATION OF FIRMS (IF APPLICABLE) AND SELECTION OF FIRMS TO BE INVITED TO TENDER

ISSUE TO SELECTED FIRMS OF INVITATIONS TO TENDER, AND OF CONTRACT DOCUMENTS (EITHER WITH INVITATIONS OR ON REQUEST FROM INVITEES)

RECEIPT OF TENDERS

VERIFICATION OF INFORMATION PROVIDED ON FIRMS' QUALIFICATIONS[48]

EVALUATION OF OFFERS: LOWEST PRICE OR MOST ECONOMICALLY ADVANTAGEOUS OFFER (EXCLUDING ABNORMALLY LOW OFFERS)

AWARD OF CONTRACT

REASONS FOR DECISIONS (ON REQUEST)

DESPATCH OF CONTRACT AWARD NOTICE TO THE *OFFICIAL JOURNAL*

---

[48] Optional, and may be done after, or alongside, evaluation of offers.

MAIN STEPS IN THE NEGOTIATED PROCEDURE WITH ADVERTISEMENT – PUBLIC SECTOR REGULATIONS

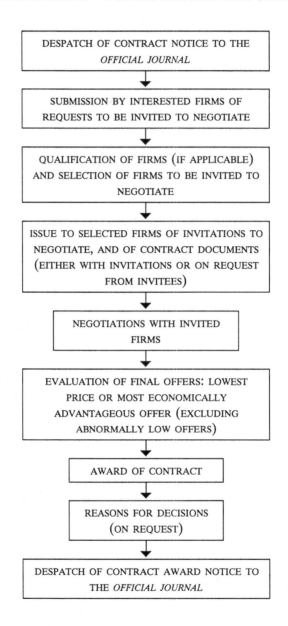

MAIN STEPS IN THE NEGOTIATED PROCEDURE WITHOUT ADVERTISEMENT – PUBLIC SECTOR REGULATIONS

(i) Where the provider is already selected:

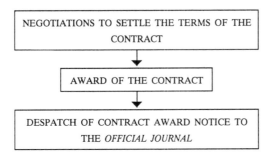

(ii) Where the provider is not already selected:

MINIMUM TIME-LIMITS FOR RESPONSE BY PROVIDERS – PUBLIC SECTOR REGULATIONS

OPEN PROCEDURE

despatch of   deadline for
contract   ←→   offers
notice

generally 52
days[49]

RESTRICTED PROCEDURE

despatch of   response   issue of invita-   deadline for
contract   deadline   tions   offers
notice

generally 37   generally 40
days (with   days (with
reduction to   reduction to
not less than   not less than
15 in cases of   10 in cases of
urgency)   urgency)[49]

NEGOTIATED PROCEDURE WITH ADVERTISEMENT

despatch of   response   issue of invita-   deadline for
contract   ←→ deadline   tions   ←→   offers
notice

generally 37   no time-limits
days (with
reduction to
not less than
15 in cases of
urgency)

---

[49] Subject to extension for bulky documents which cannot be supplied within the usual time-limits, and for inspections of documents or site; or reduction for prior publication of PIN.

CHAPTER 7

THE PUBLIC SECTOR: QUALIFICATION

1. INTRODUCTION

For a variety of reasons a purchaser may wish to exclude certain enterprises from participating in a contract. Most obviously, it will wish to ensure that any contracting partner has the ability to complete the contract. This will generally entail checks on the firm's technical ability to perform – for example, whether it has access to sufficiently skilled personnel -- and on its financial position. A purchaser may also seek to exclude a provider for reasons not directly related to its ability to deliver the goods or services: for example, because the firm has criminal convictions or because it does not follow equal opportunities guidelines. This process of deciding which firms are eligible to participate can be referred to as "qualification". This chapter explains the rules on qualification for contracts covered by the public sector regulations.[1]

In carrying out the qualification process public purchasers are, first, subject to the rules in the Community Treaties, as outlined in Chapter 4. This means, in particular, that such purchasers may not impose requirements on providers from other Member States which are not imposed on domestic providers, or which are more onerous than for non-domestic providers. Similar obligations also apply in relation to firms from certain other states under other international agreements, notably the WTO Agreement on Government Procurement (GPA), the European Economic Area Agreement and the Europe Agreements with a number of Central and Eastern European states.[2] In most cases (although not under the GPA) these rules apply to all contracts and not just those above the thresholds in the regulations.

In addition, for award procedures subject to the regulations, authorities' discretion is significantly curtailed by the regulations. These lay down a number of specific grounds on which providers may be excluded from participation.

First, it is stated in regulation 15 of each set of regulations that providers may be rejected where they lack economic and financial

---

[1] The history and background to these regulations are examined in Chap. 3; their scope in Chap. 5; and other aspects of the rules under these regulations in Chaps. 6 and 8 (award procedures) and 11 (specifications). Remedies and enforcement are dealt with in Chap. 18.

[2] See further Chap. 15.

standing (see section 2. below). Secondly, regulation 16 provides that they may be excluded for lack of technical capacity, or, with services, also for lack of "ability" (see section 3.). In these cases, as well as providing a power to reject providers, the provisions regulate the procedural rules and criteria for assessments and the information which purchasers may demand. Thirdly, regulation 14 of each set of regulations lays down a number of miscellaneous grounds for exclusion, some of which are relevant to the ability to perform – such as the existence of a winding up order – and others which concern "secondary" matters extraneous to the contract – such as previous failure to pay taxes.

Except to the extent authorised by these provisions there is generally no power to exclude providers from award procedures.[3] Thus, in open procedures, the bid of any firm which is not disqualified on the above grounds must be admitted into the bid evaluation process under Works Regulation 20, Supply Regulation 21 and Services Regulation 21.[4] In restricted and negotiated procedures all firms which are not disqualified on such grounds must be considered as potential participants.[5] Firms cannot, therefore, generally be disqualified for failing to comply with social or other secondary criteria, such as equal opportunities targets.[6]

The analysis below will consider, first, exclusion for lack of economic or financial standing, secondly, exclusion for technical reasons, and, thirdly, exclusion under regulation 14. It is also proposed to consider separately certain rules concerning the qualification process in general. Specifically these are: the provisions which regulate recognition of other states' official lists of providers; the use of domestic approved lists; rules on the legal status of providers; confidentiality of information; and the application of the Community Treaties to qualification.

2. ECONOMIC AND FINANCIAL STANDING[7]

(1) GENERAL PRINCIPLES

Purchasers are generally concerned to see that a potential contracting partner is likely to remain in business for the period of the contract, and that it has adequate financial resources to perform the contract alongside its other commitments. As already noted, in making this assessment

---

[3] See pp. 229–231.
[4] *Ibid.*
[5] It is probably not necessary to invite all such persons to bid, however, where the number of interested and qualified providers exceeds the number needed for adequate competition: see pp. 215–216.
[6] On this issue see also Chap. 16.
[7] See further Triantafyllou and Mardas, "Criteria for Qualitative Selection in Public Procurement: a Legal and Economic Analysis" (1995) 4 P.P.L.R. 145.

authorities must comply with the Community Treaties and other international agreements.[8] This assessment is also regulated by the public sector regulations, under Works Regulation 15, Supply Regulation 15 and Services Regulation 15. These regulations make it clear that providers who do not meet minimum requirements of "economic and financial standing" may be excluded. However, they also regulate to some extent the process by which this may be done. These rules are designed to ensure that authorities provide fair opportunities for participation and that procedures for checking standing are not unduly burdensome and do not provide opportunities for authorities to conceal discriminatory practices. The rules do not *require* authorities to carry out such checks, which are a question of protecting national financial interests and are not of concern to the Community; they merely regulate the way in which this is done *if* authorities decide to make such checks.

It has been explained in Chapter 6 that in open procedures economic and financial standing is considered once bids have been submitted, since there is no possibility of limiting participation to firms which have been "qualified" prior to bid evaluation.[9] In restricted and negotiated procedures, on the other hand, an authority is permitted to assess financial standing before issuing invitations to participate and may decline to issue invitations to firms without adequate standing. Indeed, as explained in Chapter 6, the regulations *require* an authority which seeks to exclude providers on economic and financial grounds to lay down the relevant standards at this stage, and to limit invitations to firms which appear to be qualified (although it may leave until later the verification of factual information).[10]

In restricted and negotiated procedures authorities may sometimes wish to invoke the *relative* economic and financial standing of providers as a means of selecting invitees. This is permitted, subject to the same procedural and other limitations which apply in assessing minimum requirements as outlined in sections (2)–(4) below. It was suggested in Chapter 6, however, that this applies only to the extent that there is genuine concern over the risk of completion and that relative standing cannot be used as a method of choosing between providers who are all clearly capable of fulfilling the contract.[11]

On the other hand, economic and financial standing cannot be used as a relative criterion in assessing bids, which is weighed against other criteria such as quality or price. Once a firm has been admitted to the

---

[8] See Chaps. 4 and 15.
[9] See pp. 229–231. It was suggested that it is permitted to *allow* firms to submit to an assessment of their qualifications before the procedure if they choose to do so (for example, by registration on a list); but that this cannot be required.
[10] See pp. 229–231.
[11] See pp. 217–222.

procedure as a qualified provider, its bid must be assessed solely on the content of the bid, in accordance with the rules on bid evaluation.[12]

Under regulations 15(3) of each set of regulations, where providers are to be excluded on the basis of financial or economic standing or selection is to be made on this basis in inviting providers to bid, the information required from providers for making the assessment must be stated in the contract notice in open procedures,[13] and in either the contract notice or the invitation to tender in restricted procedures.[14] The position is less clear for negotiated procedures – regulation 15(3) refers only to an "invitation to tender" which might be construed as excluding an invitation to "negotiate". However, it is appropriate in a negotiated procedure with adertisement to allow the information to be included in the invitation rather than the notice and "invitation to tender" should be construed to include an invitation to negotiate.[15] It can be noted that the requirement above applies only to the information required of providers which is listed in regulation 15, as set out below. In addition to the information listed authorities may call for information to "supplement" or "clarify" that in regulation 15,[16] but it is not necessary to list this additional information in the notice or invitation.

"Economic and financial standing" is not expressly defined, but its meaning is important since only exclusions made on these grounds are authorised under regulation 15. It is submitted that a measure relates to economic or financial standing when it seeks to ensure that the firm has adequate financial resources to remain in business during the contract period, to complete the contract, and to meet any legal liability to the authority arising from performance (for example, for breach of contract or negligence, or in providing any indemnities for liability incurred by the authority itself as a result of the provider's work).

---

[12] See pp. 230–231.
[13] The requircment is also stated in the model contract notices: see pp. 197–202.
[14] In addition to regulation 15(3), regulation 12(10) of each set of regulations lists this information (where not included in the contract notice) amongst that to be included in the invitation to tender. The model notices also refer to this information, although they do not state expressly that this information is required only where it is not to be included in the invitation to tender: see the model notices on pp. 208–213. This is surprising since with contract award criteria, where a similar option exists, the notice itself states that the information is required only where not in the invitation to tender.
[15] It has been suggested that in relation to award criteria the reference to "tender" in the directive is intended to include a reference to negotiation as well (see p. 277). It is true that the model notices indicate that this information must be included in the notices without referring to the alternative of inclusion in the invitation; but this is also true of the notices for restricted procedures, where it is clear from regulation 15(3) that such an alternative is available. It can also be noted that there is no equivalent of regulation 12(10) on restricted procedures, which lists the information – including that relating to financial standing – to be included in the notices; but as explained at p. 276 it seems that the directives themselves do require this information to be included for negotiated procedures, and that its omission from the regulations is an error.
[16] See p. 317.

(2) THE CRITERIA AND PRINCIPLES FOR ASSESSMENT

As regards the scope of an authority's discretion, it is clear, first, that regulation 15 only authorises measures which are genuinely directed at assessing economic and financial standing in relation to the relevant contract(s). This is made clear in Works Regulation 15(1), Supply Regulation 15(3) and Services Regulation 15(1), which indicate that an authority is limited to seeking information which "it considers it needs" to assess economic and financial standing. Thus, for example, minimum levels of business turnover could not be set with the objective of excluding certain suitable firms, in order to favour a particular provider.[17]

Secondly, these same provisions seem to indicate that authorities must determine in advance how the assessment is to be made: they may not require providers to submit a range of information, and then decide at a later point which information is to be used in making the assessment.

Thirdly, the question arises as to which criteria may be considered. Here it may be noted that certain criteria which authorities may take into account are contemplated expressly in the regulations, which give a list of specific evidence which may be sought from providers (as explained in section 3. below). For example, it is expressly stated that authorities may call for evidence of a firm's turnover, which indicates that turnover is a relevant factor in assessing standing.[18] However, the relevant criteria are not limited to those contemplated in the list. This was made clear by the European Court of Justice in the joined cases of *CEI* and *Bellini*.[19] One issue in these cases concerned Belgian legislation which generally prohibited the award of works contracts to firms which had already undertaken other work exceeding a set amount. One purpose of this was to ensure that firms did not over-commit themselves in the light of their available resources (the total figure being different according to the "class" in which a firm had been placed). The Court held that the existing commitments of providers was a relevant criterion even though the list of permitted evidence in the Works Directive did not refer to any evidence relating to total works undertaken. This was because, in the view of the Court, the list of evidence in the directive was not exhaustive of the evidence which could be sought by authorities, and the criteria which could be taken into account thus need not be limited to those matters which could be deduced from the evidence listed. The regulations are based closely on the directive and do not limit the

---

[17] This would also be a breach of the principle of equal treatment of providers laid down by the Court of Justice: on this see further pp. 180–181.

[18] See pp. 308–309

[19] Joined cases 27–29/86, *S.A. Constructions et Entreprises Industrielles (CEI) and others v. Société Co-operative "Association Intercommunales pour les Autoroutes des Ardennes" ("CEI and Bellini")* [1987] E.C.R. 3347, paras.11–18 of the judgment.

evidence or criteria which may be used. However, the criteria which can properly be considered to relate to economic and financial standing will be for determination by the Court of Justice.

Another principle laid down by the Court is that it is for authorities themselves to set the financial *standards* which firms must meet[20] – for example, the size of turnover required for a particular value of contract, or the maximum value of commitments which a firm of a certain size may undertake at any one time. Thus, even if a provider has adequate standing for a particular contract in its own state, it need not be recognised as having standing to compete for similar contracts in the United Kingdom.[21]

Provided an authority acts within the restrictions above, it is unclear whether there is any further possibility for judicial control of assessments, through implied limitations on the power in regulation 15. One possible argument is that authorities must assess a provider's suitability on the facts of each case and may not rely solely on general rules concerning minimum levels of turnover, value of works undertaken, etc.[22] This would ensure that specific providers are not unfairly excluded as unsuitable, and, in particular, that the rules do not unfairly favour large firms as against small- and medium-sized enterprises (SMEs), which is likely to happen where absolute minimum requirements are set. This is particularly significant in view of the importance attached by the Community to the participation of SMEs in public procurement.[23] On the other hand use of general formulae minimises the degree of discretion and hence the opportunities for discrimination; allows firms to know in advance whether they should participate (particularly important in open procedures where suitability is not assessed until after bids are submitted); and enables an assessment to be conducted more speedily. In relation to the evaluation of bids and the exclusion of abnormally low bids, the Court of Justice has ruled that general formulae may not be applied mechanically, which might indicate that the Court may require authorities to consider the specific situation of each provider in the context of qualification as well. However, in *CEI and Bellini*, the Court of Justice indicated that it is permitted to adopt a general rule fixing the maximum value of works which providers may carry out at any one

---

[20] *CEI and Bellini*, above, paras. 26–28 of the judgment; case 31/87, *Gebroeders Beentjes B.V. v. The Netherlands* [1988] E.C.R. 4635, para. 17 of the judgment (on the Works Directive). There is nothing in the United Kingdom Regulations imposing greater restrictions on United Kingdom authorities.

[21] *CEI and Bellini*, above, paras. 27–28 of the judgment, holding that the position is not affected by the provisions in the Works Directive

[22] On this issue see further Tryantafyllou and Mardas, above. Some support for such a view can be found, in relation to technical standing, in the Opinion of Advocate General Lenz in case C–362/90, *Commission v. Italy* [1994] 3 C.M.L.R. 1: on this see further p. 329.

[23] On this see pp. 67–68.

time.[24] This seems justified, since the arguments for and against general rules appear to be much more finely balanced in the context of assessing standing than in relation to low bids or bid evaluation.[25]

The Court of Justice might also imply that any financial requirements set must be proportionate to the objectives achieved: "proportionality" is a general principle of Community law which may be implied in interpreting Community legislation.[26] Such a requirement may limit the discretion of the authority to apply relevant criteria in an arbitrary way – for example, it may prohibit limits on the total value of work which firms undertake which are general and do not relate to the size or capability of the particular class of firm.[27] It might also allow financial standards to be struck down if wholly excessive in light of the work to be carried out, but it is likely that the courts would grant authorities a wide margin of discretion here.

(3) FINANCIAL STANDING OF COMPANIES IN GROUPS

In *Ballast Nedam*[28] the Court of Justice considered how financial standing should be assessed in relation to companies in groups. The case concerned a company designated as unqualified to participate in certain works contracts in Belgium because it was a holding company with no resources to carry out works itself. The company sought annulment of this decision in the Belgian courts, arguing that under the Works Directive the government was obliged to take account of the resources of the firm's subsidiaries, which it was able to control and which would

---

[24] *CEI and Bellini*, above, paras. 12–18 of the judgment. Under English administrative law the courts have recognised that authorities may not absolutely fetter their discretion to make decisions on the facts of individual cases by adopting rigid rules; however, the degree to which authorities may rely on rules or guidelines varies according to the nature of the case. (On these cases see Craig, *Administrative Law* (3rd ed., 1994), pp. 392–393.) If judicial review applies to procurement (as to which see pp. 33–37) this could preclude reliance on rigid rules in assessing financial standing even if this is not prohibited under European law itself, so that authorities must be prepared to consider arguments by providers that they are qualified even if they cannot meet the minimum standards in certain respects. However, it is unlikely that the courts will confine the exercise of the legislative discretion in this way when that discretion has been conferred in implementing a European rule which does not take such a restrictive approach.

[25] It can, however, be pointed out that the WTO Agreement on Government Procurement (GPA) requires conditions for participation to be limited to those which are "essential to ensure the firm's capability to fulfil the contract in question". It might be suggested that this requires an approach where providers are considered for exclusion on an individual basis; and if this is the case the Court of Justice may interpret the directives in a similar manner to ensure consistency between the Community rules and the GPA. (See GPA Article VIII. This is subject to certain exceptions, but covers conditions relating to financial matters.)

[26] See Craig, *Administrative Law* (3rd ed., 1994), pp.418–421.

[27] The legislation considered in *CEI and Bellini*, above, took this into account.

[28] Case C–389/92, *Ballast Nedam Groep NV v. The State (Belgium)* [judgment of April 14, 1994].

actually carry out the relevant contracts. In response to a request for a preliminary ruling the Court of Justice ruled that in considering the position of a company in a group account must be taken of companies belonging to the group where the applicant "actually has available the resources of those companies for carrying out the work".[29] Whether those resources are in fact available is, according to the Court, a matter for national law.

It appears that the Court intended to indicate that in certain circumstances a relationship between two companies is such that they must effectively be treated as a single company – that is, that it is necessary to "pierce the corporate veil". This was certainly the view of Advocate General Gulmann who (unlike the Court, which preferred to leave the matter solely to the national courts) indicated that this would always apply in a case, like *Ballast Nedam*, where the applicant company had 100 per cent ownership of the other relevant companies, as well as the right to take all decisions connected with those companies. This would mean that where an authority sets absolute minimum requirements for participation (for example, relating to turnover or manpower), the resources of all the relevant companies must be considered.

In addition, it is submitted that where authorities choose to make an assessment of a provider on an individual basis, it must consider all resources which the provider is actually able to use, including those of other companies in the group or even subcontractors on whom the provider can rely, even if the relationship between the companies is not sufficiently close actually to treat them as the "same" company.

(4) INFORMATION FOR PROVING ECONOMIC AND FINANCIAL STANDING

The regulations deal expressly with the information which may be demanded from providers to prove financial requirements. Regulation 15(1) of each set of regulations provides that authorities may demand the following[30]:

(i) Appropriate statements from the provider's bankers.

(ii) Statements of accounts relating to the provider's business, or extracts from such accounts. This applies, however, only where publication of the statements is required under the law of the state in which the provider is established.[31]

---

[29] Para. 18 of the judgment.
[30] Works Regulation 15(1); Supply Regulation 15(1); Services Regulation 15(1).
[31] These provisions refer to the law of the "relevant state" in which the provider is established, since it is only providers from certain relevant states who may rely on the regulations at all. On this see further p. 908.

(iii) A statement of the turnover of the firm's business as a whole, in the firm's previous three financial years.

(iv) A statement of the firm's turnover in its previous three financial years in the area of the contract concerned. In the case of a works contract this means its turnover in relation to works. For a supply contract it means its turnover in relation to goods "of a similar type" to goods to be acquired under the contract. With a services contract, this means turnover in respect of "services of the type to be provided" under the contract. What constitutes a "type" of goods or services is not defined. It is submitted that the meaning of a "similar type" of goods here is not the same as "type" of goods in relation to aggregation,[32] but is wider: authorities should be able to use a wide variety of previous contracts for assessing matters such as general reliability.

(v) For services contracts only, evidence of relevant professional risk indemnity insurance.[33]

Where an authority calls for information of the type listed above, it must obviously do so within the limitations set out in these provisions. Thus, for example, if it seeks information on turnover, it may consider only turnover in the last three years (as stated under (iii)). This means accounts may be demanded only where publication is required by law – which in many states is not required for partnerships.

An authority may also require information not listed.[34] However, this applies only where the listed information "is not appropriate in a particular case".[35]

This probably means that there is no discretion to call for other evidence where the documents listed are capable of providing the information required. It also means that the authority may not *require* firms to be registered on an "approved" list as evidence of their turnover or profitability but must accept accounts or other evidence listed as an alternative.[36] This allows firms to avoid the burden of seeking registration, or other more burdensome methods which the authority might choose.

On the other hand, the information listed will not be "appropriate" where the facts the authority seeks cannot be ascertained from the listed

---

[32] On this see pp. 168–171.

[33] Insurance for liabilities to be incurred under the contract may be appropriate for works and supply contracts also; and may in fact be considered under the principles discussed in the text below, even though not expressly listed under the works or supply rules.

[34] Works Regulation 15(2); Supply Regulation 15(2); Services Regulation 15(2).

[35] *Ibid.* This condition for the use of other evidence is not expressly stated in any of the directives, but is implied, since it is the purpose of the directives to allow firms to offer these listed means of proof if these provide adequate evidence of the matters which the authority wishes to consider.

[36] On lists see further pp. 344–346.

ECONOMIC AND FINANCIAL STANDING: SUMMARY OF THE MAIN PRINCIPLES

1. Authorites are not *required* to consider economic and financial standing.

2. Authorities *may* set minimum standards of financial and economic standing. In this case:
   — Standards are within the discretion of the authority.
   — Authorities may consider any criteria relating to economic and financial standing, and are not limited to those criteria reflected in the evidence listed in the regulations.
   — Standards may be set by means of general rules; it is not necessary to evaluate the position of each provider individually.

3. Authorities probably may consider relative economic and financial standing in selecting providers to participate from amongst those meeting minimum standards, if this reflects a bona fide concern over the possibility of completion.

4. Relative economic and financial standing may not be considered in the bid evaluation process.

5. As regards evidence of standing:
   — Authorities may demand the evidence listed in the regulations, or other evidence where that listed is not appropriate. Supplementary evidence may also be demanded.
   — Providers may offer other appropriate evidence instead of that demanded where there is a valid reason to do so.
   — In either qualifying or rejecting a provider authorities may probably also consider other evidence given by providers, or otherwise in the authority's possession.
   — Authorities must accept facts which are evidenced by registration in an official list.

6. The information required on economic and financial standing must be stated in the contract notice or invitation.

documents – for example, information on the firm's existing commit-ments.[37] This means that an authority may, for example, call for evidence of insurance for contracts under the Works or Supply Regulations even though – in contrast with the Services Regulations – insurance is not expressly mentioned there.

An important proviso to the right to demand specific information – whether that listed in the regulations, or that which is specified because the information listed is not "appropriate" – is that providers must be permitted to produce other evidence where they have a "valid reason" for not producing the information demanded.[38] This only applies where the authority considers such alternative information to be "appropri-ate".[39] However, to render the rules effective, it is probably to be implied that authorities may not unreasonably deny the use of alternative evidence.

Under regulation 17 of each set of regulations an authority may also call for information to "supplement" or "clarify" the information called for. It may also use information which it could have demanded, but which is obtained by other means.[40]

In addition, whatever the information specified by the authority, it is specifically stated in Works Regulation 18,[41] Supply Regulation 19 and Services Regulation 18 that as an alternative to producing that informa-tion a provider may rely on registration in an official national list of registered providers, where such registration is based on the facts which the authority seeks to establish. For example, if registration in a national list depends on showing a minimum turnover in certain previous years, the fact of registration in that national list constitutes proof that the provider's turnover met that minimum level in the years in question. The operation of official lists is considered further in section 5, below.

Finally, regulation 14 of each set of regulations contains certain provisions which may be relevant to a firm's financial position. These identify certain situations where a provider is in danger of collapsing without being able to meet its obligations: they include where there is a winding-up order, or where a receiver, manager or administrator has been appointed on behalf of a creditor. In such cases regulation 14 confers a power to exclude firms automatically, without entering into any other financial or technical assessment. These automatic grounds for disqualification are considered in further detail below.[42]

The provisions described above limit to a significant extent the information which an authority may *require* from providers. They do not,

---

[37] It was held in *CEI and Bellini*, above, that the Works Directive allows an authority to seek such information although it is not expressly listed, since the Directive assumes that the list is not exhaustive.

[38] Works Regulation 15(4); Supply Regulation 15(4); Services Regulation 15(4).

[39] *Ibid.*

[40] *General Building and Maintenance v. Greenwich B.C.* [1993] I.R.L.R. 535.

[41] As amended by Utilities Supply and Works Contracts Regulations 1992, S.I. 1992 No. 3279, reg. 32(10)(e).

[42] See pp. 331–342.

on the other hand, preclude the authority from considering information which it may not require, but which a firm may choose to provide to prove its standing. Thus, for example, it can operate an approved list, registration on which provides evidence of compliance with financial requirements (including those which could have been obtained from bank statements, accounts, etc.) for firms which choose to use the list system.[43] It is less clear whether the authority may *exclude* providers on the basis of information which it has no right to demand under the rules above, but which it happens to have in its possession. This issue is discussed further below under technical capacity since it is more likely to be important in that context.[44] It is suggested there that an authority should be permitted to use such information.

3. TECHNICAL CAPACITY AND ABILITY

(1) GENERAL PRINCIPLES

Another consideration is whether a potential contracting partner has the technical ability to perform the contract – that is, the skills, tools, manpower, etc., to provide the goods or services as specified in the contract. In making this assessment, like any other, an authority must comply with the Community Treaties and with other relevant international agreements[45] which, in particular prohibit direct or indirect discrimination against providers from certain other states.[46] In addition, with contracts subject to the regulations, assessment on technical grounds is subject to rules laid out in Works Regulation 16, Supply Regulation 16 and Services Regulation 16. As with the provisions on financial status, these provisions make it clear that firms may be excluded for failing to meet technical requirements: all three sets of regulations allow the exclusion of firms which do not have adequate "technical capacity", and the Services Regulations additionally allow exclusion on the basis of lack of "ability". However, the provisions limit the way in which the technical assessment may be carried out, and the criteria which may be used and in these respects are more stringent than the rules on financial standing.

As with the financial rules the purpose of the rules on technical standing is to provide fair opportunities for participation and to ensure that qualification procedures are not unduly burdensome and do not provide an opportunity to hide discriminatory practices. Again, there is no *requirement* to carry out an assessment; the rules merely regulate the process which applies where authorities choose to do so.

---

[43] On such lists see further pp. 344–348.
[44] See pp. 327–328.
[45] See Chaps. 4 and 15.
[46] On the application of the E.C. Treaty in this context see further Chap. 4.

It has been explained in Chapter 6 that in open procedures the technical assessment will be carried out after submission of bids since there is no opportunity prior to this to require firms to submit to a qualification procedure.[47] In restricted and negotiated procedures, on the other hand, an authority may carry out an assessment of technical, as well as financial, standing prior to issuing invitations and may refuse to invite unqualified firms. Indeed, as with financial standing it may be *required* to lay down the relevant standards at this point and to limit invitations to those who are qualified (although verification of factual information may be left until later).[48]

In restricted and negotiated procedures authorities may wish to invoke relative technical, as well as financial, standing as a method of selecting between interested providers in issuing invitations. Again, this is permitted subject to the rules which apply in assessing minimum requirements such as the limitations on permissible evidence and assessment criteria. However, as with financial matters it is suggested that this applies only to the extent that there is genuine concern over the risk of completion, and that this criterion cannot be used as a method of choosing between providers who are all clearly capable of completing.[49] It should also be emphasised that this criterion may be used at this stage only in so far as it concerns providers' ability to meet the minimum contract requirements. It is not permitted, for example, to use relative technical capacity to anticipate which providers will offer the best value for money in relation to the award criteria (for example, the cheapest, or best-quality product) and to select those persons to bid.[50]

It should also be noted that technical capacity and ability, like financial standing, cannot be used as relative criteria in evaluating bids, which are weighed against other criteria such as quality or price.[51] However, at the evaluation stage it is permitted to consider whether a provider is able to meet the terms of its own bid to the extent that these exceed the minimum requirements in the specifications – for example, by offering a product which exceeds the specified quality threshold.[52]

Under regulations 16(2) of each set of regulations the technical information required from providers must be stated in the contract notice in open procedures[53] and in either the contract notice or the

---

[47] See pp. 229–231. As with the financial assessment, firms may submit to this process in advance if they choose to do so.
[48] See pp. 229–231.
[49] See pp. 217–222.
[50] See further pp. 230–231.
[51] See further pp. 236–239.
[52] See pp. 236–239.
[53] The requirement is also stated in the model contract notices: see pp. 197–202.

"invitation to tender" in restricted procedures.[54] As with financial standing "invitation to tender" should be broadly construed to include an invitation to negotiate as well.[55]

The Court of Justice has stated in *Beentjes* that it is necessary to refer not only to the information required of providers but also to any "specific" substantive conditions which providers must meet.[56] It is not clear what this refers to: the Court indicated that it did not apply to a requirement that providers should have specific past experience, on the basis that this was not a specific condition of suitability, but "inseparable from the very notion of suitability". Possibly what the Court had in mind was a requirement to state any absolute standards required to be met by all providers – which must be stated in advance – in contrast with criteria used to assess each provider on its own individual merits – which need not be stated.

(2) THE MEANING OF TECHNICAL CAPACITY/ ABILITY

Authorities may only invoke regulation 16 to exclude providers on the basis of lack of "technical capacity" or "ability". These concepts are not, however, defined in the directives or regulations. In broad terms, they obviously refer to the capability of the provider to perform the contract. However, there may be some debate about what precisely "contract performance" involves.

Clearly it refers, most significantly, to the provision of the goods, works or other services in accordance with the contract requirements. It is submitted that it also includes the ability to carry out the contract in accordance with the terms of the provider's own bid. Thus, if an authority uses the "most economically advantageous offer" principle, and quality is one of the factors to be considered, where a provider

---

[54] In addition to regulation 16(2), regulation 12(10) lists this information (where not included in the contract notice) amongst that to be included in the invitation to tender. The model notices also refer to this information, although they do not state expressly that this information is required only where it is not to be included in the invitation to tender: see the model notices on pp. 208–213. This is surprising since with contract award criteria, where a similar option exists, the notice itself states that the information is required only where not in the invitation to tender.

[55] It has been suggested that in relation to award criteria the reference to "tender" in the directive is intended to include a reference to negotiation as well (see p. 277). It is true that the model notices indicate that this information must be included in the notices without referring to the alternative of inclusion in the invitation (see pp. 208–213); but this is also true of the notices for restricted procedures where it is clear from regulation 15(2) that such an alternative is available. It can also be noted that there is no equivalent of regulation 12(10) on restricted procedures, which lists the information – including that relating to technical standing – to be included in the notices; but as explained at p. 276 it seems that the directives themselves do require this information to be included for negotiated procedures and that its omission from the regulations is an error.

[56] Case 31/87, *Gebroeders Beentjes B.V. v. Netherlands* [1988] E.C.R. 4635, para. 34 of the judgment.

offers a product of exceptional quality, the authority should be permitted to assess the provider's ability to deliver a product of that high quality, rather than simply his ability to meet the minimum quality standards in the specifications.

More difficult is the issue of compliance with requirements which do not relate to this primary objective of obtaining the goods and services. One question is whether technical capacity covers the ability to comply with legal requirements, including under regulatory legislation, which applies in the course of contract performance, but does not relate to the primary objective of the contract – for example, legislation on health and safety or environmental protection. An authority may also wish to impose additional conditions – as contract terms or otherwise – relating to "secondary" policies, to be complied with in performing the contract: for example, to require providers to meet quotas for employing ethnic minorities or the long-term unemployed which are not required by law but which the authority considers to be desirable.[57] Is the ability to comply with such secondary conditions in performance of the contract an aspect of technical capacity/ability?[58]

These issues were raised in *General Building and Maintenance Ltd v. Greenwich Borough Council*[59] in which a contractor excluded from bidding on a council contract for the repair and maintenance of dwellings for alleged inadequacies in its health and safety policy contended that the exclusion breached the Works Regulations. In the High Court Sir Godfrey Le Quesne, Q.C. held that the exclusion was permitted on the basis that health and safety was an aspect of technical capacity; this he defined as "the ability competently to carry out the necessary operations of the contractor's trade", which included the ability to do so "with proper regard for the health and safety of those whom they employ and members of the public whom they affect".[60] The judgment does not make it clear whether the judge considered that technical capacity covers only compliance with *legal* requirements arising outside the contract or whether requirements imposed by the authority itself are included. Also relevant, however, is the decision of the Court of Justice in *Beentjes*.[61] In this case the court held that ability to comply with a "condition" relating to employment of long-term unemployed persons – which was not required by law – did *not* relate to technical capacity,[62] perhaps suggesting that technical capacity is confined to compliance with

---

[57] On this issue see further Chap. 15.
[58] It is submitted that technical capacity certainly could not not cover compliance with secondary conditions where this does not affect performance of the contract itself – for example, exclusion of firms which have business interests in states of which the contracting authority disapproves, where these do not affect performance of the contract with the authority.
[59] [1993] I.R.L.R. 535.
[60] p.543 at 40.
[61] Note 56 above.
[62] para. 28 of the judgment.

~~legislative requirements. This would mean that in the United Kingdom it~~
is not permitted to exclude providers on the basis of conditions such as
that in *Beentjes* since exclusion is limited to the grounds in regulations
14–16. On the other hand, a distinction might be drawn between
provisions relating to the make-up or conditions of the workforce, which
would not come within technical capacity, and those relating to the way
in which delivery is carried out (for example, impact on the environment) which would. These issues are considered further in Chapter 16.[63]

(3) INFORMATION AND CRITERIA FOR ASSESSMENT

(a) THE POWER TO DEMAND INFORMATION: GENERAL PRINCIPLES

(i) INFORMATION ON TECHNICAL CAPACITY

The procurement regulations list, in Works Regulation 16(1), Supply
Regulation 16(1) and Services Regulation 16(1), certain information
which may be demanded from providers for the purpose of assessing
technical capacity. The Works and Supply Regulations provide that *only*
this information may be demanded for assessing technical capacity. This
principle is also implicit in the Services Regulations[64] – although under
these regulations it is subject to an exception where the authority seeks
to assess "ability", as is explained at (ii) below. This principle contrasts
with the position relating to economic and financial standing where, as
explained above, it is permitted to demand and consider information
beyond that which is expressly listed.

Thus, for example, it was held in case 71/92, *Commission v. Spain*,[65]
that a Spanish provision requiring suppliers who are legal persons to
produce a document attesting registration in the register in which their
legal personality is formalised, and also a certificate from the Spanish
Embassy in their state of origin attesting to their legal personality,

---

[63] See in particular pp. 823–828.

[64] Supply Regulation 16(2) states expressly that *only* this information may be demanded;
Works Regulation 16(1) states that only the listed information may be *considered*, and in
regulation 16(2) clearly implies that authorities will seek only that information from
providers. The provisions of the directive which these regulations seek to implement
(Supply Directive 23 and Works Directive Article 27) do not expressly state that the list
of information therein is exhaustive of that which may be sought, but the Court of
Justice has held that the information listed is exhaustive in all cases except for financial
and economic standing: case 76/81, *S.A. Transporoute v. Minister of Public Works* [1982]
E.C.R. 417 and *CEI and Bellini,* above (on the Works Directive); case C–71/92,
Commission v. Spain, judgment of November 17, 1993 (concerned with the Supply
Directive). Services Regulation 16 does not expressly limit the authority to this
information, but this is to be implied as a general principle since Article 32 of the
Services Directive, which deals with this issue, is worded in a similar way to the
provisions of the Supply and Works Directives which, as noted, the Court of Justice has
interpreted as being exhaustive.

[65] Above, note 64.

contravened the Supply Directive since such documents were not mentioned in the relevant list. For the same reason, authorities may not insist on registration in mandatory lists of "approved" providers – this is also not a method of proof of technical capacity referred to in the relevant provisions.[66] The exact information which may be required is listed in section (c) below.

As well as the information listed in regulation 16, regulation 17 of each set of regulations permits authorities to demand additional information to "supplement" or "clarify" that expressly listed in the regulations. The scope of this provision is also considered further in section (c) below.

Finally, a limit on an authority's right to require production of any of the above information – that is, either the information listed or relevant "supplementary information" – is provided in Works Regulation 18, Services Regulation 18 and Supply Regulation 19 which allow providers to adduce evidence of registration in official lists of their own state as an alternative way of meeting the authority's requirements in certain cases. These provisions are considered further in section 5. below.[67]

(ii) INFORMATION ON "ABILITY"

In addition, under the Services Regulations, authorities may demand information additional to that in the lists where this is necessary to assess providers', "ability". This is made clear in Services Regulation 16(1), which confers a general discretion to assess the ability of service providers, without limiting the information or specific criteria which may be considered. In other words, "ability" is treated as distinct from technical capacity, and assessment of ability is not subject to the restrictive rules governing technical capacity in general. "Ability" is stated to involve, in particular, "skills, efficiency, experience and reliability".

It has been debated whether this correctly implements the Services Directive. Article 32(1) of the directive first provides that the ability of service providers may be evaluated "in particular with regard to their skills, efficiency, experience and reliability", and then, in Article 32(2), sets out the information which may be used to assess "technical capability". An argument can be made that "ability" is envisaged as one aspect of general "technical capability" and may thus be assessed only in accordance with the evidence listed in Article 32(2) (and Services Regulation 16(2)).[68] This is suggested by the fact that, under all three sets of regulations, the information expressly listed in the regulations is

---

[66] See further pp. 318–325.
[67] See pp. 341–344.
[68] See, for example, Lee, *Public Procurement* (1992), p. 151.

appropriate in assessing those criteria which the directives and regulations on services categorise as relating to "ability". Further, these criteria are also relevant in many supply and works contracts, and are subsumed under "technical capacity" in the works and supply rules.

However, this cannot explain why the separate concept of ability was introduced into the Services Directive. The regulations are based on the view that this was done in recognition of the subjective nature of assessment of service providers which may need to be based on a very wide range of factors, varying according to the nature of the contract and which are not capable of being enumerated in general rules. It is submitted that this is a correct interpretation. Although there is indeed an overlap between "technical capacity" and "ability", in that the latter is a subdivision of the former, it appears that where a factor relates to "ability" it is intended to be brought outside the usual restrictive rules on technical capacity. Since many aspects of technical capacity relate to "ability", the rules on technical capacity are thus much less important in relation to services than works and supplies.

Although, however, authorities are not limited in the information which they may demand to assess ability it is arguable that they must always accept any "reasonable" evidence which providers offer as an alternative to that demanded. Such a rule can be deduced from the general purpose of the qualification provisions in seeking to preclude authorities from placing unreasonable burdens on providers and finds support in case C–71/92, *Commission v. Spain*, in which the Court indicated that it is not permitted to require registration on approved lists as evidence of qualification even where the directives do not *expressly* limit the evidence which authorities may demand.[69]

Authorities may also be subject in assessing ability to Works Regulation 18, Services Regulation 18 and Supply Regulation 19 which allow providers to adduce evidence of registration in official lists of their own state as an alternative means of proof in certain cases, as explained in section 5 below.

(b) SUBSTANTIVE CRITERIA FOR ASSESSMENT OF TECHNICAL CAPACITY/ABILITY

(i) TECHNICAL CAPACITY

As regards the criteria for assessing technical capacity, the general view is that the list of permitted information limits not only the *information* which firms may be required to provide for the assessment, but also the

---

[69] See further pp. 344–346

substantive criteria which may be taken into account.[70] For example, since completion of previous contracts is listed as relevant information under all three sets of regulations, such previous experience may be taken into consideration in assessing technical capacity; but criteria which cannot be applied on the basis of the listed information cannot be considered.

Such an approach might leave some unforeseen gaps, and since the Court of Justice has held only that the *information* required is exhaustive, but has not considered expressly the question of applicable criteria, an argument may be open that authorities can take account of other *criteria*, provided these relate to "technical capacity" as defined in section (2), above.[71] However, it seems that this is unnecessary since the listed information can reasonably be interpreted to cover all matters which authorities may want to consider.

(ii) ABILITY

As noted above, in relation to services contracts, there are no express limits on either the information or criteria which may be used in assessing providers by reference to their "ability". Thus, where ability is in issue, it appears that authorities may consider any criteria which relate to "ability".

(c) THE INFORMATION AND CRITERIA LISTED FOR ASSESSING TECHNICAL CAPACITY

(i) THE PROVISIONS IN THE LISTS

The information which can be demanded from providers, and thus the criteria which can definitely be taken into account,[72] is as follows.

Public works contracts
(a) Where the contractor is an individual, the contractor's educational and professional qualifications; and in all cases the educational and qualifications of (i) the contractor's managerial staff and (ii) the persons(s) responsible for carrying out the works under the contract

---

[70] This was stated by Advocate General Darmon in case 31/87, *Gebroeders Beentjes B.V. v. Netherlands* [1988] E.C.R. 4635, para.29 of the opinion, and by the English High Court in *General Building and Maintenance v. Greenwich B.C.* [1993] I.R.L.R. 535. This view is also endorsed, for example, by Trepte, *Public Procurement in the E.C.* (1993), p.56; Winter, "Public Procurement in the EEC" (1991) 28 C.M.L.Rev. 741. Such a view is also clearly taken in the Services Regulations which refer in regulation 16 to the actual *criteria* which may be considered rather than (as in the Works and Supply Regulations) referring simply to the information which can be required and limiting the relevant *criteria* merely by implication from the rules on information.

[71] If such an approach were adopted, authorities could at best rely on information obtained by their own efforts in applying such criteria, since they could not require production of relevant information by providers.

[72] As to whether other information can be taken into account see (b) above.

(Works Regulation 16(1)(a)). It can be implied that details of other staff are not relevant.

(b) A list of the works carried out over the last five years (Works Regulation 16(1)(b)). This implies that the authority may not consider experience beyond the previous five years.

The provision deals further with the evidence which may be called for to prove the facts alleged. In this respect it states that the list may be accompanied by certificates of satisfactory completion for the most important of the works, indicating the value of the consideration; when and where the works were carried out; and whether they were carried out according to the rules of the trade or profession and properly completed. Alternatively, the authority may require the certificate to be sent to the authority directly by the certifying body. It is submitted that the authority should be permitted to consider information on the contractor's experience of the specific type of work in question, rather than simply of works generally.[73]

It was held by the High Court in *General Building and Maintenance v. Greenwich B.C.*[74] that reference to satisfactory completion allowed the authority to check whether work had been carried out in accordance with health and safety requirements, which it was suggested may be an aspect of technical capacity.[75]

The Court also held in *Greenwich* that to assess the health and safety issue authorities could demand a firm's health and safety policy statement, under Works Regulation 17, which allows authorities to seek information which is "supplementary" to that listed. By implication, this indicates that authorities may demand other information to prove compliance with similar requirements relating to the contract performance (such as environmental protection provisions), although as explained above it is not clear whether this is limited to external legal requirements governing such matters. However, it is difficult to see how a provision in the regulation regarding past performance of contracts can be used to justify the admission of any evidence which does not concern past performance.[76] Thus, it might be suggested, authorities should be limited to considering health and safety only in so far as evidenced by previous contracts, or by the grounds listed in regulation 14, notably

---

[73] In *Beentjes*, above, the Court of Justice indicated that "specific experience relating to the work to be carried out" was an acceptable criterion for assessing technical capacity (para. 24 of the judgment), although the Court did not discuss what is meant by "specific experience".

[74] Above, note 70.

[75] See pp. 315–316

[76] Indeed, if the view is taken that authorities may demand additional information relating to any matter which is evidenced by past contract performance, this undermines the whole structure of the rules: all aspects of technical capacity are evidenced by past performance, and such an approach would thus simply allow the authority to seek any information it chooses on technical capacity, rather than being restricted to specific matters listed in the legislation.

conviction of a criminal offence, or a previous act of gross misconduct. These are often, however, not the most suitable methods for assessing whether providers will comply with regulatory requirements in the future. The difficulty may have arisen because the question of compliance with legal requirements was not really contemplated in drafting the rules.

(c) A statement of the tools, plant and technical equipment "available" for carrying out the work (Works Regulation 16(1)(c)).

A broad approach should be taken to the concept of "availability", to ensure that the authority is able to take into account everything which could affect the ability to complete. For example, threats of strike action at the contractor's place of work which might make it difficult to do the job, or civil unrest which might prevent the provider delivering relevant materials or labour to the work site are probably relevant under this heading.

In case 71/92, *Commission v. Spain*[77] the Court of Justice held unlawful Spanish legislation stating that "preferably" consideration should be given to whether personnel, equipment and financial assets were held permanently on Spanish territory. The Court's reasoning was based on the fact that the legislation does not refer to any distinction between assets which are and are not in the territory of the awarding state.[78] However, it is submitted that the location of equipment (including, of course, whether it can be moved) is in principle relevant in deciding whether the equipment is "available" for carrying out the work, even though the provision says nothing expressly about location. Authorities should thus be able to seek such information on this matter as supplementary information under regulation 17 and to take it into account. The decision in case 71/92 is, however, justified, on the basis that a preference for equipment, etc., which is permanently in the awarding state is arbitrary and does not relate to the actual needs of specific contracts.[79]

(d) A statement of the contractor's average annual manpower, and a statement of the contractor's number of managerial staff over the previous three years (Works Regulation 16(1)(d). It can be implied that numbers of managerial staff in previous years are not relevant.

(e) A statement of the technicians or technical services which the contractor may call upon for carrying out the work (Works Regulation 16(1)(e)).

---

[77] Case 71/92, above, note 64, paras. 48–51 of the judgment.
[78] para. 50 of the judgment; and see also para. 86 of the Opinion of Advocate General Gulman.
[79] See pp. 328–329.

Public supply contracts

(a) A list of deliveries in the past three years of goods of "a similar type" to the goods to be supplied under the contract (Supply Regulation 16(1)(a)). As in relation to financial standing "type" of goods is not defined. As noted there, probably this has a wider meaning than "type" of goods under the aggregation rules.[80]

The list may be required to specify the date of delivery, the consideration received and the identity of the purchaser. Where the purchaser was itself a "contracting authority" under the Supply Regulations,[81] the details may be required to be attested by a certificate issued or countersigned by the purchaser. In other cases a supplier may as an alternative merely make a declaration attesting those details.

Case 362/90, *Commission v. Italy*,[82] raised the question of whether it is permitted to take account of a supplier's experience in delivering to public authorities in particular rather than to purchasers in general. Italy argued that proof of satisfactory deliveries to public authorities was a better guarantee of reliability than proof of other deliveries and that this consideration is contemplated by the directives in that they refer separately to public and private bodies, as outlined above. However, as the Advocate General pointed out, the separate reference to public and private bodies appears to be concerned merely with the different means of proof which may be required of contracting authorities[83]; it does not authorise any substantive distinction. It is submitted that such a distinction is in fact impliedly prohibited – it is an arbitrary criterion and, further, gives preference to previous suppliers to public authorities, contrary to the whole aim of the legislation.

As explained in relation to works contracts, authorities may probably seek and consider evidence on the extent to which suppliers have complied with legislative requirements, such as health and safety regulation, in previous contracts.[84]

(b) A description of the supplier's technical facilities in relation to the goods to be supplied (Supply Regulation 16(1)(b)). It is submitted that information relating to the availability of all these facilities could be sought, including to the extent that availability might be affected by external factors such as civil war or blockade. "Technical facilities" should also be widely construed, to include "facilities" for the delivery of the finished product.

(c) A description of the supplier's study and research facilities in relation to the goods (Supply Regulation 16(1)(b)).

---

[80] See p. 309.
[81] On this definition see pp. 106–115.
[82] Judgment of March 31, 1992. See further the note by Arrowsmith and Fernández Martín, (1993) 2 P.P.L.R. CS2.
[83] The Court did not consider this issue since the action was ruled inadmissible.
[84] See pp. 320–321.

(d) An indication of the technicians or technical bodies who would be involved with production, particularly those responsible for quality control (Supply Regulation 16(1)(c)). This is expressly stated to include the case where these are independent of the contractor.

(e) Samples, descriptions or photographs of the goods to be supplied. These may be required to be accompanied by certification of their authenticity (Supply Regulation (16)(1)(b)). It must be emphasised that samples may be used only to assess whether firms are able to meet the minimum contract standards: the relative quality of samples which reach the standard cannot be used to select which suppliers should be invited to bid in restricted and negotiated procedures, since it is not permitted to make this selection by considering which firms are likely to make the most favourable offer.[85]

(f) A description of the supplier's measures for ensuring quality in relation to the goods (Supply Regulation 16(1)(b)). An enterprise may also be required to provide certification "by official quality control institutes or agencies of recognised competence" attesting that the goods conform with the authority's standards and technical specifications.[86] Authorities may not insist on certificates from national authorities: this breaches the specific rules on technical capacity since the above provision does not contemplate that certificates must be obtained from any particular authority, and, further, is a breach of Article 30 E.C.[87]

(g) Checks in certain cases on the supplier's production capacity, study and research facilities and quality control measures (Supply Regulation 16(1)(f)). This applies only where the goods are "complex" or are "required for a special purpose". The checks must be made either by the contracting authority itself, or on its behalf by "a competent official body" of the state in which the provider is established.

Public services contracts[88]

(a) Where a provider is an individual, his educational and professional qualifications; and in all cases the qualifications of i) the contractor's managerial staff and ii) the person(s) responsible for providing the services (Services Regulation 16(1)(b)(i)). As with supplies, consideration of qualifications of other staff is excluded.

---

[85] See further pp. 217–222.

[86] "Standards" and "specifications" are defined elsewhere in the regulations: see pp. 573–575 and p. 597.

[87] Case 71/92, *Commission v. Spain* judgment of November 17, 1995 holding that under the Supply Directive Spanish authorities could not require quality certificates to be issued only by the competent *Spanish* authorities. The Spanish government conceded that this was also a breach of Article 30 E.C.

[88] The Services Regulations differ from the Works and Supply Regulations in expressly listing the factors which can be taken into account rather than the information on those factors which is to be provided (for example, the Services Regulations refer to "qualifications" rather than the "list of qualifications" referred to in Works Regulations); but this has no significance for interpretation.

(b) The "principal services" provided in the past three years which are of "a similar type" to the services to be provided under the contract (Services Regulation 16(1)(b)(ii)). As with financial standing, there is no express provision on the interpretation of "similar type". Again, it is submitted that the concept is wider than the similar concept referred to in the context of the aggregation rules.[89]

The provider may be required to specify the date of delivery, the consideration received and the identity of the purchaser. Where the recipient was itself a "contracting authority" under the Services Regulations the details may be required to be attested by a certificate issued or countersigned by the recipient; in other cases a service provider may as an alternative merely make a declaration attesting those details himself. It was suggested above in relation to the similar provision for supplies that authorities must consider total deliveries, and may not make a distinction according to whether they were made to public or private bodies.

As with works and supply contracts, authorities may probably seek and consider evidence on the extent to which suppliers have complied with legislative requirements in carrying out previous contracts.[90-91]

(c) The technicians or technical bodies who would be involved in the service provision, particularly those responsible for quality control – including where they are independent of the service provider (Services Regulation 16(1)(b)(iii)).

(d) The service provider's average annual manpower, and the number of managerial staff over the previous three years (Services Regulation 16(1)(b)(iv).

(e) The tools, plant and technical equipment available to the services provider for performing the contract (Services Regulation 16(1)(b)(v)). The scope of a corresponding provision in the Works Regulations was discussed above; the same principles will apply in the context of services.

(f) A description of the supplier's technical facilities in relation to the goods to be supplied (Services Regulation 16(1)(b)(vi)).

(g) A description of the supplier's study and research facilities in relation to the goods (Services Regulation 16(1)(b)(vi)).

(h) The measures for ensuring quality (Services Regulation 16(1)(b)(vi).

(i) A certificate that the services of the service provider conform to the British Standard BS 5750 (Services Regulation 16(1)(b)(viii)). Alternatively, providers may submit a certificate to attest conformity to quality assurance standards based on the EN 29,000 series (on which BS 5750 is based), where provided by an independent body from another relevant

---

[89] On this see p. 309.
[90-91] See pp. 320–321.

state which conforms to the EN 45,000 European standards series. The right of authorities to require these quality assurance certificates has been criticised as unduly burdensome, since obtaining certificates can be difficult and costly. In particular, such requirements may deter the participation in public contracts of small and medium-sized enterprises, whose participation the Community is particularly keen to promote.

There is an exception where providers have "no access" to such certificates. This will probably apply where the provider's own state has not made any provision for such certificates. There is also an exception where a provider cannot obtain a certificate "within the relevant time-limits" (which means, presumably, in time to participate in the award procedure). In these cases authorities must accept "any other evidence of conformity to equivalent quality assurance standards".

(j) Any proportion of the contract which the service provider intends to subcontract to another (Services Regulation 16(1)(b)(ix)).

(k) Finally, there is provision for actual checks in certain cases on the service provider, in relation to the services to be provided, and also in relation to study and research facilities and quality control measures (Services Regulation 16(1)(b)(vii)). This applies only where the services are "complex" or are "required for a special purpose". The checks must be made either by the contracting authority itself, or on its behalf by "a competent official body" of the state in which the provider is established.

It should also be noted that under Services Regulation 20, where the services provider is not an individual he may be required to indicate in the tender, or in the request to be selected or negotiate, the names and relevant professional qualifications of the staff who will be responsible for performing the services.[92]

(ii) INTERPRETATION OF THE LISTED PROVISIONS

It can be seen that there are differences in the information which may be required under each set of regulations. These are explained mainly by the different nature of works, goods and services. For example, the supply rules refer to photographs and samples; however, there is no similar provision in the services rules since photographs or samples are not generally appropriate for services.[93] The differences can be criticised, however, since they assume that goods are provided under supply contracts only, works under works contracts only, and services only under services contracts. This is not the case: thus a contract for computer hardware (supplies) and bespoke software (services) includes both supplies and services, though it must be classified as a supply or services

---

[92] Services Regulation 20(2).

[93] Although they might be in some exceptional cases – for example, consultants engaged to produce a report might usefully be asked to provide samples of previous writing. This does not seem to be permitted under the regulations.

contract (on the basis of the relative value of the two elements[94]). If it is a services contract, samples and photographs of the supplies element might be appropriate, although not mentioned in the Services Regulations. The Court of Justice may adopt a purposive interpretation of the directives to allow such information, however, which would be followed by the domestic courts.

There is uncertainty over how far authorities may request information which relates to the general information or criteria contemplated in the lists above, but which gives more detail than referred to there. For example, whilst average manpower is referred to in general terms, an authority may seek a more detailed breakdown of the workforce according to tasks performed; or, in relation to available tools, plant or equipment, it may seek details of their age, condition or location. It is submitted that it is too narrow an interpretation of the rules to limit the information which can be demanded, and the criteria which can be applied, to the bare generalities referred to in the regulations. The right of authorities to demand such additional details is supported by regulation 17 of each set of regulations, which allows authorities to demand information to "supplement" or "clarify" that referred to in regulations 14, 15 and 16.

Another question is the extent to which an authority may seek further evidence, or proof, of certain factual information which it is entitled to demand. In some cases, the means of proving the accuracy of information given is dealt with expressly. For example, as explained, the authority can insist that satisfactory completion of previous contracts is evidenced by a declaration from a public purchaser or, in the case of contracts between the provider and a purchaser who is not a contracting authority, can insist on a declaration by the provider. Such express rules are probably exhaustive of the evidence which may be required. In other cases, however, there are no express provisions on evidence. For example, it is stated that authorities may require information on the qualifications of certain staff, but it is not stated whether the authority may seek evidence of this – for example, the relevant certificates. Arguably, such evidence could be sought under regulation 17 which allows consideration of supplementary information. On the other hand, since the purpose of the provisions is to minimise the burdens on providers, it is also plausible to argue that specific evidence of information provided cannot be required unless this is expressly stated. Whatever the position regarding the furnishing of evidence by providers, it appears an authority may check information by other means (for example, through evidence which they obtain through their own investigations), as explained at (d) below. It can also be noted that under regulation 14 in each set of regulations providers can be excluded for future contracts where they are found to be guilty of serious misrepre-

---

[94] See pp. 142–144.

sentation in supplying information,[95] which provides a strong incentive to ensure providers give accurate information.

It seems clear that "supplementary" information must relate to the specific information and criteria contemplated in the list itself. Thus, it was suggested above that in seeking information supplementary to certificates or declarations of completion of past contracts, authorities can only seek information which concerns the completion of those contracts.[96]

(d) THE RIGHT TO USE INFORMATION WHICH COULD NOT BE DEMANDED UNDER THE REGULATIONS

As explained above, in assessing technical standing an authority may use the information listed in the regulations, supplementary information under regulation 17, and, in the case of services, any information at all which relates to "ability". The regulations make it clear that this information, and only this information, may be *demanded* from providers. It may also be used if it happens to come into the authority's possession in some other way. In addition, however, an authority may also wish to make use of information which it possesses, but which could *not* have been demanded from providers. This may be because it is voluntarily supplied by providers; because it has such information by chance; or because it has acquired the information through its own investigations.

As with financial standing, there can, first, be no objection to using such information to prove that providers *are* qualified: the regulations are relevant only where it is sought to reject providers. For example, the authority may call for evidence on previous deliveries of widgets over the past three years; but not for information on deliveries of other types of goods. However, a firm which is a new entrant to the widgets market may wish to put forward evidence of its reliability in delivering other types of goods to prove technical capacity, and this, it is submitted, may be considered. The possibility is, indeed, implicit in the rules on official lists, which contemplate that registration in a list – which cannot be *demanded* of providers – *may* be used to prove qualification.[97]

It is not so obvious, on the other hand, whether such additional information may be used to reject providers. If the main objective of the qualification rules is to minimise burdens on providers in qualifying for a contract, then it is acceptable to allow the use of information obtained in other ways, since providers themselves are not burdened – provided, presumably, that this information relates to substantive criteria which the

---

[95] See further pp. 337–338.
[96] See pp. 320–321.
[97] On these lists see pp. 344–348.

authority is permitted to consider. On the other hand, it can be argued that another objective of the rules is to limit the type of information which can be taken into account, as a way of safeguarding against arbitrary exclusion, and of rendering decisions more open to scrutiny. From this perspective it can be argued that additional information – for example, past deliveries going back beyond the time stated in the regulations – should not be relevant.

Although it is true that one purpose of the rules is to prevent arbitrary behaviour this is already achieved by the general principle that providers cannot be excluded on an arbitrary basis, as outlined in section (4) below. It would be too inconvenient not to allow the use of all available and relevant information, and it is therefore suggested that such information should be permitted to be considered, provided that it is revealed to providers where reasons are sought for a decision to reject.[98]

(4) OTHER RULES GOVERNING THE ASSESSMENT

It has been explained that – with the exception of assessments relating to the "ability" of service providers – the criteria which may be taken into account in assessing technical capacity are probably confined to those referred to, expressly or impliedly, in the lists of information and assessment criteria contained in Works Regulation 16(1), Supply Regulation 16(1) and Services Regulation 16(1). It has also been explained that the rules regulate the evidence which may be used for assessing whether such criteria are met. Certain further principles relating to the exercise of the authority's discretion must also be considered. These apply both to assessment of technical capacity in general and to assessment of ability under the services rules.

First, the permitted criteria may be used as the basis for exclusion or for selecting invitees to bid only where the *actual* objective is to assess technical capacity or ability. This is made clear under Works Regulation 16(1), Supply Regulation 16(2) and Services Regulation 16(2) which permit the authority to call for such information as it "considers it needs" to make the technical assessment. Thus, for example, the extent of staff qualifications is a permitted criterion, but it is not permitted to insist that providers hold a particular qualification with the aim of protecting the interests of a particular profession rather than because the authority considers that such qualifications are essential to guarantee satisfactory completion.

Secondly, these same provisions indicate that authorities must determine in advance how the assessment is to be made. Thus they may not require providers to submit a whole range of information, and then decide at a later point which information is to be used in making the assessment.

---

[98] A provider has the right to demand reasons: see pp. 281–283.

Thirdly, it can be noted that for technical standing, as with economic and financial standing, the Court of Justice has stated that under the directives it is for individual states to set the *levels* of standing required of providers.[99] Under the United Kingdom regulations, individual authorities retain this discretion – for example, to decide which qualifications must be held by the staff of providers.

As with financial standing, the scope for judicial control of the assessment based on other grounds is less clear. In relation to financial standing it was explained above that one view might be that the legislation limits the discretion of providers to make decisions on standing by reference to general rules – for example, setting minimum annual turnover requirements – and requires instead that specific consideration be given to the standing of each individual provider. In relation to financial standing such a view has been rejected by the Court of Justice.[1] However, Advocate General Lenz in his Opinion in case C–362/90[2] has suggested that even if rigid minimum requirements may be set in relation to financial criteria the position may be different in relation to technical capacity. It was also suggested above that it is to be implied that decisions to exclude, or exclusory rules, must meet the proportionality test, and cannot involve the application of criteria in an arbitrary way which does not reasonably relate to the actual capacity of providers, and this will clearly apply to technical capacity as well as financial standing.

It was also mentioned in considering financial standing that in *Ballast Nedam* the Court of Justice held that authorities must where appropriate consider the resources of other companies in the same group in assessing a provider's standing.[3] That decision was directed at the qualification process in general, and applies equally to the assessment of technical capacity and ability.

---

[99] *Bellini,* above, para. 26 of the judgment; *Beentjes,* above, para. 17 of the judgment.
[1] See pp. 306–307.
[2] Above.
[3] See pp. 307–308.

TECHNICAL CAPACITY/ABILITY
SUMMARY OF THE MAIN PRINCIPLES

1. Authorites are not *required* to consider technical capacity/ability.

2. Authorities *may* set minimum standards of technical capacity/ability. In this case:
   — Standards are within the discretion of the authority.
   — Authorities may probably take into account only those criteria relating to technical capacity/ability which can be deduced from the evidence listed in the regulations (except, possibly, in assessing "ability" under the Services Regulations).
   — It is not clear whether standards may be set by means of general rules or whether it is necessary to evaluate the position of each provider individually.

3. Authorities probably may consider relative technical capacity/ability in selecting providers to participate from amongst those meeting minimum standards, if this reflects a bona fide concern over the possibility of completion.

4. Relative technical capacity/ability in meeting *minimum* specifications may not be considered in the bid evaluation process.

5. As regards evidence of standing:
   — Authorities may demand only the evidence listed in the regulations, and supplementary evidence. Possibly there is an exception in assessing "ability" under the Services Regulations whereby any evidence may be demanded, although reasonable alternative evidence offered will also have to be accepted.
   — In either qualifying or rejecting a provider authorities may probably also consider other evidence given by providers, or otherwise in the authority's possession.
   — Authorities must accept facts which are evidenced by registration in an official list.

6. The information required on technical capacity/ability must be stated in the contract notice or invitation.

4. EXCLUSION UNDER REGULATION 14

(1) GENERAL PRINCIPLES

Works Regulation 14, Supply Regulation 14 and Services Regulation 14 provide for exclusion of providers on a number of grounds. Some of these relate mainly to the provider's ability to complete the contract – for example, the existence of a winding-up order; others – such as non-payment of taxes or social security contributions – are directed mainly at matters not connected with contract performance. The significance of regulation 14 is, first, that it permits exclusion where the listed grounds are made out and, secondly, that in some cases it limits the way in which this is carried out.

It has been explained in Chapter 6 that in open procedures any relevant regulation 14 criteria will be considered once bids have been submitted, since there is no possibility of limiting participation to firms which have been "qualified" prior to bid evaluation.[4] In restricted and negotiated procedures, on the other hand, authorities may evaluate providers under regulation 14 before issuing invitations and may limit invitations to those who are not excluded under the regulation 14 criteria. Indeed, as explained in Chapter 6, it appears that in the United Kingdom any exclusory criteria must be set out at this stage[5] and invitations denied to those who do not appear to meet the criteria, although verification of factual information provided may be left until a later point.[6] Failure to comply with regulation 14 criteria may also provide grounds for deciding who should be invited to bid or negotiate from amongst a number of participants.[7] On the other hand, a provider's position in relation to the regulation 14 criteria cannot be used as a criterion in the award process (for example, to be weighed against quality or price in selecting a provider): once a firm has been admitted to the procedure as a qualified provider, its bid must be assessed on the content of the bid alone.[8]

Where an authority seeks to reject a provider for reasons related to financial or technical standing, it must give certain information on its requirements in the contract notice or invitation to tender. However, there are no such information requirements where the authority wishes to reject providers under regulation 14.

Generally, it may require a provider to furnish "such evidence as it needs" to make an evaluation under regulation 14,[9] although in some

---

[4] See pp. 229–231. It was suggested that it is permitted to *allow* firms to submit to an assessment of their qualifications before the procedure if they choose to do so (for example, by registration on a list); but that this cannot be required.
[5] See pp. 229–231.
[6] See pp. 229–231.
[7] See pp. 217–222.
[8] See pp. 230–231.
[9] Works Regulation 14(2); Supply Regulation 14(2); Services Regulation 14(2).

cases it is expressly provided that certain specified evidence must be accepted as conclusive proof that certain criteria are met, as outlined below. Authorities may also, under regulation 14, call for further information to "supplement" or "clarify" any information sought. In light of the purpose of the disqualification rules in eliminating unreasonable burdens on providers it can be argued (as with assessment of ability)[10] that, even for grounds where authorities are not expressly restricted in the information which they may require, they are always obliged to accept any "reasonable" evidence which providers offer as an alternative to that requested. Support for this approach can be found in case C–71/92, *Commission v. Spain*, in which the Court indicated that registration on approved lists can never be required, even where the directives do not *expressly* limit authorities' discretion regarding the evidence which they may call for.[11]

Authorities cannot reject providers for failing to furnish documents which are not contemplated under regulation 14, unless they fall within some other specific grounds for rejection listed in the regulations (such as regulations 15 or 16). Thus, for example, it was held in *Commission v. Spain*,[12] that providers who are legal persons could not be required, in order to prove their legal capacity, to produce a document relating to the register in which their constitution as a legal person is formalised.[13] This is because "legal capacity" is not mentioned, as such, in regulation 14, and authorities are thus not free to call for any evidence on this matter; they may only establish legal capacity in so far as this can be ascertained by reference to the specific matters mentioned in the regulations, notably registration on a trade or professional register or (where registers do not exist) through declarations from providers that they are engaged in the trade or profession concerned. (See (3)(g) below).

(2) REGULATION 14 AND GROUPS OF COMPANIES

It is unclear whether a provider may be rejected when one of the regulation 14 grounds applies not to the provider himself but to another company in the same group. As explained above, the Court of Justice held in *Ballast Nedam*[14] that providers may in appropriate cases rely on the resources of such associated companies to prove financial and technical capacity. It would seem that in those cases where the associ-

---

[10] See pp. 317–318.
[11] See further pp. 344–346
[12] Judgment of November 17, 1993
[13] See also case 76/81, *S.A. Transporoute v. Minister of Public Works* [1982] E.C.R. 417, in which it was held contrary to the Works Directive to require providers to produce an "establishment permit" issued by the state awarding the contract, which attested to the provider's "qualifications and good standing". (This was also held contrary to Article 59 E.C.)
[14] See pp. 307–308.

ated company must be treated as the "same" company for the purposes of assessing such capacity, an authority would be able to disqualify that provider where the relevant associated company does not meet one of the regulation 14 criteria.[15] Arguably this should apply where the provider does not actually rely on the resources of the associated company, but the relationship is such that it would be entitled to do so. This is particularly appropriate for cases of failure to comply with tax or social security obligations, criminal convictions or gross misconduct, where the misconduct of one company should be considered to taint the other. It is interesting that under the Northern Ireland legislation designed to remove religious discrimination, the criminal convictions of one firm can lead to associated firms being disqualified from government contracts,[16] which would be legal only if the procurement rules do allow the "piercing of the corporate veil" for the purpose of disqualification under regulation 14. However, regulation 14 probably does not permit disqualification of providers simply because the regulation 14 grounds are not satisfied by their proposed subcontractors, where there is no close connection with these subcontractors such as would allow the courts to treat them as effectively the "same" company for the purpose of regulation 14.[17]

(3) THE GROUNDS AND PROCEDURES FOR EXCLUSION

(a) BANKRUPTCY, INSOLVENCY, WINDING-UP, etc.

Regulation 14(1) permits exclusion/non-selection of providers in certain specified cases which involve an obvious threat to the viability or continuation of the business. These are as follows:

(i) Where the provider is an individual, where that individual[18]
– is bankrupt;
– has had a receiving order or administration order made against him;
– has made any composition or arrangement with or for the benefit of his creditors, or has made any conveyance or assignment for the benefit of his creditors;
– appears unable to pay, or to have no reasonable prospect of being able to pay, a debt within the meaning of section 286 of the Insolvency Act 1986 or article 242 of the Insolvency (Northern Ireland) Order 1989;

---

[15] This was the view of Advocate General Gulman in Case C–389/92, *Ballast Nedam Groep N.V. v. The State (Belgium)*, above note 28, para. 16 of the Opinion.
[16] See further pp. 804–806.
[17] This will apply even where the resources of subcontractors are relied on for showing that the provider has resources "available" to carry out the contract, for the purpose of the technical assessment.
[18] Works Regulation 14(1)(a); Supply Regulation 14(1)(a); Services Regulation 14(1)(a).

– in Scotland, has been granted a trust deed for creditors or become otherwise apparently insolvent, or is the subject of a petition presented for sequestration of his estate;
– is the subject of "any similar procedure" under the law of any other state.

(ii) Where the provider is a company, where the company[19]:
– has passed a resolution, or is the subject of an order by the court, for the company's winding-up (other than for the purposes of bona fide reconstruction or amalgamation), or is the subject of proceedings for this purpose;
– has had a receiver, manager or administrator on behalf of a creditor appointed in respect of the company's business or any part of it, or is the subject of proceedings for this;
– is the subject of "similar procedures" to the above under the law of any other state.

(iii) Where the provider is a partnership constituted under Scots law, where that partnership[20]:
– has granted a trust deed or become otherwise apparently insolvent;
– is the subject of a petition presented for sequestration of its estate.

Where the provider is from a state of the European Community or from another state to which the benefit of the E.C. regime has been extended,[21] an authority must accept as conclusive evidence that a firm does not fall within the above categories an extract from the judicial record of the state concerned or, where the state concerned does not maintain such a record, a document issued by the judicial or administrative authority designated as competent for this purpose by the state of establishment.[22] Where – as in the United Kingdom itself – such documentary evidence is not issued in relation to the matters in question, the authority must accept as an alternative a declaration on oath made by the provider before either (i) an authority designated by the state of establishment or (ii) a notary public or commissioner for oaths in the state of establishment.[23]

In addition, for providers entitled to rely on the regulations authorities must also accept as evidence of the above matters, registration on an official list of the provider's state of establishment, to the extent that registration on that list depends on proof that the provider is not subject

---

[19] Works Regulation 14(1)(c); Supply Regulation 14(1)(c); Services Regulation 14(1)(c).
[20] Works Regulation 14(1)(b); Supply Regulation 14(1)(b); Services Regulation 14(1)(b).
[21] On this see Chap. 15.
[22] Works Regulation 14(2) and (3), as amended by Supply Regulation 31(1); Supply Regulation 14(2) and (3); Services Regulation 14(2) and (3), as amended by Supply Regulation 31(2).
[23] Works Regulation 14(1) and (3), as amended by Supply Regulation 31(1); Supply Regulation 14(1) and (3); Services Regulation 14(1) and (3), as amended by Supply Regulation 31(2).

to any of the above orders or proceedings.[24] This use of official lists is considered in more detail below.[25]

(b) CONVICTION RELATING TO THE BUSINESS OR PROFESSION

A provider may also be rejected where convicted of an offence relating to the conduct of the firm's business or profession.[26] This allows exclusion of providers convicted, for example, of offences under legislation on trade descriptions, health and safety, environmental standards or equal opportunities legislation. It will not apply, on the other hand, where an individual provider is convicted of, for example an assault or a driving offence not related to the business.

This provision allows authorities to consider convictions in ascertaining technical capacity, including whether providers are likely to comply with regulatory legislation in the course of doing work for the authority. It also effectively allows authorities to use their contracting power in support of government policies embodied in criminal legislation, irrespective of any connection which this may have with the contracts to be awarded.[27] For example, providers could be excluded from contracts for past breaches of environmental legislation, as an additional sanction (alongside any criminal sanctions) to encourage compliance with the legislation.[28]

For providers from states which can claim the benefit of the regulations, authorities must accept as conclusive evidence that a firm has received no conviction an extract from the judicial record of the state concerned or, where the state concerned does not maintain such a record, a document issued by the judicial or administrative authority designated by the state of establishment for this purpose.[29-30] Where – as in the United Kingdom – such documentary evidence is not issued the authority must accept as an alternative a declaration on oath made by the provider before either (i) an authority designated by the State of establishment or (ii) a notary public or commissioner for oaths in the state of establishment.

In addition, for such providers authorities must also accept registration in an official list of the state of establishment as evidence that the

---

[24] Works Regulation 18, as amended by Supply Regulation 31(1); Supply Regulation 19; Services Regulation 18, as amended by Supply Regulation 31(1).

[25] See pp. 344–348.

[26] Works Regulation 14(1)(d); Supply Regulation 14(1)(d); Services Regulation 14(1)(d).

[27] If it was intended to limit use of this ground to ascertain whether providers can perform the current contract, it is submitted that either this would have been expressly or the provision would have been incorporated into the rules on financial and technical standing.

[28] On this see further Chap 16.

[29-30] Works Regulation 14(2) and (3), as amended by Supply Regulation 31(1); Supply Regulation 14(2) and (3); Services Regulation 14(2) and (3), as amended by Supply Regulation 31(2).

provider has not received of a criminal conviction for a particular offence, where registration depends on proof that the provider has not been convicted of the type of offence in question.[31] The detailed rules relating to this use of official lists are considered further below.[32]

(c) GRAVE MISCONDUCT IN THE COURSE OF THE BUSINESS OR PROFESSION

An authority may also reject a provider who has committed an act of grave misconduct in the course of the business or profession.[33] This allows the exclusion of those who have committed a criminal act but have not been convicted of an offence, provided the misconduct is "grave". It is not clear whether this would cover all acts which are, technically, criminal: arguably there must be misconduct which is culpable, and possibly which is serious in its effects. The provision would also seem to cover certain acts which are not criminal: for example, a significant breach of a code of professional ethics. It was suggested by Advocate General Gulmann in his opinion in one case that it could also cover the deliberate breach of a previous contract.[34] Unfortunately, there is much uncertainty as to what conduct is "grave", and this may be a serious disincentive to use of this provision.

As with grounds discussed above, for firms from states which benefit from the regulations, authorities must accept the registration on an official list of the firm's state of establishment as evidence that a firm has not been guilty of grave misconduct, where registration depends on proof that the conduct in question has not occurred.[35] The use of lists in this way is examined further below.[36]

(d) NON-PAYMENT OF SOCIAL SECURITY CONTRIBUTIONS

The regulations also allow firms to be rejected where they have failed to fulfil obligations relating to social security contributions which exist under (i) the law of the United Kingdom or (ii) the law of the state in which the firm is established.[37]

For providers entitled to claim the benefit of the regulations, an authority must accept as conclusive evidence that such obligations have

---

[31] Works Regulation 18, as amended by Supply Regulation 31(1); Supply Regulation 19; Services Regulation 18, as amended by Supply Regulation 31(2).

[32] See pp. 344–348.

[33] Works Regulation 14(1)(e); Supply Regulation 14(1)(e); Services Regulation 14(1)(e).

[34] Opinion in case 71/92, *Commission v. Spain*, judgment of November 17, 1993, para. 95 of the Opinion.

[35] Works Regulation 18, as amended by Supply Regulation 31(1); Services Regulation 18, as amended by Supply Regulation 31(2)

[36] See pp. 344–348.

[37] Works Regulation 14(1)(f), as amended by Supply Regulation 31(1); Supply Regulation 14(1)(f); Services Regulation 14(1)(f), as amended by Supply Regulation 31(2).

been fulfilled a certificate issued by the competent authority designated for this purpose by the state of establishment.[38] Where such documentary evidence is not issued, the authority must accept as an alternative a declaration on oath made by the provider before either (i) an authority designated by the state of establishment or (ii) a notary public or commissioner for oaths in the state of establishment.[39]

(e) NON-PAYMENT OF TAXES

Rejection is also allowed for failure to meet obligations relating to the payment of taxes.[40] In the case of the works and services rules this applies only to non-payment of taxes under United Kingdom law; under the Supply Regulation it applies (as with the non-payment of social security contributions) to non-payment of taxes either under United Kingdom law *or* under the law of the state of establishment. There is no sensible explanation of this difference between the regulations, nor of the different treatment in this respect of tax and social security obligations.

For providers benefiting from the regulations, an authority is obliged to accept as conclusive evidence that such obligations have been fulfilled a certificate issued by the competent authority designated for this purpose by the state of establishment.[41] Where such documentary evidence is not issued, it is required to accept a declaration on oath made by the provider before either (i) an authority designated by the state of establishment or (ii) a notary public or commissioner for oaths in the state of establishment.[42]

(f) SERIOUS MISREPRESENTATION IN SUPPLYING INFORMATION

Another ground for exclusion/rejection is the fact that a provider is guilty of "serious" misrepresentation in supplying information, under regulation 14 itself, under regulation 15 (economic and financial standing), regulation 16 (technical capacity) or regulation 17 (supplementary information).[43] This provision is important to discourage providers from giving misleading information, especially since in relation to certain matters covered by regulations 14, 15 or 16 authorities must accept

---

[38] Works Regulation 14(2); Supply Regulation 14(2); Services Regulation 14(2).
[39] Works Regulation 14(2) and (3); Supply Regulation 14(2) and (3); Services Regulation 14(2) and (3).
[40] Works Regulation 14(1)(g); Supply Regulation 14(1)(g); Services Regulation 14(1)(g).
[41] Works Regulation 14(2) and (3), as amended by Supply Regulation 31(1); Supply Regulation 14(2) and (3); Services Regulation 14(2) and (3), as amended by Supply Regulation 31(2).
[42] Works Regulation 14(2) and (3), as amended by Supply Regulation 31(1); Supply Regulation 14(2) and (3); Services Regulation 14(2) and (3), as amended by Supply Regulation 31(2).
[43] Works Regulation 14(1)(g); Supply Regulation 14(1)(g); Services Regulation 14(1)(g).

statements or declarations from providers as conclusive evidence. It is not clear whether a "serious" misrepresentation would need to be a deliberate one.

The literal wording of the provisions suggests that exclusion from supply contracts is limited to the case where there is misrepresentation in relation to other *supply* contracts, exclusion from works contracts for misrepresentation relating to works contracts and exclusion from services contracts for misrepresentation relating to services contracts. This is anomalous. It also appears that firms cannot be excluded for misrepresentation in relation to contracts outside the scope of any regulations.

Under the Services Directive it is expressly stated that exclusion is permitted where a provider is guilty of serious misrepresentation in *failing* to supply required information,[44] which presumably refers to the case where material information is omitted. This is not stated expressly in the Services Regulations, which refer simply to misrepresentation in "providing" information, but this could be interpreted to include omissions. The Supply and Works Directives, as well as the regulations, refer merely to misrepresentation in "supplying"[45] information, but these provisions also should be treated as embracing the omission of material information.

With providers who benefit from the regulations, authorities must accept the registration on an official list of the firm's state of establishment as evidence that a firm has not been guilty of misinformation, to the extent that registration on that list depends on proof of this fact.[46]

(g) NON-REGISTRATION ON A PROFESSIONAL OR TRADE REGISTER

An authority may limit contract awards to providers who are registered on certain specified trade or professional registers in their state of establishment.[47] The list of registers in which registration may be required[48] is set out in the table on page 340.

In the United Kingdom and Ireland there are no such professional or trade registers. It is thus stated that providers established in these states shall be treated as registered on a trade or professional register where the provider is certified by the Registrar of Companies as being incorporated or is certified as having declared on oath that he is carrying

---

[44] Services Directive Article 29(g).
[45] Works Directive Article 24(g) and Supply Directive Article 20(g).
[46] Works Regulation 18, as amended by Supply Regulation 31(1); Supply Regulation 19; Services Regulation 18, as amended by Supply Regulation 32(1). For further detail on the status of these lists see section 5 below.
[47] Works Regulation 14(1)(i), as amended by Supply Regulation 31(1); Supply Regulation 14(1)(i); Services Regulation 14(1)(j), as amended by Supply Regulation 31(2).
[48] These are generally listed in Works Regulation 14(4), as amended by Supply Regulation 31(1); Supply Regulation 14(4); and Services Regulation 14(4), as amended by Supply Regulation 31(2).

on business in the trade in question, at a specific place of business, and under a specific trading name.[49] Providers established in Ireland may, where applicable, show that they are certified as registered with the Registrar of Friendly Societies.[50]

Providers established in states (other than the United Kingdom and Ireland) which are "relevant" states under the regulations[51] and which have "equivalent" professional or trade registers not expressly listed in the regulations, must be treated as satisfying any registration requirement imposed under regulation 14 on production of a certificate of registration in those equivalent registers.[52] Where no relevant register exists in these states, providers must be regarded as satisfying any registration requirements where the provider makes a declaration on oath that he exercises the trade or profession in question.[53] Where the state makes no provision for a declaration on oath, the purchaser must accept a solemn statement made by the provider that he exercises this trade or profession, where such a declaration is made before the relevant judicial, administrative or competent authority or before a notary public or Commissioner for Oaths in the state of establishment.[54-55] These provisions are relevant, in particular, to Greece in the case of services (where no register is listed except in the case of certain research and development services); to Liechtenstein (for works and services); and to various Central and Eastern European States, which are relevant states under the regulations since they are entitled to benefit from the regulations under the Europe Agreements concluded with the Community, but for which no registers are listed.

---

[49] Works Regulation 14(5); Supply Regulation 14(5); Services Regulation 14(5).
[50] *Ibid.*
[51] On this concept see pp. 908–909.
[52] Works Regulation 14(6), as substituted by Supply Regulation 31(1); Supply Regulation 14(7); Services Regulation 14(7), as inserted by Supply Regulation 31(2).
[53] *Ibid.*
[54-55] *Ibid*; and Works Regulation 14(3); Supply Regulation 14(3); and Services Regulation 14(3).

Professional and trade registers recognised under regulation 14

Austria: the *Firmenbuch*, the *Gewerberegister* or the *Mitglieder-verzeichnisse der Landeskammern*.

Belgium: the *registre du commerce/Handelsregister*, or in addition, under the Services Regulations, the *ordres professionels-Beroepsorden*.

Denmark: the *Ehrvs-* and *Selskabsstyrelsen* (Services Regulations) or the *Aktieselskabsregstret*, *Foreningsregistret* or *Handelsregistret* (Supply and Works Regulations).

Finland: the *Kaupparekister* or the *Handelsregistret*.

France: the *registre du commerce* or the *répertoire des métiers*.

Germany: the *Handelsregister* or the *Handwerksrolle*, or, under the Services Regulations, in addition the *Vereinsregister*.

Greece: the Μητρώο Εργοληπτικὼν Επιχε'ργσεων (the register of contractors' enterprises) of the Ministry for Environment, Town and Country Planning and Public Works (Works Regulations); βιοτεχνικό βιομγχανιΚό ή ΕμποριΚό ΕπιηελγΤηριο (Supply Regulations); or Μγτρώο Μελετγτὼν and Μγτρωό Τραφειων Μελετὼν (Services Regulations).[56-57]

Iceland: the *Firmaskrá* or, in addition under the Services Regulations, the *Hutafélagaskrá*.

Italy: the *Registro della Camera di commercio, industria, agricultura e artigianato* (Works, Supply and Services Regulations), the *registro delle commissione provinciali oer l'artigianato* (Supply and Services Regulations) or the *Consiglio nazionale degli ordini professionali* (Services Regulations).

Liechtenstein: the *Gewerberegister* (Supply Regulations only).

Luxembourg: the *registre aux firmes* and the *rôle de la Chambre des métiers*.

Netherlands: the *Handelsregister*

Norway: the *Foretaksregistret*.

Portugal: the *Commissão de Alvaras de Empresas de Obras Públicas Particulares* ("CAEOPP") (Works Regulations) or the *Registo nacional das Pessoas Colectivas* (Supply and Services Regulations).

Spain: the *Registro Oficial de Contratistas del Minsterio de Industria y Energia* (Works Regulations); the *Registro Mercantil* (Supply Regulations)[58]; or the *Registro Central de Empresas Consultoras y de Servicios del Ministerio de Economiá y Hacienda* (Services Regulations).

Sweden: the *Aktiebolagsregistret*, the *Handelsregistret* or (Works and Supply Regulations only) the *Foreningsregistret*.

[56-57] This is listed in Services Regulation 14(6)(a), and applies only in the case of services under para. 8 of Sched. 1 to the regulations (which refers to certain research and development services). For other services Greek providers are subject to the rules which are applicable when no register is listed, as described above: Services Regulation 14(6)(b), as substituted by Supply Regulation 31(2).

[58] An individual established in Spain (where a separate system applies to individuals) must be treated as registered in a professional or trade register if he is certified as having declared on oath that he exercises the trade or profession in question.

(h) ABSENCE OF REQUISITE LICENCE

Under the Services Regulations authorities may reject service providers who are not recognised as competent to carry out the services concerned in their state of establishment. (Such providers cannot normally be subject to the domestic regulatory requirements which apply to service providers established in the United Kingdom[59]; thus it is generally necessary to refer to licences, etc. held in the home state to ensure that service providers are properly qualified.) Services Regulation 14 provides for rejection where the service provider does not have a licence to provide the relevant service which is legally required by the state of establishment.[60] Rejection is also allowed where the provider does not belong to an organisation of which membership is required by the state of establishment for the provision of the services in question.

Authorities must accept registration in an official list of the state of establishment as evidence that the provider possesses the required membership and licences, where registration there depends on proof of these requirements.[61]

5. USE OF OFFICIAL LISTS OF PROVIDERS KEPT BY OTHER STATES

It is the practice of some purchasers to maintain lists of firms which have demonstrated their qualification to participate in particular types of contracts. This avoids any need for firms to demonstrate their qualification separately on each occasion on which they wish to participate in a contract.[62] Works Regulation 18, Supply Regulation 19 and Services Regulation 18 permit providers to use the fact of their registration on "official lists" in their own state to prove to United Kingdom authorities that they satisfy certain conditions for participation which those authorities may have laid down under regulations 14, 15 and 16. The purpose of these provisions is to minimise the procedural burdens on non-domestic providers.

The lists may be used to prove compliance with any conditions laid down under regulation 14, except those concerning tax and social security obligations.[63] They may also be used in proving any criteria

---

[59] See Chap. 4.
[60] Services Regulation 14(1)(i), as amended by Supply Regulation 31(2).
[61] Works Regulation 18, as amended by Supply Regulation 31(1); Supply Regulation 19; Services Regulation 18, as amended by Supply Regulation 31(2).
[62] Lists have also been used to provide authorities with information about potential providers to enable them to choose parties to bid or negotiate contracts without public advertisement. However, for contracts covered by the regulations it is not permitted to limit participation to those on lists: see further section 6 below.
[63] Works Regulation 18(a), as amended by Supply Regulation 31(1); Supply Regulation 19(a); Services Regulation 18(a), as amended by Supply Regulation 31(2).

relating to economic and financial standing, or relating to technical capacity[64] which in the latter case probably includes those criteria relating to the concept of "ability" under the Services Regulations.[65] A provider wishing to invoke the fact of registration on a list to prove any of these matters must obtain a certificate of registration from the authority which administers the list. This must specify the information which was given to the authority to enable the provider to be registered on the list, and must also state any classification given.

In relation to regulation 14, the effect of registration is that an authority must accept that the provider does not fall within any of the grounds for exclusion to the extent that the certificate deals with the ground in question, and also that it may not demand from providers any information which could normally be required under regulation 14[66] (nor any information supplementary to this under regulation 17).[67] Thus, for example, if the registration has depended on proof that the provider is registered in a trade or professional register, or has not been convicted of an offence, the authority must accept that the provider is enrolled in such a register and does not have a conviction, and may not request from the provider the evidence normally applicable to such matters (such as a certificate of registration in the relevant trade register, in the former case, or an extract from the judicial record in the latter). On the other hand, if registration on the official list does not depend on any investigation into the provider's criminal record, the fact of registration in that list will not exempt the provider from proving that he has no convictions where absence of such convictions is a condition for participating in a contract.

In relation to proof of criteria relating to economic/financial standing or technical capacity, it is provided that, to the extent that the certificate of registration in the official list deals with those criteria, an authority may not require a provider to produce any of the evidence which could normally be demanded under regulations 15 or 16 (nor any supplementary information under regulation 17). Further, it is to be implied that authorities must accept the provider's registration on the list as evidence of facts dealt with in the certificate, which cannot be questioned by any

---

[64] Works Regulation 18(b), as amended by Supply Regulation 31(1); Supply Regulation 19(b); Services Regulation 18(b), as amended by Supply Regulation 31(2).

[65] It is not stated that these provisions apply to assessing ability. Since, however, most of the matters mentioned in relation to ability, such as skills and efficiency, are clearly in general aspects of technical capacity and are treated as such under the works and supply rules (which contain no separate provisions on ability), ability may be treated as an ordinary sub-category of technical capacity for the purpose of these provisions, and as such subject to the rules on official lists.

[66] Both these consequences are expressly stated in Works Regulation 18, Supply Regulation 19 and Services Regulation 18.

[67] Works Regulation 18, Supply Regulation 19 and Services Regulation 18.

other evidence obtained from other sources.[68] Thus, for example, if registration on a list requires providers to prove a certain volume of turnover in previous years, the fact of registration must be taken as evidence that the provider had such a turnover and the authority may not call for any further evidence of turnover in that period.

The provisions on official lists, do not, however, affect the discretion of national authorities to determine their own *criteria* for participation in contracts, nor to set their own *standards* regarding the qualification criteria. For example, in relation to turnover, it is for national law or the relevant administrative authorities to determine whether to impose any minimum turnover requirements and, if so, to decide the level of turnover required for certain types of contract.[69] That this discretion is not affected by the directives was made clear by the Court of Justice in joined cases *CEI and Bellini*.[70] The judgment concerned a contractor registered on an Italian official list deemed eligible to participate in works contracts of a certain value in Italy; however, the contractor was considered ineligible for such contracts in Belgium, since it did not meet the minimum conditions relating to resources, number of workers and number of managerial staff. The Court of Justice, in response to a request for a preliminary ruling from the Belgian Council of State, ruled that registration on the Italian list did not exempt the contractor from meeting these requirements. The directive, according to the Court, merely prevents authorities from questioning "information" which can be deduced from the fact of registration.[71] This appears to refer purely to factual information concerning the provider's position.

There may, of course, be some debate over the information which can properly be deduced from the certificate. For example, where a certificate purports to depend on the registering authority's conclusion that the provider has not been guilty of any "grave misconduct" it could be argued that this is evidence of the fact that there has been no misconduct of any kind. On the other hand, it could be argued that the information which can be deduced is limited to that which has actually been investigated by the registering authority.

There is no definition of an "official list" in either the directives or regulations. This concept should be interpreted to cover all lists maintained by public bodies which are designed to provide evidence of the

---

[68] These two points are not stated in the regulations but are clear from the directives: Works Directive Article 29(3); Supply Directive 25(3); Services Directive 35(3).

[69] Likewise, where providers are assessed on an individual basis rather than by reference to general conditions of an objective nature, it will be for the authority itself to evaluate each provider, based on the factual information available.

[70] Joined cases 27–29/86, *S.A. Constructions et Entreprises Industrielles (CEI) v. Société Cooperative "Association Intercommunale pour les Autoroutes des Ardennes"* [1987] E.C.R. 3347.

[71] Paras. 25–28 of the judgment.

criteria covered by regulations 14–16 for the purpose of qualification for government contracts.[72]

The rules only apply in respect of registration on official lists in the state of establishment. Thus, for example, a French enterprise may only rely on matters which are proven by its registration on an official list maintained by French authorities; it may not rely on, for example, the fact of its registration on a Belgian list.

6. RULES GOVERNING DOMESTIC "APPROVED LISTS"

(1) THE USE OF APPROVED LISTS

As already noted above, it is the practice of some purchasers to maintain lists of firms considered by the purchaser to be qualified to undertake certain types of contract. These are sometimes referred to as "approved lists" or "qualification lists". Sometimes participation in contracts has been limited to registered firms – either all firms on the list are invited to bid or negotiate, or a restricted number of those on the list are selected. In other cases, participation is not limited to those who are registered, but registration is used to eliminate the need for qualification of registered firms each time a contract is awarded, thus reducing the procedural burden both for the purchaser and for registered firms. Qualification through registration on a list often involves an enterprise demonstrating compliance with all the conditions imposed for participation in particular types of contract – for example, financial stability, technical ability to do the type of work and any applicable "secondary" conditions (such as payment of taxes). However, in other cases there may be qualification processes in addition to registration – either because the list covers only some of the criteria set or because it is necessary to update the information.

(2) APPROVED LISTS UNDER THE REGULATIONS

(a) THE CURRENT STATUS OF APPROVED LISTS

Under the public sector directives and regulations it is no longer permitted to exclude a firm from participation because it is not

---

[72] In the case of *Transporoute*, Advocate General Reischl considered that an "establishment permit" which the Luxembourg government purported to require from providers to attest to their qualifications and good standing, could not constitute an "official list", since it was not limited to firms in the government markets but applied to all firms doing business in Luxembourg. He also stated that a number of permits issued simultaneously could not be described as a list. This last conclusion seems doubtful since the form of the process for categorisation should not be important.

The concept of an "official list" is sometimes used in a narrower sense to refer to lists on which providers must be registered but does not appear to have this meaning in the directives and regulations since authorities are not permitted to operate mandatory lists: see pp. 344–348.

registered on an approved list. This was stated clearly by the European Court of Justice in case 71/92, *Commission v Spain*.[73]

In relation to technical capacity this is clear from the wording of the directives and regulations, since authorities may demand only the means of proof expressly listed, and these do not include registration on an approved list.[74]

In relation to economic and financial standing[75] authorities must accept the documents listed in the regulations (such as bank statements) when these are appropriate to provide the information which the authority seeks, and this rules out registration on approved lists as a requirement for proving matters which can be deduced from the listed documents. Although the rules allow for authorities to call for other references in respect of matters for which the listed documents are not appropriate, it has been suggested that they are obliged to accept any reasonable evidence offered as an alternative,[76] thus again ruling out compulsory registration as proof of the matters in question.

So far as concerns regulation 14, for some of the grounds for exclusion under this regulation (such as the existence of criminal convictions), as with technical capacity specified forms of evidence are required to be accepted, implying that it is not possible to insist on registration on a list.

For certain grounds under regulation 14, however, it has been explained that authorities may generally use any relevant evidence; and the same appears to apply to the assessment of services providers' ability under the Services Regulations. In this case it might appear that registration on a list might be one method of proof which authorities may require. However, in case 71/92 both the Court and Advocate General Gulmann indicated that registration on lists could not be required at all.[77] Thus it appears that such a limitation is to be implied from the general purpose of the qualification provisions. If this is correct, it can be suggested that the limitation on the use of approved lists is best regarded as an illustration of an implied principle that authorities must always accept alternative evidence to that demanded from providers where the alternative offered is reasonable.

In limiting the use of approved lists the public sector rules differ from the utilities rules, which expressly permit purchasers to confine participa-

---

[73] Judgment of November 17, 1993, para. 45 of the judgment; and see also para. 81 of the Opinion of Advocate General Gulmann in the case. This is deduced from the provisions in the directives and regulations dealing with permissible evidence, as explained below. It can be noted that the directives expressly state that official lists must be adapted to the qualifications rules in the directives: Works Directive 29(1); Supply Directive 25(1); Services Directive 35(1).

[74] On this see pp. 316–317.

[75] That registration cannot be required for financial standing, as well as technical capacity, was made clear in case 71/92 (see para. 45) although the Court did not examine the actual provisions in the directives.

[76] See above pp. 302–307.

[77] See para. 45 of the judgment and para. 81 of the Opinion.

tion in contracts to those registered on a list.[78] However, the use of such lists in the utilities sector is carefully regulated to prevent abuse.[79]

Although participation in contracts covered by the public sector rules may not be *restricted* to those registered on lists, an authority may still keep lists as a means for registered firms to prove their qualification for contracts, should those firms wish to do so.[80] Providers who are not on the list, however, must still be considered for participation, provided that they are able to prove their qualification in accordance with the rules outlined earlier.

It is also required that firms registered on a list should not be treated more favourably than those which are not registered. Thus in *Commission v. Spain*,[81] the European Court of Justice held that a Spanish provision allowing the government to exempt registered enterprises from the requirement to provide a guarantee in tendering for public works contracts infringed the Works Directive.[82] This decision can be seen as illustrating a general principle that registration can operate only to exempt a firm from satisfying conditions which have been met by the provider to obtain registration on the list; it may not confer any other advantages. Thus it is not permitted to apply more stringent qualification criteria, standards or procedural requirements for firms which are not on a list, than were applied to providers who have qualified for the contract in question through registration on a list.[83]

It was held in case C–71/92, *Commission v. Spain* that where lists are maintained, an authority may not require a non-registered enterprise to produce a certificate from the Spanish consultative committee on public procurement to state that the enterprise is not registered and has not had its registration suspended or revoked – a requirement designed to prevent enterprises previously rejected from seeking a second chance to qualify.[84] Such a certificate, the Court held, was not referred to in the directives.

It should also be noted that the directives state expressly that in compiling lists the authorities must follow the rules on permissible criteria and evidence laid down in the directives:[85] in other words, these

---

[78] See pp. 532–539.
[79] *Ibid.*
[80] This is implied by the fact the express requirement in the directives for authorities to accept registration in the lists of other states as one way for a provider to prove certain factual information: see section 5 above.
[81] Case C–71/92, judgment of November 17, 1993, noted by Fernández Martín [1993] 2 P.P.L.R. CS 73.
[82] Paras. 55–60 of the judgment.
[83] Such a rule can be derived from the prohibition on requiring registration on a list: it follows from the principle that providers must be given the choice of proving registration by other means, that they should not be treated less favourably where they do so, as was pointed out by Advocate General Gulmann. Such a rule also finds support in the more general principle of the equal treatment of providers laid down by the Court of Justice in the *Storebaelt* case (as to which see pp. 180–181).
[84] Paras. 44–47 of the judgment.
[85] Works Directive 29(4); Supply Directive 25(4); Services Directive 35(4).

rules apply to qualification through lists equally as to qualification on an ad hoc basis for individual contracts. This is not stated in the United Kingdom regulations but may be implied from the more general provisions in the regulations which govern qualification.

Further, no additional proof or statements can be required of providers from other states for the purpose of registration than are required from national providers – a rule which follows from the E.C. Treaty provisions but has also been repeated in the directives.[86]

Where lists are maintained other states entitled to take the benefit of the procurement legislation must be informed of the address of the body to which applications for registration must be sent.[87]

It can be noted that an alternative view of the effect of the directives on approved lists is that these may be maintained for domestic providers but not for those from other states which benefit from the directives. However, this view seems inconsistent with the general philosophy of the procurement regime under which domestic purchasers are permitted to enforce the rules, and with the general principle of equality which underlies the directives. It was assumed in *General Building and Maintenance v. Greenwich L.B.C.*[88] that the regulations' provisions on qualification, from which the principles on approved lists are deduced, apply equally to domestic providers.

(b) THE DEVELOPMENT OF STANDARDS FOR APPROVED LISTS

It would considerably reduce the burden on providers who wish to compete for government contracts in other states, if recognition of approved lists of other states were extended further than is currently provided for in the Community directives, to cover, in particular, the standards and criteria for qualification to be on the lists. In April 1993 the European Community placed a mandate with CEN and CENELEC, the European standardising institutions,[89] to consider developing a "standard" for the qualification of providers for works contracts. Such a standard, once developed could be used by some or all European states, who would then find it acceptable to recognise each others' lists of providers to the extent that qualification to be on those lists would be based on the same standard. If a standard for works is successful, standards might also be developed for supplies and services. Such standards might ultimately be made mandatory and incorporated into the procurement directives. This would be a significant step in improving access to non-domestic markets for many providers.

---

[86] *Ibid.* To do so would also be contrary to the Community Treaties or, in the case of non-Community states entitled to the benefit of the directives, to other relevant international agreements.

[87] Works Directive 29(5); Supply Directive 25(5); Services Directive 35(5).

[88] [1993] I.R.L.R. 535.

[89] On these see further pp. 579–580.

(3) APPROVED LISTS FOR CONTRACTS OUTSIDE THE REGULATIONS

It is not clear whether registration on approved lists can be made mandatory for contracts outside the regulations. It could be argued that it is more burdensome for providers established in other states to register on these lists than domestic providers, since domestic providers are likely to have a much greater proportion of their business with the government, making the formalities of registration more worthwhile for such persons. However, such a requirement might not be considered to discriminate directly or indirectly against providers from other states where they are given a sufficient opportunity to register; and at the very least an open list might be justified on grounds of general interest. It should be pointed out that the validity of such lists under the Treaty where fairly and openly operated is assumed by the Utilities Directive which expressly permits such lists.[90]

7. THE LEGAL STATUS OF PROVIDERS

(1) BIDS BY CONSORTIA

Works Regulation 19, Supply Regulation 20 and Services Regulation 19 expressly allow providers to form consortia to submit bids. For this purpose a "consortium" is defined to mean two or more persons, at least one of whom is a contractor/supplier/services provider,[91] who act jointly for the purpose of being awarded a contract.[92]

These rules provide that a tender cannot be treated as ineligible simply because it is submitted by a consortium which has not formed a legal entity for the purpose of tendering; nor can an authority decline to select a consortium to tender or negotiate for a contract on this basis.[93] However, an authority may insist that a consortium which is awarded a contract should form a legal entity before entering into the contract, or as a term of the contract.[94]

In relation to the conduct of the award procedure under the regulations, it is to be noted that any reference to a contractor, supplier or service provider includes a reference to each individual member of a consortium.[95]

---

[90] An alternative view might condemn such lists as unnecessarily restrictive of trade on the basis that providers can adequately prove standing by other means, as envisaged by the procurement directives.

[91] On the meaning of these terms see pp. 907–908.

[92] Works Regulation 19(1); Supply Regulation 20(1); Services Regulation 19(1).

[93] Works Regulation 19(2); Supply Regulation 20(2); Services Regulation 19(2).

[94] Ibid.

[95] Works Regulation 19(3); Supply Regulation 20(3); Services Regulation 19(3).

(2) THE FORM OF PROVIDERS UNDER THE SERVICES RULES

Services Regulation 20 contains express provisions on the form of services providers. This states that providers cannot be treated as ineligible, or excluded from those from whom persons are selected to tender for or negotiate a contract, on the basis that the law generally requires persons providing the services in question to take a specific legal form (such as an individual or corporation), *if* the services provider is authorised to provide services in that form in the state in which he is established.[96]

Where the services provider is not an individual, he may be required to indicate in the tender, or in the request to be selected or negotiate, the names and relevant professional qualifications of the staff who will be responsible for performing the services.[97]

(3) REQUIREMENT FOR LEGAL CAPACITY

Authorities may wish to ensure that providers have legal capacity, so that they can be held legally responsible for their acts or omissions. In case C–71/92, *Commission v. Spain*,[98] the Commission accepted that the possession of legal capacity is a condition which authorities may set for participation. However, the Court of Justice held that authorities may only require proof of such a requirement by reference to the information contemplated in the directive – that is, the provisions found in regulations 14–16. Thus, authorities could not require providers to furnish certificates from their domestic administration, certified by the Spanish embassy, to attest the possession of legal capacity. Generally, authorities will be able to ascertain capacity from the provider's registration in a national professional or trade register, or an equivalent declaration, as permitted under regulation 14.

8. CONFIDENTIALITY OF INFORMATION

Supply Regulation 18 and Services Regulation 30 require contracting authorities to comply with requirements on confidentiality of information which are requested by providers, where these requirements are reasonable. There is no equivalent provision in the directive or regulations on works, which is clearly anomalous.

---

[96] Services Regulation 20(1).
[97] Services Regulation 20(2).
[98] Judgment of November 17, 1993.

9. QUALIFICATION UNDER THE E.C. TREATY

The rules in the E.C. Treaty on free movement and freedom of establishment which were explained in Chapter 4 are important in the context of qualification. These rules not only limit the discretion of authorities under the regulations but also apply in qualifying providers for contracts which are not covered by the regulations.

It was suggested in Chapter 4 that Article 30 E.C. prohibits any discrimination against providers from other Member States when qualifying providers for public supply contracts[99] since this involves indirect discrimination against imports. Article 59 E.C. covers measures which discriminate, directly or indirectly, against providers who are nationals of or established in other Member States in relation to contracts for construction or other services. Article 52 E.C., on freedom of establishment, is also infringed by any discrimination against nationals of other states established in the United Kingdom, whether in relation to supplies or services.

These provisions prohibit the government from imposing conditions for qualification for contracts which apply to non-nationals or providers established outside the United Kingdom but not to domestic providers. This would include, for example, setting higher qualification standards (higher turnover levels, etc.) for foreign providers, requiring additional guarantees, or requiring such providers to obtain special permits to do business with government.

These provisions may also be infringed by applying procedural or substantive criteria which are more difficult for foreign providers to meet than domestic providers.

An important issue here, which arises mainly in relation to construction and other services, particularly professional services, is the extent to which an authority may require parties to government contracts to meet conditions which it lays down for the provision of services in its territory, notably rules on qualifications, rules of professional conduct or other requirements, such as obtaining permits or licences. Obviously, the government will, at the very least, wish to apply the legal rules and standards which govern persons operating in the United Kingdom generally, and indeed will often be obliged to do so by law. For example, if a specific qualification or a licence is required to practice a particular profession in that state, then such a qualification or licence will be required of providers undertaking contracts with the government. To apply such requirements to non-United Kingdom providers, however, creates difficulties for those providers, who will not generally possess the relevant qualifications or licences, but only those required in their own

---

[99] See p. 82.

state. Service providers are often also subject to professional rules of conduct or are required to be members of professional organisations: again, to comply is burdensome for outside providers.

In relation to qualifications, the Community has adopted a number of directives requiring states to recognise each others' qualifications in some areas.[1] Where providers established in other states possess qualifications recognised to be equivalent to United Kingdom qualifications under these provisions, they may not be excluded from United Kingdom markets – including the government market. On the other hand, where there is no express provision for recognition, it is permitted to exclude a provider – a rule which constitutes a serious barrier to trade in services.

Rules of professional conduct,[2] although constituting a barrier to trade which discriminates indirectly against services providers from other states, are permitted under Article 59 where justified by the need to protect the general interest. However, the usual principle of proportionality applies in assessing the justification for such rules under Article 59, and justification will not be shown where the service provider is subject to rules in his own state which adequately protect the interests concerned.[3] Since this is the case with most professions, in practice it is difficult to insist that service providers comply with domestic rules of professional conduct. Similar rules will apply to other conditions or procedural requirements which burden foreign providers more than domestic providers. An example in the context of procurement is seen in *Transporoute*[4] in which the government of Luxembourg required providers who sought to participate in government contracts to obtain an "establishment permit", which was required of all firms doing business in Luxembourg, and evidenced qualifications to engage in the business concerned. The Court held this to be contrary to the Works Directive and also indicated that it infringed Article 59.[5]

The rules are different, on the other hand, for firms established in the United Kingdom, which must rely on Article 52 rather than Article 59. Such firms, whatever their nationality, may be required to meet the conditions laid down by law for the exercise of a particular profession or trade.

---

[1] Originally this problem was approached by adopting directives relating to specific professions. However, Directive 89/48 [1989] O.J. L19/16 lays down general principles for mutual recognition of certain professional qualifications, for qualifications based on at least three years post-secondary education and training. The obligation to accept another state's qualifications also applies where this recognition has been given under the regulating state's own domestic rules: case 11/77, *Patrick v. Ministre des Affaires Culturelles* [1977] E.C.R. 1199. See generally Steiner, *Textbook on EEC Law* (1992), pp. 209–212.

[2] Steiner, above, pp. 212–215.

[3] Case 279/80, *Webb* [1981] E.C.R. 3305; case 205/84, *Commission v. Germany* [1986] E.C.R. 3755.

[4] Case 76/81, *S.A. Transporoute v. Minister of Public Works* [1982] E.C.R. 417.

[5] Para. 14 of the judgment.

The discussion above concerns the minimum requirements for providers in the United Kingdom market in general, but many requirements for contract qualification are directed specifically at qualification for the contract(s) in question – such as minimum turnover requirements, or special qualifications needed for the job under the contract (rather than the minimum qualifications required to exercise the profession in question). Some conditions of this kind, though also applicable to both domestic and non-domestic providers, may be a greater burden to the former and thus give rise to a possibility of infringing Articles 52 or 59.

It was explained in Chapter 4 that Article 30 applies to some measures, notably those concerned with the characteristics of products (such as safety standards) which do not discriminate between domestic products and imports either directly or indirectly, but affect both equally; and it appears that Article 59 also applies to some measures of this kind.[6] It is not clear, however, whether this is the case with measures concerning qualification for government contracts, whether those relating to methods of proof or even substantive standards and criteria for qualification.

In case C–71/92, *Commission v. Spain*[7] the Commission contested a number of restrictive measures concerning methods of proving qualification, some of which appeared to affect all providers equally, and argued that all such measures were covered by Article 59 and required justification; and this was accepted by Advocate General Gulmann.[8] However, the Court did not consider this issue but based its judgment solely on the fact that the measures infringed the directives. If the approach of the Commission and Advocate General is correct, then even for contracts not covered by the regulations, including contracts of low value, authorities may be considerably restricted in their methods for assessing providers' standing, which will be subject to the scrutiny of the Court of Justice to ensure that they go no further than necessary. Further, such scrutiny might even be extended to substantive qualifications and criteria. However, this would be controversial. It can be pointed out that the Opinion (and judgment) in this case occurred just before the decision in *Keck*,[9] in which the Court made it clear that many types of measures other than those relating to product characteristics are *not* "caught" at all by Article 30 where there is neither direct discrimination nor any discriminatory effect. Following this decision, it may be that the application of both Article 30 and Article 59 to such measures of equal effect is limited to those setting legal requirements for product and service standards and to those relating to the specifications for government contracts but does not extend to rules on qualification.

---

[6] See Chap. 4.
[7] Judgment of November 17, 1993.
[8] See in particular paras. 75 and 81 of the Opinion.
[9] Cases C–267 and C–268/91, *Keck and Methouard* [1993] I–E.C.R. 6097.

CHAPTER 8

PUBLIC SECTOR REGULATIONS: SPECIAL PROCEDURES

1. INTRODUCTION

The previous chapters have examined the procedures under the Works Regulations, Supply Regulations and Services Regulations for contract awards by bodies which are "contracting authorities". The regulations also lay down certain other rules. First, they deal with the position of concession contracts: these are not subject to the same rules applicable to other contracts, but to a special regime, which imposes some obligations on private concessionaires as well as public bodies. Secondly, there is a special scheme applying to works contracts relating to public housing schemes. Thirdly, certain obligations are imposed on suppliers of public bodies who are not contracting authorities but enjoy "special or exclusive rights" in providing services. Fourthly, the regulations control the award of certain subsidised contracts made by bodies which are not contracting authorities and whose contracts are not therefore ordinarily subject to regulation. Finally, they control the conduct of "design contests" carried out by contracting authorities. The scope and application of these special provisions are examined in this chapter.

2. CONCESSION CONTRACTS

(1) PUBLIC WORKS CONCESSIONS

(a) THE SPECIAL TREATMENT OF CONCESSION CONTRACTS

One arrangement for the realisation of public works is the contract of concession whereby a contractor is remunerated by being permitted to exploit the work built.[1] This approach has sometimes been used, for example, to procure the construction of roads or of structures such as tunnels and bridges: a provider undertakes to build the work and is

---

[1] For an overview of this method of procurement see Ruiz Ojeda, "The Concession of Public Works: Options for the Financing and Management of Public Infrastructures" (1994) 3 P.P.L.R. 47.

permitted to collect tolls as all or part of his remuneration. Concessions have also been employed in the provision of infrastructure for rail and other transport services – for example, with the Manchester Metro Link Tram system, which has been set up by means of an agreement for the private sector to design, build, operate and maintain the system under a fifteen-year concession arrangement. Such arrangements have become increasingly important in all sectors in the United Kingdom since the start of the government's "Private Finance Initiative", launched in autumn 1992, which seeks to promote private sector involvement in the provision of public services and infrastructure.[2]

Concession contracts need to be considered separately, since they are treated differently from other works contracts. First, where such contracts are awarded by bodies which are contracting authorities, the rules which regulate their award are different from those applying to other contracts (see (c) below). Secondly, parties holding a public works concession contract – "concessionaires" – are subject to certain obligations in the award of their own contracts, even though they are not contracting authorities (see (d) below).

(b) DEFINITION OF A PUBLIC WORKS CONCESSION CONTRACT

(i) THE DEFINITION OF "PUBLIC WORKS CONCESSION"

The special rules considered in this section apply where there is a public works concession contract. This is defined in Works Regulation 2(1) as "a public works contract under which the consideration given by the contracting authority consists of or includes the grant of a right to exploit the work or works to be carried out under the contract". Thus to decide whether a contract is a public works concession contract it must first be considered whether it meets the usual definition of a "public works contract", which was considered in Chapter 5,[3] and, secondly, whether the consideration involves the grant of a right to exploit the work.

(ii) CONCESSIONS INVOLVING BOTH WORKS AND SERVICES

A contract may be a public works concession where only part of the consideration consists of the right of exploitation, and the other part consists of some other form of payment (which will usually be a lump sum); this is spelt out directly in the Works Directive[4] and is implicit in

---

[2] See generally H.M. Treasury, *Breaking New Ground* (November 1993); and on major transport projects currently being implemented through this approach see Department of Transport, *Building Tomorrow's Transport Network* (November 1994).
[3] See pp. 124–130
[4] Works Directive Article 1(b).

the definition of public works concession in the Works Regulations, given above. Thus a contract is a concession contract even if the right to exploit the work constitutes only a small part of the consideration.[5]

Exploitation of the works may involve provision of a service which the party awarded the contract is under a contractual duty to provide. For example, a firm might agree to build a leisure centre or housing estate and then to manage and operate it for a certain period of time on behalf of the authority, taking the fees paid by users by way of payment for its work. Such a contract involves acquisition by the authority of both works (construction of the centre or estate) and non-construction services (the management services). Concessions for building and operating transport networks (railways, trams, etc.) also involve both works – the provision of the infrastructure – and services – the operation of the public network. Generally, such a "mixed" contract must be classified as either a public works contract, to which the Works Regulations apply, or a public services contract, to which the Services Regulations may apply. As explained in Chapter 5 the Court of Justice in *Gestion Hotelera Internacional*[6] found that such a contract is generally a services contract where the works are "incidental" to the services. It was also explained that it is not absolutely clear how this test is to apply: one view is that a contract is a works contract where the works is the "main object" of the contract, whilst another view is that it is a works contract where the economic value of the works exceeds that of the services.[7] The classification is important where the contract in question is in the form of a concession, since if it is a works contract it is subject to regulations under the provisons discussed in this section, whereas if it is a services contract it is probably exempt from regulation.[8]

If the "main object" test is applied, then where the work in question is to remain, or to be transferred into, public use at the end of the concession period, the contract is likely to be regarded as a works concession. This will apply, for example, to most transport infrastructure concessions. On the other hand, where the work is to remain for the use of the provider at the end of the concession period, the concession is generally a services concession. Some cases, however, are more difficult to classify – for example, where the authority has an option to purchase the structure at the end of the concession period.

---

[5] If, however, a limited right of exploitation were conferred on the contractor without commercial motivation solely in order that the contract could be treated as a concession contract under the regulations, the courts are no doubt required to treat the classification as a sham and to regard it as an ordinary public works contract. A contract might also not be a concession where the right to exploit is of negligible value, by virtue of an implied *de minimis* principle.

[6] Case C-331/92, *Gestion Hotelera Internacional SA v. Comunidad Autonoma de Canarias* [1994] E.C.R. 1-1329.

[7] See the discussion at pp. 144–145.

[8] See p. 366.

(iii) CONCESSIONS INVOLVING WORKS PLUS PAYMENT

In some cases, the consideration given by the provider in return for the right to exploit a work will involve not merely the carrying out of works (and possibly also services), but will also require payments to be made to the authority, whether a fixed sum or a proportion of revenue raised from exploiting the work. For example, in relation to a new transport network, a provider, in return for the right to exploit the network for, say a ten-year period by collecting fares, might undertake (i) to build the network, (ii) to operate it for the concession period, and (iii) to pay to the public purse 20 per cent of passenger revenues. With these three different elements of the consideration, there are three possibilities: that the contract is one for works under the works rules; that it is one for services under the services rules (in which case, as a concession, it is unregulated); or that it is neither, but is a contract for raising revenue, and as such untouched by the procurement rules.

The contract could be classified by applying either a "relative value" test or, as is more likely, a "main object" test – whether the acquisition of a work, the acquisition of service, or the raising of finance. If the main object test is correct, in the case of a transport network to be returned to the authority at the end of the concession period, the acquisition of the network is likely to be the main object: hence, it is a works concession contract. On the other hand, a case can be envisaged where the main purpose of an arrangement is to raise revenue. For example, an authority running a hospital may, in order to raise funds, decide to lease part of its premises to a private provider, to enable that provider to build and use a clinic for private patients. Even though the agreement may provide for the authority to have use and ownership of the building when the concession period ends, when the purpose of the transaction is to raise revenue, rather than to acquire a building for public use,[9] such a contract is arguably not a works contract. However, it may be difficult on the facts to decide whether the acquisition of the building is the objective of the transaction or simply an incidental benefit of it, especially if it is planned to put the building to some use at the end of the concession. This is perhaps a case where there is no single object, and illustrates the difficulties of applying the "main object" test.

---

[9] This might be shown if the authority's intention was to lease the building to another private provider on expiry of the existing agreement. On the other hand, it could be argued that in this case the object of the contract is to acquire a building for renting out for a profit – so that acquisition of the work is to be considered the object of the contract.

(c) THE REGULATION OF CONCESSIONS AWARDED BY CONTRACTING AUTHORITIES

(i) THE SCOPE OF REGULATION

Bodies which are "contracting authorities" are, in awarding most public works contracts, subject to the very detailed rules which were explained in Chapter 6. In awarding a contract which is a "public works concession contract" such a contracting authority is not subject to all these rules[10]; however, it must follow certain limited obligations concerning advertising and time-limits for response (Works Regulation 25) and subcontracting (Works Regulation 26). These rules apply to all public works concession contracts except those within the exclusions in Works Regulation 6, and those falling below the thresholds in Works Regulation 7.[11] These exclusions and thresholds, which were explained in Chapter 5,[12] generally apply in the same way for public works concession contracts as for other public works contracts.

In relation to thresholds, it is expressly provided that the estimated value of the contract for the purpose of applying the threshold rules is "the value of the consideration which the contracting authority would expect to give for the carrying out of the work or works if it did not propose to grant a concession".[13]

There is nothing in the regulations or directives to exempt an authority from applying the rules set out below, even though the circumstances are such that were the contract not a concession arrangement it could be awarded by negotiation without advertisement – for example, circumstances of urgency. It would be desirable to include exemptions to cover this kind of case.

(ii) ADVERTISEMENT FOR THE CONTRACT

The authority must, under Works Regulation 25(2), publicise its intention to seek offers for a concession by sending, as soon as possible after it forms this intention, a notice to the Office of Official Publications of

---

[10] This is a consequence of regulation 5. This states that the obligations in the Works Regulations apply where it is proposed to award a "public works contract", but that the definition of a public works contract is not to include a "public works concession contract" for the purposes of Parts II, III, IV and V of the regulations and also regulations 24, 27 and 28. This effectively means that the only procedural obligations applying to concession contracts are those in regulations 25 and 26. In the 1971 Works Directive public works concession contracts were considered to be excluded (apart from an express provision stating that there was to be no discrimination on grounds of nationality): instead they were subject to a Voluntary Code of Practice adopted by representatives of all Member States at a Council meeting in 1971: see [1971] O.J. C 82/13; English Special Edition, Second Series, January 1974, IX. Legal regulation of concession contracts in the above form was first introduced in the 1989 Works Directive.

[11] Works Regulation 5.

[12] See pp. 150–175

[13] Works Regulation 7(5).

the European Communities.[14] Like notices advertising non-concession contracts, such notices must be published in the *Official Journal of the European Communities* in hard copy and in the TED data bank, in full and in the original language, with a summary of the important elements of the notice in the other official languages of the Community.[15] It must be published within 12 days of despatch by the authority.[16] Publication of a notice on the concession in the national press is not permitted until the above notice has been despatched (although it is not necessary to wait until it is actually published), and may not contain more information than found in the *Official Journal* notice.[17] Provided these rules are followed, however, notices may be published elsewhere, and it is also probably permitted to approach specific known contractors.[18]

The form of the notice must correspond, substantially, with that set out in Part F of Schedule 2 to the Works Regulations, and must contain all the information specified in that model. This model is set out on page 359. Like other notices under the regulations, it must not contain more than 650 words.[19-20] The Commission is likely shortly to adopt a recommendation for use of the CPV nomenclature in such notices.

(iii) TIME-LIMITS FOR RESPONSE

Works Regulation 25(3) provides that the last date for response to the notice is to be fixed at not less than 52 days from despatch of the notice. Since there may be a 12-day delay after despatch before publication, the actual notice to interested firms may be less than 52 days. In the case of a procedure where parties are invited to submit bids directly this 52-day period will apply to the time for submission of bids. With procedures where firms are merely permitted to contact the authority to express their interest, and the authority is to select a limited number to bid or negotiate the 52-day period relates to the time for firms to express their interest.

(iv) THE NATURE OF THE AWARD PROCEDURE

The requirements to publicise concession contracts do not entail any obligation to follow formal tendering procedure or even to use competitive procedures of any kind (such as competitive negotiations) for the contract award. Thus, once the contract has been publicised it is still open to authorities to negotiate an agreement with a single pre-selected

---

[14] This must be sent by "the most appropriate means": Works Regulation 30(1). Authorities must retain evidence of the date of despatch: Works Regulation 30(3).
[15] Works Directive Article 11(9).
[16] Works Directive Article 11(10).
[17] Works Regulation 30(4).
[18] See further the discussion at p. 196
[19-20] Works Regulation 30(2). The directive itself states that notices must not be more than one *Official Journal* page or approximately 650 words: Works Directive Article 11(13).

provider, provided that it acts within the confines of the Community Treaties and other relevant international agreements, which includes avoiding discrimination on grounds of nationality.[21]

There is no justification for this exclusion of concession contracts from the obligation to use competitive procedures. Even if special procedures may be appropriate for the award of certain concessions – for example, because of their complexity and the cost of bidding, or the need for an ongoing partnership between the authority and concessionaire in carrying out the project – in general such awards should be subject to much more stringent regulation than is presently the case.

PUBLIC WORKS CONTRACTS REGULATIONS 1991, SCHEDULE 2, PART F – PUBLIC WORKS CONCESSION CONTRACT NOTICE

1. The name, address, telegraphic address, telephone, telex and facsimile numbers of the contracting authority

2. (a) The site.
   (b) The subject of the concession and extent of the services to be provided.

3. (a) Final date for receipt of canditatures.
   (b) The address to which they must be sent.
   (c) The language or languages in which they must be drawn up:

4. Personal, technical and financial conditions to be fulfilled by the candidates.

5. The criteria for the award of the contract.

6. Where applicable, the minimum percentage of the works contracts awarded to third parties.

7. Other information.

8. Date of despatch of the notice.

---

[21] See Chap. 4 and Chap. 15.

(v) SUBCONTRACTING

Works Regulation 26(1) contains special rules on subcontracting. Basically, these require authorities to take one of two measures relating to the subcontracting of work by the concessionaire.[22]

The first is to *require*, as a term of the concession contract, that the concessionaire shall subcontract some or all of the work(s) to persons who are not affiliated to the concessionaire.[23] The amount of works subcontracted is to be not less than 30 per cent,[24] and may be a greater amount (to be specified in the contract) at the option of either the contractor or concessionaire. Authorities may sometimes wish to require subcontracting in order, in particular, to promote the participation of small and medium enterprises (SMEs) in a project.[25]

Alternatively, rather than requiring some of the works to be sub-contracted, an authority may simply request that a contractor shall indicate the proportion of the work(s), if any, which he would intend to subcontract to persons not affiliated to him, if he were awarded the concession contract.[26] This does not require that any works be sub-contracted, or even require the authority to take this possibility into account. Indeed, the rules on concession contracts do not prevent authorities from insisting that providers should not subcontract any of the work (which authorities may sometimes prefer to do to retain closer control over the project).[27]

(vi) OTHER OBLIGATIONS

The regulations do not impose any other obligations on contracting authorities in awarding concession contracts – for example, there are no rules on the qualification of providers, evaluation of bids or technical specifications. Contracting authorities are, however, also bound by the rules in the Community Treaties, as outlined in Chapter 4, which, inter alia, preclude any direct or indirect discrimination against providers from other Community Member States. They are also subject to rules in other international agreements, such as the European Economic Area

---

[22] Under the voluntary code operating before 1989 subcontracting of certain works was required: see [1971] O.J. C82/13; English Special Edition, Second Series, January 1974, IX.

[23] Works Regulation 26(1)(b). "Affiliated" is defined in Works Regulation 26(5). The definition is discussed below at pp. 363–364.

[24] This percentage is assessed by reference to the value of the consideration which the authority would expect to give in return for the work(s) if it had not granted a concession: Works Regulation 26(1)(2).

[25] On SMEs see further pp. 67–68.

[26] Works Regulation 26(1)(a). Again, "affiliated" has the definition given in Works Regulation 26(5), as discussed below.

[27] Whilst the provisions may, as noted above, be invoked to promote subcontracting and help SMEs they were not designed for this specific purpose; they derive from the Voluntary Code on concessions referred to in note 10 above and predate Community policy for promoting SMEs.

Agreement and Europe Agreements with central and eastern European states, which give similar rights to providers from a number of countries outside the E.C.[28]

(d) THE REGULATION OF CONTRACTS AWARDED BY CONCESSIONAIRES

(i) CONCESSIONAIRES WHO ARE CONTRACTING AUTHORITIES

A party who has entered into a public works concession contract with a contracting authority is referred to as a concessionaire.[29] A concessionaire is normally a private body, but in some cases may itself be a "contracting authority" under the Works Regulations. In this event, Works Regulation 26(2) makes it clear that the concessionaire authority must comply with the Works Regulations in relation to the public works contracts which it makes for subcontracting the works. The Works Regulations will, in fact, apply to such contracts in the same way as to any other "non-concession" public works contracts – that is, the authority must follow the detailed procedures set out in Chapter 6,[30] where the contract exceeds the relevant threshold and is not an excluded contract. The "lighter" regulatory regime applying to contracting authorities who *award* a concession does not apply to authorities who award contracts as *holders* of a concession.[31]

(ii) CONCESSIONAIRES WHO ARE NOT CONTRACTING AUTHORITIES

In most cases a concessionaire is not a "contracting authority". Subcontracts awarded by such firms are not, in principle, subject to the public sector regulations. However, by way of exception to this general position, Works Regulations 26(3) imposes some limited obligations on firms holding public works concessions, relating to the advertising of contracts and the time-limits for response by interested subcontractors.

(I.) Scope of the rules

The obligations under Works Regulation 26(3) apply whenever a concessionaire seeks offers for the purpose of subcontracting any of the

---

[28] See Chap. 15. The WTO Agreement on Government Procurement does not, however, appear to cover concessions.

[29] "Concessionaire" is defined in this way in Works Regulation 2(1).

[30] The contracting authority is also bound to comply with the Supply Regulations and Services Regulations where it makes relevant public supply contracts and public services contracts. The express provision in regulation 26(2) in fact appears redundant, and is inserted merely to emphasise that there is no exemption from the regulations just because a contract is awarded pursuant to a concession, and to make a contrast with the position of concessionaires who are not contracting authorities.

[31] Unless, of course, the contract which it awards is itself a concession contract.

work or works which are to be carried out under the public works concession contract,[32] and the contract to be awarded would fall within the definition of "public works contract" if awarded by a contracting authority.[33] Only works contracts are covered: the rules do not apply to contracts for goods and for non-construction services which are awarded in connection with the concession – for example, a contract to purchase building materials.

The Works Directive does not impose obligations on concessionaires in relation to contracts which would be below the threshold or would be "excluded" contracts if awarded by a contracting authority.[34] However, a literal interpretation of the Works Regulations suggests that the rules on concessionaires apply under the regulations to all public works contracts awarded by such bodies. This was clearly not the intention of the regulations, which merely sought to implement the obligations in the directive, and they should be narrowly construed to achieve the intended result.[35]

The rules do not apply in the following cases[36]:
(i) Where the open or restricted procedures have been used and there have been no tenders, or no "appropriate tenders".
(ii) Where for technical or artistic reasons, or reasons connected with the protection of exclusive rights, the works(s) may only be carried out by a particular person.
(iii) When, if it is strictly necessary, for reasons of extreme urgency, the time-limits normally applying in open and restricted procedures cannot be applied, provided that the event giving rising to urgency was unforeseeable by, and not attributable to, the concessionaire.[37]
(iv) Where the works in question are unforeseen works which are additional to other works, where for technical or economic reasons they cannot be carried out separately from the original works without great inconvenience; or, where they could be carried out separately, but are strictly necessary to the later stages of the original contract. This exception cannot be invoked when the consideration for the works exceeds 50 per cent of the consideration under the original contract.
(v) Where the works are a repetition of works under a previous contract under the same project, and are awarded to the same contractor –

---

[32] Works Regulation 26(4)(a).
[33] On the definition of public works contract see pp. 124–130.
[34] Works Directive Articles 4–6. On the thresholds and exclusions see pp. 150–175.
[35] To the extent that they may be construed to cover contacts not within the directive they may in any case by *ultra vires* since s.2 of the European Communities Act 1972 under which they were adopted only authorises measures required to implement Community obligations.
[36] Works Regulation 26(4)(c).
[37] The reference to open and restricted procedures is curious since these procedures do not as such apply to concessionaries. It appears, however, that the intention is to exempt concessionaries from the rules which do normally apply to them, in circumstances where they could not be expected to use an open or restricted procedure if they were a contracting authority.

provided that the possibility of such an award without an advertisement was referred to in the original advertisement; and provided that the procedure for the new contract is begun within three years of the start of the original contract.

These are all cases in which a contracting authority awarding a works contract is permitted to use a negotiated procedure without advertisement – that is, cases where for some special reason it is inappropriate to require advertisement of the contract. The exact circumstances covered by these exceptions was considered in Chapter 6.[38]

(II.) The exemption for contracts with affiliated persons

Under Works Regulation 26(4)(c) there is also an exception for contracts awarded to persons "affiliated to" the provider. Section 26(5) defines what is meant by affiliated. X is treated as affiliated to Y if either exercises, directly or indirectly, a dominant influence over the other. X is also treated as affiliated to Y where a third person exercises, directly or indirectly, a dominant influence over both X and Y. It is stated that a person shall be taken to exercise a dominant influence over another where he either (i) possesses the greater part of the issued share capital of that person; (ii) controls the voting power attached to the greater part of the issued share capital of that person; or (iii) may appoint more than half the individuals who are ultimately responsible for managing that person's affairs. This covers the case, for example, where a concessionaire wishes to award a contract to a subsidiary company of which it is fully or mainly the owner, or to its own parent company. Regulation 26(5) also provides that X and Y are affiliated where they are both members of a consortium formed for the purpose of performing the public works concession contract. This means that it is possible for firms to join together to bid on major projects, and to allocate the work amongst themselves according to their own investment and expertise – for example, a firm with expertise in building may join with a firm with expertise in operating that type of work.

Where a concessionaire is a utility covered by the Utilities Regulations, it appears that works contracts awarded to affiliated persons are subject to those regulations, which do not provide any special exemption for such affiliates. Thus, in contrast with other concessionaires, utilities are not free to award contracts to their affiliates without advertising. This causes practical problems where firms wish to join together in consortia, for the purpose of obtaining concessions in the utilities fields. This is common, for example, with transport concessions where the design, construction and operation elements of the concession may be assigned to different firms in a consortium. The consortium itself will be a utility, and the application of the Utilities Regulations to the consor-

---

[38] See pp. 265–268

tium will mean that separate contracts for these different elements cannot simply be given by the consortium to its members, but must be awarded in accordance with the procedures in those regulations. The inability to do this may deter firms from forming consortia to bid in the utilities areas. It may be possible to avoid this difficulty by entering into contractual arrangements for division of the works prior to the actual award of the concession, at which point it may be argued that there is no utility in existence for the purpose of the Utilities Regulations. However, it is not clear whether this would be accepted by the European Court.

(III.) The obligations on concessionaires

Under Works Regulation 26(3), concessionaires must publicise relevant contracts by sending a notice to the Office of Official Publications of the European Communities.[39] Like notices from contracting authorities, such notices must be published in the *Official Journal of the European Communities* in hard copy and in the TED data bank, in full and the original language, with a summary of the important elements of the notice in the other official languages of the Community.[40] They must be published within 12 days of despatch by the authority.[41] Publication of a notice on the concession in the national press is not permitted until the above notice has been despatched (although it is not necessary to wait until it is actually published), and may not contain more information than found in the *Official Journal* notice.[42]

The form of the notice must correspond, substantially, with that set out in Part G of Schedule 2 to the Works Regulations, and must contain all the information specified in that model. This model is set out on page 365. Like other notices under the regulations, it must not contain more than 650 words.[43-44] The Commission is likely shortly to adopt a recommendation for use of the CPV nomenclature in such notices.

There are also rules on time-limits for firms to respond, designed to give firms from all states a reasonable opportunity to participate. Where the notice in the *Official Journal* calls directly for tenders, the date for submitting tenders must be no less than 40 days from despatch of the notice, and must be specified in the notice (in para. 4(a) of the model notice).[45] Where an authority seeks applications from persons wishing to be invited to tender or negotiate, the date for applications must be no later than 37 days from the despatch of the notice (and again must be specified in the notice).[46] In such a case, the rules also prescribe a time-

---

[39] This must be sent by "the most appropriate means": and authorities must retain evidence of the date of despatch: Works Regulations 26(3)(b), 30(1) and 30(3).
[40] Works Directive Article 11(9).
[41] Works Directive Article 11(10).
[42] Works Regulation 26(3)(b) and 30(4).
[43-44] Works Regulation 30(2). The directive itself states that notices must not be more than one Official Journal page or approximately 650 words: Works Directive Article 11(13).
[45] Works Regulation 26(3)(c).
[46] Works Regulation 26(3)(d)(i).

limit for receipt of tenders after selection: this date must be no less than 40 days from the date of despatch of the invitation, and must be specified in the invitation itself.[47]

PUBLIC WORKS CONTRACTS REGULATIONS 1991, SCHEDULE 2, PART F — NOTICE OF WORKS CONTRACT AWARDED BY CONCESSIONARIES

1. (a) The site.
   (b) The nature and extent of the service to be provided and the general nature of the work.

2. Any time-limit for the completion of the works.

3. Name and address of the service from which the contract documents and additional document may be requested.

4. (a) The final date for receipt of requests to participate and/or for receipt of tenders.
   (b) The address to which they must be sent.
   (c) The language or languages in which they must be drawn up.

5. Any deposit and guarantees required.

6. The minimum standards of economic and financial standing and technical capacity required of the contractor.

7. The criteria for the award of the contract.

8. Other information.

9. Date of despatch of the notice.

---

[47] Works Regulation 26(3)(d)(ii).

(2) PUBLIC SERVICES CONCESSIONS

Concession arrangements may involve the provision of services as well as the construction of works. For example, a firm managing a public leisure facility may be remunerated through fees taken from the public in addition to, or instead of, by a lump sum payment. Such arrangements are expressly excluded from the Services Regulations: Services Regulation 2(1) provides that the definition of "public services contract" does not include "a contract under which a contracting authority engages a person to provide services to the public lying within its area of responsibility and under which the consideration given by the contracting authority consists of or includes the right to exploit the provision of the services".[48] Under this provision, a services concession arrangement appears to be excluded even where the exploitation of the service constitutes only a very small part of the consideration.

This provision is intended to reflect the position believed to apply under the Services Directive. The Commission's original proposals for a directive on services expressly covered concessions;[49] however, these provisions were removed by the Council, and it can thus be concluded that concessions are intended to be exempt.[50]

It may be noted, however, that, so far as the concessionaire is concerned, Supply Regulation 24 requires that any party providing a service to the public under special or exclusive rights is forbidden from discriminating in awarding supply contracts. This provision is considered under (4.) below.

A concession contract may involve provision of both work and services: for example, a contract to both build and operate a leisure facility, which is remunerated through the right to exploit the facility. The classification of such "mixed" contracts has already been considered above.[51]

3. PUBLIC HOUSING SCHEME WORKS CONTRACTS

Works Regulation 24 makes special provision for exemption from some provisions of those regulations for a "public housing scheme works

---

[48] Regulation 2(1), definition of public services contract, exclusion (e).
[49] See [1991] O.J. C23 and [1991] O.J. C250.
[50] It can be pointed out that on a literal reading of the Services Directive concessions do appear to be covered: the definition of public service contract (to which the directive's rules apply) covers all contracts for pecuniary interest between a contracting authority and service provider except those expressly excluded, which concession contracts are not. It is possible that the European Court could bring concessions within this definition if it wished to do so despite the legislative history, by a wide interpretation of the concept of pecuniary interest.
[51] See p. 355.

contract" – that is, a public works contract which relates to the design and construction of a public housing scheme.[51a] This applies where in view of the size and complexity of the scheme and the estimated duration of the works involved it is necessary that the planning of the scheme is based "from the outset on a close collaboration of a team comprising representatives of the contracting authority, experts and the contractor".

The existence of these circumstances do not wholly exempt the authority from following the regulations but merely provide that the authority may depart from them "insofar as it is necessary to do so to select the contractor who is most suitable for integration into the team"[51b] In light of the general principles for interpreting derogations in Community measures[51c] this will be strictly construed by the courts and the burden placed on the authority to show that departure from the usual procedures was indeed necessary for the reason referred to in the regulation (and not for any other reason).

Further, it is expressly provided in regulation 24(2) that authorities must in any case follow the obligations in Works Regulation 12(1)–12(5) governing the restricted procedure – that is, the obligations relating to advertisement of the contract (regulation 12(2)); those on time limits for the expression of interest in response to the advertisement (regulation 12(3)); the rule precluding exclusion of providers from the selection process for reasons other than financial or technical status or those under regulation 14 (regulation 12(4)); the rules concerning selection of providers (regulation 12(5)); and the requirements for financial and technical assessments and those under regulation 14 are to be carried out in accordance with the procedural and substantive requirements of regulations 14–17 (regulation 12(4) and (5)). It is also provided, in regulation 24(3), that authorities must include in the contract notice a "job description" which is as accurate as possible. This must enable contractors to (i) form an idea of the scheme and (ii) to form an idea of the economic and financial standing and the technical capacity which will be expected of the successful contractor.

4. BODIES WITH SPECIAL OR EXCLUSIVE RIGHTS TO CARRY ON A SERVICE

Under Supply Regulation 24 certain bodies which are not contracting authorities[52] are subject to limited regulation in the award of their supply

---

[51a] See the definition in Works Regulation 2(1).
[51b] Article 24(1).
[51c] See p. 256.
[52] Supply Regulation 24 is expressly stated not to apply to contracting authorities; obviously it is unnecessary for it to do so, since their contracts are covered by other, extensive, provisions.

contracts. This applies where a contracting authority[53] has granted to a body which is not such a contracting authority, special or exclusive rights to carry on a service for the benefit of the public. In such a case, the contracting authority is required to impose an express duty on the body enjoying such rights not to discriminate in seeking offers for a contract for the purchase or hire of goods, or in awarding such a contract. The discrimination which is forbidden is discrimination on grounds of nationality against a person who is a national of and established in[54] a state which is a "relevant state" for the purpose of the regulations.[55-57] The same obligations must also be followed in relation to states which are not "relevant" states under the regulations, but which are entitled to benefit from the regulations under agreements concluded with those states and the European Community. Although this is not stated in the Supply Regulations, the Supply Directive (Article 2(2)) requires the duty to be imposed in the instrument granting the special or exclusive right in question.

The regulations do not confer rights on aggrieved providers and nor do the directives require this; thus enforcement is left to the relevant contracting authority.

5. THE REGULATION OF SUBSIDISED CONTRACTS AWARDED BY PRIVATE BODIES

Works Regulation 23 requires application of the Community procurement rules to private bodies awarding contracts for certain types of works, where those contracts are subsidised by contracting authorities, whilst Services Regulation 25 requires these procedures to be applied to subsidised services contracts relating to such works – for example, contracts for the design of the works. It was explained in Chapter 5 that bodies whose activities as a whole are financed mainly by contracting authorities are themselves within the definition of contracting authorities; in this case all their contracts are subject to the regulations, regardless of how the particular contract is funded. Works Regulation 23 and Services Regulation 25 are concerned with the case where the awarding entity is not in *general* financed by public money, but lets a particular *contract* which is publicly funded. Such arrangements have

---

[53] This does not apply where the right is awarded by a contracting authority which is covered by the Supply Regulations because it is a "GATT contracting authority". On this see pp. 111–112.

[54] A person who is not a private individual is a national of a relevant state where that person is formed in accordance with the laws of a relevant state, and has its registered office, central administration or place of business in a Member State; whilst "established in" has the same meaning as in the E.C. Treaty: Supply Regulation 2(1).

[55-57] On which states are "relevant" states: see pp. 908–909.

become increasingly common – for example, private bodies have sometimes been appointed to undertake urban renewal projects which are largely funded with public money.

Works Regulation 23 requires the procedures in those regulations to be applied to contracts which would be within the definition of a public works contract if awarded by a contracting authority[58]; and which are for one of a number of specified activities. These are[59];

(i) the activities specified in Group 502 of the NACE nomenclature, as listed in Schedule 1 to the Works Regulations. Schedule 1 is set out on pages 126–127. As explained there, Group 502 covers, in general, "civil engineering: construction of roads, bridges, railways, etc."; and

(ii) the carrying out of building work for: hospitals; facilities intended for sports recreation and leisure; school and university buildings; and buildings for administrative purposes.

Thus it does not cover, for example, subsidised contracts for the building of private homes, which are not included in this list. It also applies the regulations only to contracts which would be covered if awarded by a contracting authority[60] – that is, which meet the thresholds set out in Works Regulation 7 (normally above 5 million ECUs),[61] and which are not caught by the exclusions in Works Regulation 6.[62]

Services Regulation 25 requires application of the rules in the Services Regulations to contracts which would be public services contracts if awarded by a contracting authority,[63] and which are made "in connection with the carrying out" of works specified under (i) or (ii) above.[64] For example, the regulations will apply to contracts for the planning or design of a school or hospital. However, they do not apply to contracts for the design of a housing estate, since such works are not mentioned, nor do they apply to any services contracts which are not connected at all with the carrying out of works.

Works Regulation 23 and Services Regulation 25 apply to the above contracts wherever a contracting authority undertakes to contribute more than half of the consideration "to be or expected to be paid".[65] This probably covers only those cases where the contracting authority gives a direct subsidy towards the price of the contract, and not where indirect subsidies are provided, such as interest-free loans.[66]

For works or services contracts covered by these provisions, contracting authorities must make it a condition of their contribution that the

---

[58] Works Regulation 23(2).
[59] Works Regulation 23(2).
[60] Since Works Regulation 23(1) requires subsidised bodies to be made to comply with the Regulations as if they were contracting authorities.
[61] On these thresholds see pp. 159–160.
[62] On these exclusions see pp. 159–160.
[63] Services Regulation 25(2).
[64] Services Regulation 25(2).
[65] Works Regulation 23(1); Services Regulation 25(1).
[66] The directives themselves, in Works Directive Article 2(1) and Services Directive Article 3(3) require the rules to be applied only where contracting authorities "subsidise directly" such a contract.

subsidised body will follow the requirements of the regulations in the same way as if the subsidised body were a contracting authority.[67] Thus the subsidised body must be required by the contracting authority to follow all the usual award procedures in the regulations, as set out in Chapter 6 of this book – for example, advertising the contract, and following (apart from exceptional cases) the restricted or open procedure. (The services contracts covered are generally "Part A" services contracts and so subject to the full regime of the regulations.) As explained in Chapter 6, the regulations include specific obligations that certain decisions – such as the selection of invitees and the issue of tenders – should be made without discrimination on grounds of nationality. This is unnecessary for contracting authorities since such obligations in any case arise under the free movement provisions of the Community Treaties, but is important in relation to subsidised authorities which may not be caught by the Treaties.

The regulations do not impose an obligation directly on the subsidised body, but merely require the contracting authority to enforce the rules through the inclusion of the specified condition.[68]

The obligation has no application when the recipient of the subsidy is itself a contracting authority.[69] In this case the contract is already, of course, subject to the Works or Services Regulations simply because it is awarded by a body classified as a contracting authority, so that there is no need to apply Works Regulation 23 or Services Regulation 25. Expressly excluding this case simply means that the subsidising authority is not given any responsibility for ensuring the rules are followed by the recipient of the subsidy – enforcement is left to the usual methods applying under the regulations, notably proceedings by affected providers, or action by the European Commission.[70] Although it is not required to do so, however, the authority providing the subsidy may still choose to make payment or retention of the subsidy conditional on compliance with the regulations.

There are no corresponding obligations applying to subsidised supplies, nor to subsidised works or services contracts falling outside the above provisions.

6. DESIGN CONTESTS

(1) INTRODUCTION

Where authorities seek designs or plans for new projects, they may sometimes search out ideas by holding a competition, in which firms are

---

[67] Works Regulation 23(1); Services Regulation 25(1).
[68] On this point, and the remedies available for securing enforcement of the obligation by either the contracting authority or an interested party, see pp. 916–917.
[69] Works Regulation 23(1) and Services Regulation 25(1) apply to contracts entered into by "a person other than a contracting authority".
[70] On these methods of enforcement see pp. 920–936.

invited to submit their designs or plans to be judged against each other. Such a competition may often form the basis for a subsequent contract award – for example, a contract to elaborate on and/or build the winning design may be awarded automatically to the contest winner if the design meets the authority's approval; or the authority may indicate that it will negotiate with some of the firms submitting suitable designs. To provide an incentive for firms to make submissions, prizes may be awarded to one or more firms who submit the winning design(s), and/or remuneration may be paid to those who participate, regardless of whether or not the designs are ultimately used by the authority. Such "design contests" are not infrequently used, for example, to come up with designs for "prestige" public building such as town halls or new concert houses. Such contests are very common in some Community Member States.

The Services Regulations contain special rules to deal with design contests where these are held by contracting authorities.[71] These, first, regulate the way in which such contests are conducted, to ensure that they are carried out in a fair and transparent manner, whether or not such contests are connected with any subsequent contract award procedure. In addition, there are special provisions to allow a design contest which has been conducted in accordance with the regulations to be used as the basis for awarding a subsequent contract.

We will first consider the definition of a design contest (section (2)), and which contests are subject to regulation (section (3)). We will then outline the rules governing such contests (section (4)). Finally, we will explain the way in which design contests may be incorporated into contract award procedures (section (5)).

(2) THE DEFINITION OF "DESIGN CONTEST"

The definition of a design contest for the purpose of all the rules on design contests is given in Services Regulation 2(1). It refers to a competition in which an authority invites the entry of plans and designs which under the rules of the competition are to be judged by a jury and as a result of which the authority is to acquire the use or ownership of the plans or designs which the jury selects. The definition applies regardless of whether or not prizes are to be awarded to the winners.

It is stated that the definition refers "particularly" to plans or designs in the fields of planning, architecture, civil engineering and data processing, which are the main subject areas for contests. However, the regulations apply to contests in other areas also, where these are held.

The directive and regulations are not entirely clear as to whether the rules on design contests are to apply to those for Part B services.

---

[71] They must also be applied to subsidised contracts of private bodies which are caught by the services rules (as to which see pp. 368–370) but in practice this situation is unlikely to arise.

However, it seems most likely that contests relating to these services are not intended to be covered, [72] in line with the general approach to Part B services contracts.

(3) THRESHOLDS FOR APPLYING THE REGULATIONS

Where a design contest is "organised as part of a procedure leading to the award of a public services contract", the regulations apply wherever the estimated value of that contract exceeds the threshold for applying the regulations to the award procedure, as laid down in Services Regulation 7.[73] At the time of writing the regulations generally apply to any contract of not less than 200,000 ECUs. The contest must no doubt be considered to be "part of" a contract award whenever the authority relies on the provisions discussed in section (5) below to make use of the negotiated procedure. The regulations also apply to contests which are part of an award procedure where the estimated value of the prizes or payments for the contest itself is not less than 200,000 ECUs, regardless of the value of any contract to be awarded under the procedure.

Where a design contest is not organised as part of a procedure relating to a contract award, the regulations will apply to that design contest where the aggregate value of the prizes or payments for the contest is not less than 200,000 ECUs.

The Commission has issued a Proposal to alter the contract thresholds in the Services Directive in light of the GPA, to the ECU equivalent of 200,000 SDR, or of 130,000 SDR for certain central/federal authorities.[74] The same Proposal suggests that the thresholds for design contests should be adjusted accordingly, to apply where the value of any relevant

---

[72] Article 8 provides that all the rules in Titles III–VI apply to Annex IA *contracts* (equivalent to Part A contracts under the regulations) and Article 9 that only the rules in Articles 14 (specifications) and 16 (award notices) apply to Annex IB *contracts* (equivalent to Part B contracts under the regulations). The rules on award procedures for design contests, except for the rules on result notices under Article 16, are found in Article 13 in Title III – which in general applies only to Annex IA services. It could be suggested that the rules in Article 13 are general in application since it is only Annex IB *contracts* which are excluded from their application under Article 8; Article 8 does not mention design contests at all. However, it seems likely that the references to "contracts" in Articles 8 and 9 were actually intended to cover design contests as well. Services Regulation 5(2) states that Part B *contracts* are covered only by obligations specified in a list in regulation 5(2), which does not mention the design contest rules in regulation 24. Presumably this is intended to refer to both contracts and design contests. A problem with this interpretation of the regulations, however, is that it does not appear to require publication of an award notice for Part B design contests (since the rules on award notices are contained in regulation 24), although such a notice appears to be required by the directive.

[73] Services Regulation 24(1)(a). On these thresholds see pp. 162–163.

[74] See pp. 162–163.

contract on prizes is the ECU equivalent of 200,000 SDR, or of 130,000 SDR for central/federal authorities.[75]

(4) THE PROCEDURE FOR CONDUCTING DESIGN CONTESTS

(a) ADVERTISEMENT OF THE DESIGN CONTEST

Under Services Regulation 24(2) authorities must publish their intention to hold a design contest by sending a notice to the Office of Official Publications of the European Communities.[76] This ensures that the contest is publicised throughout Europe. The notices, as with notices advertising contract award procedures, must be published by the Office of Official Publications no later than 12 days after their despatch.[77] They must be published in full in the *Official Journal of the European Communities*, in hard copy and in the Tenders Electronic Daily databank, in the original language; and a summary of the important elements of the notice must be published in each of the languages of the Community.[78] As with other notices under the regulations, the cost of publication is borne by the Community.[79] The United Kingdom regulations did not originally contain any prohibition on notices being published beforehand in the national press or containing information additional to that contained in the notice sent to the Office of Official Publications, such as are included for contract notices.[80] However, the Services Directive, Article 17(6) require these limits to be applied to design contest notices and this has now been done by an amendment to the Services Regulations[81]

The notice must be in substantially the same form as the model notice set out in Part F of Schedule 2 to the Services Regulations, and must contain all the information specified in that notice. The model notice is set out on page 376. Like other notices, the notice must not contain more than 650 words.[82-83] The Commission is likely shortly to adopt a recommendation that the CPV nomenclature should be used in drawing up notices for design contests.

---

[75] Proposal for a European Council and Parliament directive amending Directive 92/50 relating to the co-ordination of procedures for the award of public service contracts, Directive 93/36/EEC co-ordinating procedures for the award of public supply contracts, and Directive 93/37/EEC concerning the co-ordination of procedures for public works contracts, COM (95) 107 Final, Article 1(4).
[76] The notice must be sent by the "most appropriate means": Services Regulation 29(1). Authorities must retain evidence of the date of despatch: Services Regulation 29(3).
[77] Services Directive Article 17(5).
[78] Services Directive Article 17(4).
[79] Services Directive Article 17(8).
[80] See, for example, p. 195.
[81] Utilities Regulation 35(2), amending Services Regulation 29(4).
[82-83] Services Regulation 29(2). The directive is slightly different, stating that the notice shall not exceed one page of the *Official Journal*, or approximately 650 words: Services Directive Article 17(8).

(b) PUBLICITY FOR THE RULES OF THE DESIGN CONTEST

The rules which are to apply to a design contest must be made available to all providers who wish to participate.[84] The model notice for advertising the procedure, set out on page 376, indicates that some of the rules must be publicised in the notice itself – for example, the criteria for selecting participants, the proposed number of participants and evaluation criteria. Information on other relevant rules, however, will also need to be provided to interested parties.

(c) SELECTING FIRMS TO PARTICIPATE IN THE CONTEST

The model notice indicates that authorities must state in the notice a deadline for receipt of requests from persons wishing to participate in the contest. Authorities may allow any interested firms to compete,[85] or may restrict the number.[86]

Where participation is restricted, the number of persons selected to participate must be set taking into account the need to ensure adequate competition in the contest.[87] The model notice for advertising the contract, set out on page 376, indicates that the number of participants envisaged must be stated in the notice.

The selection of those to be invited must be made on the basis of "clear and non-discriminatory criteria",[88] which the model notice indicates must be stated in the notice. It is clear that the discretion of the authority in excluding and selecting participants here is much greater than in selecting candidates to participate under restricted or negotiated procedures. For example, authorities may presumably select those providers with the best reputation, who the authority thinks are likely to come up with the best designs.[89] It also appears that authorities may select some participants in advance of the notice: this is implied by the model notice which requires the names of any such preselected persons to be stated in the notice. There are, however, some limits on selection

---

[84] Services Regulation 24(3).

[85] The requirement to indicate a date for receipt of requests to participate indicates that authorities must seek such requests before actually requesting submission of designs or plans, even where the opportunity to compete is to be open to everyone. However, it could be argued that it is open to authorities to call for designs or plans through the notice itself, and the requirement to state the date for receipt of requests applies only where such requests are required under the authority's rules (although it is true that certain other provisions of the model notice are expressly stated to apply only "where applicable").

[86] Supply Regulation 24(4).

[87] Services Regulation 24(5).

[88] Services Regulation 24(4).

[89] It is perhaps more questionable, however, whether authorities could use non-commercial criteria, such as compliance with secondary policies: it appears anomalous to allow this where it is precluded under contract award procedures.

criteria. First, it is stated that authorities may not exclude firms because of their legal form (for example, whether individual or corporate), where they are permitted to provide services in that form in their state of establishment.[90] It is also expressly stated in the Services Directive, although not in the regulations, that participants may not be limited by reference to the territory, or part of a territory, of a state.[91] No specific provision to implement this has been included in the Services Regulations. However, where contracting authorities specify a territorial limit which includes the United Kingdom this is likely to infringe the rules in the Community Treaties as tending to favour domestic providers.[92] Authorities must also comply with any relevant obligations under the Community Treaties as discussed in Chapter 4.

---

[90] Services Regulations 24(6) and 20.
[91] Services Directive Article 13(4).
[92] See Chap. 4. An express provision is still, perhaps, needed to cover subsidised authorities which run design contests and also stipulations by contracting authorities which refer to territory which does not include the United Kingdom, but both these situations are unlikely to arise in practice.

PUBLIC SERVICES CONTRACTS REGULATIONS 1993, SCHEDULE 2, PART F — DESIGN CONTEST NOTICE

1. Name, address and telephone, telegraphic, telex and facsimile numbers of the contracting authority and of the service from which additional information may be obtained.

2. Project description.

3. Nature of the contest: open or restricted.

4. In the case of open contests: final date for receipt of plans and designs.

5. In the case of restricted contests:
   (a) the number of participants envisaged;
   (b) where applicable, names of the participants already selected;
   (c) criteria for the selection of participants;
   (d) final date for receipt of requests to participate.

6. Where applicable, an indication of whether participation is reserved to a particular profession.

7. Criteria to be applied in the evaluation of projects.

8. Where applicable, names of the persons selected to be members of the jury.

9. Indication of whether the decision of the jury is binding on the contracting authority.

10. Where applicable, number and value of the prizes.

11. Where applicable, details of payments to all participants.

12. Indication of whether follow-up contracts will be awarded to one of the winners.

13. Other information.

14. Date of despatch of the notice.

(d) COMPOSITION OF THE JURY

The jury for any contest must be composed of individuals who are independent of the parties competing.[93] In addition, when participants in the contest are required to possess a particular professional qualification, then at least one third of the jury members are required to possess that qualification, or an equivalent qualification.[94]

(e) SELECTING THE WINNING DESIGNS

The proposals of the participants must be submitted to the jury without any indication of who submitted each proposal.[95] The proposals will then be judged by the jury. The criteria which are to apply in judging must be set out in the model notice, as is indicated by the model. In principle, it is for the authority to set these criteria. Often, with designs of buildings or other works, they will relate primarily to the aesthetic merits of the design, although other factors such as practicability, potential cost, innovation or environmental considerations may be relevant. The authority is expressly required to ensure that the decision is taken by the jury solely in accordance with the criteria stated in the notice.[96] It is also required to ensure that the jury acts "independently" in making its decision.

The model notice advertising the contest indicates that authorities must state whether or not the jury's decisions are binding on the authority. This indicates that the authority may reserve the right to override the view of the jury in selecting the winner(s). In making its own decision, however, the authority must also adhere to the stated evaluation criteria.

(f) REQUIREMENT TO PUBLISH A NOTICE OF THE JURY'S DECISION

No later than 48 days after the jury has made its selection, authorities must publicise the results of the design contest by sending a notice to the Office of Official Publications for the European Communities.[97] This must be in a form substantially corresponding to the model notice in Part G of Schedule 2 to the Services Regulations,[98] which is set out on page 380 and, as with other notices, should not contain more than 650 words.[99] This notice must be published in full in all the official languages

---

[93] Services Regulation 24(8).
[94] *Ibid.*
[95] Services Regulation 24(7).
[96] Services Regulation 24(9).
[97] Services Regulation 24(10). The notice must be sent by "the most appropriate means" (Services Regulation 29(1)) and authorities must retain evidence of the date of dispatch (Services Regulation 29(3)).
[98] *Ibid.*
[99] Services Regulation 29(2).

of the Communities in both the hard copy *Official Journal of the European Communities* and the TED data bank.[1] The Commission is likely shortly to adopt a recommendation for the use of the CPV nomenclature in such notices.

(g) OTHER REQUIREMENTS

As indicated above, details of the contest rules must be made available to participants. It may be presumed that authorities must adhere to these rules, even where this is not expressly stated in the regulations (as it is, for example, in relation to the use of the stated evaluation criteria). However, in construing the rules it must be implied that some are not mandatory: for example, as with award procedures, it is submitted that authorities should be able to waive non-compliance by providers with formalities.[2]

In the case of *Storebaelt* the Court of Justice laid down the principle that those bidding for contracts under the directives should be treated "equally" by contracting authorities.[3] No doubt the same principle will apply to the conduct of design contests. Thus, for example, if formalities are waived for one provider, they must be waived for all others who are in a comparable position.

(5) CONTRACT AWARD PROCEDURES BASED ON A DESIGN CONTEST

As explained in Chapter 6, contracts covered by the Services Regulations must generally be awarded by the formal open or restricted procedures. These procedures do not themselves allow authorities to give any precedence to firms which have bid in a related design contest. However, Services Regulation 10(2)(f) allows authorities to bypass these usual procedures. This provision allows use of the negotiated procedure without advertisement[4] for a services contract where a design contest has been conducted under the regulations, and the contest rules state that a contract is to be awarded to the successful contestant(s), provided that negotiations are carried out with all those who were successful under the rules of the contest.[5] In other words, a contract, or the possibility of

---

[1] Services Directive Article 16(2) and Article 17(3). The original language alone is authentic: Services Directive Article 17(3).

[2] On this see p. 235

[3] See pp. 180–181.

[4] Services Regulation 13(1)(a).

[5] The provision states that negotiations must be carried out with all successful contestants. It is suggested that the definition of a "successful" contestant for this purpose is, however, to be determined by the rules of the design contest itself. Thus, if there are three prizewinners, but the rules state that the contract is to be negotiated with the first prize winner alone, then it is submitted that the first prize winner is the only "successful" contestant for the purpose of the rules on negotiated procedures.

being considered for a contract, may be a "prize" in the competition. This is not considered to be anti-competitive, since a fair and open competition has already been held to select the participant(s) for the negotiations. The rules of this negotiated procedure without advertisement – which are few and flexible – were explained in Chapter 6.[6]

Under this procedure authorities could select the design through the contest, and then negotiate the terms of a contract – for example, to expand the design – based on that design with the winning party. Alternatively, the authority may negotiate with a number of winners, and make a contract award taking into account both their designs and other factors such as cost. It is possible under this procedure to negotiate with providers the alteration of their designs, since negotiations need not take place on the basis of any set specification. It is, further, not necessary for negotiations to be carried out with each provider based on the provider's own design – authorities could, for example, pick one preferred design and negotiate with all providers in relation to that design.

As noted above, the effect of this rule is, effectively, to provide a special "two-stage" procedure for the award of services contracts – the first stage consisting of a design competition, and the second stage consisting of negotiations to fix the contract terms and/or choose the provider.

The provision may not be relied on where the contract which is to be awarded following the design contest is not a services contract but a works or supply contract. In this case, the Works Regulations or Supply Regulations must be followed in the normal way. This precludes authorities from awarding contracts to supply or build the design based on the contest without holding a competition under the normal procedures of the Works or Supply Regulations.

---

[6] See pp. 279–281.

PUBLIC SERVICES CONTRACTS REGULATIONS 1993, SCHEDULE 2, PART G—DESIGN CONTEST RESULT NOTICE

1. Name, address and telephone, telegraphic, telex and facsimile numbers of the contracting authority.

2. Project description.

3. Number of participants.

4. Number of participants established outside the United Kingdom.

5. Winner(s) of the contest.

6. Where applicable, the prize(s) awarded.

7. Other information.

8. Reference to publication of the design contest notice in the *Official Journal of the European Communities*.

9. Date of despatch of the notice.

CHAPTER 9

THE UTILITIES REGULATIONS: SCOPE[1]

1. INTRODUCTION

This chapter examines the scope of the Utilities Contracts Regulations 1996[2] ("the Utilities Regulations"), which regulate procedures for the award of major contracts in the utilities sectors of water, transport, energy and telecommunications. As explained in Chapter 3, the regulations on utilities were first adopted in order to implement the European Community directives on procurement, which seek to open up utilities procurement markets in Europe. The regulations have now also been adapted to implement the government's obligations under international agreements to open up its utilities markets to certain states outside the European Community, notably under the Association Agreements with various central and eastern European states.[3]

To determine whether a contract is covered by the regulations, the first question is whether the purchaser is a body which is covered by the regulations (referred to as a "utility"). In this respect the Utilities Regulations cover, for their "utilities" activities, all bodies which are subject to the public sector regulations, and also many entities which are not subject to the public sector rules, including some purely private entities which enjoy special privileges. Contracts of utilities are only covered by the utilities rules, however, where they are made in connection with one of the relevant "utility" activities listed in the regulations – water, energy, transport and telecommunications – so that it is also necessary to consider whether the contract in question is made in connection with a relevant activity. (Contracts made by the utility for other purposes are either unregulated, or – where the purchaser is also

---

[1] See Brown, "The Extension of the Community Public Procurement Rules to Utilities" (1993) 30 C.M.L.Rev. 721; Bickerstaff, "The Utilities Supply and Works Contracts Regulations 1992: An Analysis of the Implementation of the Utilities Directive in United Kingdom Law" (1993) 2 P.P.L.R. 117; O'Loan, "An Analysis of the Utilities Directive of the European Communities" (1992) 1 P.P.L.R. 175; Cox, *The Single Market Rules and the Enforcement Regime after 1992* (1993), Chap. 5; Geddes, *Public Procurement* (1993), Chap. 4; Digings and Bennett, *E.C. Public Procurement: Law and Practice*, B4; Weiss, *Public Procurement in European Community Law* (1993), Chap. 8; Lee, *Public Procurement* (1992), Chap. 4; Trepte, *Public Procurement in the E.C.*, esp. Chap. 1–2 and 4.

[2] S.I. 1996.

[3] On these agreements see pp. 782–786. The regulations are also likely to be applied shortly to contracts covered by the World Trade Organisation Agreement on Government Procurement. This issue is considered separately below: see pp. 563–564.

an authority caught by the public sector regulations – subject to the stricter public sector rules.) The definition of a utility and the precise scope of the relevant activities are considered in section 3. Certain exemptions which apply only to specific relevant activities are also considered here.

Where it is established that the body is a utility acting in connection with relevant utility activities it is then necessary to consider whether the particular award is covered. Here a number of issues arise.

First, as with the public sector regulations the rules apply only to "a contract in writing for consideration". This is considered in section (3).

Secondly, it is relevant for certain purposes – in particular, for the application of the thresholds in the regulations – to know whether the contract is a works contract, supply contract or services contract. This is considered in section (4).

It must then be considered whether any exemptions apply. The general exemptions under the regulations are examined in section (5).

Finally, only contracts above certain financial thresholds are regulated, and these thresholds are explained in section (6).

2. WHICH PURCHASERS AND ACTIVITIES ARE COVERED?

(1) GENERAL PRINCIPLES

The Utilities Regulations generally apply to an entity which is a "utility" under the regulations,[4] when it acts for the purpose of carrying out one of the activities specified in the regulations.[5] Thus it is necessary to consider (i) whether an entity is a utility for the purpose of the rules, and (ii) whether the contract in question is made for the purpose of carrying out one of the listed activities.

So far as concerns the purchasers who are covered, the rules apply to all those bodies which are "contracting authorities" under the public sector rules, such as government departments and local authorities. This means that in carrying out activities in the utilities sectors, these authorities are subject to the utilities rules, rather than to the stricter public sector rules which apply to most of their contracts.[6]

In addition the utilities rules apply to many types of bodies not caught at all by the public sector rules: in addition to contracting authorities under those public sector rules the utilities rules also cover all bodies – including commercial bodies – which are subject to a dominant govern-

---

[4] Utilities Regulation 5.
[5] Utilities Regulation 6(a).
[6] See Chap. 5 and 6.

ment influence or which enjoy special or exclusive, rights such as a monopoly right to provide a particular service. This is a broad approach and means that the rules apply in the United Kingdom even to those utilities which are now in the private sector, such as the water companies and electricity generators. The decision to apply the utilities rules so widely was designed to bring within the Community procurement regime all those entities which might be influenced by government pressure to "buy national",[7] either because of the influence of the government over the entity itself, or because of the entity's dependence on the state for the privileges on which its business rests. Such pressures are particularly effective where the entity does not operate in a competitive environment and is therefore not subject to the usual commercial pressures in its purchasing; this also applies with many of the utilities either because entry to the market is restricted by law, or because of the physical barriers to market entry, such as the high cost of establishing networks to provide the service. There are, in fact, exemptions from the rules for certain situations where open competition exists and it is felt that as a consequence entities are of their own accord likely to procure on a commercial basis.[8]

In defining the scope of the entities and activities covered, the approach of the Utilities Directive on which the regulations are based is first to define in general terms the bodies which are subject to the directive.[9] It applies to three types of body[10]:

(i) Public authorities. This refers to those bodies which are "contracting authorities" under the public sector directives.

(ii) Public undertakings. This refers to all bodies, including commercial bodies, over which public authorities exercise a dominant influence.

(iii) Bodies which enjoy "special or exclusive rights" from government relating to one of the utility activities. This covers, for example, privatised utilities operating under an exclusive licence.

Bodies within the definition for each Member State are listed in Annexes I-X of the directives,[11] although these are for guidance only: those within the general definition must apply the rules even if omitted from the Annexes.[12]

---

[7] For detailed discussion see Commission communication, *Public Procurement in the Excluded Sectors* (accompanying the original proposals for legislation on this subject), Bulletin of the European Communities, Supplement 6/88.

[8] It is envisaged that further exemptions may be adopted as other utility markets become more competitive: the Community itself is currently trying to open up markets on a cross-border basis in sectors such as electricity and telecommunications services, which have previously been a matter of national monopoly. The United Kingdom has already made progress in opening domestic markets in some of these fields.

[9] In the Utilities Regulations these are referred to as "utilities" as noted above; the directive uses a different term, "contracting entities".

[10] See generally Article 2 and the definitions in Article 1.

[11] Under Utilities Directive Article 2(6) Member States are to notify the Commission of amendments, and the Commission is to revise the Annexes in accordance with the procedure in Article 40 of the directive, which involves the participation of the relevant Advisory Committees.

[12] Conversely, it seems that bodies which are included but are not in law within the definition need not apply the rules.

As regards the second issue, the activities to which the rules apply, the directive states that covered entities are subject to its rules except where the relevant awards are "for purposes other than the pursuit of" the activities listed in the directive.[13]

Thus, under the directive it is necessary simply to ask (i) whether the entity is within categories (i)–(iii) above and (ii) whether the contract is for the purpose of one of the listed activities.

The United Kingdom regulations adopt a slightly different approach. Generally, for each separate relevant activity, the regulations specify in Schedule 1[14] the bodies in the United Kingdom which exercise that activity, and are considered to be within the directive, either by naming them expressly, or by reference to the possession by the entity of a particular type of licence. Column 1 of the Schedule lists the bodies to be covered, and a second column opposite the list of entities specifies the activity covered by the regulations in respect of which the entity must apply the rules. An example – covering the utility activity of supplying electricity through a fixed network (which is dealt with in Part D of Schedule 1) is as follows:

Utility   **Activity**

PART D

| A person licensed under section 6 of the Electricity Act 1989. | 6. The provision or operation of a fixed network which provides or will provide a service to the |
| A person licensed under article 10(1) of the Electricity (Northern Ireland) Order 1992. | public in connection with the production, transport or distribution of electricity. |

Thus, to determine the application of the rules in the United Kingdom it is necessary to consider, first, whether an entity is listed in column 1. If it is, it is then necessary to consider whether the contract is made for the purpose of one of the activities listed in column 2 of the same Part of the schedule.

In addition to the list of specific bodies, for many activities there is also included in column 1 a general "catch-all" provision, designed to apply the rules to other entities caught by the directive which for some reason – for example, the difficulties of identification, or the possibility of new entities being created – cannot be expressly named. Such catch-all provisions generally apply the rules to any other "relevant person", a term which basically covers the three categories of bodies – public

---

[13] Article 6(1). The relevant activities are listed in Article 2(2).
[14] Utilities Regulation 1(2) states that "utility" is to have the meaning given by regulation 3, and regulation 3 that it refers to those bodies listed in the first column of Schedule 1.

authorities, public undertakings, and bodies with special or exclusive rights – which are referred to in the directive, or to one or more of the three categories. The intention of the regulations is to implement exactly the requirements of the directive, but at the same to specify more precisely, where possible, exactly who is covered in each sector, in order to provide the most detailed information possible for purchasers and providers.

Since the regulations adopt this "sector by sector" approach, it is convenient to adopt this approach in outlining the scope of the rules. It is proposed thus to consider separately the sectors of water, transport, energy and telecommunications, examining in each case both the precise type of activity covered and the entities which must follow the rules. This will be done in section (3) below. Section (2) will first, however, examine in more detail the definitions of a "relevant person", and of "public authority", "public undertaking" and "special and exclusive rights", since these concepts are referred to across the board.

(2) DEFINITIONS

(a) "RELEVANT PERSON"

The definition of "relevant person" for the purpose of interpreting Schedule 1 of the Utilities Regulations is given in a list of definitions attached to the end of Schedule 1. It covers:
(i) public authorities;
(ii) public undertakings; and
(iii) persons not within (i) or (ii), who carry out a relevant activity[15] "on the basis of a special or exclusive right".

The concepts of public authority, public undertaking, and "special or exclusive right" are all further defined in the definitions given at the end of Schedule 1.

(b) "PUBLIC AUTHORITY"

"Public authority" is defined in the definitions at the end of Schedule 1 as referring to a body which is a "contracting authority" for the purpose of the public sector regulations.[16] Thus, such bodies, whilst in general subject to the public sector regulations, are subject to the Utilities Regulations in making contracts connected with utility activities. The precise definition of "contracting authority" has been considered in

---

[15] This includes all activities listed in the Schedule except those in paras 2 and 3 which relate to water.
[16] The definition in the schedule refers specifically to the definition of "contracting authority" in regulation 3(1) of the public sector Works Regulations, but the same definition now also applies under the public sector Supply Regulations and Services Regulations.

Chapter 5 where the public sector regulations are discussed in detail.[17] Briefly, it covers government departments, local authorities and a number of other bodies specifically listed in the regulations, as well as other non-commercial bodies established to meet public needs and which are financed or appointed mainly by another contracting authority, or supervised by such an authority.

(c) "PUBLIC UNDERTAKING"

The definition of "public undertaking" in Schedule 1 is for practical purposes identical to that in the directive itself.[18] It is stated to refer to a person over whom one or more public authorities are able to exercise (directly or indirectly) a dominant influence, by virtue of either:
(i) their ownership of that person;
(ii) their financial participation; or
(iii) the rights accorded to them by the rules which govern it (which could include, for example, the case where legislation gives a Minister a right to step in to direct the activities of an entity).

It is expressly stated that this condition of dominant influence by a particular authority is to be considered[19] as met when "directly or indirectly" the authority possesses a majority of the issued share capital or controls the voting power attached to such a majority. Thus, for example, Nuclear Electric, the entity responsible for generating electricity at nuclear power stations, would be considered a public entity because its shares are wholly owned by the government. Dominant influence is also deemed to exist when the public authority may "directly or indirectly" appoint more than half of those "ultimately responsible" for managing the undertaking's affairs; more than half its members; or, where the undertaking consists of a group of individuals, more than half of the group.

Unlike the concept of a public authority, the concept covers bodies which are of an "industrial or commercial nature",[20] as well as those which are not.

The concept of a "public undertaking" is not confined to bodies which are outside the definition of "public authority", and the two definitions

---

[17] See pp. 107–118.

[18] Although there are some inconsequential differences in wording. The definition in the directive is itself intended to reflect the concept of a public undertaking as it is used elsewhere in Community law, in particular in Article 90 E.C. On Article 90, and on whether the definitions in the directive is identical with the meaning of public undertaking in Article 90, see pp. 100–103.

[19] The word "considered" is used as opposed to the word "presumed" which is found in the Directive. "Considered" suggests that the condition is always to be regarded as met; "presumed" is ambiguous and might be interpreted as merely creating a rebuttable presumption that dominant influence exists, although this seems unlikely.

[20] Bodies of an industrial or commercial character are excluded from the definition of "contracting authority" under the public sector regulations, and hence from the definition of public authority: see pp. 110–111.

thus appear to overlap. Thus, for example, a body which is established for public purposes and is not industrial or commercial, and which is, say, financed by a public authority, is itself a "public authority". It will also be a "public undertaking" when the financial input of the other public authority is given in circumstances which allow that authority to exercise control – such as where the funding is purely discretionary and could be withdrawn for non-compliance with the funding authority's wishes. The category of public undertaking also overlaps with that of undertakings enjoying special or exclusive rights. This does not create any problems, however; there are no cases where conflicting rules apply to the different classes of undertaking.

(d) "SPECIAL OR EXCLUSIVE RIGHTS"

A "special or exclusive right" is defined in the list of definitions in Schedule 1 as "a right deriving from authorisations granted by a competent authority where the requirement for the authorisation has the effect of reserving for one or more persons the exploitation" of one of the "utilities" activities listed in Schedule 1. This would apply, for example, to a utility which is the sole entity licensed to provide a particular service to the public. The definition also expressly provides that a person shall be considered to enjoy a special or exclusive right under the above definition when that person is allowed to take advantage of a procedure for the use or expropriation of property in order to construct a network or facilities of the kind listed in the Schedule; or where it is permitted to place network equipment on, under or over a highway. Such rights are enjoyed in practice by most entities which provide products and services to the public relating to energy, water and telecommunications.

The concept of special and exclusive rights must be interpreted in accordance with the directive, and it appears that it is probable that the concept in the directive was intended to bear the same meaning as the concept of "special or exclusive rights" under Article 90 E.C. This definition – in particular, the issue of whether a licence or other right which is also open to certain other individuals may be regarded as "special" – was discussed further in Chapter 4 in the context of Article 90.

It is clear that special rights may be conferred by any method: the Utilities Directive states that it applies whether these rights are conferred by "law, regulation or administrative action". It is submitted that the provision will apply where relevant rights are enjoyed by virtue of a contract also – for example, if a water authority provides a service involving use of special or exclusive rights and contracts the running of the service to another entity which itself exercises such rights, that other entity may be covered by the procurement rules. It can also be noted that Article 2(3) of the Utilities Directive provides that entities supplying to networks operating on the basis of special and exclusive rights are themselves considered to have such rights – a provision which probably goes beyond the concept of special and exclusive rights under Article 90 E.C.

The category of undertaking enjoying special or exclusive rights overlaps with the categories of both public authority and public undertaking, but, as with the overlap between "public authorities" and "public undertakings" this causes no difficulties since there are no conflicting rules applying to the two categories.[21]

It can be noted that entities which are within the utilities rules because they enjoy special or exclusive rights are covered only in relation to the activity to which the special or exclusive rights relate. This is given effect to in Utilities Regulation 6(9) which states that the regulations apply only to contracts for the activity against which a particular utility is listed in Schedule 1, combined with the definition of "relevant person" in the Schedule, which covers only persons who have special or exclusive rights relating to the activity against which it is listed.

(3) THE WATER SECTOR

The Utilities Regulations apply in the water sector in the cases set out below. For the entities covered in this sector, there is a special exemption for the purchase of water which is also explained below.

(a) ACTIVITIES CONNECTED WITH THE SUPPLY OF DRINKING WATER

The regulations cover, first, various activities concerned with the supply of drinking water to the public through a fixed network.

Provision or operation of a fixed network for the supply of drinking water: First, they apply to the provision or operation of a fixed network which provides (or will provide) a service to the public in connection with (i) the production (ii) the transport, and (iii) the distribution, of drinking water.[22] The reference to fixed networks excludes those supplying water by other methods, notably those involved in the sale of bottled water.

So far as these activities are concerned, the regulations apply in England and Wales to any company which holds an appointment as a "water undertaker" under the Water Industry Act 1991.[23]

---

[21] Whether an entity with special or exclusive rights is, in addition, within the category of either public authority or public undertaking is, however, significant in the context of the World Trade Organisation Agreement on Government Procurement (GPA). This issue is considered further below.

[22] Utilities Regulations Schedule 1, Part A, no. 1 of second column.

[23] Utilities Regulations Schedule 1, Part A, para. 1 of first column. The Schedule also refers to the relevant bodies in Scotland and Northern Ireland.

Supply of drinking water to a fixed network: The regulations also cover contracts in connection with activities relating to the supply of drinking water *to* such a fixed network.[24] They do not, on the other hand, apply to those who supply water to the network operator where the water is not yet itself in the form of drinking water.

The Schedule does not identify precisely the entities covered in relation to this activity, but provides for the regulations to apply to such contracts when made by any entity which is a public authority or public undertaking, or which enjoys special or exclusive rights in relation to an activity specified in the Schedule.[25]

In addition, the regulations apply to contracts made by *any other person* supplying water to a fixed network of the type specified above, but only in cases where that network operator itself is covered by the regulations (which in England and Wales means, as explained above, that the operator must be a "water undertaker" within the meaning of the 1991 Water Industry Act).[26] This is intended to give effect to Article 2(3) of the Utilities Directive that entities supplying to networks operating on the basis of special and exclusive rights are themselves to be considered to have such rights. In this limited respect the regulations thus extend to purely private entities which do not even enjoy any special or exclusive rights. It appears that the provision will apply to entities which have an intention to supply a relevant network in the future, even if not engaged in supplying to a network at the time of the procurement.[26a]

Some entities produce water as a by-product of some other activity, and may wish to sell the excess to a network. In the case of entities which are *not* public authorities and which are involved in the supply of water to a fixed network because their consumption is necessary for carrying out another activity, and which only supply the excess to a network, there is an exemption given from the principle above that contracts connected with the supply of water are subject to the regulations. In this case, the supply of drinking water is treated as an activity falling within the regulations only if the amount supplied in the previous 36 months[27] exceeds 30 per cent of the total produced by the utility in that period.[28]

---

[24] Utilities Regulations Schedule 1, Parts B and C. This refers to a network referred to in Part A.

[25] *Ibid.*

[26] Utilities Regulations Schedule 1, Part B, para. 2 of column 1 and Part C, para. 2 of column 1.

[26a] See p. 413.

[27] This period is calculated as ending on the date on which a contract notice would be sent to the *Official Journal* under the regulations if a contract notice were required under the regulations: Schedule 1, Part C, column 2 and Utilities Regulations 10(19).

[28] Utilities Regulations Schedule 1, Part C, which lists an entity as a "utility" by virtue of its producing drinking water because its consumption is necessary for an activity not specified in the Schedule. In this case the supply of drinking water by it is only a relevant activity in the circumstances defined in the text. Persons supplying water who fall within Part C are specifically excluded from Part B – hence the fact that Part C effectively creates an "exemption" from the usual rules (which are set out in Part B).

The exception only applies if the activity of which the water is a by-product is not itself an activity listed in the Schedule; if the entity supplies drinking water as an incidental consequence of some other listed activity, the regulations will apply to the supply of that water to a network. For example, listed entities engaged in coal mining may supply excess to a fixed water networks. Such entities may not take advantage of the exemption, since extraction of coal is itself a relevant activity.

As was noted above, the exemption for water supplied as a by-product of an activity does not apply to bodies which are public authorities. Thus the contracts of these bodies connected with the supply of drinking water, even as a by-product of another activity, are covered in principle by the Utilities Regulations. However, where the contract is *mainly* for the purpose of a "non-utility" activity (rather than another "utility" activity) and only partly attributable to the supply of drinking water, then the public sector regulations rather than the Utilities Regulations will apply.[29]

(b) HYDRAULIC ENGINEERING, IRRIGATION AND LAND DRAINAGE

In relation to water undertakers under the 1991 Water Industry Act[30] (although not to any other bodies in England and Wales), the regulations are required to be followed for contracts connected with hydraulic engineering, irrigation and land drainage in cases where more than 20 per cent of the total volume of water made available by the activity in question is intended for the supply of drinking water.[31] This requires the regulations to be applied in such circumstances to all contracts of these entities which relate to the engineering, irrigation or land drainage activities themselves – *not* just to contracts which are concerned with making available the drinking water which results from those activities. This is to give effect to a requirement in the directive that these activities shall be covered in the circumstances outlined above, where they are carried out by bodies which are also engaged in the supply of drinking water through a fixed network.

(c) THE DISPOSAL AND TREATMENT OF SEWAGE

In the case of water undertakers under the Water Industry Act 1991[32] (but again not in any other case for England and Wales) the regulations apply to the activities of the disposal or treatment of sewage.[33] This is

---

[29] This is a contract partly for "utility" activities and partly for others: see further pp. 411–413.
[30] And relevant bodies in Scotland and Northern Ireland, as listed in Schedule 1, Part A.
[31] Utilities Regulations Schedule 1, Part A, no. 2 of column 2.
[32] And relevant bodies in Scotland and Northern Ireland, as listed in Schedule 1, Part A.
[33] Utilities Regulations Schedule 1, Part A, para. 1 of column 1, no. 3 of column 2.

again to give effect to a requirement in the directive that these activities shall be covered where carried out by bodies which are also engaged in the supply of drinking water through a fixed network.

Where these activities are carried on by bodies subject to the public sector regulations, contracts in connection with the activity will be subject to the requirements of those public sector regulations where the public body carries out that activity as a principal. (Such bodies are not "water undertakers" in the 1991 Act). In England and Wales some of the water services companies contract out their functions relating to sewage treatment to local authorities under statutory powers to enter into agreements to this effect which are contained in section 97 of the Water Industry Act 1991, and contracts in relation to such sewage treatment will therefore be subject to the public sector regulations where the local authority is operating as a principal. On the other hand, a local authority may sometimes simply act as agent for a water undertaker in carrying out these functions. In that case it seems that it is the Utilities Regulations which apply to the principal, the water undertaker – which will apply.

(d) EXEMPTION FOR PURCHASES OF WATER

For utilities engaged in activities in the water sector, as outlined above, regulation 6(f) exempts them from the regulations for the purchase of water itself. This exemption is given, according to the preamble to the directive (recital 15), because of the "need to procure water from sources near the area it will be used". Since little would thus be gained by Europe-wide tendering it is considered unduly burdensome to apply the usual rules to this case.

Article 9(2) of the Utilities Directive provides for the Council to re-examine the exemption in the future, following the submission to it of a report and proposals from the Commission. It seems unlikely, however, that this exemption will be revised, since the nature of the water supply industry still makes competition inappropriate.

(4) THE ENERGY SECTOR[34]

In relation to the energy sector, the regulations apply to the entities and activities discussed below. There is a specific exemption for entities in this sector which covers the purchase of energy, or of fuel for the production of energy; and certain entities in the sector may also apply to the Commission for a special exemption from the rules. These exemptions are also discussed below.

---

[34] See Hancher, "The New Utilities Directive and the Energy Sector" (1991) 9 *Journal of Energy and Natural Resources Law* 167.

(a) ACTIVITIES CONNECTED WITH THE SUPPLY OF ELECTRICITY

The regulations cover various activities connected with the supply of electricity to the public through a fixed network.

Provision or operation of a fixed network for the supply of electricity: The regulations apply to the provision or operation of a fixed network which provides (or will provide) a service to the public in connection with (i) the production, (ii) the transport or (iii) the distribution of electricity.[35] They apply in England and Wales only when this activity is carried out by a person licensed under section 6 of the Electricity Act 1989.[36] A list of such persons is available from OFFER, the electricity regulatory agency.

Supply of electricity to a fixed network: The regulations also generally apply to contracts awarded in connection with the supply of electricity *to* a fixed network of the type mentioned above.[37] As with the activity of supplying water to a fixed network, the Schedule does not identify precisely the entities engaged in such activities, but states generally that the regulations apply to this activity when made by any public authority or public undertaking, or any body which engages in one of the scheduled activities on the basis of special or exclusive rights.[38] This provision covers, for example, Nuclear Electric, which is responsible for generating electricity at nuclear power stations, since it is at the time of writing wholly owned by the government and is therefore within the definition of a public undertaking.

The regulations also cover other persons – those who are neither public authorities or undertakings nor enjoy special or exclusive rights as such – where these persons supply electricity to a fixed network, but only where the network is provided or operated by a person licensed under section 6 of the Electricity Act. This is intended to give effect to Article 2(3) of the Utilities Directive that entities supplying to networks operating on the basis of special and exclusive rights are themselves considered to have such rights. This covers the privatised generators such as National Power and Powergen, which supply electricity to the national grid. Probably the provision applies to those intending to supply to a network, as well as those which actually do.[38a]

As with water, some entities produce electricity as a by-product of another activity and may wish to sell the excess amount to a network. For examples, ICI and certain other large private companies produce

---

[35] Utilities Regulations Schedule 1, Part D, no. 6 of column 2.
[36] Utilities Regulations Schedule 1, Part D, first para. of column 1. Also included are persons licensed under article 10(1) of the Electricity (Northern Ireland) Order 1992.
[37] Utilities Regulations Schedule 1, Parts E and F.
[38] Utilities Regulations Schedule 1, Part E and Part F, para. 1 of column in each part.
[38a] See p. 413.

electricity for their own business and sell the surplus for distribution through the national grid. Where an entity produces electricity only because its use is necessary in an activity which is not an activity listed in Schedule 1, the regulations only apply when the electricity supplied in the previous 36 months[39] has exceeded 30 per cent of the total produced by the entity in that period.[40] If this figure is not exceeded the entity is not covered. As with the similar exemption for water, this does not apply to bodies which are public authorities, nor to those producing electricity as a by product of some other relevant "utility" activity.

(b) ACTIVITIES CONNECTED WITH THE SUPPLY OF GAS OR HEAT

Activities connected with the supply of gas and heat are also covered by the regulations.

Provision or operation of a fixed network for the supply of gas or heat: The regulations apply to contracts connected with the provision or operation of a fixed network which provides (or will provide) a service to the public in connection with (i) the production, (ii) the transport or (iii) the distribution of either gas[41] or heat.[42] The requirement for the activity to be linked to a fixed network excludes the application of the regulations to other forms of supply – for example, the sale of gas in cannisters.

In the case of a network for the supply of gas, the bodies to which the regulations apply are those falling within the definition of a "public gas transporter" under section 7(1) of the Gas Act 1986.[43]

In the case of networks for the supply of heat, the regulations apply to,[44] first, local authorities[45] and, secondly, persons licensed under section 6(1)(a) of the Electricity Act 1989, whose licence includes the provisions referred to in section 10(3) of that Act.

The supply of gas or heat to a fixed network: The regulations also apply to public authorities, public undertakings, and bodies engaged in an activity in the schedule on the basis of special or exclusive rights, where those persons supply gas or heat to a fixed gas or heating network.[46] They also

---

[39] This period is calculated as ending on the date on which a contract notice would be sent to the *Official Journal* under the regulations if a contract notice were required under the regulations: Schedule 1, Part F, column 2 and Utilities Regulations 10(19).

[40] Utilities Regulations Schedule 1, Part F.

[41] Utilities Regulations Schedule 1, Part G, no. 9 of column 2.

[42] Utilities Regulations Schedule 1, Part J, no. 12 of column 2.

[43] Utilities Regulations Schedule 1, Part G, para. 1 of column 1. In Northern Ireland this applies to an undertaker for the supply of gas under Article 14(1) of the Gas (Northern Ireland) Order 1977.

[44] Utilities Regulations Schedule 1, Part G, column 1.

[45] "Local authority" is defined in the definitions section of Schedule 1 by reference to the definition for England and Wales in Works Regulation 3(2), as to which see p. 108, and the corresponding definitions in Works Regulation 3(3)–(4) for Scotland and Northern Ireland.

[46] Utilities Regulations Schedule 1, Parts H, I, K and L.

apply to other persons – that is, private bodies with no special or exclusive rights in the ordinary sense – who supply gas or heat to such networks, but only where these networks are operated by persons themselves covered by the regulations in the operation of the networks.[47] As with water and electricity networks, this is intended to give effect to Article 3(2) of the Utilities Directive that entities supplying to networks operating on the basis of special and exclusive rights are themselves to be considered to have such rights.

It can be noted that amongst persons supplying gas to fixed networks are a number who are also involved in the exploration and extraction of gas offshore, who process and distribute the gas once this is brought onshore. Such persons are in principle caught by the regulations in their activities of extraction and exploration, as outlined in section (c) below, on the basis that they enjoy (or are deemed to enjoy) special or exclusive rights in relation to this activity. However, they may be able to claim an exemption from some of the detailed requirements of the regulations by virtue of Article 3 of the directive, discussed in section (e) below, which may apply to their supply activities as well as to their activities of exploration and extraction.

As with water and electricity the above provisions on supply to a network apply only to a limited extent to certain persons who produce gas or heat as a by-product of some other activity. Basically, it is provided that[48] where the gas or heat is produced as an "unavoidable" consequence of an activity which is not listed in the Schedule, and where it is supplied for the sole purpose of the economic exploitation of the product, then the regulations will apply only when the total consideration payable for gas, or for the heat, in the previous 36 months[49] exceeds 20 per cent of the total turnover for the utility. Here the question is not, as with water and electricity, what proportion of the commodity produced is supplied to a network, but what proportion of the entity's total business derives from this activity. If it is less than the specified proportion, then the activities of that person in supplying gas or heat to the network are exempt from regulation. This provision does not apply to bodies which are public authorities.

(c) EXPLORATION AND EXTRACTION OF ENERGY SOURCES

In the energy sector the regulations also cover persons involved in exploring for, or extracting, oil, gas or solid fuels.

---

[47] *Ibid.*
[48] See Utilities Regulations Schedule 1, Parts I and L.
[49] This period is calculated as ending on the date on which a contract notice would be sent to the *Official Journal* under the regulations if a contract notice were required under the regulations: Schedule 1, Part F, column 2 and Utilities Regulations 10(19).

Exploring for and extracting oil or gas: The regulations cover "the exploitation of a geographical area for the purpose of exploring for or extracting oil or gas".[50] In relation to this activity they cover any person licensed under the Petroleum (Production) Act 1934.[51] There may be some debate over precisely which activities are comprised within this; in particular, it is not clear whether the regulations cover transport on-shore of oil or gas extracted off-shore, or even storage or other terminal facilities. In relation to the regulated activity of provision of terminal facilities for air carriers and other operators, it is explained below that the rules cover at least activities which are "indispensable" for the activity referred to in the directive,[53] and it is probably correct to argue that any form of transport to the shore, at least, is "indispensable" for the extraction and therefore covered. Thus, the laying of an undersea pipe network for transportation to shore would be covered. Probably, however, the relevant activity will cease once the product reaches the shore or any on-shore installation, so that the operation of any on-shore storage or terminal facilities is not covered.

Exploring for and extracting solid fuels: Also covered is the activity of "the exploitation of a geographical area for the purposes of exploring for or extracting coal or other solid fuel".[54] In relation to this activity the regulations cover, in England and Wales, any licensed operator within the meaning of the Coal Industry Act 1994.[55]

(d) THE EXEMPTION FOR PURCHASES OF ENERGY AND FUEL

Under Utilities Regulation 6(g) there is an exemption for utilities engaged in activities in the energy sector, as outlined above, for the purchase of energy itself, and for the purchase of fuel for the production of energy. It was thought inappropriate to include such purchases within the directives since the nature of the markets themselves is such that there is little competition for cross-border supply, and requirements for competitive procurement would therefore have little relevance.[56] This absence of competition arises, for example, from the fact that entities in one Member State do not have easy access to networks in other states to enable them to supply products and services such as gas or electricity on a competitive basis in other Member States. The Community is currently

---

[50] Utilities Regulations Schedule 1, part M, column 2.
[51-52] Utilities Regulations Schedule 1, part M, column 1. Also covered are persons licensed under the Petroleum Production (Northern Ireland) Act 1964.
[53] See pp. 403–405.
[54] Utilities Regulations Schedule 1, part N, column 2.
[55] Utilities Regulations Schedule 1, part N, column 2. Also covered are the Department of Economic Development of Northern Ireland and persons holding a prospecting licence, mining lease, mining licence or mining permission as defined by the Mineral Development Act (Northern Ireland) 1969.
[56] See recital 17 to the preamble to the Utilities Directive.

developing programmes to liberalise these markets, however,[57] and if it is successful then it may be appropriate to introduce competitive procurement in the future. There is a specific provision in Article 9(2) of the Utilities Directive providing for the Council to re-examine the exemption in the future, following the submission to it of a report and proposals from the Commission.

The exemption applies only to purchases of fuel for the production of energy, and not to purchases made for other reasons – for example, of purchases of petrol for transport purpose – made by entities in the energy sector. This is because a competitive market exists for the latter type of purchase.

It can also be noted that arrangements for the purchase of energy are sometimes made on a non-contractual basis, so that it might be argued that the purchaser does not seek to make a "contract" for the purpose of applying the procurement regulations. This issue is considered further below,[58] where it is suggested, however, that the crucial point is the substance of the transaction, and not whether or not the transaction is characterised as a contract in domestic law.

(e) THE "ALTERNATIVE REGIME" EXEMPTION FOR EXPLORATION AND EXTRACTION UNDER UTILITIES DIRECTIVE ARTICLE 3

(i) GENERAL PRINCIPLES

Article 3 of the Utilities Directive provides for the possibility of an exemption from many of the detailed procedures under the directive for entities involved in exploration and extraction of gas, oil and other fuels which are, prima facie covered by the provisions outlined above. The exemption is intended to apply to entities which operate in a competitive environment in that they are competing against other entities for licences to carry out these activities. When the directive was adopted it was argued by the industries concerned and Member States with important energy industries, including the United Kingdom, that fair and open competition for licences should ensure that the entities in question were under pressure to engage in competitive procurement. Similar arguments, based on the fact of operation in a commercial environment, have led to the inclusion of certain exemptions from the directive in the case of bus transport services, telecommunications services and purchases for re-sale, as described elsewhere in this chapter.[59] However, the Council was not prepared to accept that competition for licences could

---

[57] On competition in the energy sector in general, and current proposals, see Slot, "Energy and Competition" (1994) 31 C.M.L.Rev. 511.
[58] See p. 414.
[59] See pp. 407–408 (bus transport), 409–410 (telecommunications services) and 433–434 (re-sale).

fully ensure open procurement by entities in the energy sector and in the end a "compromise" position was adopted. In essence, the directive provides that an exemption may be granted by the Commission if it can be shown that there are fair and open procedures for the award of licences – procedures which Member States are now in any case required to implement under the new "Hydrocarbons Licensing Directive", discussed below.[60] However, the exemption is not a complete one: entities taking advantage of the exemption are still required to show that they adhere to certain minimum standards of "non-discriminatory" and "competitive" procurement. This alternative, less detailed, procurement regime, is sometimes referred to as the "alternative regime" (or "parallel mechanism").

The possibility for United Kingdom entities to rely on such an exemption where it is granted by the Commission is provided for in Utilities Regulation 9, which also contains provisions on procedures which must be followed by those entities to satisfy the requirements of the "alternative regime". The United Kingdom had previously been granted an exemption on a temporary basis for all entities in this sector, but this expired on July 14, 1994.[61] As is explained below, the United Kingdom has implemented the Hydrocarbons Licensing Directive, and it has now made a new application for exemption, which at the time of writing was still being considered by the Commission.

The details of this exemption and the conditions and procedures for invoking it are as set out below.

(ii) SCOPE OF THE EXEMPTION

Article 3(1) of the Utilities Directive states that, under that provision, the Commission may provide (i) that exploitation of geographical areas to explore for or extract oil, gas or coal or other solid fuels shall not be considered a relevant activity under the directive, and (ii) that entities shall not be considered as operating under special or exclusive rights within the meaning of Article 2(3)(b) the directive "by virtue of carrying on one or more of these activities".

The first part of this provision effectively means that the Commission may provide that entities exercising such activities will not be required to follow the usual rules in the directive in respect of those exploration and extraction activities. The entity enjoying an exemption will, instead, be required only to follow certain limited rules, and the general requirements for non-discriminatory and competitive procurement, as outlined in section (iv) below.

The second part means that entities are not to be considered as operating under special or exclusive rights within the meaning of Article

---

[60] Directive 94/22, [1994] O.J. L164/3.
[61] See Commission Decision 93/425, [1993] O.J. L196/55.

2(3)(b). Article 2(3)(b) is the provision stating that entities supplying to fixed energy networks (and other networks) are deemed to enjoy special and exclusive rights in relation to that supply activity. The effect of an Article 3 exemption for exploration and extraction activities thus seems to be that any supply activity resulting from the exploration and extraction is also covered by the exemption.[62] This is an important point in practice since entities involved in, for example, extraction of gas, frequently supply the end product directly to a fixed network.

(iii) LICENSING CONDITIONS

The Commission is only permitted to provide for an exemption where the national provisions relating to the activities in question satisfy a number of conditions laid down in Article 3(1) of the Utilities Directive. These ensure that the exemption can only apply when the system of licensing under which utilities in that state operate is transparent, open and non-discriminatory: as explained, the justification for the exemption is that the utility is under competitive pressures in its purchasing because of the competition for licences.

Since the revised Utilities Directive was adopted, however, a new Community directive, the Hydrocarbons Licensing Directive,[63] has been adopted to govern licensing of rights to explore for oil, gas and other solid fuels. This directive, which came into force on July 1, 1994,[64] aims to ensure that all such licensing systems operate in a transparent, open and non-discriminatory manner, in order to enhance competition in these economic sectors. These provide for all the requirements listed in the Utilities Directive as conditions for obtaining the Article 3 exemption, as well as a number of others (for example, that the geographic area of the licence and length of the licence should not exceed what is necessary). Thus, compliance with the licensing conditions referred to in Article 3 is no longer merely an option for states who wish to take advantage of the Article 3 exemption in procurement, but is an absolute requirement of Community law.

The Licensing Directive, in Article 12, itself adds a new paragraph to Article 3 of the Utilities Directive, as Article 3(5). This new Article 3(5) provides that as from the date from which any Member State has complied with the Licensing Directive's provisions on the conditions for

---

[62] This assumes that the entity is not a public authority or public undertaking, in which case its relevant activities are subject to the directive regardless of the existence of any special or exclusive rights; and also that it does not enjoy any special or exclusive rights which arise outside article 2(3)(b).

[63] Above, note 60. On the directive's impact on procurement see also Trepte, "Directive 94/22/EC: Upstream Licensing" (1995) 4 P.P.L.R. CS45.

[64] The directive was not required to be actually implemented in the United Kingdom until July 1995, but had effect from July 1994 for the purpose of allowing states to rely on compliance seek exemption from the Utilities Directive under Article 3, in those cases where it was implemented before the required date.

granting and using authorisations under the directive, the conditions set out in Article 3(1) of the Utilities Directive for the Commission to grant an exemption shall automatically be deemed to be satisfied. The United Kingdom has implemented the Licensing Directive[65] and in applying for an exemption may now rely on such compliance, rather than attempting to show specifically that it has complied with the conditions in Article 3(1) of the Utilities Directive. The procedure which will apply in such an application is considered at (v) below. As noted above, at the time of writing the United Kingdom had made an application for an Article 3 exemption which was being considered by the Commission.

It can be noted that a condition stated in both Article 3(1) and in the Hyrocarbons Licensing Directive is that utilities may not be required to provide information on their intended or actual sources of procurement. The only exception is where this is required by national authorities with a view to meeting the objectives in Article 36 E.C. (which may include the need to maintain a reliable source of supply for certain energy needs, under the national security derogation in Article 36).[66]

(iv) IMPLICATIONS FOR PROCUREMENT PROCEDURES

As noted above, within the scope of any Article 3 exemption, a utility is not required to comply with all the usual obligations in the Utilities Directive. Such an exemption is provided for in the United Kingdom by Utilities Regulation 9(1), stating that where the Commission has given an exemption a utility need not comply with the obligations on award procedures contained in the directive.[67]

However, as noted above, the utility is nevertheless required to follow principles of "non-discrimination" and "competitive procurement" in procedures falling within the exemption. Adherence to such principles is required under Utilities Regulation 9(2). This regulation specifically provides that such principles entail, in particular, that the utility shall hold a competition, "unless it can objectively justify not doing so", and also that decisions shall be made "objectively on the basis of relevant criteria" when making information available to providers, specifying requirements to providers, establishing and using a qualification system, selecting providers to tender or negotiate, holding a design contest and awarding a contract.

There is much room for debate over exactly what constitutes a competitive and non-discriminatory procurement procedure, even within

---

[65] See the Hydrocarbons Licensing Directive Regulations 1995, No. 1434; the Petroleum (Production) (Seaward Areas) (Amendment) Regulations 1995, S.I. 1995 No. 1435; and the Petroleum (Production) (Landward) Areas Regulations 1995, S.I. 1995 No. 1436.

[66] On this see further pp. 84–86.

[67] The regulation actually states that the utility need not comply with the obligations in Parts II–V of the regulations, nor those in regulations 24–27 or 29 and 31; this covers all the relevant substantive obligations. The only exception is for regulation 27(2)(a), as explained in the text above.

the limitations set out in regulation 9(2), and utilities enjoying the benefit of an exemption will need to give careful thought as to whether the Court of Justice will uphold practices which are a departure from the detailed procedures of the directives. As regards information about requirements, for example, it is not clear whether advertisement in the *Official Journal* is required or whether other international publications may suffice, especially if it can be shown in practice that there has previously been a low rate of response to *Official Journal* advertisements for the requirement in question. Regarding the number of persons invited to participate it is unlikely that there is any difference between the (non-specific) requirements of the directive, and the requirements of a competitive procurement under regulation 9. It is also very likely that the Court would insist on reasonable time-limits for the various stages of the procedure, although these could probably be shorter than those in the directive if warranted by the nature of the purchase. Another issue of debate may be the extent to which utilities can take account of the desire to build up a long-term "partnering" relationship with a specific provider in deciding who should receive a contract: could the prospects for long-term co-operation in research and development, for example, be a legitimate criterion for an award, and one which is "relevant" under regulation 9(2)? (Certainly it appears to be "objective" within the terms of regulation 9(2).) It is not clear whether such considerations – which many utilities would like to take into account – can be regarded as consistent with "competitive procurement" as referred to in the directive, which may envisage a competition limited to the particular procurement in question. Given the uncertainty, many utilities operating under the exemption may in any case decide to follow the procedures in the directives.

In addition to following the general principles in regulation 9, utilities are under certain obligations with respect to the provision of information, set out in regulation 9(3).[68] For contracts exceeding 5 million ECUs the utility must send certain detailed information on the nature of the contract and the award procedure to the Commission, no later than 48 days after the award.[69] In the case of supply or services contracts valued

---

[68] These requirements have been laid down by the Commission, pursuant to Utilities Directive 3(2)(b): see [1993] O.J. L129/25.

[69] Utilities Regulation 9(3)(a). The value of contracts for this purpose is calculated using the valuation rules in regulation 10, which apply to the valuation of individual contracts for the purpose of the regulations' general thresholds; these are described at pp. 443–451. The information required is: (i) the utility's name and address, (ii) whether it is a supply, works or services contract and whether it is a framework agreement, (iii) a "clear indication" of the nature of the goods, work(s) or services (for example, by using the Classification of Products by Activity (CPA) nomenclature), (iv) whether the contract was advertised and in which publication, and, if not, the award procedure or method used to determine the provider, (v) the number of offers received, (vi) the date of the award, (vii) the name and address of the awardee, (viii) the contract value (as calculated under Utilities Regulation 10), (ix) the expected contract duration, (x) any share which is/may be subcontracted (where more than 10 per cent of the contract value), (xi) the origin of goods (supply contracts) or principal place of performance (works and services contracts), (xii) the main criteria for the award decision (where most economically advantageous offer is used) and (xiii) whether a variant was accepted.

between 400,000 and 5 million ECUs, the utility need only supply more limited information to the Commission and this need only be done every three months,[70] unless the Commission requests that the information be supplied earlier for a specific contract, in which case it must be sent "forthwith" to the responsible Minister, for onward transmission to the Commission.[71] For these smaller contracts, the information in question must also be retained by the utility itself for not less than four years after the date of the award.[72] Utilities must also follow the obligations in Utilities Regulation 27(2)(a) requiring the utility to send a report to the responsible Minister on particular contracts, where this is requested for the purposes of providing information for the Commission.[73]

(v) PROCEDURE FOR OBTAINING AN EXEMPTION

The Utilities Directive effectively provides that Member States wishing to take advantage of the Article 3 exemption must obtain a decision from the Commission giving permission to invoke the exemption.[74] An exemption could be sought for one sector or activity, or for several, or all.

Article 3(4) provides that Member States making an application must inform the Commission of any measure[75] relating to compliance with the applicable licensing conditions. However, Article 3(5), as inserted by Article 12 of the Hydrocarbons Licensing Directive, provides that this is not required where the state concerned has complied with the requirements of that Licensing Directive. In the case of compliance with that directive the licensing conditions of Article 3 are automatically satisfied, as explained above. The practice is for an application for an exemption to be submitted to Directorate General XV (which is responsible for public and utilities procurement), which will defer to Directorate General XVIII (which is responsible for administering the Licensing Directive) on the question of whether the Licensing Directive has been properly implemented.

Article 3(4) also requires states to provide details of measures relating to compliance with the principles of non-discrimination and competitive

---

[70] Utilities Regulation 9(3)(b). The information which must be sent is that in items (i)–(ix) of the list in note 69 above. It must be sent to the Commission no less than 48 days after the end of the three-month period ending the last day of March, June, September or December in which the contract was awarded: Utilities Regulations 9(1)(b)(ii)(bb).

[71] Utilities Regulation 9(1)(b)(ii)(aa). The responsible Minister is the one whose area of responsibility is most closely connected with the utility's functions, as conclusively determined by the Treasury: Utilities Regulation 28(1)–(2), and the duty to send the report is enforceable by mandamus (Utilities Regulation 28(3)).

[72] Utilities Regulation 9(2)(b)(i).

[73] This obligation is stated in Utilities Regulation 27(2)(a) to apply to contracts falling within the exemptions in the regulations, and Utilities Regulation 9(1) makes it clear that the general exemption given in regulation 9(1) from the requirements of the regulations does not apply to regulation 27(2)(a).

[74] See Utilities Directive Article 3(1) and 3(4).

[75] Article 3(4) actually refers to any "law, regulation or administrative provision, agreement or understanding".

401

procurement by entities which will be covered by the exemption. Article 3(2) requires states to take steps to ensure compliance with these principles by exempt entities, which (since such provision must be enforceable by affected entities in accordance with the Utilities Remedies Directive[76]) must generally be in the form of enforceable legislation. As noted above, such provision has been made in the United Kingdom in Utilities Regulation 9. Presumably the Commission will not be prepared to grant an exmption unless such legal measures are in place.

Article 3(4) also provides that the Commission must take a decision in accordance with the procedure laid down in Article 40(5)–(8) of the directive, which requires the Commission to obtain advice from the Advisory Committee for Public Contracts and to take account of its opinion. The Commission's decision on the exemption and the reasons for it must also, under Article 3(4), be published in the *Official Journal*.

(vi) WITHDRAWAL AND LAPSE OF THE EXEMPTION FOR NON-COMPLIANCE WITH THE RELEVANT CONDITIONS

An unresolved question is whether an exemption given under Article 3 will automatically lapse, because of a failure to comply with the licensing conditions. This could arise either because the relevant legal or other measures are not adequate, or because of a failure to comply with these measures in practice. The principles of legal certainty would suggest, however, that formal revocation of the exemption by the Commission should be required before the exemption ceases to have effect: it would be wholly unsatisfactory if individual purchasing entities were expected to monitor the law and practice of the system on a day-to-day basis in order to know which procedures they should apply, particularly since the question of how far lapses must in practice go to put a state in breach of the conditions is likely to be a matter of degree. Thus it is submitted that the exemption should not lapse automatically, but that failure by a state to comply with the licensing conditions will give rise to a power – or even a duty – on the part of the Commission to revoke the exemption. The preamble to the Hydrocarbons Licensing Directive expressly contemplates the possible removal of the exemption in those cases where the exemption was originally granted on the basis of compliance with the Licensing Directive, stating that the condition for the exemption applies "from the moment when and for as long as" a state complies with that directive.[77]

It may similarly be questioned whether failure to comply with the conditions of non-discrimination and competitive procurement should

---

[76] See Chap. 18.

[77] Since this refers to the condition for the exemption and not the exemption itself, it is consistent with the view that the exemption does not lapse automatically.

have any effect on the exemption. Here, it is suggested that a failure to provide for enforceable legal measures – such as those in Utilities Regulation 9 – to regulate entities subject to the exemption, could result in a revocation by the Commission. However, as with failure to comply with the licensing conditions it is submitted that for reasons of legal certainty this should not be automatic. It is also submitted that the Commission could withdraw the exemption for persistent failure of entities in the sector to follow the rules, although here again, and even more so than in the case of inadequacy of legislative measures, legal certainty requires a specific revocation. Individual breaches will be subject to redress based on the fact that the principles of non-discrimination and competitive procurement are enforceable in the national courts, and by the European Commission in the Court of Justice, in the same way as the other, more specific, procurement rules under the regulations.

(5) THE TRANSPORT SECTOR

(a) PROVISION OF AIR TERMINAL FACILITIES

In the transport sector the regulations cover, first, "the exploitation of a geographical area for the purpose of providing airport or other terminal facilities to carriers by air".[78]

It is not wholly clear which activities constitute the provision of airport or terminal facilities to carriers. Clearly this covers activities directly concerned with the transportation of passengers and cargo – for example, the movement of passengers around the airport, provision of facilities for arrival and departure, refuelling of aeroplanes, handling of passenger baggage, or storage and distribution of freight. Provision and development of the infrastructure for these activities in terms of building and machinery, and the management and maintenance of that infrastructure (for example, cleaning) are clearly covered.[79] In addition to these activities, however, within the geographic area of the airport additional services are often provided for the convenience of passengers or crew, such as refreshment facilities, shops, hotels and car parking, and it is less clear whether these facilities are covered. In the Advisory Committee Guidelines issued in relation to Directive 90/531,[80] which is the same as the current Utilities Directive in this respect, it is suggested that

---

[78] Utilities Regulations Schedule 1, part O, column 2.
[79] This is envisaged in guidelines published by the Commission relating to the scope of this activity under directive 90/531/EEC, the predecessor to the current Utilities Directive where the scope of the relevant activity is the same: see Advisory Commitee on the Opening Up of Public Procurement and the Advisory Committee on Public Procurement, *Policy Guidelines on Non-Relevant Airport Activities under the "Utilities Directive"* (CC/92/23 (rev. 1) Final and CC/92/24 (rev. 1) Final (1992), para. 5.
[80] Note 79, above.

provision of retail and catering facilities at an airport is covered, since these "contribute to the smooth functioning of the airport facilities".[81] On the other hand, the guidelines suggest that hotel services are excluded because they are not "indispensable to the pursuit of air transport activities".[82] Here the guidelines appear to use two different tests: in relation to hotels the test of "indispensability", and in relation to other facilities whether they are necessary for the "smooth functioning" of travel. This is inconsistent. On the first test of whether a service is indispensable, it is probable that refreshment facilities could be included, but it is difficult to see that car parking and shopping facilities should be covered if hotels are not. On the second test of "smooth functioning" it is submitted that all these services are covered. (If hotels are not covered, what would be the position of shower and sleeping facilities rented on an hourly basis within the terminal buildings?)

It is likely that the Court of Justice will adopt one of these two tests in interpreting the provision, but it is not clear which. It has been suggested by Trepte[83] that the Court's decision in case C–247/89, *Commission v. Portugal*,[84] indicates a wide interpretation. In that case the Court was required to interpret a provision in the original Supply Directive, directive 77/62,[85] which excluded those administering "transport services" from the operation of the Supply Directive (at a time when the rules on utilities were not yet in force). The Court appeared to indicate that the scope of this exclusion was intended to parallel the scope of the activity of the provision of terminal facilities eventually included in the Utilities Directive,[86] which makes the decision of relevance in the present context. Support for the broad view may be found in the fact that the Court defined transport services as those linked to the administration of the infrastructure. On the other hand, it can be pointed out that the case itself concerned the provision of a telephone exchange as part of the infrastructure, which can be considered to meet the "indispensability" test. It can also be noted that the Court emphasised the fact that transport cannot be realised without the "necessary" infrastructure: this may indicate that the Court contemplated the inclusion only of that part of the infrastructure which is "necessary" for transport provision. Thus the case is not clear on this point, and the scope of the provision remains uncertain pending further clarification by the Court of Justice.

It can be noted that where facilities such as hotels are provided away from the airport site they are clearly not covered, because of the requirement for exploitation of a "geographic area", which contemplates

---

[81] *Ibid*, para. 6.
[82] *Ibid*, para. 5.
[83] Trepte, *Public Procurement in the E.C.* (1993), p.25.
[84] [1991] E.C.R. I–3659.
[85] The case concerned the provision as it stood prior to an amendment by the "revising" Supply Directive 88/295 (as to which see pp. 53–56).
[86] See para. 41 of the judgment.

the inclusion only of airport services provided on the airport site. Activities on the airport site itself are also clearly excluded where they are not concerned in any way with the provision of transport facilities, as where buildings on the site are developed for commercial reasons, for the purpose of resale or letting to third parties for those parties own purposes.[87]

As regards the entities covered in relation to this activity, the schedule specifically mentions in relation to England and Wales[88] (i) local authorities,[89] and (ii) those who are "airport operators" within the meaning of the Airports Act 1986 and who have the management of an airport subject to economic regulation under Part IV of that Act. In addition, it is provided that the regulations apply to any other "relevant person" engaged in such activities – that is, any entity which is a public authority, public undertaking, or enjoys relevant special or exclusive rights.[90]

It can be noted that those providing transport as such – air carriers – are not covered by the rules. It is assumed, as stated in the preamble to the Utilities Directive, that in due course such markets will become fully competitive following the implementation of the Community's general air transport policy and that this competition will be adequate to achieve open procurement. However, other sectors in which eventual liberalisation is envisaged, such as the energy sectors, have still been subject to the directive pending liberalisation, as noted above.

(b) PROVISION OF PORT AND SIMILAR FACILITIES

Another activity within the regulations is the exploitation of a geographical area for the purpose of providing maritime or inland port facilities, or other terminal facilities, to carriers by sea, or carriers using inland waterways.[91] As with the provision on airports, this will cover both carriage of passengers and transportation of goods. Similar difficulties may arise as with airports, as discussed above, in deciding whether particular facilities provided for the convenience of those using the transport facilities, such as shopping facilities, are covered by the regulations. Obviously the Court of Justice is likely to take the same approach in both cases.

---

[87] This view is endorsed by the Advisory Committee Guidelines cited above, note 79.

[88] Utilities Regulations Schedule 1, part O, column 1. Also specified are Highland and Islands Airport Ltd, any subsidiary of the Northern Ireland Transport Holding Company within the meaning of the Aerodromes (Northern Ireland) Act 1971 and any "aerodrome undertaking" within the meaning of that Act.

[89] "Local authority" is defined in the definitions section of Schedule 1 by reference to the definition for England and Wales in Works Regulation 3(2), as to which see p. 108, and the corresponding definitions in Works Regulation 3(3)–(4) for Scotland and Northern Ireland.

[90] On the precise definition of relevant person see pp. 385–388.

[91] Utilities Regulations Schedule 1, part P, column 2.

As regards the entities covered, the legislation refers specifically to[92]: a harbour authority under section 57 of the Harbours Act 1964[93]; the British Waterways Board; and a local authority.[94] In addition, however, the regulations also apply to any person who is a "relevant person" as defined in the schedule.[95]

As with air transport, the activity of transportation as such is not covered by the provisions, but only the operation of facilities.

(c) THE OPERATION OF TRANSPORT NETWORKS

(i) DEFINITION OF A NETWORK

The regulations also apply to the operation of various types of transport network. In relation to the transport field, "network" is defined[96] to mean "a system operated in accordance with conditions laid down by or under the law in any part of the United Kingdom including such conditions as to the routes to be served, the capacity to be made available and the frequency of the service". This definition applies in the case of all the networks considered in section (ii) below.

(ii) TYPES OF NETWORK COVERED

Operation of a railway network: The regulations cover, first, the operation of a network providing a service to the public in the field of transport by railway. In contrast with the provisions on air and water transport this covers the operation of the transport service itself. It will also cover contracts made in connection with provision of facilities for operating the network, such as provision of stations. Here the same difficulties arise as with air transport in deciding exactly which facilities for users (for example, shopping facilities) are covered, as discussed in the section on air transport above.

The regulations list a number of specific entities[97] covered in relation to this activity, notably British Railways Board, Railtrack and local

---

[92] Utilities Regulations Schedule 1, part P, column 1.
[93] Also included is a harbour authority as defined by section 38(1) of the Harbours Act (Northern Ireland) 1970.
[94] "Local authority" is defined in the definitions section of Schedule 1 by reference to the definition for England and Wales in Works Regulation 3(2), as to which see p. 108, and the corresponding definitions in Works Regulation 3(3)–(4) for Scotland and Northern Ireland.
[95] On the definition see pp. 385–388.
[96] See the definition of "network" in Schedule 1 to the regulations.
[97] Apart from those referred to in the text the others presently listed are: any subsidiary of British Railways Board under Transport Act 1962, s.25; Northern Ireland Transport Holding Company; Northern Ireland Railways Company Ltd; London Regional Transport; Docklands Light Railway Ltd; Strathclyde Passenger Transport Executive; Greater Manchester Passenger Transport Executive; Greater Manchester Metro Ltd.; Brighton Borough Council; South Yorkshire Passenger Transport Executive; and South Yorkshire Supertram (no. 2) Ltd.

entities such as London Underground Ltd and Tyne and Wear Passenger Transport Executive. The list includes a number of private companies which are not subject to government ownership or control but operate under concession arrangements, such as Eurotunnel plc. In addition to the entities listed, the regulations also apply to "any other relevant person".[98]

Operation of a network for transport by automated systems, tramway, trolleybus or cable: The regulations also apply to "the operation of a network providing a service to the public in the field of transport by automated systems, tramway, trolleybus or cable.[99] As regards entities covered, the regulations again list certain specific entities who are known currently to operate tramways, etc.[1] They also contain the catch-all provision applying the regulations to "any other relevant person" – that is, to all other bodies which are public authorities or undertakings or enjoy special or exclusive rights and who carry on this activity.[2]

Operation of a bus network: Also covered is "the operation of a network providing a service to the public in the field of transport by bus".[3] As covered entities in England and Wales the regulations list London Regional Transport (LRT) or a subsidiary of LRT within section 36 of the Transport Act 1985, and also any person providing a London bus service as defined in section 34(2)(b) of the Transport Act 1985 under an agreement entered into by LRT under the London Regional Transport Act 1984.[4] As with networks for tramways, etc., there is also a catch-all provision stating that any other "relevant person" is also covered.[5]

For the bus transport sector there is, however a special exemption. As noted above, one reason for regulating the utilities was that in general these bodies are susceptible to government pressure to "buy national" because they do not operate in fully competitive markets and are therefore not under the usual commercial contraints to purchase efficiently. However, sometimes bus transport operators do operate in a competitive market, being allowed to compete freely over the same routes, and it was felt that in these circumstances an exemption from the directive was appropriate for this activity. This exemption is given effect in Utilities Regulation 6(h) which provides that the regulations do not apply to relevant entities involved in provision of bus transport "when

---

[98] On the definition of "relevant person" see pp. 385–388.

[99] Utilities Regulations, Schedule 1, Part R column 2.

[1] Utilities Regulations, Schedule 1, Part R column 1. These are: Greater Manchester Passenger Transport Executive; Greater Manchester Metro Ltd; Blackpool Transport Services Ltd; Aberconwy Borough Council; South Yorkshire Passenger Transport Executive; and South Yorkshire Supertram (no.2) Ltd.

[2] Utilities Regulations, Schedule 1, Part R column 1. For the precise definition of "relevant person" see pp. 385–388.

[3] Utilities Regulations, Schedule 1, Part S column 2.

[4] Utilities Regulations, Schedule 1, Part S column 1.

[5] For the precise definition of relevant person see pp. 385–388.

that activity is provided in a geographical area in which other persons are free to provide the service under the same conditions as the utility.[6] It is not clear whether the question of the freedom of others to provide the services refers to the fact that others are permitted in law to do so, so that the exemption will apply where, for example, licences are freely available to all who wish to apply, or whether other entities will not be considered to operate under similar conditions where one or more parties dominate the market in practice so that the *de facto* operating conditions are different for different entities. A similar exemption applies to providers of certain telecommunications services and similar questions concerning the meaning of the exemption in that context are currently being considered by the European Court, as is explained in the next section on telecommunications. In the United Kingdom there is in fact no licensing system as such, and operators compete in a free market for subsidies granted by bodies responsible for securing the provision of public transport services. In these circumstances it appears that the exemption will generally apply to bus transport operators in the United Kingdom.

(6) THE TELECOMMUNICATIONS SECTOR

(a) PROVISION AND OPERATION OF A TELECOMMUNICATIONS NETWORK

In the telecommunications sector the regulations cover, first, "the provision or operation of a public telecommunications network".[7] A public telecommunications network is defined as[8] "an infrastructure for the use of the public which enables signals to be conveyed by wire microwave, optical means or other electromagnetic means between physical connections which are necessary for access to an efficient communication through the network". This covers, primarily, public telephone networks provided by, in particular, British Telecommunications plc.

It is provided that the entities covered in respect of this activity are those who are public telecommunications operators under the Telecommunications Act 1984.[9] British Telecommunications plc is the main provider and operator caught by these provisions.

---

[6] This implements the provision in Article 2(4) of the Utilities Directive allowing an exemption where "other entities are free to provide those services, either in general or in a particular geographic area, under the same conditions as the contracting entities".

[7] Utilities Regulations, Schedule 1, part T, column 1.

[8] This definition is found in Utilities Regulation 2(1) and is applied in the context of Schedule 1 by the definitions section of that schedule.

[9] Utilities Regulations, Schedule 1, Part T, column 1.

(b) PROVISION OF TELECOMMUNICATIONS SERVICES

In addition, the regulations cover the provision of "one or more public telecommunications services".[10] These are defined as[11] "services which consist in whole or in part in the transmission and routing of signals on a public telecommunications network by means of telecommunications processes other than radio broadcasting and television". This covers, for example, the provision of mobile telephone services.

With this activity, as with provision or operation of a network, it is provided in principle that the entities covered are those who are public telecommunications operators under the Telecommunications Act 1984.[12]

The provisions above appear to apply the regulations quite widely to a number of entities providing a variety of services. However, the above provisions in Schedule 1 are heavily qualified by a specific exclusion in Utilities Regulation 7(1).[13] In the original Utilities Supply and Works Contracts Regulation of 1992 the parallel exclusion provided that the regulations were to apply only to two specific operators under the 1984 Act, British Telecommunications plc ("BT") and Kingston Communications (Hull) plc ("Kingston"), and not to the other operators in the United Kingdom. Further, even for these two operators the rules were to apply only to certain specified types of telecommunication service, and only where these services are provided within the geographical area for which the entity in question is licensed as a public telecommunications operator. (The specified services were: basic voice telephony services (ordinary telephone services); basic data transmission services; the provision of private leased circuits; and maritime services). The purpose of these significant limitations was to give effect to an exclusion in Article 8(1) of the Utilities Directive which applies to both provision and operation of networks and provision of public telecommunications services where "other entities are free to offer the same services in the same geographical area and under substantially the same conditions". This was included in the directive because it was thought that dangers of nationalistic purchasing are minimal in markets where entities are

---

[10] Utilities Regulations, Schedule 1, Part T, column 2.
[11] This definition is found in Utilities Regulation 2(1) and is applied in the context of Schedule 1 by the definitions section of that schedule.
[12] Utilities Regulations, Schedule 1, Part T, column 1.
[13] Utilities Regulation 7(1). Utilities Regulation 7(2) provides that entities invoking the exclusion must, when requested by the Commission, notify the Commisison of any public telecommunications services which it provides which it considers to be excluded under regulation 7. Utilities Regulations 7(3) states that the utility may indicate that any information included in its report is commercially sensitive and should not be published. Such reports may be requested by the Commission and the Minister must send the relevant report to the Treasury for onward transmission to the Commission: Utilities Regulation 28(6).

"directly exposed to competitive forces in markets to which entry is unrestricted". The United Kingdom took the view that, apart from the case of BT and Kingston in the limited areas mentioned above, such open competition does exist in telecommunications services markets; hence the complete exclusion of most operators. The failure to apply the exclusion in all fields to BT and Kingston reflected the government's view that the exclusion cannot apply when an entity is in reality in a dominant market position in a particular market, regardless of the availability of licences to other persons.

As soon as the original Utilities Regulations were made, however, BT challenged the failure to include it within the exclusion. A request for a preliminary ruling from the Court of Justice to clarify certain other matters relating to these provisions was subsequently made by the Queen's Bench Division.[14-15] At the time of writing no judgment had yet been given, but the opinion of the Advocate General[16] took the view that it is for individual entities to decide whether or not they fall within the exclusion, and that this should not be set out in the legislation. In recognition of the fact that the Court of Justice is likely to take the same view, the new version of the Utilities Regulations has merely set out the exclusion in the directive in regulation 7, leaving entities to apply it themselves. The exemption applies only to contracts intended exclusively to entitle provision of the excluded services.

(7) THE POSITION OF "NON-UTILITY" ACTIVITIES CARRIED OUT BY UTILITIES

(a) THE GENERAL PRINCIPLE: NON-APPLICATION OF THE UTILITIES RULES

Entities which are "utilities" under the Utilities Regulations are frequently involved both in "utility" activities – those listed in the regulations – and in other activities. For example, some of the United Kingdom companies involved in supplying electricity through a fixed network – a listed activity – are also involved in selling electrical household goods through high-street stores – a non-listed activity.

Since the Utilities Regulations do not apply to the "seeking of offers in relation to a contract other than for the purpose of carrying out an activity specified in the Part of Schedule 1 in which the utility is specified", contracts by utilities which are made in connection with non-

---

[14-15] (1993) O.J. C287/6. See further Brown, "Case C–392/93: Reference to the Court of Justice concerning United Kingdom Implementation of the Utilities Directive in the Field of Telecommunications" (1994) 3 P.P.L.R. CS 30.
[16] Opinion of November 28, 1995.

listed activities are not subject to the Utilities Regulations.[16a] In the case of bodies which are "contracting authorities" under the public sector regulations, these non-listed activities are subject to regulation under the stricter regime of the public sector regulations. This arises because the public sector regulations apply generally to the activities of these contracting authorities, and the Utilities Regulations apply to their utility activities only because such activities are expressly excluded from the public sector regulations and brought within the utilities rules instead.[17] In the case of bodies which are not subject to the public sector rules – for example, as is the case with the electricty companies mentioned above – their "non-utility" activites are not subject to regulation at all. However, the Commission may request utilities to notify it of any activities which those utilities regard as excluded on the basis that they are non-utility activities.[18]

(b) CONTRACTS PARTLY FOR UTILITY ACTIVITIES AND PARTLY FOR OTHER ACTIVITIES

Bodies involved in both utility activities and other activities may sometimes wish to make contracts which relate to both groups of activities. For example, the different activities may be managed from a central headquarters so that equipment, such as computer systems, purchased for the headquarters will be used for both utility and non-utility activities. Similarly, certain types of services, such as auditing services, are often purchased in relation to the activities of a company as a whole. What is the position of contracts which relate both to utility and non-utility activities? In the case of bodies caught by the public sector

---

[16a] This provision is intended to reflect Article 6(1) of the Utilities Directive, which provides that the directive does not apply to awards made for "purposes other than *the pursuit of* relevant activities (emphasis added). It has been suggested that this may require the Directive to be applied to other activities in the same *sector* as the activity listed (for example, to an electricity company selling electrical appliances). It could also be suggested that it might cover other activities which *facilitate or relate to* the listed activity – for example, where the supplier of a product or service through a fixed network (such as telecommunications) uses the network or the opportunity it provides to pursue other (non-listed) activities, such as the provision of cable television services. However, this does not appear to have been the intention: see, further, Green, "Utilities Directive 93/38: the Extent to which it Applies to Contracting Entities" (1994) 3 P.P.L.R. 173. Of course, there may sometimes be a problem determining the "scope" of the activity itself – that is, what is within the activity and what is merely incidental to it: see, for example, the discussion of transport services, above.

[17] See pp. 151–152.

[18] Utilities Directive Article 6(3). It is also provided that it may periodically publish in the Official Journal lists of exclusions (provided that it respects any "sensitive commercial aspects" of the information which are pointed out to it when the information is forwarded by the utility).
This is a much less stringent provision than that in the original proposal which required notification *and* verification by the Commission, and publication of, all contracts excluded on this basis, in order for utilities to take advantage of such exclusions: see the original proposal in Bulletin of the European Communities, Supplement 6/88, Article 3.

rules, if such contracts are not within the utility rules they will be caught by the public sector regime instead; with other utilities, the consequence of holding the contract to be outside the utilities rules is that it is unregulated. There is nothing in the Utilities Regulations or directive which expressly indicates the extent to which contracts relating to both utility and non-utility purchases are caught by the utilities rules.

In relation to bodies not covered by the public sector rules, this problem was expressly dealt with in the original proposal for a directive on utilities, where it was provided that contracts would only be excluded where made *exclusively* for non-utility purposes[19] – a stringent requirement designed to ensure that the rules could never be evaded by packaging utility requirements along with purchases made for non-utility purposes. This provision was not included in the final version of the Utilities Directive. It is, however, still possible to interpret the directive and implementing regulations, as applying *whenever* the contract relates to a utility activity in any way: it could then be considered to be for the "purpose" of that activity. This would be appropriate if the courts wished to adopt a stringent approach to the regulation of bodies not covered by the public sector rules. Under this approach, where such bodies purchase general items such as computers or office buildings these will always be covered if used (however marginally) for "utility" purposes.

Such an approach is, however, less suitable for bodies which are subject to the public sector rules: the effect of applying the test in this case would be that a large number of public authority contracts relating to general services and supplies would be subject to the lighter utilities regime, simply because some small part of the purchase is to be used for a utilities activity. However, it is possible to take the view that any contracts relating to a utility purpose, even in a minor way, are in general within the utilities rules, whilst at the same time excluding most public sector contracts from these rules: this result can be achieved by interpreting the Utilities Directive and Utilities Regulations as applying to any contract relating to a utility activity, whilst interpreting the "utilities" exclusions in the public sector directive and regulations so as to exclude only contracts which are *mainly*[20] for utilities purposes.

Alternatively, a general test might be adopted which classifies the contract for the purpose of considering whether it is "for the purpose of" one of the utility activities according to either its "predominant objective" of, or according to the basis of whether the greater part of the use or value is intended to relate to utility or non-utility activities. On this basis a contract would be for the "purpose of" a utility activity under the regulations only where its main purpose (the reason for the purchase being made) or, alternatively, the main part of its consideration – relates

---

[19] See the original proposal published in Bulletin of the European Communities, Supplement 6/88, Article 3.

[20] This could refer either to a "predominant objective" test, or a test of whether the acquisition is intended to be used more for utility purposes or non-utility purposes.

to the utility activity. Thus "general" contracts for computer systems, etc., which are made by bodies which are not also "contracting authorities" would be subject to regulation only where their main use or purpose is the utility activity: in other cases, the utility would be free to follow its own procedures. It is submitted that if this approach is followed, a test of value or intended use is preferable to one of predominant purpose, since it provides much greater certainty.[21]

(8) PURCHASERS NOT YET ENGAGED IN UTILITY ACTIVITIES ("GHOST UTILITIES")

An important question in practice is whether the regulations cover an entity which is not yet an entity engaged in a utility activity, or does not yet enjoy any special or exclusive rights (and is not a public authority or undertaking), but which makes purchases in anticipation of its future activities as a utility. This will arise with any entity which is first setting up business in a particular field. Thus an entity seeking to establish itself as a power generator will need to buy power generation equipment before it can actually engage in the activity in question. The situation also often arises when an entity enters into contracts in preparation for the performance of a particular concession – for example, the building and operation of a tramway or other transport network – which that entity hopes to be awarded in the future. Under such arrangements the delivery of products, works or services under the contracts will generally be conditional on success in obtaining the concession. At the time such contracts are made the awarding entity may not actually be a "utility" for the purpose of the rules, either because the entity is not yet engaged in the activity in question, or because whilst it carries on the relevant activity it will only obtain special or exclusive rights if the concession is awarded. This situation is especially likely to arise in the case of a consortium of different entities which have banded together to bid for a particular concession in the utilities field, which may bring the consortium and/or its members into that particular utility field for the first time.

Whilst the regulations refer to an entity which "carries on" a utility activity (Utilities Regulation 3), and the activities which "have" as one of their activities a relevant utility activity, it is likely that the rules will be construed in a broad way to cover contracts which are entered into with a view to carrying on a utility activity, even if no such activity is carried on at the time the contract is made. Any other construction would exclude many important utility contracts from the scope of the rules.

---

[21] On this issue see the discussion at pp. 427–429, concerning the classification of contracts which are partly for works and partly for services.

3. REQUIREMENT OF "A CONTRACT IN WRITING FOR CONSIDERATION"

(1) REQUIREMENT FOR A CONTRACT

The Utilities Regulations apply when a contracting authority seeks offers in relation to a proposed "works contract", "supply contract" or "Part A services contract".[22] This involves a requirement for a proposed arrangement which is a "contract".[23]

(a) THE PROVISION OF SERVICES THROUGH NON-CONTRACTUAL ARRANGEMENTS

As explained in the context of the public sector rules, certain needs may be procured through arrangements which are not classified as contractual by domestic law, and this raises the question of whether such procurements are outside the scope of the procurement rules. This issue has already been discussed above in the context of the public sector rules,[24] and the Court of Justice will no doubt adopt the same approach in interpreting the rules in the utilities sector.

(b) AWARDS IN-HOUSE AND TO AFFILIATED ENTITIES

Where work is awarded to an in-house service provider which is legally part of the purchasing organisation, there is in law no contract, and the work may thus be awarded to the in-house unit without following the regulations. This applies even if the in-house unit operates in practice on a largely independent basis, and even where it is normally required to compete for such work with the private sector. As with the public sector, the degree of market openness in different states will obviously be affected significantly by the extent to which work is contracted out – when it must be advertised Europe-wide – or retained in-house.

If for specific work the purchaser does seek external offers, a contract is in contemplation and there is then a "proposed contract" for the purpose of the regulations[25]; the regulations must then be followed. Thus, as under the public sector rules, the regulations apply where an in-house unit is required to compete for work with outside bidders.

Where work is awarded to any provider which is a separate legal entity, the award will take the form of a contract, and the regulations

---

[22] Utilities Regulation 5(1).

[23] See the definitions in works contract, supply contract and services contract in Utilities Regulation 2(1).

[24] See pp. 116–118.

[25] The regulations then require the in-house bid is to be treated in the same way as external bids: Utilities Regulations 21(9).

must thus normally be followed. Where the provider is closely connected with the utility but is legally separate – for example, a closely controlled subsidiary – a utility might seek to avoid the application of the procurement rules by entering into an informal and non-contractual supply arrangement: it may not need the protection of a formal contract where it has a reasonable degree of control over the provider. However, it is likely that the Court of Justice will interpret the rules to require such an arrangement to be treated as a contract where this is appropriate given the substance of the relationship, rather than looking at whether technically there is a contract for the purposes of domestic contract law. There is, on the other hand, a specific exemption from the regulations for certain services contracts awarded to entities "affiliated" to the undertaking, and this is discussed further below.[26] There is also an exemption which effectively allows states to set up arrangements whereby public sector bodies are given exclusive rights to provide services to bodies (whether in another part of the public sector or not) carrying out utilities activities, and this is also considered below.[27]

(c) RENEWALS, EXTENSIONS AND AMENDMENTS

Another important question is when a proposed extension, renewal or amendment to a contract is a new "contract" for the purpose of the regulations. Where this is the case, it is not permissible simply to place the work with the existing contracting party: it must be awarded in accordance with the regulations. As with the public sector rules, the utilities rules do not give any specific guidance on this point, and nor has the position been clarified by any case law.

This question has already been extensively discussed in the context of the public sector regulations.[28] It was suggested that mutually agreed extensions and amendments may often constitute new contracts, although the position will vary according to the nature and practice of the particular market. It is clear that the same principles should be applied in both utilities and public sectors, and readers are therefore referred to the discussion of this matter in the chapter on the public sector.

It can be noted that even in a situation where an agreed renewal or extension is to be treated as a new contract, there is sometimes scope for a utility to negotiate with an existing provider to enter into such a new contract without any requirement for a call for competition under the regulations. This applies in the case of works or services contracts where the utility wishes to enter into an arrangement for an existing provider to carry out additional works or services unforeseen when the contract was

---

[26] See pp. 436–439.
[27] See pp. 435–436.
[28] See pp. 119–123.

made, either where – for technical or economic reasons – it is unduly inconvenient for a different provider to do this work, or where the new work is necessary to the later stages of the existing contract.[29] Such negotiation without competition is also possible for a new works contract (although not for a new services contract) for a repetition of foreseen works relating to the same project where the possibility of such an extension was mentioned in the original contract documents.[30] For supply contracts such negotiation with the existing provider is possible for an addition to, or partial replacement of, existing goods or an existing installation where this is required to avoid incompatibility or technical difficulties.[31]

(2) REQUIREMENTS FOR WRITING AND CONSIDERATION

The definitions of works, supply and services contracts cover only contracts which are in writing and for consideration.[32] The requirements here are the same as under the public sector regulations and have already been discussed in Chapter 5.[33]

4. THE SCOPE OF "WORKS", "SUPPLY" AND "SERVICES" CONTRACTS

(a) INTRODUCTION

As noted above the Utilities Regulations apply to any proposed "works contract", "supply contract" and "Part A services contract".[34]

It is important to know whether a contract falls within one of these definitions, and so potentially is subject to the Utilities Regulations. It is also necessary to ascertain into which of the three categories a particular contract falls to determine precisely how the regulations apply to that contract; in particular, different thresholds and exclusions apply to each of the three categories. Of particular importance is the distinction between works, on the one hand, and supplies or services on the other, since the threshold for the regulation of works contracts is much higher than other types of contracts.

---

[29] See further pp. 485–486.
[30] See further p. 487.
[31] See further p. 485.
[32] Utilities Regulation 2(1).
[33] See pp. 123–124.
[34] Utilities Regulation 5.

(b) WORKS CONTRACTS

"Works contract" is defined in Utilities Regulation 2(1) to cover (i) contracts for the carrying out of a work or works, and (ii) contracts under which the utility engages a person to procure a work "by any means".

(i) THE CARRYING OUT OF WORKS OR A WORK

First, the definition covers a contract for the "carrying out" of "works" or "a work".

"Works" is defined in Utilities Regulation 2 as meaning any of the activities specified in Schedule 3 to the regulations. This schedule is identical to Schedule 1 of the public sector Works Regulations which lists the activities covered as "works" under those regulations. This Schedule was set out in Chapter 5 and the scope of the activities covered has already been examined in that chapter.[35]

The regulations cover, as indicated, any contract for carrying out such activities. This clearly does not require that the contractor should do the works itself – merely that it is responsible for securing that the works are carried out which may be done wholly or partly through subcontractors.[36]

"Carrying out" is defined in Utilities Regulation 2 to refer not merely to construction itself,[37] but also to design and construction, making it clear that contracts involving both design and construction are covered. (A contract solely for the design of works is covered as a Part A services contract).

"Work" means the *outcome* of any of the above works such as is of itself "sufficient to fulfil an economic or technical function".[38] As with the public sector this will cover, for example, a complete public building, such as a theatre or town hall, but clearly does not cover part of building such as a roof or foundations for a building. This definition was

---

[35] See pp. 124–128.

[36] Case C–389/92, *Ballast Nedem Groep NV v. The State (Belgium)* [1994] 2 C.M.L.R. 836 (concerning the public sector but equally relevant in the utilities context). In case C–331/92, *Gestion Hotelera Internacional SA v. Communidad Autonoma de Canarias* [1994] ECR I–1329 (also concerning the public sector rules), Advocate General Lenz stated that the agreement in that case for a firm to renovate a hotel to an amount of 1 million pesetas could not be a contract for works. One relevant factor was stated to be that the winning bidder was not permitted to realise the renovation itself, but only through other parties. It is not clear from the report whether the contracts to do the work were to be concluded with the contracting authority itself or the winning bidder; it is submitted that the Advocate General's remark on this particular issue is compatible only with the first possibility.

[37] It is interesting that regulation 2 in defining "carrying out" refers to the construction of the works. Here "works" is being used to refer to the end product of the activities in Schedule 3, whereas in the definition of "public works contract" and the definition of "works" itself, "works" is used to refer to an activity (such as construction itself), not the end product of the activity.

[38] Utilities Regulation 2(1).

considered further in Chapter 5 on the public sector.[39] As in that sector, the precise definition of "work" is not in fact important in relation to the first part of the definition of public works contract – as one for the carrying out of works or a work – since the reference to a "work" here does not add anything to the reference to "works": carrying out a "work" involves, by definition, the carrying out of "works". However, the concept of a "work" is relevant to the second part of the definition ((ii) below), and also for the application of the threshold rules.[40]

(ii) PROCUREMENT OF A WORK BY ANY MEANS

Also within the definition of a works contract under Utilities Regulation 2(1) is a contract under which a utility "engages a person to procure by any means the carrying out for the utility of a work corresponding to specified requirements". This brings within the works rules any arrangement whereby the purchaser draws up a specification for a work, and the contractor is entrusted with the task of providing it. This provision is the same, *mutatis mutandis*, as the corresponding provision concerning procurement of a "work" under the public sector Works Regulations, the scope of which has already been examined in Chapter 5. As noted there, the provision was intended to bring within the category of works contracts a contract for an external provider to act as agent for a purchaser in letting contracts in connection with a particular work,[41] and it also seems to catch an arrangement where a builder or developer arranges for the construction of a work on land not owned by the purchaser, and undertakes to transfer or lease the land and structure to the purchaser at a later point. For further consideration of these points readers are referred to the relevant discussion in Chapter 5.[42]

(c) SUPPLY CONTRACTS

"Supply contract" is defined in Utilities Regulation 2(1). It covers a contract for the purchase of goods or the hire of goods. It also covers a contract for the purchase or hire of goods, together with the siting or installation of those goods – for example, a contract for a plumbing firm for that firm to fit washrooms with fittings supplied by the plumber (as opposed to fittings already acquired by the utility under a separate contract). A contract for installation works or services alone is in general classified as a works contract, but this provision probably has the effect

---

[39] See pp. 128–130.
[40] See pp. 449–450.
[41] This refers to the case where the contracts let by the agent are let *on behalf of* the utility, so that the utility itself becomes the principal contracting party. Where the provider managing the work lets the contracts on his own behalf, this is probably an ordinary contract for the carrying out of works, done through subcontractors.
[42] See pp. 128–130.

of placing in the category of supply contracts contracts involving installation which have as their main object the supply of products.[43]

"Purchase" includes both the case where the consideration is given in installments and where it is not.[44] It includes a purchase conditional upon the occurrence of a particular event. This could be an external event, or the exercise of an option by the buyer or seller under the contract.

"Hire" is expressly stated to cover both the case in which the utility becomes the owner of the goods after the period of hire (for example, a contract of hire purchase) and where it does not.

As with the public sector regulations, the Utilities Regulations do not attempt an exhaustive definition of "goods",[45] but regulation 2(1) states that "goods" *include* electricity; substances, growing crops and things attached to and forming part of the land which are agreed to be severed before the purchase or hire under the supply contract; aircraft; vehicles; and ships.[46] It is also expressly provided in that regulation that in the case of entities in the telecommunications sector the expression "goods" covers telecommunications software services, "software services" being defined as the design or adaption of software.[47] It has already been explained in considering the equivalent definition of "goods" under the public sector Supply Regulations that there is some debate over whether something should be classified as goods where it is a concrete item which is the product of an activity other than simple manufacture, and that it is possible that *bespoke* software is not goods, so that its purchase is considered the subject-matter of a "services" contract.[48] This express provision above, however, makes it clear that all telecommunications software is to be regarded as goods in the cases mentioned, whether it is bespoke or "off the shelf". The distinction between goods and services is of particular importance where the alternative to defining the item as "goods" is that its provision is treated as a service in the non-priority category; if it is treated as goods, regulation will be much more stringent.

"Goods" does not naturally include land, and the express reference to things severed from the land further indicates that land itself is not included.[49]

---

[43] See further pp. 426–427 and 431.

[44] Utilities Regulation 2(1).

[45] The term "goods" and the similar term "products" have been used in other English statutes. However, domestic definitions are unlikely to be helpful, since the meaning of goods in this context is probably, a matter of European law to which existing domestic definitions are not relevant.

[46] "Ship" is further defined in the same regulations as a boat or other description of vessel used in navigation.

[47] Utilities Regulation 2(1) (definitions of "goods" and "software services").

[48] On this debate see further pp. 130–131.

[49] On the position of contracts for land see pp. 439–440.

(d) SERVICES CONTRACTS

(i) CONCEPT OF A SERVICES CONTRACT

A services contract is defined under Utilities Regulation 2(1) as one under which a utility "engages a person to provide services".[50] "Services" are not expressly defined.

Certain contracts are expressly excluded from the definition, and thus are not "services contracts" even though they may involve provision of services.

First, works contracts and supply contracts are excluded from the definition of service contracts.[51] Thus, although the carrying out of works clearly involves the provision of services, contracts for works are not "services contracts". Contracts which are for goods are not covered, as these are supply contracts.[52]

Also excluded is "a contract of employment or other contract of service".[53] There is a parallel exclusion from the definition of "public services contracts" under the public sector Services Regulations. Its scope has already been examined in considering those regulations in Chapter 5, and readers are referred to that discussion.[54]

There is also an exclusion for a contract under which a utility "engages a person to provide services to the public lying within its responsibility and under which the consideration given by the utility consists of or includes the right to exploit the provision of the services"[55] – that is a services "concession". The issue of concession contracts is considered further below.[56]

Finally, it may be noted that contracts for certain services, such as voice telephony and arbitration services, are specifically excluded from the regulations. These exclusions are also considered further below.[57]

---

[50] The Utilities Directive itself does not define public service contracts by reference to provision of services, but simply provides that the concept shall apply to all contracts which are not works or supply contracts and are not otherwise expressly excluded (Utilities Directive Article 1(4)(c)). This approach – which is also adopted in the public sector Services Directive – is curious, since it seems to bring within the ambit of the directive, contracts which do not involve procurement, such as contracts to settle legal disputes, which were obviously not intended to be covered. The Court of Justice must construe the directive as excluding contracts which do not involve provision of services since the legal basis of the relevant provisions in the directive is the rules on provisions of services.

[51] Utilities Regulation 2(1), definition of "services contract".

[52] Strictly speaking, there could be an overlap between "goods" and "services", since they are not defined as mutually exclusive. It is not necessary to consider this point; anything which is goods is covered under the supply rules because of the express provision to this effect, so that the only question in defining the relationship between the two sets of regulations is the definition of "goods". In practice, "services" is likely to be construed to cover only things which are not goods.

[53] Ibid.

[54] See pp. 131–132.

[55] Definition of "services contract" in Utilities Regulation 2(1).

[56] See p. 460.

[57] See p. 424.

(ii) THE DISTINCTION BETWEEN "PART A" AND "PART B" SERVICES CONTRACTS

I. Nature and effect of the distinction

The Utilities Regulations do not apply in the same way to all services contracts: like the public sector Services Regulations, they apply in their entirety only to contracts designated "Part A services contracts".[58] Other contracts – those for "Part B" services – are subject only to very limited regulation.

A Part A services contract is a contract for the services listed in Part A of Schedule 4 to the regulations.[59] The classification used is the United Nations Central Products Classification (CPC). Part A covers, *inter alia*, maintenance and repair of equipment and vehicles; some transport services; financial services; research and development for the utility's own purposes; accounting services; management consultancy; computer services; architectural and planning services; advertising; building cleaning and property management; publishing and printing; and sewerage and sanitation services. The list is similar to (although not identical with) that for Part A services contracts under the public sector Services Regulations. Details of which services are considered by the Community to fall into these categories may be ascertained by consulting the Community's draft Common Procurement Vocabulary (CPV).[60] Part A services are also sometimes referred to as "priority services".

The other type of public services contract is a "Part B services contract". This is defined as a contract for those services listed in Part B of Schedule 4[61] (sometimes referred to as "non-priority services"). Since this list includes a reference to "other services" (item 27 of the Schedule), in the sense of all services not expressly listed in the Schedule, a service which is not listed in Part A automatically falls within Part B. The only obligations applying to the award procedure for Part B contracts[62] are those in regulation 12 on technical specifications[63]; those in regulation 23 on contract award notices[64]; and those under regulation 27(2) concerning submission of statistical and other reports,[65] for transmission to the Commission.[66]

Part A services are those on which the open market regime is likely to have the most impact, taking into account factors such as the potential

---

[58] Utilities Regulation 5(1).
[59] Utilities Regulation 2(3)(a).
[60] On the CPV see pp. 69–70.
[61] Utilities Regulation 2(3)(b).
[62] See Utilities Regulation 5(2).
[63] See Chap. 11.
[64] See pp. 547–549
[65] On this see pp. 552–553. Also relevant is Utilities Regulation 29, containing the rules on notices. Regulation 29(5) provides that an authority may send a notice to the *Official Journal* relating to a services contract, even though this is not required.
[66] It is expressly stated in Utilities Regulation 5(2) that the rules in Regulation 28 on responsibility for obtaining reports are to apply.

for cross-border trade, economic importance, and the availability of savings. Another relevant factor was the extent of information available about each service. It was noted in Chapter 5 that in its review of the public sector Services Directive under Article 43 of that directive the Commission is obliged to consider the possibilities for applying all the provisions of the directive to Part B services. However, whilst there is also an obligation under Article 44 of the Utilities Directive to review that directive after four years of operation, there is no specific mention of a duty to consider the extension of that directive to Part B services.

II. Classification of contracts involving both Part A and Part B services

General

Where a contract involves both Part A and Part B services, its classification is determined by ascertaining the value of the consideration attributable to the Part A services on the one hand, and to the Part B services on the other. If the value of Part A services is greater than the Part B services it is a Part A contract; if equal to or less than the value of the Part B services, it is a Part B contract.[67]

Some criticism can be made of this approach, as was explained in Chapter 5 in considering the equivalent rule in the public sector.[68]

Contracts divided into lots

An award may sometimes be divided into lots in such a way as to give firms the choice of bidding/negotiating either for both the Part A and Part B services, or for the Part A or Part B services alone. In this case it appears that there are several possible "proposed contracts" for the purpose of the regulations – the "mixed" contract, which will be either a Part A or Part B contract, depending on the relative value of the different services; a separate Part A services contract, for the Part A services alone; and a separate Part B contract for the Part B services alone. If the value of the Part A services exceeds that of the Part B services, the "mixed" contract is a Part B contract and subject only to limited regulation; but it appears that the Part A services must nevertheless be advertised under the regulations as a separate Part A contract.[69]

III. Packaging and separation of Part A and Part B services

As in the public sector, the different treatment of Part A and Part B services may appear to create some, limited, opportunities for reducing

---

[67] Utilities Regulation 2(3).
[68] See pp. 136–137.
[69] It is submitted that this case is different in principle from the case where it is the nature of the purchases – rather than the nature of the contract – which is not known at the start of the award procedure: on the former case see p. 432.

the impact of the regulations, through the way in which contracts are packaged.

First, where for commercial reasons a purchaser would normally wish to advertise both types of services in a single contract, with the value of Part A services exceeding the value of Part B services, it may be tempted to advertise the Part B services separately, to avoid the full application of the rules to the Part B services. There seems to be nothing in the regulations to prevent this and it does not infringe the policy of the procurement rules, which do not seek to ensure the full regulation of non-priority services.[70] Of course, if it is done in order to favour a domestic service provider (for example, to award the Part B services to a specific domestic firm for industrial development reasons), this could be a breach of the E.C. Treaty or of Utilities Regulation 4(3) prohibiting discrimination.

A second way in which a utility may utilise the Part A–Part B distinction is by packaging Part A services, which are valued above the threshold and would otherwise have been purchased separately, along with Part B services of the same or greater value. (Opportunities for such packaging are of course limited in practice, but may occasionally arise.) There is nothing in the regulations which expressly prohibits such packaging. The Court of Justice may, however, be willing to adopt a purposive approach to the rules and imply such a limitation by analogy with the principle embodied in Utilities Regulation 10(18)[71] which prohibits *splitting* contracts to avoid the regulations: this is simply the reverse of joining contracts together for this purpose. Of course, it will often be difficult to prove that purchases have been joined together simply to avoid the rules; but it may be possible, in particular where the packaging involves a departure from the utility's own previous practice.

(iii) EXCLUDED SERVICES

As with the public sector Services Regulations, contracts for certain types of services are excluded from the Utilities Regulations. Thus, as with the public sector, services contract are divided into three types – those for Part A services, which are subject to full regulation; those for Part B services, which are subject to very limited rules; and those for "excluded" services which are not subject to regulation at all.

---

[70] A provision which might be cited in favour of a contrary view is Utilities Regulation 10(18), which provides that a utility shall not enter into separate contracts with the intention of avoiding the application of the regulations to those contracts. On a literal reading this could be interpreted to cover the deliberate split referred to above: "avoiding the application" of the regulations could be construed to cover avoiding the application of certain parts of the regulations to a contract, as well as the regulations as a whole. However, it was argued in the context of the public sector Services Regulations that the equivalent provision in those regulations, Services Regulation 7(11) does not have this effect: see pp. 137–138. The points made there apply equally in the utilities context.

[71] On this provision see p. 452.

Exclusions, which have the same scope as parallel exclusions in the public sector[72] are exclusions of contracts for the "acquisition, development, production or co-production of programme material for radio or television by a broadcaster or for the purchasing of broadcasting time" (Utilities Regulations 6(k)); contracts for voice telephony, telex, radio-telephony, paging and satellite services (Utilities Regulation 6(l)); contracts for arbitration services, and conciliation services (Utilities Regulation 6(m)); and contracts for central banking services (Utilities Regulation 6(o)).

Utilities Regulation 6(p), again like the public sector Services Regulations, further excludes contracts for research and development services, a provision which aims to exclude from the rules research activities funded or assisted by utilities for public benefit. The exclusion does not apply, however, where the benefits of the research and development are to accrue exclusively to the utility for use in its own affairs *and* the services are to be wholly paid for by the utility. The scope and purpose of these provisions has been explained in Chapter 5.[73]

Utilities Regulation 6(n) also excludes contracts for the issue, purchase, sale or transfer of securities or other financial instruments. This exclusion is narrower than that applying in the public sector, since, unlike the public sector exemption,[74] it does not extend to all contracts *connected* with the issue, etc, of securities or other financial instruments. This suggests that transactions by financial intermediaries are themselves covered, although the general methods for placing such contracts do not fit well with the rules prescribed in the Community rules.

As with the public sector, neither the relevant directive nor regulations give express guidance on the treatment of contracts involving both excluded and non-excluded services. This issue has already been considered in Chapter 5 on the public sector.[75] Clearly the same approach should be adopted in both public and utilities sectors.

(e) CONTRACTS FOR TWO OR MORE OF GOODS, WORKS AND OTHER SERVICES

(i) INTRODUCTION

A single contract may be one for both goods and services; for both goods and works; for works and other services; or even for goods, works and other services together. In all these cases the contract must be classified as a supply contract, works contract or services contract to determine precisely which rules apply: a contract cannot fall within more than one of these categories.

---

[72] See comment see pp. 138–140.
[73] See pp. 139–140.
[74] See p. 139.
[75] See pp. 140–141.

(ii) THE BOUNDARY BETWEEN SUPPLY AND SERVICES CONTRACTS

As has already been explained in the context of the public sector, contracts often involve the purchase of both goods and non-construction services: for example, a contract for both the supply of products – for example, vehicles – and their maintenance. Classification of such a "mixed" contract as either a supply contract or a services contract may affect whether the contract is subject to regulation at all and may also affect procedures: in particular where the services are Part B services, if the contract is a services contract it is classified as a Part B contract and regulated only in a very limited way.

The general rule is that the contract is a supply contract if the value of the consideration attributable to the goods (or the goods plus installation) is equal to or greater than the value attributable to the services.[76-77] If, on the other hand, the value of the goods (or goods plus installation) is less than or equal to the value of the services, the contract is a public services contract.[78] Thus, for example, a contract involving the provision of machinery worth 300,000 ECUs and maintenance services worth 200,000 ECUs is a supply contract; but if the position is reversed and the maintenance services are worth 300,000 ECUs and the machinery only 200,000 ECUs, it is a services contract. If both are worth 250,000 ECUs, it is a services contract.

This classification rule applies regardless of whether the services are Part A or Part B services.[79]

One consequence of this is that where goods of a value above the threshold are purchased along with Part B services of greater value, the purchase of goods is subject only to the limited regulation applicable to Part B services contracts. This position was criticised in Chapter 5 in the context of the public sector regulations as unduly lenient,[80] and the same criticism is valid in relation to the utilities sector. As was suggested in that sector, it is likely, at least, that if utilities deliberately packaged contracts solely to take advantage of this rule, then the more stringent regime covering goods would apply.[81] The position may be different

---

[76-77] Definition of supply contract in Utilities Regulation 2(1) which provides that where services as well as goods are provided a contract is only a supply contract where the value attributable to the goods (or goods plus their installation) is equal to or greater than that attributable to the services. Where the contract is not a supply contract under this definition – as where the value of the services exceeds the value of the goods (or goods plus installation) – it falls under the definition of a services contract which as explained above, covers any contract involving some provision of services which is not a supply or works contract (or other excluded contract).

[78] Untilities Regulation 2(1).

[79] Utilities Regulation 2(1) does not distinguish in setting out the rule between Part A and Part B Services. It appears that this faithfully implements the intention of the directive, which also makes no distinction, although there is no specific provision to make the position clear, such as appears in Article 2 of the public sector Services Directive.

[80] See p. 143.

[81] See p. 143.

under the WTO Agreement on Government Procurement: under that Agreement a contract for non-regulated services (which are equivalent to Part B services), together with regulated goods which alone exceed the threshold value for supply contracts, are probably regulated under the Agreement, even where the value of the non-regulated services exceeds that of the goods.[82]

Theoretically, a single contract might involve goods, Part A services, and Part B services. The literal wording of the Utilities Regulations (and the relevant provisions of the Utilities Directive) suggest that such a contract must first be classified as either a supply contract or a services contract, according to whether the predominant element is the goods (or goods plus installation), or the services (the Part A services and Part B services together). Where the value of the services is greater, so that the contract is a services contract, the wording of the rules indicate that its classification as a Part A or Part B services contract is then determined by the respective value of the Part A and Part B services.

It is possible in such a case that the value of the Part A services plus the goods – elements upon which the Community seeks to apply the full rules – is greater than the value of the Part B services – that is, the element which the Community does not seek to regulate fully; however, the outcome is that the contract is not subject to full regulation, but only to the limited regime applying to Part B services. It was suggested in Chapter 5 in relation to the public sector that the Court of Justice may seek to avoid such a conclusion by departing from the literal wording of the rules, and classifying such a contract as a Part A services contract[83]; and the same may apply in the utilities context.

A firm may be permitted to bid for goods and services in separate lots, as well as together: for example, with an award for the supply and maintenance of equipment, firms may be given the choice of bidding for both, or bidding for either supply or maintenance only. In such a case it appears that there is a separate proposed supply contract (for the equipment) and services contract (for the maintenance), as well as the "mixed" contract (for both the equipment and its maintenance). Thus, for example, where the mixed contract is a services contract because the services element predominates, the contract is a services contract; but if the goods may be bid for separately, the rules on supply contracts will apply to the purchase of the goods. This is significant where the services are Part B services, since a Part B services contract is subject to only light regulation.

As in the public sector, a contract which is for the supply and installation of goods (where the installation does not constitute works) is probably in general to be treated as a supply contract, even if the value of the installation services exceeds that of the goods, since it is expressly

---

[82] See note 12 on p. 137.
[83] See further p. 143.

stated that a contract for supply plus installation is a supply contract. This will apply unless the goods are an insignificant element of the contract so that its object cannot be said to be the supply of goods – for example, a contract for the installation of electrical wiring.

(iii) THE BOUNDARY BETWEEN WORKS/SERVICES CONTRACTS AND WORKS/SUPPLY CONTRACTS

I. The works/services boundary
Whether a contract involving both works and non-construction services is a works contract or a services contract is an important question since the threshold for regulation is much higher for works contracts than for services contracts.

As explained above, the regulations define works contracts as con-tracts for carrying out works or a work, and the procurement of a work to the utility's specification; whilst services contracts are those for the provision of services which are not works or supply contracts nor otherwise specifically excluded from the definition. There is nothing in the regulations themselves to deal with the classification of contracts for both works and non-construction services, to parallel the provision discussed in the previous section which governs contracts for both services and supplies.

However, the directive itself states in the definition of works contracts in Article 1(4)(b) that such contracts "may" in addition to work(s) cover "supplies and services necessary for their execution". This makes it clear that the provision of non-construction services under the contract will not prevent it from being a works contract; and the provision appears to indicate that this will be the case not only when their value is less than that of the works but also where their value exceeds those of the works themselves. This means that a contract involving 1 million ECUs of works and 2 million ECUs of non-construction services which are necessary to the works is a works contract, and as such free from regulation as it does not meet the threshold for applying the regulations to works contracts. It is unregulated even though the value of non-construction services to be provided is greater than the works, and in isolation exceeds the threshold for applying the regulations to supply or services contracts.

Such a rule might lead utilities deliberately to package non-construction services along with works in order to avoid applying the regulations to those supplies or non-construction services. However, it is to be noted that Article 4(1)(b) of the directive only refers to supplies or services which are "necessary" to the execution of the works. Thus, this provision of the directive cannot be relied upon unless this condition is met; if it is not met, it is necessary to resort to the general principles of classification as outlined below.

Where the non-construction services are not "necessary" to the execution of the works under Article 4(1)(b), what is the position? A literal reading of the directive and regulations suggests that a contract involving works is a works contract even if *other* services are also provided and are of greater value and greater importance than the works, since the contract falls within the definition of a works contract, and there is no express provision to take it out of that category and classify it as a services contract. However, it was explained in Chapter 5 that in the context of the public sector rules the Court of Justice has indicated in the case of *Gestion Hotelera* that in general the classification depends on whether the services are incidental to the works, or the works incidental to the services,[84] and this test might also be applied in the utilities sector. It was explained in Chapter 5 that it is not clear, however, what is meant by "incidental" – whether the test is the primary purpose of the contract, or whether the test is one of the relative value of the works and services, or whether both are appropriate in different circumstances.[84a]

Where the relevant rules entail the conclusion that the contract is a works contract, because of the higher works threshold the services would, under the normal threshold rules, be unregulated, even though the services themselves exceed the threshold for services contracts. For example, a contract for 1 million ECUs of works plus 500,000 of services operating the works which is classified as a works contract – for example, a contract both to build sanitation facilities and then to operate and manage them – appears not to be covered, since its value of 1,500,000 ECUs is well below the works threshold; thus under the normal threshold rules the services need not be advertised, although alone they exceed the services threshold. This would indeed be the result in the public sector. However, Utilities Regulation 10(15) provides that where the works contract is below the normal "works" threshold and goods and services which are not "necessary" for the execution of the works are to be provided under the contract, the threshold for the contract is to be calculated as if it were a supply or services contract, as appropriate,[85] the consideration being that which the utility expects to give for the goods or services. Thus, whilst such a contract is still technically a works contract, for threshold purposes it is treated as a supply or services contract.[86] The test is not whether the utility packaged the contract in this way with the intention of evading the rules, but whether objectively the goods or

---

[84] See pp. 144–145.

[84a] See further pp. 145–146.

[85] This clearly refers to the method used for determining whether a contract for both supplies and services is a supply or services contract which, as explained above, depends on which element represents the greater part of the contract in value terms.

[86] This makes it less important what is meant by "incidental", since the contract is regulated at the services threshold regardless of whether it is technically a works or a services contract. However, this may make a difference in that where it is a works contract only the services element is calculated as part of the consideration, whereas if it is a services contract the incidental works are also included in valuing the contract.

services were "necessary" for the execution of the works. Thus in the example given above of the contract both to build and to operate a sanitation facility, the contract would need to be advertised since the value of operating services (500,000 ECUs) exceeds the "services" threshold, and they cannot be said to be "necessary" for the works. A works contract may fall within this provision even if it were shown to be convenient and justifiable from a commercial viewpoint to package works along with certain supplies or services, although these latter are not "necessary" for the works themselves.[87] This seems an appropriate solution since the contract may attract interest amongst service providers rather than just construction firms, and this makes it valuable to apply the directive's procedures to the services at the lower threshold.

On the basis of the above, the principles governing "mixed" works and non-construction services contracts may be summarised as follows:

(i) Where the services are "necessary" for the execution of the works, the contract is always a works contract.

(ii) Where the services are not necessary for the execution of the works (for example, a contract both to build and operate a work), the contract is a services contract where the works are "incidental" to the services. This may involve a test based on the main object of the contract, or alternatively, may relate to the respective value of the two elements.

(iii) Where the services are not necessary for the execution of the works, but are "incidental" to those works the contract is a works contract. However, where the contract does not meet the "works" threshold, the regulations will still apply in this case where the value of the services meets the "services" threshold (although technically the contract is still a works contract).

It can be seen that the applicable rules may be slightly different from those applying under the public sector regulations, where there is no equivalent of Article 4(1)(b), nor of the special provision applying to thresholds for services which are not necessary for the execution of the works. It is difficult to see, however, that there is any justification for different rules in the public sector and utilities rules and, as argued in Chapter 5, it is desirable that the utilities rules should apply in the public sector as well.

---

[87] This is intended to implement Utilities Directive Article 13(12) which expressly prohibits utilities from adding supplies and services to a works contract with the result that the application of the Utilities Directive is avoided. It is submitted that this provision is not intended to have the effect that to package works with non-necessary supplies and services is as such a breach of the regulations; this would be unfortunate since such contracts may be commercially convenient. Rather, its effect is merely to render it unlawful not to follow the procedures under the regulations where awarding the contract, where those procedures would apply if the supplies/services were not packaged with the works. This effect is clearly provided for by the United Kingdom regulations, as explained above, which are signficantly clearer than the directive itself in spelling out what is required of utilities.

II. The works/supply boundary

As noted above, the Utilities Directive states in the definition of works contracts in Article 1(4)(b) that such contracts "may" in addition to work(s) cover "supplies and services necessary for their execution". Thus, it appears that a contract involving works and also supplies "necessary" to the execution of those works – for example, the bricks and roofing materials used in construction – are always works contracts, even where the supplies are of a greater value than the construction services. For example, a contract involving 1 million ECUs of labour and 2 million ECUs of supplies used in the construction is a works contract, and as such free from regulation as it does not meet the threshold for applying the regulations to works contracts. This is a sensible solution since such contracts are of interest solely to construction firms supplying their own products.[88] As noted above, the same principle applies with contracts for both works, on the one hand, and services necessary to the execution of those works on the other.

It is necessary also to consider the position where any supplies provided are not "necessary" to the works – for example, where a builder is asked also to provide certain fittings and attachments for the building to be constructed, but will not install these himself. This is, of course, a less likely scenario. It has been explained above that a contract involving the carrying out of works, or the procurement, by any means, of a work to the utility's specifications is a works contract, whilst a contract for the acquisition of goods, or of goods plus installation, is a supply contract. Thus a contract involving both works and goods falls prima facie within both the works and supply categories where the goods in question are not actually necessary to the execution of the works. However, it is unlikely that this was intended and probably the Court of Justice will apply the "incidental" test: a contract will be a works contract where the goods are incidental to the works and a supply contract where the works are incidental to the goods. However, even where supplies are incidental to works and the contract is therefore a works contract, the contract will be regulated where the supply threshold is met, by virtue of Utilities Regulation 10(15). As explained above, this provides that where the works contract is below the normal "works" threshold and goods and services which are not "necessary" for the execution of the works are to be provided, the threshold for the contract is to be calculated as if it were a supply contract,[89]

---

[88] It will not directly interest those who are suppliers of products who would not in practice think of bidding on the contract and providing the products whilst subcontracting the construction work.

[89] This clearly refers to the method used for determining whether a contract for both supplies and services is a supply or services contract which, as explained above, depends on which element represents the greater part of the contract in value terms.

the consideration being that which the utility expects to give for the goods.[90]

On the basis of the above, the principles governing "mixed" works and supplies contracts are probably the same as mixed works/non-construction services contracts, and may be summarised as follows:

(i) Where the supplies are "necessary" for the execution of the works, the contract is always a works contract.

(ii) Where the supplies are not necessary for the execution of the works, the contract is a supply contract where the works are "incidental" to the supplies. This may involve a test based on the main object of the contract, or alternatively, may relate to the respective value of the two elements.

(iii) Where the supplies are not necessary for the execution of the works, but are "incidental" to those works the contract is a works contract. However, where the contract does not meet the "works" threshold, the regulations will still apply in this case where the value of the supplies meets the "supplies" threshold (although technically the contract is still a works contract).

Again, the applicable rules appear at present to be different from those applying under the public sector regulations, although there is no reason to adopt a different approach under the two regimes. It was suggested in Chapter 5 that the utilities rules should in fact be applied to the public sector.

The fact that a contract for supply of goods plus installation is expressly stated in the supply rules to be a supply contract, as noted above, would appear to indicate that, whatever the general test, a contract of which the object is the supply of goods is a supply contract even if the value of any installation works exceeds the value of the goods.

(iv) CONTRACTS FOR SUPPLIES, WORKS AND OTHER SERVICES

Some contracts involve provision of goods, works *and* other types of services – for example, a contract for the design and construction of a work, along with its management for a specified period. Where the goods or services provided are "necessary" for the works, the contract will probably be a works contract by virtue of Article 1(4)(b) of the Utilities Directive, referred to above.

Where this is not the case – for example, with services for managing the completed work – the Court of Justice will no doubt apply the same test as is adopted for delimiting the works/services and works/supply

---

[90] This makes it less important to define what is meant by "incidental", since the contract is regulated at the supply threshold regardless of whether it is technically a works or a supply contract. However, this may make a difference in that where it is a works contract only the supply element is calculated as part of the consideration, whereas if it is a supply contract the incidental works are also included in valuing the contract.

boundary in other cases where the services/supplies are not "necessary" for the works (either a "main object" or "relative value" test). However, the technical classification of the contract is, again, relatively unimportant, since, under Utilities Regulation 10(15) as outlined above, even where the contract is classified as a works contract the supplies and services are regulated where their value together exceeds the supply/services threshold.[91]

(v) POSITION WHERE THE NATURE OF THE CONTRACT IS NOT KNOWN AT THE START OF THE PROCEDURE

It is possible that it is not known at the start of the award procedure whether the contract will be a supply, works or services contract. This may be the case, for example, in a procedure to purchase computer software, where the specifications allow for variations and the purchaser's needs could be met by either off-the-shelf software (goods) or bespoke software (which might in some cases be services). The Utilities Directives and Regulations assume, however, as do the public sector rules, that contracts can be classified prior to commencing the award procedure. As was suggested in Chapter 5 on the public sector, it would appear acceptable to classify the contract by means of the category into which it is most likely to fall.[92]

(f) ASSET SALES AND OTHER TRANSACTIONS INVOLVING WORKS/SUPPLIES/SERVICES PLUS OTHER CONSIDERATIONS

Chapter 5 on the public sector discussed the question of whether the procurement rules apply where an entity wishes to enter into a procurement contract which is part of some larger transaction – for example, where on a sale of a business previously carried out by the entity, that entity guarantees to the purchaser of the business future work with the entity in order to help the business get started in its new hands. The position in this case will be the same in both the public and utilities sectors, and readers are therefore referred on this point to the discussion in Chapter 5.[93]

---

[91] It may be assumed that the "appropriate" threshold for the purpose of the Utilities Regulations is the supply threshold where the value of the supplies is greater than that of the services, and the services threshold in other cases.

[92] Another view might be that where one of two types of contract is possible, the rules relating to both should be followed, similar to the principle which it was suggested earlier should apply to contracts in lots where two different types of contract may be awarded, as to which see pp. 421–422.

[93] See pp. 148–150.

5. GENERAL EXCLUSIONS

(1) GENERAL PRINCIPLES

Certain exemptions from the Utilities Regulations which relate to specific utility sectors have already been considered in section 2 of this chapter, in outlining the coverage of the regulations for each of the sectors concerned. These cover: purchases of energy and fuel for energy by entities in the energy sector[94]; purchases of water by entities in the water sector[95]; certain transport entities who operate under competitive conditions[96]; certain telecommunications services[97]; and energy utilities with an exemption granted by the European Commission pursuant to Article 3 of the Utilities Directive.[98]

In addition, Utilities Regulation 6 provides for a number of general exemptions from the regulations, and there is also an exemption provided in Utilities Regulation 8 for certain contracts awarded to entities connected to the utility (the "affiliated" undertakings exemption). In accordance with the usual principles applying to derogations from Community law rules, these derogations must be interpreted strictly.[99]

(2) ACTIVITIES OUTSIDE THE COMMUNITIES

Utilities Regulation 6(c) exempts from the regulations any contract "for the purpose of carrying out any activity outside the territory of the Communities".

However, this does not apply where the carrying out of that activity involves the physical use of a network or geographical area within the Communities. Thus whilst exploration for and extraction of oil, for example, is an activity generally covered by the directives, a utility engaged in such activities in the North Sea need not follow the procurement rules when making contracts for similar activities in the Middle East.

(3) ACQUISITIONS FOR SALE, REHIRE, ETC

Under Utilities Regulation 6(c) there is an exemption for contracts which are made for the purpose of acquiring goods, services or works in

---

[94] See pp. 395–396.
[95] See p. 391.
[96] See pp. 407–408.
[97] See pp. 409–410.
[98] See pp. 398–403.
[99] Case C–328/92, *Commission v. Spain* [1994] E.C.R.–I 1569; case C–324/93, *R. v. Secretary of State for the Home Department, ex p. Evans Medical*, judgment of March 28, 1995, para. 48.

order to resell them or to hire or provide them to another. This was included because it was felt that in carrying out such activities a utility will generally be operating in a competitive market and, being under clear commercial pressures, is not likely to be susceptible to government pressure to favour national industry. To require utilities to follow the procurement rules in relation to such activities would place them at a competitive disadvantage in operating in these markets. It was desired to ensure, however, that the exemption cannot be relied on in those cases where ordinary competitive pressures do not exist, and thus it is provided that the exemption does not apply where the utility has a special or exclusive right to sell, hire or provide the goods/works/services, or where other persons are not free to sell, hire, or provide them under the same conditions. In practice, many situations in which utilities engage in such activities – for example, the case of a United Kingdom electricity supplier which may also sell electrical goods to consumers – are not caught by the rules even apart from this exemption since they are not "utility" activities for the purpose of the rules.[1-2]

The Commission may request a utility to notify it of any activities excluded under this exemption.[3]

(4) SECRECY AND SECURITY EXEMPTIONS

Utilities Regulation 6(d) contains exemptions concerned with secrecy and security. These cover (i) contracts "classified as secret" (ii) the case where the work, goods or services provided under the contract "must be accompanied by special security measures in accordance with the laws, regulations or administrative provisions of any part of the United Kingdom"; and (iii) the case when the "protection of the basic interests of the security of the United Kingdom require" an exclusion. Identical exemptions apply in the public sector, and their scope and application has already been discussed in Chapter 5.[4]

It may be noted that there is no specific exemption for contracts falling within Article 223 of the E.C. Treaty, which contains a general exemption from the Treaty for certain activities relating to military equipment. Such an exemption – which is found in the public sector regulations – was no doubt omitted from the Utilities Regulations because it was considered irrelevant for utilities. This issue is considered further in Chapter 17 on defence procurement.

[1-2] Utilities making contracts for the purposes of "non-utility" activities are not covered: see pp. 411–413.

[3] Utilities Directive Article 7(2). It is also provided that it may periodically publish in the Official Journal lists of exclusions (provided that it respects any "sensitive commercial aspects" of the information which are pointed out to it when the information is forwarded by the utility).

[4] See pp. 152–153.

(5) CONTRACTS PURSUANT TO INTERNATIONAL AGREEMENTS INVOLVING OTHER STATES

Utilities Regulation 6(e)(i) excludes certain contracts entered into pursuant to an international agreement to which the United Kingdom and a state which is not a "relevant state" under the regulations are both party.[5] This applies where the contract is for the purchase of goods, works or other services which are for the joint implementation or exploitation of a project pursuant to that agreement, and where procedures different from the Community procedures apply to the contract. A similar exemption applies under the public sector regulations, and matters relating to this exemption have already been considered in Chapter 5 on the public sector.[6]

(6) CONTRACTS PURSUANT TO INTERNATIONAL AGREEMENTS ON THE STATIONING OF TROOPS

Utilities Regulation 6(e)(ii) excludes a contract entered into pursuant to an international agreement relating to the stationing of troops where awarded under different procedures from the Community procedures, an exemption which again is found in the public sector regulations. Such contracts are still, however, generally subject to the rules in the E.C. Treaty, where relevant.

(7) CONTRACTS OF INTERNATIONAL ORGANISATIONS

Utilities Regulation 6(e)(iii) further excludes agreements made in accordance with the contract award procedures of organisations of which only states – or states plus international organisations – are members, such as the United Nations. This exemption also appears in the public sector regulations and has been considered in that context.[7]

(8) PROVISION BY A CONTRACTING AUTHORITY PURSUANT TO EXCLUSIVE RIGHTS

Utilities Regulation 6(i) excludes from the regulations a contract under which services are provided by a body which is a contracting authority

---

[5] On which states are relevant states see pp. 908–909. Certain other states are also entitled to benefit from the regulations, but are not referred to since their rights were conferred after the regulations were adopted. Thus the exemption cannot be relied on in relation to these states.
[6] See pp. 154–155.
[7] See p. 155.

with the meaning of the public sector Services Regulations, and which has either (i) an exclusive right to provide the services or (ii) an exclusive right which is necessary for their provision. This right must be given pursuant to any published law, regulation or administrative provision (which must be compatible with the E.C. Treaty). A similar exemption for purchases from contracting authorities with such rights applies for services contracts subject to the public sector regulations, and its application was considered further in Chapter 5 on the public sector.[8] The inclusion of the exemption in the Utilities Regulations means that utilities, also, may be "tied" to centralised agencies with exclusive rights to supply certain services. It should be emphasised, however, that the exemption can only be used for purchases from a "contracting authority". As with the public sector rules there is no similar exemption for any exclusive right relating to provision of supplies or works.

(9) CONTRACTS AWARDED TO AFFILIATED UNDERTAKINGS AND JOINT VENTURE PARTNERS

(a) GENERAL PRINCIPLES

It is common in the utilities sector, especially with privately owned utilities, for activities to be carried on by a group or association of entities acting together. Often it is convenient for certain activities relating to the "group" enterprise, or enterprises, to be carried on by a separate legal entity – for example, for tax or management reasons. For these reasons separate entities are sometimes formed for the sole reason of providing a particular service – for example, accountancy or computer services – to another entity, or to a number of other entities in the same group. Alternatively, the group structure may arise as a result of the acquisition of one company by another.

Joint ventures, where different entities come together for a single project or activity are also common. Generally these involve entities with different expertise and skills, which each provide different services in connection with the project.

Both types of arrangement involve the provision of services by one legal entity to another under contractual arrangements, even though the different entities may for practical purposes be acting as a single economic unit. Clearly it would significantly undermine the possibilities for such convenient business arrangements if the contracts in question were required to be awarded in accordance with the Utilities Directive and Regulations: the work could not then be placed directly with other companies in the group or with the joint venture partner, but would have

---

[8] It may be noted that the exemption in the utilities sector, unlike that in the public sector, applies not just to a contract which is a "services contract", but to any contract under which services are provided, which could, in theory be a supply or works contract.

to be awarded through a competition held under the Community rules. In view of the practical importance and convenience of such arrangements in the utilities sector, it was decided to include an exemption to cover these situations.

The exemption is contained in Utilities Regulation 8. This provision exempts from the regulations a contract which it is proposed to award to: (a) a "relevant affiliated undertaking"[9] (that is, another entity in the same group); and
(b) a joint venture partner.[10]
The scope of the exemptions is closely defined, and is elaborated below.

In both cases the exemption applies only to services contracts, and not works or supply contracts. Thus the exemptions could not be used, for example, to allow a company within the group to provide car rental services to others, since such rental transactions are classified as supply contracts.

(b) THE EXEMPTION FOR "RELEVANT AFFILIATED UNDERTAKINGS"

For the purpose of the exemption for affiliated undertakings, an "affiliated undertaking" is defined, first, by reference to seventh Council Directive 83/349/EEC.[11] This directive provides for the consolidation of accounts for certain entities within the same corporate group. For utilities falling within this directive, an affiliated undertaking is one of which the accounts are, under the directive, consolidated with those of the utility.[12]

For utilities which do not fall within Directive 83/49, an affiliated undertaking is defined as one which is either a "parent undertaking", a "subsidiary undertaking" or a "fellow subsidiary undertaking" of the utility.[13] A "parent undertaking" is further defined as one over which the utility exercises a dominant influence, directly or indirectly. It is stated that a utility exercises a dominant influence over another undertaking if it possesses the greater part of that undertaking's issued share capital; controls the voting power attached to the greater part of that other's share capital; or may appoint more than half the individuals who are ultimately responsible for managing the affairs of that other undertaking. An undertaking is stated to be a subsidiary of a utility if the utility exercises a dominant influence over that other (applying the same definition of dominant influence as above). An undertaking is a fellow subsidiary of another if both are subsidiaries of the same parent.

It can be noted that these definitions are quite rigid, and that

---

[9] Utilities Regulation 8(2)(a).
[10] Utilities Regulation 8(2)(b).
[11] (1983) O.J. L193/1, as am. by Directive 90/605/EEC, [1990] O.J. L317.
[12] Utilities Regulation 8(1)(a)(i).
[13] Utilities Regulation 8(1)(a)(ii).

connected entities may frequently act together as a single unit even though the relevant definitions are not satisfied. In such cases it is not possible, however, to rely on the exemption.

The exemption applies only for affiliated undertakings which are "relevant" affiliated undertakings. This means an undertaking "which has as one activity the provision of services, and provides those services 'principally' to one or more affiliated undertakings".[14] This condition seeks to ensure that the exemption from the Community rules applies only when provision of services to others in the group is the *raison d'etre* of the service provider – where it can for practical purposes be regarded as a "branch" of the entity awarding the contract – and that it does not also obtain substantial business in the free market outside the group. It is conclusively provided that the condition is satisfied when an undertaking has been in existence for 36 months or more, and in the preceding 36 months 80 per cent or more of the undertaking's average turnover within the Member States of the provision of services of "the type or similar" to those to be provided under the proposed contract, was levied from the provision of such services to affiliated undertakings. This also applies where 80 per cent of the turnover of the service provider *plus its affiliated undertakings* satisfies this "80 per cent" condition. There is no guidance on the meaning of "similar" services for this purpose. These specific provisions are "without prejudice" to the general meaning of "principal activity".

(c) THE EXEMPTION FOR JOINT VENTURE PARTNERS

The exemption for joint venture partners applies in the case of a joint venture which is formed for the purpose of carrying out any of the activities listed in Schedule 1. The exemption covers any contract which the joint venture proposes to award to one of its members which is a utility within the meaning of the regulations, or to a "relevant affiliated undertaking" of such a utility.[15] "Relevant affiliated undertaking" has the same meaning as under (b) above.[16]

This exemption covers contracts between entities which do not have any "group" connection, but which have joined together for the purpose of a particular activity. This could be for a one-off project, a project extending over a period of years (for example, the operation of a transport concession over a fixed long term period), or even a collatoration in a particular utility activity which is envisaged to be of indefinite duration – for example, ongoing collaboration in the exploration for and extraction of fuel.

---

[14] Utilities Regulation 8(1)(b).
[15] Utilities Regulation 8(2)(b).
[16] Utilities Regulation 8(1).

It is important to note that this exemption applies only to services contracts awarded by the joint venture, and not to contracts awarded by the joint venture partners to the joint venture itself, or by partners to each other.

(d) INFORMATION REQUIREMENTS

A utility relying on the exemptions for relevant affiliated undertakings or joint ventures must, if requested by the Commission, send to the relevant Minister[17] for transmission to the Treasury[18] the names of the affiliated undertakings involved; the value of the consideration and the type of services to be provided under any services contracts excluded under these provisions; and any information which is necessary to justify the use of the exemption (which could involve, for example, information to show that provision of services to the group is the principal activity of a particular affiliated undertaking).

(e) INTRA-GROUP TRANSACTIONS WHICH ARE NOT COVERED BY THE EXEMPTION[19]

Since the regulations apply only to a contract in writing, where there is a close relationship, as with companies in the same group or parties to a joint venture, it is possible that the entities concerned might seek to avoid the various restrictions applying to the regulation 8 exemption by entering into arrangements which do not involve any formal contract. In this way it might be sought, for example, to award supply or works contracts to group members without following the Utilities Regulations, or to award services contracts to group members which do not satisfy the "principal activity" condition, discussed under (b) above. It was suggested above, however, that in determining when a "contract" exists for the purposes of the Community rules the courts are likely to look to the substance of the transaction, and not at whether it constitutes a contract under the domestic law of the relevant Member State, and thus it may be prepared to hold that certain transaction of this type are in fact subject to the Community rules.[20-21] Similarly, if a contract were not put in writing merely to evade the application of the Community rules, the Court of Justice – which does not, of course, apply the literal approach to interpretation adopted by English courts – may nevertheless apply the

---

[17] Utilities Regulation 8(3). The relevant Minister is the Minister of the Crown whose areas of responsibility are most closely connected with the functions of the utility, as conclusively determined by the Treasury: Utilities Regulation 28(1) and (2). The obligations to send the report is enforceable by the responsible Minister by mandamus: Utilities Regulation 28(3).

[18] Utilities Regulation 28(6).

[19] See further Kunzlik, "Intra-Group Transactions under the Utilities Procedurement Directive" [1993] Utilities Law Review 209.

[20-21] See pp. 414–416 and the references given here.

rules to that transaction, perhaps drawing on the analogy of the anti-avoidance provision which prohibits splitting contract for the purpose of escaping the rules.

(10) CONTRACTS FOR THE ACQUISITION OF LAND

Utilities Regulation 6(j) provides that the regulations do not apply to contracts "for the acquisition of land, including buildings and other structures, land covered with water, and any estate, interest, easement, servitude or right in or over land". It appears, however, that a contract for the construction of a work to a utility's own specification, followed by the transfer of that building and the land on which it stands, is not to be regarded as a contract "for" the acquisition of land, but as a works contract: this intention is indicated by the specific provision in the works rules which brings within the definition of a "works contract" the procurement of a work by any means.[22]

A contract for the acquisition of land plus a work of construction when at the time of the contract the work has not yet been built, but where it is built to a specification already set by the developer rather than one drawn up by the utility, probably falls within the above exclusion, which refers to contracts for the purchase of any buildings (and not just existing building, as with the public sector Services Regulations).[23]

6. FINANCIAL THRESHOLDS

(1) PURPOSE OF THE THRESHOLDS

As with the public sector rules, the utilities rules apply only to contracts above certain thresholds. These have been set with a view to identifying contracts for which there is a potential for cross-border competition, since it is with cross-border competition alone that the Community is concerned.

(2) THE APPLICABLE THRESHOLDS

In the Utilities Regulations the applicable thresholds are set out in regulation 10. The threshold figures are generally stated in the directives and regulations in European Currency Units (ECUs),[24] rather than in

---

[22] See p. 418.
[23] See p. 156.
[24] An "ECU" is defined in Utilities Regulation 2(1) as meaning the European Currency Unit as defined in Council Regulation 3180/78/EEC [1978] O.J.L 379/1, as amended by Council Regulation 2626/84/EEC [1984] O.J.L 247/1 and Council Regulation (EEC) No. 1971/89, [1989] O.J.L 189/1.

pounds sterling. The sterling equivalent (as well as the equivalent in other Community currencies) is calculated every two years and published in the *Official Journal*.[25]

As explained in Chapter 15, some utilities procurement is now covered by the World Trade Organisation Agreement on Government Procurement, and a Commission Proposal to align the Utilities Directive with that Agreement proposes amending the directive to state the thresholds in SDR, as is done in the WTO Agreement.[26]

(a) WORKS CONTRACTS

(i) THE GENERAL THRESHOLD

For works contracts the Utilities Regulations generally apply only to contracts with an estimated value of 5 million ECUs or more, net of Value Added Tax[27] – the same as for the public sector. For 1994–95 the sterling equivalent was £3,743,203, but this was to be revised again as from January 1, 1996, in accordance with the revision arrangements already noted.

Under the new WTO Agreement on Government Procurement (GPA), works contracts awarded by utilities have been regulated for the first time, with a threshold of 5 million SDR.[28] A Commission Proposal for adjusting the directives to take account of the GPA[29] proposes changing the thresholds on works in the Utilities Directive to bring it into line with the GPA threshold: this will involve expressing the threshold in terms of SDR ECU-equivalents, rather than ECUs.[30] It is proposed that this change will apply to all works contracts covered by the

---

[25] Utilities Regulation 2(5), referring back to the method of calculation set out in Utilities Directive Article 38, as published in the *Official Journal*. Under Article 38 the rates are based on the average of the daily exchange rates between each currency and the ECU over a period of 24 months prior to the date the rate is set, terminating on the last day of August immediately preceding the revision date; the thresholds for supply and services contracts are to be revised every two years from the date provided in the Supply Directive, and that for works contracts from the date in the Works Directive, which in both cases is from January 1 in even years. Article 38 also require the new exchange rate to be published in the *Official Journal of the European Communities* in the November before the changes take effect.

[26] The WTO Agreement does not apply to the relationship with the Community states *inter se*: but this amendment is proposed in order that the same rules should apply under the WTO and Community regimes.

[27] Utilities Regulation 10(1) and 10(2)(c).

[28] On the GPA see further pp. 774–781.

[29] On the reasons for amending the directives see further pp. 61–63.

[30] Proposal for a European Council and Parliament Directive amending directive 93/38/EEC co-ordinating the procurement procedures of the entities operating in the water, energy, transport and telecommunications sectors, COM (95) 107 Final, article 1(1)–(4), proposing amendments to Article 14 of the Utilities Directive.

The Proposal provides that the value of the threshold in ECU and in national currencies is to be revised every two years with effect from January 1, 1996. The calculation of values is to be based on the average daily value of the ECU expressed in SDR, and of the national currencies expressed in ECU, over the last 24 months, terminating on the last day of August immediately preceding the January 1 revision.

directive, with the exception of telecommunications, and not just in those sectors and for those entities covered by the GPA itself[31] and also to Part B and research and development services which are not covered by the GPA. This will not involve a significant change in the sterling value of contracts covered.

(ii) THE SPECIAL THRESHOLD FOR CONTRACTS WHICH INCLUDE NON-NECESSARY SUPPLIES OR SERVICES

Even when a contract is technically a works contract, where goods or services are included within that contract which are not necessary for the execution of the works, the contract is regulated where the value of the goods and services included within the contract meet the threshold for the regulation of supply or services contracts (which is much lower, as explained below). This is provided for in a special provision in Utilities Regulation 10(15), which is designed to ensure that supplies and services are not taken out of the procurement regime simply because they are packaged along with works in a single contract, unless there is very good justification for such an arrangement. This provision was considered in further detail above, in the context of the dividing line between works contracts and supply/services contracts.[32]

(b) SUPPLY AND SERVICES CONTRACTS

For supply and services contracts, for most utilities the regulations cover contracts valued at 400,000 ECUs or above.[33] However, there is a higher threshold for entities in the telecommunications sector[34]: the supply and services contracts of these entities are covered only if they are of a value of 600,000 ECUs or above. For 1994–95 the sterling threshold figures were £299,456 and £449,184 respectively, but these were to be revised from January 1, 1996, in accordance with the arrangements for revision already noted above. It will be noted that these thresholds are higher than those for supply and services contracts in the public sector, reflecting the generally less stringent approach to the regulation of utilities as opposed to the public sector.

Under the new GPA, supply and services contracts of utilities are also regulated for the first time. As with works, the Commission Proposal for adjusting the directive in light of the GPA proposes that – with the exception of telecommunications – the thresholds for supply and services contracts should be expressed in terms of the ECU equivalent of SDRs,

---

[31] On the sectors and entites covered see pp. 778–780.
[32] See pp. 427–431.
[33] Utilities Regulation 10(1) and 10(2)(a).
[34] Utilities Regulation 10(1) and 10(2)(b). This covers entities specified in Part T of Schedule 1 to the Utilities Regulations.

rather than simply in terms of ECUs.[35] Thus it is proposed that the general thresholds for these contracts will be the ECU equivalent of 400,000 SDR, rather than 400,000 ECUs. Apart from telecommunications, where the threshold is to remain at 600,000 ECUs, it is proposed that these changes should again apply to all entities and sectors, and not just those covered by the GPA itself, and also to Part B and research and development services, which are excluded from the GPA.

(3) VALUATION OF CONTRACTS

(a) GENERAL PRINCIPLES

The value of the contract for the purpose of the threshold rules is its *estimated value* net of value added tax,[36] the time for estimation being the *time at which a contract notice would be sent to the Official Journal* if such a notice were required.[37]

As a general rule the estimated value refers to the "value of the consideration" which the authority expects to give under the contract[38] – that is, the expected price. This must be estimated at the time of the notice, even though this may be difficult – as, for example, with a contract for the design and execution of the work, where the value of the contract depends upon the nature of the design. For cases where the value is difficult to estimate because of the unknown *duration* of the contract certain special provisions are made, as outlined below.

In the case of a works contract, where the utility intends to provide any goods or services to the contractor for the purpose of carrying out the contract, the value of the consideration is to be calculated as including the estimated value of those goods or services.[39] Thus, for example, if a utility is to supply building materials worth 1 million ECUs and expects to pay the contractor 4,500,000 ECUs the contract would be subject to the regulations, even though the anticipated price is less than the 5 million ECUs threshold, since the value of the price plus the goods – 5,500,000 ECUs – exceeds the threshold. There is, however, no provision for taking account of the value of goods or services provided by the utility in relation to a supply or services contract, which is anomalous.

---

[35] Commission Proposal, above, note 30, Article 1(1)–(4). It is proposed that the value of the threshold in ECUs and in national currencies is to be calculated as set out in note 30 above.

[36] Utilities Regulation 10(1).

[37] Utilities Regulation 10(19). A contract notice is not actually required for all such contracts, since generally a call for competition may be made by other methods, and for some no call for competition is required at all.

[38] Utilities Regulation 10(3).

[39] Utilities Regulation 10(14). The value of these goods or services is to be estimated as at the time the contract notice would be published in the *Official Journal* if required: Utilities Regulation 10(19). A similar provision in the public sector rules provides for consideration only of goods supplied, not services; the utilities rule is clearly preferable.

In the case of a services contract, it is expressly stated that, where appropriate, the utility shall, in determining the value, take account of the premium payable for insurance services; the fees, commissions or other remuneration payable for banking and financial services; and the fees or commission payable for design services.[40] There is, anomalously, no express requirement for works or supply contracts although such fees, etc., could be payable under such contracts, including those with any non-construction services provided under the contracts. Presumably such fees etc payable under works and supply contracts are in any case included by implication.

For contracts under which both goods and services are to be provided it is expressly stated that the estimated value of the contract shall be the aggregate of the consideration to be given in relation to both the provision of goods and the provision of services, although the value of the goods or services alone is less than the threshold for applying the rules[41] (in which case they would not, of course, be subject to regulation if purchased under separate contracts). The same position would apply, however, even without this express provision, since the general valuation principle states in any case that it is the value of the consideration given under the contract which is relevant.

In a procedure under which firms may bid for all or part of a requirement, the relevant value will be that of the whole of the requirement: there is a proposed contract for that requirement, even if such a large contract will not necessarily be awarded.

(b) OPTIONS

For supply and services contracts there is special provision for certain cases where the precise value of the consideration is not known because the contract includes one or more options.[42] In this case, the estimated value is the highest amount which could be payable[43]: in other words, the consideration is calculated on the assumption that all the options will be exercised. Thus, for example, the regulations will cover a contract for purchase by a transport utility of five vehicles at 50,000 ECUs each (total 250,000 ECUs), with an option to purchase a further five at the same price (overall total 500,000 ECU). Although the value of the purchase to which the utility is bound – 250,000 ECUs – is below the 400,000 ECU threshold, the regulations apply since the value of the contract if the option is exercised – 500,000 ECUs – is above this threshold. There is no

---

[40] Utilities Regulation 10(4).
[41] Utilities Regulation 10(16).
[42] In practice, this is almost always an option for the purchaser to purchase additional goods or services, though the provision will equally apply should the contracting authority be given an option regarding their supply.
[43] Utilities Regulation 10(13).

corresponding provision for works, presumably because option provisions are not common; however, such a provision would be useful for completeness.

(c) HIRE AND SERVICES CONTRACTS OF INDEFINITE DURATION

There are also special provisions for supply contracts for hire which are of indefinite duration, or when the duration is not fixed at the time of the contract (for example, because the hire is to terminate on the happening of a certain event, or is for an indefinite period subject to termination at the option of one or both parties). Rather than requiring a speculative estimate of the likely length, and hence value, of the contract, the estimated value is to be the value of the consideration which the utility expects to give in the first four years of hire.[44] In other words, the contract is treated as one of four years' duration. There is a similar provision for services contracts under which services are to be provided over an indefinite period: in this case the estimated value is the value which the utility expects to give in respect of each month of the period multiplied by 48.[45]

Where there is a contract for the hire of goods or provision of services for a definite period along with an option to renew for an indefinite or uncertain period, the value of the contract is assessed as if the option were exercised, as explained at (b) above. Thus the contract is one for an indefinite or uncertain period, and the "four-year" rule applies to valuation. For example, a contract for the hire of goods for six months, with an option for the hirer to extend the period indefinitely, falls within this provision, and the consideration is thus calculated by taking the estimated value over the first four years. If the option did not exist, the consideration would, of course, be calculated as the value of the hire for six months.

Where a "contract" is indefinite because it is provided that it may be renewed on the agreement of both parties, it has been argued that in general it constitutes a new contract for the purpose of the regulations, and must be readvertised (unless such agreed renewals are the normal commercial practice and the possibility for renewals does not extend beyond a reasonable period).[46] In addition, such a renewal does not appear to fall under this provision on indefinite/uncertain contracts.[47]

---

[44] Utilities Regulation 10(5). This is slightly different from the similar provision in the public sector rules which refers to the value of the first month's hire multiplied by 48, and thus does not take into account any increase in hire charges over the first four years.

[45] Utilities Regulation 10(6).

[46] See pp. 119–121.

[47] This is not expressly stated. However, it may be deduced from the fact such a contract is in essence a new contract, and also from the fact that the aggregation rules are expressly stated to apply to renewable contracts: this would not be appropriate if such contracts were treated as single contracts of indefinite duration.

Instead it is treated as a separate contract, and is subject to the aggregation rules which are discussed at (4) below.[48] Thus, with a hire contract for supplies for six months, renewable on the agreement of parties, the value of the consideration is merely six months' hire charge; however, if the agreement is renewed, the consideration under the new agreement must be added to the consideration under the original agreement, in accordance with the aggregation rules.

There is no provision corresponding to that set out in the first sentence of this section for *supply* contracts of *purchase* (as opposed to hire) of indefinite or uncertain duration; thus it is necessary to estimate the likely actual duration of the contract.

As explained above, where the indefinite or uncertain nature of the contract arises because of the existence of an option for one party to extend and the extension period is fixed, it must be assumed that the option is exercised to its maximum effect. Thus, a six-month hire contract with an option for renewal by one party for a further four and a half years is treated as a five-year hire contract, and the estimated value is the value of five full years' hire payments.[49]

A "contract" of purchase which is of uncertain or indefinite duration because of the stated possibility of renewal on mutual agreement appears, like a hire contract of this kind, to be regulated under the aggregation rules discussed below.[50]

(d) SERVICES CONTRACTS WHICH EXCEED FOUR YEARS

For a services contract under which services are to be provided for a period which exceeds four years, even where the duration is certain, the estimated value of the contract is to be the value of the consideration which the utility expects to give in each month, multiplied by 48.[51] Thus such a contract is effectively treated as one for a shorter period than the actual period. This applies only when the contract itself does not indicate a total cost. There is no equivalent provision for supply contracts lasting for more than four years.

---

[48] This means that a *renewable* contract is treated differently from one which is of *indefinite duration subject to termination by either party*, though it is effectively similar in its substance, since a contract subject to termination by either party does appear to be caught by the "four-year" rule.

[49] If this were a services contract then probably it must be treated as a contract extending over more than four years, and thus valued at 48 x the monthly consideration, in accordance with the rule set out at (d) below.

[50] As with hire, this means that such a contract is treated differently from one which is indefinite or uncertain because both parties have an option to terminate.

[51] Utilities Regulation 10(6).

(4) REQUIREMENTS FOR AGGREGATION OF THE VALUE OF SEPARATE CONTRACTS

(a) PURPOSE OF THE AGGREGATION RULES

In principle, the estimated value for threshold purposes is based on the value of each contract but, as under the public sector rules, in certain cases a purchaser must add together the value of purchases under a number of separate contracts, and the regulations will apply if the value of these purchases together exceeds the threshold. The purpose and general effect of these "aggregation" rules was considered in more detail in the context of the public sector: in brief, these rules seek to prevent purchasers deliberately avoiding the application of the regulations by splitting contracts, and also reduce the possibility of the regulations being rendered inapplicable by *inefficient* purchasing through lots of small contracts. As with the public sector, these rules are potentially important since contract splitting, whether deliberately to avoid the rules or otherwise, has been a serious problem in practice. However, as with the public sector rules, their actual impact appears significantly reduced by the uncertainty which surrounds their application, as set out below.

(b) AGGREGATION: GOODS AND SERVICES[52]

Rules on aggregation apply where a purchaser has a requirement over a period of time for goods and services of a particular "type", and enters into a series of contracts to obtain those goods or services.[53] This applies, for example, when a purchaser buys paper clips each month, placing a new contract each time. In this case the value of the separate contracts must be "aggregated" together, and if the collective value exceeds the threshold, then all the purchases must be awarded according to the regulations, even though each individual contract is below the threshold. The same principle applies where there is a single contract which is stated to be "renewable" (referring to the case where the renewal needs the consent of both parties, in contrast to where there is an extension through exercise of an option)[54]; thus renewals are treated, for the purpose of the aggregation rules, as a series of separate contracts. In these respects the principles applicable are the same as those on

---

[52] A process of aggregation of similar goods or services is also required for deciding whether utilities should publish a Periodic Indicative Notice. On the relationship between the basis of agreggation for the purpose of such a notice and for the purpose of applying the regulations' award procedures, as discussed in the present section, see pp. 465–467.

[53] Utilities Regulation 10(10) and 10(11).

[54] *Ibid.* Where a contract is extended through the exercise of an option, the provision on aggregation of contracts is redundant, since the *whole* value of purchases under the option is already taken into account under the express provision on options discussed above.

aggregation in the public sector. In addition, the same aggregation principles apply in the case of a supply contract which is for the purchase of goods over an indefinite period.[55] (These provisions do not apply to the *hire* of goods nor to the provision of services, since these cases are dealt with by special rules already discussed above.)[56]

The "aggregation" which must occur in the situations listed above may be carried out in one of two ways.[57]

(i) The first method provides for aggregating the value of the consideration given for the acquisition of goods or services of that "type" in the previous year, adjusted to take account of any expected changes in quantity and cost in the next twelve months (commencing from the time that notice for the present contract would be published in the *Official Journal*, if required).[58] The previous year may be taken either as the twelve months ending immediately before the time the notice would be published, or the last financial year ending before this time. This method is relevant only where the utility has had previous requirements for the same type of product.

(ii) The second method is by estimating that amount of the consideration to be paid in the next twelve months, where the contract is for an indefinite term, or is for a definite term of twelve months or less. The twelve-month period is calculated from the time of the first date for delivery under the contract. Under this second method, when the contract is for a definite term of more than twelve months, it is necessary to take account of the consideration during the whole period of the contract, not just during one year. For example, a utility may place two contracts for certain office equipment, each to run for three years, with a sum of 150,000 ECUs to be paid out under each contract each year. Under this valuation method it is necessary to take the value of both contracts over the three year period, to decide whether the purchases are subject to the regulations: in this example, the regulations do apply, since the total consideration is 900,000 ECUs (6 × 150,000 ECUs) – above the thresholds. If the one year amounts were aggregated the contract would not be above the threshold. (The value would be 2 × 150,000 ECUs – that is, 300,000 ECUs.)

Which of these two methods is to be used is a matter for the utility to decide.[59] However, it is expressly provided that a utility is not to choose

---

[55] Utilities Regulation 10(10) and 10(11).
[56] See pp. 444–446. These rules effectively require valuation over a four-year period whereas for supply purchases, as explained below, it is only in general necessary to consider the value of supplies to be purchased over a year.

There is no similar express provision for indefinite supply contracts under the public sector rules, so that it thus seems to be required that the total value, and hence duration, of the contract must be estimated.
[57] Utilities Regulation 10(11).
[58] Utilities Regulation 10(11) and 10(19).
[59] Utilities Regulation 10(10) simply says that the value "shall be the amount calculated" by applying one of these methods, but it seems obvious that the choice is intended to be left to the utility and this is assumed by the wording of regulation 7(10), discussed in the text immediately below.

the method with the intention of avoiding the application of the regulations.[60]

The rules discussed above apply, as indicated, only to purchases of goods or services of the same "type".[61] This same concept is used in the public sector rules, and will doubtless be given the same meaning in both public and utilities rules. This question was considered in Chapter 5 on the public sector where it was suggested that the test should be whether the goods or services in question are typically available from the same supplier or service provider.[62] However, as was explained in that chapter there is considerable uncertainty over this issue, a situation which, in view of the practical importance of the aggregation rules, constitutes a serious defect in the procurement regime.

The rules also only require the aggregation of purchases under contracts "which have similar characteristics". The appropriate test here appears to be whether a single provider would be likely to be interested in the different contracts. This could depend on many factors – for example, on whether the contract is for hire or for purchase (which may, in some industries, be covered by different providers), or on the applicable terms, which may be very different for regular needs and for one-off special projects and may thus attract different types of provider. Another factor might be whether additional subject-matter is included – for example, a contract for both supply and maintenance may interest different providers than a simple supply contract.[63]

In addition, the regulations provide that where the utility proposes to enter two or more supply contracts at the same time to purchase or hire goods of a "particular type" the value of the separate contracts must be aggregated.[64] This ensures that the aggregation rules are applied to contracts awarded at the same time, as well as those awarded at different times. It is also provided that where the utility has a "single requirement" for services and a number of services contracts have been/are to be entered into to fulfil that requirement, the value of the contracts must be aggregated.[65] This will cover different contracts for the same type of services which are awarded at the same time, and could also cover

---

[60] Utilities Regulation 10(18).
[61] See further Brown, "Getting to Grips with Aggregation under the E.C. Public Procurement Rules" (1993) 1 P.P.L.R. 69.
[62] See pp. 168–171.
[63] It can be noted that the utilities rules, unlike the public sector rules, do not expressly limit purchases of goods to be aggregated to those purchases made under supply contracts, nor the aggregation of services to those services purchased under services contracts. Thus goods provided under services contracts, for example, may need to be aggregated with those provided under supply contracts. This applies only where the contracts have similar characteristics, as just explained; but this will cover the case where the contracts are differently characterised only because they have a slightly different balance between supplies and services. In practice, utilities will not generally need to aggregate goods of the same type supplied under works contracts, since such contracts clearly do not have similar characteristics to supply contracts for this purpose.
[64] Utilities Regulation 10(7).
[65] Utilities Regulation 10(7).

contracts for different types of service, if they constitute part of the same "requirement".

(c) AGGREGATION: WORKS

There is no equivalent for works contracts of the requirement for supplies and services for purchases of the same "type" to be aggregated. This means, for example, that – on the assumption that exterior maintenance constitutes works – purchasers need not aggregate separate maintenance contracts, even where these are for identical work on different buildings. This is, however, subject to the general prohibition on splitting contracts to avoid the regulations,[66] discussed below.

It is provided, however, as with the public sector rules, that a utility must aggregate the value of separate public works contracts entered into for the purpose of carrying out a single "work".[67] For example, a utility erecting a new headquarters which lets separate contracts for different phases of the building must aggregate the value of each separate contract; thus it must advertise them if the total cost of the building exceeds the 5 million ECUs threshold, even if the value of each separate contract is below that amount. Where a management contract (for a firm to let contracts on behalf of the utility) is awarded, the value of this contract must be aggregated with the value of the contracts for carrying out the work in relation to that project. Clearly the definition of a "work" is important in this context.[68]

There is an exception to this aggregation requirement where the value of any particular contract relating to the "work" is valued at less than 1 million ECUs. In this case the value of that contract may be calculated without taking into account the value of other contacts relating to the same work.[69] The authority may take advantage of this exemption for contracts worth up to 20 per cent of the total value of the work.[70] A similar exemption applies under the public sector rules and its precise scope and practical application was considered further in the chapter on those rules.[71] The exemption may encourage utilities to retain some part of their work for small and medium-sized enterprises (SMEs),[72] which the Community itself has sought to promote and support.

It may be noted that there is no exemption for services contracts divided into lots, although such an exemption exists under the public sector rules.

---

[66] See p. 452.
[67] Utilities Regulation 10(8).
[68] On this see p. 128.
[69] Utilities Regulation 10(9).
[70] *Ibid.*
[71] See pp. 172–173.
[72] See pp. 67–68.

(d) THE AGGREGATION RULES AND DISCRETE OPERATIONAL UNITS

A utility which is a single legal entity may sometimes function in practice as a number of independent units. To aggregate the purchases of all independent units in such a case may cause considerable inconvenience: either procurement will need to be centralised, or the units will be required to follow the regulations in awarding their contracts, even though separately these are only for small amounts. The issue is likely to arise only with supplies and services.[73]

The directives do not deal expressly with this, but the Utilities Regulations effectively provide that the aggregation rules are not to require the aggregation of contracts awarded by independent units.[74] This applies where the following conditions are met:

(i) there is a purchase by a "discrete operational unit" (DOU). It is not clear what this means, but it probably covers only a unit with budgetary and managerial autonomy.

(ii) the goods or services are acquired solely for the purpose of that unit;

(iii) the decision over whether to purchase has been wholly devolved to the unit; and

(iv) that decision is taken independently of any other part of the utility (which probably involves a requirement that any purchasing decision should not be subject to approval).

There is some debate over whether these provisions on DOUs are lawful.

It can be pointed out that, like the public sector regulations, the aggregation rules in the utilities regulations do not state clearly that aggregation must be carried out at the level of the utility rather than the purchasing unit: it is merely provided, for example, that "regular" contracts must be aggregated, and it could be suggested that contracts are only "regular" where awarded by the same unit of the purchaser. It was argued above, in considering the DOU provisions in the public sector, that policy considerations indicate that aggregation at the level of an independent purchasing unit should be permitted. This issue is expressly addressed in policy guidelines published by the Commission,[75]

---

[73] Aggregation of works is required only where contracts relate to a single work, and autonomous units do not each tend to let different contracts relating to the same work!

[74] Utilities Regulation 10(12). The exception is relevant both for aggregation rules relating to contracts made over a period of time and renewable contracts, and also to contracts made at the same time. The issue is likely to arise only in the context of the rules relating to separate contracts over a period of time; contracts are in practice only awarded at the same time where this is done by a common purchaser.

[75] European Commission, *Policy Guidelines on Contracts Awarded by Separate Units of a Contracting Entity under Dir. 90/531/EEC (Utilities)*, January 20, 1993 (favourably considered by the Commission's Advisory Committee on the Opening Up of Public Procurement and Advisory Committee on Public Procurement). The document concerns directive 90/531, but the relevant provisions of the current Utilities Directive 93/38 are effectively identical.

which indicate that aggregation on the basis of the unit is acceptable under conditions of the kind laid out in the United Kingdom legislation.

Another view, however, is that the directives require aggregation of all purchases made for the purpose of its "utilities" activities by a utility which is a single legal entity, and that the United Kingdom provisions on DOUs are incompatible with the directives. The Commission indicated in 1993, in reply to a question from the European Parliament, that this is the case.[76] If this is correct, purchasers are obliged to ignore the provisions on DOUs, and if they fail to do so may be the subject of legal action.[77]

It is to be hoped that the Court favours an interpretation which does not require aggregation of the purchases of separate units both in the but it may be reluctant to do so without a specific provision in the directives. It would thus be desirable to adopt provisions to introduce an exemption for DOUs when the directives are reviewed.

(5) THE PROHIBITION ON CONTRACT SPLITTING

Utilities Regulation 10(18) states that a utility shall not enter into separate contracts with the intention of avoiding the application of the regulations. This is directed at a case where a purchaser which might have awarded one single contract of a value above the threshold for the application seeks instead to award two or more distinct contracts, to avoid applying the regulations. In practice, many situations which result from this sort of conduct are now caught by the aggregation rules. This provision, however, may catch some deliberate "splits" which are not caught by those rules. Obviously, however, it is difficult in practice to prove a purchaser's motive in packaging work in a particular way.

7. FRAMEWORK ARRANGEMENTS UNDER THE UTILITIES RULES[78]

(1) THE NATURE OF FRAMEWORK ARRANGEMENTS

As explained in Chapter 5 on the public sector, "framework arrangement" is a general term used in this book to refer to various types of arrangement whereby a purchaser and seller agree the terms of future dealings between them without committing themselves to any specific

---

[76] [1993] O.J. C207/38.
[77] Since most of the regulations have direct effect aggrieved providers can mount a challenge in the United Kingdom courts based on the directive itself: see pp. 902–903.
[78] See further European Commission, draft *Policy Guidelines on Framework Agreements under Directive 90/531/EEC*, December 18, 1992.

orders. Such arrangements are useful where a purchaser has a recurring need for an item or service: framework arrangements allow those needs to be met simply by placing orders under the arrangement, without the cost of negotiating a new agreement on each occasion. As previously explained, they are used, for example, for the purchases of equipment (such as photocopying machines) where additional or replacement equipment, or spares, are likely to be required later, or for the procurement of services or works, such as maintenance services, over a period of time.

For the purpose of the Utilities Regulations framework arrangements are divided into two types. These can be referred to as "framework contracts", which are ordinary supply, works or services contracts under the regulations; and "framework agreements", arrangements which are not themselves contracts governed by the regulations and to which certain special rules apply.

(2) FRAMEWORK CONTRACTS

The term "framework contract" is not actually used in the regulations but is a convenient term to use to describe those framework arrangements which are ordinary works, supply or services contracts under the regulations. This covers, first, an arrangement whereby, although no exact quantities are specified, the purchaser is committed to obtaining its requirements when they arise (or a certain amount or proportion of these) from the provider, and the provider is committed to delivery – for example, an agreement for a utility to buy all the paper clips which it requires over the next year from that provider under which the provider promises to deliver that requirement. This is a legally binding contract under which consideration is provided on both sides. As such it is clearly a "contract for consideration" under the regulations, and is subject to the regulations in the same way as any other contract. Placing a specific order under the arrangement does not itself constitute the award of a new contract, and hence the regulations do not apply to such an order. Thus, the utility is free to place orders under a framework contract which has itself been properly awarded, without advertising those orders or following any other rules, and does not need to publish a specific contract award notice to cover each order.

A second type of arrangement, although unusual in practice, could be where a utility commits itself to purchase certain needs, should these arise, from a particular provider, but that provider does not commit itself to supply any orders made. Such an arrangement would not in general be binding under English contract law since the provider gives no consideration, but could be binding if made under seal or if the provider paid for the purchaser's promise. It is not clear whether or not such a binding arrangement – under which the purchaser but not provider gives consideration – is a contract "for consideration" for the purpose of the regulations, or whether a contract under the regulations only arises when orders are placed under the arrangement. A third possible type of arrangement, whereby the provider promises to supply, but the utility makes no promise to purchase, is probably not a contract under the regulations so that here the contract does arise only at the later point when orders are made.[79-80]

The regulations do not contain any specific provisions to control or regulate framework contracts. However, the directives and regulations themselves may contain implied restrictions on contracts of unreasonable duration, and such contracts may also infringe Article 85 E.C. on restrictive agreements; and contracts which are unreasonably wide in their scope of coverage may also infringe Article 85.[81]

(3) FRAMEWORK AGREEMENTS

(a) GENERAL PRINCIPLES

Certain types of framework arrangement, on the other hand, are clearly *not* themselves works, supply or services contracts within the meaning of the regulations. This is the case with an arrangement between a utility and a provider which neither commits the utility to purchase its requirements from the provider, nor the provider to supply any requirements which the utility might have, but which merely set out the terms of possible future contracts. For example, the parties may agree the price, terms and conditions for their dealings should the utility decide to buy certain stationery items from the provider, but without either side undertaking any obligations. Should the purchaser decide to make a purchase of the products covered by the arrangement, he may choose to place the order under the framework arrangement, but is not obliged to do so – he may, for example, go to other providers, or choose to deal with the original provider only on terms which differ from the arrangement; whilst the provider is not bound to accept orders placed under the arrangement. A purchaser may prefer to enter into an agreement of this type, which does not tie him to a specific provider, rather than a framework contract, which does, so that he is able to look elsewhere if the arrangement no longer offers value for money – for example, because a new and competitive provider has entered the market. At the same time, the arrangement still offers some security of supply for the purchaser, and some expectation of business for the provider, as well as saving transaction costs.

Whilst such an arrangement is not itself a contract under the regulations, orders placed under it clearly are. Thus any stationery order placed under the arrangement referred to above, which is accepted by

---

[79-80] It is assumed that this is not itself a contract under the regulations in the Commission's draft policy guidelines, cited at note 78, paras. 2–4.
[81] See Chap. 4.

the provider, is a supply contract, and as such must generally be advertised, etc., where its value – taking into account the aggregation rules – exceeds the relevant threshold. As has been explained in Chapter 5, under the public sector regulations it is not clear whether in order to comply with the regulations each contract awarded under the arrangement must be separately advertised and awarded in accordance with the relevant procedures – in which case any framework arrangement is irrelevant since the purchaser cannot rely on it; or whether it is sufficient that the framework arrangement itself has been awarded under these procedures. It was suggested that the latter is probably the case[82] but there is still some uncertainty on this issue.

Under the utilities rules there is no such uncertainty: these rules provide expressly that it is sufficient to follow the award procedures for the framework arrangement alone. They also make certain ancillary provision for the application of the rules – for example, the aggregation rules – to framework arrangements. In addition, they contain specific provisions designed to prevent the abuse of such arrangements, by providing that they should not operate to hinder or distort competition. Non-binding arrangements which fall within the scope of these special provisions are referred to in the directive and regulations as "framework *agreements*".

(b) THE DEFINITION OF FRAMEWORK AGREEMENTS

A framework agreement is defined in Utilities Regulation 2(1) as "a contract or other arrangement which is not in itself a works, supply or services contract but which establishes the terms (in particular the terms as to price and where appropriate quantity) under which the provider will enter into contracts with a utility in the period during which the framework agreement applies".

Clearly this covers an agreement of the type noted above – that is, where neither the utility nor the provider undertakes any obligation to the other, but the arrangement merely sets out terms on which they may choose to enter contracts in the future. Such agreements are very common in practice, in view of their advantages as outlined above.

In addition, it was suggested above that an arrangement whereby the provider promises under seal to meet certain orders from the utility, without any corresponding promise by the utility to order any requirements from that firm, is not a contract caught by the regulations, even though it is an arrangement which is binding on the provider. Such an

---

[82] See pp. 177–179.

arrangement would thus seem to fall within the above definition of a framework agreement.[83]

Obviously, the definition excludes any agreement which is a contract subject to the regulations. Thus "framework contracts", as described above, are not affected by these provisions but remain subject to the regulations as individual contracts in the ordinary way.

The definition envisages that the agreement must establish the terms on which future dealings are to take place. It is submitted that this means, first, that all important matters to be dealt with in the contracts, apart from the scope and timing of the particular orders, must be included from the outset. If this is not the case, then the award of a framework agreement can be used simply as a device to authorise negotiations with a particular favoured provider. For example, the favoured provider could bid a very low price to beat off the competition and, once the bid was accepted, the parties could then negotiate on matters not expressly covered by the agreement, such as delivery times or the scope of exemption clauses, to reach an overall deal which is satisfactory to both. Secondly, in respect of matters which are covered, a degree of certainty will be required as to the precise obligations which are to be undertaken. It is likely that these terms must be agreed with sufficient certainty for the obligations to meet the test for certainty which applies for an obligation to be contractually binding in English law: thus, there must be no necessity for further negotiation on the matters covered should the parties decide to enter into a contract, in order for that contract to be sufficiently certain to be binding. It is arguable, on the other hand, that such a degree of certainty, whilst necessary, may not be sufficient. For example, an agreement to pay a reasonable price is sufficiently certain for contractual purposes but may not be adequate in the present context, as leaving too much for negotiation between the parties. It is arguable that these provisions on the need to establish terms mean that the terms cannot be changed by mutual agreement for the purpose of actually placing contracts under the agreement.[84]

---

[83] This is the view suggested in the Commission's policy guidelines, above, note 78, paras. 2–4. The inclusion of this situation can explain the reference in the United Kingdom definition to a "contract", as well to as non-contractual arrangements. (It can be noted that the definition in Article 1(5) of the Utilities Directive simply refers generally to "agreements" meeting the conditions set out.) If a promise made under seal by the utility to purchase from a particular provider certain requirements which may arise is not itself a contract under the regulations – which it was suggested above is not clear – then this type of arrangement, also, could be a framework agreement. Such a scenario is not mentioned in the draft policy guidelines.

[84] To allow such freedom is more open to abuse than allowing parties to change the terms of an existing contract – which appears to be permitted to some degree – since the terms actually agreed do not (for most framework agreements) involve the imposition of any legal obligations on the parties. Thus there is nothing to prevent both parties entering into the original agreement without any intention of carrying it out – something which is less likely to happen where an agreement is legally enforceable.

On the other hand, it could be argued that to ensure that framework agreements are sufficiently flexible to meet the parties' needs over a reasonable period of time, minor amendments should be permitted.

(c) APPLICATION OF THE RULES ON AWARD PROCEDURES

As indicated above, where a utility awards a framework agreement in accordance with the regulations, it need not subsequently follow the award procedures under the regulations for contracts awarded under that agreement. This is made clear by Utilities Regulation 11(1) which provides that a utility may choose to treat a framework agreement as a contract to which the regulations apply.[85] Since orders placed under the agreement will, by virtue of this provision, be deemed to arise under a "contract" awarded under the regulations, the regulations will not need to be followed again in placing those orders – they may simply be placed with the firm which has won the competition for the framework arrangement. This is reinforced by an express provision in Regulation 16(1)(i), stating that there is no requirement for a call for competition for a contract awarded under a regulation 11 framework agreement in accordance with the regulations.[86]

In relation to contract award notices, in draft policy guidelines on the subject of framework agreements the Commission has suggested that in the case of such agreements the section of the notice relating to the value of the contract should either be left blank or the estimated value should be included, it being made clear that the value in question is an estimate.[87]

The Commission also suggests that notices should be published not only for the agreement, but also for individual contracts awarded under the agreement.[88] Clearly, this would be useful; but it is not actually required under the directive or regulations.

To exempt from the regulations contracts awarded under framework agreements, the agreement itself must be awarded in accordance with the regulations. If it is not, individual contracts falling withing its scope must be advertised and awarded in the usual way.[89] The rules are likely to be interpreted to require strict compliance with all requirements in

---

[85] It is also provided that "accordingly", in respect of such an agreement, reference in the regulations to a contract shall include references to a framework agreement.

[86] This view is also stated in the Commission's draft policy guidelines, note 78, above, para. 9. The Commission mentions as a reason for this general principle only the statement in the directive (in Article 15(2) of Directive 90/531; now in Article 20(2) of Directive 93/38) that there is no call for competition requirements for contracts awarded under a relevant framework agreement. However, strictly this provision gives an exemption only from the call for competition requirement and not from other provisions of the directive.

[87] Draft Policy Guidelines, note 78, para. 13.

[88] Ibid.

[89] This is not expressly stated, but is to be implied. In the Utilities Directive itself Article 5(3) expressly states that there is no exemption from the call for competition requirement where the agreement has not been awarded in accordance with the directive, but there is also no exemption from other obligations since the general conditions for regarding orders placed under a framework agreement as having been placed under a "contract" are not met: thus those orders remain ordinary contracts to which the regulations apply in the usual way.

the award of the arrangement; if these are infringed in any way then the agreement probably cannot be relied upon.

(d) AGREEMENTS WHICH HINDER OR DISTORT COMPETITION

Utilities Regulation 11(2) provides that a utility which chooses to treat a framework arrangement as a contract shall not use the framework agreement to "hinder, limit or distort competition". As already noted, one feature of a framework agreement which is inimical to competition – uncertainty in the terms of the agreement – may lead to the conclusion that the arrangement is not properly classified as a framework agreement for the purpose of the regulations. Regulation 11(2) means that other aspects of a framework arrangement which unduly impede competition, may also lead the court to conclude that the exemption cannot be invoked.

It was explained in Chapter 5 that certain framework agreements which adversely affect competition may be caught by Article 85 E.C., which provides that restrictive agreements (whether or not legally binding) which have the effect or object of preventing, distorting or hindering competition shall be void (unless the subject of an exemption from the Commission).[90] This could cover, for example, agreements which cover all or a large part of a requirement, for longer than can be justified on a commercial basis. It seems clear that an agreement which infringes Article 85 will also contravene Utilities Regulation 11(2). One view could be that the scope of Article 85 is in fact co-extensive with that of regulation 11(2) and that only agreements under Article 85 are caught by that regulation. However, it was argued in Chapter 4 that this is not the case, since there is a *de minimis* rule applicable under Article 85 which was not intended to be introduced into the directive. Thus contracts which would not come under Article 85 because the part of the common market affected is too small – for example, a long-term supply agreement for stationery requirements – could be caught by regulation 11(2).[91] It is not clear, on the other hand, whether and how far the requirements imposed by Regulation 11(2) may be more stringent than those of Article 85 in other respects. In view of the directive's objectives of close regulation to ensure regular competition it is possible that the courts will in many respects apply criteria which are more stringent than the rules in Article 85. As yet, however, the Court of Justice has given no guidance on the application of this provision.

Article 85 states expressly that agreements which infringe that article shall be void. The regulations do not state what is the legal effect if any agreement contravenes regulation 11(2) but it seems clear that the

---

[90] See pp. 178–179.
[91] On these arguments see pp. 95–99.

agreement could not be relied upon in such a case.[92] The law has sometimes been reluctant to hold a concluded contract to be invalid when this infringes some public law rule, because of the interests of legal certainty,[93] but the same objections do not apply to a framework agreement where it does not have binding legal effect. However, it may be noted that "call offs" under the "ineffective" agreement will not necessarily be legally unenforceable. The effect of the utility not being able to rely on the agreement is that any subsequent contract awarded under the agreement is awarded in breach of the regulations – but a breach of the regulations does not generally render a contract invalid.[94]

(e) THE THRESHOLD RULES FOR FRAMEWORK AGREEMENTS

The Utilities Regulations, as explained, apply only to contracts above a certain threshold, and where a framework agreement is treated as a contract for the purposes of the regulations, the award procedures will therefore only apply to agreements the value of which exceeds the relevant threshold. Where a framework agreement is treated as a contract for the purposes of the regulations, it is provided in Regulation 10(17) that the estimated value of the agreement is to be the aggregate of the values of all the contracts which could be entered into under the framework agreement.[95]

Even without this express provision the value of the different contracts awarded under the regulations would need to be aggregated to determine if these contracts – and hence the framework agreement – should be awarded under the regulations, because of the general aggregation rules.[96] However, aggregation under this express provision may sometimes produce a different result from that which would apply without it. In particular, where a framework agreement is made by a consortium and is for the use of several purchasers, who will each "call off" contracts under the agreement, the ordinary aggregation rules would arguably require the aggregation only of the contracts of individual purchasers.[97]

---

[92] This conclusion is valid even if the view is taken under the public sector rules that framework agreements may be relied on by implication from the general effects of the regulations, without the need for specific authorisation such as is found in the utilities rules (as to which see pp. 178–179). This is because the provisions on framework agreements under the utilities rules do not operate merely to *authorise* such agreements, but also to restrict the conditions of their operation.

[93] See pp. 895–897.

[94] See pp. 913–915.

[95] The same provision states that the values of these contracts are to be estimated in accordance with the general provisions of the regulations on valuation of contracts.

[96] These would apply at least if the different contracts under the agreement were for goods or services of the same type, but this is normally the case; and if they are not it may be argued that the agreement in any case infringes the prohibition on agreements which hinder or distort competition, discussed below.

[97] This would mean that the contract would need to be advertised only where the contracts of at least one purchaser would need in isolation to be awarded under the regulations. If the agreement were not awarded under the regulations that purchaser would not be able to rely on it in respect of his own contracts. There is, however, an argument for the view that in this case aggregation of all the contracts is necessary: on this see p. 177.

However, under Utilities Regulation 10(17) it appears necessary to aggregate all call-off contracts which could be awarded under the agreement, even where these would be awarded by different members of the consortium.

(4) FRAMEWORK ARRANGEMENTS CONCLUDED PRIOR TO THE REGULATIONS

Framework *agreements* concluded before the utilities rules came into effect will not generally have been awarded in accordance with the rules' requirements.[98] However, where orders are placed under a framework *contract* which was awarded before the rules took effect, these need not be awarded in accordance with the regulations as they are not new contracts for the purpose of the regulations.

8. CONCESSION CONTRACTS UNDER THE UTILITIES RULES

Neither the Utilities Regulations nor the Utilities Directive contain specific rules on concession contracts – that is, contracts under which the provider is paid, in whole or in part, by being permitted to exploit the work or service provided under the contract. As has been explained, under the public sector Works Regulations works concession contracts are dealt with expressly, and are subject to special rules.[99] With services, the Services Directive is silent, but the Services Regulations provide expressly that such contracts are excluded from the regulations, it being assumed that this was the intention of the directive since provisions on services concessions were originaly included but dropped before the Services Directive was adopted.[1] It may be argued, as with the Services Directive, that the silence of the Utilities Directive indicates that concession contracts of all types are outside the scope of the rules. On the other hand, it could be argued – as is also possible with the Services Directive – that a concession contract falls within the general definitions of supply/works/services contract, which cover contracts for consideration for the provision of goods/work/services, and is therefore covered by the utilities rules like any other contract. The position at the present time remains unclear.

---

[98] However, framework arrangements for services awarded before the regulations came into effect in 1994 may have been awarded in accordance with the Utilities Directive which has applied since July 1994, and arguably may thus be invoked.

[99] See pp. 353–365.

[1] See p. 366.

CHAPTER 10

THE UTILITIES REGULATIONS: AWARD PROCEDURES[1]

1. INTRODUCTION

This chapter explains the rules which must be followed by a utility in awarding a contract which is subject to the Utilities Contracts Regulations 1995,[2] including the rules on qualification of providers. The rules on specifications are considered separately in Chapter 11.

The procedures in these regulations are likely shortly to be amended, to introduce new procedural obligations which apply in dealings with certain third country providers under the new WTO Agreement on Government Procurement (GPA).[2a] Even before these amendments are made, however, those utilities which are covered by the GPA[2b] must apply these obligations as from January 1, 1996 when the GPA comes into force. The Commission has also proposed a directive to apply these procedures applying under the GPA to Community, as well as third country, providers.[2c] Whilst this directive has not yet been adopted, in the United Kingdom Community providers may nevertheless benefit from these additional rules as from January 1, 1996 by virtue of Utilities Regulation 4(3), which states that providers who are nationals of and established in a Member State are to be treated no less favourably than those who are not. Because of the above rules, utilities covered by the GPA thus need to apply not merely the rules set out in the regulations themselves, but also any additional procedural rules deriving from the GPA. These additional GPA rules, as well as those in the regulations, will be noted in the course of this chapter.

---

[1] See further Brown, "The Extension of the Community Public Procurement Rules to Utilities" (1993) 30 C.M.L.Rev. 721; Bickerstaff, "The Utilities Supply and Works Contracts Regulations 1992: An Analysis of the Implementation of the Utilities Directive in United Kingdom Law" (1993) 2 P.P.L.R. 117; O'Loan, "An Analysis of the Utilities Directive of the European Communities" (1992) 1 P.P.L.R. 175; Cox, *The Single Market Regime and the Enforcement Regime after 1992* (1993), Chap. 5; Geddes, *Public Procurement* (1993) Chap. 4; Digings and Bennett, *E.C. Public Procurement: Law and Practice* Chap. B4; Weiss, *Public Procurement in European Community Law* (1993), Chap. 8; Lee, *Public Procurement* (1992), Chap. 4; Trepte, *Public Procurement in the E.C.* (1993), esp. Chaps. 3 and 5.
[2] The definition of utility and the question of which contracts are covered by the regulations were considered in Chap. 9. The background to the regulations is discussed in Chap. 3 and the issue of enforcement in Chap. 18.
[2a] On this Agreement see pp. 774–781.
[2b] Not all utilities are covered by the GPA: as to those which are see pp. 778–780.
[2c] See further pp. 661–663.

In addition to the specific obligations set out in the directives and implemented in the United Kingdom regulations, Article 4(2) of the Utilities Directive states as a general principle that there shall be no "discrimination" between providers. Probably this was originally intended to articulate a principle that there shall be no discrimination on grounds of nationality, so ensuring that this principle applied even to those utilities which may be outside the scope of the non-discrimination obligations in the Community Treaties. Further, as noted in Chapter 6, the Court of Justice has indicated in the case of *Storebaelt*, that there is a general principle of the equality of bidders underlying the public sector directives.[2d] It seems clear that this will also apply in the utilities sector, either by implication or by virtue of a wide interpretation of Article 4(2) to cover all unjustified differences of treatment of providers, and not merely discrimination on grounds of nationality. The United Kingdom has implemented these rules by providing in Utilities Regulation 4(3) that "When these Regulations apply a utility shall not treat any provider more or less favourably than any other provider." This must be interpreted in light of the above requirement(s) in the directive. Clearly regulation 4(3) imposes certain requirements and restrictions on utilities going beyond the specific rules set out in the regulations and – like the requirements of the Treaties themselves – must be kept in mind in the conduct of any award procedure under the regulations.

2. PERIODIC INDICATIVE NOTICES

(1) THE REQUIREMENT FOR A PERIODIC INDICATIVE NOTICE

Utilities must publicise each contract which they propose to award under the regulations in one of the ways outlined in section 4(2) below. This publicity is referred to as a "call for competition". In addition, there is also a requirement, as with the public sector, to publish a notice in the *Official Journal* giving advance notice of future requirements. This aims to ensure that the market has as much time as possible to prepare for participation. In the Utilities Regulations these advance notices are referred to as "periodic indicative notices",[3] the same terminology as is used in the Utilities Directive. (Under the public sector regulations they are referred to as "prior information notices".) The relevant obligations are found in Utilities Regulation 14.[4]

In addition to fulfilling this obligation, publication of a periodic indicative notice is also one way of satisfying the requirements for

---

[2d] Case C–243/89, *Commission v. Denmark*, judgment of 22 June 1993. See further pp. 180–181.
[3] Utilities Regulation 14.
[4] Implementing Article 22 of the Utilities Directive.

publicising a particular award – that is, it may also serve as one way of making a "call for competition" – in a restricted or negotiated procedure (although not in an open procedure). If a periodic indicative notice is to be used as a call for competition it must meet certain additional requirements which do not apply where it is merely being used as an advance notice under regulation 14. These are examined in the section on the call for competition.[5]

The publication of a periodic indicative notice covering a particular purchase may in certain cases also permit a utility to shorten the usual period for the award procedure for that purchase. This is considered further below.[6]

As with the public sector, publication of a periodic indicative notice does not bind the utility to go ahead with the purchases in question.

As was noted in relation to the public sector, there may be some difficulty for providers affected by non-publication to obtain an effective remedy, and it is necessary to rely on policing by the European Commission to ensure that these rules are adhered to.[7]

The requirements on periodic indicative notices have caused some concern amongst those utilities operating in a competitive environment, since it is felt that they may require the utility to reveal sensitive commercial information about its future plans.[8]

(2) PERIODIC INDICATIVE NOTICES FOR WORKS

For works contracts a periodic indicative notice must be published at least once every twelve months. This must cover all works contracts which the utility expects to award which are above the threshold for the application of the Utilities Regulations to works contracts,[9] and must contain certain specified information relating to these contracts. It is not clear whether the obligation is limited to contracts which are expected to be put out to tender in the next twelve months (as is the case with supplies and services, as explained below); works large enough to fall within the directive may well be anticipated more than a year in advance and meaningful preparation can be made for bidding that far ahead, but, on the other hand, it would be pointless to include works anticipated many years ahead. There is no express provision to exclude the requirement in relation to works contracts which are generally excluded from the regulations under regulations 6–7.[10] However, such contracts are probably excluded since both regulations 6 and 7 state that the

---

[5] See pp. 479–480.
[6] See pp. 491–492 and pp. 502–503.
[7] See pp. 904–905.
[8] See further Trepte, *Public Procurement in the E.C.* (1993), p.142.
[9] Regulation 14(1)(b) and 14(2)(b). For this purpose the value of contracts is to be that as estimated at the time of despatch of the notice: Regulation 14(2)(b).
[10] On these exclusions see Chap. 9.

regulations generally shall not apply to the "seeking of offers" in connection with such contracts.[11]

The notice must be sent to the Office of Official Publications of the European Communities,[12] which may be done at any time and not necessarily be at the start of the financial year. The notice will be published in the hard copy of the *Official Journal of the European Communities* and also in the TED electronic data bank, in full in the original language and in summary form in the other official Community languages.[13] The expense is borne by the Community.[14] The Office of Official Publications is in general required to publish the notice within 12 days of despatch.[15]

Whilst it is expressly stated that contract notices (those advertising individual contracts) may not be published elsewhere before despatch to the *Official Journal*, nor contain additional information, there are no similar express limitations for periodic indicative notices.[16]

It can be noted that the obligation is less onerous than the requirements on Prior Information Notices in the public sector, which requires a notice for each individual works contracts as soon as a work is planned.[17]

(3) PERIODIC INDICATIVE NOTICES FOR SUPPLIES AND SERVICES

(a) THE BASIC PRINCIPLES

With respect to supply and services contracts, a utility is required to send a notice to the *Official Journal* at least once every twelve months containing certain specified information on the contracts which it expects to award in the next twelve months.[18] As with works, the notice may be sent at any time; this contrasts with the position under the public sector supply rules where it must be sent as soon as possible after the start of the financial year. The notice must be sent to the Office of Official Publications of the European Communities.[19] It will be published in the

---

[11] Clearly this is the intention since the Utilities Directive which these provisions seek to implement states quite clearly that the directive does not apply to all to such contracts: see Utilities Directives Arts. 6–14.

[12] Utilities Regulation 29(1). The notice must be sent by "the most appropriate means" (Utilities Regulation 29(1)) and the utility must retain evidence of the date of despatch (regulation 29(2)).

[13] Utilities Directive Article 25(2).

[14] Utilities Directive Article 25(4).

[15] Utilities Directive Article 25(3). There is provision for publication within five days in "exceptional" cases, on request (Utilities Directive Article 25(3) and Utilities Regulation 29(3)), but this condition is hardly likely to be met for periodic indicative notices.

[16] Utilities Directive in Article 25(5) clearly limits these requirements to contract notices and notices of design contests.

[17] See pp. 182–184.

[18] Utilities Regulation 14(1)(a).

[19] Utilities Regulation 29(1). The notice must be sent by "the most appropriate means" (Utilities Regulation 29(1)) and the utility must retain evidence of the date of despatch (regulation 29(2)).

hard copy of the *Official Journal of the European Communities* and also in the TED electronic data bank in full in the original language and in summary form in the other official Community languages,[20] at the expense of the Community.[21] The Office of Official Publications is in general required to publish the notice within 12 days of despatch.[22]

Whilst it is expressly stated that contract notices (those advertising individual contracts) may not be published elsewhere before despatch to the *Official Journal*, nor contain additional information, there are no similar express limitations for periodic indicative notices.[23]

(b) THRESHOLDS AND EXCLUSIONS

In relation to supply contracts the obligation applies only where a utility expects the value of its supply contracts for goods within "the same product area" to exceed 750,000 ECUs.[24]

This raises the question of when particular products may be considered to fall within the same "product area": for example, is a pen within the same product area as a pencil? The same terminology is used in relation to Prior Information Notices in the public sector and the issue has already been discussed in that context.[25] It was suggested there that the general test of whether a product is in the same area as another is whether a typical supplier would provide both products. The application of this test has been suggested for the utilities sector in a draft document published by the Commission.[26] This document also suggests that this can generally be achieved by aggregating at the level of four digits in the *Classification of Products According to Activities* (CPA) (the Community's general nomenclature for products[27]), which may be a helpful starting point, although this test should not be applied in a rigid manner. It was suggested in Chapter 9 that this same test should also be adopted in deciding whether products are products of the same type for the purpose of applying the rules on aggregation relating to individual contract award procedures.[28]

The notice must be subdivided to give separate information relating to

---

[20] Utilities Directive Article 25(3). The original language only is provided to be authentic.
[21] Utilities Directive Article 25(4).
[22] Utilities Directive Article 25(3).
[23] Article 25(5) of the Utilities Directive clearly limits this requirement to design contests.
[24] Utilities Regulation 14(2). The sterling equivalent for 1994–1995 was £561,480, but this was to be revised from January 1, 1996. (The value is revised every two years from January 1, 1988). It is calculated based on the average daily value of each currency expressed in ECUs over the 24 months ending on the last day of August prior to the date for revision: Utilities Directive 38(1). The new amount must be published in the *Official Journal* at the beginning of November prior to the date the revision takes effect: Utilities Directive Article 38(1).
[25] See pp. 186–191.
[26] *Policy Guidelines Defining the Term "Product Area" in Periodic Indicative Notices for Directive 93/38/EEC*, para.7.
[27] This is based on the United Nations *Central Products Classification* (CPC).
[28] See pp. 447–449.

each product area covered. In contrast with the public sector rules, however, there is no obligation for purchasers themselves to use the CPA nomenclature in notices.

In relation to services contracts the obligation applies only to Part A services contracts.[29] It is only necessary to publish a notice where the value of services contracts in the relevant financial year in a particular category of Part A services is expected to be greater than or equal to 750,000 ECUs.[30] A "category" of services here refers to the categories used in Part A of Schedule 4 to the regulations. The notice must be divided to give separate information for each category of services. As under the public sector rules it is submitted that when used in PIN notices these categories are too broad to provide useful information to providers. In categorising services for this purpose (whether for aggregation purposes, or for the purpose of organising information in the notice) it would be better to apply the test suggested for supplies – that of whether a typical service provider would be interested in all the services in question. The reader is referred on this point to the discussion in the chapter on the public sector.[31]

For both supply and services contracts the value of contracts for the purpose of applying the threshold rule is the value which the utility expects to give at the date of despatch of the notice.[32]

It is expressly provided that the obligation relating to periodic indicative notices does not apply to contracts which are excluded from the Utilities Regulations under regulations 6, 7 and 8,[33] nor to those which are excluded because they fall below the thresholds set out in regulation 10. Thus these contracts need not be publicised through a periodic indicative notice, nor need they be taken into consideration when calculating whether the threshold of 750,000 ECUs is reached.

For the purposes of the threshold rules relating to periodic indicative notices it is the value of the contracts of the utility as a whole which must be aggregated. In deciding whether specific contracts are covered by the regulations this is not necessarily the case: where the utility is divided into several "discrete operational units" which make their purchases separately, purchases may be aggregated at the level of the individual unit rather than the utility as a whole.[34] However, there are no special provisions on discrete operational units for periodic indicative notices. Thus in deciding whether the 750,000 ECUs threshold is met, the value of the contracts of all units must be counted, provided that they are above the thresholds for application of the regulations. Some practical

---

[29] Utilities Regulation 14(2)(a).
[30] Utilities Regulation 14(2)(a). On the calculation of the sterling equivalent see note 24.
[31] See pp. 188–189.
[32] Utilities Regulation 13(2).
[33] Utilities Regulation 14(2). On these exclusions see Chap. 8.
[34] This assumes that the regulations' provisions on discrete operational units are valid, a point on which there is some debate: see pp. 450–451.

illustrations of the significance of this point are provided in the chapter on the public sector, where the same principle applies.[35]

It can also be noted that the regulations provide for the threshold to be calculated by reference to the value of the total consideration to be provided under the supply, or services, contracts entered into, rather than by reference to the value of *goods or services* purchased.[36] Thus in considering whether the figure of 750,000 ECUs is reached for supply contracts, utilities must take into account the value of services provided under supply contracts, as well as the value of goods. It also means that the value of goods provided under services or works contracts is not to be taken into account. The same principles apply, *mutatis mutandis*, for services contracts. The application of these rules is illustrated by reference to some practical examples in the chapter on the public sector, where similar principles apply.[37] This approach, involving the valuation of contracts rather than products or services as such, appears to be a correct interpretation of the Utilities Directive which refers to "the total of the contracts for each product area", in the case of supply contracts, and "the estimated total value of the service contracts", for services contracts.[38]

(4) THE FORM OF NOTICES

The notices must be in a form which "substantially corresponds" to the model notice in Part A of Schedule 5 to the Utilities Regulations and must contain the information specified therein.[39] The model is set out on pages 468–469. The requirement in the public sector that notices should not exceed 650 words does not apply.

In relation to supply contracts, a single notice may refer to a variety of products, but as indicated above, the notice must be subdivided to give separate details of each "product area."[40-41] It is not, however, necessary to indicate the nature of the contract – for example, whether the goods are to be purchased or hired.

In relation to services, as was also noted above, it is necessary only to indicate the categories of services to be purchased and the estimated value of each category, information which is often of limited use to providers. In practice, it will be useful for authorities to break down services into more detailed classes within each category.

---

[35] See pp. 189–191.
[36] See Utilities Regulation 14(2)(b).
[37] See pp. 190–191.
[38] Utilities Directive Article 32(1)(a).
[39] Utilities Regulation 14(1).
[40-41] For supply contracts it is necessary under the public sector rules to provide details only of goods supplied and for services contracts of the services provided: see p. 185. The utilities' model notice, on the other hand, requires in relation to supply contracts reference to the quantity or value of each type of goods *or* services to be supplied (although in relation to services contracts only services are referred to).

UTILITIES CONTRACTS REGULATIONS 1995, SCHEDULE 5, PART A – FORM OF PERIODIC INDICATIVE NOTICE

A. For supply contracts

1. The name, address, telegraphic address, telephone, telex and facsimile numbers of the utility and of the service from which additional information may be obtained.

2. For each type of goods or services the total quantity or value to be supplied under the contract(s).

3. (a) Estimated date of the commencement of the procedures leading to the award of the contract(s) (if known).

   (b) Type of award procedure to be used.

4. Other information (for example, indicate if a call for competition will be published later).

5. Date of despatch of the notice.

B. For works contracts

1. The name, address, telegraphic address, telephone, telex and facsimile numbers of the utility.

2. (a) The site.

   (b) The nature and extent of the services to be provided, the main characteristics of the work or where relevant of any lots by reference to the work.

   (c) An estimate of the cost of the service to be provided.

3. (a) Type of award procedure to be used.

   (b) Estimated date for initiating the award procedures in respect of the contract or contracts.

   (c) Estimated date for the start of the work.

   (d) Estimated timetable for completion of the work.

4. Terms of financing of the work and of price revision.

5. Other information (for example, indicate if a call for competition will be published later).

6. Date of despatch of the notice.

C For services contracts

1. The name, address, telegraphic address, telephone, telex and facsimile numbers of the utility and of the service from which additional information may be obtained.
2. Intended total procurement in each of the service categories listed in Part A of Schedule A.
3. (a) Estimated date of the commencement of the procedures of the award of the contract(s) (if known).

   (b) Type of award procedure to be used.
4. Other information (for example, indicate if a call for competition will be published later).
5. Date of dispatch of the notice.

The Commission is likely shortly to adopt a recommendation that products and services should be described in PIN notices by reference to the Community's Common Procurement Vocabulary (CPV) which currently exists in draft form.[42]

(5) CONTRACTS REFERRED TO IN A PREVIOUS NOTICE

In all cases there is no need to repeat in a periodic indicative notice information which has already been included in a previous notice, provided that the second notice clearly states that it is an additional notice.[43] This situation is most likely to be relevant in relation to works planned more than a year ahead which may be referred to in one notice and may still be pending at the time of a subsequent notice.

(6) PERIODIC INDICATIVE NOTICES AND FRAMEWORK AGREEMENTS

A utility may place contracts pursuant to a "framework agreement", which is a non-binding understanding setting the terms of possible future contracts, provided that the framework agreement itself, which is not actually a contract, is *treated* as a contract for the purposes of the

---

[42] On the CPV see pp. 69–71.
[43] Utilities Regulation 14(4).

regulations.[44] One consequence of this is that a PIN notice must give details of framework agreements to be entered into, as well as contracts.

It is also necessary that the value of framework agreements is taken into account in calculating whether the threshold for publication of a periodic indicative notice has been met. The principles for calculating the estimated value of a framework agreement is set out in Utilities Regulation 10(17), and these will need to be followed in calculating the value of such an agreement for the purposes of a periodic indicative notice.

3. THE THREE AWARD PROCEDURES

(1) THE THREE TYPES OF PROCEDURE

Utilities must use one of three types of procedure. These are:

(i) *The "open" procedure.* This is a formal tendering procedure, under which the contract is publicly advertised and all interested parties are able to tender.

(ii) *The "restricted" procedure.* This is also a formal tendering procedure, whereby the contract is publicly advertised to invite potential providers to express an interest. Tenders are then invited from a limited number of persons selected by the authority.

(iii) *The "negotiated" procedure.* Under this procedure, the utility simply selects potential providers with whom to negotiate, and awards the contract to one of these firms without necessarily following any formal tendering procedure. This may be either a competitive or, in exceptional cases, a non competitive, procedure.

The choice between the three procedures and the detailed requirements of each procedure are explained in the text below. An outline of the main steps of each procedure is set out in the tables on pp. 565–572.

(2) THE CHOICE OF PROCEDURE

Under the public sector regulations contracting authorities are generally required to use either the open or restricted procedure. The more flexible negotiated procedure is available only in limited and specified cases, and a contracting authority must justify its use on the facts of each case. Under the Utilities Regulations, on the other hand, a utility has a free choice between the three different procedures: Utilities Regulation 13 simply states that "a utility shall use the open, the restricted or the negotiated procedure". In practice, utilities will often choose the negotiated procedure which offers useful flexibility. This procedure may be

---

[44] See pp. 454–460.

chosen even if the utility prefers some kind of formal tendering to informal negotiations: a formal tendering stage can be incorporated into the negotiated procedure, but the choice of the negotiated procedure offers the utility more flexibility than the restricted or open procedures in setting the rules of the tendering process. In general the form of negotiated procedure is, however, a competitive one following a call for competition – only in exceptional cases may negotiations be conducted with a selected provider or providers without a prior advertisement.

4. THE REQUIREMENT FOR A CALL FOR COMPETITION: OPEN, RESTRICTED AND NEGOTIATED PROCEDURES

(1) THE CALL FOR COMPETITION REQUIREMENT

In addition to the obligation to give advance notice of a utility's general requirements, there is a requirement to give publicity to each contract which falls within the regulations. This publicity is referred to as the "call for competition". The purpose of the call for competition is to enable interested providers from throughout Europe to obtain information on award procedures and so to give them an opportunity to participate. It applies to all contracts within the regulations unless the award falls within one of a number of specific exemptions – for example, for cases of urgency, or where there is only one supplier who can meet requirements – where publicity would be unduly inconvenient or redundant.

The call for competition requirement fulfils the same purpose as the requirement under the public sector regulations to publish a contract notice in the *Official Journal* for each proposed contract.[45] The call for competition requirement for utilities is, however, much less onerous than the comparable obligations under the public sector rules. It does not require an individual contract notice to be published for each contract; instead, the utility may choose other methods whereby steps are taken to publish the utility's *general* requirements, firms are invited to express interest in meeting these requirements, and contracts are then awarded by the restricted or negotiated procedure to firms who have indicated an interest.

Essentially, there are three possible methods of making a call for competition[46]:

(i) by advertisement of the individual contract;

---

[45] On this see Chap. 6.
[46] See Utilities Regulation 15(1) (requirement of a call for competition) and 15(2) (methods of making a call for competition).

471

(ii) by inclusion of details of the particular contract in a periodic indicative notice;

(iii) by advertisement of a qualification system, and the award of the contract pursuant to the qualification system.

In the case of an award made by an open procedure, only the first method may be used. In the case of awards by restricted or negotiated procedures, on the other hand, the utility may choose either of the three methods.

We will first consider the three methods of publicity. We will then outline the limited circumstances in which no call for competition need be made.

(2) MAKING A CALL FOR COMPETITION

(a) ADVERTISEMENT OF THE INDIVIDUAL CONTRACT

The first method of making a call for competition is by sending a notice about the contract to the *Official Journal* for publication.[47] This notice is referred to as a "contract notice".[48] This is the only method available for contracts awarded under the open procedure.[49] It may also be used for restricted and negotiated procedures. A utility may choose this method for a contract even where other methods are easily available – for example, where there already exists a qualification system covering the product in question – if the utility considers such a notice appropriate for the particular award.

The notice must be sent to the Office of Official Publications of the European Communities.[50] It will be published in the hard copy of the *Official Journal of the European Communities* and also in the TED electronic data bank, in full in the original language and in summary form in the other official Community languages,[51] at the expense of the Community.[52] The Office of Official Publications is in general required to publish the notice within 12 days of despatch.[53] In "exceptional" cases a utility may request that the notice be published within five days of despatch, provided that the utility sends the notice by electronic mail,

---

[47] Utilities Regulation 15(2)(b).
[48] See the definition of "contract notice" in Utilities Regulation 2(1).
[49] Utilities Regulation 15(2)(a) (which provides that the other methods discussed below are available only for the restricted and negotiated procedure).
[50] Utilities Regulation 29(1). The notice must be sent by "the most appropriate means" (Utilities Regulation 29(1)) and the utility must retain evidence of the date of despatch (regulation 29(2)).
[51] Utilities Directive Articles 21(5) and 25(2). It is provided that the original language is authentic.
[52] Utilities Directive Article 25(4).
[53] Utilities Directive Article 25(3).

telex or facsimile,[54] and in this case the Office of Official Publications must endeavour to publish the notice within this period.[55]

The utility may also publish the information in other ways, for example, in the national press,[56] but this may not be done until the *Official Journal* notice has been despatched and national publicity material may not contain more information than the *Official Journal* notice.[57] The fact that this limitation refers to the date of despatch rather than the date of receipt by the *Official Journal* or the date of publication means that in practice nearly two weeks may elapse between the appearance of a national notice and the appearance of the notice in the *Official Journal*. This may give a significant advantage to national providers in view of the importance of advance notice of contracts. If the rule were deliberately exploited, however, this could be a breach of the E.C. Treaty or the general prohibition on discriminatory behaviour in the Utilities Regulations.[58]

Schedule 5 to the Utilities Regulations sets out model notices for these advertisements, which differ slightly for the open, restricted and negotiated procedures.[59] These models are set out on pages 474–479. The notices sent must be in a form "substantially corresponding" to those in the schedule and must contain all the information specified in the models.[60] The Commission is likely shortly to adopt a recommendation that the subject-matter of the contract should be described in contract notices by reference to the Community's Common Procurement Vocabulary (CPV) which currently exists in draft form.[61-62]

---

[54] Utilities Regulation 29(3).
[55] Utilities Directive Article 25(3).
[56] It was explained above that this would not normally be a breach of the E.C. Treaty: see pp. 195–196.
[57] Utilities Regulation 29(4).
[58] See Chap. 4 and p. 462.
[59] The notices for the three procedures are found respectively in Parts B, C and D of Schedule 5.
[60] Utilities Regulation 15(2)(b).
[61-62] On the CPV see pp. 69–71.

UTILITIES CONTRACTS REGULATIONS 1995, SCHEDULE 5, PART B – FORM OF OPEN PROCEDURE NOTICE

1. The name, address, telegraphic address, telephone, telex and facsimile numbers of the utility.
2. Nature of the contract (supply or services; where applicable, state if it is a framework agreement).
   Category of services within the meaning of Schedule 4 and description (CPA classification).
3. Place of delivery, site or place of performance of services.
4. For supplies and works:
   (a) nature and quantity of the goods to be supplied: or the nature and extent of the services to be provided and general nature of the work.
   (b) Indication of whether the suppliers can tender for some and/or all of the goods required. If, for works contracts, the work or the contract is subdivided into several lots, the size of the different lots and possibility of tendering for one, for several or for all of the lots.
   (c) For works contracts: information concerning the purpose of the work or the contract where the latter also involves the drawing up of projects.
5. For services:
   (a) Indication whether the execution of the services is by law, regulation, or administrative provision reserved to a particular profession.
   (b) Reference of the law, regulation or administrative provision.
   (c) Indication whether legal persons should indicate the names and professional qualifications of the staff to be responsible for the execution of the services.
   (d) Indication whether services providers can tender for a part of the services concerned.

6. Authorisation to submit variants.
7. Derogation from the use of European specifications, in accordance with Regulation 12(4).
8. Time-limits for delivery, completion or duration of services contract.
9. (a) Name and address from which the contracts documents and additional documents may be requested.
   (b) Where applicable, the amount and terms of payment of the sum to be paid to obtain such documents.
10. (a) The final date for receipt of tenders.
    (b) The address to which they must be sent.
    (c) The language or languages in which they must be drawn up.
11. (a) Where applicable, the persons authorised to be present at the opening of tenders.
    (b) The date, hour and place of such opening.
12. Any deposits and guarantees required.
13. Main terms concerning financing and payment and/or reference to the provisions in which these are contained.
14. Where applicable, the legal form to be taken by a grouping of providers to whom the contract is awarded.
15. Minimum standards of the economic and financial standing and technical capacity required of the provider to whom the contract is awarded.
16. Period during which the tenderer is bound to keep open his tender.
17. The criteria for the award of the contract. Criteria other than that of the lowest price shall be mentioned where they do not appear in the contract documents.
18. Other information.
19. Where applicable, the date of publication in the *Official Journal* of the periodic indicative notice which refers to the contract.
20. Date of despatch of the notice.

UTILITIES CONTRACTS REGULATIONS 1995, SCHEDULE 5, PART C – FORM OF RESTRICTED PROCEDURE NOTICE

1. The name, address, telegraphic address, telephone, telex and facsimile numbers of the utility.
2. Nature of the contract (supply, works or services; where applicable, state if it is a framework agreement). Category of services specified in Schedule 4 and description (CPA classification).
3. Place of delivery, site or place of performance of services.
4. For supplies and works:
   (a) Nature and quantity of the goods to be supplied; or the nature and extent of the services to be provided and general nature of the work.
   (b) Indication of whether the suppliers can tender for some and/or all of the goods required. If, for works contracts, the work or the contract is subdivided into several lots, the size of the different lots and the possibility of tendering for one, for several or for all of the lots.
   (c) For works contracts: information concerning the purpose of the work or the contract where the latter also involves the drawing up of projects.
5. For services:
   (a) Indication whether the execution of the services is by law, regulation, or administrative provision reserved to a particular profession.
   (b) Reference of the law, regulation or administrative provision.
   (c) Indication whether legal persons should indicate the names and professional qualification of the staff to be responsible for the execution of the services.
   (d) Indication whether services providers can tender for a number of the services concerned.

6. Authorisation to submit variants.

7. Derogation from the use of European specifications, in accordance with Regulation 12(4).

8. Time-limits for delivery, completion or duration of service contracts.

9. Where applicable, the legal form to be taken by a grouping of providers to whom the contract is awarded.

10. (a) The final date for receipt of requests to participate.
    (b) The address to which they must be sent.
    (c) The language or languages in which they must be drawn up.

11. The final date for despatch of invitations to tender.

12. Any deposits and guarantees required.

13. Main terms concerning financing and payment and/or reference to the provisions in which these are contained.

14. Information concerning the provider's personal position and minimum standards of economic and financial standing and technical capacity required of the provider to whom the contract is awarded.

15. The criteria for the award of the contract where they are not mentioned in the invitation to tender.

16. Other information.

17. Where applicable, the date of publication in the *Official Journal* of the periodic indicative notice which refers to the contract.

18. Date of despatch of the notice.

UTILITIES CONTRACTS REGULATIONS 1995, SCHEDULE 5, PART D – FORM OF NEGOTIATED PROCEDURE NOTICE

1. The name, address, telegraphic address, telephone, telex and facsimile numbers of the utility.
2. Nature of the contract (supply, works or services; where applicable, state if it is a framework agreement). Category of services specified in Schedule 4 and description (CPA reference).
3. Place of delivery, size or place of performance of services.
4. For supplies and works:
   (a) Nature and quantity of the goods to be supplied; or the nature and extent of the services to be provided and general nature of the work.
   (b) Indication of whether the suppliers can tender for some and/or all of the goods required. If, for works contracts, the work or the contract is subdivided into several lots, the size of the different lots and the possibility of tendering for one, for several or for all of the lots.
   (c) For works contracts; information concerning the purpose of the work or the contract where the latter also involves the drawing up of projects.
5. For services:
   (a) Indication whether the execution of the services is by law, regulation, or administrative provision reserved to a particular profession.
   (b) Reference to the law, regulation or administrative provision.
   (c) Indication whether legal persons should indicate the names and professional qualifications of the staff to be responsible for the execution of the services.
   (d) Indication whether services providers can tender for a part of the services concerned.

6. Derogation from the use of European specifications, in accordance with Regulation 12(4).
7. Time-limit for delivery, completion or duration of services contract.
8. Where applicable, the legal form to be taken by a grouping of providers to whom the contract is awarded.
9. (a) The final date for receipt of requests to participate.
   (b) The address to which they must be sent.
   (c) The language or languages in which they must be drawn up.
10. Any deposits and guarantees required.
11. Main terms concerning financing and payment and/or references to the provisions in which these are contained.
12. Information concerning the provider's personal position and minimum standards of economic and financial standing and technical capacity required of the provider to whom the contract is awarded.
13. Where applicable, the names and addresses of providers already selected by the utility.
14. Where applicable, date(s) of previous publications in the *Official Journal*.
15. Other information.
16. Where applicable, the date of publication in the *Official Journal* of the periodic indicative notice which refers to the contract.
17. Date of despatch of the notice.

It may be noted that the models, whilst referring to the need for all factors relevant to the award to be set out, do not indicate specifically that these should be in order of importance, as required under the regulations.[63] This must be remembered in filling out the notice.

(b) PUBLICITY THROUGH A PERIODIC INDICATIVE NOTICE

In the case of a contract to be awarded by the restricted or negotiated procedure, a second method of making a call for competition is by publication of a periodic indicative notice which indicates an intention to award the particular contract.[64] (As mentioned above, this method is not,

---

[63] See pp. 509–510.
[64] Utilities Regulation 15(2)(a).

however, available for contracts awarded under the open procedure where a contract notice must always be published.) A periodic indicative notice is, as explained above, a notice of which the basic function is to give advance notice to the market of a utility's general requirements.[65] To use a periodic indicative notice to meet the obligations to publicise a specific contract, as well, a number of conditions must be met. First, the periodic indicative notice must refer specifically to the goods or services which are to be the subject of the proposed contract.[66] This would seem to require that the subject matter of the contract should be described with the same specificity as would be required in an individual contract notice, so enabling providers to identify whether the particular contract will be of interest. Secondly, the notice must make it clear that offers are to be sought using the restricted or negotiated procedure *without publication of a further notice*.[67] Thirdly, the notice must request those interested to express that interest in writing.[68] These last two conditions ensure that interested providers are aware that they must respond to the notice. The utility must also send all those who express an interest in response to the notice "detailed information" on the contract.[69] Before beginning the selection it must invite them to confirm their wish to participate.[70] In addition, the notice can be relied upon only if it is published not more than 12 months before the date of the invitation to confirm is sent.[71]

(c) PUBLICITY THROUGH ADVERTISEMENT OF A QUALIFICATION SYSTEM

A third way in which a call for competition may be made is by advertising in the *Official Journal* the existence of a qualification system.[72] A qualification system is a system whereby firms interested in supplying the needs of a utility may apply to be registered as potential providers. The utility then selects from these a number who are designated as approved (or "qualified") providers, who effectively form a suitable pool from which the utility may draw those who are to be invited to bid or negotiate on future contracts. Where a utility proposes to award a contract through a restricted or negotiated procedure and selects firms to bid or negotiate for the contract only from those who have qualified under an advertised system, the fact that the system itself has been advertised is considered sufficient to constitute a call for competition for that contract. This method is available only where the potential bidders are all to be drawn from the qualifications list; if the

---

[65] See pp. 462–463.
[66] Utilities Regulation 15(2)(a) and 15(3)(a).
[67] Utilities Regulation 15(2)(a) and 15(3)(b).
[68] *Ibid.*
[69] Utilities Regulation 15(2) and 14(3)(c).
[70] *Ibid.*
[71] Regulation 14(2)(a) and 14(3)(d).
[72] Utilities Regulation 14(2)(a).

utility wishes to invite participation from any firms not qualified under the system then it is required to advertise the contract by an individual advertisement or in a periodic indicative notice as outlined above.[73]

Qualification systems for the purpose of these provisions must be run in accordance with certain requirements set out in Utilities Regulation 18; these are described further below.[74] These include requirements concerning the advertisement of the system which are set out in Utilities Regulation 18(12).[75] These require that the system should be advertised in the *Official Journal* when first established. If the system has already operated for more than three years or if it is expected to operate for more than three years in the future, it must then be readvertised on an annual basis. Thus new entrants to the market or those who have improved their performance are given regular opportunities to be considered or reconsidered.

The notice advertising the system must be sent to the Office of Official Publications of the European Communities,[76] which must publish the notice within 12 days of despatch.[77] As with other notices, it will be published in the hard copy of the *Official Journal* and in the TED electronic data bank, in full in the original language and in summary form in the other official Community languages.[78] As also with other notices, the cost is borne by the Community.[79]

The notice is required to be in a form which "substantially" corresponds with the model notice set out in Part E of Schedule 5 to the Utilities Regulations.[80] This model is set out at page 482.

The advertisement of a qualification system is an available method of publicity only for contracts awarded by the restricted or negotiated procedure,[81] and not for those awarded by an open procedure which, as noted above, require publication of a contract notice for each award.

The provisions permitting a call for competition through the advertisement of a qualification system provide a method for a utility to award contracts by the restricted or negotiated procedure without the bureaucracy of publicising every major contract separately, as is required under the public sector rules. A qualification procedure of this kind can also reduce the administrative burdens of qualification, since participation in individual award procedures is limited to parties already qualified. This again contrasts with the position in the public sector where the requirement to consider any party responding to a general

---

[73] Regulation 14(92)(a) and 14(4), imposing the condition that firms invited must be limited to those qualified in accordance with the system.
[74] See pp. 532–539.
[75] See Utilities Regulation 14(2)(a).
[76] Utilities Regulation 29(1). It must be sent by the most appropriate means (regulation 29(1)) and the utility must retain evidence of the date of despatch (regulation 29(2)).
[77] Utilities Directive Article 25(3).
[78] Utilities Directive Article 25(2).
[79] Utilities Directive Article 25(4).
[80] Utilities Regulation 18(12).
[81] As stated in Utilities Regulation 14(2)(a).

advertisement means that an authority may in practice need to examine the qualifications of a variety of "new" providers on each occasion.

(3) EXCEPTIONS TO THE REQUIREMENT FOR A CALL FOR COMPETITION

(a) THE NEED FOR EXCEPTIONS

In a number of circumstances a utility is exempt from the usual requirement to make a call for competition, either because this would be redundant (for example, there is only one possible provider) or because competition would be impractical (for example, in cases of urgency). In these cases the utility is free to conclude the contract, without advertisement, with any firm it chooses, using any of the three procedures under the regulations. In practice, this will almost invariably be the negotiated procedure, since the very circumstances which make award without a call for competition appropriate will also preclude the use of the restricted or open procedures.

In practice, a utility invoking the exceptions to the call for competition requirements basically is in the same position as an authority subject to the public sector rules which uses the "negotiated procedure without advertisement". As would be expected, in the same situations in which the public sector rules allow the use of the negotiated procedure without advertisement – including, for example, urgency – a utility is similarly allowed to enter into a procurement without a call for competition. However, in addition utilities are permitted a number of additional exemptions from making a call for competition which have no parallel in the public sector rules exempting authorities from advertising requirements.

UTILITIES CONTRACTS REGULATIONS 1995,
PART 5, SCHEDULE E – FORM OF NOTICE OF A
QUALIFICATION SYSTEM

1. The name, address, telegraphic address, telephone, telex and facsimile numbers of the utility.
2. Purpose of the qualification system.
3. Address where the rules concerning the qualification system can be obtained (if different from the address mentioned under 1).
4. Where applicable, duration of the qualification system.

The exceptions to the call for competition requirement are contained in Utilities Regulation 16, and are as listed below.

(b) UNSATISFACTORY OUTCOME OF A CALL FOR COMPETITION

Utilities Regulation 16(1)(a) permits an award without a call for competition where there has already been a procedure with a call for competition but this has produced either no tenders at all, or no "suitable" tenders. This applies only where the terms of the contract remain substantially unaltered from the original procedure. The scope of this exemption is considered further below in the general discussion of unsatisfactory award procedures.[82]

(c) RESEARCH AND DEVELOPMENT

Under Utilities Regulation 16(1)(b) a call for competition is also not required "where the contract is to be awarded purely for the purposes of research, experiment, study or development", except where the contract "has the purpose of ensuring profit or of recovering research and development costs". It appears that this is intended to have the same scope as an almost identical provision in the Supply Regulations,[83] an exemption which has already been discussed.[84]

(d) TECHNICAL REASONS, ARTISTIC REASONS AND REASONS CONNECTED WITH EXCLUSIVE RIGHTS

Utilities Regulation 16(1)(c) provides that a call for competition is not required when "for technical or artistic reasons, or for reasons connected with the protection of exclusive rights, the contract may only be performed by a particular person". This is identical to the provision permitting the use of a negotiated procedure without advertisement under the public sector regulations and will no doubt be given the same interpretation. Readers are thus referred to the previous discussion on the public sector provision.[85]

---

[82] See pp. 521–523.
[83] The utilities provision is different in that the exception to the application of the exemption is stated to apply where the purpose of the contract is "ensuring profit", whilst under the Supply Regulations the provision allowing use of negotiated procedures for certain research and development contracts applies where the purpose is to "establish commercial viability". It appears, however, that the meaning of these provisions is intended to be the same.

It may be noted also that the Supply Regulations provision covers only goods, but the utilities' exception applies whatever the subject matter in question.
[84] Supply Regulation 10(3)(c) and 13(1).
[85] See p. 258.

(e) URGENCY

As is explained below, the Utilities Regulations provide for minimum time-limits for certain phases of all three award procedures. Circumstances of urgency, however, may indicate that a shorter period is required than that provided for in these regulations and Utilities Regulation 16(1)(d) provides an exception to the call for competition requirement for such cases of urgency. This may be invoked only when, if it is "strictly necessary" for "reasons of extreme urgency", the time-limits which normally apply in the three award procedures cannot be met. It also required that these reasons must have been brought about by events which were "unforeseeable" by the purchaser. The meaning of these various requirements has already been discussed in the context of the urgency exception in the public sector rules.[86] In the public sector rules there is also an additional requirement that the events leading to urgency should not be attributable to the purchaser, but this requirement does not appear in the Utilities Regulations or Utilities Directive. This is probably due to an oversight.

In the case of the restricted and negotiated procedure the regulations suggest an "ordinary" minimum period for the phases between advertisement and expression of interest, and between issue of invitations and deadline for bids (five weeks and three weeks respectively), and also a "shorter" minimum period (22 days (or 15 days in "exceptional cases") and 10 respectively) for cases where it may be appropriate to shorten the usual procedure, including in cases of urgency. It is only where even this "shorter" minimum period cannot be met that the utility will be exempt from competition altogether under the urgency exception in regulation 16.

(f) FURTHER CONTRACTS WITH AN EXISTING PROVIDER

In certain cases the regulations provide for use of the negotiated procedure for concluding a follow-on contract with an existing contracting partner. It was explained in Chapter 9 that as a general principle it is not permitted simply to negotiate a new agreement with an existing partner. This is possible only where this is the usual commercial practice with that type of contract *and* the possibility has been referred to in the contract notice.[87] In other cases, a new open, restricted or negotiated procedure involving competition between providers must be used to select a new provider. However, Utilities Regulation 16 provides for some exceptions to that principle in certain defined cases, where there is a special justification for continuing the relationship with the old provider.

---

[86] See pp. 260–263.
[87] See pp. 415–416.

(i) ADDITIONAL PURCHASES FROM A PREVIOUS SUPPLIER

Utilities Regulation 16(1)(e) provides for an exception to the call for competition requirement in the case of supply contracts, where the goods to be acquired are a partial replacement for or addition to existing goods or an existing installation. The derogation applies when to obtain the goods from a party other than the original supplier would entail the acquisition of goods with different technical characteristics, and this would entail either (i) incompatibility with the existing goods or installation, or (ii) disproportionate technical difficulties. This exemption effectively identifies certain objective circumstances where it is very likely that the previous supplier will offer the best value for money. It is not necessary that the need for replacements or additions should be unforeseen for the utility to invoke the exemption.

The derogation applies only to supply contracts. Thus it may not be used where the utility seeks to acquire goods under a services contract, which seems anomalous.

Where the other party to the contract is the only party able to meet the needs of the utility then the utility may invoke the exemption considered under (d) above.

This provision is similar to a provision under the public sector supply rules allowing use of a negotiated procedure without advertisement in such circumstances.[88] However, in contrast with the public sector provision[89] there is no requirement that the new contract should be for a term of three years or less, reflecting the fact that contracts in the utilities sector are often of longer duration.

(ii) ADDITIONAL WORKS OR SERVICES WHICH WERE UNFORESEEN

Under Utilities Regulation 16(1)(f) a utility may award a new works or services contract to an existing provider without a call for competition where this is for work or services additional to that in a previous works or services contract, and where the new works or services have become necessary through "unforeseen circumstances" (which refers to the fact that they were unforeseen at the time the original contract was made). The exemption applies only in the following two cases.

The first is where, for "technical or economic reasons" the new works or services cannot be carried out separately without "great inconvenience" to the purchaser. In accordance with the general rule on interpreting derogations "great inconvenience" will be narrowly construed.

---

[88] See pp. 264–265.
[89] See pp. 264–265.

The second case is where the new works or services *can* be carried out separately but they are "strictly necessary" to the later stages of the original contract.

In these cases the objective circumstances make it almost certain that the existing provider will offer best value for money for the additional work, and it thus appears inappropriate to require the contract to be publicised.

A similar provision allowing exemption from advertisement under the public sector rules can only be relied upon where the consideration for the additional works does not exceed 50 per cent of the value of the consideration under the original contract, but this limitation does not apply under the Utilities Directive and Regulations. However, under the GPA, competition may be dispensed with for construction services only where the value of any contracts for the additional services does not exceed 50 per cent[90] of the original contract. For purchasers covered by the GPA this limitation must be adhered to from January 1, 1996 when the GPA comes into effect.[90a] A Commisison Proposal for a new directive to amend the Utilities Directive in light of the GPA proposes to apply this limitation under the directive,[90b] to ensure that the Community rules are as favourable as the GPA rules. The Proposal envisages applying this to all utilities covered by the directive, not just those which are subject to the GPA, but it is not clear that this will be accepted.[90c] It is also proposed to apply the limitation to non-construction services contracts. In fact, the GPA itself does not contain any exception of this type for non-construction services, and it thus appears that entities covered by the GPA may not therefore rely on this exception at all in relation to non-construction services. In this respect, compliance with the directive does not appear to involve automatic compliance with the GPA rules, a point which has been overlooked in the Commission's Proposal.

Where the need for the works or services was foreseen, then, as noted above, this provision cannot be relied upon. In this case, where it is considered that it may be appropriate to award the later work to the same provider, the utility should indicate this in the contract notice, and use the derogation for additional work referred to in the contract notice, described at (iii) below. If it fails to do so, it may be able to use derogation (d) above, which applies where for technical reasons the existing provider is the *only* party able to carry out the new work.

---

[90] GPA, Article XV(1)(f).

[90a] In the United Kingdom this limitation may be relied upon by both GPA providers (under the GPA) and Community providers, under Utilities Regulation 4(3): see further pp. 461–462.

[90b] Proposal for a European Parliament and Council Directive amending Directive 93/38/EEC, co-ordinating the procurement procedures of entities operating in the water, energy, transport and telecommunications sectors, COM (95) 107 Final, Article 1(6).

[90c] See further pp. 463–464.

(iii) ADDITIONAL WORKS REFERRED TO IN THE CONTRACT NOTICE

Utilities Regulation 16(1)(g) permits utilities to award a contract to a previous provider without a call for competition where it seeks to obtain works which are a repetition of those under the previous works contract, and which relate to the project for the purpose of which the original contract was made. This might apply, for example, where a contractor has been awarded a works contract to build houses in the first phase of development of an office complex, to allow the utility to award that contractor the work building identical houses under a second phase of the development. Probably it is not necessary for the work to constitute a "repetition" that it should be identical to previous work in every detail, but it must no doubt be substantially similar. There may also be debate as to what constitutes a single "project"; there is as yet no guidance on this in the case law.

The provision applies only when the original was itself awarded following a call for competition.[91] It is also essential that the utility should mention the possibility of the additional work being awarded to the same provider without a call for competition when it invited firms to tender or negotiate for the original contract.[92] This enables firms to know the exact scope of work which they may receive, and hence to judge whether it is worth submitting a bid.[93]

As already noted, it is generally not possible to simply negotiate a contract with a previous provider even where this possibility is referred to in the contract notice: to allow this as a general rule would create unlimited scope for extending the relationship with an existing favoured provider, and hence such an "extension" is normally treated as a new contract.[94] The present exception allows for this, however, in a limited case, where it is commercially reasonable and the limiting conditions preclude much scope for abuse.

In contrast with the public sector rules,[95-96] this exemption from competition, reflecting the Utilities Directive, only covers works and does not extend to services. This appears to be an anomalous difference between the two regimes. The utilities rules are in fact consistent with the GPA on this point, whereas the public sector rules are not, since the GPA does not allow such an exemption for services.

It is also provided that in determining the value of the original contract for the purpose of applying the thresholds in the regulations under regulation 10, the utility must take into account the value of the consideration which it expected to pay for the additional works.[97]

---

[91] Utilities Regulation 16(1)(g) and 16(2)(a).
[92] Utilities Regulation 16(1)(g) and 16(2)(b).
[93] *Ibid.*
[94] See pp. 415–416.
[95-96] See pp. 263–264.
[97] Utilities Regulation 16(1)(g) and 16(2)(c).

(g) GOODS QUOTED AND PURCHASED ON A COMMODITY MARKET

An exemption from a call for competition is also provided, in Utilities Regulation 16(1), for supply contracts for the purchase or hire of goods which are quoted on a commodity market, where the goods are purchased on that market. A commodity market is a market where tangible assets are bought and sold for future delivery through an exchange subject to international regulation, prices being set through the exchange. Such markets exist, for example, for precious and non-precious metals, grain, livestock, coffee, tea and cocoa. They are designed to ensure suppliers and purchasers can obtain a secure advance price for their transactions in markets where there are inherent price fluctuations; the existence of the exchange market means that these fluctuations are borne largely by speculators. This exemption allows utilities to purchase directly from the exchange without advertising. This is usually cheaper than buying through middlemen who have themselves bought directly through the market.

There is no parallel provision in the public sector rules exempting bodies from advertising contracts for products quoted on a commodity market. Thus purchases of these products must generally be made under the open or restricted procedures, following advertisement in the *Official Journal*. This may preclude public bodies from taking advantage of more favourable prices on the markets.

(h) ESPECIALLY ADVANTAGEOUS BARGAINS

There are also provisions in Utilities Regulation 16(j) and (k) which allow an authority to take account of bargains arising out of certain special circumstances, without the need for any call for competition.

(i) PURCHASES ON INSOLVENCY OR A CLOSING DOWN SALE

Utilities Regulation 16(1)(k) provides an exemption where a contract is made to "take advantage of particularly advantageous conditions for the purchase of goods in a closing down sale or in a sale brought about by insolvency". This provision recognises that a closing down sale or sale by a liquidator may provide opportunities for a particularly favourable purchase which may be lost if the normal procedures are followed. To invoke this derogation, as with others such as the urgency provision[98] the court will doubtless require the utility to prove that the relevant conditions are met, notably that the conditions of the purchase are "particularly favourable". It would seem that favourable conditions need not be confined to a favourable price.

---

[98] See p. 484.

What is meant by a "closing down sale" is not expressly defined in the regulations. The concept must be interpreted in accordance with the directive, which refers to a purchase from a supplier "definitively winding up his business activities".[99]

Insolvency is not defined. The Utilities Directive itself states that this exemption applies to purchases from "the receivers or liquidators of a bankruptcy, an arrangement with creditors or a similar procedure under national laws or regulations",[1] which suggests that the concept of insolvency in the regulations should be construed broadly and not in any technical sense.

(ii) SHORT-TERM BARGAINS

Utilities Regulation 16(1)(j) gives an exemption from the requirement for a call for competition for "bargain purchases" of supplies where the following strict conditions apply:

(a) the purchase takes advantage of a "particularly advantageous opportunity";

(b) the opportunity is available "for a very short period of time"; and

(c) the price is "considerably lower than normal market prices."[2]

This allows utilities to take advantage of short-term opportunities which do not fall within the specific confines of the insolvency/closing down exemption.

There are no similar provisions applying in the case of works and services.

There is no equivalent of either of these provisions in the public sector rules to allow a public body to take advantage of such favourable market circumstances by awarding a contract through the negotiated procedure without advertisement.

(i) PROCEDURES FOLLOWING A DESIGN CONTEST

Under Utilities Regulation 16(1)(l) utilities may dispense with the requirement for a call for competition where a design contest has been held to select potential providers, and the contract is negotiated with those providers who were successful in the contest. This provision is considered further in the section on design contests.[3]

(j) FRAMEWORK AGREEMENTS

A framework agreement is a non-binding agreement between a utility and a provider establishing the terms for possible future contracts

---

[99] Utilities Directive article 20(2)(k).

[1] Utilities Directive Article 20(2)(k).

[2] There is no reference to advantage other than price; thus the utility may not use the provision to take advantage of other favourable terms.

[3] See p. 562.

between the parties. Where a framework agreement is itself advertised in accordance with the regulations it is permitted to award contracts pursuant to that agreement without a further call for competition. This is provided by Utilities Regulation 16(2)(i).[4] The rules on framework agreement are considered in Chapter 9.[4a]

5. PROCEDURES FOLLOWING A CALL FOR COMPETITION: OPEN AND RESTRICTED PROCEDURES

(1) OBTAINING TENDERS: OPEN PROCEDURES

(a) GENERAL

As explained above, the open procedure is one under which any interested party may submit a bid, and the only method to satisfy the call for competition requirement for such a procedure is by a contract notice advertising the individual contract in the *Official Journal*. The rules governing this contract notice were explained above.[5] Following the notice, interested parties will need to obtain the documents which are needed to enable them to submit their bids, and must then submit these bids by the deadline stated in the notice.

(b) THE DESPATCH OF CONTRACT DOCUMENTS

To ensure firms can take advantage of the periods specified for them to prepare their tenders,[6] the regulations require the contract documents[7] to be sent within six days of receipt of a request.[8] A fee may be charged for the documents, which must be stated in the contract notice.[9] The

---

[4] It may be suggested that this would be the case even without this specific provision, since if the framework has been subject to a call for competition the contract itself has already been subject to a call for competition so that no specific exemption is needed. Based on this approach it has been suggested that framework agreements may thus be used in the public sector even though there is no express provision in the public sector rules to allow their use: see pp. 177–179.

[4a] See pp. 452–460.

[5] See pp. 471–482.

[6] As to which see pp. 491–492.

[7] The contract documents refer here to the contract conditions, the specifications or descriptions of the subject matter of the contract and any supplementary documents: see the definition of "contract documents" in Utilities Regulation 2(1).

[8] Utilities Regulation 17(6). The day of receipt itself is not counted in calculating this period:

Utilities Regulation 2(6)(a). If the day on which the period would expire is not a working day it must be extended to include the next working day: Utilities Regulation 2(6)(c), and the period must include at least two working days: Utilities Regulation 2(6)(b).

[9] See the model notice at pp. 474–475 above.

obligation to supply the documents applies only where the request is accompanied by any relevant fee.[10]

The obligation applies only where the request is received "in good time".[11] If a date for receipt of requests is stated in the contract notice and this date is reasonable then presumably a request is not in good time if it is not received by that date. However, there is no requirement to state any such date in the notice.

(c) OBLIGATION TO PROVIDE FURTHER INFORMATION

Any further information relating to the contract documents which is reasonably requested by a provider must be supplied not less than six days before the date for receipt of tenders, again provided the request is made in good time.[12] As with a request for the contract documents this applies only where any stipulated fee accompanies the request.[13]

(d) TIME-LIMITS FOR RECEIPT OF TENDERS

It will take interested firms some time to obtain the documents and to prepare a tender, and this time period is likely to be longer for non-domestic firms – for example, there may be a need to obtain translations of documents. The rules prescribe a minimum time period for submission of tenders, to prevent authorities from setting a short period which would constitute an unreasonable barrier to participation by non-domestic firms. In general, the last date for receipt of tenders must be not less than 52 days from the date of despatch of the contract notice,[14] the same period as for open procedures under the public sector regulations.

However, it is provided that in fixing the time-limit utilities must take into account the time required for any examination of voluminous documentation (such as lengthy specifications) or any inspection of site or documents.[15] Thus the usual 52 day period may need to be lengthened where such examinations or inspections are needed.

There is also provision for a reduction of the period when the utility has already published a periodic indicative notice, which relates to the contract in question.[16] In this case it is provided that the 52-day period may be reduced to 36 days (extended as necessary for voluminous documents, inspections, etc., in accordance with the provisions just outlined).

---

[10] Utilities Regulation 17(6).
[11] Utilities Regulation 17(6).
[12] Utilities Regulation 17(9). The time period is calculated as set out in note 8 above.
[13] Utilities Regulation 17(9).
[14] Utilities Regulation 17(1). The time periods are calculated as stated in note 8.
[15] Utilities Regulation 17(5).
[16] Utilities Regulation 17(2).

In relation to these reduced periods, the WTO Agreement on Government Procurement (GPA), in force from January 1, 1996, imposes more stringent requirements for utilities covered by the Agreement. First, advance notice allows reduction of the standard period only when the advance notice is published no more than 12 months, and at least 40 days, before the notice advertising the specific contract.[17] In addition, to be relied on for reducing the time limits the PIN must contain certain additional information on the specific contract which is not normally required in a PIN. As with the public sector, the Commission's Proposal for aligning the Community utilities regime with that under the GPA[17a] includes a provision requiring the advance notice to be published within the same time limits and to contain the relevant additional information if it is to be relied on to reduce the time limits for tendering under the Community regime.[17b] It is proposed that these additional requirements will apply to all utilities and not just those covered by the GPA, although it is not clear this will be accepted.[17c] It can be noted that, even though no amendment has yet been adopted, the more stringent obligation under the GPA will need to be adhered to by utilities covered by the GPA as from January 1, 1996, and can be relied upon both by GPA providers, under the GPA, and Community providers, under Utilities Regulation 4(2).[17d]

(e) PROPOSAL ON THE FORM OF TENDERS

As with the public sector rules Commission's Proposal for aligning the Utilities Directive with the GPA includes provisions for certain rules on the form of tenders.[18] This is largely to incorporate the rules found in the GPA.[19]

First, it is proposed that all tenders should be in writing and that telephone bids should not be acceptable.

Secondly, it is proposed to state expressly that *if* the authority chooses to permit bids by telegram, telex, facsimile or electronic means they must include all information necessary for tender evaluation; and, for open or

---

[17] GPA Article XI(3).
[17a] On this Proposal see generally pp. 563–564.
[17b] Proposal for a European Parliament and Council Directive amending Directive 93/38/EEC co-ordinating the procurement procedures of entities operating in the water, energy, transport and telecommunications sectors, COM (95) 107 Final, Article 1(11). It may be noted that the relevant date, as under the GPA, is to be the date of publication of the notice, instead of the date of despatch which is usually the relevant date for time limits under the directives. The relevant additional information is such of the information listed in the restricted procedure model notice which is available at the time the advance notice was published.
[17c] On this see pp. 563–564.
[17d] See pp. 461–462.
[18] Proposal for a European Parliament and Council Directive amending Directive 93/38/EEC co-ordinating the procurement procedures of entities operating in the water, energy, transport and telecommunications sectors, Article 1(13).
[19] GPA Article XIII(1).

restricted procedures must, in particular, include a statement that the bidder agrees to the terms, conditions and provisions of the invitation. This is curious, since there is no corresponding express requirement for tenders submitted by letter or directly in writing, but it is difficult to see why the rules on these matters should vary according to the method of tender.

Thirdly, it is proposed that where tenders are submitted by the above means, with the exception of electronic mail, they must be confirmed by letter dispatched before the time limit for receipt of tenders.

(2) OBTAINING TENDERS: RESTRICTED PROCEDURES

(a) GENERAL

As noted earlier, the restricted procedure is a formal tendering procedure in which bids may be submitted only by those specifically invited to tender. It was explained above that a call for competition under a restricted procedure may be made in one of three ways: through an individual contract notice; through a periodic indicative notice which refers to the specific contract; or through the advertisement of a qualification system. The rules applicable to this call for competition have been set out above.[20]

Once the call for competition has been made the purchaser will issue invitations to a limited number of interested firms, who must then submit their bids by the stated deadline.

(b) ASCERTAINING INTEREST IN THE CONTRACT

Invitations will be issued to those expressing interest in the contract. The exact steps involved in ascertaining who is interested may vary according to the way in which the call for competition was originally made.

Where the call for competition was made through publication of a contract notice in the *Official Journal*, interested firms will submit requests to be considered in response to the notice. The notice will expressly call upon firms to express their interest in the contract, and it must indicate the final date for receipt of requests to participate.[21]

Where the call for competition is made through a periodic indicative notice, the notice must, as we have seen, refer specifically to the contract in question and must call for expressions of interest to be submitted in writing.[22] The notice must also make it clear that there will be no further

---

[20] See pp. 471–482.
[21] Utilities Regulation 17(3); and see the model contract notice at pp. 476–477.
[22] Utilities Regulation 15(3)(b) There is no minimum time limit laid down for this initial response.

493

call for competition.[23] Utilities must then send all those who respond detailed information on the contract, and invite them to confirm whether they still wish to be selected to tender.[24] To fulfil the purpose of the requirement, which is to enable firms to know if they are interested in participating, the communication will probably need to contain the same sort of information as is found in contract notices. In fact, the GPA, which comes into force on January 1, 1996 and must be adhered to from that date for contracts subject to the GPA, expressly provides for inclusion of most of this information.[24a] A Commission Proposal for a new directive to align the Utilities Directive with the GPA proposes adding a provision to the directive requiring inclusion of all the information which would have been contained in the contract notice had the call for competition been made by such a notice.[24b] The communication must be sent within (or on the last day of this period) twelve months of the date on which the periodic indicative notice was published,[25] and must state the date by which these expressions of continued interest must be received.[26] The confirmation of continuing interest is effectively equivalent to the request to be invited to tender submitted in response to a specific contract notice.

As with open procedures the rules provide for minimum time-limits for the procedure to ensure that firms from other states are not disproportionately disadvantaged if they wish to participate. For this reason it is provided that the date for receipt of requests to be invited to tender, following either a contract notice or a request for confirmation of interest, must "in general" be at least five weeks from the date of despatch of the contract notice, and in all cases not less than 22 days from the despatch of the notice.[27] It is no doubt envisaged that specific justification should be advanced for a period of less than five weeks. Obviously urgency could be one such justification, but shorter periods could also be justified in some other cases, such as where the contract is for simple off-the-shelf items for which little preparation time is

---

[23] *Ibid.*

[24] Utilities Regulation 15(3)(d).

[24a] GPA, Article IX(6). This provision may be relied on not just by providers entitled to invoke the GPA but also by Community providers, by virtue of Utilities Regulation 4(3): see pp. 461–462.

[24b] Proposal for a European Parliament and Council Directive amending Directive 93/38/EEC, co-ordinating the procurement procedures and entities operating in the water, energy, transport and telecommunications sectors, COM (95) 107 Final, Article 1(7). Like the rest of the Proposal it is envisaged that this will apply to all contracts covered by the directive and not just those subject to the GPA, but it is not clear this will be accepted: see pp. 563–564.

[25] Utilities Regulation 15(3)(d).

[26] Utilities Regulation 16(3).

[27] Utilities Regulation 17(3). In theory the time-limits are calculated as set out in note 00 above but these rules will not be significant for these time-limits since the limits are slightly flexible in any case.

needed.[28] The Commission's Proposal for aligning the Community utilities regime with that under the GPA proposes to lengthen the period slightly to 37 days, as under the GPA itself.[28a] It is proposed that this will apply to all utilities and not just those covered by the GPA, although it is not clear that such a wide application of the amendment will be accepted.[28b] Even before any amendment is adopted, the longer GPA period must be adhered to by utilities covered by the GPA as from January 1, 1996, and can be relied upon both by GPA providers, under the GPA, and Community providers, under Utilities Regulation 4(2).[28c]

These time limits may be departed from only in an exceptional case where the utility requests the *Official Journal* to publish the notice within five days of despatch instead of the normal 12 day period.[29] In such an exceptional case the utility may allow only 15 days for a reply.[29a] This provision may no doubt normally be used only in cases of exceptional urgency.

As regards the form of requests, it is expressly provided that an "application to be invited to tender"[30] shall not be refused on the grounds that it is made by letter; nor because it is made by telegram, telex, facsimile or telephone, provided in these cases that it is confirmed by letter received prior to the closing date for receipt of request.[31] Apart from this, there are no express provisions on the form of requests. As was suggested for the public sector, it seems there is nothing to prevent an utility specifying in the contract notice the form of the request (for example, the language to be used) and to reject requests which do not meet these formalities. It should be possible to waive these, however, since they are specified for the benefit of the utility, provided, however, that all persons making requests are treated equally.[32] It is not clear whether requests to be invited to tender may be excluded from consideration for failure to meet formalities (such as language requirements)

---

[28] Under the public sector rules a general period of 37 days (similar to five weeks) is prescribed, with an exception allowing reduction of the period to 15 days where there is urgency; but there is no possibility under the public sector rules of shortening the procedure for other reasons.

[28a] Proposal for a European Parliament and Council Directive amending Directive 93/38/EEC co-ordinating the procurement procedures of entities operating in the water, energy, transport and telecommunications sectors, COM (95) 107 Final, Article 1(12).

[28b] On this see pp. 563–564.

[28c] See pp. 461–462.

[29] See Utilities Regulations 29(3). In this case the utility must send the notice by electronic mail, telex or facsimile: Utilities Regulation 29(3).

[29a] Utilities Regulation 17(3).

[30] The Utilities Directive refers to "requests for participation": Article 28(5). It seems clear that these provisions are intended to cover both requests following a contract notice, and also confirmations of interest where the contract has been publicised through a periodic indicative notice.

[31] Utilities Regulation 17(10).

[32] This arises from the fundamental principle of the equality of treatment of providers, laid down in case C–143/89, *Commission v. Denmark*, jugdment of June 22, 1993 (see pp. 180–181) which will certainly be applied in the utilities sector as well as in the public sector.

where these have not been stated in the contract notice. This could be implied on the basis of the rules underlying the purpose of eliminating unstructured discretion which might be abused. It could at least be implied that firms should be permitted to alter their requests to comply where the formalities have not been stated in advance.[33]

Where the call for competition is made through an advertisement of a qualification system there are no requirements concerning the way in which requests to be invited to tender should be made. In this case there is nothing in the rules requiring a utility to seek such requests; it may simply invite firms directly from the lists. Alternatively, in some cases the utility may still invite all or some of the firms on its list to indicate an interest in those particular contracts before issuing invitations.

In the case of contracts publicised through a contract notice or periodic indicative notice, the utility may also seek providers by additional methods – for example, by approaching providers known to be interested in this kind of work – and may consider these providers for the receipt of invitations. In the case of contracts publicised through advertisement of a qualification system, however, only providers who have been accepted onto the qualification lists may be considered.[33a]

(c) SELECTING PROVIDERS TO BE INVITED TO TENDER

Once it has followed the steps in (b) above a utility will have a list of firms which may be interested in submitting a tender. The question then arises as to which of these firms are to be issued with invitations to bid.

(i) THE NUMBER OF INVITATIONS

As with all purchasers a utility will wish the set number of firms to be invited to bid by balancing the advantages of a larger number in terms of wider competition against the disadvantages, such as costs of preparation and assessment. On this issue Utilities Regulation 19(5) states that the utility must take account "of the need to ensure adequate competition" in determining the number to be invited to bid. It is also stated expressly in regulation 19(3) that the criteria for selection may be based on the need to reduce the number selected "to a level which is justified by the characteristics of the award procedure and the resources required to complete it", which indicates clearly that the utility is not required to

---

[33] It is not clear how this principle would operate in relation to method of transmission, on which there are express provisions noted above. One view is that these merely limit the purchaser's discretion to reject on certain grounds, but do not affect any obligation to state these grounds in the contract notice if they are to be relied on; but another might be that they *confer* a discretion to reject certain forms of request where not confirmed by letter, even where the requirement for a letter is not stated in the contract notice.

[33a] Utilities Regulation 15(4).

consider all interested and qualified providers.[34] Apart from this there are no express constraints on numbers.

(ii) THE METHODS FOR SELECTING INVITEES ("SHORTLISTING")

(I.) General principles

As explained in considering the public sector rules, there are a variety of methods and criteria for drawing up a shortlist.[35] These include:

(i) whether providers meet minimum standards of financial and economic standing, and also the relative position in this respect of those reaching the minimum standards;

(ii) external factors such as strikes or political unrest[36];

(iii) approximation to the award criteria (such as which firms are likely to offer the best price or quality);

(iv) other factors relating to purchasing efficiency such as the possibilities for a long-term relationship or the need to preserve competition for future purchases;

(v) secondary factors (that is, those unrelated to the economic advantage of the contract) such as firms' equal opportunities policies;

(vi) random selection (for example, drawing lots); and

(vii) rotation between interested firms.

Which of these factors may be considered? The Utilities Regulations contain two main provisions concerning compilation of the shortlist. First, regulation 19(1) states that providers shall be selected on the basis of "objective criteria and rules". Secondly, regulation 19(2) states that the criteria for "deciding not to select a provider" may include a specific list of factors, such as bankruptcy, and conviction of a criminal offence relating to the conduct of the business (outlined further at II below). In addition, as noted above, it is expressly provided in regulation 19(3) that (without prejudice to the generality of regulation 19(1)) the criteria may take into account the need to reduce the number in line with the nature of the procedure and the resources needed.

It seems clear that the general concept of "objective" criteria includes at least all commercial criteria which are capable of being articulated and monitored in accordance with clear rules. Thus, utilities may take account of factors (i)–(iv) above. In this respect the utilities rules are much more flexible than those in the public sector which are widely considered to exclude consideration of commercial criteria other than financial and economic standing (although they are not unambiguous).[37]

---

[34] The public sector rules are more ambiguous although it was argued above that they should not be interpreted to require all qualified firms to be invited: see pp. 217–222.

[35] For more detailed explanation see pp. 217–222.

[36] In the context of the public sector regulations such factors may in fact come within the legal concepts of financial and economic standing: see Chap. 8.

[37] On the public sector rules see pp. 217–222.

It may be argued, however, that *relative* financial and technical standing of those who might reach the general *minimum* requirements may only be considered to the extent that there is some risk of non-completion amongst those who meet the minimum standards set; if this is not the case, relative standing appears to be a purely arbitrary criterion, which, as explained below, may not be permitted.

There is nothing specifically, on the other hand, to suggest that objective criteria are limited to those which relate to commercial benefit. Thus, it is arguable that social factors such as equal opportunities – which may not be taken into account in shortlisting under the public sector rules – may be considered in the utilities sector. This view is supported by the fact that some of the criteria specifically listed in regulation 19(2), which are put forward as illustrations of "objective criteria", relate to non-commercial secondary factors (for example, non-payment of taxes). However, the view that non-commercial criteria may be applied as a general principle is somewhat controversial and awaits clarification by the Court of Justice.

Even if the wide view that non-commercial criteria may be applied is correct, it is likely that the concept of "objective" criteria will be interpreted to exclude factors regarded as "arbitrary" or "irrational", or based on bad faith, even if these are factors capable of articulation and independent verification. Thus, it is unlikely that the courts would accept shortlisting decisions based on the hair colour of the firm's director. It was suggested above that relative financial and economic standing could also fall within the category of arbitrary criteria in certain cases. In practice, the use of non-commercial criteria, especially by utilities in the private sector, will be relatively uncommon.

The concept of objective criteria also seems to cover random methods or rotation which are also capable of objective application.[38] Certainly the concept *should* be interpreted to cover such possibilities, since this may sometimes be the only convenient and inexpensive way of reducing a very large number to a manageable shortlist. Regulation 19(3), which as explained emphasises the importance of a manageable shortlist, may provide support for such a view.

In addition to complying with the restrictions in the regulations, a utility which is subject to the E.C. Treaty is also bound by the Treaty rules and all utilities are also subject to the general prohibition against discrimination. Thus, for example, if "secondary" criteria are generally permitted as "objective" criteria under regulation 19(1), purchasing on the basis of national preference would not be outlawed by that provision; but it is still unlawful because of these other provisions.

---

[38] A possible argument to the contrary could be that such methods are not "criteria", but the inclusion of such selection methods is clearly a reasonable interpretation of the term and it is doubtful that any narrower meaning was intended.

(II.) The criteria in Regulation 19(2)

As explained above, regulation 19(2) expressly lists certain criteria which are included within the concept of "objective criteria" in that they provide a reason for declining to select a provider for consideration in a restricted procedure. These are the same as the "Regulation 14" criteria in the public sector: that is, those criteria which, along with absence of financial and technical standing, are the only substantive criteria which may be used to exclude providers from consideration for contracts under the public sector rules. It appears that these provisions were included to make it quite clear that the utilities rules were no narrower than the public sector rules in this respect, and it is submitted that they are not intended in any way to limit the concept of "objective criteria". Thus, for example, regulation 19(2) covers the case where a provider has committed an act of "grave misconduct" in his business or profession; but this should not mean that an act of misconduct which is not "grave" within the meaning of this provision cannot provide grounds for exclusion. On the other hand, it is possible that the court may interpret them more restrictively, as confining the discretion of the utility in the particular area to which they apply.

The full list of the regulation 19(2) criteria is as follows:

(i) Where the provider is an individual, where that individual[39]:

– is bankrupt;

– has had a receiving order or administration order made against him;

– has made any composition or arrangement with or for the benefit of his creditors, or has made any conveyance or assigment for the benefit of his creditors;

– appears unable to pay, or to have no reasonable prospect of being able to pay, a debt within the meaning of section 286 of the Insolvency Act 1986 or article 242 of the Insolvency (Northern Ireland) Order 1989;

– in Scotland, has been granted a trust deed for creditors or become otherwise apparently insolvent, or is the subject of a petition presented for sequestration of his estate;

– is the subject of "any similar procedure" under the law of any other state.

(ii) Where the provider is a company, where the company[40]:

– has passed a resolution, or is subject of an order by the court, for the company's winding-up (other than for the purposes of bona fide reconstruction or amalgamation), or is the subject of proceedings for this purpose;

– has had a receiver, manager or administrator on behalf of a creditor appointed in respect of the company's business or any part of it, or is the subject of proceedings for this;

– is the subject of "similar procedures" to the above under the law of any other state.

---

[39] Utilities Regulation 19(2)(a).
[40] Utilities Regulation 19(2)(c).

(iii) Where the provider is a partnership constituted under Scots law, where that partnership[41]:
– has granted a trust deed or become otherwise apparently insolvent;
– is the subject of a petition presented for sequestration of its estate.
(iv) Has been convicted of a criminal offence relating to the conduct of his business or profession[42]:
(v) Has committed an act of grave misconduct in the course of his business or profession[43].
(vi) Has failed to fulfil obligations relating to social security payments under United Kingdom law, or of the state in which the provider is established.[44]:
(vii) Has failed to fulfil obligations relating to payment of taxes under United Kingdom law, or of the state in which the provider is established.[45]
(viii) Is guilty of serious misrepresentation in providing information to the utility.[46]

In relation to these matters there are under the public sector rules some limitations on the evidence which may be called for by providers. However, no such limitations are found in the Utilities Regulations which, as explained further below, do not in general place constraints on providers in the way in which providers' qualifications are assessed in the same way as the public sector regulations.[47]

(III.) Application and notification of the selection criteria

Regulation 19(1) states that selection by the utility of those invited to tender shall be on the basis of "objective criteria and rules which it determines and which it makes available to providers who request them". It is submitted that this means that the selection criteria must be determined, and given to providers, *before* the shortlisting process occurs, an obligation which greatly improves the transparency of the process.

Since the provision makes reference to objective criteria *and* rules, to avoid challenge it may be necessary to do more than state under which criteria will apply; it is probably also necessary to make clear the principles on which these criteria are to be applied and how they are to operate. For example, a utility which wishes to take account of the extent to which bidders are likely to offer best value in the tendering process will need carefully to identify the factors which it proposes to consider at the award stage (for example, price, quality and reliability) and the order

---

[41] Utilities Regulation 19(2)(b).
[42] Utilities Regulation 19(2)(d).
[43] Utilities Regulation 19(2)(e).
[44] Utilities Regulation 19(2)(f).
[45] Utilities Regulation 19(2)(g).
[46] Utilities Regulation 19(2)(h).
[47] See further pp. 540–547.

of preference, and to explain how providers are to be assessed by reference to these criteria at the shortlisting stage.

(d) SENDING THE INVITATIONS TO TENDER

Invitations must be sent to each firm selected to bid and must be in writing.[48] They must be issued simultaneously to all those selected[49] to ensure that no provider selected is unfairly disadvantaged. Although this requirement is designed for the benefit of providers it is submitted that providers should not be able to waive the requirement: this could lead to abuse with purchasers sending early invitations to favoured firms and leaving others to accept a late invitation or none at all.

The invitation must be accompanied by the contract documents[50] – that is, the invitation to tender itself; the proposed contract conditions; the specifications, or description of the subject-matter of the contracts; and any "supplementary" documents.[51] The following information must also be included with the invitation:

(i) an address to which requests for further information should be sent; the final date for requesting such information; and the amount of any fee for this, along with methods of payment[52];

(ii) the final date for receipt of tenders[53];

(iii) the language of tenders[54];

(iv) a reference to any contract notice[55];

(v) an indication of any information which is to be included in the tender[56];

(vi) the contract award criteria (unless the contract has been advertised by a contract notice and this information was included in that notice)[57];

(vii) any other "special contract condition".[58-59] This appears to refer to other significant contract conditions which have not already been made available.

(e) OBLIGATION TO PROVIDE FURTHER INFORMATION

Any further information relating to the contract documents which is reasonably requested by a provider must be supplied not less than six

---

[48] Utilities Regulation 17(7).
[49] Utilities Regulation 17(7).
[50] Utilities Regulation 17(7).
[51] See the definition of contract documents in Utilities Regulation 2(1).
[52] Utilities Regulation 17(8)(a).
[53] Utilities Regulation 17(8)(b).
[54] Utilities Regulation 17(8)(b).
[55] Utilities Regulation 17(8)(c). This refers only to a notice advertising the individual contract, not a PIN, even if used as a call for competition: see the definition of contract notice in Utilities Regulation 2(1).
[56] Utilities Regulation 16(8)(d).
[57] Utilities Regulation 16(8)(e).
[58-59] Utilities Regulation 16(8)(f).

days before the date for receipt of tenders, again provided the request is made in good time.[60] As with a request for the contract documents this applies only where any stipulated fee accompanies the request.[61]

(f) TIME-LIMIT FOR RECEIPT OF TENDERS

The deadline for receipt of tenders in a restricted procedure which follows a call for competition is to be fixed by agreement between the utility and those invited to tender.[62] The deadline must be the same for all firms.[63] If no agreement can be reached, the utility must fix the deadline, which must "as a general rule" be at least three weeks from despatch of the invitation to tender, and, in all cases, at least ten days from the date of despatch.[64] A shorter period than three weeks may probably be used in the same circumstances as the shorter period for submission of requests to tender, discussed above.[65] As explained, this could be, for example, circumstances of urgency, or other circumstances, such as the simplicity of the purchase.

It is provided that in fixing the time-limit, utilities must take into account the time required for any examination of voluminous documentation (such as lengthy specifications) or any inspection of site or documents.[66] Thus, where there is no agreement the general three-week period may need to be lengthened where such examinations or inspections are needed.

The Commission's Proposal for a new directive to align the Utilities Directive with the rules in the GPA proposes some changes to these time limits.[66a] First, it is provided in line with the GPA that a general time limit of 40 days shall apply in procedures involving a call for competition. However, this 40 day period does not have much significance since it is provided that this general time period may still be shortened by agreement between all the invitees and the purchaser. Even when agreement is not possible the period set by the contracting entity need only be 24 days as a general rule, and may even be reduced to ten (although it is no doubt implied that such a short period would have to be justified by the particular circumstances). It is specifically provided that any time period set should be long enough to take account of the need for inspection of voluminous documents etc.

---

[60] Utilities Regulation 17(9). The time period is calculated as set out in note 8 above.
[61] Utilities Regulation 17(9).
[62] Utilities Regulation 17(4). Under the public sector rules there is no express provision allowing time-limits to be set by agreement, and it is not clear whether the usual periods may be shortened in this way: see pp. 224–226.
[63] *Ibid.*
[64] *Ibid.*
[65] See pp. 494–495.
[66] Utilities Regulation 17(5).
[66a] Proposal for a European Parliament and Council Directive amending Directive 93/38/EEC co-ordinating the procurement procedures of entities operating in the water, energy, transport and telecommunications sectors, COM (95) 107 Final, Article 1(12).

The Proposal also provides, as does the GPA itself, that the 40 day period may be reduced to one of 24 days as a general rule when there has been prior publication of a periodic indicative notice.[66b] Again, in such a case the period may be further reduced from 24 days to no less than 10 days (although again justification of such a shorter period is presumably required).

The commission has proposed that these alterations shall apply not merely to utilities which are subject to the GPA, but to all utilities covered by the Utilities Directive. However, this is controversial and the amendments may eventually be confined only to those entities subject to the GPA itself.[66c]

For those entities which are covered by the GPA, the GPA's more stringent requirements must be adhered to as from January 1, 1996, even before any amendments are made to the directive or regulations.[66d]

(g) PROPOSALS ON THE FORM OF TENDERS

The Commission Proposal for aligning the Utilities Directive with the GPA contains some proposals concerning the form of tenders. These have already been explained above in the context of open procedures.

(3) OPENING OF TENDERS

In open procedures purchasers must indicate in the contract notice the date, time and place for the opening of tenders.[67] There is no equivalent provision for restricted procedures.

As regards the opening of tenders, the question may be raised whether tenders must be opened in public or whether, at least, providers have a right to attend the opening. The regulations contain some reference to attendance: the model contract notice for open procedures requires utilities to indicate who may be present at the tender opening *where applicable*.[68] In his Opinion in case C–359/93, *Commission v. Netherlands*[69] Advocate General Tesauro considered the position under the public sector Supply Regulations, in which the model contract notice contains a similar provision with the omission of the words "where applicable". In this case the Advocate General seemed to suggest that providers must be permitted to be present because of the importance of

---

[66b] The same conditions apply as with the use of a PIN for shortening the time limit in the public sector, namely that the PIN must have been published between 40 days and not more than twelve months before the call for competition and must contain certain specified information about the contract.

[66c] See further pp. 563–564.

[66d] Further, these rules may be enforced by both GPA and Community providers: see pp. 461–462.

[67] See the model notices at pp. 492–493.

[68] See the model notice at pp. 474–475.

[69] Judgment of January 21, 1995.

transparency and openness under the Community procedures.[70] However, it is difficult to see that such a principle can be implied into the Utilities Directive in view of the phrase "where applicable", which seems to indicate that utilities may refuse to allow attendance.[71]

(4) CHOOSING THE PROVIDER FOLLOWING RECEIPT OF TENDERS

(a) THE GENERAL PRINCIPLES

Once the closing date for receipt of tenders has passed, the utility will proceed to select between those providers who have submitted tenders. This process is carefully regulated: the authority must make its choice in accordance with objective criteria, designed to ensure that there is no discrimination, and that any utility inclined to discriminate cannot easily hide its discriminatory decisions.

The utility will need to exclude providers who have submitted bids but are regarded as unqualified, or ineligible, to obtain the contract (see section (b)). In this area the utility has quite a wide discretion, since in contrast with the public sector regulations the Utilities Regulations do not contain detailed restrictions on the criteria for eligibility. Offers which do not respond to the specifications and conditions may also be rejected (see section (c)).

The utility must then proceed to evaluate the bids of all firms not excluded under these rules (see section (d)). At this stage it is required to choose either the lowest price bid or that which is the "most economically advantageous". In the latter case, it must be stated in advance that this basis will be used and the specific factors which it is intended to take into account (for example, price, quality or delivery date) must also be stated in advance. There is an exception in that the utility may refuse to accept any bid which is "abnormally low", and there are also limited exceptions for bids which offer products from certain countries outside the European Community. In conducting the evaluation, the purchaser must consider the bids as submitted: these may not be altered in post tender negotiations (see section (e)).

This does not mean that the utility is bound to award a contract to the best bidder: it may choose to cancel the award procedure. However, if it does to wish to go ahead, it must make the award in accordance with the rules outlined above, or must commence a new award procedure.[72]

---

[70] Para. 8 of the Opinion of November 17, 1994.
[71] The public sector Works and Services Regulations also contain the phrase "where applicable" and it was suggested earlier that the difference in wording of the different public sector regulations is purely fortuitous: the correct view is that in all types of procedures the decision whether to permit providers to attend the opening is not affected by the directives and regulations.
[72] See pp. 422–423.

(b) EXCLUSION OF UNQUALIFIED PROVIDERS

In contrast with the position in the public sector, where there are strict limitations on which bidders may be excluded as unqualified, under the Utilities Regulations a utility has a wide discretion in deciding which providers are to be considered as eligible for the contract. Probably, using reasoning by analogy, the utility may exclude providers for any of the reasons which are "objective criteria" for the purpose of the provisions on selection in restricted procedures, as considered above.[73-74] This could mean that providers may be excluded not only for commercial reasons, notably failure to meet financial and technical standards, but also, possibly, on the basis of secondary concerns, such as the firm's equal opportunities record although, as explained, it is not clear whether such concerns may be regarded as "objective" criteria. This is, of course, subject to the general principle prohibiting discrimination and with any requirements under the Community Treaties where these apply to the utility in question.

In an open procedure the utility only has the opportunity to consider a provider's qualification once bids have been received, since an open procedure is by definition a procedure in which any interested party may submit a bid. Thus, in general, the qualifications of providers in relation to financial and technical standing, and in relation to any other matters which the utility wishes to consider, will be considered at this stage. However, whilst the utility may not insist on qualification before submission of bids, a utility and provider may agree between them that the provider's qualifications should be assessed before a bid is submitted, in order to avoid a waste of effort in preparing the bid if the provider turns out to be unqualified. It should be pointed out that there is no *obligation* in the regulations to set any qualification standards for providers, but utilities will normally wish to consider at least financial and technical standing.

In a restricted procedure a utility may exclude providers regarded as unqualified before invitations are issued. This will normally be done in practice since it is useful for both parties if unqualified providers are excluded at the earliest possible stage. However, there is nothing in the directives or regulations to compel such an approach and qualification may be left until after the receipt of tenders if this is thought appropriate. Even where some steps have been taken to qualify firms prior to issuing invitations a utility may wish to carry out another check at the time of award to see if there has been any change in circumstances, or may leave until this stage the verification of factual information supplied by the providers.

These issues of qualification, together with matters concerning the procedures and standards for assessment, are considered further in the separate section on qualification.[75]

[73-74] See pp. 498–500.
[75] See pp. 540–547.

It should be noted that, as under the public sector rules, the criteria for qualification may not in general be considered as *relative* factors to be weighed alongside the award criteria in deciding who should receive the contract.[76] For example, a utility awarding a contract for basic supplies on the basis of price only, may decide that it is worth taking a risk on a firm whose financial resources are borderline only if that firm quotes a *much* cheaper price (for example, at least 10 per cent cheaper) than firms whose financial standing is clearly adequate. Under the regulations this is not possible: providers must be assessed against each other solely by reference to the merits of their bids,[77] as outlined at (d) below. Thus, in the scenario envisaged above, the utility must decide whether or not the firm has adequate resources to be considered at all; and if it does, its bid must then be accepted if it is the lowest, however small the margin of advantage. This principle would also forbid, for example, an approach whereby firms with sound equal opportunities records are given a preference if their bid is within 10 per cent of the best bidder; if it is desired to use procurement to promote equal opportunities policies this must be done by excluding all providers whose record is considered inadequate (if this is allowed under the regulations, which is not clear); or by promoting the policy solely by including conditions which concern contract performance.[78] There is, however, one exception to this principle, for bids offering products from certain non-Community countries. This is considered further below.[79]

(c) NON-RESPONSIVE OFFERS

(i) NON-COMPLIANCE WITH SPECIFICATIONS AND OTHER SUBSTANTIVE REQUIREMENTS

Tenders are sometimes submitted which do not comply with substantive requirements of the contract – that is, which offer products or services which are not in accordance with the specifications, or which do not comply with other requirements relating to contract peformance, such as provision of a performance bond. This may arise where enterprises have misunderstood, or cannot meet, the utility's requirements. It may also

---

[76] This is permitted only to the extent that the criteria for qualification overlap with those used at the award stage. For example, the provider's capacity to provide a product of the quality in the specifications may be a qualification criterion, and quality may also be an award criterion.

[77] This sharp distinction between the processes of qualification (assessment of suitability) and bid evaluation was highlighted in relation to the public sector by Advocate General Darmon in case 31/87, *Gebroeders Beentjes B.V. v. Netherlands* [1988] E.C.R. 4635 and by Advocate General Gulmann in case C-71/92, *Commission of Spain*, judgment of June 30, 1993, para. 63 of the Opinion. The same principle applies to utilities in view of the self-contained nature of the rules on award criteria, discussed at (d) below, which are the same as those relating to the public sector.

[78] On these issues see further the detailed discussion in Chap. 16.

[79] See pp. 511–513.

arise either when products are "equivalent" to those sought but are made to different technical specifications; or where enterprises proffer solutions which differ from those in the specifications, but which the tenderer believes are superior.

(I.) The discretion to accept non-responsive offers

A utility may sometimes wish to accept a non-responsive offer – for example, where an offer is in some respects so much better than the others submitted that the utility decides to waive its specified minimum requirements on some other aspects of the contract.

It was held by the Court of Justice in case C–243/89, *Commission v. Denmark*[80] (the *Storebaelt* case) that under the public sector regulations it is generally prohibited to accept such a non-compliant tender. This conclusion was based on a general principle of the equality of bidders which the Court considered was implied into the public sector Works Directive. It seems clear that a similar principle will be implied into the Utilities Directive and regulations, and that the *Storebaelt* principle regarding non-responsive bids will apply equally in the utilities sector. The precise scope of the *Storebaelt* principle in this respect was considered in the chapter on the public sector and readers are referred to the discussion there,[81–82] as it is equally relevant to utilities.

(II.) The discretion to exclude non-responsive offers

Although, as explained above, a utility is not normally *permitted* to accept non-responsive bids in some cases the utility is actually required to accept tenders which differ in detail from the specifications in the contract documents. This applies, under the regulations, to tenders drawn up in accordance with "European specifications" or by reference to certain types of national standards and who under the E.C. Treaty to other bids offering "equivalent" products or services to those in the specifications. These rules are considered in further detail in Chapter 11.

(ii) NON-COMPLIANCE WITH FORMALITIES

Offers may fail to comply not only with substantive requirements but also with the tendering formalities. For example, they may be submitted late; they may fail to meet requirements relating to the form of bids, such as language or number of copies; or may omit required information. This situation raises the questions of, first, whether the utility may choose to accept a non-compliant bid, and, secondly, whether there is ever any obligation to do so. This issue has been discussed in detail in the context of the public sector rules. It was suggested there that in

---

[80] Judgment of June 22, 1993; noted by Férnandez Martín in (1993) 2 P.P.L.R. CS 153.
[81–82] See pp. 232–233.

general purchasers are permitted to waive compliance with formalities (although this will not be possible for certain formalities expressly referred to in the regulations, such as bid deadlines), but that they may insist on compliance and thus reject non-compliant bids should they wish. In all cases, bidders must be treated equally, on the basis of the principle in *Storebaelt*.[83] The discussion on the public sector appears equally applicable in the context of utilities, and readers are thus referred to that previous discussion[84] for further consideration of this issue.

(d) EVALUATION OF OFFERS

(i) THE BASIC PRINCIPLE: LOWEST PRICE OR MOST ECONOMICALLY ADVANTAGEOUS OFFER

The process of selecting the successful bid from those which are not excluded is regulated by Utilities Regulation 21. The basic principle is the same as that applying in the public sector: the contract must be awarded either (a) to the enterprise which offers the lowest price or (b) to the enterprise whose bid is "the most economically advantageous" to the purchaser.[85] Thus it is sought to ensure that contracts are awarded on the basis of objective commercial criteria, and that discriminatory decisions cannot be disguised. In an open procedure, the utility must state in the contract notice whether the award is to be based on lowest price or most economically advantageous offer.[86] In a restricted procedure, this must be stated in either the contract notice or the invitation to tender.[87]

(ii) LOWEST PRICE

Where the applicable principle is "lowest price", the bidder offering the lowest price must be awarded the contract. The "lowest price" basis is rarely used in practice, except for simple, off-the-shelf supplies.

There are exceptions to this principle for bids which are abnormally low and bids offering products from certain third countries. These are considered further below.[88]

(iii) MOST ECONOMICALLY ADVANTAGEOUS OFFER

(I.) Factors relevant to economic advantage

Where the utility chooses the most economically advantageous offer as the basis for the award it may take into consideration other factors as

---

[83] See p. 234.
[84] See pp. 234–236.
[85] Utilities Regulation 21(1).
[86] See the model notices for the open procedure at pp. 474–475 above.
[87] Utilities Regulation 17(8)(e).
[88] See, respectively, pp. 511–513 and 515–519.

508

well as (or instead of) price: for example, quality, delivery date or product life. As in the public sector, this is the award principle chosen for most contracts, especially for complex products or services, where there is wide variation in what is offered from different providers or where it is not appropriate to compare what is available on the basis of price alone.[89] By way of illustration, the regulations list a number of criteria which may be taken into account where "most economically advantageous offer" is used as the basis for the award. In addition to price these are "delivery date or period for completion, running costs, cost effectiveness, quality, aesthetic and functional characteristics, technical merit, after-sales service and technical assistance, commitment with regard to spare parts and security of supply".[90] This covers the same criteria as are mentioned in the public sector regulations, with the addition of the provisions on spare parts and security of supply.

As in the public sector the provision makes it clear that the list is not exhaustive and that other matters relating to economic advantage may be considered. It is clear that the provisions are in this respect to be interpreted in the same manner as the analagous provisions in the public sector rules, as covering only criteria which relate to the *contract awarded*.[91] Thus a purchaser may not take into account, for example, the potential benefits of developing a long-term relationship with a particular firm – for example, prospects for collaborative research of mutual benefit, or the award of discounts on the firm's other products.

It is also forbidden under the regulations, to consider the *relative* financial and technical status of firms at this stage: once firms have been deemed to be qualified as providers, their bids must be evaluated solely by reference to the merits of the bid.[92]

(II.) Requirement for advance notice of factors to be considered

When a utility intends to use "most economically advantageous offer" as the basis for the award it must state the specific factors to be taken into account (price, quality, etc.) in advance where possible in descending order of importance.[93] This must be done in either the contract notice or the contract documents.[94] (In the restricted procedure it is thus not necessary to include this detail at the earlier stage of the invitation to tender, although, as explained above, it must be stated in either the contract notice or invitation to tender as to which of the two basic

---

[89] For examples see the discussion on the public sector at pp. 236–239.
[90] Utilities Regulation 21(2).
[91] For further discussion and the relevant legal authority see pp. 237–239 on the public sector.
[92] See pp. 230–231.
[93] Utilities Regulation 21(3). Provision is also made for this in the model contract notices, set out at pp. 474–479 above.
[94] *Ibid.*

criteria – lowest price or most econmically advantageous offer – is to be used.) It appears that the utility is then bound by these criteria in making the award.[95] This requirement seeks to make it difficult to disguise discriminatory decisions. It also has the result of enabling enterprises and interested persons to formulate their bid in the most appropriate manner.

If the utility fails to state the relevant criteria, then if it wishes to continue with the procedure it is probably required to award the contract to the lowest bidder (subject to the rules on abnormally low bids).[96] It is possible as an alternative to commence a new procedure,[97] but obviously this will delay the procurement.

(III.) The obligation to exercise a discretion

A further issue is the extent to which a utility's discretion to determine and apply the relevant criteria may be limited in advance. This issue has been considered in detail in relation to the public sector rules on which there have been some judicial decisions.[98] It was explained there that the cases indicate that criteria must be set by reference to the specific type of contract and that purchasers probably may not simply state a long list of factors without reference to the particular subject-matter in question (for example, listing all the factors in the regulations). It was also explained that purchasers must consider the merits of the bids submitted and cannot rely on general formulae for determining the winning bidder – for example, by selecting the bid which is closest to the average price submitted by bidders. These principles will be appplicable to bid evaluation by utilities.

(IV.) The difficulty of enforcing the rules

It has already been noted in the context of the public sector that even where the rules are properly applied it is difficult to prove whether a particular decision has actually been based on the listed criteria. Often decisions involve subjective judgment, and there is more than one

---

[95] The relevant provisions state that the utility must state the factors which the utility *intends* to consider. Probably this must be interpreted to mean that the utility must adhere to the factors which it lists in the notice or contract documents and must apply them in the order stated, and cannot later change its decision, to add or remove criteria from the list. This view is supported by the Commission's *Guide to the Community rules on open public procurement*, above, at 36. Consistently with this the utility could not later change the order of preference of the criteria. This allows the stated criteria to be used as a benchmark against which to review the utility's decision where it is alleged that an improper motive has influenced the decision. If it were permitted to change either the criteria or their order it would be too easy to rationalise discriminatory decisions *ex post facto*.

[96] See the opinion of Advocate General Darmon in case 31/87, *Gebroeders Beentjes B.V. v. Netherlands* [1988] E.C.R. 4635, para. 38 of the opinion; and also para. 35 of the judgment of the Court of Justice. The case concerns the public sector but the utilities provisions are the same.

[97] See p. 523.

[98] See further the discussion on the public sector at p. 240.

"reasonable" choice available. For example, where both price and quality are relevant, firm A may offer the lowest price and firm B a higher price but a better quality product. Here, an award to either A or B might be a reasonable commercial choice, and if the decision *is* based on some non-commercial factor, this will be hard to prove. This makes it difficult to challenge an evaluation decision.

(V.) The special rules on "third country" offers

Introduction

Exceptions to the bid evaluation rules, which have no parallel in the public sector provisions, apply for bids which offer products from certain "third countries" – that is, countries outside the European Community. These exceptions allow, and sometimes require, utilities to treat offers which include products originating in these countries less favourably than those bids which offer products originating in the Community.

In principle, the Community has indicated that it is willing to offer access to Community procurement markets to states prepared to offer access on a reciprocal basis to Community industry. Thus the provisions providing for discrimination against third countries were, ostensibly, adopted for protectionist reasons but also to provide a bargaining tool to persuade other states to open up their own markets – the restrictions which they contain do not apply to states which have agreed to open their own markets in this way. These policy issues are considered further in Chapter 15 on third country acccess.

It should be mentioned that there are some doubts over the legality of these provisions, in that they may infringe the principle of free movement, which is in general binding on the Community itself as well as on the Member States under Article 30 E.C. If these doubts are correct, then utilities are free to disregard the third country provisions and to treat products from third countries in exactly the same way as those from Community states; and, indeed, in many cases may be bound to do so. These issues are also considered further in Chapter 15.[99]

The rules on third countries are found in Article 36[1] of the Utilities Directive and are implemented in Utilities Regulation 22. There are two separate rules: a discretionary preference and a mandatory preference.

The discretionary preference rule

The first, in regulation 22(2) *permits* utilities to reject an offer for supplies which is of third country origin, should it choose to do so. In practice, utilities generally decline to do so, preferring the offer which provides best value for money.

---

[99] See pp. 789–792.
[1] Prior to consolidation of all the utilities rules in Directive 93/38 these rules were found in Article 29 of Directive 90/351, and are still sometimes referred to as the "Article 29" provisions.

The mandatory three per cent price preference for non-third country offers

The second rule, in regulation 22(3), effectively provides for a *mandatory* preference for non-third country offers over offers of third country origin where the price difference between them does not exceed three per cent.[2] In a procedure based on most economically advantageous offer this rule applies only where the non-third country offer is – disregarding the question of price – at least as economically advantageous as the third country offer.[3]

> **Example:**
> A utility receives a non-third country offer of £500,000 and a third country offer of £490,000 (a two per cent price difference). Both are equally advantageous in other respects.
>
> Where the procedure is based on lowest price the non-third country offer must be accepted since the price difference does not exceed three per cent.
>
> Where the procedure is based on most economically advantageous offer the non-third country offer must again be accepted because the difference does not exceed three per cent and the bids are otherwise the same. However, if in this case quality was a relevant award criteria and the third country bid offered better quality, the utility could accept the third country bid. This would apply however marginal the difference in quality.

There is stated to be an exception to this rule where not to accept the third country offer would oblige the utility to acquire goods with "different technical characteristics" from existing goods, or an installation resulting in "incompatibility, technical difficulties in operation and maintenance or disproportionate costs". This exception is of little relevance since the specifications should be drafted in practice to eliminate the need to accept offers which will lead to such problems, and offers which do not comply with the specifications are eliminated from consideration altogether.[4]

This requirement to give preference to non-third country offers has caused some controversy: most utilities, prefer to accept the offer which gives best value for money and are not keen to pay a price premium in order to promote the Community policy of reciprocity.

---

[2] Utilities Regulation 22(3), providing for preference where the offers are "equivalent"; Utilities Regulation 22(4) and (6), defining offers as equivalent in a procedure based on lowest price where the price difference does not exceed three per cent; Utilities Regulation 22(5) and (6), defining offers as equivalent in a procedure based on most economically advantageous tender where the difference does not exceed three per cent and offers are otherwise equally advantageous.

[3] It may be implied that in considering whether offers are equally advantageous a utility may only consider those factors which are relevant criteria in the award of the contract.

[4] See pp. 506–507.

The definition of "offer of third country origin"

The above rules both refer to an "offer of third country origin". This is defined in regulation 22(1) as an offer under which more than 50 per cent of the goods offered (by value) originate in third countries. The origin of goods is determined by reference to Council Regulation No. 802/68.[5] This involves complex rules which are difficult for individual purchasing entities to apply in practice. It appears that often utilities do not investigate the origin of products but simply accept assurances from providers on this issue.

States are not treated as third countries for this purpose where they have concluded an agreement with the Communities ensuring "comparable and effective access" for Member States' firms to markets of those states, or where the benefits of the Utilities Directive have been extended to the state in question.[6] Agreements falling within this provision include the WTO Agreement on Government Procurement and the European Economic Area Agreement,[7] and products from states benefiting from these agreements are thus not treated as third-country products insofar as the contract in question is covered by one of the agreements. However, it is doubtful if various agreements concluded by the Community with central and eastern European states fall within these provisions since these particular agreements do not provide for access for Community firms which is "comparable" to that provided by the Community to its own markets, nor, at present, is the access provided to the Community "effective".[8]

States which are not treated as third countries are treated exactly like Community Member States for the purpose of these rules. Thus if 30 per cent of the value of goods offered originate in the United Kingdom, 30 per cent in Norway (a member of the European Economic Area) and the other 40 per cent in a third country with which there is no agreement, etc., the offer is not a third-country offer. Even if 60 per cent of the products originate in Norway and 40 per cent in a third country not covered by an agreement, etc., the offer is not treated as a third country offer. In such a case it is entitled to the benefit of both mandatory and discretionary preference rules, even though there may be no Community products in the offer at all!

These rules apply only to products, and not to services, contained in an offer.[9]

---

[5] [1968] O.J. L148/1, as amended by Council Regulation No. 3860/87, [1987] L363/30.
[6] Utilities Regulation 22(1).
[7] On these agreements see Chap. 15.
[8] On this issue see p. 784.
[9] Article 37 of the Utilities Directive provides for the Commission to adopt measures on services if Community firms are excluded from access to the market of specific states: see further pp. 793–796.

(VI.) The exception for abnormally low offers

An exception to the above rules allows the authority to reject offers which, whilst appearing to be the most economically advantageous, are "abnormally low". The rules on such offers are considered at (e) below.

(VII.) Alternative offers

As under the public sector rules there appears to be nothing to prevent providers from submitting more than one tender. Thus, for example, where price and quality are both relevant factors, a provider might seek to improve its chances of winning by offering both a good-quality product at a high price, and a lower quality product at a lower price. It appears that in such a case the authority is required to consider both tenders, unless it specifically states as a rule of the tendering process that only one bid may be submitted.

(iv) PROCEDURES INVOLVING SEPARATE LOTS

Contracts are sometimes advertised in lots, with bidders able to bid for one or more lots. For example, a purchaser may have a requirement for three different types of machine, A, B and C. There may be some firms in the market which specialise in one type of machine, but some which make two or all three. In this case the purchaser is likely to advertise its requirements for all three in a single procedure, allowing providers to bid to supply all three types, just two, or just one.

In evaluating bids here it is submitted, as was suggested also for the public sector, that it is generally required to accept that combination of bids which offers either the lowest overall price or (where the most economically advantageous offer basis is used) the best overall "economic advantage". However, as an alternative a purchaser should be permitted to evaluate each lot as a wholly separate contract (or to retain a discretion to do so) where this is indicated in the documents setting out the award criteria. It appears that a purchaser could give a preference to a single bid covering the whole requirement (which it may wish to do because of a saving on administration costs) – *i.e.* choose between the two alternatives in its discretion – only if it indicates this possibility in advance. In other words, the award procedure must effectively proceed as two (or more) procedures in parallel – one for a series of separate contracts and one for a single (or several) larger contract(s).

(v) TREATMENT OF IN-HOUSE BIDS

A bid by another part of the same utility – that is, by an in-house provider – is required to be treated as an "offer" for the purpose of the evaluation rules.[10] Thus, it must be evaluated against external bids in accordance with the rules outlined above.

However, as explained below,[11] the regulations do not preclude utilities from terminating an award procedure, even where the reason is that the utility wishes to keep the work in-house. There is nothing in the rules on evaluation of in-house bids to affect the position in this respect. Thus, if an in-house bid is not the "winning" bid in accordance with the rules on bid evaluation outlined above, it is still possible to terminate the procedure, and instead award the work in-house.[12] This does not require a new award procedure as would be necessary if the work were still to be given to an external provider, since the in-house award is not a "contract".[13]

(iv) THE PROCEDURE FOR EVALUATION

Under open procedures, a utility may proceed by, first, evaluating all bids received in accordance with the bid criteria, and then assessing the qualifications of the provider submitting the most favourable bid. If this provider is not qualified, the utility will then consider the qualification of the next most favourable bidder and so on. Alternatively, it may prefer first to assess the qualifications of all bidders, and then to evaluate the bids, taking into consideration only those submitted by qualified providers. Either approach is permitted: the procurement legislation does not regulate the order in which qualification and evaluation processes are carried out.[14]

Similarly, where under restricted procedures utilities wish to carry out a qualification after submission of bids this may be done before or after the bids are evaluated.

(e) ABNORMALLY LOW OFFERS

(i) THE PROBLEM OF ABNORMALLY LOW OFFERS

As explained in considering the public sector procurement rules, a purchaser may be reluctant to accept a very low offer, fearing that it offers the provider little profit and that thus the contract will not be properly performed or the provider will later demand an increase in price. Low offers may also arise because the provider is in receipt of

---

[10] Utilities Regulation 21(9).

[11] See p. 723.

[12] This is not possible if the work is covered by compulsory competitive tendering legislation, since that legislation will require the award to go ahead: see Chap. 14. However, such legislation will rarely be relevant to a contract covered by the utilities rules.

[13] See pp. 414–415.

[14] *Beentjes*, above (para. 16 of the judgment). This case concerns the public sector but appears to apply equally to utilities.

unlawful state aid and the contract could be jeopardised by the provider's being required to repay the aid. It was also noted, however, that an offer which appears to be low may result in a reasonable profit – for example because the bidder has obtained materials at a bargain price – and that, even where no reasonable profit is possible, acceptance of the offer may not not pose a threat to the interests of the purchaser – for example, where a firm is seeking to keep its workforce temporarily employed at a loss rather than to lay them off. As with the public sector regulations, the Utilities Regulations contain specific provisions on "abnormally low offers".

(ii) THE OBLIGATION TO SEEK AN EXPLANATION

First, before rejecting any abnormally low offer, a purchaser must request in writing an explanation of the offer or of those parts which it considers contribute to the offer being abnormally low,[15] to ensure the utility is appraised of the full facts.[16] The utility may set a period for reply, which must be "reasonable",[17] and may presumably reject the bid without further consideration if no reply is received within that time.

This provision was included to ensure that utilities do not reject bids from other states which appear low in the awarding state but reflect the cost advantages of that other state, which would defeat the object of the procurement rules.[18]

(iii) DISCRETION TO ACCEPT OR REJECT ABNORMALLY LOW OFFERS

It is less clear what are the purchaser's substantive obligations in dealing with such bids. It is stated as a general principle in Utilities Regulation 21(6) that where the offer is abnormally low the purchaser may reject it. However, this apparent discretion over when, and whether, to reject such a bid appears to be qualified, as set out below.

(I.) Awards based on the lowest price criterion

Where the principle for the contract award is lowest price, generally an offer must be accepted if it is the lowest received. However, the express

---

[15] Utilities Regulation 21(6).
[16] The Court of Justice has rejected an argument that it is not necessary to seek explanations in a case where the tender is so low as to bear no relation to reality: it is not for purchasers to decide when it would be useful to seek explanations, but they must be sought in all cases: case 76/81, *S.A. Transporoute v. Minister of Public Works* [1982] E.C.R. 417, [1984] C.M.L.R. 382. For discussion see Arrowsmith, *A Guide to the Procurement Cases of the Court of Justice* (1992) at 3.3.2. The case concerns the public sector but will apply equally to the utilities.
[17] *Ibid.*
[18] See the Commission proposal for a Directive on the excluded sectors, Supplement 6/88 of the Bulletin of the European Communities, p.94, section 103.

provision that abnormally low offers may be rejected, referred to above, provides an exception to this principle. It is further provided, however, that the offer may only be rejected where the purchaser has examined the details of all offers, taking into account any explanations given to it of any abnormally low offers.[19] It is also stated in regulation 21(6) that in considering the explanation the purchaser "may take into account explanations which justify the offer on objective grounds", including the economy of the construction or production method, or method of service provision; the technical solutions suggested; the exceptionally favourable conditions available for the performance of the contract, or the originality of the goods, works or services proposed. Such an examination may reveal that the offer is the most favourable, in that it is the lowest and there is no default risk; this will be the case when there is an "objective" explanation of the type noted above. In such a case there is no commercial justification for rejecting the offer and to do so would be contrary to the very purpose of the legislation which seeks to ensure that the most competitive provider wins the contract. Thus, although it is not expressly provided that the purchaser *must* accept the low offer – merely that explanations must be taken into account – not to accept it is an abuse of its apparent discretion.[20]

On the other hand, the offer may also be the lowest, and there may be no risk of default, in circumstances which do not reflect an advantageous competitive position, such as where the bidder is pursuing the contract at a loss to damage the position of competitors. Since it is not the purpose of the rules to support such enterprises, presumably a purchaser may choose to reject the bid (although it may often choose to accept it).

Where, on the other hand, consideration of the reasons for the low bid lead to the conclusion that there is an unacceptable risk of non-performance, it is clear that in general the general discretion to reject the bid applies.[21]

A special provision in Utilities Regulation 21(7) deals with the case where the bid is abnormally low because the provider is in receipt of state aid within the meaning of Article 92 E.C. Here it is provided that the bid may not be rejected where the provider has shown that the aid has been notified to the Commission pursuant to Article 93(3) or has received the Commission's approval. Thus firms with authorised aid are

---

[19] *Ibid.*
[20] The original proposal for the directive did expressly state that such bids could not be rejected: see the proposal cited at note 18 above, Article 22(5) of the original proposed Directive.
[21] It might even be argued that the bid should be rejected. On the other hand, there is no requirement to assess firms' financial and technical standing, and to reject on those grounds; thus it could be accepted that likewise there is no requirement to reject a provider because the nature of the bid itself suggests a risk of default. If, however, a purchaser is required to reject such a bid where the most advantageous offer criterion is used (as to which see the text, below), for consistency the same rule should apply where the criterion is lowest price.

treated as enjoying a legitimate competitive advantage. Probably the same position in fact applies under the public sector rules, although there are no express provisions on state aid in the public sector rules. The purchaser must consult with the provider to determine the status of any aid.[22] When the aid is not approved or notified, on the other hand, it appears that the bid may be rejected,[23] a position which again also appears to apply under the public sector rules. As under the public sector rules there is nothing, however, to *require* rejection of a bid which is affected by receipt of unlawful state aid, and this case the general discretion to choose to adopt on abnormally low bid seems to apply.

In all cases where the utility rejects a bid in an award procedure based on the lowest price criterion, it is required to send to the responsible Minister a report justifying the reasons for its decision.[24] This must be sent to the Treasury for onward transmission to the Commission.[25]

It should also be noted that in deciding whether a bid should be rejected, the purchaser may not take this decision based on the application of an objective mathematical formula – for example, by rejecting all bids which fall below the average price offered by more than a certain percentage[26]; it must consider the explanations offered by the bidder in the individual case, and take a decision based upon all the specific facts. This applies even though a formula is more objective and precludes any discrimination against individual bidders, since such a formula cannot properly take account of the exact merits of individual cases.

(II.) Awards based on most economically advantageous offer

Where the principle for the contract award is most economically advantageous offer, the utility must take into account any explanation given for the low nature of the bid in assessing which offer is the most advantageous.[27] In particular, as with the case of the lowest price criterion, it must consider the various "objective" factors justifying the low offer, such as the economy of the method, which were referred to above.[28]

---

[22] Utilities Regulation 21(7).

[23] Utilities Regulation 21(7).

[24] Utilities Regulations 21(8) and 28(1). The responsible Minister is the Minister of the Crown whose areas of responsibility are most closely connected with the functions of the utility, a question which is to be determined conclusively by the Treasury: Utilities Regulations 28(2). The duty to send the report is enforceable by mandamus by the Minister.

[25] Utilities Regulation 28(6).

[26] Case 103/88, *Fratelli Costanzo v. Commune di Milano* [1989] E.C.R. 1389, [1990] 3 C.M.L.R. 239 and case 295/89, *Impresa Dona Alfonso di Dona Alfonso et Figli s.n.c.v. Consorzio per lo sviluppo industriale del Commune di Monafalcone*, judgment of June 18, 1991.

[27] Utilities Regulation 21(6).

[28] *Ibid.*

Where the purchaser concludes that the offer is the most advantageous, the normal rules on evaluation, prima facie, require acceptance of the offer. However, as noted above, regulation 21(6) expressly states that an abnormally low bid may be rejected, raising the possibility that such a bid may be rejected, by way of exception to the usual rule. As with the case where lowest price is the criterion, it is suggested that this permits a rejection of the bid where it does not reflect an objective competitive advantage. On the other hand, where the low price does reflect such an advantage, such as those referred to above, it can again be argued that it is an abuse of discretion not to accept the offer.

Where consideration of the reasons for the low offer lead to the conclusion that there is an acceptable risk of non-performance, clearly the discretion to reject the offer will apply. It might be suggested that the bid *must* be rejected in such a case, on the basis that such an offer cannot be the most economically advantageous. On the other hand, the concept of most economically advantageous offer encompasses only factors relating to the content of the offer, not the prospects of performance. Thus it appears that it is for the purchaser to decide whether such a bid should be accepted, in the same way as it is for the purchaser itself to decide whether or not to disqualify bidders on financial or technical grounds.

Again, Utilities Regulation 21(7) specifically states that a bid which is low because of receipt of state aid can only be rejected after consultation with the provider and may not be rejected where it is shown that the state-aid receipt has been notified to the Commission or authorised by the Commission under Article 93(3).

As with an award based on lowest price, the purchaser must consider the facts of each case, and cannot reject bids by, for example, applying a general mathematical formula relating the bidder's price to the general average bid price.[29]

There is no requirement to submit a report to the responsible Minister where an abnormally low bid is rejected in a procedure based on the most economically advantageous offer, as there is in a procedure based on lowest price.

(iv) THE MEANING OF "ABNORMALLY LOW"

Neither the regulations nor directives on which they are based indicate what is meant by an "abnormally low" offer, for the purpose of the above rules. It is submitted, in light of the purpose of the rules, that such an offer is one which appears to offer the particular bidder no reasonable opportunity of making a profit.

---

[29] See the discussion at p. 246.

(f) ALTERATIONS TO OFFERS PRIOR TO THE AWARD ("POST-TENDER NEGOTIATIONS")

Although this is not expressly stated in the regulations, once the deadline for submission of bids has passed, it can be implied, as under the public sector regulations, that there is no *general* power for the purchaser to allow alterations to bids: if this were the case, the open and restricted procedures would be barely distinguishable from the negotiated procedure. Thus bids cannot be treated merely as a basis for negotiations between the purchaser and bidders. A minute statement has been made on this subject by the Council and Commission of the European Community.[30] This relates to the public sector Works Directive but is also likely to be applied to open and restricted procedures under the utilities rules. This confirms the view that, in general, negotiations are not permitted, although it indicates that discussions may be acceptable for the purpose of clarification of bids. This statement and the general question of post-tender negotiations in restricted and open procedures are considered further in the chapter on the public sector.[31] In general, a utility which contemplates the possibility that it may wish to enter into discussions after bids have been received is advised to use the negotiated procedure, which is freely available under the utilities rules in contrast with the position in the public sector.

The position may also arise where the utility itself wishes to change its requirements after the bid deadline. This issue is dealt with in Chapter 11 on specifications, where it is suggested that changes to the specifications are permitted at this stage, provided that they are not "substantial".[32] In this case it will be necessary to give all bidders a reasonable and equal opportunity to revise their bids.

(g) NEGOTIATIONS WITH THE MOST FAVOURABLE BIDDER

As explained in relation to the public sector, it is not clear whether purchasers may negotiate with the winning bidder. Such negotiations are not open to abuse in the same way as negotiations with several bidders; there is no opportunity to favour a particular provider. As with the public sector rules, there is nothing specific in the Community legislation to prevent negotiations once the winning bidder has been selected, and such negotiations appear to be permitted. However, since the rules clearly require the contract to be awarded to that bidder, if at all, if negotiations are not successful, the only option for the purchaser is to commence a new award procedure.

---

[30] Statement concerning Article 7(4) of Public Works Directive 93/37 [1994] O.J. L111/114.
[31] See pp. 247–249.
[32] See pp. 617–618.

On the other hand, any agreement prior to the contract which benefits the provider – for example, an increase in price – must, by implication, be ruled out. This would enable favoured firms to win contracts by submitting very favourable bids, based on an understanding with the purchaser that these would later be revised in the provider's favour.

The position where the purchaser itself wishes to alter the specifications at this point – for example, because of changed requirements – is considered more fully in Chapter 11 on specifications. It is suggested that non-substantial changes are permitted, and that the parties may then negotiate to change the terms of the agreement to reflect the changes.[33]

(5) PROCEDURES WHICH FAIL TO PRODUCE SATISFACTORY BIDS

In some cases an open or restricted procedure fails to produce a result which is satisfactory for the purchaser. This may be because no offers are submitted at all; or because those submitted are either non-responsive (for example, do not meet the specifications), are from unqualified providers, or are rejected as abnormally low. In other cases the purchaser may be dissatisfied because of a very limited response – for example, if only one or two bids are received – or simply because those received do not offer sufficient value for money.

(a) ABSENCE OF TENDERS

Where a utility receives no offers at all under an open or restricted procedure it is permitted to find a provider through a new procedure, without any new call for competition.[34] Since a procedure with a call for competition has been made which has failed to produce an adequate response, it is considered inappropriate to require that the authority advertise the contract again (although it may, of course, choose to do so). However, the utility remains under an obligation to consider the need for adequate competition when entering into a new procedure so that, even where a negotiated procedure is used, it may not be adequate simply to negotiate a contract with a single provider if more than one interested provider is available.

It is possible to dispense with the call for competition, however, only if the terms of the contract remain "substantially unaltered" from those orginally advertised.[35] Where substantial alterations occur, it is necessary to begin a new competition which is subject to the regulations in the ordinary way. This is consistent with the more general rule which, it is

---

[33] See pp. 617–618.
[34] Utilities Regulations 16(1)(a).
[35] *Ibid.*

submitted, applies in open and restricted procedures, that a purchaser must always open a new procedure if it wishes to make a substantial change to the specifications or other terms.[36] What constitutes a substantial change should be the same for both purposes.[37-38]

It is also provided that this provision may be relied on only where the award procedure which produced no tenders itself followed a call for competition. If this was not the case, the second procedure can only be held without a call for competition if one of the other grounds for dispensing with the competition still applies. For example, if the urgency ground was used but the risk has now passed, a call for competition will be needed for the second procedure for the same project, even where no bids were received under the first.

(b) WHERE ALL BIDS ARE NON-RESPONSIVE, FROM UNQUALIFIED PROVIDERS OR ABNORMALLY LOW

A utility may also wish (or be required) to reject all bids because they are all either non-responsive, from unqualified providers or abnormally low. Where this is done it appears that it is not necessary to make a new call for competition since Utilities Regulation 16(1)(a) also allows an award without a call for competition where no "suitable" bids are received. This would seem to cover all three of these cases. As with (a) above the provision only applies where the contract is substantially unaltered from the original procedure and the first procedure was held following a call for competition.[39]

(c) WHERE THE BEST BID DOES NOT GIVE SUFFICIENT VALUE FOR MONEY

A purchaser may be dissatisfied with an award procedure because the best bid does not offer good value for money. This is especially likely where it is felt that the number of bids actually received provides inadequate competition – for example, where there is only a single responsive bid. Although, as noted above, the regulations permit utilities to award a contract under a new procedure without a call for competition where there are no "suitable" tenders, it does not seem that tenders can be considered unsuitable simply because the authority is not satisfied with the value for money offered.

It was suggested above that it is arguable that in these circumstances the utility may negotiate with the winning bidder for an improvement to the bid.[40] On the other hand, it is not permitted to negotiate with other

---

[36] See pp. 617–618.

[37-38] A situation of this type following an open or restricted procedure is hard to envisage in practice, since the negotiated procedure will generally be used in the first place in a procedure without a call for competition.

[39] On these conditions see the discussion at (a) above.

[40] See pp. 520.

providers.[41] Thus if the negotiations with the winning bidder are not successful, the only option is to decline to award the contract to any of the bidders.[42-43] If the authority still wishes to go ahead with the project and to search for new providers, it must then commence a new procedure under the regulations, and a call for competition will be required.

If a utility wishes to retain the freedom to negotiate with bidders if it is dissatisfied with the bids submitted then, as already noted, it is advisable to choose the negotiated procedure, where such negotiations are permitted, instead of the open or restricted procedure.

(6) TERMINATION OF THE PROCEDURE WITHOUT AN AWARD

For a variety of reasons a purchaser may wish to terminate an award procedure without awarding a contract: for example, it may decide to abandon the project altogether or make radical changes to requirements, or it might decide to begin a new procedure because it is dissatisfied with the offers in the first procedure. There is nothing in the legislation to prevent termination of the procedure in such cases.

Another reason for failing to award a contract may be that the utility decides to do the work in-house instead of contracting it out. This will normally happen following a market-testing exercise in which the in-house provider submits the most advantageous bid. However, a purchaser may also eventually decide to retain the work in-house for strategic reasons, even where there is no in-house bid, or where that bid is not the most favourable. The position in this case was discussed further above, where it was explained that, under the regulations, there is generally nothing to prevent a procedure being terminated so that the work can be kept in-house.[44]

There is no obligation to send a notice to the *Official Journal* where the utility decides that it will neither award a contract nor seek new offers. Such an obligation applies in the public sector.[45]

6. NEGOTIATED PROCEDURES

(1) GENERAL

As noted above, the negotiated procedure is a relatively informal procedure under which no formal tendering need be carried out,

---

[41] See pp. 520.
[42-43] See below.
[44] See pp. 414–415. This will not apply to contracts subject to CCT when the CCT legislation will effectively require an award to the best bidder, but this legislation will rarely apply to a contract governed by the Utilities Regulations.
[45] See p. 255.

although a utility may, should it wish, incorporate a formal tendering stage under a procedure which is to be operated as a negotiated procedure under the regulations.

In most cases the negotiated procedure will be operated following a call for competition under the regulations. As explained above, this may be carried out in one of three ways: through an individual contract notice; through a periodic indicative notice; or through advertisement of a qualification system. The rules applicable to the call for competition have already been set out above.[46] Once the call for competition has been made the utility will issue invitations to a number of firms to negotiate for the contract, with a view to ascertaining which one is able to offer the best value for money.

We have seen, however, that in some exceptional cases a call for competition is not required,[47] and in such cases the negotiated procedure without a competition will generally be the procedure used to award the contract. Many of the situations where there is an exemption from the normal competition requirement are cases where there is one pre-determined provider – for example, with contracts following on from existing contracts which are made with the same provider, or where there is only one possible provider for technical or other relevant reasons. In this type of case the negotiated procedure will have a very different complexion from the more usual "call for competition" case where negotiations are conducted with a number of providers in competition with each other. However, even where no formal call for competition is made some form of competitive negotiations with a number of firms may be appropriate. For example, in an immediate emergency it may still be possible to talk briefly to two separate firms to see which one can offer the best price for the emergency work.

(2) ASCERTAINING INTEREST IN THE CONTRACT

Invitations will be issued to those expressing interest in the contract. The exact steps involved in ascertaining who is interested will vary according to whether any call for competition was made and, if so, the way in which that call was made.

(a) PROCEDURE FOLLOWING A CALL FOR COMPETITION

In a procedure involving a call for competition the rules are effectively the same as under a restricted procedure.

Where the call was made through publication of a contract notice firms will submit requests to be considered in response to the notice,

---

[46] See pp. 471–482.
[47] On these see pp. 482–490.

which should have called upon firms to express their interest in the contract and should have indicated the final date for receipt of request.[48]

Where the call was made through a periodic indicative notice, the notice must have referred specifically to the contract and called for expressions of interest to be submitted in writing.[49] The notice should also have made it clear that there would be no further call for competition.[50] Utilities must then send all those who respond detailed information on the contract, and invite them to confirm whether they still wish to be selected to tender.[51] This invitation must be sent within twelve months (or on the last day of this period) of the date the periodic indicative notice was published,[52] and must state the date by which these expressions of continued interest must be received.[53]

The time-limits for response are the same as for restricted procedures. The date for receipt of requests to be invited to tender, following either a contract notice or a request for confirmation of interest, must "in general" be at least five weeks from the date of despatch of the contract notice, and in all cases not less than 22 days from the despatch of the notice.[54] As with restricted procedures, no doubt specific justification must be advanced for a period shorter than five weeks. This could, for example, be reasons of urgency, or because the contract is for simple off-the-shelf items for which little preparation time is needed.[55] In fixing the time-limit utilities must always take into account the time required for any examination of voluminous documentation (such as lengthy specifications) or any inspection of site or documents,[56] and this may in some cases require that the five-week period be extended. In "exceptional" cases where the utility has requested rapid publication by the *Official Journal* a 15 day period may apply.[56a] As with restricted procedures, the Commission Proposal for aligning the Community directive with the GPA proposes a slight extension of the general period to 37 days.

As regards the form of requests, an "application to be invited to tender"[57] cannot be refused on the grounds that it is made by letter; nor

---

[48] Utilities Regulation 17(3); and see the model contract notice at pp. 478–479.
[49] Utilities Regulation 15(3)(b).
[50] *Ibid.*
[51] Utilities Regulation 15(3)(d).
[52] Utilities Regulation 15(3)(d).
[53] Utilities Regulation 16(3).
[54] Utilities Regulation 17(3). In theory the time-limits are calculated as set out in n. 8 on p. 490 above but these rules will not be significant for these time-limits since the limits are slightly flexible in any case.
[55] Under the public sector rules a general period of 37 days (similar to five weeks) is prescribed, with an exception allowing reduction of the period to 15 days where there is urgency; but there is no possibility of shortening the procedure for other reasons.
[56] Utilities Regulation 17(5).
[56a] Utilities Regulation 17(3) and 29(3).
[57] The Utilities Directive refers to "requests for participation": Article 28(5). It seems clear that these provisions are intended to cover both requests following a contract notice, and also confirmations of interest where the contract has been publicised through a periodic indicative notice.

because it is made by telegram, telex, facsimile or telephone, provided in these cases that it is confirmed by letter prior to the closing date for receipt of tenders.[58] Apart from this, there are no express provisions on the form of requests. It was suggested in the section on restricted procedures that there is nothing to prevent an authority specifying in the contract notice the form of the request (for example, the language to be used) and to reject requests which do not meet these formalities; but that it should be able to waive these provided, however, that all persons making requests are treated equally.[59-60]

Where the call for competition is made through an advertisement of a qualification system there are no requirements concerning the way in which requests to be invited to tender should be made. In this case there is nothing in the rules requiring a utility to seek such requests; it may simply invite firms directly from the lists. Alternatively, in some cases the utility may still invite all or some of the firms on its list to indicate an interest in the particular contracts before issuing invitations.

As with restricted procedures, in the case of contracts publicised through a contract notice or periodic indicative notice the utility may seek providers by methods additional to those required by the regulations, such as national advertisements or by approaching known firms; but this is not possible with contracts where the call for competition requirement is satisfied by publicising a qualification system. In this case only those qualified through the system may be considered.[61]

(b) PROCEDURE WITHOUT A CALL FOR COMPETITION

When a negotiated procedure is conducted without a call for competition under the regulations there are no formal rules to govern the way in which interest in the contract is to be ascertained. In practice, as noted above, the reason for dispensing with the requirement for a call for competition is that the provider is already predetermined, and negotiations are then conducted merely to establish the price, and not the provider. Where this is not the case – for example, where the requirement is dispensed with for reasons of urgency – the utility may ascertain interest by any means it thinks fit.

---

[58] Utilities Regulation 17(10).
[59-60] This arises from the fundamental principle of the equality of treatment of providers, laid down in case C–143/89, *Commission v. Denmark*, judgment of June 22, 1993 (see pp. 180–181) which will certainly be applied in the utilities sector as well as in the public sector.
[61] Utilities Regulation 15(4).

(3) SELECTING PROVIDERS TO BE INVITED TO NEGOTIATE

Having followed the steps set out at (2) above, the utility must proceed to select from those interested in the contract which firms are to be invited to participate in the negotiations.

(a) NUMBER OF INVITATIONS

The rules governing the number of invitations to be issued are the same as those applicable in restricted procedures. Thus the utility is subject to Utilities Regulation 19(5) which states that the utility must take account "of the need to ensure adequate competition" in determining the number of providers to be invited to bid. Also applicable is regulation 19(3) that the criteria for selection may be based on the need to reduce the number selected "to a level which is justified by the characteristics of the award procedure and the resources required to complete it", which indicates clearly that the utility is not required to consider all interested and qualified providers.[62]

These provisions are not specifically limited to procedures which follow a call for competition, and thus appear applicable in all types of negotiated procedure.[63] In the case of procedures without a call for competition they will have no practical relevance in the case where the provider is already pre-determined – for example, where the call for competition does not apply because the contract is a follow-on from a previous contract. However, they will be relevant where this is not the case, as where the call for competition is dispensed with for reasons of urgency, and in such a case it is thus necessary to consider whether it is appropriate to negotiate with more than one provider.

(b) THE METHOD FOR SELECTING INVITEES ("SHORTLISTING")

The rules applicable to the selection of parties to negotiate are the same as those which apply in restricted procedures. The applicable rules are those in Utilities Regulation 19(1), requiring selection on the basis of objective criteria and rules, determined by the purchaser and made known to providers; regulation 19(2), stating certain specific criteria which are permissible; and the general requirements of the E.C. Treaty (where relevant) and the general principle prohibiting discrimination.

---

[62] The public sector rules are more ambiguous although it was argued above that they should not be interpreted to require all qualified firms to be invited: see pp. 217–222.

[63] This is not specifically stated, in contrast with some other provisions which indicate expressly that they apply to negotiated procedures *with or without* competition; but in the absence of any limitations it appears they must be applied to all negotiated procedures.

These rules on selection were examined in detail in the context of restricted procedures.[64]

They apply to negotiated procedures both with and without a call for competition.[65] However, they will have no practical relevance in those cases of a procedure without a call for competition where the provider is already settled, such as follow-on contracts with the same provider or where there is only one possible provider available.

(4) SENDING THE INVITATIONS TO NEGOTIATE

Invitations to negotiate must be sent to each firm selected to bid and must be in writing.[66] They must be issued simultaneously to all those selected[67] to ensure that no provider selected is unfairly disadvantaged. Although this requirement is designed for the benefit of providers it is submitted that providers should not be able to waive the requirement: this could lead to abuse with purchasers sending early invitations to favoured firms and leaving others to accept a late invitation or none at all. These requirements are expressly stated to apply to procedures both with and without a call for competition.[68]

The invitation must be accompanied by the contract documents[69] – that is, the invitation to tender itself; the proposed contract conditions; the specifications, or description of the subject-matter of the contracts; and any "supplementary" documents.[70] The following information must also be included with the invitation:

(i) an address to which requests for further information should be sent; the final date for requesting such information; and the amount of any fee for this, along with methods of payment[71];

(ii) the final date for receipt of tenders[72];

(iii) the language of tenders[73];

(iv) a reference to any contract notice[74];

(v) an indication of any information which is to be included in the tender[75];

(vi) the contract award criteria (unless the contract has been advertised by a contract notice and this information was included in that notice)[76];

---

[64] See further pp. 496–500.
[65] This is expressly stated in Utilities Regulation 19(1).
[66] Utilities Regulation 17(7).
[67] Utilities Regulation 17(7).
[68] Utilities Regulation 17(7).
[69] Utilities Regulation 17(7).
[70] See the definition of contract documents in Utilities Regulation 2(1).
[71] Utilities Regulation 17(8)(a).
[72] Utilities Regulation 17(8)(b).
[73] Utilities Regulation 17(8)(b).
[74] Utilities Regulation 17(8)(c). This refers only to a notice advertising the individual contract, not a periodic indicative notice, even if used as a call for competition: see the definition of contract notice in Utilities Regulation 2(1).
[75] Utilities Regulation 16(8)(d).
[76] Utilities Regulation 16(8)(e).

(vii) any other "special contract condition".[77-78] This seems to refer to any significant contract conditions not already notified to providers.

Again, the rules apply to procedures both with and without a call for competition.[79]

Some of the information referred to above relates to "tenders" to be submitted by the provider. However, with some negotiated procedures there may be no formal tendering stage. In these cases the rules should be read as referring to offers rather then tenders.[80]

(5) OBLIGATION TO PROVIDE FURTHER INFORMATION

The utility has an obligation to provide any further information relating to the contract documents which is reasonably requested by a provider not less than six days before the date for receipt of offers, provided the request is made in good time[81] and that any stipulated fee accompanies the request.[82] This applies to procedures both with and without a call for competition.

(6) TIME-LIMITS FOR RECEIPT OF OFFERS

As with open and restricted procedures the Utilities Regulations lay down minimum time-limits for the receipt of offers,[83] to ensure that non-domestic providers are not placed at a disproportionate disadvantage in participating in a procedure. These rules apply, however, only to negotiated procedures involving a call for competition; there are no minimum periods in procedures without a call for competition.

As with restricted procedures, the deadline for receipt of offers following a call for competition is to be fixed by agreement between the utility and those invited to tender.[84] The deadline must be the same for all firms.[85] If no agreement can be reached, the utility must fix the deadline, which must "as a general rule" be at least three weeks from despatch of the invitation, and, in all cases, at least ten days from the date of despatch.[86] The shorter period may probably be used in the same circumstances as the shorter period for submission of requests to be

---

[77-78] Utilities Regulation 16(8)(f).

[79] Utilities Regulation 17(7) states this expressly.

[80] The word "tender" is the one used in the directive but is inappropriate in English for offers submitted in a negotiated procedure.

[81] Utilities Regulation 17(9). The time period is calculated as set out in n. 8 on p. 490.

[82] Utilities Regulation 17(9).

[83] The regulations actually refer to "tenders" but, as mentioned above, this is inappropriate for some negotiated procedures, and it must be read as referring to offers in general.

[84] Utilities Regulation 17(4).

[85] *Ibid.*

[86] *Ibid.*

invited to negotiate, as discussed above, such as urgency, or the simple nature of the procurement.[87]

In fixing the time-limit, utilities must take into account the time required for any examination of voluminous documentation (such as lengthy specifications) or any inspection of site or documents.[88] Thus, where there is no agreement the general three-week period may need to be lengthened for examinations or inspections.

The Commission has proposed certain changes to these limits to align the Utilities Directive with the rules in the GPA. These proposed changes are the same as for restricted procedures and have already been considered above.[88a]

(7) CHOOSING THE PROVIDER FROM THOSE INVITED TO NEGOTIATE

As already noted, in some negotiated procedures without a call for competition the question of choosing a provider from amongst a number of contenders does not arise, since negotiations are conducted with only one provider – for example, where only one is available for technical reasons. In this case the contract will be awarded to that provider provided that satisfactory terms can be agreed between the parties. In most cases, however, there will be several providers in competition in the negotiations. This can apply, as explained, either in a procedure following a call for competition, or in a procedure where no such call for competition is required, such as where negotiations are conducted with more than one party in a situation of urgency.

In selecting the provider the utility must comply with the same rules on evaluation of offers as apply in open and restricted procedures, set out in Utilities Regulation 21. The basic principle is that the contract should be awarded on the basis of either lowest offer or "most economically advantageous" offer, with exceptions for abnormally low bids and offers containing third-country products. In negotiated procedures the offers which are to be evaluated are not necessarily identified through a formal tender process[89] but are those which emerge from each invitee at the end of the period of negotiations. The meaning of most economically advantageous offer was discussed above in relation to open and restricted procedures[90] and exactly the same provisions

---

[87] See pp. 525–528.
[88] Utilities Regulation 17(5).
[88a] See pp. 525–526.
[89] The provisions of the directive itself on evaluation refer to "tenders" which seems apt only in relation to open and restricted procedures; since negotiated procedures need not involve "tenders" in the traditional sense; but it is clear that the same principles of evaluation were intended to apply to negotiated procedures. The regulations refer to "offer".
[90] See pp. 508–509.

apply in negotiated procedures. The same rules also apply in negotiated procedures as in open and restricted procedures to the treatment of third-country products,[91] abnormally low offers,[92] and in-house bids.[93]

As in restricted procedures, the utility must state in any contract notice or the invitation which basis – lowest price, or most economically advantageous offer – is to be applied.[94] As with other procedures, where the most economically advantageous offer basis is used, the utility must state in either the notice or the contract documents which precise criteria (price, quality, etc.) are to be taken into account, in order of preference where possible.[95]

There are no express rules on how negotiations will be conducted, either in a procedure with a call for competition or one without. Often, these may take the form simply of informal discussions with each invitee. However, as has been mentioned, a utility may equally prefer to use a tendering procedure involving formal submission bids to a deadline. For example, where the reason for using the procedure is that the specifications cannot be precisely defined the utility could ask bidders to submit their own proposals and follow consideration of these proposals with either a formal tendering procedure based on a favoured proposal, or a formal request for "final" offers with each provider making a bid on the basis of its own proposal. Should utility choose a form of tendering it is not bound by the precise rules applying to open and restricted procedures – for example, the rule forbidding post-tender negotiations with bidders.

In all types of negotiations, however, constraints may arise from the operation of the general principle of "equality of treatment" for providers articulated in the *Storebaelt* case,[96] which will clearly apply in the utilities sector as well as the public sector. For example, it would probably be a breach of this principle to provide information for one invitee concerning the utility's budgetary constraints, but not to make this information available to other providers. Further, where the utility does choose to conduct a formal procedure as part of the "negotiations" behaviour which would infringe the equality principle in open and restricted procedures may also infringe that principle in negotiated procedures – for example, extending the tender deadline for one provider only. It should not, on the other hand, be considered a breach of this principle to select the providers with the best proposals and to negotiate on price with those providers alone in a second stage of negotiations: here the different treatment is based on a material distinction between providers.

---

91 See pp. 511–513.
92 See pp. 515–519.
93 See pp. 514–515.
94 Utilities Regulation 17(8)(e).
95 Utilities Regulation 28(3).
96 See pp. 180–181.

(8) UNSATISFACTORY AWARD PROCEDURES

A utility may be dissatisfied with the result of a negotiated procedure, as any other (although this is less likely, since the wide scope for negotiation between the parties makes it easier to reach a mutually acceptable agreement). Where this happens because no offers have resulted from the negotiations, the utility may seek to award the contract without a new call for competition, provided that the original procedure involved a call for competition and provided also that the terms of the contract remain substantially unaltered.[97] There is no exemption provided for the case where the terms are substantially altered,[98] since in such a case a new call for competition could bring in providers who were not interested in the original contract. It is also possible to commence a new procedure without a call for competition where offers are received but none are suitable.[99] This would cover the case where the only providers submitting offers turn out to lack the technical or financial standing to carry out the contract, or lack other qualifications set by the utility. It is submitted that it does not, however, cover the case where the utility is simply dissatisfied with the offers. In such a case it may, under the negotiated procedure, continue discussions with providers to persuade them to improve their offers. If they refuse to do so, however, it is submitted that a new procedure *with* a call for competition is necessary.

(9) TERMINATING THE PROCEDURE WITHOUT AN AWARD

As with an open or restricted procedure a utility may wish to terminate a negotiated procedure without awarding a contract. There is nothing in the regulations to prevent the utility from terminating the procedure at any time and for any reason.

7. THE OPERATION OF QUALIFICATION SYSTEMS

(1) NATURE AND SIGNIFICANCE OF A QUALIFICATION SYSTEM

One way of meeting the requirement for a call for competition is to set up and publicise a qualification system. This is a system whereby

---

[97] Utilities Regulation 15(1)(a).
[98] On this concept see also pp. 617–618.
[99] Utilities Regulation 15(1)(a).

interested providers may indicate to the utility their interest in future contracts and apply for registration on a list of potential providers. A number of firms are then selected by the provider for registration on the list, and participants in future restricted and negotiated procedures are then selected from those on the lists.

For utilities, this provides a less burdensome method for advertising contracts than publication of a contract notice for every separate award procedure (as is required under the public sector rules) or reference to each separate contract in a periodic indicative notice – the two main alternatives.[1] It can also help cut down the burden for providers of finding out what contracts are available.

Use of a qualification system in accordance with the regulations also enables purchasers to limit participation in contracts to those who have already qualified in advance under the system. Probably this is not permitted except in a procedure publicised by reference to such a system in accordance with the rules in the regulations.[2] (On the other hand, utilities may operate a qualification list which is optional for providers, without following these rules.)[3]

To take advantage of these possibilities it is necessary to comply with certain detailed rules laid down in the Utilities Regulations, contained mainly in regulation 18, concerning the operation of qualification systems. Where the system does not comply with these rules a call for competition must be made by one of the other methods in the regulations, and the procedure probably cannot, as mentioned, be restricted only to registered providers.

(2) ADVERTISEMENT OF THE SYSTEM

As regards publicity for the system, it must be advertised by sending a notice of the system to the Office of Official Publications of the European Communities, as laid down in regulation 18(2). These requirements concerning publicity have already been considered in detail above in the section on the call for competition.[4]

(3) CRITERIA FOR QUALIFICATION

Regarding the criteria for qualification, the basic principle, stated in Utilities Regulation 18(2), is that the utility shall use "objective rules and criteria". This phrase is also used in Utilities Regulation 19(2) in relation

---

[1] See pp. 472–482. The utility can also avoid making reference to every separate contract by advertising large contracts in lots, or by making use of framework agreements (as to which see pp. 452–460).
[2] See further pp. 544–545.
[3] See pp. 544–545.
[4] See pp. 479–482.

to the methods for selecting firms for participation in individual restricted and negotiated procedures from amongst those interested. It was suggested there[5] that "objective" criteria and rules refers, in general, to all criteria and rules which are capable of articulation and the application of which may be verified. It covers all commercial criteria, but may also include secondary factors such as firms' equal opportunities and environmental policies although this is not entirely clear. In relation to selection of participants regulation 19(2) expressly lists certain criteria, some of them secondary criteria (such as non-payment of taxes) which may be considered, but no such list is contained in regulation 18. However, it appears that such criteria could all nevertheless be considered in relation to qualification systems as "objective" criteria, even though not expressly listed in this context; the omission of the list is merely a drafting anomaly.

In practice a utility will generally wish to give some consideration to a firm's financial standing and technical capability to carry out contracts covered by the system. For this purpose it may wish to divide the system into lists of different types, or values, of contract, or to operate totally different systems for different contracts.[6] Consideration of financial and technical aspects at this stage need not entail that the provider is definitely deemed suitable for certain types of contract (although the utility may decide that this will be the case); utilities may choose to qualify all providers meeting certain thresholds, and consider qualifications for specific contracts separately, according to the nature of the contract, or they may at least wish to check that a provider's standing remains current at the time a particular contract is awarded. It is submitted that it is even permitted to register providers without consideration of standing at all, although this is certainly unlikely for complex products or services. The utility may also consider other commercial criteria, such as the prospects for developing long-term partnerships with particular providers[7] or the question of which providers are likely to offer the best value for money.[8] In practice utilities, particularly those in the private sector, will not often wish to take account of secondary criteria.[9]

---

[5] See pp. 498–500.

[6] Utilities Regulation 18(9) concerning written records specifically envisages divisions into different categories.

[7] On this consideration see pp. 290–295. This fact does not mean that qualification systems offer opportunities for partnering in the sense of a "guaranteed" business relationship, (as to which see pp. 290–295) since it is always necessary for registered providers to compete with others on the list for individual contracts.

[8] The latter concept overlaps with technical standing. The latter is concerned with whether firms are able to meet minimum standards for specific contracts, and "value for money" with the merits of a particular bid but factors such as the quality of a firm's products or services are, of course, relevant to both issues.

[9] However, there is an increasing tendency in private business for secondary concerns, such as firms' environmental records, to be taken into account. This has arisen partly as a result of pressure from consumers – for example, consumer groups may urge a boycott of firms who deal with other firms which are regarded as politically undesirable. Thus utilities may occasionally consider such matters to be relevant in their procurement.

Some utilities have related the qualification process to the process for selecting invitees for specific award procedures, by grading firms on qualification in relation to various qualification factors (for example, degree of reliability, quality of different firm's current product, etc.). Firms which score the most highly in the qualification exercise may then be given priority in the process of selection for participation in particular procedures.

It was suggested that in relation to selection for individual procedures "objective" criteria should include random selection methods such as the drawing of lots. Such methods seem less appropriate for general qualification systems, however, and are unlikely to be used.

As regards the number of firms on qualification lists, sufficient firms need to be included to ensure that there are enough providers to participate in individual award procedures under the system. Here it is necessary to bear in mind the utility's obligation in choosing the number to invite to consider the need for adequate competition.[10] This does not necessarily require the inclusion of a very large number of firms on the list, however. With complex products or services in particular, a utility may prefer to limit its qualification lists to a few top-performing providers, so that those providers have a reasonable expectation of future business with the utility, and the utility can build up an on-going working relationship to mutual advantage with a few competent providers.[11] However, there are limitations on the extent of co-operation arising from the fact that a competition for each contract must normally be held between several firms on the list, in accordance with the procedures outlined in the previous part of this chapter – business cannot be guaranteed to one or two favoured firms.

Within the general principles outlined above, utilities are subject to certain specific limits in setting qualification criteria. First, Utilities Regulation 18(1) specifically states that utilities may not impose conditions of an administrative, technical or financial nature on some providers which are not imposed upon others. This is a rule which probably applies to all qualification processes under the regulations in any case by virtue of the principle of equality of treatment of providers laid down in the *Storebaelt* case.[12] Secondly, the utility is subject to the rules in the Community Treaties, where applicable, which prohibit criteria in qualification which have the effect of discriminating against firms from other Member States,[13] and also in some cases to similar rules under international agreements.[14] In addition, the process of qualifying providers for lists is subject to rules on qualification in Utilities Regulation 20, which apply not merely to qualification lists but to

---

[10] See p. 496.
[11] On the advantages of such close, long-term arrangements see pp. 290–295.
[12] See pp. 180–181.
[13] On the application of such rules in the context of qualification see pp. 350–379.
[14] See Chap. 15.

qualification under the regulations in general. These rules prohibit utilities from refusing qualification simply because an entity is to take the form of a consortium, or refusing qualification to a service provider in certain cases because of the legal form taken by the service provider. These rules are considered further in the section on qualification at (8.) below. They state that a utility may not decline on the grounds listed to include a provider "amongst those persons from whom [the utility] will make the selection of persons to be invited to tender for or to negotiate a contract"[15]; this covers inclusion on a qualification list, which establishes which persons are to be invited to participate in contracts covered by the list.

Utilities Regulation 18(2) states that the qualification system is to be based on objective rules and criteria "using European standards as a reference where appropriate". This seems to suggest that where relevant European standards exist for matters covered by qualification these should be referred to. There are special provisions in Utilities Regulation 19(4) on the use of BS 5750 and equivalent standards for assessing technical capacity, which will apply where technical capacity is assessed in the context of qualification systems as well as in other cases. This provision is also considered further in the general section on qualification at (8) below.

Utilities Regulation 18(4) provides that an application for qualification may be refused only if the applicant fails to meet the criteria which have been laid down in accordance with Utilities Regulation 18(2).

(4) EVIDENCE OF QUALIFICATIONS

The public sector rules contain very detailed provisions concerning the evidence which may be demanded for the purpose of assessing the financial and technical qualifications of providers.[16] No such provisions apply in the utilities sector. However, in Utilities Regulation 18(6) it is stated that in the context of qualification systems[17] a utility may not require "the application of tests or the submission of evidence which duplicates objective evidence already available". This indicates a general principle that utilities must accept any evidence forwarded by providers which is equivalent to that specified by the utility. This ensures that the burden on providers in qualification is reduced to that which is absolutely necessary for ascertaining whether that provider meets the required standards. This applies in relation to all the qualification criteria which may be set by the utility.

---

[15] Utilities Regulation 20(2); Utilities Regulation 20(4).
[16] See Chap. 7.
[17] It is suggested below that this limitation in fact applies to qualification in general under the Utilities Regulations: see pp. 543–544.

(5) PROCEDURAL ASPECTS OF QUALIFICATION

(a) PUBLICITY FOR QUALIFICATION CRITERIA

Utilities Regulation 18(3) requires that the rules and criteria for qualification shall be made available to providers on request. Further, if a provider should request it, amendments to the rules and criteria must be sent when these amendments are incorporated.[18]

(b) INFORMATION FOR PROVIDERS ON QUALIFICATION DECISIONS

The utility must inform providers who have applied for qualification of the success or failure of their application "within a reasonable period"[19] of that decision. If the decision will take longer than six months from the date of the application the utility must inform the applicant within two months of the application of the reason for the delay and of the date by which the decision will be made.[20]

Where an application is refused the utility must inform the applicant of this fact and of the reasons for the decision.[21] Where reasons for decisions are required by legislation the courts will imply that these reasons must be adequate and intelligible and provide sufficient information for a party to decide whether to challenge the decision.[22] This requirement for provision of reasons for a procurement decision is unusual under the Utilities Regulations; whilst reasons must be given on request for most types of procurement decisions under the public sector regulations,[23] no such requirements generally apply in the utilities sector (although there is currently a proposal to introduce such a requirement for utilities, in order to align the European rules with the GPA).[23a]

(c) TIME-LIMITS FOR QUALIFICATION DECISIONS

In general, it appears that a utility is expected to complete the qualification process within six months of an application unless there are special reasons why this cannot be done. This may be deduced from the provision in Utilities Regulation 18(5) stating that if a qualification decision will take longer than six months the utility must inform the applicant within two months of the application of "the reasons justifying a longer period".

---

[18] Utilities Regulation 18(3).
[19] Utilities Regulation 18(5).
[20] Utilities Regulation 18(5).
[21] Utilities Regulation 18(7).
[22] See Craig, *Administrative Law* (3rd ed., 1994), at pp. 312–313.
[23] See pp. 281–282.
[23a] See pp. 553–554.

(d) WRITTEN RECORDS

The utility must keep a written record of qualified providers.[24]

(e) CANCELLATION OF QUALIFICATION

In the same way as a utility may only refuse an application for qualification if the relevant criteria are not met, so it may only cancel the qualification if the provider does not continue to meet the qualification criteria which have been laid down.[25] Before cancellation is permitted, the utility must notify the provider beforehand in writing of its intention and of the reason(s) for the proposed cancellation.[26] It is not expressly stated that the provider must be given an opportunity to make representations, but this may perhaps be implied from the requirement that notification should be given before the decision is taken. If general principles of judicial review apply to the exercise of procurement powers, it appears that a provider will have a right to a hearing in such a case under the principle of natural justice,[27] but recent cases indicate that judicial review does not normally apply.

(f) OPERATION OF QUALIFICATION SYSTEMS BY OTHER BODIES ON BEHALF OF THE UTILITY

Utilities Regulation 18(4) provides that it is permitted for the utility to establish a system whereby a provider may qualify under the system of a person other than the utility or be certified by another person. The operation of systems of qualification which go beyond specific utilities – for example, by a central body, or by one utility acting for others – can be useful for both utilities and providers in reducing the administrative burdens of operating a number of different systems.

Where this is done, the regulations requires that the utility must inform providers who apply of the name of that other person.

(g) QUALIFICATION IN STAGES

It is expressly stated that a qualification system may involve different stages.[27a] For example, firms could first be questioned to establish their financial standing, with tests on aspects of technical ability applied at a later time only to those who meet the utility's financial requirements.

---

[24] Utilities Regulation 15(9).
[25] Utilities Regulation 18(10).
[26] Utilities Regulation 18(11).
[27] See the discussion of the *Enfield* case on p. 34.
[27a] Utilities Regulation 18(2).

(h) PROPOSAL TO ALLOW QUALIFICATION AT ANY TIME

The Commission's proposal for aligning the Utilities Directive with the rules in the GPA includes a provision to state expressly that providers must be allowed to apply for qualifications at any time.[27b] For entities covered by the GPA itself, this requirement must be adhered to as from January 1, 1996 even if it is not yet included in the directive or regulations.

(6) USE OF THE SYSTEM TO SELECT PARTICIPANTS IN AWARD PROCEDURES

As has already been noted, where a utility wishes to make use of a qualification system to avoid the need for a call for competition through a contract notice or periodic indicative notice, it must select firms to participate in that award procedure *only* from amongst those on the list[28] – unregistered firms may not be considered. The utility may issue invitations to all firms or may issue them directly just to some firms on the list, either with or without first seeking confirmation of these firms' interest in the contract. The criteria which may be applied in selecting which providers to invite are the same as in procedures not based on a qualification list, and have been considered above.[29] As has already been observed, these selection criteria may be closely tied in with the qualification system by giving preference in issuing invitations to those providers scoring most highly on the qualification criteria.

It has also been noted that a qualification system may be used only in relation to restricted and negotiated procedures. Where the open procedure is used the only permissible method of calling for competition is a contract notice,[30] and it appears that qualification cannot be limited to those on a qualification list.

The fact that a utility operates a qualification system for a particular type of contract does not preclude that utility from running a procedure for a contract of that type without relying on the system. In such a case the utility may not, of course, rely on the system as providing a call for competition, and may not limit participation in the procedure to those registered on the list.

[27b] Proposal for a European Parliament and Council Directive amending Directive 93/38/EEC Co-ordinating the procurement procedures of entities operating in the water, energy, transport and telecommunications sectors, COM (95) 107 Final, Article 1(12).

[28] Utilities Regulation 15(4).

[29] See pp. 497–500.

[30] See p. 472.

8. QUALIFICATION OF PROVIDERS

(1) INTRODUCTION

The term "qualification" is used here, as in relation to the public sector rules, to refer to the process of deciding which firms are eligible to participate in a contract award procedure. As noted in Chapter 7 on the public sector rules, a purchaser may wish to exclude providers for a variety of reasons. Almost invariably purchasers will wish to ensure that any contracting partner has the ability to complete the contract, entailing checks on his technical ability to perform and on his financial position; and purchasers may also sometimes seek to exclude a provider for reasons not directly related to the ability to perform for example, because the firm does not follow equal opportunities guidelines.

Aspects of the qualification process have already been touched on in considering the steps to be taken in the three different award procedures, and in examining the operation of qualification systems. However, it is useful to consider separately the general rules on qualification under the regulations. In carrying on the qualification process utilities are subject to general rules prohibiting discrimination and unequal treatment, including the rules in the Community Treaties, where applicable. There are also some specific rules in the regulations. However, these are much less detailed and prescriptive than the rules on qualification found in the public sector regulations, giving utilities more freedom both over the substantive grounds for excluding providers and the evidence which may be used to assess qualification.

(2) GENERAL PRINCIPLES ON NON-DISCRIMINATION AND EQUALITY

For utilities which are subject to obligations under the Community Treaties,[31] the general obligations in the Treaties will apply to the qualification process. The E.C. Treaty, for example, imposes obligations not to discriminate in the qualification process against providers from other Member States. Thus, for example, purchasers may not impose on firms from other Member States conditions not imposed on domestic providers or conditions which are more onerous for non-domestic providers (for example, higher annual turnover requirements for measuring financial standing). The application of the E.C. Treaty in the context of qualification was considered in more detail in Chapter 7.[32] There is also a general prohibition on discriminatory conduct in the exercise of functions subject to the regulations. Similar obligations also apply in

---

[31] On the scope of the relevant E.C. Treaty obligations in this respect see pp. 86–88.
[32] See pp. 350–352.

some cases to providers from other states under international agreements concluded by the Community.[33]

The general principle prohibiting discrimination between providers[34] will also apply to the qualification process. This principle will in general prevent utilities from imposing on some providers conditions which do not apply to others or from imposing different conditions on different providers where there is no reasonable justification for such different treatment. It is expressly stated in Utilities Regulation 18(6) that in determining qualification under a qualification system a utility may not impose conditions of an administrative, technical or financial nature on some providers which are not imposed on others but although stated only in the context of qualifications systems it is submitted that the same rule applies to all types of qualification, by virtue of the *Storebaelt* principle.

(3) CRITERIA FOR QUALIFICATION UNDER THE REGULATIONS

The Utilities Regulations contain no express provisions which refer to the criteria for qualification at a general level, However, in relation both to qualification through registration on a qualification list, and qualification for the purpose of being included amongst those from whom a utility will select persons to invite to participate in restricted or negotiated persons, the regulations state that "objective" criteria and rules must be applied.[35] These provisions cover most qualification decisions, but they do not expressly apply to open procedures.

It seems very likely, however, that the Court of Justice, which adopts a broad and purposive approach to interpretation where it considers this appropriate, will apply the same principles by analogy to open procedures. The absence of express provision to cover this case is certainly a product of untidy and unsystematic drafting rather than of any intention to create different qualification principles for the different cases.

What are "objective" criteria and rules has already been considered above. It was suggested that this concept covers criteria which may be articulated and monitored.[36] It certainly covers commercial criteria, notably the economic and financial standing of firms, and possibly also non-commercial criteria, such as a firm's equal opportunities policies, although this is an arguable point. The concept of objective criteria does not, on the other hand, cover criteria which appear arbitrary or irrational, such as financial requirements which have no relationship to the specific contract or contracts under consideration.

---

[33] See Chap. 16.
[34] On this principle see pp. 461–462.
[35] Utilities Regulation 18(2) (qualification systems) and Utilities Regulation 19(1).
[36] See pp. 497–498.

(4) STANDARDS FOR QUALIFICATION UNDER THE REGULATIONS

There is nothing specific in the regulations on the standards to be set for qualification – for example, the amount and types of previous experience which is required, or the level of annual turnover required for participation in particular contracts. It is clear that these matters are in principle for the utility to determine.

(5) THE USE OF QUALITY ASSURANCE STANDARDS

There is an express provision in Utilities Regulation 20(4) concerning the imposition of a requirement for providers to conform to BS 5750 and equivalent standards relating to quality assurance. The provision states that utilities may ask that a provider seeking a services contract[37] submit a certificate to attest conformity to quality-assurance standards based on the EN 29,000 series (on which BS 5750 is based), where provided by an independent body from another relevant state, which conforms to the EN 45,000 European standards series. There is an exception, however, where providers have "no access" to such certificates. This will probably apply where the provider's own state has not made any provision for such certificates. There is also an exception where a provider cannot obtain a certificate "within the relevant time limits" (which means, presumably, in time to participate in the award procedure). In these cases the provision states that utilities must accept "any other evidence of conformity to equivalent quality-assurance standards". These same rules apply to the use of quality-assurance standards under the public sector rules.

This provision appears to give a special status to such quality-assurance standards: in general, it appears that utilities may not require specified evidence of matters which providers are able to prove by other objective means, whilst this provision allows providers to produce evidence which is an alternative to the relevant quality-assurance certificate only in those limited cases where such a quality assurance certificate cannot be obtained.

(6) THE LEGAL STATUS OF PROVIDERS

(a) BIDS BY CONSORTIA

As do the public sector rules, Utilities Regulation 20 expressly permits providers to form consortia to participate in contracts. For this purpose

---

[37] The provision refers only to service providers, defined in Utilities Regulation 4 as covering only those seeking services contracts. Thus this provision does not apply to supply and works contracts.

a "consortium" is defined as meaning two or more persons, at least one of whom is a provider (in other words – a potential contracting party), who act jointly for the purpose of being awarded a contract.[38]

These rules provide that a tender cannot be treated as ineligible simply because it is submitted by a consortium which has not formed a legal entity for the purpose of tendering; nor can an authority decline, for that reason, to include a consortium amongst those from whom it will choose persons to tender or negotiate for a contract.[39] However, a purchaser may insist that a consortium which is awarded a contract should form a legal entity before entering into the contract, or as a term of the contract.[40]

In relation to the conduct of the award procedure under the regulations, it is to be noted that any reference to a contractor, supplier or service provider includes a reference to each individual member of a consortium.[41]

(b) THE FORM OF SERVICE PROVIDERS

Utilities Regulation 20(4) contains express provisions on the form of services providers.[42] This states that such providers cannot be treated as ineligible, or excluded from the group from whom persons are selected to invite or negotiate a contract, on the basis that the law generally requires a person providing the services in question to take a specific legal form (such as an individual or corporation), *if* the services provider is authorised to provide services in that form in the state in which he is established.[43]

Where the services provider is not an individual, he may be required to indicate in the tender, or in the request to be selected or negotiate, the names and relevant professional qualifications of the staff who will be responsible for performing the services.[44]

(7) EVIDENCE OF QUALIFICATION

It has been explained in Chapter 7 that under the public sector regulations the evidence which authorities may demand from providers as evidence of the permitted criteria for qualification is limited, in particular in relation to technical capacity.[45] For many criteria only the

---

[38] Utilities Regulation 20(1). "Provider" is defined in Utilities Regulation 2(1) as any supplier, contractor or services provider, terms defined further in Regulation 2(1) as persons seeking supply, works or services contracts.

[39] Utilities Regulation 20(2).

[40] Utilities Regulation 20(2). This would appear to cover the registration of persons on a qualification list as well as decisions relating to specific award procedures.

[41] Utilities Regulation 20(3).

[42] This refers to persons who seek services contracts: see Utilities Regulation 4.

[43] Utilities Regulation 20(4).

[44] Utilities Regulation 20(5).

[45] See pp. 316–328.

evidence stated in the regulations may be called for, and it was also suggested that there is a general principle that authorities may not insist on evidence of matters which are adequately proven by other means. In the Utilities Regulations there are in general no closed lists of evidence which may be demanded, even for technical capacity.

However, in relation to the operation of qualification systems, it is expressly provided in Utilities Regulation 18(6) that utilities may not require the application of tests or the submission of evidence "which duplicates objective evidence already available". This suggests that providers may submit their own evidence which is equivalent to that demanded for criteria set for admission onto formal qualification systems. There is no express provision equivalent to this for the assessment of qualification outside the context of such a system. However, it is illogical to make a distinction between qualification under the different procedures. As was suggested earlier may be the case with the *criteria* for qualification,[46] the Court of Justice may well adopt a purposive approach and apply this limitation on evidence to qualification processes other than in relation to a formal qualification system.

The use of quality assurance standards may provide a limited exception to this principle of evidence, as explained in section (5) above.

(8) THE USE OF APPROVED LISTS

It was explained in Chapter 7 on the public sector rules that for contracts covered by those rules purchasers may not generally require providers to register on lists of qualified providers – often referred to as "approved lists" or "qualification lists" – as a condition of participating in contracts. Under the Utilities Regulations, however, there is an express provision for the use of qualification lists – referred to as "qualification systems". Not only is such a system permitted, but advertisement of the system in accordance with the regulations exempts a utility from the need to publicise specific contracts by either a contract notice or periodic indicative notice. However, to take advantage of these provisions the system must be run in accordance with a number of detailed rules in the regulations, which have been explained above.[47]

It appears, however, that apart from the operation of qualification systems in accordance with the rules in the regulations, utilities may not insist on registration on a list as a method of qualification for contracts covered by the utilities rules. This is indicated by Utilities Regulation 18(1) which states that utilities may establish and operate a system of qualification of providers *if* that system complies with regulation 18. This does not specifically say that a list operated in accordance with the regulations could not be used in a procedure under the regulations which

---

[46] See p. 541.
[47] See pp. 532–540.

did not use the list as a call for competition; thus it might be argued that a utility operating a restricted procedure following a contract notice could limit compliance to those on the list, even though the list itself had not been advertised. However, this is quite clearly not the intention of the regulations, and it seems clear that the list itself may only be used where the system provides the basis for the call for competition. This principle will also follow if the suggestion in section (7) above is correct that utilities may not insist on particular means of evidence of qualification where the provider has offered adequate alternatives.

There is, however, nothing to prevent utilities from setting up approved lists which providers may use if they choose this as a method of qualification, as an alternative to specific qualification for particular contracts in response to a notice.

(9) PROCEDURAL ASPECTS

(a) OPEN PROCEDURES

Since open procedures are open to any party wishing to bid, utilities may not insist on the qualification of every provider before bids are submitted. Once bids have been received, the utility will then find it necessary to assess the providers' qualifications according to the criteria which that utility has set. As has already been noted, it may do this either before or after, or at the same time as, the evaluation of bids: although the substance of these two processes is different there are no limitations on the order in which they may be carried out.[48]

Although utilities may not *require* a provider to qualify before the submission of the lists, it is submitted that there is nothing to prevent a provider seeking qualification on a voluntary basis beforehand. Such a process may save time and effort for both purchaser and provider by ensuring that those who are not qualified do not waste their efforts by submitting a bid.

The model contract notice for the open procedure provides that information on the minimum standards of financial and economic standing and technical capacity must be stated in the notice.[49] There is, however, no provision for other qualification criteria to be listed in the notice, even though it was suggested that other criteria, both commercial and non-commercial, may be taken into consideration by the utility. However, it may be noted that, as in the case of *Beentjes*,[50] that where a secondary condition is to be included in the contract – for example (as in that case), a requirement to employ the long-term unemployed on the contract – this must be stated in the contract notice under the public

---

[48] See further pp. 504–505.
[49] See the model on pp. 474–475.
[50] Case 31/87, *Gebroeders Beentjes B.V. v. The Netherlands* [1988] E.C.R. 4635.

sector directives, to fulfil the purpose of the notice in giving all key information, even though such a condition is not included in the model notice. The same principle might be applied to require utilities to include in the contract notice information on qualification criteria which relates to matters other than financial or economic standing.

In contrast with the public sector,[51] there is no obligation under the directive to give reasons to providers concerning their qualification, but this is required for some utilities under the GPA and there is a Proposal to introduce an obligation to give reasons into the directive.[51a]

(b) RESTRICTED AND NEGOTIATED PROCEDURES

In restricted and negotiated procedures the procedure for qualification varies according to the way in which a call for competition has been made.

(i) USE OF A CONTRACT NOTICE

Where the call for competition has been made by publication of a contract notice, persons to be invited to bid are selected from those replying to the notice. As mentioned above in considering the steps under the restricted and negotiated procedure, generally purchasers will wish to check the qualifications of those replying to the notice before issuing an invitation but may leave verification of some matters until later, or may make additional checks later to ensure that a provider's status has not changed. Utilities may, if they wish, even leave the whole process until the evaluation stage, but this is unlikely for complex contracts. Again, there is no obligation to give reasons for qualification decisions.

The model contract notices for these procedures indicate that utilities must include in the notice information on minimum standards on technical capacity and financial and economic standing and also require information on the provider's "personal position".[52] This reference to "personal position" is also used in the public sector directives where it appears to refer to the miscellaneous criteria for exclusion in Regulation 14 of each of the public sector regulations.[53] These criteria may also form the basis for exclusion under the utilities rules, as noted above. However, grounds for exclusion in these rules are not confined to these matters and financial and economic concerns. It was suggested in the previous section on open procedures that, based on the analogy of *Beentjes*, the Court of Justice might imply that other proposed grounds for exclusion should also be stated in the notice. This might apply to restricted and negotiated procedures also, a result which could be achieved either by implying such

---

[51] See pp. 281–283.
[51a] See pp. 553–554.
[52] See the model notices at pp. 476–479.
[53] See further pp. 331–342.

a requirement, or by interpreting "personal position" widely in this context to refer to all conditions relating to the provider's position.[54]

(ii) USE OF PERIODIC INDICATIVE NOTICE

Where the contract is advertised through a periodic indicative notice persons to be invited to bid are again selected from those replying to the notice, following a later confirmation of interest, and the options for qualification are the same as for procedures conducted following a contract notice. Again, there is no requirement to give reasons for decisions. In this case there are no specific provisions as to when providers should be informed of the qualification requirements. However, it is required that providers be sent "detailed information" on the contract when asked to confirm their interest,[55] which probably must include information on qualification conditions.

(iii) USE OF A QUALIFICATION SYSTEM

Where an award procedure is publicised through a qualification system, many aspects of qualification will have been considered prior to registration. The procedural aspects of this process have been discussed above in the section on qualification systems.[56] Utilities may, however, want to consider qualification issues further for particular contracts, either to update the position or because of special requirements for the particular contract.

9. INFORMATION AND RECORD KEEPING

(1) OBLIGATION TO PUBLISH A CONTRACT AWARD NOTICE

Under Utilities Regulation 23 a utility which has awarded a contract under a procedure covered by the regulations must send a contract award notice to the *Official Journal*[57] within two months of the award[58] – a longer period than the 48 days for award notices under the public sector rules. This obligation applies to awards under all three types of

---

[54] The Court might accept that such qualification conditions could instead be included in the invitation to tender, although it is perhaps hard to see why a distinction should be made between different types of qualification conditions for the purpose of drawing up the contract notice.

[55] Utilities Regulation 15(3)(c).

[56] See pp. 532–539.

[57] The notice must be sent by the most appropriate means (Utilities Regulation 29(1)) and the utility must retain evidence of the date of despatch (Utilities Regulation 29(2)).

[58] Utilities Regulation 23(1).

procedure – open, negotiated and restricted – and applies regardless of whether the procedure involved a call for competition. The notice will be published in the hard copy of the *Official Journal* and in the TED electronic database in full in the original language and in summary form in the other official languages of the Community.[59] The notice sent must be in the form of the model contained in Part F of Schedule 5 to the regulations and must contain the information specified in that model.[60] The model is set out on pages 549–550.

In the case of notices on works contracts, supply contracts and Part A services contracts, it is open to the utility to indicate that any of the information in paragraph 6 of the model notice – the number of tenders received – and paragraph 9 of the model – the name and address of succesful providers – is of a commercially sensitive nature and may not be published.[61] There are also further specific exemptions from publication requirements for Part A research and development services.[62] Where contracts for such services are awarded without a call for competition pursuant to Utilities Regulation 16(1)(b), which allows utilities to dispense with a call for competition for certain research contracts awarded solely for the purposes of research, study, etc.,[63] only the title of the category of the services need be published.[64] Where a contract for Part A research and development services is awarded with a call for competition the utility is permitted to include only "limited" information concerning the nature of the goods, work or services (that is, the information referred to in paragraph 3 of the notice) if the information on those matters is of a commercially sensitive nature.[65] However, the information provided in this last case must be no less detailed than that already provided for in the call for competition or in that recorded in the written records of any relevant qualification system which are kept under Utilities Regulation 18(9).[66]

In the case of contracts for Part B services, the utility must simply state in the notice whether it agrees to publication.[67] It appears from this that the choice of whether to publish is left to the utility. This interpretation is supported by the fact that there are no express exemptions for commercially sensitive information relating to Part B services contracts which would be needed if the utility did not have a free choice over publication.

---

[59] Utilities Directive Article 25(3), which also states that the original language alone is authentic.
[60] Utilities Regulation 23(1).
[61] Utilities Regulation 23(2).
[62] These are the research and development services listed in category 8 of Part A to Schedule 4 of the Utilities Regulations – that is, those where the benefit accrues exclusively to the utility for use in its own affairs and which are to be wholly paid for by the utility.
[63] On the scope of this exemption see p. 483.
[64] Utilities Regulation 23(3).
[65] Utilities Regulation 23(3).
[66] Utilities Regulation 23(3).
[67] Utilities Regulation 23(2).

(2) RECORDS OF THE AWARD PROCEDURE

UTILITIES CONTRACTS REGULATIONS 1995, SCHEDULE 5, PART F – FORM OF CONTRACT AWARD NOTICE

I. Information for publication in the *Official Journal*
 1. Name and address of the utility.
 2. Nature of the contract (supply, works or services; where applicable, state if it is a framework agreement).
 3. At least a summary indication of the nature of the goods, works or services provided.
 4. (a) Form of the call for competition (notice on the existence of a qualification procedure; periodic indicative notice; contract notice).
    (b) Date of publication of the notice in the *Official Journal*.
    (c) In the case of contracts awarded without a prior call for competition, indication of the relevant sub-paragraph of Regulation 16(1) relied upon.
 5. Award procedure (open, restricted or negotiated).
 6. Number of tenders received.
 7. Date of award of the contracts.
 8. Price paid for bargain purchases under Regulation 16(1)(j).
 9. Name and address of successful provider(s).
 10. State, where applicable, whether the contract has been, or may be, subcontracted.
 11. Optional information:
    – value and share of the contract which may be subcontracted to third parties
    – award criteria
    – price paid (or range of prices).

II. Information not intended for publication
 12. Number of contracts awarded (where an award has been split between more than one provider).
 13. Value of each contract awarded.

---

14. Country of origin of the product or services (EEC origin or non-EEC origin; if the latter, broken down by third country).
15. Was recourse made to the exceptions to the use of European specifications provided for under Regulation 12(4)? If so, which?
16. Which award criteria was used (most economically advantageous; lowest price)?
17. Was the contract awarded to a bidder who submitted a variant, in accordance with Regulation 21(4)?
18. Were any tenders excluded on the grounds that they were abnormally low, in accordance with Regulation 21(6) and (7)?
19. Date of despatch of the notice.
20. In the case of contracts for services specified in Part B, Schedule 4, agreement by the utility to publication of the notice.

(a) CONTRACTS COVERED BY THE REGULATIONS

For contracts covered by the Utilities regulations, Regulation 26(2) requires a utility to keep information on each contract such as is sufficient to justify its decisions taken in connection with the following matters:

(i) the qualification and selection of providers;
(ii) the award of contracts;
(iii) the recourse to derogations from the requirement that relevant European specifications be used[68]
(iv) the use of a procedure without a call for competition pursuant to the regulations.[69]

These records must be kept for at least four years from the date of the award of the contract.[70] The information in these records may be requested by the Commission within that period.[71]

(b) RECORDS OF DECISIONS CONCERNING CONTRACTS EXCLUDED FROM THE REGULATIONS

A utility must also, under Utilities Regulation 26(2), keep "appropriate information" which is sufficient to justify its decision not to apply

---

[68] This is the derogation stated in regulation 12(4) of the Utilities Regulations. On this issue see pp. 590–596.
[69] On this see further pp. 482–490.
[70] Utilities Regulation 26(3).
[71] Utilities Directive Article 41(2).

the regulations to a particular contract pursuant to the following regulations:

(i) regulation 6, containing miscellaneous exclusions (for example, of contracts for purchase for re-sale, of contracts by certain entities for the purchase of energy, and of contracts to which secrecy grounds apply)[72];

(ii) regulation 7, excluding certain contracts in the telecommunications sector.[73] On request, a report describing the services excluded under this provision must be sent to the Minister responsible for the utility for onward transmission to the Commission via the Treasury[74];

(iii) regulation 8, covering contracts excluded because they are awarded to affiliated undertakings.[75] Again, a more detailed report on the use of the exclusion may need to be sent to the Treasury for onward transmission to the Commission where requested.[76]

(iv) regulation 10, setting out the thresholds for application of the regulations. Certain statistics are to be collected on contracts excluded under these provisions, as outlined at (3) below.

These records must be kept for at least four years from the date of the award of the contract.[77] The information in these records may be requested by the Commission within that period.[78] The information may also be needed to provide reports to the Commission in accordance with the requirements considered under (3) below.

(3) REPORTS ON EXCLUDED CONTRACTS

Under Utilities Regulation 27(2), when requested by the responsible Minister[79] in a particular case a utility must send a report on any of the matters listed below. This report will be passed to the Treasury for onward transmission to the Commission[80] at its request. These reports cover matters relating to the exclusion of certain contracts from the directive and regulations and will enable the Commission to monitor the use of the exclusions, which may be open to abuse.

These matters are:

(i) Information specified by the Minister in respect of a particular contract, including contracts excluded or exempt from the regulations under Regulations 6–10.

---

[72] On these exclusions see Chap. 9.

[73] See pp. 409–410.

[74] Utilities Regulation 7(3); Utilities Regulation 28(1); Utilities Regulation 28(6). The report may indicate that material in it is of a sensitive nature and may not be published: regulation 7(3). The reponsible Minister is the one whose area of activity is most closely connected with the utility's functions, as determined by the Treasury: regulation 28(2).

[75] See pp. 436–439.

[76] Utilities Regulation 8(3).

[77] Utilities Regulation 26(3).

[78] Utilities Directive Article 41(2).

[79] The responsible Minister is the one whose area of activity is most closely connected with the utility's functions, as determined by the Treasury: Utilities Regulation 28(2).

[80] See Utilities Regulation 18(6).

(ii) A statement of which of its activities the utility considers are not activities specified in the Part of Schedule 1 in which the utility is specified, or which it considers are outside the territory of the Communities and do not involve the physical use of a network or geographical network within the Communities (cases in which contracts connected with the activity may be excluded from the regulations).

(iii) A statement of the categories of goods, works or services which the utility acquires in order to sell, hire or provide them to another (in those cases where it does not have a special or exclusive right to do so and others are free to do so under the same conditions). In this last case the utility may indicate in its report that the information is of a sensitive commercial nature and request that it should not be published,[81] although it is not clear whether the Commission must accede to the request or may make its own judgment.

(4) STATISTICAL REPORTS

The obligations of utilities to provide statistical information on their procurement for the use of the Commission are, under the current Utilities Directive, much less onerous than the obligations imposed on the public sector in this respect.[82] Statistics are automatically collected only on the value of contracts excluded from the regulations as below the thresholds in regulation 10. Utilities Regulation 27(1) requires utilities to supply to the responsible minister each year, by a date notified by the minister, a report specifying the aggregate value of the consideration payable under contracts excluded by regulation 10 which were awarded in the previous year.[83] Separate reports must be prepared for the different categories of "utility" activities.[84]

However, the GPA imposes much more onerous statistical obligations for utility contracts falling within its scope, and these must be adhered to for contracts falling under that Agreement. The Commission's Proposal for adjusting the Utilities Directive in light of the GPA contains proposals to require certain utilities to provide this extra statistical information to the Commission in line with the provisions under the GPA.[84a] The relevant statistical information is to be provided to the

---

[81] Utilities Regulation 27(3).

[82] On the public sector obligations see pp. 288–290.

[83] The responsible Minister is the one whose area of activity is most closely connected with the utility's functions, as determined by the Treasury: Utilities Regulation 28(2).

[84] These reports are to be used to prepare statistical reports for the Commission each year. The responsibility for procedures relating to these reports lies with the Commission as assisted by the Advisory Committee for Public Contracts or, with telecommunications procurement, the Advisory Committee for Telecommunications Procurement: Utilities Directive Article 42(1) and Article 40(4)–(8). For administrative simplification certain contracts of lesser value may be excluded from these reports provided that the usefulness of the statistics is not affected: Utilities Directive Article 42(2).

[84a] Proposal for a European Parliament and Council Directive amending Directive 93/38/EEC co-ordinating the procurement procedures of entities operating in the water, energy, transport and telecommunications sectors, COM (95) Final, Article 1(19).

Commission by October 31 each year, commencing October 1997. The information which must be provided is as follows:

(i) statistics on the estimated value of contracts above the threshold, broken down by category of activity, and into works/supply/services contracts;

(ii) statistics on total value of contracts above the thresholds, broken down by category of activity, where the utility has relied on the exemptions from the requirement for a call for competition;

(iii) statistics, broken down by category of activity, on the total value of contracts awarded under derogations to the GPA.

Entities are also to provide other information necessary for the GPA, as determined by the Advisory Committees, in accordance with the procedure in Article 40 of the Utilities Directive.

The Commission's Proposals on this matter are, unlike some of the other aspects of its Proposal, limited to those sectors of utility activity which are actually covered by the GPA – that is, water, electricity, urban transport, ports and airports, but not telecommunications, energy and other transport fields. Further, the proposals on statistics do not apply to non-priority services nor research and development services, which are not covered by the GPA. On the other hand, the Proposal does suggest applying the additional statistical obligations to all entities in the covered sectors, and not just those entities covered by the GPA (the GPA applying only to public authorities and public undertakings, and not entities which are under the Community rules merely because they enjoy special or exclusive rights). The reason given by the Commission is that statistical obligations confined to the GPA entities would be useful only for GPA purposes, and not for the Community's own statistical purposes.[84b]

(5) REASONS FOR DECISIONS

There is currently no obligation in the Utilities Directive or Regulations to give reasons to providers concerning procurement decisions. However, such obligations exist under the GPA, and the Commission Proposal for aligning the Utilities Directive with the GPA proposes the introduction of such obligations in the directive. Utilities covered by the GPA must in fact adhere to these obligations as from January 1, 1996, regardless of whether they have yet been specifically incorporated into the directive or regulations. Further, the duty to give reasons applies in respect of both GPA providers (under the GPA itself) and Community providers (by virtue of Utilities Regulation 4(3) requiring that Community providers shall be treated no less favourably than others). Under the Community Proposal it is proposed to apply the duty to give reasons

---

[84b] See the Explanatory Memorandum to the Proposal, p.8.

not merely to utilities and contracts actually covered by the GPA, but to all utilities covered by the Community Utilities Directive; but this is controversial and it looks likely that the duty to give reasons under the directive will in the end be confined to those cases where it is required by the GPA.[84c]

Under the Commission Proposal[84d] and the GPA, the utility must give providers (within 15 days of a request) written reasons for rejecting their application or tender. In the latter case this must include reference to the characteristics and relevant advantages of the tender selected as well as the name of the successful tenderer. However, information may be withheld if it would impede law enforcement or otherwise be contrary to the public interest, or would prejudice the legitimate commercial interest of particular enterprises, public or private, or might prejudice fair competition between providers. Where a call for competition is made but it is decided either not to award the contract or decided to recommence the procedure, the utility must also inform providers who have been candidates or bidders in a procedure of the reasons why, where this is requested in writing.

10. DESIGN CONTESTS

(1) INTRODUCTION

As explained in relation to the public sector, purchasers sometimes search out ideas by holding a competition in which firms are invited to submit their designs or plans to be judged against each other, which may then form the basis for a subsequent contract award.[85] Prizes may be awarded to one or more firms who submit the winning design(s), and/or remuneration may be paid to those who participate, regardless of whether or not the designs are ultimately used by the purchaser. The Utilities Regulations, like the public sector Services Regulations, contain special rules on design contests. These are found in Utilities Regulation 31. Like the public sector rules, these provisions regulate the way in which such contests are conducted, to ensure that they are carried out in a fair and transparent manner (whether or not connected with any subsequent contract award procedure) and they also allow a design contest which has been conducted in accordance with the regulations to be used as the basis for awarding a subsequent contract without further competition.

[84c] See generally pp. 563–564.
[84d] Proposal for a European Parliament and Council Directive amending Directive 93/38/EEC co-ordinating the procurement procedures of entities operating in the water, energy, transport and telecommunications sectors, COM (95) Final, Article 1(18).
[85] On the concept of design contests see further p. 371.

We will first consider the definition of a design contest (section (2)), and which contests are subject to regulation (section (3)). We will then outline the rules governing such contests (section (4)). Finally, we will explain the way in which design contests may be incorporated into contract award procedures (section (5)).

(2) THE DEFINITION OF "DESIGN CONTEST"

The definition of a design contest for the purpose of all the rules on design contests is given in Utilities Regulation 2(1). It refers to a competition in which an authority invites the entry of plans and designs which, under the rules of the competition, are to be judged by a jury and as a result of which the utility is able to acquire the use or ownership of the plans or designs which the jury selects. The definition applies regardless of whether or not prizes are to be awarded to the winners.

It is stated that the definition refers "particularly" to plans or designs in the fields of planning, architecture, civil engineering and data processing, which are the main subject areas for contests. However, the regulations also apply to contests in other areas, where these are held.

The directive is not entirely clear as to whether the rules on design contests are to apply to those for Part B services. It is, however, clear that utilities must publish a notice giving the result of a contest. It would perhaps be surprising if Part B services were covered apart from this, since this would be out of line with the approach to Part B services contracts, which are generally exempt from the detailed regulations in the directive, but for which an award notice must be published. The regulations, however, assume that all the rules on design contests – and not just those on result notices – should be applied to contests for both Part A and Part B services, since the obligations concerning design contracts are not specifically excluded for Part B services.[86] In practice, this is not important since design contests are unlikely to be held for Part B services.

(3) THRESHOLDS FOR APPLYING THE REGULATIONS

Under Utilities Regulation 31(1) where a design contest is "organised as part of a procedure leading to the award of a services contract", the regulations apply wherever the estimated value of that contract (calculated in accordance with the rules set out in regulation 10) is not less than 400,000 ECUs or 600,000 ECUs in the case of utilities in the telecommunications sector – that is, the thresholds above which the contracts themselves fall within the regulations. The contest must no

---

[86] See pp. 421–422.

doubt be considered to be "part of" a contract award whenever the utility relies on the conduct of a design contest, as discussed in section (5) below, to make use of a procedure without a call for competition. The regulations also apply to contests which are part of an award procedure where the estimated value of the prizes or payments for the contest itself is not less than 400,000 ECUs, or 600,000 ECUs for contests relating to the telecommunications sector, regardless of the value of any contract to be awarded under the procedure.

Where a design contest is not organised as part of a procedure relating to a contract award, the regulations will apply to that design contest where the aggregate value of the prizes or payments for the contract is not less than 200,000 ECUs.

It was explained in Chapter 9 that the Commission's Proposal for adjusting the Utilities Directive in light of the GPA proposes changes to the directive's thresholds for award procedures for services contracts, from 400,000 ECUs to the ECU equivalent of 400,000 SDR (although no changes are proposed to the 600,000 ECUs threshold for telecommunications).[87] Corresponding changes are also proposed for the thresholds for the rules on design contests, which it is proposed should apply where the value of prizes, or of any subsequent contract (where the contest is part of an award procedure), is not less than the ECU equivalent of 400,000 SDR[87a] (with the threshold remaining unchanged again for the telecommunications sector). As with the general thresholds, this Proposal envisages that the changes should apply to all contracts covered by the directives (except for telecommunications contracts) and not just to those sectors and entities covered by the GPA itself.

(4) THE PROCEDURE FOR CONDUCTING DESIGN CONTESTS

(a) ADVERTISEMENT OF THE DESIGN CONTEST

Under Utilities Regulation 31(2) utilities must publish their intention to hold a design contest by sending a notice to the Office of Official Publications of the European Communities.[88] This ensures that the contest is publicised throughout Europe. The notice must be sent to the Office of Official Publications of the European Communities. It will be published in the hard copy of the *Official Journal* of the European

---

[87] See pp. 440–442.

[87a] Proposal for a European Parliament and Council Directive amending Directive 93/38/EEC co-ordinating the procurement procedures of entities operating in the water, energy, transport and telecommunications sectors, COM (95) 107 Final, Article 1(10).

[88] Utilities Regulation 29(1). The notice be sent by "the most appropriate means" (Utilities Regulation 29(1)) and the utility must retain evidence of the date of despatch (Utilities Regulation 29(2)).

Communities and also in the TED electronic data bank, in full in the original language and in summary form in the other official Community languages,[89] at the expense of the Community.[90] The Office of Official Publications is in general required to publish the notice within 12 days of despatch.[91] In "exceptional" cases a utility may request that the notice be published within five days of despatch, provided that the utility sends the notice by electronic mail, telex or facsimile,[92] and in this case the Office of Official Publications must "endeavour" to publish the notice within this period.[93]

The Utilities Directive states that utilities may also publish the information in other ways, for example, in the national press,[94] but this may not be done until the *Official Journal* notice has been despatched and other publicity material may not contain more information than the *Official Journal* notice.[95] This is not expressly stated in the regulations but utilities must adhere to this rule in the directive.

The notice must be in substantially the same form as the model notice set out in Part G of Schedule 5 to the Utilities Regulations, and must contain all the information specified in that notice.[96-97] The Commission is likely shortly to adopt a recommendation that the CPV nomenclature (which currently exists in draft form) should be used in drawing up notices for design contests.

(b) PUBLICITY FOR THE RULES OF THE DESIGN CONTEST

The rules which are to apply to a design contest must be made available to all providers who wish to participate.[98] The model notice for advertising the procedure, indicates that some of the rules must be publicised in the notice itself – for example, the criteria for selecting participants, the proposed number of participants and evaluation criteria. Information on other relevant rules, however, will also need to be provided to interested parties.

---

[89] Utilities Directive Articles 21(5) and 25(2). It is provided that the original language is authentic.
[90] Utilities Directive Article 25(4).
[91] Utilities Directive Article 25(3).
[92] Utilities Regulation 29(3) provides for this only for contract notices but Article 25(3) envisages this possibility of notices on design contests also.
[93] Utilities Directive Article 25(3).
[94] It was explained above that this would not normally be a breach of the E.C. Treaty: see p. 196.
[95] Utilities Directive Article 25(5).
[96-97] Utilities Regulation 31(2).
[98] Utilities Regulation 31(3).

(c) PROCEDURE FOR OBTAINING ENTRIES TO THE CONTEST

Utilities may allow any interested firms to compete in a contest or may restrict the number.[99] The model notice makes it clear that utilities must state in the notice whether the contest is open or restricted.

In an open contest, the model notice makes it clear that utilities must state in the notice the final date for receipt of plans or designs.

In a restricted contest the model provides that utilities must state in the notice a deadline for receipt of requests from persons wishing to participate. Where participation is restricted, the number of persons selected to participate must be set taking into account the need to ensure adequate competition in the contest.[1] The model notice for advertising the contract indicates that the number of participants envisaged must be stated in the notice. The selection of those to be invited must be made on the basis of "clear and non-discriminatory criteria",[2] which the model notice indicates must be stated in the notice. It appears that utilities may select some participants in advance of the notice: this is implied by the model notice which requires the names of any such preselected persons to be stated in the notice.

There are some specific limits on selection criteria. As with the award of contracts, utilities may not exclude firms because of their legal form (for example, whether individual or corporate), where they are permitted to provide services in that form in their state of establishment.[3] It is also expressly stated in the Utilities Directive[4] that participants may not be limited by reference to the territory, or part of a territory of a state. No specific provision to implement this has been included in the Utilities Regulations but the rule must be followed, and in any case where utilities specify a territorial limit which includes the United Kingdom this is likely to infringe the rules in the Community Treaties as tending to favour domestic providers. Utilities must, where applicable, always comply with any obligations under the Community Treaties, where applicable, in selecting providers, and also with the general obligation to avoid discrimination.

---

[99] Utilities Regulation 31(4).
[1] Utilities Regulation 31(5).
[2] Utilities Regulation 31(4).
[3] Utilities Regulations 31(6) and 20(4).
[4] Utilities Directive Article 23(4).

UTILITIES CONTRACTS REGULATIONS 1995, SCHEDULE 5, PART G – FORM OF DESIGN CONTEST NOTICE

1. Name, address, telegraphic address, telephone, telex and facsimile numbers of the utility and of the service from which additional information may be obtained.

2. Project description.

3. Nature of contest: open or restricted.

4. In the case of open contests: final date for receipt of plans and designs.

5. In the case of restricted contests:

    (a) the number of participants envisaged;
    (b) where applicable, names of the participants already selected;
    (c) criteria for the selection of participants;
    (d) final date for receipt of requests to participate.

6. Where applicable, an indication of whether participation is reserved to a particular profession.

7. Criteria to be applied in the evaluation of projects.

8. Where applicable, names of the persons selected to be members of the jury.

9. Indication of whether the decision of the jury is binding on the utility.

10. Where applicable, number and value of the prizes.

11. Where applicable, details of payments to all participants.

12. Indication of whether follow-up contracts will be awarded to one of the winners.

13. Other information.

14. Date of despatch of the notice.

(d) COMPOSITION OF THE JURY

The jury for any contest must be composed of individuals who are independent of the parties competing.[5] In addition, when participants in the contest are required to possess a particular professional qualification, then at least one-third of the jury members are required to possess that qualification, or an equivalent qualification.[6]

(e) SELECTING THE WINNING DESIGNS

The proposals of the participants must be submitted to the jury without any indication of who submitted each proposal.[7] The proposals will then be judged by the jury. The criteria which are to apply in judging must be set out in the model notice. In principle, it is for the utility to set these criteria. Often, with designs of buildings or other works, they will relate primarily to the aesthetic merits of the design, although other factors such as practicability, potential cost, innovation or environmental considerations may be relevant. The utility is expressly required to ensure that the decision is taken by the jury solely in accordance with the criteria stated in the notice.[8] It is also required to ensure that the jury acts "independently" in making its decision.

The model notice advertising the contest indicates that utilities must state whether or not the jury's decisions are binding on the utility. This indicates that the utility may reserve the right to override the view of the jury in selecting the winner(s). In making its own decision, however, the utility must also adhere to the stated evaluation criteria.

---

[5] Utilities Regulation 31(8).
[6] *Ibid.*
[7] Utilities Regulation 31(7).
[8] Utilities Regulation 31(9).

UTILITIES CONTRACTS REGULATIONS 1995,
SCHEDULE 5, PART H – FORM OF DESIGN
CONTEST RESULTS NOTICE

1. Name, address and telegraphic address, telephone, telex and facsimile numbers of the utility.
2. Project description.
3. Number of participants.
4. Number of participants established outside the United Kingdom.
5. Winner(s) of the contest.
6. Where applicable, the prize(s) awarded.
7. Other information.
8. Reference to publication of the design contest notice in the *Official Journal*.
9. Date of despatch of the notice.

(f) REQUIREMENT TO PUBLISH A NOTICE OF THE JURY'S DECISION

No later than two months after the jury has made its selection, authorities must publicise the results of the design contest by sending a notice to the Office of Official Publications for the European Communities.[9] This must be in a form substantially corresponding to the model notice in Part N of Schedule 5 to the Utilities Regulations.[10] The notice must be published in full in the original language and in summary form in the other official languages of the Communities in both the hard copy *Official Journal of the European Communities* and the TED data bank.[11] The Commission is likely shortly to adopt a recommendation for the use of the CPV nomenclature (which currently exists in draft form) in such notices.

(g) OTHER REQUIREMENTS

As indicated above, details of the contest rules must be made available to participants. It may be presumed that authorities must adhere to these

---

[9] Utilities Regulation 31(10). The notice must be sent by "the most appropriate means" (Utilities Regulation 29(2)) and authorities must retain evidence of the date of dispatch (Utilities Regulation 29(2)).
[10] *Ibid.*
[11] Utilities Directive Article 25(3). The original language alone is authentic.

rules, even where this is not expressly stated in the regulations (as it is, for example, in relation to the use of the stated evaluation criteria). However, in construing the rules it must be implied that some are not mandatory: for example, as with award procedures, it is submitted that authorities should be able to waive non-compliance by providers with formalities.[12]

The general obligation not to discriminate between providers will mean that if formalities are waived for one provider, they must be waived for others in the same position.

(5) CONTRACT AWARD PROCEDURES BASED ON A DESIGN CONTEST

Contracts covered by the Utilities Regulations must generally be awarded only following a call for competition. However, Regulation 16(2)(1) provides for an exemption for services contracts from the usual call for competition requirement where a design contest has been conducted under the regulations, and the contest rules state that a contract is to be awarded to the successful contestant(s), provided that negotiations are carried out with all those who were successful under the rules of the contest. In other words, a contract, or the possibility of being considered for a contract, may be a "prize" in the competition. This is not considered to be anticompetitive, since a fair and open competition has already been held to select the participant(s).

Thus utilities may, if they so choose, select a winning design through the contest, and negotiate the terms of a contract – for example, to expand the design – solely with the winning party. Alternatively, the utility may negotiate with a number of winners, and make a contract award taking into account both their designs and other factors such as cost. It is possible also to negotiate with providers the alteration of their designs, using the negotiated procedure. It is not necessary for negotiations to be carried out with each provider based on the provider's own design – utilities could, for example, pick one preferred design and negotiate with all the providers on the basis of that design.

The provision may not be relied on where the contract which is to be awarded following the design contest is not a services contract but a works or supply contract, since the above provisions refer only to the award of services contracts.

11. CONFIDENTIALITY OF INFORMATION

Utilities Regulation 30 provides that where a utility makes information available to a provider pursuant to the regulations it may impose

---

[12] On this see pp. 507–508.

requirements on him for the purpose of protecting the confidentiality of that information. This might apply, for example, when a contract is connected to a proposed new business venture of a utility which it wishes to keep secret from the market; or where the contract involves research on new products or processes which it again desires to keep from competitors.

12. THE IMPLICATIONS OF THE GPA

As already noted in this chapter, the new World Trade Organisation Agreement on Government Procurement (GPA), in force from January 1, 1996, imposes obligations on some utilities which go beyond those in the Utilities Regulations. The most significant[13] concern: additional requirements for use of indicative notices as a call for competition[14]; additional conditions for relying on an indicative notice to shorten time periods in an open procedure[15]; slight differences in the time periods for restricted and negotiated procedures[16]; an obligation to provide continuous access to qualification systems[17]; a requirement to give providers reasons for decisions on requests[18]; limits on use of the exemption from a call for competition for contracts with an existing provider to supply additional works to where the new contract does not exceed 50 per cent of the original[19]; and additional provision of statistical reports.[20] For the sectors and entities covered, these additional obligations must be followed by purchasers as from January 1, 1996 when the GPA comes into effect. They may be invoked both by providers from GPA countries under the GPA itself, and also by Community providers by virtue of Utilities Regulation 4(3) which states that providers who are nationals of and established in the Community shall be treated no less favourably than providers from other states.

A present, these additional rules under the GPA do not apply to all utilities but only those covered by the GPA.[21] Thus they apply only to bodies which are public authorities and public undertakings under the Utilities Directive, and not those which are covered merely because they enjoy special or exclusive rights; and only to the sectors of water, electricity, urban transport and ports and airports, and not to telecommunications, supply of gas or heat, exploration or extraction in the energy sector, or the rest of the transport sector.

---

[13] Others are an express prohibition on assistance with specifications (see pp. 615–616) and express rules on tenders submitted other than by mail.
[14] See p. 494.
[15] See p. 492.
[16] See pp. 495 and 502–503.
[17] See p. 539.
[18] See pp. 553–554.
[19] See p. 486.
[20] See pp. 552–553.
[21] On the scope of the GPA see pp. 778–780.

As explained in Chapter 3, the European Commission has issued a Proposal for a directive to amend the Utilities Directive in light of the GPA.[22] The main purpose of the Proposal is to ensure that the rules in the directive governing the access of Community providers are as favourable as those in the GPA relating to third country providers (a position which already applies in the United Kingdom under Utilities Regulation 4(3)). For this purpose it is necessary to amend the Community rules only for those limited sectors covered by the GPA itself. However, the Commission's original Proposal goes further than this, suggesting (with a few exceptions) that the more stringent procedures should apply to all sectors and entities; this would ensure simplicity in the directive, and also that all sectors and entities are treated equally. This was considered important by the Commission, since different entities in the same sector, and even different sectors (such as electricity – which is covered by the GPA – and gas and heat – which are not) are in competition. However, there has been considerable opposition to this approach by some Member States, who prefer to limit the amendments to those which are strictly necessary to align the Community rules with the GPA – that is, to the sectors and entities covered by the GPA – and it looks likely that this view may prevail in the Council.

In some respects it appears that the detailed rules in the Commission's Proposal actually fall short of aligning the GPA and Community rules, so that compliance with the Utilities Directive will not always involve compliance with the GPA. For example, there is an exemption in the directive from the call for competition for certain additional services or works placed with an existing contracting partner which does not apply under the GPA.[23] In anticipation of this possibility the Proposal does, however, include a "catch-all" provision stating that Member States "shall apply in their relations conditions as favourable as those which they grant to third countries in implementation of the GATT Agreement". This obligation is already applied in the United Kingdom, by Utilities Regulation 4(3).

---

[22] Proposal for a European Parliament and Council Directive amending Directive 93/38/ EEC co-ordinating the procurement procedures of entities operating in the water, energy, transport and telecommunications sectors, COM (95) 107 Final.
[23] See p. 486.

MAIN STEPS IN THE OPEN PROCEDURE – UTILITIES REGULATIONS

Despatch of contract notice to the *Official Journal*
↓
Submission of requests for documents by interested firms
↓
Despatch of documents
↓
Receipt of tenders
↓
Qualification of providers[24]
↓
Evaluation of offers: lowest price or most economically advantageous offer (excluding abnormally low offers) (and third country offers where applicable)
↓
Award of contract
↓
Despatch of contract award notice to the *Official Journal*

---

[24] Optional, and may be done after, or alongside, evaluation of offers.

MAIN STEPS IN THE RESTRICTED PROCEDURE – UTILITIES REGULATIONS

(i) Restricted procedure advertised by contract notice

Despatch of contract notice to the *Official Journal*
↓
Submission by interested firms of requests to be invited to tender
↓
Qualification of firms (if applicable) and selection of firms to be invited to tender
↓
Issue to selected firms of invitations to tender and contract documents
↓
Receipt of tenders
↓
Completion of qualification procedures if applicable[25]
↓
Evaluation of offers: lowest price or most economically advantagous offer (excluding abnormally low offers) (and third country offers where applicable)
↓
Award of contract
↓
Despatch of contract award notice to the *Official Journal*

---

[25] Optional, and may be done after, or alongside, evaluation of offers.

(ii) Restricted procedure advertised by periodic indicative notice

Despatch of periodic indicative notice to the *Official Journal*
↓
Submission of expressions of interest by interested firms
↓
Issue to interested firms of detailed information and request for confirmation of interest
↓
Confirmation of interest by interested firms
↓
Qualification of firms (if applicable) and selection of firms to be invited to tender
↓
Issue to selected firms of invitations to tender and contract documents
↓
Receipt of tenders
↓
Completion of qualification procedures if applicable
↓
Evaluation of offers: lowest price or most economically advantageous offer (excluding abnormally low offers) (and third country offers where applicable)
↓
Award of contract
↓
Despatch of contract award notice to the *Official Journal*

(iii) Restricted procedure advertised by advertisement of qualification system

Despatch of notice advertising qualification system to the
Official Journal
↓
Qualification and registration of firms
↓
Selection of firms to be invited to tender from those
registered
↓
Issue to selected firms of invitations to tender and contract
documents
↓
Receipt of tenders
↓
Completion of qualification procedures if applicable[26-27]
↓
Evaluation of offers: lowest price or most economically
advantagous offer (excluding abnormally low offers) (and
third country offers where applicable)
↓
Award of contract
↓
Despatch of contract award notice to the *Official Journal*

[26-27] Optional, and may be done after, or alongside, evaluation of offers.

MAIN STEPS IN THE NEGOTIATED PROCEDURE WITH A CALL FOR COMPETITION – UTILITIES REGULATIONS

(i) Negotiated procedure advertised by contract notice

Despatch of contract notice to the *Official Journal*
↓
Submission by interested firms of requests to be invited to negotiate
↓
Qualification of firms (if applicable) and selection of firms to be invited to negotiate
↓
Issue to selected firms of invitations to negotiate and contract documents
↓
Negotiations (including tendering if desired)
↓
Evaluation of offers: lowest price or most economically advantageous offer (excluding abnormally low offers) (and third country offers where applicable)
↓
Award of contract
↓
Despatch of contract award notice to the *Official Journal*

(ii) Negotiated procedure advertised by periodic indicative notice

Despatch of periodic indicative notice to the *Official Journal*
↓
Submission of expressions of interest by interested firms
↓
Issue to interested firms of detailed information and request for confirmation of interest
↓
Confirmation of interest by interested firms
↓
Qualification of firms (if applicable) and selection of firms to be invited to negotiate
↓
Issue to selected firms of invitations to negotiate and contract documents
↓
Negotiations (including tendering if desired)
↓
Evaluation of offers: lowest price or most economically advantageous offer (excluding abnormally low offers) (and third country offers where applicable)
↓
Award of contract
↓
Despatch of contract award notice to the *Official Journal*

(iii) Negotiated procedure advertised by advertisement of qualification system

Despatch of notice advertising qualification system to the
Official Journal
↓
Qualification and registration of firms
↓
Selection of firms to be invited to negotiate from those
registered
↓
Issue to selected firms of invitations to negotiate and
contract documents
↓
Negotiations (including tendering if desired)
↓
Evaluation of offers: lowest price or most economically
advantageous offer (excluding abnormally low offers) (and
third country offers where applicable)
↓
Award of contract
↓
Despatch of contract award notice to the *Official Journal*

MAIN STEPS IN THE NEGOTIATED PROCEDURE WITHOUT A CALL FOR COMPETITION – UTILITIES REGULATIONS

(i) Where the provider is already selected:

Negotiations to settle the terms of the contract
↓
Award of the contract
↓
Despatch of contract award notice to the *Official Journal*

(ii) Where the provider is not already selected:

Negotiations with firms chosen by the utility (including tendering if desired)
↓
Evaluation of final offers: lowest price or most economically advantageous offer (excluding abnormally low offers)
↓
Award of contract
↓
Despatch of contract award notice to the *Official Journal*

CHAPTER 11

THE E.C. RULES ON SPECIFICATIONS

1. INTRODUCTION

The detailed description of the product or service which a purchaser wishes to obtain is referred to as the specifications. Normally these take the form of a written document issued to interested firms, sometimes on payment of a fee,[1] which then forms the basis for submission of offers. In the case of products, the specifications describe the characteristics of what is to be purchased, usually covering such matters as safety, quality, durability, and compatibility with existing equipment. With services, the specifications set out what exactly is required of the service provider: for example, with a building cleaning contract, it will detail matters such as the premises to be cleaned, the tasks to be performed (whether windows are included, for instance), the hours in which work is to be carried out and the standards to be attained. Where possible such requirements are usually defined by reference to general industry standards. These are mainly standards approved by recognised standardising bodies such as the British Standards Institution (BSI), but sometimes "*de facto*" industry standards are used which have not received any formal approval.

This chapter explains the impact of European Community rules on the drafting and use of specifications in public sector and utilities contracts. The most significant, deriving both from the Treaties and procurement regulations, are designed to ensure that specifications do not operate as barriers to trade. These are examined in section 3. The regulations also lay down a number of other rules on specifications, including publicity requirements and limitations on changing specifications during an award procedure, and these are considered in section 4. Further rules on specifications are found in the legislation on CCT examined in Chapter 14.[2]

2. THE DEFINITION OF "TECHNICAL SPECIFICATIONS"

The rules on specifications in the regulations discussed in sections 3 and 4 below frequently refer to the concept of "technical specifications".

---

[1] The possibility of requiring payment of a fee is expressly contemplated in the Community rules: see for example, p. 203.
[2] See pp. 714–715.

(1) THE PUBLIC SECTOR

"Technical specifications" are defined in the Works and Services Regulations[3] as the technical requirements which define, in objective terms, the characteristics of the work(s) and of the materials and goods used in the work(s) – such as their quality, performance, safety or dimensions – to ensure they fulfil the purpose for which they are intended by the purchaser. In the Supply Regulations technical specifications are defined as the technical requirements which define the characteristics of goods, so that the goods are described objectively in a manner which will ensure they fulfil their intended purpose.[4] In relation to works, the Works Regulations and Services Regulations give as examples of such technical requirements those relating to design and costing; testing, inspection and acceptance; and the methods or techniques of construction.[5] Examples given in all three regulations in relation to goods are requirements on quality, performance, safety, dimensions, quality assurance, terminology, symbols, tests and testing methods, packaging, marking and labelling.[6]

These definitions indicate that the rules on specifications are concerned only with requirements relating to the services or products purchased; they do not cover requirements on other matters, such as workforce health and safety provision. This means, for example, that the regulations' obligation to use European standards where they exist[7] refers only to European standards relating to the product or service itself, and does not obligate the use of any European standard on workforce health and safety, although a purchaser might wish to specify conditions on these matters.[8]

A literal interpretation of the definitions of technical specifications may be inadequate to cover all the specifications in a particular contract. The Works and Services Regulations, following the directives, refer only to requirements relating to work(s) and goods used in works, and not to services other than works. Services other than works are, however, the main element of a services contract – and some services may also be included in works contracts.[9] The supplies rules refer only to requirements relating to goods, although supplies contracts also often involve provision of services – for example, a contract for delivery *and* mainte-

---

[3] Works Regulation 8(1), Services Regulation 8(1).
[4] Supply Regulation 8(1).
[5] Works Regulation 8(1); Services Regulation 8(1); Utilities Regulation 12(1).
[6] Works Regulation 8(1); Services Regulation 8(1); Supply Regulation 8(1); Utilities Regulation 12(1).
[7] See pp. 586–590.
[8] (As to which see Chap. 16.) Likewise, in qualifying firms for the contract, an authority need not make reference to any European standards which might be developed for qualification processes (as to which see p. 347).
[9] The inclusion of this reference to works rather than services in the Services Directive (on which the regulations are based) appears to have been an oversight, with the definition being copied directly from the Works Directive without making the appropriate adjustments.

nance of equipment.[10] It would be more appropriate for all three sets of rules to include requirements relating to goods, works *and* services.[11] However, the Court of Justice is likely to adopt a purposive approach to the construction of the rules and to conclude that the definition of technical specifications does cover all three elements of a contract, and the regulations will then need to be interpreted accordingly.

(2) *THE UTILITIES SECTOR*

In the Utilities Regulations technical specifications are defined as the technical requirements which define the characteristics of the work(s), materials, goods or services to be supplied or used, so that these work(s), materials, goods or services are described objectively in a manner which will ensure they fulfil their intended purpose.[12] In relation to works examples given of technical requirements are those relating to design and costing; testing, inspection and acceptance; and the methods or techniques of construction.[13] Examples given in relation to goods, materials and services are requirements on quality, performance, safety, dimensions, quality assurance, terminology, symbols, tests and testing methods, packaging, marking and labelling.[14]

3. THE USE OF STANDARDS IN CONTRACT SPECIFICATIONS

(1) *INTRODUCTION*

The way in which specifications are formulated has in the past had an important impact on competition for contracts and, in particular, on the ability of non-domestic firms to participate. The difficulties in this area have arisen largely, although not entirely, from the use of different standards in different Member States, whether mandatory (imposed by governments) or voluntary (simply used by purchasers out of habit). Thus, for example, reference to a BSI standard in a United Kingdom contract – whether in the public or private sector – may effectively exclude non-domestic firms, whose manufacturing processes are likely to be geared to producing goods which meet their own national standards.

---

[10] The omission of any reference to services here follows a general pattern in the regulations whereby it is always assumed that supply contracts cover *only* supplies.

[11] That this is the intention is supported by the fact that the obligation under the Services Regulations to include technical specifications in the contract documents refers to "technical specifications" which the *services* must meet: see Services Regulation 8(2).

[12] Utilities Regulation 12(1).

[13] *Ibid.*

[14] *Ibid.*

The European Community has implemented a variety of general measures – affecting both the public and private sectors – to eliminate the barriers created for free trade by differing national standards. In addition, there are a number of rules designed to eliminate restrictive specifications which are directed specifically at public and utilities purchasing.

This section begins by explaining the use of standards and the way in which these create barriers to trade. We will then outline the European Community's general policies on standards, and finally consider the measures specific to regulated procurement.

(2) THE USE OF STANDARDS

A "standard" refers here to a requirement which a product or service must meet. Typically, standards for products cover matters such as performance levels, durability, and health and safety requirements. They may also specify the technical characteristics of products, such as dimensions, in order to ensure the compatibility of equipment made by different producers (as, for example, with standards for compact disks and audio cassettes), to encourage manufacture in a way which is economically efficient, or to further other interests such as environmental protection or energy conservation. Most standards are for products, but they have also been developed for some services – for example, the British Standards Institution (BSI) has recently developed a standard for grounds maintenance (BS 7370). Most of the standards in use in the United Kingdom are those approved by the BSI, an independent body established by Royal Charter which is funded for its work on standardisation by government grants and members' subscriptions. Many of the standards which it adopts are based on those of European and international standardisation bodies, which seek to harmonise standards on an international basis.[15]

A standard may be "mandatory" in that it is specified by law for products or services placed on the market. Thus, for example, United Kingdom law requires all motorcycle helmets sold in the United Kingdom to meet the BSI standard BS 5361. Other standards are "voluntary" – they are widely used but are not legally required for products and services on the general market. This is the status of most BSI standards: they are commonly adhered to by manfacturers, and are often expected by consumers (who may in practice often decline to purchase a product which does not meet the standard), but do not constitute legal requirements.

For many standards, whether voluntary or mandatory, rules are laid down concerning the way in which compliance is to be attested. These

---

[15] See further pp. 579–580.

may take a variety of forms – for example, obligations to notify the product design; sample testing of products by a third party; or third-party approval of the manufacturer's own production processes. More than one method may apply to a single standard; and in many cases manufacturers may choose from amongst a number of possible methods. For some standards, requirements to show conformity are obligatory, whilst with others they are merely an option for producers, to demonstrate compliance.

(3) STANDARDS AS BARRIERS TO TRADE

Both the legal requirement to adhere to mandatory standards for products or services, and the use in practice of voluntary standards in industry, can operate as barriers to trade. These barriers are of three main types.

(i) **Legal barriers**. Whenever a mandatory standard applies in state X, but state Y applies no standard or a different standard, it is quite likely that products manufactured in state Y will not meet the standard set by state X, since production will be geared up mainly to the home market. Where this is the case, products from state Y might not lawfully be able to obtain access to the market of X. This is a legal barrier to trade.

(ii) **Commercial barriers.** Even where state X has no mandatory standard, industry may in practice operate to a voluntary standard, which may differ from that used in state Y. In such a case, the products of state Y can lawfully be sold in state X. However, in practice, purchasers in state X may, out of habit and familiarity, seek products which meet state X's voluntary standard. In the case of goverment, national standards have also sometimes been used deliberately, in order to favour domestic firms. Products from state Y may thus find it difficult to gain access to X's market. This problem, arising from the practice of using voluntary standards to specify requirements, may be referred to as a "commercial" barrier to trade.

(iii) **Technological barriers.** The existence of different standards – voluntary or mandatory – often leads to a situation where products from different states are incompatible. Thus, for example, industry in state X and Y is likely to be geared up to producing rolling stock for use on its own railway system. If different gauges are used in the two states, rolling stock produced in state X cannot be used in state Y and vice versa. This is a "technological" barrier to trade, which may persist even though legal and commercial barriers have been broken down.

The barrier to trade created by differing standards is one of the most significant problems which the E.C. has faced in attempting to create a single European market. Since commercial and technical barriers are particularly prevalent in markets for complex, high technology equipment, the public and utilities markets have been particularly affected.

This also means that efforts to tackle the barriers existing in regulated markets are of special importance for the single market as a whole.

(4) GENERAL COMMUNITY MEASURES ON STANDARDS[16]

Leaving aside the measures specific to the regulated procurement market, which are considered at (5) below, Community policies directed at the trade barriers created by differing national standards can be considered in four categories: the development of detailed standards in directives; the "new approach" directives; the mutual recognition principle of *Cassis de Dijon*; and the use of voluntary standards.

(a) DETAILED LEGISLATIVE STANDARDS

The Community first sought to tackle the problem of standards as barriers to trade largely by promulgating *mandatory* Community-wide standards. These aim, first and foremost, to supersede restrictive national requirements which might otherwise be imposed within the limitations to, and derogations from, Article 30 E.C. (for example, those protecting health and safety). Such standards eliminate any legal barriers to trade for the product concerned. They may also help to reduce commercial barriers by reducing the need for voluntary national standards concerned with other features of a product, and will also assist with the removal of technological barriers where the standards cover "compatibility" features of products (dimensions, etc.).

Obtaining agreement on detailed standards is a slow process, however, and relatively few products and services have been covered.[17] Further, detailed standards often stifle innovation, and where it does occur, they may date very quickly.[18]

(b) THE NEW APPROACH DIRECTIVES

The difficulties with detailed directives led the Community to adopt an alternative legislative strategy from the mid 1980s, in the drive to

---

[16] See further Weatherill and Beaumont, *E.C. Law* (1993), Chaps. 16 and 17; van Voorst and van Dam, "Europe 1992: Free Movement of Goods in the Wider Context of a Changing Europe" (1988) 25 C.M.L.Rev. 693; Swann (ed.), *The Single European Market and Beyond* (1992).

[17] The process has, though, been made easier by the adoption of Article 100a E.C., which dates from the Single European Act of 1987, allowing many standards to be adopted in the Council by a qualified majority.

[18] Such standards also stifle cultural diversity in favour of a uniform approach which, in some fields in particular, is considered a serious disadvantage.

complete the internal market by 1992.[19] Under this new approach, directives set out broad performance requirements – referred to as "essential requirements" – for products, rather than detailed specifications. (For example, a directive may specify the degree of fire resistance required of a product, rather than the material from which it is to be made.) These directives harmonise requirements relating to those matters on which States may legislate consistently with Article 30. In so doing they normally preclude national legislation and thus eliminate legal barriers to trade. Other interests may also be the subject of essential requirements, so reducing the role of national standards, and helping to eliminate commercial barriers – purchasers may become inclined to accept any product complying with the directive, rather than insisting on compliance with voluntary national standards. Examples of these "new approach" Directives are the Construction Products Directive,[20] implemented through the Construction Products Regulations 1991,[21] setting essential requirements for products to be incorporated into works, and Directive 91/263/EEC on telecommunications terminal equipment,[22] implemented through the Telecommunications Terminal Equipment Regulations 1992.[23]

In addition to formulating essential requirements, the Community has mandated European standardising bodies to develop detailed voluntary standards for the products covered, which meet the essential requirements. Manufacturers may use these standards if they choose, although firms may also comply with the essential requirements through a method of manufacture which differs from the detailed standard. The adoption and use of European standards further reduces commercial barriers to trade – purchasers across Europe will tend to accept products meeting the European standard – and will also reduce technological barriers to trade where the detailed standard is formulated with compatibility in mind.

The following European bodies are entrusted with the development of voluntary standards:

(i) The European Committee for Standardisation (CEN). CEN deals with standards for most products and services. Its members are the national standardising bodies of the E.C. and EFTA countries, including

---

[19] This was suggested by the Commission in its 1985 White Paper to the Council concerning completion of the internal market, and endorsed in a Council Resolution of May 7, 1985, [1985] O.J. C136/1. Community legislation is now largely limited to areas where measures are required to protect the interests recognised under Article 36 E.C. or as mandatory requirements – in other cases, products can trade freely in any case, since Member States cannot impose technical requirements to protect other interests. Legislation may also be needed, however, to eliminate technological barriers, since these are not dealt with by the rule in *Cassis de Dijon* nor even by all the new approach directives.

[20] Directive 89/106/EEC, [1989] O.J. L40/12.

[21] S.I. No.1620 of 1991.

[22] [1991] O.J. L128/1.

[23] S.I. No.2423 of 1992.

BSI. It issues two main types of standard. One is the European standard (EN), which members are required to implement into national law, by giving it a national number and promulgating it as an approved standard of the national body concerned. (British standards implementing European standards are prefixed with the letters "BS EN".) Existing national standards conflicting with the new standard must be withdrawn. The other type of standard is a Harmonisation Document (HD); here, there is no requirement for national implementation, but national bodies must announce the CEN standard and withdraw any conflicting national standard.

(ii) The European Electro-technical Committee (CENELEC). CENELEC issues standards for electric and electronic equipment, again in the form of either EN standards or HDs. It is composed of the electro-technical committees of the E.C. and EFTA states (including the Electro-technical Standards Council of BSI).

(iii) The European Telecommunications Standards Institute (ETSI). This body issues standards in the telecommunications field, generally in the form of European Telecommunications Standards (ETS). Its membership is diverse, drawn from (*inter alia*) national administrations, telecommunications operators, manufacturers and users, both within the E.C. and EFTA and also from other European states.

(c) MUTUAL RECOGNITION: THE *CASSIS DE DIJON* PRINCIPLE

Most products and services are still not covered by mandatory common rules, under either detailed directives or "new approach" directives. An important step was taken, however, to deal with trade barriers in these areas, in the Court of Justice decision in *Cassis de Dijon*.[24] This case concerned the interpretation of the various limitations on and derogations from Article 30 E.C., discussed in Chapter 4,[25] which make possible national regulations on matters such as safety and consumer protection which operate as legal barriers to trade. In *Cassis de Dijon* the Court established a presumption that, despite these exceptions, products lawfully produced and marketed in one Member State should generally be admitted into circulation in other Member States also. It is thus now difficult to persuade the Court that the protective requirements set by the Member State from which the product is imported are not adequate, or that the interests in question could not be protected by some other means (such as warnings or other information for consumers): the case

---

[24] Case 120/78, *REWE Zentral A.G. v. Bundesmonoplverwaltung für Branntwein* [1979] E.C.R. 649 ("*Cassis de Dijon*"). Historically, this decision preceded the new approach directives, and like the new approach was a response to the slow progress made in adopting Directives setting out detailed standards.
[25] See pp. 84–86.

has reduced the scope for Member States to retain their own legislative requirements, requiring them generally to recognise standards promulgated by other E.C. states. This principle of "mutual recognition" of national standards has also been adopted in some specific Community legislation.[26] Such mutual recognition eliminates legal barriers to trade. It affects, of course, regulated markets as well as the market as a whole, since regulated purchasers are now able to purchase products which might otherwise have been unavailable in the domestic market. Recent cases relating to services indicate that the Court will also adopt a similar approach in relation to the provision of services under Article 59 E.C.[27]

(d) DEVELOPMENT OF VOLUNTARY EUROPEAN STANDARDS

As well as developing voluntary standards to meet the requirements of the new approach directives, CEN, CENELEC and ETSI develop voluntary standards for a variety of products not covered by Community legislation. Adoption of such standards, as explained at (b) above, helps to eliminate both commercial and technological barriers to trade by providing a single standard for general use throughout Europe. Even though use is optional, industry will frequently make use of the standard in practice, especially since the national standards previously used are withdrawn once the European standard is adopted.

(5) THE RULES ON SPECIFICATIONS IN REGULATED PROCUREMENT

Having considered the Community policies on standards which affect the market as a whole, we may now turn to the special rules governing the procurement of government and utilities. These derive from three main sources: i) the European Community Treaties; ii) the procurement directives and implementing regulations; and iii) other Community measures, in particular the "IT Standards Decision".

(a) IMPACT OF THE E.C. TREATY

Like other purchasers, regulated purchasers may only buy products and services which comply with national legal rules. It has already been explained that these rules may restrict intra-Community trade, but that the barriers created by such rules are reduced by the operation of the

---

[26] See Directive 89/106/EEC, [1989] O.J. L40/12 (the Construction Products Directive), Article 4(2)–(3), providing for mutual recognition where there are no harmonised standards or procedures for the issue of European Technical Approvals.
[27] Case 205/84, *Commission v. Germany* [1987] 2 C.M.L.R. 69; Case C–384/93, *Alpine Investments B.V. v. Minister van Financiën* [1995] 3 C.M.L.R. 209.

E.C. Treaty provisions, especially following the decision in *Cassis de Dijon* which limits the scope for national regulatory measures. In addition, the Treaty has a further impact for government and some utilities, which does not generally apply to private entities. This arises from the fact that the Treaty rules on free movement apply to government purchasing decisions as well as to regulatory measures, as was explained in Chapter 4.[28]

In the context of specifications the effect of these rules is, first, to prohibit authorities from formulating their requirements in such a way that they are more difficult for firms from other states to meet than for domestic firms. This is made clear by the Court of Justice decision in *Dundalk*,[29] which concerned a contract to be awarded by an Irish municipality for construction of a water main. The specifications provided that certain pipes to be used in the construction should be asbestos cement pipes certified as complying with an Irish Standard, and the municipality rejected one tender on the grounds that the pipes to be supplied (manufactured by a Spanish firm) did not conform with the Irish standard. In proceedings under Article 169 E.C. the Court ruled that the "Irish standard" clause infringed Article 30 E.C.[30] since it restricted the access of imported products to the Irish government market. Ireland contended that the clause was justified to ensure that the pipes were compatible with the existing network, but this argument was rejected. It was stated that this concern could be met by allowing firms to supply pipes which met the Irish standard *or equivalent*[31]: manufacture to the Irish standard was merely one way, but not the only way, of meeting the authority's operational requirements. The same reasoning will apply to requirements concerned with other characteristics, such as safety or quality – a purchaser cannot require adherence to a particular national standard, but must accept any product which meets the purchaser's performance requirements.[32] The general effect of this principle is to substantially reduce the commercial barriers to trade in public markets, by preventing reliance on national standards where this is not necessary to safeguard the purchaser's interests.

The clause in *Dundalk* rendered access to the market more difficult for non-domestic products than for Irish products. As well as applying to regulatory measures which are discriminatory in effect, however, Article

---

[28] See general Chap. 4

[29] Case 45/87, *Commission v. Ireland*, [1988] E.C.R. 4929.

[30] A similar rule will also apply under Article 59 in the few cases where national standards relating to service provision are used.

[31] See paras. 21–22 of the judgment.

[32] The Irish government in *Dundalk* also argued that the standard was necessary to ensure the pipe met health standards, but this was rejected since these health requirements were the subject of a quite separate requirement in the specifications in any case. Had this not been the case, the municipality would have been required to accept other products which met the same health standards as the Irish standard. On this see further pp. 583–584.

30 applies also to measures concerning product requirements which *hinder equally the sale and production of domestic products*, as explained in Chapter 4. On this basis it appears that any restrictive specification may contravene Article 30, even if it does not tend to favour domestic products. This view was accepted by the Court of Justice in its recent decision in case C–359/93, *Commission v. Netherlands* (the "UNIX" case).[33]

In this case a Netherlands authority advertised a contract for the supply and maintenance of a weather station which referred to UNIX as the required operating system for connecting computers used in the project. UNIX is a specific make of software system developed in the United States which, whilst not recognised as a formal standard, is referred to and used in the industry as a *"de facto"* standard. Its use had the effect, however, of excluding providers offering other systems which could still meet the authority's needs.[34] Although the specification did not favour products from the Netherlands, the Court held that it nevertheless constituted a restriction on trade in breach of Article 30 E.C.[35] The Court was of the view that, as in *Dundalk*, the authority should have indicated that it was willing to accept "equivalent" products.[35a] The UNIX case itself will apply only to those purchasers who are subject to the relevant Treaty provisions, which may not include all utilities[36]; but arguably the same rule will apply under Utilities Regulation 4(3) which prohibits different treatment of providers.[37]

This case implies a general principle that specifications must not be drawn up in such a way as to exclude products which meet the authority's performance requirements. Compliance with such a rule can be achieved by formulating specifications in terms of performance rather than detailed requirements. For example, an authority might refer to the degree of heat resistance required from a product, rather than require the manufacture to be from a specified heat-resistant material. Use of performance specifications wherever possible is in any case considered best procurement practice, since it both maximises competition and encourages industrial innovation. However, it is not essential to adopt the performance requirements approach: it is permitted under the Treaty to use detailed specifications or even refer to particular product makes provided the purchaser indicates that it is willing to accept

---

[33] Judgment of January 24, 1995
[34] In fact, the authority had accepted a bid from a provider offering a different but equally suitable system. However, this did not affect the legal position since the mere reference to the UNIX system could deter those offering other systems from bidding at all and hence was capable of restricting trade: see para. 27 of the judgment.
[35] Para. 27 of the judgment.
[35a] Para. 28 of the judgment (where the Court pointed out that this was also required by the Supply Directive).
[36] See pp. 86–88.
[37] See p. 381.

"equivalent" products.[38] It should be noted, however, that for contracts covered by the regulations reference to particular makes of product, as in the UNIX case, is generally prohibited under the regulations themselves.[39]

An important issue, which arises both with specifications which have a discriminatory effect and those which do not, is what constitutes an "equivalent" product for the purpose of the principle established in *Dundalk* and the UNIX case.

One view, which appeared to be endorsed by Advocate General Darmon in *Dundalk*,[40] is that it is presumed that a product is "equivalent" to that specified whenever it meets the standards for entry to the market of the Member State of origin. This view is based on the premise that Article 30 E.C. applies to government decisions concerning the performance requirements (safety, durability, etc.) of its purchases; that such requirements are thus permissible only where justified by reference to mandatory requirements or the derogations under Article 36 E.C.; and that the rule in *Cassis de Dijon*[41] applies to create a presumption that requirements are not justified where they are not considered necessary in the state of origin. On this view there would have been a presumption that Dundalk should have accepted pipes made to the Spanish standard, even if this did not provide the same level of safety as the Irish standard, in the same way that the Irish government is compelled to permit such pipes to be sold in the Irish market generally. Such an approach entails that the government's consumer choice on matters such as product quality and safety, as well as its freedom to regulate, is limited in the interests of free trade.

However, it is submitted that this is not the correct approach, since it would limit the government's policy choices to an unacceptable degree. First, the limitations on Article 30 do not embrace many of the legitimate considerations relevant to procurement decisions: for example, aesthetic considerations probably may not be taken into account under Article 30. Moreover, even if all relevant interests could be accommodated within the limitations on Article 30, it seems unwarranted to subject the government's choices on all these matters to review

---

[38] It appears that this general Treaty rule will even prohibit a requirement that products should comply with voluntary European standards, since this will prevent participation by persons whose products meet the same performance requirements but are not manufactured in accordance with the standard. The procurement directives, on the other hand, expressly require the use of European standards where they exist for contracts covered by the directives. It appears that this was intended to prohibit acceptance even of equivalent products, but may now be interpretated merely to require use of European Standard without prohibiting acceptance of equivalent products: see pp. 588–589.

[39] See pp. 601–602.

[40] It was also accepted by the Irish government in argument and has been accepted by the Commission, for example, in its original proposal for the Utilities Directive: *Public Procurement in the Excluded Sectors*, Bulletin of the European Communities, Supplement 6/88, p.89.

[41] See pp. 580–581.

by the Court of Justice.[42] A better view is that a product is only "equivalent" to that specified where it matches exactly (or exceeds) the performance requirements set. On this view, an Irish municipality would be required to accept a pipe manufactured to a Spanish standard only where that standard provided for levels of health protection, quality, etc., at least equal to those of the specified product. This can be explained on the basis that a government's procurement choices do not restrict the domestic market – they are part of the process of creating that market, and it is only when the decision has been taken on what to procure that Article 30 can come into operation. On this approach the government retains its discretion in its choices on the level of product standards, so that, for example, it may exceed for its own products the minimum safety levels which it is permitted to impose for the market as a whole under the *Cassis de Dijon* principle. This should apply even if the result of the choice is discriminatory in its effects: for example, because the government's choice reflects a national tradition of high-quality standards, and national firms are therefore more geared up to making products to these standards than those from some other Member States, or because the product which is selected to fulfil a particular need is one which domestic firms are best able to supply.[43]

If this is the correct approach the motive in setting the specification will be crucial – a decision motivated by protectionism rather than a genuine assessment of requirements is not a decision which establishes what the market is, but one which restricts access to the market. Here Article 30 applies, and there is no possibility of justifying the decision in view of the protectionist motive. Because of the difficulties of proving such a motive the argument in court is likely to revolve around the government's reasons for the particular standard of safety, quality, etc., which has been set (as it did in *Dundalk*). However, this should not disguise the fact that the key question is the bona fides of the decision, and not its objective justification; and that reasons other than those recognised as mandatory requirements and derogations from Article 30 are permitted to form the basis of purchasing decisions.

For contracts subject to the regulations these rules are bolstered in certain cases by provisions forbidding purchasers from rejecting tenders merely because they are drawn up in accordance with national specifications of other states, where these products are nevertheless suitable for the required purpose. Thus, even if the authority does not use the correct specifications, in some cases at least bidders are free to submit tenders in accordance with such specifications.[44]

---

[42] Government decisions on some of these issues are, however, limited under the regulations by the requirement to use European standards: see pp. 586–590.

[43] For example, if the government were to choose to purchase more helicopters as an alternative to more lifeboats for sea rescue, it could surely not be suggested that this decision would have to be justified before the Court of Justice simply because the state in question has a competitive helicopter industry but is not so good at making lifeboats.

[44] See pp. 605–607.

(b) THE RULES UNDER THE PROCUREMENT REGULATIONS[45]

(i) INTRODUCTION

Important rules on specifications are also contained in the procurement directives and regulations. Their main objective is to improve competition in regulated markets by eliminating in these markets the "commercial" barrier to trade – that is, the use of restrictive specifications. In addition, by requiring the use of European standards where these are relevant they seek to increase the use of European standards in the wider market, as a result of the indirect effect of regulated purchasing on industry in general. In this way, in the long term the procurement rules may help to reduce commercial and technological barriers in all Community markets.

The rules apply only to contracts within the scope of the regulations.[46] Contracts below the threshold are, however, subject to the rules in the E.C. Treaty which, as explained above, have a significant effect in prohibiting restrictive specifications. Some contracts below the thresholds are also affected by other Community measures, notably the IT Standards Decision.[47]

In the case of services contracts the regulations' rules on specifications apply, unlike most of the other rules in the regulations, to Part B services contracts as well as to Part A contracts.[48]

The rules on specifications are set out mainly in Works Regulation 8, Supply Regulation 8, Services Regulation 8, and Utilities Regulation 12. The rules for the public sector and the utilities can be considered together, since many of the rules apply in the same way in both sectors. There are also, however, some small differences, most of which are hard to justify.

(ii) THE REQUIREMENT TO USE RELEVANT EUROPEAN SPECIFICATIONS

I. The obligation to use European specifications

The first requirement of the regulations is that purchasers must draw up technical specifications by reference to "European specifications"

---

[45] See also Bickerstaff, "Applying the E.C. Rules on Standards and Specifications in Public and Utilities Procurement" (1994) 3 P.P.L.R. 153; Trepte, *Public Procurement in the E.C.* (1993) Chap. 6.
[46] On this see Chap. 5.
[47] See pp. 607–614.
[48] On this distinction see pp. 132–138.

wherever these are relevant.[49] This obligation is subject only to a few carefully defined exceptions.[50] The concept of European specifications covers three types of standard – (i) British standards implementing European standards; (ii) European technical approvals; and (iii) common technical specifications.[51]

(i) British standards implementing European standards. These are the most important type of European specification in practice. A European standard is a standard, either mandatory or voluntary, which has been approved by CEN or CENELEC in the form of an EN or HD,[52] according to the common rules of those organisations[53] and, under the Utilities and Services Regulations, a standard issued by ETSI in the form of an ETS.[54] The ETS is not mentioned in the supply and works rules, which is anomalous, since, although supply and works contracts will less frequently include products and services covered by these standards, this is certainly possible. As has been explained, ENs are implemented in the United Kingdom by the BSI, and it is this BSI standard which must be referred to. Products and services from other states which comply with other national standards which implement the European standard will, however, automatically comply with the British standard.

The concept of European standards does not include published draft standards ("pre-standards") issued by CEN, CENELEC and ETSI. Thus regulated purchasers are not required to use these standards, although they may choose to do so.

This rule on European standards means that regulated purchasers must use these standards where applicable, even where their use for the non-regulated sector is purely voluntary. It appears that the intention of these provisions was that purchasers should not be able to *accept* products which do not meet these European standards, even where these products are exactly equivalent in terms of performance requirements.[55] Thus, for example, where a product is covered by a "new approach" directive,[56] and is also the subject of a detailed European standard, it

---

[49] Works Regulation 8(3); Supply Regulation 8(3); Services Regulation 8(3); Utilities Regulation 12(3). On the definition of technical specifications for this purpose see pp. 573–575.

The public sector Directives do not use the phrase "European specifications", but it is found in the Utilities Directive and adopted in the United Kingdom public sector regulations, as well as those on utilities, as a convenient term to cover the three types of standard which purchasers are required to use.

[50] See (ii) below.

[51] See the definition of European specifications in Works Regulation 8(1); Supply Regulation 8(1); Services Regulation 8(1); Utilities Regulation 12(1).

[52] On these bodies and standards see pp. 579–580.

[53] See the definition in Works Regulation 8(1); Supply Regulation 8(1); Services Regulation 8(1); Utilities Regulation 12(1).

[54] Definition of European standard in Services Regulation 8(1) and Utilities Regulation 12(1). On ETSI see p. 580.

[55] On this point see European Commission, *Policy Guidelines on the interpretation of the obligation to refer to European standards in the framework of the Public Procurement Directives* CC/91/61 (rev.2) final of December 16, 1992.

[56] On these directives see pp. 578–580.

may have been intended that only products which meet the European standard will generally be acceptable – the authority may not purchase other products, even though they meet all the "essential requirements" of the directive. By way of express exception, however, as explained further below,[57] authorities must accept as an alternative to products meeting European standards those which (i) have obtained a European Technical Approval or (ii) are manufactured in accordance with "common technical specifications".

The requirement to use European standards ensures that domestic firms or products are not favoured above those from other Member States: it eliminates the application of the commercial barrier in government markets. In addition, such a rule may help to eliminate technological barriers to trade, where the European standards in question have been designed to ensure compatibility. Although there is an exception to the rule where use of these standards would lead to incompatibility with existing equipment, this applies only on a temporary basis pending the purchaser's switch to the European-based standard.[58]

The use of European-based standards by regulated purchasers seeks also to encourage providers, and as a consequence, some non-regulated purchasers, to switch to these standards, improving the competitiveness of industry as a whole. This effect will be particularly marked where regulated purchasers account for a large share of the market. Thus it is hoped that in the long term the rules on European Standards in regulated procurement will tend to reduce the commercial and technological trade barriers in the whole Community market. Such an approach was first introduced for information technology and telecommunications procurement in the "IT Standards Decision"[59] and was extended to other procurement in the revision of the public sector supplies and works rules in 1988 and 1989.[60]

On the other hand, the rule may in the short term reduce competition for some contracts, since, as explained, providers offering exactly equivalent products which do not conform to the detailed European standards will be unable to compete. This restrictive effect on trade of insisting on European standards means that for States to insist on such standards on their own initiative may infringe Article 30 E.C.[61] It is not clear whether it is acceptable for the Community to impose such measures despite their immediate restrictive effect, on the basis that they are designed to promote free movement in the long term.[62] In any case,

---

[57] See pp. 589–590.
[58] See further pp. 590–591.
[59] On this see pp. 607–614.
[60] On this revision process see pp. 54–56.
[61] See above Chap. 4.
[62] Although the Community is obliged to respect the free movement of goods in adopting its own measures, exceptions are made for certain common measures where their ultimate objective is to promote free movement – see further Oliver, *Free Movement of Goods in the EEC* (1988) 4.08–4.09.

even if this is permissible it is possible that in the light of the UNIX principle prohibiting restrictive standards in general, the Court of Justice might interpret the directives as meaning that, whilst purchasers must *refer* to relevant standards implementing European Standards, they may accept equivalent products or services offered by providers. If so, purchasers will be bound to accept such products or services, under the Treaty, as established in the UNIX case.

It may also be observed that the European standards rule is quite burdensome for purchasers, who are required to keep up to date with the development and revision of standards, although there is no single publicly available information source to provide information on these matters. The rule also to an extent reduces a purchaser's choice as a consumer: for example, it precludes the possibility of specifying a higher standard of safety than is embodied in a European standard – even a voluntary one – although such an option is open to a private purchaser. These drawbacks were recognised when the rules were adopted but it was considered that they were outweighed by the benefits.[63]

Whatever, the position where European Standards are directly relevant, it is submitted, on the other hand, that other standards may be referred to to supplement European standards when these do not deal at all with a particular characteristic which is important for the purchaser. For example, if the purchaser wishes to impose requirements relating to aesthetic characteristics and the relevant standard does not refer to these, then requirements relating to such characteristics should be able to be included as an additional requirement. This is assumed in the Utilities Regulations which contain express rules for specifications designed to "complement" relevant European standards.[64]

(ii) European technical approvals. Also classified as "European specifications", and thus required to be used by regulated purchasers, are "European technical approvals"[65] (ETAs). These are approvals for products satisfying the "essential requirements" of the Construction Products Directive (Directive 89/106/EEC),[66] which are given under a procedure provided for in that Directive. Under the Directive, Member

---

[63] See the Commission guidelines, note 55 above.

[64] Utilities Regulation 12(9).

[65] Defined in Works Regulation 8(1); Supply Regulation 8(1); Services Regulation 8(1); Utilities Regulation 12(1). The Works, Supply and Services Regulation provisions define an ETA in general terms as "an approval of the fitness for use of a product, issued by an approval body designated for that purpose by a Member State, following a technical assessment of whether the product fulfils the essential requirements for building works, having regard to the inherent characteristics of the product and the defined conditions of application and use"; there is no specific reference to the Construction Products Directive. However, the provisions are effectively limited to building products, since there is in practice no other approval process for building products which would fulfil the definition. Thus clearly the provisions are directed at products approved as satisfying this directive's requirements. The parallel reference in Utilities Regulation 12(1) is limited expressly to this directive.

[66] On this see pp. 578–579 above.

States designate national bodies to issue ETAs and in the United Kingdom this is the British Board of Agreement.

ETAs are designed mainly for products not yet covered by detailed European standards, although it is planned that detailed standards will eventually be produced for these products. However, even where detailed European standards exist it is proposed that ETAs may still be given for products which differ "significantly" from the standard. ETAs will generally not be given where there are national standards which have been recognised under a mutual recognition procedure set out in the directive for products meeting the directive's essential requirements.

(iii) Common technical specifications. A common technical specification is defined as "a technical specification drawn up in accordance with a procedure recognised by member States with a view to uniform application in all member States and which has been published in the Official Journal".[67]

II. Exceptions to the requirement to use European specifications[68]

The exceptions

(i) Incompatibility and disproportionate costs or technical difficulty
New equipment may need to be used in conjunction with existing equipment, or operated by existing staff, and the requirement to procure equipment which meets European specifications may cause difficulties in this respect. The directives and implementing regulations provide exceptions to take account of this.[69] These cover the following cases:

– Where use of European specifications would require the authority to use or acquire goods or works which are incompatible with existing goods or works.

– Where use of European specifications would entail disproportionate costs.
Cost could be incurred, for example, where equipment meeting European specifications could be used with existing equipment only after

---

[67] Works Regulation 8(1); Supply Regulation 8(1); Services Regulation 8(1); Utilities Regulation 12(1).

[68] In defining the scope of the exceptions in the various provisions discussed below, the Works Regulations refer to specifications relating to work or goods and the Supply Regulations merely to goods. The Services and Utilities Regulations refer to goods, works and services. It was suggested above at pp. 574–575 that the obligation to use European specifications should apply to the goods, work, and services elements of all three types of contract, although the literal wording of the rules does not provide for this. If this is correct, then clearly the scope of the exceptions should be construed in the same broad manner.

[69] Works Regulation 8(4); Supply Regulation 8(4); Services Regulation 8(4); Utilities Regulation 12(4).

adaptations. No guidance is given on what would be *disproportionate* cost; but it is clear that the provision does envisage that *some* costs may be forced on purchasers. However, since these must be in proportion to the objective sought, it can be argued that costs above the *de minimis* level are generally sufficient to bring the exception into play where adaptions are required: the objectives of the standards rules, in particular in encouraging purchasers to move to European standards, will not be significantly affected by allowing exceptions, since these are permitted only temporarily pending the conversion to these standards, as explained below. Costs of training staff to use the new equipment will not generally be relevant, on the other hand, since this will be required anyway on conversion.

– Where use of European specifications would involve disproportionate technical difficulty.
This may apply, for example, where equipment meeting European specifications could be used with existing equipment, but this would reduce the performance of the equipment. Again, it is suggested that a low level of technical difficulty should suffice for the exception, given its temporary nature.

As indicated above, these exceptions are of a temporary nature: this is because they may be invoked only when the purchaser can demonstrate a strategy for changing over to European specifications.[70] This strategy must be clearly defined and recorded, and must provide for a set period for the changeover.[71] Thus in the long term all regulated purchasers are effectively forced by the specifications rules to change over to equipment and systems based on European specifications. As has already been mentioned, this may ultimately encourage the use of such specifications in industry as a whole.

(ii) Problems establishing conformity
Further exceptions apply to the rules on European specifications where there are problems in ascertaining whether these specifications are met.

First, there is an exception under both public sector and utilities rules where it is technically impossible to establish conformity in a satisfactory manner.[72] This situation sometimes arises, for example, with standards which set acceptable error levels for computerised control systems, where it may be impossible to demonstrate the chance of error in particular systems.

Secondly, the public sector rules make an exception where the European specifications themselves do not include provision for estab-

---

[70] Works Regulation 8(5); Supply Regulation 8(5); Services Regulation 8(5); Utilities Regulation 12(5).
[71] *Ibid.*
[72] Works Regulation 8(4)(b); Supply Regulation 8(4)(b); Services Regulation 8(4)(b); Utilities Regulation 12(4)(b).

lishing conformity to their requirements.[73] This is often the case in practice. This exception seems unduly wide: there is no reason why a European specification with no provision to establish conformity should not be used where there is some reasonable way in which conformity can be ascertained. There is no equivalent exception in the utilities rules.

(iii) Incompatibility with national rules[74]

European specifications also need not be used where United Kingdom law requires specifications to be drawn up by reference to different technical requirements which are mandatory in the United Kingdom.[75] Obviously, this only applies where these different requirements themselves are valid under European Community law.[76]

This is designed to deal with situations where there are valid reasons for national differences in standards. These may arise, for example, because of different national practices which are difficult to alter (driving on the left rather than the right), language differences (which require differences in keyboards, for example) or different national conditions, such as climate or terrain which may make different demands on products.

In practice, however, this derogation rarely applies since European specifications are devised to provide adequate protection for any interests which may lawfully form the object of restrictive national legislation (that is, those based on mandatory requirements and derogations from Article 30 E.C., such as health and safety).[77] Where there is a valid reason for national variation from the European "norm" this is taken into account in drawing up the specification itself and is generally incorporated in European standards as an "A type variation". National legislation protecting the interests recognised under Article 30 is then generally not permitted, since the interest has been protected through the standard. Where the standard is voluntary, national legislation will often in practice adopt the levels of protection reflected in the European specification. Where this is not done, such legislation will generally be ineffective when applied to imports, since the *Cassis de Dijon* rule[78] will demand recognition of products meeting the European specification. National legislative requirements which are not based on the interests recognised under Article 30 will, of course, constitute unlawful restrictions on trade, and so may not be relied upon.

The exception may, however, apply in rare cases, where it can be shown that the European specification is not adequate to protect recognised interests. This is more likely to arise because of changed

---

[73] Works Regulation 8(4)(b); Supply Regulation 8(4)(b); Services Regulation 8(4)(b).
[74] See also the guidelines cited in note 55, section 3.
[75] Works Regulation 8(4)(a); Supply Regulation 8(4)(a); Services Regulation 8(4)(a); Utilities Regulation 12(4)(a).
[76] *Ibid.*
[77] See pp. 84–86.
[78] See pp. 580–581.

conditions, than because such interests were not protected by the original standard. In such a case, the European specification will, in practice, be swiftly revised. It should be emphasised that the fact that the purchaser *perceives* the European specification to be inadequate does not suffice – this exception may be invoked only where the different specification is a *legal* requirement in the United Kingdom.

(iv) Priority of other Community provisions
A further exception to the requirement to use European specifications applies in some cases where to do so would conflict with other Community rules prescribing standards to be used by purchasers.

In the case of the Supply and Services Regulations, an exception applies[79] where to use European specifications would conflict with the application of Council Directive 91/263/EEC, which deals with the standards for telecommunications terminal equipment[80] or with Council Decision 87/95/EEC (the "IT Standards Decision"), relating to standards for information technology and communications equipment.[81] The IT Standards Decision, and its relationship with the procurement regulations, is discussed further below.[82] An exception also applies where there would be a conflict with other Community measures dealing with specific services or goods.

The Works Regulations do not contain any exceptions for either Directive 91/263 or the IT standards decision, nor any other specific Community measures on standards. Presumably this was because it was considered that there are no conflicting measures in the area of works standards. However, contracts governed by the Works Regulations may include elements of supplies and services as well as works, and it thus seems that such exceptions should be included in the Works Directive.

The Utilities Regulations also provide for an exception where there is a conflict with the Directive 91/263, and with the IT Standards Decision.[83] There is no exception for other conflicting measures which may exist.

(v) Innovative projects
An authority is not required to use European specifications where the project or work is of a "genuinely innovative nature" and because of this existing European specifications would be inappropriate.[84] The reference

---

[79] Supply Regulation 8(4)(c); Services Regulation 8(4)(c).

[80] [1991] O.J. L128/1. The directives and implementing regulations actually refer to Directive 86/361/EEC, [1986] O.J. L217/21, but this has been superseded by the 1991 Directive (which is the one referred to by the utilities rules, discussed below).

[81] [1987] O.J. L36/31.

[82] See pp. 607–614.

[83] Utilities Regulation 12(4)(c).

[84] Works Regulation 8(4)(d); Supply Regulation 8(4)(e); Services Regulation 8(4)(e); Utilities Regulation 12(4)(f). The Works Regulations refer to work(s) of an innovative nature; the Supply Regulations to the innovative nature of the project for which goods are acquired; and the Services Regulations and Utilities Regulations merely to a project of an innovative nature.

to *genuine* innovation suggests that this exception will apply only to wholly new technology, and not to adaptations or improvements on existing technology[85] or to technology which is very different from that referred to in the standard but which is now well established. An example of a case which could be covered is the use of a wholly new technology in an experimental telephone network. With experiments involving adaptations of existing standards, or new developments which have gone beyond the purely experimental stage, utilities may be able to invoke exception (vi) below, but such an option is not available to public bodies.

(vi) Where European specifications lag behind technical development

There are two further exceptions in the utilities rules which have no counterpart in the public sector. One is where the European specification does not take account of developments since its adoption.[86] When new technical developments occur, it may take many years before a new standard is approved, and this exception allows utilities to take advantage of such improvements during this period. This exception may be used by utilities to take account of developments which are not sufficiently radical to be considered genuine innovations under exception (v) above. Such a possibility is not open under the public sector rules, and this is an unfortunate gap in the rules.

A utility invoking this provision must inform the appropriate body as to why the European specification should not apply and must request its revision.[87] It is not clear whether a failure to do so at the time the contract is publicised would "taint" the decision not to use the European specification, so that, for example, the procurement could be held up until this notification has been given. This is not required where the project or work is an innovation falling within (v) above.

(vii) Where European specifications are inappropriate

A second exception for utilities which does not apply under the public sector rules is where the European specification is "inappropriate for the particular purpose".[88] This could cover the case where an existing standard does not cover some uses of a product at all, or where a standard is not used in practice in the industry and products made to the standard are therefore unavailable. The provision might also be applied to other situations as yet unforeseen where serious difficulties might arise in using European specifications. It would be useful to include a similar exception in the public sector regulations.

A utility invoking this exception must, as with (vi) above, inform the "appropriate standardising organisation" or "other body empowered to review the European specification" why it seeks to do so, and request a revision of the standard.[89]

---

[85] This is emphasised in the Commission guidelines referred to in note 55.
[86] Utilities Regulation 12(4)(e).
[87] Utilities Regulation 12(6).
[88] Utilities Regulation 12(4)(e).
[89] Utilities Regulation 12(6).

Conditions for invoking the exceptions

Under the public sector regulations, except for the case where the use of European specifications would be incompatible with United Kingdom law,[90] a purchaser departing from the obligation to use European specifications must state in the contract notice which exception is invoked.[91] Where it is impossible to include the information in the contract notice, it may be included in the contract documents.[92] The information is also to be put in the contract documents in the case of services contracts listed in Part B of the Services Regulations[93] (since with these contracts there is no requirement to publish a contract notice at all). The purchaser must keep a record of its reasons[94] and, when requested by the Commission or another relevant state,[95] must send this record to the Treasury (in the case of a Minister or government department) or the Minister responsible for the authority[96] for transmission (in the latter case via the Treasury) to the Commission or state concerned.

For contracts governed by the Utilities Regulations, where relevant European specifications are not used the utility must specify the reason in any contract notice, or in any periodic indicative notice or notice advertising a qualification system which acts as a call for competition for the contract.[97] The utility must keep a record of the reasons for its decision[98] for at least four years from the date of the contract award.[99]

The rules governing specifications where an exception is invoked

When one of the above exceptions is invoked, European specifications need not be used, but some Community rules still apply. In particular, the purchaser is still subject to the provisions of the Community Treaties,[1] and also to the rules in the regulations prohibiting reference to specific makes, sources and processes, discussed below.[2]

Arguably a purchaser must also apply the rules explained at (iii) below, which apply where no European specifications exist. The directives provide that such rules are to apply "in the absence" of European specifications,[3] which could cover the situation where a specification has

---

[90] As to which see pp. 592–593.
[91] Works Regulation 8(6); Supply Regulation 8(6); Services Regulation 8(6).
[92] *Ibid.*
[93] Services Regulation 8(6).
[94] Works Regulations 8(6) and 29(1); Supply Regulations 8(6) and 26(1); Services Regulations 8(6) and 28(1).
[95] On the definition of "relevant state" see pp. 908–909.
[96] Works Regulation 8(6); Supply Regulation 8(6); Services Regulation 8(6).
[97] Utilities Regulation 12(7).
[98] Utilities Regulation 26(1)(b).
[99] Utilities Regulation 26(3). There is no specific provision for forwarding on the information, even though the forwarding of information under Regulation 26 is referred to expressly in regulation 28(6).
[1] See Chap 4.
[2] See pp. 601–602.
[3] Works Directive Article 10(5); Supply Directive Article 8(5); Services Directive Article 14(5); Utilities Directive Article 18(3).

been adopted but is not mandatory for the regulated purchaser, as well as where none exists at all. It is appropriate to apply the same rules in both cases, and the European Court may be prepared to adopt a broad interpretation of the legislation to achieve that result. In fact, many of the rules under (iii) are not relevant where European specifications exist – for example, they often contemplate the use of national standards not based on European standards, but such national standards will have been withdrawn where European standards exist. However, they could be important in some cases: for example, where a utility declines to apply a European standard as inappropriate or lagging behind technological development, the rules would require reference to other standards in common use[4] – for example, third country standards employed by Community industry as an alternative to an outdated European standard.

(iii) POSITION WHERE NO EUROPEAN SPECIFICATIONS EXIST

I. Introduction
For most products and services there are still no standards which constitute "European specifications". In this case purchasers must follow the rules outlined below. These differ between the public and utilities sectors, which are thus examined separately.

As explained above, it is not clear how far these rules also apply where European specifications exist but are not required to be used.[5]

II. The public sector
Where there is no relevant European specification, purchasers must use British technical specifications complying with the "basic requirements" of harmonising Council Directives, under the procedure established under those Directives.[6] This is stated to apply "in particular" to the Construction Products Directive,[7] but also applies to other harmonising directives. Whilst British technical specifications must be used to describe the requirement however, under the Community Treaties and under other international agreements imposing similar obligations[8] a purchaser must also accept – and indicate that it is prepared to accept[9] – other "equivalent" products.

---

[4] See pp. 599–600 below.
[5] See pp. 595–596.
[6] Works Regulation 8(7)(a); Supply Regulation 8(7)(a); and Services Regulation 8(7)(a). The provisions refer "in particular" to the Construction Products Directive 89/106/EEC, but cover other "new approach" Directives also.
[7] *Ibid.*
[8] On this see Chaps. 4 and 15.
[9] See p. 583.

The regulations also provide that an authority *may* define the technical specifications by reference to British technical specifications relating to the design and method of calculation and execution of work(s), and the use of material and goods.[10] Again however, the authority must indicate its willingness to accept equivalent products if offered.

The regulations provide further that the authority *may* use certain other standards, in the following order of priority: i) British standards implementing international standards; ii) other British standards and technical approvals; and iii) "any other standards".[11]

(i) British standards implementing international standards. "International standard" is not defined as such. However, "standard" is defined generally as "a technical specification approved by a *recognised standardising body* for repeated and continuous application, compliance with which is not compulsory"[12] (emphasis added). The main international standardising bodies[13] are the International Organisation for Standardisation (ISO), a federation of standardising bodies from around 90 countries, which sets standards in most fields; the International Electro-technical Committee (IEC), which sets standards relating to electric and electronic equipment; and the International Consultative Committee for Telephones and Telegraph (CCITT), which sets standards in the telecommunications field. ISO and IEC work together in the field of information technology standardisation.

"British standards" also is not defined, but in view of the definition of standards above refers only to specifications approved by recognised standard-setting bodies. The recognised standard-setting bodies in the European Community are listed in the annex to Directive 83/189.[14] The definition of a standard in the regulations does not cover specifications issued by bodies which are not recognised standard-setting bodies, even though these may be widely used in industry.[15] For example, CCTA, a government agency responsible for providing advice and support in relation to information technology in government, issues specifications for computer management contracts which are widely used by public authorities, but these are not "British standards".

Where such British standards are used, the Treaty and relevant international agreements will again also require authorities to indicate that they will accept any "equivalent" tender.

---

[10] Works Regulation 8(7)(b); Supplies Regulation 8(7)(b); Services Regulations 8(7)(b).

[11] Works Regulation 8(7)(c); Supply Regulation 8(7)(c); Services Regulation 8(7)(c).

[12] Works Regulation 8(1); Supply Regulation 8(1); Services Regulation 8(1).

[13] Exactly which bodies are covered by this definition is not important; if a British standard based on the standard of another body is not caught in category i) it will fall into category ii) in any case, with the same effect – that reference to such a standard is required in priority to reference to any other type of standard.

[14] [1983] O.J. L109/8.

[15] This view of the definition of a standard is taken in the Policy Guidelines on "Standards having currency in the Community", discussed in the next section below.

(ii) Other British standards or technical approvals. The meaning of "British standard" has been considered under (i) above. There is no definition of a technical approval. By analogy with the definition of European technical approval,[16] however, this may probably be taken to refer to an approval of a product as meeting performance requirements set out in legislation in accordance with an approval process which is recognised nationally. This would apply, for example, to agreement certificates to certify compliance with the Construction Products Directive, which are currently being issued pending recognition of the process for European technical approvals. As always, the Treaty and other international agreements will, however, oblige authorities to accept any "equivalent" product and to refer to this fact in the specifications.

(iii) "Any other standards". Where there is no European specification, "basic requirement" approval, or British standard or technical approval, an authority may rely on other standards. It has been explained above that "standards" comprise only specifications set by recognised standardising institutions. This category of "other standards" will include standards of the ISO, IEC or CCITT which have not been implemented through British standards, and standards set by standardising institutions in other states, such as those set by the American National Standards Institute (ANSI), which are sometimes referred to in practice in European industry.

These provisions do not appear to *require* authorities to use the above standards – they merely provide for an order of priority where an authority chooses to do so. This permissive wording simply repeats that in the directives themselves. However, it is possible that the intention of directives was to require the use of such standards where they exist, which seems in accordance with the directives' policy of providing information in an accessible manner. If there is no requirement to refer to the above standards, it appears that an authority is always free to refer to any specifications which are not recognised standards, or to design its own, even where British standards (or other recognised standards) do exist.

In practice an authority will generally prefer to make use of existing standards of which it is aware, whether those of recognised bodies or other industry standards. This both makes the authority's job easier and makes the specifications more accessible to providers. There may, however, be cases where these are inappropriate – for example, because they are outdated.[17] Of course, for some purchases there will be neither recognised standards nor other specifications in common use, and an authority must then inevitably design its own.

---

[16] As to which see pp. 589–590.
[17] Since there is no obligation to use recognised standards which are not European specifications, there is no need for express exceptions to deal with this kind of case, such as apply in relation to the rule on European specifications.

The advantages of established, as compared with ad hoc, specifications have lead to the inclusion in the utilities rules (considered immediately below) of a provision requiring the use, wherever possible, of recognised standards in use in the Community (or in other states which participate in the open European procurement market). Further, no priority is laid down for different types of standards. These utilities rules are both more simple and more sensible than those in the public sector. They also oblige an authority to use performance-based rather than design-based specifications and this rule, also, could usefully be added to the public sector directives.[18]

III. The utilities sector

Obligation to use other standards "in common use"

Under the Utilities Regulations, where there are no European specifications then specifications must be defined, "as far as possible", by reference to standards "in common use within the relevant states" (being certain other States entitled to take the benefit of the directives, both those within and outside the Community).[19] "Standard" is defined, under the public sector rules, as "a technical specification approved by a recognised standardising body for repeated and continuous application, compliance with which is in principle not compulsory".[20] Recognised bodies for this purpose will include the bodies listed in Directive 83/189,[21] the international standardising bodies ISO, IEC and CCITT,[22] and also those in third countries, such as ANSI. *De facto* standards set by non-recognised bodies, on the other hand, are clearly not included and the defintion also appears to exclude draft standards. Thus, whilst utilities may still choose to use these where no formal standards are available, they are not obliged to do so.

When is a standard "in common use" in the Community? This phrase implements a provision in the Utilities Directive which refers to "standards having currency within the member states of the Community" (which is adapted by later international agreements to cover also certain other States which participate in the Community's open procurement market).[23] This appears to cover all standards which are frequently used in any of the relevant states – even if just in one state – and not just those used throughout the Community and other relevant states.[24] Thus

---

[18] On this rule see pp. 600–601.
[19] Utilities Regulation 12(8). On relevant states see further pp. 908–909.
[20] Utilities Regulation 12(1).
[21] [1983] O.J. L109/8.
[22] On these see p. 597.
[23] Utilities Directive Article 18(3).
[24] European Commission, *Policy Guidelines on "Standards having currency in the Community"* CC/92/80, final. The document was favourably considered by the Advisory Committee on the opening up of public procurement on October 14, 1992, and by the Advisory Committee on Public Contracts on October 21, 1992.

national standards, international standards and those of third countries are all included, where used in practice and set by recognised bodies.

No order of priority is given between the different standards which may be in common use at the same time. Thus, a utility may choose between, for example, a national standard used only in the home state, or a United States standard used in a number of relevant states. Whatever standard is chosen, the utility must generally comply with the general principle in the regulations which prohibits discrimination, and with the Community Treaty obligations where these apply to the utility. Thus if a British standard is used, it must be indicated that "equivalent" products will be accepted.[25]

The fact that such standards need be used only "as far as possible" indicates some limit on the obligation to refer to standards in common use. It is submitted that this qualification will in fact allow exceptions from this obligation similar to the express exceptions which are provided to the requirement to use European specifications – for example, for incompatibility, or where the standard lags behind technology. Clearly, however, these cannot be directly transplanted to the "common use" rule: for example, where incompatibility would arise from using, say, British standards, the utility could not be expected to show a plan to convert to such standards as a condition for invoking the exception.

It is unclear whether the fact that such specifications need be used only "as far as possible" would relieve a utility of an obligation to use standards of which it could not reasonably have been aware.

The obligation to use performance requirements

The utilities rules further provide that in laying down specifications apart from European specifications or other standards, the utility must if possible use "specifications that indicate performance requirements rather than design or description characteristics".[26] Thus, for example, requirement for a storage facility for containing toxic chemicals would have to be defined by reference to its function – to contain chemicals for a certain period of time, at certain levels of safety, rather than the product details, such as materials of manufacture, sealing processes, etc. Specifying products in this way widens the range of potential suppliers, ensuring that all those who are able to meet the authority's objective needs are able to participate and is also often favoured by governments because it encourages innovative solutions, and may thus produce wider benefits for the economy. The same objectives are now promoted to a significant extent for purchasers covered by the Treaty by the principle in the UNIX case, discussed above,[27] which requires such purchasers to

---

[25] See pp. 581–585.

[26] Utilities Regulation 12(9). The rules apply where further specifications are laid down to "complement" European or other standards; this clearly should include, however, the case where no recognised standards exist.

[27] See pp. 581–585.

accept (and to indicate that they will accept) products and services which do not meet the detailed specification, but can fulfil its performance requirements; and arguably this applies also under the prohibition on discrimination under the Utilities Regulations.

The obligation to use performance specifications does not apply where this would be inadequate for some reason.[28]

(iv) PROHIBITION ON REFERENCES TO A SPECIFIC MAKE, SOURCE OR PROCESS

Under both the public sector and utilities rules purchasers are prohibited from using technical specifications which refer to goods of a specific make or source or to a particular process.[29] This is expressly stated to include – though it is not limited to – references to trademarks, patents, types, origin or means of production.[30] Thus in the "UNIX" case,[31] which has already been discussed above,[32] the Court of Justice held that (subject to the possibility of limitations and exceptions discussed below) it is prohibited under the directives as well as under the Treaty to specify that the "UNIX" software system should be provided by a supplier, since this is a reference to a particular make. It was irrelevant that the specification in question had been drawn up by an unofficial body of consumers and producers and had become a *de facto* industry standard, nor that it was understood in the industry that other "equivalent" products were generally acceptable.[33] The prohibition also means that authorities may not generally insist that a product is produced according to a particular process, even though the process is not protected by any intellectual property rights; nor, for example, that goods should be made from material quarried from a particular site.

A qualification to this prohibition is that it applies only where the specification will have the effect of "favouring or eliminating" particular goods or firms (under the public sector regulations) or particular firms alone (under the Utilities Regulations).[34] Thus, a reference to a particu-

---

[28] Utilities Regulation 12(9).

[29] Works Regulation 8(8); Supply Regulation 8(8); Services Regulation 8(8); Utilities Regulation 12(10). The utilities rules refer only to *materials* and *goods* under the contract. However, the exceptions to the rules discussed immediately below refer generally to the "subject-matter" of the contract (Services Regulations and Utilities Regulations), the "works" (Works Regulations) and goods (Supplies Regulations). Probably, to give effect to the objective of the directives, the rule, and the exceptions, should be construed as applying to all elements (works, supplies and services) of all types of contract.

[30] Works Regulation 8(8); Supply Regulation 8(8); Services Regulation 8(8); Utilities Regulation 12(10).

[31] Case C–359/93, *Commission v. Netherlands*, judgment of January 24, 1995.

[32] See pp. 581–585.

[33] The Court did not expressly refer to this point but it was put in argument, and implicitly rejected in the Court's ruling.

[34] Works Regulation 8(8); Supply Regulation 8(8); Services Regulation 8(8); Utilities Regulation 12(10). The Commission in its proposal for the Utilities Directive, considered it was not appropriate to exclude reference to particular goods, since it would be appropriate to exclude some goods because of their characteristics.

lar process might be acceptable where all firms use that process, or where a product which can meet the authority's requirements is made by only one manufacturer. However, to rely on this provision an authority would have to be sure that no alternatives are available, which may be virtually impossible in practice.

Another question is whether reference to a particular make or source may be considered not to favour particular firms or products where the words "or equivalent" are added. It appears, however, that the limitation was not intended to be used in this kind of case: this can be deduced from the fact that there is a separate provision permitting reference to a particular source, make, etc., where the words "or equivalent" are added *where there is no other way to describe the product*, as explained below. In the UNIX case the Court indicated that the reference to UNIX would have been acceptable if the phrase "or equivalent" was included, but this is probably explained on the basis that this was the only way to adequately describe the authority's requirements.[35]

---

[35] Para. 25 of the judgment.

THE RULES ON USE OF STANDARDS UNDER THE REGULATIONS — PUBLIC SECTOR

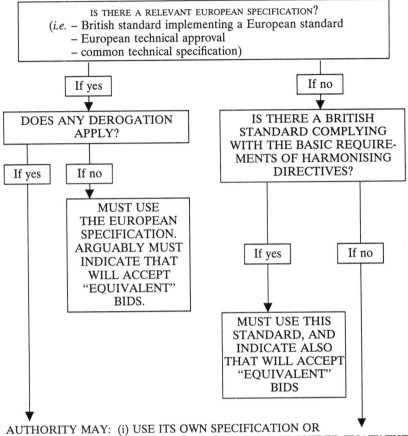

IS THERE A RELEVANT EUROPEAN SPECIFICATION?
(*i.e.* – British standard implementing a European standard
– European technical approval
– common technical specification)

If yes

If no

DOES ANY DEROGATION APPLY?

IS THERE A BRITISH STANDARD COMPLYING WITH THE BASIC REQUIRE-MENTS OF HARMONISING DIRECTIVES?

If yes

If no

MUST USE THE EUROPEAN SPECIFICATION. ARGUABLY MUST INDICATE THAT WILL ACCEPT "EQUIVALENT" BIDS.

If yes

If no

MUST USE THIS STANDARD, AND INDICATE ALSO THAT WILL ACCEPT "EQUIVALENT" BIDS

AUTHORITY MAY: (i) USE ITS OWN SPECIFICATION OR
(ii) USE OTHER STANDARDS, PROVIDED THAT[36] THE FOLLOWING ARE USED IN THE STATED ORDER OF PRIORITY
– British standards implementing international standards
– other British standards or technical approvals
– other standards

IN BOTH CASES: (i) THE AUTHORITY MUST INDICATE THAT IT WILL ACCEPT "EQUIVALENT" PRODUCTS OR SERVICES
(ii) IT MAY NOT REFER TO A SPECIFIC MAKE, SOURCE OR PROCESS *UNLESS* THIS IS JUSTIFIED BY THE SUBJECT-MATTER OR IS THE ONLY WAY TO DESCRIBE THE SUBJECT-MATTER

[36-37] It is not entirely clear whether these particular restrictions in the directives and regulations apply where there is a derogation from the requirement to use European specifications, as opposed to the case where no relevant European specifications exist.

THE RULES ON USE OF STANDARDS UNDER THE
REGULATIONS — UTILITIES SECTOR

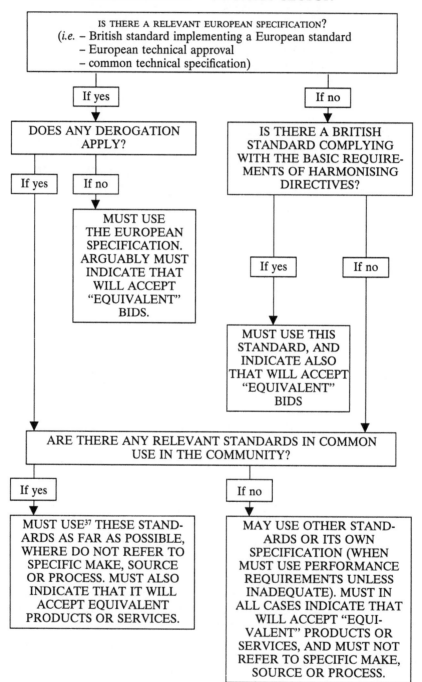

IS THERE A RELEVANT EUROPEAN SPECIFICATION?
(*i.e.* – British standard implementing a European standard
– European technical approval
– common technical specification)

If yes

If no

DOES ANY DEROGATION APPLY?

IS THERE A BRITISH STANDARD COMPLYING WITH THE BASIC REQUIRE-MENTS OF HARMONISING DIRECTIVES?

If yes

If no

If yes

If no

MUST USE THE EUROPEAN SPECIFICATION. ARGUABLY MUST INDICATE THAT WILL ACCEPT "EQUIVALENT" BIDS.

MUST USE THIS STANDARD, AND INDICATE ALSO THAT WILL ACCEPT "EQUIVALENT" BIDS

ARE THERE ANY RELEVANT STANDARDS IN COMMON USE IN THE COMMUNITY?

If yes

If no

MUST USE[37] THESE STAND-ARDS AS FAR AS POSSIBLE, WHERE DO NOT REFER TO SPECIFIC MAKE, SOURCE OR PROCESS. MUST ALSO INDICATE THAT IT WILL ACCEPT EQUIVALENT PRODUCTS OR SERVICES.

MAY USE OTHER STAND-ARDS OR ITS OWN SPECIFICATION (WHEN MUST USE PERFORMANCE REQUIREMENTS UNLESS INADEQUATE). MUST IN ALL CASES INDICATE THAT WILL ACCEPT "EQUI-VALENT" PRODUCTS OR SERVICES, AND MUST NOT REFER TO SPECIFIC MAKE, SOURCE OR PROCESS.

604

There is also an exception where the subject of the contract makes the use of a reference to a particular make, source, etc. "indispensable".[38] This allows reference to specific makes or requirements where this is the only way in which the authority's functional needs can be met: for example, where this is necessary to ensure compatibility with existing equipment. Probably it cannot be used where the purchaser's functional needs could be met by another product but this would cause extra difficulty or expense (for example, staff retraining). In this case the additional costs would, however, have to be taken into account in evaluating tenders.

There is also a further exception where this is the only way in which the subject-matter of the contract can be described in a way which is sufficiently precise and intelligible, provided, however, that the words "or equivalent" are appended to the description.[39] As noted above, it appears that it was accepted in the UNIX case that the use of UNIX could be justified on this basis, and that this may thus be referred to where the words "or equivalent" are added.

(v) LIMITATION ON THE POWER TO REJECT TENDERS REFERRING TO ALTERNATIVE STANDARDS

Works Regulation 20(5), Supply Regulation 21(6), Services Regulation 21(6) state that purchasers may not reject a tender on the ground that the technical specificiations in the tender have been defined by reference to (i) European specifications[40] or (ii) to the national technical specifications referred to in Works Regulation 8(7)(a) and (b)/Supply Regulation 8(7)(a) and (b)/Services Regulation 8(7)(a) and (b). The national technical specifications referred to in these provisions are: (i) British technical specifications complying with the basic requirements of Council Directives on technical harmonisation, such as the Construction Products Directive,[41] which are recognised as complying in accordance with the procedures laid down in the directive; and (ii) British technical specifications relating to design and method of calculation and execution of work(s) and use of materials and goods.

Utilities Regulation 20(5) states that utilities may not reject a tender on the ground that the technical specifications are drawn up in accordance with (i) European specifications or (ii) national technical specifications recognised as complying with the essential requirements of the

---

[38] Works Regulation 8(10)(a); Supply Regulation 8(10)(a), Services Regulation 8(10)(a); Utilities Regulation 12(12)(a).
[39] Works Regulation 8(10)(b); Supply Regulation 8(10)(b); Services Regulation 8(10)(b); Utilities Regulation 12(b). On the wording of these exceptions see further the comment in note 29.
[40] On the definition of European specifications see pp. 586–590.
[41] Council Directive 89/106/EEC, [1989] O.J. L40/12.

Construction Products Directive. (Unlike the public sector rules these regulations do not refer also to other "new approach" directives.)

It appears that the equivalent provisions in the directives were intended to make it clear that authorities may not reject tenders *on the sole basis* that a bidder has described the product in question by reference to different technical specifications, in certain cases where the product or service offered is adequate to meet the performance requirements of the authority. In other words, the authority must assess the product on its merits, and not reject it merely because it is not drawn up in accordance with the specifications actually used in the contract documents.

In the case where bids are drawn up by reference to European standards purchasers will in any case be in breach of the regulations if they have not referred to these standards in the first place, where applicable. Thus the above provisions make it clear that there is a requirement to accept such a product or service even where the correct specification has not been used by the purchaser.

As regards the reference made to British national technical specifications in the public sector regulations, this appears to have been an error. The provisions should include a reference to the national technical specifications of *other* relevant states also,[42] as does the provision in the Utilities Regulations which refers simply to "national" specifications, and must be construed in this way by the courts. The intention here is to make it clear that where a product or service is described in terms of the national standard of some other relevant state rather than the standard used in the tender documents it may only be rejected where it is unsuitable for a specific reason – that is, where it is not "equivalent". Again, an obligation to refer in the contract notice to the possibility of accepting "equivalent" products or services to those specified is in any case imposed by the Treaty and by Utilities Regulation 4(3). Thus this provision again merely clarifies that purchasers must accept such tenders even where the correct specifications have not been adopted.

Further, even in the cases not covered by the express rules above it appears that purchasers must accept products or services which meet their performance requirements but do not comply with the specifications. As explained, it will breach the Treaty, and in some cases (for example, where brand names are used) the regulations, to draw up tender documents which exclude suitable products, and an aggrieved provider may obtain a remedy to strike down the call for tenders or (for contracts covered by the regulations) an order for the authority to amend the documents.[43] It is a corollary of the Treaty obligations not to

---

[42] The relevant provisions in the directives refer to "national standards" in general, and are not intended to be confined to the national standards of the awarding state: see Works Directive Article 10(5) and Article 19; Supply Directive Article 5 and Article 16(1); Services Directive Articles 14(5) and Article 24(1).

[43] On these remedies see pp. 904–905.

refer to restrictive specifications that an obligation must arise not to *reject* suitable tenders – that is, those which comply with the specifications which the authority should have used. If this is correct then the provisions in the regulations referred to above are merely illustrations of a more general principle.

(c) COUNCIL DECISION 87/95 (THE "IT STANDARDS DECISION")[44]

(i) INTRODUCTION

In the fields of information technology and telecommunications rules on specifications are also contained in Council Decision 87/95,[45] the "IT Standards Decision". This Decision requires public sector authorities making information technology purchases to use, in certain cases, either European standards *or* accepted international standards. This obligation was introduced primarily to deal with the urgent need for compatibility in information technology markets, which was necessary to remove technological barriers to trade; to ensure that the benefits of information technology were maximised; and also to challenge the near monopoly of IBM in some of the relevant markets. The Decision slightly pre-dated the requirements in the procurement directives to use European standards in procurement, which were discussed above[46]: these general provisions were introduced for the first time only in the 1988 Supply Directive and 1989 Works Directive. These were modelled on the earlier provisions in the IT Standards Decision, although they differed to some extent: in particular, as explained below, it is arguable that the directives' obligation to refer to European standards in all cases in priority to international standards does not apply under the IT Standards Decision.

The Decision also imposes obligations on providers of public telecommunications networks. These seek to ensure that such networks can be connected with services designed for exchange of information and data between IT systems.

(ii) REQUIREMENT TO USE EUROPEAN OR INTERNATIONAL STANDARDS IN INFORMATION TECHNOLOGY PROCUREMENT

I. Scope
An obligation to use European or international standards applies to contracts for pecuniary interest made in writing for the purchase, lease,

---

[44] See also O'Connor, *A Guide to the Requirements of the IT Standards Decision and the Revised Supply Directive* (2nd ed. 1990), a report commissioned by the European Commission.
[45] [1987] O.J. L36/31.
[46] See pp. 586–596.

rental or hire purchase of products,[47] which are made by authorities subject to the Supply Directive,[48] for the supply of equipment relating to information technology. Information technology is defined as covering "the systems, equipment, components and software required to ensure the retrieval, processing and storage of information in all centres of human activity (home, office, factory, etc.), the application of which generally requires the use of electronics or similar technology".[49] The obligation does not apply, however, to all aspects of the specifications, but only so far as to ensure that the standards stipulated in the Decision "are used as the basis for the exchange of information and data for systems interoperability".[50] This clearly covers Open Systems Interconnection standards, the very purpose of which is to ensure systems interchange and interoperability, and also some physical media such as diskettes. It will not, on the other hand, apply to matters such as keyboard characteristics or safety requirements which do not affect interoperability.[51]

The obligation is not limited to supplies but may apply also to information technology services which are included in a contract covered by the Decision. It is not clear, however, whether the Decision covers only contracts which are governed by the Supply Directive or also covers those subject to the Services Directive. Probably it should apply regardless of the way in which the contract is classified.[52]

The provision covers IT purchases of such authorities which relate to all their activities – that is, both those activities generally covered by the public sector procurement regulations, and those activities subject to the Utilities Regulations.

There are no exemptions based on security or secrecy grounds like those which apply under the procurement directives.[53] However,

---

[47] Decision Article 5(1) and Article 1(14), which defines the scope of the relevant rule by cross-reference to contracts defined as "public supply contracts" in the directive.

[48] *Ibid.* This must be read as reference to the consolidated Supply Directive 93/36/EEC; see Article 33 of that directive.

[49] Decision Article 1(13).

[50] Decision Article 1(5).

[51] On what is covered see further O'Connor, above, p.16 and Annex 2.

[52] Article 5 states that the provision applies to public procurement orders relating to IT. "Public procurement orders" are defined in Article 1 of the Decision as those under Article 1 of the Supply Directive which are "concluded for the supply of equipment". Article 1 of the Supply Directive refers to "public supply contracts" which are effectively defined in that directive as all contracts involving the acquisition of products. However Article 2 of the Services Directive then states that contracts mainly for services are under the Services Directive, thereby removing them from the Supply Directive. "Mixed" contracts predominantly for services could still be regarded as "caught" by Article 1 of the Supply Directive, but then removed from the directive's application; alternatively, it could be suggested that such contracts are not under Article 1 of the Supply Directive at all. However, the fact that a derogation is included in the Services Directive and Regulations from the obligation to use European specifications in the case of conflict with the Decision (as to which see pp. 612–613 below) suggests that the decision does apply to services contracts.

[53] See pp. 152–154.

contracts for equipment designed for military use will be exempt insofar as provided for by Article 223 E.C.[54]

The Decision applies in general to purchases of a value[55] of 100,000 ECUs and above.[56] However, authorities may not decline to apply it to lower-value purchases where these lower-value purchases will prevent the use of the required standards in relation to contracts above 100,000 ECUs. This is directed, in particular, at the case where not to apply the Decision to lower-value purchases might lead to the procurement of equipment which is not compatible with purchases which are subject to the Decision (in which case the Decision allows for a derogation, as explained below). There are no detailed rules for calculating the value of contracts comparable to those found in the procurement directives themselves, but the Court of Justice will no doubt apply very similar rules in determining how the value of contracts is to be calculated.

II. The requirement to use European or international standards

For those matters referred to above, Article 5 of the Decision requires Member States to take the steps to ensure reference is made to European Standards or European pre-standards *or* to international standards accepted in the state awarding the contract.

A European standard[57] is defined as a standard approved pursuant to the statutes of the standardising bodies with which the Community has concluded agreements, namely CEN, CENELEC and ETSI.[58] A European pre-standard is defined as a "standard adopted under the reference 'ETS' in accordance with the procedures of the same bodies."[59] In requiring reference to pre-standards where applicable the Decision differs from the directives and regulations which do not require pre-standards to be used. However, even under the Decision, pre-standards need not be referred to unless stable.[60] It can be noted that, in light of the objective of seeking maximum interoperability in the IT sector, including with equipment from outside Europe, it is provided elsewhere in the Decision that in drawing up standards pursuant to the Decision the standardising bodies should generally adopt international standards unaltered, and that where it is necessary to supplement or clarify

---

[54] See pp. 857–863.
[55] The Decision does not refer to estimated value, as do the directives, but simply to value. However, it must be implied that the specifications are to be determined by reference to the estimated value.
[56] IT Standards Decision Article 5(7).
[57] "Standard" is defined in Article 1 of the IT Standards Decision as "a technical specification approved by a recognised standards body for repeated or continuous application, compliance with which is not compulsory". European standards will meet this definition of standard in any case.
[58] IT Standards Decision Article 1(7). On these bodies see pp. 579–580.
[59] IT Standards Decision Article 1(8).
[60] See further p. 612.

international standards in European standards (and the international standard cannot therefore be adopted unaltered) the European standard should not diverge from the international standard.

In recognition of this same objective the Decision also gives recognition to international standards. These must certainly be referred to if no European standard exists. The wording of the directive itself implies that international standards may be referred to instead of relevant European standards at the option of the purchaser, since no indication is given of any priority between them. However, another view – which would render the Decision more consistent with the directives – is that relevant European standards have priority.

An international standard is defined as one adopted by a recognised international standardising body. The main ones are ISO, IEC and CCITT,[61] although others are relevant to IT in specific fields such as energy and transport. Draft international standards are not within this provision, although authorities may of course use these if they choose to do so (and there are not relevant European standards which must be used instead). It is expressly stated that Member States themselves may *require* reference to draft international standards.[62]

(iii) OBLIGATIONS RELATING TO TELECOMMUNICATIONS PROCUREMENT

The IT Standards Decision is also concerned with specifications in contracts awarded by "telecommunications administrations" of Member States. This appears to cover all telecommunications bodies whether they are in the public sector or private sector.[63] Indeed, it appears to cover even those telecommunications bodies which are exempt from the Utilities Regulations because they operate in a competitive environment.[64]

Article 5(2) of the Decision requires states to take steps to ensure that telecommunications administrations "use functional specifications for the means of access to their telecommunications networks for those services specifically intended for exchange of information and data between information technology systems which themselves use the standards mentioned in [Article 5(1)]". The standards mentioned in Article 5(1) are European standards and pre-standards, and international standards, which it was explained above are required by the Decision to be used in certain IT procurement. A "functional

---

[61] On these bodies see p. 597.
[62] IT Standards Decision Article 5(4).
[63] The definition of "telecommunications authorities" in Article 5(1) of the IT Standards Decision refers to "recognised authorities or private enterprises in the Community which provide public telecommunications services". There is no definition of "telecommunications administrations" but it would substantially reduce the impact of the Decision if private bodies were not included within its scope.
[64] See pp. 409–410.

specification" means "the specification which defines, in the field of telecommunications, the application of one or more open system interconnection standards in support of a specific requirement for communication between information technology systems (standards recommended by such organisations as the Comite international télégraphique et téléphonique (CCITT) or the CEPT)".[65]

The Decision again applies to purchases of a value[66] of 100,000 ECUs and above,[67] except that authorities may not decline to apply it to lower value purchases where this would affect standards in contracts meeting the threshold.

(iv) DEROGATIONS

I. The availability of derogations

Derogations from the requirements to use European standards, international standards or functional specifications may be justified by reference to the following circumstances[68]:

(i) the need for operational continuity in existing systems. This is designed to cater for similar circumstances to the derogation in the procurement directives for cases of incompatibility.[69]

Like those provisions it may be invoked only where there is a clearly defined and recorded strategy for subsequent transition to international or European standards.

(ii) the genuinely innovative nature of certain products. A similar derogation is found in the regulations.[70] The derogation covers only products, not services, although the Decision may apply to services in supply contracts or even in services contracts.[71]

(iii) where the standard or functional specification is technically inadequate for its purpose for one of the following reasons:
– it does not provide the appropriate means of achieving information and data exchange or systems interoperability. This may apply, for example, where an existing standard has been adopted for use in a factory environment but is not appropriate for use in an office, for which a different standard is being developed. Another possible case is where no products conforming to the standard yet exist. Under the directives and regulations such problems may allow a utility to derogate from the

---

[65] IT Standards Decision Article 1(10).
[66] The Decision does not refer to estimated value, as do the directives, but simply to value. However, it must be implied that the specifications are to be determined by reference to the estimated value.
[67] IT Standards Decision Article 5(7).
[68] Listed in IT Standards Decision Article 5(3).
[69] On these see pp. 592–593.
[70] See pp. 593–594.
[71] See note 29 above.

utilities rules on the grounds that the standard is not "appropriate", but there will often be no available derogation from the public sector rules.

– the means (including testing) do not exist to establish to a satisfactory extent that the product conforms to the standard or functional specification. Arguably this covers only the case where testing is impossible and not simply the case where no Community-wide provision for conformance testing exists.[72]

– in the case of European pre-standards, the standard lacks the necessary stability for application.

(iv) where it is found that important reasons of cost effectiveness make use of the standard or functional specification inappropriate. This applies only where there has been a "careful consultation of the market". The procurement directives and regulations contain a derogation for cases of disproportionate costs or technical difficulties, and this derogation is likely to be interpreted in a similar way. Under the regulations it is provided that a strategy to change over to European specifications is in place to invoke the derogation, but there is no such provision in the IT Standards Decision.

II. The requirement to keep a record of derogations
Authorities invoking the derogations listed above must record their reasons for invoking the derogation, if possible, in the tender documents.[73]

They must also record the reasons in their internal documentation. The relevant information must be supplied on request to tenderers or to the Senior Official Group on standardisation in the field of information technology (SOGITS), which was set up to assist the Commission in its activities pursuant to the Decision.[74] This is, however, subject to requirements of commercial confidentiality.[75]

(v) RELATIONSHIP BETWEEN THE IT STANDARDS DECISION AND THE REGULATIONS

Some IT and telecommunications specifications fall within the scope of both the IT Standards Decision and the procurement regulations, usually the Supply Regulations. In this case the obligations in both the Decision and relevant regulations will generally apply. Thus, for example, where the regulations impose obligations which are not imposed at all under

---

[72] On the similar derogations under the regulations see pp. 591–592.
[73] IT Standards Decision Article 5(5).
[74] See IT Standards Decision Article 7. It is provided in Article 5(3) that it shall be open to other Member States to demonstate to the Committee that the derogations under (iii) and (iv) above have not been properly invoked on the basis that equipment conforming to the relevant specification has been used satisfactorily. (In relation to (iv) it must be shown that it has been used satisfactorily "on a normal commercial basis".)
[75] IT Standards Decision Article 5(5).

the Decision (such as the prohibition on use of proprietary names which applies under the regulations even where no formal standards exist), these will apply to procurements covered by the Decision as well as those procurements which are not.

However, in relation to the specific obligation to use European standards, there is a derogation in the regulations stating that they are not to apply where there is a "conflict" with the IT Standards Decision.[76] One view of the effect of this provision is that the regulations' obligation to use European specifications does not apply where the specification in question is already covered by an obligation in the IT Standards Decision – that is, the obligation to use European or international specifications.[77] If it is correct that the IT Standards Decision allows a purchaser to choose between European and international standards[78] then the effect of the above view on the priority of the Decision is that a purchaser enjoys more flexibility in relation to these IT specifications than in procurement generally. On this view of the priority of the Decision it also appears that the relevant derogations are those in the Decision and that those in the directives are not relevant. An alternative view is that no "conflict" exists between the Decision and regulations merely because the latter are more stringent, but only where the two impose mutually inconsistent obligations. On this view, procurement subject to both sets of provision is covered by both sets of rules on the use of European standards, which means such standards must (because of the regulations) always be referred to. If this second view were correct, however, it would be expected that the rules on procurement in the Decision would have been repealed and the matter left to the directives.

(vi) THE FUTURE OF THE IT STANDARDS DECISION

One of the main objectives of the IT Standards Decision was to break the monopoly in certain areas of government IT procurement which was held in the 1980s by IBM proprietary products. This situation has already come about, however, largely as a result of other developments in the industry. The obligation to refer to European standards in IT is now regarded by many purchasers as inconvenient, since the standards in question are less satisfactory to use than *de facto* industry standards, including those based on the proprietary system UNIX. In particular, the

---

[80] Supply Regulation 8(4)(c); Services Regulation 8(4)(c); Utilities Regulation 12(4)(c). There is no such provision in the Works Regulations or directive, presumably because it is assumed that the IT Standards Decision is not relevant to public works contracts, although theoretically this is possible.

[77] This view is taken by O'Connor, above, note 00, pp.17 and 28.

[78] As to which see p. 610. If, on the other hand, the view is preferred that authorities must always use European specifications where they exist, the question of whether the procurement directives apply as well as the Decision is less significant.

de facto standards are more detailed and precise, enabling them to be used to describe very specific requirements, and they also deal with other characteristics of IT products, as well as the problem of interoperability. Such standards have become widely used by other major purchasers, notably the United States defence procurement entities, and are now preferred in practice by European industry on both the supply and demand sides. However, governments and utilities in Europe, under the IT Standards Decision or the directives, are still required to define their requirements by reference to more unwieldy and lesser-known European standards.

It is possible that the IT Standards Decision may be revised or repealed in order to deal with the issue of IT Standards in procurement in a way which takes account of the developments which have occurred in the industry in the last 15 years. Alternatively (and perhaps more likely) it may be sought more generally to revise the existing European standards regime concerning information technology.

4. OTHER REQUIREMENTS CONCERNING CONTRACT SPECIFICATIONS

(1) THE REQUIREMENT TO DRAW UP SPECIFICATIONS

Although it is not expressly stated in the regulations, it is clear that a purchaser using an open or restricted procedure is required to draw up specifications for the contract, to provide the basis for the submission of formal bids. However, these may leave scope for considerable discretion for the bidder in deciding how the purchaser's basic requirements should be met, and it is also permitted to accept bids which propose some variations to the specifications.[79] On the other hand, it appears that it is not necessary to formulate precise specifications where a negotiated procedure is used. Support for these propositions can be found in the fact that under the Services Regulations one of the situations in which the use of the negotiated procedure is permitted is where it is not possible to formulate specifications with sufficient precision to use open or restricted procedures.[80]

---

[79] See p. 233.
[80] See p. 265.

(2) OBLIGATION TO INCLUDE SPECIFICATIONS IN THE CONTRACT DOCUMENTS

Where an authority wishes to lay down technical specifications relating to goods, services or works to be procured, the regulations generally require these to be included or referred to in the contract documents.[81]

The effect of this rule is to ensure that interested parties receive this information in writing, and also that its provision is subject to the rules concerning the supply of contract documents, such as the time-limits for despatch in response to a bidder's request.[82] It also has the effect that where specifications are required, these must be ready at the latest at the time the contract documents are made available to bidders (which in the open procedure is the time of advertisement and in the restricted procedure the time of issue of invitations).[83]

(3) THE PARTICIPATION OF BIDDERS IN ESTABLISHING SPECIFICATIONS

Purchasers may in some cases wish to consult with experts, including potential providers, before establishing specifications for a contract, especially in complex procurements (for example, the procurement of a sophisticated IT system) where the purchaser may have insufficient expertise to draw up the specifications itself. Consultation with persons interested in the contract, however, gives rise to a danger that these persons may influence the formulation of the specifications in a way which will improve their own chances of winning the contract. Such persons may also be advantaged by receiving more notice of the authority's requirements than other potential providers.

Where, as a result of such a consultation (or otherwise) specifications are drawn up with the effect of eliminating certain providers who are able to meet the authority's performance requirements, this infringes the general principles in the E.C. Treaty and may also breach the provisions

---

[81] Works Regulation 8(2), Services Regulation 8(2); Supply Regulation 8(2); Utilities Regulation 12(2). For supply contracts the Regulation appears to impose this requirement only for technical specifications relating to goods, whilst the Works Regulations refer only to requirements relating to the work(s) and goods used for the work(s); this follows both from the wording of Supply Regulation 8(2) and Works Regulation 8(2), and the definition of technical specifications, explained above. The Services Regulations refer only to the specifications for the services to be provided (Services Regulation 8(2)), which refers to "technical specifications" which the services must meet. As explained earlier, the definition of technical specifications given does not, read literally, cover requirements on non-works services, but obviously must be interpreted to cover such requirements. As with the definition of technical specifications, arguably this particular rule on specifications should be construed to cover the supplies, services and works elements of all contracts (as it does under the Utilities Regulations).

[82] See pp. 202–203.

[83] On the despatch of contract documents see pp. 202–203 and pp. 223–224.

of the directives and regulations, as explained above. These rules were considered above.[84] It is also probable that to involve one provider in establishing the specifications before the contract is advertised, so that that provider received greater notice of the authority's requirements, might be a breach of the general principle of equality under the directives.[85]

In its Proposal designed to align the Community directives with the WTO Agreement on Government Procurement the Commission is now also proposing a specific provision in the directives to deal with this issue. This states that contracting authorities and utilities "shall not seek or accept, in a manner which would have the effect of precluding competition, advice which may be used in the preparation of specifications for a specific procurement from anyone that may have a commercial interest in the procurement".[86]

The exact impact of this provision is not entirely clear. Clearly it may be infringed where, as a result of consultation, the specifications are set in a restrictive way so as to infringe the Treaty. One view, however, is that it may go further than the existing Treaty rules by affecting the position not merely where the specifications eliminate certain providers who can meet the authority's performance requirements: it may be construed as applying where advice is received which affects what the performance requirements should be, rather than merely the technical question of how requirements should be described. However, it is rather unlikely that this latter case is intended to be covered. The proposed provision could also be invoked where as a result of consultation on the specifications one firm received greater notice of the procurement than other interested parties. However, as noted above, such conduct may in any case infringe the general principle of equality of treatment of providers.[87]

Generally, any consultation will occur before the contract is advertised. However, in some restricted or negotiated procedures the authority may seek to consult with providers only once it has established who is interested in the contract. It has already been explained that it is unclear whether consultations with interested providers are permitted in a restricted procedure prior to issuing invitations, or whether the procedure must be conducted wholly on the basis of documents.[88] In a negotiated procedure, on the other hand, discussions are permitted on this matter, as on any others, provided that all providers are treated equally in accordance with the general principle of equality of treatment.

---

[84] See pp. 581–602.
[85] On this principle see pp. 180–181.
[86] COM (95) 107 Final, 95/0079 (COD), Article 1(5) (adding to Article 14 of the Services Directive), Article 2(3) (adding to Article 8 of the Supply Directive) and Article 3(3) adding to Article 10 of the Works Directive) and 95/0080 (COD), Article 1(5) (adding to Article 18 of the Utilities Directive).
[87] On this see pp. 180–181.
[88] See pp. 223–224.

(4) OBLIGATION ON UTILITIES TO SUPPLY ADVANCE INFORMATION

Under the utilities rules, there is an obligation for a utility to supply to providers who request it a copy of any technical specifications which are regularly laid down as terms of its contracts[89] and with copies of specifications to be used in contracts which have already been the subject of a periodic indicative notice.[90] Although a PIN must give a reasonably precise indication of the subject-matter of a contract in order to qualify as a call for competition,[91] it is submitted that this does not necessarily entail that all the detailed specifications are available at the time of the PIN; and in this case, it is suggested, the obligation is to provide detailed specifications as soon as they have been drawn up. Where specifications are based on documents available to firms, the utility need only tell firms what these are[92] and need not supply a copy; this would apply, for example, where the utility uses standards approved by recognised standardising institutions, which are available from these bodies. There is nothing to stop utilities charging a fee for providing documents which it does supply,[93] in the same way as a fee may be charged for contract documents.

The information supplied will enable firms to determine in advance whether they are likely to be interested in contracts with the utility, and to prepare themselves for competition. A rule requiring a purchaser to supply specifications which it uses regularly would be useful in the public sector, also.

(5) THE POWER TO CHANGE SPECIFICATIONS DURING THE AWARD PROCEDURE

After a contract has been advertised a purchaser may wish to change the specifications – for example, because new technology has made the old specifications obsolete, or because budgetary or other considerations have led the purchaser to change its requirements. The regulations do not deal expressly with this issue. However, it is submitted that changes to the specifications are permitted, provided that these are not "substantial", in the sense that the altered specifications are so different that they would be likely to attract providers who did not consider bidding on the original contract. Such a test strikes an appropriate balance between the

---

[89] Utilities Regulations 12(13).
[90] *Ibid.*
[91] See pp. 479–480.
[92] Utilities Regulation 12(14).
[93] This was the view of the Commission in making its original proposal for the Utilities Directive: see *Public Procurement in the Excluded Sectors*, Bulletin of the European Communities, Supplement 6/88, p.90.

need to ensure that all requirements are publicised under the regulations, and the need to avoid the burden which would be imposed on both the purchaser and providers participating in the procedure if it were necessary to re-open the procedure for every minor alteration.

Support for such a test is provided by the analogy of the rules on the use of the negotiated procedure following the failure of an open or restricted procedure. These rules allow the use of a negotiated procedure without advertisement where no tenders are received or all those received are irregular or from unqualified providers, but only where the terms of the contract remain "substantially" unaltered.[94] Thus, with a failed procedure it is permitted to proceed without advertising the contract, even where changes are made, provided that these are not substantial. It would be odd if it were not also permitted to proceed without re-advertising where such small changes are made in an open or restricted procedure which has *not* failed.

This test is appropriate regardless of the stage of the award procedure at which it is decided to alter the specifications – whether before the tender deadline, after bids have been received, after they have been opened, and even after the award has been announced. This test should also be applied where the contract has actually been concluded with a provider. In other words, it should be permitted to negotiate non-substantial changes to the contract once it has been made without the need to award a new contract under the regulations' procedures.[95]

(6) THE RULES ON VARIATIONS

The general rule under both the public sector and utilities regulations is that purchasers may not accept bids which do not comply with the specifications.[96] One exception is that purchasers using specifications which contravene the Treaty or regulations are compelled to accept bids which comply with the specifications which the authority should have referred to.[97]

Other provisions in the regulations which concern this problem are those on the acceptance of "variations". A variation may be defined as a proposal for a product or service which is designed to provide a solution to the purchaser's needs which differs from the solution which the purchaser has specified in the contract documents. Purchasers are often willing to consider variations submitted by providers, which may offer a superior approach to the one contemplated by the purchaser itself. For example, an authority seeking to provide a river-crossing for traffic may, on the basis of its own knowledge, determine that a bridge of a

---

[94] See pp. 250–251.
[95] See pp. 232–234 on the meaning of "contract" for the purpose of the regulations.
[96] Case C–243/89, *Commission v. Denmark* ("Storebaelt"), judgment of June, 22 1993.
[97] See p. 583.

particular design would provide the best solution. However, providers may be able to suggest solutions – for example, a bridge of a radically different design – which may be more effective. In this case the authority may wish to advertise a contract for the bridge according to a design set out in the specifications, but may also indicate its willingness to consider other proposals for providing the traffic-crossing. In such a case it will be useful to indicate the essential requirements which any crossing will need to meet, such as the volume of traffic which must be catered for.

The consideration of variations under the regulations is dealt with in Works Regulation 20(4), Supply Regulation 21(4), Services Regulation 21(4) and Utilities Regulation 21(4). These expressly allow consideration of variations where the basis of the award is to be most economically advantageous offer.

Where variations are to be used the Works Regulations provide that the willingness to consider variations must be considered in the contract notice. The Supply, Services and Utilities Regulations, on the other hand, provide that the purchaser must state in the notice where applicable that it is *not* prepared to accept variations. There is no sensible reason for this discrepancy between the different regulations. In practice, it is desirable for purchasers to state in every notice their intention in relation to variations, to avoid doubts which may arise where nothing is included in the notice, as discussed below.

The purchaser must state any minimum requirements in the contract documents. It may subsequently accept only those variations which meet the minimum requirements.

The purchaser must also state in those documents any specific requirements for the presentation of offers involving variations.

It is not clear what is the position where the required information is not given to bidders. In particular, if variations are not mentioned in the contract notice and no minimum requirements are specified, is the purchaser permitted, or required, to accept such variations? It could be argued that this is required under the Supply, Services and Utilities Regulations since under those provisions the purchaser must specifically indicate where it does *not* intend to consider variations, but not under the Works Regulations. However, it is doubtful if different rules were intended and the same approach should apply to all the regulations.

One possibility is to neither require nor permit variations in any case where minimum requirements are not specified. Another is to permit providers to request, or seek a remedy, for amendment of the documents to require the purchaser to include its minimum requirements, and to require variations to be considered where this has been done, but not otherwise. A third approach is to require the authority to consider variations but on the basis that there are no definite minimum requirements. It is not clear which interpretation is correct.

CHAPTER 12

CONTRACTING OUT, MARKET TESTING AND COMPULSORY COMPETITIVE TENDERING

1. INTRODUCTION

In considering how their needs for services or goods are to be met governments must decide whether to provide or manufacture these "in-house" – with their own employees – or to obtain them from outside sources – either from the private firms, or, occasionally, from other public bodies. Traditionally governments have tended to rely more heavily on in-house provision than has the private sector. A variety of services have been provided in-house, both those needed to support government functions (for example, accounting and office cleaning), and those involving provision of a service directly to the public (such as refuse collection and street cleaning). Public bodies have also often employed their own construction and maintenance teams, particularly for routine or minor work. It is less common for governments to run manufacturing establishments, but this is not unknown, particularly in the defence sector.[1]

Traditional practices on in-house provision have in the last fifteen years been challenged by the Conservative central government. This is one aspect of a wider drive towards competition in government and the economy, which has led to a number of activities being privatised altogether.[2] With activities for which the government does remain responsible, public bodies have been required to conduct a review to determine whether these should be carried out in-house, or would be better contracted out to external providers. Such a review introduces an element of competition into deciding who is to perform the services, so that they cease to be an area of the economy immune from competitive pressures. For central government the policy has been implemented through guidelines or administrative direction. With local government, on the other hand, legislation has been enacted, which requires market

---

[1] See p. 849.
[2] See generally, Ascher, *The Politics of Privatisation* (1987). Contracting out policy is placed in this wider context in *The Government's Guide to Market Testing* (1993), section 1, which instructs managers to consider first whether any existing function should not be ceased completely or privatised, before addressing the question of whether contracting out is appropriate. On this wider context see also Craig, *Administrative Law* (3rd ed., 1994), Chap. 3, *passim*.

testing of specified functions, and regulates the process in detail. This regime for local authorities is referred to as "compulsory competitive tendering" (CCT).

This chapter considers the general issues arising in this area of law. First, it outlines the objectives of the government's policy on contracting out and market testing, and notes some of its wider legal and constitutional implications. Secondly, an overview is given of the development and current application of government policy. Finally, the chapter examines the impact on contracting out of the European Community's Acquired Rights Directive. The detail of the legislative regime relating to CCT is considered separately in Chapters 13 and 14.

2. THE OBJECTIVES OF GOVERNMENT POLICY

In some cases contracting out may be preferred to in-house provision for strategic reasons: for example, where management of an in-house operation is considered to detract unduly from the "core function" of policy making.[3] In other cases, strategic concerns may point to in-house provision, as with most policy-making functions. In many cases, however, the decision whether or not to contract out is now based mainly on the relative cost and/or efficiency in delivering the service of the in-house unit, on the one hand, and external providers, on the other. Generally, a formal review is carried out to compare the two, a process referred to as "market testing". Frequently, this takes the form of a tendering procedure, in which the in-house team bids for the work in competition with the private sector.

A market testing exercise often helps public bodies to obtain better value for money as a result of efficiency gains. Private enterprise may offer better value because of the spur of operating in a competitive market (which means, for example, that it makes better use of resources or is more innovative) or because its operation in a wide market provides it with economies of scale and other advantages over an in-house unit. Market testing reveals this information, thus allowing savings to be exploited. In some cases the in-house team may potentially be the most efficient, but is not meeting its potential because its in-house market is guaranteed; here the competition of market testing provides a spur to efficiency, and again savings are achieved. In-house units have in fact won most competitions, but in many cases only after improving their

---

[3] A significant number of cases subject to market testing or contracting out between 1992 and 1994 under its "Competing for Quality" initiative for central government services (as to which see the text below) have been contracted out on a strategic basis, without an opportunity for an in-house bid: see *The Civil Services: Taking forward Continuity and Change* (1995) Cm. 2748, p.34.

own performance.[4] A report commissioned by the Department of the Environment and published in 1993 on the impact of CCT in local government found average costs savings of around 7 per cent across the range of activities subjected to competition under the Local Government Act 1988 (and over 10 per cent in building cleaning, grounds, maintenance and refuse collection).[5] These were ascribed mainly to improvements in productivity and work methods.[6] Whilst such figures are difficult to ascertain with precision (as acknowledged by the authors of the Department of the Environment's study), and whilst some of the savings following CCT may arise from improvements in technology which cannot be attributed to CCT,[7] it seems clear at least that the savings made are significant.

Savings often arise, however, not only from efficiency gains, but as a result of changes to the terms and conditions of the workforce.[8] In the United Kingdom blue-collar wages have traditionally been less favourable in the private than the public sector, because of the combination of union power and "fair employment" policies in public employment.[9] Private firms have therefore often been able to win work from an in-house unit, because of lower labour costs, and have also sought to cut back on costs in competing for the work against each other; whilst public bodies seeking to retain work in-house have in some cases responded by adjusting the pay and conditions of their own employees. Thus one effect of strategic contracting out or market testing is financial savings at the expense of worker protection. During the period in which the modern contracting out and market testing policies have been developed, the government has generally promoted a free labour market, and it is no coincidence that its former policy of requiring "fair wages" to be paid by firms doing work for the central government was abolished in 1983,[10] the same year in which the government began to pursue contracting out and

---

[4] See for example, Shaw, Fenwick and Foreman, "Compulsory Competitive Tendering for Local Government Service: the Experiences of Local Authorities in the North of England 1988–92 (1994) 72 *Public Administration* 201, p.207, reporting an in-house success rate of 85 per cent in the cases studied but only following significant changes in the in-house unit; see Walsh and Davies, *Competition and Service: the Impact of the Local Government Act 1988* (1993).

[5] Walsh and Davies, *Competition and Service: the Impact of the Local Government Act 1988* (1993), p. 143.

[6] *Ibid*, pp.145–147.

[7] This point has been made by the Audit Commission. The competition introduced by CTT may in some cases itself, however be a spur to innovation.

[8] *Ibid*. On this consideration see also, for example, H.M. Treasury, *Using Private Enterprise in Government* (1986) (a review of contracting out in government departments) and Public Service Privatisation Research Unit, *Privatisation: Disaster for Quality* (1992). Savings have been attributed not mainly to changes in basic pay but to other changes such as reduction of overtime and bonus schemes, increased part-time working (savings on national insurance contributions and other worker benefits), and decreased holiday and sickness benefits.

[9] On fair wages policies in public employment, see pp. 805–807.

[10] See p. 807.

market testing with particular vigour. From the central government's point of view this aspect of the policy is thus seen as a benefit.[11] Recently, however, the possibility for such savings has been substantially diminished by the European Community's Acquired Rights Directive which, as recently interpreted, has the effect of firms taking over activities which were previously carried on in-house in many cases having to retain the in-house employees on the same terms as they enjoyed as government employees. This is considered further below.

A more disputed issue is the impact of contracting out and market testing on quality of service provision. The potential for quality improvements is often cited as a benefit of such policies.[12] This may arise because such processes require a careful definition of the services for the contract specification; this may lead to greater attention to formulating and monitoring quality standards, to be met by both external and internal providers.[13] Quality may also be improved by the fact that monitoring is carried out by a body external to the service provider: where an authority is responsible for providing the service as well as monitoring it, it is unlikely to be so critical of defects. On the other hand, defects of quality are difficult to prove, making a threat of contractual sanctions risky, and it may in any case be inconvenient in practice to terminate the contract. In addition, problems have occurred with contracting out new services where firms inexperienced in certain activities or in the scale of operations required, have bid too low or otherwise been too ambitious, and have been unable to deliver what was promised (although these problems may diminish as the private sector gains more experience).

The competition introduced through contracting out or market testing can also provide benefits for the economy as a whole, similar to those sought under the European Community's policy on open procurement, which seeks to promote other aspects of competition (fair competition between firms from different Member States).[14] Thus both in-house units and private enterprise may be stimulated to innovation and efficiency,

---

[11] The need for in-house units to lower wages and conditions to retain jobs has also undermined centralised bargaining and the power of the public sector unions, another factor regarded as a benefit by government.

[12] The study by Walsh and Davies, above, Chap. 12, claims that the quality specification for services subject to CCT under the LGA 1988 improved in a quarter of cases above the previous level of service provision, and was maintained in others; and that the service was delivered in accordance with the specification in 85–90 per cent of cases. The central government has maintained that with services contracted out between 1992 and 1994 under the "Competing for Quality" initiative, as to which see below, quality improved in a third of cases, and was maintained in others: *The Civil Service: Taking forward Continuity and Change* (1995), Cm.2748.

[13] See Harden, *The Contracting State* (1992), Chap. 7. Under the CCT legislation internal providers winning an award are now required to provide the service in accordance with the specification. More generally, the Citizen's Charter Initiative has since 1991 sought to improve the definition and monitoring of standards of public services, whether carried out in-house or by external contractors.

[14] See pp. 45–50.

whilst the larger market made available to private enterprise may allow such enterprise to take advantages of economies of scale which benefit the rest of the market as well as government. The government may also gain indirectly from contracting out, in ways which are often not measured in a market testing exercise, notably through payment of taxes by the private sector on the work done.

On the other hand, apart from the issue of quality control, there are a number of other potential costs and difficulties. These include the resource costs of running a tendering process and of monitoring outside service providers[15] – which should, however, diminish with increased public sector experience – and the loss of morale for government employees, leading to difficulties in retaining and recruiting staff. The point has also been made that a rigid structure involving periodic retendering of contracts may be detrimental to the kind of long-term co-operative relationship which may be the most effective framework for the delivery of complex services.[16] For certain services this possibility is already excluded by the tendering obligations under the European Community procurement rules, but the CCT legislation also imposes rigid tendering obligations in relation to certain services – such as legal services – which are not heavily regulated under Community law, and for which a "partnering" approach may bring great benefits.[17] Further, in those cases where the TUPE labour protection rules do not apply or have not been followed, it has been argued that public welfare, costs, such as the cost in unemployment benefits, may greatly exceed any efficiency sawings from CCT.[18]

All these factors must be considered in assessing the success and desirability of policies on contracting out and market testing, and the way in which such policies should be operated. Much of the criticism of recent government policy has focused on its detrimental effect on wages and conditions, and the "hidden agenda" of reduction in the power of the public service unions. At local government level, complaints have also been made over the particular manner of implementation of CCT policy, as will be explained below. However, such criticisms should not obscure the potential efficiency benefits which may be realised from a well-designed market testing programme.

---

[15] See Walsh and Davies, above, note 5, pp.147–48, who found that although such costs existed they were probably not significant.

[16] See further Vincent-Jones, "The Limits of Contractual Order in Public Sector Transacting" (1994) L.S. 364.

[17] See Chaps. 3–11.

[18] See Equal Opportunities Commission, *The Gender Impact of CCT: Calculation of the National Costs and Savings of CCT* (1995).

3. LEGAL AND CONSTITUTIONAL IMPLICATIONS OF THE CONTRACTING OUT OF SERVICE PROVISION[19]

(1) GENERAL PRINCIPLES

The move towards contracting out of service provision has wider implications of constitutional interest.

First, the application of a number of legal and administrative doctrines for the protection of citizens may potentially depend on whether a person involved in carrying out a particular service is the employee of government or of an external provider. These issues are particularly important in cases where external firms provide services – such as refuse collection – directly to the public, or otherwise come into direct contact with citizens – for example, in providing prison management services. In general it is submitted that such legal and administrative doctrines should be interpreted to preserve the protections afforded to citizens. As *Craig*, has argued, where a public body chooses to fulfil its statutory functions by contracting out to a private undertaking "it would be contrary to principle for the citizens' protection to be reduced as a result of this organisational choice.[20] As he points out, protections can be preserved either by preserving the public law responsibility of the public body itself, or by subjecting the provider himself to public law doctrines.

One issue, for example, is the availability of redress through the Commissioners for Administration ("Ombudsmen").[21] For example, it is clear that excessive delay in processing benefit claims can be "maladministration" and so subject to the jurisdiction of the Parliamentary Commissioner for Administration when this activity is carried out by a government department or agency, but could a complaint be made to the Commissioner if a benefit scheme were administered by an external provider? In fact, the Acts conferring jurisdiction on the Commissioners provide for investigations of actions of those acting for *or on behalf of* the public bodies which are subject to the Commissioners' jurisdiction.[22] It appears that this is to be construed to apply to action taken by independent contractors in administering functions on behalf of government, as well as to actions by government employees.[23]

---

[19] See further Craig, *Administrative Law* (3rd ed., 1994), pp.93–96, 112–113 and 734–738; Freedland, "Privatising *Carltona:* Part II of the Deregulation and Contracting Out Act 1994" [1995] P.L. 21; Department of Trade and Industry, *Deregulation and Contracting Out Act 1994: An Explanatory Guide* (November 1994).

[20] Craig, *Administrative Law* (3rd ed., 1994), p.112.

[21] See generally Craig, above, pp.127–141.

[22] Parliamentary Commissioner Act 1967, s.5(1); Local Government Act 1974, s.26; National Health Service Act 1977, s.115.

[23] This view has been taken by the Parliamentary Commissioner himself (see the *Annual Report for 1992,* p.2, para. 5) and also by the Commissioners for Local Administration.

Another such issue is the application of judicial review to actions by such external providers. It is submitted that the right of review against the public authority which has contracted out the function is maintained: the duty to ensure compliance with these principles is an absolute duty which attaches to the authority regardless of the instrument (employee or independent contractor) chosen for performance of the function. It is also arguable that the provider himself is subject to judicial review, on the basis that in carrying out a service for which government has a statutory responsibility the provider is himself exercising a public law function.[24] A similar question of whether an external provider, or that provider's own employees, may be said to exercise a public function also arises in the context of the special public law tort of misfeasance in public office, which imposes liability for the exercise of a "public" power in a manner which is knowingly unlawful, or malicious.[25] It is submitted that here also there is an exercise of a public function by the private party where action is taken in the course of a function for which responsibility is conferred by statute on a public body, and that thus liability may be imposed on the private party with the appropriate knowledge or malicious intention.[26] Some responsibility for the actions in question might also be placed on the authority itself, as explained in the next paragraph.

As well as the application of special public law doctrines there is the question of attribution of responsibility under general legal principles of tort and the criminal law. Here, to change the relationship of service providers from employees of the government to independent contractors may have legal consequences. For example, in tort government is vicariously liable for the torts of its own servants but is not generally liable for the torts of the employees of its independent contractors carrying out functions or providing services on the government's behalf, since there is in general no vicarious liability for the torts of independent contractors. In certain exceptional cases, however, there is responsibility for the torts of independent contractors by virtue of a non-delegable duty to ensure that no tortious act is committed by an independent contractor, and this concept might be used to impose liability for tort of such contractors carrying out functions on behalf of government where there are special policy reasons to do so. In *S. v. Walsall M.B.C.*,[27] which concerned the liability of a local authority for the negligence of foster parents towards a child placed in their care by the authority, the court

---

[24] That bodies which are in form wholly private may exercise "public law" functions for the purpose of judicial review was accepted by the courts in *R. v. Panel on Take Overs and Mergers, ex p. Datafin plc* [1987] Q.B. 87.

[25] On this tort see Arrowsmith, *Civil Liability and Public Authorities* (1992), pp.226–234.

[26] There is also a "public law" tort principle allowing exemplary damages for "oppressive, arbitrary or unconstitutional" action by government servants: *Rookes v. Barnard* [1967] A.C. 1129. It also seems appropriate that this should cover independent contractors carrying our statutory functions.

[27] [1985] 1 W.L.R. 1150.

rejected the view that there is any *general* liability for the negligent actions of independent contractors carrying out statutory functions for others, a view which appears correct in principle. However, liability might be imposed in special cases, which could include the case of liability for the special public law tort of misfeasance in public office, where private firms are less likely to have appropriate insurance.[28]

Finally, the question also arises not merely of the extent to which providers share the "burdens" of public law – such as susceptibility to judicial review and liability in misfeasance – but also of their participation in the "benefits" of public status, such as the application of Crown immunities. The particular question of Crown immunities was discussed in Chapter 2 where it was suggested that these may be invoked only where this is specifically authorised by the Crown.[29] In relation to the right of access to confidential information, which may by law be limited to the government bodies to which the information is provided, it can be noted that the matter is dealt with expressly and comprehensively by the Deregulation and Contracting Out Act 1994, section 75 and schedule 15, which provides for any external provider exercising a governmental function[30] to have access to information where this is necessary or expedient. At the same time, the Act providers for such external providers to be subject to the same safeguards against disclosure as apply to the government.[31]

This need for appropriate development of legal principles is mirrored by the requirement for government itself to develop and adapt its own accountability mechanisms to take account of the changed framework for service provision. For example, it is necessary to ensure – for example, through appropriate drafting and supervision of contracts – that control is retained over policy issues which the government does not desire to relinquish to an outside operator, and that provision for redress of complaints from members of the public is not diminished.

---

[28] There may also be a non-delegable duty where an independent contractor acts on behalf of the authority in exercising special powers not generally held by private persons, at least in the case of powers of entry onto land: see *Darling v. Att.-Gen.* [1950] 2 All E.R. 793, and the discussion in Arrowsmith, *Civil Liability and Public Authorities* (1992) at pp.194–195. And see also the decisions of the Court of Appeal in *Murphy v. Brentwood D.C.* [1992] 2 W.L.R. 944 (rev'd by H.L. on other grounds), holding that an authority owes a non-delegable duty to ensure that reasonable care is taken by an external provider in inspecting building plans for the authority: see Arrowsmith, above, p.196. (It is not clear that in the latter case there is a tort by the independent contractor himself, since the careless action involves merely a failure to prevent damage, for which a private party is not generally liable, although liability is (according to the decision in *Anns v. Merton L.B.C.* [1978] A.C. 728) placed on the authority by virtue of its statutory responsibilities).

[29] See pp. 42–43.

[30] These provisions are of general application and are not limited to functions contracted our pursuant to the 1994 Act.

[31] Deregulation and Contracting Out Act 1994, s.76 and Sched. 15, para. 9. And see also Sched. 15, para. 8, placing an implied contractual obligation on the provider to take all reasonable steps to prevent unauthorised disclosure.

(2) THE EXPRESS PROVISIONS RELATING TO FUNCTIONS CONTRACTED OUT PURSUANT TO THE DEREGULATION AND CONTRACTING OUT ACT 1994

Whatever the general principles relating to the matters discussed above, special rules may apply in the case of functions which have been contracted out pursuant to a specific order under sections 69 or 70 of the Deregulation and Contracting Out Act 1994 (which provide for contracting out certain functions previously required to be performed in house).[32] Section 72(2) of the Act provides that, in such a case, acts and omissions by the independent contractor or his employees in, or in connection with, the exercise (or purported exercise) of the function shall for all purposes be treated as the acts or omissions of the Minister, office holder or local authority to which the function is entrusted. This indicates that the public body in question will be held responsible if that public body would have borne a legal responsibility had the acts and intentions of the provider been those of the public body or its employees, and that this will apply regardless of whether the provider himself is subject to any legal responsibility for his conduct. Thus, for example, if no hearing is given to a citizen before the provider takes a decision, but such a hearing would be required under the principles of natural justice if the public body itself had taken the decision, the public body itself will be amenable to judicial review, even if (contrary to what was suggested above) the provider himself would not be amenable to judicial review. Similarly, if a citizen is injured by the negligence of the provider it appears the public body will be held directly (not vicariously) liable, as if the negligent act had been that of that body or its employees. Since it appears irrelevant whether the provider himself is liable, liability under public law rules, such as the tort of misfeasance, may be imposed on the public body for the conduct of the provider even if (again contrary to the argument made above) this tort does not apply to external providers exercising public functions.[33]

It is not clear whether the above provision removes any liability which the provider himself would have under general legal principles, but it is submitted that this is not the case: the provision operates merely to create an additional liability, on the part of the government contracting out the function in question.

Section 72(3)(b) provides for an exception to the principle in section 72(2) for criminal proceedings brought in respect of the acts or omissions of the external provider, making it clear that the public body does not bear criminal responsibility for the acts of the provider.

---

[32] See further pp. 26–27.

[33] On the other hand, it can be argued that no liability will arise on the part of the public body if the public body enjoys relevant immunities, even if these immunities are not shared by the provider. This appears to be a loophole in the provision.

It is also provided, in section 72(3)(a), that section 72(2) shall not apply "for the purposes of so much of any contract made between the [provider] and the Minister, Office Holder or local authority as relates to the exercise of the function". The meaning of this exception is unclear, but probably it seeks merely to provide that the independent contractor's acts or omissions are not to be treated as those of the Minister etc so far as concerns the provider's own obligations under the contract.

These provisions attaching responsibility to public bodies where it might not otherwise arise apply, as indicted, only to functions contracted out pursuant to the Act, and not to all cases where providers exercise statutory or other public functions for government. The Act refers to cases closely associated with the idea of "core" government functions, for which it is therefore particularly important to retain governmental accountability for those directly affected by the function.

4. THE IMPACT OF MARKET TESTING FOR INTERNATIONAL COMPETITION

Another point of interest is the impact of market testing in the context of the procurement liberalisation policy. Market testing exposes services to competition from all states which have access to the United Kingdom procurement market, since if an external award is contemplated the procedures in the procurement regulations must be followed, and access must be given under such procedures to bidders from the European Community and a variety of other states. In the case of CCT, an authority is legally obliged to award the contract to the best bidder, regardless of nationality. With other authorities, domestic legislation does not preclude a decision to retain the work in-house, even following a market testing exercise in which the in-house unit fails to offer the best bid,[34] but in practice this is unlikely, and would obviously contravene Community law and other international obligations if the motive was simply to keep the work within the United Kingdom. In practice, market testing thus increases the openness of the United Kingdom market to providers. This is felt, in particular, with construction, and with other services which are "priority" services under the Community services regime[35] and which are covered by the WTO Agreement on Government Procurement with effect from January 1, 1996.[36] More generally, a state's policy on contracting out inevitably has a significant effect on the degree of market openness, and differences between states may (unless taken into account in negotiations) give rise to a lack of reciprocity in market

---

[34] This may, however, be subject to some constraints under an implied contract between the government and bidders: see pp. 37–40.
[35] On the concept of priority services see pp. 132–135.
[36] On this see pp. 774–781.

access. Under the European Community regime, Article 43 of the Services Directive which provides for a review of the directive by 1996 expressly provides that the Commission shall consider the effect on market-openness of the in-house provision of services.

5. AN OVERVIEW OF CURRENT POLICY

(1) CENTRAL GOVERNMENT

Within government departments and other bodies for which government Ministers are responsible, including those of the National Health Service, the government's philosophy on contracting out dates from when the Conservative government took office in 1979. In contrast with the position in relation to local government, it has been enforced through guidance and administrative direction, rather than legislation.

First, in the early 1980s managers were encouraged, though generally not required,[37] to consider contracting out and to employ market testing. Many did so, mainly in relation to blue-collar support services such as cleaning and catering, and also construction and maintenance, and significant contracting out occurred as a result. From 1985 the policy became more prescriptive, with departments being required to contract out certain services, beginning with cleaning, laundry, and some security and maintenance, and later extending to other services. In November 1991 the policy received a new impetus with the publication of a White Paper, entitled "Competing for Quality: Buying Better Public Services",[38] which suggested that the widest possible range of activities should be market tested, and identified a wide range of (mainly white-collar) activities considered to offer scope for such market testing.[39] The Paper indicated that the onus would be on managers to justify decisions to retain functions in-house without testing the market, and Departments and "Next Steps" Agencies were to be required to set targets for "testing" areas of activity. A presumption was also adopted that new activities should be contracted out in preference to creating an in-house capability.[40] In June 1992 it was announced that departments would be directed to adopt market testing for certain further functions. Contracting out is now not limited to "support" services but, as in local government, has been extended to service areas where external providers are in direct contact with citizens

---

[37] As far back as 1983, however, managers in the Health Service were directed by administrative circular to test the market for certain designated services: circular HC(83)18, "Competitive Tendering in the Provision of Domestic Catering and Laundry Services".

[38] Cm. 1730 of 1991.

[39] The Paper also highlighted possibilities for further measures in the National Health Service.

[40] See *The Government's Guide to Market Testing* (1993) at 1.7.

– the most notable, and controversial being prison operation and management.[41] The effects of the general policy are difficult to evaluate, but the government has claimed significant savings. For example, it has stated that savings of £400 million were achieved between April 1992 and September 1994 as a result of a review of over £2 billion worth of activities under the "Competing for Quality" initiative.[42]

The government remains committed to its policy of competition through market testing and contracting out. Recently, the Deregulation and Contracting Out Act 1994 was enacted to facilitate further contracting out. As has been explained in Chaper 2, this Act provided for the removal of legal barriers to contracting out certain activities, and, as noted in Chapter 2, orders have already been made under its provisions allowing for the contracting out of certain additional government functions.[43] The Act also contains provisions to facilitate external service provision, both in relation to functions contracted out specifically under the Act, and others, most notably concerning the access of external providers to confidential information.[44] Between October 1994 and September 1995 it was proposed to review further activities to the value of £860 million, with candidates for market testing and contracting out including several functions for which contracting out has been facilitated by the 1994 Act – for example, administration of civil service pensions and collection of business statistics.[45]

However, in a July 1994 White Paper, *The Civil Service: Continuity and Change*,[46] the government announced its intention to retreat slightly from its previous prescriptive approach, and to give individual managers more freedom to determine how to achieve benefits through competition. A prescriptive approach is considered less necessary now that departments have gained experience of market testing and have had an opportunity to examine the benefits, and the most inefficient in-house capability has been dismantled. Following responses to the White Paper it has announced, in January 1995, that it proposes to carry out a broad policy evaluation of the "Competing for Quality" initiative,[47] in which the policy for the future will be considered.

General advice to departments and agencies on the procedures for market testing is contained in a government paper, *The Government's Guide to Market Testing*, issued in 1993. Information on specific con-

---

[41] As of May 1995 six prisons were privately managed with plans to extend this to ten by the year 2000: *The Times*, May 19, 1995.
[42] *The Civil Services: Taking forward Continuity and Change* (1995) Cm. 2748, at 3.9.
[43] See pp. 000–000.
[44] Deregulation and Contracting Out Act 1994, s.75 and Sched. 15. Section 76 and Sched. 16 of the Act contain further facilitating and adjustment provisions. They mainly provide for consequential amendments to other legislation which has been drafted on the assumption that the government may not contract out certain functions.
[45] See Department of Trade and Industry, *Deregulation and Contracting Out Act 1994: an Explanatory Guide* (November 1994).
[46] Cm. 2627.
[47] *The Civil Services: Taking forward Continuity and Change* (1995) Cm. 2748, at 3.9.

tracts, and on award procedures which have been conducted, is published in the government's monthly *Market Testing Bulletin*, and, in the case of award procedures subject to the European Community procurement rules, is also found in the *Official Journal of the European Communities*.

(2) LOCAL GOVERNMENT: AN OVERVIEW OF CCT[48]

In the case of local authorities, stringent obligations relating to market testing have been imposed by legislation, under the Local Government Planning and Land Act 1980 (LGPLA 1980), and the Local Government Act 1988 (LGA 1988). This is the regime of "compulsory competitive tendering", or "CCT". Essentially, the CCT regime requires authorities to compare the relative cost and efficiency of internal and external service provision, by means of a formal tendering procedure in which the internal unit must submit a bid in competition with outside providers. To ensure a fair comparison, the in-house provider must keep separate accounts for the service in question, and is required to meet financial targets set by government, which are intended to be similar to those achieved by the private sector.

The first provisions adopted were those of the 1980 Act, which covers construction and maintenance. These provisions, adopted before the government had undertaken any general commitment to market testing, were designed to fulfil a specific pledge in the Conservative Party's 1979 election manifesto: it had, in response to complaints by industry, promised to improve competition in the construction sector by eliminating "unfair" competition from local authority construction units. When the government's commitment to competition became a more general policy, in particular after the 1983 general election, local authorities were strongly encouraged to extend market testing to other activities. However, the response was very limited and in 1986 it was announced that market testing would be required by legislation. This was introduced through the Local Government Act 1988, which applied CCT to refuse collection, cleaning, catering, grounds maintenance, and repair and maintenance of vehicles, under a regime similar to, though not identical with, that under the 1980 Act. Management of sports and leisure facilities was added in 1989. The value of services covered by the 1980 Act, and the original activities under the 1988 Act, totalled in 1993 about £4 billion and £2.3 billion respectively.[49]

---

[48] See, in general, Cirell and Bennett, *CCT: Law and Practice*; Sparke, *The Compulsory Competitive Guide* (1993); Greenwood and Wilson, "Towards the Contract State: CCT in Local Government" (1994) 47 *Parliamentary Affairs* 403; Painter, "Compulsory Competitive Tendering in Government: the First Round" (1991) 69 Public Administration 191; Radford, "Competition Rules: the Local Government Act 1988" [1988] M.L.R. 51.

[49] Department of the Environment, *CCT and Local Government: Department of the Environment Annual Report 1993*.

Since 1988 the government has pressed ahead with its policy on CCT, and, in contrast with its attitude to market testing in central government, shows no sign of relaxing its prescriptive approach.[50] Following completion of the initial process of market testing for the services covered by the 1988 Act, in a White Paper of November 1991, outlining future plans on market testing for the public sector as a whole, the government announced its intention to extend further the scope of local authority CCT, and to tighten the procedural rules.[50a] On the same day, a Consultation Paper was published by the Department of the Environment, putting forward detailed proposals for achieving these two aims.[51] These proposals have now been substantially implemented.

First, the scope of CCT has been extended to cover a few new blue-collar activities and, more significantly, a wide range of white-collar services, by adding to the list in the 1988 Act. The additional services now covered are supervision of parking, security work, vehicle management, housing management, legal services, construction and property services, information technology, finance and personnel services. The value of all these additional services is estimated at about £6 billion.[52]

Secondly, the procedural rules for market testing have been tightened. The original Acts of 1980 and 1988 merely provided a broad framework for market testing. They required contracts to be advertised, and laid down some rules about the procedure – for example, governing the type of advertisement and the minimum numbers of bids to be solicited. They did not, however, contain rules on most aspects of the solicitation of bids, nor on bid evaluation,[53] and although there has been since 1988 a general prohibition on "anti-competitive behaviour" this remained for a long time undefined. Since 1992, however, new legislation has been adopted to regulate in further detail a whole range of tendering decisions, including under a new power derived from the 1992 Local Government Act which allows the Secretary of State to define in regulations what constitutes anti-competitive behaviour. This increased stringency has occurred in response to perceived attempts by authorities to evade the spirit of the CCT regime in conducting tendering procedures.[54]

There is thus now in existence a detailed tendering regime, which applies whenever an authority is contemplating in-house provision of

---

[50] However, the Labour Party has indicated that if it should be elected it will abolish the CCT regime and, further, where a decision to tender work is taken will even *require* that the in-house unit be given a fair opportunity to bid: the Labour Party, *Renewing Democracy, Rebuilding Communities* (1995), pp.8–9.

[50a] H.M. Treasury, *Competing for Quality: Buying Better Public Services* (November 1991).

[51] Department of the Environment, *Competing for Quality: Competition in the Provision of Local Authority Services* (November 1991).

[52] Department of the Environment, *CCT and Local Government: Department of the Environment Annual Report 1993*.

[53] Although the 1988 Act introduced a requirement for both regimes that non-commercial considerations should not be taken into account: see pp. 830–849.

[54] See, *Competing for Quality: Buying Better Public Services*, n.50a, Chap. 5.

certain services. The details of this regime are considered in Chapter 13, which deals with the exact scope of the regime, and Chapter 14, which examines the applicable tendering procedures together with related provisions on accounting, financial targets for in-house service providers, and reporting requirements. The system of remedies and enforcement, which depends mainly on the use of ferocious enforcement powers by the Secretary of State, is considered in Chapter 18.

Some criticisms of the CCT regime involve the general issues referred to earlier, such as the adverse impact on workforce conditions and the difficulties of quality control. Further criticisms have also been made, over the particular way in which market testing has been applied to local authorities. It has been suggested that the regime is now unnecessarily prescriptive, and is built on an assumption of lack of co-operation which is unjustified so far as most authorities are concerned. It can be argued that the rules go, in some respects, further than necessary to achieve efficiency or cost gains (for example, financial targets for in-house units appear unduly stringent, and the rules on the costs which may be taken into account in bid assessment are very narrow[55]); and that in this respect the rules may reflect a "hidden agenda" of an ideological commitment to weakening the public sector and its unions. Criticism has also been directed at the fact that in the initial rounds of CCT under the 1988 Act, authorities were given inadequate time to prepare for tendering, and in particular to draft adequate contract specifications; however, the government has been more sensitive to this issue in implementing white-collar CCT.

The rules are also badly drafted, and unduly complex in the way they are scattered over many different pieces of legislation, as will become apparent from Chapters 13 and 14. It is difficult to disagree with the description given by Cirell and Bennett of the provisions on construction and maintenance as a "Frankenstein's monster style jumble of legislative provisions which are clumsily composed and difficult to understand"[56]; and this description would equally well fit the legislation relating to other services. The approach contrasts sharply with that adopted in implementing Community rules, where the regulations have been consolidated with each major change. Consolidating legislation is urgently required in the CCT context. The difficulties with the CCT legislation are exacerbated by the slight differences in the rules under the 1980 Act and 1988 Act, which are mostly difficult to justify, and problems are also created by the parallel application of the separate European Community rules on tendering.[57] Some substantive adjustments have been made already to

---

[55] See further pp. 724–733.
[56] Cirell and Bennett, p.A11.
[57] On the inter-relationship of these regimes see further Boyle, "Regulated Procurement: a Purchaser's Perspective" (1995) 4 P.P.L.R. 105 at pp.108–112; Bennett and Cirell, "The Interrelationship of E.C. Public Procurement and Compulsory Competitive Tendering in the United Kingdom" (1992) 1 P.P.L.R. 281.

bring the CCT and E.C. regimes into line – in particular, by harmonisation of the time periods for response to advertisements and invitations to bid[58] – but, whilst clearly differences must remain given the differing objectives of the rules, further adjustments would be useful, both to reduce complexity and iron out consistencies (for example, the requirement to use approved lists under the LGPLA 1980, which conflicts with Community obligations).[59] On the other hand, justifiable differences in scope and procedure between the two regimes indicate that consolidation of both in a single code on procurement is not necessarily appropriate.

A final point to emphasise is that the CCT tendering procedures apply only where in-house provision of a service is under consideration: they have no application where a decision has already been taken to contract out. In this event, there are no detailed legislative procedures to regulate tendering, except to the extent that the European Community rules apply; generally the only obligation is to provide for some tendering procedures in the authority's standing orders.[60] The stark absence of regulation of the process for choosing between external providers, in contrast with the prescriptive regime under CCT might be seen as a reflection of the hidden agenda in CCT. However, it can be justified by the need to correct an inherent tendency to favour an in-house organisation, in the same way as European Community legislation is seen as necessary to correct another kind of favouritism – national favouritism. Where such special difficulties do not exist, it is submitted that value for money is best obtained by entrusting trained and professional purchasers with a wide discretion (as is generally done in the private sector), rather than by detailed legal regulation.

6. IMPACT OF THE "ACQUIRED RIGHTS DIRECTIVE"[61]

(1) INTRODUCTION

As already mentioned, the processes of contracting out and market testing have recently been affected by the European Community's

---

[58] See, for example pp. 718–719.
[59] See p. 717.
[60] See p. 29.
[61] See further McMullen, "Contracting Out and Market Testing: the Uncertainty Ends?" (1994) 23 I.L.J. 230; Napier, *CCT, Market Testing and Employment Rights* (1993); Sutcliffe, "Contracting Out Public Services: U.K. Policy v. E.C. Law" (1993) 22 Anglo Am L. Rev. 337; de Groot, "The Council Directive on the Safeguarding of Employees Rights in the Event of Transfers of Undertakings: an Overview of the Case Law" (1993) 30 C.M.L.Rev. 331; O'Loan, "Further Developments on the Acquired Rights Directive (77/187) and Implementation in the United Kingdom" (1994) 3 P.P.L.Rev. CS 195; O'Loan, "New United Kingdom law on Transfer of Undertakings" (1993) 2 P.P.L.R. CS 142; O'Loan, "Acquired Rights and the Contracting Out of Services in the U.K." (1993) 2 P.P.L.R. CS 174.

"Acquired Rights Directive" (Council Directive 77/187[62]; also referred to as the "Business Transfers Directive"), which seeks to protect the interests of employees where a business is transferred. It has been implemented in the United Kingdom through the Transfer of Undertakings (Protection of Employment) Regulations 1981[63] ("TUPE Regulations"). The regulations apply wherever there is "a transfer from one person to another of an undertaking" (or part of an undertaking).[64] In such a case, the transferee becomes responsible for the obligations of the transferor towards the employees of the undertaking, which arise out of their employment contracts or under legislation, and is also bound by any existing collective agreements.[65] This generally means, *inter alia*, that the transferee must continue to employ the existing workforce, and that the existing wages and other conditions of employment continue to apply. If employees are dismissed, the new employer will be liable to pay compensation for unfair dismissal, or for the applicable redundancy payments, as appropriate.[66] Employees are also given rights to be consulted about the transfer.

These rules are most obviously applicable where a complete business – comprising fixed assets, goodwill, etc. – is sold by its owner to a third party. However, they are also relevant in relation to contracting out, where this involves the transfer of a task from one party to another: for example, where a local authority transfers its street-cleaning functions from an in-house service organisation to an outside firm. The application of the rules in this kind of case has the important consequence that the external bidder must engage the authority's former employees on the same conditions as they enjoyed under the authority itself, making it impossible for firms to cut costs by changing the conditions of the workforce.

Although the directive was adopted in 1977, its real impact in this context has been felt only in the last few years. One reason was that the TUPE Regulations formerly provided that the regulations should not apply to an undertaking not "in the nature of a commercial venture", which was interpreted to exclude their application to contracting out by government.[67] However, the Court of Justice ruled in 1992 in *Redmond Stichting*[68] that the directive does not permit such a limitation, and it

---

[62] [1977] O.J. C 61/26. In 1994 the Commission proposed a new directive to replace the existing directive (see [1994] O.J. C 274). The significance of the proposals in the present context is considered at pp. 647–648.

[63] 1981 S.I. No. 1794; as amended by the Transfer of Undertakings (Protection of Employment) (Amendment) Regulations 1987, S.I. No. 442 and Trade Union Reform and Employment Rights Act 1993 ss.32 and 33.

[64] TUPE Regulations, Regulation 3(1).

[65] TUPE Regulations, Regulations 5 and 6.

[66] On the consequences of a transfer see further *The Government's Guide to Market Testing* (1993), section 5; McMullen, *Business Transfers and Employment Rights* (2nd ed., 1992), especially Chaps. 5–10; Upex, *Law of Termination of Employment* (4th ed., 1994), especially pp.80–85.

[67] *Expro Services Ltd v. Smith* [1991] I.C.R. 577.

[68] Case C–29/91, *Dr Sophie Redmond Stichting v. Bartol* [1992] I.R.L.R. 366.

became apparent that contracting out by government was covered.[69] The TUPE Regulations were amended in 1993[70] to make this clear.[71] In addition, the acquired rights rules have become important because of a very expansive interpretation in recent cases of what constitutes a transfer of an undertaking; this means that a transfer is to be found in most cases where a function is contracted out, whereas at one time it was thought that the rules were relevant only in very limited "contracting out" situations. This is discussed further in section (2) below.

As noted above, a transfer of an undertaking may take place where the government contracts out to the private sector a function previously carried out in-house.[72] Such a transfer may also apply where work previously carried out by outside firm A is subsequently placed with firm B[73] – firm B must then engage the relevant employees on the conditions which they enjoyed in firm A. Presumably it will also apply in the rare case that a purchaser takes back in-house a service formerly contracted out.

(2) THE MEANING OF TRANSFER OF AN UNDERTAKING

A very important issue is the exact circumstances in which the transfer of the task of performing an activity in the context of contracting out actually constitutes the "transfer of an undertaking". The basic test laid down by the European Court of Justice is whether the function which has been transferred retains its identity.[74]

This does not necessarily apply in every case where an in-house function is contracted out to the private sector, or where an authority replaces one outside provider with another. However, as recently

---

[69] This was emphasised in case C–209/91, *Rask v. ISS Kantinservice* [1993] E.C.R., where it was held that the contracting out of a canteen service by a public body could be covered. In case C–382/92, *Commission v. United Kingdom* [1994] E.C.R. I–2435, the Court held that the "commercial venture" limitation in the TUPE Regulations had been unlawful.

[70] Trade Union Reform and Employment Rights Act 1993, s.33. This was done before the Court of Justice delivered formal judgment holding the previous limitation to have been unlawful: see note 69 above.

[71] Many who lost their jobs or were re-employed on less favourable terms following the contracting out of services by government, but should have been protected by the Acquired Rights Directive, have now made claims for damages against the government for its failure properly to implement the directive in the United Kingdom, under the principle established in *Francovich* (as to which see p. 915) which recognised the possibility of damages for failure to implement a Directive. However, in that case no steps had been taken at all towards implementation, and culpability may be an issue; if so, damages might not be awarded against the United Kingdom if it is considered that at the relevant time it was not clear whether the Directive applied to government.

[72] *Rask*, above; *Wren v. Eastbourne B.C.* [1993] I.R.L.R. 425.

[73] *Foreningen v. Daddy's Dance Hall* [1988] I.R.L.R. 315; *Kenny v. South Manchester College* [1993] I.R.L.R. 265; *Dines v. Initial Health Care Services* [1994] I.R.L.R. 336.

[74] Case 24/85, *Spijkers v. Gebroders Benedik Abbatoir CV* [1986] E.C.R. 1119; *Rask*, above; case C–392/92, *Schmidt v. Spar- und Leihkasse der früheren Amter Bordesholm, Kiel und Cronshagen* [1994] E.C.R. I–1311.

interpreted, the "retention of identity" test is satisfied, at the very least, whenever the employees of the old service provider are engaged by the new provider, and the task performed is substantially the same – which applies to many cases in practice.

This was made by clear by the Court of Justice in *Schmidt*.[75] This case concerned an individual cleaner, responsible for a particular branch of a bank, whose tasks were contracted to an outside firm. She was offered employment with that firm, doing mainly the same work, but with a larger area to clean. The Court ruled that the directive applied, so that the cleaner's terms and conditions could not be altered by the new employer: the activity of cleaning the particular branch was an undertaking, which retained its identity as an activity when transferred, even though ancillary to the banks' functions, and even though carried out by only one individual. It was confirmed, as had been made clear in previous cases, that it is not necessary for any relevant assets to be transferred from the original service provider to the new provider[76] (a principle now expressly stated in the TUPE Regulations[77]). According to the Court, the "retention of identity" test is satisfied by the fact that the new employer continues or resumes "the same or similar activities".[78] In the United Kingdom the test was held to be satisfied in *Dines v. Initial Health Care Services*,[79] where a contract for cleaning services for a health authority, previously held by one provider, was awarded to another.

A gloss on this was added by the most recent case of *Rygaard*,[80] in which the Court of Justice ruled that where one provider takes over a specific works project started by another, there is no relevant transfer simply because that work is transferred, since the directive envisages a transfer relating to a "stable economic entity", the activity of which is not limited to "one specific works contract".[81] Such situations are unusual, however, and it appears that the directive applies whenever there is a transfer of the performance of an ongoing activity, such as cleaning or maintenance.

In some cases there may be debate over whether the service performed by the new provider is indeed "the same or similar" as before. A service may, on contracting out, be provided or carried out in a different place: for example, with school catering, it may be decided that meals should be prepared off, instead of on, the premises. Alternatively, the way in which the service is organised may be altered, as where vehicle management and vehicle maintenance activities previously carried out

---

[75] Above.
[76] *Rask*, above; *Schmidt*, above; applied in the United Kingdom in, for example, *Wren*, above, *Dines*, above, and *Birch v. Nuneaton and Bedworth Borough Council* [1995] I.R.L.R. 518.
[77] Above note 63.
[78] Para. 17 of the judgment.
[79] Above.
[80] Case C–48–94, *Rygaard v. Strø Mølle Akustik*, judgment of September 19, 1995.
[81] Para. 20 of the judgment.

management and vehicle maintenance activities previously carried out within different units of an authority are combined in a single contract. In the context of construction, it is submitted that there is no transfer of an undertaking where some members of a Direct Labour Organisation which was previously responsible for construction are engaged by an outside firm awarded a specific project (for example, construction of a road). However, a transfer of an undertaking will exist if a contract to perform general maintenance work as it arises, on particular structures or more generally, is awarded to an outside firm, where such work was previously performed by an in-house unit. In the case of contracting out of white-collar services, including under the new regime of compulsory competitive tendering for the white-collar services of local authorities, it is possible that the services will not retain their identity, if certain parts of the service carried out by single individuals are contracted out, whilst other parts are retained in-house.

The nature or manner of performance may also change. In *Dines*, however, the Court of Appeal was prepared to hold that the hospital cleaning service did not lose its identity on transfer, even though the Court did not know what equipment was used by the new service provider, or whether any changes in cleaning methods were introduced, on the basis that hospital cleaning "is not an operation which lends itself to the employment of many different techniques".[82] It was also held in *Kenny v. South Manchester College*[83] which concerned the transfer of the function of the education of prison inmates from one external provider to another by the Home Office, that it was immaterial under the TUPE Regulations that the Home Office did not control the context of what was taught and thus that this could differ with different providers.[84] However, a substantial change in organisation might mean that the activity does not retain its identity. For example, if a commercial refuse collection and disposal function formerly performed by an authority by collecting waste were (if this were lawful) to be performed by requiring persons to bring their own waste to a central site, then this would probably not constitute the same service.

Another question is whether the position is affected by the fact that the new provider does not seek to engage the employees of the previous provider. Where there is a transfer of an undertaking under the rules, the employer must do so; but it appears that the agreement of the new provider to take on at least some of the old workforce is a factor which is itself relevant to whether a transfer of an undertaking exists in the first place.[85] It is not clear, however, whether this is an *essential* factor in those cases where the only other connection between the old and new provider is that the service provided is the same or similar (for example,

---

[82] *Per* Neill L.J., at para. 51.
[83] Above.
[84] And see also *Porter v. Queens Medical Centre* [1993] I.R.L.R 486.
[85] *Spijkers*, above.

where there is no transfer of assets): in both *Schmidt* and *Dines* the service was to be provided by the employee(s) of the previous provider so that this question did not arise.[86] In *Kenny v. South Manchester College*,[87] where no provision had been made for the transfer of employees, the High Court held that this was not essential and granted a declaration that the employees of the previous provider would become employees of the new provider. However, in that case the same premises and equipment, provided by the Home Office, were used by both providers, which may provide an additional factor for suggesting that the activity retained its identity; it is not clear that this would be the case where the activity is carried out by different employees using the provider's own premises and equipment. It is difficult to see, however, that voluntary engagement should be crucial: this would defeat the object of the legislation, by discouraging transferees from taking on the former employees. On the other hand, it seems artificial to speak of a transfer of an "undertaking" when all that is transferred is the performance of a function. In the context of market testing this issue is important, since government guidance indicates that purchasers should not *require* providers to take on former government employees, unless there are sound operational or economic justifications.[88]

Factors, such as a transfer of assets, which are not *essential* where the service provided is fundamentally the same, are probably relevant in borderline cases. Thus in *Rygaard*, discussed above, the Court indicated that the "retention of identity" test might be satisfied in a case which involves a transfer only of one specific project, *if* significant assets are also transferred.[89] This could apply where there is some difference in the way the service is carried out by the new provider. In such cases, these factors (which have been repeatedly held by the Court of Justice to be relevant, though not crucial) can tip the balance in favour of the view that there is a transfer of an undertaking.

It is clear that the fact that an authority retains the statutory responsibility for providing a particular service (as in the case, for example, of refuse collection) does not preclude the possibility of a "transfer" under the regulations where an outside provider is engaged to actually carry out the service.[90]

---

[86] *Schmidt* does not give a clear indication on this point. In paras. 12 and 14 of the judgment, the Court implies that its pronouncements are concerned with the case where the employees are engaged by the transferee independently of the effect of the directive itself. In para. 17 the Court indicates that the similarity of the new function is "indicated" by the fact of re-engagement.

[87] Above.

[88] Department of the Environment Circular 10/93 and Welsh Office Circular 40/93, para. 41; Department of the Environment, *Guidance on the Avoidance of Anti-Competitive Behaviour: Legal, Construction & Property and Housing Management Services* (June 10, 1994) (hereafter "White Collar Guidance"), paras. 61–62. New guidance with which the government proposes to replace the existing guidance (as to which see pp. 708–709) does not mention this point specifically, but it is likely that such behaviour will continue to be regarded as anti-competitive.

[89] Note 80 above; para 21 of the judgment.

[90] *Rask*, above; *Wren*, above.

The concept of a "transfer of an undertaking" has clearly been defined very widely. The definition has been criticised by United Kingdom government, amongst others, because of the detrimental effect which the directive consequently has on market testing policy, and on competition in general, as explained in section (3). A recent proposal for replacing the existing directive with a new directive *may* have the effect of narrowing the definition, although this is not clear. The proposal is discussed further in section (4), below.

(3) IMPACT ON GOVERNMENT POLICY

The directive has significant consequences for contracting out and market testing policy. Most obviously, it reduces the potential for savings. It was explained above that savings have been partly achieved through alteration to the pay rates and conditions of the workforce, but this is no longer possible where the regulations apply. However, other potential benefits of market testing remain, notably gains from greater efficiency and quality of service provision,[91] and this is now the main basis on which bidders will compete. This is welcomed not only by many public bodies, but also by some providers who prefer to compete on this basis, rather than on the basis of workforce conditions, either because they, also, wish to act as good employers, or because they believe firms who win contracts by offering poor terms and conditions are often unable to deliver, so that honest firms are unfairly disadvantaged.

From the perspective of the European Community's free market policy, the directive makes it difficult for firms from other Member States to win contracts by taking advantage of more competitive wages and conditions prevailing in their own states. This is in conflict with the Community's general policy on open procurement, and may be an unintended effect of the directive, which was not initially envisaged as applying to contracting out by government. Where the directive does not apply, for a public body to insist on an external service provider applying pay and conditions as favourable as those enjoyed by authority employees, or to take on the authority's former employees, is probably a breach of Articles 48 and 59 of the E.C. Treaty where this would disadvantage firms from any other Member States compared with domestic firms.[92]

---

[91] Transferees may be able to dismiss employees in consequence of a reorganisation of the work force: a dismissal is not necessarily an "unfair dismissal" if this results from "economic, technical or organisational reasons" in the workforce (TUPE Regulations, Regulation 8(1)). In this case the dismissal is not unfair if it is "reasonable" under the Employment Protection (Consolidation) Act 1978, s.57(3) – although it may constitute a redundancy.

[92] See Chap. 4.

(4) TUPE ISSUES IN THE TENDERING PROCESS

The possible application of TUPE raises a number of important issues relating to the conduct of the tendering process.

As indicated above, the directive's application depends on the organisation of the service once it is contracted out, whether assets of the authority are used by the new provider, and (possibly) the extent to which the new provider engages the authority's employees – factors which the purchaser might control. The government has been concerned to minimise the impact of the directive on its attempts to achieve cost savings through market testing, and in particular to prevent abuse by purchasers who might seek to protect their employees by deliberately arranging a contract in such a way as to render the directive applicable. In relation to CCT, current government guidance indicates that it will be considered anti-competitive behaviour (and thus a breach of the CCT legislation) for an authority to place constraints on the way in which the service is organised, to require a provider to engage the authority's former employees, or to include any similar restrictive condition so that the directive will apply, unless there is an "economic or operational justification" for such restrictions.[93] In relation to central government, *The Government's Guide to Market Testing*[94] generally indicates that purchasers should not require (or indeed allow) the use of government assets[95]; and that they should use broad performance specifications, thus leaving organisation of these service to the provider – a point specifically reiterated in the guidance given on the TUPE Regulations in that publication.[96]

The uncertainty over when exactly the regulations will apply gives rise to practical difficulties in tendering, which are not unique to award procedures involving an internal bidder, but arise also where contracts are transferred from one outside provider to another. In considering these, it should be remembered that the application of the regulations may depend on how a particular provider proposes to organise the services and on his plans relating to assets and employees; thus the regulations may apply for some providers only, and their application may not be known until the winning bid is selected.

---

[93] Department of Environment Circular 10/93 and Welsh Office Circular 40/93 (hereafter referred to collectively as Circular 10/93), paras. 41–43; Department of Environment, White Collar Guidance, above, paras. 61–62. Requirements for providers to use local authority assets are, even apart from these provisions, treated as anti-competitive: see p. 744. Proposed replacement guidance (as to which see pp. 708–709) states the general principle that method of service delivery should not be specified in detail but that the subject matter of the contract should be specified in terms of outputs, which implies the same results as the present guidance: see Department of the Environment draft *Guidance on the Conduct of Compulsory Competitive Tendering*, para. 8.

[94] Above.

[95] Section 4 at 4.8 and section 9 at 9.10. This position in the latter respect contrasts with that relating to local authorities, which are generally required to make their assets available to ease the position of potential providers: see pp. 742–744.

[96] Section 4 at 4.2; and section 5 at 5.28.

First, it is important for bidders to know whether they will be affected by the regulations, since this may significantly affect their workforce costs and hence the bid price. Where there is uncertainty it may also be useful to know the view likely to be taken by the purchaser. The purchaser will wish to ensure that its own view on the applicability of the regulations to a bid is shared by the bidder.

To help meet these concerns, it is useful for the authority to require bidders to state whether or not their bid is based on an assumption that the TUPE regulations apply.[97] It may also be useful for the purchaser to state its own preliminary view on whether TUPE is likely to apply – although, as indicated above, this cannot be definitive, since the position may depend on individual bidders' own proposals. Previously, guidance issued to local authorities for CCT procedures indicated that to state a view in advance would be considered anti-competitive behaviour[98]; the government feared that authorities might, by doing this, try to impose the regulations where not strictly applicable, in order to protect their workforce. However, because, apparently, of firms' reluctance to bid without some guidance, the government has now stated that authorities may indicate such a preliminary view provided, however, that they make it clear that the application of the regulations depends on the exact proposals of the bidder, and that the preliminary view is taken in good faith and based on a careful consideration of the activity.[99] In the government's own advice to departments and agencies, on the other hand, it is indicated that a preliminary view should not be given, because of the difficulties of taking such a view without reference to the way in which individual bids are formulated.[1] It seems unsatisfactory that different guidance has been given to different authorities. The same issue may arise outside a market testing situation, and here also the purchaser may wish to give bidders its own view on whether the rules are

---

[97] This is specifically recommended in guidance given to local authorities on the application of CCT: Issues Paper, "Handling of TUPE Matters in Relation to CCT", circulated by the Department of the Environment and Welsh Office to local authorities on January 21, 1994 (hereafter "the TUPE Issues Paper"). This supplements guidance given in circular 10/93, above, on the question of what constitutes anti-competitive behaviour under the LGA 1988 and LGA 1980. In proposed new guidance to replace this existing guidance (as to which see pp. 708–709) a similar provision is proposed to be included: see Department of the Environment, draft *Guidance on the Conduct of Compulsory Competitive Tendering*, para. 35. Unlike the circular, the Issues Paper does not itself have the effect of "statutory guidance" which is *required* to be taken into account in deciding whether an authority has acted in an anti-competitive manner, but indicates factors which the Secretary of State will take into account in practice in making his decisions on this matter. (On the concept of statutory guidance see pp. 708–709 above.)

[98] Circular 10/93, above, para.43.

[99] The TUPE Issues Paper, above note 97, para. 22. Some difficulty arises over the legal status of this new advice, however; since, as explained, in note 97, the circular containing the original advice has "statutory" status and the Paper does not, it might be argued that the Secretary of State is still legally obliged to take notice of the advice in the original circular.

[1] *The Government's Guide to Market Testing* (1993), section 5, at 5.28.

likely to apply. Uncertainty could be avoided by including contract terms over the method of service provision and other matters to ensure that TUPE applies, but the government will not contemplate this in practice because of the detrimental effect on competition, as explained above.

In all cases where a bidder is uncertain about the application of the rules to his own bid, perhaps the best solution is to submit parallel bids, one on the basis that TUPE applies and one on the basis that it does not, and for the purchaser to evaluate the bid which conforms with its own view of the application of TUPE to the proposal which has been submitted. Guidance to local authorities in relation to CCT procedures indicates that this should normally be allowed[2] and guidance to central government also contemplates that departments might want to consider this possibility.[3] It will also be appropriate in contract award procedures which do not involve market testing.

Where the parties do proceed on a common assumption regarding the application of TUPE it is, however, possible that this may turn out to be incorrect. The parties may in this case desire to include a term in the contract for one to indemnify the other for loss incurred as a result of failure to fulfil the relevant obligations. The guidance issued to central government in relation to market testing does not favour this practice, suggesting that departments should avoid potential liability by carrying out required consultations with the workforce in all cases of doubt (removing the need for any indemnity) and that indemnities should not be given to external providers.[4] However, guidance issued to local authorities in the context of CCT indicates that authorities may seek indemnities where appropriate on the facts of the case, and may likewise provide for indemnities to external providers where this is appropriate.[5]

The case may still, however, arise, where a firm submits a single bid based on what the purchaser believes is an erroneous view on the application of TUPE. Guidance issued to local authorities in the context of CCT suggests that where this happens the authority should inform the bidder of its own view, and allow a reasonable time for the bid to be revised accordingly.[6] It is stated that other bidders should be informed of this and permitted a reasonable time to revise their own bids.[7] This is a sensible approach which might also be useful outside the context of CCT and is probably consistent with the European Community rules on procurement.[8]

---

[2] TUPE Issues Paper, above, para. 22.
[3] *The Government's Guide to Market Testing* (1993), section 5, para. 5.28.
[4] *The Government's Guide to Market Testing* (1993), section 5, para. 5.29.
[5] TUPE Issues paper, above, paras. 4–7. The cost of the indemnity may be taken into account in assessing the respective merits of external and in-house service provision, provided it is based on a reasonable assessment of the risk. (If not, it would be anti-competitive to add the cost into the evaluation in favour of the in-house organisation: see p. 728.)
[6] TUPE Issues Paper, above, para. 14.
[7] TUPE Issues Paper, para. 16.
[8] See pp. 247–249.

A further issue is what is to be done where a bidder insists on maintaining what the authority considers is an erroneous view of TUPE. Where the purchaser, but not the bidder, believes that TUPE does apply, the purchaser will generally wish to reject the bid because of a risk of default by the bidder if the TUPE rules are later enforced, and to avoid being complicit in a breach of the law. Where a public purchaser's decision is based on an erroneous view of the law – for example, the purchaser wrongly takes the view that an asset transfer is necessary for TUPE to apply – it is probably subject to challenge by way of judicial review.[9] The application of the general legal principles to the circumstances of the case, however, is probably a question of fact,[10] and here the court may be willing to accept the authority's view provided that there is some reasonable evidence on which this view could be based.[11] In the context of CCT the decision is subject to challenge not only before the court, but also by the Secretary of State.[12] Here guidance issued to local authorities whilst accepting that authorities may reject an erroneous bid indicates that to do so may be regarded as anti-competitive if the result is that the work is awarded in-house and the decision to reject the external bid on "TUPE" grounds cannot be positively justified before the Secretary of State.[13] Where a tendering procedure is subject to the Works and Services Regulations, it is also necessary to ensure that the rejection is justified under the regulations, which allow bids to be rejected only on a limited number of specified grounds. However, the purchaser may probably reject the bidder for lack of technical capacity, which covers the case where the bidder is unable to perform the contract in accordance with requirements imposed by law,[14] which would include TUPE requirements. Another possibility, where a risk of default is perceived, is that the bid may be rejected as abnormally low, in which cases procedures applicable to such rejection (including giving a hearing to the bidder) must be followed.[15]

In the opposite case where a bidder believes that TUPE applies and an authority does not, it is likely that other bidders will share the authority's view and that the TUPE-based bid is then unlikely to win the contract. Where it does, a purchaser is unlikely to seek to reject it. Where the Works Regulations or Services Regulations apply, there does not appear to be any lawful ground for rejection, where the bid is the best bid according to the relevant award criteria.

---

[9] *Page v. Hull University Visitor* [1993] 1 All E.R. 97.
[10] See, for example, *Wren v. Eastbourne B.C.* [1995] I.R.L.R. 425.
[11] On this issue see Craig, *Administrative Law* (3rd ed., 1994), pp.365–368.
[12] See pp. 945–954.
[13] TUPE Issues Paper, above, paras. 18–20, where it is emphasised that the decision should be based on detailed consideration of the tenderer's proposals, and that the authority must show, if challenged, that it has been "thorough, specific and reasonable". Proposed new guidance (as to which see pp. 708–709) does not deal expressly with these issues, but they may later be dealt with in a separate paper on TUPE issues.
[14] See pp. 314–315.
[15] See pp. 243–247.

Where any bids are to be submitted on the basis that TUPE is applicable, bidders need to know in practice details of the staff of the existing provider as well as their terms and conditions of employment. Where the work is presently carried on in-house, relevant guidance provides that the details must be given to interested outside bidders whenever TUPE *may* apply, and local authorities will be considered to act in a manner which is anti-competitive under the LGA 1988 and LGPLA 1980 where such information is not given in relation to award procedures which are subject to CCT.[16] Normally it is possible to give the relevant information within the confines of the Data Protection Act 1984, by keeping anonymous the position relating to identifiable individuals.[17]

Where, on the other hand, a service is presently being provided by an external provider, that provider is likely to be unwilling to reveal workforce information, which will clearly give other bidders some competitive advantage. To ensure that other providers are able to bid, it is thus desirable now to include terms in all services contracts which require information relevant to the application of TUPE to be produced when the contract is retendered.[18]

(5) PROPOSALS FOR REFORM

In 1994 the Commission made a Proposal for a new directive on acquired rights, to replace the existing directive.[19] Under the Proposal, the broad principles of Community policy remain the same, but certain clarifications and amendments are suggested: for example, the definition of employee is to be clarified, and specific rules adopted to deal with the application of the directive on insolvency.

The new proposal provides in express terms that it shall apply to public undertakings,[20] confirming the European Court's approach on this point. However, it is possible that in the context of contracting out by public bodies, the scope of operation of the acquired rights rules may be

---

[16] *The Government's Guide to Market Testing* (1993), section 5 at 5.28 (and see also the Market Testing Guidance Notes of August 18, 1993 and September 27, issued by the Cabinet Office Efficiency Unit); Circular 10/93, above, note 97, para. 44, White Collar Guidance, above, note 00, para. 64 and TUPE Issues Paper para. 13 (and see also TUPE Issues Paper, paras. 8–9 and Annex A for details regarding the information which may need to be provided). In new draft guidance which it is proposed will replace the existing guidance (as to which see pp. 708–709) similar provisions are included: see Department of the Environment, *Guidance on the Conduct of the Compulsory Competitive Tendering*, paras. 28 and 36.

[17] This view is taken in the above guidance. For further details on this issue see the Guidance Note of August 18, above.

[18] This is advised in *The Government's Guide to Market Testing* (1993), section 5 at 5.26; TUPE Issues Paper, para. 10.

[19] [1994] O.J. C 274. This followed a report by the Commission to the Council highlighting problems in the operation of the directive: SEC (92) 857.

[20] Article 1(3) of the proposal.

narrowed by the new directive, by virtue of express provisions contained in the Proposal to define what constitutes a transfer of an undertaking. These state that a transfer only of an activity of an undertaking does not itself constitute the transfer of an undertaking; but, however, that a transfer of an undertaking does take place where, together with the transfer of an activity, an economic entity which retains its identity is also transferred.

Where a function is contracted out by a public body, or transferred from one provider to another, clearly this involves a particular activity, rather than the transfer of the undertaking as a whole. Under the definition in the Proposal, the question thus then arises as to whether the transfer of the activity also involves the transfer of "an economic entity which retains its identity". The decision in *Schmidt* states that in the circumstances of that case there was a transfer of a "business" which retained its identity. On this basis it could be suggested that under the Proposal there is, in the circumstances of that case, indeed a transfer of an "economic entity" which retains its identity, so that the definition of a transfer of an undertaking remains very wide.

On the other hand, the effect of these provisions may be to narrow the definition, and the concept of an "economic unit" could provide a basis for a narrower interpretation of the directive in the future – in particular by confining it to cases where significant numbers of employees and/or assets are transferred. Further, a particular issue which arises from the new provisions is the position where a function which retains its identity is contracted out without the transfer of either assets or employees. It was suggested above that, in light of the present case law, it would be anomalous not to apply the directive to this case. However, the Commission's Proposal appears to indicate that transfer of the function alone does not constitute a transfer of an undertaking, the existence of an "economic unit" being a requirement separate from and additional to the transfer of the function itself.

It is thus open to debate what the effect of the Proposal would be in the context of contracting out by government; the only thing which is clear is that adoption of these provisions are likely to produce even more uncertainty in the law.

CHAPTER 13

COMPULSORY COMPETITIVE TENDERING: SCOPE OF THE RULES

1. INTRODUCTION

This chapter explains which authorities and activities are subject to the rules on compulsory competitive tendering (CCT).[1] The first part of the chapter considers the scope of the rules under the Local Government Planning and Land Act 1980 (LGPLA 1980) which deals with construction and maintenance. The second part of the chapter examines the application of the Local Government Act 1988 (LGA 1988) which governs other "CCT" services, both manual and professional.

2. THE LOCAL GOVERNMENT PLANNING AND LAND ACT 1980 (CONSTRUCTION AND MAINTENANCE)

(1) GENERAL PRINCIPLES

Under the Local Government Planning and Land Act 1980 (LGPLA 1980) CCT applies to "local authorities" or "development bodies" (defined at (2) below), where they carry out activities of construction and maintenance (defined at (3) below) which relate to their own functions ("functional work" – defined at (4) below). The main obligations relating to work covered by the LGPLA are laid down by the LGPLA itself. However, the obligations under this Act are now also supplemented by further requirements, imposed either under legislation or in guidance issued by the Secretary of State. These obligations are described fully in Chapter 14.

---

[1] The background to these rules was examined in Chap. 12. The procedural rules themselves are considered in Chap. 14, and the remedies for enforcing the rules in Chap. 18.

The chapter deals only with that work designated under the legislation as "functional work" which, broadly speaking, is that work carried out by local authorities in connection with their own functions, rather than as providers for other bodies. It is only functional work which concerns the authority as a purchaser, other work concerns the activities of the authority specifically as a provider. On the distinction between functional work and other work see pp. 662–664 and 700–701.

The obligations fall into two main categories – those on award procedures for market testing, and those on the keeping of accounts and financial performance of in-house units.[2-3] Generally, these two categories of obligation apply to the same authorities and activities, and the scope of exemptions from each is the same. However, emergency work and work carried out as an extension of an existing agreement with the DLO, whilst exempt from the usual tendering procedures is still subject to accounting, reporting and financial obligations.

CCT came into effect some years ago for all contracts covered by the LGPLA 1980, and continues to apply: as the expiry dates arrive for agreements previously awarded under CCT procedures – whether with an internal or external provider – they must generally be re-tendered under the CCT rules if the authority wishes to do the work in-house. The only exception is for certain cases where CCT has been suspended pending local government re-organisation.

(2) BODIES COVERED

As mentioned, the LGPLA 1980 covers bodies which are either "local authorities" or "development bodies",[4] concepts which are both defined in section 20(1) of the Act. In relation to England and Wales "local authority" covers[5] a county council; a district council; a London borough council; a joint authority established by Part IV of the Local Government Act 1985; the Council of the Isles of Scilly; and the Common Council of the City of London, but in this latter case only when the Council acts in its capacity as local authority or police authority. "Development body", in relation to England and Wales, covers the Commission for the New Towns;[6] development corporations established under the New Towns Act 1981[7]; and urban development corporations established under the LGPLA 1980 itself.[8] It can be noted that this list is narrower than the list of authorities subject to CCT under the LGA 1988; in particular, the LGPLA does not cover parish and community councils, nor most police and fire authorities.

Bodies caught by the Act are also generally caught by either the public sector Works Regulations, Supply Regulations and Services Regulations,

---

[2-3] LGA 1988, ss.17–19 also prohibit consideration of non-commercial considerations. However, these obligations are not limited to contracts within the CCT regime, but apply to virtually all local government procurement contracts, so that it is not appropriate to consider them in the CCT chapter. They are considered further at pp. 830–845 in Chap. 16.

[4] LGPLA 1980 s.9(1), 10(1), 12(1) and 13(1).

[5] LGPLA 20(1), definition of "local authority", (a) and (b), as substituted by LGA 1988, s.32 and Sched. 6 paras. 1, 10(1) and 4.

[6] LGPLA s.20(1), definition of "development body, (a)(i).

[7] LGPLA s.20(1), definition of "development body", (a)(ii) (as substituted by the New Towns Act 1981, s.81 and Sched. 12, para. 28).

[8] LGPLA s.20(1), definition of "development body", (a)(iii).

or, in those few cases where they are involved in "utilities" activities, by the Utilities Regulations. Thus, in awarding major contracts involving an in-house bidder, they may need to follow two sets of rules.

(3) ACTIVITIES COVERED[9]

(a) APPLICATION TO CONSTRUCTION AND MAINTENANCE WORK

The obligations under the LGPLA 1980 apply in general to "construction or maintenance work" undertaken by a local authority or development body.

(i) THE GENERAL DEFINITION OF CONSTRUCTION AND MAINTENANCE WORK

"Construction and maintenance work" is defined by section 20(1) of the LGPLA, to cover the following activities.

(a) **Building or engineering work involved in (i) either construction, improvement, maintenance, or repair of buildings and other structures and ii) the laying out, construction, improvement, maintenance or repair of highways and other land** (section 20(1)(a)). It can be seen that it is not any work which constitutes construction, improvement, maintenance, etc., which is covered but only "building" and "engineering" work which is involved in construction, maintenance, etc. Thus a twofold test applies: first, is the work building or engineering work, and, secondly, is it construction, improvement, maintenance, etc.? None of these general concepts is further defined – in contrast with the activities covered by the LGA 1988, which are defined in detail in a schedule to the Act. This position has been criticised because of the uncertainty created.[10]

As to what constitutes building work, in the Court of Appeal decision in *Wilkinson v. Doncaster Borough Council*[11] Sir John Donaldson MR, with whom the other members of the court agreed, suggested that work is generally building work where it is "work of the type done by a builder".[12] Presumably, this refers only to work of a type which some builders are normally prepared to undertake as a separate activity: it would not include, for example, cleaning, which may be undertaken by builders after a job but is not generally undertaken separately and is clearly not intended to be caught by the LGPLA. Obviously work such as laying foundations, building walls and roofing is covered, as it is clearly

---

[9] On this see also Cirell and Bennett *Compulsory Competitive Tendering: Law and Practice*, Chap. 7.
[10] Cirell and Bennett, above, Chap. 3 at 3.6 and 3.7.
[11] (1986) 84 LGR 257.
[12] *Ibid*, at 261.

building work and involves construction or maintenance, but some activities are less easily categorised. In *Wilkinson* itself it was held that house painting was caught by the definition of building work under the above definition, since builders do undertake house-painting contracts; this applies even though the painting is not connected with any other type of work (for example, painting a wall after it has been built or restored by the builder). Since painting is also either "construction" or "maintenance" (depending on whether it is new or a renewal) house painting is caught by the Act. Interior decorating by itself may, on the other hand, not be covered. Another uncertainty is whether installation work – for example, the installation of kitchen or bathroom fittings – is "building work".

In relation to work on roads, clearly the laying of new roads and pavements, and resurfacing is covered: this is again building or engineering work, and involves construction or maintenance. At the other extreme it is generally accepted that sweeping and cleaning is not covered. (This is now subject to CTT under the LGA 1988[13].) However, the status of some activities is again uncertain – for example, painting road markings. The Department of Transport has suggested that a general distinction is to be drawn between work requiring supervision or instruction by a competent engineer, which is subject to the LGPLA, and other work on highways, which is not; and to avoid uncertainty, it has further suggested that all work should in practice be regarded as subject to the Act with the exception of grass cutting and sweeping and cleaning of gullies and signs, unless exclusion of a particular job can be specifically justified.[14] The position of work on matters not on the road surface itself, such as erecting traffic signs or street lighting, is also unclear. The debate with regard to street lighting was expressly resolved in 1988 where this was added as a separate category (see below).

In practice, most work relating to roads will now be subject to CTT as involving either construction or maintenance, or cleaning.

(b) The gritting of or clearing of snow from highways (section 20(1)(b).

(c) The maintenance of street lighting (section 20(1)(c).[15]

(ii) EXCEPTIONS TO THE GENERAL DEFINITION OF CONSTRUCTION AND MAINTENANCE

Certain activities which fall prima facie within the general definition of construction and maintenance above, are specifically excluded from the definition. The result is that these activities are entirely outside the scope

---

[13] See pp. 670–671.
[14] Department of Transport, Trunk Road Management and Maintenance Notice 4/83, of July 29, 1983, para. 6; see further Cirell and Bennett, at 7.0.2. This guidance relates to trunk roads, but if it is correct the same will apply under the Act to all types of roads.
[15] Added by LGA 1988, s.32 and Sched. 6, paras. 1, 10(1)–(2).

of the LGPLA 1980 – they are subject to neither the tendering procedures under the Act, nor the obligations on accounts and financial returns (although some of them are now caught by the CCT regime under the LGA 1988).[16]

I. Parks, playing fields, allotments, etc.

First, the Act expressly states that work relating to "parks, gardens, playing fields, open spaces or allotments" falls outside the definition of construction and maintenance, except where the work relates to a building or structure.[17] Thus, for example, the Act probably does not cover the resurfacing of paths in municipal gardens, parks or allotments, the turfing of grassed surfaces or the construction of a pond. However, it covers the construction or repair of pavilions, cafes, allotment sheds, etc., which are clearly buildings or structures. There is some debate over the exact scope of "building or structure"[18] – for example, whether it would cover a bridge or an outdoor swimming pool which are arguably "structures".

Some of these matters excluded from the 1980 Act are now subject to the CCT under the 1988 LGA as grounds maintenance – for example, returfing work.[19]

II. Docks and harbour undertakings

Also outside the definition of construction and maintenance is work undertaken by a local authority "for the purposes of or in connection with" a dock or harbour undertaking, where the carrying on of this dock or harbour undertaking is authorised by enactment.[20]

III. Routine maintenance by caretakers

Section 20(2) of the LGPLA is designed to exclude from the Act routine maintenance carried out by caretakers as part of their general duties. Caretakers are often appointed to undertake a variety of duties, such as cleaning, security, reception work, etc., in relation to specific premises, of which routine maintenance is often one, and it was felt appropriate to allow this practice to continue without the need to put the maintenance work out to tender.

Thus the Act excludes from the definition of construction and maintenance "routine maintenance" of specific buildings and structures

---

[16] See, for example, p. 674 (which covers some matters under I.).

[17] LGPLA 1980, s.20(2).

[18] Some authorities appear to have taken the view that it may even cover paths and driveways, but this seems incorrect, for these are not included within the natural meaning of the word "structure", and in any case it may be argued that "structure" should be construed *ejusdem generis* with building: see Cirell and Bennett, *Compulsory Competitive Tendering: Law and Practice* at 8.0.6.

[19] See p. 674.

[20] LGPLA 1980, s.20(3).

which is carried out by a person employed to perform duties in relation to the building(s) or structure(s).[21] This applies only where the greater part of the employee's work is work which is *not* routine maintenance or other construction and maintenance work (as defined under the Act).[22] Thus the exemption does not cover persons employed specifically to undertake maintenance and renewal work (for example, the employment of crews of workers to maintain housing estates), but only those for whom maintenance is not a predominant part of their duties.[23] The section does not specify what proportion of the employee's duties must relate to the building(s) or structure(s) on which the work is carried out. It is suggested that the test should be whether this is more than half the work of the employee.

The same problems in defining a building and, particularly, a structure arise here as in relation to the exemption for parks, playing fields and allotments, as discussed at **I.** above.

The exemption applies only to maintenance work, not new construction.[24] It also applies only to "routine" maintenance work. Thus it probably does not cover, for example, the wholesale renewal of windows and doors, even if done periodically for reasons of maintenance rather than for aesthetic reasons.

IV. Work pursuant to training schemes

A further exemption applies to work done pursuant to government training schemes. If such work were required to be subject to CCT, this would jeopardise the possibilities for the provision of training, which would not be available were the DLO to lose the contract.[25] The exemption applies where a local authority or development body undertakes work pursuant to an agreement with the Secretary of State under the Employment and Training Act 1973, which specifies the work to be undertaken, and where the Secretary of State bears at least part of the cost.[26] The exemption does not, however, cover other training schemes implemented by local authorities, nor does it apply simply because work is carried out by apprentices.

---

[21] LGPLA 1980, s.20(2) as amended by Local Government Act 1992, s.11 and Sched. 1, para. 8.

[22] *Ibid.*

[23] This limitation was introduced by the 1992 amendment.

[24] On the definition of this, see *R. v. Hackney L.B.C., ex p. Secretary of State for the Environment* (1989) 88 L.G.R. 96, discussed at pp. 752–753.

[25] It is, however, permitted to take into account the cost of certain training schemes implemented by the DLO in comparing the bids from the DLO with those of external bidders: see pp. 725–726.

[26] LGPLA 1980 s.20(4), substituted by the Employment Act 1989, s.29(3) and Sched. 6, para. 27 The exemption operates by excluding such work from the definition of construction and maintenance.

(b) EXEMPTIONS FROM THE ACT

(i) THE COMPETITION-FREE ALLOWANCES

Previously, for all types of work caught by the LGPLA there were "competition-free" allowances, which permitted authorities to carry out certain smaller jobs or a percentage of those jobs without putting these out to tender. However, these have now nearly all been abolished. There remains only an exemption for works relating to the construction and maintenance of a sewer, of a value of below £50,000.[27]

(ii) SMALL DIRECT LABOUR ORGANISATIONS

Section 21 of the LGPLA provides an exemption for authorities with small DLOs. Currently the exemption allows the obligations to be disregarded in any financial year when in the previous financial year the authority did not at any time employ more than 15 persons on construction and maintenance work.[28] Those engaged wholly or mainly on the "design, development or control" of construction or maintenance work are not included[29]; thus supervisors and engineers who do work related to construction and maintenance are not counted, but blue-collar staff actually engaged in the construction and maintenance activities are. All this latter group are included, even if only partly engaged in such work.[30]

In addition, the Secretary of State may allow a body to take advantage of this exemption where he is satisfied that the figure of 15 has been exceeded only because this was necessary in order to carry out urgent construction or maintenance work, the necessity for which could not have been foreseen by the body concerned.[31]

These provisions give a general exemption from the requirements of Part III of the Act – that is, those relating to both award procedures, and accounting and financial obligations.[32] Even where the DLO is not sufficiently large to take advantage of these general obligations, there are in addition provisions for less stringent accounting obligations for certain

---

[27] The Local Government (Direct Labour Organisation) (Competition) Regulations S.I. 1989 No. 1588, reg. 8(1)(b). And see reg. 2(2) which effectively prevents the splitting of work naturally falling within one contract so as to avoid this £50,000 threshold.

[28] LGPLA s.21(1); LGPLA s.21(8), as added by the Local Government (Miscellaneous Provisions) Act 1982, s.47(1), Sched. 6, para. 8; Local Government (Direct Labour Organisations) (Specified Number of Persons) Order 1989 (substituting a figure of 15 for the original 30).
The Secretary of State is empowered to change the stipulated figure by order by way of statutory instrument, which is to be subject to annulment by either House of Parliament: s.21(3)–(5).

[29] LGPLA 1980, s.21(2).

[30] LGPLA 1980, s.21(1).

[31] LGPLA 1980, s.21(6).

[32] LGPLA 1980, ss.11(1) and 21(1).

DLOs at the smaller end of the non-exempt group. These are explained further below in the section on accounting obligations.[33]

(iii) EMERGENCY WORK

There is also an exemption from the usual tendering procedures for "emergency work", provided for in the Local Government (Direct Labour Organisations) (Competition) Regulations 1989.[34] This recognises that in an emergency there is insufficient time to undertake a market testing exercise. This exclusion, unlike the others discussed above, does not, however, cover the obligations relating to accounts and financial objectives.

"Emergency work", in relation to work to be done on or after April 1, 1990,[35] is defined to cover work which meets the following conditions[36]:

(a) It is required that the necessity for the work "could not reasonably have been foreseen" by the local authority or development body. The concept of foreseeability is obviously a difficult one to apply, but this will at least preclude the application of the exemption to occurrences which, whilst individually unpredictable, or of a type likely to occur periodically, such as burst pipes resulting from cold weather or fallen tiles from high winds. An event which is unforeseeable, on the other hand, might be a flood or the slipping of a mud bank.

(b) The work must be required to avert, alleviate or eradicate in the purchaser's area (or part of it), the effects or potential effects of any "emergency or disaster".

(c) The emergency or disaster must involve, or be likely to involve, either risk of injury or danger to life or health; or must involve, or be likely to involve, *serious* damage to or destruction of property. Thus, for example, the exemption could not be invoked where the consequence of a disaster is that a road is blocked off, where the road may easily be closed and the only consequence is inconvenience for travellers being forced to take an alternative route.

(d) The work must be required to be put in hand as a matter of urgency within 48 hours of the emergency or disaster occurring.

(e) The work must be on a scale or of a nature not normally undertaken by the authority. If it is of a scale and nature normally undertaken, it would be expected that the authority would already have in place arrangements for dealing with this kind of problem, which have been entered into under the CCT rules. Events such as burst pipes in council dwellings would probably be excluded since this is work of both a scale

---

[33] See p. 754.

[34] reg. 9(1)(a).

[35] For work to be done before this date the regulations provide for the test to be as it stood before the 1989 Regulations, which amended the test to make it more stringent: see part (i) of the definition of emergency work under reg. 2(1).

[36] 1989 Regulations, reg. 2(1).

and nature which is generally undertaken by the authority. On the other hand, work required to deal with a one-off major flood would be covered.

If urgent work is required in circumstances where these strict conditions are not met, it should be remembered that it is not necessarily required that the authority should go through the CCT tendering procedure set out in the Act; the work may be placed quickly with a private contractor without following the CCT procedure, since CCT applies only in the case where the authority is considering placing the work with the DLO.[37] The strictness of the rules on emergencies may be seen to reflect the government's presumption in favour of contracting out rather than in-house provision. What is surprising is that there is any exemption at all for emergency work; an alternative approach might have been to require contracting out automatically in cases where it is not feasible to hold a competition between the DLO and external bidders.

(iv) EXTENSION OF EXISTING ARRANGEMENTS WITH THE DLO

Regulation 9 of the Local Government (Direct Labour Organisations) (Competition) Regulations 1989 (the "1989 Regulations")[38] allows for the award of work to the DLO without following CCT procedures in certain cases where the work is a minor extension of an existing arrangement[39] with the DLO which the DLO has already won under CCT. This allows for small adjustments to existing arrangements, which are often needed in practice, especially to cope with unforeseen situations, without the necessity for a whole new award procedure, which would clearly be unduly onerous.

This possibility does not apply at all to maintenance work,[40] but only to construction work covered by the Act. In the case of maintenance, if it is expected that an extension might be needed beyond the existing scope

---

[37] Thus the urgency exemption has a different significance from the "urgency" exemptions from the Works, Supply and Services Regulations. Under those regulations the effect of the "urgency" provisions is to allow authorities to use a negotiated procedure. If the urgency provisions cannot be invoked, the restricted or open procedures must be applied which will be quite lengthy: see Chap. 5. These regulations do not, however, restrict the possibility for an authority to do the work in-house to deal with an emergency situation: this possibility is affected only by the CCT rules themselves.

[38] Local Government (Direct Labour Organisations) (Competition) Regulations 1989 S.I. 1989 No. 1588.

[39] Referred to in the regulations as a "job".

[40] 1989 Regulations, reg. 9(1)(c)(i), which applies the exemption to three of the four categories of work covered by the 1980 Act, but omits mention of maintenance, the fourth category. The definition of "maintenance" work, and the other three categories of work, for this purpose is that discussed at pp. 752–753 below in the section on accounting provisions and financial obligations, since that is the main context in which the distinction between the different categories of construction and maintenance work is relevant.

or duration of the contract, then an authority should provide expressly in the existing agreement for the possibility of an extension of the work arrangement, either by agreement[41] or at the sole option of the client side. The maximum duration of any such extension – as well as the maximum duration of any fixed term for the original contract – is inherently limited, however, by a general requirement that authorities should not act in an anti-competitive manner in awarding work to the DLO,[42] which entails that the period of the arrangement with the DLO must not exceed what is reasonable.[43]

Extensions to construction arrangements are permitted only under the following strict conditions:

(a) The work under the extension must be of a "similar description" to work under the existing arrangement[44] and must be carried out on the same site or surface as the original work or on an adjacent site or surface.[45]

(b) The estimated value of the extension must not exceed by more than 10 per cent the estimated cost of the original arrangement.[46]

(c) The estimated value of each item of work in the new arrangement must not exceed by more than 10 per cent any corresponding item of work in the original arrangement.[47]

(d) Previous work to which the extension has been made must have been undertaken by the DLO in the previous 12 months.[48]

(e) The original work must have been won in a competition in which at least three external bidders (not including other local authorities and development bodies) were invited to tender.[49]

(f) The bid of the DLO in the original competition must have been the lowest bid submitted.[50] It is difficult to see any justification for this limitation. It is appropriate to preclude the application of the "extension" provisions in cases where the DLO has not won the original contract on commercial grounds – for example, where the DLO bid has been chosen even though it is not the most advantageous (in which case the authority will also have infringed the general prohibition on anti-competitive behaviour) – and this is probably the intention behind this provision. However, it is not apt to achieve such a result. Often it is not

---

[41] The concept of agreement has little meaning where the work is ultimately awarded to the DLO which is part of the same authority as the purchaser. However, the distinction between a unilateral option and provision for an agreed extension will be reflected in the specifications since this would have been a point of significance if the work had been awarded to an external bidder.

[42] See further pp. 745–747.

[43] See p. 712.

[44] 1989 Regulations, reg. 9(1)(c)(ii).

[45] 1989 Regulations, reg. 9(1)(c)(iii).

[46] 1989 Regulations, reg. 9(1)(c)(ii).

[47] 1989 Regulations, reg. 9(1)(c)(ii).

[48] 1989 Regulations, reg. 9(1)(c)(ii).

[49] 1989 Regulations, reg. 9(2)(a).

[50] 1989 Regulations, reg. 9(2)(b).

appropriate to apply "lowest price" as the award criterion for the contract and the DLO will often quite properly win the contract against other eligible bidders as a result of the application of other award criteria. Further, the lowest bidder may sometimes be rejected because the bid is adjudged abnormally low (in the sense that the bidder is unlikely to complete for the price submitted) or because it transpires following submission of bids that the lowest bidder does not have the requisite financial or technical capacity. Where for these kinds of reasons the DLO has won the competition despite the fact that its bid is not the lowest the extension provisions should apply. Conversely, where the DLO has submitted the lowest bid but its tender should not have been accepted on commercial grounds (for example, because it was not the most advantageous taking other concerns into account) the extension provisions should *not* be available; but the provision does not achieve this effect.

In applying the provisions on extensions it is necessary to consider whether particular work arises under an "extension" or whether it may merely be treated as an application of the existing arrangement with the DLO. Probably a provision for renewal of the arrangement which is referred to in the specifications, whether this is a renewal at the option of the client or by agreement,[51] may be treated as an application of the existing arrangement.[52] As noted above, the duration of an arrangement with the DLO which involves a variation in its scope or duration is inherently limited by the general requirement that the authority should not act in a manner which is anti-competitive. For contracts covered by the regulations implementing the European Community procurement rules authorities will also need to consider the limitations on extension of existing arrangements which are contained in those regulations.[53] These do not affect the extent of arrangements with the DLO as such, since they are not concerned at all with the decision on whether or not a function should be contracted out in the first place, and thus have no application where work is awarded in-house without any market testing exercise (as may be done with functions not covered by CCT). However, they do limit the possibility of including provisions for extensions of contracts in any market testing exercise which is caught by the regulations. Thus where a particular award procedure is caught by the

---

[51] On this see note 41.

[52] This is expressly contemplated by reg. 9(2)(c) of the 1989 Regulations, discussed below, which provides for one extension only *unless the possibility of further contracts is referred to in the invitation to tender.* This assumes that where such a reference is made the further arrangement is simply an application of the existing agreement. An alternative interpretation of the provisions could be that that where the possibility of further work is mentioned in the invitation further work may be awarded *in accordance with the conditions set out above* but in such a case is not limited merely to one extension. However, it is unlikely that this is the intended effect of the provision: the better view is that it is based on an assumption that the extra work is not in this case an "extension" at all.

[53] See pp. 119–123.

Community procurement rules as well as by the CCT rules the limitations in the Community rules must be respected in terms of what is included on duration of contracts in the contract specifications. These specifications will then govern the relationship with the DLO should it win the work.

Only one extension of an arrangement is possible under the above provisions,[54] unless the additional work is expressly contemplated in the original invitation to tender.[55] In the latter case, it is submitted, the work does not constitute an extension at all but is merely an application of the existing agreement.[56]

As with emergency work, this exemption permits the award of work to the DLO without a tendering procedure, but the rules relating to accounting and financial objectives still apply to any such work carried out by the DLO.

The CCT rules do not affect the possibility for authorities to extend contracts entered into with external providers. This is merely a reflection of the general principle that CCT does not seek to regulate the authority's discretion to contract work out rather than choosing in-house provision nor the manner of choosing between different external providers.[57] However, for procedures falling within the regulations implementing the Community directives some limitations on extensions may, as indicated above, arise under those regulations,[58] and provision for retendering with reasonable regularity might also exist under the authority's own standing orders on the use of competitive procedures.

(v) WORK FOR A CROWN COURT

There is also an exemption, recently added, for any work undertaken for the purposes of a Crown Court.[59]

(vi) TEMPORARY EXEMPTIONS PENDING LOCAL GOVERNMENT REORGANISATION

Pending the reorganisation of local authorities, authorities which are being reorganised are being given certain temporary dispensations from the requirement to apply market testing to construction and maintenance work. Such authorities are given an exemption from the CCT

---

[54] 1989 Regulations, reg. 9(2)(c).

[55] *Ibid.*

[56] See note 52.

[57] The absence of limits on extensions with outside providers is criticised by Cirell and Bennett, *Compulsory Competitive Tendering: Law and Practice*, Chap. 8, at 8.0.17, as tending to discriminate against the DLO. This is simply an aspect of the absence of more general regulation of local authority tendering, as noted in the text, rather than a criticism relevant specifically to the issue of extensions.

[58] See pp. 119–123.

[59] The Local Government (Direct Labour Organisations) (Competition) (Amendment) Regulations 1995, S.I. 1995 No. 1377.

tendering rules for 18 months after the authority comes into being.[60] Thus during this period the DLO may do the work without competing with outside bidders. However, the authority is still required to prepare a detailed specification against which the DLO must submit a bid[62] and the accounting and reporting rules and those on financial objectives still apply, to ensure that the DLO is performing efficiently in doing the work. The temporary exemption does not apply to work undertaken under a single arrangement which is to be completed within a year, or which has an annual cost of less than £200,000.[62]

(c) WORK WHICH CANNOT BE SEPARATED FROM CONSTRUCTION AND MAINTENANCE

Under section 20(5) of the LGPLA[63] authorities may choose to treat as construction or maintenance work, work which in the authority's opinion cannot effectively be undertaken separately from construction and maintenance. Such work could be either work which is not otherwise subject to CCT at all, or work which would otherwise be subject to CCT under the LGA 1988.

This provision prevents the need for authorities to separate artificially work which can only efficiently be carried out under a single contract or by a single unit of the authority. For example, an authority might choose to include interior decoration of premises (which as, explained above, may not fall within construction and maintenance) as construction and maintenance where it would be convenient to let both construction and decoration under a single contract. This would mean, for example, that should the DLO win the contract the costs and the "price" of the part of the "job" which relates to interior maintenance could be included in its accounts, as well as the details of the work relating specifically to construction and maintenance. Where the authority considers it necessary to include within a single contract work which is otherwise subject to CCT under the 1988 LGA together with construction or maintenance work, this provision means that it may choose to let the work all together under the LGPLA, rather that being required to follow the (slightly different) procedures under the LGA for the part of the work falling under the latter Act. Alternatively, the authority may in such a case be able to treat the whole of the work as falling within the LGA 1988, as is explained below.[64]

---

[60] The Local Government Changes for England (Direct Labour and Service Organisations) Regulations 1994 S.I. 1994 No. 3167 (as amended by the Local Government Changes for England and Local Government Act 1988 (Competition) (Miscellaneous Amendment) Regulations 1995), reg. 5(3).

[61] *Ibid.* reg. 5(4).

[62] *Ibid.* reg. 5(1). But see the anti-avoidance provision in reg. 5(5).

[63] As inserted by LGA 1988, s.32 and Sched. 6, para. 10(6).

[64] See pp. 667–668.

These provisions apply only where the work *cannot efficiently* be carried out separately. They do not apply merely because it is *more convenient* to carry them out together. The latter test would give authorities more flexibility to adopt arrangements which are commercially convenient, and appears preferable to the current provision.

(d) THE DISTINCTION BETWEEN FUNCTIONAL WORK AND WORK UNDER WORKS CONTRACTS

(i) SIGNIFICANCE OF THE DISTINCTION

The discussion in this chapter and Chapter 14 on CCT is concerned primarily with work which an authority proposes to do through its DLO which is connected with the implementation of the authority's own functions. This is referred to in the LGA 1988 as "functional work". For example, an authority responsible for provision of libraries or leisure centres will be responsible for the construction and maintenance of such structures, and work done in connection with these structures is clearly "functional work". The principle behind the CCT regime is that authorities should not be able to perform such work themselves when it would be more efficient for the private sector to do so. This is achieved through the rules on tendering of work, which regulates the local authority in its role as procurer of services, combined with strict accounting requirements and financial objectives for the DLO, as described in Chapter 14.

In addition to its functional work an authority may also wish to undertake, through its DLO, work for other bodies. For example, it may wish to do work for others – either public or private bodies – to utilise spare capacity of the DLO. Here also, the government has taken the view that a local authority DLO should not undertake work where it would be more efficient for this to be done by the private sector. The LGPLA seeks to achieve this by requiring that the body which wishes to *purchase* the services from the DLO has put these services out to tender to the private sector, so that, as in relation to the authority's own work, the DLO must compete with the private sector to win the work. Accounting and financial requirements are again imposed on the DLO to ensure that the work is carried out only if won in fair competition. Here the legislation seeks to control an authority's activities not as a procuring entity but as a provider of services only. Where the authority engages in work for another this is referred to as work under a "works" contract, as opposed to "functional work".

This book is focused on the role of the authority as a procurer, as opposed to a provider. These present chapters are thus concerned mainly with the rules governing functional work. The rules on works contracts are, however, relevant to an authority's procurement activity in that these must be followed where an authority is contemplating engaging a provider who is another local authority, and are considered briefly at the end of Chapter 14.

(ii) THE DISTINCTION BETWEEN FUNCTIONAL AND NON-FUNCTIONAL WORK

"Functional work" is defined in section 8 of the LGPLA 1980. Subject to exceptions discussed below, it covers construction and maintenance work undertaken by a local authority or development body in the following cases:

(a) Where the work is in performance of or in connection with the authority's own functions.[65] Thus, if an authority has a responsibility for providing and maintaining library buildings and services, construction and maintenance work in connection with its libraries is functional work.

(b) Where the work is in performance of or in connection with an authority's discharge of the functions of a Minister of the Crown, a sewerage undertaker, or a local authority (within the meaning of Part VI of the 1972 Local Government Act), where this is done pursuant to obligations under any agreement, arrangement or requirement made under an enactment.[66]

For bodies which are caught under the label "local authorities",[67] however, the Act excludes from this definition all work done under a "works contract". A "works contract" is defined in section 5 of the LGPLA to cover various types of agreement under which a local authority may carry out construction or maintenance for *other* persons rather than for its own purposes. These are:

(a) An agreement under section 5(3)(c) of the London Government Act 1963.[68] This provides for agreements between certain London authorities for maintenance work by one on land or buildings for which another is responsible.

(b) An agreement under section 1 of the Local Authorities (Goods and Services) Act 1970.[69] This provides for agreements between local authorities and certain other public bodies for local authorities to carry out certain works of maintenance for those authorities.[70]

(c) An agreement made by virtue of any other enactment which provides for the carrying out by a local authority of any construction or maintenance work. This might include, for example, work carried out for other bodies pursuant to the power in section 111 of the Local Government Act 1972 permitting work incidental to the authority's own functions, which might permit it to use its spare capacity to do other

---

[65] LGPLA 1980, s.8(1)(a).
[66] LGPLA 1980, s.8(1)(b), as amended by the Water Act 1989, s.190(1) and Sched. 25, para. 6(1).
[67] This does not apply, however, to bodies which are caught as "development bodies" under the Act.
[68] LGPLA 1980, s.5(1)(a)(i).
[69] LGPLA 1980, s.5(1)(a)(ii).
[70] The 1970 Act itself precludes the possibility of covered authorities themselves carrying out construction (as opposed to maintenance) work for other bodies unless specifically authorised under some legislative provisions. This is why section 5 refers to maintenance work only, and not construction also.

work – for example, by bidding to carry out maintenance contracts tendered by other local authorities.

Section 5(2) of the LGPLA, however, provides that work is not a works contract under the above provisions only by reason that it is, or comprises, an agreement under which the functions of a Minister or other public body[71-72] fall to be discharged by a local authority. This kind of work is not excluded from the definition of "functional work" and thus falls to be treated as functional work. This appears to contemplate the case where the authority is vested with legal responsibility for the function in question, rather than merely carrying out the work as an independent contractor for another body – in other words, where the authority has the "client" responsibility, as well as where it proposes to carry out the "provider" role of actually performing the work. Thus, in general, it appears that work is functional work where the authority acts as both purchaser and bidder, and is works under a works contract where the authority seeks to do work on a contract let by another.

The definition of functional work above prima facie includes the case where an authority acts for another body not only by actually carrying out work but also merely by placing contracts for work on behalf of that other entity. This situation is, however, excluded from the definition of functional work by section 8(2) of the LGPLA. This provides, for both local authorities and development bodies, that where such bodies carry out construction or maintenance in the situations listed at (a), (b) or (c) above by placing a contract for the doing of work by another person, this is not to be treated as functional work. Such activity in simply letting contracts is regulated neither as functional work nor as work done under a works contract. However, this is not the case where the work is dependent upon, incidental to or preparatory to other construction or maintenance work which *is* to be undertaken by the DLO.

3. CONTRACTS COVERED BY THE LOCAL GOVERNMENT ACT 1988 (OTHER ACTIVITIES)

(1) GENERAL

The CCT rules under the Local Government Act 1988 apply to bodies which are "defined authorities" (defined at (2) below), in relation to activities designated as "defined activities" under the Act (see (3) below). As with the Local Government Planning and Land Act 1980, the rules applicable to contracts falling within the Act are partly laid down in

---

[71-72] As defined in the Local Authorities (Goods and Services) Act 1970.

rules applicable to contracts falling within the Act are partly laid down in the statute itself but are also supplemented by rules contained in delegated legislation and in statutory guidance.[73] As with construction and maintenance there are are two main types of obligations, those on the procedures for the award of contracts within the Act and those concerning the accounting, reporting and financial obligations of the in-house organisation (the DSO).[74]

(2) BODIES COVERED

The rules under the LGA 1988 generally apply, as mentioned, to bodies designated as "defined authorities" under the Act.[75] The meaning of defined authority is set out in section 1(1) of the Act. Generally, it covers most bodies subject to the LGPLA 1980 and in addition a number of other bodies of a local nature which are not covered by the 1980 Act – in particular, parish and community councils, and police and fire authorities.

More specifically in relation to England and Wales the concept of a "defined authority" covers:

(a) A local authority (section 20(1)(a)). In relation to England and Wales this covers a county council, a district council, a London borough council, a parish council, a community council, the Council of the Isles of Scilly, and the common council of the City of London in its capacity as local authority or police authority.

(b) An urban development corporation established by an order under section 135 of the LGPLA 1980 (section 20(1)(b)).

(c) A development corporation established for the purposes of a new town (section 20(1)(c)).

(d) The Commission for the New Towns (section 20(1)(d)).

(e) A police authority constituted under section 2 of the Police Act 1964, or as mentioned in section 3(1) of the 1964 Act; or a police authority established by section 24 or 25 of the Local Government Act 1985 (section 20(1)(d)).

(f) A fire authority constituted by a combination scheme and a metropolitan county fire and civil defence authority (section 20(1)(f).

(g) The London fire and civil defence authority (section 20(1)(g)).

(h) A metropolitan county passenger transport authority (section 20(1)(h)).

(i) An authority established by order under section 10(1) of the Local Government Act 1985 (which provides for local authorities engaged in

---

[73] On the main sources see pp. 706–709.
[74] On these see 14.
[75] LGA 1988, s.6(1) (obligation to follow the prescribed tendering procedure); s.9(1) (obligations relating to accounts); s.10(1) (obligations on financial reporting); s.12(1) (provision of information to interested persons); and s.13(1) and s.14 (notices and directions by the Secretary of State).

waste disposal to set up a separate entity for this purpose) (section 20(1)(i)).

(j) A joint education committee established by an order under paragraph 3 of Part II of Schedule I to the Education Act 1944.

In relation to England and Wales, where two or more bodies which are "defined authorities" under the above definition arrange under section 101 of the Local Government Act 1972 for the discharge of their functions by a joint committee, that committee is also a defined authority for the purpose of the Act.[76]

Bodies regulated under the 1988 Act will, like those covered by the LGPLA, be regulated also by either the public sector Works, Supplies or Services Regulations, or, in limited cases, the Utilities Regulations, which will also have to be followed where major contracts are awarded.

(3) ACTIVITIES COVERED

(a) GENERAL PRINCIPLES

The obligations under the LGA 1988 apply only to work which relates to the activities listed in section 2(2) of the Act – referred to by the Act as "defined activities".[77]

Originally, section 2(2) listed seven defined activities. However, it also provides for the Secretary of State to add new activities to the list by order[78] and a number of activities have been added subsequently to the list pursuant to this provision. The activities originally listed are refuse collection; the cleaning of buildings; other cleaning (effectively, street cleaning); school and welfare catering; other catering; grounds maintenance; and the repair and maintenance of vehicles. Activities subsequently added by order of the Secretary of State are the management of sports and leisure facilities; the supervision of parking; vehicle management; security; housing management; legal services; construction related and property services; personnel services; financial services; and information technology services. The scope of each activity is set out in detail at (d) below.

---

[76] LGA 1988, s.20(4).

[77] LGA 1988 s.2(1), providing for the section to apply in respect of Part I of the Act; s.2(2), listing "defined activities"; s.6(1) providing for stated tendering procedures to apply in relation to functional work "falling within a defined activity" (also s.9(1), 10(1), 11(1) and 12(1), referring to "defined activity" in relation to other obligations under the Act).

[78] LGA 1988 s.2(3), as amended by LGA 1992, s.11 and Sched. 1, para. 10. The power is exercisable by statutory instrument which must be laid before and approved by each House of Parliament (LGA 1988, s.15(1)). In exercising the power the Secretary of State must consult with "such representatives of local government as appear to him appropriate". LGA 1988, s.6(3), as amended by LGA 1992 s.11 and Sched. 1, para. 12, makes it clear that for each defined activity the Act may be applied to only a proportion of that activity as has been done in the case of many of the professional services, as explained further below.

(b) WORK WHICH CANNOT BE SEPARATED FROM A DEFINED ACTIVITY

Section 2(7) of the Act provides that where work which is not within the definition of a defined activity cannot in the view of the authority be carried out efficiently separately from a particular defined activity, the authority may treat that other work as falling within the defined activity also. This may be used to combine work falling within defined activity X with (i) work falling within another defined activity; (ii) work falling under the LGPLA 1980; and (iii) work which is not subject to CCT at all. This provision prevents the need for authorities to separate work, partly covered by the Act and partly not, which is more conveniently treated as a single package. It allows such work to be treated as a single activity for the purpose of, for example, letting contracts, DSO accounts and the application of thresholds for exemption.

The provision is most likely to be invoked in situation (i), where an authority seeks to combine two defined activities together. For example, authorities may wish to let a single contract and run a single DSO to cover all catering, both for schools and welfare (one defined activity) and for other purposes (a separate defined activity). Authorities may also, for example, wish to combine the defined activities of refuse collection and street cleaning.

Situation (ii) is rather unlikely to arise now that so many of an authority's activities which are suitable for contracting out are now subject to CCT in their own right.

As regards situation (iii), where an authority considers it necessary to include within a single arrangement both construction and maintenance within the meaning of the 1980 LGPLA and work under a defined activity under the 1988 Act it is submitted that the effect of this provision is that it may choose to treat all the work under the LGA rather than applying the LGPLA to the construction or maintenance element of the work. Alternatively, the authority may in such a case be able to treat the whole of the work as falling within the LGPLA 1980, as was explained above.[79]

As was noted in considering the LGPLA, these provisions apply only where the work *cannot efficiently* be carried out separately and probably cannot be used simply because it is *more convenient* not to separate them. In combining work in this way authorities must also bear in mind the need to avoid anti-competitive behaviour in the way contracts are packaged, and to ensure maximum competition it may be necessary to allow bidders to bid for one element of the contract alone as well as for the whole package.[80]

In preparing accounts relating to the work of the DSO for each defined activity under the Act authorities must expressly identify work

---

[79] See pp. 661–662.
[80] See further pp. 710–711.

included in the accounts which is included by virtue of a decision under this provision.[81]

(c) WORK RELATING TO MORE THAN ONE DEFINED ACTIVITY

Section 2(5) of the LGA 1988 provides that where work falls within more than one defined activity it shall be treated as falling within one only, as determined by the authority in question.

In preparing accounts relating to the work of the DSO for each defined activity under the Act authorities must expressly identify work included in the accounts which is included by virtue of a decision under this provision.[82]

(d) SCOPE OF THE DEFINED ACTIVITES[83]

(i) THE COLLECTION OF REFUSE

The first defined activity is collection of refuse.[84] In relation to England and Wales, this is defined exhaustively in paragraph 1 of Schedule 1 to the LGA 1988 to cover[85] (a) the collection of household waste[86] and (b) the collection of commercial waste.[87]

(ii) THE CLEANING OF BUILDINGS

The second defined activity is the cleaning of buildings, which is defined in paragraph 2 of Schedule 1 of the LGA 1988[88] to cover:
(a) the cleaning of the windows of any building, both inside and outside and
(b) the cleaning of the interior of any building.

It appears that this is not an exhaustive definition, but that other types of building cleaning not listed above may be included.[89] However, the

---

[81] LGA 1988, s.11(2)(d).
[82] LGA 1988, s.11(2)(c).
[83] For more detail on what is involved in practice in these defined activities, and strategic considerations in letting contracts, see Cirell and Bennett, *Compulsory Competitive Tendering: Law and Practice,* Chap. 7.
[84] Listed in LGA 1988 s.2(2)(a).
[85] LGA 1988 s.2(2) and Sched. 1, para. 1.
[86] Household waste has the meaning in section 75 of the Environmental Protection Act 1990, except that sewage is excluded, so that the disposal of sewage is not within the defined activity.
[87] Commercial waste has the meaning in section 75 of the Environmental Protection Act 1990, except that sewage is excluded so that again disposal of sewage is not subject to CCT.
[88] LGA 1988 s.2(2) and Sched. 1, para. 2(1).
[89] This is not absolutely clear: LGA s.2(2) merely says the schedule is to have effect in interpreting section 2, and the relevant para. of the schedule itself merely says that the above things "fall within" the definition. However, the non-exhaustive nature of the definition can be deduced from the exclusion of exterior cleaning apart from windows – which would be unnecessary if the definition were confined to the list mentioned, since it is not included in that list.

Schedule expressly excludes the cleaning of the exterior of buildings apart from the windows.[90]

There are also exclusions for cleaning of the following:

(a) A "dwelling".[91] This is defined to mean "a building or part of a building occupied as a person's home or as other living accommodation (whether the occupation is separate or shared with others)".[92] The concept of a dwelling does not, however, cover any part not so occupied,[93] the cleaning of which must thus be included in work to be tendered in accordance with the Act.

(b) A "residential establishment".[94] This is defined to mean,[95] in relation to England and Wales, a building or part of a building under which residential accommodation is provided under section 21 or 29 of the National Assistance Act 1948; Schedule 8 to the National Health Service Act 1977; or section 81 of the Child Care Act 1980 (now repealed).

(c) A regional "police establishment".[96] In relation to England and Wales this means a building or part of a building used by two or more police forces for the joint discharge of functions relating to the investigation of crime pursuant to section 13 of the Police Act 1964.[97] Previously there was a wider exemption covering all buildings used by police forces for police functions, but this was removed in 1995. However, for work previously covered by this general exemption it is still permitted to retain 20 per cent of the value of the work in-house, it being recognised that a certain "core" amount of such work may need to be kept in-house for strategic reasons.

A further exemption also applies in the case of small schools which have opted out of local authority control, to allow such schools to pursue their own arrangements with respect to the cleaning of the school – which might be either through in-house provision, or through a private contractor. The exemption also applies in relation to ground maintenance, as explained at (vii) below. However, it does not apply in relation to other activities relating to the school such as building maintenance or catering. This exemption is contained in the Local Government Act 1988 (Defined Activities) (Exemption) (Small Schools) Order 1992.[98] More specifically, it applies to building cleaning and ground maintenance, where carried out in a school which is conducted by a governing body with a delegated budgetary authority (that is, delegated in accordance with Chapter III of Part I of the Education Reform Act 1988).[99] It only

---

[90] LGA 1988, Sched. 1, para. 2(2)(a).
[91] LGA 1988, Sched. 1, para. 2(2)(b).
[92] LGA 1988, Sched. 1, para. 2(3).
[93] *Ibid.*
[94] LGA 1988, Sched. 1, para. 2(2)(b).
[95] LGA 1988, Sched. 1, para. 2(4).
[96] LGA 1988, Sched. 1, para. 2(2)(b), as amended by the Local Government Act 1988 (Competition) (Defined Activities) Order 1995, 1995 S.I. No. 1915, Article 3(1).
[97] LGA 1988, Sched. 1, para. 2(b), as substituted by Local Government Act 1988 (Competition) (Defined Activities) Order 1995, above, Article 2(3).
[98] S.I. 1992 No. 1626.
[99] Article 1(2) and Article 3(1) of S.I. 1992 No. 1626.

applies where it is estimated that in the financial[99a] year in question the total amount of building cleaning and ground maintenance work will not exceed the equivalent of three full-time employees[99b] – an estimate which must be made by the authority itself, having regard to the advice of the school governing body, and the number of persons required to carry out the activity in previous years.[1]

The application must be considered at the start of each financial year, although contracts for these activities are required to be let for a period of at least three years. Hence, contracts with external contractors must take into account the possibility that schools exempt in one year may need to be covered by the contract in future years.

(iii) OTHER CLEANING

Certain cleaning which does not fall within the heading of "building cleaning", discussed above, constitutes a defined activity, within the category listed in section 2(2) of the LGA 1988 as "other cleaning".[2] The kind of cleaning falling within this heading is set out in an exhaustive list in Schedule 1 to the Act.[3] It covers the following:

(a) The removal of litter from land.[4] "Litter" is not defined exhaustively, but is expressly stated to include leaves. On the other hand, derelict vehicles, derelict vessels and scrap metal are expressly excluded.[5]

(b) The emptying of litter bins.[6] "Litter bin" is defined, in relation to England and Wales, as a "receptacle provided in a street or public place for refuse or litter".[7]

(c) The cleaning of streets (by sweeping or otherwise).[8]

(d) The emptying of gullies.[9]

[99a] Local Government Act 1988 (Defined Activities) (Cleaning of Police Buildings) (England and Wales) Regulations 1995, S.I. 1995 No. 1973, providing for CCT to apply to only 80 per cent of this work. A further deduction from the 80 per cent is also permitted for a limited period for work already won by the authority in a voluntary competitive tendering exercise.

[99b] Article 3(2). A full-time employee is defined as an employee whose average weekly working hours including overtime do not over the year exceed the standard working week for a full-time employee as specified for the time being by the National Joint Council for Local Authorities Services (Manual Workers): Article 1(2). Article 3(2)(b) of the Order requires that an authority must include in the calculation work in the cleaning of buildings and maintenance of ground which would normally be outside the defined activities of building cleaning and ground maintenance by virtue of the exemptions provided in s.2(6) LGA (covering certain work incidental to other duties – see further pp. 697–699) and in Article 4 of S.I. 1988 No. 1372 (the exemption for "tied work": see further p. 699).

[1] Article 3(3).

[2] LGA 1988 s.2(2)(c).

[3] LGA 1988, Sched. 1, para. 3.

[4] LGA 1988, Sched. 1, para. 3(1)(a).

[5] LGA 1988, Sched. 1, para. 3(2).

[6] LGA 1988, Sched. 1, para. 3(1)(b).

[7] LGA 1988, Sched. 1, para. 3(2).

[8] LGA 1988, Sched. 1, para. 3(1)(c). "Street" has, in relation to England and Wales, the meaning given to it by section 329(1) of the Highways Act 1980.

[9] LGA 1988, Sched. 1, para. 3(1)(d).

(e) The cleaning of traffic signs and street name plates.[10]

(iv) CATERING FOR PURPOSES OF SCHOOLS AND WELFARE

"Catering for purposes of schools and welfare" is another defined activity,[11] and an exhaustive definition of what this category covers is given in paragraph 4 of Schedule 1 to the LGA 1988. The functions covered are as follows.

(a) Providing ingredients for, preparing, delivering and serving meals for consumption in schools[12]; and providing refreshments for consumption in schools.[13] There is an exception for special schools, and schools "on whose premises some or all of the pupils reside" (*i.e.* boarding schools), provided that, in England and Wales, the school is maintained by a local education authority and also that all the meals are prepared on the premises.[14]

(b) Providing ingredients for, preparing and delivering (though not serving) meals, in residential establishments and day centres[15]; and providing refreshments for consumption in residential establishments or day centres.[16] There is an important exception, however, in that the rules do not apply to establishments and centres maintained by a local authority[17] where meals are prepared on the premises.[18] Thus where the meals at, for example, an old people's home or day centre, are prepared on the premises the CCT rules do not apply, and the meals may continue to be prepared by local authority staff (which may of course be those involved in other aspects of the establishment).

(c) Providing ingredients for and preparing meals (though not serving and delivering meals) for provision under the local authority "meals on wheels" service.[19]

---

[10] LGA 1988, Sched. 1, para. 3(1)(e). "Traffic sign" has the meaning given to it by section 64(1) of the Road Traffic Regulation Act 1984, except that in the present context it is not to include a line or mark on a road: Sched. 1, para. 3(2).

[11] LGA 1988 s.2(2)(d).

[12] LGA 1988, Sched. 1, para. 4(1)(a).

[13] LGA 1988, Sched. 1, para. 4(1)(b).

[14] LGA 1988, Sched. 1, para. 4(2).

[15] LGA 1988, Sched. 1, para. 4(1)(c).

[16] LGA 1988, Sched. 1, para. 4(1)(d). "Residential establishment" has the same meaning for these purposes as it does in relation to the cleaning of buildings (LGA 1988, Sched. 1 para. 4(4)), as outlined at pp. 669–670, above. "Day centre" is defined in relation to England and Wales as premises, other than residential premises, where facilities are provided under either section 29 of the National Assistance Act 1948; section 45 of the Health Services and Public Health Act 1968; schedule 8 to the National Health Service Act 1977; or part II of schedule 9 to the Health and Social Services Adjudications Act 1983.

[17] "Local authority" here has the same meaning as under section 1(1), which defines this term in the context of "defined authority" for the purposes of the CCT rules generally: see p. 665.

[18] LGA 1988 Sched. 1, para. (3).

[19] More precisely, this refers to the provision of meals to persons in their own homes under statutory schemes under section 45 of the Health Services and Public Health Act 1968, section 2(1)(g) of the Chronically Sick and Disabled Persons Act 1970, or Part II of Schedule 9 to the Health and Social Services and Security Adjudications Act 1983.

(v) OTHER CATERING

Catering other than for schools and welfare is also covered, as the defined activity of "other catering".[20] This is defined in paragraph 5 of Schedule 1 to the LGA 1988 to cover all catering (providing ingredients for and preparing and serving meals, and providing refreshments),[21] except catering for schools, residential establishments, day centres and meals on wheels.[22] Within this defined activity falls, for example, provision of meals and refreshments for the public at facilities such as leisure centres and museums, provision of catering services for local authority employees, and catering at local authority functions.

Specifically excluded, with respect to England Wales, is catering for institutions of further education, but this exclusion is now of little importance since such institutions have now been largely removed from local authority control.[23]

(vi) MANAGING SPORTS AND LEISURE FACILITIES

Managing sports and leisure facilities is another defined activity, which was added to the list by statutory instrument in 1989.[24] The scope of this activity is elaborated in paragraph 8 of Schedule 1 to the 1988 Act, in a paragraph added by the 1989 statutory instrument.[25] This provides that the activity includes management of swimming pools; skating rinks; gymnasia; tennis, squash and badminton courts; pitches for team games; athletics grounds; tracks and centres for bicycles (motorised or otherwise); golf courses and putting greens; bowling greens; bowling centres; bowling alleys; riding centres; courses for horse racing; artificial ski slopes; riding centres; flying centres; ballooning or parachuting facilities; and boating or water sports centres, whether on coastal or inland waters.[26]

The Act does not make it clear whether or not this list is exhaustive. Some paragraphs of the schedule indicate expressly that the definition in that paragraph is exhaustive (for example, the definition of refuse collection) which might suggest that where this is not done the definition is *not* exhaustive; but, on the other hand, there are other paragraphs of the schedule in which no express indication is given but in which it seems clear that the definition is intended to be complete. Thus the presence or absence of express indication is not really conclusive. In fact, it seems

---

[20] LGA 1988 s.2(2)(e).
[21] LGA 1988, Sched. 1, para. 5.
[22] Sched. 1, para. 5(2) and (3).
[23] The meaning of "institution for further education" is defined in Sched. 1, para. 5(3) and (4).
[24] LGA 1988, s.2(2)(ee), added by the Local Government Act 1988 (Competition in Sports and Leisure Facilities) Order 1989 SI 1989 No.2488, s.2(1).
[25] LGA 1988, Sched. 1, para. 8, added by Article 2(2) of the 1989 order.
[26] LGA 1988, Sched. 1, para. 8(1).

likely that this particular definition was intended to be comprehesive, since if the words are interpreted in a general manner this would bring with the defined activity many "leisure" facilities which do not involve physical exercise, yet it seems the provision is intended to cover only sporting facilities. However, if the definition is intended to be exhaustive, it may be that some relevant facilities have been mistakenly omitted – for example, climbing walls, which are maintained by some authorities.[27]

"Managing" is defined to include[28]: instruction and supervision of sports and activities; catering; hiring out of equipment for use at the facilities (although it appears hire for use elswhere is not covered); marketing and promotion; taking bookings; collecting, and accounting for, fees and charges; security; cleaning and maintenance (excluding the maintenance of the outside of buildings); and the assumption of responsibility in relation to heating, lighting, and other service charges relating to the facility. The definition given is stated to be without prejudice to the general concept of "management".

Management of facilities is excluded if the facilities are provided on premises which are not used predominantly for sport or physical recreation.[29] For example, a badminton court in a Community hall mainly used for other activities (youth clubs, meetings, fetes etc.) would be excluded.[30] However, where the predominant use of premises is for sport or physical recreation, the application of the Act is not affected by the fact that part of the premises are used for other purposes.[31] It has been suggested that the test of predominant user is using "more than 50 per cent of the realistically usable time".[32]

The provisions are also inapplicable to facilities on the premises of educational institutions.[33] Thus they would not apply in relation to a swimming pool on a school site, regardless of whether the public uses the pool for more hours than the school.

A further exemption applies to certain facilities provided under section 53 of the Education Act 1944,[34] a section which allows *education* authorities to provide sports and leisure facilities not necessarily limited to educational use. Such facilities may not be on educational premises but could be in a separate location altogether, so that the exemption referred to in the previous paragraph for facilities on the premises of educational institutions would not apply. The exemption applies where there is use of such facilities by the education authority itself which amounts to 600 hours in the preceding financial year.

---

[27] See Cirell and Bennett, *Compulsory Competitive Tendering: Law and Practice*, at 8.26.
[28] LGA 1988, Sched. 1, para. 8(4).
[29] LGA 1988, Sched. 1, para. 8(2)(a).
[30] This exception is also capable of covering use of facilities on school premises but there is in any case a special exemption to cover this specific case, considered in the next paragraph, which does not even require consideration of the issue of dominant user.
[31] LGA 1988, Sched. 1, para. 8(1).
[32] Cirell and Bennett, above, at 8.2.1.
[33] LGA 1988, Sched. 1, para. 8(2)(b).
[34] LGA 1988, Sched. 1, para. 8(3).

(vii) MAINTENANCE OF GROUND

A further activity covered by the LGA 1988 is "maintenance of ground".[35] This is defined in Schedule 1 to the LGA 1988, paragraph 6, as covering the following activities only.

(a) The first is cutting and tending grass. This is expressly stated to include returfing and reseeding, but not to include initial turfing and seeding. These latter activities are thus in practice largely excluded from the CCT regime.[36]

(b) The other activity covered under this heading is planting and tending trees, hedges, shrubs, flowers and other plants. However, "landscaping" is expressly excluded, and thus the provision does not seem to cover the initial laying out of lines of trees, flower beds, etc.[37] There has been some debate over whether nursery activity (for example, directed towards the rearing of plants to be used in public parks) is covered. It is submitted that both planting and tending nursery beds are indeed covered, since the rearing of plants in a place other than the intended destination cannot reasonably be regarded as "landscaping".[38]

Expressly excluded from the defined activity is any activity of which the primary purpose is "research or securing the survival of any kind of plant".[39]

In practice, these activities of planting and tending grass, trees, plants, etc. largely relate to work in public parks and gardens, and to school grounds and playing fields. Related activities, such as tree felling and maintenance of boundary fencing, do not appear to be covered.[40]

In the case of school grounds, there is a special exemption for small schools which have opted out of local authority financial control; these may make their own arrangements for ground maintenance, and also for the cleaning of the building, free from the CCT regime. The details of this exemption have already been considered above in relation to building cleaning.[41]

---

[35] LGA 1988 s.2(2)(f).

[36] Whilst prima facie they are construction or maintenance works caught by the LGPLA 1980, works relating to parks, gardens, playing fields, open spaces or allotments are expressly excluded from the 1980 Act so that initial turfing and seeding in relation to these venues will be excluded: see p. 653.

[37] This activity might again be considered construction and maintenance activity within the LGPLA 1980, but if so is again in any case largely excluded by the exclusion of work relating to parks and gardens: see p. 653.

[38] This view has been taken by the Department of Environment: see Circular 8/88. For a contrary view see Cirell and Bennett, *Compulsory Competitive Tendering: Law and Practice* at 8.19.

[39] LGA 1988, Sched. 1, para. 6(2).

[40] They might, however, by caught by the LGPLA 1980 as construction and maintenance work, if not within the exclusion for work relating to parks, gardens, etc., considered above. It was noted above that the exclusion from the 1980 Act does not apply to work relating to a building or structure, but it is not clear whether "fencing" may be considered a "structure".

[41] See pp. 669–671.

(viii) SUPERVISION OF PARKING

A further defined activity[42] is "supervision of parking, added in 1994. CCT applies to this activity for most defined authorities but not for Waste Regulation Authorities (or County Councils acting as such), Urban Development Corporations or the Commission for New Towns,[43-44] or for fire authorities or metropolitan County Passenger Transport Authorities.

The activity covers certain activities of local authorities in the enforcement of on-street parking controls. Powers to carry out some of these activities which were formerly carried out by traffic wardens under the control of the police, may now be conferred upon local authorities, on application to the Secretary of State, under the Road Traffic Act 1991. (The requirement to apply CCT to such activities may, of course, inhibit authorities from applying for these powers.) CCT does not apply to all authorities' parking activities; in particular, it has no application to their activities relating to off-street parking, although authorities may choose to put these out to tender.

More precisely, "supervision of parking" is defined exhaustively in paragraph 6A of Schedule 1 to the LGA 1988, to cover the following:[45]
(a) the fixing or giving of penalty charge notices under section 66 of the Road Traffic Act 1991;
(b) the fixing or removal, or authorisation of the fixing or removal, of immobilisation devices under section 69 of the Road Traffic Act 1991;
(c) the removal, or the making arrangements for the removal, of vehicles, in pursuance of regulations under section 99 of the Road Traffic Regulation Act 1984, in cases where this removal is effected or arranged by "parking attendants";[46] and
(d) the making of arrangements for the custody, release or disposal of vehicles whose removal is effected or arranged under 3 above. This will include in practice the operation of vehicle compounds.

The CCT rules do not extend to setting penalties. Authorities are generally likely to choose to retain this function, setting out in the contract specifications the penalties to be levied.

(ix) REPAIR AND MAINTENANCE OF VEHICLES

"Repair and maintenance of vehicles" is also a defined activity.[47] This activity is defined in Schedule 1, paragraph 7(1), as covering "the repair

---

[42] LGA 1988, s.2(2)(ff), as inserted by Local Government Act 1988 (Competition) (Defined Activities) Order 1994, S.I. 1994 No. 2884, Article 2(2).
[43-44] It is proposed that this will be provided for under an order made under LGA 1988, s.2(9).
[45] As inserted by Local Government Act 1988 (Competition) (Defined Activities) Order 1994, S.I. 1994 No. 2884, Article 2(1)(a).
[46] As defined under s.63A of the Road Traffic Regulation Act 1984.
[47] LGA 1988, s.2(2)(g).

and the maintenance of any motor vehicle or trailer". The definition does not provide expressly that it is exhaustive of the activities covered, but it is probably intended to be so.

"Motor vehicle" is further defined in paragraph 7 as a "mechanically propelled vehicle intended or adapted for use on roads or otherwise on land" thus excluding, for example, water-borne motorised craft. The concept of "vehicle" is not itself further defined, but probably does not include *all* motorised landcraft. It has been suggested by Cirell and Bennett that it covers only items which are driven to the work site under their own power (thus excluding, for example, man-driven lawn mowers) and further that it does not include certain more specialised items (such as a mobile asbestos decontamination unit)[48] even where these are fully mobile. This view seems to be correct. Within the definition will be ordinary cars and vans used in local authority work (for transport of dignitaries and staff, or transport of materials), as well as a variety of specialised vehicles, such as those used by the authority in refuse collection or street cleaning.

"Trailer" is defined for this purpose in paragraph 7 as "a vehicle intended or adapted to be drawn by a motor vehicle".

Repair of damage caused by an accident is expressly excluded by paragraph 7(2), although in practice authorities may often wish to include this along with other repair and maintenance. A general exclusion of emergency work from the CCT requirements, considered below,[49] will also be of particular relevance for this activity.

Also excluded, under paragraph 7(3), is the repair and maintenance of police vehicles.[50]

An exemption also covers motor vehicles and trailers used only for the discharge of a fire service function.[51] In 1992 the Department of the Environment has recommended market testing of such services, except where carried out by firefighters, but has not required the application of the strict CCT regime.[52]

---

[48] Cirell and Benett, above, at 8.20.

[49] See pp. 698–699.

[50] A police vehicle is defined, in relation to England and Wales, as a vehicle used *only* in connection with the discharge of police functions of an authority falling within section 1(1)(e) of the Act (that is, a "police authority") or of the Common Council of the City of London (LGA 1988, Sched. 1, para. 7(5)). In 1992 the Department of the Environment proposed extending CCT to 40 per cent of such work with a later review to see if a further proportion should be covered: Department of the Environment, Consultation paper, *Extension of Compulsory Competitive Tendering* (November 1992), paras. 14–15.

[51] The Local Government Act 1988 (Defined Activities) (Exemptions) (England) Order S.I.1988 No. 1372, Article 5; the Local Government Act 1988 (Defined Activities) (Wales) Order S.I. 1988 No. 1469, Article 5.

[52] *Extension of Compulsory Competitive Tendering*, above, para. 17.

(x) MANAGEMENT OF VEHICLES

"Management of vehicles" is a further defined activity added in 1994.[53] CCT applies to this activity for most defined authorities but not for Waste Regulation Authorities (or County Councils acting as such), Urban Development Corporations or the Commission for New Towns,[54-55] or for fire authorities.

The activity is exhaustively defined, in paragraph 7A of Schedule 1 to the LGA 1988[56] as covering the following:

(a) Arranging for motor vehicles to be available to meet the authority's requirements from time to time. This will involve procuring the vehicles, and also ensuring that they are made available as required. However, it is not intended to cover the drawing up of specifications for the procurement nor the scheduling of vehicle use[57] but merely the application of the management process once the issues of policy have been determined by the authority.

(b) Ensuring that statutory provisions on registration, licensing, safety and insurance are complied with in respect of the vehicles made available, and that drivers are licensed; and

(c) Arranging for provision of fuel, cleaning, repair and maintenance for such vehicles.

A motor vehicle for this purpose includes a trailer.[58]

As with vehicle maintenance, vehicles to be used exclusively for the purposes of a defined authority's functions as a police or fire authority are excluded.[59] It was originally also proposed to exclude vehicles used for home to school transport (under section 55(1) of the Education Act 1944), since a proposal was under consideration for designating provision of home and school transport as a separate defined activity which would include any vehicle management. However, since this proposal was not adopted at the time of the addition of vehicle management to the list of defined activities school vehicles have not been excluded.

In practice, this activity will often be packaged in a single contract with either vehicle maintenance or with an activity to which the vehicle relates – for example, the management of refuse collection vehicles with refuse collection. This may be permitted under the provisions of section 2(7) of the LGA 1988.[60]

---

[53] LGA 1988, s.2(2)(gg), as inserted by Local Government Act 1988 (Competition) (Defined Activities) Order 1994, S.I. 1994 No. 2884, Article 2(1)(a).

[54-55] It is proposed that this will be provided for under an order made under LGA 1988, s.2(9).

[56] As inserted by Local Government Act 1988 (Competition) (Defined Activities) Order 1994, S.I. 1994 No. 2884, Article 2(2).

[57] This is indicated by the Department of the Environment in its guidance *CCT for the Further Manual Services* (December 1994), para. 9.

[58] The definition of both motor vehicle and trailer are the same as that given in relation to the function of repair and maintenance of vehicles, considered at pp. 675–676. See LGA 1988, Sched. 1, para. 74(3).

[59] LGA 1988, Sched. 1 para. 7A(2).

[60] See pp. 667–668.

(xi) SECURITY WORK

"Security work" is another defined activity added in 1994.[61] An exhaustive definition of the activity is given in paragraph 10 of schedule 1 to the LGA 1988.[62] CCT for this activity will not apply to Waste Regulation Authorities (or County Councils acting as such), Urban Development Corporations or the Commission for New Towns.[63]

The definition covers certain types of security work relating to land:
(a) operation of security controls in relation to persons entering or leaving land, or moving between different parts of land; and
(b) operating security controls in respect of such land.

The land referred to is any which is occupied by a defined authority or land in which a defined authority has an interest. Such land will include, for example, buildings such as offices, schools and housing; construction sites; depots; and recreation grounds. Expressly excluded, however, is any work relating to libraries, museums or art galleries[64] and to any police establishment.[65] In the case of work falling under (a), there is also an exemption for any work relating to a dwelling or residential establishment.[66] This means, in particular, that staff employed in nursing homes, children's homes, etc., may carry out work relating to entry and exit security without the need for such work to be put out to CCT.

The activity is clearly not intended to cover the development of a security policy which remains for the authority.[67] It also does not include installation and maintenance of security systems.[68]

There is a specific exclusion from the scope of the defined activity for certain work which is carried out by an authority's employees which involves the exercise of special powers to enforce legislation.[69-70] This applies to work carried out by an employee whose work may involve the exercise of a power to deal with a breach of legislation in a "controlled

---

[61] LGA 1988, s.2(2)(i), as inserted by Local Government Act 1988 (Competition) (Defined Activities) Order 1994, S.I. 1994 No. 2884, Article 2(1)(b).

[62] As inserted by Local Government Act 1988 (Competition) (Defined Activities) Order 1994, S.I. 1994 No. 2884, Article 2(2)).

[63] It is proposed that this will be provided for under an order made under LGA 1988, s.2(9).

[64] For England and Wales this reference covers any library museum or art gallery maintained under the Public Libraries and Museums Act 1964: LGA 1988, Sched. 1 para. 10(3)(a).

[65] This means a building or part of a building used by police for the performance of their functions, whether as a police station, police training establishment or otherwise: Local Government Act 1988 (Competition) (Defined Activities) Order 1991, S.I. 1995 No. 1915, Article 3(3).

[66] For England and Wales these terms have the same meaning as in relation to building cleaning, as to which see pp. 668–669.

[67] See Department of Environment, *CCT for the Further Manual Services* (December 1994) para. 17.

[68] *Ibid.*

[69-70] The Local Government Act 1988 (Security Work) (Exemption) (England) Order 1995, S.I. 1995 No. 2074, Article 2.

place", namely an airport,[71] a burial ground,[72] a common,[73] a country park,[74] education premises,[75] a harbour, housing amenity land,[76] a market, an open space,[77] a park, a picnic site, [78] a pleasure ground,[79] a port, a recreation ground, or a road playground.[80] It applies to powers of enforcement conferred under section 40 of the Local Government (Miscellaneous Provisions) Act 1982, under any local Act of Parliament, or under any byelaws made under, or by virtue of a power in, any general or local Act of Parliament. The exemption only applies when the power in question cannot be exercised by anyone other than either an employee of the authority or a constable. It also applies only where the greater part of the employee's work is carried out in relation to a controlled place.

There is also an exemption for security work carried out in relation to a court house.[81] This is not subject to any specific restrictions.

(xii) HOUSING MANAGEMENT

I. Services Covered

Housing management is another defined activity under the LGA 1988,[82] added in 1994. The functions falling within this activity are set out exhaustively in paragraph 9 of Schedule 1 to the LGA 1988. Generally, the philosophy of the rules is to require the day-to-day management function to be subject to CCT whilst permitting the authority to retain in-house policy decisions relating to housing management, such as the decision to allocate accommodation The approach adopted here is different to that for most white collar activities under the CCT rules, which have been defined in a comprehensive manner to include even some functions which are unsuitable for contracting out. In these areas it is for authorities to decide which functions should be contracted out, by making use of a right to retain a high percentage of the defined activity in-house, without applying CCT. With housing management, on the

---

[71] As defined in the Airports Act 1986 s.82(1).
[72] As defined in the Open Spaces Act 1906 s.20.
[73] As defined in the Commons Act 1899 s.15.
[74] Meaning a country park provided under the Countryside Act 1968 s.7.
[75] Meaning premises to which the Local Government (Miscellaneous Provisions) Act 1982 s.40 applies.
[76] Meaning land in relation which bye laws may be made under the Housing Act 1985 s.23(2).
[77] As defined in the Open Spaces Act 1906 s.20.
[78] Meaning a site provided under the Countryside Act 1968 s.6(2).
[79] Meaning land held under the Public Health Act 1875 s.164.
[80] Defined as a road in relation to which an order has been made under the Road Traffic Regulation Act 1984 s.29.
[81] The Local Government Act 1988 (Security Work) (Exemption) (England) Order 1995, S.I. 1995 No. 2074, Article 3.
    It can also be noted that there are exemptions in the same Order for certain security work carried out by the Common Council of the City of London relating to the Guildhall (Article 4) and for security relating to the Woolwich ferry (Article 5).
[82] LGA 1988, s.2(2)(h), as inserted by the Local Government Act 1988 (Competition) (Defined Activities) (Housing Management) Order 1994, S.I. No. 2279, Article 2(b).

other hand, only 5 per cent of the work may be retained in-house without competition, but functions which would widely be regarded as unsuitable for contracting out are excluded from the initial definition of the defined activity.

More specifically, in relation to England and Wales housing management covers the following with respect to all local authority housing[83]:

(a) dealing with applications, from the time the property has been allocated until immediately after the tenancy agreement has been entered into, and dealing with assignments under section 92 of the Housing Act 1985;

(b) informing tenants of the terms of their tenancies and taking steps to enforce these terms;

(c) collecting rent, services charges[84] and service charge loan payments; keeping suitable records of sums collected; collecting arrears and negotiating agreements for the payment of arrears; and monitoring compliance with such agreements;

(d) arranging for the vacating of the property when the tenancy or licence has terminated;

(e) inspecting vacant property,[85] determining the need for works before the next letting, ensuring that these are carried out and reporting on progress to the landlord;

(f) taking steps to prevent vandalism and unlawful occupation of vacant property,[86] including by ensuring necessary works are carried out, and reporting on progress to the landlord;

(g) taking steps to remove unlawful occupants;

(h) assessing the condition of the common parts; assessing the necessary maintenance, repair, cleaning (including disinfestation) and clearance; and ensuring that necessary works are carried out and progress reported to the landlord;

(i) assessing requests for repairs; ensuring that necessary work is carried out; and reporting on progress to the landlord;

(j) carrying out inspections and surveys to ascertain the physical condition or state of repair of the property and whether it is occupied;

(k) assessing claims for compensation under regulations under section 96 of the Housing Act 1985 and making recommendations to the landlord;

---

[83] "Local authority housing" means housing accommodation provided by a local authority under the 1985 Housing Act, including garages, parking spaces and outhouses provided in connection with this accommodation and usually enjoyed with it, and common parts of buildings with two or more dwellings: para. 9(3) of Sched. 1. It excludes provision of accommodation in hostels as defined in section 622 of the Housing Act 1985: para. 9(3) of Sched. 1.

[84] "Service charge" means an amount payable by a tenant of premises which is payable, directly or indirectly, for services, repairs, maintenance or insurance or the landlord's costs of management: LGA 1988, Sched 1, para. 9(3).

[85] "Vacant property" means housing accommodation (including garages, parking spaces and outhouses provided in connection with the accommodation and usually enjoyed with it) which is unoccupied whether by reason of termination of a secure tenancy or otherwise: LGA 1988, Sched. 1, para. 9(3).

[86] On the definition of "vacant property" see note 85 above.

(l) assessing applications for payment under regulations under section 99A of the 1985 Housing Act (concerning compensation for improvements) or under section 100 of the Act (concerning reimbursement for work which adds value to the property), and making recommendations to the landlord;

(m) operating reception and security services at the entrance to the property;

(n) taking action to control any disturbance in local authority housing or to resolve disputes between occupants, including dealing with appropriate bodies (such as dispute resolution agencies).

Certain of these functions are not covered where the tenant(s) or prospective tenant(s) in question are not all private individuals; where the tenancy is a "long tenancy"[87]; where the tenancy is a lease granted in pursuance of the right to acquire on rent to mortgage terms conferred by Part V of the Housing Act 1985; where the tenancy is a lease granted on payment of a premium calculated by reference to a percentage of the value of the demised premises or the cost of providing them; or where it is a tenancy under which the tenant or his personal representative will or may be (directly or indirectly) entitled to a sum calculated by reference to the value of the demised premises.[88] The functions not covered in these circumstances are those in (a) (dealing with applications and assignments); (d) (arranging for vacating of property); and (g) (taking steps to remove unlawful occupants); and assessing whether housing is occupied under (j).

A "tenancy" for the purpose of the above provisions has the same meaning as in section 621 of the Housing Act 1985 and includes a secure tenancy[89]; and "tenant" is to be construed accordingly.

Housing management work is not treated as a defined activity for certain authorities when the work relates to houses in respect of which the authority has delegated its housing management functions to other organisations, where the work is being carried out by staff of the relevant organisation subject to the direction of its committee or board of directors.[90] The exemption expires on either April 1, 2001 or April 1, 2002, according to the authority. Whilst the effect of this exemption is to exclude such work from the defined activity, so that no aspects of the CCT regime apply to such work, it should be noted that the value of this work must nevertheless be taken into account in calculating the value of

---

[87] Within the meaning of Housing Act 1985, s.115.

[88] LGA 1988, para. 9(2).

[89] LGA 1988, para. 9(3). Secure tenancy is defined in the same provision as having the same meaning as under the Housing Act 1985, s.622.

[90] Local Government Act 1988 (Defined Activities) (Exemption) (Housing Management) (England) Order 1995 No. 1182. The exemption applies to a district council, London Borough Council the Common Council of the City of London in its capacity as a local authority and the Council of the Isles of Scilly, where the work relates to houses in respect of which the authority has delegated functions to any organisation under the Housing Act 1985, s.27, where approved by the Secretary of State before April 1, 1994, of a housing management organisation within s.27 AB (8) of the same Act.

housing management work for the purpose of deciding whether this value meets the threshold of the CCT regime.

II. The excluded element

An authority is not required to put the whole of its housing management activities out to CCT but may retain a proportion in-house without the need for any competition. For most authorities the requirement to subject the activity to CCT is being phased in, with authorities being required to apply CCT to an increasing proportion of this activity as time goes on; but once the CCT regime is fully applicable the proportion to which CCT need not be applied will be a mere 5 per cent.[90a] To determine the amount of housing management services to which CCT applies, an authority must ascertain the total cost of such services over the forthcoming year and then deduct the 5 per cent (or whatever other proportion is applicable at the time in question). In calculating this amount the authority need not take into consideration any work which has already been contracted out to the private sector, since the CCT regime applies only to work carried out by the authority itself.

(xiii) LEGAL SERVICES

I. Services covered

"Legal services" is another defined activity designated as such in 1994[91].

The provision of such services is covered, where they are provided by "legal staff."[92] This covers solicitors, legal executives, barristers, advocates, and licensed and qualified conveyancers[93] and also any persons under their management or control.[94] Legal work done by other staff, such as enforcement work by trading standards officers, which is not supervised by persons with legal qualifications, is not covered.

[90a] Local Government Act 1988 (Competition) (Housing Management) (England) Regulations 1994, S.I. 1994 No. 2297. Authorities may also exclude from the figure to which CCT applies the amount equal to the value of any work which the authority is carrying out which it has won in a voluntary competitive tendering exercise, which ensures that it is not expected to compete again for work which it has already won in a fair competition: S.I. 1994 No. 2297, above, reg. 2. For most other white collar services there is, as explained below, also a minimum amount of work expressed in financial terms which the authority may retain in-house, even if it exceeds the percentage amount normally allowed to be kept in-house without competition. There is no such absolute amount provided for housing management: the figure must not exceed the 5 per cent. For housing management CCT does not apply at all unless the total annual value of the activity exceeds £500,000, but if it does exceed this amount CCT will apply to the whole activity bar 5 per cent: see further pp. 694–696.
[91] LGA 1988, s.2(2)(j), as inserted by Local Government Act 1988 (Competition) (Defined Activities) Order 1994, S.I. 1994 No. 2884, Article 2(1)(b).
[92] LGA 1988, Sched. 1, para. 11, as inserted by Local Government Act 1988 (Competition) (Defined Activities) Order 1994, S.I. 1994 No. 2884, Article 2(2).
[93] Within the meaning of the Administration of Justice Act 1985 (for England and Wales).
[94] Inserted by Local Government Act 1988 (Competition) (Defined Activities) Order 1994, S.I. 1994 No. 2884, s.2(1)(b).

No exhaustive definition of "legal services" is given, but a list of activities which definitely fall within the concept is set out in paragraph 11 of Schedule 1 to the LGA 1988.[95] These are as follows:

(a) the provision of legal advice to a defined authority; to its elected members; to any committee or subcommittee of a defined authority, or any other group of persons which reports to a defined authority or one of its committees or subcommittees; to any officer of defined authority; or to any department of a defined authority; or to any other person, where the advice is related to the discharge of the authority's functions;

(b) legal work in, or in connection with, any criminal or civil proceedings before a court or tribunal or at an inquiry;

(c) conveyancing work relating to property of any kind;

(d) legal work in connection with: contracts or agreements of any kind; matters relating to property of any kind; insurance arrangements; statutory notices, orders and bye-laws; and local or personal Bills;

(e) legal work in connection with the provision of a legal service for a defined authority, otherwise than by a member of its own staff.

The scope of legal services for the purpose of the CCT rules is deliberately very wide. It is recognised that it includes some activities which are not appropriate for contracting out at all – for example, activities relating to the tendering process itself, or involving the provision of strategic advice, or where there is unlikely to be relevant private sector expertise. However, this is not problematic because of the existence of the 55 per cent exemption, which allows the authority to retain such activities in-house without competition. The definition of the defined activity does not, in fact given any specific guidance to authorities on which type of legal work should be subject to CCT, and which the authority should bring under the exemption. However, the authority's choice may be constrained by the prohibition on anti-competitive behaviour[96]: for example, because of this prohibition, it probably will not be permitted to include within the part subject to CCT those services in which the private sector is unlikely to be interested.

Some legal services are provided in support of specific activities of the authority which are themselves activities subject to CCT – for example, legal services relating to housing management. In this case, they fall within both that defined activity and the activity of legal services. Authorities may in this case, under section 2(5) of the LGA 1988, choose within which activity they are to be included.[97] Even where a legal service does not fall within another defined activity and it might usefully be packaged with it on some occasions, using the power in section 2(7) of the LGA 1988.

---

[95] LGA 1988, Sched. 1, para. 11(3), as inserted by Local Government Act 1988 (Competition) (Defined Activities) Order 1994, S.I. 1994 No. 2884, Article 2(2).

[96] See further pp. 645–646.

[97] See further pp. 667–668.

II. The excluded element

With most blue-collar services the whole of the activity in question is required to be subject to CCT. However, it is not proposed that authorities shall be required to put all legal services out to CCT. This would be inappropriate both because certain services are inherently unsuitable for contracting out and also because it was desired to retain a reasonable amount of work in-house for other reasons – such as the need to provide proper training for the authority's "core" staff. Thus, authorities are permitted an exemption for 55 per cent of this activity, with only 45 per cent the total being subject to CCT.[98] For all authorities it is, further, permitted to retain in-house legal services amounting to £300,000 per annum. This is relevant for those smaller authorities for whom the 55 per cent in-house figure may not reach £300,000: for these authorities the £300,000 minimum figure allows them to retain this amount (the "competition-free allowance") in-house even if it means that less than 45 per cent of their total is subjected to CCT. Of course, authorities may market test more than the amount actually required should they choose to do so.

To determine the amount of legal services to which CCT applies, an authority must ascertain the total cost of legal services over the forthcoming year, and then deduct 55 per cent (or £300,000, as appropriate).[99] In calculating this amount the authority need not take into consideration any work which has already been contracted out to the private sector, since the CCT regime applies only to legal work which is carried on by the authority itself.[99a]

The authority may, additionally, exclude an amount to represent any work within this defined activity which it is carrying out after conducting a voluntary competitive tendering procedure – referred to in the legislation as a "competitive process" — in which at least three persons who are not defined authorities under the LGA 1988 were invited to bid.[1] For work awarded after April 1, 1994 this means that all the requirements of the LGA 1988 must have been followed in respect of the procedure.[2] This means that there is no need for the authority to

---

[98] Local Government Act 1988 (Competition) (Legal Services) (England) Regulations 1994, S.I. 1994 No. 3164 (the "Legal Services Regulations").

[99] This means the "estimated total annual cost including overheads": Legal Services Regulations, above, regs. 2 and 3. The authority may use the new local authority accounting mechanism, the Statement of Support Services Costs (SSSC) to assist in this; this mechanism is based on the same definition of "legal services" as the CCT regime. However, this can only be used as a guide, since the SSSC refers to the actual cost at year end, whereas the CCT regulations refer to estimated cost. On the problems of using the SSSC mechanism to calculate the cost of legal services see Cirell and Bennett, *Competitive Tendering for Professional Services* at C.11.22.

[99a] See the definition of functional work in LGA 1988 s.3(4), as am. by Local Government Act 1988 (Competition) (Defined Activities) Order 1994, S.I. 1994 No. 2884, Article 3(2).

[1] Legal Services Regulations, above, reg. 2.

[2] For work awarded before this date there is room for debate over exactly what kind of tendering procedure is adequate to constitute a competitive process under the regulations.

compete again for work which it has already won in a competitive bidding process. The exemption is applicable until March 31, 1999, or at the end of a period five years after the work was awarded, if earlier than March 31, 1999.

The authority may also, further, exclude an amount equal to the cost of legal services carried out by the authority on behalf of a school with a delegated budget under section 33 of the Education Reform Act 1988.[3] It appears that the concession is intended to apply only when the budget for legal services has itself been delegated, although the wording of the legislation does not make this absolutely clear. It will apply, however, regardless of whether the school's legal services are actually provided centrally, or by its own separate staff. The concession is based on the view that where there is a delegated budget the school in question is already subject to adequate commercial pressure regarding the way the money is spent.

It may also – until April 1, 1999 – exclude an amount equal to the value of legal services carried out in connection with functional work falling within the activity of housing management. This provision has been introduced to facilitate authorities in combining legal and housing management functions in a single contract, where appropriate. Since in some cases housing management will not be subject to CCT until after legal services, it would sometimes be possible to combine activities from both only by bringing forward competition for the housing management functions which it is desired to include in the contract along with the legal services. To avoid the need for this authorities have been given an exemption for the value of work carried out together with housing management where the housing management activity is not itself subject to the LGA 1988.[4] Thus the joint package will not need to be put out to tender until the date that the housing management element comes within the CCT regime.

There is also an exemption for an amount equivalent to the value of legal work done in connection with other functional work which relates to defined activities under the LGA 1988 or construction and maintenance work under the LGPLA 1980, where other work is being carried out in accordance with the relevant CCT regime.[5] This provision has been included because it is considered that, where work is being done for the DLO/DSO, competition has already been introduced by the fact that the cost of the work is built into the DSO/DLO's own "bid". The provision is not expressly limited to legal services provided to the DLO/DSO, and the provision could be interpreted to cover *all* legal services concerned with the activity in question, even those which are on the "client" (purchaser) side: for example, the services involved in drafting

---

[3] Legal Services Regulations, above, reg. 2.
[4] Legal Services Regulations, above, reg. 2.
[5] Legal Services Regulations, above, reg. 2.

CCT tender documents. It is clear, however, that this is not the intention of the legislation and that any such effect results from a defect in drafting.[6]

The specific exemptions discussed in the previous paragraphs are in addition to the "55 per cent/£300,000" exemption. Thus to find the total of legal services covered by CCT the authority must estimate the total cost of such services over the coming year, as noted above and then deduct 55 per cent. The authority may then deduct from the 45 per cent remaining the value of work awarded by competition, carried out on behalf of a schools with a delegated budget etc, to reach the figure to which CCT will apply.

Example: an authority's estimated cost for legal services for the next year is £1 million. Of this, £100,000 is being carried out by the authority having been won in a previous competition carried out under the same rules as apply with CCT. From the £1 million the authority may first subtract £550,000 (55 per cent), leaving £450,000. From this it may then subtract a further £100,000 to represent the work won in competition, leaving £350,000 of work subject to CCT.

(xiv) CONSTRUCTION AND PROPERTY SERVICES

I. Services covered

Construction and property services were also added as a defined activity under the LGA 1988 in 1994.[7] The precise services covered are set out in what appears to be an exhaustive definition in paragraph 12 of Schedule 1 to the LGA 1988. This refers to services in the following fields:
(a) architecture, including landscape architecture;
(b) engineering;
(c) valuation;
(d) property management;
(e) surveying, including quantity and building surveying.
This applies when,[8] and only when, the services consist of or are provided for the purposes of or in connection with, the following[9]:
(a) giving advice to a defined authority, its elected members, a committee or sub-committee of a defined authority; to a group of persons reporting to such an authority, commitee or subcommittee; or to any officer or department of a defined authority;

---

[6] See further Cirell and Bennett, *Competitive Tendering for Professional Services,* (looseleaf) at 2.3.
[7] LGA 1988, s.2(2)(k), as inserted by the Local Government Act 1988 (Competition) (Defined Activities) (Construction and Property Services) Order, S.I. 1994 No. 2888.
[8] This is, however, subject to specific exclusions for certain services provided by authorities on behalf of other bodies. These exclusions cover services in pursuance of section 6 of the Highways Act 1980 (which provides for the delegation of functions concerning certain roads from other public bodies to local authorities) and services for the purpose of or in connection with sewerage functions carried out on behalf of sewerage undertakers in pursuance of arrangements under Water Industry Act 1991, s.97: LGA 1988, Sched. 1, para. 12(4).
[9] LGA 1988, Sched. 1, para. 12(3).

(b) giving advice to any other person in relation to the discharge of any functions of a defined authority;

(c) establishing and managing capital and revenue programmes for the development and maintenance of "relevant land" (as defined further below);

(d) the design and planning of development projects and maintenance work, including feasibility studies, investigatory work and the preparation of plans, costings and reports;

(e) management of such projects and work, including contract and finance management;

(f) management of "relevant land" (as defined below). There is an exception here for local authority housing as defined in the context of housing management,[10] which is subject to CCT under the separate activity of housing management, as explained above;

(g) procuring, monitoring and supervising the above services and arranging payment for their provision, where they are provided to a defined authority.

"Relevant land" for the above purposes is widely defined, covering virtually all land in which the authority has an interest or for which it has responsibility. More precisely, it refers in England and Wales to land occupied by a defined authority; land in which a defined authority has an interest or is seeking to acquire an interest; land for the maintenance or management of which the authority assumes responsibility by agreement; and highways for which the defined authority is the highway authority and which are maintainable at public expense.[11] It can be seen that the definition does not cover activities relating to land which is not the authority's own direct responsibility.

As with legal services, the definition of the defined activity is very wide and includes some activities which may not be suitable for contracting out; but an authority may keep such activities in-house by relying on the exclusions discussed at II. below.

II. The excluded element

As with other white-collar services it is not thought appropriate that the whole amount of construction and property services should be subject to CCT, but it is considered desirable that an authority should be able to guarantee the retention of a minimum in-house capability. Authorities are permitted an exemption of 35 per cent for this activity, with only 65 per cent therefore being subject to CCT.[12] For all authorities it is permitted to retain in-house without applying the CCT rules work worth £450,000 per annum, even if this means less than 65 per cent of the

---

[10] On this definition see note 83 above.

[11] LGA 1988, Sched. 1, para. 12(5).

[12] Local Government Act 1988 (Competition) (Construction and Property Services) (England) Regulations 1994 S.I. 1994 No. 3166, reg. 2 ("Construction and Property Services Regulations").

relevant work is subject to CCT. As with other professional services, to determine the value of services to which CCT applies, an authority must ascertain the total cost of the relevant service over the forthcoming year, excluding any services already contracted out to the private sector,[13] and then deduct the exempt portion of 35 per cent (or £450,000)[14].

An authority is also given exemptions for amounts equal to: (i) the value of any functional work within this defined activity which it is carrying out after conducting a voluntary competitive tendering procedure: (ii) the value of any such work carried out on behalf of a school with a delegated budget; (iii) (until April 1, 1999) the value of such work carried out in connection with other functional work falling within the defined activity of housing management; and (iv) the value of such work done in connection with other functional work which relates to "CCT" activities under either the LGA 1988 or LGPLA 1980.[15] The purpose and scope of these exemptions is the same as the parallel exemptions which apply in relation to legal services, which have already been discussed above.

In addition, for certain types of construction and property services, namely the design and planning of development projects or maintenance work, and project management, an exemption is allowed for the value of work being carried on in-house which has been "started" at the time the CCT regime for construction and property services takes effect.[16] This avoids the need to include work which it would be disruptive or otherwise inconvenient to hand over to the private sector because it relates to a particular project or programme which is partly complete. In the case of design and planning of development projects and maintenance work, the exemption comes to an end when the work is completed, whilst for project management the exemption ceases when the document certifying completion of the work is issued.[17]

(xv) FINANCIAL SERVICES

I. Services covered

Financial services were added as a defined activity in 1995.[18] The services covered are set out in paragraph 13 of Schedule 1 to the Local

---

[13] This is because the CCT regime applies only to work done by the authority itself: see the definition of functional work in LGA 1988 s.3(4), as am. by Local Government Act 1988 (Competition) (Defined Activities) (Construction and Property Services) Order 1994, S.I. 1994, No. 2888.

[14] This means the "estimated total annual cost including overheads": Construction and Property Services Regulations, above, regs. 2 and 3. The authority may use the new local authority accounting mechanism, the Statement of Support Services Costs (SSSC) to assist in this; this is based on the same definition as the CCT regime. However, as with legal services it can be a guide only, since the SSSC refers to the actual cost at year end, whereas the CCT regulations refer to estimated cost.

[15] Construction and Property Services Regulations, reg. 2.

[16] *Ibid.*

[17] *Ibid,* including the definition of "allowable period" under reg. 2.

[18] LGA 1988, s.2(2)(1), as inserted by Local Government Act 1988 (Competition) (Defined Activities) Order 1995, S.I. 1995 No. 1915, Article 2.

Government Act.[19] in a list which is expressly stated to be exhaustive.[20] The list covers any services which consist of the following, or which are provided for the purposes of or in connection with the following:

(a) financial advice to: a defined authority, its elected members, its committees or sub-committees; any other group of persons reporting to such an authority or its committees or sub-committees; any officer or department of such an authority; any other person in relation to the discharge of the functions of a defined authority.

(b) accounting services. This includes "in particular" (though is not limited to) the completion of statutory accounts and the maintenance of appropriate financial records.

(c) the administration of taxation (direct and indirect) for a defined authority.

(d) the development and maintenance of financial information and management systems.

(e) audit services. This includes "in particular", though is not limited to, liaison with external auditors and other appropriate bodies.

(f) the administration, collection and recovery of non-domestic rates, council tax, water and sewerage charges or rates, community charges and general rates.

(g) the provision of pay roll facilities.

(h) the determination, administration and making of payments, including arranging abatements and rebates. This activity is expressly excluded from the defined activity, however, where it relates to certain educational awards and allowances (such as grants for univerity and college students) and to certain other grants and benefits.[21]

As with legal services, the definition of financial services is comprehensive and includes many activities which may not be suitable for contracting out, such as those carried out on a decentralised basis rather than through the finance office, and sensitive tax collection functions which most authorities will prefer to retain in-house. However, as with most other professional services, authorities will not be required to subject the whole of this activity to CCT, but only a proportion, as explained further below, and this provision will give sufficient scope for authorities to retain functions in-house where appropriate for strategic reasons.

With this particular activity authorities will frequently wish to rely on the exemption in section 2(6) of the LGA 1988, discussed further below,

---

[19] As inserted by Local Government Act 1988 (Competition) (Defined Activities) Order 1995, S.I. 1995 No. 1915, Article 4.

[20] LGA 1988, Sched. 1, para. 13(1).

[21] LGA 1988, Sched. 1, para 13(2). More precisely, excluded for England and Wales are: mandatory and discretionary awards made pursuant to the Education Act 1962; education maintenance allowances payable pursuant to the Scholarship and Other Benefits Regulations 1977; clothing grants pursuant to the Education (Miscellaneous Provisions) Act 1948, s.5; free school meals and milk provided under Education Act 1980; and board and lodging fees payable under Education Reform Act 1988, s.111.

which applies to work carried out by persons who spend less than 50 per cent of their time on financial work. This can be used, for example, to exempt work done by general managers who spend only a small part of their time on financial matters relating to their area of responsibility.

II. The excluded element

As with the other recently added professional services, only part of the activity will be required to be subject to CCT, allowing the authority considerable freedom to retain certain parts of the function in-house.

Other excluded elements similar to those applying to other new white collar services, will also be permitted to be added to the competition free allowance. At the time of writing, however, the regulations on this matter had not yet been made.

(xvi) INFORMATION TECHNOLOGY SERVICES

I. Services covered

Information technology services were also added as a defined activity in 1995.[22] The activities covered are set out in paragraph 14 of schedule 1 to the Local Government Act.[23] These are defined in paragraph 14(2) as "services which are designed to secure for a defined authority the availability or application of information technology". "Information technology" is defined in paragraph 14(4) as meaning "any computer, telecommunications or other technology the principal use of which is the recording, processing and communication of information by electronic means".

Paragraph 14(3) states – although without prejudice to the generality of the above definition – that the defined activity includes services which consist of, or which are provided in connection with or for the purpose of, the following:

(a) giving advice in relation to information technology to: a defined authority or its members; any committee or sub-committee of a defined authority; any group of persons reporting to the authority or one of its committees or sub-committees; or any officer or department of a defined authority.

(b) giving advice to any person as to the application of information technology.

(c) assessing a defined authority's requirements for information technology, and keeping those requirements under review, including appraising any technology in use for the time being.

---

[22] LGA 1988, s.2(2)(m), as inserted by Local Government Act 1988 (Competition) (Defined Activities) Order 1995, S.I. 1995 No. 1915, Article 2.
[23] As inserted by Local Government Act 1988 (Competition) (Defined Activities) Order 1995, S.I. 1995 No. 1915, Article 4.

(d) arranging for information technology to be made available to meet a defined authority's requirements.

(e) developing information technology.

(f) maintaining equipment used in connection with information technology.

An order will shortly be made to exempt from the scope of this defined activity information technology services relating to certain activities of fire authorities.

II. The excluded element

As with the other recently added professional services, only part of the activity is required to be subject to CCT, allowing the authority considerable freedom to retain certain parts of the function in-house. Authorities are permitted an exemption of 30 per cent for this activity, with 70 per cent therefore being subject to CCT.[24] For all authorities it is permitted to retain in-house without applying the CCT rules work worth £300,000 per annum, even if this means less than 70 per cent of the relevant work is subject to CCT. As with other professional services, to determine the value of services to which CCT applies, an authority must ascertain the total cost of the relevant service over the forthcoming year, excluding any services already contracted out to the private sector,[25] and then deduct the exempt portion of 30 per cent (or £300,000).[26]

An authority is also given exemptions for amounts equal to: (i) the value of any functional work within this defined activity which it is carrying out after conducting a voluntary competitive tendering procedure; (ii) the value of any such work carried out on behalf of a school with a delegated budget; (iii) (until April 1, 1999) the value of such work carried out in connection with other functional work falling within the defined activity of housing management; and (iv) the value of such work done in connection with other functional work which relates to "CCT" activities under either the LGA 1988 or LGPLA 1980.[27] The purpose and scope of these exemptions is the same as the parallel exemptions which apply in relation to legal services, which have already been discussed above.

---

[24] Local Government Act 1988 (Competition) (Information Technology) (England) Regulations 1994, S.I. 1995 No. 2813, reg. 2 ("Information Technology Regulations").

[25] This is because the CCT regime applies only to work done by the authority itself: see the definition of functional work in LGA 1988 s.3(4), as am. by Local Government Act 1988 (Competition) (Defined Activities) Order 1995, S.I. 1995 No. 1915, Article 5(2).

[26] This means the "estimated total annual cost including overheads": Information Technology Regulations, above, regs. 2 and 3. The authority may use the new local authority accounting mechanism, the Statement of Support Services Costs (SSSC) to assist in this; this is based on the same definition as the CCT regime. However, as with the legal services it can be a guide only, since the SSSC refers to the actual cost at year end, whereas the CCT regulations refer to estimated cost.

[27] Information Technology Regulations, above, reg. 2.

(xvii) PERSONNEL SERVICES

I. Services covered

Personnel services were, along with financial and IT services, also added as a defined activity in 1995.[28] The services covered within this activity are set out in paragraph 15 of schedule 1 to the Local Government Act,[29] in a list which is expressly stated to be exhaustive.[30] As with most other white collar services, the definition is very broad and includes some activities which it is accepted will not generally be suitable for CCT; but an authority is expected to retain these services for in-house provision by relying on the provision which allows it to exclude a significant proportion of the activity, as discussed further below.

The list covers any services which consist of, or are provided for the purposes of or in connection with, the following:

(a) personnel advice to: a defined authority, its elected members, its committees or sub-committees; any other group of persons reporting to such an authority, or its committees or sub-committees; any officer or department of such an authority; any other person in relation to the discharge of the functions of a defined authority.

(b) conducting organisational and method studies and work studies including in particular (although not limited to) conducting management service reviews and preparing business plans.

(c) human resource management, including though not limited to, recruitment, monitoring, assessment and appraisal.

(d) personnel research.

(e) developing and maintaining statistical and managerial information systems.

(f) training a defined authority's employees, including arranging, monitoring and evaluating training and development programmes. This does not, however, include activities relating to the "ordinary supervision" of trainees or other employees (that, is, on-job training), nor the training of fire fighting members of fire brigades.[31]

(g) developing and maintaining employee relations, policies, practices and procedures.

(h) personnel work in connection with: pay and other employee benefits including, in particular, superannuation benefits; terms and conditions of employment; health and safety policies and procedures; employee welfare policies and procedures including occupational health services; and redundancy arrangements and agreements.

(i) procuring, monitoring and supervising any of the above services which are provided for a defined authority by any person.

---

[28] LGA 1988, s.2(2)(n), as inserted by Local Government Act 1988 (Competition) (Defined Activities) Order 1995, S.I. 1995 No. 1915, Article 2.

[29] As inserted by Local Government Act 1988 (Competition) (Defined Activities) Order 1995, S.I. 1995 No. 1915, Article 4.

[30] LGA 1988, Sched. 1, para. 15(1).

[31] LGA 1988, Sched. 1, para. 16(2).

II. The excluded element

As with other white collar services it is not thought appropriate for all services to be subject to CCT. Generally, authorities are permitted an exemption of 70 per cent for this activity, with only 30 per cent therefore being subject to CCT[32]; for fire and civil defence authorities 85 per cent of the activity is exempt.[33] For all authorities it is permitted to retain in-house without applying the CCT rules work worth £400,000 per annum, even if this means less than 30 per cent of the relevant work (or 15 per cent for fire and civil defence) authorities is subject to CCT.[34] As with other professional services, to determine the value of services to which CCT applies, an authority must ascertain the total cost of the relevant service over the forthcoming year, excluding any services already contracted out to the private sector,[35] and then deduct the exempt portion of 70 per cent (or £400,000).[36]

An authority is also given exemptions for amounts equal to: (i) the value of any functional work within this defined activity which it is carrying out after conducting a voluntary competitive tendering procedure; (ii) the value of any such work carried out on behalf of a school with a delegated budget; (iii) (until April 1, 1999) the value of such work carried out in connection with other functional work falling within the defined activity of housing management; and (iv) the value of such work done in connection with other functional work which relates to "CCT" activities under either the LGA 1988 or LGPLA 1980.[37] The purpose and scope of these exemptions is the same as the parallel exemptions which apply in relation to legal services, as discussed at (xii) above.

There is also an exemption for an amount equal to the cost of covered training work (that is, those falling within (f) above), where this work is wholly or partly funded by a grant under section 1 of the Education (Grants and Awards) Act 1984.[38]

---

[32] Local Government Act 1988 (Competition) (Personnel Services) (England) Regulations 1995 S.I. 1995 No. 2101, reg. 2 ("Personnel Services Regulations").

[33] Local Government Act 1988 (Competition) (Personnel Services) (Fire and Civil Defence Authorities) (England) Regulations 1995 S.I. 1995 No. 2100, reg. 2.

[34] Personnel Services Regulations, above, Local Government Act 1988 (Competition) (Personnel Services) (Fire and Civil Defence Authorities) (England) Regulations 1995, above, reg. 2.

[35] This is because the CCT regime applies only to work done by the authority itself: see the definition of functional work in LGA 1988 s.3(4), as am. by Local Government Act 1988 (Competition) (Defined Activities) Order 1995, S.I. 1995 No. 1915, Article 5(2).

[36] This means the "estimated total annual cost including overheads": Personnel Services Regulations, above, reg. 2. The authority may use the new local authority accounting mechanism, the Statement of Support Services Costs (SSSC) to assist in this; this is based on the same definition as the CCT regime, although it can be a guide only, since the SSSC refers to the actual cost at the year end, whereas the CCT regulations refer to estimated cost.

[37] Personnel Services Regulations, above, Local Government Act 1988 (Competition) (Personnel Services) (Fire and Civil Defence Authorities) (England) Regulations 1995, above, reg. 2.

[38] As am. by Education Act 1993, s.278.

(xviii) FURTHER DEFINED ACTIVITIES?

As was explained in chapter 12, the recent initiatives to extend CCT to a range of new white collar services derived from the government's 1991 Consultation Paper, *Competing for Quality: Competition in the Provision of Local Services*. This Paper considered the possibility of applying CCT to a number of other services which have not, as yet, been added to the list of defined activities under the LGA 1988. One group of services considered in this Paper was a group referred to as "corporate and administrative" services, which included, for example, secretarial and clerical services, public relations and procurement. Following consultation, however, the government decided in 1994 that it would not, after all, seek to extend CCT to these services.[39] The Consultative Paper, further, contemplated applying the CCT regime to the management of theatre and arts facilities and library services. Although the government has not announced any intention to abandon consideration of these services, as yet no firm proposals have been put forward for extending CCT to these activities.[40]

(e) THRESHOLD FOR THE APPLICATION OF THE RULES

The rules on CCT described in Chapter 14[41] generally have no application where the total amount of work falling within a defined activity for a particular authority does not exceed £100,000 per annum. This ensures that authorities with a small amount of work to let are not troubled by CCT requirements; in such a case the burden of applying the procedures is considered to outweigh any benefits to be gained. In relation to England and Wales the limitation is generally provided for in the Local Government Act 1988 (Defined Activities) (Exemptions) (England) Order 1988[42] and a similarly named Order for Wales[43] (hereafter "the exemptions orders"). In the case of building cleaning work relating to public buildings which is carried out by a police authority the relevant figure is £125,000[44] and for housing management it is £500,000.[45]

---

[39] For discussion of the background see Cirell and Bennett, *Competitive Tendering for Professional Services* at C15.

[40] For discussion of the Consultation Paper and progress so far, see Cirell and Bennett, above, Chaps. C7 (theatre and arts facilities) and C8 (library services).

[41] This covers both the rules on award procedures and those concerning accounting requirements and financial objectives: the exemption is a complete exemption from the operation of the CCT regime.

[42] Local Government Act 1988 (Defined Activities) (Exemptions) (England) Order 1988 SI 1988 No. 1372.

[43] Local Government Act 1988 (Defined Activities) (Exemptions) (Wales) Order 1988, SI 1988 No. 1469.

[44] Local Government Act 1988 (Defined Activities) (Cleaning of Police Buildings) (Exemption) (England and Wales) Order 1995, S.I. 1995 No. 2449.

[45] S.I. 1988 No. 1372, above, as am. by Local Government Act 1988 (Defined Activities) (Exemption) (England) (Amendment) Order 1994, S.I. 1994 No. 3296.

The relevant figure in deciding whether this threshold is met is the estimated gross amount of carrying out the particular defined activity in-house in the *immediately preceding* financial year.[46] In calculating the figure the authority must include such proportion of its administrative expenses as are attributable to the work,[47] except those which would be incurred regardless of whether the activity were carried out in-house or externally.[48] The cost is the cost of providing services across the authority as a whole – the authority cannot apply a separate threshold for particular units of the authority even if these units act in a wholly independent manner. The Department of the Environment has also indicated that capital costs (for example, cost of the purchase of vehicles in the activity of vehicle management) should not be included in calculating the annual value of the work.[49]

The authority need not include the amount of work which is of such a nature that it is exempt from the regime altogether – that is, work carried out under the "incidental work" exemption, "tied housing" exemption or the "training" exemptions, discussed below. Thus, for example, if an authority carries out £105,000 of catering work over a year and £10,000's worth is exempt from CCT because it is carried out pursuant to relevant training schemes, the whole of the work is exempt, since the covered part is worth only £95,000, which is below the £100,000 threshold. It also appears that work which is exempt from the award procedures because of an emergency situation (also discussed below) need not be included in the calculation, since it is stated by section 2(8) of the 1988 Act that this is not to be treated as work falling within a defined activity. This is surprising, since this is work which is in principle appropriate for CCT procedures but has merely been excluded on a one-off basis because of special circumstances, and it might thus be expected that it would be counted for this purpose. In relation to housing management the authority must take into account work which is excluded from the scope of the housing management activity because it is being carried out by another organisation to which housing management functions have been delegated.[49a]

Since it is included in a Statutory Instrument rather than the Act itself, the figure of £100,000 may easily be revised to take account of inflation, but this has not been done, so that the scope of the exemption has been steadily reduced in practice since 1988 as a result of inflation. This is in line with the general tendency seen in expanding the scope of CCT and reducing the ambit of exemptions.

---

[46] s.3(2).

[47] Exemptions orders, above note 42 and 43, s.3(3)(a)

[48] Exemptions orders, note 42 and 43, s.3(3)(a).

[49] Department of Environment, *CCT for the Further Manual Services* (December 1994), paras. 14 and 25.

[49a] Local Government Act 1988 (Defined Activities) (Exemption) (Housing Management) (England) Order 1995, S.I. 1995 No. 1182.

As noted above, where the general annual figure for the application of CCT is exceeded – as it is in most cases – for certain white-collar services there is also an exemption from the CCT regime for a *proportion* of the services in question and, for smaller authorities, for services up to a certain minimum amount.[50] For blue-collar services, leisure management and housing management, on the other hand, if the total of an authority's work within the defined activity exceeds the threshold figure, stated above, *all* the relevant work is subjected to the rules: there is no exemption for the first £100,000/£125,000/£500,000.

(f) EXEMPTIONS

(i) EFFECT OF THE EXEMPTIONS

There are several general exemptions from the CCT regime which provide that the exempt work shall not constitute a "defined activity" for the purpose of the LGA 1988. These cover work which is incidental to non-CCT work done by a particular employee; certain work done by those in "tied housing"; and work done pursuant to training agreements. The scope of these exemptions is discussed below. The work covered by these provisions need not be put out to tender under the usual CCT rules governing award procedures described in Chapter 14.[51] In addition, this work need not be considered in complying with the rules on accounting and financial objectives contained in section 9–12 of the Act, also described in Chapter 14, which refer only to work falling within a defined activity.[52] Work falling within these exemptions is also discounted in determining whether the threshold figure is met for applying the regime, since this figure covers only work which is in general appropriate for CCT.[53]

There is also an exemption from the CCT tendering procedures for emergency work, the scope of which is also discussed below. This work is exempt from tendering procedures under the LGA 1988 since in such a case it would be too time consuming to go through such procedures. In addition, since work is excluded by providing that it does not fall within a "defined activity" it appears that such work can be discounted in calculating the threshold for applying the CCT rules although, as explained above in relation to the LGPLA 1980, this is perhaps surprising.[54] For the same reason it appears to be excluded from the rules on accounting and financial obligations,[55] although emergency work is subject to these obligations under the LGPLA 1980.[56]

---

[50] See pp. 684–693.
[51] See pp. 710–746.
[52] See pp. 751–760.
[53] This is provided expressly in the exemption orders, above, note 42 and 43, s.3(3)(c) for the second two, whilst incidental work is excluded because under LGA 1988, s.2(6): it does not fall within a "defined activity". This is also the case for work under the other two exemptions so that the express provisions in s.3(3)(c) of the order seem unnecessary.
[54] See p. 657.
[55] See pp. 751–760.
[56] See pp. 656–657.

(ii) INCIDENTAL WORK

I. The exemption for blue-collar CCT and leisure management

Section 2(6) of the LGA 1988 provides that work carried out by an employee is not to be considered as falling within a defined activity where the work is "incidental to the greater part of the work which [the employee] is employed to do and the greater part does not constitute a defined activity". This exemption applies to all defined activities except for the white collar activities of housing management, construction and property services and legal services, financial services, information technology services and personnel services, for which the exemption is differently worded and considered at II. below.

This exemption is designed to cover the case where the main reason for engaging the employee is for that employee to carry out other types of work, which may not be suitable for contracting out. It may be inappropriate or impossible to employ a person solely to carry out that part of the work which is unsuitable for contracting out – for example, because there is insufficient work of that kind to keep the employee occupied full-time – and therefore useful to combine that work with other work carried out on the same premises. When the exemption was adopted the main work envisaged was security work, such as the work carried out by the caretaker of a residential building; the exemption permitted the employee engaged in security work also to carry out other work such as building cleaning, without this other work being subject to CCT. However, the provision is less significant now that security work has itself been added to the LGA 1988 as a defined activity. However, it is still relevant: for example, the Department of Environment has suggested that authorities may wish to use it where a social services manager spends part of his time on the management of the fleet of vehicles used for social service activities, which in general are not defined activities; in this case the exemption could be used to allow that employee to continue with this activity without the need for that particular work to be subject to CCT.[57]

As to what is meant by incidental, Cirell and Bennett have suggested that work may be incidental even though it takes more than 50 per cent of an employee's time, on the basis that the test is the primary reason for employment.[58] This seems sensible with regard to the policy behind the provision. Another interpretation, however, could be that work is incidental only where the non-CCT work constitutes the greater part of the employee's work and this appears to be the view of the Department of the Environment.[59]

---

[57] Department of the Environment, *CCT for the Further Manual Services* (December 1994), para. 12.

[58] Cirell and Bennett, *Compulsory Competitive Tendering: Law and Practice*, at 8.2.

[59] See, for example, Department of the Environment, *CCT for the Further Manual Services* (December 1994), para. 12, which makes this assumption.

II. The exemption for other CCT services

In relation to housing management section 2(6) does not apply, but is replaced by a more specific exemption contained in section 2(6A).[60] This provides an exemption for housing management work carried out by a particular employee only where work falling within a defined activity occupies less than 25 per cent of his working time. This a stricter test than that in section 2(6) which, as explained, will at the very least permit the exemption to apply where CCT work occupies less than 50 per cent of the employee's time. The "25 per cent" test applies, however, only to employees normally employed for more than 30 hours a week. For other employees the exemption in section 2(6A) applies where such work occupies less than 50 per cent of the employee's time.[61]

In relation to construction and property services, financial services, information technology services and personnel services, legal services special provision is also made: it is stated that in all cases an exemption for such work is given only where the work carried out by the employee which does not fall within a defined activity occupies less than 50 per cent of his time.[62]

These very precise provisions on white-collar CCT were included because it was feared that the incidental work exemption was particularly open to abuse in this context, by authorities arranging their workforce to exempt as much work as possible from the CCT regime. If this could be proven it would, of course, constitute anti-competitive behaviour, but it was thought easier to deal with the problem by tightening up the objective scope of the exemption.

(iii) EMERGENCY WORK

Under LGA 1988, s.2(8), certain emergency work is deemed not to be a defined activity. This exemption applies where the work is to "avert, alleviate or eradicate" the effects of an "emergency or disaster". It applies, however, only where the emergency or disaster involves danger to life or health or *serious* damage to or destruction of property. These conditions are almost identical to the basic conditions for invoking the emergency exemption relating to construction and maintenance under the LGPLA, discussed above.[63]

---

[60] As inserted by the Local Government Act 1988 (Competition) (Defined Activities) (Housing Mangement) Order 1994, S.I. 1994 No. 2297, Article 3.

[61] *Ibid.*

[62] The Local Government Act 1988 (Competition) (Defined Activities) (Construction and Property Services) Order 1994, 1994 S.I. No. 2888, Article. 3(1) and Local Government Act 1988 (Competition) (Defined Activities) Order 1994, 1994 No. 2884, Article 3(1), and Local Government Act (Competition) (Defined Activities) Order 1995, S.I. 1995, No. 1915, Article 5(1) which operate by inserting a "special" s.2(6) in the LGA 1988 which applies for the purpose of these activities only.

[63] See the discussion at pp. 656–657.

The LGPLA exemption also involves a number of other conditions added in 1989 – that the emergency/disaster could not reasonably be foreseen; that work needs to commence within 48 hours; and that it is on a scale not normally undertaken by the authority. These do not apply to the exemption under the LGA 1988.

(iv) THE TIED HOUSING EXEMPTION

There is also an exemption for certain work done by local authority employees living in "tied" housing. This is contained in paragraph 4 of the Local Government Act 1988 (Defined Activities) (Exemptions) (England) Order 1988,[64] and paragraph 4 of a similar Order applying in Wales.[65] It provides that work is not to be treated as a defined activity "so long as it constitutes work carried out through an employee who is required as a condition of his employment to live in particular accommodation for the better performance of his duties, and the work forms part of his duties". An example would be where an employee performing security duties is required to live on the premises for the better performance of those security duties.

(v) WORK DONE PURSUANT TO TRAINING AGREEMENTS

Certain statutory schemes provide for local authorities to engage trainees to carry out work with the objective of providing those persons with training or work experience. An exemption from CCT is provided for work done under certain training schemes, to enable authorities to continue with these schemes which could not be carried on by the authority if the work were won by the private sector. The exemption is contained in paragraph 6 of the Local Government Act 1988 (Defined Activities) (Exemptions) (England) Order 1988,[66] and paragraph 4 of a similar Order applying in Wales.[67] To qualify the scheme must be one carried out pursuant to an agreement with either the Secretary of State or the Training Commission under the Employment and Training Act 1973, which must specify the work to be done by the authority. It is also a condition that the Training Commission or Secretary of State has agreed to pay the whole or part of the cost of the work.

---

[64] S.I. 1988 No. 1372.
[65] Local Government Act 1988 (Defined Activities) (Exemptions) (Wales) Order 1988, S.I. 1988 No. 1469.
[66] S.I. 1988 No. 1372.
[67] Local Government Act 1988 (Defined Activities) (Exemptions) (Wales) Order 1988, S.I. 1988 No. 1469.

(vi) TEMPORARY EXEMPTIONS PENDING LOCAL GOVERNMENT REORGANISATION[68]

Some local government authorities are currently undergoing reorganisation and a temporary exemption from CCT has been granted to such authorities.[69] This has been done so that new authorities can make decisions on the organisation of local service provision unconstrained by previous arrangements, and to ensure that existing authorities do not waste resources on setting up arrangements which may be short lived in the light of reorganisation.

For the CCT activities contained originally in the 1988 Act and for sports and leisure management authorities are given an exemption for 18 months from the time of their creation, for the tendering rules under the 1988 Act.[70] An authority is still, however, required to submit its own written bid to a detailed specification,[71] and to comply with accounting and reporting requirements and financial objectives, so that it can be ensured that the DSO is operating efficiently.

The exemption does not apply to work under a single arrangement which is to be completed in less than a year or is worth less than £200,000 a year.[72] Nor does it apply where bids have been submitted prior to the date of the reorganisation order.[73]

Similar provisions apply to housing management, except that in certain circumstances the exemption is for two years, and no detailed specification is required.[74]

(g) THE DISTINCTION BETWEEN FUNCTIONAL WORK AND WORKS CONTRACTS

As already explained in the context of construction and maintenance work under the LGPLA 1980, the CCT legislation as such applies only to work done by the Direct Service Organisation which relates to the authority's own functions and responsibilities – that is, where the authority itself is acting as the "purchaser" of the services. This is

---

[68] For further details on this issue see Cirell and Bennett, *Compulsory Competitive Tendering: Law and Practice* Chap. 9.

[69] The Local Government Changes for England and Local Government Act 1988 (Competition) (Miscellaneous Amendment) Regulations, S.I. 1995 No. 1325; Local Government Changes for England (Direct Labour and Service Organisations) Regulations 1994 S.I. 1994 No. 3167; and the Local Government Act 1988 (Defined Activities) (Competition) (Supervision of Parking, Management of Vehicles and Security Work) (England) Regulations 1994, S.I. 1994 No. 3165.

[70] The Local Government Changes for England (Direct Labour and Service Organisations) Regulations 1994, S.I. 1994 No. 3167 (As amended by the Local Government Changes for England and Local Government Act 1988 (Competition) (Miscellaneous Amendment) Regulations 1995, S.I. 1995 No. 1326), reg. 14(3).

[71] *Ibid.*, reg. 14(4).

[72] *Ibid.*, reg. 14(1) but see the anti-avoidance provision in reg. 14(5).

[73] *Ibid.*

[74] S.I. 1994 No. 3167, above.

referred to as "functional work". The CCT award procedures do not apply where the DSO seeks to do work for *another* body – for example, by bidding on a contract put out to tender by another public authority. Such work done for another – where the authority acts only as provider and not purchaser – is referred to in the legislation as work done under "works contracts".[75] A similar distinction is made under the LGA 1988: CCT is relevant only to work for which the authority acts as "purchaser".

More specifically, for the purpose of the CCT rules under the LGA 1988 functional work is defined prima facie as all work carried out by the authority.[76] However, work carried out under a "works contract" – that is, work carried out pursuant to an agreement with another[77] – is then excluded from the definition of functional work,[78] with the result that the concept of functional work only covers the authority's own work.

Work pursuant to an agreement for the authority to discharge the functions of a Minister of the Crown, another defined authority or a sewerage undertaker is not within the definition of "works contract". Thus work done in this case is treated as functional work – the authority's own work – and so is subject to CCT. This refers to the case where the authority is not merely carrying out the activity in question – for example, the actual collection of refuse for another authority – but has taken over the general responsibility for that function, so that it takes over the function of *purchaser* from the other body as well as acting as potential *provider*.

As under the LGPLA 1980, however, certain tendering procedures similar to those under CCT apply under separate provisions of the LGA 1988 when a body other than the authority itself wishes to engage a local authority DSO to carry out services as a provider. These provisions are considered briefly at the end of Chapter 14.

---

[75] Whilst it is not subject to the usual CCT procedures there is a requirement in the act for the purchaser of such services to follow a procedure designed to ensure that a local authority DSO cannot be selected to do work unless it really is the most commercial option for the purchaser: see further pp. 000–000.

[76] LGA 1988, s.3(4)(a). It also includes work not actually carried out by the authority but which is "dependent upon, incidental or preparatory to" other functional work (s.3(4)(b)). This ensures that work placed with the private sector need not be included in evaluating the total cost of these services, for the purpose of deciding the amount of services which the authori y is permitted to retain in-house without following a CCT exercise. However, in the case of legal services construction and property services, financial services, information technology services and personnel services see the Local Government Act 1988 (Competition) (Defined Activities) (Construction and Property Services) Order 1994, S.I. No. 2888 art. 3(2), the Local Government Act 1988 (Competition) (Defined Activities) Order 1994, S.I. 1994 No. 2884, art. 3(2)) and the Local Government Act 1988 (Competition) (Defined Activities) Order 1995, S.I. 1995 No. 1915, Article 5(2).

[77] See the definition of "works contract" in LGA 1988, s.3(2).

[78] *Ibid.*

(4) COMMENCEMENT OF CCT FOR DEFINED ACTIVITIES[79]

The first round of CCT has already been completed for the defined activities originally listed in the LGA 1988, the commencement date for CCT for these activities being between August 1, 1989 and January 1, 1992. The dates were established, for most authorities, by the Secretary of State in regulations.[80] Generally the date for particular defined activities was different for different authorities, since it was feared that if many authorities were to place work on the market at the same time, this would saturate the market and mean that adequate competition would not be available. This was especially so because significant private sector markets for some types of work did not already exist. This was achieved by dividing authorities into groups – six for England and five for Wales – and giving each group a different start date for a particular defined activity[81] (and with authorities in the same area being placed in different groups, to take account of the regional nature of some markets). A different approach was adopted to grounds maintenance: here it was decided that, since interested firms were likely to be small firms able to cope with only small amounts of work, each individual authority should be encouraged to split its work and put it out to tender in successive stages. Thus authorities were permitted to put the work out in five annual stages, with at least 20 per cent of the total work being added each year. The dates given were merely the latest start dates; authorities were free to market test as much as they wished at any time. For sports and leisure management, added in 1989, a similar approach was adopted as with ground maintenance with authorities being required to put work out to CCT in "tranches", of at least 35 per cent in the first year, a second 35 per cent in the second, and the final 30 per cent in the third year.

With these activities, on the expiry of the existing contract or arrangement with the DLO, the CCT regime must continue to be followed where the authority is considering placing work with the in-house organisation.[82] Work will generally be staggered in practice

---

[79] For a detailed explanation see Cirell and Bennett, *Compulsory Competitive Tendering: Law and Practice,* Chap. 9.

[80] Local Government Act 1988 (Defined Activities) (Competition) (England) Regulations 1988 S.I. 1988 No. 1371; Local Government Act 1988 (Defined Activities) (Competition) (Wales) Regulations 1988 S.I. 1988 No. 1468.

[81] For further details of this process see Cirell and Bennett, *Compulsory Competitive Tendering: Law and Practice,* Chap. 9 at 9.2–9.7.

[82] It is suggested by Cirell and Bennett, above, Chap. 9 at 9.6.2. that new regulations are needed to regulate future rounds of CCT, but this seems unnecessary, since the legislation provides that CCT is to come into effect on the date provided in the original regulations. New regulations seem unnecessary thereafter, on the basis that once CCT has come into effect it remains in effect, precluding authorities from awarding any work to the DSO at any time in the future, until the CCT provisions are revoked or suspended.

because of the original staggering arrangements. As noted above, however, local authorities which are subject to reorganisation have been given a temporary exemption from the application of CCT and will not need to apply the regime until after reorganisation.

CCT for the blue-collar services added to the LGA 1988 in 1994 – that is, parking supervision, security and vehicle management – was required to be implemented in England by London Boroughs and metropolitan authorities by January 1, 1996, and must generally be implemented by October 1, 1997 by other authorities which are not subject to reorganisation in the review of local government.[83] CCT for legal services and construction and property services will be required to be implemented by April 1, 1996 for the former group and October 1, 1997 for the latter.[84] For personnel and finance services the dates are October 1, 1996 and April 1, 1998[84a]; and for information technology April 1, 1997 and April 1, 1999.[84b] Authorities which are undergoing reorganisation have been given a temporary exemption from CCT in general,[85] and in accordance with this policy in general need not apply CCT for the new services until after reorganisation. There is a delay of 18 months after the reorganisation order takes effect for the blue collar services; 24 months for construction and property and legal services; and 32 months for information technology and personnel services.[86]

For housing management the provisions are quite complex with provision for staggering of implementation and also for the gradual introduction of CCT in "tranches" as occurred with management of sports and leisure facilities.[87] Again provision has been made for a later application of the CCT provides for authorities undergoing reorganisation.[88]

---

[83] The Local Government Act (Defined Activities) (Competition) (Supervision of Parking, Management of Vehicles and Security Work) (England Regulations) 1994, S.I. 1994 No. 3165, reg. 2, as amended by The Local Government Act 1988 (Defined Activities) (Competition) (Amendment) (England) Regulations 1995, S.I. 1995 No. 2546, reg. 4.

[84] The Local Government Act 1988 (Competition) (Legal Services) (England) Regulations 1994, S.I. 1994 No. 3164 reg. 3, as amended by S.I. 1995 No. 2546, above, reg. 3; The Local Government Act 1988 (Construction and Property Services) (England) Regulations 1994, S.I. 1994 No. 3166, as amended by S.I. 1995 No. 2546, above, reg. 5.

[84a] Local Government Act 1988 (Competition) (Personnel Services) (England) Regulations 1995, S.I. 1995 No. 2101, reg. 3. The same plans have been announced for finance services.

[84b] Local Government Act 1988 (Competition) (Information Technology) (England) Regulations 1995, S.I. 1995 No. 2813, reg. 3.

[85] See pp. 700.

[86] See the regulations cited in notes 80, 83 and 84 above.

[87] The Local Government Act 1988 (Competition) (Housing Management) (England) Regulations 1994 S.I. 1994 No. 2297.

[88] The Local Government Changes for England and Local Government Act 1988 (Competition) (Miscellaneous Amendment) Regulations, S.I. 1995 No. 1326.

CHAPTER 14

COMPULSORY COMPETITIVE TENDERING: AWARD PROCEDURES[1]

I. INTRODUCTION

(1) SCOPE OF THE CHAPTER

Chapter 12 examined the objectives of government policy on compulsory competitive tendering (CCT) and Chapter 13 explained which contracts are covered. This chapter outlines the tendering procedures which must be followed in order to ensure a fair comparison between the in-house team and the private sector. It also considers briefly the financial objectives and accounting and reporting requirements imposed on the in-house organisation to support this process. The chapter covers both construction and maintenance work under the Local Government Planning and Land Act 1980 (LGPLA 1980) and other work under the Local Government Act 1988 (LGA 1988), for which the procedures are similar, although not identical. As has been explained, the award procedures are relevant only where an authority is contemplating that the work should be done in-house: they have no application where it has already been decided to contract out the work.[2]

(2) THE DIRECT LABOUR ORGANISATION (DLO) AND DIRECT SERVICE ORGANISATION (DSO)

In this chapter frequent reference is made to authorities' Direct Labour Organisations (or DLOs) and Direct Service Organisations (DSOs). DLO is the term used to describe that part of a local authority which is engaged in construction and maintenance work covered by the LGPLA 1980; whilst the term DSO is used to designate a unit of the authority engaged in a particular defined activity under the LGA 1988 – for

---

[1] See generally Cirell and Bennett, *Compulsory Competitive Tendering: Law and Practice*; Cirell and Bennett, *Compulsory Competitive Tendering for Professional Services*; Sparke, *The Compulsory Competitive Tendering Guide* (1993).
[2] See p. 636.

example, the unit responsible for grounds maintenance, or for building cleaning.[3]

The degree to which those responsible for "CCT activities" are constituted as a distinct and separate unit of the local authority varies between authorities. Not every part of a defined activity is necessarily carried out by the same unit of a workforce, whilst individual units might be involved in more than one defined activity (or partly with defined activities and partly with others). For example, maintenance of refuse collecting vehicles might be the responsibility of the refuse collection unit or of a special vehicle maintenance unit. In relation to each defined activity, there are also differences in the extent to which individuals involved in actually carrying out the work are separated from those who are responsible for defining the authority's needs and implementing the policy (which will include letting the work and supervising performance). The fair conduct of the CCT regime appears to require separation of these functions. This has occurred in practice, and it is also now required to some extent by specific legislation, discussed below.[4] Authorities are also, in general, required to keep separate accounts for each defined activity under the 1988 Act.[5]

(3) SOURCE OF THE RULES

The CCT procedures and related rules derive from three main sources – (i) the CCT statutes; (ii) delegated legislation made under these statutes; and (iii) "guidance" issued by central government.

(i) **The CCT statutes.** The framework of the procedure to be followed is laid down for construction and maintenance work in the LGPLA 1980, and for other activities in the LGA 1988. These statutes require authorities which are considering giving work to the DLO/DSO[6] to solicit bids from outside firms, and for the DLO/DSO to submit a competing bid. They also lay down rules relating to the financial

---

[3] Direct Labour Organisation is not expressly defined and is not a term of art. However, the LGPLA uses the heading "Direct Labour Organisation" as a heading for that Part of the statute dealing with CCT, and also uses the phrase "DLO revenue account" to refer to the account which must be kept in respect of construction and maintenance work carried out by the authority: see pp. 752–755 (and see also LGA 1988 s.7(6) which for procedures under the LGA requires a written bid to be prepared by the Direct Labour Organisation or "similar" organisation). "Direct Service Organisation" is used as a term of art in the Local Government (Direct Service Organisations) (Competition) Regulations 1993, 1993 S.I. No. 848, in the context of rules which prohibit giving information to the Direct Service Organisation which is not given to others; here it is defined as "that part of the local authority's workforce which is equipped to carry out the work" (reg. 1(2)). The terms "DLO" and "DSO" are frequently used by the Secretary of State in guidance issued on CCT, and by others, in the general sense used in the text above.

[4] See pp. 747–749.

[5] See pp. 755–756.

[6] On the meaning of these terms see pp. 704–705 above.

objectives to be met by DLOs/DSOs. The award procedure contained in the statutes is, however, skeletal only: for example, there are no detailed rules on bid evaluation or qualification. However, both Acts do contain general provisions which prevent an authority doing anything, in connection with a decision to award a contract to its DLO/DSO, which has the effect of, or is intended or likely to have the effect of, "restricting, distorting or preventing competition"[7] (the prohibition on "anti-competitive behaviour"). This means that even in those areas where the detail of the tendering procedure is not expressly set out, authorities must ensure that outside firms are fairly treated.

(ii) Delegated legislation. The statutes also provide for delegated legislation to be made to regulate the award procedure. Section 8 of the LGA 1988 and section 9(4)(aa) of the LGPLA 1980 confer upon the Secretary of State the power to make regulations on a number of specific procedural matters. In addition, section 9 of the LGA 1992 gives him a power to make regulations providing that specified conduct shall be regarded (or shall not be regarded) as anti-competitive behaviour under the LGA 1988 and LGPLA 1980. This is a wide power, which allows the Secretary of State to make regulations on virtually all aspects of CCT procedure. The skeletal statutory procedure has gradually been filled out by various regulations adopted under these powers, in particular the Local Government (Direct Service Organisations) (Competition) Regulations 1993[8] (hereafter the 1993 Competition Regulations).

Section 8 of the Local Government Act 1992 allows the Secretary of State by order (by Statutory Instrument approved by each House) to make provision either to facilitate or to require separate procedures for CCT for professional services: that is, any defined activity which consists in or involves "professional advice", "other professional services" or the "application of any financial or technical expertise".[9] These separate procedures may concern (i) the evaluation of the quality of services which interested bidders can provide; (ii) the fitness of firms to provide the services; and (iii) the evaluation of the financial terms on which the work will be carried out.[10] Such provision may include a power to modify the 1988 Act itself.[11]

(iii) Guidance. Since the inception of CCT the government, through the Department of the Environment, of England, the Welsh Office, for Wales, and the Scottish Office Environment Department, has also issued guidance to authorities on the operation of the rules, generally in the

---

[7] L.G.A. 1988, s.7(7); L.G.P.L.A. 1980, s.9(4)(aaaa), as inserted by LGA 1988 s.32 and Sched. 6, paras. 1 and 3.
[8] S.I. 1993 No. 848.
[9] LGA 1992, s.8(2).
[10] LGA 1992, s.8(1).
[11] And see also LGA 1988, s.8(5) for further elaboration of what may be included. At the time of writing, however, this provision had not been brought into force.

form of circulars. This has included guidance on what constitutes "anti-competitive" behaviour.

Generally such guidance has no legal effect; authorities are free to ignore it if they consider that it does not accurately reflect the legal position, and have often done so. However, under the 1993 Competition Regulations, the Secretary of State now has an express legislative power to issue guidance on the avoidance of anti-competitive behaviour, and it is provided that contravention of this guidance must be taken into account in deciding whether anti-competitive behaviour has occurred.[12] This effectively means that the Secretary of State may fill out the statutory CCT procedures not merely through the formal means of a statutory instrument, but also through guidance issued in any form.

At the time of writing there was a variety of guidance applicable. The main guidance was issued in Joint Circular DoE 10/93, Scottish Office Environment Department 13/93 and Welsh Office 40/93 1993 (hereafter "Circular 10/93"), which covers "blue-collar" CCT. Further guidance was also issued in December 1994 to deal with specific issues relating to the services added to the regime in 1994 (that is, supervision of parking, security work and vehicle management).[13] (These services are also, though, subject to the general guidance in Circular 10/93.[14]) Separate guidance to cover CCT for professional services was issued in December 1994 dealing with legal services, construction and property services and housing management services, which were the first of the "new" white collar services to be subjected to CCT.[15] This guidance has sought to deal with a variety of matters including the meaning of anti-competitive behaviour, the interpretation of other provisions in the CCT legislation, and the application to CCT of the TUPE rules.[16]

In October 1995, however, the government issued a consultation draft of new statutory guidance on CCT, intended to cover CCT for all services, and called for comment by December 15, 1995.[17] It is proposed that this will replace the guidance in Circular 10/93 and the guidance on blue collar and white collar CCT issued in December 1994, as well as covering those services recently included in the CCT regime for which

---

[12] LGA 1992, s.9, conferring a power to make regulations defining anti-competitive behaviour provides that this is to include a power to make regulations i) giving the power to issue guidance and ii) requiring such guidance to be taken into account in deciding if anti-competitive behaviour has occurred: s.9(3)(e) and (f). Regulations have now been made under these provisions giving the Secretary of State a general power to issue such guidance and also providing that it shall be taken into account in deciding if there has been anti-competitive behaviour in connection with functional work: 1993 Competition Regulations, reg. 15(1) and (2).

[13] Department of the Environment, *CCT for the Further Manual Services* (December 1994).

[14] *CCT for the Further Manual Services,* above, para. 24.

[15] This "White Collar" Guidance replaces the provisions in Circular 10/93 in respect of the professional services covered in the White Collar guidance.

[16] On the TUPE rules see pp. 636–648.

[17] *Guidance on the Conduct of Compulsory Competitive Tendering* (draft), sent to local authority Chief Executives by the Department of Environment, accompanied by a letter dated October 11, 1995.

no guidance has yet been issued (that is, financial, information technology and personnel services). The guidance is less detailed than that which currently exists. It simply lays down five "key principles", with some limited elaboration of how these should or might be implemented. The proposed principles are[18]:

(i) "Ensuring that the competition process is conducted, and is seen to be conducted, in a fair and transparent manner". It is suggested that one way to secure this objective is to provide elected members of the authority with a detailed report at appropriate stages of the competition, and, where the in-house bid wins, on the subsequent performance.[19]

(ii) "Taking steps to identify the way in which the market operates for the service in question, and removing obstacles to competition where feasible and where compatible with authorities' key objectives for the service".

(iii) "Specifying the service output to be achieved rather than the way in which the service is to be performed in detail . . .".

(iv) "Adopting clear procedures for balancing quality and price".

(v) "Acting fairly between contractors to ensure that the conduct of tendering does not put external contractors at a disadvantage".

It is also proposed, however, that the new guidance will be supplemented by further guidance documents, issued in a numbered series, which deal with specific issues (for example, performance bonds and guarantees).[20]

The guidance in Circular 10/93 in so far as it deals with the scope of anti-competitive behaviour, and the proposed new guidance just referred to, is, or is to be, issued as "statutory guidance" pursuant to the 1993 Competition Regulations. This means that it is required to be taken into account by the Secretary of State and the courts in determining what constitutes anti-competitive behaviour. The guidance issued in December 1994 on blue collar and white collar CCT services recently included in the regime was not issued pursuant to these provisions since it was intended merely to be temporary. Guidance issued by the government which is concerned with matters other than the definition of anti-competitive behaviour, or which is concerned with anti-competitive behaviour but not issued pursuant to the 1993 Competition Regulations, does not have the same legal status. This is the case, for example, with the December 1994 guidance, and the proposed new guidance on specific areas of CCT referred to above. However, this non-statutory guidance is still useful as an indicator of the kind of conduct which may lead to action being taken against an authority by the Secretary of State.

---

[18] *Guidance on the Conduct of Compulsory Competitive Tendering,* above, para. 8.
[19] *Ibid,* paras. 12–13.
[20] See pp. 741–742.

2. PACKAGING AND SPECIFICATIONS

(1) PACKAGING THE WORK: THE SIZE AND MIX OF CONTRACTS

In deciding how to package work for tendering, and in drawing up the specifications for individual contracts, authorities must take care to act in such a way as to make the work attractive for private sector firms. Should an authority act with the intention of making it difficult for private firms to handle the work, or should this be the effect of its conduct even if not intended, its actions may be regarded as anti-competitive and thus unlawful. Five per cent of the 157 complaints of anti-competitive behaviour made to the Department of the Environment in 1993 concerned packaging of work.[21] The government guidance suggests that as a general principle work "should be packaged in such a way as to bring it within the scope of as wide a range of contractors as practicable".[22] However, in determining what is anti-competitive, it is necessary to balance the number and nature of competitors with other commercial considerations, such as administrative cost.[23] Thus, for example, where reasonable competition is available for work let in medium-sized lots, it should not be necessary to advertise in lots suitable for the very smallest firms, if savings from greater competition will be outweighed by the higher costs of awarding and administering many small contracts.

Allegations of anti-competitive behaviour may arise because of the size of contracts or because of the mix of work.

In relation to size of contracts, the greatest danger is advertising contracts which are too large for the private sector. The existing government guidance on blue-collar CCT has suggested that this needs to be considered, in particular, with activities such as grounds maintenance, building cleaning and jobbing maintenance where most private firms are small.[24] Where some large firms exist, these may be able to take on larger packages of work and offer economies of scale. However, this possibility can be covered, whilst at the same time taking advantage of the competition from smaller firms, by advertising in small packages and allowing firms to bid for more than one package.[25] On the other hand,

---

[21] Department of Environment, *CCT and Local Government: Department of Environment Annual Report 1993.*

[22] Circular 10/93, para. 7; and White Collar guidance, para. 12.

[23] See generally the section on anti-competitive behaviour at pp. 745–747 below.

[24] Circular 10/93, para. 7; and see also the White Collar Guidance, para. 12 and, for housing management specifically, para. 16.

[25] Circular 10/93, para. 8. In practice, an authority may not wish to allow a single firm to take on the whole of a particular defined activity, since the authority will not then have alternative firms to call upon in case of default.

as noted above, the greater administrative costs of supervising lots of small contracts may outweigh any savings through greater competition, and this also needs to be taken into account.

Authorities must also ensure that the mix of work is such that it is likely to be attractive. In some cases the authority may wish to mix work relating to different defined activities where firms exist which can do both; but this may also have the effect of excluding specialist firms. To avoid anti-competitive behaviour it may be necessary to permit firms to bid separately for the different elements should they wish. Similar problems may arise in packaging work which all falls within the same defined activity; again some firms may be able to carry out all the work, but others only part of it, and it would seem appropriate to adopt the same strategy of permitting bids for the whole or just parts. There may even be work within a single defined activity which is normally the province of specialist firms only. An example might be leisure management; this includes golf course management, which tends to be carried out by specialist firms. A package which includes both golf course management and general leisure management may be unattractive both to golf course management specialists and those with more general interests; thus perhaps the two should be separated, and if they are combined, firms should again be permitted to bid on parts of the contract only.[26]

As suggested by the existing guidance and the proposed new draft guidance, authorities may wish to consult interested parties – such as service providers or their associations or recipients of the services – on the appropriate packaging of the work.[27]

The new draft guidance, with which the government is proposing to replace the existing detailed guidance on CCT, simply emphasises that authorities should seek to achieve a "good competitive response" by considering the range of suppliers and their likely response to the proposed package, and that they should be able to demonstrate that their packaging of the work has taken full account of the market.[28]

(2) DURATION OF CONTRACTS

Authorities must also ensure that contracts are not rendered unattractive by being either too long or too short.[29] For most activities covered by the

---

[26] This example has been given in Circular 10/93, para. 10.
[27] Circular 10/93, para. 11; White Collar Guidance, para. 13; draft *Guidance on the Conduct of Compulsory Competitive Tendering,* para. 16. The guidance points out that authorities must have regard to their obligations under the procurement directives, as to which see pp. 615–616.
[28] Department of the Environment, draft *Guidance on the Conduct of Compulsory Competitive Tendering,* para. 15 (and see para. 17 for specific guidance on the service of housing management).
[29] See Circular 10/93, above, para. 12.

LGA 1988 maximum and minimum periods are in any case laid down by legislation. The minimum periods seek to ensure that contracts are long enough to be attractive – for example, to allow recovery of any start-up costs (such as the purchase of street cleaning or refuse collecting equipment). The maximum ensures that the efficiency of the DSO is tested against the market with reasonable regularity, so allowing the authority to take advantage of any new developments in the market.

It seems unlikely that a contract which complies with the periods set out in the legislation could be considered anti-competitive. However, it might transpire that the periods set in the legislation are not in all circumstances satisfactory to attract competition, and arguably compliance with the legislation would not then preclude the existence of anti-competitive behaviour. This is the view adopted by the Secretary of State in the proposed new statutory guidance on CCT.[30] On the other hand, it might be suggested that the legislation intends to regulate this area exhaustively, and that in such a case there should be no role for the rule on anti-competitive behaviour.

The periods which apply to contracts awarded in England on or after October 19, 1995 are as set out below.[31] The periods which applied to contracts awarded prior to this date were shorter for most defined activities. However, it was decided in 1995 to lengthen both maximum and minimum periods. It was hoped that this would attract more firms to bid for contracts, and also that it would encourage greater investment in the services in question, thus leading to cost reductions and better quality service provision.

Different periods apply for some activities, according to whether or not the work under the contract is to be done "at or in connection with an educational establishment"[32]; for this work, the periods are in some cases shorter than those which apply to other contracts.

---

[30] Draft guidance on CCT, above, para. 20, suggesting that authorities must consider what would achieve "full competition" within the period in the legislation.

[31] These periods are set out for most activities in Local Government Act 1988 (Defined Activities) (Specified Periods) (England) Regulations 1995, S.I. 1995 No. 2484 (the "Specified Periods Regulations), which disapply the previous provisions for contracts for contracts awarded on or after October 19, 1995 (reg. 4) and set out the new periods (reg. 5 and the Schedule). The periods for parking supervision, vehicle management and security work are laid down in the Local Government Act 1988 (Defined Activities) (Supervision of Parking, Management of Vehicles and Security Work) Regulations 1994, S.I. 1994 No. 3165, reg. 3; and for the cleaning of police buildings in Local Government Act 1988 (Defined Activities) (Cleaning of Police Buildings) (England and Wales) Reguations 1995, S.I. 1995 No. 1973, reg. 5.

[32] "Educational establishment" means a county school, a voluntary controlled school, a voluntary aided school, a special agreement school, a special school, a nursery school or a pupil referral unit within the meaning of the Education Act 1944 and the Education Act 1993. The special shorter periods apply whenever all or part of the work is undertaken at or in connection with such an establishment (Specified Periods Regs., above, reg. 5(2)), except that the general periods apply when the hours of work at or in connection with the establishment are less than 40 per cent of the total (reg. 5(3)).

Work not at or in connection with an education establishment

Activity	Minimum period (yrs)	Maximum period (yrs)
Refuse collection	6	10
Building cleaning	4	6
Other cleaning	5	10
Schools/welfare catering	4	6
Other catering	4	6
Ground maintenance	5	7
Vehicle repair/maintenance	5	7
Sports/leisure management	5	10
Supervision of parking	4	6
Vehicle management	4	6
Security work	4	6

Work at or in connection with an education establishment

Activity	Minimum period (yrs)	Maximum period (yrs)
Refuse collection	6	10
Building cleaning	3	4
Other cleaning	5	10
Schools/welfare catering	4	5
Other catering	4	6
Ground maintenance	3	4
Vehicle repair/maintenance	4	6
Sports/leisure management	4	6
Supervision of parking	4	6
Vehicle management	4	6
Security work	4	6

No minimum or maximum periods are specified for services subject to the LGPLA 1980 or for white-collar services under the LGA 1988 (that is, legal services, construction and property management services and housing management services). However, authorities must have regard to the obligation not to act in an anti-competitive manner. The guidance on white-collar CCT suggests that for on-going services, such as housing management, the maximum period should not generally exceed five years (subject to provision for tasks still ongoing at the end of the fixed period), and that contracts for performing a specific task should be defined by reference to completion of that task.[33]

---

[33] White Collar Guidance, para. 17. The new draft *Guidance on the Conduct of Compulsory Competitive Tendering* includes a similar provision.

(3) SPECIFICATION OF THE SERVICE

The rules of both the LGA 1988 and LGPLA 1980 require that interested firms be provided with a detailed specification for the service.[34] Government guidance emphasises that this should be as precise as possible[35]: a lack of precision may advantage the DSO or DLO which already has a detailed knowledge of the service. With professional services it may be difficult to specify the exact work, since this may be unpredictable, and this is recognised in the guidance which suggests that in this case the authority should simply indicate the expected range and volume of work.[36] It is unclear, however, how far authorities must go to satisfy the legal requirement of a "detailed" specification. In the context of the Services Regulations implementing the European Community Services Directive it is recognised that in purchasing some services it is impossible to define specifications with sufficient precision to enable firms to submit bids on the basis of a specification, as required by the open and restricted procedures under those regulations; and in this case authorities may invoke the negotiated procedure, which effectively allows bidders to submit proposals based on their own suggested specifications.[37] It is unclear if this derogation allowing use of the negotiated procedure could ever be invoked in relation to a CCT procedure, because of the requirement for a detailed specification. It is submitted, however, that the concept of a "detailed" specification in CCT should not be rigidly interpreted, but should only entail that requirements be specified *as far as possible*. Thus there may be cases where this obligation is satisfied, but the specification is still not suffcently precise for the conduct of an open or restricted procedure under the Services Regulations.

The guidance also indicates that specifications should be defined in terms of performance requirements or outputs as far as possible, rather than by reference to work methods or procedures.[38] For example, it is suggested that it may be acceptable to specify for a wheeled bin system for refuse collection but not to specify the type of equipment to be used or manning levels. It is also suggested the authority should consider the proposals for organisation of the service which differ from that previously adopted by the DLO/DSO.[39] Where broad performance criteria are not adopted and the authority unreasonably refuses to accept variants proposed by providers, there is a danger that the authority may be considered to have acted anti-competitively. It can be noted that the

---

[34] LGA 1988, s.7(3)(b); LGPLA 1980, s.9(4)(a), as amended by LGA 1992, s.11, Sched. 1, para. 2(2).

[35] Circular 10/93, para. 18; White Collar Guidance, para. 23.

[36] Para. 24.

[37] See pp. 265–267.

[38] Circular 10/93, para. 19; White Collar Guidance, paras. 24 and 26.

[39] *Ibid.*

application of the rules on transfer of undertakings[40] may depend on whether or not the service is substantially reorganised when it is contracted out, and it will certainly be anti-competitive if it is decided to preclude any reorganisation simply because the authority wishes to ensure that the rules on transfer of undertakings apply.[41] The government's new draft guidance, with which it is proposed to replace the existing guidance, likewise places great emphasis on the importance of output based specifications as a general principle in CCT.[42]

The rules on anti-competitive behaviour will also prohibit unreasonable requirements concerning the type of equipment to be used by a provider where the in-house organisation already possesses the specified equipment. It will also generally be anti-competitive to require providers to use the authority's own equipment, or to deny it the use of equipment which the authority has.[43] Authorities must also take care to comply with the rules on specifications in the Works Regulations and Services Regulations.[44]

It is also required that the detailed specification which is sent to firms should state the period during which the work is to be carried out.[45]

The specification will need to be adhered to by any external provider as part of his contractual obligations, subject to the possibility of the parties later agreeing non-substantial variations to these specifications.[46] Section 7(8) of the Local Goverment Act 1988 specifically provides that where the authority itself performs the work it must adhere to the detailed specification.[47]

(4) PUBLICITY FOR THE SPECIFICATION

A provision introduced in 1992 in section 10 of the Local Government Act 1992 requires authorities to keep a copy of the specification and a summary of its main requirements at the authority's principal office, for inspection by members of the public at "all reasonable hours".[48] The authority is also required to publicise these arrangements "as they think sufficient" to draw them to the attention of interested members of the

---

[40] See pp. 636–648.
[41] On when the rules apply see pp. 638–641.
[42] See Department of the Environment, draft *Guidance on the Conduct of Compulsory Competitive Tendering,* paras. 17–18.
[43] See pp. 742–744.
[44] See generally Chap. 11
[45] LGA 1988 s.7(3)(c).
[46] On this see p. 737.
[47] The Department of the Environment's proposed new draft guidance, above, para. 13, suggests that the best way for an authority to demonstrate compliance with this condition is to submit regular reports on the matter to the relevant local authority committee.
[48] Local Government Act 1992, s.10(1) and 2(a). On what should be included in the summary see Department of the Environment, *Letter to local authorities concerning the Local Government Act 1992: Commencement (No.2) Order 1992,* para. 7.

public.[49] Thus the public are informed of the standards of service which they may expect of a provider, whether this is an in-house or external provider.

3. OBTAINING TENDERS

(1) PROCEDURES UNDER THE LGPLA 1980

(a) USE OF A RESTRICTED PROCEDURE

The LGPLA 1980 envisages that the procedure used for obtaining tenders will be a form of restricted procedure – that is, the authority must seek expressions of interest from potential bidders, and then invite a number of those interested to submit bids, rather than advertise for bids to be submitted directly by any interested party, as in an open procedure. This is implicit in the requirement that the authority must have "invited offers" from at least three persons, discussed below, which contemplates that invitations will be issued to limited persons only.[50]

(b) ADVERTISING THE CONTRACT

In contrast with the position for contracts governed by the LGA 1980, there are no rules on how contracts are to be advertised. Since, as is explained below, the rules require that generally bids be solicited from those on the authority's approved lists, it is probably assumed that the contract will not be advertised at all, but invitations simply issued to persons known because of their registration on a list. However, it is permissible for the authority to solicit expressions of interest from those on its lists if it wishes, before deciding which of those persons should receive invitations. This could be done either by an advertisement or, more likely in practice, by contacting those on the list individually.

However, with contracts subject also to the Works Regulations or Services Regulations which implement the European Community procurement directives, an advertisement in the *Official Journal of the Communities* is required for this purpose.[51] Further, invitations cannot in these cases be confined to those on approved lists, as explained at (c) below.

---

[49] Local Government Act 1992, s.10(1) and 2(b).
[50] It is not clear whether an authority might argue that the conditions in the statute may be satisfied also through a procedure by which *any* qualified party is directly invited to bid without any intermediate process of issuing invitations to specific bidders – that is, by an open procedure. Probably this would not be permitted, but the same effect can be achieved simply by issuing invitations to all who respond.
[51] See Chap. 5.

(c) CHOOSING PROVIDERS TO BE INVITED TO TENDER

The LGPLA 1980 requires an authority to invite to tender at least three persons,[52] who are not themselves local authorities or development bodies.[53] This is a minimum requirement – authorities may always invite more, and it may be anti-competitive behaviour not to do so where it would be appropriate to issue more invitations to secure adequate competition.[54] The Secretary of State has a power to alter this minimum number by regulations.[55]

The invitees must be selected from persons who are "included in a list maintained by the authority or body seeking to undertake the work of persons who are willing to undertake such work".[56] Normally inclusion on a list will in practice involve a process to assess the qualification of a firm; thus the provision arguably intends to refer to a list of *qualified* firms. However, this is not stated expressly and it may be that the list could be open to anyone expressing an interest in the authority's work. The requirement to use a list appears to suggest that those interested in local authority work which is covered by the LGPLA should generally ensure that they are registered to be eligible (although persons could perhaps be admitted to a list after the contract has been advertised).

In the case of contracts covered by the Works and Services Regulations the requirement for inclusion on an approved list appears inconsistent with those regulations, which do not allow authorities to insist on registration on such lists.[57] Since this rule derived from Community law takes precedence over national legislative provisions, authorities must disregard the list requirement for these contracts, and must consider for shortlisting all firms responding to the advertisement in the *Official Journal*. Alternatively, the courts might seek to interpret this requirement in a manner which is consistent with the Community rules: this could be done by confining the concept of an "approved list" to a list of qualified firms drawn up for the individual contract, following the advertisement of the contract. However, it seems clear that this was not the intention when the provision was enacted.

No provision is made for the case where there are not three persons available to bid. In this case it is probably to be implied that all interested persons (or at least all those qualified) are to be invited to bid.

There are no specific rules on the criteria for deciding which of those firms interested are to be invited to bid, but in making this decision the

---

[52] LGPLA 1980 s.9(4)(a).
[53] LGPLA 1980 s.9(4)(a), as substituted by LGA 1988, s.32, Sched. 6, paras. 1 and 3.
[54] See Circular 10/93, paras. 52–53.
[55] LGPLA 1980 s.9(5).
[56] LGPLA s.9(4), as substituted in part by LGA 1988, s.32, Sched. 6, paras. 1 and 3.
[57] See pp. 344–347.

authority is subject to the general obligation not to act in an anti-competitive manner. Probably all firms who are unqualified for lack of minimum financial or technical capacity may be eliminated. (Indeed, it is submitted that the qualification of providers in these respects *must* be assessed at this stage, to ensure that sufficient bids are received from *qualified* providers to provide competition for the DLO: not to do this might constitute anti-competitive behaviour.) An authority could also use other commercial criteria – for example, selection of the most competitive firms or random methods (provided these are consistent with its obligations under other legislation, notably the Works or Services Regulations[58]). The requirement that the authority must not act anti-competitively clearly precludes, on the other hand, any conduct aimed at improving the chances of the DLO – for example, deliberately choosing the most uncompetitive firms.

The Secretary of State has a power to prescribe what information should be included in invitations to tender,[59] but has not yet exercised this power.

(d) TIME-LIMITS FOR SUBMISSION OF EXPRESSIONS OF INTEREST AND SUBMISSION OF BIDS

No specific time-limits are yet prescribed for the various stages of the tendering procedure, although the Secretary of State has a power to set down such limits.[60] This contrasts with the position for work under the LGA 1988, where minimum time periods are set for bidders' response to an initial advertisement (37 days), and also to the invitation to tender (normally 40 days).[61] However, setting an unrealistic time for response may constitute anti-competitive behaviour. Circular 10/93 has suggested that authorities should generally have regard to the limits set for procedures under the 1988 Act, even though these do not strictly apply.[62] Where there is no advertisement of the contract, or other specific request for expressions of interest, it is not clear whether 40 days would normally be an appropriate period for submission of bids, or whether the period should be longer to take account of the fact that invited bidders have not received any prior notice of the work.

---

[58] On permissible criteria under these provisions see pp. 217–222.
[59] LGPLA 1980, section 9(4)(aaa). Circular 10/93, however, indicates that authorities should include certain details relating to the use of local authority assets: see para. 59 and para. 63.
[60] LGPLA 1980 s.9(4)(aa).
[61] See pp. 721 and 723.
[62] Circular 10/93, paras.15–16. The circular does indicate that the fairly long time periods in the 1988 Act might not, though, be appropriate in the case of smaller contracts (under one year in duration or £100,000 in value: para. 16).

Contracts subject to the European Community regime under the Works and Services Regulations are, of course, subject to the 37 day and 40 day time-limits under that regime.[63]

(e) SUBMISSION OF A BID BY THE DLO

The purpose of the procedure under the 1980 LGPLA is to compare the value for money offered by the DLO with that offered by external bidders. Thus the DLO must in all cases submit a formal "bid" in the award procedure[64] which is to be compared with the external bids in the manner explained later in this chapter.[65] The amount of this bid is dictated by the fact that the DLO must adhere to certain financial objectives on an annual basis, and the amount charged in the bid must be sufficient to ensure that these objectives are met.[66] It is in theory possible that for a particular contract the DLO could submit a bid which is less than the cost of doing the work, and "subsidise" this by other work. However, it is arguable that such conduct might constitute anti-competitive behaviour.

(f) THE PROHIBITION ON GIVING ADDITIONAL INFORMATION TO THE DLO

The 1993 Competition Regulations provide that it is anti-competitive behaviour for authorities to make available to the DLO information which is not available either in the notice advertising the contract or in the other contract documents, where this information is not available to external providers.[67]

(2) PROCEDURES UNDER THE LGA 1988

(a) USE OF A RESTRICTED PROCEDURE

The LGA 1988 contemplates that authorities will use a restricted procedure, according to which the contract is advertised, and bids then solicited from those expressing an interest.[68]

---

[63] See pp. 213 and 224–226.
[64] LGPLA 1980, s.9(2), requiring the preparation of a "written statement", which effectively constitutes a bid, which must correspond to the contract specifications (see s.9(6), as amended by LGA 1988, s.32, Sched. 6, paras. 1 and 3).
[65] See pp. 723–737.
[66] See further pp. 756–757.
[67] Local Government (Direct Service Organisations) (Competition) Regulations 1993 S.I. 1993 No. 848.
[68] An open procedure would probably not be consistent with the rules: for example, the advertisement of the contract must state that interested persons should notify the authority and that it will issue invitations. An authority seeking the widest competition could, of course, invite all qualified persons expressing an interest.

(b) ADVERTISING THE CONTRACT

To advertise the contract the authority must place an advertisement in both (i) a local newspaper (a "newspaper circulating in the locality in which the work is to be carried out"), and (ii) a trade journal (a "publication circulating among persons who carry out work of the kind concerned").[69] The CCT regime does not preclude an authority from advertising the contract elsewhere in addition, or from informing particular firms which it believes may be interested. Contracts which are subject to the E.C. regime must, of course, be publicised in the *Official Journal*; this is in addition to the publications stipulated in the 1988 Act. In such a case, care must be taken to ensure that the work is not advertised in the local and trade publications before the notice has been despatched to the *Official Journal*,[70] which would be a breach of the E.C. rules.

The LGA 1988 lists certain information which must be provided in all advertisements, to ensure that firms have sufficient information to decide whether they are interested in the contract. First, the advertisement must include a "brief description" of the work.[71] It must also state that the specifications may be inspected, and provide details of the time, place and period when this may be done[72]; and that a copy may be obtained on request on payment of the appropriate, specified, charge.[73] Secondly, the advertisement must make it clear that the authority intends to invite bids,[74] and that interested persons must notify the authority within a specified time.[75] Since it is a breach of the regulations which implement the Community directives to include information in a domestic publication which is not included in the *Official Journal*,[76] any information published in accordance with the Act must also be included in the *Official Journal* notice.

(c) THE AVAILABILITY OF SPECIFICATIONS

The detailed specification of the work must be made available for inspection by interested parties, free of charge.[77] The place, time and period for inspection must be reasonable,[78] and must be publicised in the advertisement, as noted above; and the authority must adhere to the times, etc., stated there.[79] It is also required that copies should be made

---

[69] LGA 1988, s.7(1).
[70] See p. 206.
[71] LGA 1988, s.7(2)(a).
[72] LGA 1988, s.7(2)(b).
[73] LGA 1988, s.7(2)(c).
[74] LGA 1988, s.7(2)(e).
[75] LGA 1988, s.7(2)(d).
[76] See p. 206.
[77] LGA 1988, s.7(3)(b) and 7(2)(b).
[78] LGA 1988, s.7(3)(a).
[79] LGA 1988, s.7(3)(b).

available during the same period to firms who request it, on payment of a specified fee.[80] This fee must be reasonable.[81] Government guidance suggests that it must be limited to the amount necessary to cover the reasonable costs of distributing the specification and producing copies, and that the cost of drawing it up cannot be included.[82]

(d) TIME-LIMITS FOR BIDDERS' RESPONSE

The 1993 Competition Regulations provide that the period for firms to respond to the advertisement inviting expressions of interest must, as a general rule, be not less than 37 days, beginning on the date the notice is published.[83] This provision does not apply, however, to contracts subject to the E.C. works and services rules[84]; these contracts are governed instead by the periods stated in the appropriate regulations. The period specified in the 1993 Competition Regulations is in fact similar to the time-limit applying under the E.C. rules, which is generally 37 days, although the latter is counted from the date of despatch of the notice to the *Official Journal* rather the date of publication.

(e) THE ISSUE OF INVITATIONS TO TENDER

Where more than three persons (who are not defined authorities) notify their interest in bidding, at least three of them must be invited to bid.[85] Where three or less notify their interest, all three must be invited.[86] This appears to require three persons to be invited even where there are not three *qualified* bidders. However this would clearly be unsatisfactory, wasting the time of both the authority and the bidder. Further, for contracts covered by the Works and Services Regulations it is generally required that only providers appearing qualified should be invited.[87] It is to be hoped that the courts will construe this provision as requiring bids only from eligible persons. Where notification of interest is received from a body which is a defined authority under the Act[88] (for example, another local authority), the awarding authority has a discretion whether to invite that body to bid.[89] Thus an authority may decline to invite such a body even if there are less than three other interested parties. The

---

[80] LGA 1988, s.7(3)(b).
[81] LGA 1988, s.7(3)(a).
[82] Circular 10/93, para. 17; White Collar Guidance para. 29. A similar provision has been included in the new draft guidance, note 17 above, para. 29.
[83] Above note 67, reg. 2(2). Previously, as provided by the LGA 1988, s.7(3)(a), the period was merely required to be "reasonable".
[84] 1993 Competition Regulations, reg. 2(1), as am. by the Local Government (Direct Service Organisations) (Competition) (Amendment) Regulations 1995, S.I. 1995 No. 1336, reg. 4.
[85] LGA 1988, s.7(4)(b).
[86] LGA 1988, s.7(4)(c).
[87] See p. 219.
[88] On the definition of defined authorities see pp. 665–666.
[89] LGA 1988, s.7(4)(d).

specified figure of three is a minimum and where more than three persons express an interest it may be necessary to invite more than three, to avoid accusations of anti-competitive behaviour. The appropriate number will depend on the nature and size of the contract and factors such as the costs of preparing and assessing bids. Government guidance suggests, however, that between four and six invitations should generally be sent.[90]

For the blue collar CCT services and for sports and leisure management invitations to tender must generally be issued not less than three and not more than six months from the date of publication of the advertisement.[91] The minimum period ensures that providers have adequate time to prepare for the contract.

These periods do not, however, apply to housing management services, construction and property services, legal services, financial services, information technology services or personnel services. For these activities authorities may apply a period shorter than three months before issuing tenders/invitations for the activity, where appropriate, although within the time period chosen it is necessary to comply with the legal requirements for minimum time periods for replies to the advertisement (generally 37 days) and also to allow sufficient time for assessing the qualifications of those who reply, where relevant. For this group of services authorities may also choose a period longer than six months, although an unduly long period which could deter participants may be regarded as anti-competitive behaviour.[92]

The Secretary of State has a power to make regulations specifying matters to be included in the invitation to tender.[93] This power has not been exercised, but government guidance has indicated that authorities should include, at least, certain information relating to the bidders' right to use the local authority's assets in the contract.[94]

Where, following the advertisement, no firms express an interest in bidding for the work, an authority may award the work to the DSO without further procedural requirements.[95]

---

[90] Circular 10/93, para. 53; White Collar Guidance para. 75. This is also stated in para. 38 of the draft *Guidance on the Conduct of Compulsory Competitive Tendering*, which it is proposed should replace the existing guidance.

[91] LGA 1988, s.7(4)(a).

[92] Local Government Act 1988, s.7(4)(a) as applied by the Local Government Act 1988 (Competition) (Defined Activities) (Construction and Property Services) Order 1994 (S.I. 1994 No. 2888), Article 3(3); Local Government Act 1988 (Competition) (Defined Activities) Order 1994 (S.I. 1994 No. 2884), Article 3(3); Local Government Act 1988 (Competition) (Defined Activities) Order 1995, S.I. 1995 No. 1915, Article 5(2).

[93] LGA 1988, s.8(2)(a).

[94] Circular 10/93, paras. 59 and 63; White Collar Guidance para. 83. On use of assets see pp. 724–744.

[95] This follows from the fact that the rules concerning issue of invitations to tender apply only where some person has notified the authority of an interest in participating: LGA 1988, s.7(4).

(f) TIME-LIMITS FOR THE SUBMISSION OF BIDS

The 1993 Competition Regulations provide a minimum time of not less than 40 days from the date of the invitation for firms to submit a bid.[96] Again the period does not apply to contracts governed by the E.C. works and services rules. These are subject instead to the periods laid down by those rules, which is in any case normally 40 days from despatch of the invitation.[97] Government guidance emphasises, however, that periods must be appropriate to the particular contract,[98] and in some cases the minimum period might not be considered adequate for competition.

(g) SUBMISSION OF A BID BY THE DSO

As with the LGPLA 1980, the purpose of the procedure under the LGA 1988 is to compare the value for money offered by the in-house provider with that offered by external bidders, and the DSO must submit a formal bid to allow a comparison to be made.[99] As under the LGPLA, the amount of this bid will be dictated by the fact that the DLO must adhere to certain financial objectives.

(h) PROHIBITION ON GIVING ADDITIONAL INFORMATION TO THE DSO

The 1993 Competition Regulations state that it shall be regarded as anti-competitive behaviour for authorities to make available to DSOs information additional to that available in the contract notice or documents, which is not available to others who have requested to be invited to bid on the contract.[1]

4. THE PROCEDURE FOLLOWING THE RECEIPT OF TENDERS (LGA AND LGPLA)

(1) EVALUATION OF BIDS

(a) ORIGINS AND PURPOSE OF THE RULES ON BID EVALUATION

Prior to 1993 there were few legal rules dealing with the process of bid evaluation, whereby tenders received from the DLO/DSO and private

---

[96] 1993 Competition Regulations reg. 2(1). Previously the period was merely required to be reasonable under LGA 1988, s.7(3)(a).
[97] See pp. 224–226.
[98] Circular 10/93, para. 15; White Collar Guidance, para. 21.
[99] LGA 1988, s.7(6).
[1] Competition Regulation 5(b) and (c).

firms are compared against each other.[2] However, the authority's discretion under both the LGPLA 1980 and LGA 1988 has been constrained since 1988 by the general prohibition on anti-competitive behaviour.[3] This will generally require the authority to give preference to an external bid which is more economically advantageous than that of the DSO/DLO, unless there is a special reason to prefer the in-house bid. Since the inception of CCT an increasing amount of guidance on exactly how bids should be compared has been included in government circulars, but this had no formal status and was sometimes disregarded by authorities who disagreed with the Secretary of State's approach.

As a result the government decided to adopt binding legal provisions to deal with this issue. Largely this has been done through the 1993 Competition Regulations which designate certain conduct in the bid evaluation process as "anti-competitive".[4] The rules in the regulations have been elaborated in guidance, in particular in circular 10/93 and in the equivalent guidance for white-collar CCT[5] – although as explained above this guidance is likely soon to be replaced by less detailed statutory guidance.[6] Unless otherwise stated, these rules apply to procedures under both the LGPLA 1980 and the LGA 1988.

The rules are directed at ensuring a fair comparison between the internal and external bids. They are not concerned at all with the process of comparing external bids against each other; this is consistent with the whole purpose of CCT procedure, which is solely to measure the relative merits of internal and external service provision. Thus the prohibition on anti-competitive behaviour applies only in relation to an award to the internal bidder – it cannot be claimed that an authority acted anti-competitively in the choice made between outside bidders; and the more specific rules in the regulations relate only to the comparison of internal and external bids. This choice may, however, be subject to other rules, notably the E.C. rules where these apply[7] or the prohibition on taking account of non-commercial considerations imposed under section 17 of the LGA 1988.[8]

(b) THE EVALUATION PROCESS

(i) ASCERTAINING THE COST OF THE IN-HOUSE BID

The 1993 Competition Regulations deal, first, with the question of how the effective cost, or "price", of the DLO/DSO bid is to be calculated,

---

[2] The main exception was the rule in LGA 1988, s.17 prohibiting non-commercial considerations: see further pp. 830–845.
[3] See generally pp. 745–747.
[4] Under the power given by LGA 1992, s.9: see pp. 745–747.
[5] See pp. 707–709.
[6] See pp. 707–709.
[7] See Chap. 5.
[8] See pp. 830–845.

for the purpose of comparing it with external bids. The starting point is the amount of the "bid".[9] This bid is a written statement, put forward by the authority in advance of the award procedure,[10] which indicates the amount to be credited to the relevant DLO/DSO account if the in-house unit should do the work – effectively, the "price" of the internal bid. Because the in-house unit is obliged to meet certain financial objectives (as is explained further below), this bid will in practice need to reflect the costs which will be included in the other side of the relevant account (materials used in performing the work, the cost of use of assets, etc.), and also an amount for achieving a certain rate of return on capital used, which the legislation requires to be included.[11] It is intended that through comparing this figure with bids submitted by the private sector the relative merits of internal and external service provision can be compared.

In making the comparison certain sums may, however, be effectively added or subtracted from the authority's basic bid price, as set out below.

I. Addition of the cost of a performance bond

First, there is a provision to deal with the fact that outside firms may be asked to provide a performance bond or guarantee, to protect the authority in case the firm should default. The cost of securing such a bond or guarantee will be reflected in the firm's bid price, but the DLO/DSO itself will not incur such a cost. The regulations require allowance to be made for the fact that the internal bidder enjoys this advantage over its private sector rivals. This is done by providing for the amount of the lowest-cost performance bond/guarantee obtained by bidders to be added to the amount of the DLO/DSO bid for the purposes of comparison.[12]

II. Deduction of costs of providing opportunities for the disabled and trainees

On the other hand, the internal bidder may incur costs which are not applicable to an external provider because of the authority's policy of giving employment to the disabled or providing training. In order not to discourage authorities from providing these opportunities provision is made for certain costs attributable to these matters to be effectively deducted from the internal bid.[13] These costs are referred to in the jargon of the regulations as "allowable costs".

---

[9] 1993 Competition Regulations, reg. 6(a).
[10] See pp. 719 and 723.
[11] See pp. 756–757.
[12] Competition Regulation 6(b); Competition Regulation 7(2); and the definition of "notional premium" in reg 1.
[13] Competition Regulations, regs. 6(d) and 7(a)(1); and regs. 9 and 10 (defining allowable costs in relation to the disabled, and provision of training, respectively).

In the case of disabled persons, regulation 9 generally allows authorities to deduct all costs which arise from, or are attributable to, the
employment of disabled persons,[14] where these would not be incurred if
the employee were not a disabled person.[15] This might include, for
example, the costs of providing special facilities for a disabled worker.
The authority must, however, deduct the amount of any grant from the
Department of the Environment which is paid towards the cost of
employing disabled persons.[16]

The costs allowable for trainees are detailed in regulation 10. A
"trainee" in relation to England and Wales is[17] any person employed
under arrangements made by the Secretary of State under section 2 of
the Employment and Training Act 1973.[18] The regulation also covers all
trainees or apprentices of the authority who are employed under
arrangements made by the authority for training persons in their
employment.[19] The regulation allows deduction of certain costs which
arise out of, or are attributable to, the employment of trainees.[20] Only
costs relating to the matters specified in regulation 10(2) may be
considered. These are costs relating to management of the arrangements
(expressly stated to include advertising, recruiting, setting up projects,
and placement); overheads (including the provision of premises and
equipment, and necessary outgoings, including loan charges); the provision of instruction required under the relevant arrangements, and the
registration of qualifications; and the provision of financial support
required by the schemes above (in the case of those employed under
such schemes), or by the authority, in the case of its other trainees. From
these costs must be deducted any aid from the Department of Employment for the training arrangements.[21] For those not engaged pursuant to
one of these arrangements, the authority must also deduct the costs
which would be incurred in any case for the work to be done by non-
trainees.[22] (Such costs need not be deducted for persons employed under
the specific schemes mentioned above.)

No provision is made for taking into account the extent to which such
costs are incurred by external providers. This would in many cases be
precluded under section 17 of the LGA 1988[23] which prohibits consideration of criteria relating to the composition of the workforce as well as
matters relating to the provision of training by providers. It is also

---

[14] A disabled person means any person who is a disabled person within the meaning of s.1
of the Disabled Persons (Employment) Act 1944: 1993 Competition Regulation 9(1).
[15] 1993 Competition Regulations, reg. 9(1)(a) and 9(2). The authority can include also
costs which would be incurred if the internal bid were succesful: reg. 9(1)(b) and 9(2).
[16] 1993 Competition Regulation 9(2).
[17] 1993 Competition Regulations, reg. 10(1) and 10(4)(a)–(b).
[18] As substituted by the Enployment Act 1988, s.25(1).
[19] 1993 Competition Regulations, reg. 10(1) and 10(4)(c).
[20] 1993 Competition Regulations, reg. 10(1)–(3).
[21] 1993 Competition Regulations, reg. 10(3)(a) and 3(b)(i).
[22] 1993 Competition Regulations, reg. 10(3)(b)(2).
[23] See pp. 830–845.

prohibited by the European Community rules on the evaluation of bids, which permits authorities to consider only the economic merits of a bid.[24] Thus providers who support such social policies may find themselves at a competitive disadvantage against both the internal bidder and other external bidders. It is, however, open to authorities to require the engagement of trainees or disabled persons to work on the contract under a contractual condition.[25]

(ii) TREATMENT OF COSTS INCURRED FROM CONTRACTING OUT

Prior to the 1993 Competition Regulations there was much controversy over the extent to which an authority comparing the merits of accepting the in-house or external bid could take into account costs which would be incurred by removing work from a DLO/DSO, such as redundancy costs. The Competition Regulations now define exhaustively which of these costs may be considered: to take account of others is designated anti-competitive conduct.[26] The term used by the regulations to describe these relevant costs is "prospective costs". These are as follows.

– Redundancy costs: When accepting an external bid would lead to the redundancy of authority employees, the authority may take into account redundancy payments which it would be liable to make to such employees under Part VI of the Employment Protection (Consolidation) Act 1978.[27] Authorities which have generally pursued a policy of making discretionary compensation payments pursuant to regulations on this subject,[28] and would make such payments if job losses occurred from loss of the advertised work, may also take those payments into account.[29]

The current statutory guidance makes it clear that redundancies of both service and support staff will have to be shown to be clearly related to the work lost, and to be based on an authority's standard policy on redundancies. It is stated that authorities may be expected to furnish the Secretary of State with details of the way in which the calculations were made.[30] The guidance also provides that redundancy costs should not normally be taken into account in relation to contracts of one year or less, or with an estimated value of £100,000 or less, on the basis that these will not normally involve redundancies.[31] It is also generally stated

---

[24] See pp. 236–239.

[25] See Chap. 16.

[26] Competition Regulations, regs. 5(a)(iv), 6(e) and 5(a)(iii).

[27] Competition Regulations, regs. 12(1), (2) and (3)(a), as am. by the Local Government (Direct Services Organisations) (Competition) (Amendment) Regulations 1995, S.I. 1995 No. 1336, reg. 8.

[28] The regulations under which such discretionary payment may be made are set out in Competition Regulation 1(1).

[29] The amounts which may be taken into account are set out in Competition Regulations 12(2) and (3).

[30] See paras. 47–49 of Circular 10/93; White Collar Guidance, paras. 67–69.

[31] Circular 10/93, para. 46; White Collar Guidance, para. 66.

that redundancy costs should be taken into account only where it is "appropriate" to do so in the particular case.[32] Where, however, such costs would demonstrably be incurred as a result of the work, it is difficult to see why it would not be appropriate to consider them.

– Payments during period of notice of dismissal: Under regulation 13 authorities may take into account the amount of the gross wages and salaries which would be payable to employees who would be excused from their contractual duties on the grounds of redundancy.[33] This is, effectively, the amount payable in lieu of notice. This applies only when the work commences within twelve weeks of accepting the tender (reg. 13(2)(a)); and the authority would be likely to excuse the staff in question at any time between work commencing and twelve weeks from the tender (reg. 13(2)(b)).

– Costs of terminating contracts relating to the service: An authority can take into account, in accordance with Regulation 14, the costs of terminating certain other contracts made by the DLO/DSO, where this is a consequence of accepting an outside tender. This applies to contracts for the lease or maintenance of land or a building; for the hire or maintenance of other things such as plant or equipment; or for the purchase of goods. The authority may here take into account any amount which would be payable because of the early termination of the contract.[34]

– Indemnity against TUPE: When an award procedure goes ahead on the basis that the legislation on transfer of undertakings (TUPE)[35] applies, the regulations provide that an authority may take into account as a prospective cost any "reasonable amount" which providers require from the local authority by way of indemnity against costs which would be incurred from the application of the regulations to the authority's staff who would be dismissed by the authority as redundant if the authority accepted one of the external bids.[36] Since this is a cost which would be incurred if the authority were to accept an external bid, clearly it is appropriate that it should be taken into account in determining the economic advantage of the outside bids.

Generally, it is provided that it is anti-competitive to calculate the amount of the above "prospective costs" *after* the opening of bids.[37]

---

[32] *Ibid.*
[33] Competition Regulations, reg. 13.
[34] Competition Regulations, reg. 14.
[35] On this legislation see pp. 636–648.
[36] Competition Regulations, reg. 14A, as inserted by Local Government (Direct Service Organisations) (Competition) (Amendment) Regulations 1995, 1995 S.I. No. 1336, reg. 9(1). This applies where the bid is evaluated on the understanding that TUPE does not apply.
[37] Competition Regulations, reg. 5(a)(i). See circular 10/93, para. 50; White Collar Guidance, para. 70. The Secretary of State has also suggested in the statutory guidance that authorities should inform contractors when inviting them to tender of which such costs are to be taken into account, although it is not necessary to provide details of what these costs are.

This does not apply, though, to prospective costs arising from the provision of an indemnity against the application of TUPE,[38] since the potential application of TUPE is not known until the bid has been opened and the service providers plans for the organisation of the service are known.

Costs of losing the work other than those listed above may *not* be taken into account – for example, costs of supervising the outside contractor[39] or extra payments needed to deter existing staff from leaving before the contract start date. The government's current guidance also emphasises that authorities may not take into account any perceived losses arising out of the disposal of assets which were used for the performance of the work by the DSO, and have been sold as a result of the loss of the work.[40] The government's refusal to allow costs such as these to be taken into account has been interpreted by some as an attempt to favour external bidders where this is not warranted on economic grounds, and thus as evidence of the ideological preference for the private sector (involving concerns such as the desire to weaken public sector unions) which is seen by some commentators as underlying the CCT regime. Another interpretation, however, might emphasise the government's desire to ensure that significant economic costs are considered, whilst avoiding the possibilities for abuse by authorities who might seek to exaggerate certain more minor cost elements. In fact, it appears that government policy is influenced to some degree by both considerations, and that this policy sometimes appears unduly harsh towards in-house units since in cases of debate the tendency is to favour the external bidder.

It can be noted that the draft statutory guidance which it is proposed to issue to replace the existing statutory guidance[41] does not contain the same detailed provisions on costs as the existing guidance. It is not clear whether this will result in any greater flexibility for authorities within the confines set by the 1993 Competition Regulations.

(iii) THE REQUIREMENT TO TAKE ACCOUNT OF LONG-TERM SAVINGS FROM CONTRACTING OUT

Where the price quoted in an external bid is lower than that in the internal bid, in comparing the two bids the authority must take into account the possibility of long-term savings from contracting out the work, which may extend beyond the life of the particular contract.[42] The way in which these are calculated is set out in the Schedule to the

---

[38] Local Government (Direct Service Organisations (Competition) (Amendment) Regulations 1995 S.I. 1995 No. 1336, reg. 9(1).
[39] On the significance of these costs see p. 625.
[40] See circular 10/93, para. 68; White Collar Guidance, para. 87.
[41] As to which see pp. 708–709.
[42] Competition Regulations, regs. 6(c) and 7.

Competition Regulations.[43] It involves working out the cost of the internal bid as explained above (*i.e.* subtracting allowable costs but adding any sum required to represent a performance bond[44]), and then determining the difference between the internal bid and any lower outside bid over each year of the contract. The differences for each year are then expressed in constant prices, and the annual average difference determined. It is assumed in the Schedule that these savings will extend over a ten-year period, and the total of savings arising from contracting out is then calculated on this basis, and expressed in present prices. This savings figure is referred to in the regulations as the "present value of savings".

These savings must then be taken into account in determining whether the internal or external bid offers best value for money. This ten-year savings period appears unrealistically long, weighting the evaluation unjustifiably in favour of outside bidders – another illustration of the tendency of government policy to lean towards contracting out rather than in-house provision.

(iv) SAVINGS RESULTING FROM THE AVAILABILITY OF ASSETS

When an asset is made available to external bidders free of charge the in-house bid need not include a charge for use of the asset, nor need the bid reflect a rate of return for the use of that asset.[45] However, if an external provider who submits a bid does not wish to make use of assets offered free of charge, there will be a saving if this bid is selected arising from the fact that the asset will be available for the authority's use. Statutory government guidance provides that it is anti-competitive not to take this saving into account in favour of the outside bid when it is compared with that from the DLO/DSO.[46] The credit which must be given is the open-market disposal value of the asset[47] and account must be taken of any redevelopment or alternative use potential.[48]

It is not proposed to include these detailed rules in the proposed new statutory guidance,[49] however.

---

[43] Competition Regulations, reg. 8 and the Schedule.
[44] For the present purpose a proportion of the cost of such a bond is attributed to each year of the contract period.
[45] Circular 10/93, para. 63.
[46] Circular 10/93, para. 63; White Collar Guidance, para. 82.
[47] Circular 10/93, para. 63; White Collar Guidance, para. 83.
[48] Circular 10/93, para. 63; White Collar Guidance, para. 83. These principles apply even if the authority decides to retain the assets, when the value must be calculated unencumbered by the effect of the authority's own use: circular 10/93, para. 66 (where, however, it is accepted that an exception may be made where assets need to be retained to meet emergencies); White Collar Guidance, para. 86.
[49] On this new guidance see pp. 708–709.

(v) THE NATURE OF THE EVALUATION PROCESS

The rules above are concerned with determining the relevance, and the value of certain financial costs and benefits which authorities may wish to take into account in bid evaluation. The other main financial considera- tion is, of course, bid price. In addition, an authority will also generally wish to consider non-financial criteria relating to the content of the bid, such as quality, delivery date, or availability of after-sales services. The contract specifications will lay down minimum requirements for many of these factors, and only providers able to meet these requirements will generally be considered. However, where a bidder offers a service which exceeds the minimum standards on these matters, an authority may wish to consider this as a variable to be weighed against price and the other financial considerations noted above.[50]

How must the different factors – financial and non-financial – be weighed in comparing the internal bid with external bids?

The most straightforward case is where the authority is comparing the in-house bid with a private bid which offers a lower financial cost – that is, where the amount of the in-house bid, taking into account the allowable costs and cost of performance bond, exceeds the price offered in the external bid. Such a lower bid by an outside contractor is referred to as a "qualifying bid". In this case the authority must calculate the "prospective costs" of accepting the outside bid, and weigh these against the "present value of savings" to be obtained in accepting the outside bid,[51] in accordance with the rules outlined earlier. The difference between these two figures shows which option – contracting out to the qualifying bidder or retaining the service in-house – is the most favourable in *financial* terms.

However, the Competition Regulations do not require the authority to accept the bid which is the cheapest in accordance with these calcula- tions. First, the authority retains any discretion which it otherwise has under the law to eliminate firms which are unsuitable (for example do not meet minimum conditions relating to financial and technical stand- ing) or do not comply with the contract specifications. It also retains in principle its discretion to take non-price factors into account as variables to be weighed against the financial considerations. Thus, for example,

---

[50] Secondary policy factors may also in principle be considered as a variable in the evaluation process, although in practice consideration of these factors is generally forbidden under other rules (in particular, section 17 of the LGA 1988). It is also possible that *relative* financial and technical ability (*i.e.* the degree of likelihood that each bidder will successfully complete the contract) might be thought relevant, and taken into account as a variable in relation to external bidders. However, if external bidders meeting minimum requirements are unfavourably compared with the in-house bidder and the authority's assessment is regarded as erroneous, this may be anti-competitive behaviour: *R. v. Secretary of State for the Environment, ex p. Haringey* (1994) 92 L.G.R. 538. It should also be pointed out that consideration of these factors is not permitted under the Works Regulations or Services Regulations: see the discussion at pp. 230–239.
[51] Competition Regulations, reg. 8(2).

the work could be retained in-house despite a cheaper outside bid if it was felt this was outweighed by the better quality of the in-house service provision.

Existing government guidance on blue-collar CCT in Circular 10/93 states that to reject a lower-priced external bid in favour of the internal bid will be consistent with the duty to avoid anti-competitive conduct "only in very limited circumstances", and that authorities taking such action are expected to have "specific and well-founded reasons for such a decision".[52] Authorities have complained that the rule is applied unduly strictly in practice by the Secretary of State, and that this may reflect a desire to restrict the genuine discretion of local authorities to balance different considerations and instead to push down costs of local service provision at the expense of quality. However, this emphasis on price is not reflected in the new draft statutory guidance which the government has proposed as a replacement for the existing guidance: the new guidance seeks to prevent abuse merely by stating that authorities should inform providers of which factors other than price are to be taken into account (something which is anyway required under the E.C. rules for contracts falling within that regime), and that evaluation decisions should be recorded.[53]

In the case of white-collar CCT, on the other hand, the current guidance already indicates that it is for authorities to determine the balance between price and service quality and that no presumption in favour of a lower-priced bid is adopted.[54] It is also provided that the procedure for evaluating the respective merits of the in-house and external bid must be "rigorous and even handed" and decisions fully documented.[55]

A different question is whether it is *permitted* to accept an external bid which is *higher* in terms of its financial cost than the in-house bid. The 1993 Regulations do not deal with the calculations of prospective costs and of savings in this event; it is merely stated that these must be considered in relation to any "qualifying tender",[56] which refers only to external bids which are *less* favourable on this financial analysis. This omission may, perhaps, suggest an assumption that a tender which is financially more expensive than the in-house bid cannot be considered. However, this is not stated expressly and further, the prohibition on anti-competitive behaviour has no relevance where the internal bid is rejected. There thus seems to be nothing to prevent the authority from considering such a tender if the higher price is offset by non-financial considerations.[57]

---

[52] Circular 10/93 para. 35.
[53] Department of the Environment, draft *Guidance on the Conduct of Compulsory Competitive Tendering*, para. 27.
[54] White Collar Guidance, para. 54.
[55] White Collar Guidance, para. 54.
[56] 1993 Competition Regulations, reg. 8(2)(b).
[57] This is also the view of Cirell and Bennett, *Compulsory Competitive Tendering: Law and Practice*, at 13.62.

There is also no obstacle to choosing one external bid on the basis of quality above another, lower-priced, external bid. The question of anti-competitive behaviour again cannot arise, since it is relevant only when the work is awarded to the internal bidder.

(vi) CONTRACTS DIVIDED INTO LOTS

A contract may be divided into lots to allow bidders to bid for the whole requirement or just for part of it. In such a case, it is submitted that an authority is likely to be acting anti-competitively unless it accepts that combination of bids which offers the best value for money overall.

However, in deciding which bid(s) to accept the authority is entitled to insist that bidders adhere to such reasonable rules on submission of bids in lots as are set out in the tender documents. This issue was considered in the case of *Re Ettrick and Lauderdale D.C.*[58] In this case the authority advertised a requirement for grounds maintenance in lots, reserving a right to accept part of each bid only, and requiring that each of the lots be separately costed in each bid. Only two bids were received, one from the DSO, which offered the best value for money for all but one item, and one from Brophy, which so far as individual lots were concerned offered the best value for the grass cutting lot only, but also offered better value than the DSO when all the lots, including grass cutting, were added together. The best combination was to accept the Brophy bid for grass cutting and the DSO bid for the other lots. However, Brophy refused to proceed on the basis of the grass cutting lot alone and declined to sign the contract for grass cutting. The authority therefore awarded all the work to the DSO.

Brophy then complained to the Secretary of State, who issued a direction to the authority on the basis of his powers under the Local Government Act 1988, on the grounds that the authority had acted in an anti-competitive manner in awarding the work to the DSO when better value would have been obtained by awarding all the work to Brophy. The court ruled, however, that the behaviour in question could not in law constitute anti-competitive conduct. It is submitted that this is a correct view. Whilst Brophy's total bid offered better value than the DSO's total bid, the best solution overall was to split the work; this was not possible only because Brophy refused to accept it, even though the tender documents provided that bids must be submitted on the basis that it was open to the authority to accept part of a bid only. In fact, the court concluded that since Brophy's bid for the grass cutting had already been accepted, Brophy was under a contractual obligation to perform that part of the work. This is not crucial to the decision, however: even if Brophy had purported to withdraw its separate bid for the grass cutting before the bid was accepted, it would not have been anti-competitive to

---

[58] Judgment of May 25, 1995.

refuse to accept Brophy for the whole contract. Its decision to withdraw its separate bid for the grass cutting amounted, effectively, to an attempt to renegotiate the terms of the tendering exercise, which is not generally permitted: an authority is entitled to set rules for the tendering exercise (provided that the rules themselves are not anti-competitive), and to insist that bidders adhere to these rules.

(vii) IMPACT OF THE WORKS AND SERVICES REGULATIONS ON BID EVALUATION

The Works Regulations and Services Regulations which have been enacted to implement the European Community directives on procurement will apply to many contracts which are subject to the CCT regime. It may be noted that the directives themselves do not regulate the comparison of in-house and external bids, since the directives are concerned only with the choice between different external providers and not with the decision as to whether the work should be contracted out at all. However, under the Works and Services Regulations the United Kingdom government has effectively provided that the rules on the evaluation process are to apply to in-house bids.[59] Thus the evaluation of in-house and external bids under CCT, as well as the evaluation of external bids against each other, must be conducted in accordance with the rules in the regulations.

The application of the Works and Services Regulations in CCT procedures limits authorities to consideration of either lowest price or "the most economically advantageous offer". This may prevent authorities from considering certain factors relating to the relative merits of the external and internal bids which are *not* prohibited under the CCT rules. For example, CCT does not prohibit authorities from taking into account the *relative* technical standing of bidders, but this is not permitted under the Works or Services Regulations.[60] It also seems debatable whether it is permitted under these regulations to take into account costs attributable to the employment of trainees or disabled persons by the in-house unit, since these do not relate to economic advantage. If this is correct it is surely an unintended consequence of the Works and Services Regulations.

The CCT rules themselves are concerned only with comparing in-house and external bids. Whilst, as explained, the Works and Services Regulations have an impact on the process of comparing internal and external bids where those regulations apply alongside the rules on CCT, the CCT rules have no application in any award procedure in comparing different external bids.

---

[59] See further p. 242.
[60] On this point see pp. 230–231.

(2) THE DISCRETION TO REJECT NON-RESPONSIVE BIDS

In some cases an authority may need to consider how it should treat an external bid which does not comply with procedural requirements, such as the deadline for submission of bids or the number of copies to be submitted. This question has not raised any problems in the context of CCT and has not been the subject of guidance from central government. However, it should be pointed out that to decline to consider the bid of an external provider for non-compliance with minor requirements, or to refuse to allow external bidders to amend their bids to comply with the specifications where there is no corresponding adjustment of the price, might be considered as anti-competitive behaviour by the authority.

In waiving formalities in procedures covered by the Works or Services Regulations authorities must, of course, comply with the rules contained in those regulations.[61] It is submitted that it should not be treated as anti-competitive behaviour to decline to permit a change or grant a waiver, where the grant or waiver in question is of a type prohibited by these regulations – for example, accepting a late bid – even if the CCT procedure in question is not itself covered by the regulations (for example, because it falls below the threshold).

(3) CLARIFICATION AND POST-TENDER NEGOTIATIONS

The ability of authorities to enter into discussions and negotiations with bidders once bids have been submitted is always a controversial question. Government guidance on CCT states that "post-tender negotiations" (not defined) may be anti-competitive, since they undermine the integrity of the formal tendering process.[62] In other words, it is indicated that bidders can normally expect the contract to be awarded on the basis of the bids as submitted, and it will be anti-competitive to award a contract to the DLO/DSO following negotiations. However, there are a number of limitations to this general prohibition on post-tender discussions.

First, government guidance accepts that discussion may be held for the purposes of clarification – for example, of the terms offered or the quality or performance available from the bidder[63] – which might not be clear from the bid. Regulation 5 of the 1993 Competition Regulations specifically provides that it shall be considered anti-competitive behaviour to give the DSO an opportunity to explain or provide further information about its bid without giving an equivalent opportunity to

---

[61] See pp. 234–236.
[62] Circular 10/93, para. 36; White Collar Guidance, para. 55.
[63] Circular 10/93, para. 37; White Collar Guidance, para. 55.

each of the external bidders.[64] This must surely, however, merely refer to the requirement to treat like situations alike – thus this provision appears to be relevant only if clarification of outside bids is needed but is denied.

In addition, the guidance on blue-collar CCT indicates that negotiations may be acceptable where the evaluation does not present "overwhelming evidence" in favour of one bidder.[65] This seems to suggest that bidders, including the DLO/DSO, may in such a case be allowed to make improvements to their initial bid in order to win the work. However, this is probably not permitted for procedures falling within the E.C. regime where it appears the awards must be made on the basis of the bids as submitted.[66] If such revisions are to be permitted to the in-house bidder, then obviously equal opportunities for revisions will need to be given to all other bidders.[67] In such a case it may be sensible to provide for this through a second formal tendering process, to avoid accusations that the in-house unit has been unfairly advantaged in the way informal negotiations are conducted.

Government guidance on the application of the "TUPE" rules has also suggested that providers may be permitted to revise bids which have been based on an erroneous view of the application of the TUPE regulations. This issue was considered in Chapter 12.[68]

The guidance also indicates that discussions may be held with the in-house unit where the unit's is the only bid received.[69] However, this is permitted only where the authority has taken all reasonable measures to attract competition. If it has not, this in itself is presumably anti-competitive behaviour and the authority will need to recommence the procedure rather than considering an in-house award. It is also stated that authorities should not significantly amend the specifications on which bids were invited.[70] This is because it may be possible to attract competition with an amended specification, so that in such a case it is not appropriate simply to award the contract to the in-house unit on the assumption that no competition exists.

Apart from the cases noted above, it appears that it will be anti-competitive for the internal bidder to be allowed to amend its bid even where the same opportunity is given to any other bidders. For example, it is probably not permitted to allow bidders to make revisions because it is felt that none of the bidders offers sufficient value for money. If this occurs and the contract is later awarded to the in-house unit then a complaint may be made to the court or Secretary of State. However, if

---

[64] Competition Regulations, reg. 5(a)(2).
[65] Circular 10/93, para. 37.
[66] See pp. 247–249.
[67] Circular 10/93, para. 37.
[68] See p. 646.
[69] Circular 10/93, para. 38; White Collar Guidance, 56.
[70] *Ibid.*

an external bidder and *not* the in-house unit is permitted to revise or discuss a bid, then it is unlikely that the authority's conduct could be regarded as anti-competitive, since the rules are concerned only with the possibility of unfair advantages for the internal bidder, and not with fairness between outside bidders. On the other hand, it is submitted that it is not anti-competitive to *refuse to allow* an external bidder to improve his bid in order to beat that of the DLO/DSO. This view is supported by the approach taken in *Re Ettrick and Lauderdale*, discussed above.[71]

(4) AMENDING THE SPECIFICATIONS

Authorities may wish to amend specifications after bids have been received – for example, because of changed requirements, the development of new technology or suggestions for improvements made by bidders. The existing guidance on white-collar CCT indicates that changes may be made provided all bidders are given the opportunity to revise their bids or to submit a new bid.[72] However, where the change to the nature of the work is "substantial" it is stated that the contract should be readvertised since different providers may be interested in the revised project.[73] A similar freedom to make non-substantial changes exists under the Works and Services Regulations. The concept of a "substantial" change for the purpose of CCT should be interpreted in the same way as under those regulations since the purpose of the requirements – to ensure publicity for specifications which might attract different bidders – is the same in both cases. The same principles should be applied to both blue-collar and white collar CCT.

(5) TIME-LIMITS FOR ANNOUNCING THE AWARD DECISION

In general the winning bidder must be announced no later than 90 days from the date by which bids are required to be submitted.[74] For housing management the period is 120 days.

(6) TIME-LIMITS FOR COMMENCING WORK

For the blue collar CCT services, and for sports and leisure management and housing management, the period between announcing the winning

---

[71] See pp. 733–734.
[72] White Collar Guidance, para. 57.
[73] *Ibid.*
[74] 1993 Competition Regulation, reg. 5(b) as am. by the Local Government (Direct Service Organisations) (Competition) (Amendment) Regulations 1995, S.I. 1995, No. 1336, reg. 7(1) and (2) (deeming a failure to do so to be anti-competitive behaviour).

bidder and commencing the work is required by regulation 3 of the 1993 Competition Regulations to be between 30 and 120 days. This allows sufficient time for preparing the contract, but also ensures that bidders are not discouraged by an unduly long wait. A breach of this principle is deemed by the regulations to be anti-competitive conduct. There is no similar requirement in the regulations for procedures covered by the LGPLA 1980. However, the current statutory guidance in Circular 10/93 suggests that the same time periods should be respected for procedures under that Act, where appropriate.[75] No such rules apply to legal services, construction and property services, financial services, personnel services or information technology services, since such a rigid timetable is not felt to be appropriate in these cases.

(7) DECISION TO ABANDON THE PROCEDURE OR OPEN A NEW PROCEDURE

Under the regulations implementing the European Community directives on procurement an authority may in general abandon an award procedure and retain the work in-house for any reason,[76] even if the in-house bid is much less favourable than the best external bid. However, this is not possible where the CCT rules apply: as explained, it is anti-competitive to award the work in-house where this is not the most advantageous bid.

It is, however, possible that having begun an award procedure the authority no longer wishes to conclude a contract: for example, because the work will cost more than expected, or simply because of a change of heart about the project (although the latter cannot apply where the authority has a statutory responsibility for providing the service as with street cleaning or refuse collection). There is nothing in the CCT rules to limit the authority's discretion to abandon the project altogether.

Another possibility which an authority might wish to consider, for a variety of reasons, is a new tendering exercise. The government guidance on CCT states that an authority must have "sound reasons" for re-tendering where the in-house organisation is a bidder in the second tendering exercise.[77] Certainly it will be anti-competitive behaviour to re-tender a contract simply because the in-house bid was not successful in the first round. Sound reasons to re-tender, however, may be that the original bids exceeded the budget; to allow the work to be repackaged to attract more competition; or because some mistake was made in the first

---

[75] Para. 16. As with other time-limits it is recognised that the same periods may not apply with smaller contracts, that is, those less than one year in duration or less than £100,000 in value; here a shorter time-limit, both maximum and minimum might be appropriate.
[76] See pp. 254–255.
[77] Circular 10/93, para. 39; White Collar Guidance, para. 59.

procedure (for example, a failure to draw up the specifications with sufficient clarity). The existing statutory guidance states that when re-tendering does occur, the in-house bidder should not be given any information which might give it an advantage in re-tendering and should not be told of the contents of the bids submitted by other firms nor any other information which would give it an advantage in the new pro-cedure.[78] The guidance also states that an opportunity to re-tender should be given to those participating in the first round.[79] Such detailed provisions on re-tendering are not included in the government's new draft statutory guidance, which is to replace the existing guidance,[80] but it still seems likely that similar principles will apply.

There is nothing in the CCT rules to prevent an authority from awarding the contract to a provider who has not participated in the tendering procedure at all – provided, of course, that this provider is not the DLO/DSO, which can only be awarded the work after participating in a tendering procedure.

5. QUALIFICATION OF PROVIDERS

(1) THE NEED FOR QUALIFICATION

The term "qualification" is used in this book to refer to the process whereby an authority ensures that firms meet certain minimum require-ments which it has set for participation in a contract. Normally standards are set relating to the firm's financial position and also its technical ability to carry out the contract requirements. Providers have also sometimes been excluded for failing to meet "secondary" requirements – that is, those which do not relate to the ability to deliver the goods or services required but to other matters such as the provision of equal opportunities or their policy towards the environment. However, exclu-sion for secondary reasons is generally prohibited for authorities subject to CCT procedures under section 17 of the Local Government Act 1988, adopted at the same time as the CCT rules.[81]

(2) THE PROCESS OF QUALIFICATION

Authorities will often wish to eliminate unqualified firms before issuing invitations to tender. Under the LGPLA 1980 invitations are in fact

---

[78] *Ibid.*
[79] *Ibid.*
[80] See pp. 708–709.
[81] See pp. 830–845. Exclusion may also be prohibited under the Works or Services Regulations: see Chap. 16.

confined to firms on approved lists[82] and these firms will normally have been vetted before inclusion. However, this may not always be the case. Further, as was explained above, for procedures caught by the Works and Services Regulations it is not permitted to limit invitees to those on approved lists, but it is necessary advertise for potential bidders. For procedures covered by the LGA 1988 the authority must always advertise the contract.[83] In this case the authority may wish to consider the qualifications of providers before selecting providers to bid.

The CCT legislation and guidance neither expressly forbids nor requires assessment of qualifications at this stage. However, as mentioned above, it is arguable that in general an assessment *must* be carried out at this early stage, to ensure that an adequate number of *qualified* bidders emerge to challenge the internal bid: to fail to do so may be considered anti-competitive behaviour if the internal bidder should go on to win the contract. For contracts covered by the Works or Services Regulations those regulations in any case require qualifications to be assessed before invitations are issued in a restricted or negotiated procedure, although verification of factual information from bidders may be left until later time.[84]

The *relative* financial and technical status of firms may also be considered in deciding which firms should be selected to receive invitations to tender; there is nothing in the CCT rules to prevent this (although there are limits to the possibility of considering this under the Works and Services Regulations).[85] The probability of a particular firm's being able to complete the contract might also be considered as a variable alongside the merits of bids, although this is not permitted for contracts covered by the Works and Services Regulations.

(3) APPLICABLE STANDARDS AND MEANS OF PROOF

Under the CCT rules an authority in principle retains its discretion to set its own standards for qualification – for example, acceptable levels of financial turnover, or extent of prior experience – and the means of proof which may be demanded from providers. However, to set unreasonably high standards for qualification for outside bidders or to reject adequate evidence that relevant standards have been met will constitute anti-competitive behaviour.[86] In this respect, the existing

---

[82] See pp. 717–718.
[83] See. p. 720.
[84] See Chap. 7.
[85] See pp. 230–231.
[86] This is indicated by *R. v. Secretary of State for the Environment, ex p. Haringey,* above (concerning anti-competitive behaviour in weighing technical and financial capacity as a variable to be compared with the economic advantage of the bid).

statutory government guidance indicates specifically that it will be anti-competitive to insist on certification to European quality assurance standards (BS 5750 or equivalent)[87]: a judgment "should be made on the ability to perform the work to the specified standards based on all the available evidence.[88] (This contrasts with the position under the Works and Services Regulations which allow authorities to insist upon these quality assurance standards except in limited circumstance.)[89]

6. PERFORMANCE BONDS OR GUARANTEES

Where there is a risk of default by a provider a purchaser may sometimes require a performance bond or guarantee. This will provide security in case of default, which may involve the purchaser in considerable costs – for example, in finding a new provider at short notice or in making good defects. Such bonds or guarantees may be sought in CCT procedures, but subject to provisions on their use laid down in statutory guidance.[90] This was felt to be necessary since such requirements impose costs on providers (which may be passed on to purchasers) and if applied in an unreasonable way may affect the ability or willingness of providers to submit tenders. The current statutory guidance provides, in particular, that bonds or guarantees should not be sought automatically but only where necessary in the particular case,[91] and that the amount should be linked to the expected costs of default, which must be carefully calculated in advance.[92] In the draft guidance recently issued by the Department of the Environment which it is proposed will replace the existing statutory guidance[93] the same principle is stated that the need for bonds or guarantees must be assessed in light of the risks associated with the specific contract.[94] The Department has also issued a consultation paper setting out its proposals for more detailed guidance in the specific area of performance bonds and guarantees.[95]

---

[87] Circular 10/93, paras. 32–34; White Collar Guidance, paras. 51.
[88] Circular 10/93, para. 34; para. 52. No such specific provisions are included, however, in the new draft statutory guidance which it is proposed will replace the current guidance (as to which see pp. 708–709).
[89] See pp. 324–325.
[90] Circular 10/93, paras.28–31; White Collar Guidance, paras. 42–49.
[91] Circular 10/93, para. 28; White Collar Guidance, paras. 42–43.
[92] Circular 10/93, para. 29; White Collar Guidance, paras. 46.
[93] See pp. 708–709.
[94] Department of the Environment, draft *Guidance on the Conduct of Compulsory Competitive Tendering*, para. 34.
[95] Department of the Environment, *Local Government Act 1992: Statutory Guidance on Performance Bonds and Guarantees in CCT* (1994).

7. THE AVAILABILITY OF ASSETS AND SERVICES TO EXTERNAL BIDDERS

(1) OBLIGATION TO MAKE ASSETS AVAILABLE

A DLO/DSO which has previously undertaken work in connection with a defined activity will generally own or lease various premises and items of equipment used to perform the work. Premises may include, for example, vehicle depots and kitchens used for catering. Equipment may range from small items such as brooms and buckets for cleaning through to items which represent considerable capital expenditure – for example, vehicles used for street cleaning, refuse collection or construction. To allow potential bidders to use these assets may increase competition for the work, particularly with premises which may not otherwise be immediately available in the locality, and also with expensive capital equipment.

The central government has long been in favour of allowing external bidders to use local authority assets, but this has been bitterly opposed by many authorities, either for commercial or for other reasons. Thus authorities may wish to choose the time to dipose of the asset (particularly with real property) which is not possible if it is tied up in the contract; or they may wish to deploy the asset for other local authority purposes. To allow a provider to use an asset may also involve difficulties of supervision (for example, to ensure proper maintenance) or may increase the complexity of administering the asset, since decisions on repair or replacement must be made in liaison with the provider. It also makes attribution of defects in contract performance more difficult, since this might be due to defects in the asset. Further, premises used for the defined activity may also be used for other local authority purposes and in this case authorities are often particularly reluctant to allow access. On the other hand, in some cases these concerns have been exaggerated and the reluctance has in reality reflected a desire to avoid assisting external bidders.

Whether to make assets available to external providers has for the last few years been required to be determined in accordance with statutory guidance which indicates that in certain cases failure to allow use of assets is anti-competitive behaviour.[96]

The guidance on blue-collar CCT states that the availability of assets is in principle a matter for authorities, but that to fail to make such assets available may amount to anti-competitive conduct.[97] Specific guidance is

---

[96] Circular 10/93, above, para. 56. In the proposed new statutory guidance on CCT which is to replace the existing guidance use of assets is dealt with much more briefly: see Department of the Environment, draft *Guidance on the Conduct of Compulsory Competitive Tendering*, paras. 40–42.

[97] Circular 10/93, paras. 56–57.

given on, first, depots, and second, vehicles – the two assets which are of most interest to contractors. Here, it is stated that it will normally be regarded as anti-competitive not to make those assets available.[98] This applies even where the authority has alternative uses for the asset or wishes to dispose of it; the possible alternative use must instead be reflected in the charge made, not by withdrawing the asset.[99] It is expressly stated that in cases where a depot is also still used by the authority itself, the government will not regard general "security" or "industrial relations" reasons as grounds for refusing to make it available.[1] Thus, it is effectively indicated that employees of private firms cannot be considered a greater security risk than the authority itself. There is no specific guidance on other assets. However, where non-availability of assets is likely to have a significant effect on competition, an authority would be wise to follow the guidelines for depots and vehicles; it appears that these are dealt with expressly simply because availability is almost always an issue in practice with these particular assets.

For white-collar CCT the guidance simply provides that authorities are to determine themselves which assets need to be made available to provide a good show of competition,[2] and it is likely that an unreasonable decision on this point will be regarded as anti-competitive conduct. The problem of asset use is less likely to arise with white-collar CCT but may do so where authorities include specific requirements on assets in the contract, such as an obligation to use local premises. In this case authorities are normally expected to make their own assets available.[3]

For all CCT it is provided that terms for the use of assets should not be onerous; in particular charges should generally be based on the commercial rental or hire charge.[4] In practice, assets are often made available free of charge, since any charge will generally be added to the bid price in any case. Normally, the in-house organisation is required to include the cost of use of the assets (like its other costs) in its bid price, and to achieve a certain rate of return on the assets used.[5] However, this does not apply where the asset is made available free of charge to the private sector as well as to the DLO/DSO, since the two are then in the same position.[6] However, if a provider does not use the asset this must be taken into account in evaluating bids, as explained earlier – the availability of the asset to the authority is a benefit which will follow

---

[98] Circular 10/93, paras. 58 and 60.
[99] Circular 10/93, paras. 59 and 60.
[1] Circular 10/93, para. 58.
[2] White Collar Guidance, para. 79.
[3] White Collar Guidance, para. 79.
[4] Circular 10/93, para. 62; White Collar Guidance, para. 81. In calculating this, authorities may take account of potentially more valuable uses, to reflect the full opportunity costs of the use by the provider: circular 10/93, para. 65 and White Collar Guidance, para. 83.
[5] Circular 10/93, para. 62; White Collar Guidance, para. 81.
[6] Circular 10/93, para. 63.

from the award of the contract to the external bidder, as compared with an award to the DLO/DSO.[7] The invitation to tender must give the amount of any credit to be given where an asset is offered free but the provider declines its use.[8]

Any terms applicable, and the length of time for which assets will be made available, should be indicated in the invitation to tender.[9]

Many authorities have criticised the rules on use of assets. It is true that to retain assets and make them available is not the usual practice in the private sector. However, special rules may be justified for local authorities since the market for many of the CCT services is small or non-existent and special measures are warranted to ensure the availability of competition. Further, even in the private sector the market may sometimes lead to assets being made available to firms providing contractual services. The existing guidance has taken the view that to determine when asset use is appropriate in light of these considerations cannot be left entirely to local authority discretion, since this may be abused to favour the internal bidder.

It can be noted that no detailed guidance on making assets available is included in the new draft statutory guidance with which the government is proposing to replace the existing guidance.[10]

(2) REQUIREMENTS TO USE LOCAL AUTHORITY ASSETS

Clearly in general firms must be free to make the arrangements which they consider to be the most efficient, either through use of their own existing assets, or otherwise. Circular 10/93 also provides that it is generally anti-competitive conduct to require a contractor to make use of local authority assets.[11] To similar effect the guidance on white-collar CCT provides that a provider should only be required to use assets where this is "essential" for efficient and effective delivery of the service.[12] Although not expressly stated, the same principles will apply under the new draft guidance which is to replace the existing, by virtue of the general emphasis on "output" specifications.[13]

---

[7] See pp. 730–731.

[8] Circular 10/93, paras. 63–64; White Collar Guidance, para. 83.

[9] Circular 10/93, para. 59 (in relation to depot facilities).

[10] As to which see pp. 708–709. The draft guidance (para. 40) merely requires relevant assets to be made available when contractual conditions are included on use of local premises or other assets.

[11] Circular 10/93, para. 61. The legislation also provides expressly for providers to provide their own ingredients for catering, should they wish, since the provision of ingredients is specifically stated to be subject to competition: see pp. 671–672.

[12] White Collar Guidance, para. 80. It is specifically stated that requirement for firms to use the authority's own information technology systems is not generally permitted.

[13] On this see pp. 708–709; and see also paras. 40–41 of the draft guidance which assume that conditions relating to asset use may be imposed only when justified by reference to operational requirements.

8. THE OBLIGATION TO AVOID ANTI-COMPETITIVE CONDUCT

It has already been noted that in making a decision to award a contract to the in-house team there is a general obligation to avoid conduct which has the effect of, or is intended or likely to have the effect of, "restricting, distorting or preventing competition"[14] – generally referred to as "anti-competitive" conduct. Section 9 of the Local Government Act 1992 confers upon the Secretary of State a wide power to make regulations defining what conduct is, or is not, anti-competitive. Section 9(3) lists – without prejudice to the generality of the provision – matters falling within the scope of this very wide power, which includes, for example, the prescription of matters which may *not* be taken into account by authorities and also prescription of the extent to which certain matters *should* be taken into account. It is also specifically provided in section 9(3)(e)–(f) that the Secretary of State may confer upon himself a power to issue *guidance* on how anti-competitive behaviour is to be avoided and that he may provide that such guidance must be taken into account in deciding whether anti-competitive behaviour has occurred. This has been done through regulation 15 of the Competition Regulations, which now allows the Secretary of State to issue guidance in this area which is required to be taken into account in law. In other words, the Secretary of State now has a power to prescribe what conduct is anti-competitive behaviour not merely through formal legislation but also through merely informal instructions issued to authorities without the necessity for any procedural formalities or parliamentary scrutiny.

Pursuant to these provisions the definition of anti-competitive behaviour in CCT proceedings has already been filled out both by formal regulations and informal guidance. Of particular significance, as already noted, are the 1993 Competition Regulations[15] and the guidance contained in Circular 10/93 on blue-collar CCT and guidance issued in December 1994 to deal with white-collar CCT,[16] as well as special guidance on the application of the TUPE Regulations.[17] Most of these specific provisions have already been discussed in the analysis of the tendering procedures above. They include requirements to package contracts in such a way as to ensure that competition is available[18]; a prohibition on giving information to the internal bidder which is not available to outside providers[19]; and a prohibition on considering costs of

---

[14] LGA 1988, s.7(7) (for procedures covered by the LGA); LGPLA 1980, s.9(4)(aaaa) (for procedures covered by the LGPLA).
[15] Above, note 67.
[16] Above, pp. 707–708.
[17] See pp. 636–648.
[18] See pp. 710–711.
[19] See pp. 719 and 723.

contracting out (such as supervision costs) other than those provided for in the Competition Regulations.[20] (As noted above, however, this present detailed guidance is shortly to be replaced with more general "principle-based" statutory guidance.)[21]

The general prohibition on anti-competitive conduct may, however, cover a variety of conduct which has not been the subject of any specific regulations or guidance. This must be born in mind at all stages of the tendering procedure.

The prohibition applies only to conduct which occurs in taking a decision *that the authority itself should carry out the work*. This limitation reflects the general purpose of the CCT rules which is to provide for a comparison of the merits of in-house and external service provision, rather than to regulate the way in which a choice is made between potential external service providers. This suggests that no legal action is possible once an award has been made to a bidder other than the DLO/DSO. However, the question may be raised as to whether a judicial review action can be brought *before* the award decision is made in order to prevent the continuation of a procedure which has been affected by anti-competitive conduct. At this point it is, of course, not known whether the alleged behaviour will lead to an award to the DLO/DSO. It would, however, be very inconvenient to all parties involved in the procedure if a challenger was forced to wait for the procedure to be completed before initiating proceedings, and it is submitted that an action should be permitted prior to the award.

Another issue is whether a provider may complain of conduct relating to that provider's treatment as compared with another external bidder, which does not in any way advantage the DLO/DSO. An example might be where an authority permits bidder X to revise its tender but does not give the same opportunity either to bidder Y *or* to the in-house team. This clearly distorts competition in general, but it does not distort competition between the in-house and the external bidders. In light of the purpose of the CCT rules, as outlined above, it is arguable that the reference to distortion, etc., of competition under the anti-competitive conduct provisions refers only to an effect on the in-house/external competition which favours the internal bidder, and does not cover any conduct which affects only the competition between external bidders *inter se*.

A final question is whether an action may be brought by persons within the DLO/DSO[22] itself where it feels that it has been discriminated against compared with outside bidders. (This is likely only if no award has been made, since if an award has been made and it is made to the DLO/DSO that body is unlikely to complain over its treatment). Since

---

[20] See pp. 724–728.
[21] See pp. 708–709.
[22] The DLO/DSO itself cannot sue as it is not a legal entity separate from the awarding authority.

anti-competitive conduct covers only conduct which tends to favour the internal bidder as against external providers, it appears that there can in fact be no question of anti-competitive conduct in such a case. Whatever the position on this point, however, it appears that persons from the in-house unit do not have standing to bring an action to enforce the rules on anti-competitive behaviour,[23] since the rules are not intended to benefit such persons.

Issues of either a factual or legal nature concerning the designation of particular conduct by an authority as anti-competitive behaviour may fall to be determined either by a court, or by the Secretary of State in exercising his enforcement powers in relation to CCT. The scope of the Secretary of State's discretion in determining what constitutes anti-competitive behaviour, in relation both to factual and legal issues, and the extent to which this discretion is reviewable by the courts in judicial review proceedings, is considered in Chapter 18.[24]

9. SEPARATION OF "CLIENT" AND "PROVIDER" FUNCTIONS

It was observed earlier that the degree to which individuals involved in carrying out a defined activity are responsible also for policy making and policy implementation for that activity, may vary between different authorities. Since CCT came into effect, however, it has become clear that for a single individual to be involved in both aspects of service provision may lead to unacceptable conflicts of interest. In practice, the effect of the introduction of CCT has been for authorities to separate these functions, so that the DLO/DSO has increasingly become a separate and independent unit.[25] The function of carrying out the work is now generally referred to as the "contractor" function, and that of defining, awarding and monitoring it the "client" function. In some cases this separation has been achieved by setting up completely separate council committees for each of the two functions, with a separate chairperson; in others it is less marked, with both sides answerable to the same chairperson (or even to the same person further down the line). The Audit Commission has provided guidance on this question, in which it has made it clear that it considers the "ideal" situation to be complete separation of functions through different committees.[26]

---

[23] *Kershaw v City of Glasgow D.C.* (1992) *Scots Law Times* 71, concerning title to sue for an interdict. The same principle would probably be applied in England and Wales. The position of the DLO/DSO was also raised in *R. v. Walsall M.B.C., ex p. Yapp* [1994] 1 I.C.R. 528 but not considered by the court.

[24] See pp. 750–751.

[25] For more detailed discussion of these issues see Sparke, *The Compulsory Competitive Tendering Guide* (1993), Chap. 7; Cirell and Bennett, *Compulsory Competitive Tendering: Law and Practice*, section B Chap. 5.

[26] Audit Commission, Occasional Paper No. 7, *Preparing for Compulsory Competition* (1989).

The most serious possibility of a conflict of interest is now dealt with expressly in the 1993 Competition Regulations. In the same way as a conflict of interest may arise where a local government official has an interest in a private company bidding on a contract, officials involved in both the work of a DLO/DSO and the evaluation of bids may be, or may appear to be, biased in favour of the internal bidder. To avoid this Competition Regulation 4 provides that it shall normally be considered anti-competitive for individuals both to undertake responsibility for, or do work on, certain matters relating to the contract award procedures[27] and to undertake also any work or responsibility relating to either the DSO generally or the preparation of the particular bid.

Exceptions are made for:

(i) the head of paid service[28] (or, in his absence, his authorised deputy)[29]

(ii) the chief officer who is directly accountable for the procedure (or, in his absence, the deputy chief officer directly accountable to him)[30]; and

(iii) persons employed by the authority to provide legal, financial or other professional advice relating to the authority's business.[31] This exception was included to allow those responsible for providing such advice to the authority to give advice both to the DLO/DSO and the "client" (purchaser) side of the authority. It does not apply, on the other hand, where the provision of legal, financial or other advice is itself the subject of the contract (for example, under CCT for the defined activity of legal services). Thus it is specifically stated that the exemption does not apply where the advice provided is "advice within the description of the work for which tenders are invited".[32]

(iv) In the case of a police authority, an officer of the rank or status of assistant chief constable (or assistant commissioner) or above.[33]

The rules do not cover elected Council members.[34] However, the statutory guidance indicates that elected members should, in relation to their "interests" in or responsibility for the DSO, follow the principles in the National Code of Local Government Conduct which governs con-

---

[27] That is, selecting the publication for advertising the work under the 1988 Act; selecting the persons to be invited to tender, sending the tender documents to invitees; calculating or estimating prospective costs; receiving, opening or evaluating bids; and choosing between internal and external bids (reg. 4(1)).

[28] Defined in 1993 Competition Regulations 4(1) as the officer designated in accordance with s.4(1) of the Local Government and Housing Act 1989 or, where no such officer has been designated, the chief executive or other officer responsible for general management.

[29] 1993 Competition Regulations, reg. 4(3)(a)(i).

[30] 1993 Competition Regulations, reg. 4(3)(a)(ii).

[31] 1993 Competition Regulations, reg. 4(3)(a)(iii), as am. by the Local Government (Direct Services Organisations) (Competition) (Amendment) Regulations 1995, S.I. 1995 No. 1336, reg. 6(1)(a).

[32] Local Government (Direct Service Organisations) (Competition) (Amendment) Regulations 1995, S.I. 1995 No. 1336, reg. 6(1)(b).

[33] Local Government (Direct Service Organisations) (Competition) (Amendment) Regulations 1995, S.I. 1995 No. 1336, reg. 6(1)(a).

[34] Ibid, reg. 4(3)(a)(iv).

flicts where members have interests in outside organisations, even though the Code itself does not apply to agreements with a DSO.[35]

10. EXTERNALISATION AND THE CCT RULES[36]

An authority may, for a variety of reasons, take a decision to sell off its DLO or DSO. This may be because it wishes to concentrate on its "core" function of enabling service provision; because it feels the unit would be more competitive in the private sector, and thus offer the authority better value for money; or simply to raise revenue. The advent of CCT, requiring in-house units to compete with the private sector, has contributed to an increase in sales of in-house units by threatening the viability of some units. This may arise either because the unit is relatively inefficient in public hands or because, although efficiently run, its competitiveness is hampered by the strictures of the law applying to public sector service providers, under both CCT and other rules, such as the legal requirement to meet stringent financial objectives, or the fact that it is largely forbidden from competing for outside work and thus cannot take advantages of economies of scale, etc. In these circumstances the authority may wish to sell the unit rather than disband it, either for revenue reasons, to preserve an additional competitor in the market, to preserve the jobs and conditions of its workers, or to enable it to continue to deal with known staff (albeit as part of a private entity, rather than within the authority). It may seek to bolster these objectives by placing its work directly with the buyer of the in-house organisation. This is not generally precluded by the CCT procedures, which apply only where an authority seeks to place work in-house; thus a sale may appear to offer a way to preserve the authority's relationship with its workforce and the position of that workforce despite the CCT rules.

Often the in-house unit is sold to the unit's senior management team or, more rarely, to the employees generally, with or without some participation from existing private sector organisations. In this case a separate company is usually set up to make the purchase. Alternatively, the in-house organisation may simply be sold to an existing private buyer.[37] Usually the agreement involves a transfer of assets, and also an agreement that some or all of the existing employees will be retained.

In addition, the agreement also usually provides for the authority to place work with the privatised unit for a certain period. This is generally

---

[35] Circular 10/93, para. 13; White Collar Guidance, para. 19.
[36] See further Cirell and Bennett, *Compulsory Competitive Tendering: Law and Practice*, section B, Chap. 6A; Sparke, Chap. 8; Audit Commission, Management Paper No. 6, *Management Buy-Outs: Public Interest or Private Gain?* (1990).
[37] On the different types of sale see further Cirell and Bennett, and Sparke, above.

necessary to make the purchase attractive and so facilitate the deal. Where one of the motives for the sell-off is to preserve the position of the in-house workforce or to allow the authority to continue its own dealings with a known workforce the authority may seek to provide work for the unit for longer than is strictly necessary to achieve the sale.

There may, however, be legal difficulties over providing a guarantee of work to the buyer in the sale transaction, or of subsequently placing work with the buyer without subjecting it to competition, even though the CCT regime itself may not apply because the work is not being placed in-house.

First, work covered by the Works Regulations or Part A of the Services Regulations may be required to be subject to tender under the procedures in those regulations, even if placement of the work forms part of a larger transaction. This issue was discussed in Chapter 5 on the scope of the regulations.[38] It was suggested there that at present such work would probably be required to be put out to tender, although this is not certain, unless it can be shown to be strictly necessary, to place the work without competitive tendering, to facilitate the transaction. However, tenders are not required in the case of services contracts falling within Part B of the Services Regulations.

Secondly, the authority may be in breach of other rules on tendering such as those in its standing orders, or may breach its general fiduciary duty to the ratepayers, if it is clearly not seeking value for money. The Audit Commission, in a paper issued to local authorities on the subject of management buy-outs, recognises that some guarantee of work may be necessary to secure the buy-out deal, which itself may be in the authority's interest, but emphasises that work should only be placed without competition to the extent required for such legitimate purposes.[39] It is indicated that contracts should normally only be placed for one or two years, unless special justification can be shown for a longer period.[40] Even then, it is suggested that it will be very difficult to justify any contract which is for a longer period than provided for that type of contract under the CCT legislation.[41]

Finally, it should be noted that the CCT rules may be relevant if the decision to privatise is taken following a specific award procedure in which the DLO/DSO has participated but has not submitted the best bid. In this case, if it were decided not to go ahead with the award in order that the DLO/DSO could be privatised, and was then awarded the contract to the privatised entity without recourse to CCT procedures, the decision not to award the contract to the best bidder in the CCT procedure could be regarded as anti-competitive behaviour.

---

[38] See pp. 148–150.
[39] Audit Commission Management Paper No. 6, Management Buy-Outs: Public Interest or Private Gain (1990), paras. 47–48.
[40] Audit Commission, above, note 39, para. 48.
[41] Audit Commission, above, note 39, para. 49.

11. FINANCIAL OBJECTIVES AND ACCOUNTS

(1) OVERVIEW

As explained, the market testing process under CCT requires the in-house organisation to bid against the private sector for work with the objective of determining whether the in-house team or an external provider offers the most efficient method of service provision. For a fair comparison to be made it is considered necessary to ensure that the amount of the in-house bid reflects the proper costs of in-house provision. This is achieved by requiring the DLO/DSO to meet certain financial objectives in each area of CCT activity. These objectives are intended to mirror the targets which a private concern would expect to meet in order to stay in business. In general the financial objective is to achieve a six per cent rate of return on capital used or, where no capital is used, to break even. In other words, the "prices" submitted by the DLO/DSO must be sufficient to cover the costs incurred in performing the work and also, in relevant cases, to cover the required rate of return. To ensure that compliance with these requirements can be monitored, there are requirements to prepare clear accounts relating to each CCT activity and to prepare various reports and statements on financial performance for the benefit of the Secretary of State, the authority's auditors, and also members of the public.

For the purpose of these obligations concerning financial objectives each "defined activity" under the LGA 1988 is treated separately. Thus a separate account must be prepared for each activity, and the financial objectives must be achieved for each one. There is no distinction made between functional work (work done for the authority itself) and work done by the DSO for other authorities[42]: thus a single account is prepared for both, and work of both kinds is taken into consideration in deciding if financial objectives are met. For the LGPLA 1980, construction and maintenance work is divided into four different categories, each of which is again treated as separate activity for the purposes of preparation of accounts and achievement of financial objectives. Again, no distinction is made between functional work and work done under works contracts for others.

These obligations on accounts and financial objectives are explained in further detail below, whilst the reporting requirements are outlined in section 12.

---

[42] On this distinction between functional work and works contracts see further pp. 662–664 and 700–701.

(2) ACCOUNTS

(a) PROVISIONS UNDER THE LGPLA 1980

(i) NATURE AND SCOPE OF THE ACCOUNTS

Section 10 of the LGPLA 1980 requires an authority to keep accounts – referred to as "DLO Revenue Accounts"[43] – for all work covered by the Act. These accounts must cover all work which is construction and maintenance work under the Act.

Such work is for the purpose of these accounts provisions divided into four categories,[44] and section 10 requires a separate account to be kept for each of the categories. These categories are:[45]

(a) General highway works and work in connection with the construction or maintenance of a sewer. "General highway works" means construction and maintenance work for the purpose of laying out, construction, improvement, maintenance or repair of highways (other than construction work which is connected with new construction – which falls under (b) or (c) below); the gritting and clearing of snow from highways; and the maintenance of street lighting.[46]

(b) Works of new construction, other than general highway work or works in connection with the construction of a sewer, of which the estimated cost does not exceed £50,000. Works of new construction are defined to mean building or civil engineering works of any description which are not works of maintenance under section 1(4) of the Local Authorities (Good and Services) Act 1970.[47] The 1970 Act does not give an exhaustive definition of works of maintenance but merely states that they shall "include minor renewals, minor improvement and minor extensions". In *R. v. Hackney, ex p. Secretary of State for the Environment*[48] Schiemann J. held that maintenance could include replacements of roofs, windows and doors, where this was done for reasons of maintenance rather than for aesthetic reasons (for example, because the owners wished to change the style of the windows), even if the work is not of a "minor" nature. On the other hand, the judge noted that the

---

[43] In respect of functional work the Secretary of State may also direct authorities to keep other accounts: LGPLA 1980, s.10(1)(b)(ii).

[44] Laid down in LGPLA 1980, s.10(2).

[45] The Secretary of State has a power (exercisable by statutory instrument) to amend these categories or to introduce new ones: LGPLA 1980, s.10(4). All work by a covered authority must be included, even where carried out by separate units of the authority: *ILEA v. Department of the Environment* (1985) 83 L.G.R. 235.

[46] LGPLA 1980, s.10(3), as substituted in part by the Local Government (Direct Labour Organisations) (Accounts) Regulations 1981 (S.I. 1981 No. 339).

[47] This definition is included in the 1970 Act for the purpose of defining the scope of the power of authorities to carry out work for other authorities pursuant to s.1(1) of the 1970 Act; this power, covers, *inter alia*, "works of maintenance".

[48] (1989) 88 LGR 96.

mere fact that work solves a maintenance problem does not entail that it is maintenance: for example, he suggested that to add an extra storey to a house could not be considered maintenance even if adding that storey solved the problem of a leaking roof. It would appear that the test could be either whether maintenance is the primary objective, or alternatively, whether maintenance should be regarded as the most significant result of the work in objective terms. On the facts of the case the judge held that the replacement of a roof with a pitched roof – a different type from that in place before – could be maintenance. Where work is minor it appears that it can be considered a work of maintenance even if the main motive or result is not maintenance as such, but an "improvement": this is indicated by the express reference to "minor improvements" contained in section 1(4) itself.

(c) Works within the description in (b), of which the estimated cost exceeds £50,000.

(d) Works of maintenance other than those in connection with highways or the maintenance of a sewer. Maintenance here is as defined under section 1(4) of the Local Authorities (Goods and Services) Act 1970.[49]

Section 11(1) of the LGPLA 1980 exempts the authority from the obligation to keep a separate account for a particular category where the authority did not at any time in the previous financial year employ more than 15 persons who were engaged in carrying out work in the category in question.[50] This figure of 15 is to be calculated excluding persons engaged wholly or mainly in the design, development or control of construction or maintenance work.[51] It has already been noted in Chapter 13 that where the total number of persons employed does not exceed 15 in all categories of construction and maintenance work taken together, the authority is not required to prepare accounts at all.

As noted above, a single revenue account may at present cover both functional work and work carried out for others under "works contracts".[52] However, the Secretary of State may now specify the form of the account should he choose to do so,[53] which could require a distinction to be made.

---

[49] On this definition see further *Hackney*, above.

[50] The original number of persons specified was thirty; the new figure of 15 was inserted by the Local Government (Direct Labour Organisations) (Specified Number of Persons Employed) Order 1989 (S.I.1989 No. 1589), made pursuant to a power in LGPLA 1980 allowing the Secretary of State to specify by order a number less than 30.

[51] LGPLA 1980, s.7(2).

[52] LGPLA 1980, s.10(1) specifies that account must be kept for both types of work, and the Act does not anywhere require separate accounts for the two types. For work done for other authorities pursuant to powers in s.1 of the Local Authorities (Goods and Services) Act 1970 there are general requirements in s.2(2) of that Act for keeping specific accounts of work done under its provisions, which previously included maintenance work, but LGPLA, s.14(2) provides that such separate accounts need not be kept for such maintenance work, now it is covered by CCT accounts, thus avoiding any requirement for separate accounts.

[53] LGPLA 1980, s.13(5)A, inserted by LGA 1988, ss.32, 41 and Sched. 6 paras. 1 and 5 and Sched. 7, Part III.

Accounts need not be kept in respect of work relating to parks, playing fields, allotments, etc., or to dock or harbour undertakings, nor to routine maintenance work done by caretakers or work done under certain assisted training schemes, since as explained in Chapter 13 this work is excluded from the Act's definition of "construction and maintenance work".[54] As just noted, the obligation to keep accounts also does not apply where in the previous year there were fewer than 15 persons employed by the authority in construction and maintenance work; in this case, as explained, none of the CCT provisions of the LGPLA apply.[55] However, the accounts must cover work classified as "emergency work" for the purpose of exemption from the Act's tendering procedures under section 7(1)[56]: although an exemption from section 7(1) is given for such work, no exemption is provided from the other CCT provisions of the LGPLA, relating to accounts, financial objectives and reporting.

(ii) INFORMATION IN THE ACCOUNTS

For each financial year the authority must produce a revenue account for each of the above four activities (or, where permitted as outlined above, a combination of these activities), which must provide a "true and fair view" of the financial result for each year with respect to the activity or activities in question.[57] The account is designed to compare the costs incurred by the DLO in carrying out the work with the amount which it has "earned" by carrying out that work: it is stated in section 13(6) that the account must give the information necessary to show that the DLO has complied with its financial obligations under section 16(1) of the Act.

As regards the credit side – the amount "earned" by the DLO from its own authority for performing work of the type in question – it is expressly provided in relation to functional work that the amount which the authority may credit is the amount of its written "bids" for the work as prepared under the CCT rules.[58] No other amount may be included.[59] As regards the costs incurred by DLOs, the Secretary of State has a power to give directions on which matters shall be included; how such amounts shall be calculated; the method to be used to determine the cost of construction and maintenance work; and the extent to which the costs of support services (professional, technical and administrative) shall be counted as part of the costs of the construction and maintenance work.[60] In the Local Government Planning and Land Act 1980 Financial Objectives Specifications 1994, which were issued attached to an explan-

---

[54] See pp. 652–654.
[55] See pp. 655–656.
[56] See pp. 656–657.
[57] LGPLA 1980, s.13(1).
[58] See LGPLA, s.12(1)–(4). On this contents of this "bid" (that is, the written statement prepared under s.9(4) of the Act) see p. 790.
[59] LGPLA 1980, s.12(1).
[60] LGPLA 1980, s.12(5).

atory Joint Circular DoE 12/94 and Welsh Office 39/94 (hereafter Circular 12/94) it is directed that the account must be charged with expenditure in accordance with the Code of Practice on Local Authority Accounting in Great Britian, issued by the Chartered Institute of Public Finance and Accounting.[61]

(b) PROVISIONS UNDER THE LGA 1988

(i) NATURE AND SCOPE OF THE ACCOUNTS

Accounts must also be kept under the LGA 1988, under section 9 of that Act, for all functional work caught by the Act.[62] Accounts are to cover a single financial year, and separate accounts must generally be kept for each defined activity in respect of which the authority has carried out work in that year.[63] As mentioned above, accounts may cover both functional work and works contracts: there is no requirement for separate accounts to be kept for the different types of work.[64]

The accounts need not include details of work covered by the "incidental work exemption" from the Act, the "tied housing exemption" or the "training exemption".[65] It also appears that work exempted from the CCT tendering procedures because of an emergency situation need not be included, a position contrasting with that applying under the LGPLA where such work must be included in the accounts.[66]

(ii) INFORMATION IN THE ACCOUNTS

With all functional work, the authority must credit the account with the amount representing the value of the "written bid" submitted by the authority in the tendering procedure.[67] No other items may be credited to the account.[68] As under the LGPLA 1980, the Secretary of State has powers to specify further items to be entered into the accounts and the method of determining the value of items entered.[69] In the Local

---

[61] Local Government Act 1988 Financial Objectives Specifications 1994, para. 2.

[62] LGA 1988, s.9(1)(a) (works contracts) and 9(1)(b) (functional work).

[63] LGA 1988, s.9(2).

[64] For work done for other authorities pursuant to powers in s.1 of the Local Authorities (Goods and Services) Act 1970 there are general requirements in s.2(2) of that Act for keeping specific accounts of work done under its provisions, but LGA 1988, s.9(7) provides that such separate accounts need not be kept for work for which accounts must be kept under the LGA 1988. There is no general provision for the Secretary of State to specify the content of accounts as there is under the LGPLA 1980, but only a provision (in LGA 1988, s.9(5)) allowing him to specify the time to be included and the method of calculation, which does not seem to allow him to specify for a division into functional work and work done under works contracts.

[65] See p. 699.

[66] On this exclusion, which appears anomalous, see pp. 698–699.

[67] LGA 1988, s.9(4).

[68] LGA 1988, s.9(6). There is an exception for items specifically authorised by the Secretary of State pursuant to the power discussed in the text immediately below.

[69] LGA 1988, s.9(5).

Government Act 1988 Financial Objectives Specifications 1994, which were issued attached to an explanatory Joint Circular DoE 12/94 and Welsh Office 39/94 (hereafter Circular 12/94) it is directed that the account must be charged with expenditure in accordance with the Code of Practice on Local Authority Accounting in Great Britain, issued by the Chartered Institute of Public Finance and Accounting.[70-71]

(3) FINANCIAL OBJECTIVES

For work done under the LGPLA 1980 the financial objectives are established in accordance with section 16 of the Act. Previously this required that for each of the four categories of work for which separate accounts must be kept, the authority must make a positive rate of return on capital, with the exact rate to be specified by the Secretary of State.[72] However, the Local Government Act 1992 has now replaced this with a more flexible provision which requires the authority to meet such financial objectives as shall be specified by the Secretary of State, which he may define by reference to "such factors as he thinks fit".[73] Currently financial objectives are dealt with in the Local Government Planning and Land Act 1980 Financial Objectives Specifications 1994, which were issued attached to an explanatory Joint Circular DoE 12/94 and Welsh Office 39/94 (hereafter Circular 12/94). For each of the categories of construction and maintenance work for which accounts are required, these require that revenue properly recorded in the revenue account shall not be less than total expenditure properly recorded in that account[74] – in other words, the DLO must break even for each activity. The need for a positive rate of return specified in the Act is ensured through the fact that the accounts must include provision for a capital financing charge of six per cent per annum,[75] for any capital employed. There is no provision for separate treatment of functional work and work done for others under works contracts. Thus the financial objectives must simply be met for each of the different accounts. The authority must for each financial year produce a statement showing whether it has met its financial objectives.[76]

In relation to work under the LGA 1988, section 10 of the Act requires that, for each defined activity, the authority shall meet the

---

[70-71] Local Government Act 1988 Financial Objectives Specifications 1994, para. 2.
[72] LGPLA 1980, s.16(1). This must always be calculated on a current cost accounting basis: LGPLA 1980, s.16(3).
[73] LGPLA 1980, s.16(1), as am. by LGA 1992 s.11 and Sched. 1, para. 4(1), and s.16(1)(A) as inserted by LGA 1992, s.11 and Sched. 1, para. 4(2) (also repealing LGPLA 1980, ss.16(2) and (3)).
[74] Local Government Planning and Land Act 1980 Financial Objectives Specifications 1994, (hereafter "LGPLA Financial Objectives"), para. 4.
[75] LGPLA Financial Objectives, above, para. 4.
[76] LGPLA 1980, s.13(2)(c) and 3(6). LGA 1992, s.11, and Sched. 1 para. 3, amending s.13(2)(c), and s.29 and Sched. 4, deleting s.13(6).

financial objectives specified by the Secretary of State. The financial objectives for work under this Act are presently the same as for construction and maintenance and are stated in the Local Government Act 1988 Financial Objectives Specifications 1994, which like the 1980 Act Specifications are annexed to Circular 12/94. For the LGA 1988, as with the LGPLA 1980, there is a general obligation to break even and also a provision for six per cent rate of return on capital where capital is used, by virtue of a requirement for including a capital financing charge as an element of costs.[77] As with work under the LGPLA 1980 there is no provision for separate treatment of functional work and work done for others under works contracts. Thus the financial objectives must be met simply for each of defined activity.

The financial objectives set for DLOs and DSOs have been criticised as unduly harsh, on the basis that the many private firms bidding for the contracts do not anticipate such a rate of return. It can also be suggested that the rate of return approach is not particularly useful for many of the activities covered by CCT, since the use of capital is low (a criticism which might perhaps suggest the need for a more stringent approach towards the in-house unit). Further, it has been pointed out that this approach which emphasises the rate of return on capital is open to manipulation in that authorities may seek to reduce the obligations placed on them by using as small an amount of capital as possible in carrying out particular activities.[78]

12. INFORMATION AND REPORTING OBLIGATIONS

(1) OBLIGATION TO PROVIDE WRITTEN STATEMENTS ON REQUEST

Under both the LGPLA 1980 and LGA 1988, authorities must provide any person requesting it with a written statement concerning work awarded under CCT procedures.

Under the LGPLA the obligation is contained in section 9(8) of the Act. It requires statements to be provided on request in relation to any functional work covered by CCT,[79] and not just work awarded to the

---

[77] Local Government Act 1988 Financial Objectives Specifications 1994, para. 2.
[78] See Audit Commission, *Preparing for Compulsory Competition* (Occasional Paper No. 7, 1989). At one time the only requirement for some activities was a rate of return on capital used and there was no requirement of any sort where no capital was employed; thus some authorities were able to continue to make a loss by avoiding use of capital. As indicated in the text, however, this loophole has now been closed since authorities must break even and this applies where no capital is employed, although here the obligation is less onerous than that expected of private firms in a normal economic climate.
[79] This obligation does not apply in connection with emergency work which is required to be included within the accounts and subject to financial objectives but to which the award procedures under the Act do not apply.

authority itself. The statement must show who was awarded the work and the price of each offer. It must also state the estimated cost of the work which means, where the DLO won the work, the amount to be credited to the DLO[80] (effectively the DLO's bid price) or, where an external bidder won the work, the contract price.[81]

For procedures covered by the LGA 1988 the obligation is contained in section 12(1). This obligation, like that under the LGPLA, applies to all functional work covered by the Act.[82] However, in this case it applies only to work which the authority has decided to carry out itself. The statement under this Act must show[83]: the authority's decision to carry out the work; the amount of each offer made in response to the invitation to tender; and the financial provisions of the authority's own written bid. It is not clear how this last item is to be interpreted; a wide interpretation could require details of all the elements of the authority's tender.

The provision is most likely to be used by those participating in the procedure. However, the right to demand a written statement applies to anyone, and could be invoked by firms seeking information on CCT contracts in which they might wish to participate in future.

(2) ANNUAL REPORTS

Under both the LGPLA 1980 and the LGA 1988 authorities must prepare annual reports relating to work covered by CCT. The purpose of these reports is to provide readily available information for the Secretary of State and the authority's auditors, so they may monitor compliance with the legislation, and also to members of the public.

Annual reports for work covered by the LGPLA are dealt with in section 18 of that Act. This requires authorities to prepare annual reports, for each financial year, for each of the four categories of activity for which separate accounts must be prepared (that is, general highway and sewer works; works of new construction below £50,000; works of new construction above £50,000; and other maintenance works), covering both functional works and works contracts.[84] This applies only where the authority itself has carried out some work in the relevant category during the financial year.

The report must include the revenue account for the relevant activity and the statement of compliance with financial objectives, documents which are required to be prepared under section 13 of the Act.[85] The

---

[80] Under the statement of credit made under section 9(2): see p. 719.
[81] LGPLA 1980, s.9(9).
[82] The obligation applies also to work done for others under works contracts. In this the position is different from the LGPLA where no similar obligation exists for work under works contracts.
[83] LGA 1988, s.12(2).
[84] LGPLA 1980, s.18(1).
[85] LGPLA 1980, s.18(1A)(b), inserted by LGA 1988, s.32, and Sched. 6, paras. 1 and 8.

report must also identify any work which has been counted as construction and maintenance work for the purpose of the Act by virtue of section 20(5) LGPLA (that is, work which the authority has decided cannot be carried out efficiently separately from construction and maintenance).[86] The Secretary of State is also given a power to direct that other information shall also be included in the report for any of the four categories of activity.[87] None have yet been specified, but in October 1992 the Secretary wrote to local authorities requesting that a variety of other information about CCT should be included in the reports on a voluntary basis – for example, the number of occasions on which the lowest bid was rejected.

Under the LGA 1988 the annual report is dealt with in section 11.[88] The authority is required to prepare a report for each financial year, relating to each of the defined activities, where the authority has itself carried out work relating to that activity.[89] (As with the LGPLA, reports are not necessary where all the work has been contracted out.) This applies to all functional work covered by the rules on award procedures in section 6.[90] The report must contain[91] a summary of the account kept for that activity under section 9[92]; this summary must "fairly" reflect the financial result of the work in the year concerned, and must be in the form specified by the Secretary of State.[93] The report must also include a statement showing whether the financial objectives under section 10 have been met for the defined activity.[94] It must also identify any work which is within the activity by virtue of section 2(5) or 2(7) of the LGA 1988.[95] The Secretary of State may specify further matters to be included and also the form of the report.[96] He may also require the inclusion of information, in a specified form, which relates to work carried out in a previous financial year.[97] The authority itself has a discretion to include any further information it thinks fit.[98] At the present time no further information has been required, but as explained in relation to the LGPLA 1980 the Secretary of State has requested authorities to provide certain additional information on a voluntary basis.

Under both the LGPLA and LGA the report must be prepared by September 30 of the year following the financial year to which the report

---

[86] LGPLA 1980, s.18(1A)(a), inserted by LGA 1988, s.32, and Sched. 6, paras. 1 and 8.
[87] LGPLA 1980, s.18(2). In contrast with the LGA 1988 there is no express power to give directions regarding the form of the report.
[88] LGA 1988, s.11(1).
[89] LGA 1988, s.11(1) and (2).
[90] It also applies to work done pursuant to works contracts.
[91] LGA 1988, s.11(2).
[92] See pp. 755–756.
[93] LGA 1988, s.11(3).
[94] LGA 1988, s.11(2).
[95] On these provisions see pp. 667–668.
[96] LGA 1988, s.11(4).
[97] LGA 1988, s.11(5).
[98] LGA 1988, s.11(6).

relates.[99] In both cases it must be sent, first of all, to the Secretary of State, which must be done by October 31 of the year following the financial year to which the report relates.[1] The information in the report will enable the Secretary of State to establish whether the financial objectives set by the Act have been met. The power to demand the inclusion of additional information means that the reports might also be used in making judgments about the existence of anti-competitive behaviour.

The report must also be sent by the same date to the authority's own auditors.[2] The auditor must consider the authority's statement showing whether the financial objectives have been met and send a written statement on this matter both to the Secretary of State and to the authority.[3]

Any person is permitted to inspect the report, and to obtain a copy on payment of a reasonable fee set by the authority.[4] The authority must publicise in at least one newspaper circulating in the area the place and time where the report may be inspected, as well as the fact that the report is available to purchase and the price per copy.[5] These provisions have been criticised as effectively allowing competitors of the DLO/DSO to have access to valuable commercial information which will help them prepare their own bids in the future.

13. THE RULES APPLYING TO WORK DONE UNDER "WORKS CONTRACTS"

As mentioned, as well as the rules described above which govern the case where an authority wishes to carry out its own work in-house ("functional work"), the LGPLA 1980 and LGA 1988 also contain rules which apply where an authority's in-house unit wishes to do work as a provider for *another* body – referred to in the legislation as work done under a "works contract".[6] Most commonly this involves one local

---

[99] LGPLA 1980, s.18(2); LGA 1988, s.11(7).

[1] LGPLA 1980, s.18(2A), as inserted by LGA 1988, s.32 and Sched. 6, paras. 1 and 8; LGA 1988, s.11(7).

[2] *Ibid*. The relevant auditor is the person appointed under any enactment to audit the authority's accounts for the financial year for which the report is prepared: LGPLA 1980, s.18(5) as added by LGA 1988, s.32 and 6 paras. 1 and 8; LGA 1988, s.11(9).

[3] LGPLA 1980, s.18(2B), inserted by LGA 1988, s.32 and 6 paras. 1 and 8; LGA 1988, s.11(8).

[4] LGPLA 1980, s. 18(3); LGA 1988, ss. 12(4) and (5). LGA 1988, s. 12(5) expressly states that for reports under the LGA inspection must be free of charge, and this can probably also be implied into the LGPLA.

[5] LGPLA 1980, s.18(4); LGA 1988 s.12(6) and (7). Reports of the Commission for the New Towns under the LGA 1988 must be publicised in a national newspaper: LGA 1988, s. 12(7).

[6] On the precise distinction between functional work and work done under a works contract see pp. 662–664 (on the LGPLA 1980) and pp. 700–701 (on the LGA 1988).

authority wishing to work for another, although authorities may sometimes also seek to carry out work for other types of public body or for private entities.[7] The rules in the LGPLA and LGA on this subject provide that in-house units may not do such work for others unless the work has been won in a competitive procedure similar to that applying where the DLO/DSO seeks to do work for its own authority. This ensures that the in-house unit does not work for other bodies unless it is efficient enough to obtain the work by competition.

These rules apply whoever is the purchaser of the services – whether another authority or a private body. In practice, the need to follow these statutory procedures before work can be awarded to an authority is likely to deter bodies from seeking or accepting bids from such authorities where they are not already obliged to follow such procedures under other legislation.

The legislation places an obligation on the authority which seeks to do the work, stating that such authorities shall not undertake work unless the procedures in the legislation are complied with.[8]

Under the LGPLA 1980 the rules apply where construction or maintenance work[9] is to be done under a works contract with another by any body which is a "local authority".[10] Under the LGA 1988 the rules apply where work is to be done by a body which is a "defined authority"[11] and which relates to an activity which is a "defined activity" under the 1988 Act.[12]

Both Acts lay down requirements for publicising the contract and obtaining competitive tenders. Under the LGPLA 1980 it is required that the offer in question must have been accepted following an invitation to submit offers[13] and at least three persons who are not local authorities or development bodies[14] were invited to submit offers also.[15] Under the LGA 1988 two procedures are permitted.[16] One is a procedure similar to that contemplated by the 1980 Act, where the purchaser has accepted an offer following the issue of invitations, and has invited at least three persons, willing to carry out work of the kind concerned, who are not defined authorities.[17] The other is an open

---

[7] In addition to complying with the procedural requirements under the LGPLA and LGA, authorities wishing to do work for others must also comply with the substantive legal limits on their ability to undertake such activity, under the general *ultra vires* doctrine and under specific statutory restrictions. On these see Sparke, *The Compulsory Competitive Tendering Guide* (1993), Chap. 10.

[8] LGPLA 1980, s.7(1) and LGA 1988, s.4(1), discussed below.

[9] LGPLA s.5(1). On the definition of construction and maintenance work see pp. 651–654.

[10] On the definition of local authority see p. 650.

[11] On these definitions see pp. 665–666.

[12] On what is a defined activity see pp. 666–699.

[13] LGPLA 1980, s.7(1), 7(2), 7(3) and Local Government (Direct Labour Organisations) (Competition) Regulations 1989 S.I. 1989 No. 1588, reg. 5.

[14] On the definition of development bodies see p. 650.

[15] *Ibid.*

[16] LGA 1988, s.4(1).

[17] The number of persons invited and the number who are not defined authorities may be varied in regulations made by the Secretary of State: LGA 1988 s. 4(3).

procedure, where the contract must be advertised in at least one newspaper circulating in the locality in which the work is to be carried out, and also in at least one trade publication (that is, a publication circulating amongst persons who carry out work of the kind concerned). It seems that unless three relevant persons are known to be interested in the award procedure the method of public advertisement will have to be used. The procedures for functional work which have been outlined under these Acts, and delegated legislation under the Acts, also contain other provisions, such as a requirement for the authority to perform to the detailed specification set out[18] and time limits for response by providers,[19] but such further requirements do not apply in the case of works contracts.

It is also provided under both Acts that in entering into the contract, or in doing anything in connection with it prior to the award, the purchaser should not have acted in a manner which has the effect, or is intended to have or likely to have the effect, of restricting, distorting or preventing competition.[20] As has been explained above, a general obligation to avoid such "anti-competitive" behaviour also applies to an authority awarding a contract for functional work to its own DLO or DSO. In that context, the notion of anti-competitive behaviour has been extensively defined in regulations, notably the 1993 Competition Regulations, and in "statutory guidance" issued by the Secretary of State.[21] However, although the Secretary of State has powers to define anti-competitive behaviour in the context of works contracts,[22] the provisions of these instruments have not been formulated to apply to works contracts but only for award procedure relating to functional work.[23] It is not clear how far the courts will use the definitions applying to functional work in construing the concept of anti-competitive behaviour in the context of works contracts.

Under the LGPLA 1980 it is stated that the authority is not prohibited from undertaking the work if, at the time it was proposed to enter into the contract, the authority was not aware that there had been "anti-competitive" behaviour in breach of the above provisions.[24] This does not seem to apply, however, to a breach of the specific tendering rules, as opposed to the general requirement to avoid anti-competitive

---

[18] See p. 715.
[19] See pp. 718, 721 and 723.
[20] LGPLA 1980, s.7(1)(A), as inserted by LGA 1988 s.32, Sched. 6, paras. 1 and 2; LGA 1988, s.4(1) and (5).
[21] See pp. 707–709.
[22] LGA 1992, s.9(2)(a) and (c).
[23] The specific provisions in the regulations purport to apply only to functional work, whilst the relevant guidance states in general that it is limited to functional work only: see, for example, Circular 10/93, para. 2.
[24] LGPLA 1980, s.7(1)(B), as inserted by LGA 1988, s.32, Sched. 6 paras. 1 and 2. This is amended by LGA 1992, s.11 and Sch. 1, para. 1, to refer to awareness before the contract is made, permitting action to be taken before conclusion of the contract; but this was not in force at the time of writing.

behaviour. Under the LGA 1988 it is provided in general that there is no prohibition on the work where the authority is unaware of the breach of the provisions.[25]

---

[25] LGA 1988, s.4(6).

CHAPTER 15

THIRD COUNTRY ACCESS[1]

1. INTRODUCTION

The right of access of firms and products from the other Member States of the European Community to procurement in the United Kingdom has already been considered. It was explained in Chapter 4 that firms from other Member States and products imported from those states have rights of access to United Kingdom markets on the same terms as firms and products from the United Kingdom, under the provisions of the E.C. Treaty. Further, the European Community has adopted directives requiring states to implement fair and open procedures for the award of contracts, designed to ensure that this free access becomes a reality. These directives have been implemented in the United Kingdom by the Works Regulations, Supply Regulations, Services Regulations and Utilities Regulations, which were described in detail in Chapters 5–11. As is required by the directives themselves, the rules in the regulations may be enforced by all providers who are nationals of and established in the European Community.[2]

This chapter considers the position of countries *outside* the European Community – generally referred to as "third countries". It is necessary in this respect to consider the position of third country *firms* wishing to participate in contracts – for example, where a firm from the United States submits a tender. It is also necessary to examine the position of products and services which originate in third countries. These might be offered in a tender by either a third country *or* a Community firm – a tender offering machinery made in the United States could be submitted by a British or French firm, for example, as well as a firm from the United States itself.

In both respects the position is significantly affected by the United Kingdom's membership of the European Community. This is because rules affecting third countries in trade matters are found in the E.C.

---

[1] See further Arrowsmith, "Third Country Access to E.C. Public Procurement: an Analysis of the Legal Framework" (1995) 1 P.P.L.R. 1; Eeckhout, *The European Internal Market and International Trade: a Legal Analysis* (1994), Chap. 9; Footer, "External Aspects of the Community's Public Procurement Policy in the Utilities Sectors" (1994) 3 P.P.L.R. 187; Bovis, "Public Procurement within the Framework of the E.C. Common Commercial Policy" (1993) 2 P.P.L.R. 210; Halford, "An Overview of E.C.–United States Trade Relations in the Area of Public Procurement" (1995) 4 P.P.L.R. 35.

[2] See further pp. 907–909.

Treaty itself, and because the Community also has significant powers to take decisions and conclude agreements on trade relations which are binding on all Member States. The Community has exercised these powers in the area of procurement and the current position in the United Kingdom regarding third countries is, for the most part, now a reflection of a policy determined at Community level.

For most of the Community's major trading partners, the position on access to procurement markets is to a large extent governed by specific access agreements, which have been concluded by the Community and are applicable in all Member States. These agreements – such as the World Trade Organisation Agreement on Government Procurement and the European Economic Area Agreement – are considered in section (2) of this chapter. The position which applies where the matter is not governed by any specific agreement is considered in section (3.).

2. AGREEMENTS GOVERNING ACCESS TO PROCUREMENT

(1) THE DIVISION OF POWERS BETWEEN THE COMMUNITY AND MEMBER STATES

As mentioned above, under the E.C. Treaty Member States of the E.C. have conceded much of their power in the field of trade relations with third countries to the Community. The most important provision is Article 113 E.C. which confers on the Community both a power and a duty to pursue a common policy in commercial matters relating to third countries. This policy is referred to as the "common commercial policy". It includes a power to take unilateral measures on trade (referred to as "autonomous" commercial policy) – for example, to impose a ban on imports from a particular country. It also includes a power to conclude agreements on trade with other countries (referred to as "conventional" commercial policy) – for example, agreements on quotas for imports between a third country and the states of the Community. Where this provision applies the measures in question are within the *exclusive* competence of the Community. This means that only the Community may act and that Member States may not take their own measures in the area concerned.

Agreements concerning the liberalisation of procurement in *goods* clearly fall within Article 113.[3] Thus it is for the Community, and the Community alone, to negotiate agreements with third countries in this

---

[3] There has been some debate over whether procurement measures are a type of measure falling within within Article 113, but it is now generally accepted that this is the case: see Arrowsmith, above, note 1, pp. 2–4.

field; Member States may not conclude their own agreements, even if such agreements do not conflict with Community policy. The powers under Article 113 are exercisable by the Council by a qualified majority, following the submission of proposals by the Commission.[4] In the case of negotiations for agreements with third countries the Commission makes recommendations to the Council and it is for the Council then to authorise the Commission to conduct the negotiations, pursuant to a framework set out by the Council.[5] Once agreement is reached the practice is for the Commission to initial the text, but the agreement must be formally concluded by a Decision of the Council.

The Community may also conclude agreements under Article 238, which authorises it to conclude "association agreements" with third states. These are agreements which may involve "reciprocal rights and obligations, common action, and special procedures" – they cover, for example, agreements to extend to third countries rights and obligations similar to those applying between Member States, with a view to the future of accession of those states to the Community.[6] As explained below, a number of association agreements have been concluded with states from central and eastern Europe which include provisions on procurement,

It is not clear how far Article 113 E.C. covers agreements relating to procurement of services as well as procurement of goods. There has for many years been debate over whether Article 113 E.C. is in general limited to trade measures relating to goods or whether it also covers trade in services. In 1994 the Court of Justice stated in Opinion 1/94 that Article 113 will in general apply to trade in services *only where no movement of persons is involved.*[7] This would be the case, for example, where a consultant produces a report from his home base which is sent to the recipient. It does not, on the other hand, apply to the case where a service provider from outside the European Community seeks to enter the Community in order to provide a service or establish a branch there (or where the consumer of the services travels across borders to receive it). Thus, in general Article 113 gives the Community exclusive power to conclude agreements on trade in services only to the extent that these do not touch upon movement of persons. This reflected a policy decision by the court that such issues were too sensitive to remove from the purview of Member States at present. General agreements on market access to

---

[4] Article 113(2) and 113(4).

[5] Article 113(3). In carrying out negotiations the Commission must act in consultation with a special committee appointed by the Council. This provides an opportunity for input from the individual Member States and provides the Commission with views on the acceptability to states of the options being considered.

[6] Case 12/86, *Meryem Demirel v. Stadt Schwabisch Gmund* [1987] E.C.R. 3719. Advocate General Darmon suggested that the provision is confined to agreements concluded with a view to accession, but no such limitation was mentioned by the Court of Justice.

[7] Opinion 1/94, 15 November 1994. See Footer, "Opinion 1/94 on Community and Member States' Competences under the WTO: Implications for Public Procurement" (1995) 4 P.P.L.R. CS14.

services are unlikely to be so limited that they do not contemplate any possibility of cross-border movement, so that Article 113 is unlikely to be suitable as a sole basis for agreements on services.

The position of agreements dealing with procurement is not specifically dealt with in Opinion 1/94. One view may be that, to the extent that persons *may* need to cross Community borders to gain access to procurement governed by an agreement, Article 113 does not apply. On this basis, Article 113 would not generally provide a basis for such agreements, since obviously cross-border movement is common during the performance of government contracts. On the other hand, it can be pointed out that agreements on procurement, such as the WTO Agreement, are frequently subject to the more general rules which apply to market access of third countries to the services markets of Member States. For example, the right of providers to provide financial services under government contracts in the Community will generally be made subject to any rules governing the right to provide financial services in the Community generally. Where this is the case, it may be argued that the agreement on procurement should fall within Article 113 since it does not, as such, deal with any issues of cross-border movement. This, it is suggested, is the better view; but the matter awaits resolution by the Court of Justice.

To the extent that Article 113 does not apply, the Community must rely on other Treaty provisions.[8] In general, the Community may rely on Article 235 E.C. which authorises Community action, in the course of the operation of the common market, to achieve any objective of the Treaty, where there is no other Treaty power available. The exercise of this power, unlike that under Article 113, requires unanimity in the Council and also consultation with the European Parliament. Another

---

[8] It can also be noted that where the Community has power to act in the internal sphere to attain a particular objective, and a power to act in the external sphere, also, is *necessary* to attain that "internal" objective, a power to act in the external sphere will be implied: Opinion 1/76, [1977] E.C.R. 741. The Community has extensive powers to regulate services in the internal market, including in relation to government procurement, under Articles 57(2), 66 and 100a E.C. It might be argued that the exercise of powers over services in the external sphere is necessary to achieve the objectives of the internal market, since absence of a common external policy may give rise to distortions of competition internally, and thus undermine the functioning of the internal market. However, the case law does not support the view that such effects render the exercise of external powers *necessary* to the internal market; and this is probably too wide a view of the implied powers doctrine: Eeckhout, above, p.40. Exclusive implied powers also arise where the Community has actually exercised powers in the internal sphere, and the external measure which is envisaged (for example, the conclusion of a particular international agreement), "alters" or "affects" those internal measures: case 22/70, *Commission v. Council* [1971] E.C.R. 263 (the AETR case); joined cases 3, 4 and 6/76, *Kramer* [1976] E.C.R. 1279; Opinion 2/91, [1993] 3 C.M.L.R. 800. However, it is difficult to see that measures relating to external relations in procurement will normally "affect" or "alter" the internal Community procurement regime: the only effect of external measures is to affect competitive conditions in the different national markets. This does not alter or affect the internal market rules themselves – it merely affects the practical conditions in which these rules operate.

possibility[8a] is to include provisions on services procurement in an association agreement made under Article 238, and indeed the existing association agreements with central and eastern European states include provisions on services, as well as goods, procurement.[9] Until such time as the Community has actually adopted a policy under these provisions, Member States remain free to conclude their own agreements since, unlike Article 113, these provisions do not give exclusive power to the Community in their field of operation.

(2) THE GENERAL PRINCIPLES OF COMMUNITY POLICY

The Community's policy towards third countries in general has since the late 1980s been based in general (although not entirely) on the principle of "reciprocity" – that is, the Community has indicated its willingness to open up Community markets to third countries provided that they are willing to make equivalent concessions to Community firms and products. During the 1980s there was some debate over this.[10] The E.C. Treaty envisages, in the Preamble and in Article 110, that the common commercial policy will be a liberal one, formulated with a view to removing barriers in international trade. However, after a period of liberalisation in the 1950s and 1960s, the 1970s and 1980s saw a more protectionist approach, in particular in action by individual Member States[11] and during the 1980s it was argued by some that the Community as a whole should adopt a protectionist policy: at least it was suggested that this was needed to promote new high technology industry until it could become competitive in world markets. Prior to 1985 the Community gave little express attention to strategy in the external field, but the internal market programme ultimately gave impetus to the formulation of a clear external trade policy.[12] This happened because completion of the internal market would improve opportunities for third countries (for example, this is one consequence of increased market transparency and technical standardisation) and a positive decision was needed as to

---

[8a] And see also Article 59(3), second para., which allows the Council, acting on a qualified majority, to apply measures concerning freedom to provide services in the internal market to third country firms established in the E.C.

[9] See pp. 782–786. The Court of Justice held in *Demirel*, above, that Article 238 may be used to adopt measures for which there is no other specific power in the Treaty.

[10] See generally Pearce and Sutton, *Protection and Industrial Policy in Europe* (1985).

[11] See, for example, Tsoukalis, *The New European Economy* (revised 2nd ed. 1993), Chap. 9; Pearce and Sutton, above.

[12] For consideration generally of the impact of 1992 on external relations see Eekhout, "The External Dimension of the E.C. Internal Market – A Portrait" (1991) 2 World Competition 5; McMahon, "Fortress Europe: the External Dimension of the Internal Market" (1993) 44 Northern Ireland Legal Quarterly 130; Redmond (ed.), *External Relations of the E.C.: the International Response to 1992* (1992); Milner and Allen, "The External Implications of 1992" in *The Single European Market and Beyond* (Swann ed. 1992); Tsoukalis, above.

whether these benefits of the Community's open market policy should be allowed to accrue to third countries as well as E.C. Member States. It was also necessary to formulate a common policy for the proper functioning of the internal market.[13] Further, the issue was placed firmly on the agenda as a result of the fears voiced by the Community's major trading partners and competitors, notably the United States and Japan, that the single market would result in protectionism at the European level – the creation of a "Fortress Europe".

The Community's response was to announce its intention to support international liberalisation of trade, in line with the original objectives of the E.C. Treaty.[14] However, unsurprisingly, access to European markets was not to be automatic – it would be given only on the basis of the principle of "reciprocity". In other words, Community markets should be opened only to those states which are prepared to allow the Community access to their own markets (subject to existing international obligations, and also to special provision for developing countries). It was envisaged that this approach would work as an instrument of liberalisation, inducing third countries to open their markets where they have not done so previously pursuant to liberalisation agreements with the Community. However, where existing rules and practices confer access to E.C. markets on states which will *not* reciprocate, the principle may also be applied to justify measures which restrict market access.

Policy on procurement has reflected these general trends. Thus, prior to the 1980s, virtually no attention was given to the issue, and the early directives on procurement, adopted in the 1970s to regulate public sector works and supplies,[15] did not address the problem of external access.[16] The only significant measure was the conclusion of the Agreement on Government Procurement in 1978, under the auspices of GATT, to regulate supplies procurement in central government.[17] During the revision of the internal procurement regime in the late 1980s, however, the question of external access was more closely addressed,[18] and since that time the Community has sought to implement a general policy of access based on reciprocity in the procurement field. In the last five years

---

[13] See Cremona, "The Completion of the Internal Market and the Incomplete Commercial Policy of the European Communities" (1990) 15 E.L.Rev. 283.

[14] See, in particular, the Commission Memorandum of 1988, "Europe 1992: Europe World Partner", Commission Press Release P 117 of October 19, 1988.

[15] See pp. 52–54.

[16] It may be observed, though, that as early as 1980 the Council did adopt a Resolution noting the need for a common policy in this area and calling upon the Commission to make proposals for such a policy, which it was stated should be based on the principle of reciprocity: see Council Resolution of July 22, 1980, [1980] O.J. C211, concerning access to Community public supply contracts of products originating in third countries, and also the earlier Resolution on the same subject, [1977] O.J. C11/2.

[17] See pp. 774–782.

[18] Indeed, the 1988 "Europe World Partner" statement referred expressly to the need for negotiations with trading partners on the basis of reciprocity in the area of utilities procurement, which was at that stage being examined as part of the internal market initiative.

this policy has been pushed forward through a number of bilateral and unilateral agreements providing for access to public and utilities procurement, either as part of more general agreements on trade liberalisation concluded by the Community or in the form of specific agreements on procurement.

The main agreements are:

(i) the European Economic Area Agreement, which opens up procurement with members of the European Free Trade Association;

(ii) the World Trade Organisation Agreement on Government Procurement, which seeks eventually to open up procurement on a world-wide basis;

(iii) the association agreements with certain central and eastern European states, designed to prepare for the ultimate accession of these states to the Community, and which contain specific provisions on procurement; and

(iv) a bilateral agreement with the United States.

These are considered below. Together they represent a substantial move towards liberalisation of procurement between the Community and its major trading partners.

(3) THE EUROPEAN ECONOMIC AREA AGREEMENT

(a) GENERAL PRINCIPLES

The European Economic Area Agreement (EEA Agreement),[19] which was concluded on May 2, 1992, is a wide-ranging agreement which provides for the states of the European Free Trade Association (EFTA) to be brought together with the Community Member States in a single market regime which mirrors that of the Community. In the field of procurement, the Agreement creates an open market regime based on the same rules as the Community regime.[20] This means, first, that Member States of the Community must open up their markets to these EFTA states in the same way as to other E.C. states: they must follow general rules similar to those of the E.C. Treaty for all contracts and must also allow firms from the participating EFTA states to invoke the detailed rules of the procurement directives in respect of major contract awards. Secondly, it means that these EFTA states must, for their part, effectively follow the same rules in their own procurement, with the effect of giving access to their markets both to each other and to the Community Member States.

---

[19] [1994] O.J. L1/1; and see also EEA Council Decision 1/95, [1995] O.J. L86/58 on the accession of Liechtenstein.

[20] See generally Norberg, "The Agreement on a European Economic Area" (1992) 29 C.M.L.Rev. 1171; Laredo, "The EEA Agreement: an Overall View" (1992) 29 C.M.L.Rev. 1199; O'Keefe, "The Agreement on the European Economic Area" (1992) Legal Issues in European Integration 1.

At the time the agreement was signed the members of EFTA were Austria, Finland, Iceland, Liechtenstein, Norway, Sweden and Switzerland. Switzerland, however, ultimately rejected the Agreement in a referendum, and it went ahead without Switzerland's participation.[21] The Agreement was of some significance at that time: although the size of EFTA public procurement markets was estimated at only about 10 per cent of those of the E.C.[22] these states are near neighbours and significant trading partners of the United Kingdom. Subsequently, however – from January 1, 1996 – three of the members of EFTA, Austria, Finland and Sweden, have acceded to the European Community and ceased to be members of EFTA, and the EEA agreement is now relevant only to the relationship between the Community Member States and Norway, Iceland, and Liechtenstein. Whilst this development renders the Agreement itself of diminished current significance, it was important in easing the transition of Austria, Finland and Sweden into full membership of the Community.

(b) APPLICATION TO PROCUREMENT[23]

The EEA Agreement contains provisions on free movement and competition which parallel those in the E.C. Treaty. For example, Article 4 EEA prohibits within the scope of the EEA Treaty, discrimination on grounds of nationality, parallel to Article 6 E.C.; Article 11 prohibits restrictions on the free movement of goods, paralleling Article 30 E.C., whilst Articles 31 and 36 guarantee the freedom to establish and freedom to provide services, paralleling Articles 52 and 59 E.C. The effect of these provisions is that Community Member States may not generally impede the import of products from participating EFTA states or the right of persons from these states to establish or provide services in the Community; whilst the EFTA states must provide the same rights for Community firms and products. In relation to procurement these provisions have the effect of prohibiting the government from adopting measures which restrict the access of firms and products from the EFTA states to United Kingdom procurement markets. This applies to all contracts, not just those falling within the Community directives. These provisions are directly applicable and have direct effect – that is, they may be enforced against the United Kingdom in the national courts.[24]

So far as concerns the rules in E.C. secondary legislation, rules on the single market adopted at the time of the EEA Agreement were applied automatically in the EFTA states. Rules in subsequent directives apply only if specifically adopted by the EEA Joint Committee. This Com-

---

[21] The position of Switzerland is dealt with in Protocol 4.
[22] EFTA, *Public Procurement in the EEA* (Geneva, 1992).
[23] See further Bock, "The EEA Agreement: Rules on Public Procurement" (1993) 2 P.P.L.R 136; Toikka, "Public Procurement in the EEA" (1993) 2 P.P.L.R. CS123.
[24] See pp. 941–942.

mittee has already adopted a package of measures which includes the rules in the Services Directive and Utilities Remedies Directive, adopted by the Community later in 1992, and the "consolidating" Works, Supply and Utilities Directives rules, adopted by the Community in 1993.[24a]

The EEA Agreement provides for adaption of the E.C. rules to cover the EEA states, since the wording in the rules is based on the assumption that they only apply to E.C. Member States. Certain general ("horizontal") adaptions are contained in Protocol 1 to the EEA Agreement and the procurement rules must be read in light of these adaptations where the EEA is concerned.[25] Thus, for example, it is stated that if a rule in a Community measure is directed at an E.C. Member State – such as the obligation to publish notices under the procurement rules – it applies also to participating EFTA states, and where it is stated that a rule confers a right on a Member State or a national of that state, the same right applies in respect of participating EFTA states and their nationals.[26] There are also some special provisions modifying, in the context of the EEA, the usual application of the rules.[27] In particular, EFTA states may not send procurement notices to the *Official Journal* in their own language, but must use one of the official languages of the E.C.[28]

Article 6 EEA provides for the reception of all the relevant case law of the Court of Justice which applies to the interpretation of the provisions of the EEA Agreement which are "identical in substance" to those of European Community law. Thus the EEA Treaty provisions on free movement and the rules on award procedures which derive from the E.C. Directives are to be applied and interpreted in the light of the existing European Community case law. It is anticipated that in the future a uniform approach will be adopted for the interpretation of the provisions of the EEA Agreement and the parallel provisions of European Community law.

(c) IMPLEMENTATION IN THE UNITED KINGDOM

To give effect to its obligations to apply to all EEA states the benefits of the Community directives, the United Kingdom has included relevant provisions in United Kingdom implementing regulations – that is, the Works Regulations, the Supply Regulations, the Services Regulations and the Utilities Regulations.[29] First, it has been provided that these

---

[24a] EEA Joint Committee Decision 7/94, [1994] O.J. L160/1.

[25] Article 65(1) and Annex B XVI, applying to the measures on procurement the general principles ("horizontal adaptations") of Protocol I.

[26] *Ibid*

[27] Article 65(1) and Annex XVI (headed "sectoral adaptations").

[28] *Ibid*.

[29] For the Supply Regulations these necessary modifications were introduced in the new version of the Supply Regulations which were adopted in 1995 (see pp. 64–66). The Supply Regulations also amended the Works Regulations and Services Regulations so as to apply those regulations to the EFTA States also: see Supply Regulation 31. For utilities the express provisions were introduced for the first time in the 1996 version of the Utilities Regulations.

regulations are to be enforceable not only by providers who are nationals of, and established in, Community states, but also by providers in other "relevant" states,[30] in accordance with the same remedies as apply to Community providers. The definition of "relevant state" includes Norway, Iceland and Liechtenstein.[31-32] Secondly, certain adjustments have been made to the substantive provisions of the regulations to reflect the fact that these provisions now also apply to these states. For example, the provisions permitting rejection of providers who are not registered on domestic professional or trade registers have been adjusted to refer not merely to the registers of "Member States" but to those of "relevant states"[33]; whilst the rules which benefit providers by allowing them to deduce evidence of registration on certain domestic lists to prove certain matters to United Kingdom authorities have been amended to include express recognition of certain registers of providers in Norway, Iceland and Liechtenstein.[34]

(4) THE WORLD TRADE ORGANISATION AGREEMENT ON GOVERNMENT PROCUREMENT (GPA)[35]

(a) INTRODUCTION

Another important agreement concluded by the Community on behalf of the United Kingdom and other Member States is the World Trade

---

[30] Works Regulations 4(1), as amended by Supply Regulation 31(1), and Works Regulation 31(1); Supply Regulation 4(1); Services Regulation 4(1), as amended by Supply Regulation 32(1), and Services Regulation 32(1); Utilities Regulation 4(1).

[31-32] See the definition of "relevant state" in Works Regulation 2(1), as am. by Supply Regulation 31(1) and Utilities Regulation 35(1), and Works Regulation 4(1), as am. by Utilities Regulation 35(1); Supply Regulation 2(1) and 4(1), as am. by Utilities Regulation 35(1); Services Regulation 2(1), as am. by Supply Regulation 32(1) and Utilities Regulation 35(1) and Services Regulation 4(1), as am. by Utilities Regulation 35(1); Utilities Regulations 2(1) and 4(2). The provisions in the Works, Supply and Services Regulations state that Liechtenstein is to be included within the definition of "relevant state" only from the time that the EEA Agreement comes into force for Leichtenstein, but this has now occurred.

[33] Works Regulation 14(1), as am. by Supply Regulation 31(1); Supply Regulation 14(1); Services Regulation 14(1), as am. by Supply Regulation 32(1).

[34] Works Regulations 14(4), as amended by Supply Regulation 31(1); and Services Regulation 14(4), as amended by Supply Regulation 32(1).

[35] See further Jones, "The GATT-MTN System and the European Community as International Frameworks for the Regulation of Economic Activity: the Removal of Barriers to Trade in Government Procurement" (1984) 8 Maryland Journal of International Law and Trade 53; Bourgeois, "The Tokyo Round Agreements on Technical Barriers and on Government Procurement in International and EEC Perspective" (1982) 19 C.M.L.R. 5; de Graaf and Trepte, "The Revised GATT Procurement Agreement" (1994) 3 P.P.L.R. CS70; de Graaf and King, "Towards a More Global Government Procurement Market: The Expansion of the GATT Government Procurement Agreement in the Context of the Uruguay Round" (1995) 29 Intl. Lawyer 435; Hoekman and Mavroidis, "The WTO's Agreement on Government Procurement: Expanding Disciplines, Declining Membership?" (1995) 4 P.P.L.R. 63; Brown and Pouncey, "Expanding the International Market for Public Procurement: the WTO's Agreement on Government Procurement" [1995] Int. T.L. Rev. 69.

Organisation (WTO) Agreement on Government Procurement (GPA).[36] This is the successor to an agreement referred to as the "GATT" Agreement on Government Procurement, and seeks to liberalise procurement on an international basis.

The original GATT Agreement on Government Procurement[37] was negotiated under the auspices of GATT – the General Treaty on Tariffs and Trade – during the Tokyo Round between 1973–1979, and came into force on January 1, 1981.[38] This Agreement was, however, narrow in scope, covering only supplies contracts and only central/federal government entities. In parallel with the Uruguay round of GATT talks a much more extensive agreement was concluded. This forms part of the World Trade Organisation Agreement, concluded at the end of the Uruguay round, which sets up the World Trade Organisation as a new institution for regulation and development of world trade. The WTO package includes a new version of the GATT itself, and also a number of other agreements, such as the General Agreement on Trade in Services and the TRIPS agreement concerning intellectual property rights. The Agreement on Government Procurement is another part of the package and is contained in Annex IV of the general WTO Agreement. Most parts of the WTO Agreement came into force on January 1, 1995, but the Agreement on Government Procurement took effect for most states, including the United Kingdom and other Community Member States, on January 1, 1996. This supersedes the old Agreement for those states party to the new Agreement.

The new Agreement is, as mentioned, much wider than the old. It covers works and other services as well as supplies; it embraces certain activities in the utilities sector which were previously excluded; and it now applies to many subfederal and local entities, and certain public undertakings, as well as to central/federal government. As a result, procurement subject to the GPA regime will increase tenfold.[39] The new Agreement also includes for the first time a requirement to provide legal remedies for enterprises affected by a breach which should considerably enhance its effectiveness. The applicable principles and award procedures on the other hand remain largely unchanged from the original Agreement.

States which accede to membership of the WTO are required in general to accept all its measures and cannot opt out of parts of the package. However, this is not the case for the GPA, which WTO members may choose to accept or reject. (Thus this Agreement is

---

[36] [1994] O.J. L336/3, p.273, (approved on behalf of the Community by Council Decision 94/800, [1994] O.J. L336/1).

[37] Approved on behalf of the E.C. by Council Decision 80/271/EEC, [1980] O.J. L71/1.

[38] The Agreement was slightly amended in 1987 by a Protocol, approved on behalf of the E.C. by Council Decision 87/565/EEC of November 16, 1987 [1987] O.J. L345/24, which came into force on February 14, 1988.

[39] European Commission Press Release, Memo/94/29, "E.U.–U.S. Negotiations on Public Procurement" (April 21, 1994), p.1.

referred to as a "plurilateral" rather than multilateral agreement.) States which choose not to accede are not required to follow the obligations in the GPA but nor do they enjoy its benefits of access to the procurement markets of the signatory states. Most WTO members have yet to commit themselves to the GPA: the only parties at present apart from the Community and its Member States are Norway (a member of the EEA); Canada; Israel; Japan; South Korea; the United States; and Switzerland.[40] However, the membership of the United States and Japan, in particular, means the Agreement is important for the Community. It is hoped that in future more states will accept the Agreement. For adherence to the GPA, states must be in a position to implement the transparent award procedures of the Agreement, and in this context it is pertinent to note that the United Nations has recently endorsed a Model Law on Procurement of Goods, Construction and Services, together with a guide to its enactment, drawn up by its Commission on International Trade Law (UNCITRAL), which is designed to provide guidance for countries wishing to adopt legislation governing the award of public contracts or to improve existing legislation.[41] One aim of the Model Law is to enable states to obtain better value for money, but an additional objective is to facilitate further international liberalisation of procurement markets. Should the Model Law prove successful in encouraging the regulation of procurement, this will open the way for greater participation in the GPA. However, at present procurement is not a priority on the trade agenda for most states, and many may be reluctant to give up the possibilities for using procurement as a tool to promote national industrial development.[42]

(b) OBLIGATIONS UNDER THE GPA

The approach of the GPA to liberalisation of procurement is similar to that of the Community.

---

[40] These are the same as the parties to the old agreement except that South Korea was not formerly a party and Hong Kong and Singapore, who did sign the previous GATT Agreement on procurement, are not yet party to the new GPA. However, Singapore has already made an offer with a view to accession to the new GPA. The old Agreement will continue to govern the relationship between Hong Kong and Singapore with the European Communities (and other signatories to the old Agreement) pending accession to the new GPA or withdrawal from the old Agreement.

[41] UNCITRAL Model Law on Procurement of Goods, Construction and Services (1994); United Nations Commission on International Trade Law, Guide to Enactment of UNCITRAL Model Law on Procurement of Goods, Construction and Services. For analysis see Wallace, "UNCITRAL Model Law on Procurement of Goods and Construction" (1994) 3 P.P.L.R. CS2; Wallace, "The UN Model Law on Procurement" (1992) 1 P.P.L.R. 406; Myers, "UNCITRAL Model Law on Procurement" (1993) 21 International Business Lawyer 179; Westring, "Multilateral and Unilateral Procurement Regimes: to which Camp does the Model Law Belong?" (1994) 3 P.P.L.R. 142; Wallace, "The UNCITRAL Model Law: the Addition of Services" (1994) 3 P.P.L.R. CS218.

[42] On the accession of developing countries see Hoekman and Mavroidis, above, note 35, pp. 73–78.

First, Article III of the Agreement contains certain general principles. One is a principle of national treatment: with respect to all procurement covered by the Agreement the parties must give to (i) the providers and (ii) the products and services[43] of other signatory states, the same treatment as is afforded to national providers and products.[44] In addition, parties must give to (i) the providers and (ii) the products and services[45] of other parties treatment no less favourable than that afforded to other parties (the 'most favoured nation" principle).[46] In relation to the United Kingdom this has the effect that, for procurement falling within the scope of the Agreement,[47] the providers of third country signatories must be able to take advantage of the procedures in the procurement regulations implementing the Community regime – which are available to national firms and firms from certain other states. Article III of the Agreement also prohibits discrimination against local firms based on the degree of foreign affiliation or ownership, or based on the country of production of the goods or services where these have been produced in one of the states which is party to the Agreement. In contrast with the general principles under the E.C. Treaty these principles under the GPA do not apply to minor procurement but only to procurement falling above the thresholds for the application of the Agreement (set out further below) – smaller procurements remain wholly unregulated.

The Agreement also lays out detailed procedures which must be followed in awarding contracts within its scope. These have similar objectives to the procedures under the Community directives, being designed to ensure transparency and to facilitate participation by overseas firms through advertising, reasonable times for response to notices, etc. The procedures are, in general, less stringent than those applying under the Community's public sector directives and are more akin to those applying in the utilities sector in the Community. The relationship between the GPA and Community procedures is considered further below.[48]

---

[43] To apply these provisions it is necessary to decide whether products or services are "of" a particular third country. Rules governing this question in international trade are generally referred to as "rules of origin". These are dealt with in Article IV of the GPA, providing that parties shall not apply rules which are different from the rules of origin applied in the normal course of trade and at the time of importation to imports of the same products or services from the same parties. Rules on the origin of goods are not required in Community law itself since the principle of free movement of goods under Article 30 (which fulfils the function of the GPA requirement to treat products of third countries no less favourably than national products) applies not only to goods originating in other Member States but to all products in free circulation those states regardless of origin: see further pp. 790–791.

[44] GPA Article IIII(1).

[45] See note 43 above.

[46] *Ibid.*

[47] The principle that signatories must be treated no less favourably than other parties is effectively modified in relation to the scope of coverage of the GPA, since coverage is effectively arranged as series of bilateral agreements between the different signatories: see pp. 778-780.

[48] See pp. 781–782.

Article XXIII provides for certain general exceptions to the Agreement. Thus there are certain exemptions dealing with national defence and security,[49] and also for measures to protect "public morals, order or safety, human, animal or plant life or health, [or] intellectual property", or measures relating to the products or services of handicapped persons, philanthropic institutions or prison labour.

The GPA deals only with access specifically to the government procurement market: the principles of access to the market of states in general is dealt with under other agreements, notably the GATT (on the import of goods) and the GATS (on access to services markets). Article III(3) of the GPA makes it clear that the right of access to government procurement under the GPA is subject to the rules which govern access to the general market of the signatory states. This provides that the general principles of Article III as set out above "shall not apply to customs duties and charges of any kind imposed on or in connection with importation, the levying of such duties and charges and other import regulations and formalities, and measures affecting trade in services other than laws, regulations, procedures and practices regarding government procurement covered by this Agreement". Thus, if a firm submits a tender on a major contract advertised by a United Kingdom government department which includes machinery made in Japan, under the GPA that tender could not be treated by the purchaser less favourably than a tender offering United Kingdom-made machinery. However, any import duties on machinery of that type from Japan would need to be paid: the GPA does itself not prohibit imposing such a duty, even though its imposition gives an advantage to United Kingdom machinery in government contracts.

(c) PROCUREMENT COVERED BY THE AGREEMENT

The detailed scope of the new GPA with regard to the entities covered, the type of procurement and monetary thresholds is set out mainly in Appendix I to the Agreement.[50]

So far as the Community is concerned, the Agreement applies in principle to all bodies which are "contracting authorities" for the purposes of the public sector directives.[51] In the utilities sector the Agreement applies to entities which carry out one or more of certain listed "utility" activities, where these entities are either "public authorities" or "public undertakings", in the sense of the Utilities Directive.[52] The GPA does not, on the other hand, cover another group of entities covered by the directives and implementing Utilities Regulations – that is, those operating in the utilities sector on the basis of "special and

---

[49] See further the discussion at pp. 874–875.
[50] GPA Art. I(1) and (4), providing that coverage shall be as stated in the Appendix.
[51] GPA, E.C. Annex I and Annex II.
[52] GPA, E.C. Annex III.

exclusive rights". The listed utility activities are; (i) activities connected with the provision of water through fixed networks; (ii) activities concerned with the provision of electricity through fixed networks; (iii) the provision of terminal facilities to carriers by air; (iv) the provision of terminal facilities to carriers by sea or inland waterway; and (v) the operation of public services in the field of transport by automated systems, tramway, trolley bus, or bus or cable. In principle the provision of public transport services by rail is included, but there is an exclusion for entities listed in Annex VI of the Utilities Directive, designed to exclude non-urban services. This list does not cover all activities which are within the E.C. utilities regime: it does not apply to activities connected with the distribution of gas or heat; those connected with fuel exploration or extraction; telecommunications; nor some of the transport activities which are covered by the E.C. rules.

The threshold for the E.C.'s application of the GPA to works contracts is SDR 5 million, for all entities.[53] For supplies and services it is SDR 130,000 for central government[54]; 200,000 for local government[55]; and 400,000 for all contracts in the utilities sectors (including those awarded by central and local government).[56]

This is the general scope of coverage for the E.C.; but the position is, however, qualified by certain important derogations. For central/federal government works and supply contracts the position is quite straight-forward: generally the Agreement applies in respect of all other signatories to the Agreement, to all central government works and supplies contracts as outlined above.[57] However, for services contracts, certain contracts in the utilities sector, and for contracts awarded by other levels of government (such as local and regional authorities), the issue is more complex. This arises from the fact that many signatories have been unable, or unwilling, to offer for coverage all of their entities or contracts in these categories. For example, whilst the E.C. has been willing to open up the markets of all subfederal entities, this was difficult for some states – for example, the United States – because of the independent constitutional position of these entities which necessitated their agreement in political terms, at least (although perhaps not required by law). Given the divergence, coverage based on what each signatory state was able to offer was unacceptable; this would have resulted in great imbalances of coverage between states, which the E.C. was not prepared to contemplate in view of the policy of reciprocity. On the other hand, to define coverage of the revised GPA on the basis of the minimum

---

[53] See E.C. Annexes I, II and III (hereafter "E.C. Annexes").

[54] E.C. Annex I.

[55] E.C. Annex II.

[56] E.C. Annex III.

[57] There are some minor derogations: for example, the benefit of the remedies provisions is not available to small- and medium-sized enterprises from Japan, Korea and the United States, until such time as those countries cease to discriminate in favour of small or minority businesses.

common denominator of all signatory states would have taken matters little further than coverage of federal/central government works and supplies. Thus, it was decided that each signatory should effectively negotiate with each other signatory, to come to a satisfactory agreement on coverage based on reciprocity on a bilateral basis.

As a result of this policy, the wide coverage of E.C. entities and activities is expressly limited in respect of many of the signatory states, by a list of derogations attached to the E.C. Annexes to Appendix I; these mirror limitations which those states have imposed on access to their own markets. Thus, for example, coverage in the utilities sector does not apply to Canada,[58] since that country did not commit itself to opening its own markets to the E.C. (When the Agreement was first concluded in December 1993 there was also no coverage for utilities with respect to the United States, but there have since been modifications to the E.C.-U.S. coverage as a result of a subsequent E.C.–U.S. bilateral agreements, discussed below.) Also outside the Agreement in the utilities sector are, in relation to Japan, urban transport and electricity; in relation to South Korea, urban transport and airports; and, in relation to Israel, urban transport.[59] There are also significant derogations for certain categories of services[60] and for specified types of equipment.[61]

Thus, in the scope of its coverage the GPA gives the appearance of a series of bilateral agreements rather than a multilateral arrangement and involves a significant compromise of the "most favoured nation" principle (that concessions extended to one state should be extended to all others) which underlies many international trade agreements. States joining the GPA in future will need to reach separate agreement on the scope of coverage with all existing parties to the Agreement – a need which complicates the accession process.

(d) REMEDIES FOR ENFORCING THE RULES

A significant feature of the new GPA is that Article XX requires states to give aggrieved providers a right to enforce the rules. The rules actually set out in the GPA provide a minimum standard for states to meet on remedies. However, the general principles of national treatment and the most favoured nation principle referred to in section (b) above mean that, as well as satisfying the specific requirements of the GPA, states must make available any existing domestic remedies to GPA providers. For the United Kingdom, this means that the remedies generally available for enforcing the Community rules, provided pursuant to the Community Remedies Directives, must also be available for third country providers seeking to enforce the GPA. In addition, there is

---

[58] See Item 1 of the list of derogations from the E.C. Annexes.
[59] Item 1 of the list of derogations from the E.C. Annexes.
[60] Item 1 of the list of derogations from the E.C. Annexes.
[61] See in particular items 3 and 5 of the list of derogations from the E.C. Annexes.

an inter-governmental dispute resolution procedure which may be invoked to resolve disputes relating to the GPA.

This issue of remedies, both for providers and through the dispute resolution mechanism is considered further in the general chapter on remedies.[62]

(e) IMPLEMENTATION OF THE GPA IN THE UNITED KINGDOM

In order to give effect to its obligations under the GPA the United Kingdom is obliged to put in place in the United Kingdom contract award procedures complying with the requirements of the GPA for contracts covered by the Agreement, and to render these provisions enforceable by providers from third countries in accordance with the GPA obligations on remedies.[63]

So far as concerns the applicable award procedures, contracts covered by the GPA are, in general, already subject to detailed legal procedures under the Community's own internal market regime, as implemented by the Works Regulations, Supply Regulations, Services Regulations and Utilities Regulations. As indicated above, it is probably necessary under the terms of the GPA itself that third country providers, as well as firms from any other Member States, should be permitted to take advantage of these procedures – as well as any other legal rules on procurement – since under Article III of the GPA third countries who are party to the GPA must be treated no less favourably than national providers. Thus it is necessary at the very least to make these procedures available to all "GPA" providers. Further, as was also mentioned above the same general principle indicates that the remedies available to enforce the procedures should be no less favourable for third country GPA providers than for national providers. Thus it is necessary, in effect, that for contracts covered by the GPA, GPA providers should be able, at least, to enforce all the existing United Kingdom procurement regulations, on both remedies and procedure.

At the time of writing none of the regulations give an express right to enforce their provisions to providers covered by the GPA, and indeed appear to limit rights of enforcement to providers from the E.C. and from certain states covered by Europe Agreements. However, it is the intention of the government in due course to confer such an express right to enforce the regulations on GPA providers, in the case of those contracts covered by the GPA; indeed it has an obligation to do so to ensure that United Kingdom legislation (which presently seems to exclude GPA providers) is consistent with the GPA. Pending adoption of relevant legislation, the rules in the regulations may probably still be

---

[62] See pp. 938–941.
[63] See further pp. 938–941.

enforced by GPA providers for contracts covered by the GPA, on the basis that the access rules under the GPA have direct effect.[63a]

Since the GPA rules are in certain respects more stringent than the Community rules (for example, on the effect of Prior Information Notices in shortening award procedures) relevant purchasers in the United Kingdom must, as from January 1, 1996, also follow these more stringent rules, as well as the rules in the regulations. As explained in Chapter 3, the Commission has put forward a Proposal for a directive to amend the existing Community directives to ensure that they are as stringent as the GPA rules, and that compliance with the Community rules, as implemented in domestic law, will automatically mean compliance with the GPA.[63b] At the time of writing this proposed directive had not been adopted, and nor had the United Kingdom regulations been independently amended to reflect these more stringent obligations. This does not, however, affect the obligation of purchasers to comply with these additional rules for GPA providers from January 1, 1996, when the GPA comes into affect. Further, since the regulations provide expressly that Community provisions shall be treated no less favourably than third country providers,[63c] Community providers will also obtain the benefit of these obligations.

(5) THE ASSOCIATION AGREEMENTS WITH CENTRAL AND EASTERN EUROPE[64]

(a) THE REQUIREMENTS OF THE ASSOCIATION AGREEMENTS

Under Article 238 E.C. the Community has concluded association agreements ("Europe Agreements") with a number of the former socialist states of eastern and central Europe, which deal expressly with liberalisation of procurement markets. It is anticipated that these states will eventually become members of the Community, and also that they will accede to the GPA.

Agreements are presently in force with Hungary and Poland (in force from February 1, 1994), and with the Czech Republic, the Slovak

---

[63a] See pp. 938–941.
[63b] See pp. 61–63.
[63c] Works Regulation 4(2), Supply Regulation 4(2), Services Regulation 4(2), Utilities Regulation 4(2).
[64] See also Arrowsmith, above, note 1; Footer, "Public Procurement and the Wider Europe: a Review of some Recent Europe Agreements" (1995) 4 P.P.L.R. CS115; and on developments on procurement within the central and eastern European States, see Servenay and Williams, "Introduction of a Regulatory Framework on Public Procurement in the Central and Eastern European Countries: The First Step on a Long Road" (1995) 4 P.P.L.R. 237.

Republic, Romania and Bulgaria[65] (in force from February 1, 1995) (referred to hereafter as the "association states"). Agreements, on the same line as the other association agreements, have also been signed with Lithuania, Latvia and Estonia although at the time of writing these were not yet in force.[66]

In relation to trade in goods, the agreements provide, first, for the Community to abolish quantitative restrictions and measures of equivalent effect, with respect to most products originating in the association states.[67] This is to take effect from the date of entry into force of the agreements. Restrictions on access to government procurement markets are caught by this general provision, since they are measures equivalent to quantitative restrictions; thus exclusion of association states' products from E.C. public procurement, or any other discrimination against such products in procurement, is in principle prohibited. In addition, the Agreements specifically provide for companies from the association states to be given access to contract award procedures in the Community pursuant to Community procurement rules, under conditions no less favourable than Community companies.[68] This means, in effect, that companies from these states wishing to supply goods to E.C. governments – which will generally be goods from the association states themselves – can rely on the directives to obtain access, as well as on the general prohibition against discrimination. In return, E.C. companies are generally to be given access to award procedures in the association states within 10 years (or earlier if possible), the delay being designed to give industry in these states an opportunity to become competitive.[69] Community firms established in the association states, on the other hand, have immediate access.[70]

---

[65] See Council and Commission Decisions 93/742/Euratom, ECSC, E.C. [1993] O.J. L347 (approving the Europe Agreement with Hungary); 93/743/Euratom, ECSC, E.C. [1993] O.J. L348 (Poland); 94/907/Euratom, ECSC, E.C. [1994] O.J. L357/1 (Romania); 94/908/ Euratom, ECSC, E.C. [1994] O.J. L358/1 (Bulgaria); 94/909 Euratom, ECSC, E.C. (Slovak Republic) [1994] O.J. L359/1; 94/909/Euratom, ECSC, E.C. [1994] O.J [1994] O.J. L360/1 (Cezch Republic). The texts of the Agreements are published in the Official Journal attached to the relevant decisions. The Agreements express the parties' views that liberalisation in procurement should be brought within the GPA framework if possible.

[66] These were signed on June 5, 1995. Free trade agreements with these States came into force on January 1, 1995: see [1994] O.J. L373/2 (Estonia); [1994] O.J. L374/2 (Latvia); [1994] O.J. L375/2 (Lithuania).

[67] Article 9(4) of the Polish and Hungarian Agreement; Article 10(4) in the other Agreements. The provision covers all products listed in Chaps. 25 to 97 of the combined nomenclature, except for products listed in Annex I, and also textiles and ECSC products, which are subject to special arrangements.

[68] Article 66 of the Hungarian Agreement; Article 67 of the Polish Agreement; Article 68 of the other agreements. Article 48 of the Polish and Hungarian Agreements and Article 49 of the other agreements define Hungarian/Polish/Romanian/Bulgarian/Czech/Slovak companies as companies/firms set up in accordance with the law of that state, and which have either their central administration or principal place of business in that state, or have their registered office in that state, and also a "real and continuous link" with the economy of that country.

[69] Article 66 of the Hungarian Agreement; Article 67 of the Polish Agreement; Article 68 of the other agreements.

[70] Ibid.

It is not clear how the above provisions fit with the rules in Article 36 of the Utilities Directive, contained in regulation 21 of the Utilities Regulations, which provides for certain preferences for Community products, as explained below. The directive provides for the Council to disapply the preference rules for products from states which agree to give "comparable and effective" access to Community products in that sector. However, this does not apply to the association states since the Europe Agreement provisions do not provide for *immediate* Community access to contracts of these states.[71] Thus it would appear that amendment to the directive is required to give access to these states.[72] The reference in the Europe Agreements to Community treatment for firms from the association states suggests that the E.C. has an obligation to make such an amendment.

In relation to services, both Agreements provide for the Association Council to take, progressively, the measures necessary to open up markets between the Community, on the one hand, and the association states on the other.[73-74] So far as access to government procurement of services is concerned, companies may also rely on the provisions just discussed, giving access to contract award procedures. Thus, firms from the association states may, effectively, take advantage of the directives' rules in relation to provision of works and other services, as well as supplies and, again, may probably enforce these rules in the E.C. courts (whilst, as with goods, E.C. firms must wait for access to markets of those states, unless they are established there). However, it is expressly provided that this access is subject to the general provisions on freedom to provide services.[75-76] Thus, so long as general restrictions continue to exist on the cross-border provision of services between the Community and the association states, such restrictions will apply to public contracts as well as to other areas of the market.

(b) IMPLEMENTATION AND APPLICATION IN THE UNITED KINGDOM

As with its obligations under the EEA Agreement, to give effect to its obligations to apply to the association states the benefits of the Community directives the United Kingdom has included relevant provisions in United Kingdom implementing regulations.

As indicated above, it has been provided that these regulations are to

---

[71] Once the transitional period has expired, however, access is likely to be comparable and effective, since both states will have in effect legislative Codes prescribing fair and open award procedures for major procurements, similar to those of the E.C.

[72] The same would apply in relation to future measures giving access to developing states in order to aid their development.

[73-74] Article 55 of the Polish and Hungarian Agreements; Article 56 of the other agreements.

[75-76] Article 66 of the Hungarian Agreement; Article 67 of the Polish Agreement; Article 68 of the other agreements.

be enforceable not only by providers who are nationals of, and established in, Community states, but also by providers in other "relevant" states,[77] in accordance with the same remedies as apply to Community providers. "Relevant state" is defined in all four sets of regulations to include Hungary, Poland, the Czech Republic, the Slovak Republic, Bulgaria and Romania as well as the Community states and the states benefiting under the EEA Agreement (that is, Norway, Iceland and Liechtenstein).[78-79] In addition, similar adjustments have been made to the substantive provisions of the regulations as for the EEA states. For example, as indicated the rules on rejecting of providers who are not registered on domestic professional or trade registers have been adjusted to refer to the registers of all "relevant states"[80]; whilst the rules which benefit providers by allowing them to deduce evidence of registration on certain domestic lists to prove certain matters to United Kingdom authorities have been amended to include express recognition of "equivalent registers" of certain other relevant states and have also made express provision for the case where no register exists.[81-83] Should any new association agreements be concluded the definition of relevant state is likely to be extended to the new association states. In the meantime providers from these states may in any case enforce these rules since it appears that the procurement rules in the association agreements are directly applicable and have direct effect in the United Kingdom.

As indicated above, the association agreements impose obligations going beyond those in the Community directives themselves – for example, a general requirement not to discriminate against products from the association countries, which will apply to procurement both below and above the directives' thresholds. These obligations are also directly applicable and have direct effect and thus are enforceable in the United Kingdom courts. The one exception to this principle, however, appears to be the rule in the Utilities Directive and Regulations requiring and permitting preferences for Community products. An amendment to the directive appears necessary, as explained above, to disapply this for the association states, and in light of this it appears that to the extent that the Community preference rules apply the Europe Agreement obligations were not intended to have direct effect.

---

[77] Works Regulations 4(1), as amended by Supply Regulation 31(1), and Works Regulation 31(1); Supply Regulation 4(1); Services Regulation 4(1), as amended by Supply Regulation 32(1), and Services Regulation 32(1); Utilities Regulation 4(2).

[78-79] See the definition of "relevant state" in Works Regulation 2(1), as am. by Supply Regulation 31(1) and Utilities Regulation 35(1), and Works Regulation 4(1), as am. by Utilities Regulation 35(1); Supply Regulation 2(1) and 4(1), as am. by Utilities Regulation 35(1); Services Regulation 2(1), as am. by Supply Regulation 32(1) and Utilities Regulation 35(1) and Services Regulation 4(1), as am. by Utilities Regulation 35(1); Utilities Regulation 2(1) and 4(2).

[80] Works Regulation 14(1), as am. by Supply Regulation 31(1); Supply Regulation 14(1); and Services Regulation 14(1), as am. by Supply Regulation 32(1).

[81-83] Works Regulation 14(4), as am. by Supply Regulation 31(1); and Services Regulation 14(4), as am. by Supply Regulation 32(1).

(6) THE BILATERAL AGREEMENT WITH THE UNITED STATES[84]

In April 1993 the E.C. and U.S. concluded an agreement[85] providing for mutual access to all major central/federal government contracts, under which the E.C. extended access to the U.S. for such contracts based on the provisions of the directives. It also provided for mutual access to works and supply contracts in the electricity sector. From January 1, 1996, however, it was superseded by the new GPA to which the European Community and the United States are both party, as noted above. Some agreement had been reached between the two on the extent of mutual access under the GPA provisions when negotiations for the new GPA were first concluded in December 1993 including for procurement covered by the agreement reached in April 1993, but for many entities and sectors no satisfactory agreement had resulted. The parties then continued to negotiate for further coverage up until April 1994 when the WTO Agreement was formally signed, and at that time they concluded a further "bilateral" agreement on procurement.

This agreement has provided for some extensions to the coverage originally negotiated for the GPA. First, it provides for some opening of sub-federal procurement, which under the GPA as originally negotiated had not been opened up at all between the E.C. and U.S. The agreement on coverage in this field involves a "dollar for dollar" approach (that is, procurement of equal monetary value is opened up on each side). It involves the United States opening up the procurement of 37 state governments in accordance with the general principles of the GPA, for works, supplies and services, as well as some other concessions based on "out of state" or "out of city" treatment (where the Community is treated as favourably as industry from the United states outside the purchasing state or city, but not necessarily as favourably as local industry). The E.C. for its part will open up supply procurement for all sub-federal entities in the E.C. (which includes, for example, United Kingdom local authorities), but not works and services. Secondly, the agreement providers for substantial mutual liberalisation in the ports sector; and, thirdly, it provides for the opening up of services in the electricity sector (to add to the agreement on supplies and works reached earlier).

The Agreement also attempts generally to improve transparency, by providing for both sides to ensure that contract notices indicate clearly where the GPA applies to a procurement.

---

[84] See further Halford, "An Overview of E.C.–U.S. Relations in the Area of Public Procurement", (1995) 4 P.P.L.R. 35; Trepte, "The E.C.–United States Trade Dispute: Negotiation of a Partial Solution" (1993) 2 P.P.L.R. CS82; de Graaf, "The E.C.–United States Agreement on Government Procurement" (1994) 3 P.P.L.R. CS179.

[85] Approved by Council Decision 93/323/EEC, [1993] O.J. L125/1.

The agreements referred to above have provided a partial solution to ongoing difficulties between the two countries over access to procurement, which were rendered more serious following the E.C.'s adoption of a "Community preference" clauses in the Utilities Directive.[86] The E.C. continues to complain of "Buy America" restrictions on other contracts, and the U.S. about difficulties of access to E.C. utilities not covered by the WTO rules or the existing E.C.–U.S. bilateral agreement and, in particular, the utilities preference rules. Telecommunications services, in particular, are an important area of dispute in which agreement has so far proved impossible. The U.S. complaints have lead the U.S. to impose sanctions on Community industry under Title VII of the United States 1988 Omnibus Trade and Competitiveness Act. Not wishing to undermine the access agreements already concluded, the U.S. sanctions were confined to excluding Community industry from federal contracts not covered by existing agreements – that is, those of a low value. The Community has now imposed similar sanctions in retaliation under Regulation 1461/93.[86a] The Regulation applies to works, supplies and services contracts awarded by central government entities,[87] but only to supplies contracts below the thresholds of the current GPA, and to services and works contracts below the thresholds of the E.C. Directives (except in the case of contracts for services which are "non-priority" services under the Services Directive, to which the sanctions apply whatever the contract value). The sanctions require exclusion of all firms which are established in, and operating from, the United States. Thus, in contrast with the Community preference rules in Article 36 of the Utilities Directive, the measure addresses the position of the tenderer, rather than the origin of the products themselves. The sanctions were imposed before conclusion of the 1994 bilateral agreement, but remain in effect since that agreement did not resolve all differences.

3. THE POSITION WHERE NO AGREEMENTS APPLY

(1) INTRODUCTION

The agreements above provide for significant liberalisation of procurement on a reciprocal basis between the United Kingdom and other Community states, and their major trading partners. However, there will be cases where bidders (whether domestic or foreign) seek to offer to

---

[86] See pp. 781–790.
[86a] [1993] O.J. L146/1, as am. by Council Decision 1836/94, [1995] O.J. L183/4, extending sanctions to relevant contracts awarded by Austria, Sweden and Finland.
[87] Coverage is set out in Article 1 of the Regulation. Article 2 provides for exceptions for certain reasons of public interest.

the United Kingdom government and utilities products and services from outside the Community which are not covered by these agreements, as well as cases where participation is sought by firms from third countries who are unable to obtain the benefit of an agreement. This may arise either because the products, services or firm in question are from a state with which no agreement exists; or because the agreement with that state does not cover the procurement in question – for example, where a provider from a GPA state with whom there is no other agreement seeks to participate in a procurement below the GPA threshold.

In this section we will consider, first, the position of third country products and, secondly, the position of third country services.

(2) THIRD COUNTRY PRODUCTS

The position of products from third countries is relevant mainly to supply contracts, but also where products are provided in performing works or other services contracts – for example, products used in construction of a building. In practice, third country products will often be used in bids submitted by non-E.C. firms bidding from third countries. They are also common in bids submitted by E.C. subsidiaries of third country producers (such subsidiaries often being set up to provide easier access to E.C. markets), but may also be supplied by E.C. firms with no third country connection.

(a) THE RELEVANT LEGISLATIVE PROVISIONS

For contracts covered by the public sector procurement regulations there are no express provisions to deal with the treatment of third country products. The regulations do, however, prevent authorities from taking account of third country products through means of price preferences – for example, through a rule which would favour bids involving Community products where these are no more than 5 per cent more expensive than the most favourable bid. This arises from the fact that the rules on award criteria require that bids be evaluated on the basis of the lowest price or most economically advantageous offer criteria, which do not permit consideration of the origin of products as one of the award criteria.[88] Apart from this, there is nothing in the regulations themselves to stop authorities including provisions in the specifications of the contract that certain third country products should be excluded. The restrictions in the regulations do not, of course, affect contracts not covered by those regulations.

The Utilities Regulations contain express provisions on third country

---

[88] See further pp. 736–739.

products in Utilities Regulation 21. First, it is provided that utilities *may* in all cases, if they choose, reject third country offers – that is, those which offer products which originate more than 50 per cent in certain third countries. Secondly, it is stated that utilities *must* reject third country offers where the price advantage of these offers over the next best offer is less than 3 per cent (and the next best offer is equally advantageous in other ways). These provisions were considered in detail in the context of award procedures by utilities.[89] The provision was adopted in the original Utilities Directive, in 1990, at a time when the Community was negotiating for the inclusion of utilities within the GPA. It was anticipated that the practical effect of the E.C. Utilities Directive would be to open up Member States' markets to third countries as well as to other Member States, even though this was not an objective of the directive: in particular, the directive would be enforceable by all firms which are nationals of and established in the E.C., including E.C. subsidiaries of foreign firms.[90] As a result, it was envisaged that third countries would be unwilling to agree to measures for opening their own markets to the Community – they would have nothing to gain, since access to Community markets would already be available. Thus the main reason for including these provisions was to secure the Community's bargaining position in international negotiations and to ensure access to E.C. markets only on the basis of reciprocity. It would appear that these provisions are intended to exclude any scope for action by individual states against third country products in contracts covered by the regulations, except within the confines of these provisions.

Apart from these provisions, the only other main legislation relevant to third countries is section 17 of the Local Government Act 1988. This provision, which is considered in further detail in Chapter 16, prohibits local authorities from taking into account non-commercial considerations in the exercise of their procurement functions, and this includes a prohibition on consideration of the country or territory of origin of a provider's supplies. This was aimed at preventing authorities from discriminating against certain countries on political grounds, but will also apply should local authorities wish to act against third countries for trade reasons (although it is rather unlikely that such action would be taken at a local level).

---

[89] See pp. 511–513.

[90] The directive may also improve access to third country products in other ways. Thus the requirement to advertise in the *Official Journal* makes it easier for third country firms to find out about and bid on E.C. contracts; and the requirement to use European specifications may also assist third countries as well as suppliers from other member States, where European specifications correspond with international specifications (or simply because overseas firms find it worthwhile to manufacture to such specifications for the large European market). These considerations may benefit even firms which cannot enforce the directives, since in practice it is unlikely that utilities will normally wish to discriminate against them – now that it is not possible to discriminate in favour of *national industry*, purchasers will generally prefer to buy "best value".

This legislation imposes some limitations on the discretion of author-ities to discriminate against third country products, but does not curtail this freedom for all purchasers and for all contracts and in one case – the utilities preference rule – actually requires exclusion of certain third-country bids pursuant to Community policy. Thus it may appear there is still scope for the government or for individual purchasers to adopt discriminatory policies. However, this may not be the case, because of the effect, first, of the E.C. principle of free movement of goods and, secondly, because of the effect of Article 113 on the power of national authorities to adopt measures affecting trade in goods without authority from the E.C.

(b) THE IMPACT OF ARTICLE 30 E.C.

The first problem is the effect of Community rules on free movement of goods. For Member States these problems arise from Article 30 E.C., the scope of which was considered in Chapter 4. The difficulty arises from the fact that Article 30 applies not only to goods of Community origin, but to all goods in "free circulation" in the Community. A product generally enters into free circulation once it has complied with import formalities, and applicable import duties or equivalent charges have been paid[91]; and where it meets all requirements for its lawful marketing in the state of import (for example, it must comply with legal requirements on matters such as product safety). Thus, an American-made computer which has been legally imported, and complies with all requirements for sale on the Belgian market, is a product in free circulation; it is protected by Article 30, and the U.K. may not restrict its access to the U.K. market.

Since restrictions on access to public procurement fall under Article 30, it appears to follow that Member States are prevented from excluding such third country products from their own procurement.[92] Thus, it appears, U.K. entities could not refuse to purchase the American computer imported into Belgium because of its American origins. This does not prevent an authority from discriminating against third country products imported directly – for example, the government could (subject to relevant international agreements) refuse to purchase American computers imported through the U.K. since this does not affect trade in computers within the Community. However, such a policy could be evaded by suppliers of third country products by the simple

---

[91] Article 10 E.C.

[92] The need for Member States' measures in the procurement field to comply with Article 30 was recognised by the Council in its Resolutions of 1976 and 1980 on the subject of third country access to supply contracts, discussed in the text below; and it seems that the authorisation in those measures was intended to be confined, in so far as it concerned national measures restricting trade (as opposed, for example, to liberalisation agreements) to measures taken under an exception to Article 30 in Article 115, the scope.

expedient of offering products imported through other Member States.[93] Thus it appears impossible in practice for the United Kingdom government or purchasers to adopt a policy of discriminating against third country products.

The question arises as to whether the restrictions under Article 30 apply even where the policy in question is a policy authorised by the Community, as with the voluntary preference provisions in the Utilities Regulations which appear expressly to authorise utilities to discriminate in their purchasing. In fact, there is nothing to prevent Article 30 applying in such a case,[94] and it thus appears that the apparent authorisation of such discrimination in the directive may be invalid.

Finally, the question arises of the position of measures of common Community policy adopted by the Community itself pursuant to Article 113. The 3 per cent preference provision in the Utilities Directive is a measure of this kind. In principle the free movement of goods principle does bind the Community as well as Member States, which might suggest that the preference rule is unlawful. However, the principle does not impose on the Community exactly the same restrictions as on Member States.[95] Some of the cases indicate that the Community may adopt measures which restrict trade between states, where these measures apply in a uniform manner to all Member States and are designed to promote a general Community interest.[96] Thus the Court of Justice may develop a concept of Community interest, which justifies restrictions on trade being imposed by the Community institutions, similar to the concept of mandatory requirements, which justify restrictive measures by Member States to protect certain national interests. Liberalisation of trade is stated in the Treaty as an objective of Community policy, and arguably an exception to the usual free movement principle might be made for a measure such as Article 36 of the Utilities Directive, provided that it can be shown that this seeks to promote the goal of liberalisation and is not merely protectionist in nature.[97] However, it is far from clear that the Court would take this view and it may prefer to give priority to the application of the free movement principle, and thus hold that the preference rule is invalid.[98]

---

[93] The authority could not avoid this by insisting that the product supplied should be imported through the U.K. - this would constitute a restriction on trade contrary to Article 30 E.C.

[94] There is an exception under Article 115 E.C. for national measures seeking to prevent deflection of trade caused by different national policies, provided that these measures are authorised by the Community. However, it does not appear that this can be used to authorise discrimination against third country products in procurement: see Arrowsmith, "Third Country Access to E.C. Public Procurement: an Analysis of the Legal Framework" (1995) 4 P.P.L.R. 1, pp.13–16.

[95] For discussion of the case law generally see Oliver, *Free Movement of Goods in the EEC* (2nd ed., 1988) 4.08–4.19.

[96] Case 46/76, *Bauhuis v. Netherlands* [1977] E.C.R. 5; Case 10/73, *REWE-Zentral v HZA Kehl* [1973] E.C.R. 1175.

[97] See further Arrowsmith, above, note 1, pp.19–20.

[98] This view is taken by Eeckhout, above, note 1.

If the Court takes this approach the Community could make it more difficult for third country products to obtain access to Community markets only by restricting the access of firms likely to supply such products, and not by restricting access of the products as such. This is the approach adopted in applying sanctions against the United States, as explained earlier: these operate by excluding United States firms, not United States products, and thus there is no danger of infringing Article 30. More generally, participation could be limited to firms which are nationals of and established in the Community, with a real link with the Community economy: this would "eliminate the submission of tenders by mere mailbox subsidiaries"[99]. Such an approach would not, however, be as effective as a policy which operates against third country products directly, since such products could still be supplied by firms meeting the above criteria.

(c) THE IMPACT OF ARTICLE 113 E.C.

A second difficulty, which applies to national policies which discriminate against third country products, is that policy on third country products is in principle a matter for the Community under Article 113 E.C. It has been explained that where the Community enjoys powers over external trade under Article 113 E.C., Member States no longer have any power to act, even if the Community itself has not yet exercised its powers and established a common policy. On this basis it is arguable that E.C. Member States no longer have the power to discriminate against third country products in procurement, unless authorised by the Community. This will apply at least where the action is taken for trade reasons, although there may be debate over action taken for non-trade reasons – for example, where procurement is used to put pressure on another state in the context of a human rights dispute.[1]

At present, there are two E.C. measures which may give authority to adopt measures against third countries. One is Article 36(2) of the Utilities Directive permitting discrimination against third country offers in contracts covered by the Utilities Directive, which has already been considered above. The other is a 1980 Council Resolution concerning public supply contracts. This was first adopted by the Council in 1976 during the negotiations for the original GATT Agreement on Government Procurement and was superseded by a second Resolution adopted in 1980 following the entry into force of that Agreement.[2] Accession to the GATT Agreement on Procurement GPA constitutes a measure of

---

[99] Eeckhout, above, note 1, p. 314.

[1] See Arrowsmith, above, note 1 on p. 765, pp. 2–4.

[2] Council Resolution of December 21, 1976, [1977] O.J. C11/1, concerning access to Community supply contracts for products originating in non-member countries; and Council Resolution of July 22, 1980, [1980] O.J. C211, concerning access to Community public supply contracts for products originating in third countries.

common policy in relation to third countries which are signatory to the Agreement, but the Council was aware in 1980 that, as noted above, no common policy was in place in relation to non-signatory states.[3] The Resolution recognises a need for such a common policy and calls upon the Commission to make proposals to this end. It also provides, however, that in the meantime, Member States may continue to apply *existing* measures of commercial policy in respect of public supply contracts. This appears to authorise states to continue with existing measures relating to use of third country products in supply contracts (though not, illogically, works or services contracts); this could include measures involving direct discrimination against such products.[4] The scope of the authorisation is open to debate; in particular, it is unclear whether it would cover only actual measures of discrimination in existence in 1980, or would allow new acts of discrimination. If the latter is the case, however, it might be relied upon by United Kingdom entities which seek to discriminate.

Where no authority to discriminate is given under these provisions it is arguable, as suggested above, that no discrimination is permitted without seeking a specific authorisation, at least where such measures are motivated by trade considerations. If such an authorisation were to be sought – for example, if the United Kingdom were to seek authority to exclude products of a particular state because of a trade or other dispute with that state – it is likely that the Community would prefer to deal with the matter on a Community level, rather than authorising unilateral action.

The importance of the rules on Community authorisation depend on the impact of Article 30 E.C. If, as was argued above, the Community may not authorise conduct which contravenes Article 30 E.C., then the rules discussed in this section are of little significance.

(3) THIRD COUNTRY SERVICES AND SERVICE PROVIDERS

(a) THE RELEVANT LEGISLATION

The public sector directives and implementing regulations do not contain specific provisions on services originating in third countries.[5] As with goods, the rules on award criteria do prevent the operation of any

---

[3] Nor, indeed, was there any common policy in relation to products supplied under contracts not covered by the agreement, such as small contracts, and contracts for works and services.

[4] On this see also Eeckhout, *The European Internal Market and International Trade* (1994), pp.302–303.

[5] It was originally proposed to include in the Services Directive a provision similar to that on exclusion of third country service providers which is contained in the Utilities Directive, as discussed in the text below; but this was eventually omitted.

preference policies since bids must be evaluated solely on the basis of lowest price or most advantageous offer, and this does not allow consideration of the third country content of the offer. However, there is nothing in the regulations themselves to prohibit purchasers from including prohibitions on services of third country origin. So far as third country providers are concerned the right to invoke the directives is apparently limited to Community providers and others benefiting from the rules under international agreements.[6]

The issue of third country access was, however, addressed in the Utilities Directive as it was in the case of goods. Whilst it was concluded that specific provisions for excluding third countries were not appropriate since access of third country service providers did not pose the same threat as access of third country products,[7] it was decided to include, in Article 37 of the Utilities Directive, a provision for excluding certain third countries in the future, should it be determined that they did not provide reciprocal access for E.C. industry. The Article provides for the Commission to make proposals to the Council for action against third countries when it establishes that, in relation to services contracts,[8] one of the following conditions apply. The first will be the most common basis of action in practice.

(i) That Community undertakings do not enjoy "national treatment" or "the same competitive opportunities as are available to national undertakings".[9] This is a normal minimum requirement for reciprocal access arrangements, and forms the main basis of most arrangements – as for example, between the Member States of the E.C. under the Treaty.

(ii) That third country undertakings receive treatment more favourable than Community undertakings.[10] Thus, even if E.C. firms are treated as well as national firms, the Commission may propose action if firms from other countries are given privileges above those enjoyed by national firms. This is unlikely in practice.

(iii) That Community undertakings do not enjoy "effective access comparable to that granted by the Community to undertakings from that country".[11] This will apply where Community firms are given national treatment, but opportunities for both national firms and Community firms are rather limited. For example, a third country may not offer any

---

[6] See pp. 766–787.

[7] In the original proposal for a Utilities Directive, covering works and supplies contracts, the Commission proposed that the "third country" rules, which *inter alia* authorise Member States entities to exclude third country tenders, should apply to the works and services content of works and supplies contracts as well as the supply content and had such a provision been included it would doubtless have been applied to non-works services contracts also, when the Directive was extended to cover these in 1993. However, the third country provision was eventually confined to products only.

[8] The provision does not apply to works contracts, nor supply contracts (although non-construction services are often provided under supply contracts).

[9] Utilities Directive, Article 37(3)(b).

[10] Utilities Directive, Article 37(3)(c).

[11] Utilities Directive, Article 37(3)(a).

access to private firms because all work is done "in-house". If such work were generally contracted out in the Community access is not "comparable" to that which exists in the Community, nor "effective".

Where one of these conditions is satisfied, the Commission may propose:

(i) To suspend or restrict the award of services contracts to undertakings governed by the law of the third country. As indicated above, such firms are, by definition, not E.C. nationals and hence are not covered by Article 59 E.C.

(ii) To suspend or restrict the award of services contracts to undertakings affiliated to those governed by the law of a third country, which have their registered office in the Community but no direct and effective link with the economy of a Member State. As already explained, the links which such firms have with third countries may cause them to "import" services, so that despite their E.C. nationality, there is no benefit to the E.C. economy. These firms we have also seen are not protected by Article 59 E.C.

(iii) To suspend or restrict the award of services contracts in respect of tenders which have as their object services originating in the third country concerned. This provision concentrates on the nature of the service rather than the nature of the service provider – an approach similar to Article 36 of the Utilities Directive on third country products. This provision is useful in the situation where the Community economy is damaged as a result of firms which are E.C. firms under Article 59 E.C. providing services of third country origin. Its application will, however, involve the difficult question of how the origin of services is to be determined.[12]

Although it is for the Commission to propose action, it is for the Council to decide – by a qualified majority – whether to take action.[13] There is an obligation on Member States to inform the Commission about any difficulties – legal or factual – which their own undertakings encounter in obtaining access to service contracts in third countries.[14]

The exercise of this power, like the preference rules in Article 36, is without prejudice to the Community's obligations.[15] It should also be noted that where problems arise the Commission has a duty to negotiate

---

[12] The provision on third country services which was included in the original Utilities Directive provided for exclusion of offers where over half the price represented the value of products manufactured outside the Community or "services performed outside the Community", or a combination thereof. The value of services performed outside the Community was stated to include "the value of all activity performed on the territory of third countries that contribute to the rendering of the services covered by the contract" (proposed Article 24(4)(b)).

[13] Utilities Directive, Article 37(4). Once a proposal has been made, the Council is required to act "as soon as possible". The period of any suspension or restriction referred to is to be determined by a Council decision.

[14] Utilities Directive, Article 37(1).

[15] Utilities Directive, Article 37(5). The Commission may take action on its own initiative or on the suggestion of Member States: Article 37(4).

with the third country concerned to achieve a remedy.[16] However, there is no express provision to bar a suspension or restriction of access, as detailed above, whilst negotiations take place.

It is submitted that Article 37 lays down, by implication, a common policy for the Community in the field of its application, and implies that third countries shall not be excluded *except* in accordance with its provisions: it signals the Community's clear intention to deal with discrimination against individual Member States on a Community-wide basis, and as such it must surely also be intended to remove any power of Member States to take independent action.

For local authorities the prohibition on non-commercial considerations under the Local Government Act 1988 may again be relevant, as with goods, since section 17(5)(e) provides that local authorities may not take account of the location or territory of a provider's business.

(b) THE IMPACT OF THE FREE MOVEMENT PROVISIONS

In the context of third country products it was noted that the free movement of goods principle under Article 30 E.C. appears to provide an obstacle to the exclusion of third country products from government contracts. So far as service providers are concerned, it can be noted that there is nothing in the Treaty to prevent exclusion of providers from third countries. However, under Article 59 E.C. all providers who are nationals of the Community must be admitted to Community contracts and this will include Community providers who are owned by third country nationals. These firms, as well as Community owned firms, may sometimes wish to provide services which originate in third countries. This raises the question of whether measures may be adopted which exclude services of third country origin, regardless of who provides such services. Could a purchasing authority insist that all the activity relating to its services contracts be carried out within the E.C.? The answer to this question is not clear. Certainly such a measure would restrict the ability of firms to provide services in other Member States. However, such a measure would be equally applicable to domestic service providers and to those from other Member States and does not tend indirectly to favour domestic providers; and, although some restrictions of this kind appear to be within Article 59 (and hence prohibited unless specifically justified) it is unclear whether all restrictions of this type will be caught. It is submitted that the Court ought not to bring a non-discriminatory restriction relating to the origin of services within Article 59; but it is difficult to predict the approach which the Court will take.[17] If such a restriction *is* within Article 59, it is unlikely to be capable of justification, since it relates to an economic objective.

---

[16] Utilities Directive, Article 37(3).
[17] Certain non-discriminatory restrictions are caught by Article 59: see Chap. 4.

(c) THE IMPACT OF ARTICLE 113

To the extent that the power to discriminate against third country services and providers is not curtailed by the directives, by domestic legislation or by the Treaty's free movement provisions, it may also be affected if access to procurement services markets is covered by Article 113. As was noted earlier, it is not clear how far this is the case. To the exent that Article 113 does cover services procurement, then policy in this field will be an issue exclusively for the Community and, as with goods, it is submitted that states may not discriminate against third countries, at least not for trade reasons. However, if Article 113 does not apply, Member States retain the power to develop their own policies in this field until such time as the Community chooses to adopt common measures, and thus States will remain free to discriminate.

CHAPTER 16

INDUSTRIAL AND SOCIAL CONCERNS IN PUBLIC PROCUREMENT[1]

1. INTRODUCTION

The "primary" objective of a procurement may be defined as the acquisition of goods or services fulfilling a particular function on the best possible terms.[2] Most questions surrounding a procurement are concerned with this objective. However, the exercise of procurement power is also affected by industrial, social or political concerns – "secondary" factors – which are unconnected with this primary objective. For example, the choice of provider may be influenced by the desire to support domestic industry; the government may promote social objectives by contracting only with firms which comply with policies such as the provision of fair employment opportunities for minorities; or it may monitor a provider during the performance of a contract to ensure compliance with environmental or labour standards. This concern with economic and social issues in procurement is not unique to government: for example, some private individuals do not purchase from firms from states of which they disapprove or from firms with a poor record on environmental issues. However, such secondary factors have been of particular importance in the public sector or sectors subject to government influence, because of the government's special concern for social and economic matters, and because of its ability to harness and co-ordinate such a considerable purchasing power in pursuit of social and industrial objectives.

The first part of this chapter explains the way in which procurement may be affected by such secondary concerns, with particular reference to

---

[1] See also Arrowsmith, "Public Procurement as a Tool of Policy and the Impact of Market Liberalisation" (1995) 111 L.Q.R. 237, on which some of the material in this chapter is based.

[2] This division into primary and secondary objectives assumes the prior existence of decisions concerning the levels of purchasing, and the type of goods and services to be acquired. Of course, these prior decisions themselves may also be influenced by considerations going beyond the simple acquisition of goods and services to fulfil a specified function. In particular, overall expenditure decisions are influenced by macroeconomic considerations, such as their potential impact on general economic development and growth. Individual purchasing decisions may also be made on the basis of social and economic considerations. For example, a decision to undertake a particular project may be justified not merely by virtue of the need of the public for the project but also on the basis of its contribution to employment in a depressed region, and in this case job creation might be seen as, in some sense, a "primary" or foremost objective of the procurement.

practices in the United Kingdom, and the constitutional concerns raised by such activity. The remainder of the chapter examines the legal provisions which regulate the powers of governments and utilities in this field. These now significantly limit the extent to which secondary objectives may be considered.

2. THE USE OF PROCUREMENT TO PROMOTE INDUSTRIAL AND SOCIAL OBJECTIVES

(1) PRACTICE IN THE UNITED KINGDOM

Procurement has traditionally been an important tool of national industrial policy. Its significance arises from a number of factors: the sheer size of the markets of government (and sectors subject to government influence); the high dependence on government orders of certain industrial sectors, which makes them especially susceptible to government action; and the technological importance of these markets, particularly in the defence and utilities sectors.

The United Kingdom has never adopted a comprehensive "Buy National" policy, unlike the United States, where there has been a federal "Buy American" policy since the Buy American Act of 1933.[3] In a study published in 1972, however, Hindley concluded that "although the extent of the bias is difficult to determine, there is no doubt that discrimination against foreign sellers is an important element in British procurement policy".[4] This was particularly apparent in the nationalised industries, including the utilities (which are some of the most technologically advanced and economically important sectors[5]), and also in defence purchasing until the 1980s.[6] Alongside a general preference for national industry, there are also many past examples of strategies aimed at development of particular sectors, such as telecommunications, pharmaceuticals and the computer industry. Procurement was also used from the 1930s until 1991 to support depressed regions. Under the "General Preference Scheme" government bodies were encouraged to let contracts to firms in development areas, provided, however, they offered value for money; whilst the Special Preference Scheme provided that where supplies tenders from firms in these areas equalled others in all but price, firms in these areas should be permitted 25 per cent of an order provided the price was lowered. A scheme in Northern Ireland

---

[3] For an overview see Greenwold and Cox, "The Legal and Structural Obstacles to Free Trade in the U.S. Procurement Market" (1993) 2 P.P.L.R. 237.
[4] Hindley, *Britain's Position on Non-Tariff Protection* (London, 1972), p.21.
[5] Baldwin, *Non-tariff Distortions of International Trade*, Chap. 3, p.65.
[6] See further pp. 850–854.

provided for a 5 per cent price preference for bids benefiting employ-ment in Northern Ireland. The government has also sometimes sought to place contracts strategically in order to maintain competition in a particular sector, and thus to ensure that value will be preserved by the effects of a competitive market in the future.[7]

Industrial policies have also been implemented by international institutions such as the European Space Agency (ESA), which places research and development contracts relating to the use and exploration of space for civil purposes.[8] Indeed collaborative projects, which are generally prompted by the need to share costs in areas of high technology, are the very kind of projects likely to be important for industrial development. Not surprisingly, organisations such as ESA have a carefully formulated industrial policy.[9] More specifically, the ESA Convention provides that members' industry is to be given preference over that of non-members, and that members are to participate in an equitable manner with regard to their contribution to the Agency's programmes.[10] This principle of "fair returns" has been applied with increasing stringency, since states' willingness to participate has become increasingly dependent on the guarantee of industrial benefits.[11-12] Industrial development concerns have also generally been prominent in collaborative projects in the defence field.

The policies above have all involved domestic preference or strategic placing of contracts, but this is generally no longer possible because of limitations imposed by European Community law and the World Trade Organisation Agreement on Government Procurement (GPA), and such policies are thus generally no longer pursued within the United King-

---

[7] This policy is emphasised again recently in the White Paper, *Setting New Standards: a Strategy for Government Procurement* (1995) Cm 2840 (see especially paras. 3.13–3.15); but it is doubtful if this is permitted for contracts covered by the E.C. procurement directives: see further Chap. 16.

[8] Other members are Austria, Belgium, Denmark, Germany, Ireland, Italy, the Nether-lands, Norway, Sweden and Switzerland. Finland has Associate status. There is also collaboration with states outside Europe notably Canada, the United States, Russia and Japan. ESA is concerned only with research and development contracts, and not with the procurement of equipment once developed. On procurement in ESA see Kahn, "Advanced Technology Projects and International Procurement: the Case of the European Space Agency" (1993) 2 P.P.L.R. 13.

[9] The development of an industrial policy is one of ESA's objectives: ESA Convention, Article II d.

[10] Article VII. The "fair returns" principle is also dealt with in more detail in Annex V, Article IV. The detailed application of the principle is determined by guidelines set at ESA Council meetings.

[11-12] The ESA Convention itself provides for proposals for measures to rectify any imbalance once a State's "return co-efficient" (its percentage share of all contracts awarded, divided by its percentage share of all contributions) falls to 0.8 or below (1 being the ideal figure); this figure has been steadily adjusted upwards, and the 1994–96 threshold set at the 1993 Council meeting in Granada now stands at 9.6. For recent developments in the policy see unpublished ESA paper by Morel de Westgaver and Imbert, "Fair Return: Constraint or Means to European Integration?"; European Space Agency Industrial Policy Committee, "Introduction to deliberations on industrial policy following the Granada ministerial Council meeting", ESA/IPC (93)51.

dom. These restrictions do not cover military equipment and some states have continued to use procurement in this area to pursue industrial objectives. As is explained in Chapter 17 on defence procurement, the United Kingdom has since 1983 generally preferred a commercial approach and has eschewed strategic use of procurement, although there are some recent signs that there may be a swing back to a more strategic approach.[13]

The requirements for open and competitive procurement under the European Community and GPA rules are, of course, themselves rules of industrial policy which seek to promote industrial efficiency, although on a Europe-wide or world-wide basis rather than at national level.[14] In addition, there are still ways in which national governments can use procurement to enhance their own industrial development, which do not involve discrimination. For example, ensuring that specifications are drafted by reference to recognised standards or by reference to performance requirements can improve the competitiveness of industry.[15] Measures can also be taken to encourage or facilitate participation in government contracts by small businesses[16] and this is a policy pursued in the United Kingdom although such businesses are not given any preferential treatment. Even where contracts are open to foreign firms, such policies largely benefit domestic industry, which will win most contracts even under open competition. In both these areas – efficient use of standards and the promotion of smaller firms – the Community itself has also played a role as an aspect of its own industrial policy, as explained in Chapter 3.[17]

Governments can also use contract power to induce compliance with regulatory policies aimed at industrial objectives, one illustration being the "blacklisting" in the 1970s of providers who failed to comply with guidelines on wage settlements.[18] Procurement is also currently used to support initiatives relating to late payment of debts. The government has pledged itself to measures to tackle this problem[19] and has already taken

---

[13] See pp. 850–854.

[14] On the way in which such rules aim to promote industrial development see pp. 45–50.

[15] See Turpin, *Government Procurement and Contracts* (1989) at 67–68; *Competitiveness: Helping business to win* (1994) Cm. 2563, pp.154–158.

[16] On U.K. small firms policy see Turpin, above, p.75. This policy is currently under review with a view to improvement: see *Competitiveness: Helping business to win*, above, at p.158 and Department of Trade and Industry Consultation Paper, *Review of Government Procurement from Small and Medium Enterprises* (1994).

[17] See further pp. 66–71.

[18] See further Ferguson and Page, "Pay Restraint: the Legal Constraints" (1978) 128 New Law Journal 515; Ganz, [1978] P.L. 333 (comment); Daintith, "Legal Analysis of Economic Policy" (1982) 9 Journal of Law and Society 191; Daintith, "Regulation by Contract: the New Prerogative" [1979] 32 C.L.P. 41.

[19] Proposals include developing a British Standard for prompt payment, requiring large companies to publish information on payment performance, and improved procedures for debt recovery: *Competitiveness: Helping business to win*, above, p.106. The possibility of legislation for interest on late payments, considered in a DTI consultative document, *Late Payment of Commercial Debt* (Nov. 1993), and favoured by many, will be put on hold for two years to see if the new measures work.

measures to secure prompt payment in its own projects and encourage the private sector by example.[20] Thus prompt payment is required from government departments, and from 1993–94 details on this have been provided in their reports. In addition, contract clauses require prompt payment of subcontractors, whether or not the main contractor has himself been paid.

Procurement decisions have also frequently been influenced by social and political concerns. Two of the main areas linked with procurement have been equal opportunities and fair working conditions, but purchasing decisions have been influenced by a wide range of policies. For example, when use of procurement as a policy tool became popular with local government in the 1980s, many authorities refused to deal with providers who had business dealings in South Africa, and/or refused to oallow South African materials to be used in contracts, whilst others refused to contract with firms which had been engaged in civil or military nuclear work.[21] The pursuit of such controversial policies was one significant factor in the government's decision to substantially outlaw the pursuit of secondary policies under the Local Government Act 1988, which is considered further below.[22]

As mentioned, one area in which procurement has been invoked is that of equal opportunities for disadvantaged groups, including women, ethnic and religious minorities and the disabled, and it has been used extensively in these areas in the United States.[23] However, in the United Kingdom such measures have been much more limited and sporadic.

In relation to opportunities for women and ethnic minorities, "contract compliance" policies have been pursued by a number of local authorities. The most serious attempt was a joint endeavour of the Greater London Council and Inner London Education Authority,[24] instituted in 1983. The policy required that providers should not merely refrain from unlawful acts of discrimination against these groups, but should implement practices which give fair access to employment,[25] based on personnel practices in the Codes issued by the Commission for Racial Equality and the Equal Opportunities Commission. Firms were required, for example, to demonstrate a fair recruitment policy; to devise

---

[20] See further Arrowsmith, "The United Kingdom Government Policy on Prompt Payment of Government Contractors and Sub-contractors" (1993) P.P.L.R. CS124 and also *Setting New Standards: a Strategy for Government Procurement* (1995) Cm. 2840, at 7.13–7.14 and also the statement of good practice at p.41.

[21] For details of the application of such policies in the 1980s see Institute of Personnel Management, *Contract Compliance: the United Kingdom Experience* (London 1987) esp. p.29.

[22] See pp. 830–845.

[23] See Institute of Personnel Managment, above, pp.7–12; Carr, *New Roads to Equality: Contract Compliance for the United Kingdom* (Fabian Society no. 517).

[24] See further, ILEA Contract Compliance Equal Opportunities Unit, *Contract Compliance: a Brief History* (London 1990); Institute of Personnel Management, *Contract Compliance: the United Kingdom Experience* (1987), pp.27–28; Carr, above, p.10–16.

[25] See, in particular, "Contract Compliance and Equal Opportunities" IR-RR December 2, 1986 p.3.

fair and open procedures and criteria for promotion; to establish and publicise procedures for dealing with complaints of discrimination and harassment; and to provide training on equal opportunities. The policies were vigorously enforced by special compliance units. Compliance was established by requiring firms admitted to "approved" lists to fill in a questionnaire and through detailed reviews of the practices of selected listed contractors and those involved in performing major contracts.[26] The approach was conciliatory; the emphasis was on encouraging contractors to comply and providing advice, rather than on sanctions of termination of contracts or debarment, although some firms who refused to co-operate were ultimately debarred.[27] The experiment inspired a number of other authorities and by 1986 19 authorities had contract compliance units.[28] A number continue to use contract in the equal opportunities field, but such policies are now much less effective as a result of legal restrictions arising from European Community law and from the Local Government Act 1988, as explained below.

The central government, on the other hand, has not made any serious attempt to use its procurement contracts to combat race and gender discrimination. Since 1969 a term has been inserted into contracts requiring providers to refrain from unlawful racial discrimination and to take reasonable steps to ensure that their servants, agents and sub-contractors observe this requirement, but there have been no attempts to monitor compliance and it does not appear that sanctions have ever been imposed.[29] There is no equivalent clause to require firms to observe the law on gender discrimination.

The government has, however, used procurement to support its policy for combatting religious discrimination in Northern Ireland under the Fair Employment (Northern Ireland) Acts of 1976 and 1989, and associated orders. This legislation, as well as prohibiting direct and indirect religious discrimination, imposes obligations designed to secure fair employment opportunities regardless of religious belief. It requires public sector employers and many in the private sector to register with the Fair Employment Commission and to monitor the composition of their workforce and (with firms having over 250 employees) job applications, and to make an annual report on this to the Commission. Firms must also engage in a periodic review of employment practices, and where imbalances are revealed must take steps to correct them. Where appropriate, the Commission may seek an undertaking that action will

---

[26] On enforcement and implementation see, in particular, "Contract Compliance Assessed" *Equal Opportunities Review* no. 31 May/June 1990, p.26; Carr, above, pp.13–16.

[27] For example, the first annual report of the Unit stated that 9 works contractors and 13 suppliers had been excluded Reported in "Contract Compliance and Equal Opportunities", above, at p.5.

[28] Figures from a survey on contract compliance carried out by the Association of Authorities in 1986; cited in *Contract Compliance: the United Kingdom Experience*, p.16.

[29] This was the position in 197 according to Carr, above, p.9.

be taken; if it is refused, or there is a breach of an undertaking, it may give directions.[30] The Commission may enforce its directions and any undertaking given through the Fair Employment Tribunal for Northern Ireland,[31] which, in case of non-compliance may impose a financial penalty, or certify the matter to be dealt with by the High Court as if there had been a breach of a High Court order.[32] Firms which fail to register[33] or to submit proper returns[34] are also subject to criminal penalties.

Disqualification from participation in government contracts is a further sanction,[35] governed by the legislation itself.[36] This provides for the Fair Employment Commission to make a disqualification order[37] against those convicted of an offence for failing to register or provide returns, or who have been subject to a penalty for failing to comply with an order of the Tribunal or High Court,[38] as well as against certain persons connected with them.[39] The effect is to debar the party who is subject to the order from consideration for contracts awarded by Northern Ireland Government Departments.[40] The Commission is obliged to bring any order to the attention of the relevant authorities,[41] which are prohibited from contracting with the party subject to the order and in some cases must also take "all reasonable steps" to ensure that no work is done on the contract by a disqualified party.[42] There is, however, no provision for terminating existing contracts.

Procurement has also been used to secure fair working conditions, both directly, for those working for government providers, and indirectly, by providing a model for the private sector. This use of procurement is covered by International Labour Organisation Convention No. 94,[43] which provides for inclusion of labour clauses in contracts of central government (except for those for standard supplies) and also in those of other public agencies where so extended by the ratifying state.[44] Such labour clauses are to provide for wages, hours of work and other

---

[30] Fair Employment (Northern Ireland) Act 1989 (hereafter the FEA), ss. 12–14.
[31] FEA, s.16.
[32] FEA, s.17(1) and (3).
[33] FEA, s.23(5) and s.24(2).
[34] FEA, s.27(5) and s.28(2)(f)(i).
[35] There is also provision for denying government financial assistance to firms which do not comply: see FEA, s.43.
[36] FEA, ss.37–42.
[37] FEA, s.38(2).
[38] FEA, s.38(1).
[39] FEA, s.39.
[40] For the authorities covered see FEA, s.25 and Fair Employment (Specification of Public Authorities) Order 1989 (1989 No. 475), and the Fair Employment (Specification of Public Authorities) Amendment Orders 1990 and 1993 (1990 No. 453 and 1993 No. 4).
[41] FEA, s.38(3).
[42] FEA, s.41(4).
[43] See Nielsen, "Public Procurement and International Labour Standards" (1995) 4 P.P.L.R. 94.
[44] Article 1. It is envisaged that this will apply only to contracts above certain thresholds, which are set by states themselves.

"conditions of labour" for employees of providers on government contracts which are no less favourable than those established – by collective bargaining or other recognised mechanism, or by law or arbitration award – for work of the same character in the relevant trade or industry in the district where the work is carried out.[45] The clauses are to be incorporated as contractual obligations[46] and adequate sanctions are to be provided,[47] a suggestion – though not a requirement – being withholding of contracts.

In the United Kingdom a policy in this area was first formalised within central government in 1891 in a House of Commons "Fair Wages Resolution",[48] and was extended and developed until 1983, when it was finally abandoned by the Conservative government.[49] This first Resolution, adopted in response to investigations and a public outcry over the conditions of "sweated" labour,[50] was concerned mainly with wages, providing that in letting contracts departments should "make every effort to secure the payment of wages at a level generally accepted as current for a competent workman in his trade". This was extended thereafter to include, from 1909 hours of work, and 1946, other working conditions. The 1946 Resolution also embraced the recognition of a worker's right to join a trades union, and provided for reference to be made to collective agreements in determining "acceptable" working conditions. It sought to protect all those employed by government providers, and in 1909 was extended to require contractors to ensure the conditions were applied to those working for subcontractors as well as to their own workforce. The earlier Resolutions provided for labour conditions for those engaged on government work which were more favourable than those required under the general law.[51] The Resolutions purported to apply only to those actually engaged on government work. However, in practice it is difficult for firms to adopt different practices for different groups of workers, and the Fair Wages Committee, set up to advise on the Resolutions, suggested that payment of low wages on private work might justify debarring a provider, although not covered by the Resolutions.

---

[45] Article 2.

[46] Article 2.

[47] Article 5.

[48] A practice of including Fair Wages clauses in government contracts had been adopted even before this in relation to works and maintenance contracts by the Office of Works.

[49] For a detailed account see Bercusson, *The Fair Wages Resolutions* (1978). On the legal issues see also Kahn-Freund, "Legislation through Adjudication: the Legal Aspects of Fair Wages Clauses and Recognised Conditions" (1948) 11 M.L.R. 274.

[50] For a history see Bercusson, above. Chap. 1.

[51] However, protection similar to that provided under the resolutions effectively operated from 1940 for many other workers as a result first of war time legislation and later of the development of the general law on collective bargaining: on this see Bercusson, p. 247.

Ultimately the government extended the protection provided for its own contracts by providing for the application of the Fair Wages Resolutions as a condition of certain grants and subsidies: for example, under the Independent Broadcasting Act 1973, Films Act 1960, Public Passenger Vehicles Act 1981, Housing Act 1957. Health authorities and nationalised industries were also later encouraged to follow the resolutions.

The policy was largely ineffective, however, because of inadequate enforcement.[52] There was no centralised policy; enforcement was left to individual departments, who relied almost wholly on the complaints of individuals, who were unaware of their rights. Enforcement was also hampered by a lack of sanctions. Compliance was required as a contract condition, often with an express right of termination for breach, but this was not exercised in practice, because of the inconvenience and also the possible legal difficulties, given the vagueness of the policy's requirements.[53] Debarment was rare, and the effectiveness of this sanction hampered by disputes between departments on whether a particular provider was in breach. Further, the courts ruled that the provisions could not be enforced by providers' employees[54] and the government often did not compel providers to make back-payments to workers who had been underpaid. The Fair Wages Resolutions were abandoned with effect from 1983, and the ILO Convention (which the government had formerly ratified) denounced at the same time. Subsequent policy has been to leave conditions to the free market – although this policy is now affected by the Community's "Acquired Rights Directive", as is explained in Chapter 12.[55]

Local authorities often followed similar policies until enactment of the Local Government Act 1988: by 1982 over 87 per cent of authorities had adopted some policy on conditions for those working on procurement contracts.[56] Some authorities also included contractual provisions on the right of providers' employees to join a trade union and several actually required use of unionised labour.[57] Procurement power was also used to impose or encourage standards on other employment-related issues such as training (for example, requiring firms to adopt a training policy and to pay levies to the relevant industry training board)[58] or the use of labour-only subcontracting.[59] All these policies are now affected by the 1988 Act and other legal provisions.

---

[52] See generally Bercusson, above; Chap. 4 and pp.136–146, from which the following summary is taken.

[53] A problem avoided in some works contracts by including schedules specifying the wages to be paid.

[54] *Simpson v. Kodak* [1948] 2 KB 104, where the court rejected the argument that the terms were to be implied in a contract between employer and employee.

[55] See pp. 636–648.

[56] M. Ingham and A. Thomson, *Dimensions of Industrial Relations in Local Authorities* (1982), Table 5A.

[57] The latter type of provision was made unlawful generally (that is, not just in the public sector) under the 1982 Employment Act, s. 12. Between 1927 and 1946 requirements for contractors to employ union labour (or non-union labour) were unlawful for public bodies only: s.6(2) Trade Disputes and Trade Union Act 1927. Such policies are now prohibited by the general provisions of the 1988 Local Government Act, discussed below at pp. 830–845.

[58] See Institue of Personnel Management, above note 21, pp. 24–25.

[59] *Ibid* pp. 25–26.

The central government has also supported job opportunities for the disabled and those in prison,[60] by placing its contracts with workshops set up to employ these groups. Under a scheme previously know as the "Priority Suppliers Scheme" registered workshops were given preferential treatment, where they could supply at a commercial rate. This meant that with low-value contracts not put out to tender, departments purchased selectively from those Priority Suppliers whose products were available on "commercial terms". With tendered contracts, Priority Suppliers were favoured by being invited to tender where possible and by being offered contracts even if theirs was not the lowest tender if they were able to match the lowest. In August 1994 the government announced its intention to abandon the policy in recognition that it contravened the E.C. Treaty and directives,[61] but has now introduced a more limited policy confined to contracts below the directives' threshold and which is open to workshops from other states.

Finally, many purchasers impose requirements relating to health and safety,[62] requiring contractors to comply with safety legislation, and to submit a copy of their health and safety policy statement, which by law must be drawn up by all companies with more than five employees. In the past authorities have also sometimes gone beyond the law – for example, requiring statements from firms with fewer than five employees.[63] It is also common for purchasers to concern themselves with compliance by a provider with other legislation, such as that on environmental matters.

(2) THE DIFFERENT APPROACHES TO USE OF PROCUREMENT AS A POLICY TOOL

As is apparent from the description of United Kingdom practice, there are a variety of ways in which industrial and social concerns may affect procurement decisions. The different types of strategy raise different constitutional concerns, and are also important in considering the legality of policies, as will be explained below.

The first strategy is the strategic placement of contracts with individuals or groups which the government seeks to promote: for example, workshops for the handicapped, firms in deprived regions or specific firms which the government seeks to establish as a "national champion". Such strategic placement is most significant in the area of industrial policy.

---

[60] Details of this scheme, which commenced in 1979, were set out in a booklet, *The Priority Suppliers Scheme*. The scheme, which began in 1979, was originally publicised through papers PPC (79) 5 and PPC (79) 8 issued through the Treasury's Public Procurement Committee.

[61] See pp. 815–828.

[62] See Institute of Personnel Managment, above, note 21, p. 24; Robson, "Contract Compliance" *The Safety Practitioner* Sept. 1985, 9.

[63] Institute of Personnel Managment, above, note 21, p. 24.

As an alternative, the government may simply give some form of preference to the favoured group. This may take the form, for example, of a price preference (as with the 5 per cent price preference formerly adopted by tenderers who could benefit employment in Northern Ireland), or preferential treatment in being invited to tender or in being allowed to supply part of the requirement by matching the best tender after bids are received (as under the old Priority Suppliers scheme). Such methods have the advantages of widening competition, and of setting specific limits to the additional costs (if any) which the government is prepared to pay to support the favoured group.

Procurement is also used as a method of "regulating" behaviour: the government's purchasing power is employed as a means of providing sanctions, or rewards, to uphold norms promulgated by the public authority.

In this regulatory role procurement may be used, first, simply as a supplementary sanction for enforcing rules which are also subject to other sanctions, such as criminal penalties. An example is the use of procurement in support of the rules in the Northern Ireland Fair Employment legislation. Under this legislation the use of the procurement sanction is dependent on the existence of a criminal conviction, but this is not always the case. Thus, as noted above, government providers are required to comply with the law on race discrimination, but in this case the exercise of contractual sanctions is not dependent on conviction of any offence, or even any formal determination by a body other than the purchaser that a breach of the law has occurred.

As well as supplementing other sanctions procurement has also been used to promote compliance with norms not implemented in any other way. In this case, the norms in question are often those devised by the purchasing authority itself. Examples include the use of procurement power by local government authorities in the 1980s to promote their own objectives ranging from equal opportunities policies which went much further than supporting existing legal requirements, to anti-nuclear policies. Such "secondary" policies implemented by central government purchasing authorities are often devised at Cabinet or Parliamentary level: for example, the anti-inflation policy of the 1970s and the "fair wages" policies which were formulated in Parliamentary Resolutions. Generally, policies of this kind have not been embodied in legislation, which is not necessary under the British constitution where the sanctions involved are purely contractual.

Another distinction between different regulatory policies is one between those which are concerned only with the way in which the contract itself is performed, and those which involve consideration of the provider's conduct in his business more generally. As explained above the Northern Ireland legislation to combat religious discrimination uses contract as a sanction to enforce legal rules which apply to the provider's business in general. Further, contract compliance as carried out in the area of equal opportunities by authorities such as the GLC sought to impose requirements going *beyond* the requirements of the law in firms' general conduct of their business, and was not confined to the provision of opportunities for those engaged in work on public contracts. The Fair Wages Resolutions, on the other hand, purported to apply only to work done for the government. Further, many authorities are concerned with whether a provider complies with the law – for example, on health and safety – in contracts actually carried out for that authority, but are not interested in monitoring its activities on other contracts (except to the extent that this may be relevant to deciding whether that firm is likely to adhere to the law in its contracts with the government).

As regards sanctions, the most successful policies have tended to rely on the possibility of debarment from future public sector business. Another possibility is to include a clause permitting termination of the contract if rules are breached. However, authorities are likely to be reluctant to do this (as shown by experience in the context of Fair Wages Resolutions) because of the inconvenience which it causes. The recovery of damages for breach of a contractual condition on secondary issues is not, on the other hand, a viable possibility since the authority will generally be unable to demonstrate any actual loss from breach for the provision, and the court have held that there is no implied contract between the provider and any persons affected by the breach, such as employees who do not receive the required wages.[64] Further, it is not possible under English law to enforce clauses providing for "penalty" payments.[65]

A number of constitutional questions have been raised over the use of procurement in the ways described above.[66]

First, where it is used to encourage behaviour not otherwise required by law, an issue is whether it is legitimate to regulate only one group of society, namely those who contract with the government. An answer is that contract compliance is a particularly efficient policy instrument in some fields when compared with, for example, criminal sanctions. As one commentator has noted in relation to equal opportunities "the individual complaint and adjudication model of tackling discrimination is fundamentally flawed by problems of legalism, tortuous procedure and satisfying the legal burden of proof. Contract compliance, in contrast, is not handicapped by these problems. It evades the inherent deficiencies of individual adjudication or institutional investigation . . .".[67] This justifies concentrating resources on this enforcement method. Such a use of procurement may also encourage others by example, without the costs of regulatory legislation.

---

[64] *Simpson v. Kodak*, above.

[65] Treitel, *The Law of Contract* (9th ed., 1995).

[66] For further discussion see Carr, *New Roads to Equality*, above, note 23; Morris, "Legal Regulation of Contract Compliance: an Anglo-American Comparison" (1990) 19 Anglo-Am. L. Rev. 87.

[67] Morris, above, at pp. 88–89. These assertions are supported by evidence from the United States.

Another issue is whether it is appropriate to regulate – whether in relation to policies in legislation or those devised by contracting authorities – without the safeguards of the criminal process. This may be relevant either to determination of "guilt" (an issue which does not arise where contractual sanctions depend on a criminal conviction) or to the decision on what sanction to apply. However, contractual sanctions, like other administrative decisions, should merely entail the application of the ordinary mechanisms of control which apply to government action (such as natural justice); they do not require the mechanism of the criminal law where there is no stigma of a criminal conviction resulting from the government decision. One problem in English law is that the mechanisms of control applying to procurement activities appear inadequate: as explained in Chapter 2, generally the "Ombudsmen" have no jurisdiction over procurement and there are doubts as to whether judicial review principles apply.[68] However, the solution here is to extend such mechanisms to procurement, and not to limit the way in which procurement may be used.

In relation specifically to the use of procurement to support policies in legislation (for example, health and safety requirements), it might be queried whether it is not appropriate to leave enforcement solely to the mechanisms in that legislation, ruling out contract compliance where this is not expressly referred to. However, it is submitted that the imposition of criminal sanctions does not imply any restriction on contract compliance powers which the government otherwise enjoys, but merely indicates that the policy is one for which a criminal sanction is *also* appropriate. Further, to allow providers who breach the law to benefit from government contracts can undermine both the legislative policy which has been breached, and the public perception of government in general. Thus the argument for allowing secondary concerns to be considered in public procurement appears particularly strong where this is done in support of existing regulatory provisions.

Finally, where procurement is used to enforce policies not contained in legislation, concerns may arise over the way in which such policies are formulated, and whether both the content of such policies and the safeguards for those affected by them have been adequately addressed. As explained below, since the Crown has the same power to contract as a private person it appears that such policies may be given effect without Parliamentary consent, a position which should give some cause for concern. As far as statutory authorities are concerned, on the other hand, their procurement powers are limited to those contemplated by their enabling legislation and it has become clear that this significantly, and properly, limits their power to pursue their own regulatory agenda through contract, as is also explained below.

---

[68] See pp. 33–37.

3. LEGAL LIMITATIONS ON SECONDARY OBJECTIVES IN PROCUREMENT

Legal limitations on the ability to use procurement as a tool of industrial or social policy derive from a variety of sources. First, authorities which derive their powers from legislation enjoy a capacity to contract only to the extent conferred by the legislation, and may not use their contract power for "secondary" purposes except to the extent contemplated by that legislation. Secondly, significant restrictions, affecting both industrial and social policies, derive from the E.C. Treaty and directives, and also from liberalisation agreements concluded between the European Community and third countries. In addition, the Local Government Act 1988 generally prohibits local authorities from taking into account "non-commercial" considerations in relation to procurement contracts. Authorities seeking to take into account secondary factors in procurement will need to ensure that none of these restrictions are violated.

(a) THE CAPACITY TO PURSUE SECONDARY OBJECTIVES

(i) THE CROWN AND CROWN AGENTS

It was explained in Chapter 2[69] that the Crown has at common law the same capacity to contract as any natural person. Under English law a natural person may take into account any social or other concerns in contracting, subject only to specific restrictions imposed by law, such as the criminal law. It has thus generally been assumed that the Crown, likewise, is free to take account of any secondary consideration in contracting. On this view Parliamentary authority is not required for policies pursued through the application of contractual sanctions, although legislation would be necessary if policies were promoted by means of powers which are not held by private individuals – for example, through a fine or imprisonment. The government may choose to place its procurement policies on a legislative footing (as it has done under the Northern Ireland fair employment legislation),[70] but in some important cases it has not done so – for example, in its use of procurement in the 1970s to promote wage restraint. In this case the Parliamentary scrutiny which normally applies to governmental regulation, and helps both to safeguard the interests of affected individuals and to promote effective policy making in the public interest, is not required.[71] However, in

---

[69] See pp. 10–11.

[70] See pp. 804–805.

[71] It has been suggested that the details of the policy whereby contract was used to promote wage restraint would never have been approved by Parliament, because of the width of the discretion given to ministers, and the fact that the criteria which firms were required to meet were both unpublished and subject to fluctuation: see Daintith, "Legal Analysis of Economic Policy", (1982) 9 J. Law and Society 191 at pp. 216–217. On Parliamentary approval see also Arrowsmith, "Government Contracts and Public Law" (1990) 10 Legal Studies 231, pp.232–235; Harris, "The 'Third' Source of Authority for Government Action" (1993) 103 L.Q.R. 626.

practice there is sometimes discussion in Parliament, as with the "Fair Wages" policy, which was embodied in House of Commons Resolutions; and procurement policies may also be the subject of Parlimentary questions or subject to consideration by relevant Parliamentary Select Committees. Procurement powers are also excluded from the jurisdiction of the Parliamentary Commissioner for Administration, so that defects in the administration of secondary policies cannot be brought to the attention of Parliament through investigations of the Commissioner.[72]

A more restrictive view of the Crown's powers to implement secondary policies could be put forward based on the GCHQ case[73] in which it was established that the common law principles of judicial review apply in principle to the common law powers of the Crown. On this basis, it might be argued that, by analogy with the approach applied to the construction of statutory powers, secondary policies would, at least in some cases, be "irrelevant considerations" in the exercise of the common law power to make procurement contracts – that these are conferred only for the purpose of enabling the government to obtain the goods and services which it requires on the best possible terms. However, probably the "irrelevant considerations" rule cannot be applied in the same way to common law as to statutory powers: the rule as applied to statutory authorities derives from the requirement of positive statutory authorisation for their activities, its scope depends on the particular statute, and in this light it does not provide a general body of principles which can be used to limit the scope of the common law powers of the Crown. It is only those principles, such as natural justice and the rules against bad faith, which are applied presumptively to all statutory powers, whatever their nature, which should be applied to regulate the common law powers of the Crown. Thus it is submitted that the recognition of the availability of judicial review does not affect the scope of the Crown's common law powers to promote secondary objectives through contract.

It could also be suggested that where powers to contract are conferred by statute on Ministers or on other agents of the Crown, these confer a capacity to contract which impliedly restricts the scope of the Crown's common law power relating to the subject-matter covered by the statutory powers. It could then be argued that the statutory procurement power can be exercised only for the purpose for which it was given by the legislation.[74] It was suggested in Chapter 2, however, that the effect of such statutes is merely to confer authority on these agents to act for the Crown.[75] It is submitted that these provisions should not themselves be construed as giving Ministers authority to exercise the Crown's own power to promote secondary objectives through procurement, but that authority to follow such policies must be found elsewhere – for example,

---

[72] See pp. 40–41.
[73] *Council of Civil Service Unions v. Minister for the Civil Service* [1985] A.C. 374.
[74] See p. 34.
[75] See pp. 111–113.

in other legislative provisions conferring powers upon the Minister, or in a decision of the cabinet.

Although the Crown has a wide power to use contract as a tool of policy under domestic law this power is now, however, significantly limited, in relation to major contracts, by restrictions deriving from European Community law, as explained below. Where these restrictions apply, the Crown may not pursue secondary policies even with the authorisation of Parliament, since this would infringe Community law obligations.

(ii) STATUTORY PUBLIC AUTHORITIES

Statutory public authorities which are not agents of the Crown generally have only those powers conferred upon them by statute, and may exercise those powers only for the purpose contemplated by the statute.[76] Authorities have express or implied powers to enter into procurement contracts for the purpose of obtaining the goods and services which they need.[77] However, where the exercise of procurement powers is influenced by a "secondary" policy the question arises as to whether the use of procurement for this purpose is contemplated by the relevant legislation.

This question was raised in *R. v. Lewisham L.B.C., ex p. Shell U.K.*[78] In that case the local authority had adopted a policy of refusing to purchase the products of Shell U.K. where equivalent products were available elsewhere on reasonable terms. The reason for the policy was Shell's membership of a multi-national group of companies with trading links with South Africa (although Shell U.K. itself did not trade in South Africa). The Court indicated that the policy would have been lawful had it been adopted solely from a desire to promote good race relations within the area, since under section 71 of the Race Relations Act 1976 the authority was obliged to consider the need to promote good relations between persons of different racial groups. However, the Court found that the policy had also been influenced by the desire to put pressure on Shell to cease its trading links with South Africa, and this the Court held to be an "extraneous and impermissible purpose".[79]

The Court did not, however, make it clear exactly what secondary considerations are prohibited.[80] One view could be that there is a presumption that procurement powers are conferred solely to allow the government to acquire goods and services on the best possible terms and that thus any secondary considerations are generally prohibited. This

---

[76] See pp. 13–15.
[77] See pp. 13–15.
[78] [1988] 1 All E.R. 938.
[79] [1988] 1 All E.R. 938 at 952.
[80] On this issue see also *Shell Canada Products v. City of Vancouver* judgment of February 24, 1994, noted by Arrowsmith (1994) 3 P.P.L.R. CS 174.

would be subject only to express contrary provisions (such as those in the Race Relations Act). Proponents of this view might also accept that authorities can include conditions requiring firms to comply with the law during the performance of the contract. Another approach, however, is to permit the use of procurement power in pursuit of any policies entrusted to the authority by other legislative provisions, even if the possibility of using contract to support such policies is not expressly contemplated. For example, on this view, authorities could refuse to contract with firms which fail to abide in general by regulatory legislation which the authority is responsible for enforcing. This approach is consistent with *Shell*.

The exact scope of the *Shell* principle is now, however, of little significance, in light of the express legal restrictions on the use of contract for secondary purposes which have been imposed by the 1988 Local Government Act and by European Community law, as discussed below.

(iii) OTHER PURCHASERS

Other entities taking a variety of legal forms are also subject to regulation in their procurement, as explained in Chapters 5–11. These include, for example, private companies which are more than 50 per cent owned by government, or private entities which carry out utilities activities on the basis of "special or exclusive rights". The extent to which these entities have a power to consider secondary matters in contracting will depend on the terms of the specific legal instruments by which they are created and governed (for example, in the case of a company incorporated under the Companies Acts, the Articles and Memorandum of Association).

(b) RESTRICTIONS UNDER THE E.C. TREATY

As explained in Chapter 4, Articles 30, 52 and 59 E.C. Treaty prohibit government measures, including those in the field of procurement, which have the effect of discriminating against products and firms from other Member States, unless such measures can be justified under specific derogations or limitations.[81] Most attempts to promote national industry through procurement inevitably involve discrimination, and thus the free movement rules virtually eliminate the power of government to use procurement as a tool of industrial development.

Thus the rules prohibit, for example, bans on foreign participation; set-asides of any part of the national requirement for domestic indus-try[82]; price preferences for domestic products or firms; and all other

---

[81] See pp. 84–86 and 92–94.
[82] Case C–21/88, *Du Pont de Nemours Italiana SpA v. Unita Sanitaria Locale No. 2 di Carrara* [1990] 1–ECR 889, discussed below in the context of regional policy.

kinds of preference – for example, preferential treatment for domestic bodies in deciding who to invite to tender.[83] It should also be noted that they cover not merely measures directed at those seeking government contracts directly, but also discriminatory provisions relating to sub-contractors, or to the workforce of a main contractor or subcontractor. This is illustrated by case C–360/89, in which the Court of Justice held contrary to Article 59 E.C. an Italian requirement that a proportion of public works should be reserved by the contractor for undertakings with their registered office in the region of the works.[84] An obligation to employ nationals, or a requirement which favours national labour, is also unlawful: it contravenes Article 52 and 59, in discriminating against providers from other States who wish to use their existing labour force,[85] and also infringes Article 48 E.C. on the free movement of workers.[86] "Indirect offsets" – requiring the buyer to provide the purchaser with benefits unconnected to the contract – would also be covered (although to require opening of subcontracts to competition might not, even if it benefits mainly domestic firms, since this does not hinder the normal course of trade). Such policies will not generally be capable of justification.[87]

The government is forbidden not merely from supporting domestic industry in general, but also from using procurement to promote specific

---

[83] Case C–360/89, *Commission v. Italy*, July 3, 1992, not yet reported.

[84] Above, note 84. The Court did not specify the nature of the discrimination but Advocate General Lenz suggested that the measure discriminated against potential subcontractors from outside Italy, and also favoured main contractors in these areas since only they can excecute the work themselves.

[85] Case C–113/89, *Rush Portuguesa v. Office national d'immigration* [1990] E.C.R. 1485, where a requirement for foreign nationals working on contracts in France to hold a special permit or to be recruited through the national immigration office was held contrary to Article 59 EEC. The same will apply to restrictions which relate only to public contracts.

[86] There was no infringement in *Rush Portuguesa*, since under the Treaty of Accession with Portugal this provision was not yet in effect.

[87] Case 95/81, *E.C. Commission v. Italy* [1982] E.C.R. 2187; case 288/33, *E.C. Commission v. Ireland* [1985] E.C.R. 1761 (concerned with Article 36). In fact, it is submitted that a general concept of "economic" objectives is not useful. The Court has allowed measures directed at economic ends – the effectiveness of fiscal supervision, for example, which is recognised as a mandatory requirement under Article 30, and the right to mint and protect coinage, one of the rare objectives within "public policy" under Article 36 (case 7/78, *R. v. Thompson, Johnson and Woodiwiss* ([1978] E.C.R. 2247). That such a prohibition is too broad is also illustrated by case 238/82, *Duphar v. The Netherlands* [1984] E.C.R. 523, which concerned a ban on state reimbursement of certain medical products on efficiency grounds (that cheaper and equally effective alternatives existed). The efficient use of state resources, though an economic matter, *should* be capable of justifying this kind of measures, even if domestic products provide better value for money, and the list can thus be said to favour domestic products. The measures would now probably be wholly outside Article 30, as non-discriminatory measures not concerned with the characteristics of the products; but at the time this was not clear and the Court assumed that such measures required justification. In the end it concluded they were outside Article 30 if they met certain conditions, the legal basis for which was not articulated; in fact, the Court merely applied the normal conditions for justification under mandatory requirements. Clearly this "economic" objective should have been openly admitted as a mandatory requirement.

Even if there is no blanket prohibition on economic justifications, however, it is clear that most will not be admitted.

policies such as restructuring, technology promotion or regional development, where these involve preferential treatment for national industry
(as is almost inevitably the case, since individual government actions
tend to be concerned only with support for domestic enterprise). In
relation to regional preference the Court of Justice ruled in 1990 in *Du
Pont de Nemours*[88] that Italian legislation requiring certain authorities to
reserve 30 per cent of their supplies contracts for firms with establishments and fixed plant in the underdeveloped *Mezzorgiorno* region, and
which offered products processed partly in the region, contravened
Article 30 E.C.[89] The Court rejected the view that regional policy
constituted a ground for derogation from Article 30, and also rejected an
argument that preferential procurement to promote regional development could be excluded from Article 30[90] on the grounds that it
constituted a "State Aid" under Articles 92–93.[91] The use of procurement to promote domestic technology is also affected: placement of
technology contracts to retain spin-off within the domestic economy, or
to establish a new industry, for example, clearly restricts trade. Such
measures would almost certainly also fall outside the grounds of
justification, even if directed at establishing viable industries; in view of
its restrictive approach to economic objectives, the Court is likely to take
the view that such policies – and others, such as restructuring – should
be implemented only through measures which do not interfere with
trade or which are expressly permitted (such as state aids). This is
reinforced by Article 130(1) E.C., entrusting the Community and
Member States with securing the conditions for the competitiveness of
Community industry; this is to be done "in accordance with a system of
open and competitive markets". However, it may be noted that the
Court of Justice decision in *Campus Oil*[92] indicates that strategic

---

[88] Above, note 82.

[89] para.16 of the judgment. The Court did not consider whether regional development
could be a mandatory requirement, but simply pointed out that any such mandatory
requirement could not in any case apply here since the measure was distinctly applicable
(para. 5 of the judgment). Advocate General Lenz, however, considered that it could not
be a mandatory requirement, since the objective was adequately provided for under the
Treaty provisions on State Aids.

[90] The reason given was that as a restriction on the free movement of goods the measure
was incapable of authorisation – the fact that it might be said to be within Article 92
could not exempt it from Article 30. A literal reading of the judgment suggests that all
assistance to industry which impedes free movement (of goods at least) is prohibited; but
this would render the state aids provisions virtually redundant. A narrower interpretation would be that the free movement provisions apply, and the measure cannot be
authorised, *wherever the aid goes further than necessary to achieve its objective as an aid*; in
other words provisions which restrict free movement may be authorised where they pass
a proportionality test. Whatever the basis for the decision, however, it indicates that the
aid provisions may not be invoked to justify the use of procurement to promote regional
development. Following these decisions, the U.K. abandoned its own regional preference schemes.

[91] See further Arrowsmith, *A Guide to the Procurement Cases of the Court of Justice* (1992)
at pp.99–103; Fernández Martín and Stehmann, "Product Market Integration versus
Regional Cohesion in the Community" (1991) 16 E.L. Rev. 216.

[92] Case 72/83, [1984] E.C.R. 2727, discussed further at pp. 864–865.

purchasing to maintain a national base in a vital industry may be permitted under the security derogations to the free movement provisions.

In addition, there is a major exception to the free movement rules under Article 223 E.C., which exempts from the Treaty measures relating to the procurement of military hardware.[93] One view is that this enables states to continue to use such military procurement to promote industrial objectives. However, an alternative view is that the derogation may be invoked only on security grounds, and not for economic reasons. Further, European states have in any case now concluded an informal agreement for the creation of a European Defence Equipment Market (EDEM), under which they have agreed to accept substantial limitations on their ability to use defence procurement to promote industry. This is considered further in Chapter 17.[94]

There is still also scope for industrial policies which do not interfere with competition: for example, national governments can use procurement to promote innovation through the way in which standards are formulated and can improve competitiveness by using international standards. The Community itself may have a role in encouraging the use of procurement to promote industry in Europe as a whole, in accordance with Article 130(1) E.C. which entrusts the Community, as well as Member States, with securing the conditions necessary for the competitiveness of European industry. One objective of this industrial policy is to strengthen the scientific and technological base of Community industry.[95] The primary responsibility is on Member States, but the Community has a co-ordinating and "complementing" role – so far largely pursued through co-ordination and planning of research, funding of private research, and through research undertaken directly by the Community.[96] So far as procurement is concerned, one of the very aims of the single market policy is to contribute to development of technology, by providing opportunities for the most innovative firms and through changes in market structure. More specifically, the Community has sought to harness procurement to promote industry by *requiring*, in the directives, use of European and other international standards when available. It can also be observed that Article 130f(2) E.C. expressly provides that, in pursuing the aim of strengthening the scientific and technological base of industry, the Community shall encourage enterprises to co-operate to take advantage of the opportunities of the single market, *in particular* those provided (*inter alia*) through the opening up

---

[93] On the scope of this exemption see pp. 857–863.
[94] See pp. 869–874.
[95] Article 130f; and see also Article 130(1).
[96] See further Elizalde, "Legal Aspects of Community Policy on Research and Technology Development (RTD)" (1992) 29 C.M.L.R. 309; Swann, *The Economics of the Common Market* (1992) Chap. 10. For an outline of the Treaty provisions see Lane, "New Community Competences under the Maastricht Treaty" (1993) 30 C.M.L.R. 919.

of public markets; and the Community has taken a number of initiatives in this respect, particularly in relation to small- and medium-sized enterprises as has already been explained.[97] Article 130(g) also provides that the Community shall promote *co-operation* in the field of technological development; here the Community might act by encouraging collaboration in procurements of high technology interest.

Measures taken by Community Member States in collaboration with other states would also seem to be covered by the free movement provisions where they restrict the flow of trade within the Community, including purchasing by international institutions, where trade within the Community is affected. Thus the division of contracts by the European Space Agency according to the principle of "fair returns" may possibly conflict with obligations under Article 30 E.C. This also creates difficulties for collaboration with States outside the ambit of the E.C. regime which may not be willing to accept a principle of open procurement.

The rules contained in agreements concluded by the Community for reciprocal access to procurement markets, such as the GPA and the Association Agreements with central and eastern European states[98] have a similar effect to the E.C. provisions, by preventing individual states from adopting policies which favour national industry. Individual Member States have already given up this possibility under the E.C. Treaty. However, the other agreements have the effect of limiting the possibility for using procurement to promote industry from a *Community* perspective – for example, by limiting access to a high technology contract to Community firms – except in so far as limitations and derogations apply.

Social policies, as well as industrial and economic policies, may also infringe the E.C. Treaty where they operate in a manner which is directly or indirectly discriminatory.

To require providers to comply with regulatory legislation is unlikely to infringe the Treaty in the case of a supply contract since such legislation tends to be concerned only with activities in a State's own territory, and the activity connected with the contract will take place elsewhere.[99] However, legislation on matters such as safety and the environment may affect providers from other states operating in the United Kingdom: for example, on a works contracts. Here, the legality under the E.C. Treaty of procurement measures requiring compliance with the legislation will depend on the validity of the legislation itself under Articles 52 and 59 E.C. The issue is most likely to cause controversy in cases where the legislation is applied to "posted workers" (those imported by a provider from another Member State) to fulfil the contract in question. In *Rush Portuguesa*[1] the Court of Justice held that

---

[97] See pp. 67–71.
[98] On these see pp. 774–786.
[99] Of course, legislation governing the characteristics of the products will normally be applicable.
[1] Note 85, above.

to prevent enterprises importing their own labour force to provide services in another Member State would normally breach Article 59 E.C., since not being able to use their existing labour force would place such firms at a disadvantage; and it would also breach Article 48 on free movement of workers. However, the Court also stated that there would be no breach of the Treaty in requiring observance of national legislation on working conditions.[2]

Where procurement is used to promote standards of behaviour going beyond those otherwise required by law, there will be a breach of the E.C. Treaty if compliance is more difficult for firms from other Member States.[3] This point was made in *Beentjes*,[4] which concerned a requirement for a Dutch public works contract that contractors should provide work for the long-term unemployed. Beentjes had submitted the lowest tender, but this was rejected, one reason being that the firm was unable to meet this requirement. The Court of Justice stated that the requirement could infringe the Treaty if it could be satisfied only by tenderers from the awarding state, or if tenderers from other states would have more difficulty in complying.[5]

Special problems may arise in promoting equal opportunities and fair labour conditions since, in contrast with regulatory legislation which tends to be limited to activities in the awarding state, in imposing standards purely through contract compliance states may wish to concern themselves with providers' activities elsewhere. This avoids the appearance of unfair competition between firms competing for particular contracts (although the same disparities arise from differences in *regulatory* measures in different states, these are not an immediate focus of concern to individual providers); and, further, enforcement presents no practical problems.

So far as equal opportunities are concerned, policies applying to all providers will be lawful if care is taken to avoid discrimination. However, this may not be easy. For example, one useful way of implementing such a policy, adopted by many local authorities,[6] is to require firms to adhere to codes of practice on recruitment produced by the Commission for

---

[2] para. 18 of the judgment. This view has been stated by the Commission: see para. 58 of the Communication *Public Procurement Regional and Social Aspects*, COM (89) 400 Final. The application of local conditions to posted workers may be *required* under a proposed new Directive: see COM (91) 230 final [1991] O.J. C255/6. The application of some other conditions to posted workers could, however, disadvantage foreign firms – for example, measures imposing ethnic minority quotas would disadvantage states with a lower proportion of minorities, and, in the light of *Rush Portuguesa*, might infringe Article 59 E.C., unless capable of justification. The possibility of justification is considered below in relation to non-legislative standards.

[3] Policies which are non-discriminatory are unlikely to be caught.

[4] Case 31/87, *Gebroeders Beentjes B.V. v. The Netherlands* [1988] E.C.R. 4365; discussed Arrowsmith, *A Guide to the Procurement Cases of the Court of Justice* (1992) at 8.

[5] Para. 30 of the judgment. The Court referred only to Article 7, but the specific provisions on free movement would apply.

[6] This must now be done in accordance with s.18 of the Local Government Act 1988: see pp. 730–745.

Racial Equality and Equal Opportunities Commission. This may, however, favour domestic firms, which are more likely already to follow these codes. This would certainly be the effect if the authority required such standards to be followed in the providers business as a whole, including outside the host state. It would also apply if the provider were merely required to adhere to such policies in relation to workers employed on the contract; this would make it more difficult for contractors to use their existing workforce which would, according to *Rush Portuguesa* infringe Articles 59 and 48 E.C. Where the policy is limited to workers recruited in the host state, it will probably not have a discriminatory effect – it would be no different from a requirement to comply with legislative provisions regulating recruitment in that state. Another way to avoid indirect discrimination may be to accept compliance with similar codes of other Member States – but this could prejudice firms from states where no codes exist. Even a simple requirement to demonstrate fair recruitment practices could be discriminatory, if there are widespread differences between states; and in any case, such an approach is not as effective as insisting on adherence to clear guidelines.[7] There would, however, be no objection to requiring a contractor to comply with *legal* requirements of his own state – although, these, of course, may be very limited.

It is possible that equal opportunities objectives might be recognised as mandatory or general interest requirements. Even if this is the case, however, it is not clear what approach the Court would take in balancing the objective of equal opportunities against those of free trade. For example, the principle of proportionality might require the recognition of all reasonable equal opportunities strategies, as opposed to insistence on precise compliance with domestic codes – even though, as noted above, this may not be such an effective way of securing fair opportunities. Reliance on mandatory or general interest requirements is also open to the objection that it is not a proper concern of governments to protect the interest of citizens and consumers of *other* Member states,[7a] although this could be counteracted by an argument that secondary policies need to be applied to all firms to ensure fair competition.

Within the Community context, one way forward might be to develop codes or similar guidelines at Community level; if widely adopted, these could be used as a basis for effective and non-discriminatory contract compliance. Alternatively, States could be encouraged to develop their own codes, which could be recognised by other Member States. The fact

---

[7] An alternative to codes, which tend to concentrate on recruitment practices and opportunities, might be to impose quotas; but many dislike this approach. In any case, in light of the different levels of ethnic minorities in the different States, this can also be problematic. The Commission in its Communication cited in note 2 states at para. 57 that an obligation to employ a given number of women or persons from "some other category not based on nationality" would "not appear to give rise to difficulty"; but it does note that this depends on the facts of each case.

[7a] *Alpine Investments B.V. v. Minister van Financiën* [1995] 3 C.M.L.R. 209.

that many contracts are required to be open to firms from outside the E.C. and even from outside Europe, however, introduces further complications. In practice, the most effective way to reconcile contract compliance with free movement may thus simply be to limit contract compliance policies – like regulatory legislation – to domestic contractors, or to operations in the awarding state.

In relation to working conditions, *Rush Portuguesa* indicates that it is lawful to set conditions relating to workers on a state's own territory,[8] as noted above. For workers employed elsewhere, however, the position may be different. In its 1989 Communication concerning social and regional policy in procurement[9] the Commission stated that: "it is difficult to see what justification there could be for admitting requirements which would permit national contracting authorities to export local conditions of employment to other member States. Such requirements could provoke intolerable conflicts of law and policy and also eliminate important elements of the comparative advantage of firms in States with lower labour costs, in particular, less developed regions".[10] The Commission does not explain the legal basis for this conclusion, but it appears to be largely correct. So far as concerns health and safety and other working conditions, to "export" domestic requirements may often disadvantage firms from other states; this will be the case, in particular, if the requirements are already imposed on domestic contractors under national law. Health and safety is, of course, a ground for derogation from the free movement provisions; but in relation to product safety the Court operates on a presumption that measures in other Member States are already adequate to protect safety,[11] and a similar approach is likely in the context of health and safety at work. It is unclear whether improvement of working conditions apart from safety is a mandatory requirement[12]; but if so, again the Court may well adopt a presumption that measures in other Member States give adequate protection. On the other hand, insistence on wages and conditions which are not "local" to the awarding state but which are reasonable in the light of conditions in the state of the provider's operations, or are required by law there appear acceptable. As with equal opportunities, legal objections to a policy may also be avoided by limiting it to activities carried on in the awarding state.

---

[8] *Rush Portuguese* refers specifically to conditions imposed by legislation and collective agreements, but there is no reason to distinguish between these and standards enforced through contract compliance.

[9] Note 2 above.

[10] Para. 58.

[11] Case 120/78, *Cassis de Dijon* [1979] E.C.R. 649, esp. para. 14.

[12] Article 117 E.C. recognises this as a Community objective; and its recognition as a mandatory requirement may be supported by case 155/80, *Oebel* [1981] E.C.R. 1993. However, in light of recent case law on the application of Article 30 to non-discriminatory measures, the decision can be explained as concerning a measure wholly outside Article 30, and requiring no justification.

Finally, preference schemes in the social field – such as those for workshops for the disabled – may contravene the E.C. Treaty where such preferences are limited to domestic providers. As noted above, the United Kingdom has tried to bring its own schemes in this area within the Treaty by extending them to cover similar workshops in other states. The legality of this approach may be questionable if other states do not actually have similar qualified providers since the policy will then operate to favour United Kingdom enterprises above those from certain other States. There is, on the other hand, a possibility that the Court may recognise such social objectives as mandatory or general interest requirements. Even this, however, may meet the argument that the goal could be pursued by means less restrictive of competition, in particular a subsidy. In any case, as explained below, preference schemes contravene the directives and thus (like the United Kingdom's new regime) must in any case be limited to contracts below the threshold.

(c) RESTRICTIONS UNDER THE PROCUREMENT REGULATIONS

(i) THE PUBLIC SECTOR REGULATIONS

Even where it is lawful under the Treaty to take account of secondary concerns in procurement, public authorities' ability to do so is now considerably restricted by the procurement regulations.

I. Prohibition on excluding providers for past failure to comply with government policy

Most significantly, authorities are not generally permitted to exclude providers from government contracts which are subject to the regulations, as a sanction for past non-compliance with the norms with which the authority has required the provider to comply. This is because, as explained in Chapter 6, providers can be excluded from participation in such contracts *only* on the grounds of failing to meet the "regulation 14" criteria or because of inadequate financial and economic standing or technical capacity.[13] Thus, secondary concerns can only be taken into account to the extent they are specifically contemplated by these provisions.

Regulation 14 of the Works Regulations, Supply Regulation and Services Regulations does in fact permit exclusion of providers on certain secondary grounds.

---

[13] See pp. 217–222 (explaining that providers may not be excluded on the basis of secondary considerations in selecting who is to be invited to bid in negotiated and restricted procedures) and p. 236 (explaining the basis on which bids may be excluded from consideration).

(i) First, and most significantly, it permits exclusion of those previously convicted of a criminal offence in connection with the business.[14] Thus, it is possible to use exclusion from procurement contracts as a sanction to ensure compliance with regulatory legislation provided, however, that an actual conviction has been obtained. This covers the Northern Ireland "Fair Employment" legislation where debarment operates as a sanction only where a conviction has been obtained. It is not generally permitted, however, to exclude under this provision providers whom the authority believes to be guilty of past offences but who have not actually been convicted.

(ii) Secondly, regulation 14 permits exclusion of those guilty of "grave" professional misconduct.[15] This could be relied on to exclude those who have breached criminal provisions but not been convicted, although it is not clear whether it could be applied to breaches of regulatory legislation, such as legislation on health or the environment, at least if the conduct was not intentional. Here, the vagueness of the provision is likely to be a barrier to its use by authorities, who may fear legal action if a provider is wrongly excluded. The provision might also be used to exclude those not complying with non-legal requirements stipulated by the authority, such as professional codes of ethics. Whether non-legal requirements on matters such as equal opportunities or fair wages might be included is, however, rather doubtful.

(iii) In addition, regulation 14 expressly permits exclusion for non-payment of taxes and social security contributions in certain cases, as outlined in Chapter 7.[16] In practice, authorities in the United Kingdom (in contrast with those in some continental states) have not traditionally sought to exclude providers for these reasons.

Except on these grounds, however, providers may not be excluded from contracts for past failures to comply with secondary policy. This means that the power to use a contract to enforce compliance with such policy is severely limited, since, as explained above, such debarment is generally the only effective sanction which may be used.

II. Prohibition on preferences and strategic placement

The regulations also generally prevent authorities from giving preferences to specific providers. Thus, as explained in Chapter 6, secondary concerns may not be taken into account as a factor in deciding who is to be invited to bid in restricted or open procedures.[17] This rules out, for example, policies such as the former Priority Suppliers scheme whereby workshops registered under the scheme were given preference in the issue of invitations. Nor may secondary concerns be taken into account

---

[14] See pp. 335–336.
[15] See p. 336.
[16] See pp. 336–397.
[17] See pp. 217–222.

in evaluating bids received, which must be assessed on the basis of either lowest price or most economically advantageous tender (both of which relate solely to the primary objectives of the contract).[18] This prevents authorities from giving price preferences to bids from certain tenderers, as used to be done, for example, under the Northern Ireland preference scheme.[19] Preferential treatment by allowing certain bidders whose bid is not the lowest to take part of a requirement if they are prepared to lower their price – which was also formerly part of the Priority Suppliers scheme – are also precluded, since the contract must be awarded to the lowest or most economically advantageous offer as submitted in the tender process.[20] Further, the general principle of the equality of bidders laid down in the *Storebaelt* case[21] prohibits authorities from giving any other forms of preference to bidders.

A *fortiori*, the rules prohibit placing a contract with a specific provider for strategic reasons. Thus it is unlawful to place a contract with a selected provider to maintain that provider as a competitive force in the market, and so to prevent a situation of monopoly arising. Such policies are advocated by the government in its recent White Paper on purchasing strategy,[22] but appear to be precluded by the regulations for major contracts.

III. The validity of contract conditions imposing secondary requirements

On the other hand, authorities may impose conditions in a contract which require the provider to meet secondary requirements relating to the performance of that particular contract. This was held to be lawful in the decision of the Court of Justice in the case of *Beentjes*[23] which, as noted above, concerned a condition in a works contract requiring the contractor to provide work for the long term unemployed.

All such conditions must, however, be stated in the contract notice. This is not stated expressly in any of the directives (or in the United Kingdom regulations), but it was held by the Court in *Beentjes* to be an implied requirement, on the basis that this is necessary in order for the notice to fulfil its function of enabling contractors to know which contracts are of interest to them.[24]

IV. Exclusion of providers unable to meet secondary conditions applying to contract performance

As explained above, a provider may not be excluded from a contract merely because of a failure to comply with secondary requirements of

---

[18] See pp. 236–239.
[19] See pp. 800–801.
[20] See further pp. 236–239.
[21] See the discussion on pp. 180–181.
[22] *Setting New Standards: a Strategy for Government Procurement* (1994), paras. 3.13–3.15.
[23] Above note 4.
[24] Paras. 34 and 37 of the judgment.

government in the past. A point which has caused some difficulty is the extent to which authorities may exclude from participation providers whom it is felt will in the future, whilst performing the contract, be unable to meet secondary requirements.

This question was raised before the Court of Justice in *Beentjes* in relation to the condition concerning the long-term unemployed which did not reflect the requirements of any regulatory legislation, but appears to have been written into the contract as a contractual condition. Unfortunately the Court's reasoning on this issue is not entirely clear. The Court merely notes, first, that it considers that the provision of employment for the long-term unemployed to be a matter which relates neither to technical capacity nor to financial or economic standing,[25] and then goes straight on to consider the compatibility of the provision with the Treaty without expressly examining the effect of the relevant directive; it is only in the concluding part of the judgment that the Court expressly states that the condition is not prohibited by the directive,[26] and it does not explain its reasons for this conclusion. Since in the general, introductory, part of the judgment the Court emphasises that the directive does not lay down a "uniform and exhaustive" body of rules and that within its framework states remain free to adopt their own substantive and procedural rules,[27] it might be thought that it was taking the view that the factors enumerated in the directive, such as financial standing and technical ability (which the Court has said do not cover this case) are not exhaustive of those which may be considered,[28] and that secondary matters can thus generally be taken into account to exclude a contractor provided they are compatible with other provisions of the law. This, it is submitted, is the most natural interpretation of the judgment.

A different interpretation, however, is adopted by the Commission in its 1989 Communication to the Council concerning the regional and social aspects of procurement.[29] This suggests that the effect of *Beentjes* is generally to forbid any exclusion for "secondary" reasons, except to the extent specifically referred to in the directives, on the basis that the listed criteria for exclusion of providers and selection between bids are exhaustive. This interpretation now appears generally to be accepted.

On this latter view providers can be excluded because of their anticipated inability to perform in accordance with a secondary requirement only where this is a matter of financial or technical capacity. The scope of these concepts was considered in Chapter 7. It was explained there that technical capacity probably covers the ability to perform the contract in accordance with the requirements of the general law, whether

---

[25] Para. 28 of the judgment.
[26] In para. 37.
[27] Para. 20 of the judgment.
[28] The purpose of these provisions would then be solely to regulate the manner and extent to which exclusions can be made *on these grounds*.
[29] Above note 2.

or not such requirements are additionally referred to in the contract as contract conditions.[30] On the other hand, it does not cover the ability to perform in accordance with contractual conditions referring to matters extraneous to the subject-matter of the contract – such as working conditions or wages – where these are not otherwise legally required of the provider; this can be deduced from the fact that the conditions in *Beentjes* itself was held by the Court not to relate to technical capacity. The position, on the other hand, of "non-legal" conditions relating to matters such as health and safety and environment matters is less clear, but probably these can be regarded, unlike conditions relating to the composition of the workforce, as an intrinsic part of contract performance rather than as matters extraneous to it, and thus capable of falling within the concept of technical capacity.[31]

The main argument for imposing significant restrictions on the power to exclude contractors is that discretion increases the opportunities for disguising discrimination. For this reason the discretion which authorities must obviously have to evaluate bids and to eliminate firms with inadequate finances and technical ability is closely controlled, as explained in Chapters 6–8 and most, although not all,[32] of the "secondary" factors for which exclusion is expressly permitted are capable of objective verification (for example, the requirement of a criminal conviction). Controls can also be applied, however, to other secondary factors, by requiring secondary criteria to be laid out in advance (as *Beentjes* held must be done where secondary conditions are included in a contract). Although abuse may still occur in the way that policies are applied, the risk seems small in light of the disadvantages of preventing the effective use of procurement to promote social policy. It is thus suggested that a better approach would be to permit exclusion for policy reasons.

V. The special provisions on employment protection and working conditions

Works Regulation 27 and Services Regulation 26[33] state expressly that when an authority gives information in the contract documents as to where a provider may obtain information on employment protection and working conditions which will apply in carrying out the works or services it must request providers to indicate that the provider has taken those obligations into account in preparing the tender or negotiating the contract. It is not clear whether this is intended to cover only conditions imposed by law – such as legislative requirements on health and safety matters – or whether it also extends to conditions imposed by the

---

[30] See pp. 314–316.
[31] See further pp. 314–316.
[32] For example, the case of "grave" professional misconduct.
[33] There is no equivalent provision in the supply rules.

authority itself – such as those formerly contained in the Fair Wages Resolutions.[34]

This provision has the effect of requiring authorities to give attention to providers' compliance with relevant conditions. However, this applies only where these are referred to in the contract documents, which seems to indicate that authorities may decline to give consideration to this issue altogether by declining to refer to it in the contract documents.

It is unclear if this provision authorises purchasers to consider working conditions or to exclude providers who cannot comply with applicable requirements, in a way which could not be done under the general principles outlined above. It was explained above that authorities may under the general provisions of the regulations include in the contract conditions relating to working conditions and employment protection, and may exclude firms which decline to accept such conditions[35]; hence there is no need for a special regulation to cover this issue in the context of working and employment conditions. It also appears that authorities may exclude those who cannot comply with legal requirements on secondary matters, since the ability to carry out the contract in accordance with the law is a matter of technical capacity[36]; hence for this also there is no need for a special regulation. However, authorities may not exclude providers who are willing to accept the relevant conditions but whom the authority believes are not likely to apply them in practice, when these conditions are *not* legal requirements but merely requirements laid down by the authority. It is arguable, however, that Works Regulation 27 and Supply Regulation 26 may be interpreted to permit this, by implication from the requirement to consider the matter. However, since the regulations and the directives which they implement merely refer to a requirement to ask the provider to indicate that this matter has been taken into account, and do not give a power to make any further investigations, it is perhaps unlikely that the provisions would be construed to give such a power.

(ii) THE UTILITIES REGULATIONS

I. The general provisions

So far as the utilities sectors are concerned, under the Utilities Regulations it can first be noted that the criteria for the evaluation of bids from qualified providers are the same as under the public sector regulations: that is, contracts must be awarded on the basis of either lowest price or most economically advantageous offer. This means that, as under the public sector regulations, utilities may not take into account

---

[34] The relevant provisions of the directives, Works Directive Article 23 and Services Directive Article 28, provide no assistance since they refer merely to "applicable" working conditions.

[35] See p. 825.

[36] See pp. 314–316.

secondary concerns through the application of preferences at the stage of bid evaluation.[37-38]

The regulations, and the directives which they implement, are less clear on the question of whether providers may be excluded from consideration for contracts altogether because they fail to meet secondary criteria, or whether secondary criteria may be taken into account in deciding which providers are to be invited to bid or to negotiate. In this respect the rules merely provide that providers are to be excluded, and selected, only on the basis of "objective" criteria.[39]

It is clear that this permits exclusion or non-selection of a provider who is not able to deliver the goods or services required. Thus the utility may reject firms on the basis of those matters comprised within "technical capacity" or "economic and financial standing" under the public sector rules, including the ability to perform the contract in accordance with general legal requirements such as legislation on health and safety or the environment. It is also expressly stated that in selecting providers utilities may have regard to certain criteria listed in regulation 19(2) of the Utilities Regulations, which are the criteria set out in regulation 14 of the Works Regulations, Supply Regulations and Services Regulations. These permit rejection on grounds, *inter alia*, of a criminal conviction relating to the trade or business; gross misconduct; and failure to comply with tax and social security obligations.[40-41]

However, it is not clear whether, apart from the matters specifically listed in regulation 19(2), the concept of "objective" criteria refers only to commercial criteria – that is, those relating to value for money – or whether it includes all criteria capable of objective verification and application, including secondary criteria. The doubts on these issues were considered further in Chapter 10.[42] If the broader interpretation is correct, then utilities may exclude providers for failing to comply with secondary requirements which have been set by the utility itself – for example, for past failures to meet requirements on fair wages and employment conditions which have been imposed by the utility. The broader interpretation would also permit utilities to exclude providers whom the utility feels are unable to meet conditions in the contract relating to secondary matters, such as a requirement to pay fair wages to those working on the particular contract. Neither of these possibilities is permitted for contracts subject to the public sector regulations, as explained above.

II. The special provision on working conditions and employment protection

Utilities Regulation 24 expressly provides that where a utility includes information in the contract documents as to where a contractor or

---

[37-38] See the discussion of the public sector regulations at pp. 236–239.
[39] See further p. 541.
[40-41] See further pp. 497–500.
[42] See pp. 497–498.

services provider[43] may obtain information on obligations relating to employment protection and working conditions, the utility must ask those providers to indicate that they have taken account of those obligations in preparing their tender or negotiating the contract. A similar provision is included in the Works Regulations and Services Regulations. If the view is taken that utilities may always exclude providers for secondary reasons, then Regulation 24 clearly is not needed to justify exclusion of providers for reasons relating to employment and working conditions. If, however, the view is taken that utilities may not generally exclude for secondary reasons, then, as with the corresponding provisions of the Works and Services Regulations, Utilities Regulation 24 might be construed as permitting such exclusion specifically in connection with policies in this area. However, it was suggested above that such an interpretation is rather unlikely.[44]

III. The special provision on subcontracting

Finally, Utilities Regulation 25 states that a utility may require a provider to indicate in his tender what part of the tender, if any, he intends to subcontract. This could be relevant to the issue of technical capacity, in particular, where the authority believes the likelihood of completion may be prejudiced by subcontracting, or it may be relevant to economic advantage where, for example, it is feared that the quality of the service offered by a provider may be adversely affected by subcontracting. However, the extent of subcontracting might also be of concern for a utility for "secondary" reasons in that the utility seeks to promote subcontracting in order to provide greater opportunities for small and medium-sized enterprises (SMEs).

As with other secondary considerations it seems that, quite apart from this provision, it is permitted under the regulations to include contract conditions on subcontracting and to exclude providers who will not accept the condition. As explained at I. above, it is less clear whether the utility may exclude providers who accept the conditions but appear unlikely to comply. It is not clear whether Utilities Regulation 25 might be construed to permit exclusion of providers in this case, but it is submitted that it is unlikely.

(d) THE PROHIBITION ON "NON-COMMERCIAL" CONSIDERATIONS UNDER THE LOCAL GOVERNMENT ACT 1988

(i) INTRODUCTION

For local authorities and certain other bodies the power to take account of social and economic concerns is also substantially curtailed by the

---

[43] Since the provision applies only to a "contractor" and "services provider" it does not apply at all to those seeking public supply contracts (referred to as "suppliers"), even where those persons are involved in providing some services under the supply contract.
[44] See pp. 497–498.

Local Government Act 1988 (LGA 1988).[45] This prohibits consideration of a wide range of "non-commercial considerations" in procurement. The basic restriction is found in section 17(1) providing that with respect to certain procurement functions authorities must act "without reference to matters which are non-commercial matters for the purposes of this section".

(ii) SCOPE OF THE PROHIBITION

The restriction applies to the authorities specified in Schedule 2 of the LGA 1988.[46] For England and Wales this covers any "local authority", a term defined to cover any county council, district council, London borough council, parish council, community council, the Council of the Isles of Scilly, and the Common Council of the City of London in its capacity as local authority or police authority.[47] It also applies to various other authorities, including police and fire authorities.[48]

The restriction governs all types of procurement contracts, whether for works, supplies or non-construction services. Section 17(1) states that it applies to the exercise of functions in relation to "public supply or works contracts", without mentioning services; however, the phrase "public supply or works contracts" is widely defined in section 17(3) as covering "contracts for the supply of goods or materials, for the supply of services or for the execution of works", thus including services contracts generally. The distinction between works, supply and services contracts which is made under the Works Regulations, Supply Regulations and Services Regulations to determine which set of regulations apply is not important here, since the same rules apply to all types of contract. There are no financial thresholds: the rules apply to all contracts regardless of value.

The provisions apply only to the procurement functions expressly listed in section 17(4). These functions are divided into three groups. The first deals with decisions relating to approval for contracts generally, specifiying the inclusion or exclusion of persons from an approved list[49] or the inclusion or exclusion of persons from a list of those from whom tenders may be invited.[50] ("Exclusion" is expressly defined to include removal).[51] The second covers decisions relating to the award of particular proposed contracts[52]: this specifies the inclusion or exclusion

---

[45] See further, Cirell and Bennett, *Compulsory Competitive Tendering: Law and Practice*, Chap. 16; Radford, "Competition Rules: the Local Government Act 1988" (1988) 51 M.L.R. 746 esp. pp.756–757; Morris, "Legal Regulation of Contract Compliance: An Anglo-American Comparison" (1990) 19 Anglo-Am L.Rev. 87 esp. pp.103–121; Morris, "Local Government and Contract Compliance" (1990) 154 Local Government Review 728.
[46] LGA 1988, s.17(2).
[47] LGA 1988, Sched. 2.
[48] See further the list in LGA 1988, Sched. 2.
[49] LGA 1988, s.17(4)(a).
[50] LGA 1988, s.17(4)(a).
[51] LGA 1988, s.17(8).
[52] LGA 1988, s.17(4)(b).

of a person from those from whom tenders are invited; the acceptance or non-acceptance of the submission of tenders; the selection of the persons with whom the contract will be made; and also decisions granting or withholding approval for a person to act as subcontractor, and the selection and nomination of subcontractors. The third group covers decisions relating to a subsisting contract[53]: again it specifies decisions to give or withhold approval of a subcontractor and the selection or nomination of a subcontractor; and also specifies as a relevant function the termination of the contract. The list is fairly comprehensive but omits some types of decision: for example, there is nothing to prohibit a bonus being paid to a provider upon the fulfilment of a "non-commercial" requirement.

It is expressly stated that the provisions on non-commercial considerations are to apply even when the authority is acting on behalf of the Crown.[54]

Sometimes local authorities make arrangements for other public bodies to exercise their procurement functions on their behalf – for example, where the authority participates in collective purchasing arrangements pursuant to section 101 of the Local Government Act 1972. Section 19(6) of the LGA 1988 provides that where a regulated authority arranges pursuant to this provision for another public authority to exercise on its behalf functions regulated under section 17 of the LGA 1988, section 17 is to apply as if the regulated authority were exercising the function itself. This will apply although the public authority making the procurement on the local authority's behalf is not subject to section 17 in its own purchasing. Thus a local authority cannot avoid the restrictions on non-commercial considerations by entrusting its procurement functions to a non-regulated authority.

Where a local authority engages a private body to act as its agent in placing contracts it seems clear that section 17 will still apply: the procurement function is still exercised by the authority, albeit through a third party agent rather than through its own employees.

(iii) THE MEANING OF "NON-COMMERCIAL" MATTERS

I. General

Under section 17(1) authorities must exercise their procurement functions without reference to matters which are "non-commercial matters for the purposes of this section". "Non-commercial matters" are expressly listed in section 17(5), and are outlined below. Matters not expressly listed in section 17 are not caught by the Act, even though they are matters which could be categorised as non-commercial under the natural

---

[53] LGA 1988, s.17(4)(c).
[54] LGA 1988, s.19(5)

meaning of that term. However, their consideration may still be prohibited by virtue of the general principle that procurement powers may be exercised only for those purposes contemplated by the authority's enabling statutes.[55]

It should also be noted that some of the matters listed are in fact capable of relating to the authority's "commercial" interests in the sense of value for money under the contract. For example, the conditions under which a firm's employees are employed ((i) below) may affect the stability of the workforce and hence the reliability of the firm, and an authority may wish to include provisions on working conditions for this reason. Likewise the territory of a provider's business interests ((v) below) may be relevant to reliability: the fact that a firm's factory is an area where civil war seems imminent indicates a risk that the contract may not be completed. The literal wording of section 17 suggests that even when included for commercial reasons such concerns are to be regarded as "non-commercial" under the section. A more sensible interpretation is that such considerations are only excluded to the extent that they are motivated by non-commercial considerations.

II. The list of "non-commercial" matters

The matters listed in section 17 (5) as "non-commercial" are as follows:

(i) "The terms and conditions of employment by contractors[56] of their workers or the composition of, the arrangements for the promotion, transfer or training of or the other opportunities afforded to, their workforces"[57]

The prohibited workforce matters

"Terms and conditions of employment" refers to the circumstances of employment of an enterprise's employees. Its effect, *inter alia*, is to forbid an authority from requiring a firm to meet minimum standards on matters such as wage levels, hours of work, holidays, sick pay and maternity benefits. The concept of "terms and conditions" is not limited to requirements which oblige employers to include specific terms in the contracts with their employees. Thus a requirement for providers to pay fair wages is prohibited even if there is no requirement actually to

---

[55] See p. 34. LGA 1988, s. 19(9) expressly provides that any such other right to judicial review is not affected.
[56] The Act itself makes reference throughout to "contractors". "Contractor" is defined in s.18(8) to mean (except in relation to a subsisting contract) a "potential contractor", further defined as a person seeking inclusion on an approved list (in relation to functions concerned with such a list) or a person seeking inclusion in the group from whom tenders are invited or seeking to submit a tender (in relation to functions concerning a proposed contract). This chapter, however, uses the term "provider": "contractor" is avoided since it has a narrower meaning under the regulations implementing Community law, referring merely to a person interested in a works contract.
[57] LGA 1988, s.17(5)(a)

include the "fair wages" obligation in the provider's own agreements with his employees.[58] On the other hand, in *R. v. London Borough of Islington, ex p. Building Employers Confederation*[59] the court indicated that section 17 only covers matters which are the subject of contractual conditions between employers and employees: it rejected an argument that the section covers all the "physical conditions" in which employees work. This conclusion is open to criticism, since it renders the scope of the section dependent on the matters which each provider chooses to deal with in his contracts with employees. A wider view that all matters relating to actual working conditions are covered is more logical. The court appears to be influenced in its conclusion, however, by a desire to remove health and safety matters from the scope of the provision.

The prohibition clearly covers requirements which go beyond the general law – for example, any requirement for firms to pay "fair wages", which is not a legal obligation in the United Kingdom – but it is not clear whether it might also preclude contract conditions designed to secure compliance with the law – for example, any statutory requirements limiting hours of work. In the *Islington* case it was stated, in the context of considering provisions on pay, hours of work, etc., that the statute was not intended to have the effect "that a local authority is not to include in its contracts provision requiring the contractor to comply with the general law". On the other hand, in the same decision the court held that contractual requirements for compliance with the sex discrimination *legislation* prohibiting discrimination against women in access to employment infringed section 17 because this related to the prohibited concern relating to composition of the workforce, as noted below. It is difficult to reconcile these two aspects of the decision – if compliance with the law is covered in one case it is surely covered in another. Since the section makes no specific exceptions for legal requirements the natural interpretation would seem to be that contractual conditions cannot be used to enfore compliance with the law.

The rules on non-commercial considerations in the 1988 Act were introduced at the same times as the provisions setting up a compulsory competitive tendering regime (CCT), requiring market testing of a variety of local authority services.[60] One objective of this policy was to reduce local government expenditure on services, and it was envisaged that this would arise as a result of the lower labour costs of the private sector. In support of this policy it was necessary to prevent authorities from imposing their own requirements on terms and conditions on outside providers, since to do so could eliminate the possibility of any such savings; and hence the rule in section 17 on terms and conditions of

---

[58] *R. v. London Borough of Islington, ex p. Building Employers Confederation* [1989] I.R.L.R. 383.

[59] Above.

[60] On this see further Chap. 12.

employment was an important measure in the context of CCT. The possibility for savings in this way has now been significantly affected by the European Community's Acquired Rights Directive, which in many cases requires providers to take over an authority's existing workforce on the same terms and conditions as they enjoyed with the authority. This is considered further in Chapter 12.[61]

As well as covering conditions in the sense of pay, hours worked, etc. the provision on terms and conditions of employment could also be interpreted as covering the working conditions of employees in terms of health and safety. However, the government in guidance on the provision has indicated that it is not intended to prevent consideration of a firm's health and safety record, although it does not explain how this conclusion is reached within the terms of the legislation.[62] As noted above, the court in *Islington* concluded that the section applied only to matters dealt with in contractual conditions, which would seem to exclude health and safety matters from the scope of section 17 in most cases. However, as argued above this general approach of the court lacks merit. Another way of excluding most health and safety provisions from section 17 would be to take the view that the section does not cover conditions which simply concern compliance with the law, as is the case with many health and safety provisions. However, as noted above, such a general conclusion is difficult to reconcile with the court's view that authorities may not require compliance with legislation on sex discrimination.[63] It is indeed unfortunate if the possibility of including health and safety conditions is precluded, but the section is not well drafted to avoid this result.

As well as the terms and conditions of employment, the composition of the workforce and arrangements for the promotion, transfer or training or the provision of other opportunities are listed as non-commercial matters. It was held in *Islington* that the designation of the "composition of the workforce" as a non-commercial matter means that an authority cannot take into account a provider's practices in making decisions about recruitment and dismissal – which are not expressly mentioned – as well as decisions on promotion or transfer, which *are* specifically mentioned. In *Islington* it was held that a condition requiring compliance with obligations under the Sex Discrimination Act 1975 which prohibit discrimination against women in employment matters contravened section 17. Clearly the provisions on workforce matters outlaw many policies previously implemented by local authorities through procurement: for example, promoting equal opportunities for

---

[61] See pp. 636–648.

[62] Joint circular, Department of the Environment Circular 8/88 and Welsh Office Circular 12/88 (April 6, 1988), para. 8.

[63] The court in *Islington* also held that a health and safety supervisor was not a part of the "workforce", and so could be made the subject of a requirement of the contract, another doubtful conclusion.

disadvantaged groups; encouraging employers to provide training (for example, by insisting that a certain number of trainees are employed in doing the work); or supporting local labour (a policy which is anyway contrary to the E.C. Treaty). This applies, as *Islington* indicates, even where the policy reflects a general legal requirement, although, as noted earlier, it is difficult to reconcile the decision in *Islington* on this point with other statements in the case that appear to permit requirements for providers to comply with legislation on labour conditions.

The government has indicated that it did not intend to preclude questions concerning the qualifications of the workforce to carry out the work.[64] Clearly it would be extremely inconvenient if such a matter of commercial importance could not be considered. It is likely that the courts will construe section 17 as applying only where the condition is included for a non-commercial reason, as suggested earlier,[65] or will construe "composition" to exclude the matter of qualifications.

Exception for race relations

There is an exception to the above principles, contained in section 18 of the Act,[66] which allows use of contract to a limited extent in support of equal opportunities for racial groups.[67] This was included because of section 71 of the Race Discrimination Act 1976 which requires local authorities to exercise their functions with regard to the need (i) to eliminate unlawful discrimination and (ii) to promote equality of opportunity between persons of different racial groups. It appeared to be accepted by both parties in *Shell*[68] that prior to the 1988 Act this provision had the effect of permitting such objectives to be taken into consideration in procurement (subject to general administrative law principles such as reasonableness). Further, since the provision imposes a *duty*, it could be argued that authorities were bound to take these matters into account and thus at least to *consider* whether to adopt a contract compliance policy (although clearly any such duty involves a substantial area of discretion and authorities could not be required to adopt any specific policy, or, indeed, any policy at all). Section 18 of the LGA 1988[69] now deals with the issue expressly, stating that except to the

---

[64] Joint circular, Department of the Environment Circular 8/88 and Welsh Office Circular 12/88 April 6, 1988), para. 8.

[65] See p. 833.

[66] And see also LGA 1988, s.17(9) expressly stating that the restrictions in s.17 are subject to s.18.

[67] On this see further Commission for Racial Equality, *Local authority contracts and racial equality: implications of the Local Government Act 1988*, summarised in (1989) Equal Opportunities Review no. 28 p. 32.

[68] [1988] 1 All E.R. 938, discussed at p. 34.

[69] It may be observed that section, 18 applies only to "local authorities" (which appears to refer to those bodies defined as such in Sched. 2 to the Act) and not to all bodies which are subject to the restrictions in section 17 which as we have seen include some which are not local authorities. This is because the duty in section 71 of the Race Relations Act applies only to local authorities.

extent permitted by section 18 nothing in section 71 of the Race Relations Act shall either require or authorise a local authority to take into account non-commercial matters in exercising procurement functions.[70] In essence, section 18 allows authorities some powers to use contract compliance, but subject to extensive limitations.

Basically, section 18(2) provides that nothing in section 17 shall prevent certain measures referred to in the section where these are "reasonably necessary" to secure compliance with section 71 of the Race Relations Act. First, authorities may ask specified questions seeking information or undertakings on these matters and may consider the responses.[71] They may also call for certain evidence in support of the answers.[72] Secondly, they may include in a draft contract or tender, terms or provisions relating to these matters and consider the responses received.[73] Thus the section permits authorities to obtain certain information and to require compliance with certain practices through inserting a contractual term to this effect.

As regards sanctions, section 18(3) states that the exception in section 18 does not apply to termination of a contract, thus making it clear that this remedy is not available against providers who fail to comply with the policy,[74] even where compliance is a contract condition. The section says nothing else, however, about what action may be taken, apart from the fact that a provider's "responses" may be "considered". Since, however, an express provision has been included to prevent termination as a sanction, it can be surmised that the Act does not prevent authorities from using other measures. In *Islington* the court held that a provision for suspending the contract, and for the authority itself to perform the work so far as necessary to ensure compliance with the conditions, did not contemplate "termination" and was acceptable. Another possibility is exclusion from future contracts,[75] but this is not possible for contracts covered by the Works, Supply or Services Regulations.[76]

In principle, measures may be taken both to prevent unlawful discrimination and to promote equality of opportunity, which leaves scope for authorities to promote the development of specific policies to foster equal opportunities, as well as requiring providers to comply with the law. However, in practice freedom is substantially limited by the nature of the questions which may be asked.

---

[70] LGA 1988, s.18(1).
[71] LGA 1988, s.18(2).
[72] LGA 1988, s.18(4).
[73] LGA 1988, s.18(2).
[74] There is room for debate over the meaning of "termination" for this purpose – for example, whether it includes failure to exercise an option to renew or the exercise of an express contractual power to terminate on notice prior to the expressed expiry date. It seems illogical to make a distinction between these cases and others where the contract is brought to an end.
[75] This is the view taken by the Commission for Racial Equality in, *Local authority contracts and racial equality: implications of the Local Government Act 1988*.
[76] See pp. 823–827.

Questions (which must be put in writing[77]) are limited to those laid down in writing by the Secretary of State[78] and the evidence which may be called in support of answers given is limited to that stipulated by the Secretary of State, again in writing.[79] One objective of this is to achieve standardisation and so reduce the burden on both providers and authorities, a laudable objective. However, the narrow scope of the permitted evidence and questions can be criticised.

At present six sets of questions have been approved for use, as follows:
(i) "Is it your policy as an employer to comply with your statutory obligations under the Race Relations Act 1976 and, accordingly, your practice not to treat one group of people less favourably than others because of their colour, race, nationality or ethnic origin in relation to decisions to recruit, train or promote employees?"
(ii) "In the last three years has any finding of unlawful discrimination been made against your organisation by any court or industrial tribunal?"
(iii) "In the last three years has your organisation been the subject of formal investigation by the Commission for Racial Equality on grounds of alleged unlawful discrimination?"
(iv) If the answer to (ii) above is in the affirmative, or if the Commission for Racial Equality made an adverse finding, "What steps did you take in consequence of that finding?"
(v) "Is your policy on race relations set out –
  (a) in instructions to those concerned with recruitment, training and promotion;
  (b): documents available to employees, recognised trade unions or other representative groups of employees;
  (c): recruitment advertisements or other literature?"

(vi) "Do you observe as far as possible the Commission for Racial Equality's Code of Practice for Employment, as approved by Parliament in 1983?"

The only approved evidence is in relation to question (v), which allows authorities to call for examples of the instructions, documents, recruitment advertisements or other literature.

These questions allow authorities to seek to establish whether there has been a formal finding of unlawful discrimination (questions (ii) and (iii)) and whether appropriate steps have been taken in response. No evidence is specified, and it may thus be difficult to verify the steps which the firm claims have been taken. Further, many firms may be involved in

---

[77] LGA 1988, s.18(3).
[78] LGA 1988, s.18(2); LGA 1988, s.18(5); LGA 1988, s.18(7) (definition of "approved questions" used in s.18(2)).
[79] LGA 1988, s.18(4); LGA 1988 s.18(5); LGA 1988, s.18(7) (definition of "approved request for evidence" used in s.18(2)).

unlawful practices without any official finding being made on this point, and it seems that an authority cannot make its own enquiries, nor even take account of information about unlawful practices which comes to light in other ways. The questions allow an authority to enquire about compliance with the Code of Practice, but not to obtain evidence on personnel practices and procedures (apart from the question relating to inclusion of the race relations policy in job advertisements), to prove the truth of its assertion. Nor is there anything to permit a local authority to monitor the composition of and changes to the ethnic make-up of a provider's workforce. The provision of such information may be burdensome to firms, but not to allow this seriously restricts authorities' powers to pursue effective contract compliance. In fact, as noted these powers have now in any case been severely limited under the regulations implementing Community law on procurement.

The exception in section 18 applies only in relation to the "workforce" matters specified above – that is terms and conditions of employment, the composition of the workforce and arrangements for promotion, transfer, and training and the provision of other opportunities.[80] Thus questions on other matters, such as whether the firm does business in a state which engages in racist practices, could not be approved by the Secretary of State, even when it is relevant to section 71 of the Race Relations Act.

Attention has focused on the extent of a local authority's *powers* to consider race relations matters in procurement, but the question also arises whether it still has a duty to do so. Arguably this is the case since section 71, which imposes a duty, is not in principle repealed in relation to the procurement function. Section 18(2) of the LGA limits the way in which any powers may be exercised in relation to section 71, but it does not appear to affect the duty element of section 71. This interpretation is supported by the fact that the section 18(2) powers are limited to what is necessary to "secure compliance" with section 71 of the Race Relations Act; the concept of compliance would not be relevant if there were no duty.

There are no exceptions to allow authorities to consider providers' compliance with other legislation such as obligations under the Sex Discrimination Act (as was pointed out in *Islington*) or under legislation concerned with the disabled, although some attempts were made to include such exceptions during the passage of the Act.

---

[80] LGA 1988, s.18(2) allows questions and the inclusion of c ntract terms and provisions only in relation to "workforce matters", defined in s.18(7) as including only those things mentioned above.

(ii) "Whether the terms on which the contractors contract with their subcontractors constitute, in the case of contracts with individuals, contracts for the provision by them as self-employed persons of their services only"[81]

This is designed to prevent authorities from insisting that their own subcontractors do not use "labour only" subcontractors, which had been the practice of some authorities before the 1988 Act.

(iii) "Any involvement of the business activities or interests of contractors with irrelevant fields of government policy"[82]

Government policy is stated to fall within "irrelevant fields" if it concerns "matters of defence or foreign or Commonwealth policy".[83] This particular provision was designed to prevent authorities implementing policies which contradict those of central government in these listed fields: an example would be by refusing to do business with providers who have worked on military nuclear installations, in opposition to the government's defence policy in the area of nuclear armaments. It is not clear from the wording of the provision that the list of "irrelevant" policy areas is intended to be exhaustive but this is generally assumed to be the case.[84] This seems to be the correct view, since the purpose of the provision was to designate as unlawful certain conduct which was occuring at that time rather than to state a comprehensive principle. Further, it would be difficult to give any sensible meaning to the concept of an "irrelevant" field of policy without a specific definition. On this view, action by authorities which contradicts central government policy in fields not listed will not be caught – for example, a policy to pressurise contractors not to work on civil nuclear installations.

"Business activities" are defined for the purpose of this provision as any activities comprised in the carrying on of a persons' business,[85] and are expressly stated to include receiving the benefit of performance of a contract.[86] "Business interests" are defined as "any investments employed in or attributable to", the carrying on of a persons' business.[87] The activities or interests of firms are "involved" in a policy where the firm provides goods, services or works to a persons carrying on business in that field (for example, a provider supplying materials to be used in construction of a nuclear military installation), or where it invests in any authority or person whose functions or business activities are involved in the field (for example, where a firm has invested in another company involved in nuclear work, rather than being involved directly itself).

---

[81] LGA 1988, s.17(5)(b).
[82] LGA 1988, s.17(5)(c).
[83] LGA 1988, s.18(8).
[84] For example, by Morris, above, p.111.
[85] LGA 1988, s.17(8).
[86] *Ibid.*
[87] *Ibid.*

(iv) "The conduct of contractors or workers in industrial disputes between them" and "any involvement of the business activities of contractors in industrial disputes between other persons"[88]

The reference to conduct in industrial disputes prevents authorities from using procurement as a penalty against employers who are in dispute with their employees, in order to support the cause of their employees. This phenomenon had occured in some well-publicised cases prior to the passage of the Act.

The second part of the provision ensures this is extended to prevent authorities further pressurising or penalising such employers not merely by refusing to deal with the employer himself, but by refusing to deal with firms who do business with the employer, so putting pressure on other firms also to refuse dealings with that employer. In this context it is provided that a person is "involved" in an industrial dispute between others by supplying those parties with goods, materials, services or works to parties to the dispute, or as a customer of those parties.[89]

For the purpose of this provision "industrial dispute" is stated to have the same meaning as "trade dispute" in the Trade Union and Labour Relations Act 1974.

(v) "The country of or territory of origin of supplies to" providers and "the location in any country or territory of the business activities of" providers[90]

This provision prevents authorities from using their contract power to put economic pressure on the governments of nation states or other regions to alter policies of which the authority disapproves. This provision was specifically directed in 1988 at the policy of a number of authorities of refusing to do business with firms which had business interests in South Africa, seeking to pressure the South African government to end its policy of apartheid, but it will also apply to any other case where an authority might wish to put pressure on a particular government.[91]

The provision prohibits penalising of firms on the basis of the origins of their supplies. This clearly applies regardless of whether the contractor manufactured those supplies himself. It does not appear to be limited to the case of supplies used on the contract with the authority, but extends to the case where an authority wishes to penalise a firm which

---

[88] LGA 1988, s.17(5)(d).

[89] LGA 1988, s.18(8).

[90] LGA 1988, s.17(5)(e).

[91] It also appears to preclude the use of procurement to discriminate against firms from other states for economic reasons. Discrimination against firms from any countries is in any case generally prohibited under the E.C. Treaty and under various international agreements concluded between the Community and third countries. (See pp. 771–787). However, in certain cases, Community law permits Member States to adopt measures which discriminate against "third country" products or firms, and in these cases the Local Government Act 1988 means that such an option is not open to local government in the United Kingdom.

uses supplies from the territory concerned in connection with his other business. In addition, it prevents an authority from taking account of the fact that the provider himself carries on business activities[92] in the states concerned.

(vi) "Political, industrial or sectarian affiliations" of contractors, their directors, their partners or their employees[93]

"Political, industrial or sectarian affiliations" is expressly and exhaustively defined[94] to include actual or potential membership of or support for (a) a political party (b) an employer's association or trade union or (c) "any society, fraternity or other association".

The reference to "any other association" is extremely wide. One consequence may be to preclude authorities from stipulating a requirement for membership of a trade association, although this can be an important method of ensuring that providers have the required technical standing to fulfil a contract.

It is not made clear whether a *refusal* to support one of the above bodies is included. It might be suggested that it is not, particularly since refusal is expressly mentioned in relation to the financial support provision discussed in the next section. On the other hand, such an exclusion seems illogical.

(vii) "Financial support or lack of financial support for any institution to or from which the authority gives or witholds support"[95]

(viii) "Use or non-use by contractors of technical or professional services provided by the authority under the Building Act 1984 (or in Scotland the Building (Scotland) Act 1989)"[96]

These Acts lay down requirements for local authority approval of certain work. As an alternative, builders may instead obtain approval under the National Housebuilders Registration scheme, but some authorities have taken the view that this is unsatisfactory and have insisted on their own approval. This provision under the 1988 Act ensures that authorities may not insist on this.

III. Application to subcontractors, suppliers, customers and associates[97]

Section 18(7) of the LGA 1988 provides that where any matter would be a non-commercial matter under the list above if it referred to a provider,

---

[92] "Business activities" refers to any activities comprised in the carrying on of the provider's business, including the receipt of the benefit of a contract.

[93] LGA 1988, s.17(5)(f).

[94] LGA 1988, s.17(8).

[95] LGA 1988, s.17(5)(g).

[96] LGA 1988, s.17(5)(h).

[97] "Supplier" includes any person who in the course of business supplies a provider with services or facilities of any description for the purpose of his business: LGA 1988, s.18(8). Suppliers, customers and subcontractors are defined to include prospective suppliers, customers and subcontractors. "Associated body" means any company which, within the meaning of the 1985 Companies Act, is the provider's holding company or subsidiary or is a subsidiary of the provider's holding company.: LGA 1988, s.18(8).

it shall also be deemed a non-commercial matter where referable to any one of the following:

(i) a supplier or customer of the provider;

(ii) a subcontractor, or the subcontractor's supplier or customer;

(iii) an associated body of the provider or his supplier or customer; and

(iv) a subcontractor of an associated body of the provider or his supplier or customer.

Thus, for example, a requirement for a main contractor to ensure that subcontractors pay fair wages would be a non-commercial consideration.

(iv) THE SECRETARY OF STATE'S POWER TO AMEND THE LIST OF NON-COMMERCIAL MATTERS

Section 19(1) of the LGA 1988 states that the Secretary of State may add to the list in section 17 "any other matter which appears to him to be irrelevant to the commercial purposes" of the contracts covered. This must be done by order made by statutory instrument,[98] which must be laid before both Houses of Parliament and approved by a resolution of each House; and it may include "such consequential and transitional provisions as appear to the Secretary of State to be necessary or expedient".[99]

(v) THE DUTY TO GIVE REASONS FOR DECISIONS

The duty not to consider non-commercial considerations is enforceable by providers by judicial review.[1] Enforcement is bolstered by section 20 of the LGA 1988 which requires persons affected by certain decisions covered by section 17 to be notified "forthwith" and requires a written statement of reasons for the decision where this is requested in writing within 15 days of the notification of decision.[2] The statement of reasons must be provided within 15 days of the request.[3]

The decisions to which the obligation applies are[4]: exclusion from an approved list; a decision not to issue an invitation to tender to a person requesting to be invited; a decision to accept a submission of a tender; a

---

[98] LGA 1988, s.19(1).

[99] LGA 1988, s.19(3). It includes a power to apply to any new "non-commercial" matter specified in the order the provisions of s.17(6) (which states that the listed non-commercial matters cover things which happened in the past), and the provisions of s.17(7) (which provides that matters which are non-commercial in relation to a contractor are also such in relation to suppliers, customers, subcontractors and associate bodies). It also includes a power to amend the definitions contained in s.17(8) (which are the definitions relating to the matters specified as non-commercial in the section); this power which may be exercised without any other order being made at the same time.

[1] On such actions see further pp. 942–944.

[2] LGA 1988, s.1.

[3] LGA 1988, s.20(3).

[4] LGA 1988, s.20(2).

decision not to award the contract to a person who has tendered; a decision to withhold approval for or to select or nominate particular subcontractors (whether for a subsisting or proposed contract); and a decision to terminate a subsisting contract.

The purpose of the obligation is to assist firms in deciding whether they believe a decision is affected by unlawful considerations and whether a legal challenge could succeed. According to general principles of English law concerning the interpretation of statutory rights to reasons the reasons given must be intelligible, and adequate to allow the affected party to decide whether to mount a challenge.[5]

For contracts subject to the Works, Supply or Services Regulations reasons must in any case be given for decisions under the provisions of those regulations.[6]

(vi) THE IMPACT OF SECTION 17

The introduction of these restrictions in 1988, as part of a package of measures which had begun to eat away at the policy-making and financial powers of local government, provoked considerable controversy. To some extent, the Act was a response to obviously legitimate concerns. In particular, there was disquiet over the use of contract compliance use in relation to matters over which local authorities generally have no jurisdiction, such as apartheid and nuclear policy. To this extent it is logical to forbid the consideration of such secondary matters in contracting: if authorities are not permitted to regulate behaviour or implement some policy through other methods, then it is logical that they should not be permitted to do so through contract where no specific authority to do so has been given (a principle reflected in the court's judgment in *Shell* at around the time the Act was passed[7]). In addition, the implementation of social policies through contract frequently involves some financial cost, and a desire to reduce the public expenditure attributable to these policies was one consideration. This applied especially to policies designed to support fair labour conditions, as was explained above.[8] Thus in these areas the central government has sought to limit the power of local authorities to make their own balance between financial costs and social concerns. This might be interpreted as reflecting the low value placed by the government at that time on the kind of social considerations with which local authorities had been concerned, or as reflecting the government's judgment that contract compliance is not an efficient method (or was not being used in an efficient way) for promoting these kind of policies. In addition, the strict approach of the Act was surely influenced by the government's hostility

---

[5] See Craig, *Administrative Law* (3rd ed., 1994), pp. 311–312.
[6] See pp. 281–282.
[7] See p. 34.
[8] See pp. 805–807.

to the substance of the policies adopted by some councils (such as those on nuclear policy), which led to a desire to limit the policy-making discretion available to those bodies.

Since the 1988 Act was passed it has become apparent, as explained above, that public bodies freedom to use contract as a tool of policy is now in any case substantially curtailed by Community requirements. The provisions of the 1988 Act are important mainly for contracts below the threshold for the procurement regulations implementing the Community directives, and – possibly[9] – in prohibiting consideration of providers' ability to comply with general legal requirements during the performance of the contract.

---

[9] Whether this is actually forbidden by the 1988 Act is open to debate: see p. 834.

CHAPTER 17

DEFENCE PROCUREMENT

1. DEFENCE PROCUREMENT IN THE UNITED KINGDOM

(1) THE UNITED KINGDOM DEFENCE MARKET

Procurement for defence purposes is in the United Kingdom the responsibility of the Ministry of Defence (MoD).[1] Most equipment and services are procured through the MoD's Procurement Executive, which has developed a special expertise in the procurement of complex defence equipment, such as aircraft, missile systems and tanks. In addition, for each of the three Services (which are separate units within the MoD), the Principal Accounting Officer has responsibility for procurement of some spares and maintenance services, whilst works construction and management is under the control of the Defence Works Service.[2] Research is mainly the responsibility of the Defence Evaluation and Research Agency, a "Next Steps" agency.

Defence purchasing is of great significance for the economy, and the Ministry is the largest single customer of United Kingdom industry. In 1995 expenditure on defence equipment alone was expected to be £9.560 billion,[3] and it was estimated in 1994 that MoD procurement supported 300,000 jobs.[4] This procurement is important not merely because of its volume, but also because of its high-technology nature, which makes it particularly important for economic development. Although defence procurement remains significant, however, expenditure on defence in the United Kingdom has declined steadily since the mid-1980s.[5] This decline began largely as a response to general budgetary pressures,[6] but was

---

[1] On the organisation of procurement see further MoD, *Britain's Defence Procurement*, Chap. 1.

[2] It is proposed to amalgamate this with the Defence Land Service to form a single defence property organisation.

[3] *Statement on the Defence Estimates 1995*, Cm.2800, p. 59.

[4] MoD, *Front Line First – Defence Costs Study* (1994), p.29 para. 412.

[5] See Taylor, "British Defence Policy", Chap. 6 in Taylor, ed. *Reshaping European Defence* (1994); Willett, "Introduction: the Restructuring of the U.K. and European Defence Industrial Base" (1993) 4 Defence Economics 83, p.83; Dunne, "The Changing Military and Industrial Complex in the U.K." (1993) 4 Defence Economics 91, pp. 94–97.

[6] Government policy of reducing public expenditure had existed before this period in the civil field, but could not be applied to military spending until 1984–5 because of commitments to NATO.

reinforced by decisions to reduce and reorganise the armed forces as a result of the end of the Cold War.[7]

MoD purchases many of the standard services and products bought by all public bodies; these account for about 7–8 per cent (by value) of its purchasing.[8] However, a special feature of its procurement is the significance of major individual equipment projects involving high technology and significant expenditure, which account for the vast majority of the defence procurement budget. Equipment requires constant upgrading and development to keep pace with new requirements and strategies, and with developments in technology, and expenditure on research and development is therefore high (often from around one-third to one-half of production costs). The "Eurofighter 2000" project for development of a new combat aircraft in conjunction with Italy, Spain and Germany, for example, will have cost over £10 billion for research and development, with the United Kingdom providing one third of that cost; production, should it go ahead, will involve expenditure of a further £10.5 billion. In 1994 MoD also had more than 50 other current projects which involved development expenditure of more than £40 million or production expenditure of more than £75 million.[9] Another feature of much military procurement is high life cycle costs; with major weapons systems these may substantially exceed the original procurement costs and are thus an important consideration. These features of defence procurement mean that it is a particularly difficult and complex area, creating problems in obtaining value for money; the large sums involved, however, mean that efficient procurement is particularly important for the taxpayer.

The special features of defence procurement make collaboration with other states attractive.[10] This allows savings through shared research and development costs and larger and longer production runs – though gains may be offset by transaction costs and the need for compromise which are inherent in collaborative work.[11] It also offers the possibility, through the provision of a larger market, of improving the efficiency of the European defence industry, and in the military field can provide operational benefits arising from standardisation of equipment between allies. For several years the government has sought to procure equipment in collaboration with its allies whenever this makes "economic and military sense",[12] with possibilities for collaboration considered for all

---

[7] Defence expenditure as a whole was expected to fall from a value of £25,437 million in 1990/91 to £21,307 million in 1994/95 (both figures being expressed in constant 1992/93 prices): GSS, *U.K. Defence Statistics 1994.*
[8] Ministry of Defence, *Britain's Defence Procurement* (1994), p. 17, para. 2.28.
[9] *Statement on the Defence Estimates 1994, above,* pp. 55–56, 58 and 60–61.
[10] See generally Hartley, "Evaluating International Projects", Chap. 9 in Hartley, *The Economics of Defence Policy* (1991); Hartley and Martin, "Evaluating Collaborative Programmes" (1993) 4 Defence Economics 195.
[11] For an empirical study on this issue see Hartley and Martin, above.
[12] *Statement on the Defence Estimates 1991*, Cm.1559–I, p. 65.

major equipment projects[13]; and recently it has encouraged its allies in Europe to increase opportunities for collaboration, with a view both to improving value for money and strengthening the European defence market. In April 1995, MoD was involved in 47 collaborative projects, most with European allies, although 19 included the participation of the United States.[14] About 40 per cent related to aerospace, including, for example, the joint procurement of the EH101 Merlin helicopter with Italy, now in the production phase, and the "Eurofighter 2000" project, mentioned above, which was expected to begin production in 1995. Other collaborative projects covered equipment as diverse as missiles, naval navigation systems and military satellite communications.

The government's defence needs are now largely met by private firms. Prior to the 1980s, the major suppliers of weapons and vehicles of war were owned by the government – these included British Aerospace, Rolls-Royce, British Shipbuilders, and Royal Ordnance, four of only seven firms paid over £100 million a year by the Ministry of Defence. By 1991, however, these and several others had been privatised, with the objective of improving commercial performance.[15] Many of the defence industries have traditionally been heavily dependent on MoD orders, as are many individual firms involved in those industries, although some also have civilian interests. In 1990 the Ministry accounted, for example, for about 40 per cent of the work in the shipbuilding industry, 50 per cent in aerospace and 60 per cent in ordnance.[16]

The combination of privatisations, the decline in defence spending and a more competitive approach to awarding defence work (outlined in section (3) below) has significantly affected the profitability of defence firms and has had a considerable impact on the structure of the defence industries.[17]

There has been a trend, first, towards fewer operators in equipment sectors involving high technology and high costs; as a result of mergers and takeovers within the United Kingdom in many areas there is now only one significant United Kingdom provider. Dominant firms include British Aerospace in relation to aeroplanes and missiles; Royal Ordnance (now taken over by British Aerospace), in small arms; Westland in the production of helicopters; Vickers in the manufacture of tanks, following its purchase of the tank business of the privatised Royal Ordnance; and GEC in the area of defence electronics. Several firms, including British Aerospace and GEC, have also sought to broaden their

---

[13] National Audit Office, Report of the Comptroller and Auditor General, *Ministry of Defence: Initiatives in Defence Procurement* (1991) HCP 189, para. 15.

[14] For details see *Statement on the Defence Estimates 1995, above*, p. 72. Other partners outside Europe were Canada and Australia.

[15] Only the Royal Dockyards at Rosyth and Devonport remained in public ownership at the beginning of 1995, but the government has already received initial tenders, and entered into subsequent negotiations, with a view to selling off the yards.

[16] Hartley, *The Economics of Defence Policy* (1991), p. 113.

[17] See further Dunne, above.

defence interests. Many firms have also sought to increase export earnings, and in 1993 export sales amounted to £6 billion, making the United Kingdom the second highest defence exporter after the United States. However, the decline in demand for defence equipment is worldwide, falling by a massive 45 per cent between 1987 and 1992,[18] and export opportunities may also become increasingly limited as export controls are tightened further within the European Community. Some firms have diversified into civilian markets, often using existing expertise: a notable example of successful diversification is that of Racal in the area of cellular radios.

Increasingly, British firms are looking to strengthen their position through partnerships, mergers and takeovers involving firms from elsewhere in Europe. This is a trend which is likely to continue, especially if, as looks probable, the defence equipment markets of the European states are increasingly opened up to Europe-wide competition (an issue considered further in section 4 below). It is a trend which the United Kingdom seeks to encourage, believing that international specialisation offers the best prospects for value for money for government, as well as for improving the competitive position of industry in markets outside Europe.[19]

(2) PROCUREMENT AS A POLICY TOOL AND THE DEFENCE INDUSTRIAL BASE

Two issues of special importance in defence procurement are its use as a tool to support the domestic economy, and the strategic placement of contracts for reasons of national security. These are often related, since strategic awards may be directed towards both ends. For example, restructuring of a defence sector through procurement may be prompted by the desire both to maintain a strong domestic capability out of concern for national security, and to improve the industry for economic reasons.

The options for using procurement as a tool of domestic industrial policy were noted in Chapter 16, and include maintenance of employment, regional development, restructuring, and support of particular industries or technology.[20] Procurement in the defence sector both of military products and certain dual-use products is of particular significance in this context, because of the size and high-technology nature of the defence market[21] and its importance for employment. The fact that

---

[18] Willett, above, note 5.
[19] Commitment to this approach was announced by the then Chief of Defence Procurement, Roger Freeman, in a speech on December 7, 1994: see *The Times*, December 7, 1994, "Freeman to call for more European defence deals".
[20] See pp. 800–802.
[21] It is well recognised that defence technology may have spin off benefits in in the civil sphere: see Ministry of Defence, *Britain's Defence Procurement* (1994) p. 37, para. 7.09. However, it can be noted that civil high technology industries have themselves recently increased considerably in their importance relative to the defence sector.

certain sectors and firms depend heavily on MoD also makes it easier for the government to influence developments through its own purchasing, should it choose to do so.

Generally, the pursuit of industrial objectives requires the government to purchase from domestic industry, although some objectives can be achieved through negotiation of offset benefits, whereby overseas firms or their governments guarantee work to United Kingdom firms in return for MoD business. Until 1983 there was a significant tendency in the Ministry of Defence to purchase from British suppliers, which was influenced by industrial development concerns, as well as by security factors. In the 1950s, for example, the government used its purchasing powers to promote large "national champions" in aerospace, jet engines and shipbuilding: as well as maintaining a strong British capability it was considered that large firms would be best able to compete in world markets. The use of procurement for industrial purposes often involved clear and significant costs; for example, it has been estimated that a decision to use a British engine and avionics in the Phantom aircraft involved additional costs of 28–43 per cent per unit.[22]

From 1983, however, the Ministry adopted a more commercial approach to procurement, as is explained in section 3 below. This has involved, *inter alia*, opening markets to foreign suppliers, to enhance efficiency and value for money: the MoD has claimed that there is no longer any presumption in favour of domestic firms.[23] Since that time industrial development objectives, which entail exclusion of foreign suppliers and a compromise of the competitive approach, have been much less influential.[24] The main exception has been the MoD's approach to offset benefits (or "industrial participation" as the MoD prefers to call it) – the Ministry will sometimes take account in evaluating bids of opportunities for British firms *to compete for work* from an overseas supplier – and also the continued division of work between participating nations in collaborative projects.[25]

The original change in strategy was influenced partly by a desire to purchase from the most competitive supplier regardless of nationality, but partly also by the practical difficulties in meeting objectives when secondary considerations are taken into account. These affect both the primary objective of the procurement – obtaining the required product

---

[22] Hartley, "Defence Procurement and Industrial Policy", Chap. 8 in Roper ed. *The Future of British Defence Policy* (1985), p. 80.

[23] Cm. 1559, *Statement on the Defence Estimates 1991*, vol. 1, p. 73.

[24] Commitment to this open policy was reiterated in *"Defending our Future", Statement on the Defence Estimates 1993*, Cm. 2270, p. 71, para. 71.

[25] Ministry of Defence, *Britain's Defence Procurement*, paras. 2.15–2.17. Waiver of offset requirements are negotiated where possible, pursuant to the preference for open procurement, but where other states engage in protectionism, the offsets policy provides some protection for U.K. industry. Proposals for offsets are generally considered from firms from outside the Western European Armaments Group (WEAG) on contracts over £10 million, but are not generally sought from WEAG firms, although contracts over £10 million are considered on a case-by-case basis.

on time – and the secondary industrial goals themselves. With regard to the primary objective, for example, attempts to develop domestic products, rather than purchase off the shelf from abroad, have frequently been characterised by additional costs and long delays. Indeed the new competitive approach was prompted by a series of spectacular disasters in cases where the choice of system had been influenced by industrial development concerns. The most notable example has been the Nimrod Airborne Early Warning Aircraft Project, cancelled in 1986 in favour of the purchase of the Boeing AWACS aircraft, after enormous cost escalations and with an anticipated date for operation of the mid 1990s instead of 1982. As Smith has noted, "Defence procurement is difficult enough without adding wider economic considerations which further complicate the decision process and increase the likelihood of costly mistakes".[26] Doubts have in any case been expressed about the effectiveness of past attempts to use defence procurement in achieving the intended industrial objectives.[27] Further, the government has taken the view that exposure to foreign competition will in the long term benefit domestic industry, ensuring that it maintains the competitive edge necessary to compete abroad[28]; thus the competitive approach can itself be considered a strategy for domestic industrial development.

Most recently, these justifications for preferring an open policy have been supplemented by the government's commitment to a "European" rather than a national approach to the defence industry.[29] Under this policy, it seeks to promote open competition for defence contracts throughout Europe, with the aim of improving the efficiency of the European defence industry as a whole. Obviously this entails a continuation of its own policy of allowing access to providers from allied European states.[30] There are already some limited European measures designed to open up defence procurement, as explained in section 4: dual-use products are in principle required to be subject to competition under the E.C. directives, and military equipment is dealt with under an informal agreement to create a European Defence Equipment Market (EDEM), operated by the Western European Union. However, there is still a long way to go and the United Kingdom's markets are at present more open than those of many European states.[31]

Even in the United Kingdom, however, it can be expected that where the secondary economic benefits are overwhelming or – more likely – in

---

[26] Smith, "Defence Procurement and Industrial Structure in the United Kingdom" (1990) 8 International Journal of Industrial Organisation 185, p. 195.

[27] This is something which is difficult to assess: for an overview of the competing arguments and the evidence on its effectiveness in the United Kingdom see Hartley, *The Economics of Defence Policy* (1991) Chap. 8, "The U.K. Defence Industrial Base".

[28] MoD, *Britain's Defence Procurement*, p. 9, para. 2.3.

[29] See further p. 877.

[30] Commitment to this policy does, on the other hand, raise the possibility of retaliation by the United Kingdom if its European allies fail to follow the United Kingdom's example and open up their own markets to a comparable degree.

[31] On policies in some other key European states see Taylor (ed.), *Reshaping European Defence* (1994).

cases of political sensitivity, placement of key contracts may be influenced by secondary concerns, sometimes in the face of opposition from MoD. Thus in June 1993[32] the government gave an assurance that the Rosyth Royal Dockyard would for the next twelve years be guaranteed work refurbishing Royal Navy surface vessels; this accompanied an announcement that a £5 billion contract for refitting submarines, widely expected to go to Rosyth, would be awarded on commercial grounds to Devonport. The stated aim was to allow Rosyth to develop the skills to compete for work in the future, so that both dockyards could be kept open. However, the Navy had stated that two yards were unnecessary, and the main consideration appeared to be to preserve jobs at Rosyth.[33]

Another illustration of the tension which can arise is the ongoing controversy of the last few years over whether MoD should, on industrial development grounds, purchase as a transport aeroplane to replace the existing Hercules the planned European Future Large Aircraft (FLA), to be manufactured through the European Airbus consortium but not yet available, or the C–130J (a version of the Hercules) produced by the American firm Lockheed. Lockheed is prepared to provide off-set benefits, but it is feared that these will be significantly outweighed by damage to British Aerospace if the MoD chooses the American aircraft: the Airbus partners may then deny British Aerospace participation in the FLA, which the firm claims could lead to 7,500 immediate job losses and threaten its position as Europe's leading manufacturer of aircraft wings. Purchase of the FLA has always been urged by the Board of Trade, but for a while MoD appeared inclined to favour the United States option already in production.[34] In December 1994 it was announced that the government would order 25 of the United States aeroplanes, and postpone a firm decision on the remaining requirement. It has since announced that it will re-enter the FLA project if its requirements on "price and performance" are met.[34a] Any such decision can probably be justified only on industrial development grounds, because of the greater expense in maintaining a "mixed" fleet.

Strategic placement of contracts may also be considered appropriate for security reasons, whether to maintain a domestic industrial base in a sector[35] or for other reasons, such as confidentiality. Such concerns have

[32] *The Times*, June 25, 1993, pp. 1, 8 and 23.

[33] Procurement decisions affecting shipbuilding have been particularly affected by secondary concerns, because of its importance as an employer and the serious impact of individual procurement decisions: see Hilditch, "Defence Procurement and Employment: the Case of U.K. Shipbuilding" (1990) 14 Cambridge Journal of Economics 453.

[34] See *The Economist*, September 3–9, 1994, pp. 16–17.

[34a] See *Statement on the Defence Estimates 1995*, above, p. 68.

[35] On the U.K. defence industrial base see Taylor and Hayward, *The U.K. Defence Industrial Base: Development and Future Policy Options* (1989); Dunne, "The Changing Military Industrial Complex in the U.K." (1993) 4 Defence Economics 91; Taylor, "West European Defence Industrial Issues for the 1990s" (1993) 4 Defence Economics 113; Hartley, *The Economics of Defence Policy* (1991), Chap. 8; Hartley, "Defence Procurement and Industrial Policy", Chap. 8 in Roper ed. *The Future of British Defence Policy* (1985) and the comment by Hussein at pp. 183–186.

frequently been invoked in the past to justify placing contracts with British industry.[36] Recently, the MoD has stated that it is its policy to procure from domestic suppliers in a "small number" of cases,[37] and it has made it clear, for example, that it intends to maintain a national capability for building and fitting its nuclear submarines.[38] However, recent statements by the government encouraging international specialisation indicate that it is prepared to move towards the concept of a "European" rather than a national defence base. It is likely that in future industrial strategy on procurement – whether based on security or purely economic concerns – will be directed increasingly at the creation of a strong "European" defence industry, rather than a national industry as such. These issues are considered further in section 3 on the future of defence procurement.

(3) PROCUREMENT PROCEDURES: THE COMMERCIAL APPROACH OF THE MoD

Efficiency is particularly important in defence contracting because of the large sums of money involved. However, as explained above, it is difficult to achieve because of the special features of defence markets, such as the complexity of projects; the innovative nature of many projects – making it difficult to estimate costs in advance; the existence of domestic monopolies; and the influence of strategic and (until recently) industrial considerations. The pressure to obtain value for money has increased as projects have become ever more expensive with new technology and this is exacerbated by declining defence budgets which have meant smaller production runs and consequent increases in unit costs.

The key features of the present system date from reforms which began in 1983 and accelerated with the appointment of Peter Levene as Chief of Defence Procurement the following year,[39] and which involved a determined effort to implement a commercial approach to defence procurement. MoD has estimated that these initiatives have resulted in savings of £1 billion each year in the purchase of defence equipment,[40] as well as producing a more competitive domestic industry which is better placed to win orders abroad.

One of the chief reforms was to increase the use of competitive tendering,[41] and to widen the range of potential competitors. This

---

[36] For a history of government policy in this area see Taylor and Hayward, above, Chap. 7.

[37] MoD, *Britain's Defence Procurement*, Chap. 2 at 2.10. Some critics argue that the U.K. has not formulated a clear policy on the defence industrial base in the post-Cold War world: see Taylor and Hayward, above, esp. Chap. 7; Hartley, *The Economics of Defence Policy* (1991), pp.124–126; Taylor, "West European Defence Industrial Issues for the 1990s" (1993) Defence Economics 113, pp. 117–119.

[38] Speech by Roger Freeman, above, note 19.

[39] See generally National Audit Office, Report by the Comptroller and Auditor General, *Ministry of Defence: Initiatives in Defence Procurement* (1991), HCP 189; Hartley, "Competition in Defence Contracting in the United Kingdom" (1992) 1 P.P.L.R. 441.

[40] MoD, *Front Line First: the Defence Costs Study* (1994), p. 28, para. 402.

[41] See Turpin, *Government Procurement and Contracts* (1989), pp. 130–131; National Audit Office, above, paras. 6–8.

enables the government to find the best supplier, and also improves the efficiency of industry through the discipline of competition. One way in which the use of competition has been extended, for example, is by splitting the development and initial production phases – previously it was common for design and the first phase of production to be carried out by the same firm, but now it is more common for the initial production phase to be put out to tender. Steps to widen the supplier base, to create or improve competition in particular sectors, include opening the market to overseas suppliers,[42] wider advertising of contracts (through MoD's own contract bulletins or the *Official Journal of the European Communities*), and assisting new entrants to the market. Use of competitive procedures has been increased through closer scrutiny by senior officials of individual decisions to use single tendering procedures,[43] whilst it has been sought to enhance the efficiency of the process through measures such as increased use of post-tender negotiations. The result of these and other policies[44] has been that between 1983/84 and 1991/92 the proportion by value of contracts priced by competitive tendering rose from 22 per cent to 63 per cent.[45-46] It should be mentioned that contracts for military equipment are generally excluded from the E.C. procurement rules, although contracts for dual-use equipment – that is, equipment with both military and civilian uses – are covered unless some exemption applies (for example, on security grounds). However, the commitment to competitive procedures will be enhanced by the voluntary scheme for creation of a European Defence Equipment Market within the Western European Union, which is designed to open up the "hard" defence equipment market currently excluded from the Community rules.

In its *Defence Costs Study* of 1994 the MoD has reiterated that competition will remain the cornerstone of its policy.[47-48] It has also, however, begun to reduce the frequency of competition by extending the length of individual contracts.[49] This is expected to reduce the costs of running competitions, and also to provide greater opportunity for suppliers to achieve economies of scale. The Ministry has also indicated that it will be more prepared to consider single sourcing for suppliers offering innovative proposals. These recent moves may indicate a greater confidence in the efficiency of the industry, following from the earlier reforms.

Another significant change dating from the 1980s reforms has been the move away from cost-plus contracts, whereby suppliers are paid on

---

[42] See p. 851 above.

[43] National Audit Office, above, note 39, para. 7.

[44] On tendering policies see further MoD, *Britain's Defence Procurement*, Chap. 6.

[45-46] *Defence Statistics* (1992).

[47-48] MoD, *Front Line First: the Defence Costs Study* (1994), p. 28, para. 403.

[49] *Ibid.* Orders which are greater than expected have already followed – for example, an order of 259 tanks, expected to be divided into lots over a period of time, was placed with Vickers in one go in 1994.

the basis of reimbursement of costs plus a sum for profits.[50] This provides no incentive to reduce costs since the supplier does not benefit from a cost reduction. Further, where profits are paid as a percentage of costs (the most usual form of cost-plus contract) there is, indeed, an incentive to increase costs and delay completion, to secure additional work and profit. Such contracts have now been replaced wherever possible by fixed-price contracts, thus placing the risks of the project on the provider and giving the maximum incentive to cut costs, or (where it is not possible to fix an exact price at the outset) by other forms of contract which provide some incentive to efficiency.[51] The percentage, by value, of contracts awarded on a cost-plus percentage fee basis declined from 15 per cent in 1983/4 to only one per cent in 1991/92.[52] Other changes include the increased use of specifications ("Cardinal Points Specifications") which define broad operational requirements only, to encourage innovative solutions by providers and widen competition, and a greater emphasis on collaborative procurement. The government has also sought to improve efficiency by making greater use of opportunities to contract out in-house services to the private sector.[53]

2. REGULATION OF DEFENCE PROCUREMENT

(1) INTRODUCTION

Defence procurement, like other central government procurement in the United Kingdom, has not traditionally been subject to legal regulation; government has relied on administrative and Parliamentary control to secure its objectives. Thus the procedures and policies described above have been implemented through administrative means, rather than legal regulation.

Defence procurement is, however, now subject to regulation to some extent under the E.C. procurement rules and the WTO Agreements on Government Procurement (GPA), designed to open up procurement markets on an international basis.[54] Broadly, so far as purchases for defence purposes are concerned, the E.C. and GPA rules apply to dual-use products unless there is some specific reason (such as national security) for exempting a particular procurement. They do not, on the other hand, apply at all to the purchase of military equipment, such as

---

[50] On methods of pricing in government contracts see generally Turpin, above, Chap. 6; McAfee and McMillan, *Incentives in Government Contracting* (1988).
[51] For an outline of the possibilities see Turpin, above, Chap. 6.
[52] *Defence Statistics* (1992).
[53] See generally Chap. 12.
[54] These rules are discussed at pp. 774–782.

tanks and missiles, an important limitation. However, purchases of such equipment have recently been the subject of an informal agreement by Defence Ministers, designed to create an open market for defence equipment in Europe (the "European Defence Equipment Market" – EDEM). This now provides some external constraints on MoD's policy for the purchase of military hardware.

(2) DEFENCE PROCUREMENT UNDER THE E.C. PROCUREMENT RULES[55]

(a) APPLICATION OF THE E.C. TREATY

(i) GENERAL PRINCIPLES

Discrimination in procurement against firms and products from other E.C. states is generally prohibited under the E.C. Treaty, as explained in Chapter 4. There are, however, important exemptions from the Treaty which can be invoked in relation to defence procurement. First, Article 223(1)(b) E.C. excludes from the Treaty measures relating to products of a military nature, such as tanks and weapons (the "military equipment exemption"). Secondly, Article 224 provides for an exemption in various exceptional circumstances, such as war. Thirdly, states may derogate from the Treaty provisions on free movement for reasons of national security.

(ii) THE MILITARY EQUIPMENT EXEMPTION UNDER ARTICLE 223 E.C.

I. Article 223(1)(b)
Article 223 (1)(b) E.C., states as follows:

> "Any Member State may take such measures as it considers necessary for the essential interests of its security which are connected with the production of or trade in arms, munitions and war material; such measures shall not adversely affect the conditions of competition in the common market regarding products which are not intended for specifically military purposes".

II. Which products are covered by Article 223(1)(b)?
The exemption applies in principle to "arms, munitions and war material". Article 223(2) provides that the Council, acting unanimously,

---

[55] See further, Van Gerven and Gilliams, "The Application in the Member States of the Directives on Public Procurement", General Report to the 14th FIDE Conference, Madrid 1990, paras. 42–48; Wheaton, "Defence Procurement and the European Community: the Legal Provisions" (1992) 1 P.P.L.R. 432.

shall draw up a list of the products to which it applies[56] and this was done in a Council Decision of April 15, 1958 (which has never officially been published although it has been widely circulated).[57] Article 223(3) allows the Council to make changes a proposal from the Commission, again acting unanimously, but no subsequent amendments have been made.

The exact significance of the list is not stated.

One question is whether the exemption may ever be invoked for products not on the list. It could be suggested, in order to minimise abuses, that this should not be possible. On the other hand, to limit the application of Article 223 to products actually listed arguably places an undue burden on the Community in amending the list to take account of new products (and would certainly render the current list very outdated) and it is submitted that for this reason the list should not be treated as exhaustive.

A second question is whether *all* products on the list are covered, or only those which the Court of Justice itself considers to be capable of falling within Article 223(1)(b). To allow the Council to determine conclusively which products are capable of being exempt may give rise to abuse, in an area where abuse is generally considered to be particularly prevalent. On the other hand, such an approach has the advantages of certainty, and also recognises the discretion of Member States in a sensitive area, effectively leaving the scope of the exemption to be fashioned by unanimous political agreement. On balance, however, it is submitted that the dangers of abuse require that the Court of Justice should be able to decide which items may properly be included on the list. Probably it is capable of covering equipment such as tanks, fighter aeroplanes and missiles – the military hardware which, as explained, accounts for over 90 per cent of defence procurement by value – and also equipment designed solely for carrying out military operations and training, such as armoured personnel carriers, as well as products specifically adapted for military purposes. Whether it may also cover products frequently used in battle, but also with common civilian uses, such as explosives is more debatable and is considered below. Clearly purchases related to defence administration, on the other hand, such as office equipment are not included.

The second limb of Article 223(1)(b) provides that measures taken in relation to arms, munitions and war material are not to affect competition in the market for products not intended specifically for military use. Clearly this entails that measures relating to "military" products must

---

[56] This could refer to arms, munitions and war material. Alternatively, if one takes the view that the products covered by Article 223(1)(b) comprise arms, munitions and war material *minus* those products which are not intended specifically for military purposes, this list might refer to products which are covered by the provision which are not within the exception.

[57] Answer to Written Question 574/85, [1985] O.J. C287/9.

not affect competition in markets for purely civilian products. Thus, for example, it would not be permitted to pay excessive prices for military equipment to a firm which is engaged also in the manufacture of civilian products, which could then use its excess profit to subsidise its civilian activities.

As mentioned above, it is not clear whether the concept of "arms, munitions and war material" covers *only* products intended specifically for military use or whether it may also cover some products – for example, explosives – which are manufactured for both military and civilian purposes.

One possibility is that it does cover some "dual-use" products and that some measures relating to these products are thus permitted. On this view the proviso in the second limb of the article may be taken to indicate simply that the measures taken must not affect the civilian market in that product. On this view restrictive purchasing measures relating to such dual-use products are permitted provided that they do not affect the non-military market: for example, because an excessive price is paid which can be used to subsidise the civilian production of the product.

An alternative interpretation,[58] however, is that only products confined to the military market are covered as "arms, munitions and war material". On this view the proviso is intended to make it clear that Article 223 does not exempt from the Treaty *any* measures affecting products which are not purely military in nature, whether these affect the civilian *or* military markets, as well as indicating that measures relating to military products must not affect markets in purely civilian products.

This question arose in a competition case, *French state/Suralmo*.[59] Suralmo had been issued with a patent licence by the French government to work patents relating to improvements in diesel engines and in assemblies using such engines. Such engines and assemblies had both civil and military applications. The case involved a challenge to a licence clause which required approval for the grant by Suralmo of sub-licences relating to military applications, but not to civilian applications, of the patent, which it was contended infringed Article 85(1) E.C. The Commission took the view that Article 223 could not apply to the restriction although it related solely to military applications, since the products in question were dual-use products, and not products intended specifically for military purposes. (Indeed, their main applications were civilian.) This conclusion appears to rest on an assumption that Article 223 cannot be used at all for dual-use products, even where the measures in question affect only the military market for the product. However, the

---

[58] Another possibility – which would produce the same result in practice – is that "arms munitions and war material" covers some dual-use products, but that such products are then "removed" from the Article as a result of the application of the proviso.

[59] European Commission, *Ninth Report on Competition Policy* (1979) points 114–15, pp. 72–73.

question remains open to doubt pending an interpretation by the Court of Justice.

III. Application to procurement

Article 223(1)(b) removes from the scope of the E.C. Treaty measures connected with the "production of or trade" of products within its scope, which clearly may cover government decisions concerning the procurement of these products. Thus such procurements may be exempt from the usual free movement provisions, and the Community has no power to regulate procurement in this area.

One question which arises, however, is which types of procurement measures are measures "connected with" the production of, or trade in, a relevant product.

Clearly a contract for the acquisition of the product is covered. Also probably covered are research and development contracts for such products, even if the government proposes to conclude separate contracts, possibly with separate providers, for the R & D and production phases. It is also likely that Article 223(1)(b) covers acquisition of other services connected with military products, such as installation, repair and maintenance, or the design of bespoke software for product operation. If so, the exemption will again apply regardless of whether they are procured under the same contract as the products themselves. A purposive approach to Article 223(1)(b) would indicate that such contracts should be within the exemption,[60] even though their purchase might not be regarded literally as trade *in* the product concerned. For example, a contract for maintenance of military aircraft or tanks should be treated as falling within Article 223.

A distinct issue is the position of contracts which involve the acquisition of both (i) products and services which are generally covered by Article 223(1)(b) (as explained in the previous paragraph) and (ii) products or services normally outside its scope. An example might be a contract for the acquisition of a military vehicle (generally within Article 223), along with the supply of spares which are of a type commonly used also in civilian vehicles (generally outside it). If (contrary to the view stated above) purchases of ancillary services such as installation or repair are not *per se* within Article 223(1)(b), they also will often be comprised within "mixed" contracts of this type, since contracts are often made to cover both supply and installation, or supply and repair.

In this type of case, that part of the procurement which is *per se* outside the scope of Article 223(1)(b) might still be regarded as a measure "connected" with the trade (that is, the purchase) of the product, by virtue of its inclusion together with the exempt purchase in a

---

[60] It is interesting that the European Defence Equipment Market, which is designed to cover measures which are outside the scope of the Treaty, purports to cover maintenance as well as research and acquisition.

single contract. One view could be that the whole procurement should be treated as within Article 223(1)(b) whenever there is a sound commercial or operational reason for combining the purchases into a single contract. A stricter approach would be to exempt the non-military acquisitions only where it is either *essential* for these to be procured in conjunction with the exempt purchases, or, where it would involve tangible and significant costs to separate the two elements. In considering the scope of the security derogations in the directives and regulations it has been suggested that, in view of the strict approach to the interpretation of derogations to fundamental Treaty principles, the second test is more likely to be adopted by the Court of Justice.[61] The same test should be applied in relation to Article 223 as in that context. Whatever the correct test, in accordance with the same principle of the strict construction of Treaty derogations, the onus of showing a commercial reason for including the non-military acquisition within the contract will be on the purchasing authority.[62]

As noted earlier, procurement of military equipment will, however, be caught by the Treaty by virtue of the proviso to Article 223(1)(b) where it is carried out in such a way as to affect competition in markets for non-military products. Thus, for example, it is not permitted to pay excessive prices for military equipment where this could be used to subsidise production of non-military products by the same enterprise.

IV. The scope of judicial review

A final question is how far security concerns must be raised in order to invoke Article 223(1)(b). It has been widely assumed that states need not show a security justification to exempt measures relating to military products from Community rules, but that such measures are automatically outside the scope of the Treaty, irrespective of the reasons for their adoption. On this view, it is permitted to place contracts for these products with domestic industry not merely for security reasons but also for purely economic motives, such as to maintain domestic employment.

This assumption appears questionable, however, since the Article merely refers to measures which states *consider necessary for their security interests*. It may thus be argued that the Treaty applies *unless* states have taken a decision that it should not do so for security reasons. On this view the Treaty provisions apply in principle to procurement of military equipment, subject merely to an exemption on security grounds. This means that states are prohibited from favouring national industry on economic grounds, under the usual free movement provisions. It also opens up the possibility for the Community to regulate the procurement

---

[61] See pp. 153–154.
[62] The Court's general reluctance to require justification of security decisions (as to which see pp. 864–866 below) will not apply where the motivation for the challenged decision is purely commercial.

of military hardware under the directives, without the need actually to repeal Article 223 – although subject to states' option to derogate for security reasons. At the present time, it appears that the Supply Directive and Supply Regulations exclude all measures relating to Article 223 products regardless of the motive for exclusion,[63-64] so that even if it is permitted to regulate military hardware it is necessary to amend the directives to achieve this result. However, the Services Directive and Services Regulations merely exclude contracts covered by Article 223, so that if the Article is interpreted to require a security justification for its use, services contracts connected with military hardware must be advertised under the regulations unless there is a security reason why this should not be done.

Even if it is accepted that specific security grounds must be invoked to rely on Article 223, the Court of Justice is likely to give a wide margin of discretion to states in determining what their own security interests require. This has been its approach so far to the application of the "free movement" security exemptions where external security is concerned – although it is possible that a more rigorous approach may be developed, and indeed the Commission has recently argued for close judicial scrutiny of external security measures in the context of Article 224 E.C., as is explained at (iv) below. However, even if review is only permitted based on a test of whether a measure is actually motivated by security concerns, and objective justification of the measures is not required, increasing political commitment to an open European defence market, as manifested through EDEM[65] may lead to doubts over the bona fides of the United Kingdom government and other states in invoking Article 223.

The view that the application of Article 223 to measures affecting trade in military products requires reference to a specific security justification is, however, controversial, and the Court is perhaps more likely to adopt the view that exclusion of such measures is automatic. In this case a state's decision to invoke Article 223 in relation to procurement could be challenged only on the basis that the product in question is not within Article 223; that the measure adopted does not affect trade in such a product (for example, if it is contended that services related to the product are not covered); that the measure goes beyond what is necessary (for example, that a contract for the purchase of a product which has been treated as exempt wrongly includes non-exempt material); or that it adversely affects competition in civil markets in contravention of the second paragraph of Article 223(1)(b).

Where the Commission or another Member State disputes the application of Article 223, proceedings may be brought to the Court of Justice under a special procedure under Article 225. This is by way of

---

[63-64] See p. 154.
[65] See pp. 869–874.

derogation from the usual procedure applicable in actions against Member States, and involves a hearing *in camera*.[66]

Whatever the correct interpretation of Article 223(1)(b) and the scope for judicial scrutiny of decisions to invoke the exemption, it is difficult to monitor its use, especially since Article 223(1)(a) provides that states are not obliged to disclose any information which they feel is contrary to their essential security interests. However, the Commission or another Member State could bring the government of another State before the Court of Justice under the procedure in Article 225 E.C. if this power to withhold information were to be abused.

(iii) EXEMPTIONS UNDER ARTICLE 224 E.C.

Article 224 E.C. authorises[67] states to take measures which may affect the functioning of the common market in circumstances of:
(a) "serious internal disturbances affecting the maintenance of law and order";
(b) war;
(c) "serious international tension constituting a threat of war"; and
(d) in order to carry out obligations which the state has accepted for the purpose of maintaining peace and international security.

This exemption might be invoked in relation to the purchase for military purposes of products not covered by Article 223(1)(b).

It is not clear what standards will be applied in reviewing states' decisions to rely on this provision. This issue was raised in case C–120/94, *Commission v. Greece*.[68] In an application for interim measures the Commission argued for a stringent standard of review, whereby states must demonstrate by reference to objective circumstances that one of the situations outlined at (a)–(d) above actually exists, and that the measures taken are strictly necessary to deal with that situation. Greece, on the other hand, argued that the only test is one of whether the state has acted bona fide, and in this respect it was suggested that the margin of discretion is wider than that enjoyed under Article 36 E.C. The Court accepted that the Commission's view was arguable so that it had cleared the hurdle of demonstrating a prima facie case for the purpose of the rules on interim relief. In fact, as is explained below, the Court has so far proved reluctant to subject external security measures to scrutiny even under Article 36[69] and, despite this ruling, it is perhaps unlikely that it will be prepared to become significantly involved in such matters in the near future.

---

[66] See further pp. 934–935.
[67] The authorisation is implicit not express; the Article merely states that Member States shall consult each other where such measures are taken to consider steps to prevent their affecting the common market – this is taken as an implicit authorisation of such measures.
[68] Case C–120/94R, *Commission v. Greece* [1994] E.C.R. I–3037.
[69] pp. 864–866.

The Court of Justice has held that Article 224 is a general derogation which may not be invoked where a situation is covered by more specific Community rules in a directive.[70] In relation to the Treaty provisions on free movement, it is thus arguable that grounds (a)–(c) above fall to be dealt with by the specific security derogations (although this is not true of situation (iv), since Article 36 appears to cover only the internal and external security of the state concerned). The significance of this point will depend on whether the standard of scrutiny of decisions is to differ under Articles 224 and Article 36. It seemed to be assumed in *Commission v. Greece*, however, that Article 224 could apply by way of a derogation to the general free movement provisions even in situations (a)–(c); but this point was not expressly addressed.

(iv) SECURITY DEROGATIONS FROM THE FREE MOVEMENT PROVISIONS

As explained in Chapter 4 the free movement provisions of the E.C. Treaty provide for derogations on security grounds,[71] and these cover external as well as internal security.[72]

The European Court of Justice has held in *Campus Oil* that these derogations allow security goals to be implemented through economic means.[73] This raises the possibility that contracts may be placed strategically to preserve a domestic industrial base for defence purposes, even for products which fall outside Article 223(1)(b).

An important issue is the extent to which the Court of Justice may review decisions taken by Member States on such grounds. Whilst in most circumstances it will, in applying the free movement derogations, examine both the validity of the threat against which measures are directed and the justification for those measures as a response, it has shown in the *Richardt*[74] case a reluctance to review decisions involving external security. In that case, which concerned the application of Article 36 E.C. to justify restrictions on the export of "dual-use" products, the Court merely noted that the import, export and transit of strategic goods was capable of affecting security, and did not examine the need for the specific measures in question[75] (although it did accept the possibility of scrutiny on the basis of proportionality in relation to the sanction imposed for breach of the measures in question). As noted above, the scope of review of decisions purportedly based on external security has also been raised in *Commission v. Greece*[76] in the context of Article 224,

---

[70] See Case 222/84, *Johnston v. Chief Constable of the R.U.C.* [1986] E.C.R. 1561.
[71] Similar provisions are included in the directives and regulations: see pp. 867–868 below.
[72] Case C–367/89, *Ministre des Finances v. Richardt* [1992] 1 C.M.L.R. 61.
[73] See p. 85 esp. n. 42.
[74] Above, note 72.
[75] This approach has been criticised: see further Govaere and Eeckhout, "On Dual Use Goods and Dualist Case Law: the Aime Richardt Judgment on Export Controls" (1992) 29 C.M.L.Rev. 941.
[76] The question of the Court's power to scrutinise decisions purportedly based on security grounds was also raised in case C–120/94R, *Commission v. Greece* [1994] E.C.R.–I 3037, but was not determined by the Court: see p. 863 above.

where the Court accepted that the Commission's arguments for close judicial scrutiny of the use of Article 224 at least showed a prima facie case for the purpose of awarding interim measures. It is submitted that the Court is more likely at present, however, to follow the approach in *Richardt* and that it would not question a government's view on either whether a particular capability is essential for military purposes or the necessity of strategic procurement as a method of maintaining that capability. Should the Community move further towards the construction of a "European" defence base as a subsititute for individual national strategies the Court may become willing to examine national policies in the light of measures taken at European level. However, the *Campus Oil* case – in which Irish measures designed to preserve Irish oil supplies were upheld despite the fact that some moves had been taken towards a common Community policy for securing energy supplies – suggests that, even then, rigorous common measures will need to be in place for such an argument to succeed.

Another reason for invoking the security exemptions may be to conceal information which might betray military strategy, particularly in a time of tension or conflict. It was explained in Chapter 4 that, according to the decision in *Re Data Processing*,[77] in general discriminatory purchasing cannot be justified by a concern for confidentiality, since this can be achieved by imposing confidentiality duties which, the Court considered, will normally be effective irrespective of the national connections of the provider. However, in line with the approach adopted in *Richardt*, the Court might not be willing to examine the justification for the choice of measures adopted in the context of external security, and may thus accept the possibility of discriminatory purchasing. Alternatively, it may examine this issue in principle but be more willing to accept the utility of restrictions based on nationality in the particular context of defence (although such an approach could again alter with the advent of a more "European approach" to defence issues by Member States). The need to preclude unlawful diversion of equipment is another security issue in relation to which the Court of Justice, in *R. v. Secretary of State for the Home Department, ex. p Evans Medical*,[78] has indicated that strategic purchasing is unjustified, since there are other adequate safeguards – such as inclusion of security as one of the award criteria – which are less restrictive. However, again the Court may take a different approach where the issue is one of external security.

If the Court does adopt a "hands-off" approach to the derogations in the external security area, a question is whether it is even possible to review a measure for lack of bona fides. In general, the Court has

---

[77] Case C–3/88, *Commission v. Italy* [1989] E.C.R. 4035.
[78] Case C–324/93, judgment of March 28, 1995, discussed at pp. 152–153 above. This case concerned the security exemption in the directive, but it was suggested previously that the same degree of scrutiny will apply to the review of decisions under these specific exemptions as under the Treaty derogations themselves.

concentrated on the question of objective justification and permitted measures which are justified on objective terms without enquiring into motive.[79] However, should the Court take the view that it is not competent to review objective justification then a test of bona fides in the sense of whether the measure was actually motivated by security concerns may be applied.

(b) APPLICATION OF THE DIRECTIVES AND REGULATIONS

(i) EXEMPTIONS

The E.C. procurement directives and the implementing regulations[80] apply in principle to defence contracts,[81] and purchases for defence purposes are exempt only where a specific exemption applies. The thresholds which apply are generally the same as for other types of contract, subject to one exception discussed at (ii) below.

I. Exemptions based on Article 223 E.C.

So far as concerns procurement of military hardware covered by Article 223(1)(b), the Supply Regulations expressly exclude "goods to which the provisions of Article 223.1(b) apply".[82] This wording, which follows Article 3 of the Supply Directive,[83] seems to indicate that all products which are on the list of products designated as "arms, munitions and war material" under Article 223 are excluded from the procedures. If, as is the general view, such products are wholly excluded from regulation under the Treaty anyway, this exemption simply reflects Article 223 itself. However, if it is correct that the Article 223 exemption may be used only where there is a specific security justification, it appears that the exemption in the supply rules is wider than is necessary to give effect to Article 223, its effect being to exclude the application of the award procedures for all products capable of falling within that Article regardless of whether exclusion is justified by the nature of the particular procurement.

---

[79] Hence it has been suggested that a specific requirement that derogations are not to constitute a "disguised restriction on trade" merely indicates that if a motive is protectionist there is a *presumption* that the measures cannot be objectively justified: Oliver, *Free Movement of Goods in the EEC* (2nd ed.), pp. 170–171.

[80] On these rules see Chaps. 3 and 5–11.

[81] This is made clear in Supply Directive Article 3 and Services Directive Article 4(1). Such provisions were not included in the original Supply Directive; this was unnecessary, since contracts made for defence purposes, like any others, were caught by the general definition of supply contracts and thus within the rules. The express statement on this point was added later, to emphasise that such contracts are regulated. There is no such express statement in the Utilities Directive or Works Directive, but since defence contracts fall within the general definition of works, supply and services contracts covered by these two directives they are regulated where no exclusion applies.

[82] Supply Regulation 6(d).

[83] This refers to "products to which Article 223(1)(b)" applies.

The Services Regulations, following Article 4(1) of the Services Directive, exempt all contracts "to which the provisions of Article 223" apply.[84] This clearly covers all contracts which are exempt from the Treaty itself under that provision.

There are no exemptions based on Article 223 in the public sector Works Directive/Regulations or in the Utilities Directive/Regulations. In practice, contracts subject to the works or utilities rules are most unlikely to fall within Article 223(1)(b) and no doubt this is why no exemptions were included.[85]

II. Other security exemptions

Apart from the exemption for military equipment, the other exemptions most relevant to defence procurement are those in Works Regulation 6(d), Supply Regulation 6(c), Services Regulation 6(i) and Utilities Regulation 6(d). These exemptions, which were discussed in Chapter 5,[86] apply:

(i) To contracts classified as secret. This could be invoked for dual-use purchases where it is feared that to advertise details of the contracts publicly would reveal military information.

(ii) Where delivery of the goods or carrying out of work(s) or services must be accompanied by special security measures. This could be used, as in the civilian field, to ensure that equipment is not diverted.

(iii) Where exemption is necessary to protect the state's "basic security interests". It is this provision which would need to be relied on to justify strategic purchasing to preserve a domestic industrial base.

It was suggested in Chapter 5[87] that in determining principles for the use of these exemptions by Member States the Court of Justice will apply the same principles of scrutiny as it operates in the context of the free movement derogations under the Treaty. These were discussed in section (c) above, where it was suggested that the Court may be reluctant to scrutinise states' judgments. As was pointed out in Chapter 4, however, the application of the same principles does not mean that the scope for derogation is exactly the same under the regulations as under the Treaty: the regulations impose more onerous obligations, and thus the derogations from the regulations may more readily come into play than derogations from the Treaty. Thus, even if the Court were unwilling to allow a derogation from Article 59 to permit authorities to discriminate against providers from other states for reasons of confidentiality, on the basis that confidentiality duties could safeguard the secrecy of the

---

[84] Services Regulation 6(h).
[85] If military products are wholly outside the Treaty so that the E.C. may not regulate these products at all, an exemption based on Article 223 is to be implied into the directives. Thus Member States could include such an exemption in their implementing legislation (although the United Kingdom has not done so).
[86] See pp. 152–154.
[87] See pp. 152–154.

information concerning the contents of the contract from third parties, the same reasons may well justify a departure from the publicity requirements of the regulations which would allow anyone to know the gist of this information.

Exemptions from the procurement regulations also apply in the case of contracts awarded pursuant to international agreements concerned with the stationing of troops.[88]

(ii) THE SPECIAL RULES APPLYING TO SUPPLY CONTRACTS OF 200,000 ECUs OR LESS

The rules discussed at i) above apply, so far as concerns supply contracts of the Secretary of State for Defence, only to contracts of an estimated value of at least 200,000 ECUs. These contracts of 200,000 ECUs plus are all regulated by the regulations, unless covered by a specific exclusion (such as the "Article 223" and general security exclusions outlined at (i) above).

The rules also apply, however, at a lower threshold for *some* contracts made by the Secretary of State for Defence. The background to these special provisions is that until 1980 only contracts valued at 200,000 ECUs or above were covered at all by the Supply Directive (including in the civil sphere). However, in 1980 the directive was amended to change the threshold for central government contracts from 200,000 ECUs to the equivalent in ECUs of 130,000 SDR. The reason for this was that 130,000 SDR was set as the threshold for central government procurement under the GATT Agreement on Government Procurement ("the GPA threshold"), which came into effect in 1980, and it was desired to bring the E.C. rules into line with the GPA by applying the same threshold in the directive.[89-90] However, in the case of supply contracts offered by the Secretary of State for Defence (and equivalent authorities in other Member States), the directive was not adjusted simply by changing the threshold for all its supply procurement. Instead, the threshold was changed *only* for the purchase of products subject to the GATT Agreement. As is explained further below, for purchases by the Secretary of State the Agreement applied (as does the revised GPA coming into effect in 1996) only to contracts for the purchase of products on a special list annexed to the Agreement. To reflect this, the lower GPA threshold has been applied in the Supply Directive only to products on this list. This position is now provided for in Supply Regulation 6(2)(b).[91] For contracts of 200,000 ECUs plus the usual rules continue to apply.

---

[88] Supply Regulation 6(e)(ii); Works Regulation 6(e)(ii); Services Regulation (j)(ii); Utilities Regulation 6(e)(ii).

[89-90] On this point see further pp. 874–875.

[91] The list of products to which the lower threshold applies is set out in Schedule 2 to the regulations.

APPLICATION OF THE PUBLIC SECTOR PROCUREMENT REGULATIONS TO PROCUREMENT BY THE MINISTRY OF DEFENCE

TYPE OF CONTRACT	THRESHOLD VALUE	CONTRACTS COVERED BY THE REGULATIONS
Works	5 million ECUs plus	All (subject to Article 223(1)(b) and security derogations)
Services	200,000 ECUs plus	All (subject to Article 223(1)(b) and security derogations)
Supplies	200,000 ECUs plus	All (subject to Article 223(1)(b) and security derogations)
	ECU equivalent of 130,000 SDR to 200,000 ECUs	Contracts for products listed in Schedule 2 (subject to Article 223(1)(b) and security derogations)
	Below ECU equivalent of 130,000 SDR	None (although Treaty obligations may apply)

This rather complex position which applies to MoD supply contracts is summarised in the table above.

(3) THE EUROPEAN DEFENCE EQUIPMENT MARKET (EDEM)[92]

(a) ORIGINS AND OBJECTIVES

As explained above, it is the general view that the purchase of military hardware is completely outside the scope of the E.C. Treaty. If this is the

---

[92] See further, Stormanns, "Europe's Defence Industry – Single Market, Yes – but How?" (1991) E.C. Public Contract Law 75; Weber, "Integration of the European Defence Market in the Internal Market" (1992) E.C. Public Contract Law 70.

case,[93] Member States remain, under Community law, free to place their contracts as they please with national industry, including for purely economic reasons. However, the nature and size of these markets – notably their high-technology nature and the government's position as a dominant puchaser in many sectors – means that this is an area where particular benefits could be gained from liberalisation on a Europe-wide basis.[94] Concern at the inefficiencies of the European defence industry which have resulted from nationalistic purchasing has become particularly important in the present climate of declining domestic defence expenditure and of shrinking world markets for export.

An attempt has been made to address these concerns at a European level, not, however, directly by the European Union, but through the separate European Defence Equipment Market (EDEM). EDEM originated in the Independent European Programme Group (IEPG), set up in 1976 to provide a forum for collaboration amongst the European members of NATO; the aim was to provide for more effective research, development and procurement in Europe to strengthen the defence industry. In June 1987 the Defence Ministers determined a need to strengthen the defence technology base amongst the IEPG states and agreed on an "Action Plan on a Stepwise Development of a European Armaments Market",[95] involving the liberalisation of procurement, alongside more systematic co-operation in technology development.[96] The proposed approach to procurement was set out in a document attached to the Communique of the 1990 IEPG Ministerial meeting in Copenhagen ("the policy document"), and has since been elaborated in other guidelines and communiques.

In 1992 it was decided to name the IEPG the Western European Armaments Group (WEAG), and to transfer its functions, including the operation of EDEM, to the Western European Union (WEU),[97] the European pillar of NATO. An Armaments Secretariat has been established to administer the functions of WEAG, which administratively is part of the WEU organisation in Brussels, although supervised by the National Armaments Directors of the WEAG states. Apart from the United Kingdom, there are twelve other participants in EDEM and the other WEAG initiatives: Belgium, France, Germany, Greece, Italy, Luxembourg, the Netherlands, Portugal and Spain, which are all full

---

[93] For a contrary argument see pp. 859–860.
[94] On the benefits flowing from an open procurement policy see more generally pp. 45–50.
[95] The Plan followed publication of the Vredeling Report, commissioned by the Group: *Towards a Stronger Europe*, Report by the IEPG Special Study Team (1987).
[96] Such co-operation is now implemented through the programme known as "EUCLID" (European Co-operative Long Term Initiative for Defence).
[97] See WEU, Communique of the Council of Ministers, Rome, November 20, 1992, para. 5, announcing the mandate to the WEU Permanent Council to take necessary steps; Communique of December 4, 1992 following the IEPG ministerial meeting in Bonn ("the Bonn Communique), announcing the decision of the IEPG ministers for the transfer to be made "forthwith".

members of the WEU; Norway and Turkey, which are associate members of the WEU; and Denmark, which has observer status in the WEU. It can be noted that two of these states, Norway and Turkey, are not members of the European Union, whilst Ireland, Sweden and Austria, which are E.U. Member States, do not participate.

EDEM provides for opening up markets in military hardware by advertising and transparent award procedures, based on commercial criteria. However, the broad principle of an open market is qualified, in theory at least, by the concept of *juste retour*, described below, under which it is sought to achieve an equitable spread in the economic benefits arising from defence procurement.

(b) SCOPE OF THE RULES

EDEM is intended to cover that procurement which is excluded from the E.C. Treaty under Article 223(1)(b). In particular, it applies to the supply of military products, and also contracts for their development and maintenance, both of which it was suggested above are excluded from the scope of the Treaty.[98] The rules apply only to contracts above the value of 1 million ECUs (about £750,000), a threshold considerably higher than those in the E.C. directives or the new and revised GATT/WTO Agreements on Government Procurement, although easily surpassed for many military purchases.

Expressly excluded are nuclear weapons and propulsion systems; warships; anti-toxic and radioactive agents; and cryptographic equipment.[99] These are products which states normally wish to produce for themselves for security reasons or to preserve the defence base, and seem to have been excluded for this reason, although the exclusion of shipbuilding may also reflect its importance for employment. General exemptions are also provided for "emergencies" and for "national security". States may thus continue to place their procurement so as to maintain a national base in any military product or may decline to advertise it when it is considered necessary to keep the purchase confidential.

The rules have not been applied to collaborative procurements, in which it has been traditional to divide up work between the industry of the participating states in accordance with their contribution to the project. Even with these projects, however, attempts have recently been made to increase the extent of competitive procurement.

(c) CONTRACT AWARD PROCEDURES

The EDEM policy involves a commitment to public advertising of contracts covered by the scheme, in bulletins issued by the Defence

---

[98] Para. 7 of the policy document.
[99] *Ibid.*

Ministries. In the United Kingdom this is done through the Ministry of Defence Contracts Bulletin, published fortnightly by the MoD itself. In practice, the Ministry also includes details of many contracts below this threshold, in accordance with its general commitment to a commercial procurement policy. Awards are generally to be made on the basis of "the most economic solution",[1-2] similar to the European Community directives' concept of the "most economically advantageous tender"[3]; and it is also agreed that bids which are low because of state subsidies will be rejected. The competitive approach is "encouraged" even when advertisement is not required (for example, for contracts below the threshold) and also at subcontract level[4] – this is important in relation to high-cost and high-technology procurements, which involve numerous skilled subcontractors. Once a contract is awarded, whether by competitive procurement or single tender, states must publish the award in the national bulletin, the main purpose being to publicise subcontracting opportunities.

In contrast with the rules on qualification of suppliers which apply under the E.C. public sector procurement directives[5] it is accepted that potential suppliers may be required to demonstrate their standing by proof of registration on national qualification lists. However, to preclude the need for multiple qualification and thus to encourage cross-border participation, it has been sought to set up a system for states to recognise each others' lists. States have also agreed to establish "focal points", where suppliers – and other states – can obtain information and advice about each state's procurement practices and procedures.

There is an on-going process of collecting information about the practices of participating states; the aim is to build up a more detailed body of "best practice", which can be incorporated into formal (although non-legal) guidelines for common use. At present agreed statements of best practice have been drawn up on an ad hoc basis to cover particular areas. Once this body of information is reasonably complete, however, it is proposed to incorporate it all into a single volume.

Participation in the open procedures described above is open to firms from all 13 WEAG states, but the Group has also stressed that, despite the objective of improving European defence technology, it will allow competition from other states, preferably on a basis of "reciprocity".[6] These statements are particularly directed towards Europe's North American allies.[7] A number of WEAG states, including the United Kingdom, have concluded Memoranda with the United States on

---

[1-2] Para. 7 of the policy document. Factors specifically mentioned as relevant are both acquisition and life cycle costs, quality, "compliance" and security of supply.

[3] As to which see pp. 236–239.

[4] Policy document para. 7.

[5] See Chap. 8.

[6] Policy document para. 3; Communiqué of July 3, 1993 following the IEPG ministerial meeting in Brussels, p.3; Bonn Communique, above, p. 2.

[7] See further p. 879.

liberalisation of defence equipment,[8-9] but a formal trans-Atlantic agreement along the lines of EDEM has yet to materialise.

(d) THE PRINCIPLE OF JUSTE RETOUR

The principle of open competition described above is, in theory, subject to a significant qualification, under a principle referred to as *juste retour*.[10] This is similar to the doctrine of "fair returns" operated by the European Space Agency[11] and has also been applied to collaborative defence procurements within Europe: it provides that states can expect an equitable industrial return in relation to their participation in the market, and that measures should be taken to correct any "unacceptable imbalances".[12] This is to be applied, in particular, to countries still developing their defence base[13] (the "DDI countries"), notably Turkey, Portugal and Greece; these have most to lose from an open market, since viable new industries may not yet be in a position to compete.[14] It is formally envisaged that *juste retour* will apply, however, only for a transitional period; but in practice it may prove difficult to drop the principle.[15]

In theory, the principle is an important limitation in the operation of a free market. However, its significance is likely to be limited in practice, for although there is provision for collecting data to identify inequities, in contrast with the policy of the European Space Agency, there is neither any formula for determining when inequities exist, nor a mechanism to direct corrective action, which is the responsibility of each nation in its own purchasing.[16]

(e) DISPUTE SETTLEMENT AND MONITORING

In contrast with the E.C. procurement rules and also the new WTO Agreement on Government Procurement (GPA), EDEM does not require states to provide legal redress for aggrieved providers, which is not surprising given the informal and often imprecise nature of the rules themselves. The programme does, however, provide for a system of complaints to the national authority responsible for administering the

---

[8-9] See p. 879.

[10] See generally paras. 11, 12 and 13 of the policy document.

[11] See p. 801.

[12] Para. 13

[13] Para. 13 of the policy document.

[14] Para. 16 of the policy document stresses the need for technology benefits for the DDI countries.

[15] Para. 12 of the policy document.

[16] Para. 13 of the policy document. Guidance on the possible nature of corrective measures includes a suggestion for taking into consideration the scope of participation of DDI country industries in a bid where other factors are "equal", indicating that *juste retour* should be applied without prejudice to "best value" where possible (para. 13 of the policy document); although it is envisaged that corrective measures may compromise best value in some cases (see para. 11 of the policy document).

programme, which is obliged to respond fairly and objectively within a short period of time. Complaints and the responses given are required to be forwarded to the WEAG Secretariat, and to be published at regular intervals.

There is also a system for the Secretariat to monitor contract awards; thus it is hoped to monitor the practical application of EDEM, including the principle of *juste retour*. It will be difficult, however, to assess the application of the programme and its effects on markets for a considerable time because of the long-term nature (up to 20 years) of many defence equipment projects: only a small percentage of current defence expenditure relates to projects placed since EDEM was introduced.

(4) DEFENCE PROCUREMENT UNDER THE WTO AGREEMENT ON GOVERNMENT PROCUREMENT[17]

The Ministry of Defence, like other United Kingdom government departments, is listed as an authority subject to the WTO Agreement on Government Procurement (GPA).[18] However, in the case of purchases by the Ministry, a footnote provides that the Agreement only applies to purchases of products which are set out in a specific list in the Agreement[19] (referred to as "non war-like materials"). Broadly, the list covers most dual-use products which defence ministries might purchase – ranging from paper and manuscripts, to chemicals, fertilisers and vehicles – but does not cover military hardware. Thus, for example, tanks and other armoured vehicles are expressly excluded from the listed category of "vehicles", and warships from the listed category of "ships, boats and floating structures". It is interesting, however, that the list specifically excludes a variety of products commonly used for civilian as well as military purposes: examples include tractors, binoculars and explosives. It is not known whether this list is the same, or similar, to that which the Council has drawn up under Article 223(1)(b) E.C. for the purpose of applying the Community rules since, unlike the GPA list, the Community list has not been officially published. The list is relevant both to the application of the general rules in the GPA, such as those prohibiting discrimination against firms and products from other signatory states, and to the award procedures under the GPA.

The GPA also provides that it shall not prevent a party from "taking any action or not disclosing any information which it considers necessary for the protection of its essential security interests relating to the procurement of arms, ammunition or war materials, or to procurement indispensable for national security or national defence purposes".[20] This

---

[17] See generally pp. 774–782.
[18] Annex 1 of the European Community Annexes to the Agreements.
[19] This list is contained in Part 1(3) of Annex 1 of the European Communities Annex to the new GPA.
[20] GPA Article XXIII.

derogation is in addition to the limitations discussed above which apply to the purchases of specific defence authorities. In practice MoD will not need to use this exemption in relation to purchases of hard defence material since these are already covered by the exemption previously discussed, but may use it to exempt non-warlike purchases where appropriate in circumstances similar to those to which the E.C. free movement derogations might apply (for example, secrecy, or strategic placement to preserve a national defence base). Since there is no specific exemption for defence works and services related to "warlike" products, it appears that this general security provision must also be relied on to exempt procurements concerned with these matters.

It is interesting that with the other general exemptions from the GPA which have a parallel with those in the E.C. Treaty, such as protection of health, limitations similar to those in the Treaty – that measures may not constitute a means of arbitrary or unjustifiable discrimination or a disguised restriction on trade – are expressly provided for.[21] However, these same limitations are *not* applied to the "security" derogation cited above, indicating that a decision to invoke this exemption should be subject to scrutiny at best only on the basis of bona fides.

Collaborative procurement carried out by separate legal entities which are not listed in the Agreement does not appear to be covered. In practice, this procurement would generally be exempt in any case as relating to "warlike" purchases.

In practice, the operation of the GATT Agreement in the past has caused some friction between the European Community and the United States, the Community claiming recently that the US has "unjustifiably" failed to apply the Agreement to a significant amount of its "non-warlike" defence purchases.[22] As within the Community itself, the application of security derogations is difficult to monitor in practice.

3. THE FUTURE OF DEFENCE PROCUREMENT[23]

The future direction of defence procurement policy in the United Kingdom is likely to be significantly affected by developments at European level. Within Europe, there is a widely perceived need to

---

[21] GPA Article XXIII.

[22] See European Commission, *1994 Report on U.S. Barriers to Trade and Investment* (April 1994), Doc. No.I/194/94, pp. 25–27.

[23] See further Cox, "The Future of European Defence Policy: the Case for a Centralised Procurement Agency" (1994) 3 P.P.L.R. 65; Hartley, "Public Procurement and Competitiveness: A Community Market for Military Hardware and Technology?" (1987) 25 Journal of Common Market Studies 237; Walker and Gummett, "Nationalism, Internationalism and the European Defence Market", Institute for Security Studies, Chaillot Papers No. 9 (1993).

improve the efficiency of the defence industry, for both economic and military reasons, and there is a strong military argument for greater standardisation of equipment. Creation of an open procurement market in military equipment, and better harmonisation of specifications and the timing of procurements, could help advance both these objectives. The potential importance of a "European" approach to these issues is generally recognised; but there is, however, little sign of consensus on the steps which should be taken.

One issue is the appropriate institutional framework for any policy; another, closely related, that of which countries will participate. One possibility is that further action will be taken by the European Union, which already regulates dual-use products, and has well-developed mechanisms for enforcing its rules.[24] As explained above, it is generally considered that to regulate the acquisition of military hardware it is necessary to repeal Article 223 (although an alternative view is that this is possible to some extent without repeal).[25] Article 223 E.C. is, however, on the agenda for the intergovernmental conference to be held in 1996 to review the Treaty, and measures may be agreed there which would give a legal and political mandate for the Community to take steps in this field. Another possibility, however, is action through the WEU, especially WEAG. As we have seen, WEAG is already involved in liberalising military hardware markets, through EDEM, and in promoting collaborative research, through EUCLID. Developments in procurement are, of course, likely to be affected by developments in the area of substantive foreign and security policy. For example, if a common defence policy is developed, states may not be so insistent on maintaining an extensive national defence base; and this might also open the way for a centralised purchasing agency (a prospect discussed further below). In this context it may be noted that the E.U. plans to move towards a common policy in these areas.[26] Development of policy through the EU would, however, exclude Norway and Turkey, which are not members of the European Union but participate in EDEM and are associate members of the WEU; it may also raise difficulties (the degree of these difficulties depending, of course, on the form in which policy develops) over the position of Ireland and Denmark, mere observers in the WEU, and Sweden and Austria, which are members of the European Union, but have no formal association with the WEU.

Another issue which arises is the exact form of any European industrial policy. Some policy at a European level appears essential to

---

[24] See Chap. 18.
[25] See pp. 861–862.
[26] The E.C. Treaty originally made no specific provision for Community jurisdiction over defence and foreign policy matters, but the Single European Act of 1986, amending the Treaty, added *cooperation* in the field of foreign policy as a Community objective and the 1991 Treaty on European Union (more commonly known as the Maastricht Treaty) substitutes for this a reference to a *common* foreign security and defence policy (Title V, Articles J and J.1 to J.11). The way is thus open for the introduction of a common policy-making institution for all Member States.

improve the competitiveness of industry, in particular by encouraging and facilitating further cross-border mergers and increased international specialisation in certain products and technologies. This will inevitably require some degree of market liberalisation for military hardware, to parallel the Community's open market programme in the civil sector. EDEM has already begun this process in relation to the purchases of individual European states. However, the EDEM programme is limited at present, at least in theory, by the *juste retour* principle, designed to ensure that states' economic interests are not too substantially affected. This principle – which has no counterpart in the Community's open market rules for civil and dual-use products – involves some compromise of efficiency. It remains to be seen whether states will be prepared to accept a liberalisation programme for military equipment which is not subject to this limitation, especially if it is stringently enforced.

Another important issue, relevant not just to the purchase of military equipment but also of the dual-use products already regulated under Community law and the GPA, is the extent to which exemptions on security grounds will be permitted under any future open market regime. These narrow the scope of the open market, reducing the opportunities for international specialisation, and are also open to abuse. They are particularly used at present for states to maintain a domestic defence industrial base, and many states may be reluctant to give up the idea of a national defence base in favour of a "European" base, whereby essential capabilities are secured on a European basis with specialisation in different European states. As already mentioned, however, this approach may become more acceptable with increased co-operation in substantive policy matters. Further, the "national" approach is already becoming increasingly difficult to maintain in practice in view of the cross-border mergers and alliances which have already occurred, and will become more so if markets are opened further. In the United Kingdom itself the government has strongly supported a "European" approach to the defence base, even though it has indicated a commitment to maintaining autonomy in the substantive policy field.[27]

The future is certainly likely to see increased efforts to harmonise states' timing of purchases and specification of requirements to allow for greater collaborative procurement. It has already been noted that this has economic benefits – for example, economies of scale through longer production runs and the sharing of costly R & D – and also military benefits from standardisation. Ad hoc collaboration is increasing, and should be further facilitated by the EUCLID programme. A special panel of WEAG also has responsibility for identifying opportunities for collaboration, through, *inter alia*, regular meetings to review the equipment needs of the participating states. In the past, collaborative pur-

---

[27] Taylor, "British Defence Policy", Chap. 6 in Taylor, ed., *Reshaping European Defence* (1994), p. 98.

chases have generally been characterised by the same "national preference" approach as purchases by individual states, work being strictly
divided between the industries of the participating nations at both prime
and subcontract level. However, there have been some moves away from
such a strict principle of *juste retour*, especially in projects involving the
United Kingdom. Thus for the new "Horizon" frigate programme
involving the United Kingdom, Italy and France it is planned that
components will all be put out to competitive tender to firms from states
within the partnership. A truly open European market, however,
requires possibilities for the award of contracts to firms from European
states not participating in the project.

Another possible development is provision for centralised purchasing.[28] This could facilitate rational planning of a "European" defence
base, and provide an opportunity to maximise both military and industrial benefits. A central agency is certainly a realistic possibility for a
group of states sharing a common defence and security policy, when a
common organisation could be responsible for establishing equipment
needs, as well as for the acquisition process; but this is still a long way
off. Such a body could still play some role, however, even whilst
equipment needs continue to be determined largely by individual states.
In December 1991 the WEU states called in the Maastricht Declaration
for the establishment of a "European Armaments Agency" and in 1994 a
WEAG study examined the possibilities for a present role in Europe of
an international body. Whilst no steps have yet been taken to this end on
a pan-European level, in 1993 France and Germany announced an
intention to create a joint procurement agency – although mainly for the
limited purposes of defining requirements and improving management
of their joint projects.[29]

Whatever the institutional structure, and whatever the approach
adopted to achieve an open defence market, it should be noted that it is
not sufficient to deal with procurement issues alone. Matters such as the
distortion of the market by heavy state subsidy (as occurs in France and
Italy, for example), the development of a common export regime to
ensure that firms in different states operate under equal conditions, and
the improvement of the structure of competition law in the defence
sector are all issues which need to be tackled if a truly open market is to
be achieved.

A final issue is the extent to which markets are to be opened to non-
European states. For equipment not covered by Article 223 E.C.,
conclusion of agreements with third countries is within the exclusive
competence of the Community under Article 113 E.C.[30] As noted earlier,
such procurement is, subject to security derogations, covered by the

---

[28] See further Cox, above, note 23.
[29] The agency is also to evaluate research and development proposals.
[30] See pp. 766–767.

GPA. It also falls within the scope of other Community agreements covering liberalisation of procurement including the Association Agreements with Eastern Central Europe, whose coverage in the procurement field is almost identical with that of the E.C. Treaty and directives.[31] However, the application of these rules, particularly because of the security derogations, is difficult to monitor.[32]

Procurement of military equipment, on the other hand, is generally considered to be excluded entirely from the Treaty and to remain in the hands of Member States[33]; and it does not fall within the international liberalisation agreements concluded at Community level. In practice, liberalisation in this field is feasible only between military allies and is, almost exclusively, an issue of E.C.–U.S./Canada relations. A number of Community states, including the United Kingdom, have concluded Memoranda with the United States providing for mutual access to each other's defence markets where practical.[34] Further, the MoD has, as explained earlier, generally been keen to buy "off the shelf" from the United States rather than developing its own equipment or buying within Europe when the former option offers the best value for money – a policy which has sometimes attracted criticism from the United Kingdom's partners within Europe.[35] However, although the issue has been studied within NATO, it has not yet proved possible to reach agreement on a "trans-Atlantic" equipment market of the kind promoted within Europe through the EDEM programme. Factors such as declining defence spending on both sides of the Atlantic, loosening of co-operation following the end of the Cold War, and increased competition for defence markets abroad, make conclusion of such an agreement perhaps less likely in the future.

It is evident that the United Kingdom at present favours the creation of an open and competitive European defence market which is not hampered by any concept of *juste retour*, and that it continues in general

---

[31] See pp. 782–786.

[32] As noted above the Community has accused the United States of abusing the security exemption.

[33] Although an argument was made that such procurement might be within the Treaty where not specifically excluded for security reasons: see pp. 861–862.

[34] *U.S./U.K. Co-operation Memorandum* (published January 1995). This is to have effect until January 1, 2005. It requires the two states, *inter alia*, to *consider* procurement from the other state for defence products and related services (section 2.1); to provide information to each other's providers interested in defence markets (section 2.3); and – within the confines of national regulation – to evaluate each other's offers without applying price differentials or import duty (section 2.6). The need for each to maintain a defence industrial basis is recognised but it is undertaken to confine this to a small proportion of defence purchasing (section 3.2.5.). There is provision for award procedures to be publicised "to the extent practicable" in a "generally available periodical", for adequate time periods for bids, and for notification of and reasons for decisions to be given to participants (section 4).

[35] As with the United Kingdom's decision, announced in 1995, to buy 67 Apache helicopters from McDonnell Douglas, a United States firm, rather than the Tiger offered by Eurocopter. The United Kingdom's Westland will, however, co-operate in making the Apache.

to follow an open approach in its own procurement. Thus, there will be little difficulty for the United Kingdom in adjusting to a European regulatory regime for all military procurement. It is difficult, however, to know how far this liberalisation process will proceed at a European level, or the precise instruments for liberalisation. Likewise, the future extent of more radical developments which would have a significant impact for the United Kingdom, such as a centralised purchasing agency, cannot yet be predicted.

CHAPTER 18

REMEDIES AND ENFORCEMENT

1. INTRODUCTION

This chapter examines the legal remedies for enforcing the rules on procurement award procedures.[1]

In most cases, the remedies which apply are the general administrative law and private law remedies of English law, such as judicial review and damages for misfeasance in public office. However, for some breaches these are modified or supplemented by other provisions – for example, by specific statutory rules on the award and calculation of damages. Further, in addition to the legal remedies available to affected individuals, there are in some cases other enforcement mechanisms as well – for example, the possibility of action by the European Commission for a breach of Community law, or by the Secretary of State for the Environment in the case of a breach of the rules on compulsory competitive tendering.

The first part of this chapter will consider the general administrative law and private law remedies. These apply where there is a breach in the procurement process of general principles of administrative law, such as natural justice.[2] They also apply to breaches of procurement rules contained in legislation, where their application is not excluded by the legislation. In this case the general remedies will sometimes operate alongside any additional remedies provided in the legislation.

The remaining sections of the chapter examine the operation of the remedies system in specific areas of procurement law, including any special rules which supplement or modify the general remedies system. Here we will look at (i) rules deriving from European Community law[3]; (ii) the rules under the (GPA) World Trade Organisation Agreement on Government Procurement and under other agreements with third countries; (iii) the rules in Part II of the Local Government Act 1988, prohibiting local authorities from taking account of non-commercial considerations[4]; and (iv) the rules on CCT.[5]

---

[1] There are also other rules on procurement discussed in this book, which are not concerned with award procedures but with the subject matter of the contract – in particular, the *ultra vires* rule, and the rule on parliamentary appropriations. The effect of these rules and the remedies available to affected parties were considered in Chap. 2.
[2] See pp. 33–36.
[3] These rules were discussed in Chaps. 3–11.
[4] See pp. 830–845.
[5] See Chaps. 12–14.

2. GENERAL REMEDIES

(1) NON-FINANCIAL REDRESS

(a) THE FORMS OF RELIEF: DECLARATION, INJUNCTION AND THE PREROGATIVE ORDERS

Remedies generally available in English law for breach of public law or private law duties are (i) the injunction and (ii) the declaration. An injunction is normally given to restrain a breach of the law, but it is also possible to obtain a mandatory injunction, to command compliance. A declaration simply involves the court's declaring that a breach of the law has occurred or that proposed conduct would be a breach. An injunction is not available against the Crown as such, but may be obtained against a Minister who acts under legislative powers conferred upon the Minister himself.[6]

In addition, there are three remedies applicable only in the area of *public law*. These are (i) certiorari, to quash a decision, (ii) mandamus, to compel the authority to render a lawful decision, and (iii) prohibition, to prevent unlawful action – collectively referred to as the "prerogative orders".[7] They are probably not available against the Crown,[8] but, like the injunction, certiorari and prohibition may be obtained against Ministers performing functions conferred upon them by statute.[9] Since these remedies are available only in public law cases, the question arises as to whether procurement cases involve matters of public law.

With actions for breach of the substantive "public law" principles of judicial review, such as natural justice or legitimate expectations, there are, as explained in Chapter 2, doubts over whether procurement is a public law activity for the purpose of applying these principles at all.[10] If these public law principles of review *do* apply, however, it seems clear that the public law remedies of certiorari, prohibition and mandamus will be available to vindicate those public law rights.

With actions for breach of legislative rules on procurement, it is likely that where such rules apply *only* to bodies amenable generally to public law review, they are rules of public law and as such capable of being enforced by the prerogative orders.[11] Thus certiorari, mandamus and

---

[6] *M. v. Home Office* [1993] 3 All E.R. 537, changing the previous understanding of the law; see Craig, *Administrative Law* (3rd. ed., 1994), pp. 727–729.

[7] See further Craig, *Administrative Law*, above, pp. 516–530.

[8] See Wade, *Administrative Law* (7th ed., 1994), Chap. 7 though for a contrary view see Craig, *Administrative Law*, above, pp. 725–726.

[9] The position with respect to mandamus against Ministers is more doubtful: on this see Craig, pp. 725–726.

[10] See pp. 33–36.

[11] s.19 of the Local Government Act 1988 concerned with remedies for breaching the prohibition on non-commercial considerations in local authority procurement assumes the availability of judicial review in providing for express rules on standing in such actions: see p. 942.

prohibition will be available, for example, in actions to enforce the rules in the Local Government Act 1988 and Local Government Planning and Land Act 1980, since these regulate only local authorities and certain other local bodies of a clearly public nature.[12]

A more difficult case is that of legislative requirements which are not confined to bodies subject to public law review.[13] This is the case with the E.C. procurement rules: thus the Supply, Works and Services Regulations in limited cases impose duties on private firms (for example, private firms holding public works concessions),[14] whilst the Utilities Regulations apply to all bodies which are subject to a degree of public influence or enjoy special or exclusive rights, including those in the private sector whose activities may generally be outside the scope of judicial review.[15] An action to enforce a legislative rule of a general nature which applies equally to private and public bodies is not normally a matter of public law: for example, an action to enforce a safety duty placed on all employers could not be enforced through the public law remedy of prohibition, even against a public body. However, it is submitted that the rules on procurement should be regarded as "public law" rules for the purpose of the prerogative orders, even though not strictly confined to bodies subject to public law review, because their rationale is the public nature of the purchasing authority or the influence which public authorities may be able to exercise over the purchaser. This does not mean, however, that the prerogative orders should be available to enforce these rules against all regulated persons: a two-fold test should be applied, requiring both that the rule in question is a rule of public law, and that the decision-maker is otherwise subject to public law review. Thus it is submitted that the public law remedies are available against, for example, government departments which breach the regulations, but not against privatised utilities (assuming that the public law remedies do not generally apply to the activities of such utilities).

---

[12] A contrary argument has been made, analagous to that made in the context of applying substantive public law principles to procurement – that procurement is a "private" matter, and that public law remedies as well as substantive rules, do not generally apply: see Bowsher, *European Initiatives in Public Procurement*, cited in Digings and Bennett, *E.C. Public Procurement* at C1.15. However, this appears incorrect in principle even if procurement does not have the same status as other government decisions for common law review purposes, since breach of an express legislative rule of a public nature can be considered to impart the necessary element of "public law" to the case. This was accepted by the Court of Appeal in *Birmingham City Council v. Mass Energy,* September 3, 1993, in which it was held that tendering provisions under the Environmental Protection Act 1990 are enforceable by way of judicial review; and see also *R. v. Avon County Council, ex p. Terry Adams, The Times,* January 20, 1994.

[13] In the context of contract legislation on procurement should be treated as clearly of a public nature not merely where the functions of the body in general are subject to judicial review, but also where the relevant contracts relate to specific functions of the body which the themselves subject to judicial review (even if the rest of the body's activities are not reviewable).

[14] See pp. 353–365.

[15] See pp. 387–388.

(b) PROCEDURE AND TIME-LIMITS

When a case involves an issue of "public law", proceedings must normally be brought before the High Court, by way of judicial review.[16] This applies regardless of whether the applicant seeks an injunction, declaration, the prerogative orders or a combination of these. The rules governing such proceedings are found in section 31 of the Supreme Court Act 1980 and Order 53 of the Rules of the Supreme Court.

What is an issue of public law for this purpose is closely related to the question of what is a public law matter for the purpose of availability of the prerogative orders[17] – where the prerogative orders are available, an issue is one of public law for the purpose of the judicial review procedure also. Claims alleging breach of one of the general principles of administrative law, such as natural justice, must thus generally be pursued by way of the judicial review procedure, since these may be enforced through the prerogative orders. The same applies to claims alleging a breach of statutory procurement rules of a type enforceable by the prerogative orders, where brought against public authorities[18] – for example, claims against local authorities for breach of the procurement rules under the Local Government Act 1988. In addition, even if the Crown itself is not subject to the prerogative orders, the judicial review procedure will apply to similar proceedings when brought against the Crown: if such proceedings are of a public law nature when brought against public authorities generally, then they are also of a public law nature when brought against the Crown. The judicial review procedure, like the prerogative orders, will probably not, on the other hand, apply to proceedings against bodies which are not normally amenable to public law, which may include the privatised utilities.[19]

Proceedings by way of judicial review are normally heard by a single judge of the High Court.[20] A special feature of such proceedings is that leave must be sought.[21] Applications must be made[22] within three months, and must also be made "promptly", or leave may be refused.

---

[16] For further details of the procedure see Craig, *Administrative Law*, above, Chaps. 15 and 16.

[17] See further Craig, above, pp. 566–577.

[18] If the analysis in the text on the scope of the prerogative orders is incorrect, then in view of the close relationship between the scope of the prerogative orders and the judicial review procedure, it also follows that to this extent the judicial procedure likewise will not apply.

[19] Proceedings against such bodies must be thus brought in an ordinary action in the High Court. In practice, any action against a purchaser who is not subject to judicial review is likely to arise in the context of procurement only under the regulations implementing Community law, when an aggrieved provider will use the special remedies provided by the regulations.

[20] Usually this is a judge with special expertise on administrative law matters: see Craig, above, pp. 595–596.

[21] Rule of the Supreme Court, Order 53, r.3(2).

[22] The relevant provisions, set out in Order 53, r.4 and Supreme Court Act 1988, s.31(6), are not entirely clear, but were interpreted in the manner set out in the text in the House of Lords decision in *R. v. Dairy Produce Quota Tribunal, ex p. Caswell* [1990] 2 A.C. 738.

The court may hold that an application is not prompt even if made within three months, and is likely to do so in procurement cases in view of the need for prompt action to avoid disrupting government programmes. It is generally assumed that the time begins to run from when the challenged conduct occurred.[23] The court may extend the time-limit if there is "good reason"; this may apply, in particular, where the applicant could not have known of the decision.[24] However, even where good reason exists, relief may be refused at the hearing to an applicant relying on an extension of the time-limit where either (i) it would cause substantial hardship to a third party or prejudice to that party's rights or (ii) relief would be detrimental to good administration. The relevance of this discretion in procurement cases is considered further in section (d) below.

As explained in section (3) below, often an applicant is unable to obtain relief once a contract has been concluded with a third party. Often a contract will be signed within a few days of the award decision and prompt action is thus of particular importance in procurement cases, quite apart from the short time-limits set out above.

(c) STANDING TO SUE

In practice, actions relating to contract award procedures are most likely to be brought by aggrieved competitors or by their representatives, such as trade associations. They might also be brought by interested members of the public. A remedy cannot be obtained by any person who feels concerned at a breach of the law, however, but only by persons with "standing" to sue.[25]

An application for judicial review[26] may be made by a party with "sufficient interest in the matter to which the application relates", under section 31(3) of the Supreme Court Act 1981. Prior to the introduction of this provision (originally, in 1977 in Order 53 of the Rules of the Supreme Court),[27] the test for standing differed for the five different remedies, but now appears to be the same in each case.[28] Further, the test of sufficient interest is more flexible and liberal than even the most liberal of the previous rules, so that cases decided before 1977 are of limited value.[29] Whether a party has a sufficient interest to enforce a statutory rule is determined by examining the intention of the legislature,

---

[23] This assumption was made in *R. v. London Borough of Redbridge, ex p. G* [1991] C.O.D. 398.

[24] *Ibid.*

[25] See Craig, *Administrative Law* (3rd ed., 1994), Chap. 13.

[26] Claims made other than by way of judicial review are in practice likely to arise only in the context of the European Community rules and are therefore considered only in the section on Community rules.

[27] On the history see Craig, above, p. 490.

[28] *R. v. Inland Revenue Commissioners, ex p. National Federation of Self Employed and Small Businesses Ltd* [1982] A.C. 617.

[29] See the discussion of the recent cases in Craig, above.

involving consideration of the nature of the power exercised, the subject-matter of the claim, the nature of the illegality and any specific indications in the statute.

Domestic legislative rules on procurement are generally concerned to secure best value for money. In the United Kingdom one such provision is section 135 of the Local Government Act 1972, requiring local authorities to adopt standing orders on competitive procedures. It was held in *R. v. Hereford Corporation, ex p. Harrower*,[30] that a provider did not *as a competitor* have standing to obtain either certiorari or man-damus to enforce the procedures. However, this case was decided before the sufficient interest test was adopted and will probably no longer apply: generally the courts are now willing to recognise that standing is intended to be conferred on any person with a direct personal interest in a decision and thus are likely to accept that any competitor with a prospect of obtaining the contract may bring an action.[30a] The courts are also likely to recognise the standing in the area of procurement of representative trade organisations: recent decisions have given standing to groups with an "expertise" and "genuine" concern in the matter in question,[31] and the case for standing is even stronger where the group represents those who are directly affected by the type of decision which is subject to challenge. Certainly such an organisation will have standing where its members as a whole are directly affected by a measure – for example, to challenge a local authority standing order – although it is perhaps more debatable whether this would apply to a measure relating to a specific contract, which affects only one or two members, where an argument might be made that legal action should be reserved for those directly affected. Ratepayers of a local authority may sue in respect of a decision which affects public expenditure,[32] and thus might be able to challenge unlawful procurement measures by local authorities. On the other hand, a taxpayer does not automatically have standing to sue for a breach of law affecting central government expenditure,[33] and although he may do so in serious or flagrant cases this exception is unlikely to apply in the procurement context.

In practice, in most cases the procurement legislation in the United

---

[30] [1970] 1 W.L.R. 1424; and see also *McKee v. Belfast Corporation* [1954] N.I. 122.

[30a] This was assumed, for example, in *R. v. Avon County Council, ex p. Terry Adams* and in *Birmingham City Council v. Mass Energy*, n.12 above. Standing may be precluded, however, when the applicant has submitted a bid in an award procedure, but it is one which the purchaser is not permitted to accept: this seemed to be the view of Ralph Gibson L.J. in *Terry Adams*. On the other hand, it is clear, as accepted in *Terry Adams*, that standing can exist even when the applicant has not bid, if this has been caused by the purchaser's breach of the rules, such as an unlawful failure to advertise the contract or the use of unlawful specifications.

[31] *R. v. Inspectorate of Pollution, ex p. Greenpeace (No. 2)* [1994] 4 All E.R. 329; *R. v. Secretary of State for Foreign Affairs* judgment of 10 November 1994.

[32] The aggrieved provider in *Harrower*, above, was awarded standing to obtain certiorari on this basis.

[33] *R. v. Inland Revenue Commissioners*, above.

Kingdom now deals expressly with standing and the most significant provisions are considered later in this chapter under the relevant areas of law.

The question of standing will also arise in relation to the application of common law review principles such as natural justice, if these principles apply. Where the principle in question is concerned to protect the interests of the applicant, as with the natural justice or legitimate expectations principle, he will have standing. Where it is claimed that the authority acted unreasonably or for improper purposes, it is necessary to consider the precise nature of the statute and the breach alleged, as with a breach of express legislative rules. Here again, however, it is very likely that the court will find standing for any person directly affected by the decision, including an aggrieved provider.

(d) THE DISCRETION TO REFUSE RELIEF

The declaration, injunction and prerogative orders are discretionary remedies. This raises the question of whether the court may in its discretion deny any remedy to reopen a contract award procedure, either because of administrative inconvenience or because of the hardship to the party who has been awarded the contract.

In practice, where an applicant wishes to reopen a procedure, he will seek interim relief to delay the procurement, an issue considered at (e) below. If this is denied, it is likely that a contract will have been made with a third party by the time the case is heard, and that performance will have commenced or even have been completed. The fact that a contract has been made is sometimes a complete bar to reopening the procedure, as explained in section (3) below, a rule itself designed to protect the interests of the administration and of third parties. When there is no such bar on the other hand, these interests may be taken into account only by virtue of the court's discretion to refuse relief.

The courts have not been entirely consistent in their views on how far administrative inconvenience or third party interests may be generally taken into account in granting administrative law remedies, and it is therefore difficult to predict the approach which they will take in the context of procurement contracts.[34] However, regardless of the general position, in actions for judicial review there is always a discretion to refuse relief on the grounds of administrative inconvenience or hardship to third parties where an action has not been brought within three months *and* promptly, as explained in section (b) above.

In practice, when the court has refused interim relief this will generally be because of the inconvenience to the administration or the hardship to the third party in holding up the procurement. To the extent that a

---

[34] For the cases see Bingham, "Should Public Law Remedies be Discretionary?" [1991] P.L.64.

discretion to refuse a remedy at trial does exist, these same considerations are likely to suggest that the discretion should be exercised to refuse a remedy at that point also. Indeed, the case for allowing the contract to go ahead may be strengthened if substantial performance has occurred – for example, with a work of construction. However, relief may well be granted if on the facts of the particular case there is little prejudice to the public interest in requiring the contract to be re-tendered. This is often the case with long-term services contracts where, pending re-tendering, an authority's needs could be met by temporary contracts.[34a] When interim relief *has* been granted it is unlikely that the court would refuse relief at trial, unless there has been a change in circumstances – for example, making the project more urgent.

(e) INTERIM RELIEF

Since it may be several months before an application is heard, a litigant will often seek interim relief to suspend the award process pending judgment. This is particularly important in view of the fact that if a contract is made the court might refuse a remedy in its discretion, or there may, in some cases, be a complete bar to setting aside the concluded contract.[35]

Interim relief may generally be obtained by way of an application for an interim injunction. It is possible to obtain a form of interim relief in the form of a "stay" where the applicant seeks one of the prerogative orders in judicial review proceedings[36]; however, probably this power applies only in relation to proceedings of a lower court or tribunal, and does not give the power to suspend administrative action such as procurement decisions.[37] It is probably not possible to obtain an interim declaration; this means that interim relief is not generally available in actions against the Crown itself, since as explained above, the declaration is normally the only remedy available (although there are specific exceptions for breach of Community law).[38]

The award of an interim injunction is discretionary.[39] In deciding

---

[34a] Relief was granted in *Terry Adams*, above, in relation to a contract for waste disposal where it appeared that the authority's need could be met on a temporary basis in other ways. The court also thought it relevant that re-tendering in accordance with the legal requirements would result in substantial cost savings which were likely to outweigh the costs resulting from the delay and re-tendering exercise.

[35] See pp. 895–897.

[36] Order 53 r.10(3).

[37] *Minister of Foreign Affairs, Trade and Industry v. Vehicles and Supplies Ltd* [1991] 1 W.L.R. 550 per Lord Oliver at p. 556.

[38] See p. 906.

[39] On the general principles governing the award of such injunctions see decisions of the House of Lords in *American Cyanamid Co. v Ethicon* [1975] A.C. 396, and *Factortame Ltd v. Secretary of State for Transport* (No. 2) [1990] 3 W.L.R. 818. Where interim relief is sought other than by way of an interim injunction it seems likely that the court would apply the same principles.

whether to grant such relief the court will consider, first, if there is a serious case to be tried and, if not, no interim relief will be given.

If there is a serious case, the court will then proceed to consider whether damages would be an adequate remedy for the applicant; if so, there is no need to award interim relief. As explained in section (2) below, damages are not, in general, available for breaches of procurement law. However, they are available where the breach is deliberate or malicious (under the tort of misfeasance in public office) or where legislation expressly provides for damages. It is submitted that damages will not be adequate where they are limited to tender costs – as is the case with damages for breach of the rules in the Local Government Act 1988 on non-commercial considerations.[40] However, damages might be adequate in cases of breach of statutory duty or implied contract where (as explained in section (2) below) damages are awarded to put the plaintiff in the position in which he would have been had there been no breach of the procurement rules.

This issue arose in *Burroughes Machines Ltd v. Oxford Area Health Authority*.[41] Burroughes was one of five parties invited to tender for a contract to supply a computer system for the authority's data centre. Although an advisory committee had recommended that Burroughes be awarded the contract, the authority had voted to award it to another firm, ICL, a decision it was claimed was made in breach of statutory duty and in breach of contract.[42] On these facts, interim relief was refused by Croom Johnson J., one reason being that damages were an adequate remedy; and this was upheld by the Court of Appeal. However, in this case it was accepted by the plaintiff that damages would be adequate to compensate for the lost contract. This may have been true on the facts, where, had the alleged breach been proven, the result would have been an award to the plaintiff. However, it is submitted that in most cases the damages remedy will not be adequate because of the difficulties of proving that the plaintiff would have succeeded in his bid had the breach not occurred which will be required to recover full lost profits.[43]

---

[40] See pp. 943–944.

[41] July 21, 1983 (transcript available on Lexis).

[42] The case appears to have involved an allegation of breach of the European Community directive on public supply contracts (which had not yet been implemented in the United Kingdom) and of breach of an implied contract governing the tendering process (although at that time the existence of such a contract had not yet been recognised by the courts). However, this is not wholly clear from the judgment.

[43] On this see pp. 892–895. An exception to this may be the case of misfeasance, if the courts are prepared to adopt a generous approach to proof and calculation of damages in such a case.

It was also conceded in *Burroughes* that damages would be adequate to compensate for loss of the possibility of future contracts with the same authority. However, the plaintiff did contend that damages would not be adequate to provide redress for possible loss of business with other, similar, authorities. The courts held the latter allegation of damage too remote to affect the adequacy of damages issue, which seems correct. In cases where future contracts must be awarded under the Community rules, it would also appear that the possibility of obtaining future contracts with the same authority also cannot be affected by loss of one particular contract.

Where damages cannot adequately compensate the plaintiff, the court will then consider whether the defendant can himself adequately be protected by requiring the applicant for relief to give an undertaking that, should his claim fail, he will pay damages for loss caused by the award of interim relief. If so, interim relief will be granted, subject to such an undertaking. If the only adverse consequence of delay to a procurement is extra expense for the purchaser, such an undertaking may indeed be sufficient. However, it will not be adequate in many cases, where delay to the procurement will involve delay to a project – for example, to the construction of a road, or the delivery of supplies (such as refuse collection vehicles) which are required to carry out a public service. In the case of some services and off-the-shelf supplies it may, however, be possible to avoid such consequences by awarding a short-term and temporary contract pending resolution of the dispute.

If an undertaking in damages would not be adequate compensation, the courts must consider the "balance of convenience" – that is, it must weigh, on the one hand, the damage resulting from a delay to the procurement against, on the other, the interests which may be prejudiced if no interim relief is given and the claim proves well founded. So far as delay is concerned, this will vary considerably, according to the nature of the project: for example, there is more urgency about a contract to rebuild a damaged hospital than to construct an ornamental archway in a public park. The courts are perhaps unlikely to grant interim relief in a case where the contract is concerned with averting an immediate and specific threat to life or health, but other cases pose more difficulty. In considering the balance of convenience the courts should also take account of the interests of other firms involved in the award procedure, who may be prejudiced by the delay, and, in particular, of the interests of any firm which may have been awarded the contract.[44]

This balance of convenience issue was also considered in *Burroughes*, where the judge held that the inconvenience which the administration would suffer by the delay to the contract was a further reason to refuse relief. The Court of Appeal not only refused to interfere with the judge's discretion on the basis that correct principles had been applied, but Griffiths L.J., with whose judgment the other members of the court agreed, stated that he would have exercised the court's discretion in the same way. Both the decision and the tenor of the judgments indicate that the courts are generally likely to refuse relief where this would cause delay to government projects.

Arguably, such an approach cannot be followed in future in the context of a breach of Community rules, because it does not comply with

---

[44] Interestingly, contractors giving evidence to a House of Lords Select Committee collecting evidence to assist in implementation of the European Community procurement rules opposed the award of interim relief because of the prejudice which could be caused to other providers involved in the procedure: see House of Lords Select Committee on the European Communities, 12th Report, Session 1987–1988, *Compliance with Public Procurement Directives*, pp. 17–18.

Community requirements on provision of effective remedies.[45] However, it is likely that this restrictive approach to interim relief will be followed in actions for breach of domestic procurement rules. Such an approach combined with the difficulty of obtaining relief at trial and the absence of a damages remedy in most cases, means that it may be difficult for an aggrieved provider to obtain effective relief.

Interim relief may also be refused on certain other grounds, one being the impossibility of supervising the order. In *Burroughes* it was held that this justified refusing an interim injunction which would prevent the authority going ahead with the award based on its unlawful decision. The reason was that, should the authority reconsider that decision and still decide to award the contract to ICL, it would be too difficult to determine in the context of interlocutory proceedings whether the second decision was in fact lawful, or tainted by the same unlawful motives as the first. If correct, this precludes interim relief in all cases where the alleged breach relates to the consideration of unlawful criteria in the award process. It is doubtful if this limitation is acceptable in the context of breach of Community law, as is explained below.[46]

If interim relief is given, the applicant will normally be required to give an undertaking in damages that, should his claim fail, he will compensate the authority for loss suffered from any delay. This will operate in practice as a considerable deterrent to applications for interim relief in cases where loss will be caused. In practice, these are the circumstances in which the courts are unlikely, in any case, to award interim relief; where, on the other hand, there will be little damage from a delay so that interim relief is a real possibility, the undertaking in damages will present less of a problem.

(2) DAMAGES

(a) DAMAGES IN TORT

(i) AVAILABILITY OF DAMAGES

In practice, damages are most likely to be sought by an enterprise which has failed to win a contract. There is, in English administrative law, however, no general right to damages for a person suffering loss as a result of unlawful administrative action.[47] Where there is breach of legislative *duties*, damages may be claimed for loss suffered under the tort of breach of statutory duty. However, this applies only where a legislative intention to give a damages remedy may be implied and the courts will rarely find such an intention, especially for breach of public

---

[45] See pp. 898–899.
[46] See pp. 909–911.
[47] See, for example, *R. v. Knowsley M.B.C., ex p. Maguire* [1992] 90 L.G.R. 653.

law duties.[48] It is unlikely that such an intention will be found in legislation regulating procurement.

Damages are available, however, under the tort of misfeasance in public office, where there has been a *deliberate* breach of public law.[49] Thus damages will be given for loss suffered from an intentional breach during a contract award procedure by a public authority,[50] whether of general administrative law principles such as natural justice[51] or of legislative requirements. Damages are also available, where expressly provided for by legislation, and such a right has been given for breach of E.C. rules and for breach of section 17 of the Local Government Act 1988.[52] Such express provisions give rise to a tort claim for breach of statutory duty.

(ii) CALCULATION OF DAMAGES

Damages for both misfeasance and breach of statutory duty are actions in tort. The general principle of damages in tort requires the plaintiff to be put in a position as if the tort had not occurred. In the present context, this requires the aggrieved provider to be put in the position in which it would have been had the purchaser complied with its obligations. Thus it is necessary to ask: what would the firm's position have been if the proper rules had been observed?

If that firm would not have obtained the contract even had the rules been followed, that firm will be no worse off as a result of the breach, and may not claim any damages. In particular, it should be emphasised that such a firm has in principle no right to recover costs incurred in preparing a bid: these would have been wasted even if the rules had been followed.

If the plaintiff firm would have obtained the contract, on the other hand, it will be able to claim damages for the amount which it has lost by not receiving the contract. This will be the difference between the

---

[48] See further Stanton, *Breach of Statutory Duty in Tort* (1986); Arrowsmith, *Civil Liability and Public Authorities* (1992), Chap. 7.

[49] *Bourgoin v. Ministry of Agriculture* [1986] Q.B. 716; and see Craig, above pp.636–638 and Arrowsmith, *Civil Liability and Public Authorities* (1992), pp. 226–234.

[50] It is not clear how far the tort will extend and, in particular, whether it will apply to the privatised utilities; but this is of little importance in light of the fact that there is an express right to damages for breach of the Utilities Regulations. (As for deliberate breaches of general administrative law principles, if these substantive principles apply at all then it is clear that the tort of misfeasance *will* apply to allow a damages action for deliberate breach).

[51] It was suggested above (see pp. 33–37) that these should apply to procurement decisions. Even if they do not, damages may be claimed under the misfeasance principle for any *malicious* action in exercising procurement powers: see *Jones v. Swansea City Council* [1990] 1 W.L.R. 54 (affirmed by H.L. [1990] 1 W.L.R. 1453).

[52] See pp. 943–944. In Northern Ireland there is also an express right to damages under s.42(2) Fair Employment (Northern Ireland) Act 1989, for breach of the rules in Northern Ireland relating to the making of contracts with firms which have failed to comply with their "fair employment" obligations (as to which see pp. 804–805). This is expressly limited to expenses incurred.

amount which it would have been paid,[53] minus the costs which would have been incurred as a result of the contract[54] – a difference which may conveniently be referred to as the "profit" from the contract. For example, if the contract price is £1 million and expenditure of £900,000 would have been incurred to complete it, the firm will be £100,000 worse off for not receiving the contract, and this is the sum which it will be able to claim. Bid costs will not be taken into account in calculating the sum – these costs, like other overheads, will have been incurred regardless of whether the bid is successful. (In practice, they will be covered from the "profit" made from successful contracts.)

Most claims will be made by firms which have submitted bids. Often it is difficult to know which bidder would have won the contract if the proper procedure had been followed, especially if subjective factors such as product quality or after-sales service are relevant, as well as price. Proof that a particular firm would have won a contract is even more difficult where it has not participated in the tendering procedure – for example, where the grievance is that it was denied this chance because the contract was not advertised. Under the usual rules of tort law a plaintiff must prove that he would have won the contract *on the balance of probabilities*. If this is established, he will then recover the full amount of the profit which would have been made; if not, he will recover nothing. However, it is likely that in the circumstances of the present case the courts will apply the so-called "rule in *Chaplin v. Hicks*".[55] This applies in certain cases where the plaintiff is deprived of a chance of a benefit, as a result of a wrongful act – for example, where the act has deprived the plaintiff of the chance to compete in a talent contest and the realisation of the benefit depends on the outcome of a hypothetical act. Under this rule, the court will assess the chance which the plaintiff had of obtaining the benefit (in the present case, of winning the public contract) and award the value of the benefit (here, the likely profit under the contract), discounted to take account of the value of the chance. For example, if the court estimates that the plaintiff has a 40 per cent chance of obtaining the benefit, it will award the plaintiff 40 per cent of its value. In the above example, where the expected contract profit is

---

[53] Where payment for the contract consists wholly or partly in exploitation of a work or service (for example, right to collect tolls from a motorway built under the contract), this amount will include the amount of revenue collected.

[54] For a different view see Bowsher, "Prospects for Establishing an Effective Tender Challenge Regime: Enforcing Rights under E.C. Procurement Law in English Courts" (1994) 3 P.P.L.R. 30, p. 40, who states that damages must be limited to tender costs. Bowsher's argument, however, involves a misapplication of the principle that the plaintiff must be put in the position as if the *wrong* had not occurred: in the context of procurement this will be, in practice, that the contract would have been awarded lawfully. Bowsher's view seeks to put the plaintiff in the position as if the tendering procedure itself (*i.e.* the activity from which the wrong arose) had not occurred, which is not the correct test.

[55] [1911] 2 K.B. 786.

£100,000, a firm whose chances of winning the contract were put at 40 per cent, would receive £40,000. Such a firm would receive nothing under the balance of probabilities rule. Until recently the courts had not established whether the *Chaplin v. Hicks* rule could ever be applied in tort. The issue was left open by the House of Lords in *Hotson v. East Berkshire Health Authority*,[56] but the recent Court of Appeal decision in *Allied Maples Group v. Simmonds and Simmonds*[56a] indicates that the principle does apply in tort and may be invoked where there is a "real and substantial" chance of obtaining the benefit.

Another difficulty is proving the amount of the likely profit. In this respect, the courts might be prepared to adopt a presumption that the amount of profit would at least have been sufficient to cover the costs incurred in seeking that profit. A similar principle is used in assessing damages for breach of contract: where the plaintiff has spent money in anticipation of contract performance, it is presumed that he would have recovered at least the amount of that expenditure from the contract. This sum may thus be recovered by way of damages, unless the defendant can prove that the plaintiff would not have recouped his expenditure.[57] A similar principle could be used in relation to expenditure made in anticipation of the performance of a legislative duty. On this basis a contractor could recover his costs of tendering, unless the government could prove that these costs would not have been recouped from contract profits. For example, if bid costs were £10,000, the disappointed enterprise would need only to show that it would have won the contract; it would then recover £10,000, unless the authority could show that the difference between the price received and the cost of performing would be less than that amount. Any expected profit in excess of £10,000 would still have to be proved by the firm itself. To the extent that damages sought are limited to costs, there seems to be no reason why a similar presumption should not apply in relation to the other uncertainy in issue – that is, whether or not the firm would have won the contract. Thus, in the above example, the disappointed contractor should *automatically* recover the amount of his costs, unless the defendant purchaser can show either that the contractor would probably have been unsuccessful, or that the profits would not have covered this sum.

These general rules are, of course, subject to any specific provision on damages in the legislation. Special rules apply to calculation of damages for breach of section 17 of the Local Government Act 1988, and

---

[56] [1987] A.C. 750. The Supreme Court of Canada rejected the possibility in *Laferriere v. Lawson* (1991) 78 D.L.R. (4th) 609. However, the Australian High Court has accepted the availability of such a claim for loss of a commercial opportunity: see *Poseidon Ltd v. Adelaide Petroleum N.L.* (1994) 68 A.L.J.R. 313.

[56a] [1995] 4 All E.R. 507.

[57] *C & P Haulage v. Middleton* [1983] 3 All E.R. 94; *CCC Film (London) Ltd v. Impact Quadrant Films Ltd* [1984] 3 All E.R. 690.

breaches of European Community law, and these are considered below.[58]

A claim for damages may be made in proceedings by way of judicial review, where combined with an application for some other remedy.[59] Damages claims may also be made in the county court, or by writ in the Queens Bench Division of the High Court, according to the amount claimed.[60] In this case, the limitation period is the usual period for tort claims of six years from the time the action accrues,[61] and not the short period applicable to judicial review proceedings.

(b) DAMAGES FOR BREACH OF AN IMPLIED CONTRACT

It was explained in Chapter 2 that in certain tendering procedures there is an implied contract governing the conduct of the procedure.[62] In some cases a breach of public law rules may coincide with the private law obligations in this contract; thus damages may be available for breach of contract. In general – although the underlying principle is different – this will give the same result as a tort claim: damages will be given to put the disappointed firm in the position in which it would have been if there had been no breach – that is, as if the purchaser had complied with its contractual obligations. However, it has been noted in section (a) that there may be some differences in the damages rules in contract and tort – in particular regarding the availability of "loss of chance" claims.

It was suggested in Chapter 2, however, that it is not possible to imply an obligation into the contract that all applicable administrative law rules and legislative provisions will be followed. Thus many of these obligations will not form part of the purchaser's contractual duties.[63]

(3) THE PROBLEM OF CONCLUDED CONTRACTS

An important question is the impact of a breach of public law on concluded contracts. If, following a defective award procedure, a purchaser concludes an agreement which would, under ordinary principles of contract law, constitute a binding contract, is its validity vitiated or affected by the defect? Two main questions arise: first, may it be challenged by a third party (for example, by way of judicial review); and,

---

[58] See pp. 911–913 and pp. 943–944.
[59] Order 53 r.7; Supreme Court Act 1981, s.31(4).
[60] Although claims involving public law issues may only be pursued through judicial review proceedings, this does not apply to claims in tort and other private law claims, even though the claim may depend on an issue of public law: *Roy v. Kensington and Chelsea and Westminster Family Practitioner Committee* [1992] 1 A.C. 624.
[61] Limitation Act 1980, s.2.
[62] See pp. 37–40.
[63] See pp. 37–40.

secondly, may the parties themselves refuse to go ahead with the agreement? These questions have already been considered in the context of contracts whose subject-matter is outside the scope of a purchaser's powers (*ultra vires* contracts).[64]

These issues are sometimes dealt with by the relevant legislation. For example, under the regulations implementing the Community procurement directives third party remedies are expressly limited to damages once the contract is concluded[65] (although there is no express provision concerning the rights of the contracting parties). It is also provided by section 135 of the Local Government Act 1972, which requires local authorities to adopt standing orders providing for competitive tendering, that breach of the standing orders does not affect the validity of a subsequent contract and by section 41(6) of the Fair Employment (Northern Ireland) Act 1989 that a contract remains valid although concluded in breach of authorities' obligations not to contract with firms who are debarred for failure to meet their "fair employment" obligations.[66] The main purpose of such limitations is to protect the other party to the contract, although they also protect the administration. On the other hand, it is expressly provided in the Environmental Protection Act 1990 that breach of its provisions on tendering shall render the contract void.[66a] For many rules, however, such as those on compulsory competitive tendering and the general principles of administrative law such as natural justice there is no express provision.

Where the matter is not governed by express provisions, a number of older cases have held that a breach of procedural requirements relating to procurement *does* affect a contract to the extent that the public authority itself may refuse to go ahead.[67] The language of these cases suggests that the agreement is wholly void and it would thus presumably also be open to challenge by third parties with standing to do so. However, in other Commonwealth jurisdictions recent decisions have tended to favour the view that breach of such provisions do not affect the contract.[68] It is submitted that as a general rule the courts should, in line with this trend, generally construe procedural requirements and breaches of general administrative law principles as having no effect on the contract. Thus, neither party should be able to evade its obligations, nor should the agreement be open to challenge by third parties. In other

---

[64] See pp. 15–18.
[65] See pp. 805–806.
[66] On this Act see further pp. 29–31.
[66a] Environmental Protection Act 1990, s.51 and Sched. 2, Pt. II, para. 20(1).
[67] *Young v. Royal Leamington* [1883] 8 AC. 517; *Rhyl U.D.C. v. Rhyl Amusements* [1959] 1 WLR 465; *Mellis v. Shirley Local Board* (1885) 16 Q.B.D. 446; *Lawford v. Billericay R.D.C.* [1903]1 KB.772.
[68] See, in particular, the decision of the High Court of Australia in *Australian Broadcasting Corp. v. Redmore* (1989) 166 C.L.R 454 (in which the authority sought to evade the contract). On the Canadian decisions see, Arrowsmith, *Government Procurement and Judicial Review* (1988), Chap. 14.

words, private law rights should not be subsumed to considerations of public interest as reflected in the procedural rules on government procurement. This is particularly so where the breach in question may well not have affected the award decision.

An exception to this rule may, however, be justified where one or both parties was aware of the defect. Where both were aware, the contract should be susceptible to challenge by third parties – subject, possibly, to the discretion of the court to refuse a remedy for reasons of hardship or public inconvenience[69] (although these arguments may receive a less sympathetic hearing where the parties are complicit in the breach, or where the contract has deliberately been concluded in order to avoid a judicial challenge). Where one of the parties was aware of the defect, arguably the other should be permitted to renounce the agreement. In the case of the public authority, this might be subject to an obligation to do so only for the purpose of upholding the public interest behind the rules which has been breached: for example, where there has been a breach of a rule on tendering, the authority should not be permitted to renounce the agreement simply because there has in the meantime been a drop in the market price, revealing that the authority has made a bad bargain.[70]

3. REMEDIES FOR BREACH OF EUROPEAN COMMUNITY LAW

(1) INTRODUCTION

A variety of mechansims exist to enforce the European Community rules on procurement. This section will consider, first, the remedies available for aggrieved individuals, consisting of legal actions in the courts (section (2) below) and, in the utilities sector, the possible use of a Community "conciliation" procedure (section (3)). Secondly, the chapter will examine the role of the European Commission in enforcing the rules, including the possibility of proceedings by the Commission in the European Court (section (4)). Finally, for the utilities sector there is also provision for a special system of "attestation" (section (5)).

---

[69] On this see pp. 887–888.

[70] Such an argument does, however, face the possible objection that the exercise of contract powers may not be subject to judicial review (as to which see pp. 33–37). It can also be pointed out that in the cases cited in note 67 public bodies were permitted to renounce the agreement for what were clearly "ulterior" motives.

(2) LEGAL REMEDIES IN THE DOMESTIC COURTS[71]

(a) GENERAL PRINCIPLES

As with other rules on procurement the Community rules may be enforced through actions by affected persons brought in the United Kingdom courts.

The remedies and procedures for enforcing Community law rules and national measures implementing those rules, such as the procurement regulations, are in principle for national law. However, this is subject to two general principles of Community law. The first, is that remedies and procedures must be at least as favourable as those for enforcing similar provisions of domestic law[72] – the principle of non-discrimination.[73] The second is that remedies provided must be effective[74] – the principle of effectiveness. This sometimes requires a *particular* type of remedy – for example, damages – to be made available.[75]

In addition, there are directives to deal specifically with remedies in the procurement field, as was explained in Chapter 3.[76] These are the Remedies Directive,[77] which applies to the public sector, and the Utilities Remedies Directive,[78] applying to the utilities sector, which were adopted as part of the drive to enhance the open procurement

---

[71] See further Arrowsmith, "Enforcing the Public Procurement Rules: Legal Remedies in the Court of Justice and the National Courts" in Arrowsmith (ed.), *Remedies for Enforcing the Public Procurement Rules* (1993), pp. 43–90; Weatherill, "Enforcing the Public Procurement Rules in the United Kingdom", Chap. 8 in Arrowsmith (ed.), above; Arrowsmith, "Enforcing the E.C. Public Procurement Rules: the Remedies System in England and Wales" (1992) 1 P.P.L.R. 92; Bowsher, "Prospects for Establishing an Effective Tender Challenge Regime: Enforcing Rights under E.C. Procurement Law in English Courts" (1994) 3 P.P.L.R. 30; Gilliams, "Effectiveness of European Community Public Procurement after *Francovich*" (1992) 1 P.P.L.R. 292; Gormley, "The New System of Remedies in Procurement by the Utilities" (1992) 1 P.P.L.R. 259; Cox, *The Single Market Rules and the Enforcement Regime after 1992* (1993), pp. 241–254; Trepte, *Public Procurement in the E.C.* (1993), Chap. 7; Arrowsmith, "The Implications of the Court of Justice Decision in *Marshall* for Damages in the Field of Public Procurement" (1993) 2 P.P.L.R. CS164.
[72] Case 33/76, *Rewe-Zentralfinanz v. Landwirtschaftskammer für das Saarland* [1976] E.C.R. 1989.
[73] This seeks to ensure that Community law is given the same priority in national systems as national rules. Before it was recognised that remedies must be effective in an objective sense, the principle ensured that a minimum level of protection was available for Community rights without interfering with the freedom of states to decide what was appropriate in the light of their own traditions.
[74] Joined cases C–6 & 9/90, *Francovich v. Italy.* [1991] I-E.C.R. 5357.
[75] *Francovich*, above.
[76] On these directives see further Arrowsmith, "Enforcing the Public Procurement Rules: Legal Remedies in the Court of Justice and the National Courts", above; Gormley, "The New System of Remedies in Procurement by the Utilities" (1992) 1 P.P.L.R. 259; Cox, above, pp. 241–254; Weatherill, National Remedies and Equal Access to Public Procurement" (1990) 10 Y.E.L. 243. On implementation of the public sector Remedies Directive in other Member States see generally Arrowsmith (ed.), *Remedies for Enforcing the Public Procurement Rules* (1993);
[77] Directive 89/665/EEC, [1989] O.J. L395/33.
[78] Directive 92/13/EEC, [1992]) O.J. L/76/14.

market following the Commission White Paper of 1985.[79] Most of their provisions are concerned to improve the enforcement system at the national level[80]; it is hoped that provision of effective national remedies will play a significant role in ensuring purchasers comply with Community rules. In relation to national remedies, the directives contain three main types of provision:

(i) First, they lay down certain general principles. Article 1(1) of each directive provides that procurement decisions shall be reviewed effectively and, in particular, "as rapidly as possible". This can probably now be seen simply as an express statement of the general Community law principles of effectiveness. In addition, Article 1(2) of each Directive requires that the benefit of remedies rules which are more favourable than those of domestic law, can be used by home contractors as well as those from other Member States.[81]

(ii) Secondly, Article 2 of each Directive requires provision of certain specific forms of relief, namely interim measures, the setting aside of unlawful decisions, and damages. The utilities rules allow states to adopt as an alternative to set aside and damages an enforcement regime based on financial sanctions, but this option has not been taken up by the United Kingdom.

(iii) Thirdly, the Directives lay down rules concerning forum and procedure – for example, that decisions must be effectively enforced (Remedies Directive Article 2(7) and Utilities Remedies Directive Article 2(8)),[82] and that review procedures shall be available to providers (Article 1(3) of each Directive).

These directives apply only to contract award procedures which are subject to the directives and implementing regulations; actions alleging breaches of Community law (for example, a breach of the E.C. Treaty) in other award procedures are, so far as Community law is concerned, subject only to the general principles of non-discrimination and effectiveness. Of course, states may, if they choose, implement a single and uniform remedies system for all award procedures. However, the United Kingdom has not done this; the special rules in the Remedies Directives (for example, requiring provision of damages) have been applied only to procedures which are subject to the regulations. Slightly different remedies systems apply in the two cases, and these are therefore examined separately, in sections (c) and (d) below.

---

[79] On the background see further Chap. 3.

[80] Other provisions concern the enforcement powers of the Commission (see pp. 933–934) and, in the Utilities Remedies Directive, conciliation and attestation (see pp. 918–920 and 936–938).

[81] The provisions state that: "Member States shall ensure that there is no discrimination between undertakings claiming injury in the context of a procedure for the award of a contract as a result of the distinction made by this Directive between national rules implementing Community law and other national rules". It is rather obscurely worded but appears designed to have the effect suggested in the text.

[82] This may anyway be inherent in the more general requirement of effective review.

(b) WHICH RULES MAY BE ENFORCED?

Before considering the remedies themselves it is necessary to consider *which* of the Community procurement rules may be the subject of an action. Most of the Community rules are legally enforceable, but in a limited number of cases legal remedies are not available.

(i) THE RULES IN THE DIRECTIVES AND REGULATIONS

I. The regulations: duties owed by contracting authorities, utilities and concessionaries

All four substantive directives on procurement have been implemented into United Kingdom law.[83] The implementing regulations expressly provide that a breach of the duties imposed by the regulations on bodies which are contracting authorities or utilities are duties owed to providers[84] and are actionable by providers who suffer, or risk suffering, loss or damage from the breach.[85] The Works Regulations also make similar provision for duties owed by concessionaries who are not contracting authorities.[86]

However, certain duties are expressly excluded from this principle of actionability.[87] These are as follows:

(i) The requirements in Works Regulation 8(6), Supply Regulation 8(6), Services Regulation 8(6) and Utilities Regulation 12(7), which require purchasers to state in the contract notice or documents the reason for not using relevant European specifications, and to keep a record on this and send it to the Treasury or relevant Minister if required[88];

(ii) The requirements in Works Regulation 10(7), Supply Regulation 10(6) and Services Regulation 10(7), concerning submission to the Treasury or relevant Minister of reports on use of the negotiated procedure[89];

(iii) The obligation in Works Regulation 20(7), Supply Regulation 21(8), Services Regulation 21(8) and Utilities Regulation 21(8) to send an explanation to the Treasury/relevant Minister where a bid is rejected as abnormally low in a procedure using the "lowest price" criterion[90];

---

[83] See pp. 93–96.

[84] Works Regulation 31(1); Supply Regulation 29(1); Services Regulation 32(1); Utilities Regulation 32(1).

[85] Works Regulation 31(3); Supply Regulation 29(2); Services Regulation 32(2); Utilities Regulation 32(1).

[86] Works Regulations 31(1) and 31(2).

[87] Works Regulation 31(1); Supply Regulation 29(1); Services Regulation 32(1); Utilities Regulation 32(1). These are all obligations which it appears are not intended under the directives to confer rights on individuals; hence it is acceptable that these rules should not be enforceable by providers or other third parties in the United Kingdom.

[88] See p. 595.

[89] See p. 288.

[90] See pp. 288 and 518.

(iv) The requirement in Works Regulation 22(3), Supply Regulation 23(3) and Services Regulation 23(3) to send to the Treasury/relevant Minister a written report on an award procedure where requested by the Commission[91];

(v) The requirements under Works Regulation 28(1) and (2), Supply Regulation 27, Services Regulation 27(1) and (2) and Utilities Regulation 27 concerning submission of statistical reports.[92]

A point separate from actionability is the extent to which a particular unlawful decision or omission may be considered to affect a specific contract award procedure, so as to render the procedure as a whole unlawful. For example, failure to publish a Periodic Indicative Notice (PIN) is an actionable breach, and publication could be enforced by a mandatory injunction; but failure to publish such a notice for particular products would probably not invalidate any subsequent award procedure relating to those products. This question is considered further below.[93]

II. The regulations: duties owed by bodies which are not contracting authorities, utilities or concessionaries

On the other hand, duties owed by other bodies which are not either contracting authorities or concessionaries are not stated to be actionable.[94]

This is relevant for bodies which are not contracting authorities or concessionaries but are caught by the rules in the Works or Services Regulations because they award contracts subsidised by a contracting authority.[95] In this case it appears that such rules are not intended to be directly enforceable by affected parties. The method of enforcement in this case is set out in Works Regulation 23(1) and Services Regulation 25(1).[96] These require that the body subsidising the work shall make it a condition of its contribution that the subsidised body complies with the regulations' provisions in awarding the contract, and that it shall ensure that the subsidising body does comply or shall recover the contribution.

Likewise, the obligation for bodies with special or exclusive rights to provide services not to discriminate in awarding public supply contracts, which is required to be imposed under Supply Regulation 24, also appears not be enforceable by aggrieved individuals.

---

[91] See pp. 286–287.
[92] See pp. 288–290 and 552–553.
[93] See pp. 904–905.
[94] Such duties are not referred to in the statements of actionability in Works Regulation 31(1), Supply Regulation 29(1), Services Regulation 32(1) and Utilities Regulation 32(1).
[95] See pp. 368–370.
[96] This is consistent with the directives which appear to place an obligation only on the subsidising contracting authority – requiring it to secure compliance by the subsidised body – and not directly on the subsidised body itself.

III. The directives: rules which have not been properly implemented

Even if regulations have been adopted to implement all the procurement directives, in some cases these may not implement the directives properly – for example, it is possible that the provisions on discrete operational units might infringe the directives.[97] If an authority or utility acts in way which is permitted under the regulations but prohibited by the directives, the question arises as to whether an individual may enforce the directive itself.

An affected party may rely on a provision in a directive which has not been properly implemented by the required date, where the directive has "direct effect".[98] To have direct effect a provision must be sufficiently clear and precise for judicial application, and establish an *unconditional* obligation which is complete and the implementation of which does not depend on further measures being taken. It appears that most of the substantive rules of the procurement directives which govern advertising and the contract award process do satisfy all the above conditions: it was ruled in *Beentjes*[99] that direct effect could be attributed to provisions on the criteria for evaluating bids, and on the criteria for, and means of proof of, technical ability and in *Costanzo*[1] that the rules on procedures rejecting abnormally low bids also had direct effect; and in *Commission v. Portugal* Advocate General Lenz indicated that the obligation to publish a tender notice is directly effective.[2]

Directives have direct effect only against the state and bodies providing a service under state control and which enjoy special powers.[3] All purchasers who are "contracting authorities" under the public sector directives will satisfy these requirements. However, it is more debatable whether they cover all entities subject to the Utilities Regulations, especially those which are caught merely because they operate on the basis of special or exclusive rights. It was explained in Chapter 4 that the High Court decision in *Griffin v. South West Water*[4] indicates that direct effect will probably apply to most United Kingdom utilities because of the extent of government regulation; but that it is not clear whether this decision is correct. Clearly, on the other hand, ordinary private bodies which are caught by the Works Directive as concessionaries are not

---

[97] See pp. 173–175.
[98] On the direct effect of directives see Wyatt and Dashwood, *European Community Law* (3rd ed., 1993), pp.71–76.
[99] Case 31/87, *Gebroeders Beentjes B.V. v. The Netherlands* [1988] E.C.R. 4635, paras. 39–44 of the judgment.
[1] Case 103/88, *Fratelli Costanzo SpA v. Commune di Milano* [1989] E.C.R. 1839, para. 32 of the judgment. The case concerned Article 29(5) as it stood prior to its replacement by a new provision in Article 1(20) of Directive 89/440, [1989] O.J. L210/1 (now Article 30(4) of the consolidated Works Directive of 1993) but there is nothing in the wording of the new provision to suggest it would not have direct effect.
[2] Case C–247/89, [1991] I-E.C.R. 3659, para. 15 of the Opinion.
[3] Case C–188/89, *Foster v. British Gas* [1990] E.C.R. I–3313.
[4] Judgment of August 25, 1994. See further p. 88.

subject to direct effect, and hence the directives cannot be enforced against such bodies where they have not been properly implemented.

IV. The rules in the Community Treaties

The Treaty rules do not need to be implemented in the United Kingdom, but are enforceable by affected individuals in the national courts provided that they are clear, precise and unconditional, and intend to confer legal rights. It is well established that the Treaty provisions which are most significant in relation to procurement, Articles 30 E.C., 52 E.C. and 59 E.C., satisfy these requirements, as do the competition rules in Articles 85–86 E.C.[5] All these Treaty provisions are thus enforcable in acordance with the rules outlined in (c) and (d) below.

(c) REMEDIES IN PROCEDURES SUBJECT TO THE REGULATIONS

(i) INTRODUCTION

This section examines the remedies available in relation to award procedures covered by the regulations. For these award procedures, special remedies provisions have been adopted in Works Regulation 31, Supply Regulation 29, Services Regulation 32 and Utilities Regulation 32, in order to satisfy the requirements of the Remedies Directive, and Utilities Remedies Directive.[6] These special provisions operate alongside the ordinary remedies of English law.

The remedies described in this section, including the special remedies under the regulations, apply in any action against contracting authorities or utilities which is based upon a breach of the regulations themselves. They also apply to actions against contracting authorities or utilities which are based upon breach of any other Community law provisions which occur during a procedure which is subject to the regulations,[7] including a breach of the E.C. Treaty.[8]

The special rules under the regulations do not, however, apply to entities which are regulated merely as public works concessionaires

---

[5] Case 127/73, *BRT v. Sabam* [1974] E.C.R 51 (subject to certain limitations which are not significant here).

[6] See pp. 904–906.

[7] This arises from the fact that the scope of the special rules is stated by reference to those duties owed under Works Regulations 31(1), Supply Regulation 29(1), Services Regulation 32(1) and Utilities Regulation 32(1); these provisions, in turn, refer to the duties in the regulations and also any other enforceable Community obligations owed in relation to contracts covered by the regulations.

[8] They will also apply to some breaches of the "IT Standards Decision", discussed in Chap. 11.

However, this Decision applies also to some contracts below the thresholds of the procurement directives and for breaches relating to these contracts the remedies described in this section do not apply. On the remedies which do apply in that case see (d) below.

under the public Works Regulations (even though the rules can be enforced directly against such concessionaires, by aggrieved providers). Remedies available against these bodies are discussed separately in section (e) below.

(ii) NON-FINANCIAL REMEDIES

The forms of non-financial relief available are a set-aside, an order to amend documents, a declaration, an injunction and the prerogative orders. The first two are remedies created specifically by the regulations; the others are remedies generally available under English law.

I. Set aside

The regulations expressly confer on the court a power to "order the setting aside of [a] decision or action" where this is taken in breach of an enforceable duty.[9] The effect is that the decision or action is devoid of legal effect, and cannot be acted on. Where such a breach relates to a contract award procedure, it will thus be unlawful to continue the procedure on the basis of that decision. For example, if a purchaser disqualifies an interested firm from bidding on a ground which is not permitted under that regulation, where that decision is set aside later decisions in the procedure – for example, selecting between bids – will be unlawful. It is submitted also that an unlawful decision or omission relating to an award procedure, will "taint" the legality of later decisions in the award procedure, regardless of whether the earlier decision has been set aside. Thus where there is a failure to advertise, or an unlawful disqualification of an interested firm, as well as those actions/omission themselves being unlawful, decisions inviting bidders or selecting bidders in that procedure will also have been taken "in breach of duty" for the purpose of the award of a set-aside, and may be set aside themselves.

Whilst most breaches occurring prior to or during an award procedure will affect the rest of the procedure this may not always be the case. For example, it is submitted that failure to publish a Periodic Indicative Notice (PIN) for particular products will not affect award procedures relating to those products. This means however, that the remedies system provides little incentive for purchasers to comply with the PIN rules; a remedy may be obtained to enforce publication of a PIN, but firms are unlikely to be able to prove that damage has been suffered in order to claim compensation. It is suggested also that a wrongful refusal by a utility to include a firm on a qualification list, or an unlawful

---

[9] Works Regulation 31(6)(b)(i), Supply Regulation 29(5)(b)(i), Services Regulation s.32(5)(b)(i) and Utilities Regulation 32(5)(b)(i). These provisions were included to ensure that United Kingdom law complies with the requirements in the two Remedies Directives. In the case of public law actions the existing remedy of certiorari was probably already adequate for this purpose; however, certiorari does not apply to all bodies subject to the regulations.

debarment from a list, would not affect the legality of all individual contracts for which the list is used as a call for competition. Further, breaches of duty after the contract award, such as failure to give reasons for the decision or to publish an award notice, will probably not vitiate the procedure.

Another question is whether a minor defect in a particular action or decision will vitiate that action or decision, so that the action or decision as a whole may be said to be made "in breach of duty" for the purpose of the set-aside remedy. For example, a minor omission from an advertisement – such as omission of a telephone number – probably will not vitiate the notice as a whole.

II. Amendment of documents

A second remedy created by the regulations enables the court to order a purchaser to amend any document where a decision or action has been taken in breach of a relevant duty.[10] This could be used in relation to specifications which do not comply with the regulations or Treaty, or to remedy other unlawful provisions – for example, where time-limits given for firms to respond to a notice are insufficient.

The power is important. If the court were limited to a power of set aside, then when an unlawful provision could not be severed from the documents the whole call for tenders or issue of invitations would have to be set aside. Unlawful specifications, for example, could not be severed, since the tender documents would be meaningless without specifications. The amendment power allows this to be avoided if the applicant prefers to seek only a more limited remedy. On the other hand, if a firm prefers it may still seek a set-aside. This might be sought, for example, where a provider has not prepared a bid because its product does not meet the unlawful specifications and it later realises that they are unlawful; here it could be unfair merely to amend the document, since presumably time periods would continue to run from the date of despatch of the notice.

III. Availability of the injunction, declaration and prerogative orders

It is expressly stated that the provisions on remedies under the regulations are "without prejudice to any other powers of the Court".[11] Thus the general remedies of the declaration, the injunction and the prerogative orders remain available.[12]

---

[10] Works Regulation 31(6)(b)(i), Supply Regulation 29(5)(b)(i), Services Regulation 32(5)(b)(i) and Utilities Regulation 35(5)(b)(i).
[11] Works Regulation 31(6), Supply Regulation 29(5), Services Regulation 32(5) and Utilities Regulation 32(5)(b)(i).
[12] See pp. 882–883.

The declaration and injunction are generally available against any purchaser, except that normally there can be no injunction against the Crown. The regulations, however, expressly provide for injunctions to be available against the Crown also.[13] This will in fact be a particularly useful remedy: for example, it may be issued to restrain a purchaser from proceeding with an unlawful contract or award procedure, and may presumably be sought in conjunction with a set-aside.[14] As was also explained, the prerogative orders are available against many of the authorities covered by the regulations, but may not lie against some of the regulated utilities and are also unavailable against the Crown. Probably these remedies are also unavailable against public bodies for breach of the competition rules in Articles 85–86 E.C. since these are treated as private law not public law rules.[15]

As with the remedy of set-aside, it is necessary to decide for the purpose of these remedies whether a particular unlawful decision "taints" a subsequent award procedure. This should be resolved in the same way as in relation to set-aside.[16]

IV. Procedure

The remedies of set-aside and order for amendment of documents are obtained in the High Court.[17] The declaration, injunction and prerogative orders, as explained above, are also sought in the High Court, but where they are sought against public authorities this *must* be done through the Order 53 procedure with its distinctive features, such as the leave requirement.[17a] This special procedure does not, however, apply to actions for a set-aside and amendment. Thus, in the case of public authorities it may not be possible to seek the set-aside and amendment and the five "general" remedies in a single action.[18]

V. Time-limits

It is provided in Works Regulation 31(5)(b), Supply Regulation 29(4)(a), Services Regulation 32(4)(b) and Utilities Regulation 32(4)(b) that

---

[13] Works Regulation 31(8), Supply Regulation 29(7), Services Regulation 32(7) and Utilities Regulation 32(9). This was included to satisfy the European law requirement that effective remedies should be provided.

[14] See Chap. 4.

[15] *Garden Cottage Foods v. Milk Marketing Board* [1984] A.C. 130, *per* Lord Diplock at 144.

[16] See pp. 904–905.

[17] Works Regulation 31(4); Supply Regulation 29(3); Services Regulation 32(3); Utilities Regulation 32(3). In Scotland such remedies are obtained in the Court of Session.

[17a] *O'Reilly v. Mackman* [1983] 2 A.C. 237.

[18] However, it could be suggested that an exception should be made to the rule in *O'Reilly v. Mackman*, above, that Order 53 is the exclusive procedure for obtaining a declaration or injunction in public law cases. The rule is based on the fact that to use the ordinary procedure is normally an abuse of process because this would circumvent the safeguards of Order 53, but this is surely not the case when the ordinary procedure can be used to obtain other forms of relief (the set aside and amendment remedies).

proceedings under the regulations must be brought promptly, and in any event within three months from when the grounds for proceedings first arose; but may be extended for "good reason". This is similar to the time-limit for judicial review proceedings. There is no specific provision allowing the Court to refuse relief on the basis of prejudice to the administration or hardship to third parties where the action is delayed, but a discretion to refuse relief for these reasons may exist under general legal principles.[19] In practice, actions will anyway need to be brought promptly, because non-financial relief is unavailable once a contract has been concluded.[20]

This time-limit applies to proceedings brought under Works Regulation 31, Supply Regulation 29, Services Regulation 32 and Utilities Regulation 32. Probably this covers all proceedings to enforce the regulations and to enforce other Community law rules which apply in award procedures governed by the regulations, including those instituted by way of judicial review.[21] As explained the time-limit for judicial review is in any case very similar.[22]

VI. Standing

The regulations state that the duty to comply with the regulations and with other Community law provisions applying to regulated procedures is a duty owed to contractors (works contracts), suppliers (supply contracts) and service providers (services contracts),[23] and that a breach is actionable by any contractor, supplier or service provider who, in consequence, suffers loss or damage.[24] The terms "contractor", "supplier" and "service provider" refer to a person who sought, or who seeks to be, or who would have wished to be, the person to whom a works/supply/services contract is awarded.[25] "Service provider" also covers a

---

[19] See pp. 887–888.

[20] See pp. 913–915.

[21] These may all be considered to be proceedings "under" the relevant regulation based on the fact that Works Regulation 31(3), Supply Regulation 29(2), Services Regulation 32(2) and Utilities Regulation 32(3) expressly provide for both duties under the regulations and under other relevant Community rules to be actionable by providers.

[22] See pp. 884–885.

[23] Works Regulation 31(3), Supplies Regulation. 29(1), Services Regulation 32(1) and Utilities Regulation 32(1). (On the limited duties which are not actionable see pp. 900–901). It is expressly stated in all regulations that the rules do not create any criminal offence.

[24] Works Regulation 31(1), Supplies Regulation 29(2), Services Regulation 32(2) and Utilities Regulation 32(2).
These rules on standing implement Article 1(3) in each of the Remedies Directives, requiring that review procedures must be available to any person having or having had an interest in obtaining a contract or participating in a design contest and who has been or risks being harmed by an alleged infringement, and must be interpreted in light of these Community provisions.

[25] Works Regulation 4(1)(a), as amended by Supply Regulation 31(1); Supply Regulation 41(1)(a); Services Regulation 4(1)(a), as amended by Supply Regulation 31(2); Utilities Regulation 4(1).

person seeking to participate in a design context under the services rules.[26]

The right to enforce the regulations under these provisions is expressly limited to those persons who are nationals of and established in certain specific countries, referred to as "relevant" states.[27]

"Relevant" states include, of course, the fifteen Member States of the European Community,[28] on whose providers rights are conferred by the Community procurement directives. In addition, "relevant" state covers Norway, Liechtenstein and Iceland,[29] whose providers are given rights equivalent to those under the Community directives by virtue of the European Economic Area Agreement,[30] and Hungary, Poland, the Czech Republic, the Slovak Republic, Romania and Bulgaria whose providers are given rights to participate in award procedures according to the directives' procedures by virtue of Association Agreements concluded between those states and the Community.[31]

For the purpose of these provisions a person who is not an individual is a "national" of a relevant state where that person is formed in accordance with the laws of a relevant state and has its registered office, central administration or principal place of business in a relevant state.[33] "Established" has the same meaning as under the Community Treaties.[34]

Providers from certain other states may have a right to enforce the rules even though not mentioned in the regulations, if they are entitled to take advantage of the rules under agreements concluded with the Community which have direct effect.[35]

It appears that these provisions are intended to define exhaustively who may sue. This means, for example, that actions may not be brought by organisations representing providers, or by interested members of the public. This contrasts with the position under section 19 of the Local Government Act 1988, which confers standing on representative bodies

---

[26] Services Regulation 4(1)(a), as amended by Supply Regulation 31(2); Utilities Regulation 4(1)(c).

[27] Works Regulation 4(1)(b), as am. by Supply Regulation 31(1)(b); Supply Regulation 4(1)(b); Services Regulation 4(1)(b), as am. by Supply Regulation 31(2)(b); Utilities Regulation 4(1).

[28] Utilities Regulation 2(1), 4(2) and Sched. 2; Works Regulation 2(1), as am. by Supply Regulation 31(1)(a) and Utilities Regulation 35(1), and Works Regulation 4(1)(b), as am. by Utilities Regulation 35(1); Supply Regulation 2(1) and 4(1)(b), as am. by Utilities Regulation 35(3); Services Regulation 2(1) as am. by Supply Regulation 31(2)(a) and Utilities Regulation 35(2), and Services Regulation 4(1)(b), as am. by Utilities Regulation 35(2).

[29] *Ibid.*

[30] See further pp. 771–774.

[31-32] See pp. 781–786.

[33] See the definition of "national of a relevant state" in Works Regulation 2(1), as am. by Supply Regulation 31(1); Supply Regulation 2(1); Services Regulation 2(1), as am. by Supply Regulation 31(2); Utilities Regulation 2(1).

[34] See the definition of "established" in Works Regulation 2(1), as am. by Supply Regulation 31(1); Supply Regulation 2(1); Services Regulation 2(1), as am. by Supply Regulation 31(2); and Utilities Regulation 2(1).

[35] See further pp. 902–903.

to sue for a breach of the rules in the Act on non-commercial considerations. It may contravene the Community law principle of non-discrimination to grant standing to such bodies for breach of domestic rules only.[36]

VII. The requirement of prior notification

Proceedings may only be brought under the regulations[37] if the aggrieved party has informed the contracting authority or utility of the breach, or apprehended breach, and of his intention to bring proceedings.[38] This is designed to encourage a settlement of the dispute without recourse to legal action if possible.[39]

VIII. Discretion to refuse relief

The non-financial remedies are discretionary, and the court may have a power to refuse relief because of prejudice to the administration or hardship to the party who has been awarded the contract.[40] In practice such discretion is unlikely to be important, since once a contract has been made there is an absolute bar on any relief other than damages.[41]

IX. Interim relief

Interim relief is important to a firm wishing to challenge an award procedure for breach of the Community rules. If it is not granted, the contract is likely to have been concluded by the time of the trial, and in such a case the only relief available is damages, as is explained below.[42] The Remedies Directives require all Member States to provide for the award of interim measures in proceedings for breach of the Community rules.[43]

As already explained,[44] the court has power to award interim relief by way of an interim injunction in applications for judicial review (including

---

[36] On this principle see pp. 898–899.

[37] Proceedings "under" the regulations probably covers judicial review actions as well as proceedings to obtain the new remedies created by the regulations.

[38] Works Regulation 31(5)(a); Supply Regulation 29(4)(a), Services Regulation 32(4)(a) and Utilities Regulation 32(4)(a).

[39] This is a general condition for administrative law actions in some European countries, although not in the United Kingdom. The government has been prompted to include such a provision here by the fact that the Remedies Directives expressly alludes to the fact that such a procedural requirement is permitted – though not required: Remedies Directive Article 1(3); Utilities Remedies Directive Article 1(3).

[40] On the declaration, injunction and prerogative orders see pp. 882–883. The legislation on set aside and amendment merely requires that the court *may* award such remedies, and they are likely to be awarded in accordance with the same discretionary principles as the other remedies.

[41] See pp. 913–915.

[42] See p. 899.

[43] Remedies Directive, Article 2(1); Utilities Remedies Directive, Article 2(1) (subject to the option in this directive of providing an "alternative" system which does not involve interim relief or set-aside remedies: see Article 2(1)(c)).

[44] See pp. 881–891.

in proceedings against the Crown where an alleged breach of Community law is in issue) and also in other proceedings for an injunction. In addition, the procurement regulations confer on the court an express power to suspend a contract award procedure where there is a breach of duty relating to the contract in question, or to suspend the implementation of any decision or action in the course of the procedure.[45] Thus a suspension may be sought prior to a set-aside or amendment of documents.[46]

The domestic rules on the award of interim relief were discussed above.[47]

It was noted there, first, that such relief will be denied where damages are an adequate remedy. For some breaches of the Community rules damages clearly are not adequate – for example, for failure to advertise a contract or unlawful exclusion of a provider from a list from which invitees will be selected. In these cases, where the provider will not have submitted a bid, he is unlikely to show a sufficient chance of obtaining a contract to obtain damages. In the case of a firm which has already bid, it was held in *Burroughes v. Oxford Area Health Authority*[48] that damages would be an adequate remedy; but it was suggested above that this will not apply in many cases because of the difficulties of proving who would have won the contract if the law had been followed.[49] It was also suggested that damages for lost bid costs only will not be adequate compensation; thus the existence of a claim for costs under the Utilities Regulations[50] does not of itself mean that the court should deny interim relief.

Burroughes also indicates that the courts will be reluctant to hold up procurements where this entails inconvenience.[51] The Remedies Directives expressly permit a review body to deny interim relief where the adverse consequences could exceed the benefits,[52] which might suggest that the *Burroughes* approach is acceptable. However, these provisions of the directives are subject to the overall obligation to provide relief which is *effective*. Since in the United Kingdom the courts may not set aside a concluded contract, it can be argued that where damages alone do not provide relief which is effective the court must be more ready to award

---

[45] Works Regulation 31(5)(a); Supply Regulation 29(5)(a); Services Regulation 32(6)(a); Utilities Regulation 32(5)(a).

[46] It appears interim measures will be available against any contract decision "affected" by a breach of rules, in the sense discussed at pp. 904–905 above. In other words, the question of which of the rules are "in relation" to a particular contract for the purpose of the legislative power of suspension should be answered in the same way as the question of which decisions may be enjoined, set aside, etc., once the case has been heard.

[47] See pp. 881–891.

[48] See the discussion of this decision at pp. 888–891.

[49] pp. 888–891.

[50] See pp. 911–912.

[51] See p. 890.

[52] Remedies Directive, Article 2(4) and Utilities Remedies Directive, Article 2(4).

interim measures to ensure some effective remedy exists. This would apply where no bid has been submitted since in this case a damages claim is generally unlikely to succeed. In view of the difficulties of proving loss in an ordinary tort action, it may even apply in cases where a bid has been submitted, unless the courts are willing to adopt a generous approach to the calculation of damages.[53]

Another feature of United Kingdom law is that a firm is normally required to give an undertaking in damages as a condition for the award of interim relief.[54] This will, however, provide a serious disincentive to actions by aggrieved firms and it is arguable that this requirement is therefore in conflict with the rule for the provision of effective remedies, at least in cases where damages alone do not provide an effective remedy.

Finally, it was explained that *Burroughes* also indicates that interim relief might be denied because of the impossibility of supervising an order where the breach relates to criteria used by the authority in the exercise of its discretion. To uphold this limitation also appears to contravene Community law, since the Remedies Directive indicates that interim measures should be available in principle for breach of all the Community procurement rules.

The regulations state that interim relief – as with all forms of non-financial relief – may not be awarded once a contract has actually been concluded.[55] There may, however, be an exception where the other party to the contract is aware of the breach.[56] It may also be necessary to make an exception for applications based on Article 85 E.C., since an agreement concluded in breach of this provision is void and interim relief may be required to give effect to this consequence in an "effective" manner. Further, it should be noted that the Court of Justice has a power to hold up a concluded contract on application by the Commission.[57]

(iii) DAMAGES[58]

The regulations, implementing a requirement in the Remedies Directive and Utilities Remedies Directive, expressly confer on the courts a power

---

[53] It might be suggested that damages are adequate in actions under the Utilities Regulations, since bid costs are available to any firm with a reasonable chance of the contract: see further pp. 911–912.

[54] See p. 891.

[55] Works Regulation 31(7); Supply Regulation 29(6); Services Regulation 32(6); Utilities Regulation 32(6).

[56] See further p. 914.

[57] See further pp. 930–931.

[58] On the issues raised in this section see further Arrowsmith, "Enforcing the Public Procurement Rules: Legal Remedies in the Court of Justice and the National Courts" in Arrowsmith (ed.) *Remedies for Enforcing the Public Procurement Rules* (1993), pp.69–78; Weatherill, "Enforcing the Public Procurement Rules in the United Kingdom", Chap. 8 in Arrowsmith (ed), above, Arrowsmith, "Enforcing the E.C. Public Procurement Rules: the Remedies System in England and Wales" (1992) 1 P.P.L.R. 92.

to award damages to any provider who has suffered loss or damage as a result of a breach of duty.[59] These provisions do not, however, state how such damages are to be calculated or assessed. Since the claim can be categorised as one in tort for breach of statutory duty, the applicable principle is that of tort which requires the provider to be put in the position as if the breach had occurred. The application of this principle in the context of procurement claims was considered in detail earlier in the chapter.[60] It was explained that to recover under the general principle applied in tort cases a provider must probably show a substantial chance that he would have been awarded the contract if the breach of duty had not occurred. He will then be able to recover any "profit" – in the sense of the difference between expenditure on the contract and the price which would have been obtained – which he would have made on the contract, discounted to reflect the value of the chance.

In addition to this general damages provision the Utilities Regulations – but not the public sector regulations – state that where a provider had a "real chance" of being awarded a contract (if that chance had not been affected by the breach of duty) the provider is entitled to damages for the costs of preparing the bid and in participating in the award procedure.[61] Like other measures based on loss of chance this contemplates recovery by more than one provider – for example, where two can each show a 40 per cent chance of success in the procedure. It does not seem to require providers to prove that, had they succeeded in winning the contract, the profit obtained would have covered their tender costs. The right given here is in addition to the general right of damages referred to in the previous paragraph.[62] Thus a provider may choose between an action for recovery of lost profits based on the extent of the chance of actually being awarded the contract, and an action for recovery of costs based merely on showing a real chance of success in the procedure. Presumably it is possible to pursue both, although any damages for costs awarded under the second principle would be taken into account in calculating any award under the first.

The specific rules on damages, as with the other rules on remedies, must be interpreted in light of the general requirement to provide a remedies system which is effective, and of the requirement that damages, where available, must not be unduly difficult or impossible to obtain.[63] Under the Utilities Regulations it could be argued that, in view of the

---

[59] Works Regulation 31(6)(b)(ii); Supply Regulation 29(5)(b)(ii); Services Regulation 32(5)(b)(ii); Utilities Regulation 32(5)(b)(ii).

[60] See the discussion at pp. 891–895.

[61] Utilities Regulations 32(7).

[62] Utilities Regulation 32(8). It is also expressly stated that this provision is without prejudice to the requirement of proof for any other type of claim, whether the general damages claim referred to in the previous paragraph, or any other type of relief: Utilities Regulation 32(8).

[63] *Francovich* above, note 74.

express provision for recovery of tender costs on proof merely of a real chance of winning the contract, the damages remedy is indeed effective: the requirements for obtaining relief are not onerous, and the amount recoverable is sufficient to provide an incentive for providers to sue and to deter breaches by utilities. Under the public sector regulations the law as it existed when the regulations were adopted appeared to require proof of success on the balance of probabilities and proof that profit would have been made from the contract may make it very difficult to succeed in obtaining damages. Further, it can be pointed out that since it will often be difficult to obtain non-financial relief (especially in view of the rules that this is not available once a contract has been concluded)[64] damages are important to make the system as a whole effective. However, following the recent decision in *Allied Maples* which allows providers to recover based on a "loss of chance" principle the law appears more satisfactory.[65]

Claims for damages under the regulations are brought in the High Court.[66] The general time-limit for proceedings under the regulations, which requires that claims be brought promptly and in any case within three months,[67] appears to apply to damages claims as well as claims for non-financial relief.[68] However, the time limit for damages claims for breaches of domestic procurement rules is six years, and to impose such a short time-limit for claims under the regulations arguably infringes the Community law principle of non-discrimination requiring that remedies for enforcing Community rules are as favourable as those for enforcing domestic rules.

As well as a damages claim under the regulations, there is no reason why providers may not seek damages if they choose for misfeasance in public office, where the purchaser knows that it is acting in breach of the rules.[69] It is not clear, however, that this tort will apply to all regulated purchasers: for example, it may not cover privatised utilities and private concessionaires.

(iv) THE POSITION OF CONCLUDED CONTRACTS

As mentioned above, once a contract has actually been concluded, the regulations state that the only remedy in the national courts is damages: it is not possible to obtain interim relief nor relief at the trial to prevent

---

[64] See pp. 913–915.
[65] On this principle see pp. 893–894.
[66] Works Regulation 31(4); Supply Regulation 29(3); Services Regulation 32(3); Utilities Regulation 32(3).
[67] See pp. 884–885.
[68] Works Regulation 31(5)(b); Supply Regulation 29(4)(b); Services Regulation 31(4)(b).; Utilities Regulations 32(4)(b). These provisions apply the time limits to all "proceedings under" the regulations.
[69] On this see pp. 891–892. It is submitted that damages are not available for breach of an implied contract governing the tendering process, since an undertaking to follow the regulations cannot be implied into any such contract. (See p. 895 above).

the parties proceeding with the contract.[70] This rule is designed to protect the interests of the party who has won the contract, as well as the interests of the administration. The Remedies Directives expressly state that this question of the effect of a breach of the rules on a concluded contract is a matter for Member States.[71]

However, this apparently general rule may be subject to exceptions.

First, there is an exception for a breach of Article 85 E.C., since Article 85(2) states expressly that a contract concluded in breach of that provision is null and void, and a Treaty provision cannot be overridden by a directive. The same consequence may also follow for an agreement made in breach of Article 86 E.C.[72] In this case both a right to set aside a decision and the possibility of interim relief must be provided, to give effect to this consequence so far as aggrieved third parties are concerned.

Secondly, it is submitted that, by virtue of the general Community law requirement of effectiveness, a more general exception must be made where the other party to the contracts knows, or, perhaps, should have known, that the contract may be unlawful. This arises because the inability of the courts to set aside concluded contracts jeopardises the provision of an effective remedy. This is acceptable in order to protect the interests in "legal certainty" of a third party, but such interests cannot exist where that party is aware of the breach. These are the rules which have been applied by the Court of Justice in the context of recovery of payments made by government to citizens which are contrary to Community law, where it has been held that national law may impose limits on recovery to protect innocent third parties,[73] but that such limits cannot be applied to recovery of unlawful state aids since recipients should be aware that such aids are unlawful.[74] This application of the effectiveness principle must override any express provision in the procurement directives since the principle derives from the Treaty itself (Article 5). Such an approach seems essential to prevent the contracting parties from rushing into contracts to avoid review, following notification by the purchaser of the possibility of legal action (as is required under the regulations). To avoid this situation it would also be useful to adopt measures to prohibit contracts from being made for a few days after notification of the award decision.

The regulations deal only with the effect of the contract in the context of a challenge by a third party, and do not state whether the existence of a defect in the award procedure may allow the parties to the contract

---

[70] See p. 911.
[71] Remedies Directive, Article 2(6); Utilities Remedies Directive, Article 2(6).
[72] Wyatt and Dashwood, *European Community Law* (3rd ed. 1993), p.492.
[73] Cases 205–215/82, *Deutsche Milchkontor v. Germany* [1983] E.C.R. 2633.
[74] Case 5/89, *Commission v. Germany* [1990] E.C.R. I–3437 (decided in the context of centralised enforcement proceedings; but the Court made it clear that the same principles apply here as apply to proceedings in the national courts).

themselves to withdraw from the agreement. It was suggested earlier, however, that in general neither party to the agreement should be able to avoid its consequences simply because it is concluded in breach of public law requirements,[75] and this general principle should be applied in the context of breach of Community law rules.

(d) REMEDIES IN PROCEDURES NOT COVERED BY THE REGULATIONS

Breaches of Community law – in particular, the E.C. Treaty – may occur in award procedures not covered by the regulations. As has been explained, the Compliance Directive and the implementing provisions do not apply to those award procedures.

In these cases the general remedies and procedures described in section 2 must be made available to enforce Community rules.[76] Thus providers may seek a declaration, injunction or (where applicable) the prerogative orders in accordance with the rules and procedures outlined in section 2. In addition, however, the usual remedies system must, if necessary, be modified by the courts to comply with the general Community obligation to provide "effective" remedies. For example, normally it is not possible to obtain interim relief against the Crown, but such relief may be required under Community law in order to ensure that an effective remedy is available, and the courts may thus be prepared to award an interim injunction against the Crown.[77] In addition, although damages are not generally available in English law for breach of rules on procurement, except for a deliberate breach (under the tort of misfeasance in public office),[78] Community law may require damages for disappointed providers, based on the Court of Justice decision in *Francovich*,[79] in which the Court ruled that damages must, in some cases at least, be made available in national courts to redress breaches of Community law. However, it is not yet clear whether damages are required for all breaches of administrative provisions deriving from Community law or only in exceptional cases (for example, when the breach is deliberate or grossly negligent).[80] Thus it is not entirely certain whether damages are generally available in award procedures not covered by the regulations.

---

[75] See pp. 15–18.

[76] See pp. 882–897.

[77] See Case C–231/89, *R.v.Secretary of State for Transport, ex p. Factortame* [1990] E.C.R. I–2433 (E.C.J.) and [1990] 3 C.M.L.R. 818 (application by the House of Lords).

[78] See p. 892. Damages are also available for breach of the general competition law rules in Articles 85 and 86 E.C., which occur in an award procedure, under the tort of breach of statutory duty: *Garden Cottage Foods v. Milk Marketing Board* [1984] A.C. 130.

[79] Above, note 72 on p. 898.

[80] See further Arrowsmith, *Civil Liability and Public Authorities* (1992), pp.254–257 and Craig, *Administrative Law* (3rd ed., 1994), pp.642–645 and the articles cited there.

(e) REMEDIES AGAINST BODIES WHICH ARE NOT CONTRACTING AUTHORITIES OR UTILITIES

The discussion above has concerned bodies which are "contracting authorities" under the public sector regulations or "utilities" under the Utilities Regulations. Rules under the public sector regulations also apply, however, to certain persons which are not "contracting authorities".

I. Concessionaires

Certain obligations under the Works Regulations apply to any person who is a concessionaire, even if not a contracting authority.[81] As with the obligations on contracting authorities, it is provided that these obligations involve duties owed by concessionaires to persons seeking to participate in contracts with the concessionaire[82] who are nationals of or established in a "relevant" state.[83] The duties owed may be enforced by such contractors in accordance with the remedies set out in regulation 31 (damages, set-aside and interim measures) and in accordance with the procedure under that regulation, as described above. The contractor may also use any other relevant remedies although judicial review will not, of course, be available against private concessionaires.

II. Contracts subsidised by contracting authorities

Contracting authorities which subsidise by more than 50 per cent certain types of works and services contracts awarded by entities which are not themselves contracting authorities are required to ensure that these entities follow the rules in the regulations when awarding the subsidised contract.[84] In this case the regulations do not place any duty directly on the awarding entity, but merely impose a duty on the contracting authority undertaking to subsidise the contract to ensure the rules are followed. In this respect it is stated that the contracting authority must make it a condition of the contribution that the regulations are followed in awarding the contract, and must ensure that the rules are followed or recover the contribution.[85]

Since there is no duty owed under the regulations by the awarding body (that is, the body receiving the subsidy) an aggrieved provider may not bring an action against that entity to force compliance with the rules. However, it is arguable that such a person would have standing to

---

[81] Works Regulation 26(3), discussed at pp. 361–365.
[82] Works Regulation 31(1) (duty is owed to a contractor) and Works Regulation 31(2)(b) (stating that the term "contractor" includes a person "who sought, who seeks, or who would have wished, to be the person to whom a contract to which Regulation 26(3) applies is awarded").
[83] Works Regulation 31(2)(b), as amended by Supply Regulation 31(1)(b).
[84] Works Regulation 23 and Services Regulation 25, discussed at pp. 368–370.
[85] Works Regulation 23(1); Services Regulation 25(1).

compel the subsidising authority to recover the contribution if the rules are not followed.

(f) ADEQUACY OF THE NATIONAL REMEDIES SYSTEM

The Remedies Directives and their implementation in the United Kingdom have certainly improved the position of providers. First, although to some extent the rights conferred under the directives are now in any case available as a result of developments in the general Community law principle of effectiveness, the directives may add some substantive rights to those under the general law. For example, as explained above, it is not clear that under general principles of Community law damages would be available for *every* breach of the procurement rules; nor is it clear that effectiveness would entail a specific right to have unlawful documents amended. Secondly – and perhaps even more important – the process of adopting this legislation has been valuable in clarifying and publicising the rights available to providers, many of whom were previously unaware of the possibility of using legal remedies.

However, it can be doubted whether the operation of the new remedies in the legislation against the existing legal background in the United Kingdom really provides a system of remedies which is adequate to encourage legal actions and thus to deter breaches of the rules. It is apparent that, since several months may elapse before cases are heard and contracts cannot generally be set aside once concluded, providers must rely on either interim or damages to obtain effective relief. However, often it may be difficult under the usual principles of domestic law to obtain either remedy, although the position is more satisfactory now that the courts have recognised the possibility of a loss of chance claim in tort. It is likely that the courts' traditional approach to some matters needs to be modified in order to meet Community law requirements to provide an effective remedy. For example, in both the public sector and utilities sector the courts may need to be more ready to award interim relief, especially where there is no prospect of damages, such as where there has been a failure to advertise a contract. The courts are required under Article 5 E.C. to interpret the law in such a way as to ensure that Community obligations are met, but uncertainty over whether, and how, this will be done probably acts as a deterrent to actions at present and it is regrettable that the regulations did not deal expressly with some of these difficulties. Of course, where there would be serious public inconvenience in holding up the procurement the courts are always unlikely to interfere, and this difficulty can be dealt with adequately only by providing a very rapid remedy and appeal system. Since the Remedies Directives require *rapid* review, the United Kingdom in fact is under an obligation to give priority to hearing urgent procurement cases, which may alleviate the difficulties of awarding interim relief in these cases.

Quite apart from the problem of implementing a remedies system which is effective for those who wish to use it, another important issue is whether providers will be prepared to take legal proceedings, fearing that this may prejudice their chances of receiving contracts in the future. It is a common perception that this has an influence on providers and this finds some support in the 1994 Department of Trade and Industry *Public Procurement Review*.[86] This is a difficult problem to deal with, although one useful reform may be to permit actions by trade associations, as is allowed for breach of the Local Government Act 1988 (and indeed, as suggested above, this may be required under the Community law principle of non-discrimination[87]). Because of this difficulty it may even be doubted whether it will ever be possible to rely on national review actions as the primary method for enforcing Community law in the procurement area, as was hoped by the Commission when the Remedies Directives were conceived. Thus suggestions such as the use of a national "ombudsman" system, introducing a compulsory Community-wide system of "audit" or "attestation",[88-89] improving the enforcement powers and resources of the European Commission (discussed below),[90] and even the application of criminal penalties, deserve serious consideration.

(3) CONCILIATION

For the utilities sector Articles 9–11 of the Utilities Remedies Directive provide for a special procedure for use in resolving disputes over the procurement rules. This is referred to as "conciliation", although its characteristics are less that of a traditional conciliation procedure – where an individual acts to encourage the parties themselves to reach agreement – than of a non-binding arbitration: essentially the procedure involves the pronouncement of a non-binding decision on the dispute by a panel of independent third parties. The procedure has the same scope as the other provisions of the Utilities Remedies Directive: it may be used by any provider who considers that he suffers or risks suffering loss or damage as a result of a breach of Community law, or national rules implementing that law, in relation to a contract falling within the Utilities Regulations.[91] This could be a breach of the regulations themselves or of some other Community law provision such as those in the Community Treaties.

---

[86] See in particular paras. 104 and 114.
[87] See pp. 898–899.
[88-89] See pp. 936–938.
[90] See pp. 920–935.
[91] Utilities Remedies Directive Article 9(1) and Utilities Regulation 33.

Utilities Regulation 33 provides that where a provider alleging a breach of duty wishes to use this procedure it shall send a request to do so to the Treasury, for transmission by the Treasury to the Commission (which transmission must under Article 9(2) of the directive take place "as quickly as possible"). The Commission will then consider whether the dispute concerns the correct application of Community law and, if so, must initiate the procedure by informing the utility of the request for use of the procedure[92] and seeking the utility's agreement to participate. Participation is voluntary on the part of both parties, and each may decide to terminate the procedure at any time.[93] If the utility declines to take part the Commission must simply inform the person who made the request that the procedure cannot be used.[94] If, however, the utility agrees the Commission must initiate the procedure.

Three conciliators are appointed, under a procedure set out in Article 10(2). One is chosen by the Commission from a list of independent persons accredited for this purpose. This is drawn up by the Commission, following consultation with the Advisory Committee for Public Contracts or, in the case of disputes concerning utilities in the telecommunications field, with the Advisory Committee on Telecommunications Procurement. Both parties must state whether they accept the conciliator; if one does not, then presumably the Commission will choose an alternative since otherwise the objecting party is likely to exercise his rights to terminate the procedure. Each of the parties must also designate a conciliator to make up the total of three. The conciliators themselves may invite up to two experts to assist them in their work, but these may be vetoed by the Commission or by either of the parties to the procedure.

The conciliators' duty, under Article 10(4), is to "endeavour as quickly as possible to reach an agreement between the parties which is in accordance with Community law". Their findings and any result must be reported to the Commission.[95]

The operation of the conciliation procedure is stated to be without prejudice to either proceedings under Article 169 E.C. by the Commission or proceedings by another Member State under Article 170 E.C.[96] It is also without prejudice to the rights of the provider requesting the procedure or the rights of the utility.[97] Thus, merely by participating in the conciliation procedure a provider does not lose his rights to take legal proceedings nor a utility its right to defend such proceedings and, indeed, the conciliation procedure may be pursued at the same time as

---

[92] Utilities Remedies Directive Article 10(1).
[93] Utilities Remedies Directive Article 10(6).
[94] Utilities Remedies Directive Article 10(2).
[95] Utilities Remedies Directive Article 10(5).
[96] Utilities Remedies Directive Article 11(2)(a). On these procedures see pp. 920–935. It is also stated that the procedure is without prejudice to intervention by the Commission under Article 8 of the directive: on this see see pp. 933–934.
[97] Utilities Remedies Directive Article 11(2)(b).

legal proceedings are pending or ongoing. However, if the parties are able to reach an agreement over the dispute as a result of the conciliation, in practice they may well choose to embody this in a contract which operates as a legally binding compromise of their dispute and precludes the possibility of legal proceedings over the issue.

Where another provider who has an interest in obtaining a contract in the disputed award procedure is pursuing review proceedings under the directive in respect of that procedure the utility must inform the conciliators. They in turn must inform that other provider of the conciliation procedure and ask him to state, within a specified time, whether he agrees to participate.[98] If not, the conciliators may decide (by a majority if necessary) to terminate the conciliation procedure, where they feel that the participation of the other provider is necessary to resolve the dispute.[99] In this event they must notify the Commission of their decision and give reasons for it.[1] It is expressly provided that the conciliation procedure is without prejudice to the rights of any person not party to the procedure.[2]

The aggrieved provider and the utility each bear their own costs and also share equally the costs of the procedure, excluding the costs of any intervening parties[3] (who, presumably, are responsible for these costs themselves).

There is no equivalent conciliation procedure for disputes relating to procedures covered by the public sector rules.

(4) ENFORCEMENT BY THE EUROPEAN COMMISSION[4]

(a) THE ROLE OF THE EUROPEAN COMMISSION

The European Commission has an important role in ensuring compliance with the Community procurement rules, which it has pursued with vigour in the last decade. It is involved in ensuring that Member States take the steps necessary to implement the directives and that there are no general national measures or practices which conflict with Community law. It is also concerned to see that individual purchasers comply with their obligations under these Community rules and under national implementing measures. If breaches of the directives or the free

---

[98] Utilities Remedies Directive Article 11(1).
[99] *Ibid.*
[1] *Ibid.*
[2] Utilities Remedies Directive Article 11(2)(b).
[3] Utilities Remedies Directive Article 10(7).
[4] See further Arrowsmith, "Enforcing the Public Procurement Rules: Legal Remedies in the Court of Justice and the National Courts" in Arrowsmith (ed.), *Remedies for Enforcing the Public Procurement Rules* (1993), pp. 4–43; Fernández Martín, "The European Commission's Centralised Enforcement of Public Procurement Rules: A Critical View" (1993) 2 P.P.L.R. 40.

movement provisions come to light, the Commission may ultimately institute proceedings in the European Court of Justice, under Article 169 E.C.

Breaches may come to light in a number of ways. Regarding implementation of the directives, states must notify the Commission of implementing measures and communicate the relevant texts, to assist the Commission in monitoring implementation. In the United Kingdom all the directives have been implemented, but the Commission could take action if it feels that any directive has not been implemented properly. Other breaches may come to the Commission's attention through monitoring: for example, through analysis of notices in the *Official Journal* and the national press. This can bring to light unlawful general practices – such as non-publication of notices, or persistent use of the negotiated procedure – as well as isolated breaches of the rules, and the Commission has frequently been successful in persuading national authorities to change unlawful practices revealed in this way.[5] The Commission's role may be particularly useful in areas where individual firms are unlikely to be interested in taking action, or cannot easily discover breaches – for example, in relation to the publication of Periodic Indicative Notices (PINs). The Commission also attempts to monitor the application of the applicable procurement rules to contracts financed by the Community's structural funds (in which case a sanction for non-compliance may be the withholding or recovery of funds provided by the Community).

Finally, breaches may come to light as a result of individual complaints. Complaining to the Commission offers a number of advantages for an aggrieved provider, including possible anonymity, assistance in investigating the complaint, absence of legal costs, and also the possibility of relief not available in national courts, notably the suspension and set-aside of concluded contracts.[6] For the last few years it has generally been the policy of the Commission to take action on all plausible complaints.

The Commission has in fact been criticised for pursuing many cases concerning small contracts right to the end, including through proceedings in the Court of Justice, rather than leaving these to the national courts: it has been suggested that it is better to concentrate resources on the monitoring of systematic abuses and to leave isolated breaches to the national courts.[7] Further, the use of enforcement proceedings under Article 169 E.C. in apparently minor cases may devalue the "political significance and symbolic value" of such proceedings.[8] On the other hand, because of the difficulties of instituting an effective remedies

---

[5] See Arrowsmith, above, note 4, pp. 6–10.
[6] See pp. 913–915.
[7] Fernández Martín, above; Department of Trade and Industry, *Public Procurement Review* (1994), para. 110.
[8] See the note by Bieber, (1993) 30 C.M.L.Rev. 1197.

system through the national courts, as discussed above, procurement is an area in which it would be especially useful for the Commission to have a significant enforcement role, including in the pursuit of individual cases. One possible way forward is to institute a new system for the pursuit and determination of complaints concerning procurement. This could be similar to the system currently applying in competition cases brought under Articles 85 and 86 E.C., which is outlined in section (d) below. Features of the "competition" system which could be useful in all procurement cases include the provision of specific investigatory powers for the Commission, the absence of which significantly hampers investigations at present; a power for the Commission itself to award interim measures[9]; the power to impose financial sanctions on undertakings which do not comply with the rules; and the fact that proceedings are brought against the party in breach rather than the Member State as such, as with Article 169 proceedings. In addition, as will be explained, cases under this competition law system are determined by the Commission itself, and are merely subject to review by the Court, a system which permits resolution of more minor cases without damaging the political significance of Article 169 proceedings.

(b) PROCEEDINGS BEFORE THE COURT OF JUSTICE UNDER ARTICLE 169 E.C.

(i) SCOPE OF THE POWER TO PROCEED UNDER ARTICLE 169 E.C.

As indicated, in cases of failure to implement the procurement directives, or failure to comply with the directives or the free movement provisions of the E.C. Treaty, where a negotiated solution cannot be achieved the Commission may take proceedings before the Court of Justice of the European Communities. Normally proceedings are brought under a procedure set out in Article 169 E.C.[10] Proceedings can be brought in respect of any breach of Community law, including the Treaties, the directives and other secondary legislation, such as the IT Standards Decision.[11] Where, however, a State relies on Article 223 or Article 224 E.C. to justify its conduct, a special procedure applies under Article 225 E.C.; this is considered in section (c) below. There is also a special system for dealing with breaches of the competition rules in Articles 85-86 E.C. which is outlined in section (d).

---

[9] Such a power was in fact originally included in the public sector Remedies Directive but was dropped because of opposition from Member States.

[10] Under Article 170 E.C., proceedings may also be brought before the Court of Justice by other Member States. Only one such procedure has been instituted; in practice, other Member States normally leave the matter to be dealt with by the Commission. Other persons, including individual firms or persons affected by a breach, have no power to bring proceedings before the Court of Justice: they must pursue the other remedies available to them, as described in this section.

[11] On this see pp. 607–614.

Proceedings under Article 169 E.C. are brought against the United Kingdom as a Member State, and not against a particular purchasing entity which has breached the rules. States are responsible for the conduct of all institutions which are of a "public" nature including, for example, local authorities and state universities[12] In fact, it appears that the government will be responsible under Article 169 for the actions of all bodies defined as "contracting authorities" under the public sector Regulations[13] which are all bodies funded, controlled or appointed by government. Probably the same will apply to all bodies which are either "public authorities" or "public undertakings" under the Utilities Regulations, since these are all entities which are subject to general governmental control.

It is not clear, however, that the government is responsible under Article 169 for all bodies which are subject to obligations under the regulations. First, it might not be accountable for entities which are subject to the Utilities Regulations merely because they enjoy special or exclusive rights. As explained in Chapter 4, *Griffin v. South West Water*[14-15] indicates that many such bodies are sufficiently associated with the state for the purpose of the rules on the direct effect of directives where the service which they provide is closely regulated.[16] However, it has been suggested by Advocate General Lenz that the test for direct effect may be wider than that for responsibility under Article 169 E.C.,[17] and it is possible that the activities of such bodies are not in general within Article 169. Secondly, obligations under the public sector rules apply to certain entities which hold public works concessions or which award certain subsidised works or services contracts,[18] even though these entities are purely private in form and substance so that their activities are quite clearly not normally attributable to the state. However, in all these cases accountability might possibly arise under Article 169 where the state exercises some influence over the particular contract in question.[19] In particular, the procurement rules confer upon a contracting authority concerned with a concession or subsidised contract a responsibility for ensuring the rules are complied with,[20] and this might suffice for the state to be held responsible under Article 169 for the relevant award procedures, as, indeed, might the grant of the subsidy itself.

---

[12] Case C-24/91, *Commission v. Spain*, [1994] 2 C.M.L.R. 621.
[13] On the definition of contracting authorities see pp. 106–115. This seems to be the view of Advocate General Lenz in case C-24/91, *Commission v. Spain*, [1994] 2 C.M.L.R. 621 (paras. 8–13 of the Opinion), and in case 247/89, *Commission v. Portugal*, judgment of July 11, 1991 (para. 37 of the Opinion.).
[14-15] [1995] 1 I.R.L.R. 15.
[16] See p. 88.
[17] Case 247/89, *Commission v. Portugal*, above, paras. 16–20 of the Opinion.
[18] See pp. 386–388.
[19] See the comments of Advocate General Lenz in *Commission v. Portugal*, above.
[20] See pp. 916–917.

(ii) PROCEDURE

Prior to instituting proceedings under Article 169, the Commission must first follow certain procedural steps. These comprise "administrative" or "pre-litigation" phase of the proceedings.

First, the Commission must give the government an opportunity to submit observations; this requires an "adequate and realistic" opportunity to respond,[21] including a reasonable time to submit any reply.[22] This formal requirement is fulfilled in practice by sending a letter referred to as a "letter of infringement", setting out the allegations.[23] Where the breach relates to a specific contract award, the Commission is likely to give only a short time period for response. For major contracts there is a special procedure for Commission intervention ("the corrective mechanism", discussed below) requiring a state to respond to a notice of alleged breach within 21 days, and it is the Commission's practice to treat written notice given under this procedure as equivalent to a letter of infringement, allowing only the 21-day period for reply. For award procedures outside the corrective mechanism, one month is generally allowed in practice. These periods appear reasonable.[24]

If the Commission is not satisfied with the response and wishes to institute proceedings, it must deliver a "reasoned opinion" – that is, a formal and reasoned explanation of why it considers a breach to have occurred – specifying a reasonable time-limit for rectifying the breach.[25] Only if this is not done may proceedings be instituted. Where a complaint concerns a specific award procedure, a one-month time-limit is normally specified. This was challenged as too short in *Commission v. Portugal*,[26] which concerned a failure to publish in the *Official Journal* a notice for a supply contract.[27] The Court held the period acceptable, but

---

[21] Case 31/69, *Commission v. Italy* [1970] E.C.R. 25, [1970] C.M.L.R. 175. For further discussion of the formal requirements of this stage of the proceedings see Wyatt and Dashwood, above, note 14, at pp. 396–397.

[22] Case 293/85, *Commission v. Belgium* [1988] E.C.R. 305, [1989] 2 C.M.L.R. 527.

[23] In practice, the Commission will first initiate informal discussions, and proceed with a formal letter only if dissatisfied with the initial response.

[24] The view that this is a reasonable period was expressly stated by Advocate General Tesauro in his Opinion of November 17, 1994, in case C–359/93, *Commission v. Netherlands* (jugdment of January 4, 1995).

The 21-day or 30-day period for response in the directive cannot override any discretion which the Commission might otherwise enjoy under the Treaty to specify such shorter period as it thinks fit, since the "corrective mechanism" does not derogate from or replace the powers which exist under Article 169 E.C.: see case C–359/93, *Commission v. Netherlands*, above. However arguably a time period shorter than 21 days could *not* generally be justified – there is no urgent need for earlier action to forestall conclusion of a contract, since the Court of Justice may suspend a procurement even though the contract has been concluded.

[25] On the formal requirements see further Wyatt and Dashwood, *European Community Law* (3rd ed., 1993), pp. 397–398 and 403–405.

[26] Above, note 13.

[27] It seems the Commission took issue with general measures under which the award had been made, but the action was based only on the breach relating to an individual contract: see para. 21 of the judgment. There was held to be no breach since the entity concerned was not then covered by the Supplies Directive.

did point out, first, that the matter had been brought to the attention of the government many months earlier and, secondly, that the existence of any breaches had been denied[28] (the significance of this being that as a consequence no remedial action had even begun).[29] However, a one-month period would probably be reasonable even without these factors.

As to what constitutes compliance, it is submitted that normally it will be necessary to reopen the procedure.[30] As to whether an opinion may be issued and proceedings brought when it is no longer possible to redress the breach – for example because the contract has been performed or the procedure abandoned – the jurisprudence is conflicting. In case 199/85, *Commission v. Italy*,[31] the Court held proceedings admissable in respect of an award procedure for a works contract, even though the procedure had subsequently been abandoned: it was held that compliance with the reasoned opinion required that the breach should be "remedied" through an admission that the breach had occurred, and failure to make such an admission rendered the action admissable. In the later case C–362/90[32] however, also an action against Italy, the Court held that proceedings were not admissable because the contract, for the supply of beef, had already been performed and the subject-matter consumed, and the breach, therefore, could not be remedied. It could be argued on the basis of case 199/85, however, that the breach was still capable of remedy, by an admission that it had occurred. It is submitted that proceedings should in fact be allowed where the authority will not acknowledge that any breach has occurred.

There is no fixed time-limit for instituting proceedings, nor any obligation on the Commission to act promptly in doing so.[33]

(iii) INTERIM MEASURES

I. Availability of interim measures

As already explained, interim relief is important where specific award procedures are challenged since if no such relief is available, by the time the matter is resolved the contract may already have been performed.

---

[28] para. 25 of the judgment.

[29] These factors have been held in other cases to be relevant to the question of what is a reasonable time period: see, for example, case 74/82, *Commission v. Ireland* [1984] E.C.R. 317; case 85/85, *Commission v. Belgium* [1986] E.C.R. 1149; case 293/85, *Commission v. Belgium* [1988] E.C.R. 305.

[30] On what constitutes compliance see further Arrowsmith, above, note 4, pp. 14–19. It is submitted that, in principle, the same steps are required as those which would be necessary to comply with a judgment of the court under Article 171 E.C. Thus it is suggested that where a contract has already been made when the reasoned opinion is issued, whether the contract must be set aside depends on whether the court would require this to be done under Article 171, as to which see pp. 932–933.

[31] [1987] E.C.R. 1039; see further Arrowsmith, *A Guide to the Procurement Cases of the Court of Justice* (1992), section 5.

[32] See the note by Arrowsmith and Fernández Martín, (1993) 2 P.P.L.R. CS2.

[33] Case C–359/93, *Commission v. Netherlands*, above, where the Court of Justice rejected an argument that proceedings could be inadmissable on such grounds.

This is very likely in the context of Court of Justice actions where the average length of proceedings is over 20 months.[34] The Court may award interim measures in relation to such proceedings under a power contained in Article 186 E.C. An application may not be made, however, until proceedings under Article 169 have actually been instituted. Applications are made to the President of the Court, who may hear the matter himself or refer it to the Court.

II. Requirement for a prima facie case

To obtain interim relief the Commission must first show a prima facie case.[35] This merely requires proof that the action is not "manifestly without foundation".

III. The requirement of urgency

It is also necessary to show urgency,[36] which means that serious and irreparable harm will be suffered if interim measures are not given. There is some debate about what this requires in Article 169 proceedings. One view is that the Commission must, like any other applicant, show specific damage to a particular interest,[37] although this may be any Community interest (such as damage to the free market) and need not involve damage to the Commission itself. In procurement cases, arguably this might require concrete damage to the open market – which would be difficult to show in cases concerning a single contract. Alternatively, it might suffice to show damage to providers – although this is open to the objection that adequate remedies are available in the national courts. The second view is that it is not necessary to show concrete damage, but only a potentially irreversible breach of Community law.[38] If this view is correct, it could be explained on the basis that "serious and irreparable damage" is not required in Article 169 cases (in other words, "urgency" merely requires that the breach is irreversible). Alternatively, it could be explained on the basis that the existence of an irreversible breach itself constitutes serious and irreparable damage to the Community interest.

This issue was raised in *Dundalk*,[39] in which the Commission sought to suspend an award procedure carried out by an Irish municipality for a contract for the construction of a water pipeline. Ireland argued that the condition of urgency was not met, since the Commission had not shown the possibility of damage to a specific interest. However, the President

---

[34] In 1993 it was 22.9 months and in 1994 20.8 months: *Proceedings of the Court of Justice and of the Court of First Instance of the European Communities* No. 34/94, p. 36.
[35] Rules of Procedure of the Court of Justice, Article 83(2).
[36] Rules of Procedure of the Court of Justice Article 83(2).
[37] See Borchardt, "The Award of Interim Measures by the European Court of Justice" (1985) 22 C.M.L.Rev. 203 at pp. 21–219.
[38] See the discussion in Usher, *European Court Practice* (1983) at pp. 285–286.
[39] Case 45/87R, *Commission v. Ireland* [1987] E.C.R. 1369. See also the *ex parte.* Order, reported at [1987] E.C.R. 783, where relief was granted. The Court's judgment at the hearing is reported in [1988] E.C.R. 4929.

ruled that the damage which might be caused to the Commission as "guardian of the interests of the Community" would suffice. This could refer either to the damage to affected providers (which was one argument put forward by the Commission), or simply to the harm from the existence of an irreversible breach of Community law. In two subsequent procurement cases – *La Spezia*[40] and *Lottomatica*[41] – interim measures were awarded, but the question of serious and irreparable damage was not expressly considered. In the most recent case, however, *Wallonia Buses*,[42] the issue was again expressly raised; here it was argued by Belgium, as by Ireland in *Dundalk*, that a simple breach of Community law deemed to constitute prejudice to the Commission as "guardian of the Treaties" could not suffice. In response, the President pointed to the damage which would occur both to "the Community legal order" *and* to competing bidders,[43] holding the condition of urgency thus to be satisfied. This might suggest that either type of interest can be relied on, thus supporting the view that the Commission can obtain interim relief without pointing to concrete damage to Community policy.[44]

As is clearly recognised by the Court in all these cases, any damage which might occur will generally be irreversible, since by the time the case is finally resolved the contract will generally have been executed.

IV. The balance of interests

Once an applicant has shown an arguable case and urgency, the Court must consider the "balance of interests", a concept similar to that of the "balance of convenience" in domestic law. This involves weighing the need for interim measures, on the one hand, against, on the other, the harm which will be caused to the party against whom such measures are awarded. As to the first, the Court must consider the possible damage to the open procurement policy by a breach of the rules and the need for some deterrent to breaches; and it seems also that the interests of interested providers may also be considered.[45] On the other side, it must take into account prejudice to the public interest from a delay to the

---

[40] [1988] E.C.R. 4547 (report of the *ex parte* application); [1988] E.C.R. 5647.

[41] Case C-272/91R, Orders of January 3, 1992 and June 12, 1992. (The judgment of the Court was given on April 26, 1994).

[42] Case 87/94R, *Commission v. Belgium* ("Wallonia Buses"), order of April 22, 1994. See the notes by Arrowsmith, (1994) 3 P.P.L.R. CS130 and Fernández Martín (1994) 3 P.P.L.R. CS200.

[43] Para. 1 of the order.

[44] If this is correct, it is not clear whether this is an approach which the Court will adopt generally in Article 169 actions, or whether there are special features of the area of procurement which justify such an approach in this specific area.

[45] Third party interests are not normally relevant at this stage in awarding interim measures, but an exception is made in the context of actions by the Commission under Article 169 since the Commission acts as guardian of all interests under the Treaties. Although contractors often have a right to damages in the national courts if a breach is proven, it is submitted that it cannot always be assumed that their interests can be adequately protected in this way, because of difficulties of proof.

procurement. Probably the interests of other providers interested in the procedure should also be considered; in particular, the Court should take account of the possible prejudice to a provider to whom the contract has been awarded.

It is difficult to predict whether the Court will award interim relief in any particular case, because of the wide variety of factual circumstances.

The first interim measures case was *Dundalk*,[46] which, as mentioned, concerned an award procedure for the construction of a water pipeline. This case suggested that the Court might be reluctant to award such measures; relief was refused on the basis that an existing shortage of water posed a threat to health and safety. In an earlier case, case 118/83R, *CMC Co-operativa Muratori e Cementisti v. Commission*,[47] the Court had also shown itself unwilling to delay a procurement in a different context. This case concerned an Ethiopian government contract for the construction of a hydro-electric dam, which was subject to the supervision of the Commission under the Rome Convention. One of the bidders alleged illegality arising out of unfairness in the treatment of its bid, and sought interim measures *against* the Commission to require it the Commission, *inter alia*, to attempt to secure suspension of the procedure. These were refused. The Court emphasised the prejudice to the public interest in holding up the construction, and seemed to indicate that the Court would not generally countenance measures which would delay government projects.

In two recent cases, however, interim measures were awarded. The first, *La Spezia*,[48] concerned a contract for the renovation of a waste disposal plant. Here the President awarded interim measures despite accepting that damage to both public health and the environment might result. A factor which was noted as distinguishing this case from *Dundalk* was that the urgency of the renovations was due to the fault of the government in not acting earlier, and it may be that interim measures would have been refused but for this fact. Nevertheless, the case does indicate a willingness to delay a procurement in the face of serious prejudice to the public interest; certainly it showed the Court's commitment to the open procurement policy, and could be seen to pave the way for interim relief in cases of less serious prejudice even in the absence of fault. Interim measures were also awarded in *Lottomatica*,[49] to suspend a contract for computerisation of the Italian national lottery system, awarded in breach of Community rules. Italy argued that the balance of interests required the application to be refused because of, first, the potential loss of revenue, and, secondly, the fact that delay to the computerised system would delay the government's fight against illicit gambling. However, these arguments were briefly dismissed, the Presi-

---

[46] Above, note 39.
[47] [1983] E.C.R. 2583.
[48] Above, note 40.
[49] Above, note 41.

dent declining even to examine them in detail, and noting simply that the interests of the Community should prevail over those of Member States. The Order could be interpreted to indicate that considerable weight should be given to the need to enforce the open procurement policy, and on the basis of *La Spezia* and *Lottomatica* it might be suggested that *Dundalk* was an exceptional case. On the other hand, *Lottomatica* might also be interpreted as turning on the fact that the breach in that case was "manifest", in the sense that the legality of the action was unarguable.[50]

In the most recent case, *Wallonia Buses*,[51] relief was again refused. Proceedings here concerned an award procedure for delivery of a number of public transport buses in which the Commission contended that there had been infringements of the Utilities Directive. Its application to suspend the procedure was refused, however, one reason being the balance of interests.[52] This was based on the fact that the age of the existing fleet meant that replacement was urgent to protect the safety of passengers and staff. It was pointed out that the award of interim relief would mean at the very least rescission of the existing contract and a new award procedure, which would hold up each delivery by thirteen months. Relief was denied despite the fact that the government itself was largely responsible for the urgency – the buses should have been replaced at least every twelve years and many were already much older. Whilst recognising, as in *La Spezia*, that fault could affect the balance of interests the President considered that the procurement should not be delayed here because the safety risk was particularly serious.[53]

Decisions on the the balance of interests inevitably depend on their own facts. However, it is difficult to see that the position in *La Spezia*, which by the President's own admission involved a "serious" threat to health, differed much from that in *Wallonia Buses*. Furthermore, the danger in the *Wallonia Buses* case could be avoided by withdrawing the buses from service, and whilst this would cause disruption to public services, it is arguably not as as serious as a threat to safety. *Wallonia Buses* probably indicates a current reluctance to suspend procurements, even where the state is at fault, in cases where substantial damage or inconvenience will occur.

V. Interim measures in relation to a concluded contract

Interim measures may only be obtained once Article 169 proceedings have actually been instituted. Because of the pre-litigation phase,

---

[50] The general legislation which had been applied in this case had already been held unlawful in *Re Data Processing* (case C-3/88, *Commission v. Italy* [1989] E.C.R. 4035, as pointed out in para. 37 of the order. However, it can be pointed out that Italy did raise defences specific to this type of contract, and it is not clear that the Court treated these contentions as wholly unarguable.

[51] Above.

[52] Another reason was the dilatory conduct by the Commission: see p. 930 below.

[53] para. 41 of the Order.

proceedings cannot actually be commenced for several weeks and a contract may have been concluded by this time. The availability of interim measures to suspend a contract once concluded is thus of vital importance. In *Lottomatica*[54] the Court of Justice held that interim measures may be granted in these circumstances and this was confirmed in the *Wallonia Buses* case.[55] This is despite the fact that the Remedies Directive expressly permits Member States to deny the possibility of suspending concluded contracts in actions brought in their own courts, an option which has been taken up by the United Kingdom.[56] It can in fact be argued that interim measures are available in the Court of Justice only when national law itself permits a suspension of a concluded contract which would mean that such measures would not generally be possible in relation to United Kingdom authorities; but this has not been stated by the Court of Justice.[56a]

It was also held in *Wallonia Buses*, however, that if interim measures are to be given to suspend a concluded contract, the Commission must "quickly and unequivocally" inform the state concerned of its intention to seek a suspension. In *Wallonia Buses* the Commission had not indicated its intention to do so until its reasoned opinion, delivered three months after it received a complaint and two months after the letter of infringement, and it was held that relief should be denied because of the delay. Probably the Commission will have to make known its intention as soon as it has concluded that there is an arguable case for proceedings; this should be done even before the formal letter of infringement if, as is the practice, the letter is not sent immediately but only following initial informal discussions. This rule is designed to protect the interests in legal certainty of the parties to the contract.

It is submitted, however, that measures should not be refused on grounds of delay where no contract has yet been signed; delay should not in itself be grounds for refusing relief, but should be relevant only where the applicant's dilatory conduct has actually caused prejudice to other interests. This alone should suffice to encourage prompt action by the Commission. It is more arguable whether delay should preclude relief where the contract has actually been made, but no work has begun. In *Wallonia buses* the work had commenced and this was specifically mentioned.[57] However, the emphasis which the President placed on the analogy of the provision in the Remedies Directive relating to concluded contracts could indicate that simply making the contract will suffice.

---

[54] Above, note 41.
[55] Above, note 42.
[56] See pp. 913–915.
[56a] In the *Lottomatica* case there is no mention of the point. In *Wallonia Buses* the Court mentioned that concluded contracts could be challenged in Belgian law, but did not consider the significance of this point for its own powers to award interim measures.
[57] para.37 of the Order.

VI. *Ex parte* applications

There is normally a delay of one to two months before a hearing on an application for interim measures. There is however, provision for *ex parte* orders[58] – orders without notice to the other party – which may be heard almost immediately. These may be cancelled or varied, and will in practice be reconsidered once a hearing is held to consider the issue of interim measures Such orders were made with little discussion in the cases of *Dundalk*[59] and case 194/88.[60] It might be argued that in view of the fact that the Court's power to suspend a contract even once concluded is now established, that there is now no "urgency" justifying the award of *ex parte* measures prior to a hearing on interim relief, unless it is likely that substantial performance or completion will quickly occur. Since such performance might bar a remedy later on, in this case *ex parte* suspension may still be warranted.

(iv) THE EFFECT OF A JUDGMENT UNDER ARTICLE 169[61]

When in Article 169 proceedings the Court finds a breach of Community law has occurred, judgment is given in the form of a declaration that the state is in breach of its Community obligations. The Court cannot *order* the state to act, or refrain from acting, in a particular way to redress the breach. However, an obligation to take steps to eliminate the consequences of its unlawful action is imposed by Article 171 E.C. which states: "If the Court of Justice finds that a Member State has failed to fulfil an obligation under this Treaty, the State shall be required to take the necessary measures to comply with the judgment of the Court of Justice". The necessary steps must be taken immediately and must be completed in the shortest possible time.[62]

This obligation generally requires that any unlawful measures be set aside.[63] Thus, where the judgment concerns legislative practices or general administrative measures which do not conform to the procurement rules, these must be repealed or amended. Where it concerns an unlawful award procedure, it seems clear that this must normally be reopened. Where the breach consists of the fact that unlawful clauses were included in the tender documents – for example, clauses requiring use of local labour, or unlawful specifications – and bids have been submitted on that basis, it is probably not sufficient merely to delete the

---

[58] Rules of Procedure Article 87.
[59] Case 45/87R, *Commission v. Ireland* [1987] E.C.R. 783.
[60] Case 194/88R, [1988] E.C.R. 4547 and [1988] E.C.R. 4559.
[61] See further Arrowsmith, above, note 4, pp. 14–19 and 41–43.
[62] See, for example, case 131/84 *Commission v. Italy* [1985] E.C.R. 3531, [1986] 3 C.M.L.R. 693.
[63] In the context of Article 171 see joined cases 314–316/81, *Procureur de la Republique v. Waterkeyn* [1982] E.C.R. 4337.

clause and continue with the existing competition. It is unclear, however, whether it is adequate merely to permit alteration of bids or whether it is necessary to recommence the whole procedure. Probably a new procedure is necessary, since the unlawful clauses may have deterred many firms from bidding in the first place.[64]

Presumably it is not required to reopen the procedure where the contract has already been performed.[65] More debatable, however, is the position where the contract has been signed, or work begun, but it has not been completed.

One view is that Article 171 generally requires such a contract to be set aside (subject to the Commission's discretion to provide for the contrary in its reasoned opinion, as explained below). It can be argued that this view is implicit in cases awarding interim measures to suspend a concluded contract: it would be odd if the court could order a suspension, but states could then choose to proceed with the unlawful contract later. An alternative view, however, is that Article 171 does not require states to take action which could not be required by domestic law; thus if national law does not permit an authority to set aside a concluded contract, as in the United Kingdom,[66] this is not required by Article 171. This is the approach adopted by the Court of Justice to the recovery of unlawful state aids, where states are under a duty to recover only as required by national law.[67] It is submitted that this latter approach is correct in principle: since Community law imposes an obligation on national governments to provide effective national remedies in such cases, by definition adequate protection is already given to Community interests through the operation of national law rules. If this view is correct, it could likewise be argued that the powers of the Court of Justice to award interim measures when a contract has been concluded is limited to the case where this possibility is accepted in national law.

Whatever the general rule concerning Article 171, it is submitted that it should be open to the Commission in its reasoned opinion in the

---

[64] Case C–243/89, *Commission v. Denmark* ("Storebaelt"), judgment of June 22, 1993, para. 26 (concerning the steps necessary to comply with a reasoned opinion, which it is submitted involves the same requirements as Article 171 E.C.).

[65] In case 199/85, *Commission v. Italy* [1987] E.C.R. 1039, Advocate General Lenz assumed that in such a case the procedure need not be reopened in order to comply with a reasoned opinion. The steps generally required for compliance with a reasoned opinion should be the same as those required to comply with Article 171 E.C.

[66] See pp. 913–915.

[67] See, for example, case C–5/89, *Commission v. Germany* [1990] E.C.R I–3437. Centralised enforcement proceedings by the Commission in this context are not brought under Article 169, but under a special enforcement procedure under Article 93 E.C.; but it is submitted that the same rules apply concerning the steps required to redress a breach.

It can also be noted that in case 199/85, above, Advocate General Lenz stated that to comply with a reasoned opinion relating to an award procedure of an Italian municipality, the government should "urge" the municipality to rescind the contract; but did not mention that this was *required*. The author's own previous interpretation of this statement was that rescission is required: see Arrowsmith, above, note 4, pp. 16–17. However, this was based on an assumption that national rules cannot affect obligations under Article 171, a view which the author has, on further consideration of the issue, now come to reject.

original action to specify that only more limited steps are required of a Member State – for example, admission of a breach. This allows factors such as prejudice to the administration and third parties to be taken into account in deciding whether a procedure should be reopened; the court cannot do this in giving judgment, since the court does not itself specify the steps which must be taken.

If the measures required are not taken, the Commission may bring the state before the Court, in further Article 169 proceedings, for failure to comply with its obligation under Article 171. If it is found in this second action that this obligation to take necessary measures has not been complied with, the Court may impose penalty payments under a power contained in Article 171(2).[68]

(v) THE "CORRECTIVE MECHANISM" UNDER THE REMEDIES DIRECTIVES

Under Article 3 of the public sector Remedies Directive (89/665/EEC),[69] and Article 8 of the Utilities Remedies Directive (92/13/EEC),[70] there is a special procedure for the European Commission to intervene in award procedures,[71] which is sometimes referred to as the "corrective mechanism". It may be invoked when the Commission concludes that there has been a "clear and manifest" breach of the law in procedures covered by the procurement directives, except once a contract has been concluded.[72] The Commission must notify both the relevant state *and* the contracting authority of the reasons for its conclusion that such a breach exists, and request correction of the alleged infringement.[73] The Member State must reply within 21 days of receipt of notification in the public sector, or 30 in the utilities sector, and must either confirm that the infringement has been corrected or give an explanation as to why not (unless the procedure has been suspended, in which case it must simply notify the Commission of this fact).[74]

---

[68] There is no power to impose a penalty merely because judgment is given under Article 169; it is limited to the case where a state subsequently fails to comply with that judgment.

[69] [1989] O.J.L 395/33.

[70] [1992] O.J.L 76/14.

[71] The breaches to which the mechanism applies are generally those covered by the Remedies Directives, as discussed at pp. 898–899 above. However, there has been an oversight in respect of public sector services: when the Services Directive was adopted in 1992 it was mistakenly omitted to amend Article 3 of the public sector Remedies Directive to render it applicable to contracts covered by the Services Directive.

[72] Remedies Directive Article 3(1); Utilities Remedies Directive Article 8(1). The limitation in respect of concluded contracts seems to be based on the assumption that suspension of the award procedure is not possible in such a case, and that a state cannot be required under Article 171 to set aside a concluded contract. However, it now appears this assumption is incorrect (see pp. 930–931) and that thus it is not appropriate to limit the mechanism in this way. In practice, the point is unimportant since the mechanism adds little to the Commission's existing powers.

[73] Remedies Directive Article 3(2); Utilities Remedies Directive Article 8(2).

[74] Remedies Directive Article 8(3); Utilities Remedies Directive Article 8(3).

Failure to give a satisfactory reply does not, however, attract any specific sanctions and nor is the Commission given any special powers of enforcement. Nor does the mechanism in any way restrict or replace the Commission's general powers of enforcement under Article 169 and the rules which govern their exercise.[75] Thus if a satisfactory reply is not received the Commission will simply institute proceedings under Article 169 in the normal way.[76-77] It was originally proposed that the Commission should be able to suspend the award procedure on its own intitiative, which would have added significantly to its powers; but this proposal was dropped because of opposition from the Member States. The mechanism is thus of little practical importance. Its only formal effect is to place states in breach of Community law if they fail to reply within 21 days to the Commission's notification of breach.

(c) PROCEEDINGS BEFORE THE EUROPEAN COURT OF JUSTICE UNDER ARTICLE 225 E.C.

Where the Commission (or another Member State) believes that a state has made improper use of its powers under Article 223 or 224 E.C., Article 225 provides for a special procedure for actions before the Court of Justice by way of derogation from the usual procedure under Article 169 E.C. (or Article 170 E.C. in the case of proceedings by another Member State). This would be used, for example, should a state seek to avoid applying the open procurement rules to a purchase on the grounds that the product in question falls within the category of "arms, munitions and war material" under Article 223, and the Commission disputes that the product is within this category.

Under the Article 225 procedure an action may be brought directly to the Court of Justice without the need to follow the usual procedural steps of the letter of infringement, reasoned opinion, etc., as are required for proceedings under Article 169 and Article 170. Interim measures may still be ordered under Article 186 E.C.,[78] and the usual principles for awarding such relief derived from Article 83(2) of the Rules of Procedure are applicable.[79] Article 171, requiring a Member

---

[75] This was held by the Court of Justice in case C-359/93, *Commission v. Netherlands,* above, para. 13 of the judgment and confirmed in case C–79/94, *Commission v. Greece,* judgment of May 4, 1995. In the *Netherlands* case the Court specifically rejected an argument that the mechanism implied an obligation for the Commission to act swiftly in those cases to which it applied in order that Member States may take action before the contract is concluded, and that it limited the power of the Commission to bring court proceedings (*i.e.* restricted the discretion to act under Article 169) where the Commission failed to do so.

[76-77] As mentioned above, it is the Commission's practice to treat a notification of a breach given under the corrective mechanism procedure as a "letter of infringement" for the purpose of the Article 169 procedure, so that a reasoned opinion will be issued if there is no satisfactory reply within the 21-day period.

[78] Case C–120/94R, *Commission v. Hellenic Republic* [1994] E.C.R. I–3037, para. 42 (rejecting an express argument that interim measures are not available under the Article 225 procedure).

[79] *Ibid.* para. 44.

State to take steps to comply with the judgment of the Court, appears to apply to a judgment under Article 225 in the same way as to a judgment under Article 169.

(d) PROCEEDINGS FOR BREACH OF ARTICLES 85–86 E.C.[80]

Procurement decisions which infringe Article 85 or 86 E.C. are not dealt with in accordance with the Article 169 procedure outlined above but under a special system applying to competition cases. This is set out in Regulation 17,[81] enacted under Article 87 E.C. Regulation 17 gives the Commission responsibility for investigating breaches, taking decisions and imposing sanctions, with the Community Courts enjoying merely a supervisory role.

Breaches may be brought to the Commission's attention in a variety of ways, but of particular significance for procurement is the provision in Article 3(2) for a complaint by any person claiming a "legitimate interest" in the matter. This could include a provider complaining about an award made to another provider, or a provider who contends that a purchaser or provider has abused a dominant position in setting the terms of a contract between the parties. The regulation gives the Commission significant fact finding powers for investigating such complaints which are exercisable against any undertaking, including a power to order production of documents under Article 11, and to enter premises and take copies of documents or conduct an oral examination, under Article 14.

If it appears that a breach has occurred the Commission may formally initiate proceedings against the undertaking in breach (rather than, as with Article 169 proceedings, the relevant Member State). This is done by a "statement of objections" setting out the facts and reasons for the Commission's view. The Commission itself has a power to award interim measures pending its final decision on the matter,[82–83] which is rendered following a formal hearing (Article 19).

Where a breach is found to exist, the Commission may order its termination. For a breach of Article 85 it is clear that this may include the rescission of a concluded contract, since Article 85(2) states expressly that such a contract is null and void. No such express rule is included in the Treaty for Article 86 but arguably the same rules apply. An order for periodic penalty payments may be attached to the Commission's order to ensure that the order is enforced. For negligent or intentional infringements of the rules, as well as ordering a termination of the breach the Commission has a power to impose a fine.

---

[80] See generally Wyatt and Dashwood, *European Community Law* (3rd ed., 1993), Chap. 16.
[81] O.J. 1962 204; O.J. 1959–62, 87.
[82–83] Case 792/79R, *Camera Care v. Commission* [1980] E.C.R. 119.

The Commission's decisions pursuant to this procedure may be challenged before the Court of First Instance by way of a review action under Article 173 E.C., with a possible appeal to the Court of Justice.

(5) ATTESTATION

The Utilities Remedies Directive makes provision, in Articles 3–7, for entities to have access to a system whereby they may submit their procurement to independent scrutiny to determine whether it is being carried out in accordance with Community rules. This is referred to as "attestation". The submission to an attestation process is purely voluntary. It was envisaged that it would provide a way for the utility to demonstrate to the market that it complies with the rules and so perhaps encourage providers to participate in award procedures run by that utility. It may also provide a useful method for utilities who seek to comply with the rules to check that the procedures which they have devised are adequate, and help them avoid the threat of legal actions by aggrieved providers. At present there is no measure on attestation in the public sector, but the system may be extended to the public sector in due course.

The responsibility for provision of a system of attestation lies not with the Community itself but with Member States, who under Article 3 must make such a system available. Under Article 4, it is provided that the system must cover all award procedures covered by the Utilities Directive and must involve assessment for compliance with all relevant Community rules (thus covering those in the Treaty as well as the directives). It must involve a review "periodically" of both "procedures" and "practices" of the utility, which appears to require examination of any relevant procurement rules or guidelines within the organisation and also an assessment of what is done in practice (including whether purchasers follow the guidelines).

Article 6 requires that "attestors" shall be independent of purchasers and "completely objective" in carrying out their duties, and must demonstrate relevant professional qualifications and experience. It is specifically stated that Member States may identify persons, professions or institutions whose staff are considered by them to possess such qualifications and experience. They may require professional qualifications[84] or alternatively may organise or recognise for this purpose other examinations of professional competence.

Under Article 5 attestors must make a report on their examination to the purchaser, in writing. They may not award an "attestation" of compliance unless satisfied both that any irregularities identified in practices and procedures have been corrected *and* that measures have been taken to ensure that they are not repeated. Article 5(2) makes

---

[84] These must be at the level at least of a higher education diploma within the meaning of Directive 89/48/EEC, [1989] O.J. L19/16.

provision for purchasers who have received an attestation to publish a notice to that effect in the *Official Journal of the European Communities.*[85]

When these provisions were adopted it was envisaged that a European "standard" for an attestation system would be developed, which could be used by Member States in devising a system for use in their own jurisdictions. In contemplation of this Article 7 of the directive expressly provides that the provisions in Article 4–6 of the directive concerning, respectively, scope, procedure and the qualifications, etc. of attestors, are to be essential requirements for the development of any European attestation standards. Following adoption of the directive, at the end of 1992 the Commission gave a mandate to the European Committee for Standardisation (CEN) to develop a European standard and at the time of writing it looked likely that this would be approved in November 1995.[86]

The United Kingdom has as yet made no provision for an attestation system, either in the regulations or otherwise,[87] and to this extent is in default of its obligations under the directive. The adoption of a European standard, however, may prompt the provision of such a system.

Until attestation systems are actually in place it is not possible to know how far utilities will take advantage of such systems. Whilst at present there is some scepticism over the value of achieving voluntary attestation, should the option be taken up by a number of the larger utilities this may lead to attestation becoming the normal practice in the industry.

Provision for systematic and independent scrutiny of an entity's award procedures is a potentially valuable way of monitoring compliance with the rules. It provides an opportunity for a more searching examination than can be carried out by the Commission with its present powers, in particular in relation to less obvious breaches arising out of the exercise of discretion such as abuses in applying the award criteria. *Compulsory* attestation could thus be a useful supplement to other methods of enforcing the procurement rules,[88] either as an aid to the Commission in

---

[85] This is to take the form of a statement that "The contracting entity has obtained an attestation in accordance with Council Directive 92/13 that, on . . ., its contract award procedures and practices were in accordance with Community law and the national rules implementing that law" (Article 5(2)).

[86] On development of the standard see Gjonnes, "Attestation of Conformity with the E.C. Procurement Rules for Utilities" (1993) 2 P.P.L.R. CS119.

[87] Since the provisions on attestation do not seem intended to confer any legal rights on providers it is not necessary to enact legislation on this issue, but practical steps must be taken to make an appropriate system available.

[88] The original proposals on attestation had something of this character: the system was to be compulsory in cases where set aside and interim relief were precluded and a state relied instead on the "dissuasive payments" system of remedies, to supplement this latter system. It can be noted that the Department of Trade and Industry (DTI) has suggested that attestation for compliance with general principles of fair procurement could be a useful substitute for detailed procurement rules: see DTI, *Public Procurement Review* (1994), paras. 89–92.

its own enforcement activities (by requiring attestors' reports to be submitted to the Commission) or more directly, if specific sanctions, or the possibility of sanctions, were to be attached to a failure to obtain an attestation.

4. REMEDIES FOR BREACH OF THE GPA AND THE ASSOCIATION AGREEMENTS

(a) REMEDIES FOR BREACH OF THE GPA[89]

(i) REMEDIES IN THE NATIONAL COURTS

The World Trade Organisation Agreement on Government Procurement (GPA)[90] is binding on Member States.[91] The procedural rules which it contains appear, like those of the directives, to be clear and precise and not to be subject to the adoption of any further measures – that is, they are "directly applicable". Thus, Member States are under an obligation in Community law to follow the procedures which they lay down in awarding their contracts.

It is not clear whether the original "GATT" Agreement on Government Procurement – the predecessor to the existing GPA – was intended to confer rights on affected persons, including providers from third countries who seek to rely on the rules – that is, whether its rules had "direct effect". With internal Community legislation the fact that a provision is sufficiently clear, precise and unconditional to be directly applicable is generally enough to render that provision enforceable by affected persons under the doctrine of direct effect. However, this is not the case with international agreements where, in addition to showing that the provision is capable of being judicially applied, it is further necessary to demonstrate that the provision is one actually intended to create legal rights, which involves consideration of the "spirit, general scheme and terms" of the agreement.[92] So far provisions of GATT have not been held to create legal rights, the Court of Justice pointing, in particular, to the existence of an inter-governmental mechanism for settling disputes whose provisions may be prejudiced if national remedies are given.[93] It seems unlikely that the original GATT procurement agreement was such as to confer rights on third country providers.

---

[89] See further Footer, "Remedies under the New GATT Agreement on Government Procurement" (1995) 4 P.P.L.R. 80.

[90] On the GPA see pp. 774–781.

[91] See joined cases 21–24/72, *International Fruit Co N.V. v. Produktschap voor Groenten en Fruit* [1972] E.C.R. 1219.

[92] *International Fruit*, above. See further Cheyne, "International Agreements and the European Community Legal System" (1994) E.L. Rev. 581, at pp. 588–594.

[93] *International Fruit*, above; case C–280/93, *Germany v. Council*, judgment of October 5, 1994. See further Castillo de la Torre, "The status of GATT in E.C. Law Revisited" (1995) 29 Journal of World Trade 53.

Under the new GPA, however, which is in force from January 1, 1996, express provision is made for remedies for aggrieved third country providers,[94] and it is thus more likely that to the extent that the rules in the GPA are clear, precise and unconditional they will be treated as having direct effect. As indicated above, the procedural rules governing the award of contracts, like those in the directives, pass this test.[95] On the other hand, it can be pointed out that there is a general statement in the pre-amble to the Council Decision accepting the WTO Agreement that its rules are not intended to have direct effect, which might apply to the GPA as well as the other WTO Agreements.

The requirements of the GPA system of remedies may be less stringent than those of Community law: for example, although damages are required there is an express provision permitting these to be limited to "costs for tender preparation or protest",[96-97] which, arguably, may not be permitted under Community law. However, since there is a general requirement in Article III of the new GPA that providers from signatory states should be treated no less favourably than national providers or providers from other parties, the remedies given to such providers must be just as favourable as those conferred upon Community providers. Thus these third country providers are effectively enabled to take advantage of the Community remedies system under the Remedies Directives.

It is likely that the Government will implement the GPA expressly, by providing that the existing procurement regulations may be enforced by relevant third country providers in award procedures which are covered by the GPA. It will also be made clear that such providers may use the remedies set out in the regulations. These remedies were discussed in detail in section 3 of this chapter.

(ii) THE WTO DISPUTE SETTLEMENT MECHANISM[98]

In addition to the possibility of remedies for individual providers in the relevant national courts, there is a possibility of recourse by the government of the aggrieved provider to an inter-governmental mechanism set up under the WTO Agreement, the "Understanding on Rules and Procedures Governing the Settlement of Disputes" (or DSU), set out in Annex II of the Agreement. The operation of this mechanism in

---

[94] Article XX(ii). On these remedies see further Footer, above.
[95] See pp. 902–903. In any case, the award procedures must be no less favourable than those applying to other domestic providers and those of other parties (Article III): this means that providers from signatory states may enforce the same rules as Community providers, including those in the procurement directives and regulations, which have already been recognised as being clear and precise.
[96-97] Article XX(ii)(7)(c).
[98] See further Footer, above.

procurement cases is subject to special provisions in Article XXII of the GPA.

Where a government wishes to invoke the DSU it must first consult with the state allegedly in breach and attempt to find a solution by informal means.[99] If one party fails to respond or the parties fail to reach agreement a party can request a Panel to be established. This is organised by the WTO Dispute Settlement Body (DSB), which appoints the Panel in consultation with the parties.[1] The Panel must include "persons qualified in the area of government procurement".[2] It is stated that "every effort shall be made to accelerate the proceedings to the greatest extent possible" and specifically that the panel shall attempt to provide its final report to the parties not later than four months from the time its composition and terms of reference are agreed (or seven months "in case of delay".[3] There is an appeal to a standing Appellate Body, which must normally be completed within 60 days.[4]

Once the report has been completed and "adopted" by the DSB, a government found to have breached the rules must report to the DSB the actions which it proposes to take to implement the Panel's recommendations.[5] In the case of general procurement measures this will normally involve repeal of the measures, but where the dispute concerns a specific contract the problems of public inconvenience and hardship to the selected contracting party may be considered to make this inappropriate. In recognition of this particular difficulty with procurement disputes, Article XXII(3) of the GPA provides for the DSB to authorise consultation on remedies where withdrawal of the measure is not possible. This seems to envisage the possibility of governments negotiating for compensation (although, as explained above, compensation may be available in any case through the national courts).

Article XXII(3) also provides for the DSB to authorise suspension of obligations or concessions under the Agreement. This might apply, for example, where a state refuses to withdraw general measures which restrict market access in a sector covered by the Agreement, to allow the state affected by the restrictions to suspend the access of the offending state in the same sector. In general in the WTO non-compliance under one of the Agreements permits the possibility of the state(s) adversely affected suspending their own obligations and concessions under a *different* WTO Agreement. However, under XXII(7) of the GPA it is expressly provided that the only possibility in this case is for suspension of provisions under the GPA itself.

---

[99] GPA Article XXII(II). See generally DSU Article 4.
[1] GPA Article XXII(3).
[2] GPA Article XXII(5).
[3] GPA Article XXII (6).
[4] DSU Article 20.
[5] DSU Article 21.

(b) REMEDIES UNDER THE EEA AGREEMENT AND THE ASSOCIATION AGREEMENTS

Under the European Economic Area (EEA) Agreement concluded between the Community and the states of the European Free Trade Association access to procurement in the European Community under the same terms as Community providers is conferred on Norway, Iceland and Liechtenstein, and this includes the benefits of the rules on remedies which Community providers enjoy under the Compliance Directives.[6] The substantive rules on award procedures thus clearly have direct effect in relation to providers from these states.

Subject to certain limitations the Association Agreements concluded with a number of central and eastern European countries also expressly permit providers from those states to have access to Community markets procurement under the same terms as Community providers,[7] and this is probably intended to include access to the special rules on remedies for Community providers. In any case, whilst, as noted above, it is necessary to show a specific intention to confer legal rights on affected persons in order for provisions of an international agreement to have direct effect, the Court of Justice has generally been willing to recognise direct effect in the case of the clear and precise provisions of the Community's Association Agreements.[8]

In the United Kingdom the procurement regulations which implement the directives have been amended to give effect to the rights conferred under the EEA Agreement and the Association Agreements. At the time of writing the regulations provide for access to both procedures and remedies for providers from Norway, Iceland and Liechtenstein (covered by the EEA Agreement), and Poland, Hungary, the Czech Republic, the Slovak Republic, Bulgaria and Romania (covered by Association Agreements).[9] New Association Agreements are likely to be ratified shortly,[10] and the regulations will not doubt be amended in due course to give express rights of enforcement to providers from states covered by these new Agreements.

To the extent that providers covered by such Agreements are not yet expressly included within the regulations, the question arises as to whether the requirements governing remedies themselves will have direct effect. Generally, the obligations on remedies appear to lack direct

---

[6] On the EEA Agreement see generally pp. 771–774.

[7] See generally pp. 781–786.

[8] See, for example, case C–192/89, *Service v. Staatssecretaris van Justitie* [1990] E.C.R. I–3461.

[9] Utilities Regulations 2(1), 4(2) and Sched. 2; Works Regulation 2(1), as am. by Supply Regulation 31(1)(a) and Utilities Regulation 35(1), and Works Regulation 4(1)(b), as am. by Utilities Regulation 35(1); Supply Regulation 2(1) and 4(1)(b), as am. by Utilities Regulation 35(3); Services Regulation 2(1) as am. by Supply Regulation 31(2)(a) and Utilities Regulation 35(2), and Services Regulation 4(1)(b), as am. by Utilities Regulation 35(2).

[10] On this see p. 783.

effect since they are not precise and unconditional, but involve a discretion for states over the manner of their implementation (for example, whether a concluded contract may be set aside). However, the obligations in the Association Agreements are subject to the further principle that the rights given must be equal to those conferred on Community providers; and the implementation of a system for Community providers appears to impart sufficient precision into the obligation owed to providers under these Agreements to produce direct effect. Thus it is submitted that providers from states benefiting from Association Agreements which include the same procurement rules as the existing Association Agreements may take advantage of the remedies provided by the regulations, even before they are mentioned expressly.

5. REMEDIES FOR BREACH OF PART II OF THE LOCAL GOVERNMENT ACT 1988

(1) SECTION 17 (NON-COMMERCIAL CONSIDERATIONS)

Section 17 of the Local Government Act 1988, which prohibits local authorities from taking account of non-commercial considerations in procurement, may be enforced by way of judicial review.[11] The remedies available, and the procedures and time-limits which generally apply in such proceedings, were considered in section (2) above.

The question of standing is expressly dealt with in section 19(7)(a), which provides that persons who have a sufficient interest for review shall include any potential provider "(contractor")", or, where a contract has been made, former potential provider, and also "any body representing contractors". The fact that interested parties are said merely to *include* such firms and organisations indicates that the standing of other possible litigants, such as ratepayers, is not excluded.[12]

The Act does not state expressly whether a breach of section 17 may invalidate a concluded agreement. It is clearly contemplated that a review action may be brought after conclusion of the contract, since the legislation provides that a "former potential contractor" has standing *after* a contract is made. However, such an action could be one for a declaration or simply to challenge a decision leading up to the contract, rather than the contract itself, so that this provision does not necessarily indicate an intention to invalidate concluded agreements. Indeed, the

---

[11] Judicial review is probably generally available for breaches of statutory public procurement rules, and this is assumed in LGA 1988, s.19 which makes specific provision on some aspects of review, as explained in the following text.
[12] On who else may have standing see pp. 885–887.

reference to a "former" potential contractor could indicate that an interested bidder has no prospect of obtaining the contract once an agreement has been made, suggesting that any concluded contract remains binding. It was suggested in section (2) that the courts should be reluctant to invalidate concluded contracts[13] and it is submitted that any agreement made should be treated as unaffected by a breach of section 17.

Even if the court is able to set aside a concluded contract it may be reluctant to do so, especially if work has commenced, and in some cases the work may even be completed before the case is heard. Thus the availability of interim relief is an important issue. However, it is likely that such relief will often be refused on the balance of convenience;[14] and in any case providers may be unwilling to seek such relief because of a requirement to give an undertaking to pay damages for any loss caused to the authority.[15] These difficulties, combined with the difficulty of obtaining relief at trial, mean that it is difficult for an aggrieved firm to insist on being considered for the award itself.

A right to damages is, however, provided for a breach of section 17, by section 19(7)(b). Damages for breach of a statutory duty relating to procurement will normally require a plaintiff to show that he had a real chance for the contract, and to prove the profits which would have been made; damages are then awarded for the value of the chance to obtain this profit. However, under section 19 any damages claims by persons who have submitted a tender are expressly limited to expenditure "reasonably incurred" for the purpose of submitting the tender[16-17] and the provider thus may not recover the full amount of his lost profits. Since the provision is actionable only by persons who suffer loss or damage as a consequence of the breach[18] it is still necessary, in claiming even these limited damages for costs, to show that this loss has occurred as a result of the breach in accordance with the usual tort rules. This may require the provider to show on the balance of probabilities that it would have won the contract and also that the profits made would have been sufficient to cover his costs: if not, the provider has not suffered any loss from the breach, since the expenditure would have been lost regardless of the breach. In proving his loss, however, it is arguable that the provider may be able to take account of a rebuttable presumption that he would have won the contract and recovered his costs.[19]

In proceedings for breach of section 17 a provider is aided by section 17(10). This provides that an authority is deemed to have exercised its

---

[13] See pp. 895–897.
[14] On this see p. 890. As explained there, interim relief can also be refused where damages are an adequate remedy. However, although damages are available for breach of s.17 they are not an adequate remedy since they are limited to tender costs, as explained in the text below.
[15] See p. 891.
[16-17] LGA 1988, s.19(8).
[18] LGA 1988, s.19(7)(b).
[19] On this issue see pp. 892–895.

functions by reference to non-commercial matters where it either (i) asks a question relating to a non-commercial matter or (ii) submits to any firm a draft contract or draft tender which includes terms or provisions relating to a non-commercial matter.[20] This provision obviates the need for a litigant to prove that the matter in question actually influenced the authority's decision, or even that it was considered in making the decision, allowing a judicial review action simply on proof that the relevant term or question was included. However, this does not affect the need to prove loss to maintain a damages claim; it merely creates a rule that the authority is deemed to have considered the non-commercial matter, and not that this necessarily had an influence on the choice of provider.[21]

Section 19(7) of the Act expressly states that a breach of section 17 is not a criminal offence.

(2) SECTION 20 (REASONS FOR DECISIONS)

Judicial review will also be available[22] to enforce the obligation to give reasons for procurement decisions which is set out in section 20 of the LGA 1988.[23] In this case there is no question of interfering with the contract award procedure itself. No right to damages is given for breach of this provision.

(3) SECTION 2 (PROHIBITION OF CHARGES FOR REGISTRATION)

Section 22(1) of the LGA 1988 prohibiting charges for inclusion on approved lists is stated in section 22(2) to be "actionable" by a person seeking to be included or retained in the list. Thus a decision to charge for inclusion is open to judicial review: for example, an action could be maintained to quash the decision to charge, or to require an authority to consider an application for inclusion by a firm which has not paid the charge. It is submitted that a breach would not affect the validity of award procedures for all contracts to which the list relates. However, a decision to exclude a firm from a specific award procedure because the charge has not been paid is probably an unlawful decision which could vitiate that particular procedure. Any charge paid in contravention of

---

[20] This excludes matters covered by section 18, concerning race relations matters: on this see pp. 836–839.
[21] Even if this is incorrect, and it must be taken to establish that the choice of provider would have been different but for this influence, to claim damages it will be necessary to show that the applicant would have been successful from amongst the remaining contenders.
[22] See the discussion at pp. 882–883. On the applicable remedies and procedures see section 2 of this chapter.
[23] See pp. 843–844.

this provision would be recoverable in proceedings in restitution.[24] Damages for profits from contracts which a firm might have obtained if it were included on the list will not be recoverable: if this had been intended, express reference would have been made to the right to claim damages.

6. REMEDIES FOR BREACH OF THE RULES ON COMPULSORY COMPETITIVE TENDERING[25]

(1) INTRODUCTION

The rules on compulsory competitive tendering (CCT) were explained in Chapters 12–14. Providers affected by a breach of these rules may, as with other procurement rules, seek judicial review in the courts and this possibility is considered in section (2) below. The main mechanism for enforcing the CCT rules, however, is through the intervention of the Secretary of State who enjoys stringent enforcement powers in this area. These are examined in section (3).

(2) JUDICIAL REVIEW

There have been few attempts to enforce the rules on compulsory competitive tendering by way of judicial review, probably because of the significant enforcement powers of the Secretary of State, but in principle judicial review is available.[26] The remedies available in such proceedings, and the applicable time-limits and procedures, have been outlined above.[27]

A possible difficulty for an aggrieved firm is the question of standing, since in contrast with the rules on non-commercial considerations, the legislation contains no express provision giving standing to providers. However, it was suggested above that aggrieved competitors do have standing to enforce rules to promote efficiency in public contracting, even if this is not expressly stated.[28] It is also possible that the rules are enforceable by members of the public since certain information about the contract is required to be made available to such persons.[29]

---

[24] *Woolwich Equitable Building Society v. Inland Revenue Commissioners* [1993] A.C. 70.
[25] See further, Cirell and Bennett, *Compulsory Competitive Tendering* Chaps. 15 and 17.
[26] See the discussion at pp. 882–883 above. In some cases, the existence of an alternative method for enforcing legal provisions is held to oust the possibility of judicial review actions. However, it is expressly provided in LGA 1988, s.16(2) and LGPLA 1980, s.20(7) (as inserted by LGA 1988, s.32 and Sched. 6) that the provisions conferring enforcement powers on the Secretary of State shall not prejudice other remedies.
[27] See pp. 882–883.
[28] See pp. 885–887.
[29] See pp. 715–716. At the very least, these persons could enforce the rules requiring the provision of this information.

On the other hand, it was held in Scotland in *Kershaw v. City of Glasgow D.C.*[30] that the manager of a Direct Service Organisation (DSO)[31] does not have standing to enforce the prohibition on anti-competitive conduct under the LGA 1988, where the DSO feels it has itself been unfairly treated in relation to its competitors.[32] This is because the legislation does not seek to protect the DSO, assuming that its interests will be protected by the authority itself; indeed, the very purpose of the legislation is a fear that the authority will show undue favouritism to the DSO. The same reasoning will apply to deny such persons standing in proceedings in England and Wales under the 1988 Act and under the LGPLA 1980.

Proceedings will be brought only where there is a decision to award the contract to an authority's DLO/DSO.[33] Any principle that the Court may not hold invalid a contract already made (which it was suggested above is the usual rule in English law)[34] will not apply here, since the internal bidder is not a legal entity which is separate from the awarding authority, and there is no legal contract between them. Further, the courts are unlikely to exercise any discretion which they have to refuse relief,[35] since the interests of the DSO/DLO will not be considered to deserve the same protection as those of an external provider.

In contrast with the position in relation to a breach of section 17 of the Local Government Act, there is no express right to damages for breach of the CCT rules, either under Part I of the 1988 Act or under the LGPLA. Thus damages are not available to aggrieved firms, unless the breach is deliberate when there may be a claim based on the tort of misfeasance in public office.[36] A right to damages is not necessary, however, to give an effective remedy for aggrieved firms, in view of the potential effectiveness of judicial review proceedings, as explained above, and also the enforcement powers of the Secretary of State (which may involve reopening an award procedure).

---

[30] 1992 S.L.T. 71.

[31] The proceedings were brought by the manager of the DSO, since the DSO, being legally part of the authority, was not able to bring proceedings as an entity in its own right.

[32] Probably in these circumstances no anti-competitive behaviour in fact exists: see pp. 745–747. The same reasoning applies, though, to other breaches of the CCT rules, such as the rules on advertising – but. in practice, the DSO is unlikely to complain of other breaches, since these rules have the effect of promoting the interests of its competitors.

[33] This is because the duty to follow these procedural requirements, and the definition of anti-competitive behaviour, are formulated so that a breach of duty only occurs in circumstances where work is to be done by the DLO/DSO: the breach of duty lies in the award of the work to the DLO/DSO following the conduct listed in the Act. It can be noted that the Secretary of State, also, may only intervene when the outcome of the procedure is an award to the internal bidder: see pp. 947–954.

[34] See pp. 895–897.

[35] On this see pp. 887–888

[36] See pp. 891–892.

(3) POWERS OF THE SECRETARY OF STATE

(a) INTRODUCTION

As noted above, in practice, the main way in which the rules on compulsory competitive tendering have been enforced, is through enforcement powers conferred by the CCT legislation on the Secretary of State. These powers are exercised by the Secretary of State for the Environment in England and the Secretary of State for Wales in Wales. They provide for the Secretary of State to issue a notice to an authority where he considers the CCT rules have not been followed, requiring an explanation. If he is not satisfied, he may follow up the notice with a range of sanctions, imposed through written "directions" issued under the legislation, which may include an order for work to be re-tendered and even an order barring the DSO/DLO from future work. For defined activities under the Local Government Act 1988 Act these powers were included at the time CCT was introduced in 1988. For construction and maintenance activities subject to CCT under the Local Government Planning and Land Act 1980 they were not included in the original legislation but were added to the 1980 Act by the LGA 1988.[37]

In relation to failure to comply with the rules governing individual award procedures investigations by the Secretary of State are undertaken mainly as a result of complaints from providers although complaints are also received from others – for example, opposition council members, or members of the general public.[38] A complaint to the Secretary of State is an attractive option for an aggrieved firm since, unlike the alternative of judicial review, it does not involve expense or much inconvenience, and it also provides a more effective means of ascertaining the detailed facts and reasons behind a decision. Further, in deciding whether anti-competitive behaviour exists, the Secretary of State probably also has greater powers to review the decisions of local authorities than does the court, in that he may interfere in the merits of a bid evaluation decisions, or assessments of financial or technical standing. The existence of these powers explains why judicial review proceedings against local authorities have been so rare.

(b) THE STATUTORY NOTICE

Before he may exercise his power to impose sanctions through the issue of directions, the Secretary of State must first issue a statutory notice to the authority concerned, in the form set out in section 13 LGA 1988 and section 19A of LGPLA 1980. This notice may be issued – and hence the possibility of sanctions raised – for breach of any of the rules of the CCT

---

[37] LGA 1988, Sched. 6, para. 9, inserting new sections 19A and 19B into LGPLA 1980.
[38] Department of the Environment and Local Government – Annual Report 1993, p. 11.

regime: that is, both the rules regulating specific tendering procedures and the rules concerning accounts, financial objectives and reporting requirements.[39]

As regards rules regulating the tendering procedure, a notice may be issued whenever it appears to the Secretary of State that there has been a decision to award work to the DSO/DLO and that there has been a breach of the tendering rules.[40] These include, for example, the very specific rules on methods of advertising and time-limits for submission of bids, as well as the general prohibition on anti-competitive conduct. A notice can also be issued when an in-house unit which has won the work has not carried it out in accordance with the detailed specification.[41]

Other CCT rules concern financial objectives and accounting and reporting obligations. Under the 1988 Act a notice may be issued where work falling within a particular defined activity has in a particular year been carried out by the in-house unit, and in the financial year concerned the authority has not complied, in relation to the defined activity in question, with either (i) its accounting obligations relating to that defined activity; (ii) its obligations concerning financial objectives; or (iii) its reporting obligations.[42] Similarly, under the LGPLA 1980 a notice can be issued where the in-house unit has carried out construction or maintenance work and has not complied with its accounting or reporting obligations, or has not met the financial objectives relating to work of a particular description.[43]

The LGA 1988 expressly states that the Secretary of State may serve different notices identifying the same work and the same financial year.[44] This is most likely where different breaches are alleged in a single tendering procedure. It is also possible for more than one notice to be served over the same breach – for example, if in response to the first notice it is decided to take no action, but new information later comes to light which leads the Secretary of State to change his view. The LGPLA 1980 similarly provides that the Secretary of State may serve different notices identifying the same work.[45]

---

[39] On these rules see Chaps. 13–14.

[40] LGA 1988, s.13(1)(b), as amended by Local Government Act 1992, s.11 and Sched. 1, para. 13; LGPLA 1980, s.19A1(b), as amended by Local Government Act 1992, s.11 and Sched. 1, para. 6. The amendments were introduced to make it clear that the notice may be issued before the DLO/DSO has commenced the work. The previous wording suggested no action could be taken until work had been done by the in-house unit, but this was clearly not intended since the main objective of sanctions is to stop the in-house unit doing the work when proper procedures have not been followed. On the other hand, it does not appear that any action may be taken before award decision — for example, when the authority is simply *considering* a bid by the DLO/DSO without following the proper advertising requirements.

[41] *Ibid.*

[42] LGA 1988, s.13(1)(c)–(e).

[43] LGPLA 1980, s.19A(1)(c)–(g); and see LGA 1992, s.29(2) and Sched. 4.

[44] LGA 1988, s.13(4).

[45] LGPLA 1980, s.19A(4).

The notice must[46]: identify the work; state that a breach appears to have occurred and the type of breach[47]; and state "why" it appears a breach has occurred (which will require details of both the facts giving rise to the breach and the exact legal provision which has been breached). The notice must also inform the authority of the requirement to respond and give details of the form of response required.[48]

The authority's response must be in written form, and must do one of two things.[49] First, the authority may state that it has "not acted as alleged", and justify this statement. It is submitted that this permits the authority to contend either that it did not carry out the action concerned; that an assessment which it has made (for example concerning the financial standing of a competitor) is justified; or that the Secretary of State's interpretation of the legal provisions, including the meaning of anti-competitive behaviour, is unlawful *or* incorrect (for example, that it is not anti-competitive to take certain costs into account). As an alternative, the authority may admit that it has acted as alleged but give reasons why no direction should be given. On the literal wording of the provisions it appears that it is not open to the authority to maintain both that its actions are lawful, and that, if not, no action should be taken.

It is the practice of the Secretary of State for the Environment to contact an authority informally to discuss an allegation of breach of the rules, before a formal notice is issued under the Act.[50] Issue of a notice is thus quite a serious a matter, indicating that the Secretary of State has not been satisfied by the initial explanations.

Authorities may seek judicial review of the Secretary of State's decision that a breach of the CCT rules has occurred. One situation in which such an action may be brought is where the authority disagrees with his interpretation of the legislation. Generally, judicial review is available where the court considers that a Minister has taken a decision based on an error of law in construing legislation[51] or has otherwise based the exercise of his discretion on an error of law. Thus if, for example, the Secretary of State concludes that there has been a breach of advertising requirements, but the Court considers that this is based on an erroneous view of what the statute requires by law by way of advertising, then the Secretary of State's decision may be quashed.[51a] Most of his decisions will be based on an alleged breach of the general prohibition on "anti-competitive" behaviour and this raises the question

---

[46] These requirements are set out in LGA 1988, s.13(2)(a) and (b) and LGPLA 1980, s.19A(2)(a) and (b).
[47] The notice must identify the exact parapgraph of LGA 1988, s.13(1) or LGPLA 1980, s.19A(1) which is relied on in this respect (whether s.13(1)(b), (c) etc.).
[48] LGA 1988, s.13(2)(c) and (3); LGPLA 1980, s.19A(2)(c) and (3).
[49] LGA 1988, s.13(3); LGPLA, s.19A(3).
[50] Department of Environment and Local Government – Annual Report 1993.
[51] *Page v. Hull University Visitors* [1993] 1 All E.R 97.
[51a] Errors of law on other matters which influence the decision may also lead to it being quashed: see *Re Etterick and Lauderdale District Council,* judgment of May 25, 1994.

of whether classifying a particular type of conduct as anti-competitive is a question of law for the court, or is a factual or discretionary matter within the powers of the Secretary of State.

In *R. v. Secretary of State for the Environment, ex p. Knowsley*[52] Ralph Gibson L.J. appeared to take the view that whether conduct was capable of being anti-competitive was for the court and thus it was for the court to decide, for example, which reasons for rejecting a bid could be treated as anti-competitive and which could not. Leggatt L.J., on the other hand, considered that there was some discretion for the Secretary of State over such issues.

Since *Knowsley*, however, the Secretary of State has been given an express statutory power to issue guidance on what is anti-competitive behaviour which is binding in nature.[53] Thus an action will not be available to review a decision based on such guidance, even if the court itself would have taken the view that such conduct is not anti-competitive. For example, in issuing guidance it now appears open to the Secretary of State to decide if post-tender negotiations, or the consideration of certain criteria in the award process, are anti-competitive. The guidance itself may still be reviewable on the basis of the principles of unreasonableness of improper purposes – for example, the court would strike down guidance providing that it is anti-competitive to award contracts to firms whose managing directors have red hair – since this cannot possibly relate to the issue of competition; but guidance is likely to be struck down only in exceptional cases. This same approach may also apply where a decision is taken that conduct is anti-competitive even where no guidance on that point has yet been issued: the existence of the power to give guidance might be construed as showing an intention that the Secretary of State is to have a general discretionary power to determine what behaviour can be treated as anti-competitive. On the other hand, the court may prefer the approach of Ralph Gibson in *Knowsley* on this point, and reserve this matter for the court alone until specific guidance has been issued.

Another possible basis for dispute is where the Secretary of State condemns the exercise of an authority's own discretionary assessment, such as whether a bidder's financial standing – such as the amount of his capital – or his technical capacity – such as the number of skilled personnel or extent of the firm's experience – are adequate for the contract. Another such assessment might be which of two bids, one with an earlier delivery date but the other slightly cheaper, offers better value for money. In *R. v. Secretary of State for the Environment, ex p. Haringey L.B.C.*[54] the Divisional Court took the view that assessment of financial and technical standing, and the weighing of doubts over these issues

---

[52] Judgment of July 31, 1991.
[53] See pp. 707–709.
[54] Judgment of December 22, 1992 (affirmed, C.A., (1994) 92 L.G.R. 538. This issue was not appealed).

against the financial savings to be made from a bid were also matters on which the Secretary of State is given a wide and subjective discretion. Thus the Secretary of State may determine that the authority has acted anti-competitively in the way in which these assessment have been made; and in a review action the court will not review his conclusion on its merits, but will accept it unless clearly irrational.

Finally, a disagreement may concern questions of fact – for example, whether a particular bidder had or had not failed to perform previous contracts in a satisfactory way. In *Knowsley* Ralph Gibson L.J. indicated that in accordance with the general principles applying to review of ministerial discretion[55] the court will enquire whether the facts on which the Secretary of State's decision is based do in fact exist. Probably the applicable test is whether *some* "reasonable or sufficient evidence" exists for such facts[56]: the court will not re-examine the question to determine whether the authority's view of the facts or that of the Secretary of State is the correct one.

(c) THE POWER TO ISSUE DIRECTIONS

When a notice has been served and the time-limit for response has expired, and it still appears to the Secretary of State that the authority has acted as alleged in the notice, he may issue directions. These must be given to the authority in written form.[57]

Under the LGA 1988, the following directions may be given:

(i) That the authority shall cease to have any power to carry out the defined activity to which the notice relates.[58] This effectively allows the Secretary of State to insist that the whole of a certain defined activity should be contracted out in future. In practice this is likely to mean closure of the DSO.

Alternatively, an order may be made covering only part of the work within a defined activity, to be specified in the direction.[59] This usually involves an order that the DSO may not bid for work on a particular contract which the Secretary of State feels has previously been awarded to the DSO improperly. Where an award procedure has already been held for the work, in practice the authority is then likely to award the work to the outside bidder who submitted the best offer in the tendering procedure.

(ii) That work within the defined activity to which the notice relates, or a specified part of that work, may be carried out by the authority only under certain conditions, as specified in the direction.[60] It is expressly

---

[55] See Craig, *Administrative Law* (3rd ed., 1994), pp. 365–368.
[56] For the case law and discussion of the relevant principles see Craig, *Administrative Law* (3rd ed., 1994), pp. 371–372.
[57] LGA 1988, s.15(4); LGPLA 1980, s.19B(6).
[58] LGA 1988, s.14(2)(a) s.14(5).
[59] LGA 1988, s.14(2)(b) and s.14(5).
[60] LGA 1988, s.14(2)(c) and (d), and s.14(5).

stated that this may include a condition requiring the Secretary of State to be satisfied on a matter stated in the direction, or which requires authorisation or consent of the Secretary of State.[61] It is common for a condition to be imposed that the work should be awarded to the DSO only if the contract is re-tendered.[62] So far as a disappointed bidder is concerned, this is the effective equivalent of a judicial remedy reopening the award procedure. In such a case it is also often provided that any award made to the DSO should require the consent of the Secretary of State – or, at least, should require his consent if the DSO is not the lowest bidder. Conditions can also be used, for example, to require an authority to supply information about a particular procedure, or to effectively modify[63] or supplement the procedural rules of the CCT regime for particular authorities – for example, changing the number of bids which must be sought by certain authorities from the usual number in the legislation.

Where directions have been given, new directions may be made either ending prohibitions in a previous direction,[64] or replacing an outright prohibition with a prohibition with conditions[65] – for example, replacing a ban on DSO participation by the DSO by an order which allows this where the consent of the Secretary of State is given. New directions may also provide that previous prohibitions are to apply only to particular work[66] thus, for example, allowing the Secretary of State to replace a general prohibition on work within a defined activity to apply to only part of the work within that activity. The date from which the new direction is to take effect must be specified in the new direction. The Secretary of State is also expressly empowered to agree variations of the directions with the authority.[67]

Powers to make similar directions are given under the 1980 LGPLA, by section 19B.[68] The Secretary of State may here direct that the authority shall cease to have the power to carry out any construction or maintenance work as identified in the direction (which may be all such work or just certain types) or may specify that the work identified may be carried out only subject to such conditions as are specified in the direction.[69] He may also bar the authority from carrying out certain specified construction and maintenance work altogether, whilst allowing

---

[61] LGA 1988, s.14(4A), as inserted by Local Government Act 1992, Sched. 1, para. 14.
[62] Retendering may involve some delay. If the work is carried out in the meantime by the DSO/DLO this may involve a breach of the legislation (since the work cannot be carried out internally where it is not covered by a relevant tendering exercise).
[63] It is provided that a direction may require that a condition imposed may apply instead of any other requirement which would apply under Part I of the LGA 1988; LGA 1988, s.14(4B), as inserted by Local Government Act 1992, Sched. 1, para. 14.
[64] LGA 1988, s.14(3)(a).
[65] LGA 1988, s.14(3)(b).
[66] LGA 1988, s.14(3)(c).
[67] LGA 1988, s.14(4)(c), as inserted by Local Government Act 1992, Sched. 1, para. 14.
[68] As inserted by LGA 1988, Sched. 6, para. 9.
[69] LGPLA 1980, s.19B(2).

other such work to be carried out only subject to specified conditions.[70] As with the LGA 1988, it is expressly provided that any conditions may include a requirement that the Secretary of State shall be satisfied on certain matters, or that his consent or authorisation shall be given.[71] New directions may be given to revoke previous prohibitions (whether conditional or otherwise); to replace an outright prohibition on certain work by a prohibition which is conditional; or to replace a prohibition (conditional or otherwise) by one which applies only to a certain part of the work previously covered by the prohibition.[72] There is, again as in the 1988 Act, an express power for the Secretary of State to agree variations of a direction with an authority.[73]

The decision as to whether to issue directions, and the form which the directions should take, is within the discretion of the Secretary of State. It is provided merely that the Secretary of State *may* issue directions, and thus he may not be compelled to do so (for example, by an aggrieved competitor) where he feels that this is not appropriate.

As regards the possibility of a challenge to a direction by an authority against which it is made, the Court of Appeal in *R. v. Secretary of State for the Environment, ex p. Haringey*[74] has held that there is wide discretion as to the nature of the direction appropriate in any particular case, and that they will review the Secretary of State's decision only where clearly irrational. That case involved a direction to re-tender refuse collection work without participation by the DLO, following a decision that the authority had acted anti-competitively in erroneously rejecting two external bidders on financial and technical grounds. The Court accepted that such a sanction could lawfully be imposed in a case of "blatant" anti-competitive conduct, even though it could not be shown that the authority had intentionally acted in an anti-competitive manner. Further, the court held that it was a lawful consideration to have regard to the need to deter local authorities in general from anti-competitive behaviour.

In 1993 the Secretary of State for the Environment dealt with a total of 157 cases involving allegations of anti-competitive behaviour. Most of these were resolved informally and only 20 formal notices were eventually served – five under the LGPLA 1980, and 15 under the LGA 1988.[75] As a result 12 directions were made – six under each Act. Most of these required the authority to re-tender particular work which it was felt had been awarded following a defect in the procedure; generally the in-house organisation was permitted to re-tender, but a condition was

---

[70] LGPLA 1980, s.19B(3).
[71] LGPLA 1980, s.19B(5A), as inserted by Local Government Act 1992, Sched. 1, para. 7(1).
[72] LGPLA 1980, s.19B(4).
[73] LGPLA 1980, s.19B(6), as amended by Local Government Act 1992, Sched. 1, para. 7(2).
[74] (1994) 92 L.G.R. 538
[75] Department of Environment and Local Government – Annual Report 1993.

imposed requiring the consent of the Secretary of State before the work could be awarded in-house.[76] In 1994 20 notices were served and nine directions given.[77]

Most notices which have been served, however, have concerned failure to meet financial objectives: in 1993 a total of 79 such notices were served, 40 under the 1980 Act, resulting in five directions, and 39 under the 1988 Act, resulting in six directions.[78] Action was considered unnecessary in most cases because the authority had either chosen already to close down its in-house organisation, or because the Secretary of State was satisfied with steps taken by the authority to reduce in-house costs or otherwise improve performance. In three cases, however, it was felt necessary to direct that the in-house organisation should not be allowed to bid further for any work.[79] In 1994 102 further notices were served for failure to meet financial objectives and 39 directions given.[80]

It is clear from these figures that the Secretary of State has made significant use of his enforcement powers and has shown a determination to ensure that the CCT rules are strictly applied.

---

[76] *Ibid.*

[77] Department of Environment, *CCT and Local Government in England: Annual Report 1994*, pp. 11–12.

[78] *Ibid.*

[79] *Ibid.*

[80] Department of the Environment, *CCT and Local Government in England: Annual Report 1994*, p. 13.

INDEX